THE PAPERS OF
THOMAS JEFFERSON

THE PAPERS OF
Thomas Jefferson

Volume 18
4 November 1790 to 24 January 1791

JULIAN P. BOYD, EDITOR

RUTH W. LESTER, ASSISTANT EDITOR

LUCIUS WILMERDING, JR.,

CONSULTING EDITOR

PRINCETON, NEW JERSEY

PRINCETON UNIVERSITY PRESS

1971

Printed in the United States of America by
Princeton University Press, Princeton, New Jersey

ACKNOWLEDGMENTS

As indicated in the first volume, this edition was made possible by a grant of $200,000 from the New York Times Company to Princeton University. Since this initial subvention, its continuance has been assured by additional contributions from the New York Times Company; by the grant of the Ford Foundation to the National Archives Trust Fund Board as explained in Volume 17; by the Fellowship bestowed on the Editor by the John Simon Guggenheim Memorial Foundation; and by other benefactions from the Charlotte Palmer Phillips Foundation and from such loyal supporters of the enterprise as James Russell Wiggins and David K. E. Bruce. In common with other editions of historical documents, *The Papers of Thomas Jefferson* is a beneficiary of the good offices of The National Historical Publications Commission, tendered in many useful forms through its Chairman, James B. Rhoads, its Executive Director, Oliver W. Holmes, and its dedicated staff. For these and other indispensable aids generously given by librarians, archivists, scholars, and collectors of manuscripts, the Editors record their sincere gratitude.

FOREWORD

THE PRINCIPAL but by no means the only cause of the regrettably long delay in the appearance of this volume arises from the considerable number of problems in both domestic and foreign policy that Jefferson faced during the third session of the First Congress. All of these—commercial and diplomatic relations with Great Britain, the state of the fisheries, the interrelated problems of Algerine piracy and trade with the Mediterranean, the first cases of impressment of seamen to be confronted by the new government, the beginnings of the new system of territorial government, the French protest against the tonnage acts of 1789 and 1790, and so on—had roots in the past. All, too, continued as problems during Jefferson's increasingly unhappy tenure as Secretary of State. Some, such as the Algerine threat and the important question of impressment, extended into or beyond his presidential years.

The editorial commentary required by Jefferson's reports and opinions during the winter of 1790-1791 has therefore been more demanding than for any comparable period covered in previous volumes. Because of the continuity of these problems the editorial context has been framed in the hope that some attention to both background and later developments may make it less necessary for subsequent notes on these major topics to be so detailed. In respect to some matters of great importance in foreign policy, such as the question of relations with Great Britain and France, it is prudent to emphasize that this is a hopeful intent rather than a confident expectation.

The problem of anticipating what unexplored areas may require particular attention has been present, of course, since the very beginning of this edition. But this difficulty has been greatly compounded by the fundamental divisions on policy and principle that emerged in the troubled decade of the 1790's. These divisions also affected the nature of the evidence, thus further complicating the editorial problems. For in a time when many Americans, including even Washington, began to doubt whether a nation so deeply divided could endure and when some in the United States seemed to share the hope of William Smith and other Loyalists that a reunion with Great Britain might be achieved, it was scarcely to be expected that either the public or the private record would afford an adequate representation of motives and actions. It is beyond question that the nation at large was still gripped by the immense power of its revolutionary principles. The press, as ubiquitous as it was free, was generally alert to detect and quick to challenge what Jefferson would soon brand as political heresies. Yet behind the closed doors of the Senate, whose debates the public was not privileged to hear, even the fragmentary record made it clear that the contest between Burke and Paine in England had its counterpart in the United States. It is equally obvious that elsewhere, particularly in the national administration, the contest was carried on without leaving a full expression in the documentary remains. Thus the most taxing and the most risky duty of the editor—that of probing for the evidence not overtly expressed—is made immensely more complicated in this period of ordeal for the nation. At a time when the fundamental assumptions to which the nation was formally committed were viewed with skepticism by some in office, the nature and extent of their reservations may be gauged less by the actual record than by the circumstances surrounding it. Indeed, in such a time the record itself must often be regarded as suspect or contrived.

These observations find illustration in the Appendix to the present volume—postponed from the previous one for the reasons given in its foreword—concerning the first conflict in the cabinet. On its surface this was a contest of little significance. It involved only a small amount of public funds, relatively few persons, and no pivotal decisions on policy. The obligation of the government to protect citizens against fraud and the duty of public officials to refrain from collusive support of fraud were, to be sure, the expressed or implied questions on which the issue was joined. Yet even these do not comprehend the full implications of this initial conflict. On the one level it was fought out in terms of elevated principle and on the other it was permitted to descend to the lower reaches of partisan politics. On both levels the documentary record is incomplete, confused, and in part—as indicated in the continuation of the editorial commentary set forth in the Appendix —not entitled to credence. But these deficiencies should not be permitted to obscure the symbolic meaning of the episode. For what emerges with indisputable clarity is that the contest involved two fundamentally opposing ways of looking at the American experiment and thus of regarding man and society. Given the conviction with which Jefferson had embraced the moral propositions on which that experiment was predicated, it is obvious that these opposing views were as irreconcilable as they were enduring.

This volume, like all that have preceded it, has benefited from the interest, cooperation, and scholarly contributions of Mr. and Mrs. Howard C. Rice, Jr. Soon after the edition was first projected, Professor Gilbert Chinard recommended that Mr. Rice, then Director of the United States Information Service in Paris, be designated as its representative in France. This recommendation, immediately adopted, inaugurated a happy and fruitful relationship that has extended through a full quarter of a century. While they were in France, Mr. and Mrs. Rice's investigations there and in Italy, Switzerland, Holland, and England resulted in a constant flow of copies of Jefferson documents of various sorts that they found in libraries, archives, and private collections. This useful collaboration continued after Mr. and Mrs. Rice returned to the United States in 1951, when he became head of the Department of Special Collections of the Princeton University Library and she became a member of the staff of *The Papers of Thomas Jefferson*. For their interest, assistance, and devotion to this edition through so many years, the Editors gratefully express their appreciation and extend their best wishes to them in their years of retirement, being confident in doing so that the indebtedness to them for past contributions will be augmented by others in the future, prompted by their zeal and generosity.

Since the appearance of the last volume, Mrs. Dorothy S. Eaton, another devoted and indeed irreplaceable pillar of editorial scholarship, has retired from the posts of responsibility that she had filled with distinction in the Manuscript Division of the Library of Congress from 1933 to 1966. In 1952 Mrs. Eaton was given leave to serve for six months as a special consultant to *The Papers of Thomas Jefferson* and thereafter, until her retirement, represented the Library of Congress as an adviser to this edition. Such was her zeal, fidelity, and cheerful readiness to respond to every call for assistance that it was difficult to tell where her brief period of leave as consultant ended and her long years of usefulness as adviser began. On a special occasion held in honor of Mrs. Eaton in 1966, the Librarian of Congress, L. Quincy Mumford, bestowed upon her the Library's Distinguished Service Award—its highest form of recognition, of which she was the tenth recipient—and hailed her "incomparable services to historical scholarship." This is a tribute that the Editors applaud with lasting gratitude both to Mrs. Eaton and to the national library, whose great tradition of service to learning she ornamented with such exceptional grace and intellectual competence.

JULIAN P. BOYD

30 July 1971

GUIDE TO EDITORIAL APPARATUS

1. *TEXTUAL DEVICES*

The following devices are employed throughout the work to clarify the presentation of the text.

[. . .], [. . . .]	One or two words missing and not conjecturable.
[. . .]¹, [. . . .]¹	More than two words missing and not conjecturable; subjoined footnote estimates number of words missing.
[ ]	Number or part of a number missing or illegible.
[roman]	Conjectural reading for missing or illegible matter. A question mark follows when the reading is doubtful.
[*italic*]	Editorial comment inserted in the text.
⟨*italic*⟩	Matter deleted in the MS but restored in our text.
[ ]	Record entry for letters not found.

2. *DESCRIPTIVE SYMBOLS*

The following symbols are employed throughout the work to describe the various kinds of manuscript originals. When a series of versions is recorded, *the first to be recorded is the version used for the printed text.*

Dft	draft (usually a composition or rough draft; later drafts, when identifiable as such, are designated "2 Dft," &c.)
Dupl	duplicate
MS	manuscript (arbitrarily applied to most documents other than letters)
N	note, notes (memoranda, fragments, &c.)
PoC	polygraph copy
PrC	press copy
RC	recipient's copy
SC	stylograph copy
Tripl	triplicate

All manuscripts of the above types are assumed to be in the hand of the author of the document to which the descriptive symbol pertains. If not, that fact is stated. On the other hand, the following types of manuscripts are assumed *not* to be in the hand of the author, and exceptions will be noted:

FC   file copy (applied to all forms of retained copies, such as letter-book copies, clerk's copies, &c.)

Tr   transcript (applied to both contemporary and later copies; period of transcription, unless clear by implication, will be given when known)

3. LOCATION SYMBOLS

The locations of documents printed in this edition from originals in private hands, from originals held by institutions outside the United States, and from printed sources are recorded in self-explanatory form in the descriptive note following each document. The locations of documents printed from originals held by public institutions in the United States are recorded by means of the symbols used in the National Union Catalog in the Library of Congress; and explanation of how these symbols are formed is given above, Vol. 1: xl. The list of symbols appearing in each volume is limited to the institutions represented by documents printed or referred to in that and previous volumes.

CLSU	University of Southern California Library, Los Angeles
CLU	William Andrews Clark Memorial Library, University of California at Los Angeles
CSmH	Henry E. Huntington Library, San Marino, California
Ct	Connecticut State Library, Hartford
CtHi	Connecticut Historical Society, Hartford
CtY	Yale University Library
DeHi	Historical Society of Delaware, Wilmington
DLC	Library of Congress
DNA	The National Archives, with identifications of series (preceded by record group number) as follows:

            AL   American Letters
            CD   Consular Dispatches
            DCI   Diplomatic and Consular Instructions
            DD   Diplomatic Dispatches
            DL   Domestic Letters

FL	Foreign Letters
MLR	Miscellaneous Letters Received
MTA	Miscellaneous Treasury Accounts
NL	Notes from Legations
NWT	Northwest Territory Papers
PCC	Papers of the Continental Congress
PDL	Printing and Distribution of the Laws
SDC	State Department Correspondence
SDR	A Record of the Reports of Thomas Jefferson, Secretary of State for the United States of America
SWT	Southwest Territory Papers

G-Ar	Georgia Department of Archives and History, Atlanta
ICHi	Chicago Historical Society, Chicago
IHi	Illinois State Historical Library, Springfield
IMunS	St. Mary of the Lake Seminary, Mundelein, Illinois
InHi	Indiana Historical Society, Indianapolis
MB	Boston Public Library, Boston
MBAt	Boston Athenæum, Boston
MH	Harvard University Library
MHi	Massachusetts Historical Society, Boston
MHi:AM	Adams Manuscripts, Massachusetts Historical Society
MdAA	Maryland Hall of Records, Annapolis
MdAN	U.S. Naval Academy Library, Annapolis
MeHi	Maine Historical Society, Portland
MiU-C	William L. Clements Library, University of Michigan
MoSHi	Missouri Historical Society, St. Louis
MWA	American Antiquarian Society, Worcester, Massachusetts
NA	New York State Library, Albany
NBu	Buffalo Public Library, Buffalo, New York
NcD	Duke University Library, Durham, North Carolina

NcU	University of North Carolina Library, Chapel Hill
NhD	Dartmouth College Library, Hanover, New Hampshire
NhHi	New Hampshire Historical Society, Concord
NHi	New-York Historical Society, New York City
NK-Iselin	Letters to and from John Jay bearing this symbol are used by permission of the Estate of Eleanor Jay Iselin.
NN	New York Public Library, New York City
NNC	Columbia University Libraries, New York City
NNP	Pierpont Morgan Library, New York City
NNS	New York Society Library, New York City
NjP	Princeton University Library
NjMoW	Morristown National Historical Park, Morristown, N.J.
O	Ohio State Library, Columbus
OCHP	Historical and Philosophical Society of Ohio, Cincinnati
OHi	Ohio State Archaeological and Historical Society, Columbus
PBL	Lehigh University Library
PHC	Haverford College Library
PHi	Historical Society of Pennsylvania, Philadelphia
PP	Free Library, Philadelphia
PPAP	American Philosophical Society, Philadelphia
PPL-R	Library Company of Philadelphia
PU	University of Pennsylvania Library
PWW	Washington and Jefferson College, Washington, Pennsylvania
RPA	Rhode Island Department of State, Providence
RPAB	Annmary Brown Memorial Library, Providence
RPB	Brown University Library
Vi	Virginia State Library, Richmond
Vi:USCC	Ended Cases, United States Circuit Court, Virginia State Library

ViHi	Virginia Historical Society, Richmond
ViRVal	Valentine Museum Library, Richmond
ViU	University of Virginia Library
ViU:McG	McGregor Library, University of Virginia
ViU:TJMF	Manuscripts deposited by the Thomas Jefferson Memorial Foundation in the University of Virginia Library
ViW	College of William and Mary Library
ViWC	Colonial Williamsburg, Inc.
VtMC	Middlebury College Library, Middlebury, Vermont
VtMS	Secretary of State, Montpelier, Vermont
WHi	State Historical Society of Wisconsin, Madison

4. OTHER SYMBOLS AND ABBREVIATIONS

The following symbols and abbreviations are commonly employed in the annotation throughout the work.

Second Series   The topical series to be published at the end of this edition, comprising those materials which are best suited to a topical rather than a chronological arrangement (see Vol. 1: xv-xvi)

TJ Thomas Jefferson

TJ Editorial Files   Photoduplicates and other editorial materials in the office of *The Papers of Thomas Jefferson*, Princeton University Library

TJ Papers   Jefferson Papers (applied to a collection of manuscripts when the precise location of a given document must be furnished, and always preceded by the symbol for the institutional repository; thus "DLC: TJ Papers, 4:628-9" represents a document in the Library of Congress, Jefferson Papers, volume 4, pages 628 and 629)

RG   Record Group (used in designating the location of documents in the National Archives)

SJL   Jefferson's "Summary Journal of letters" written and received (in DLC: TJ Papers)

SJPL   "Summary Journal of Public Letters," an incomplete list of letters written by TJ from 16 Apr. 1784 to 31 Dec. 1793, with brief summaries, in an amanuensis' hand except for six pages in TJ's hand listing and summarizing official reports and communications by him as Secretary of State, 11 Oct. 1789 to 31 Dec. 1789 (in DLC: TJ Papers, at end of SJL)

V   Ecu

ƒ   Florin

£   Pound sterling or livre, depending upon context (in doubtful cases, a clarifying note will be given)

s   Shilling or sou. (Also expressed as /)

d   Penny or denier

₶   Livre Tournois

℔   Per (occasionally used for pro, pre)

5. SHORT TITLES

The following list includes only those short titles of works cited with great frequency, and therefore in very abbreviated form, throughout this edition. Their expanded forms are given here only in the degree of fullness needed for unmistakable identification. Since it is impossible to anticipate all the works to be cited in such very abbreviated form, the list is appropriately revised from volume to volume.

Adams, *Works*   Charles Francis Adams, ed., *The Works of John Adams*, Boston, 1850-56, 10 vols.

Adams, *Diary*   *Diary and Autobiography of John Adams*, ed. L. H. Butterfield and others, Cambridge, 1961, 4 vols.

AHA   American Historical Association

AHR   *American Historical Review*, 1895-

Ammon, *Monroe*   Harry Ammon, *James Monroe*, New York, 1971

Annals   *Annals of the Congress of the United States: The Debates and Proceedings in the Congress of the United States . . . Compiled from Authentic Materials by Joseph Gales, Senior*, Washington, Gales & Seaton, 1834-56, 42 vols. The edition employed here is that which contains the running heads on verso and recto pages respectively: "Gales & Seatons History" and "of Debates in Congress." Another printing, with the same title-page but with running heads on both recto and verso pages reading "History of Congress," has a different pagination, so that pages cited in the edition employed here should be converted by subtracting approximately fifty-two from the number given in the citation. All editions are undependable.

ASP   *American State Papers: Documents, Legislative and Executive, of the Congress of the United States*, Washington, Gales & Seaton, 1832-61, 38 vols.

Atlas of Amer. Hist., Scribner, 1943   James Truslow Adams and R. V. Coleman, eds., *Atlas of American History*, N.Y., 1943

Bear, *Family Letters*   Edwin M. Betts and James A. Bear, Jr., eds., *Family Letters of Thomas Jefferson*, Columbia, Missouri, 1966

Bemis, *Jay's Treaty*   Samuel Flagg Bemis, *Jay's Treaty: A Study in Commerce and Diplomacy*, New Haven, 1962, rev. edn.

Bemis, *Pinckney's Treaty*   Samuel Flagg Bemis, *Pinckney's Treaty: America's Advantage from Europe's Distress, 1783-1800*, rev. edn., New Haven, 1960

Betts, *Farm Book*   Edwin M. Betts, ed., *Thomas Jefferson's Farm Book*, Princeton, 1953

Betts, *Garden Book*   Edwin M. Betts, ed., *Thomas Jefferson's Garden Book, 1766-1824*, Philadelphia, 1944

Beveridge, *Marshall*   Albert J. Beveridge, *The Life of John Marshall*, Boston, 1916

Biog. Dir. Cong.   *Biographical Directory of the American Congress, 1774-1949*, Washington, 1950

B.M. Cat.   British Museum, *General Catalogue of Printed Books*, London, 1931-; also *The British Museum Catalogue of Printed Books, 1881-1900*, Ann Arbor, 1946

B.N. Cat.   Bibliothèque Nationale, *Catalogue général des livres imprimés. . . . Auteurs*, Paris, 1897-1955

Brant, *Madison*, i   Irving Brant, *James Madison: The Virginia Revolutionist*, Indianapolis, 1941

Brant, *Madison*, ii   Irving Brant, *James Madison: The Nationalist, 1780-1787*, Indianapolis, 1948

Brant, *Madison*, iii   Irving Brant, *James Madison: Father of the Constitution, 1787-1800*, Indianapolis, 1950

Brant, *Madison*, iv   Irving Brant, *James Madison: Secretary of State, 1800-1809*, Indianapolis, 1953

Brant, *Madison*, v   Irving Brant, *James Madison: The President, 1809-1812*, Indianapolis, 1956

Burnett, *Letters of Members*   Edwin C. Burnett, ed., *Letters of Members of the Continental Congress*, Washington, 1921-1936, 8 vols.

Butterfield, *Rush*   *Letters of Benjamin Rush*, ed. L. H. Butterfield, Princeton, 1951, 2 vols.

Cal. Franklin Papers   I. Minis Hays, ed., *Calendar of the Papers of Benjamin Franklin in the Library of the American Philosophical Society*, Philadelphia, 1908, 6 vols.

Carter, *Terr. Papers*   *The Territorial Papers of the United States*, ed. Clarence E. Carter, Washington, 1934-62, 26 vols.

Cutler, *Cutler*   William Parker Cutler, *Life, Journals, and Correspondence of Rev. Manasseh Cutler*, Cincinnati, 1888, 2 vols.

CVSP   William P. Palmer and others, eds., *Calendar of Virginia State Papers . . . Preserved in the Capitol at Richmond*, Richmond, 1875-1893

DAB   Allen Johnson and Dumas Malone, eds., *Dictionary of American Biography*, N.Y., 1928-1936

DAE   Sir William A. Craigie and James Hulbert, eds., *A Dictionary of American English*, Chicago, 1938-1944

DAH   James Truslow Adams, ed., *Dictionary of American History*, N.Y., 1940, 5 vols., and index

DeConde, *Entangling Alliance*   Alexander DeConde, *Entangling Alliance; Politics & Diplomacy under George Washington*, Durham, N.C., 1958

DNB   Leslie Stephen and Sidney Lee, eds., *Dictionary of National Biography*, 2d ed., N.Y., 1908-1909

Dumbauld, *Tourist*   Edward Dumbauld, *Thomas Jefferson American Tourist*, Norman, Oklahoma, 1946

Elliot's *Debates*   Jonathan Elliot, ed., *The Debates of the Several State Conventions on the Adoption of the Federal Constitution . . . together with the Journal of the Federal Convention*, 2d ed., Philadelphia, 1901, 5 vols.

Evans   Charles Evans, comp., *American Bibliography*, Chicago, 1903-1955

Ford   Paul Leicester Ford, ed., *The Writings of Thomas Jefferson*, Letterpress Edition, N.Y., 1892-1899, 10 vols.

Freeman, *Washington*   Douglas Southall Freeman, *George Washington*, N.Y., 1948-1957, 6 vols.; 7th volume by J. A. Carroll and M. W. Ashworth, New York, 1957

Fry-Jefferson Map   Dumas Malone, ed., *The Fry & Jefferson Map of Virginia and Maryland: a Facsimile of the First Edition*, Princeton, 1950

Gottschalk, *Lafayette, 1783-89*   Louis Gottschalk, *Lafayette between the American and the French Revolution (1783-1789)*, Chicago, 1950

Greely, *Public Documents*   Adolphus Washington Greely, ed., *Public Documents of the First Fourteen Congresses, 1789-1817: Papers Relating to Early Congressional Documents*, Washington, 1900

HAW   Henry A. Washington, ed., *The Writings of Thomas Jefferson*, N.Y., 1853-1854, 9 vols.

Hening   William Waller Hening, ed., *The Statutes at Large; Being a Collection of All the Laws of Virginia*, Richmond, 1809-1823, 13 vols.

Henry, *Henry*   William Wirt Henry, *Patrick Henry, Life, Correspondence and Speeches*, N.Y., 1891, 3 vols.

Humphreys, *Humphreys*   F. L. Humphreys, *Life and Times of David Humphreys*, New York, 1917, 2 vols.

JCC   Worthington C. Ford and others, eds., *Journals of the Continental Congress, 1774-1789*, Washington, 1904-1937, 34 vols.

JEP   *Journal of the Executive Proceedings of the Senate of the United States . . . to the Termination of the Nineteenth Congress*, Washington, 1828

JHD   *Journal of the House of Delegates of the Commonwealth of Virginia* (cited by session and date of publication)

JHR   *Journal of the House of Representatives of the United States*, Washington, Gales & Seaton, 1826-

Jefferson Correspondence, Bixby   Worthington C. Ford, ed., *Thomas Jefferson Correspondence Printed from the Originals in the Collections of William K. Bixby*, Boston, 1916

JS   *Journal of the Senate of the United States*, Washington, Gales, 1820-21, 5 vols.

Ketcham, *Madison*   Ralph Ketcham, *James Madison*, New York, 1971

Kimball, *Jefferson*, I   Marie Kimball, *Jefferson the Road to Glory 1743 to 1776*, New York, 1943

Kimball, *Jefferson*, II   Marie Kimball, *Jefferson War and Peace 1776 to 1784*, New York, 1947

Kimball, *Jefferson*, III   Marie Kimball, *Jefferson the Scene of Europe 1784 to 1789*, New York, 1950

King, *King*   C. R. King, ed., *The Life and Correspondence of Rufus King, Comprising His Letters, Private and Official, His Public Documents, and His Speeches, 1755-1827*, New York, 1894-1900, 6 vols.

L & B   Andrew A. Lipscomb and Albert E. Bergh, eds., *The Writings of Thomas Jefferson*, Washington, 1903-1904, 20 vols.

L.C. *Cat.*   *A Catalogue of Books Represented by the Library of Congress Printed Cards*, Ann Arbor, 1942-1946; also *Supplement*, 1948-

Library Catalogue, 1783   Jefferson's MS list of books owned or wanted in 1783 (original in Massachusetts Historical Society)

Library Catalogue, 1815   *Catalogue of the Library of the United States*, Washington, 1815

Library Catalogue, 1829   *Catalogue: President Jefferson's Library*, Washington, 1829

Loubat, *Medallic history*   J. F. Loubat, *The Medallic History of the United States of America*, 1776-1876, New York, 1878, 2 vols.

Maclay, *Journal*, ed. Maclay   Edgar S. Maclay, ed., *Journal of William Maclay, United States Senator from Pennslyvania, 1789-1791*, New York, 1890

Madison, *Letters and Other Writings*   James Madison, *Letters and Other Writings of James Madison*, Philadelphia, 1865

Malone, *Jefferson*, I   Dumas Malone, *Jefferson the Virginian*, Boston, 1948

Malone, *Jefferson*, II   Dumas Malone, *Jefferson and the Rights of Man*, Boston, 1951

Malone, *Jefferson*, III   Dumas Malone, *Jefferson and the Ordeal of Liberty*, Boston, 1962

Malone, *Jefferson*, IV   Dumas Malone, *Jefferson the President First Term, 1801-1805*, Boston, 1970

Mayo, *IBM*   Bernard Mayo, ed., "Instructions to the British Ministers to the United States 1791-1812," American Historical Association, *Annual Report*, 1936

Miller, *Hamilton*   John C. Miller, *Alexander Hamilton Portrait in Paradox*, New York, 1959

Mitchell, *Hamilton*   Broadus Mitchell, *Alexander Hamilton*, New York, 1957, 1962, 2 vols.

MVHR   *Mississippi Valley Historical Review*, 1914-

OED   Sir James Murray and others, eds., *A New English Dictionary on Historical Principles*, Oxford, 1888-1933

Peterson, *Jefferson*   Merrill D. Peterson, *Thomas Jefferson and the New Nation*, New York, 1970

PMHB   *Pennsylvania Magazine of History and Biography*, 1877-

Randall, *Life*   Henry S. Randall, *The Life of Thomas Jefferson*, N.Y., 1858, 3 vols.

Randolph, *Domestic Life*   Sarah N. Randolph, *The Domestic Life of Thomas Jefferson, Compiled from Family Letters and Reminiscences by His Great-Granddaughter*, Cambridge, Mass., 1939

Sabin   Joseph Sabin and others, comps., *Bibliotheca Americana. A Dictionary of Books Relating to America*, N.Y., 1868-1936

St. Clair, *Narrative*   Arthur St. Clair, *A Narrative of the Manner in which the Campaign against the Indians . . . was Conducted . . .* , Philadelphia, 1812

St. Clair, *Papers*   William Henry Smith, ed., *The St. Clair Papers. The Life and Public Services of Arthur St. Clair*, Cincinnati, 1882, 2 vols.

Setser, *Reciprocity*   Vernon G. Setser, *The Commercial Reciprocity Policy of the United States*, Philadelphia, 1937

Shipton-Mooney Index   Clifford K. Shipton and James E. Mooney, comps., *National Index of American Imprints through 1800, The Short-Title Evans*, 1969, 2 vols.

Sowerby   E. Millicent Sowerby, comp., *Catalogue of the Library of Thomas Jefferson*, 1952-1959, 5 vols.

Sparks, *Morris*   Jared Sparks, *Life of Gouverneur Morris*, Boston, 1832, 3 vols.

Swem, *Index*   Earl G. Swem, comp., *Virginia Historical Index*, Roanoke, 1934-1936

Swem, "Va. Bibliog."   Earl G. Swem, comp., "A Bibliography of Virginia History," Virginia State Library, *Bulletin*, VIII (1915), x (1917), and XII (1919)

Syrett, *Hamilton*   *The Papers of Alexander Hamilton*, ed. Harold C. Syrett and others, New York, 1961–, 15 vols.

TJR   Thomas Jefferson Randolph, ed., *Memoir, Correspondence, and Miscellanies, from the Papers of Thomas Jefferson*, Charlottesville, 1829, 4 vols.

Tucker, *Life*   George Tucker, *The Life of Thomas Jefferson*, Philadelphia, 1837, 2 vols.

Turner, *CFM*   F. J. Turner, "Correspondence of French Ministers, 1791-1797," AHA, *Ann. Rept.*, 1903, II

U.S. Statutes at Large   *The Public and General Statutes Passed by the Congress of the United States of America from 1789 to 1836*, edited by George Sharswood. Second edn., Philadelphia, 1837-40, 4 vols.

Van Doren, *Secret History*   Carl Van Doren, *Secret History of the American Revolution*, New York, 1941

VMHB   *Virginia Magazine of History and Biography*, 1893-

WMQ   *William and Mary Quarterly*, 1892-

CONTENTS

CONTENTS

CONTENTS

CONTENTS

CONTENTS

CONTENTS

CONTENTS

CONTENTS

CONTENTS

CONTENTS

ILLUSTRATIONS

Following page 268

This truncated column and its pedestal, both of marble, filled two of the eighty-six crates of Jefferson's furniture and personal possessions that were packed in Paris under William Short's supervision and shipped to America in the summer of 1790. The weight of the two crates caused a revolutionary mob at Le Havre to suspect that plate or other valuables belonging to some aristocrat were being smuggled out of France under Jefferson's diplomatic passport. The mob forced the shippers to open them, along with six other crates containing busts by Houdon of Voltaire, Turgot, Lafayette, Franklin, Washington, and Jefferson (Le Mesurier & Cie. to TJ, 27 Aug. 1790). This added somewhat to the "monstrous bill of freight" and other costs that Jefferson had to pay. The immense shipment of furniture, books, wines, papers, and personal effects descended upon Jefferson at a time of extraordinary official pressures, but it did not include the additional burden of the pedestal and its column. These went by another ship to Norfolk and thence to Monticello (see note, Short to TJ, 7 Nov. 1790; TJ to Brown, 16 Dec. 1790).

The "magnificent pedestal," given to Jefferson in 1789 by the Comtesse de Tessé, contained a Latin inscription predicting that his name would "descend forever blessed to posterity" (note, TJ to Madame de Tessé, 27 Aug. 1789). During Jefferson's lifetime this gift from a cherished friend, surmounted by Giuseppe Ceracchi's massive bust of Jefferson, stood in the entrance hall at Monticello with the inscription turned to the wall. In his directions for an epitaph Jefferson suggested that the bust, "with the pedestal and truncated column on which it stands, might be given to the University, if they would place it in the Dome room of the Rotunda" (MS of Epitaph, DLC: TJ Papers, 231: 41473). Instead, the ensemble became the property of the government and pedestal, column, and bust were all destroyed in the Capitol fire of 1851.

This drawing may have been executed by Jefferson's granddaughter, Cornelia Jefferson Randolph. Another representation of the pedestal and column, a very unsophisticated pencil sketch, shows the same signs of the zodiac while failing to indicate the inscription, thus confirming travellers' comments that it was hidden from view. It also shows the bust mounted on the column (reproduced in A. L. Bush, *Life portraits of Thomas Jefferson* [Charlottesville, 1962], p. 28; this sketch appears on the verso of a letter written by Thomas Jefferson Randolph in 1826, ViU; hence the very childlike drawing has been improbably attributed to him). This is apparently the only surviving depiction of Ceracchi's likeness of Jefferson, since Robert Mills, after Congress in 1850 had refused to give him permission to execute a plaster copy of it, made daguerreotypes that apparently have been lost. A floor plan of Monticello by Cornelia Jefferson Randolph, reproduced by James A. Bear, Jr., *Report of the Curator 1961* (Thomas Jefferson Memorial Foundation, 1962), p. 12, indicates that the pedestal, column, and bust stood in the entrance hall immediately to the right as the visitor entered from the portico. (*Courtesy of The Thomas Jefferson Memorial Foundation*)

PRIVATE CHANNELS OF COMMUNICATION BETWEEN THE
UNITED STATES AND THE BRITISH MINISTRY, 1790-1791

By the opening of the third session of the First Congress, Hamilton and others friendly to the British interest in the United States were well aware that their privately expressed views of policy had brought about no sensible change in the attitudes of the ministry. Up to this point their principal channel of communication had been George Beckwith, whose communications left the British government in no doubt as to the identity of its American friends. But the mission of Gouverneur Morris, inspired by Hamilton and Jay, had failed (see Vol. 17: 35-108). Also, Jefferson and Madison were fixed in their determination to seek reciprocity in commerce through retaliatory means, a policy which Hamilton himself had advocated in *The Federalist*. The fear that they might succeed led their opponents late in 1790 to make a sudden and more direct appeal to the British ministry.

This clandestine effort to undermine the policy of the Secretary of State was aided by Robert Morris, whose business connections proved useful in gaining access to the ministry. The person chosen for the mission was William Stephens Smith, who was ambitious for diplomatic office. Both he and his sponsors sought to create the impression that he went to England on private affairs and that, showered by attentions from the ministry, he was anxiously solicited by Grenville to convey a friendly message to the American government. This view has been accepted by historians, but the cloak of Smith's private business, which was real enough, served as a disguise for public objects. What actually took place was just the reverse of what he tried to make his own government believe. It was Smith himself who solicited a meeting with Grenville, then about to succeed Leeds as Secretary for Foreign Affairs. He almost failed to get an audience but at last was granted a single interview as a result of the importunations of Patrick Colquhoun, Henry Dundas, and, most important of all, William Pulteney. At this meeting with Grenville, which lasted less than an hour, Smith made available to the minister a prepared memorandum on affairs in the United States in which he described the "two parties in the American Government, composed of the principal leading men in the Country—one set of Individuals very powerful and respectable in favour of France and another in favour of England" (undated memorandum, in Smith's hand, endorsed as received by Grenville on 15 Apr. 1791, PRO: FO 4/9, f. 222-3). This document, which in substance echoed what Hamilton and others had long been saying to George Beckwith, represented the real object of the mission.

It was an urgent appeal to the British government to sustain its American friends.

On his return Smith volunteered a report to the President in which he unwittingly revealed more than he intended. With some discreet omissions and several serious misrepresentations, he discoursed at length on the changed attitudes and the friendly dispositions he had observed in the ministry. Hamilton, Jay, and others saw and approved the report before it was transmitted to the President. But neither Washington nor Jefferson, who drafted the response to Smith, was any more deceived by this calculated misrepresentation than they had been by Hamilton's similar distortion of Beckwith's communication of the preceding summer.

A similar overture to the ministry, arising in the same quarters and prompted by the same fears, was made in 1790 through General John Maunsell, who indeed returned the next year with a written message from William Pitt to the friends of the British interest in America. But this result was inspired less by their appeals than by fear of the rising influence of the Secretary of State. For an account of the missions of Smith and Maunsell, see Editorial Note to the group of documents on commercial and diplomatic relations with Great Britain, p. 221-83.

William Stephens Smith (1755-1816). Portrait by Gilbert Stuart. (*Courtesy of Yale University Art Gallery*)

Patrick Colquhoun (1745-1820). Engraving by S. Freeman after a portrait in possession of the family. (*Courtesy of Wilmarth S. Lewis, Farmington, Connecticut*)

Henry Dundas, first Viscount Melville (1742-1811). John Kay's engraving of 1790 shows Dundas in conversation with James Fergusson (1769-1842), a Scottish legal writer. (*Courtesy of Mrs. Donald F. Hyde, Four Oaks Farm, Somerville, New Jersey*)

THE FIRST CONFLICT IN THE CABINET

The collision between Hamilton and Jefferson that occurred in May 1790 when the former sought and the latter opposed a presidential veto of resolutions designed to protect Revolutionary veterans from exploitation revealed both their contrasting personalities and their opposing concepts of government. On one level, quickly terminated by Washington's refusal of a veto, the issue was joined in terms of overarching principles (see Vol. 16: 455-70). On another, with consequences that did not come into public view until 1797, it terminated for Hamilton in personal tragedy (see Appendix). Having successfully opposed Hamilton's request for a veto, Jefferson was only an interested but passive observer of the denouement. Aside from these two principals, the following persons whose portraits are here reproduced were involved in one way or another:

Frederick Augustus Conrad Muhlenberg (1750-1801). This portrait by Joseph Wright, painted in 1790, reveals Muhlenberg as a man of impressive dignity, urbane solidity, and more than a touch of human warmth. A Pennsylvania Federalist of moderate views and accommodating disposition, Muhlenberg is seated in the chair of the Speaker of the House of Representatives, an office to which he was elected by men of varying political convictions both North and South. He is shown in the act of signing a bill, perhaps intended to represent the first to bear his name as Speaker since the words "Act to regulate the" are clearly legible in the document and since these are also the opening words of the Act to regulate the manner of administering oaths required by the Constitution for members of the Senate and the House—the first bill to be introduced and the first to be passed into law under the new government (JHR, I, 14, 21, 29, 43). The symbolism is apt both for the beginning and for the end of Muhlenberg's Congressional career. In 1796, with the nation and the Congress deeply divided over Jay's Treaty, it fell to him to break the tie in a crucial vote on the bill to provide for its execution. This was an act of courage, but it terminated his political life. Toward the end of their regime the Federalists lost the allegiance of this man of probity, moderation, and good will.

In 1792, in an effort to gain clemency for an errant clerk, Muhlenberg accidentally became possessed of information proving that speculation in soldiers' claims had somehow been aided by official collusion. When the Secretary of the Treasury seemed also to be implicated, he felt it his duty to consult two legislative colleagues, James Monroe and Abraham B. Venable of Virginia. The inquiry that posed such a painful dilemma for Alexander Hamilton was thus begun through inadvertence by a respected supporter of Federalist measures. In this as in other episodes Muhlenberg's sense of public duty triumphed over his partisan loyalties. (*National Portrait Gallery, Smithsonian Institution, Washington, D.C.; lent by Mrs. George Brooke III, through whose courtesy the portrait is reproduced*)

James Monroe (1758-1831). From the time Muhlenberg informed him of the imprisonment of James Reynolds, reportedly a constituent speculating in soldiers' claims for pay, Monroe took the leading part in the effort to trace the source of official misconduct in the Treasury. His role has been misunderstood, chiefly because the interpretation that Hamilton sought to establish has been accepted without critical examination. The clash with Hamilton that had its roots in this first conflict in the cabinet came at a time when Monroe, recalled as minister to France and vilified in the Federalist press as a hireling of that nation, was primarily engaged in preparing a justification of his own official actions. His defense, *A view of the conduct of the Executive, in the foreign affairs of the United States* (Philadelphia, 1797), is a restrained, cogently reasoned, and quite impersonal account of his mission to France. It thus stands in marked contrast to *Observations on certain documents* (Philadelphia, 1797), in which Hamilton attempted to refute charges against his own official conduct by impugning the honor of Republicans in general and Monroe in particular. Jefferson joined other friends of Monroe in urging him not to continue the dispute, despite Hamilton's misrepresentations.

This sensitive portrait of Monroe was executed during his years as minister to France, 1794-1797. It was painted by the portrait-miniaturist, Madame G. Busset. (*Courtesy of The James Monroe Memorial Foundation, Fredericksburg, Virginia*)

Abraham Bedford Venable (*1758-1811*). A graduate of the College of New-Jersey of the class of 1780, Venable was the scion of a prosperous family of planters, merchants, and public figures of Prince Edward County, Virginia. He was the same age as Monroe and followed his lead in the inquiry after Muhlenberg revealed to them the evidence he had received concerning James Reynolds' activities. Venable was the only one of the three who was still in Congress when the affair became public in 1797. His role at that time also was secondary, chiefly because Hamilton sought to place the entire responsibility upon Monroe.

The portrait of Venable, which has always been in the possession of the family, has been attributed to Rembrandt Peale (*Virginia historical portraiture, 1585-1830*, ed. Alexander W. Weddell [Richmond, 1930], p. 340-1). The family historian, Elizabeth Marshall Venable, *Venables of Virginia* (New York, 1925), p. 35, reports a family tradition that it was painted while Venable was a student at Princeton. While its provenance establishes it as of the period, the appearance of the costume, particularly the jabot, indicates subsequent overpainting (communication from E. P. Richardson, 13 May 1971). Charles Coleman Sellers (communication to the Editors, 14 May 1971) suggests that the portrait could have been painted after Venable's death in 1811 from whatever likeness the family possessed, perhaps a miniature of Venable as a student. (*Courtesy of Mrs. James Watson Morris, Virginia Beach, Virginia*)

Oliver Wolcott, Jr. (*1760-1833*). Comptroller of the Treasury, staunch Federalist, and faithful supporter of the Secretary, Wolcott was guided in his official conduct by exacting standards of probity and propriety. Unlike Hamilton, who at times lent the influence of his office to such friends as William Duer, Baron Steuben, and the widow of General Greene, Wolcott bluntly refused to allow private friendships to impinge upon his official duty. In 1792, in his effort to prevent some of the numerous frauds and impositions on the public, he instituted legal proceedings against James Reynolds and Jacob Clingman. This action resulted in acute embarrassment for Hamilton and led to the inquiry conducted by Muhlenberg, Monroe, and Venable. At Hamilton's request, Wolcott was present at the confrontation between Hamilton and the three members of Congress. When the affair became known in 1797, Wolcott urged Hamilton not to make a public response. After this prudent advice was rejected, he supplied an affidavit which sought to bolster Hamilton's defense but which, in one essential respect, contradicted it. Wolcott remained to the end one of Hamilton's most loyal friends and admirers.

The portrait of Wolcott is a miniature painted by John Trumbull about 1790. (*Courtesy of Yale University Art Gallery*)

William J. Vredenburgh (*1760-1813*). An enterprising young merchant and broker of New York City, Vredenburgh obtained from the Treasury in the autumn of 1789—very likely with the assistance of William Duer, Assistant Secretary—lists of names of officers and soldiers of the Virginia and North Carolina lines, with amounts of arrearages of pay due them. Several speculators were probably involved in this venture in which sums actually due were at times misrepresented, with claims being purchased at a fraction of their value even as understated. But it was Vredenburgh who employed as his agent one James Reynolds, son of an assistant commissary of purchases under Jeremiah Wadsworth during the Revolution. Reynolds' activities in Virginia aroused such bitter resentments as to bring about the protective legislation which Hamilton, echoing in part arguments advanced in Vredenburgh's own protests, urged Washington to veto.

The portrait of Vredenburgh is a wax medallion by an unidentified artist. It is here reproduced from the half-tone illustration in E. Reuel Smith's *Notes on the Vredenburgh and Burnett families* (New York, 1917), its present location not being known. (*Courtesy of Mrs. Sedgwick Smith, Skaneateles, New York*)

Jefferson records the Reynolds affair. On 17 Dec. 1792, two days after Muhlenberg, Monroe, and Venable confronted Hamilton, Jefferson recorded information about the affair that perhaps came to him from Monroe. It is to be noted that in this brief memorandum he merely alluded to the "affair of Reynolds and his wife," without in any sense connecting the name of Hamilton with either. Also, while he recorded the fact of Reynolds' speculations and fixed responsibility for collusion upon Duer, he did not implicate Hamilton in the speculations but merely noted that he had asked for a veto of the resolutions aimed at curbing exploitation of soldiers. This second part of the memorandum he subsequently deleted, perhaps because it may have seemed to imply an involvement in the speculation on the part of Hamilton. The deletion was possibly made in 1818 when Jefferson reviewed the contemporaneous memoranda that he began to record in 1791. At that time he "cut out from the rest" some that he deemed incorrect, doubtful, or merely personal and deleted passages in others that, as in this instance, he retained in the three bound volumes to which he gave the name *Anas* (DLC: TJ Papers, 231: 37839). The deleted passage is quoted in the Appendix, at note 102.

WILLIAM TEMPLE FRANKLIN (1762-1823)

One of the first matters that Jefferson attended to on his return to Philadelphia late in 1790 was to transmit to William Temple Franklin the manuscript of that part of Benjamin Franklin's autobiographical writings which dealt with his unsuccessful efforts to achieve peace in 1775. It is not certain which, if either, of the two known manuscripts of the narrative Jefferson had had in his possession for a few months after he received it from Benjamin Franklin. Jefferson's remembered accounts both confused the question and did injustice to William Temple Franklin, whom he suspected of having been bribed to suppress publication of the document. Disappointed in his ambition for diplomatic office, Franklin departed for England in the autumn of 1790 with the avowed purpose of seeking to publish

of being obliged to return to you my appointment; a circumstance which on every account would give me the most sensible pain. If such however should be the fate of the business, I shall entreat you to make my most unfeigned thanks, acceptable to the Honble the President and Congress for the high honor intended me by making me their Representative in these parts and to assure them when the time shall arrive when they can employ me in their Service here. I shall be proud of the honour of receiving their Appointment and to prove how much I am theirs & Sir, Your most faithfull & very obedient Servant,   THOMAS AULDJO

If Congress wants proof of the Interest of America requiring protection at this port, they will find it in the instances of the Fanney Capt. Colley, Mary Capt. Boardman, Hannah Capt. Kilkem of Newbury port and Minerva Capt. West of Boston who discharged their Cargoes here this last Summer.

RC (DNA: RG 59, CD). Recorded in SJL as received 17 Jan. 1791, but there given the erroneous date of 28 Oct. 1790. Enclosures: (1) Copy of a letter from James Mackenzie to Auldjo, 28 Oct. 1790, informing him of a conversation at the Foreign Office the day before with J. B. Burges "in the course of which he and Mr. [George] Aust the New Secretary were uncommonly civil. . . . They said very readily they approved fully of the Appointment as to its principle and of you as an officer but that a doubt had arisen which had occasioned a Suspension as to the propriety of admitting a Consul where none had ever resided for were they to admit you as an American consul there they must of course, Consuls who might be appointed by France Spain or any other foreign Country which would be opening a door which they could not shut and might have ill consequences. They said that Congress had not intimated their intention of sending Consuls to this Country, the first knowledge of which was the production of your Commission. I answered that his Majesty had approved of Mr. Johnson without any such previous intimation. They replied they had no objection to any place at which it had been usual for Consuls to reside—they wished it would not be pressed upon them as in Case of refusal for it is yet undetermined it might give offence which they were Studious to avoid." Burges and August informed him also that if Auldjo were appointed consul at Poole or at Southampton, his commission would be readily admitted even though he resided at Cowes. When Mackenzie pointed out the delay of getting a new commission, the secretaries suggested that Auldjo might act as a deputy of Joshua Johnson. "It appeared clearly," Mackenzie concluded, "that they feared that if an American Consul of whom they have no apprehension were by authority resident at Cowes, the Spaniards and French might . . . apply and to have persons resident in publick Characters So near the Seat of naval armament might prove a dangerous protected Spy. This is not what they averred but Mr. Turnbull and I could clearly infer from their answer and reasoning" (Tr in DNA: RG 59, CD, endorsed "No. 1"; accompanied by Dupl, both in Auldjo's hand). (2) Copy of a letter from Thomas Auldjo to the Duke of Leeds, dated at Cowes, 31 Oct. 1790, asking for a speedy approval of his commission and stating: "I humbly beg leave to premise to your Grace the strong reasons the United States have for fixing my Residence at the Port of Cowes are the Notoriety of its being their principal Port of Trade indeed I may affirm that it is the only one of any Consequence in the British Channel for American trade therefore I presume with all due submission they have judged a Consular Residence indispensably Necessary at this Port.— Permit me to add that I have it in Command thro' the Secretary of State for the United States to Cultivate the

Friendship and good disposition of the British Government . . . and I entreat of your Grace to believe my most strenuous endeavours will ever be exerted to the Completion of so pleasing a part of my Consular Duty" (Tr in DNA: RG 59, CD, endorsed "No. 2," in Auldjo's hand). (3) Copy of "Mr. Auldjo's Remarks on the Conversation . . . between Mr. Burgess and Mr. Mackenzie," dated at Cowes, 31 Oct. 1790. In this document Auldjo rejected as fallacious the argument that a door might be opened to French and Spanish "spies on the Arsenal at Portsmouth," since neither of those countries had any trade at Cowes; pointed out that information of what was "going forward in the Dock Yard" at Portsmouth could as readily be gathered in London as in Cowes; and hinted that Poole and Southampton were quite as near to Portsmouth as was Cowes. Auldjo concluded: "I must now strongly enforce the Necessity of a Consular Residence here from the Notoriety of the importance of the American Trade at this Port being the only one of Consequence in the British Channel where their Ships frequent. . . . The Port of Cowes has for nearly a Century past been the Rendezvous for American Shipping whether for the purpose of Clearing their Cargoes calling for Orders getting Intelligence of the State of the Northern Markets procuring Supplies repairing damages sustained in their Voyages across the Atlantic or wintering when the Season of the Year is too far advanced for their entering the North Sea. To such a port therefore it was Natural for the United States to turn their first Attention in their Arrangement of and appointment of Consuls for want of which I will affirm their Interest has suffered Materially in several instances lately. It ought to be a Matter of serious Consideration with the British Government to debar the United States of America from having an officer on their behalf for the Protection of their Trade at the only Port in the Channel where his Service is Materially required or can be usefull" (MS in DNA: RG 59, CD, in Auldjo's hand).

On 23 Nov. 1790 Auldjo sent TJ duplicates of the above and also of that of 7 Nov. 1790, with copies of enclosures (RC in DNA: RG 59, CD; endorsed by TJ as received 12 Feb. 1791 and so recorded in SJL).

From David Humphreys

SIR   Gra[ve]send Nov. 4th. 1790.

The only object of this letter is to inform you, that I have been unavoidably detained by the weather until the present moment; in which I am embarking.

Nothing has yet transpired to enable one to form a definitive conclusion, whether the great hostile preparations will terminate in war.

Notwithstanding the Public continues to be amused and deluded, with pompous accounts, in all the Papers, of the offers of powerful Assistance from the *Cherokee Ambassadors*; Yet it is merely a Ministerial fiction to divert the popular attention, for the Government has good information that the Cherokees have far from 1000 men capable of bearing arms. This I heard yesterday myself from a Mr. Tate, who has formerly been employed in the Creek and Cherokee nations—and who, from a concurrence of circumstances, I [am confident] must be the father of McGillivray's Nephew now in the care of Genl Knox. He says, he numbered the Creeks in

1773, and found them to consist of between 13 and 14,000 Souls.

Mr. Calonne's Work on the French Government, and Mr. Burke's Letters on the French Revolution have just made their appearance. I should have forwarded them to you, but found Mr Johnson had already done it. Calonne is gone to the Continent—probably to Turin. I have the honor to be, With perfect consideration Sir Your Most obedient & Most humble Servant,

D. HUMPHREYS

RC (DNA: RG 59, DD); endorsed as received 12 Mch. 1791 and so recorded in SJL. FC (same).

The CHEROKEE (and Creek) AMBASSADORS were led by the adventurer William Augustus Bowles (see J. L. Wright, Jr., *Bowles*, p. 36-70). Gren-

ville stated later that "Such of their requests as related to views of hostility against the United States . . . met with no kind of encouragement"—but they would be permitted to trade with the free ports of the West Indies (Grenville to Dorchester, 7 Mch. 1791, PRO: CO 42/73, f.15).

To Daniel L. Hylton

DEAR SIR   Monticello Nov. 4. 1790.

The inclosed letter to Mr. Eppes being of great consequence to me, and not knowing any other sure means of conveying it to him I take the liberty of inclosing it to you, and of begging the favor of you to send it by the first *sure* conveyance. I set out for Philadelphia three days hence. I hope Mrs. Hylton continues satisfied with our chaffer, and that she enjoys good health. Present my affectionate respects to her, and believe me to be Dear Sir Your friend & servt,   TH: JEFFERSON

PrC (MHi). Enclosure: TJ to Eppes, 31 Oct. 1790 and, no doubt, that of TJ to Elizabeth Wayles Eppes of the same date.

The CHAFFER with Mrs. Hylton was

an exchange by which TJ received a vis-à-vis that he had evidently admired when he stayed with the Hyltons on 4 Oct. 1790 (see note, TJ to Hylton, 1 Mch. 1791).

From George Read, Jr.

SIR

New Castle on Delaware
November 4. 1790.

I was honour'd with your letter of the 12th. of August wherein you request full and accurate information of any and what Acts Orders Proclamations or decisions, legislative executive or judiciary may have taken place within this State since the treaty with Great Britain whereby the Debts or other property or the persons of

[7]

British Subjects or American Refugees may have been affected. As I had not usually attended the Courts of Common Pleas in some of the Counties in this State in which some judiciary proceeding[s] might have had in the Case of persons above referred to I have necessarily deferred this Answer in order to be satisfactorily informed therein.—And [from the Result of all my inquiries I am induced to believe that no proceedings of any kind have taken place within this State since the Treaty of Peace tending in any manner to affect the persons or property of British Subjects or American Refugees in Contravention to that Treaty.—Whatever property any british Subject might have had within this State at or after the declaration of Independence the same hath been in no wise altered or diminished by any Act of the State Legislature, the Confiscations of Property specially declared by law extended only to Citizens and Subjects of the State.—And such outstanding Debts which british Subjects might have had within the State I have generally understood have been settled by such their Debtors as had ability to pay, in a way satisfactory to passing the Act of the 2d. of February 1788—herewith also transmitted "for repealing all Acts or parts of Acts Repugnant to the Treaty of Peace between the United States and his Britannic Majesty or any Article thereof," as that Act was framed by the late Congress in the Terms in which it is expressed and passed by our Legislature upon the special requisition of that body which was made circular to all the States then in the Union.][1]

The last regular Impression of the laws of the State was made in the Year 1752, and they are become now so scarce that I am told it was after much pains taken and search made by Order of the Legislature that a spare copy could be obtained for the Use of the person appointed by that Legislature to revise and prepare a general compilation of the laws of the State down to the present time for the purpose of reprinting. And since that period of 1752 the Acts of the respective Sessions were occasionally printed and dispersed that it hath been equally difficult for the same person beforementioned to collect a Set for the purpose aforesaid, for all the original Acts of the State and such printed Copies of them as were in the Rolls Office then kept in New Castle County were Seized upon and taken by a detachment of the british Army which, in September 1777, took possession of the Town of Wilmington, and have not since been regained. But as a Gentleman of this State under a resolve of the Legislature is engaged in preparing a Collection of it's laws for reprinting I flatter myself that it will be in my power in the course of the ensuing year to transmit to you a compleat Set within that time.

Should I obtain further or other information relative to the Creditors or their Agents. And almost the only Suits which have been brought were against persons whose circumstances were declining or against the Representatives of deceased persons but in no instance that hath come to my knowledge hath the least Clamour or Complaint been made or raised against any Man of the law for commencing such Suits or any distinction urged during their pendency in the Courts. As to the American Refugees I do not know that the property of any other of them than specially nam[ed] in the Act of Assembly of this State of the 26th. of June 1778 and transmitted with this, was seized upon and taken as forfeited and several of those persons have returned since the peace and resided without disturbance in the neighbourhood of their former dwellings tho' no instance of any restitution of their property within my knowledge. As to the State it derived no benefit from the Sales of their Estates they being made for Continental paper; and the Court of Claims, which was established sometime after in favour of the Creditors of such whose property had been declared to be forfeited under the Act aforesaid, having allowed the Debts of those creditors in Specie to an amount exceeding the Specie Value of the paper received for that property.

From every information I have heretofore had of alledged infractions of the Treaty I never understood the government in this State or any Executive departments thereof or the Conduct of it's Citizens with regard to British Subjects or American refugees were at any time included and such I am told was the decided opinion of the Legislature of this State at the time of their subject matter of your letter Sir, I shall take the liberty of communicating the same without delay.—I have the honor to be with great respect Sir your most Obedient & very humble Servt.,

GEO: READ JUNR.

RC (PP); slightly mutilated so that a few letters have been lost; endorsed by TJ as received 7 Dec. 1790 and so recorded in SJL; with one pencilled note by TJ (see note below). FC (DNA: RG 59, SDR); at head of text: "No. 15. Extract of a letter from George Read, Junr. . . . to the Secretary of State, dated Newcastle on Delaware Novr. 4. 1790"; text consists of that part indicated in note 1 below and comprises the matter set forth in Appendix No. 15 of TJ's reply to Hammond, 29 May 1792. PrC of Extract (DLC); in another clerk's hand, consisting of text identical with that of FC.

1 Matter within brackets (the first supplied, the last inserted in pencil by TJ together with the following note at this point: "add the conclusion of the letter") comprises the whole of the extract described above in FC and PrC, save the complimentary close and signature.

From Benjamin Vaughan

MY DEAR SIRS   London, Nov. 4 90.

A convention was agreed upon the 24th. ulto. at Madrid, to be signed and exchanged as the 27th: ulto. by which I trust our differences are ended.

France, I think, goes on solidly.

Austria and Prussia have *renewed* their accommodation.— Prince Potemkin is making a winter campaign against the Turks, and no thoughts of peace in that quarter.

We are said to be at *open* war with Tippoo Saib.

By the first ship I shall send a copy of Chalmers's treaties for the use of Mr. Jefferson, and I shall desire Mr. Johnson to send the like for Congress.—It is very superior to others.

Mrs. V. is this moment brought to bed of a girl: Mrs. Darby of a boy 18 hours ago. You will wonder that I end with assurances that I am, my dear sirs, Your respectful & affectionate humble sert,   BENJN. VAUGHAN

RC (DLC); evidently addressed to Vaughan's brother and TJ; endorsed as received 17 Jan. 1791 but not recorded in SJL.

George Chalmers' *Treaties* (London, 1790) was apparently not intended as a gift but as a work to be made available to TJ. A copy was given to him in 1794 by George Joy of London (TJ to Madison, 28 Dec. 1794; Sowerby, No. 1432).

John E. Howard to George Washington

Annapolis, Md., 5 Nov. 1790. Agreeably to the Act of Assembly for regulating elections, he encloses a certificate of the late election of representatives for the state.

RC (DNA: RG 59, MLR); endorsed at foot of text in TJ's hand: "The above certificate was delivered to Mr. Beckley, clerk of the house of representatives by Th: Jefferson." Washington acknowledged Howard's letter and said he had caused the certificate "to be delivered to Mr. Beckley Clerk of the House of Representatives" (Washington to Howard, 21 Dec. 1790; DNA: RG 59, MLR).

From Joshua Johnson

SIR   London 5 November 1790

I had the honor to write you the 3rd. Instant by this conveyance; Yesterday Morning a Messenger arrived from Madrid, with dispatches from Mr. Fitzherbert to the Duke of Leeds, which occasioned the publication of the extraordinary Gazette, inclosed; and which has produced many conjectures. The Effect it has on the Stocks was considerable; they rose 4 ℔ Ct. in the forepart of the day, but declined towards the close of the Market; I have exerted my best endeavors to find out whether, there was any relaxation in the Impress Service and could discover none, tho' it was conjectured that orders were issued in a day, or two, to break up the Rendezvous Houses and Press Gangs. I was informed that the Guards who had been drafted for Foreign Service, and order'd to Portsmouth for embarkation, had received counter orders to join their Regiments. This, I think, carries the appearance of an accomodation more than any thing I see in the extraordinary Gazette. The sudden confutation of the wishes and expectations of numbers has created much discontent and will in all probability draw down on the Ministry the weighty opposition of Army and Navy on the meeting of Parliament. I will be watchfull over the future movements of Government, and transmit you every information worth your attention, being always with the sincerest respect & Esteem Sir, Your most obedt & very humble Servt,

JOSHUA JOHNSON

RC (DNA: RG 59, CD); endorsed by TJ as received 17 Jan. 1791 and so recorded in SJL. Dupl (same); at head of text: "Copy ℔ the New York Packett." Recorded in SJL as received 12 Mch. 1791. FC (same). Enclosure: Copy of *The London Gazette, Extraordinary*, 4 Nov. 1790 (same). On 6 Nov. 1790 James Maury wrote

TJ: "To day's post bringing the Important Intelligence as ℔ the inclosed Handbill, I avail of the first opportunity to communicate it" (RC in DNA: RG 59, CD, endorsed by TJ as received 23 Jan. 1791 and so recorded; the enclosed handbill may have been another copy of *The London Gazette, Extraordinary*, of 4 Nov. 1790).

From Joseph Fenwick

SIR   Bordeaux 6 Novr. 1790.

I have the honor to acknowledge the receipt of your letter of 26 August containing general instructions and advice for the Consuls of the United States which I promise on my part to obey and comply with.

I have only arrived here about three or four weeks and not as yet obtained the Kings Exequator for the exercize of my functions. My Commission is now with Mr. Short at Paris for that purpose.

The last mail from Madrid brings accounts universally credited here, that an arrangement is agreed on by the English Minister, and that Court to preserve peace between the two Countries. No official promulgation of this arrangement has yet reached this place. The hostile preparations of course continue. This port has furnished the Kings docks with 5 or 6000 men say sailors, Rope and sail Makers, Coopers, Carpenters &c. and they are now daily sending off more to Rochfort and Toulon. Yet I am disposed to believe that an accomodation has taken place and that the Marines will be disarmed. I have the honor to be with highest respect Sir Your most Obedient and Most humble Servant,

JOSEPH FENWICK

RC (DNA: RG 59, CD); endorsed by TJ as received 15 Jan. 1791 and so recorded in SJL. Dupl (same).

Jefferson's Deed of Gift of Certain Slaves

Know all men by these presents that I Thomas Jefferson of Albemarle county in Virginia in consideration of the affection I bear to Thomas Mann Randolph the younger and Martha Randolph my daughter, and of the sum of five shillings to me in hand paid, have given and conveyed unto the said Thomas Mann and Martha in full and absolute property the following slaves, to wit, Suck and Philip Evans her child, Scilla and her children Suck, John, Dick and George, and Molly the daughter of Mary, to have the said slaves to their own proper use. In witness whereof I have hereto set my hand and seal and made delivery of the said slaves this sixth day of November one thousand seven hundred and ninety.

TH: JEFFERSON

Signed, sealed and delivered in presence of
  NICHOLAS LEWIS
  J. G. JEFFERSON

MS (ViU); entirely in TJ's hand except for signatures of witnesses.

From Moustier

MONSIEUR   à Paris le 6. novembre 1790

Le Roi ayant jugé à propos de me nommer en qualité de son Ministre Plénipotentiaire à la Cour de Berlin, j'ai reçu l'ordre de Sa Majesté de prendre congé de Mr. Le President des Etats-Unis en lui addressant la lettre par laquelle elle me rappelle de ma mission auprès de ces Etats. J'ai l'honneur de vous prier, Monsieur, de vouloir bien lui remettre ma lettre et de faire valoir auprès de lui l'expression de mon respect et de tous les sentimens que méritent sa dignité et son caractere personnel.

J'ai tout lieu de craindre que Mr. Le Président n'ait pas reçu deux lettres confidentielles que j'ai pris la liberté de lui écrire (conformément à la permission qu'il avoit bien voulu m'en donner), l'une à mon arrivée en France, l'autre quelque tems après. J'ai eu l'honneur de vous écrire, Monsieur, aux mêmes époques. Il m'est pénible de songer à la difficulté de pouvoir suivre ma correspondance avec un pays auquel j'ai voué l'attachement le plus sincère et dont, vû cette difficulté, je ne pourrai plus m'occuper que par des écrits publics et des souvenirs. J'ai taché de prouver que mes sentimens à l'égard des Etats-Unis s'étendoient au delà de simples protestations. Ce ne sont pas toujours ceux qui cajolent le plus et qui font le plus de bruit qui sont les amis les plus sincères et les plus utiles. Si toutes les combinaisons ne s'étoient pas reunies contre mon zèle pour assurer les intérêts reciproques, j'ose me flatter que j'aurois justifié la vérité de cette assertion. Si jamais des circonstances plus heureuses me fournissent l'occasion de prouver mon attachement pour les intérêts des Etats-Unis, je ne la laisserai point certainement échapper. On peut en croire à la parole d'un homme incapable de flatter ceux qui exercent le pouvoir dans quelques mains qu'il soit. Je ne connois que l'ordre et la justice sans acception de personnes. Tel fut mon penchant avant, tel il est pendant, et tel il sera après une révolution. Aucune ne doit influer sur un esprit sain, ni un coeur droit.

Agréez, je vous prie, mes voeux pour vos succès dans la carrière publique que vous parcourez. Je vous renouvelle à vous et à vos concitoïens ce que je vous marquois dans une des lettres que je crains qui ne soient perdues: *Vivit felices quibus est fortuna peracta jam sua. Nos jactamur in alto.*

J'ai l'honneur d'etre avec le plus sincère attachement et la considération la plus distinguée, Monsieur, Votre très humble et très obéissant serviteur   F. DE MOUSTIER

RC (DLC); in clerk's hand except for signature; endorsed by TJ as received 27 Jan. 1791 and so recorded in SJL.

From William Short

DEAR SIR   Paris Nov. 6. 1790.

My last letters to you were of the 21st. and 25th. ulto. by M. St. Triest, 27th. by the English packet, 30th. and 2d. inst. by the way of London. This last was merely to inform you that the English messenger had passed through this place, and brought despatches as well to the Spanish as English Ambassador which decided that peace would not be interrupted between those two powers. Since then nothing further is known officially, but the articles of pacification are expected daily.—It is useless to mention that the papers contained in your letter of Aug. 10. will not be shewn to M. de F.—I have said to Count D'E. what was necessary, in the manner you desired. He is fully satisfied and says he is sure something like it must happen as soon as one of the three parties shall be sufficiently enlightened to see its own interests.

I have only had a few words of conversation with the Spanish Ambassador alone, since that mentioned formerly. I was in hopes that accident would throw us together tête à tête, which I thought would be better than to have the air of seeking it.—We were again interrupted after a few words had passed in which he told me that he had been told that there was an American at London *qui intriguoit beaucoup.* I told him it was probably Miranda [to whom he alluded. He said no, that he knew Miranda, that the person he meant was a Colonel, and an American of the U.S., that he had been told his name but that he had forgotten it. He added also that he had been a long time in London. I thought then it was Miranda, whom his informant had mistaken for an American of the U.S. as he frequently gave himself for such in other parts of Europe, and I still think it more applicable to him than any other person in London. I know not what change the peace will make, but I think that if a war had taken place, the Spanish Ambassador here, who has much influence, as it is supposed, at Madrid, would have listened without much difficulty to arrangements in the nature of those you speak of in your letter to Mr. C. Even as it is, I should suppose it not amiss to have the idea set agoing by the French court by way of experiment. Should you approve of this it would be well to give instructions respecting it without loss of time. This is the most favorable moment that will probably ever occur at Paris. 1. Because M. de Montmorin who will probably remain and is talked of as prime minister, is well acquainted with the Spanish court. 2. Because he is not only personally attached to M. de la fayette, but knowing that he owes the preservation of his place to him, is fully disposed to enter into all his views. 3. Because more confidence can be had in M. de la fayette than any other person in this business; so that by his means it might be ascertained to what length the court of Madrid could be induced to go, and that without the U.S. committing themselves at all. 4. Because it is very possible that under another administration][1] our views might be thwarted instead of being promoted by this country.

No other change in the ministry has taken place since the resignation of M. de la Luzerne. It is known however that they are to go out, and that they have remained thus long only because no choice is yet made of their successors. The Marquis de la fayette desires to make M. de Montmorin prime Minister and to bring in very unknown and subordinate characters for the departments, under the idea that their being commoners will give more pleasure to the nation. In this however I fear he will be mistaken. For although they are here perfectly reconciled to the idea of pulling down all those who were considered as being elevated either by birth or by places, yet I do not believe they would see without envy inferior people placed in elevated stations. This business is now negociating between M. de la fayette, Montmorin and the court.

The rapporteur of the domanial committee tells me that he had proposed to explain the decree so as to extend the abolition of the *droits d'Aubaine* to the islands, that the committee were unanimously for it as it had been always their intention and had authorized him to report it to the assembly. I advised him to use the term *all the foreign possessions of France*; so as to express more fully their idea and to leave no ground for fiscal abuse, which he has determined to do, and intends making this report the first moment that an opportunity offers. He is sure of carrying it without any kind of opposition, as he tells me.

I intended to have set out for Amsterdam three days ago and was ready, but I have been detained until now by the pressing sollicitations of the Marquis de la fayette who insisted that I should meet a committee at his house, of several members of the assembly on the subject of our commerce. He himself is so totally absorbed by the functions of his place that I thought it advisable not to lose that opportunity of conferring with several of the leading members of the assembly collected for the purpose, and particularly as the subjects of tobacco and oil are to be treated by them in a very short time. This committee assembled yesterday evening and I had the pleasure to observe that they came by degrees to acknowlege the importance of keeping up their commercial connexions with the United States, not only because they were advantageous in themselves, but because their political connexions depended on them.

[15]

You will be surprized perhaps to find that bringing them to this point is considered as something gained; but you can have no idea of the preventions which exist in the assembly against the commerce of the U.S. It proceeds from several causes, of which however the principal is that those who are listened to on commercial matters being the deputies of the trading towns who are merchants, have either suffered themselves mediately or immediately, or been witnesses of those who have suffered in their commercial speculations with America. Another reason also is that these same persons see with an evil eye whatever regards the commerce of a people that they fear will sooner or later, lawfully or unlawfully take from them a part of their profits in the West India trade of which they consider the monopoly as their birthright. You may add to this their idea of our preference in favor of every thing English which induces us as they say, to take bills of exchange on London for the articles we sell in their ports, so that all sacrifices made to encourage our commerce become a pure loss. They say that the returns of the balance of commerce shew that this preference augments; since in 1782, the balance in favor of France with the U.S. was 10,531,000.[tt] and in 1788, the balance on the contrary was in favor of the Americans 4,84,400.[tt] I classed their several observations and answered them in a manner which satisfied several. I will not repeat to you all the details here. The outlines were that altho a sudden peace, arriving on speculations made for war, might have injured all the merchants engaged in it, that although French Merchants adventuring their capital imprudently in a commerce with which they were entirely unacquainted, or confiding it to persons unworthy of the trust, might have suffered by it, yet that did not change the nature of things and that certainly commerce with a nation that furnished raw materials and took in return those which were manufactured must be advantageous—that France could furnish many of the manufactures of which we had occasion on as good terms as England, and that her wines and brandies were sure of a market with us and that our numbers were increasing rapidly so that the market would be increased in the same proportion—that the balance of commerce appeared so much against France because our productions were brought into her ports as well by English as American vessels and the former, being on account of English houses, it suited them best to take bills on that country, or were laden with articles of exportation which entered into their balance with England; of this the last year furnished abundant proof, besides that the balance of commerce was not always a sure guide by which to judge of the advantages of commerce. I instanced the article of tobacco and supposed that if the U.S. should have sent to France for the value of eight millions annually without taking any thing but cash in return, yet if this tobacco was converted in France into a revenue of thirty millions, or was re-exported to other countries so as to produce a greater value than the eight millions, it could not be considered as a losing trade although by the rule of the balance of commerce it would appear so. The same was applicable to the other articles of exportation from the U.S. as being aliment either for the inhabitants or manufactures of France.

Their prejudices with respect to the American commerce in general removed, there still remained the difficulties with respect to the systems of the two committees relative to tobacco and whale oils, by which the one was much diminished in its consumption and still kept under a monopoly and the other prohibited altogether. —I have frequently spoken to you of the plan of the committee respecting tobacco. As soon as the report was made to the assembly there seemed little doubt of its passing for the reasons which I formerly mentioned. In order to induce the assembly however to examine this question I prevailed on Count De Moustier to publish the pamphlet which I inclose you, and to add his name to it, as among the multitude of writings which appear here daily few of those which are anonymous are attended to. I made very full notes on the subject also, and treated it in a different point of view, and had them translated and by the Marquis de la Fayette's desire converted into a speech, which he is to deliver as his own in the assembly, or put into the hands of some one of his friends if he thinks it will produce a better effect.

The plan of the committee is there combated because 1. it preserves the expense and abuse of an administration by *regie*. 2. the *regie* would send specie out of the country to purchase the tobacco. 3. it was an injustice to those parts of France which could not cultivate tobacco, as there would naturally be a tendence both in the provinces that cultivate it, and in the *regie* to keep up the price as high as possible. 4. the tobacco being free once it had passed the frontiers, and the price at which the committee supposed it would be sold, being from 40 to 48 sous the pound, it would be impossible to prevent smuggling, with so great an inducement to it and so little means of pursuing and detecting it. Thus the revenue would necessarily be much diminished and be always uncertain, whilst the expence of the *regie* would continue the same.

[17]

5. although the assembly may suppose that under the principles of the present constitution they cannot *prohibit* the cultivation of tobacco, or cannot reconcile the prohibition with the abolition of the barriers and the privileges of Alsace and Lorraine, yet it is impolitic to *invite* to this cultivation by a monopoly on foreign tobacco, as it is known that it exhausts the soil and requires more manure than any other, and will necessarily diminish the quantity of productions essential to the subsistance of the people.

In lieu of the plan of the committee it was proposed to admit the free importation of foreign tobacco subject only to such a duty on entering the Kingdom as would not endanger smuggling and after that put on the footing of home made tobacco, and if judged proper, subjected with it, to an excise. As this latter mode of taxation however was proscribed by the assembly it was supposed that only the duty on entry would be adopted. Estimating this at five sous a pound, it was thought it would at that rate prevent the cultivation in France, and of course the consumption remaining as heretofore, would produce on 23,400,000. pounds, a revenue of 5,850,000.[tt] This being free of the uncertainty and expence of the revenue promised by the *regie* was thought preferable to it, and particularly as it would probably augment; the diminution in the price tending naturally to an augmentation in the quantity consumed. Tobacco being brought to France by merchants it became their interest to take in return such articles of French manufacture and productions as suited them. The American taste would thus become accustomed to them and whilst it held out a new debouché for the manufactures of this country it prevented the exportation of specie to purchase American tobacco. This being the most considerable article of American commerce, if admitted freely into France, would draw after it other branches of that commerce, as the accessory naturally adheres to the principal.

Another plan proposed at the same time with less hopes however of success at present, although time would probably demonstrate its propriety, was to abandon altogether the idea of revenue on tobacco and to admit it free of duty, in order to secure greater advantages in another way. In support of this the following considerations were submitted. 1. There are exported annually from the U.S. 100,000,000 pounds of tobacco. These are carried almost wholly to G. Britain in the first instance, from ten to twelve millions of pounds are consumed there and the rest re-exported to foreign markets. The original value of the whole of this tobacco

may be estimated at 24,000,000.⋕ The freight of tobacco is supposed to be somewhat less than ⅓ of its value—say 7,800,000.⋕
The English have about ⅔ of the freight of our exportations to
Europe. Their proportion then of the freight of tobacco would be
5,200,000.⋕ This added to the original value makes 29,200,000.⋕
2. The article is paid for in the manufactures of England, and
thus becomes an aliment to them, and at the same time increases
the number of their sailors. 3. It also produces a revenue of
15,000,000.⋕ for the public treasury, which is more in proportion
to the number of inhabitants in England than it yielded in France
under the monopoly. 4. The manufacture of tobacco is acknowleged
to be superior in France to what it is in England.

On these data it appeared that if American tobacco should be
admitted here free of duty, the consequences would be as follow.
1. All the tobacco which now goes to England would come to
France in the first instance, because there is an high duty in the
one case and none in the other. 2. France would supply foreign
markets instead of England, notwithstanding the drawbacks there
allowed, because her manufacture is allowed to be superior. 3. This
aliment to the manufactures of England, which are both the rival
and destruction of those of France, would not only be taken from
them, but applied to vivify the agriculture and manufactures of
France, because the importation would be paid for either in their
immediate productions, or such as commerce should have brought
to France for that purpose. 4. The number of sailors necessary for
the transportation of this article (or ⅔ of them, being the English
proportion of them) might not only be taken from the English
marine, but added to that of France, as it would be easy to regulate
that it should be brought only in French or American bottoms.
5. The English would be deprived by this means of a considerable
part of their revenue on this article also, because every port in
France would then, as Dunkirk now, be tempted to smuggle it
into England. If France renounces the idea of revenue on tobacco
it is something gained without doubt to take it also from her rival.
6. The nation which has the importation of the whole or much
the greater part of the American tobacco, will have great advantages also in drawing after it the other articles of American commerce, as they are necessarily more or less connected with each
other. Hence the probability of rescuing the rising commerce of
the U.S. from the hands of a rival and of concentrating it in France.
Hence also advantages of a political nature which as they regard
the U.S. must necessarily depend on commercial connexions in a

very great degree.—It may be now asked if the promise of an uncertain revenue of 12. millions, with the preservation of a regie and the inconveniences abovementioned, is to be perferred to the advantages resulting from an admission of foreign tobacco free of duty?

These are the principal arguments which I have used on the subject of tobacco. They have been perfectly satisfactory to M. de Montmorin, who would immediately adopt the free system if it depended on him. I cannot say what effect they will have in the assembly when delivered there. The deputies extraordinary of commerce, who approved in the beginning the plan of the committee on this article, have since been brought over to the system of a duty on the entry. I send you inclosed an address they have distributed to the members of the assembly to-day on the subject. Some of their bases as you will see, are not the same which, I have adopted. They chose to exaggerate them, as they told me, in hopes of having more weight with the assembly, who would be too ignorant or too much employed to prove the contrary. This was their mode and therefore I had no objection to make to it. If the assembly adopt the principle, they may be induced to lower the duty to five sous the pound, as most of the members are of opinion that an higher duty cannot be collected without too great a temptation to smuggling.—The idea of Ships of 200. tons is altogether theirs. It will be more difficult to induce them to change it. I shall desire M. de la fayette however to try it fully as it is evident that we have a great interest in having the size of the ships reduced as much as possible.

The subject of oil was discussed also at the Marquis de la fayette's, in general terms. I had previously made notes likewise on that subject to be used in the assembly. This letter becomes too long to go into details. The outlines are 1. that by excluding the American oils a means of exchange between the two countries is taken away.—2. If that commerce were encouraged and confined to American and French bottoms it would be a better nursery of seamen than the whale fishery.—3. The *cabotage* of France is now in the hands of foreigners. If the same encouragement were given to it as to the whale fishery it would produce many more sailors and until France has a superabundance for that business, it is impolitic to use her resources in raising them at a distance, as they cost dearer, and are more exposed to be cut off by an enemy at the beginning of a war.—4. At present, a premium of 50.^{tt} a ton is allowed on vessels fitted out in France for the whale fishery. A duty of 10.^{tt} 15' a barrel is levied on the American oils. The freight, insurance and commission on oils sent from the U.S. to America may be estimated at 63.^{tt} a ton. Most of the articles for fitting out a vessel on the whale business cost the American fisherman dearer than it does the French. If these advantages are not sufficient to support the fishery in France it may be averred that it is impolitic to try it.—The Nantucket fishermen settled in France say they are not sufficient and have induced the committee to exclude American oils. They ground their petition on the *arret du Conseil* of 87 which admitted them being repealed in 88, and revived only *provisoirement* by the influence of M. de la fayette, until the national fishery should suffice. They say that it now suffices as they have large quantities of oil on hand unsold. As they had hopes however of getting the American oils excluded for some time past, they would naturally have held up their oils for a better price, so that the large quantities they say they have on hand, prove nothing.—5. Although vegetable oils may be a kind of check, as is pretended, to prevent the whale-oils getting beyond a certain price, yet the American oils being excluded, and this supply confined to a few houses at Dunkirk and L'Orient will certainly raise the price, whilst every thing should be done, on the contrary to render this article, so essential to a variety of purposes, as abundant as possible.—5. [i.e., 6] It is hoped that numbers of the Nantucket fishermen if deprived of a market for their oils will be brought to France. A greater number would certainly go to England and the English possessions in America, and of course the relative difference between the number of sailors in the two countries will become more considerable than at present. 6. [i.e., 7] The English now admit American oils on American as well as English bottoms. This comparison will produce unquestionably an evil impression on the minds of the Eastern fishermen in America. Their interests will thus become common with the English fishermen and opposed to those of the French.—All the arguments above apply equally to the admission of the American Codfish with low duties and besides, being an article of subsistance, it should be encouraged as much as possible for the advantages of population and manufactures, which in all countries depend on the low price of food.

As the committee seemed to listen with attention to these ideas, and insisted on a second meeting tomorrow evening at which a greater number of members should be assembled, I have agreed to stay, supposing it more important to make use of this opportunity of obtaining advantages for the American commerce if possible, than to arrive two days sooner at Amsterdam.

I have had already some conversations with some of the members of the committee of commerce. They had raised the duties on American salted meats, as I mentioned to you in my No. 44. to 10.^{tt} They have agreed now as you will see by the papers inclosed, which they have communicated to me, to reduce it to 5.^{tt} This is too high but they will not consent to a lower duty. Salted meats brought to France to be re-exported to their islands or elsewhere, do not pay any duty, and this has been the law as they tell me ever since the year 48.

I mentioned to you in a former letter that it would not be possible to keep it long a secret that the million and an half of florins were at my disposal, as it had been communicated to Mr. J. Van Staphorst at this place. He immediately informed Swann and Le Coulteux of it, I believe rather inadvertently than with an evil intention, although he had been desired by his house not to mention it. Besides the letters from Amsterdam on this subject had been sent through the post, and those from the Secretary of the treasury to me had been sent through the hands of M. de Montmorin. Under these circumstances I have thought it best to mention to him that the money would be paid as soon as it could be remitted from Amsterdam. I mentioned to him at the same time what you desired in your letter of Aug. 26. with which he seemed perfectly satisfied. I modified however what related to our efforts and to the colonies because this did not appear the proper time for it.—I hope my making this communication to M. de Montmorin at present under the present circumstances, instead of waiting until the subject of the colonies shall be taken up, will be approved by you. And particularly as it being known previously to him in all probability by means of the post, and certainly to Le Coulteux and Swann by means of V. Staphorst, and by their means to the committee of finance, an attempt to keep it secret to be used occasionally would have been vain.

I have written therefore to the bankers to take measures for obtaining gradually the bills necessary for this remittance. As so large a number could not be obtained all at once, and if not obtained before it were known publicly that such a remittance were to be made, would be purchased at a less advantageous exchange. I have preferred the mode of remittance because more advantageous than by draughts from this place, and more convenient.

I do not know whether Le Coulteux and Swann are going on

with their speculation with the committee of finance. If any contract is made with them by government at present it will be at least with a knowlege of the present situation of our debt. The propositions which they intended making and which I believe they had been assured of passing in the committee of finance and liquidation was to pay half a million a month in French *effects* now due, to the full amount of the whole American debt. Their profit was to arise on their purchasing these effects now below *par.* The advantage they held out to government was that by this means the whole American debt would be liquidated at fixed and certain periods and in a much shorter time than the terms at present existing.

I have had a second conversation with M. de Montmorin and one also with Rayneval on the subject of the consular convention. They are both decided in their interpretation of it. They say the word *Etats du Roi* mean strictly *la France*, and that this is proved by an infinity of treaties. I observed to them what you mentioned concerning the word *France* being changed, and your objecting to it in your correspondence. Montmorin persisted in saying that no *exequatur* could be given—Reyneval, that no correspondence could be adverted to, as the act itself must explain itself. We did not satisfy each other on that score. I mentioned the use that a consul might be of in the islands in preventing differences, or at least giving a true account of them, whereas our citizens interested would naturally be induced to exaggerate them and produce disagreeable effects in the U.S.

They observed that any merchant of confidence, settled there, and represented to this government as such, would be countenanced and might answer the same end, whereas if we had a *Consul* it would bring them into difficulties with Spain. They added that they were sure that the U.S. would not reduce them to the disagreeable necessity of refusing a demand, which would certainly be the case if they persisted in desiring a consular establishment in the islands.—They observed however that the time to speak further of this would be, if an *exequatur* should be asked for the consul appointed to Martinique. I did not bring on this conversation and of course was willing not to push it, particularly as I am persuaded this would produce a bad effect in the assembly at present, where as I have mentioned, there is much ill humour against their islands, and much jealousy of us with respect to them.

I am very well acquainted here with some of the principal

proprietors in the islands, and several of the deputies also. They do not need urging respecting the provision business. They have hopes of succeeding ultimately, but they know it will not be willingly on the part of this country, and particularly as long as the circumstances remain as at present. The merchants of Bordeaux, the deputies in the assembly from all the commercial towns, as well as the provinces in which they are, have been all forward in the revolution. They are therefore indulged at present, and no inducement could engage the leading members of the assembly to displease them although many of them acknowlege the justice and policy of allowing the islands to victual themselves on the best terms possible. They told me at the time war was expected, that they were sure of obtaining an admission of neutral vessels into the islands during the war, and they have no doubt as soon as the revolution is considered as completed here, viz. in the next legislature, of obtaining many commercial privileges that would be now refused, such as that of procuring provisions, and slaves by foreign commerce.

I inclose you a letter from one of the American captives at Algiers, and also a paper respecting them which Cathalan desires me to communicate to you. I do not answer the letters I receive from Algiers as it might be a means of injuring the prisoners in inducing a belief of a desire to ransom them, which would necessarily excite the avarice of the regency. I see no hopes of any thing being done by the Mathurins, and I have no knowlege of the attempt to ransom them mentioned in the letter.

You will receive inclosed also a memorial by M. de Calonne, and also one by the Duke of Orleans. They are both much read. It is reported that M. de Calonne has left England and is gone to join the Count D'Artois at Turin. I send you also various reports made by the committees of the assembly. And a packet sent here to your address I dont know by whom. I have the honor to be with sentiments of the most sincere attachment, Dear Sir, your obedient humble servant,   W SHORT

Nov. 7. P.S. I have learned this morning that the messenger has passed through Paris with the articles of pacification signed at Madrid. M. de Montmorin told a person from whom I have it that the principals were that the English should have a right to form an establishment any where to the north of Nootka, where the Spaniards had never had one, that they should enjoy the whale fishery in those seas and should be allowed to build *des cabanes*, (but not form an establishment) on the coasts of the Spanish possessions. This pacification gives great pleasure here, and they are now waiting with much anxiety for the arrival of a messenger who shall bring an account of their disarming in England. They have some difficulty in believing that Mr. Pitt after such heavy expences, will be satisfied with what appears to them so trifling a consideration.

PrC (DLC: Short Papers); at head of text: "No. 46." FC (DNA: RG 59, DD). Recorded in SJL as received 18 Mch. 1791. Text of Cathalan's letter to Short, dated at Marseilles 14 Oct. 1790 and enclosed in the above, is in DNA: RG 59, DD.

The COLONEL engaged in intrigues in London was William A. Bowles

(see Humphreys to TJ, 4 Nov. 1790).

[1] The passage in brackets (supplied) comprises the second page of the letter, to which TJ called Washington's attention in forwarding the entire letter (TJ to Washington, 18 Mch. 1791). See also TJ to Short, 19 Mch. 1791.

From Thomas Auldjo

SIR   Cowes 7 Novr 1790

I had the honour to write to you 4th instant to which I beg leave to refer you. Since then I have received the paper inclosed from Mr. Aust which I beg to submit to your Consideration. I have not received any answer to my letter to the Duke of Leeds, therefore I conclude that they consider the note from Mr. Aust a reply to it. They say that if my appointment was for the Port of Poole and places adjacent I should be received and that Cowes being within my district I might act here as Consul. Poole is the next port to the Westward of this and distant only 25 miles. If the Honble. the President should be pleased to honour me with a new Commission for the Port of Poole &c. I shall be happy to receive it and I could then serve the United States with Effect, the approbation of the King being essentially necessary to procure me proper attention to my applications to Kings Officers and official people on behalf of American Subjects.

In consideration I think it best to keep my present Commission till I am honoured with your Commands which I beg the favor of receiving as early as possible. I have the honor to be with great respect Sir Your most obedient & most humble Servant,

THOMAS AULDJO

RC (DNA: RG 59, CD); endorsed by TJ as received 17 Jan. 1791 and so recorded in SJL. Enclosure: George

Aust to James Mackenzie, Whitehall, 30 Oct. 1790, returning Auldjo's commission as being "objected to, not from any Reason Affecting Mr. Auldjo personally, but from such as would naturally apply to a Commission from any other Power, at that port; but that there would be no Objection to his Appointment to the Ports of Poole, Dartmouth or Falmouth" (RC in same).

To Martha Jefferson Carr

DEAR SISTER   Monticello Nov. 7. 1790.

That you may have no uneasiness from what you will hear from Peter, I will mention to you that a worthless fellow, named Rind, wrote a libel on the inhabitants of Charlottesville and neighborhood, which P. Carr and G. Jefferson were imprudent enough to suffer him to communicate to them. Rind then pasted it up in Charlottesville, and from expressions of his, the suspicions were directed on all three. Peter has I believe satisfied every body that he was innocent, and has taken proper notice of the much more scurrilous peice written against the three. The matter is over as to him. But not as to G. Jefferson. He leaves the neighborhood therefore, and I wish him to be boarded in yours, that he may be convenient to the books he is to read. If you and the boys can find a good place for him I will be obliged to you. Let it be at a reasonable rate, distant from public places, and rather distant from you: for if the account my neighbors give of him be true, the less he is with your family the safer their reputations will be. Therefore the sooner he is placed elsewhere, the better. Do not let it be delayed. I know nothing of him myself, but feel myself bound to convey to you the opinions of those who do know him. Mr. Lewis will pay his board regularly once a year.

Doctr. Walker's account against Mr. Carr will be about £30. principal. The interest may run it up to £50. As soon as Peter gets it settled, Mr. Lewis will pay it, as well as any other pressing calls you may have; for I shall still owe the estate. How does your consumption? Adieu my dear sister Yours affectionately,

TH: JEFFERSON

PrC (CSmH).

Neither the LIBEL ON THE INHABITANTS OF CHARLOTTESVILLE nor the piece written against Rind, Carr, and Garland Jefferson has been found.

RIND was probably James Rind, son of the Williamsburg printer, who was a lawyer and a duellist in Richmond between 1792 and 1804. He was known as "a clever letter writer" (communication from F. L. Berkeley, Jr., to the Editors; L. G. Tyler, *Encyclopedia of Virginia biography*, I, 313; II, 255-6). For the sequel to this episode, see Garland Jefferson to TJ, 12 Nov. 1790 and 26 Feb. 1791; TJ to Garland Jefferson, 5 Feb. 1791.

To Andrew Donald

SIR   Monticello Nov. 7. 1790.

I recieved at New York your account, but could not do any thing in it till I could come here, and have recourse to my papers. I find the balance of £27-3-9 due, which I have desired Colo. Nichs. Lewis, who takes care of my affairs, to pay you with interest from the 19th. of April 1783. This will be done as soon as money, for which judgments have been already obtained, can be collected. We hope it will be in the course of this year. Of this he will be better able to inform you hereafter. I am Sir Your very humble servt,

TH: JEFFERSON

PrC (MHi); at foot of text: "Mr. Andrew Donald at Ozborne's." PrC from another MS (CSmH).

From George Gilmer

DR SR   7 Novr 1790 Pen Park

A Call to Amherst with a wish of Col. Nicholas that I should not be out of the way the knowing woman being new with his Lady may prevent my once more being in company with you and Mr. Madison. It hurts me to intrude a long letter from Lambert to you and ask you if it would be elgible to do any thing with our present Assembly to secure what's in our treasury of Harmers Estate having had such an object in view but like not the complexion of the Assembly. When at leizure will you direct me what's best to be offered and what inter[est?] Lambert may build on. Should I not see you let me beg to hear from you may still overtake you before you get beyond Madison. May bliss attend you. Adieu.

GEO GILMER

P.S. Billy will bring back Lamberts letter.

G G

RC (MHi); endorsed by TJ as received 7 Nov. 1790 and so recorded in SJL. Enclosure not found, but for TJ's previous correspondence on the subject, see Gilmer to TJ, 23 Dec. 1787, and TJ to Gilmer, 16 Dec. 1788.

To George Gilmer

DEAR DOCTOR   Monticello Nov. 7. 1790.

I do not sufficiently recollect the case of Mr. Harmer's will to venture any opinion. When I arrive at Philadelphia I hope to find there my papers arrived from Paris, among which is your letter stating the case. I will there revise it, and write you what I think of it. I will confer with Madison on it also. Perhaps he will be able to give me a sight of the act of assembly respecting it. I wish more than I expect to fall in with you on the road tomorrow. Present me affectionately to Mrs. Gilmer. Yours sincerely,

TH: JEFFERSON

PrC (MHi).

To John Hanson

DEAR SIR   Monticello Nov. 7. 1790.

Having visited my estate with a view to settle the affairs of the year, and being now on my departure, I presume it will be desireable to you to know, as it was to myself, the prospect of making my stipulated payment of the ensuing year. The wheat and other small resource of the estate, with the outstanding debts, are found somewhat more than sufficient to pay every existing demand against me, excepting the two to Jones, and Kippen & co. They are therefore so appropriated, and the whole of the tobacco is left clear for these two demands. As nearly as can be estimated safely in the present state of the crop, my part will be about 69,000 ℔. with which £700. sterl. is to be paid. I leave directions with Colo. Nicholas Lewis, who takes care of my affairs, if 20/ sterl. can be got, to sell it in the country: otherwise to sell the 14,000 ℔ of it which is injured by firing, for what it will fetch, and to ship the residue to James Maury of Liverpool. If it is sold in the country, the proceeds shall be paid in the country: if in Britain, they shall be paid in Britain by order on Maury (not by bill of exchange). This I think the best possible arrangement for us all, for in this our interest is the same. I shall write you further at some future time, and am Dr. Sir your most obedt. hble servt,

TH: JEFFERSON

P.S. I wish you would take the whole, or your part @ 20/ sterling. If your part only, the qualities should be exactly proportioned.

[28]

PrC (MHi).

On the same date TJ wrote to James Lyle an identical letter: its PrC (CSmH) bears the following note in TJ's hand, obviously written after the press copy was executed: "To Mr. Lyle. Illegible. But verbatim the same with the letter to Hanson." The letter to Lyle, however, lacked the postscript that appears in the letter to Hanson (and the press copy, though faded, is far from being illegible).

Memorandum for Nicholas Lewis

[ca. 7 Nov. 1790]

Mr. Randolph and my daughters being to remain at Monticello, are to be furnished with whatever the plantations will furnish, to wit, corn, fodder, wheat, what beeves there may be, shoats, milch cows, fire-wood to be cut by the plantation negroes, and brought in by the mule-cart or ox-cart.

Tom or Phill to go to mill for the house as usual. They are to have also the use of the house-servants, to wit, Ursula, Critta, Sally, Bet, Wormeley and Joe. So also of Betty Hemings, should her services be necessary. To be always cloathed and fed by me.

A wash house 16. feet square to be built and placed where I pointed out to George.

Two meat-houses to be made, about the same size each, 12 feet apart and a cover over the whole: one of them for me, the other for Mr. Randolph and the passage between, for their dairy. All these to be of logs covered with clapboards.

A stable to be built on the same plan with the meat-house, the rooms 14. by 16. The passage the same, of logs, below the gate where I have pointed out to George.

The fences which inclose the house, garden and orchard to be well repaired with chesnut rails, and a partition fence run between the yard and garden as formerly.

MS (DLC); unsigned and undated, entirely in TJ's hand; at head of text: "Extracts from the memorandums I leave with Mr. Lewis." TJ probably made this extract from his general instructions to Nicholas Lewis for the use of Martha or Thomas Mann Randolph, Jr.

To James Monroe

DEAR SIR   Monticello Nov. 7. 1790.

Being just on the wing I have only time to acknowledge the reciept of your favors of the 20th. and 22d. and to express a hope of seeing yourself and Mrs. Monroe at Philadelphia where you are wanting. In the event of your election, I beg you to make me useful to you. Will you trust me to search[1] lodgings for you at which you may alight, Mrs. House's for instance, or in any other quarter you may alike?[2] Pray command me, being with great respect and attachment to Mrs. Monroe & yourself my dear Sir Your affectionate friend & servt.,

TH: JEFFERSON

RC (NN). PrC (MHi).

[1] TJ first wrote "find" and then, remembering the housing situation in

Philadelphia, altered the passage to read as above.

[2] Thus in MS.

From William Short

DEAR SIR   Paris Nov. 7. 1790

This letter accompanies my No. 46. and will be delivered to you with the several papers therein mentioned by M. Louis Ormont. He is a young man that Madame D'Houdetot insists on my recommending to what she calls your protection, viz. your counsel's advice. Notwithstanding I have on all occasions avoided sending you these kind of recommendations, yet I think you will easily see Sir that it would have been impossible to have refused Mde. D'Houdetot, and will therefore excuse me for it. His object is to go and settle in America, and serve an apprenticeship to commerce. His family is injured in their fortune, probably ruined, by the present revolution, and his father sends him therefore to the U.S. in hopes of his being soon able to provide for himself. He is well educated and above all well disposed. Mde. D'Houdetot assures me *qu'il est un jeune homme unique par sa sagesse.* I have told him however freely that my letter to you would be of much less service probably than he might imagine. That it was entirely out of your line to give him instructions respecting commerce, and also that your occupations left you no time for particular attentions. But these things substracted I did not doubt you would give him such advice and such countenance as might be in your power.—He carries letters from Le Coulteux to Mr. Morris, which he has hopes of being useful to him in his way. He has letters also from Mr. Crevecoeur and by his advice adopts his family name of Louis Ormont instead of *de la Pouillaude* which he has hitherto borne. He has from him also a good deal of written advice which I hope will be useful to him. He has made an unfortunate beginning in purchasing land of a M. Tonnelier in the country of the Oneidas. Tonnelier has since I believe, eloped from Paris, so that those to whom he sold suppose it an imposture.

I send you inclosed also my accounts with you. One is for expences in packing up your furniture and sending it to Havre, and others included in Petits account. By your order I drew on Amsterdam for this money and therefore that account as you will see is balanced. Its vouchers are Petits account of which I inclose you a copy with remarks, and also copies of the accounts of the most considerable contained in it, such as Arthurs, Piebots, &c. The originals with the reciepts remain in my hands as my vouchers. The account of the *emballeur* amounting to six thousand and odd livres after being *reglé* remains also in my hands for the same reason. I sent a list of the articles formerly but do not recollect whether the prices were annexed. In the doubt I have sent to have a copy taken of this account to be sent to you, I hope to recieve it before my letter is finished. If not, it shall be sent by another opportunity.

My other account with you as you will see is still open. It is for your servant's wages. The medal boxes made for Congress by your order as I then expected your return I thought it best that I should charge them to you as you had an account already open with Congress for them. If however you chuse that they should now enter into my account with Congress it might be done. I have not yet drawn on Amsterdam to be re-imbursed this account. However I have given notice some time ago to the bankers that I should draw for it. I then only waited until I had finally discharged de la Motte's account, and sold your horses and other things here. Your horses are at length sold but with a loss of which I had no idea. I had them put in the petites affiches and they were in perfect order, yet I have been only able to get 18. Louis for them. I could find no body to take them for their food, or I should not have thought myself warranted to take that price for them, particularly as I had been offered more on a former occasion, and did not sell them then because I thought them worth much more and still think so. I am offered so little for my cabriolet house that I hastened to leave him with my *Sellier*, who offers to take him for his food. I fear he will suffer in his hands, but it seems better than to give him for nothing.—This is a most unfortunate period for selling here, owing to the total ruin of immense numbers of people by the changes which have taken place. There are outcrys every day where all sorts of effects are purchased for almost nothing. All the papers also are filled with advertisements which gives a list of effects to be sold in the different magasines with the former cost and present prices. It is alarming and I fear will produce much disorder here ere long. It is to be observed that amongst these sufferers are for the most part the Bourgeois of Paris who have contributed much to the revolution, and hitherto to the preservation of peace and order here.

I spoke to Mazzei about your account. He does not seem much disposed to settle it in the manner mentioned. He insists it was your intention to settle it otherwise viz. to take money in America for it. I observed to him the uncertainty of that business which he could not doubt of. I mentioned the Abbe Morellets affair about the maps, and that your affairs had cost much more for packing &c. than had been expected. He promises to speak to the Abbe Morellet on this business. He is much more ready to engage others to pay than to pay himself, and if any thing can be done with the Abbé Morellets bookseller he will do it. As soon as I see that nothing can be done however which I apprehend, I will mention this matter again to Mazzei and get him to settle his own account one way or another.

Houdon is having the dress that you desired, made. I hoped to have sent it to you by this occasion but it is not ready. The Marquis de la fayettes picture is begun and will be sent to Havre as soon as finished. Your watch is now in the hands of Chanterot, and he says it will take eight days to finish it, and for greater security he would wish to keep it some time after its being finished, to try it. I am very sorry not to have recovered it in time to have been able to have sent it by this opportunity.

M. Morris has lately arrived here from England by the way of Brussels, Liege &c. He tells me that a letter which he has recieved from America says 'it is supposed here that Mr. Jefferson supports Madison warmly for Paris.' He supposes therefore that the plan is to make no appointment until Madison's time shall have expired, as there might be some doubt whether he was eligible at present, then to send him here and to keep me Chargé des affaires in Holland. Until this delay took place he was persuaded I should be appointed for Paris, as he says. This delay induces him to believe that I shall not. His inference from the delay is therefore directly the contrary to mine. I had supposed the delay and my being sent to Holland rendered it much more probable that I should be named for Paris. The trust reposed in me at present if I perform well, and the time I have already remained in Paris seemed to me arguments in my favor, and particularly as the being kept here merely because another could not be sent would have the air of being a *bouche-trou*, that would be deemed little flattering. The business to be executed in Amsterdam being of all others the most disagreeable and dangerous also when confided to one person alone, if he who is charged with it has the appearance of not having the approbation of those who employ him, it is no ground for public censure. Morris has placed these considerations very strongly before me in telling me, what I did not know, that even Mr. A. had been censured by some, though he had given no ground at all for it. This makes me wish still more that a second person had been joined with me in this business. Mr. Morris gives me to understand, or tells me indeed that he has taken care to inform his friends at N. York that he did not chuse to be employed in it.—Be this as it may, I will exert myself for the best, and I cannot conceal to myself that I have now more hopes of being named for Paris than formerly, not only from considerations which relate to myself, but because I think Madison can render much more service in America than here. It is certain let who will come, unless he has been here before he will find himself for a long time quite *depaysé*, and have to learn what no talents can supply the place of. I never have mentioned to you, because I thought it then useless, that M. de Montmorin has more than once expressed to me his desire that I should be named and his persuasion that it would be so, as you would necessarily have it in your power. This is also so fully the persuasion of the corps diplomatique, that when I express my doubts they suppose it merely a *façon de parler*. Should it be thought proper however for reasons unknown to me to send another person here, and a minister should be sent to London, I should like much to go there, though I still think I could be more useful here. The business in Holland not requiring by any means constant presence there, and having no connexion with the Hague might be done from hence and in concert with the minister residing in London if there was one there. I hope I shall not be obliged again to beg your excuse for such details. Nothing is more common than Chargés des affaires being appointed ministers and sometimes ambassadors. Yr. friend,   W: SHORT

RC (DLC); at head of text: "*Private*"; endorsed by TJ as received 18 Mch. 1791 and so recorded in SJL. PrC (PHi).

It was not until the spring of 1791

that TJ received either the various ACCOUNTS enclosed by Short in this letter or their duplicates sent in another (Short to TJ, 30 Dec. 1790). But on the 22d of October, just a month before his return to Philadelphia, the *Henrietta*, Captain Benjamin Wickes, had arrived from Le Havre with the furniture, household goods, books, and papers that he had left in Paris in 1789 in the full expectation of returning (*Federal Gazette*, 22 Nov. 1790; Le Mesurier & Cie. to TJ, 27 Aug. 1790; TJ to Delany, 15 Jan. 1791). Other effects from his house in New York had arrived by sea in mid-October. He had also sent on from Virginia a trunk by stagecoach and three boxes by the *Linnet*, the latter containing books and a harpsichord. Soon an additional box came from Charleston by the *Philadelphia* (Account Book, 12 and 15 Nov., 15 Dec. 1790; TJ to Brown, 4 Nov. 1790; Remsen's statement, 25 Nov. 1790).

These coastal shipments were not inexpensive, but on the 30th of November, when he accepted the consignment brought by the *Henrietta*, he had to pay a really "monstrous bill of freight" amounting to $544.53 (Account Book, 30 Nov. 1790). The shipment had cleared customs in France under diplomatic passport, though after a disagreeable experience with a revolutionary mob at Le Havre that added to the delay and expense (Le Mesurier & Cie. to TJ, 27 Aug. 1790; charges from Paris to Le Havre amounted to 3,023 livres and included an item of 36 livres "Lost by our Clerk out of his Pocket, during the Scuffle on board with the Mob"; invoice of Le Mesurier & Cie., 8 Sep. 1790, DLC: TJ Papers, 59: 10121). On TJ's return to America in 1789 the collector at Norfolk had permitted his sizeable amount of baggage to enter duty free but had remained doubtful about the decision. On account of that importation as well as the much larger one on the *Henrietta* —and no doubt also because he wished to reach an accommodation with the Secretary of the Treasury on the mint, the proposed standard of weights and measures, and other matters of policy —TJ called on him three days after he arrived in Philadelphia. Except for twelve cases of wine and 145 rolls of wall paper, Hamilton allowed both the 1789 and the 1790 importations to enter free (Vol. 15: 375-7; TJ to Hamilton, 24 Nov. 1790; TJ to Lindsay, 10 Jan. 1791; TJ to Delany, 15 Jan. 1791).

PETITS ACCOUNT, covering purchases of items TJ had instructed Short to make, as well as other miscellaneous expenditures between 20 Aug. and 14 Nov. 1790, amounted to 3,406 livres, including household expenses of 269 livres (Tr in DLC: TJ Papers, 59: 10123, with note by Short; original in DLC: Short Papers; Petit's account of household expenses, dated 14 Nov. 1790 and with explanatory notes by Short, is in DLC: TJ Papers, 59: 10122, 10124, being intermingled with the foregoing account of purchases; for TJ's instructions, see TJ to Short, 12 Mch. and 6 Apr. 1790). This total was slightly reduced by Petit's sale of two carriage horses, a secretary, four dumb waiters, two book presses, and a stove. One of Petit's purchases was from Piébot, a grocer, for 50 lbs. of Parmesan cheese, 25 lbs. of nectarines, 20 lbs. of raisins, 40 lbs. of almonds, 10 lbs. of mustard, 40 pints of vinegars, a barrel of olive oil, and a barrel of anchovies at a total cost of 496 livres (Piébot's invoice, 8 July 1790, DLC: TJ Papers, 59: 10116). Another purchase—the costliest of those authorized by TJ—was 145 rolls of wall paper, procured for 1,117 livres from Messrs. Arthur & Robert, "Manufacture Royale de Papiers pour Tentures et Decorations" (Arthur & Robert's receipted invoice, 29 July 1790, in DLC: Short Papers; see TJ to Short, 6 Apr. 1790; see also, Kimball, *Jefferson*, III, 113-14). Other authorized purchases included 118 livres to the bookseller Froullé for TJ's subscription to the 34th-39th instalments of the *Encyclopédie*; 377 livres to Goldsmith for books and periodicals, including Buffon's works; 649 livres to Dupuis for materials for "eight best and thickest hair mattrases" and 38 livres to Husson for making them (Froullé's invoice, 22 June 1790; Goldsmith's invoice, 20 June 1790; Dupuis' invoice, 23 June 1790; Husson's invoice, 23 June 1790—all in DLC: Short Papers; copies of invoices of Dupuis and Goldsmith are also in DLC: TJ Papers, 59: 10117-8, 10120; see Sowerby, No. 1024).

The ACCOUNT OF THE EMBALLEUR who packed TJ's books and household goods was almost twice that of Petit, totalling 6,443 livres. The *emballeur* was one Grevin, who described himself as a *maître layetier*. His invoice, dated 17 July 1790, covers 16 pages (DLC: Short Papers, in French). Short also enclosed his own two ACCOUNTS with TJ. The first covered the transactions of packing and shipping the household goods, which was balanced by Short's draft on the Amsterdam bankers as authorized by TJ. These drafts, totalling more than 13,000 livres, discharged the obligations of Petit, Grevin, and Le Mesurier & Cie. (MS in DLC: TJ Papers, 70: 12182, with notations "a" and "b" in TJ's hand designating the public and private elements: the former indicating credits totalling 636 livres for the sale of TJ's saddle horse, the old carriage, and a secretary; the latter designating the drafts on the bankers; PrC in DLC: Short Papers; Short's memoranda of bills of exchange on Amsterdam given Grand, 21 Aug. and 22 Sep. 1790; the originals that Short retained as vouchers included Petit's statement and receipt, 20 Aug. 1790, and the invoices of Goldsmith, Grevin, and others: PrC of Short's letter of advice to W. & J. Willink, N. & J. Van Staphorst & Hubbard, 21 Aug. 1790; same). The second statement of account enclosed by Short, left open, was for the period 1 Nov. 1789–2 Nov. 1790. It showed total debits of 5,063 livres against TJ, chiefly for servants' wages, medal boxes from Upton, and "two months gratification to coachman, Petit and Henri" at their discharge on 1 Aug. 1790. Against this there were credits of 611-16-0 livres for the items sold by Petit, including the two horses that fetched only 432 livres. Short appended a note to explain this item: "Pettit kept them till lately trying in vain to sell them, and has never been able to get more for them" (MS in DLC: TJ Papers, 70: 12176, 12178, with pencilled total of credits and endorsement by TJ on verso reading in part: "This account is stated on another paper and continued therefore useless"; PrC of this and also of TJ's restatement, with public and private debts separated in two columns, are in DLC: Short Papers). After reaching Amsterdam, Short sent a duplicate of this account, adding to the debit balance payments to Petit for "gunlocks ordered by you for public use" and to Charpentier for the new copying-press ordered by TJ. He drew on the Amsterdam bankers for the balance of 4,716-14-0 livres and closed the account as of 30 Dec. 1790 (Dupl of statement, DLC: TJ Papers, 70: 12179; see Short to TJ, 29 Dec. 1790). The task of packing and shipping all of TJ's effects, discharging the servants, selling some articles, purchasing others, and terminating the lease of *Hôtel de Langeac* was an onerous as-

signment. Short handled it with remarkable dispatch and efficiency.

Now, just before Congress opened, the burden of coping with such a cargo as "no other American had ever brought from France" fell upon the owner (Malone, *Jefferson*, II, 322). Grevin the *maître layetier* had made and packed 86 crates, including those for the cabriolet and the phaeton that did not arrive until the summer of 1791 (Short to TJ, 15 Aug. 1790; Le Mesurier & Cie. to TJ, 27 Aug. 1790; Remsen to TJ, 16 June 1791). Six of the crates, two of which enclosed the marble pedestal given to TJ by Madame de Tessé, were shipped on the *John* to Norfolk, being destined for Monticello along with the delayed carriages (TJ to Brown, 16 Dec. 1790). The bulk of the shipment, totalling 78 crates, came directly to Philadelphia on the *Henrietta*. TJ had instructed Short to have an exact invoice prepared specifying the contents of each crate so that it might, among other uses, serve as a customs declaration (TJ to Short, 12 Mch. 1790). This characteristic attention to detail served history as well, for it is only from the invoice of Grevin that we know what a cargo of treasures TJ brought back from France.

Crates Nos. 1-15, as Grevin's invoice shows, were filled with books, appropriately placed first in the shipment because first in TJ's estimation. "While residing in Paris," he later wrote in offering his library to the nation, "I devoted every afternoon I was disengaged, for a summer or two, in examining all the principal bookstores, turning over every book with my own hands, and putting by every thing which related to America, and indeed whatever was rare and valuable in every science. Besides this, I had standing orders during the whole time I was in Europe, in it's principal bookmarts, particularly Amsterdam, Frankfort, Madrid, and London, for such works relating to America as could not be found in Paris. So that, in that department particularly, such a collection was made as probably can never again be effected; because it is hardly probable that the same opportunities, the same time, industry, perseverance, and expence, with some knolege of the bibliography of the subject would again happen to be in concurrence" (TJ to Samuel H. Smith, 21 Sep. 1814; Fiske Kimball, *Thomas Jefferson Architect*,

p. 91, first suggested that TJ's undated list of books in MHi comprised principally the books purchased abroad in the years 1784-1789, a conjecture amply supported by the evidence adduced in Sowerby's *Catalogue of the Library of Thomas Jefferson*; another MS catalogue and list of desiderata, also in MHi, bears this notation: "√ This mark denotes the books I have. Those unmarked I mean to procure. 1783. Mar. 6. 2640. vols."—a clear indication that, on his expected voyage to France in 1783, TJ made the acquisition of books one of his primary objects; see Randolph G. Adams, *Three Americanists* [Philadelphia, 1939], p. 69-96). TJ had directed that each volume be wrapped separately in paper and then the whole covered in oil cloth (TJ to Short, 12 Mch. and 6 Apr. 1790).

Crates Nos. 16 and 17 held the 8 mattresses. *No. 18* with 6 large crimson chairs, 9 woollen blankets and a servant's mattress; *No. 19* with 6 blue chairs, 6 cotton blankets, 4 woollen blankets, and a servant's mattress; *No. 21* with 4 large blue chairs, 6 large blue damask curtains, 22 bell pulls, 8 medium-size blue damask curtains, 1 drapery, and 4 pillows for day beds; and *No. 24* with 2 large blue arm chairs, 2 crimson chairs with their cushions, 2 crimson cords and tassels, the brass lock on TJ's bedroom door, and an old mattress—these exemplified the improvement over Abigail Adams' suggestion for packing that TJ had specified for those chairs and couches upholstered in silk (TJ to Short, 6 Apr. 1790). *No. 20* with 6 chairs in red Morocco; *No. 22* with 6 chairs and a servant's mattress; and *No. 23* with 6 chairs of crimson velvet and 17 packages of wall paper, one meridian, and the base of a marble table, evidently were packed as Mrs. Adams suggested (Vol. 16: 323).

The following summary lists the principal articles in the remainder of Grevin's crates. *Crate No. 25:* 9 pictures, some paintings in a roll, a pair of large pistols in a leather case, a roll of parchment and a piece of Moroccan leather. *No. 26:* 4 large pictures from TJ's study. *No. 27:* 6 large pictures. These pictures included his likenesses of American worthies— among them Joseph Wright's unfinished portrait of Washington that Trumbull had completed in Paris. *No. 28:* a day bed, 2 rugs, an ivory duster

from the library, a library ladder, 4 screens, 1 lectern, 2 mahogany tables, a bridle and saddle. *No. 29:* 2 stoves, basins, pots, cauldrons, 12 hot water tins, 4 butler's pantry daybooks, 28 round saucepans, 2 oval ones, 2 small copper frying pans, 3 butler's pantry saucepans, 1 strainer, 1 kettle, 1 coffee mill, 3 waffle irons, 1 coffee pot, 4 tin plated pie pans, 1 sheet-iron camp stove, 2 fish kettles and 1 pair of scales, 19 copper saucepan covers, and various spoons, ladles, cleavers, knives, spits, shovels, tongs, and a poker. *Nos. 30 and 31:* 2 cast iron stoves, with their stone bases. *No. 32:* 3 busts. TJ had acquired seven of Houdon's portrait busts—Voltaire, Turgot, Lafayette, Franklin, Washington, Jones, and three copies of his own bust in plaster (Kimball, *Jefferson*, III, 116). This box, perhaps having the three copies of his own bust, was one of those the mob at Le Havre caused to be opened. *No. 33:* 2 crimson arm chairs, 2 blue easy chairs and their cushions, a fountain and its basin from the anteroom, 12 food warmers, 3 iron kettles. *No. 34:* 5 pairs of brass andirons, 3 iron pokers, 2 large tongs, 2 shovels, and 2 sconces. *No. 35:* dishes for hors d'oeuvres, 4 porcelain salt cellars, 8 crystal decanters, 12 crystal goblets, and 4 small flasks. *No. 36:* 2 stoves, a large cauldron, a barrel of olive oil, a barrel of anchovies, and 4 packages of nectarines. *No. 37:* 7 unframed mirrors. *No. 38:* 2 blacksmith's paring irons and base, 1 package of almonds, and 4 white porcelain cups. *No. 39:* 3 gaming tables, 1 wooden cover trimmed in green cloth, 1 lectern, 2 ordinary tables, 3 mahogany table legs, 2 pillows of red Morocco, and a servant's mattress. *No. 40:* a commode from TJ's bedroom, the filing cases, 2 brass locks for the secret drawers, 2 cases of macaroni, one leather bag filled with iron tools. *No. 41:* 9 master's mattresses, 2 feather beds, 2 bolsters, and 2 cotton blankets. *No. 42:* a plaster Vestal virgin, 3 cases of instruments, business papers, a thermometer, 2 white glass jars, 3 tubes and 8 cups for medicine, 2 plates and paper for the copying-press, the copying-press, 2 rules, 3 pieces of mahogany, and 2 iron weights for a pendulum. This crate included a part of the scientific instruments that TJ had ordered to be "most carefully packed." The copying-press was neither the new one made by Charpentier, which was shipped later, nor "the great copying press . . . from London," which was public property and which TJ directed to be left in Paris, but presumably the small portable copying-press which he had also acquired in London and carried with him to the south of France in 1787 (TJ to Short, 12 Mch. and 6 Apr. 1790; Short's account of 30 Dec. 1790). *No. 43*: 4 pairs of candlesticks, 2 girandoles, 1 mahogany press, 5 boxes with glassware, 1 box of tools, a small trunk of business papers from the writing desk, a double syringe, a mirror, a pair of silver-plated pistols, several books, 2 plates, 1 package of various kinds of paper, and folios for use in the copying-press. *No. 44*: a blue silk ottoman and its cushions, 4 chairs to accompany it, 2 lanterns from TJ's carriage, a wooden model for a coffee urn. This was perhaps the wooden model for the two silver coffee urns that were made by Odiot in 1789 after TJ's design (see Vol. 15: xxvii-xxix). *No. 45*: a red Morocco ottoman, 2 mahogany tables, 4 epergnes. *No. 46*: 1 day bed, 2 crimson armchairs, 1 commode, 2 servant's mattresses, 2 whips trimmed in silver, 3 swords (one of them silver), 2 maps, 2 collapsible parasols, 1 double-barreled gun, 2 carpenter's chalk strings, 1 piece of *toile de Jouy*, 1 bedspread of "Col. Onfry's" [Humphreys], 2 bolsters (with a confused description seeming to indicate that they were made of a textile print showing red partridges in a garden). *No. 47*: the marble top to TJ's commode and 4 marble tops with gilt borders. *No. 48*: 4 floor-length mirrors with gilt borders (still to be seen at Monticello). *No. 49*: 14 pictures. *No. 50*: maps, 7 pairs of TJ's shoes, 16 books and pamphlets. *No. 51*: 10 dozen porcelain plates and 2 porcelain soup tureens. *No. 52*: 2 jars of mustard, a large porcelain platter, 4 large oval platters, 42 porcelain cups, and 39 porcelain saucers. *No. 53*: 2 mirrors, 2 silver and vermillion goblets, 2 silver-plated vases and sugar bowls, 6 crystal vases, 2 of TJ's silver-plated candlesticks from his bedroom, a chiffonier, a gilt tin lamp, 1 powder horn, and various candlesticks and snuffers. *No. 54*: 2 porcelain soup tureens and 2 hot water tins. *No. 55*: a glass figurine and its base from the drawing room, 7 glasses, 4 porcelain figurines, 2 large casseroles, 2 presses, and a quarter of cheese. *No. 56*: a telescope, a violin case, 2 jalousies from the window in

the drawing room, a figurine from the mantle of the drawing room, a clock from TJ's study, a porcelain figurine, a meridian trimmed with copper, a pistol and its case, a Moroccan ammunition pouch, 3 reams of fine paper, a package of blue paper, 8 quires of coordinate drawing paper such as TJ had purchased of Corneillon in 1788. *No. 57*: TJ's clothes and linen, 23 table settings, 30 knives and 30 forks. *No. 58*: 9 pairs of TJ's sheets, 6 pairs of servant's sheets, 18 regular aprons, and 30 kitchen aprons. *No. 59*: a trunk filled with business papers. *No. 60*: 30 pictures. *No. 61*: 145 rolls of wall paper and 1 servant's mattress. *No. 62*: a roasting spit, a waffle iron, a chair, 2 nets from the carriage, bedspread ornaments, and a letter addressed to TJ. *No. 63*: a slab of marble, a vial of paint for the busts, 39 glass goblets, 16 porcelain cups, 14 white glass jars, 1 porcelain platter, 12 chocolate molds, 2 copper hot plates, 3 round platters, 2 window curtains, a carriage seat, 4 molds for ices, 2 pistol cases and various pieces of harness. *Nos. 64-72* had in each 5 dozen bottles of wine. Grevin did not particularize the contents of *No. 73*, but it presumably contained wine also, as did *No. 74* and perhaps *No. 75*, since the customs declaration for the wine and wall paper described 12 cases containing 56 2/3 dozen bottles (ViU). *No. 74*: 40 bottles of vinegar and 20 bottles of wine. *No. 75*: 2 servant's mattresses. *No. 76*: an ornament for the end of a staircase baluster. *No. 77*: one part of the marble pedestal given by Madame de Tessé to TJ, together with its base and accessory iron hooks, screws, leather thongs, straw matting, bolts, and locks. *No. 78*: two other pieces of the pedestal and base with its similar accessories. *No. 79*: a bundle of harness. *No. 80*: a bundle of jalousies. *Nos. 81 and 82*: a chest of drawers in each. *No. 83*: two marble tops for the chests. *No. 84*: TJ's cabriolet seat and cushion. *Nos. 85 and 86*: contained the phaeton and cabriolet which were delayed in getting to Virginia. The six crates sent by the *John* to Norfolk were Nos. 77, 78, 81, 82, 83, and 84 (see TJ to Brown, 16 Dec. 1790).

Grevin's charge for making the 86 crates came to 2,408-7-0 livres. The cost of packing materials and services amounted to almost twice as much. For packing materials he used 356 ells of coarse cloth, 10 lbs. of oil, 526 ells of strong packing cloth, 887 toises of rope, 79 ells of oil cloth, 8 ells of oil cloth for the carriages, 624 bundles of rye straw, 385 quires of coarse paper, 36 bundles of hay, 37 quires of "papier de Soye," 39 quires of ordinary paper, 397 lbs. of shredded paper, 32 ells of flannel for the carriages and the unframed mirrors, 122 balls of twine, 60 lbs. of hair, 6 lbs. of cotton, 40 screws for the unframed mirrors, 26 covers of "papier de Soye," and 52 covers of coarse paper for the carriages, furniture, and busts, 21 lbs. of fine and large nails for the stoves and pieces of marble. For these materials; for making 80 bags out of coarse cloth and oil cloth; for plumbing and procuring 87 seals at the customs; for his trouble, care, and packing of the furniture and other items; and for transporting the whole to Port St. Nicolas for shipment to Rouen—for all of these supplies and services Grevin charged an additional 4,215-8-0 livres, making a total of 6,623-15-0 livres. One Maris Debrie who audited the invoice for Short or Grand on 19 Aug. 1790 found it just and reasonable but deducted 180 livres —presumably the charge for making 40 of the oil cloth bags. Grevin signed a receipt for the reduced amount on the following day. Since his invoice bears the date 17 July 1790 at its head and the auditor's notation the date 19 Aug. 1790 at its foot, it is obvious that the crating, packing, and transportation to Port St. Nicolas took place in the four weeks between these dates (MS in DLC: Short Papers). In expedition and thoroughness as well as in his zeal for itemizing liberal costs, Grevin was clearly a *maître layetier*.

The immense cargo from the *Henrietta* descended upon TJ at a time when he was as embarrassed for space as he was for finances with which to pay the staggering freight bill, to say nothing of the invoices of Petit, Grevin, and Le Mesurier & Cie., yet to come. He had warned his landlord that it was essential for his house to "be in readiness by the 1st. of October" (TJ to Leiper, 4 Aug. 1790). But the shipments from New York and France were obliged to incur warehouse charges and he to seek lodgings at Mrs. House's famous boarding-house for almost a month because the house in High Street west of Eighth was far from being completed. It was not until the 11th

of December that TJ "entered into possession of the 2. rooms of 3d. story." On the 17th, after laying in oats and firewood, he took over the use of the stable. Two days later he gained a bedroom. On the 22d there arrived the first of the twenty-seven drayloads required to move the great mass of crates from the wharf. On the day before Christmas TJ "took kitchen." On the 29th and the last day of the year the final loads of crates arrived. On the 9th of January he got possession of the drawing rooms and parlour and began to dine at home. But, two months after his return to Philadelphia, half of the crates were still unopened and the house was still unfinished (Account Book under the dates given: TJ to Short, 24 Jan. 1791; see also, Dumbauld, *Tourist*, p. 160-6; Malone, *Jefferson*, II, 322-3; and Marie Kimball, "Thomas Jefferson's French Furniture," *Antiques*, XV [Feb. 1929], 123-8, the first published account to be based on Grevin's invoice).

Thus in the six weeks from the middle of December to the end of January TJ was unpacking crates, contending with carpenters and masons, and undoubtedly adding to the delay by moving in before the house was ready for occupancy. His insistence on doing so was understandable, for his official duties were pressing and Mrs. House's congenial establishment—the focal point of all activities of the Virginia delegation in Congress—afforded no such solitude as was required for the preparation of state papers. The confusion of unpacking and getting settled was also compounded because, except for the cases of books and wine that were so essential to him, chairs, sofas, pictures, blankets, tools, clothing, and food were hopelessly intermingled under a logic of packing known only to Grevin. In one crate almonds were mixed in with a blacksmith's paring irons. Anchovies and nectarines were to be found in another containing two stoves and a sprinkler. Macaroni and raisins were in still another, along with the commode from TJ's bedroom, his filing cases, and a leather bag filled with tools. Pillows and bolsters were stuffed among chairs and sofas to protect their silk coverings, while sheets, blankets and mattresses were elsewhere, so that the task of assembling even a single bed and bedding meant opening several of Grevin's solid crates and well-tied bundles. One's imagination balks at the spectacle of confusion that must have transpired in these six weeks—carpenters and plasterers trying to get on with their work, servants opening crates and removing refuse, departmental clerks coming and going on official business, and the Secretary of State, standing amid piles of Grevin's hay, straw, rope, twine, packing cloth, and mountains of ordinary paper, coarse paper, shredded paper, and *papier de soie*, trying to get at the most essential articles and at the same time to protect his books, papers, apparatus, and *objets d'art* from damage. The very thoroughness of Grevin's packing contributed to TJ's ordeal of moving.

Such was the household crisis that befell a man who took extraordinary care and pleasure in planning every detail of his domestic surroundings, who understood the problems of the carpenters at work because he was himself adept in working with wood and metal, but who, always cherishing privacy among his books and papers, was in dire need of it at this precise time. For these six weeks of household confusion—aggravated particularly for one who was hypersensitive to cold because this was in the middle of a severe winter—were the very weeks in which TJ produced, one after the other and always with his prompt and sure touch, a remarkable series of state papers of fundamental importance on foreign and domestic policy: reports and opinions on territorial government, the manufacture of textiles, the cod and whale fisheries, commercial

and diplomatic relations with Great Britain, the first determination on impressment abuses, the French protest of the tonnage acts, the supplement to the report on weights and measures, trade with the Mediterranean, the situation of the Algerine captives, and so on. Settled principles, habitual anticipation of the course of events, and an unflagging devotion to system were the traits of character that made possible this simultaneous discharge of unusually heavy duties both in household and in office. In the midst of the ordeal, TJ declared that his mind had been so totally occupied with public affairs that he had been unable "to think of anything private" (TJ to Hiltzheimer, 19 Jan. 1791). But during this time he had not failed once to write the weekly letter to the family at Monticello on his alternating plan of correspondence. That plan placed upon each of his daughters and his son-in-law the need to write only one letter to his three. The almost total silence from Virginia evoked in the records of these six weeks his only hint of distress of mind.

The concurrent pressures created by the arrival of the *Henrietta*, by the failure of the landlord to have the house in readiness, and by the extraordinary public demands upon a cabinet officer in an administration divided beyond hope of concord presented both a public and private ordeal. But they also provide a lens of crystal clarity with which to read both the state papers of this period of crisis and the character of the man who wrote them.

Subscription for Extending the Navigation of the Rivanna

[Before 8 Nov. 1790]

Whereas by an act of the General assembly passed in the year 1764. intitled 'an act for clearing the great falls of James river, the river Chickahominy and the North branch of James river' Thomas Walker, Edward Carter, Charles Lewis, Nicholas Lewis, Thomas Jefferson, Henry Fry, Nicholas Meriwether, John Walker, John Harvey, Valentine Wood and James Adams were constituted trustees for clearing the Rivanna or North branch of James river from the mouth thereof upwards, and were authorized to receive subscriptions for that purpose, and to do such other acts as were necessary for effecting the same, and the said Trustees having received considerable subscriptions proceeded to have the said river cleared from the mouth up to the mountain falls and it being now desireable that the said navigation should be extended from the said falls upwards as far as may be and the death of several of the trustees, and removal of others rendering it impracticable to procure a meeting of six as required by the act[1] for chusing others in the room of those dead and removed it is proposed to sollicit the General assembly to nominate or authorize the nomination of others. But it being expedient that in the mean time subscriptions be opened and other necessary measures taken for extending the said navigation from the said Mountain falls, upwards as aforesaid, we the subscribers do hereby oblige ourselves severally, our several heirs executors and administrators to pay into the hands of [Nicholas Lewis and George Divers][2] gentlemen the several sums of money affixed to our respective names dividing the same into four equal instalments the first of which shall be paid on the [15th.][2] day of [April 1791.][2] and the other three on the same day annually and successively the three ensuing years: and we hereby authorize the said [N.L. and G.D.][2] to demand, recover, receive and proceed to apply the same towards extending the said navigation as aforesaid in such manner as they shall think best until other persons be authorized[3] by special act of Assembly to proceed therein [in] which event we oblige ourselves to pay to the said other persons so to be specially authorized the instalments which shall not have been previously paid to the said [N.L. and G.D.][2] and we further consent that the said act of assembly may be so amended as to expedite the recovery of our subscriptions in a course of law in such way as the General assembly shall think best. In witness whereof we have hereto subscribed our names and opposite thereto have expressed the sums we severally subscribe.

Dft (MHi); undated but evidently written just before TJ left Monticello on 8 Nov. 1790.

Two decades had elapsed since TJ's first effort to organize support for clearing the Rivanna of obstructions to navigation (Vol. 1: 88n.). In this document—possibly drafted as an enterprise to challenge his son-in-law, then about the same age at which TJ had launched the earlier venture—he attempted to rely on methods that had already proved successful. But far more changes had taken place than the death or removal of trustees to make that precedent a realistic one to follow: voluntary subscriptions for public improvements had little appeal for a generation now busily engaged in organizing turnpike, canal, and manufacturing companies for operation at a profit, often with the aid of foreign capital. Later, in tracing the legislative history of this enterprise, TJ wrote: "The desire to extend the navigation from the Mountain or Milton falls upwards produced in 1791. a new subcription, and in 1794 the act [of General Assembly for clearing the North fork of James river], which it has not been in my power to see. But the rough draught of the subscription paper, still in my possession, informs me that the object was to name trustees with power to receive subscriptions and to 'extend the said navigation from the said Mountain falls upwards as far as may be.' But the subscriptions in this case, as in the former, were voluntary: no incorporation was asked, no toll, as, in the course of 10. years following it was found that sufficient funds could not be raised as a free gift, a plan was adopted of forming by subscription a company who should undertake the work, and receive a toll for reimbursement and profit" ("Notes on the several acts of assembly for clearing the Rivanna river," 1817; DLC: TJ Papers, 211: 37587). But for some years longer TJ clung to his hope of voluntary action through free gifts. His own subscription of £15 was paid

on 17 Dec. 1798 (Account Book).

On 10 Sep. 1790 Nicholas Lewis, as manager of TJ's affairs at the Monticello and other plantations, paid "Colo. G. Thompson in full" for TJ's "Subscription for clearing the N. River" (Lewis' Accounts, 1786-1792, ViU). Since Thompson was one of those in charge of the work carried on under the earlier subscription, this payment was probably made toward that and its date may indicate the approximate time at which TJ launched the new plan.

[1] TJ first wrote: "But four of the said eleven trustees being since dead and several others removed to great distances so as that a meeting of ⟨a majority⟩ six of them cannot be had to fill their numbers," and then altered the passage to read as above.

[2] Brackets in MS.

[3] TJ first wrote: ". . . may be legally authorized to take the said business out of their hands," and then altered the passage to read as above.

From Thomas MacDonogh

Boston, 8 Nov. 1790. Enclosing his commission as consul for Massachusetts, Rhode Island, Connecticut, and New Hampshire, asking him to lay it before the President. "Being desirous to have the Honour of paying my personal Respects to the President, as well as to yourself, I set off immediately after my Arrival here in the latter End of August, for New York, but was not fortunate enough to get there before his Departure for Virginia." Requests the return of his commission after it is recognized.

RC (DNA: RG 59, CD); endorsed by TJ as received 23 Nov. 1790 and so recorded in SJL. Enclosure: Copy of MacDonogh's commission, signed by Leeds and dated 18 Dec. 1789 (Tr in DLC; PrC in DNA: RG 59, CD). For MacDonogh's difficulties in delivering his commission, see Remsen to TJ, 6, 9 and 25 Sep. 1790; TJ to Remsen, 1 Oct. 1790.

To Nicholas Lewis

DEAR SIR   Monticello Nov. 9. 1790.

I omitted in my Memorandums to mention 2. boxes of books marked T.I. No. 1. and No. 2. which are packed, and a box containing a Spinet which the carpenters have to put a top to, which when done I have taken the liberty to direct shall be carried to your house, and perhaps when there you had better order the same person to go on with [them] to Charlottesville, from whence they may be better forwarded to Mr. Brown at Richmond whom I have desired to send them on to me at Philadelphia. The two boxes of books will weigh a good deal, but I imagine Colo. Bell or any other person you please in Charlottesville can get them a passage to Richmond on board some waggon. I hope, this, my dear Sir, is the last thing that will occur for me to plague you with for a year to come. I am with very sincere esteem & attachment to Mrs. Lewis and yourself Dear Sir your affectionate friend & servt.,

TH: JEFFERSON

PrC (MHi).

From George C. Fox & Sons

ESTEEMED FRIEND   Falmouth 10 Novem 1790

The enclosed Letter from our Friends James Mackensie & Co. came under our [cove]r and was immediately sent to the Agent's [offi]ce, but our Clerk informing us that it [wa]s much torn thro' an accident to the Mail, We ordered it to be taken out again, to put it under Cover, not Knowing its Consequence which we hope Thee wilt approve.

We take the Freedom to tender thee our best Services at this port and if we can at any Time be useful in forwarding thy Letters from hence, or in serving any of thy Friends who may come This way, it will give us great pleasure to obey thy Commands, being very Respectfully Thy assured Friends,

GEO C FOX & SONS

RC (DNA: RG 59, CD); at foot of text: "Thomas Jefferson New York"; slightly mutilated. Enclosure: Auldjo to TJ, 4 Nov. 1790 and its enclosure. See note, Johnson to TJ, 15 Nov. 1790.

From Thomas Mann Randolph, Jr.

DEAR SIR   Richmond November 11. 1790.

I am extremely sorry it is not in my power to forward to you Andersons account of the Hebrides as I promised: it was lent by Mr. Forster to a friend who mislaid it and as yet it has been searched for in vain. You will probably meet with it at Mr. Dobsons Bookseller 2d Str. Philadelphia.

The bargain with my Father will be droped alltogether I believe as I have been with him several times in private and he has never mentioned it. The affair has only accumulated my debt of Gratitude to you, which before, was beyond the possibility of discharge.

Perhaps it is fortunate for me that objections were made as I have since learned that a Petition is to be presented to the present Assembly for the sale of the Glebe at Varina, which would ruin my estate there, if it fell in the hands of another.—Mazzei's place with an addition of 300 acres from Coll. Carter when furnished with Stock will supply our table in abundance and those purchases will not prevent our increasing the estate at Varina.

The Dog which ran off from Monticello the day after my arrival there was seen at Varina on Sunday before 12 oClock having performed the journey in 42 hours. I have taken care to have it sent back. I am Dear Sir Your most obedt. humble Servt.,

THOMAS M. RANDOLPH

RC (ViU); endorsed by TJ as received 3 Dec. 1790 and so recorded in SJL.

ANDERSON'S HEBRIDES: TJ no doubt desired the use of James Anderson's *An account of the present state of the Hebrides* (Edinburgh, 1785) because he was preparing his report on the fisheries and needed the author's reports and testimony before a committee of parliament on the state of the fisheries of Great Britain, included in this work. See TJ's report of 1 Feb. 1791.

From John Garland Jefferson

MY DEAR SIR   Goochland 12th November 1790

I have now taken up board with one Hilton, a man with whom I am well pleased. He has the character of an honest good man, and I really believe that this is a character he justly merits. I am to give him twenty pounds by the year, for board, bed, and washing which I consider as a very reasonable price.—Convinced from the discourse you held with me a few days before your departure that you did not wish for me to have any intercourse with that unfortunate young man Rind, I formed a determined resolution from that moment to break off all further communication with him. This design I imparted to Mr. Carr, who highly approved of it. We immediately set down and wrote him a joint letter informing him how absolutely necessary it was for us to take this measure. Thus an acquaintance formed in one week was broke off in one hour, never to be revived. My only motive for wishing to befriend that young man was his forlorn and desperate situation, which I considered as truly deplorable. I put the case to myself, examined well my own breast, and considered if I was in his situation what wou'd be my sensations! Thus a simpathy which took its rise from compassion alone, had well nigh involved me in difficulties from which I shou'd not easily have extricated myself. When I arrived in Goochland I found Rind there, and delivered with my own hand the letter just mentioned. I thought I cou'd discover as he read that he was shook with the most violent emotions. As soon as an opportunity offered I observed to him that we had found it indispensable to pursue that line of conduct; to which he ironically answered that Mr. Carr and myself were prudent men: that we had acted very righ[t]ly, and that a man who wou'd not from selfish principles give up a friend, ought to be damned. I felt a little stung at his observations, and told him that my acquaintance with him was of short duration, and that altho I wou'd not attribute my misfortunes to him, that I cou'd venture to say I was under no obligations to him; I looked upon it therefore that that was a language he had no right to hold.

I have now given you a full account of the sequel of the business, and hope that you will favor me as often as convenient with a line, and by your friendly instructions pour the balm of consolation into my wounded heart; for I never before considered this matter in so serious a light, or saw the imprudence of it so plainly, and altho' I was not the author of a sentence yet by my intercourse with Rind, I laid myself open to the suspicions of the people, and incured the imputation of having done that which in my though[t]ful moments I look up with a degree of horror. I s[hall?] conclude, suffer me therefore to subscribe myself. Your most grateful hbl servt.,   J G JEFFERSON

RC (ViU); addressed: "Thomas Jefferson. Secretary o.f the united states. Philadelphia"; endorsed by TJ as re-ceived 11 Dec. 1790 but recorded in SJL under 10 Dec.

To Thomas Mann Randolph, Jr.

DEAR SIR   George-town Nov. 12. 1790.

I inclose you some wheat which the President assures me from many years experience to be the very best kind he has ever seen. He spread it through the E[aster]n shore of Maryland several years ago, and it has ever be[en c]onsidered as the very best of the white wheat of that state so much celebrated. It is said to weigh 62. 63.

64. lb to the bushel. The grain, tho' small, is always plump. The President is so excellent a farmer that I place full confidence in his recommendation. Will you be so good as to make George (under your directions and eye) set it out in distinct holes at proper distances so as to make the most seed from it possible? The richest ground in the garden will be best, and the partition fence they are to make will guard it. After harvest we will divide the produce. I imagine the rows should be far enough apart to admit them to go between them with the hoes for the purpose of weeding.—Wheat at Baltimore is at a French crown.—We are so far without any accident, and our horses as full and lively as the first day. Give my sincere love to the girls from, my dear Sir, Your's affectionately,   TH: JEFFERSON

RC (DLC); addressed: "Thomas Mann Randolph junr. esquire to be sent to Richmond and thence to Monti- cello"; franked; postmarked: "GEO. TOWN NO 15."; slightly torn. Not recorded in SJL.

From J. P. P. Derieux

MONSIEUR   Charlotte Ville 15 Novembre 1790.

La Situation de Mde. de Rieux etoit telle lors de votre depart qu'il me fut impossible de la quitter pour aller vous presenter mon respect et vous remettre les lettres dont vous me promites de voulloir bien vous charger. J'ai l'honneur de vous les adresser cy inclus, en vous demandant encore l'excuse de cette nouvelle importunité.

D'après la liberté que vous m'avés donné de vous informer de mes esperances vis-a-vis de Mr. Pierre Le Roy, mon Cousin à Bordeaux, je profitterai avec empressement de cette marque de bonté. Ce parent, du coté de ma mère, possède deux habitations considerables dans les environs du Cap-françois sur lesquelles il a plus de deux Cent negres travaillants. Il n'a presque jamais eu la moindre Liaison avec sa famille, ny encore moins avec celle de mon père. Son Sejour aux Isles depuis sa plus grande jeunesse lui a rendu indifferent toutte espèce de parentée. Cependant, à son retour de l'Amerique, il offrit à ma mère de nous faire du bien et de nous donner les moyens de reussir avantageusement dans le monde, mais elle s'y refusa, dans la Crainte que ce qu'il auroit fait pour ses Enfants ne diminua la portion de fortunne qu'elle esperoit de lui et, loin de l'encourager dans ses bonnes dispositions, fit l'impossible pour le mettre tout à fait contre nous, ce qui lui fit perdre en même tems, et l'amitié de ce parent qui ne la voit plus, et le fruit certain qu'elle en auroit retiré, en le laissant nous aider, comme il en avoit le projet. Le détail de tout ce qui s'est passé à ce sujet présenteroit d'une manière trop revoltante jusqu'à quel point les passions d'une mère injuste peuvent se manifester. Ce qu'il y a de certain suivant toutte probabilité, c'est que si ce parent n'avoit trouvé aucun obstacle à ses projets, nous n'eussions jamais connu que le bonheur et la fortunne. Il est depuis très longtems retiré à Bordeaux où il ne dépense pas le quart de son revenu. Mr. Mazzei, à son passage dans cette ville en 1783., fut le voir, mais il lui dit que tant que je resterois en France il ne feroit rien pour moi, parcequ'il etoit sûre que cela passeroit dans les mains de ma mère sans que j'en reçoive jamais un Sol, mais que quand je serois Eloigné il verroit ce qu'il auroit à faire. Ce sera un grand sujet d'esperance pour moi, Monsieur, si vous avés la bonté d'adresser ma Lettre à quelqu'un de Vos amis à Bordeaux avec un mot en ma faveur, qui pourra puet être decider ce parent à m'aider. C'est un homme d'un coeur très genereux et qui, voyant des personnes de hautte Consideration s'interesser à moi, ne refusera pas, je l'espère, de le faire Lui-même. Je me rappelle que, quelques années avant la mort de mon père, il lui donna en argent comptant une Somme de quarante mille livres, pour subvenir aux fraix d'une entreprise qu'il avoit faitte. Sa fortunne est telle, et ses revenus si bien payés, qu'il a toujours beaucoup d'argent devant lui et que, soit par lui-même, soit par Mr. Aubert, son Correspondant au Cap, il a toujours la plus grande facilité de faire toucher des fonds dans touttes les parties du monde.

Que ne vous devrai-je pas, Monsieur, si par une suitte de vos bontés, vous pouvés obtenir de ce parent qu'il me donne les moyens d'acheter quelques Nègres, c'est la seule chose qui me manque dans ce moment ici pour être parfaittement heureux. Je n'en ay jamais senti un si pressant besoin. Les louages me sont très Couteux, et je vois clairement qu'aussi longtems que je serai restrain je serai obligé de sacriffier la meilleure partie de mes recoltes pour payer le Salaire de ceux que j'y aurai employé, et que le surplus sera toujours trop mediocre pour maintenir ma famille, surtout dans les terres qui avoisinnent la Ville.

Ne pouvant refuser plus Longtems à Mde. Bellanger les détails qu'elle me demande sur la manière dont les choses sont tournées, je lui marque dans la Lettre cy joint que le Succès de mes Entreprises n'avoit pas justiffié l'idée que je m'en étois formé, que j'avois fait beaucoup de pertes considerables, et que je n'avois pas

encore pu les reparer, par le deffaut de nègres que le Bruit de leur
Liberté m'avoit empeché d'acheter dans le tems. Je lui ajoutte que
j'ai tout à fait quitté le Commerce interieur, n'y ayant trouvé
aucun encouragement et que, dans l'espoir de mieux faire et de
réparer une partie de mes pertes, j'avois fait un Envoy de farinne
aux Isles, et qu'aussitôt la rentrée de mes fonds j'acheterois un
morceau de la meilleure terre que je pourrois trouver, et les nègres
necessaires pour la cultiver, que j'étois déterminé à quitter la ville
pour embrasser tout à fait la vie Champêtre, reconnaissant par ma
propre experience qu'il n'en est point de plus heureuse et que, si
elle ne conduit pas à la fortunne, elle procure toujours l'aisance qui
feroit mon bonheur et assureroit celui de mes Enfants. De ce que
vous aurés la bonté d'écrire à Mde. Bellanger, relativement à ce
que je lui marque moi-même, dépendra l'impression plus ou moins
favorable qu'elle s'en formera, comme aussi ce que vous aurés la
bonté de lui apprendre du consentement que vous m'avés donné de
nommer mon jeune fils d'après vous, ne pourra que lui être du plus
grand encouragement pour nous accorder, ou à l'enfant, des avantages proportionés à l'idée d'être maraine avec vous, sans que cela
vous induise à aucune formalité quelconque, n'ayant d'autre objet
en flattant à cet Egard l'ambition de cette chère parente, que de
nous la rendre de plus en plus favorable, et peut-être la décider
à faire quelque chose dans ce moment ici, où je suis dans le plus
grand embarras pour faire face à mes engagements, que le retard
de mes fonds à rentrer augmente tous les jours davantage; et je
me regarderois encore une fois comme le plus heureux des hommes
si je puis voir se réaliser les esperances que je conçois des Lettres
que vous aurés encore la bonté d'écrire en ma faveur.

Mde. de Rieux, dont le rétablissement paroît encore très Eloigné,
me prie de vous presenter l'assurance de son respect. Toutte notre
famille est malade, je l'ai eté moi-même, ce qui m'a privé d'avoir
encore le plaisir d'aller voir Mr. et Mde. Randolph depuis votre
depart. J'ay l'honneur d'être, avec le plus respectueux attachement
et la plus parfaitte reconnaissance, Monsieur Votre très humble et
très obeist. Serviteur.   P. De Rieux

RC (MHi); endorsed by TJ as received 24 Dec. 1790 and so recorded in SJL.

From Joshua Johnson

SIR   London 15 Novr 1790

Finding the Packet has not Sailed, affords me the opportunity of handing you the Court Gazette and Woodfalls Papers up to the 13th. We are at present quiet, and every thing bears the appearance of Peace, which will give facility to Trade, but which will add nothing in favor of the Shipping belonging to the United States. On the Meeting of Parliament the Minister will be called on, for an Account of his Conduct, and as he renders it so I will hand it you. I am always with the greatest respect and esteem, Sir, Your most obedt & very humble Servant,   JOSHUA JOHNSON

RC (DNA: RG 59, CD); recorded in SJL as received 12 Mch. 1791. FC (DNA: RG 59, CD). This packet was forwarded by George C. Fox & Sons of Falmouth, who wrote TJ on 19 Nov. 1790: "We wrote thee the 10th Inst. by this Conveyance to which thee will be pleased to refer. The purport of the present is to inform thee, that we received by the Coach a parcel from our friend Joshua Johnson Esqr. desiring us to forward it to thee. It has been delivered to Capt. Gibson of the Colworth Packett, who we requested would take particular care of it" (RC in DNA: RG 59, CD).

From David Humphreys

SIR   Lisbon Novr. 19th. 1790.

I came on shore yesterday evening, and hearing a vessel is to sail for England before the Packet, I write with the design of sending this letter by that conveyance. We made the passage from Gravesend to the Rock of Lisbon in a fortnight, during which time we had favorable winds and fine weather, for the season.—The forms to be passed through in entering the vessel, and the impediments I shall meet with in having my baggage landed, will prevent me from waiting immediately on M. de Pinto.—But, in the mean time, I thought it proper to acquaint you, that a Convention has certainly been signed, on the 27th or 28th of last Month, by the Cte. Florida Blanca and Mr. Fitzherbert, for laying a basis to terminate the dispute between *Spain* and *Great Britain*. Intelligence of this measure, I imagine, might have arrived in the latter just about the time we left it. The English here greatly rejoice at the event; they speak of the terms as favorable; though nothing is said respecting a compensation to Britain for the expences incurred by arming. Little that is authentic seems to be known by those to whom I have access. Several articles are vaguely spoken of concerning the rights of settlements to the Northward of Nootka

Sound, Fisheries in the South Seas, and arrangements for future Trade. Two English Frigates had lately arrived in this Harbour from NewFoundland, and Admiral Peyton, from Gibralter, is now coming in with a 50 Gun Ship and two Frigates more. A great number of British Merchant vessels are also here.

There is not, at present, one American vessel in this Port; or a single Merchant from the U.S. established here. The annual Trade is, however, very considerable. Last summer more than twenty American vessels were at the same time, in the Harbour; and it is now nearly the season for some to arrive with the produce of the last Harvest. A Mr. Dorhman, a Native of Germany (actually in America) was formerly appointed Agent for the U.S. A brother of his now conducts the business as Deputy to the former, and he has appointed a Mr. Harrison (an Englishman by birth, who has been in America) as a kind of acting Vice Consul. There must be, at times, a good deal of trouble in dispatching vessels from the Custom House. For which, I am informed, they receive Consular fees, somewhat on the plan of the British establishment for this Port. I do not know exactly to what sum these amount. But I will write more fully on these subjects, when I shall have acquired farther knowledge of them. The British, whose Factory here is very opulent, and who are more extensive in their commerce with this country than the Merchants of any other Nation, have, by their expensive provisions for protecting and succouring the Trade, made the Port charges very high. They have a Hospital for Seamen of the Royal Navy, and another for those of Merchantmen. In order to prevent their own Masters of Vessels from smuggling, the Factory petitioned Government to put two Custom House officers on board of each vessel. This was done at the expense of the owners. They afterwards petitioned that these officers might be dispensed with as unnecessary and burdensome. But, instead of obtaining relief from the expense for the Trade of their own nation, the burden has been extended to the Merchant Vessels of all other nations. Every vessel is boarded by three different official Boats, with a number of Officers in each, before it can pass the Castle of the Tagus to come up to Lisbon. By the little observation I have been able to make, I am convinced that the most favored nation must be subject in its commercial intercourse here, to great embarrassments, delays and charges.

I unfortunately mislaid, among my papers, the small Memorandum you was so kind as to give me of the Book Store, at which I could find, the Privileges of the English in Portugal. I spent more than a day in searching for the Book, at almost every shop in London, without being able to procure it. If you will have the goodness to *repeat the Memorandum*, I shall be able in season to obtain the Book, together with others for which I have made arrangements through Mr. Johnson. This Gentleman gave me a letter to Messrs. John, Bulkeley & Son of this Place, who are extensively engaged in American commercial business. Letters for me may, at present, be addressed under cover to that *Mercantile House*, who will take charge of them, and to whom I have engaged to refund the postage.—Mr. Johnson has written to Mr. George C. Fox, Merchant at Falmouth, to receive and forward all such letters as may be enclosed to his care directed to or transmitted from me.

A Gentleman from Malaga informed me, that the Pirates of Morocco have been very troublesome in giving alarms on the Coasts of Spain; and that they have sometimes landed and carried off families, for whose ransome (provided the Prisoners be of any consideration) they receive large sums: but accounts arrived, at the moment, from Gibralter give reason to believe a pacification will be immediately effected between the Spaniard and Moors. The Moorish Emperor seems disposed to lay the Christian Powers under a new contribution, upon his accession to the Throne.

I shall hold myself prepared to set out for Madrid, as soon as my business in this place can be accomplished. If I should be obliged to hire Mules here to go through to Madrid (for there are no relays of Post Horses or Mules on the road) the journey will be irksome; slow and expensive. Sometimes a passage offers in a returning Carriage at a reasonable rate, but for such a contingency I shall not wait, especially as the rainy season is commencing. With the highest sentiments of esteem & respect, I have the honor to be Sir, Your Most obedient & Most humble Servant,

D. HUMPHREYS.

P.S. Finding the private conveyance I expected will not happen sooner than that by the Packet, I have opened the Seal of this letter, to put it under the same cover with my other Dispatches.

D.H.

RC (DNA: RG 59, DD); at head of text: "(No. 7)"; endorsed by TJ as received 11 Feb. 1790 and so recorded in SJL. FC (same).

From La Motte

Havre 20. 9bre. [Nov.] 1790.

J'ai recû quatre paniers de vin de Champagne et une petite
Caisse contenant deux Cilindres de Cuivre. Ces objets restent avec
ceux de vos meubles qui doivent vous être envoyés à Philadelphie
directement. Le Cape. Hathaway ne voulant pas s'engager à aller
à Philadelphie de peur d'en trouver les abords gelés, il s'expedie
pour Baltimore ou Philadelphie, de sorte que je n'ai rien pû lui donner pour vous. D'ailleurs les Ecoutilles de son Navire n'etoient point
assés larges pour charger vos voitures. Je crains d'après cela d'être
obligé de laisser passer une bonne partie de l'hyver avant de vous
envoyer ces divers objets qu'il vous feroit sans doute plaisir de
recevoir.

Vous aurés sans doute appris, Monsieur, avant que ma lettre
vous parvienne, que l'angleterre et l'espagne sont entrés dans un
arrangement qui assure la paix; on désarme de part et d'autre, et
nous françois, qui croÿons ne pouvoir éviter de devenir parties ac-
tives dans cette guerre, nous regardons maintenant la paix comme
fermement établie pour longtems en Europe.

Voici quelques papiers qui vous apprendront à quoi on en est
icy sur un objet bien interessant pour les Etats unis, l'abolition ou
la Continuation de la ferme du tabac. L'Issuë des débats renvoye
la decision de cet important article à un tems futur, mais je vous
engage à considerer ce delai comme Compensé par les dispositions
ou vous verrés qu'est l'assemblée nationale d'aviser aux moyens
d'aggrandir la sphere des relations commerciales de la France avec
l'Amerique. Il est facheux dans ces Circonstances qu'on n'ait point
à citer l'exemple d'un seul navire americain qui ait essayé de Con-
vertir en denrées de notre Crû ou de nos manufactures le montant
de son importation. Cela laisse à Croire que les Americains, ac-
coutumés aux fabriques Anglaises, ou entrainés par la conformité
de l'Idiome et par des liaisons de Consanguinité, ne nous donneront
jamais la préference, ni même l'égalité. J'ai l'honneur d'etre avec
une parfaite consideration, Monsieur Votre très humble & très
obeissant Serviteur,   Delamotte

RC (DLC); endorsed as received 3 Mch. 1791 and so recorded in SJL.

From James Maury

SIR   Liverpool 20 Novr. 1790

On the 6th Instant I had the Honor to inform you of the Convention between Spain and this Country.

On this Day the ports of Britain are Shut against the Importation of foreign Wheat and Flour at the low Duties until the 28th February:—after which they will remain so or be opened as prices shall govern. I have the Honor to be with much Respect Sir your most obt St,   JAMES MAURY

RC (DNA: RG 59, CD); endorsed by TJ as received 23 Feb. 1791 and so recorded in SJL.

From John Rutledge, Jr.

DR SIR   Charleston Novr. 20th. 1790

Since my arrival here I have received from Mr. Wedgwood, in england, some of his imitations of etruscan and roman antique lamps vases &c. Amongst the lamps he has sent me, one is fashioned and painted after an etruscan candelabras I saw at his manufactory. His copy I find a very exact one, and he has made it much more complete than the original by fitting to it Keirs patent hydrostatical lamp. This lamp I have had put on board of Captain Strongs vessel, address'd to you at Philadelphia, and I request, Sir, you will do me the favor to accept of this small token of my friendship? I enclose a paper with directions for using Keirs lamp, and another, explaining the principles of it.

Our State does not afford any news worthy of your knowing. The general election was over before I returned. I learn that it was a very quiet one, and that none of our members to Congress met with any opposition. Mr. Burk declined being continued, and the part of the state from which he came, will be represented by Mr. Barnwell, a very virtuous and good Citizen, and who I think will make a valuable member of congress. We have had lately several arrivals from europe, but none of them bring us accounts of as late a date as I suppose you will have received at Philadelphia before this letter gets there. I am very happy to observe, by some irish papers received by them, that the people of that Country are again shewing their uneasiness, and declaring their determination to attempt a political reformation. I wish to god they may be successful, and certainly they will, if there is any truth in Mr. Humes observation that there is an ultimate point of depression from which human affairs naturally return in a contrary progress, and beyond which they never decline. The irish appeared to me, when I was amongst them, to have got to this ultimate point and I never was in a country where *the people* seemed more depress'd by the yoke of servitude. Altho I am glad the spirit of liberty began in france, because I am more partial to that Country than any in europe, yet I rejoice to hear that other countries shew a disposition to cherish it. I most sincerely wish the whole nations of the earth free. Evils enough, god knows, attend humanity, altho' slavery be abolished. From the moment I was certain of the french revolutions success, I was also certain that Revolution would generate others. France counts for two much amongst the european nations not to have the glorious example she has given them imitated, and, I flatter myself, it will be followed by all of them, even by england, tho' probably she will be the last. I do not think the english will be late in reforming because a reformation is less wanted there than amongst the continental nations; but, because the english nation is, in my opinion, more a nation of tories than is generally thought. They are admirers of royalty, of nobility, of arch bishops bishops &c. not merely from the philosophical and manly idea that such gewgawry are for the benefit of the whole nation, but also for the sake of the frippery itself, and they have a veneration for those who wear it, *because they wear it*, more than on account of any good qualities belonging to their characters.

When you shall write to my friend Mr. Short, I will be much obliged to you if you will remember me to him. Since my return I have been so entirely engaged by the company of my friends and relations that it has not been in my power to perform a promise I made him of writing to him, when I should be returned, to inform him how I liked *home*. When in europe we used sometimes to fear that the wisest way of going thro' this world was not to see too much of it; and would, at times, doubt if we should not have been happier men had we remained on the spots where we were born, and attached ourselves to the objects which are there. But it is with real pleasure I find there was no occasion for these reflexions. Having seen many countries of europe has made me, if possible, more closely attached than I was before to this, independent of the happiness which being surrounded by ones friends occasions, I find here. But, my dr Sir, I am entering into a subject which would make this letter much too long for you to read. Indeed it is already very long and methinks I hear you say when will this good man have done. My father desires me to present you with his friendliest Compliments, and I request, Dr Sir, you will believe me to be with the most sincere sentiments of friendship & gratitude Your very much obliged servant,   J. RUTLEDGE JUNIOR

RC (DLC); at foot of text: "Honorable Mr. Jefferson"; endorsed by TJ as received 8 Dec. 1790 and so recorded in SJL.

From Schweighauser & Dobrée

SIR   Nantes 20. Nov. 1790.

Having just now learnt your nomination of Secretary of State, we beg leave to present you with our fellicitations and sincerely congratulate your Countrymen convinced that the greatest blessings a State can enjoy flows from a well chosen Ministry.—This Event destroys the hopes we have long entertained of seing you return to france and of bringing our unhappy affair against the Alliance to a final settlement. Permit us then to request of you to lay once more our Claim before Congress, and apprized of the whole transaction as you are we make no doubt from their resolves of the 23. Augt. 1781 and 16 8bre. 1786, that they will render us the justice we sollicit.

These advances lay extreamly heavy upon us, and causes us continual disputes with our late Partners in the house of Puchelberg & Co. who persist in leaving us the burden of the whole, and say that if we find it too heavy, we are masters to sell the arms, &c. we have in our possession belonging to the U.S.—We have till now in hopes of Justice evaded coming to this extremity. But we greatly fear that as soon as our Tribunal de Comerce is established, that they will insist on the decision of this affair. We need not remind you that the above arms &ca. are perishing and pay a constant warehouse hire, that our advances were made for the service of the *United States* and legally attested, that our Conduct towards America and the Americains has been such during the whole revolution as to procure us the most satisfactory acknowledgement from our employers, that several of them to this day owe us considerable sums of money, and lastly that this privation of our funds, proves very detrimental to us, and to our late Mr. Schweighauser's numerous familly and retards their settlement in the world. In Justice sake Dear sir take this in consideration and be assured of the lively Sence and Gratitude we will ever retain of it.

We are very respectfuly Honoured Sir! Your most humble & obt servants, most obt Ser[vt.],

SCHWEIGHAUSER & DOBRÉE

RC (DNA: RG 59, MLR); endorsed by TJ as received 12 Mch. 1791, but not recorded in SJL. Dupl (same); en- dorsed by TJ as received 21 Feb. 1791 and so recorded in SJL.

From La Motte

SIR   havre 21st. of Novber. 1790.

I have received the letter you was pleased to honour me with under date 26th. August, Containing your orders and instructions relative to my discharging the office of Vice-Consul in this and neighbouring places. You may depend on my Strict Complying to them and that I will make it my Study, not only to reach your views, but not to overpass them.

As it will take Some time before my Commission be put in force, it will be impossible for me to send you any table of the ships arrived in my district, Except from first of January to the last day of June next, and this first table, if my Commission qualifies me to Act before the end of this year, will include the Ships that will have fallen in the remainder of this year.

After having Consulted Mr. Short about the matter, I have embarked on board the brig hawke, Capt. Robert hathaway, bearer of this, a Seaman named Benjamin huls, born in blooming-grove, State of New-york, aged twenty three years, Son to Nathaniel huls and Peggy Sutherlay. This man was brought here by the brig Rambler, Capne. Richard Gillcrist who lives in New-york arrived here in the month of february last with a Cargo of 732. Bbls. of flour Shipp'd at New-york in the month of January by Mr. Conningham Nesbitt & Co. to the Consignment of Mr. Cellery & Boismarsas Agents for french government in this place. This Cape. Gillcrist had on board his owner or Supercargo John Keaquiet.

Benjamin huls having had during his passage the misfortune of being frozen, he was put on the first of March in the hospital at the rate of 1.^{lt} 10s. a day, where he has had his toes Cut off, and Cape. Gillcrist at his departure, the latter end of march was obliged to leave him, So that Mr. Cellery & Boismarsas have been till now at the expence of his board and maintenance at the hospital, which expences I will reimbourse them of and give you an account of the whole by next opportunity, together with Six Louis I have paid Cape. hathaway for passage, which Sum I would have thought myself intitled to reduce to five louis, had I been qualified to Act as Vice-Consul.

I am told that Benjn. huls is rather weak in his intellects and as he told me that he has lost his papers I have given directions to the Captain to deliver him to the head officers of the place he will arrive at, Baltimore or Philadelphia. I remain respectfully Sir Your most obedient, humble Servant, DELAMOTTE

RC (DNA: RG 59, CD); endorsed by TJ as received 3 Mch. 1791 and so recorded in SJL.

From William Nelson, Jr.

SIR   Wmsburg Novr. 22d. 1790

An indisposition of some weeks, with the uninterupted succession of courts, prevented my earlier attention to the subject of your letter, which I have answered this day. The intervention of another circumstance, which might be improperly mentioned in a public letter, has also retarded my sending before the inclosed orders and proclamations. This was the illness of my mother, who, I am happy to say, is much better. Information of this brought me from Richmond near a fortnight past. When I left that place, I left also the copies of the laws to be authenticated; but, on my return, found, that the weight of business on the clerk of the house of delegates had prevented his examining them. This therefore occasioned an additional delay.

At the end of the laws passed in Octr. 1784, which, I find from the note to your letter, is in the office of your department, is published, what is called "an act for enabling British Merchants to recover their debts from Citizens &c." On Decr. 30th. of that year, this act passed the house of delegates. The senate made certain amendments to it. These were agreed to, except one. On a conference the house of delegates acceded, and agreed to the amendment proposed by the senate with an amendment. The senate agreed to this amendment of the house of delegates to their amendment, so that the act had passed both houses; but, before the report hereupon was made from the Senate to the house of delegates, the river at Richmond became frozen over, which prevented the return of a sufficient number of members to form a house. Thus the act had the assent of both houses, and, possibly, a question may arise, whether, under our constitution this was not a law, or at least equal to one, altho it had not been reported from the Senate, nor was it signed by the Speakers. You, no doubt, remember a decision of the general court, that a resolution might repeal a law, in a case of certain Staff officers, who made a claim under an act of assembly, which the court determined was repealed by a resolution.

The last assembly passed a law, declaring that a resolution shall not be construed to repeal a law. Whether this declaration would affect this case, I cannot certainly determine, as I have not the last-mentioned law by me, and an anxiety to close my letter this evening prevents my postponing it 'till tomorrow. I suppose however, as it relates to the construction of what should be considered to be a law, that the assembly intended, that it should have a retrospective operation; however improbable it may be, that the judges would give it such a construction. It is not likely that the force of this act will *now* come into controversy, considering the treaty, the powers of the Congress under the late Government, the adoption of the new Constitution, and the operation of it's courts. Still I have had it copied, as the payment by installments, which are authorized by it, and the suspension of interest during the war will be considered as infractions of the treaty, if the act should be holden to be in force, and will send it authenticated, if you wish for it. I thought it improper to annex it to the laws which have passed thro' all the formalities as one, or to mention it in the letter directed to you officially.

With respect to adjudications, as I have never been present at one on the subject of your letter, and know of none, in which the debts, property, or persons of British-subjects have appeared on record to be included in the decision, I have been silent on that head in my answer sent with this; but will mention what I have heard of opinions in courts where I do not practice, and the arguments which have occur'd at those which I attend.

I have understood, that, at the last State-district-court at New-London, a plaintiff was nonsuited on evidence being given that he was a British-subject. I have heard also that something similar took place at the district-court holden in Charlottesville, the term before last, and at a session of the court in Fredericksburg that it was the opinion of the judges that our laws on the subject are to be repealed by the legislature of the State, before British-subjects can recover their debts.

The general court, which is now in session, made an order that the suits, suspended by the sequestration-law should be sent to the districts; but no decision is made as to the propriety of rendering judgement in them.

Some members of the bar support an opinion that the act marked No. 9 in the list enclosed, whilst in force, or if now in force, only prevents the recovery of debts which have been assigned by British subjects to Citizens. On this subject, as well as for a further answer to your letter I beg leave to refer you to my next. I am, with great Regard, Sir, yr. obedt Svt,   WM. NELSON JR

P.S. Colo. Monroe can probably give information as to the judgements said to have been given at Charlottesville and Fredericksburg.   WN

RC (DNA: RG 59, MLR); endorsed by TJ as received 3 Dec. 1790 and so recorded in SJL.

From William Nelson, Jr.

SIR   Wmsburg Novr. 22d. 1790.

I received your favor desiring information of the proceedings in this State, which may be considered by Great Britain as infractions of the treaty, and copies of all acts, orders, proclamations, and decisions, legislative, executive and judiciary, which may have affected the debts or other property, or the persons, of British-subjects, or American-refugees, and do myself the pleasure of inclosing you the following resolutions, and laws, on the subject, duly authenticated.

Passed Decr.

1st. The Resolutions for putting in execution the Statute-Staple.

1776.
[Ma]r 1777.

2d. An act for sequestering British property &c. See the collection of laws, made pursuant to the resolution of June 16th. 1783. published under the inspection of the judges of the high-court of Chancery. P. 64.

1779

3d. An act concerning escheats and forfeitures &c. P. 9-8

May

4th. An act concerning escheators 106

Octr.

5th. An act to amend the act entitled "an act concerning escheats and forfeitures" P. 110

6th. An act confirming the titles of purchasers of escheated and forfeited estates. P.[1]

Passed

7th. An act repealing part of an act entitled "an act for seques-   1780 May.
tering British property &c."

8th. An act to adjust and regulate the pay and accounts of the   1781.
officers and soldiers &c." The 5th. 6th. and 15th. sections of this   Novr.
law relate to the subject P. 145.

9th. An act to repeal so much of a former act as suspends the   1782
issuing of executions upon former judgements untill Decr. 1783   May.
P. 165.

10th. An act providing more effectual funds for the redemption
of certificates granted to the officers and soldiers &c. P. 166

The first, second and third sections of this act relate to the subject of your letter.

11th. An act to amend an act entitled "an act to repeal so much
of a former act as suspends the issuing of executions untill Decr.   Octr.
1783" P. 182.

These are the laws and resolutions previous to the treaty. Those
passed subsequent to that event on this subject are the following.

In order since the beginning of the revolution	In order since the treaty		Passed
No. 12	No. 1.	An act for the admission of emigrants and declaring their rights to Citizenship. P. 213. Passed in the Octr. session 1783.	
No. 13	No. 2	An act prohibiting the migration of certain persons to this Commonwealth	1783 Octr.
14	3	Resolutions respecting the infractions of the seventh article of the definitive treaty.	1784 June
15th	4.	An act to explain, amend, and reduce into one act, the several acts for the admission of emigrants to the rights of citizenship, and prohibiting the migration of certain persons to this Commonwealth. P. 12 of this Session.	1786 Octr.
16th	5	An act to repeal so much of all and every act or acts of assembly as prohibits the recovery of British debts. P. 25. of the acts of this session.	1787 Octr.
17.	6.	An act concerning monies paid into the public loan office,	

in payment of British debts. You will also receive with this copies of such orders of council as I have been able to procure. Those relative to sequestered property will, I presume, be found in the journals of council, now in possession of Colo. Davies, one of the commissioners for settling the accounts of the United States with the individual States. As that gentleman is in Philadelphia with the books, I must refer you to them on the subject. If you wish for copies of the returns which have been made to the assembly of the profits of these estates, you will be kind enough to inform me. In this case, these journals may probably serve in some measure as an index. I also send the following proclamations.

1st. One of July 1st. 1779. Commanding all persons, who were British-subjects, within the escheat-law to appear before the Governor in council &c.

2d. Decr. 19th. 1782. To arrest British-subjects &c.

3d. April 21st. 1783. for a cessation of hostilities.

4th. July 2d. 1783. Commanding persons who have adhered to the enemy, or voluntarily left this country, or have been expel'd by any act of the legislature, or order of the executive &c. to depart.

5th. July 26th. 1784. For the protection of those who have come into the State under the acts of Octr. 1783.

6. Octr. 14th. 1786. Commanding those whose residence is forbidden by "an act to prevent the migration of certain persons to this Commonwealth &c." to depart, and, for the preservation of the rights of foreign nations, requiring information of them to be given to the attorney-general.

As to a complete collection of the laws of this State, I have procured the revisals printed in 1733, in 1752, and 1769, which I shall send forward shortly, and I expect to procure those of an earlier date. You will be kind enough to inform me whether you wish for a list of inquests, traverses, and injunctions which may be depending relative to the estates of British-subjects. I have directed a copy of the act to prohibit intercourse with British subjects, which was passed in Octr. 1782, and shall transmit it as soon as I receive it. In the mean time I have the honor to be with great Regard yr. obedt Svt,   WM. NELSON JR

RC (DNA: RG 59, MLR); endorsed by TJ as received 3 Dec. 1790 and so recorded in SJL.

[1] The page number is omitted in MS, being the same as that preceding, 110.

From Thomas Auldjo

DEAR SIR   Cowes 23d Novemr 1790

I avail myself of the opportunity of the American Brig Two Brothers bound for New York to entreat your acceptance of some of our latest news papers which I hope you will do me the favor to receive. To them I beg leave to refer you for the news of the times.—We are here becoming quite pacifick by the late convention with Spain. The fleet is paying off and dismantling as fast as possible, but report says that our number of Guardships is to be 25 Sail of the Line which is an augmentation of 7 Sail beyond the usual peace Establishment. I beg you will dispose of me in your service in every occasion and I have the honor to be most truly Sir Your most obdt most humble Servant,   THOMAS AULDJO

RC (DNA: RG 59, CD); endorsed by TJ as received 11 Mch. 1791 and so recorded in SJL.

From John Churchman

November 23rd. 1790

John Churchmans best respects attend the Secretary of State, in company with a Variation Chart and Book of explanation, hoping they will be accepted as a token of esteem. Before the Book went to the press, he took the Liberty of introducing several articles, all of which have been a considerable credit to the work, 1st. On finding a disposition in his friend to be useful to him on this occasion he inserted his name on the respectable list of patrons. 2nd. A quotation is made from the notes on Virginia. 3rd. Two Letters are published in the appendix. For this Freedom he hopes to receive a pardon.

J.C. would be very glad to be introduced to some suitable correspondent in Paris to whom he might send some of the same kind.

RC (DLC); endorsed by TJ as received 23 Nov. 1790 and so recorded in SJL. Enclosure: Copy of Churchman's *An explanation of the Magnetic Atlas, or Variation Chart . . . projected on a plan entirely new* (Philadelphia, 1790). See Sowerby, No. 669. Churchman included in the appendix to his pamphlet the texts of TJ's letters of 8 Aug. 1787 and 18 Sep. 1789. The list of subscribers includes the following: "Thomas Jefferson, Esq. Secretary of State, late Minister Plenipotentiary of the Court of France." See TJ to Churchman, 18 Sep. 1789, note. The reference to TJ's *Notes on Virginia* (not a quotation) occurs at p. 45 of the pamphlet in a discussion of evidences of an inundation of North America in ages past. The reference to TJ, as well as to Benjamin Lincoln, Lewis Evans, and Charles Thomson, was omitted in the third (1800) edition (Shipton-Mooney, No. 37183).

From Tench Coxe

Sir   [23 Nov. 1790]

Since I had the honor of taking leave of you in New York I have made some Enquiries upon the subject of the fisheries, but from their inattention and want of facility in committing their knowledge to paper even persons concerned in the prosperity of this branch of commerce have yielded little Information. I have however collected from various sources some facts, that may assist to elucidate the subject, which are thrown together and intermingled with my own remarks in the enclosed paper, marked #. You will also find under this cover a paper translated, in abridgment, by a very well informed and judicious German merchant from a Dutch Book, which he assures me is to be relied on.

In the margin of that paper marked **, I have introduced some explanatory notes. To these I shall add in a few days some Documents made up from the Custom house returns to the Treasury Department since the establishment of the general Government, which are nearly complete; also a table of prices referred to in my notes.

On the papers now sent you I beg leave to remark that I have hazarded, without reserve, every idea (though some of them are very light) that appeared worth your examining from a reliance on your candid allowance, and because they were afterwards to undergo your consideration. I must also observe that though I have been a practical merchant, the fisheries never formed an object in the commerce of Philadelphia. You will consider me therefore as a theorist upon this subject, and will find it best to scrutinize cautiously any novelty I may have suggested.

I beg leave, Sir, to avail myself of this occasion to make a tender of any little service it may at any time hereafter be in my power to render, that will promote your individual convenience, or lessen the fatigues of your public station. I have the honor to subscribe myself, with the highest respect, Sir Your most humble & most obedient servt.,

TENCH COXE

RC (DLC); in clerk's hand, except for signature; endorsed by TJ as received 23 Nov. 1790 and so recorded in SJL. Enclosures: (1) Abridgement "from a Dutch Book" with Coxe's notes on the Dutch and Prussian fisheries, printed as Document I in group of documents on fisheries, 1 Feb. 1791; (2) Coxe's notes on the American fisheries, printed as Document II in group of documents on fisheries, 1 Feb. 1791.

From C. W. F. Dumas

Lahaie 23e. Nov. 1790.

Depuis ma dernière du 19e. au 22 Octobre, l'évenement le plus interessant pour nous est l'accommodement signé entre l'Espagne et l'Angleterre. Il faudra voir comment le Ministère Britannique se tirera d'affaires chez eux, pour les 4 millions Sterling dépensés en Armemens. L'on y trouve déjà que les Cabanes de Nootka et une pêche limitée à 10 lieues marines des possessions Espagnoles sont un pauvre dédommagement, une moquerie.

Je ne puis m'empêcher de poursuivre mon idée de Paquebots *Américains* pour ce pays-ci, dont j'ai fait l'ouverture dans mes précédentes, entre autres dans celle du 30e. 7br. Crainte d'abonder en mon sens, et aussi pour sonder un peu sur cette matiere nos amis d'Amsterdam, je leur en ai parlé comme d'une idée que je voudrois proposer. Leur réponse, que je crois devoir transcrire ici, avec mes remarques à côté, me fait conjecturer qu'ils craignent peut-être qu'un tel établissement ne leur fût préjudiciable, quoique j'en ignore et ne puisse concevoir le pourquoi.

Je suis moins crédule, je crois que Votre Excellence l'est encore moins et que nous en avons de bonnes raisons.

"We are not among those persons who are extraordinarily suspicious about the fidelity of Post-offices, which is a point that makes us less friends to your Packet-boot scheme."

Il y a eu de ces Paquebots en France; ils avoient cessé; s'ils ont recommencé tant mieux; mais je voudrois à notre Gouvernement une voie de correspondance régulière avec l'Europe, purement américaine et indépendante de tout autre Gouvernement.

"But were we so, there are Packets from France, which obviate every motive of suspicion the United States could entertain for the perfect safety of their dispatches."

Le même vent qui conduit jusqu'à Falmouth conduira les Paquebots Américains à Helvoet, tandis que les dépeches doivent aller par la poste de Falmouth par Londres à Harwich, et de là par les Paquebots Anglois à Helvoet. D'ailleurs il ne s'agit pas seulement de la plus grande expédition, mais de la plus grande sureté, surtout.

"And as to Expedition, you are terribly mistaken indeed, to think they could have the advantage in that particular over those from Falmouth at the mouth of the Channel, or the French ports in the Bay of Biscay. No, Sir, so inimical[1] is our situation for dispatch, that it is not one in twenty times perhaps, that we cannot hope for arrivals sooner from England than any of these ports."

Il ne s'agit pas de la connexion politique des Etats Unis avec ce pays-ci, mais de la politique générale de l'Europe, dont il est le foyer ordinaire. Une intelligence traitreusement interceptée, ou une fausseté artificieusement propagée

"Adding to which the little importance, in our Opinion, for American politics, what goes on in this Country, or their connexion with it under the actual system, and we have no doubt that your plan would be deemed both useless and improper."

et accréditée en Amérique, peut plus coûter à pure perte aux Etats-Unis que cent paquebots. Leur politique me paroît exiger de savoir *régulierement*, par des *bâtimens et gens entierement en leur puissance et à leur dévotion*, le vrai et le faux, le bon et le mauvais de l'Europe, afin de profiter de l'un et éviter l'autre avec sureté et connoissance de cause.

du 26 Nov.

L'insurrection Brabançonne touche à son terme. Probablement les Autrichiens seront les maîtres du pays la semaine prochaine. Une nation si bigote, et les cagots qui la gouvernent, ne pouvoient finir que par servir de risée à toute la terre.

du 27 Nov. 1790.

L'on vient me dire que Namur est prise par les Autrichiens. Cela étant, Bruxelles, Louvain, Malines et Anvers vont suivre, et tout sera dit. Je suis avec grand respect, De Votre Excellence, Le très-humble, très-obéissant & fidele serviteur

C W F Dumas

Dupl (DNA: RG 360, PCC No. 93); at head of text: "No. 70 Dup."; endorsed by TJ as received 19 June 1791 but not recorded in SJL. The RC (missing) is recorded in SJL as received 8 Apr. 1791.

[1] Thus in MS. Either Dumas' correspondents or he himself obviously erred; "inimitable" was perhaps the word intended.

To Thomas Mann Randolph, Jr.

Dear   Philadelphia Nov. 23. 1790.

I wrote you from George town inclosing some seed of the best white wheat. Our journey here was without accident, except that of retardation by the rains. Our delay happened however at the Susquehanna, where the abundance of Sheldrakes was some solace. My newly purchased horse (Brimmer) performed well; I drove him a good deal in the carriage. I do not think he lost a pound of flesh on the road, so that I have a very good opinion of him. The President will be here on the 26th. The rumours of war are pretty well blown over. Peace is made between Sweden and Russia as is believed, and consequently it will take place thro' the whole of the North and East of Europe. I cannot believe that Spain and England will go to war, tho' they shew no symptoms of disarming. It is said indeed that their fleets are retired into port. The price of wheat here is 8/6 to 8/10, say about 7/ Virginia money. This is ascribed, not to any demand from Europe (for it is pretended that that demand is very limited, and that every country there has made enough for itself) but from the notions of the farmers exalted by last years high prices and therefore holding back their wheat insomuch that enough cannot be bought for the West India demand. I cannot help believing there is some justice in this statement and consequently that towards the spring the price will fall when the farmers begin to bring in their wheat generally. I will be obliged to you to mention these circumstances to Mr. Lewis, as a reason for so selling what wheat is for sale as to ensure the best price from the time of selling till the spring, and to hasten the sale. I believe I asked your attention to the upland rice. I have received a few more grains of that of the Moluccas from Mr. Samuel Vaughan of Jamaica, with a note of which the inclosed is a copy. My furniture is arrived from Paris, except my carriages. My house here, however, will not be ready for some weeks. I shall write weekly as heretofore to yourself and the girls by turns and will hope answers on your parts, by which means I shall hear from you by some one of the family once a week regularly. I calculate thus. I will send my letters by the post of Wednesday always. They will arrive in Richmond in time for the Charlottesville post. You will receive them the Saturday (11 days after they leave this place). If answered on Sunday, the Albemarle post will carry them to Richmond immediately and they will be here before the expiration of the three weeks from the date of mine, so that writing the next day again to the same person in turn, the correspondence with each may be continued. I inclose you the newspapers to this date. I forgot to mention that I am unable to open my packages from Paris till so much of my house can be ready as will contain them. I shall then immediately send on some of the mattrasses. My cordial love to the girls, and believe me to be Dear Sir Yours affectionately,   TH: JEFFERSON

RC (DLC). PrC (DLC). Enclosure: Copy of Vaughan to TJ, 4 Oct. 1790, received the day before.

TJ arrived in Philadelphia on 20 Nov. 1790. More than fifty letters were awaiting him, including some from Europe more than a year old (SJL). BRIMMER: a former race horse of notable lineage (see TJ to Fitzhugh 21 July 1790).

Henry Remsen, Jr. to Benjamin Russell and Others

SIR   Philadelphia Novr. 23d 1790

I am directed by the Secretary of State to request that you will furnish him with an estimate of the expense that will attend the publication of the Laws of the United States in your paper. It should mention the lowest price for which you will perform this work, and on account of the meeting of Congress early in next month, be transmitted to him without delay. I am Sir &c.

FC (DNA: RG 59, PCC No. 120); at head of text: "To the Printers who publish Laws"; duplicates of this letter were sent to Benjamin Russell, Boston, editor of the *Columbian Centinel*; Childs & Swaine, New York, editors of the *Daily Advertiser*; Andrew Brown, Philadelphia, editor of the *Federal Gazette*; Augustine Davis, Richmond, editor of the *Virginia Gazette, and General Advertiser*; and to Mrs. Ann Timothy, Charleston, editor of the State *Gazette of South-Carolina*.

Although the act under which TJ exercised an authority having potential political influence directed that the laws be published in at least three newspapers in as many states, he soon extended the number to five and hoped eventually to extend it to all (see note on TJ's arrangement with John Fenno, under 20 Mch. 1790). His initial use of this patronage benefited those newspapers that tended to favor federal or national views. Thus he first chose Fenno's *Gazette of the United States*, continued to recognize Benjamin Russell's *Columbian Centinel*, avoided the partisan conflict of editors in Rhode Island, and patronized Andrew Brown whose *Federal Gazette* Benjamin Rush said had been "very instrumental . . . in circulating federal sentiments" through Pennsylvania (see Howell to TJ, 6 July 1790; TJ to Howell, 21 July 1790; Rush to TJ, 15 Aug. 1790; Fenner to TJ, 31 Aug. 1790; Carter to TJ, 24 Sep. 1790; Rush's opinion of Brown is from Rush to John Adams, 26 Jan. 1790, MHi: AM). When the government moved to Philadelphia TJ transferred the privilege from Fenno, whose partisanship had clearly emerged before the newspaper left New York, to Andrew Brown. Remsen was permitted to handle such communications as the above, but there can be no doubt that it was TJ who decided which papers were to be granted the privilege of printing the laws. Having recently found that Fenno's paper had become partisan instead of presenting general intelligence in the manner TJ had persuaded him to do for a brief period, TJ must have given Benjamin Franklin Bache the same kind of encouragement as he passed through Philadelphia early in September (see Vol. 16: 232-67). Two of the early issues of Bache's *General Advertiser* carried British arguments on weights and measures consonant with TJ's own recommendations, probably supplied by him to the paper (see documents on coinage, under 29 Dec. 1790, note 22 of Editorial Note). There soon followed reports to the National Assembly on finances by Montesquieu and on tobacco by Roederer, along with selections from the *Gazette de Leide*, certainly supplied by TJ. See also TJ to Randolph, 15 May 1791.

On the responses of the editors, see Brown to TJ, 26 Nov. 1790; Davis to TJ, 2 Dec. 1790; Russell to TJ, 5 Dec. 1790; and Childs & Swaine to TJ, 16 Dec. 1790. No answer was received from Mrs. Ann Timothy, editor of the State *Gazette of South-Carolina*. Remsen wrote her again on 11 Jan. 1791, informing her that the Secretary of State had fixed the rate of compensation for publishing the laws in five newspapers, and added: "He intends yours shall be of the number, and only waits your determination" before sending authenticated copies of employing "some other Printer in Charleston to undertake it, in case you decline" (FC in DNA: RG 59, PCC No. 120). For TJ's determination, see Remsen to the printers, 10 Jan. 1791. Texts of most of TJ's letters with printers during his tenure as Secretary of State are printed in Jessie Ryon Lucke's "Some Correspondence with Thomas Jefferson Concerning the Public Printers," *Papers of the Bibliographical Society, University of Virginia*, I (1948), 27-37. See also, J. H. Powell, *Books of a New Nation* (1957), p. 88; W. A. Katz, "An Episode in Patronage: Federal Laws Published in Newspapers," *Am. Jour. Legal Hist.*, X (July 1966), 214-23.

From William Channing

Sir   Newport November 24th. AD 1790

The letter you were pleased to honor me with of the 12th. of August, I received soon after the date, and have since attended to the objects it respected. The situation of the records of our State, made your commission a business of some difficulty, and a part of it still remains unexecuted. That part however is in a prosperous train.

Herewith are transmitted authenticated Copies of all the Acts of our Legislature, that affect either the debts, or the persons of British Subjects, or American refugees. As to the proceedings of the Judiciary of this State upon these Acts, I have to observe, that the one for confiscating of the Estates of the persons therein described, was early carried into effect, with regard to those who were contemplated by it, the American refugees; and their Estates were confiscated and sold, and the proceeds after the payment of the debts of the original proprietors, were paid into the Treasury of the State. This Act was considered by our Courts as annulled by the Treaty of Peace, and subsequent to the ratification thereof, no proceedings have been had thereon. Government during the war, were possessed of the real Estates belonging to British Subjects, but on the application of the Proprietors, they have been since restored, and the rents and Profits accounted for.

The Act of Banishment has not been formally repealed by the Legislature; but I have not known any instance, in which it has been enforced; although many persons, either named or described in the Act have since the War resided, and some of them still reside among us.

The Courts of this State have been ever open alike to the British Subject, and the American Citizen; and equally enabled either, to recover his just debt, agreeably to Contract, until the substituting and paper money Acts were made.—The first of these Acts was repealed soon after the passing of it, but the other continued to operate untill September 1789. But previous to this, in September 1787, from an Idea that the making the Paper money a Tender might be considered as an infraction of the Treaty with Great Britain, the Legislature passed the resolution, declaring the Obligation of the Treaty sacred and inviolable.

Herewith are also transmitted the Code, that contains all the existing Laws of this State up to the last revision. The subsequent laws are blended with a great deal of other matter in a great number of Schedules; and must be transmitted in manuscript. This is that part of the business which still remains unexecuted, but which is in a train to be executed. I shall exert my endeavours to have the manuscript in readiness to forward as expeditiously as the nature of the business will permit.[1]

I have the honor to be with great respect Sir Your most Obedient and most Humble Servant, WILLM. CHANNING

RC (DNA: RG 59, MLR); endorsed by TJ as received 23 Dec. 1790 and so recorded in SJL. FC (DNA: RG 59, SDR); at head of text: "No. 19. Extract of a letter from William Channing . . . to the Honble. Thomas Jefferson, Secretary of State"; extract consists of the whole of the letter save the paragraph indicated below and forms Appendix No. 19 in TJ's reply to Hammond, 29 May 1792. PrC of Extract (DLC); in another clerk's hand, and identical with text in FC.

[1] This paragraph omitted in FC and PrC.

To John Churchman

[24 Nov. 1790]

Th: Jefferson presents his compliments to Mr. Churchman and his thanks for the pamphlet and chart he has been so good as to send him. He incloses him a letter to Mr. Leroy, who will recieve and distribute such of these pamphlets and charts as Mr. Churchman may send to him. It will be proper to take care that no expence fall on him for either postage or transportation.

RC (PPAP); addressed: "Mr. John Churchman Philadelphia"; at foot of text in Churchman's hand: "came to hand 24 Nov. 90." PrC (DLC). Enclosure: TJ to Jean Baptiste LeRòy, 24 Nov. 1790, reading: "Mr. Churchman being desirous of sending to some person in Paris some of his Variation charts and pamphlets for purposes which he will explain by letter, I take the liberty of advising him to address them to you, whose zeal for the service of science has ever rendered you open to it's votaries. The importance of the object of his researches and the ingenuity he had displayed in pursuing them will I am sure interest your attention to them. I am happy in this and every other occasion of assuring you of the sincerity of those sentiments of esteem & respect with which I have the honour to be Sir Your most obedt. & most humble servt., Th: Jefferson" (PrC in DLC).

To Alexander Hamilton

Nov. 24. 1790.

Th: Jefferson presents his respectful compliments to the Secretary of the Treasury, and incloses him a note from Mr. Droz, the coiner, which he forgot to deliver to him to-day when he had the honour of waiting on him. It came to hand yesterday.

PrC (DLC); not recorded in SJL. The enclosed note from Droz was in that from Grand to TJ, 28 Aug. 1790.

To Henry Knox

Th: Jefferson presents his respectful compliments to Genl. Knox and incloses him a copy of a memoire sent him by Blanc the gunsmith who made the 6. fusils sent to Genl. Knox. It will explain to him more fully the extent of Blanc's improvements.

He incloses him also some certificates in favor of a Mr. Hastings Marks junr. of Virginia who would be glad of some commission in the federal troops to the Westward should an opening exist or occur.

PrC (DLC). Blanc's MEMOIRE has not been found, but it was probably enclosed in Short to TJ, 4 Aug. 1790 (private). For TJ's abortive effort to promote the principle of interchangeable parts in the manufacture of weap-ons, see TJ to Knox, 12 Sep. 1789. HASTINGS MARKS, JR. was married to TJ's sister Anna (or Nancy). Marks was appointed ensign in 1791 (JEP, I, 86, 88).

From James Brown

DEAR SIR   Richmond 25th: Novm 1790

I have your favors of the 29th: Ultimo and 4th: Current and thank you for the information therin contained. I have no late letters from France but the Publick Prints bespeaks a Civil War, should that take place property of every kind would be subject to certain risk and deters me from availing myself of your advice. Tobacco of New Crop may now be Purchased at and under 3 dollars at which Price it should leave a handsome profit in France even at 30£ ℔ Ct. I will be regulated in my operations by the advices I may receive, at Present I shall go on with a Purchase and promise myself the Honor of hearing from you when you receive any advices from France of consequence in the Business in question.—The Spinet and two Boxes of Books were received here ten days having the Schooner Lennet Cap. Weymore loading Wheat at Ansley to the address of Anda: Clow & Co. at Philada: I sent the three Packages on board her two days ago, and will hand you Bill Loading as soon as I receive it. The Boxes being in good order and no such thing as Oil Cloth to be got here I forwarded them as I received them. With due respect I am Dr Sir Your obt: Hbl. Sv,   JAMES BROWN

RC (MHi); endorsed by TJ as received 3 Dec. 1790 and so recorded in SJL.

From Henrietta Maria Colden

SIR   New York Novr. 25th. 1790

I feel at this moment, that it requires a share of Courage, thus, to solicit your attention, which even the liberality and benevolence of your disposition might fail to inspire; did not the anxieties of a mother surmount feelings, that in other circumstances would have prevented this intrusion; and impel me to address you on a Matter, that lays heavy on my Mind.

My Eldest Son (who arrived here soon after your departure) has conceived an insurmountable Passion for the Sea. The bias originated in childhood and has been rivetted by his Voyage to Ireland. I find that his Studies have been directed to those branches of the Mathematicks and Natural Philosophy, connected with Scientific Navigation, Naval Architecture and Tactics, with an Avidity and perseverance, that mark, the force of his predeliction for the Naval line. He has also, availed himself of the opportunities afforded him in his Voyages to make himself a practical (as well as a Theoreatical) Seaman. I am told by Gentlemen of that profession, that his endeavours to attain the Art of Seamanship have been but too successful.—The fact is, that possessed of that decisive and collected Spirit, which rests upon itself; and of considerable Mathematical talents, he feels that Nature has furnished him with materials to gratify his ruling Passion to distinguish himself as a Sea Officer and Scientific Navigator; and is determined to pursue his Object at all Risks, and to spare no pains nor study that can ensure him success. Devoted to America, his Object is to serve in her Navy; which, with the enthusiasm of Hope, and the ardour of youthful expectation, he already pictures, riding triumphant on the Ocean, and giving Laws to Europe. Fully persuaded that a very few Years, will realize his vision, and America become a Maritime Power; he is desirous in the interim, of being employed in the only naval line in the Service of the Government which now offers; and wishes to get appointed Second in Command, to one of the Revenue Cutters; which, he understands are speedily to be put in Commission. The nearer the Station to the Seat of Government the more (he thinks) it would promote his Ultimate Views, in affording him opportunities of being known to the President and other distinguished Public Characters, and of obtaining a knowledge of the Politicks of America.

I confess to you Sir, that my Son's election of a Sea life is adverse to the Views I had formed for him, and the happiness I had promised myself in his Society—but he tells me, that *his* happiness depends on being permitted to follow his bias for the Sea; and I have yielded mine to that consideration. He tells me too, that should he fail in his *first* wish, to be employed in the Service of his Country, he has determined to try his fortune in some Foreign Navy: an Alternative I anxiously wish to avoid.

I have trespass'd Sir, on your leisure with this detail to request, that should an opportunity present itself, you would have the goodness, to mention my Son to the President as a Youth of some Talents, who has resolved to dedicate himself to the Naval line, and is desirous (for the present) to serve in the Station already mentioned, on board one of Revenue Vessels. Your good Offices, on this occasion, may make him happy in the attainment of his present Object, and prevent an Alternative, in which I contemplate the extinction of all my hopes in him.

To any one but yourself Sir, the liberty I have taken would require much Apology.—Amongst the Characters who have access to the President there are some to whom I am better known, than I have the honor to be to you Sir, but there are none to whom my Mind would be more at ease, under a Sense of obligation. I have the honor to be with much Regard Sir, Your most obedt. and humble Servt., HENRIETTA M. COLDEN

RC (DLC); endorsed by TJ as received 27 Nov. 1790 and so recorded in SJL.

It is interesting that Mrs. Colden should have appealed to TJ to intercede in behalf of her elder son for an appointment on one of the revenue cutters rather than to the Secretary of the Treasury. For TJ's earlier relation with the son, see Madison to TJ 23 May 1789; TJ to Dugald Stewart, 21 June 1789.

To Alexander Donald

DEAR SIR   Philadelphia Nov. 25. 1790.

Your favor of Sep. 1. came to my hands a few days ago and gave me the first account of your safe arrival in England, on which, as well as your pleasant voyage accept my friendly congratulations. The incertainty of the footing on which the supplying the French market with tobacco will be put, induces me to believe that the surest mode of rendering you that service which I ever wish to render you, is to give a special recommendation on the subject to Mr. Short, who will best know to whom an efficacious application can be made, and who will make any use of my name in it which may seem to promise any effect. I presume he will be returning from Amsterdam to Paris about the time you will recieve this, or certainly very soon after. What business I do in Virginia myself with any mercantile house, I do with Mr. Brown for whose character, as given me by others I have great respect. With respect to my general affairs, they are in the hands of Colo. Lewis, and you know there is no delegating a trust by halves. I say to him always that when he can do business with Mr. Brown equally to his own mind, my partiality asks a preference of him. You will not expect mercantile news from me, and we have none political. I only add therefore assurances of the esteem with which I am Dear Sir your affectionate friend & servt.,

Th: Jefferson

RC (ViW); addressed: "Alexander Donald esquire of the house of Donald & Burton merchants London" and (in another hand) "⅌ Ship London"; post-marked: "JA 10" and "DOVER SHIP LRE." PrC (DLC). TJ probably enclosed his letter to Short of the same date with the above.

From William Lewis

Sir   [Philadelphia] Nov: 25th: 1790

Whether you will charge me with neglect or not, in not having Compleated the business respecting which you sometime since wrote me, I cannot say, but be that as it may, I cannot in my own mind entirely acquit myself, although I might offer some apology if I did not think it better to let you know what has realy been done and what is to be expected. Most of the Laws which you desired to have were transmitted to your office at New York. There has been much Difficulty in collecting the remainder, which could only be picked up in Pamphlets as they cou'd be found in different places, and a few of them are yet wanting although I flatter myself this will not long be the case. In order to ascertain what Laws had been passed in Pennsylvania, and what proceedings by the executive authority had taken place, which might be supposed to Contravene the Treaty with his Britainic Majesty, I have examined the Acts of the Legislature, I have applied to the British Consul for a List of real or supposed Grievances, and I have applied to the supreme executive Council for the necessary extracts from their proceedings. Being by these Means furnished with the necessary Information, I should have laid it before you in a Day or two, had I not been call'd to York-Town to try some interesting Causes.

On my return I will lay before you such Information as I have been able to Collect, and I must beg that until then you will excuse the seeming, I hope not real Inattention of Sir Your mo: obt. & mo: hble Servt,

WM. LEWIS

RC (DNA: RG 59, MLR); endorsed by TJ as received 27 Nov. 1790 and so recorded in SJL.

Lewis wrote TJ on 14 Sep. 1790 promising to attend to the request in TJ's of 12 Aug. 1790 immediately, having theretofore been impeded by engagements "in the State Convention, in the legislature and in Court."

He promised to send all the laws of Pennsylvania, ancient and modern, in a few days and, as soon as possible, "Copies of all proceedings since the treaty with Great Britain, which may be considered as infractions of the treaty" (RC in DNA: RG 59, MLR, endorsed by TJ as received 2 Nov. 1790 and so recorded in SJL).

To Paul R. Randall

SIR

Philadelphia Nov. 25. 1790.

My departure from New York having obliged me to leave unanswered several of the letters addressed to me, and of course those which were last received, your favor of Aug. 26. which was of that number, remains to be answered on my return here. This I take the liberty of doing by inclosing you the extract of a letter I wrote to one of the first applicants for the office of chief clerk, and which has been sent to the others, explaining the reasons which oblige me to consider the office of additional chief clerk as no longer existing, and consequently putting it out of my power to avail myself of your assistance. I have the honour to be with sentiments of great esteem Sir Your most obedt. & most humble servt,

TH: JEFFERSON

PrC (DLC). Enclosure: Not found, but perhaps an extract of TJ to Barton, 12 Aug. 1790.

Remsen's Account of Moving Expenses

[25 Nov. 1790]

1790	The Honorable Mr. Jefferson	Dr.	
Augt. 9th.		New York curry.	
	To cash paid for a silver Inkpot & pen 2 1/2 dollars		£1. 0.0
October 1st.	" paid Francis & Mathew 14 1/2 dollars each		11.12.0
	" paid for strapping Mr. Jefferson's cases with hoops		0.10.0

		[To cash] paid for carting Mr. Jefferson's furniture, including Francas's, to the wharf	1. 5.0
13th.	"	paid the freight of Mr. Jefferson's effects, and those of Mr. Madison, and the Servants	9.12.0
	"	paid the passages of Francis & his wife & Mathew	2. 0.0
14th.	"	paid the cartage of Mr. Jefferson's furniture, Mr. Madison's & Servants	0.16.4
Novem. 6th.	"	paid Francis & Mathew eleven dollars each	8.16.0
			£35.19.4

Cr. by cash H. Remsen junr. retained out of
Mr. Jefferson's quarter's salary 75 dollr.   30.0.0
by cash Mr. Jefferson paid for the
Richmond paper 5 dollars   2.0.0
                                                      £32.0.0   − 32. 0.0
                                                      Balance   £3.19.4

Note. Mr. Madison will pay Mr. Jefferson for the freight of his cases from New York to Philadelphia, and the cartage from the Philadelphia wharf to the Office where they were deposited, and from Mr. Jefferson's house at New York to the Sloop. He should be charged about 5d. per square foot Freight—the cartage may amount to about half a dollar.

H. REMSEN JUNR.

MS (MHi); in Remsen's hand. TJ settled this account with Remsen on 25 Nov. 1790, having just arrived in Philadelphia on the 20th. Five days later he paid for a "monstrous bill of freight" on the shipment of his books and household goods from France (Account Book, 25 and 30 Nov. 1790; see Short to TJ, 7 Nov. 1790, for note on the cargo brought by the *Henrietta* from Le Havre). In addition to the effects brought from New York and Philadelphia, TJ sent on to Philadelphia one trunk by stagecoach and three boxes shipped by the *Linnet* from Virginia. He also received an additional box from Charleston by the *Philadelphia* (Account Book, 12 and 15 Nov., 15 Dec. 1790).

To William Short

DEAR SIR   Philadelphia Nov. 25. 1790.

Mr. Donald having it in contemplation to make overtures for the purchase of tobacco for French consumption, and the public papers rendering it uncertain whether that business will be left in the hands of the farmers general, or committed to a new board, or perhaps left altogether free, insomuch that we know not here to whom application must be made, I cannot do better than recommend him as my particular friend to you, and ask for him your counsel and recommendation to the proper persons so far as may be consistent with the general interests of our country which is the first object of your office, and the rights of other individuals of it which may in justice claim your patronage also. You are too well acquainted with the solidity of Mr. Donald's house to require any information from me on that head, and I add my own testimony of his integrity and honor, already sufficiently known to you, only because it is always pleasant to bear witness to the truth. I am at all times, my dear Sir, with sincere attachment Your affectionate friend & servt,

TH: JEFFERSON

RC (ViW). PrC (DLC). Entry in SJL reads: "(for A. Donald)," and the letter was probably enclosed in that to Donald of the same date.

From William Short

DEAR SIR   Amsterdam Nov. 25th. 1790.

It has just come to my knowlege that there is a vessel bound for New-York which has been for some time waiting in the Texel for a sailing wind and that it is probable a letter sent by this evening's post may arrive in time to go by her. Under that idea I anticipate a letter I intended writing by the post of to-morrow for the English packet to inform you of my arrival at this place on the 20th. inst. I was detained at Paris much longer than I had expected by the continuation of the conferences begun at the Marquis de la fayette's as mentioned in my No. 46.—Notwithstanding my anxiety to arrive here I found it impossible to avoid postponing my departure from one day to another, as conferences were daily proposed (although frequently interrupted by the present accumulation of affairs in the assembly) and as M. de Montmorin and M. de la fayette both insisted on my continuing them.—On the whole I had no reason to be dissatisfied with these conferences as they produced an evident change in the minds and dispositions of many who have influence in the assembly. I regretted only that this business could not have been advanced to its present stage some time sooner so as not to have delayed my departure for this place.

The discussion of the report of the committee of imposition on tobacco fixed as the order of the day almost every day since my last and constantly interrupted by incidental matters, was begun on the 13th. instant as you will see by the journals of the assembly which will be forwarded to you as usual with the other papers from Paris. I have seen here the debates on it as low as the 16th. It had been then interrupted and resumed. The papers as low as the 19th. give no later account of that business. The diplomatick committee, as had been agreed on out of the assembly, asked to give their ideas on it and are to be heard. They will take up the subject on political principles, and by shewing that tobacco is the strongest commercial link between France and the United States, argue that it must be made use of so as to fortify their political connexions also, which are necessarily dependent thereon. It has been moved also and carried in the assembly that the question of the cultivation of tobacco in France should be adjourned until the committee of imposition shall have reported their plan for supplying the place of this revenue. This motion was made by a member (Barnave) who is for prohibiting the culture. Should this prohibition however be continued, and consequently the farm, considerable changes will be made in the system and particularly with a view to their commerce with the U.S. now that they consider it as worth making some sacrifices for. This was the principal advantage I expected also from de Moustier's pamphlet.

I mentioned to you in my last the reasons which induced me not to defer the payment intended to be made to the French treasury. I hope they will have met your approbation, as it seems to me the circumstances there mentioned left no alternative.

Previous to my leaving Paris it was agreed between M. de Montmorin, M. du Fresne, Directeur du Trésor Royal, and myself, that this money should be remitted to him by bills of exchange, and orders were given in consequence.—On my arrival here I found that bills for upwards of two millions of livres had been already remitted, on terms highly advantageous owing to the present rate of exchange, which is such that the 1½ million of florins will produce about three million six hundred thousand livres.—The balance would have been remitted by the two following posts; but last night I received a letter from M. Du Fresne informing me that having to pay 570.000. florins the fifth of next month at Amsterdam, on account of the loan made by France for the service of the United States, he wished I would give orders to our bankers to pay that sume here *'afin déviter les pertes du change qui sont enormes dans ce moment-ci.'* This letter was soon followed

by a visit from the French bankers charged with this business.—
I informed them that I had already given orders to our bankers
previous to my departure from Paris in consequence of my agreement with M. du Fresne—that they had already made considerable
remittances, but that if they had a sufficiency in their hands I did
not doubt they would readily comply with M. du Fresne's desire.
It had been agreed on with our bankers that the others should be
referred to them on this footing, as it would prevent my entering
into any discussions relative to the exchange which I wished to do,
as what was loss for France was gain for us. They have agreed to
day that the French bankers should receive the sum here in florins
and give an order for it in livres on M. du Fresne so that the U.S.
may be credited for it with the present benefit of exchange.—I know
not whether this will square with Du Fresne's ideas, however
it is so rigorously just that he can have no right to complain.

I will thank you to communicate this matter to the Secretary of
the Treasury.—I do not write to him by the present conveyance
because it is uncertain whether my letter will arrive in time at the
Texel, and also because as yet I have only general ideas on the
several objects to which he directed my attention.—I have not as yet
proposed a loan because I chose first to examine the ground, and
also to see whether it was proper to continue the business in the
present hands. We are to have a meeting to-morrow which will
probably decide the matter. The rate of interest will be certainly
five ℔ Ct. The commission and other charges I hope may be reduced
below 4½. I will inform the Secretary of the Treasury immediately
on any thing being concluded on. This letter is given to our bankers
to be forwarded. Tomorrow I shall write to you by the English
packet. I beg you to be assured of the attachment with which I
am, dear Sir, your obedient servant,   W: SHORT

PrC (DLC: Short Papers); at head of text: "*No. 47.*" Tr (DNA: RG 59,
DD). Recorded in SJL as received 19 Jan. 1791.

To Mercy Warren

MADAM   Philadelphia Nov. 25. 1790.

On my return to this place I receive the honour of your letter of
Sep. 23. together with the volume which accompanied it; for which
be pleased to accept my grateful thanks. A multiplicity of business
has as yet permitted me to dip but a little into it; but yet sufficiently
to foresee that it will soothe some of my moments of rest from

drudgery, and will add another illustrious name to the roll of female worthies, made for the ornament as well as vindication of their sex. I see in it too, and with peculiar pleasure, a demonstration the more (and that in behalf of the most amiable moiety of society) of the illiberality of that hypothesis which has supposed a degeneracy even of the human race on this side the Atlantic. I beg you to accept the homage of those sentiments of respect & esteem with which I have the honor to be Madam your most obedient & most humble servt,   TH: JEFFERSON

PrC (DLC).

Mrs. Warren's letter of 23 Sep. 1790 is recorded in SJL as received on 20 Nov. 1790 from "Plimouth"; it has not been found. The volume transmitted with that letter was Mrs. Warren's *Poems, dramatic and miscellaneous* (Boston, 1790); see Sowerby No. 4439.

To John Adams

DEAR SIR   Philadelphia Nov. 26. 1790.

From a letter received from the President Mr. Lear is satisfied he cannot be here to-day and doubts even the possibility of his arrival tomorrow. Of course our expedition of to-day would be certainly fruitless, and is therefore laid aside agreeably to a message I have received from Genl. Knox and the attorney General. Your's affectionately & respectfully,   TH: JEFFERSON

RC (MHi: AM); addressed: "The Vice-president of the United States at Bush-hill." Not recorded in SJL.

The EXPEDITION of the Vice-President and members of the cabinet to meet the President, perhaps at Gray's Ferry, was necessarily postponed. Washington arrived in Philadelphia about 11 in the morning of the 27th (Freeman, *Washington*, VI, 286).

From Andrew Brown

Philadelphia, 26 Nov. 1790. In response to Remsen's letter of yesterday—should he be continued as publisher of the laws—he would "perform that duty, with accuracy and expedition, at the rate of one dollar for what is equal to one page of the edition of the laws printed by Childs & Swaine"—a rate considerably under that of the state of Pennsylvania and much less than his fixed price for advertising. "I beg leave just to add that should any other reputable paper propose to undertake the business for a less sum I shall most cheerfully lower my price accordingly."

RC (DNA: RG 59, PDL). Not recorded in SJL. Remsen's letter was that of 23 Nov. 1790. For TJ's determination of the price, see Remsen to the printers, 10 Jan. 1791.

To Nathaniel Cutting

Philadelphia Nov. 26. 1790.

Your several favors of the following dates have been duly received.

At sea. Lat. 7° 40' long. 13°.	Mar. 5. 1790.
At sea. Lat. 7 20. long. 10-55.	Mar. 30.
St. Marc.	July 6.
do.	Aug. 4.
do.	Aug. 9.
Havre	Sep. 25.
do.	Sep. 26.

The cask of Mountain rice came also safely, for which precious present accept my grateful thanks. I have already distributed it into so many hands as to ensure a fair experiment whether it may not be raised in the lands and climates of the middle states, and so render it useless to poison the air with those inundations which sweep of annually so many of our fellow creatures. The accounts of the disturbances in St. Domingo, contained in your letters from that island have given us the information of them on which we rely the most. I hope their issue will be favorable to the prosperity of the islands, which I am sure must bring advantage at the same time to the mother country and to us. This is not the language, I know, of Havre or Bordeaux whose purposes are better answered by ripping up the hen, and getting all the eggs at once. I have regularly communicated these letters to the President.

When the appointment of Consuls took place, it was much wished you had been in place to receive that of Havre; but your departure thence with an intention not to return was known, nor could it be said where you would be. M. la Motte was therefore named Vice-consul, but with the general notification which went to all the Vice-consuls that whenever an approved native should go to the port, he would be named Consul, and that during his residence the exercise of the functions of the Vice-consul would cease, but revive again on his departure. Knowing the terms on which you are with M. de la Motte, I do not propose to the President to send you a commission of Consul for Havre till I hear from yourself that it would be agreeable to you. Perhaps you might prefer some other consulship. Those as yet vacant are Gottenburg, Cadiz, Lisbon, the Canaries, Neury, Lorient and Guadaloupe. I cannot say however how long they will be vacant, as they are so at present because no approved person has as yet asked them. I believe you might have any of them which should be vacant at the arrival of your demand. There would certainly be but one obstacle, which is that so many Massachusets men have already obtained Consular appointments as to endanger considerable discontent in the other states. On this ground several have been latterly refused of that state. Perhaps this might be got over, tho I could not absolutely say it could be so. Write me your wishes, and nothing but justice shall be an obstacle to them.

My elder daughter is married, very much to my mind, to a Mr. Randolph. Both of them are well and remember with gratitude your kindnesses on our route, which are duly remembered also by Dear Sir Your friend & servt, Th: Jefferson

PrC (DLC).

Cutting's application for the post of consul at Le Havre was in his letter of 8 July 1790, noted under that to TJ of 6 July 1790. The letters of 25 and

26 Sep. 1789 (missing) were received 20 Nov. 1790. The above letter conveyed to Cutting information that could not have failed to interest him—that of Martha's marriage (see note to Cutting to TJ, 30 Mch. 1790).

To Francis Kinloch

Dear Sir   Philadelphia Nov. 26. 1790.

Your favor of Apr. 26. 1789. did not come to my hands till the 4th. of the last month when it found me on my way to Virginia. It should not otherwise have been so long unanswered. I am certainly flattered by the approbation you are so good as to express of the Notes on Virginia. The passage relative to the English, which has excited disagreeable sensations in your mind is accounted for by observing that it was written during the war, while they were committing depradations in my own country and on my own property never practised by a civilized nation. Perhaps their conduct and dispositions towards us since the war have not been as well calculated as they might have been to excite more favorable dispositions on our part. Still as a political man they shall never find any passion in me either for or against them. Whenever their avarice of commerce will let them meet us fairly halfway, I should meet them with satisfaction, because it would be for our benefit: but I mistake their character if they do this under present circumstances.

The rumours of war seem to pass away. Such an event might have produced to us some advantages: but it might also have exposed us to dangers: and on the whole I think a general peace more desirable.—Be so good as to present my respects to Mrs. Kinloch and to be assured of the esteem & respect with which I am Dear Sir your most obedt. & most humble servt.,

TH: JEFFERSON

PrC (DLC).

From William Knox

Dublin, 26 Nov. 1790. On the 17th instant his appointment as consul for Dublin approved by the King and on the 24th he arrived in this city. He will lose no time in beginning his duties.

RC (DNA: RG 59, CD); endorsed as received 12 May 1791 and so recorded in SJL.

From James Monroe

DEAR SIR   Fredricksburg Novr. 26. 1790.

Since my appointment I have not before had leasure to acknowledge the receipt of your obliging favor from Monticello. The arrangement of my business in the different courts, and other affairs, has given me full employment and detain'd me so long that it will be difficult to reach Phila. by the day appointed for the meeting of the Congress. This however I shall attempt and for this purpose sit out hence on Monday, unless detain'd by bad weather which threatens much at present. I should most chearfully accept your kind offer to procure us lodgings upon our first arrival, if we were determin'd to proceed in the first instance to Phila; but tis probable we may call upon a Mr. Chs. Willing an uncle by marriage of Mrs. Monroe, where she may remain a few days, untill I shall be able to procure the necessary accomodation. If this should not be the case I shall proceed to the city tavern, from whence I shall soon be able to find you, to avail myself of your aid to better our situation. Mrs. House's would be our object, but we should only interfere with her interest, by excluding for the time more permanent lodgers. I believe we will take the rout of annapolis and the eastern shore. I hope to reach Phila. on sunday evening. I am sincerely your friend & servant,   JAS. MONROE.

RC (DLC); endorsed by TJ as received 3 Dec. 1790 and so recorded in SJL.

To Gouverneur Morris

DEAR SIR   Philadelphia Nov. 26. 1790.

I have yet to acknowledge the receipt of your two favors of Apr.
10. and July 7. By the latter it would seem as if you had written
an intermediate one which has never come to hand: and the letter
of July 7. itself was not recieved till the 14th. of October, while I
was in Virginia from which I am but just returned. The President
is not yet returned, tho' expected tomorrow.—The Declaration and
Counter declaration established with us a full expectation that peace
would be continued; perhaps this is still the most rational opinion,
tho the *English* papers continue to talk of preparations for war.
That such an event would have ensured good prices for our produce,
and so far have been advantageous, is probable. But it would have
exposed us to risks also, which are better deferred, for some
years at least.—It is not to be expected that our system of finance
has met your approbation in all it's parts. It has excited even here
great opposition; and more especially that part of it which transferred the state debts to the general government. The states of
Virginia and N. Carolina are peculiarly dissatisfied with this measure. I believe however that it is harped on by many to mask their
disaffection to the government on other grounds. It's great foe in
Virginia is an implacable one. He avows it himself, but does not
avow all his motives for it. The measures and tone of the government threaten abortion to some of his speculations: most particularly to that of the Yazoo territory. But it is too well armed to be
overawed by individual opposition. It is proposed to provide additional funds, to meet the additional debt, by a tax on spirituous
liquors foreign and home-made: so that the whole interest will be
paid by taxes on consumption. If a sufficiency can be now raised
in this way to pay the interest at present, it's increase by the increase
of population (suppose 5. per cent. per annum) will alone sink
the principal within a few years, operating, as it will, in the way
of compound interest. Add to this what may be done by throwing
in the aid of Western lands and other articles as a sinking fund,
and our prospect is really a bright one.

A pretty important expedition has been undertaken against the
Indians north of the Ohio. As yet we have no news of it's success.
The late elections of members of Congress have changed about
a third or fourth of them. It is imagined the session of Congress
which is to begin within 10. days will end on the 3d. of March,

with the federal year; as a continuance over that day would oblige them to call forward the new members. The admission of Vermont and Kentuckey into Congress, will be decided on in this session.[1] I have the honour to be with very great esteem Dear Sir Your most obedt and most humble servt,   TH: JEFFERSON

PrC (DLC).

The great and implacable foe of the national government in Virginia, of course, was Patrick Henry (see note to Nicholas to TJ, 3 Feb. 1790). The letter of 7 July 1790 was addressed to John Jay, hence the INTERMEDIATE ONE must also have been to him (for that of the 7th see Editorial Note, report on Mediterranean trade, 28 Dec. 1790).

[1] This sentence, being much crowded, was added as an afterthought at the end of the paragraph.

From John Marsden Pintard

[Madeira] 26th. November 1790.

"I beg leave to submit to your consideration, whether it would not be proper that Consuls of the United States should certify the manifests of the cargoes of American vessels, sailing from their Consulates, and bound to any ports of the United States. I think it very proper at this Island for the following reason, vizt. The clearance from the Custom house here only mentions in general terms, that the Ship or Brig (here is inserted the name of the vessel and commander) has permission to depart with a cargo of wines. The vessel may have two pipes only on board, or two hundred, and also may have a quantity of fruit and citron &c. The master of the vessel certainly has it in his power, under these circumstances, to defraud the revenue of the United States. The British Government found the inconvenience of those kind of clearances, and now oblige their vessels sailing from this port, to have the manifest of their cargo certified under the official seal of the british Consul.

The 32d. Section of the collection Act recites, that no person shall be entitled to receive the drawback allowed on any goods, wares, or merchandise, exported from the United States, until he shall produce a certificate in writing of two reputable merchants at the foreign port or place in which the same were landed &c. I would submit to your consideration whether it would not be more proper that the Consul of the United States should certify the landing of the article, under his official seal."

PrC (DLC); at head of text: "Extract of a letter from John Marsden Pintard esquire, Consul of the United States for the Island of Madeira to the

Secretary of State dated 26th November 1790"; in clerk's hand except for the name "Hamilton Alexr." at foot of text and endorsement in TJ's hand. Recorded in SJL as received 31 Jan. 1791.

As indicated by TJ's addition of the name of Hamilton to an extract of a letter addressed to himself, this was doubtless sent by him to the Secretary of the Treasury. TJ may have sent it as an enclosure of a letter to Hamilton recorded in SJL under 11 Feb. 1791 but not found. On 7 Dec. 1790 Pintard wrote a letter in almost identical terms to the Secretary of the Treasury (text in Syrett, *Hamilton*, VII, 200-1). The COLLECTION ACT referred to was that of 31 July 1789 for regulating collection of duties on tonnage and imports; that Act had been superseded by the Act of 4 Aug. 1790.

From William Short

DEAR SIR   Amsterdam Nov. 26. 1790

I wrote to you yesterday by a vessel in the Texel to inform you of my arrival here on the 20th. inst. and of the causes of my delay in Paris.—I mentioned also that the report of the committee of impositions on tobacco was now under discussion in the national assembly, but that nothing had been decided on it so low down as the 19th. I mentioned also and begged you to communicate *to the Secretary of the Treasury that on my arrival here I found nearly* $\frac{2}{3}$ *of the payment destined to France remitted and that almost the whole of the balance was to be immediately paid to the bankers of France here agreeable to the present rate of exchange.*[1]

Latest accounts from Paris say that the city has been quiet since the mob which rose suddenly on the 13th. inst. destroyed the furniture of the hotel de Castries, and then dispersed without committing any other violence. This was in consequence of M. de Lameth being wounded in a duel by M. de Castries. It proves that the people of Paris are far from losing their attachment to their present favorites, as is pretended by many. It will be fortunate if the late inexcusable excess shall convince all parties of this truth. It may perhaps thus prevent the chiefs of the democratic party from going much further than is their wish at present. It seems to me that many of them who desire the preservation of tranquillity provided no opposition is made to their organizing the government as they think proper, would rather excite disturbances, viz: call the people to their aid, than see any order of things take place which should lessen their power.

The operation of the sale of ecclesiastical lands is going on with a rapidity and success beyond their most sanguine expectations, as well in Paris as in the provinces.—This is a rich mine and if properly managed might very soon enable them to put their immense debt on a very governable footing. It is to be feared however that with such a legislature and such administrative bodies as they have at present, the facility that these sales will give them with respect to the paper money system, will have an evil tendency. You have been regularly informed of the attacks made on the ministry and their success. Du Portail has finally succeeded to the minister of war. M. de St. Priest and the Garde des Sceaux, still keep their places, more because their successors are not agreed on, than for any other reason. They must inevitably soon yield to the storm. The latter is tenacious and has written to the assembly to have the accusations against him articulated, that he may shew his innocence and give a proof of his submission to ministerial responsibility. This is putting the matter on the best possible footing, as there is nothing against him but popular clamor, which it is difficult to reduce to a precise article of accusation. You will no doubt have received before the arrival of this letter the articles of pacification between England and Spain. There seems no doubt that they will both disarm. At least this is the opinion here, where their important money connexions with every part of Europe, keep them well informed of the intentions of the several powers.

The affairs of Brabant are at present at their crisis. The negotiations at the Hague were without success. Deputies were sent there from the Belgic Congress to ask for a prolongation of the term allowed by the Emperor. This was however refused by Count Mercy and as it expired on the 21st. inst. he wrote on the 22d. to the Maréchal Bender who commands the Austrian troops, under the idea of his having passed the Meuse. In this letter he presses him to shew a perfect forgetfulness of the past, to make use of force only against such as oppose him by force, and even then to do it if possible without shedding of blood. I know not what influence such a conduct may have, but when I passed through that country there seemed a fixed determination to resist, and an hatred to the Austrians which it would not be easy to get the better of. It was evident however at the same time that they were deluded by their leaders and kept in absolute ignorance of their real situation by the Congress.—It will be a fortunate circumstance that the Imperial authority should be re-established there as it will be the best ally the people can have, although they do not think so at present, against a theocratical tyranny. It is believed here on the authority of the English Ambassador who informed Mr. Hope, that the Belgick Congress have determined to accept the offers of the Emperor and of course that they laid down their arms on the 21st.

Letters from Brussels mention it also, and that Vander Noot and Van Eupen had at length consented, so as to be comprehended in the amnesty proposed by the Emperor. This circumstance and the disposition of the Maréchal Bender will probably bring on so sudden and so total a submission as to avoid violence and bloodshed every where.

For further particulars of the present political situation of Europe and especially of the proceedings of the national assembly I refer you to the papers which will be forwarded to you regularly by the Secretary I left in Paris. You will see from them also that war still continues between Russia and the Porte, without Prussia's interfering. The Turks have undergone a signal defeat on the Cuban and Prince Potemkin is beginning the campaign agreeably to his usage in this advanced season. The circumstances of the two armies are such as cannot fail to insure him success, with this advantage.

This letter will go through the English post-office and by the English Packet. I inclose you one also for the Secretary of the Treasury, which I ask the favor of you to deliver. My late letters to you have been of Oct. 21. 25. 27. 30. Nov. 2. 6. and 7.—The meeting with the Bankers fixed for today mentioned in my letter of yesterday is to be tomorrow. No loan is yet agreed on. I shall write fully by a vessel which will sail from hence for America in a few days. In the mean time I beg you to be assured of the sentiments of attachment with which I am, dear Sir, your affectionate servant,

W: SHORT

FC (DNA: RG 59, DD); at head of text: "No.48." Recorded in SJL as received 19 Jan. 1791. PrC (DLC: Short Papers).

[1] The passage in italics is in code and has been decoded by the Editors, employing a partially reconstructed key to Code No. 10.

To William Temple Franklin

DEAR SIR

Philadelphia Nov. 27. 1790.

I am favoured with yours of Oct. 13. The President is not yet arrived. Your general desire being known, I will take care that your special preferences shall also be known should circumstances give place to it. Your grandfather sent me only one sheet of Mitchell's map, and it makes part of the testimony he was desired to give on the subject of the disputed river of St. Croix, being referred to in his letter accompanying it. I therefore take the liberty of proposing to you to give you a complete copy of the same map, or the price of it, in exchange for the remaining sheets to which the one in our possession belonged.

I am in hopes you will continue in the mind of publishing Dr. Franklin's works in 8vo. otherwise I think you will find fewer purchasers, till the Irish printers by a cheaper edition intercept the wishes of those who like books of a handy size. I am sure your delicacy needs no hint from me against the publication of such letters or papers from Dr. Franklin as Minister Plenipotiary of the U.S. as might not yet be proper to put into the possession of every body. Wishing you the best success in your pursuits I am with great esteem Dr. Sir your most obedt. and most humble servt.,

TH: JEFFERSON

P.S. I inclose herewith and deliver to Mr. Bache the M.S. of negotiations put into my hands by Dr. Franklin.

PrC (DLC). Enclosure: One of the manuscript texts of a document written by Benjamin Franklin "On board the Pennsylvania Packet, Captain Osborne, bound to Philadelphia, March 22, 1775" describing the informal discussions in 1774-1775 among Franklin, some intermediaries of the British cabinet, and members of the opposition (printed in Franklin, *Writings*, ed. Smyth, VI, 318-99, under the caption "An Account of Negotiations in London for Effecting a Reconciliation between Great Britain and the American Colonies"). This narrative was intended by Franklin as an integral part of his Autobiography and is so treated, along with other pieces, in William Temple Franklin's *Memoirs of the life and writings of Benjamin Franklin* (London, 1818), its first appearance in print. It is also included in Carl Van Doren's *Benjamin Franklin's autobiographical writings* (New York, 1945), p. 347-99. Van Doren makes the following comment on this narrative and two others, these last relating to the affair of Hutchinson's letters and the peace negotiations of 1782: "All three of them were written after the first section of the *Autobiography*, and no doubt would have been incorporated in the narrative, in whole or in part, if it had ever reached the years in which these events took place. The three should be regarded as further fragments of a work which is itself a fragment" (same, p. v). *Benjamin Franklin's Memoirs Parallel text edi-*tion, ed. Farrand (Berkeley, 1949) does not include any of these chronologically subsequent fragments. Neither does Farrand's *The Autobiography of Benjamin Franklin*, which attempts to solve by restoration an unusually complex textual problem. The most succinct and authoritative discussion of the textual problem is that of Leonard Labaree and others, *The Autobiography of Benjamin Franklin* (New Haven, 1964), which presents a faithful rendering of the original manuscript written by Franklin at various dates between 1771 and 1790 that carried the narrative of his life down to 1757. It of course excludes the text of the informal negotiations of 1774-1775 which TJ here refers to as M.S. OF NEGOTIATIONS.

Temple Franklin's GENERAL DESIRE for diplomatic office had long been known to TJ, as it was to many others (TJ to Monroe, 5 July 1785; W. T. Franklin to TJ, 18 Jan. 1786 and 17 Dec. 1789; William Smith, *Diary*, ed. Upton, I, 142). His first ambition was to be minister to France and one of the latest efforts in this direction may have been inspired by his mistress, Mme. Caillot ("Blancette" to W. T. Franklin, 20 Nov. 1787, PPAP; Le Veillard to TJ, 25 July 1790). In announcing his plans to the President, Franklin denied the rumor that he was leaving in disgust and would not return. But his failure to mention this in his letter to TJ or to declare his diplomatic ambition in that to Washington of the same date allows the unpleasant inference that he may have supposed the President and the Secretary of State would exchange such information and might be influenced in their decision by his projected plan to publish his grandfather's PAPERS—an object he took care to mention to both and about which TJ was clearly concerned (Franklin to TJ, 13 Oct. 1790; Franklin to Washington, 13 Oct. 1790, DNA: RG 59, MLR; Washington to Franklin, 25 Oct. 1790, *Writings*, ed. Fitzpatrick, XXXI, 134-5). Even if unintended, this indelicacy in intermingling public and private motives so as to permit such an interpretation must have combined with other factors to create an insuperable obstacle to his ambition.

One of Temple Franklin's private objects in going to England was to dispose of lands in the Phelps and Gorham purchase owned by Robert Morris. In this he was successful (TJ to Washington, 27 Mch. 1791; Editorial Note, commercial and diplomatic relations with Great Britain, under 15 Dec. 1790). But it was not until 1817-1818 that he finally published Franklin's papers. The fascinating story of that portion that Temple Franklin took to England—"some 3,000 items of political and philosophical interest" out of a total of about 15,000 documents—is set forth in Whitfield J. Bell, Jr., "Henry Stevens, his Uncle Samuel, and the Franklin Papers," *Mass. Hist. Soc.*, *Procs.*, LXXII, 143-211 (see also Smyth's excellent summary, Franklin, *Writings*, I, 4-8). These papers, which Temple Franklin regarded as the most important of those bequeathed to him by his grandfather, were ultimately purchased by the United States and placed in the custody of the Department of State but later transferred to the Library of Congress, where they were calendared by Worthington C. Ford (*List of Benjamin Franklin Papers in the Library of Congress* [Washington, 1905]). The available evidence sustains Henry Stevens' explanation for the long delay in publication: "William Temple Franklin was . . . an unmethodical muddler, an incompetent editor, and uncommonly dilatory in his habits" (Bell, "Henry Stevens," *Mass. Hist. Soc.*, *Procs.*, LXXII, 157; see also, Henry Stevens, *A bibliographical essay . . .* [London, 1881], p. 5-11.) It is important to note that, in addition to making a specific request of TJ (see

Franklin to TJ, 13 Oct. 1790), Temple Franklin announced his purpose to the public and requested all to assist him in the publication of his grandfather's papers. In an advertisement he described the chest of papers that had been left with Joseph Galloway while Benjamin Franklin was abroad. Some of these, after being pillaged, had been recovered. But Franklin's letterbooks and a manuscript in four or five volumes on finance, commerce, and manufactures were missing. Temple Franklin therefore requested any who had any letters or writings of Franklin to make them available as early as possible so that they might be included in the edition. He urged those who had books or maps belonging to Benjamin Franklin to return them without delay, since he was about to embark for Europe (Bache's *General Advertiser*, 6 Oct. 1790).

But the long delay in publishing bred suspicions that the British government had bribed Temple Franklin to suppress publication of the whole, particularly the remarkable M.S. OF NEGOTIATIONS here enclosed. These suspicions flourished on both sides of the Atlantic and came into the open with the Marshall-Vaughan edition of *The complete works . . . of the late Dr. Benjamin Franklin* (London, Johnson and Longman, 1806). The editors' preface charged that some emissary of the British government had approached Temple Franklin with the object of withholding "the manuscripts from the world" and that, in consequence, the papers "either passed into other hands, or the person to whom they were bequeathed received a remuneration for suppressing them." This, the editors declared, had been asserted by a number of persons, both in England and America, "of whom some were at the time intimate with the grandson, and not wholly unacquainted with the machinations of the ministry" (quoted in Stevens, *Franklin A bibliographical essay*, p. 5-6; Franklin, *Writings*, ed. Smyth, I, 27). This charge was soon reprinted in New York by James Cheetham in *The American Citizen* and accepted by him as a proven fact. "William Temple Franklin," Cheetham asserted, "without shame, without remorse, mean and mercenary, sold the sacred deposit committed to his care by Dr. Franklin to the British government!—Franklin's works are therefore lost; lost to America, lost to the world!" (*The American Citizen*, 8 Sep. 1806). Franklin branded the charge as false and the *Edinburgh Review* for July 1806 cast serious doubt upon its validity. But the suspicions continued.

As the above letter shows, TJ feared that Franklin's papers as an American minister contained matter improper to be revealed to other governments. His delicate hint—the first intimation by a Secretary of State of what would finally become fixed policy governing the publication of diplomatic records—reveals the depth of his concern. In 1790 he feared premature publication, but this fear was transformed over the years into another kind of anxiety. In 1806 he was a subscriber to both *The American Citizen* and the *Edinburgh Review*, being an admirer of the former for its Republican politics and of the latter for the quality of its criticism (TJ to Cheetham, 17 Jan., 23 Apr. 1802, 17 June 1803; Cheetham to TJ, 29 Dec. 1801, 25 July 1804, and invoices of 1 July 1806 and 1 July 1807; for his opinion of the *Edinburgh Review*, see Sowerby, Nos. 2811, 3501, 4733). It can scarcely be doubted that he read in these publications the quoted preface of Franklin's *Works*, the skeptical comment by Francis Jeffrey in the *Edinburgh Review*, and the unquestioning belief of James Cheetham. Whether he did or not, he unequivocally shared Cheetham's conviction that Franklin's papers had indeed been lost to America and to the world through the venality of Temple Franklin. He could the more readily accept the charge as valid, even as published in its extreme form by Cheetham, because it confirmed an opinion he himself had long since formed.

In 1810 in seeking to correct obvious encrustations of error in an anecdote reported to him by William Duane about the manner in which he had received M.S. OF NEGOTIATIONS from Benjamin Franklin, TJ perpetuated others. He then recalled that in passing through Philadelphia in 1790 on his way to New York, he had called on Franklin, had expressed pleasure in hearing he was at work on his memoirs, and had received from him as a specimen of it "about a quire of paper, in which he had given, with great minuteness, all the details of his negotiations (informal) in England to prevent their pushing us to Extremities." He also recalled that soon after, on learning Franklin had bequeathed his papers to Temple Franklin, he notified the latter of his possession of a manuscript regarded as "fairly his property," which he would deliver at his order; that Franklin soon called on him at New York and TJ handed the document to him; that Franklin, "while putting it in his pocket, observed that his grandfather had retained another copy which he had found among his papers"; that this remark made no impression "till suspicions were circulated that W. T. F. had sold these writings to the British minister"; that he had then "formed the belief that Dr. Franklin had meant to deposit this spare copy with me in confidence that it would be properly taken care of"; and that he "sincerely repented having given it up." TJ then added: "I have little doubt that this identical paper was the principal object of the purchase by the British government, and the unfortunate cause of the suppression of all the rest" (TJ to Duane, 16 Sep. 1810).

In the concluding passages of his Autobiography ten years later TJ repeated and elaborated upon the version given Duane. He then declared that, on learning of the bequest of the papers, he "immediately wrote to Mr. Franklin"; that Franklin "immediately came on to New York, called on me for it, and I delivered it to him"; and that, as he pocketed the document, Franklin "carelessly" remarked that he had "either the original, or another copy of it." This remark, he added, "struck my attention forcibly, and for the first time suggested to me the thought that Dr. Franklin had meant it as a confidential deposit in my hands, and that I had done wrong in parting from it." He believed that this document "established views so atrocious in the British government that it's suppression would to them be worth a great price" (TJ, Autobiography; Ford, I, 151-3). To the end of his life TJ held to the conviction that Temple Franklin had been bribed to suppress publication of this manuscript. He continued to buy works of American history and to assist Girardin, Wirt, Sanderson, and others in their writings. But he never acquired Temple Franklin's publication either in an English or an American edition, although William Duane himself brought out one in six volumes of which TJ, as a subscriber to the *Aurora*, could not have been unaware.

[89]

In his Autobiography, TJ said that he had "not yet seen the collection" Temple Franklin had published three years earlier and therefore did not know whether this document was included in Franklin's *Works*. He added: "I have been told that it is not" (TJ, Autobiography; Ford, I, 152). But Temple Franklin had printed it and Franklin's other papers as "a solemn trust . . . [and] a positive injunction" upwards of a decade before TJ died (Franklin, *Memoirs*, ed. W. T. Franklin, I, iii [3rd edn., London, 1818]).

The obvious errors and inconsistencies in TJ's two accounts—including in the Autobiography what purports to be a direct quotation from the manuscript that is discussed below—are all the more puzzling because this document and its fate made such a deep impression upon him. In matters of far less importance TJ often checked his memory against his full and systematic files. Had he done so in this instance, the above letter and that to Duane in 1810 would have revealed to him some of his more egregious errors. Also, had he been as careful to retain a copy of this manuscript as he was with respect to the outline of Franklin's Autobiography, wherein it was given the rubric "Negociation to prevent the War," he might have spared himself much anguish and others much confusion (see TJ to Le Veillard, 9 May 1786, notes and enclosures). Considering TJ's profound concern from early youth in the preservation of historical records, his special interest in Franklin's autobiographical writings, the circumstances under which this manuscript was received, and its obvious public importance, his failure to retain a copy is difficult to understand. Indeed, his first account of its return to Temple Franklin was in response to Duane's inquiry as to whether, as had been reported, he had preserved "a copy of it . . . for posterity" (Duane to TJ, 17 Aug. 1810). Because of these puzzling and uncharacteristic omissions, TJ left two accounts that collide with the facts and, in some respects, with each other.

The known facts may be briefly stated. TJ received the manuscript from Benjamin Franklin on the 17th or 18th of March 1790. Franklin died a month later. Temple Franklin came to New York in late spring or early summer. TJ saw him then and also later in Philadelphia after Congress adjourned.

On one of these occasions he informed Franklin of the manuscript. We may be certain that this was not by letter, as TJ later recalled, for in the first known reference to its existence, Franklin requested the return of "the Manuscript you mentioned to have of my Grandfathers" (Franklin to TJ, 13 Oct. 1790). TJ received this request on the 3rd of November. He returned to Philadelphia on the 20th where the manuscript probably had been left among his papers. Two days later he delivered to Benjamin Franklin Bache the above letter and its bulky enclosure. By this time Temple Franklin was on the high seas and of course TJ could not have delivered the manuscript to him. Indeed the two men never saw each other again.

It is clear, therefore, that the letter and the manuscript were handed to Bache in person by TJ. Young Bache was just establishing his *General Advertiser* and had applied to TJ for patronage that would soon be forthcoming (Bache to TJ, 20 Aug. 1790; TJ to Randolph, 15 May 1791). He alone could have told TJ that "the original, or another copy of it" was in Temple Franklin's possession. Bache thus inadvertently planted the seed of the legend that Benjamin Franklin had given the manuscript to TJ to be held in trust. Amid the bitterly divisive contests of the next few years the seed germinated and flourished in a climate of suspicion warmed by partisan animosities and by Franklin's delay in publishing Franklin's papers. The conviction was strengthened also by an anguished if mistaken sense of complicity. For if what TJ believed to be true were actually true, it not only meant that he had violated Franklin's confidence: it also meant that the world had lost a manuscript of great historical importance—"a masterpiece in the literature of diplomacy" which, it has been said, inaugurated that genre in the United States (Carl Van Doren, *Franklin's autobiographical writings*, p. 347). But the trust, in the sense that TJ came to view it, had not been bestowed. Benjamin Franklin may have urged TJ to keep the manuscript, but he certainly did not do so from any lack of confidence in Temple Franklin, whose talents and virtues he rather tended to exaggerate. Also, Franklin was as scrupulous as TJ himself in preserving his papers, if less systematic, and the extraordinarily detailed and documented narrative presented in this manuscript shows that he was fully cognizant of its value. He could safely entrust it to TJ because he knew that the original manuscript was among his own papers. These constituted the far greater trust which he confidently bestowed upon his grandson.

Indeed, the great concern Franklin had for his papers—and for the Autobiography in particular—may explain why TJ failed to take a copy of the manuscript after he knew that Temple Franklin had requested its return. On a former occasion when he feared that the letterbooks of Silas Deane might come into possession of the British government, TJ himself had made extended extracts under urgent pressures (TJ to Jay, 3 Aug. 1788; TJ to Bancroft, 2 Mch. 1789). Why, then, did he return this manuscript without comment and without retaining a copy when he had both time and clerical assistance at his disposal? Since this was a part of Franklin's memoirs, it seems plausible to assume that Franklin laid TJ under the same injunction that he imposed on others respecting its text. Only a few months earlier, when Franklin had sent copies of the unfinished narrative of his life to Vaughan and Le Veillard, he did so "under this express Condition . . . that you do not suffer any Copy to be taken of them, *or of any Part of them*, on any Account whatever" (Franklin to Le Veillard, 13 Nov. 1789; Franklin to Vaughan, 2 Nov. 1789; *Writings*, ed. Smyth, x, 49-53, 69-70; emphasis added; *Benjamin Franklin's memoirs Parallel text edition*, ed. Farrand, p. xxiv-xxvi). The injunction could not be stated in plainer or more emphatic words. It permitted no exception whatsoever, for any reason. If Franklin felt so about every part of his memoirs, it seems improbable that he would have failed to place the same restriction on the very significant part that he placed in TJ's hands.

But did TJ in fact make a copy of "any Part" of the text? The question needs to be raised because, in his reply to Duane's specific question in 1810, he gave no categorical answer either to affirm or to deny. Further, in the account given in TJ's Autobiography the allusion to "views so atrocious in the British government" contains the only part of his recollection of the contents of the document that is presented as if in direct quotation. It appears in the following passage: "I remember that Ld. North's answers were dry, unyielding, in the spirit of unconditional submission, and betrayed an absolute indifference to the occurrence of a rupture; and he said to the mediators distinctly *at last* that 'a rebellion was not to be deprecated on the part of Great Britain; that the confiscations it would produce would provide for many of their friends' " (quoted from MS; emphasis added. See Ford, I, 152). In a review of Randolph's edition of TJ's papers, the *Edinburgh Review* pointed out that the manuscript had in fact been printed by Temple Franklin and that the reader might "look in vain for the declaration stated to have been made by Lord North." The reviewer expressed the "firm opinion that Jefferson's passions have in this instance confused his recollection, and that no such declaration was ever made or stated. Any such sentiment is utterly inconsistent with Lord North's disposition; it is contradicated by the general character of the messages as reported; and, had any such wicked feeling escaped the minister, we cannot believe that Lord Howe and his sister, while acting the part of generous mediators, would have been guilty of the gratuitous mischief of repeating it" (*Edinburgh Review*, LI [July, 1830], 503-4). John Bigelow in 1875, on the other hand, regarded the whole of TJ's recollection about the manuscript as authoritative and did not challenge the statement attributed to Lord North (Bigelow, *Life of Benjamin Franklin*, II, 253n.). But in 1881, Henry Stevens, aligning himself with the *Edinburgh Review* but being far more volatile, declared flatly that TJ's treacherous memory had led him into a "contradictory and transparent misconception" and that these "wild statements of the quondam friend of Franklin" had finally been repudiated by Temple Franklin's fair editing and printing of the narrative (Stevens, *Franklin A bibliographical essay*, p. 7-9). A few years later Paul Leicester Ford simply dismissed the "atrocious . . . views" attributed to North with this comment: "Neither this expression, nor any of Lord North's, were given in Franklin's narrative" (Ford, I, 152n.). In this century Philip Marsh, declining to take the easy path of so summary a rejection, offered a hypothetical defense of TJ's attribution based upon a characteristic of one of the manuscripts of the narrative (Marsh, "The Manuscript Franklin Gave to Jefferson," Am. Phil. Soc., *Library Bulletin 1946*, p. 45-8). Such differences of opinion among serious investigators over the past century and a half concerning TJ's autobiographical comment on a highly important segment of Franklin's memoirs can best be appraised in light of the two manuscripts of the narrative that are known to exist. Both are in the Stevens Collection in the Library of Congress and neither is in its original state. For convenience they will be referred to here as *MS 1* and *MS 2*.

MS 1: This is the original manuscript in the hand of Benjamin Franklin, written by him on board the Pennsylvania packet between 22 Mch. 1775—the date given in its caption on page 1—and 5 May 1775 when he landed in Philadelphia. It measures approximately 8 x 7 inches and consists of 96 pages as numbered by Franklin without the supporting letters, memoranda, and propositions. As to these documents, Henry Stevens asserted that "the Narrative was drawn up at sea, without the many original notes, letters and memoranda" and that in 1790 Temple Franklin, having these documents in hand, was anxious to recover Franklin's original manuscript from TJ in order that it might be completed" (Stevens, *Franklin A bibliographical essay*, p. 9).

This conjectural explanation cannot be supported for two reasons. First, it is virtually certain that *MS 1* was not the text that TJ received from Franklin. That manuscript, TJ recalled, was about a quire and in folio sheets, a description quite incompatible with *MS 1*. TJ also remembered that the manuscript he received was not in Franklin's hand but "in a large and running hand very like his own." There is little reason to doubt his recollection on this score. He was very familiar with Franklin's flowing script and his memory for handwriting was so acute that, on one occasion, he identified the anonymous author of a very brief inscription some years after he had received a letter from him (TJ to Duane, 31 May 1824). Further, in 1790 *MS 1* lacked the original documents that were essential to a proper understanding of the negotiations. TJ's account makes it quite clear that the manuscript in his possession did contain the "several propositions and answers" that

were passed back and forth by the negotiators (TJ, Autobiography; Ford, I, 152). Second, it is certain that, with two exceptions, Franklin did have with him at sea all of the supporting documents. He could not have composed *MS 1*, at least in the form he gave it, if these documents had been lacking. The negotiations in London had ended only six days before he boarded the packet at Portsmouth. Franklin began the narrative on the very first day of the voyage, a clear indication that he had planned from the outset to devote the time at sea to its composition. His purpose perhaps was to publish it on landing or at least to make it available to key leaders in order to foster American unity—an object achieved far more efficaciously by the events at Lexington and Concord which occurred two weeks before he landed. In the course of composition Franklin gave a number to each of the original letters, memoranda, and propositions—there were 24 in all—and keyed them to the text of *MS 1* by such notes as those on page 11 ("Here Insert the Letters of Dec. 3 No. 1. 2.") and page 14 ("Here Insert the Hints &c."). Franklin omitted the texts of these documents from *MS 1* simply to spare himself the chore of transcription which any clerk could perform—a sensible expedient that he would have followed whether on land or sea.

Subsequently, after the manuscripts Temple Franklin carried to London had come into Henry Stevens' possession, these original documents were inserted in their appropriate places in *MS 1* as called for by Franklin's notations. A new pagination was then given to the whole, resulting in a total of 129 numbered pages, and the manuscript was bound, being now composed of Franklin's original narrative and these inserted originals in a single sequence. The first of the two documents Franklin did not have with him at sea was the petition to the King drawn by him (*Writings*, ed. Smyth, VI, p. 379-80). The second was Lord North's conciliatory motion of 20 Feb. 1775, lacking perhaps because he had already sent it to America (Franklin to Galloway, 25 Feb. 1775; same, VI, 313). At some time after he arrived in America and before *MS 2* was prepared, Franklin transcribed North's motion himself, executed a press copy from it, inserted his transcript in *MS 1*, and placed the press copy in the following manuscript.

MS 2: This is a clerk's copy of MS 1, including the texts of the documentary insertions. It is in the hand of Benjamin Franklin Bache except for corrections and additions in the hand of Benjamin Franklin. The transcript was made by Bache sometime after 1785, probably about 1788-1789. It measures approximately 9 x 8 inches and contains 196 pages numbered in red ink by Benjamin Franklin, plus a leaf at the end containing a single note each on recto and verso by the editor who assisted Temple Franklin in 1817. The note on the verso of this leaf reads: "Sent Augt. 1817." This notation, together with other editorial notes, directives to the printer, and various cancelled pagination sequences, proves beyond question that this is the text used by Temple Franklin as printer's copy for the first publication of the narrative.

Benjamin Franklin Bache, as this document demonstrates beyond all question, was a very careless copyist. As he transcribed MS 2 from Franklin's clear and flowing hand, he committed almost all of the errors of omission, repetition, and misconstruction of which an incompetent copyist is capable—including such nonsense readings as *tine pish* for *time past*. Benjamin Franklin gave the result a very meticulous reading, patiently correcting in red ink Bache's stubborn insistence upon writing *would* for *could*, *have* for *hence*, *nearly* for *merely*, and so on. The young scribe, his errant thoughts elsewhere, garbled one page in such a way as to call for the insertion of another sheet. Franklin made the necessary alterations, wrote out the continuation, and inserted the new sheet after page 58. He also put in its proper location the press copy of Lord North's motion. At various places throughout the manuscript Franklin inserted single brackets in the text and opposite each wrote in red ink "New Paragr"—at times doing so both in the text and in the margin so as to make certain that Bache would not miss the signal. He also occasionally inserted an additional comment such as that in the margin of page 22 concerning Lord Howe's sister, which reads: "This Lady, (which is a little unusual in Ladies,) has a good deal of Mathematical Knowledge." MS 2 is incomplete, lacking pages 73-102. Page 72 ends: ". . . after I receiv'd the Petition, before" (the last being the catch-word). Page 103 begins: "high Esteem I had imbib'd. . . ." The missing thirty pages of the text may be identified in Franklin, *Writings*, ed. Smyth, VI, 349-62.

It was this missing section of MS 2 that led Marsh to advance his conjectural explanation of the controverted passage. He thought it plausible to assume that Temple Franklin, having in his possession the original manuscript (MS 1), which Marsh described as "legible and whole," might have considered it sufficient for his purposes, in which case he could have treated the copy returned by TJ "carelessly and . . . as of little importance." Hence the "separated gift paper" may possibly have been lost about the time Temple Franklin departed for England and, Marsh found it reasonable to conclude, the thirty missing pages of MS 2 could have been the manuscript of about a quire that Franklin gave to TJ. If this were so, he argued, the fact impelled consideration of "the possibility that, among the insertions made by Franklin in the lost portion, there may have been a statement" approximating the expression TJ attributed to Lord North (Am. Phil. Soc., *Library Bulletin 1946*, p. 47-8). The premise on which this argument rested was the exact reverse of that of Henry Stevens and, not surprisingly, Marsh arrived at a conclusion more sympathetic to TJ.

But the hypothesis, like that of Stevens, is neither supported by the probabilities nor by the known facts. The original manuscript (MS 1) was undeniably legible but in 1790, lacking the documentary insertions, it was certainly not whole. Temple Franklin, having a choice, would scarcely have taken this as sufficient for his purposes in preference to a text that was both complete and corrected. Later, when faced with a similar problem, he gave to Le Veillard the original manuscript of Franklin's Autobiography in exchange for Le Veillard's fair copy for use with the printer. This is precisely what he did in 1817 in the case of MS 1 and MS 2 when, having both with him in London, he chose the latter to put through the press. Marsh conceded that TJ's controverted expression would have been more appropriate at the close than in that part of the negotiations covered by the missing pages of MS 2. This indeed is where TJ himself places it, for he states clearly that North's statement came "at last"—*i. e.*, at the end of the negotiations. Even so, it seems highly improbable that Benjamin Franklin would have given to TJ a fragment of the narrative torn from its context, stripped of beginning and end, and containing only about one-sixth of the whole narrative. Such a fragment would have provided a far less coherent account of the negotiations than even the original manuscript in its undocumented state. And it is scarcely conceivable that Franklin would have surrendered to TJ the whole or any part of *MS 2* that he had so laboriously corrected, amended, and authenticated as the definitive text. To have done so would have exposed him to the risk of having to cope once again with young Bache's vagaries as a clerk. It is impossible to believe that, in the last few weeks of his life, Franklin would have surrendered this authoritative text—*unless another copy equally complete and correct was also in existence.*

It is plausible to suppose that such a second copy had been made. With respect to the first part of his Autobiography, Franklin had in fact caused two copies to be executed from his original manuscript—the copies that he gave to Vaughan and Le Veillard in 1789. It seems unlikely that he would have failed to take the same precaution in the case of this very important and integral part of his memoirs. The making of such another copy, we may reasonably conclude, was the first object Franklin had in view in making his corrections, additions, and repeated calls for new paragraphs in *MS 2*. If such a copy had been needed for no other purpose, it could have served as salutary discipline for a youth who sorely needed it in the art of accurate transcription. It should also be noted that, when he returned the manuscript, TJ recalled having been told that Temple Franklin had "the original or another copy of it"—a remark that could easily have been a misconstruction of "the original *and* another copy of it." No such copy is known to exist. But this is true also of the two copies that Franklin caused to be made of the first part of his Autobiography. If, as seems plausible, *MS 2* did serve as the prototype for such an additional copy, this second copy may have been the one that Franklin gave to TJ. But all that can be said with reasonable certainty is that TJ did not have *MS 1* in his possession, that he may have been given the whole of *MS 2*, but that he did not receive a meaningless fragment torn from it. A hypothetical second copy derived from *MS 2*, if transcribed by Bache on both sides of folio sheets, could have comported better with TJ's explicit and repeated description of the physical characteristics of the paper given him than does either *MS 1* or *MS 2* in their original states.

But to account for the views that TJ attributed to Lord North one does not need to rely upon a conjectured insertion by Franklin either in the missing middle gap of *MS 2* or at the close of a probable second copy. One need only look at the concluding paragraph of all versions of this full and explicit narrative, whether in manuscript or in print. There, for all to read, is the essence of TJ's remembered attribution, superficially at variance but substantively in accord with it. This is the pertinent part of Franklin's final paragraph: "The Evening before I left London, I received a Note from Dr. Fothergill, with some Letters to his Friends in Philadelphia. In that Note he desires me to get those Friends 'and two or three more together, and inform them, that, whatever specious Pretences are offered, they are all hollow; *and that to get a larger field on which to fatten a Herd of worthless Parasites, is all that is regarded.* Perhaps it may be proper to acquaint them with D.B.'s and our united Endeavours, and the Effects. They will stun at least, if not convince, the most worthy, that nothing very favourable is intended, if more unfavourable Articles cannot be obtained' " (*MS 1*; emphasis added; Franklin, *Writings*, ed. Smyth, VI, 399). Fothergill's note, written at "1/2 past 10" and enjoining Franklin to support "this infant, growing empire with the utmost exertion of thy abilitys, and no less philanthropy," was quoted exactly by Franklin except for punctuation, capitalization, and one error in transcription—a misreading of "the most worthy" for "the most courtly" (Fothergill to Franklin, [19] Mch. 1775, DLC: Franklin Papers; all editions of the narrative have naturally copied Franklin's error; for the texts of Fothergill's note to Franklin and his letters to friends in America [James Pemberton and William Logan], see Betsy C. Corner and Christopher C. Booth, eds., *Selected letters of Dr. John Fothergill* [Harvard, 1971]. For the suggestion that it was Dr. Fothergill who prompted the negotiations, see Betsy Copping Corner and Dorothea Waley Singer, "Dr. John Fothergill, Peacemaker," Am. Phil. Soc., *Procs.*, 98 [Feb. 1954], 11-22). The ominous thrust of the passage is unmistakable. TJ erred in attributing the views to Lord North himself rather than to the ministry. But in recalling that the negotiations at the close revealed an official attitude of absolute indifference to rebellion because "the confiscations it would produce would provide for many of their friends," he was only paraphrasing the substance of the opinion that Fothergill had expressed and that Franklin had accurately reported.

What is surprising is that the superficial differences of the two versions should have obscured their substantive agreement or that this should have aroused in the *Edinburgh Review* such stately indignation. Fothergill in making the charge and Franklin and TJ in repeating it may indeed have been unjust to the character of Lord North and the British ministry. But Franklin, who had reportedly been moved to tears of anger, frustration, and sorrow at the final collapse of the negotiations, certainly did not disbelieve it. "The Doctor, in the Course of his daily Visits among the Great," he wrote in commenting upon the charge, ". . . had full Opportunity of being acquainted with their Sentiments, the Conversation everywhere at this time turning upon the Subject of America" (*MS 1*; *Writings*, ed. Smyth, VI, 399; see Van Doren, *Franklin*, p. 519-22). A month before the negotiations ended Franklin had written a frank letter to Charles Thomson, advising that further petitioning was useless, that the ministry believed the majority of the people disapproved of the proceedings of Congress, that they thought "an Army sufficient to support these Friends . . . of Government" would cause an overthrow of the leaders, and that Lord Chatham's plan of conciliation—which in substance was suggested by Franklin himself—was treated in the House of Lords "with as much contempt as they could have shown to a Ballad offered by a drunken Porter" (Franklin to Thomson, 5 Feb. 1775, cautioning him "to let no part of this Letter be copied or printed"; same, VI, p. 307). Three weeks later, he had contrasted the corruption prevalent in England with the "glorious publick Virtue so

predominant in our rising Country" and had pointed to the "Numberless and needless Places, enormous Salaries, Pensions, Perquisites, Bribes, groundless Quarrels, foolish Expeditions, false Accounts or no Accounts, Contracts and Jobbs" which devoured all revenue and produced continual necessity in the midst of plenty (Franklin to Galloway, 25 Feb. 1775; same, VI, 312).

Franklin in 1775 no less than TJ in 1821 was prepared to believe that an intransigent ministry wanted a larger field on which to fatten a herd of worthless parasites—indeed that it needed one in order to sustain itself. Such a belief was natural. After all, confiscations of rebels' estates for bestowal upon loyal friends of the crown had been a normal concomitant of rebellion for centuries, as the long history of Britain, Scotland, Ireland, and Wales amply testified. This time-honored treatment for those who dared to challenge royal authority—if no worse fate befell —was one no American leader of the day could have failed to consider as a very probable outcome of unsuccessful rebellion. Even in the narrative of the peace negotiations Franklin expressed the belief that the ministry would rather give him "a Place in a Cart to Tyburn, than any other Place whatever" (*Writings*, ed. Smyth, VI, 372). At three different points in the document he was at pains to show that ministerial hints or outright promises of office, reward, or honors had been made to him, a reiteration indicating his view of ministerial use of corrupt and manipulative methods (same, VI, 353, 372, 386). Both Franklin and TJ, at the opening of the Revolution and during its course, had reason to grasp with their compatriots the full implications of their mutual pledge of lives, fortunes, and honor should the challenge to royal authority fail. On the much controverted point of TJ's attribution of sentiments to Lord North, therefore, his remembered account seems more remarkable for its substantive fidelity to the plain meaning of Fothergill's words as accurately reported by Franklin than for its superficial variance in phraseology.

But one is forced to a very different conclusion with respect to his belief that he had violated a trust committed to him by Franklin and that he thereby became an accessory to Temple Franklin's presumed venality. TJ erred in both respects and these errors in turn proceeded from other culpabilities concerning the origin of the legend that Franklin had given him the manuscript as a confidential deposit. In 1810 when William Duane asked TJ whether he had retained a copy of it, he introduced his question with this statement: "It was mentioned to me, that on your passage thro' this city several years ago, Dr. Franklin put into your hands a manuscript, entreating you to keep it, and as the fittest person to trust it to; that you returned it, and it was put into your hands again; but that on the death of that great man, you conceived yourself bound to put the Manuscript in the hands of Mr. Temple Franklin; and thus it is lost to the world. . . ." (Duane to TJ, 17 Aug. 1810). It is not surprising that this should have fixed forever in TJ's mind the conviction that he had been given a trust. For the account as stated by Duane, despite its minor inaccuracies, was one that only TJ himself could have originated. Only he could have revealed what had transpired in 1790 during that last memorable exchange between him and the dying patriarch. Suspicions about the behavior of Temple Franklin developed independently and for different reasons on both sides of the Atlantic, but there can be little doubt as to when and why TJ initiated the version that came back to him through Duane after almost two decades of growth from the seeds that he alone could have planted.

Temple Franklin himself was an unwitting accomplice in this planting of the seeds of suspicion. In acknowledging receipt of the manuscript that TJ had forwarded through Bache, Franklin mentioned a highly secret and extremely important report of the Lords of Trade to the Privy Council concerning British commercial policy toward the United States (Franklin to TJ, 6 Apr. 1791; see Editorial Note, commercial and diplomatic relations with Great Britain, under 15 Dec. 1790). When he received this news, TJ had already gained some inkling of the contents of the report and he instantly grasped its significance. He was so anxious to procure it that he told the American consul he would "not think 50. or 100 guineas mispent in getting the whole original," though he feared it could not be obtained (TJ to Johnson, 29 Aug. 1791). This implicit authorization of bribery in an official instruction revealed the great value

TJ placed upon the document, but even so the consul—who was not without resourcefulness and who did occasionally acquire important official documents of a secret nature (see Editorial Note, report on fisheries, 1 Feb. 1791) —did not succeed in getting it. But less than a month after TJ had expressed this urgent desire, Temple Franklin sent him a comprehensive and exact transcript of all of its salient features. TJ did not repeat his desire to have the full text, perhaps because Franklin's abstract was so full as to make this no longer a desideratum.

But the significant fact is that TJ did not even acknowledge this notable service that Temple Franklin had performed at a crucial moment for the United States—an accomplishment that the Secretary of State should have welcomed all the more because of its effect on domestic politics and on foreign policy. For the revelation not only threw the Secretary of the Treasury and his supporters momentarily on the defensive: it also gave TJ the advantage of knowing precisely the ground on which the newly arrived British minister to the United States stood. Furthermore, if TJ received the complete set of MITCHELL'S MAP that Franklin had sent to him through William Stephens Smith, he did not acknowledge the gift (Franklin to TJ, 6 Apr. 1791; see also, TJ to Benjamin Franklin, 31 Mch. 1790; Benjamin Franklin to TJ, 8 Apr. 1790; Vol. 16: xxiv-xxv). Indeed, from that time forward he held no further correspondence with the man from whom he had so recently solicited and received both public and private favors (see TJ to Franklin, 20 Apr., 16 and 25 July 1790; Franklin to TJ, 27 Apr., 20 July and 1 Aug. 1790). Such an abrupt termination of a once friendly relationship inevitably brings to mind the chilling manner in which TJ parted from Charles Williamos, who was also suspected of being in the pay of the British government (TJ to Williamos, 7 July 1785). Temple Franklin undoubtedly was still hoping for the appointment as minister to France when he sent the abstract (Franklin to TJ, 6 Apr. 1791). He could justifiably have felt that his accomplishment in gaining access to so important a state paper established a claim in addition to others he and his grandfather thought he possessed (TJ to Monroe, 5 July 1785).

But TJ's abrupt termination of his

correspondence and his failure to express appreciation for this achievement suggest that he placed a very different construction upon it. Added to the remark made by Bache when TJ delivered the manuscript to him, this must have meant to him that Temple Franklin, only a few months after arriving in London, was in such intimate touch with the leaders of the British government as to be able to gain access to documents of the highest secrecy and thus perhaps, in the immemorial custom of double-dealers, was giving secrets in return. Within a short time TJ dared to express his fears to one who might be in a position to reveal the truth. "When are we to see the new edition of Dr. Franklin's works?" he asked Bache. "The delay gives me apprehensions" (TJ to Bache, 26 Dec. 1795; this question also may have been put in TJ's [missing] letter of 2 June 1795 to Bache). The apprehensions expressed in retirement had almost certainly arisen as early as 1791.

It is therefore difficult to avoid the conclusion that the most useful diplomatic service Temple Franklin ever rendered his country was the ironic cause of extinguishing the hope of preferment in diplomacy that had prompted him to perform it—a hope that had been nurtured in the ten years since Benjamin Franklin first made a direct appeal to the President of Congress in his behalf (Franklin to Huntington, 12 Mch. 1781, *Writings*, ed. Smyth, VIII, 220-2). Such a deeply disappointing silence after so useful a service may well have created in Temple Franklin the disgust that he had professed not to feel at the time he left the United States. If so, the responsibility lay with the Secretary of State who was the principal beneficiary of the revealed secret of state. In any event his initial suspicion, nourished by Franklin's continued absence abroad and the delay in publishing his grandfather's papers, became over the years a fixed and unshakeable conviction.

To Samuel Vaughan, Jr.

DEAR SIR   Philadelphia Nov. 27. 1790.

I feel myself much indebted to Mr. Vaughan your father for the opportunity he has furnished me of a direct correspondence with you, and also to yourself for the seeds of the Mountain rice you have been so good as to send me. I had before received from your brother in London some of the same parcel brought by Capt. Bligh; but it was so late in the spring of the present year that tho the plants came up and grew luxuriantly, they did not produce seed. Your present will enable me to enlarge the experiment I propose for the next year, and for which I had still reserved a few seeds of the former parcel.—About two months ago I was fortunate enough to recieve a cask of mountain rice from the coast of Africa. This has enabled me to engage so many persons in the experiment as to be tolerably sure it will be fairly made by some of them. It will furnish also a comparison with that from Timor. I have the success of this species of rice at heart, because it will not only enable other states to cultivate rice which have not lands susceptible of inundation but because also, if the rice be as good as is said, it may take place of the wet rice in the Southern states, and by superseding the necessity of overflowing their lands, save them from the pestilential and mortal fevers brought on by that operation.

We have lately had introduced a plant of the Melon species which, from it's external resemblance to the pumpkin, we have called a pumpkin, distinguishing it specifically as the *potatoe-pumpkin*, on account of the extreme resemblance of it's taste to that of the sweet-potatoe. It is as yet but little known, is well esteemed at our tables, and particularly valued by our negroes. Coming much earlier than the real potatoe, we are so much the sooner furnished with a substitute for that root. I know not from whence it came; so that perhaps it may be originally from your islands. In that case you will only have the trouble of throwing away the few seeds I enclose you herewith. On the other hand, if unknown with you, I think it will probably succeed in the islands, and may add to the catalogue of plants which will do as substitutes for bread. I have always thought that if in the experiments to introduce or to communicate new plants, one species in an hundred is found useful and succeeds, the ninety nine found otherwise are more than paid for.—My present situation and occupations are not friendly to agricultural experiments, however strongly I am led to them by inclination. But whenever I shall be more free to indulge that inclination I will ask permission to address myself to you for such seeds as might be worth trying from your quarter, freely offering you reciprocal services in the same or any other line in which you will be so good as to command them. I have the honour to be with great respect & esteem, Sir Your most obedt. & most humble servt, Th: Jefferson

PrC (DLC).

Jefferson's Memoranda for Washington

[29 Nov. 1790]

Note of letters recieved.

Mr. Short. July 16. A private letter in which he says it is true that the Queen of Portugal has appointed Mr. Freire her Minister resident for the U.S.

———

Ignatius Polyart. Phila. Oct. 5. Announcing his commission as Consul general for the Queen of Portugal in the U.S.

———

Dumas. Hague. May 26.—July 10.—July 14. Nothing new.

Nathaniel Gilman. Exeter Sep. 10.
John Neufville. Charleston. Sep. 22. } accepting their appointment as Commissioners of loans.
James Tilton. Dover. Sep 25-----

Stephen Sayre, of New York. Havre. Aug. 25. 1790. Desiring *some employment in Europe.*

Thos. Delaire of France. Rochelle. Nov. 17. 1789. Desiring to be agent there.

Robert Montgomery (of Pennsylvania) Alicant. Aug. 21. 1790. Desiring to be consul there.

Thos. Hardy (of Rhodeisland) Copenhagen. Oct. 28. 1789. Desiring to be Consul there.

Mr. Short. No. 37. July 27. & No. 38. Aug. 4
John Stokes. Newbern. Oct. 5.
Nathaniel Cutting. St. Domingo. Aug. 9. } The letters themselves for the President's perusal
Fulwar Skipwith. St. Pierre in Martinique Sep. 18 and Oct. 10.
Robert Montgomery. Alicant. Aug. 21.
Richard O'Bryen. Algiers. Sep. 23. and Dec. 12.

PrC (DLC); at foot of text: "given in to the President. Nov. 29. 1790"; recorded in SJPL as "Note of Th: J. letters received."

Jefferson's Draft of Items for the President's Message to Congress

[29 Nov. 1790]

The laws you have already passed for the establishment of a judiciary system have opened the doors of justice to all descriptions of persons. You will consider in your wisdom[1] whether improvements in that system may yet be made; and particularly whether an uniform process of execution, on sentences issuing from the federal courts, be not desireable thro' all the states.

The patronage[2] of our commerce, of our merchants and seamen, has called for the appointment of Consuls in foreign countries. It seems expedient to regulate by law the exercise of that jurisdiction, and of those functions which are permitted them[3] either by express convention, or by a friendly indulgence in the places of their residence.[4] The Consular convention too, with his most

Christian Majesty has stipulated, in certain cases, the aid of the national authority[5] to his Consuls established here. Some legislative provision is requisite to carry these stipulations into full effect.

MS (DLC); entirely in TJ's hand; undated, but entry in SJPL under 29 Nov. 1790 can only refer to this document: "Subjects of speech to Congress."

These two paragraphs were inserted in Washington's message to Congress of 8 Dec. 1790 as written by TJ (Washington, *Writings*, ed. Fitzpatrick, XXXI, 167-8).

Four days after TJ arrived in Philadelphia, Andrew Brown's newspaper listed the measures requiring action at the forthcoming session of Congress: "a *national mint*, and a *national bank* —*uniformity of weights and measures* —the *post-office*, and *post-roads*" (*Federal Gazette*, 24 Nov. 1790). The list seems almost too balanced a reflection of the aims of both the Secretary of the Treasury and the Secretary of State not to have been contrived. But if promptings came from either official, it seems more likely that they came from the former, who at this time regarded the editor as "a zealous federalist and personally friendly" though he later came to believe TJ had detached him through the use of patronage (Coxe to Hamilton, 5 Mch. 1790; Hamilton to Carrington, 26 May 1792, Syrett, *Hamilton*, VI, 291-3; VII, 431). Washington had first asked Hamilton, in a private letter, to submit suggestions for the annual message touching both his own department and general matters. But Hamilton, who had been requested by the House of Representatives to present plans for a mint, did not mention this topic. Nor did he advance the idea of a national bank, limiting himself only to a suggested sentence expressing "confidence that measures for the further support of public Credit . . . will be pursued with zeal and vigour." He did, however, urge the importance of trade with the Mediterranean—a topic he knew would be reported upon by the Secretary of State and on which his views of policy ran exactly counter to what he urged the President to recommend ("Notes of Objects for Consideration of the President," endorsed by Hamilton "Decr. 1. 1790," same, VII, 172-3; Editorial Note, documents on Mediterranean trade and

Algerine captives, under 28 Dec. 1790; Washington to Hamilton, 10 Oct. 1790, *Writings*, ed. Fitzpatrick, XXXI, 132). But John Jay anticipated the President's similar request by proffering suggestions on coinage and post roads even before he was asked (Washington to Jay, Mount Vernon, 19 Nov. 1790, same, XXXI, 155-6; Jay to Washington, Boston, 19 Nov. 1790, Johnston, ed., *Corres. . . . of John Jay*, III, 405-8). All of the circumstances appear to justify the inference that the agenda offered by Andrew Brown may have been inspired by the Secretary of the Treasury after he had talked with TJ the day before the paper appeared (TJ to Hamilton, 24 Nov. 1790).

TJ himself certainly made suggestions for the message in addition to the above items dealing with judicial reform and consular regulations. He and Madison had already visited Washington at Mount Vernon and TJ had pointedly called attention to the need of doing something about the Algerine captives and the treaty with Morocco —subjects which, if the above suggestions represent the whole of his recommendations, he also failed to mention (TJ to Washington, 27 Oct. 1790). But the above note was certainly not the whole of TJ's written suggestions for the annual message. Immediately following the entry in SJPL for 29 Nov. 1790 listing "Subjects of speech to Congress," there appears the following: "Dec. 3. G. W. to Th: J. on same subject." Following this entry, under the same date, is this: "paragraphs proposed for speech." Neither Washington's note to TJ of 3 Dec. 1790 nor the text of these additional paragraphs has been found. But that passage in the message assuming that the subjects of a militia establishment, a mint, weights and measures, post office, and post roads would be resumed as a matter of course and as being "abundantly urged by their own importance" may well have reflected TJ's missing response to Washington's note of the 3rd. And if that response touched upon any other topic, it must have been the "very important transaction" between Virginia and the District of Kentucky by which the latter, if sanctioned by Congress, would become a member of the union. This sentence in the message undoubtedly reflects the views and perhaps the hand of the Secretary of State: "The liberality and harmony, with which [that transaction] has been conducted will be found to do great honor to both the parties; and the sentiments of warm attachment to the Union and its present Government expressed by our fellow citizens of Kentucky cannot fail to add an affectionate concern for their particular welfare to the great national impressions under which you will decide on the case submitted to you"

(Washington, *Writings*, ed. Fitzpatrick, XXXI, 164-8; see Editorial Note, group of documents on admission of Vermont and Kentucky, under 4 Mch. 1791).

1 TJ first wrote: "Your wisdom will decide" and then altered the passage to read as above.
2 This word interlined in substitution for "interests," deleted.
3 At this point TJ deleted the following: "in the places of their residence."
4 TJ first wrote: "or by the sufferance of friendly powers," and then altered the passage to read as above.
5 Preceding two words interlined in substitution for "civil power," deleted.

From Sylvanus Bourne

SIR   Boston Novr 30th. 1790

I had the honour some time since to acquaint you of my intentions of embarking for Cape Francois by the middle of this month, but the want of an opportunity has hitherto prevented me and I wait yet some days for a Vessell bound to that Port.

You was pleased to suggest in your last the peculiar necessity of my departure as it related to the public and I doubt not under these circumstances your Candour will lead you to subscribe also to the necessity and propriety of the Case that Government should early in this session pass some Consular regulations and not subject their officers abroad to the uncomfortable situation of performing public Duty without the light of Law—or to the burthen of performing public service without an adequate recompense, more especially as the tenor of their Commissions excludes them from any emolument not established by the Laws of their own Country or of that where they may reside.

It appears to me it will also be necessary that the Consular Bill whenever it may pass should contain a Clause making it the duty of Masters of Vessells on arrival to make those reports to Consuls of the Vessells, Cargoes &c. which you require to be made by the Consuls to Government at home every six months as I think without such an injunction on the Captains it will be impossible for the Consuls to obtain the necessary information. The Bill as it passed the House last session did not make such the duty of Captains tho it required the semiannual returns similar to your instructions.

You once observed to me that you should furnish me with printed Copies of the Consular Convention with France which from the hurry of business you have not yet which I would thank you to transmit me with the Bill as soon as passed. I must advance as much as 50. Dolls. for Seals Books &c. necessary to establish the Consular Department within my District. Is it not proper Government should reimburse it to me? I have the honour to be with great Respect Sir Yr most Obedt Servt,

Sylvanus Bourne

RC (DNA: RG 59, CD); endorsed by TJ as received 11 Dec. 1790, and so recorded in SJL.

To Tench Coxe

Nov. 30. 1790.

Th: Jefferson returns Mr. Cox many thanks for the several communications he has favored him with and which will be of great utility to him. Can he procure him the loan of one of the latest editions of Ld. Sheffeild's book? As also Edward's answer to it.

RC (CtY); addressed "Mr. Coxe Treasury office Chesnut street"; endorsed. Not recorded in SJL. Sheffield's *Observations on the commerce of the American states* (see Sowerby, Nos. 3618, 3616) and Bryan Edwards' *Thoughts on the late proceedings of Government respecting the Trade of the West India Islands with the United States* (London, 1784) were the works that TJ desired. The latter was by a West Indian merchant and historian who argued for a free exchange in trade with the United States.

From David Humphreys

Sir   Lisbon Novr. 30th. 1790

As soon as my baggage was landed, I wrote a note to M. de Pinto, advising that I was charged with the delivery of a letter from you to him, and requesting the honor of being informed at what time it would be convenient for His Excellency to receive it. To this he gave an extremely polite answer, and fixed upon the 25th of this Month at his House in Junqueira. I accordingly waited on him, and, though he had been so much indisposed the preceding night as to refuse all other visits that morning, as soon as my name was sent in, he received me in his closet with great goodness. Upon perusing your letter he enquired kindly about your health, expressed himself strongly attached to you personally, and gave the most pointed assurances of his dispositions to promote a friendly intercourse between our two nations: at the same time declaring that he had been much mortified in not having been able to carry your former negociations into effect, but that you knew it was not owing to his fault; and adding that he was very happy to have obtained from the Queen the nomination of the Chr. de Freire as *Minister Resident* in the United States, because Mr. de Freire was so well known to Mr. Adams, yourself, and many respectable Americans, and because he was himself so fully acquainted with that Gentleman, and knew him to be a person of good understanding, strict honor, conciliating temper, and well inclined to the U.S.—I gave him the best answer of civility in my power, with assurances of the reciprocal favorable dispositions of the Executive of the United States; and that, from the partial acquaintance I had formerly had the pleasure to have with M: de Freire, as well as from the excellent reputation he universally sustained, there was no doubt he would be perfectly well received in, and highly acceptable as a *Diplomatic Character* to the U.S.: but I observed that the designation of this Gentleman *as such* was not known in America at the time when I left it: that therefore the overtures contained in the letter I had just had the honor of delivering to him originated spontaneously with the American Government in the same friendly sentiments which had influenced Her Most Faithful Majesty to make this nomination: that this was the first new arrangement of a Diplomatic nature which had been proposed since the establishment of the present Government: that His Excellency would be pleased to notice that motives of economy and difference in circumstances between our young nation and the old nations of Europe, were the reasons which operated with the Executive of the U.S. for wishing to keep only a Chargé des Affaires at this Court: that, although the President of the U. S. (with the advice and consent of the Senate) had the appointment of Diplomatic Characters, yet the pecuniary provision for their subsistence was made solely by Acts of the Legislature: and that the existing Act of the Legislature for this purpose had granted a specific appropriation of Monies to the disposal of the President, with a limitation that he might allow to a Minister Plenipotentiary and a Chargé des Affaires an annual salary not exceeding such a sum for each.— The Minister of Her Most Faithful Majesty replied, that he fully comprehended the scope of the observations in Mr. Jefferson's letter, but that he did not perceive any inconvenience could result to the U. S. on account of the pecuniary appointment, because the Salary which would support a Chargé des Affaires might also answer for a Minister Resident, whose intermediate grade between a Minister Plenipotentiary and a Chargé des Affaires would certainly give him more respectability than the latter, without subjecting him of necessity to more expense: and he named an instance of a Minister Resident, who, being a merchant, did not receive a single farthing of pay from his Court, and yet enjoyed all the privileges and favor annexed to that grade: But he laid the principal stress of the propriety of the measure of naming a Minister Resident from the Court of Lisbon to the U. S. upon their not being able to select *a sufficiently worthy and dignified Character*, who would consent to go such a distance, in only the Capacity of Chargé des Affaires. He finished by saying, that as such good dispositions prevailed on both parts, he flattered himself; there could not be a difficulty about names, rather than things; that he was not, however, enabled to give any conclusive opinion, without first consulting the Queen and her other Ministers.—Here I took occasion of enlarging as much as I could with decency, upon our situation as a new Nation in a manner dissevered from the rest of the world, the system which had been established by us, the policy and propriety there might be for European Nations to dispense with forms in regard to us; and the conduct of Spain on this subject; together with whatever other topics I judged might without indiscretion be adduced as tending to obtain the object in view. The Chr. de Pinto rejoined much to the same effect he had before; and added that he would also give the sentiments he had now expressed in writing to you, in answer to your letter; particularly on the impossibility of finding a proper Character who would be willing to go to America, merely in the quality of Chargé des Affaires.—As he appeared to be somewhat unwell, and as the ground of the business had been so much changed from what it was understood to be when I left America, by the actual appointment of the Chr. des Freire as Minister Resident to the U.S., I did not press the conversation so much at that interview as I should otherwise have done.—But before I took my leave I added, that, as he had been pleased to mention that whatever had fallen from him in the course of this conversation was not to be considered as conclusive, and as perhaps something farther would occur to make some alteration of opinion in consequence of the observations that had been or might be made, it was my desire to know at what time I might have the honor of seeing him again on the subject of this conference. He assigned this day at 12 O'Clock.

I attended at the time appointed, and the Chr. de Pinto informed me, that having considered attentively the subject of your letter, he was still fully confirmed on the sentiments he had expressed to me in our first conversation; that he greatly applauded the system of severe œconomy in which we were laying the foundations of our new government; that attention to this œconomy (as he had before observed) need however occasion no objection against our naming a Minister Resident rather than a Chargé des Affaires, because there need be no difference of expence in the grades; and that, although the Etiquette which had formerly been observed by the Court of Lisbon in not admitting Chargés des Affaires to equal privileges with Ministers might be dispensed with; yet the policy of keeping a Person of respectable Character from that Court in the U. S. had made it absolutely necessary to appoint a Minister Resident,—for he repeated the observation to me, upon his word of honor and with the greatest appearance of earnestness, that they could not find a Person who was proper to be employed in a public Character in America, and who would accept the appointment as Chargé des Affaires. He also mentioned that it was impossible for the Queen to receive a Diplomatic Character of a different denomination from that which she sent. I observed in reply, that the embarrassment of the Government[1] of the U. S. would not probably be occasioned so much by the article of expense in the present instance as by a deviation from the System to which they had wished to adhere; that it would be peculiarly unfortunate and much to be regretted if the systems of the two nations should be so incompatable, as to prevent an exchange of Diplomatic Characters, when the mutual interests and inclinations of both seemed to render it so expedient; and after recapitulating, under different points of view, several observations which had been before suggested, I remarked, that although His Excellency might have noticed it was hinted in your letter that whatever should be agreed upon with me as to the grade of Diplomatic Characters to be exchanged should be considered as settled, yet as I was not authorised to agree upon the exchange of any but in the capacity of Charges des Affaires, and as in the meantime a Minister Resident had been appointed by this Court, I did not perceive what could be done at present farther than to state the circumstances to the Executive of the U. S. He said, if I would give him leave, he would read to me the draft of a letter he was preparing for you— which he did—and which, as well as I could comprehend from a single reading, I believe, in addition to what I have already had the honor to report, will bring you sufficiently well acquainted with the purport of what passed in the conferences I was directed to hold with the Chr. de Pinto on the subject of your letter to him.—The polite attention of that Minister merits all my acknowledgments. Having made arrangements for hiring Mules, I propose to set out for Spain immediately, and to return here before it will be possible for your answer to this letter to arrive in this place.

An Ambassador Extraordinary from Vienna has just come to Lisbon, to announce to this Court the election of the Emperor of Germany.—A Portuguese Frigate, destined to carry an Ambassador to the new Emperor of Morocco, went down the River yesterday. Nothing farther is known here, respecting the terms of the Convention between Spain and England, than when I wrote to you on the 19th of this Month. With Sentiments of perfect esteem & consideration I have the honor to be Sir, Your Most obedient & Most humble Servant,   D. HUMPHREYS

RC (DNA: RG 59, DD); at head of text: "(No. 8)"; endorsed by TJ as received 11 Feb. 1791 and so recorded in SJL. Tr (same). PrC of a different Tr (DLC); this was the text that

Washington sent to the senate, 18 Feb. 1791.

[1] This word interlined in substitution for "Executive," deleted.

From Joshua Johnson

SIR   London 30th November 1790

I had the Honor to address you on the 3d. 5th and 15 Instant by the New York Packett, Copies of which be pleased to find annexed and to which I beg reference. Inclosed I hand you the Court Gazette and Woodfalls register to this day inclusive. They contain the Kings speech and proceedings of Parliament. So far, nothing else has transpired worth observation, or your attention; Mr. Pitt seems firmly fixed in his place and out of the reach of Opposition.

All I understand from the allusion in the Kings Speech to Quebec is the regulation of their Government. I will be attentively watchfull to find out if they have any other object and will inform You. It is reported that Mr. Elliott Brother to Sir Gilbert Elliott is appointed Plenipotentiary to the United States of America; I will wait on the Duke of Leeds in a day or two, when I get rid of a slight indisposition which now confines me, and know from him if it is so, or not, and which information, I will hand you by the first opportunity.

I am to inform you that since I have undertaken to act under my appointment, that neither the Courts of Justice or Commons will enter any Process for one American Seaman against another. All their disputes come before me to be adjusted and settled and as our Sailors have long been in the habit of running to the petty Attorneys, on every frivolous occasion; they, as yet, pursue this same folly and which you may readily suppose gives me much trouble, and not a little vexation; I hope Congress will very shortly form a Code of Marine Laws for the regulation of their Consuls. I am striving to obtain from the Consuls resident in England representing other Powers, what fees are allowed to each; this, I have hopes of obtaining in a short time, and which I will transmit to you, hoping it may prove usefull to Congress in forming their Table of Fees to be paid their Servants. Since the Exchange of articles of Peace, between the Courts of London and Madrid, there is an entire stagnation to the sale of American produce, and I fear when the Market opens that the Price will scarcely pay Freight and Expences. This will militate more particularly against the Southern States, and force them into manufacturing for themselves.—I have daily applications to know the value of your Public Funds, many Monied Merchants would freely receive payment from their Debtors there in transfers of your Stock could they rely on being accurately informed of their Value, as it will tend to the ease of many individuals, and probably a public good; I rest it with your better Judgement, whether it would not, be proper to hand me from the Treasurers Office, the price of each Stock on the last day of each Month preceeding the sailing of the Packet. I will write you again in a few days. In the mean time, I have the honor to remain with much respect & Esteem Sir, Your most humble &c. &c.   JOSHUA JOHNSON

RC (DNA: RG 59, CD). Tr (same); at head of text: "⅌ the Eleanor Captn. Magruder." Recorded in SJL as received 12 Mch. 1791. Dupl (same); addressed in part: "⅌ the New York Packet"; postmarked (within circle) DE 1 90"; endorsed by TJ as received 19 Jan. 1791 and so recorded in SJL. On 1 Dec. 1790 Johnson wrote TJ enclosing Dupl, the original having been sent the day before "by the Eleanor, Captain Magruder, Via George Town, Maryland" (RC and Tr in same).

From Luis Pinto de Souza

MONSIEUR   À Lisbonne ce 30me Novembre 1790.

Je viens de recevoir la lettre que Votre Excellence m'a fait l'honneur de m'ecrire en date du 7 Août, et que Mr. le Colonel Humphreys m'a donnée, et c'est avec une parfaite satisfaction, Monsieur, que je vous vois placé à la tête d'un Departement où je puis avoir l'avantage de vous communiquer avec cette confiance que vos vertus ont su m'inspirer et qui pourra devenir un jour la base des Relations reciproques d'amitié et d'interêts entre les deux Nations.

Je suis parfaitement convaincu, Monsieur, de toutes les difficultés qu'entrenne avec soi une Constitution Nouvelle, et du tems qui est necessaire pour parvenir à la maturité. Je connois encore, Monsieur, tous les pris d'une economie prudente, et combien elle est éssentiel à Votre Constitution, et je ne puis qu'y aplaudir. C'est en consequence de ces principes que je me suis élevé au dessus de toutes étiquetes en proposant à Sa Majesté La Reine un simple Ministre Resident auprès des Etats Unis d'Amerique, sans attendre même de sa part aucune nomination préalable, et le choix en est tombé sur Monsieur Freire, Secretaire de Legation à la Cour de Londres.

Je crois, Monsieur, que cette mesure remplira entièrement les vues d'une juste economie en vous metant en même de pouvoir comettre avec plus de dignité les soins des affaires publiques, ne voiant dans le titre de Résident, ou dans celui de Chargé d'Affaires, qu'une simple question de nom; mais malgré cette conviction, elle est de la derniere importance pour nous, puisqu'il a été impossible de pouvoir trouver aucune personne convenable qui voulu passer en Amerique en qualité de Simple Chargé d'Affaires, et vous devez comprendre, Monsieur, que nous ne pouvons pas nous dispenser d'exiger la réciprocité de Caractere entre les Representans des deux Nations.

Je me flatte donc, Monsieur, que votre Gouvernement verra dans sa sagesse que le titre de Ministre Resident n'altere en rien ses vues economiques, et que, donnant plus de consideration à ses Agens en Europe, il ne fairat que gagner en fait des Negotiations.

D'après ces principes, vous pouvez être persuadé, Monsieur, du plaisir avec lequel la Reine vairra paroître à sa Cour un Ministre Resident des Etats Unis, et de la part qu'il aura toujours à sa bienveillance Royale.

Après vous avoir exposer les vrais sentimens de Sa Majesté, permettés moi, Monsieur, de vous renouveller ceux de l'amitié la plus sincere, et de la parfaite consideration avec laquelle j'ai l'honneur d'être de Votre Excellence Le tres humble et tres obeissant Serviteur,   DE PINTO

RC (DNA: RG 360, PCC No. 59); in a clerk's hand except for complimentary close and signature; endorsed by TJ as received 11 Feb. 1791 and so recorded in SJL. Tr (DLC); in English, in clerk's hand. PrC of Tr (DLC).

Estimate by Nicholas Lewis of Yield of Jefferson's Estate, 1790

Mr. Jeffersons Estate

Dr

[Nov. 1790]

	[£]		
To Mr. Maury bord and tuition of Master Carr . .	30	–	–
To a balance of former Subscriptions to Mr. Maury, About	6	–	–
To the present years subscription to Mr. Maury . .	5	–	–
To Martin & Pollards Acct 63.5.7 ½ Mazies bond to be deducted will leave a balance of about	37	–	–
To county levies including what is levied for the support of the poore in Bedfor & Albemarle	18	–	–
To The State tax	36	–	–
To Carriage of Tobo	20	–	–
To Building a House for the Overseer	8	–	–
To Montgomery & Henry	200	–	–
To N. Lewis Exclusive of what is in hand and including his Smiths Acct.	35	–	–

Contra

Bedford

At the Old Quarter	34 000 ℔. Tobo.
At James Hubbards	14 000 ℔. Do.
	———————
The whole	48 000
Deducted for Mr. Randolphs Negroes which work at old Quarter & the Overseers Shares	8 000
	———————
	40 000 @

Wheat 200 Bushs. @ 4/6 45

5,000 Grose pork @ 15/ 37 10

100 Barrels Corn @ 8/1 . . . . 40 0 0[1]

money which Clark supposes may [be] collected by
June including £10.13.2 which I recd. when
last up . . . . 133 – 10 –

Albemarle

Exclusive of the Overseers Shares 29,000 ℔.

Tobo. at . . . .

Wheat 400 Bushs. 4/6 . . . .

Due for the present years Rent from Robt. Lewis,
Wm. Norris, & Robert Smith . . . . 40 – –

MS (ViU); in hand of Nicholas Lewis, except as indicated in note 1 below; endorsed by TJ: "Estimate by Mr. Lewis. Nov. 1790."

[1] The figures representing commodity prices and totals for this and preceding two items are in TJ's hand, as also is the price of wheat below.

To Thomas MacDonogh

SIR   Philadelphia Decemr. 1st. 1790

I am sorry that the short recess of the Executive happened at the time you were pleased to attend here with your Commission as Consul. I received your favour of November 8th. on the 23rd. of that month, together with your original Commission, which I exhibited to the President immediately on his return, and have now the honor to re-enclose it to you, together with the Exequatur, adding assurances of the respect with which I am Sir &c.

FC (DNA: RG 59, PCC No. 120).

To Martha Jefferson Randolph

MY DEAR DAUGHTER   Philadelphia Dec. 1. 1790.

In my letter of last week to Mr. Randolph I mentioned that I should write every Wednesday to him, yourself and Polly alternately, and that my letters arriving at Monticello the Saturday and the answer being sent off on Sunday I should recieve it the day before I should have to write again to the same person, so as that the correspondence with each would be exactly kept up. I hope you will do it on your part. I delivered the fan and note to your friend Mrs. Waters (Miss Rittenhouse that was) she being now married to a Doctr. Waters. They live in the house with her father. She complained of the petit format of your letter, and Mrs. Trist of no letter. I inclose you the Magasin des modes of July.—My furniture is arrived from Paris: but it will be long before I can open the packages, as my house will not be ready to recieve them for some weeks. As soon as they are the mattrasses &c. shall be sent on.—News for Mr. Randolph. The letters from Paris inform that as yet all is safe there. They are emitting great sums of paper money. They rather believe there will be no war between Spain and England: but the letters from London count on a war, and it seems rather probable. A general peace is established in the North of Europe, except between Russia and Turkey. It is expected between them also. Wheat here is a French crown the bushel. Kiss dear Poll for me. Remember me to Mr. Randolph. I do not know yet how the Edgehill negociation has terminated. Adieu my dear, Your's affectionately,   TH: JEFFERSON

RC (NNP). PrC (MHi).

To John Woodard

SIR   Philadelphia Dec. 1. 1790.

I recieved yesterday your favor of Nov. 24. and am sorry that I am not able to serve your wishes: but there neither is, nor has been a single vacancy in the clerkships in my office since I came to it. I found them all filled, and continued the same gentlemen as was just, so that I have not had a single appointment to make. I am Sir Your very humble servt.,   TH: JEFFERSON

PrC (DLC).

Woodard's letter, dated "Bordentown New Jersey Nov 24. 1790," declared that he was a stranger, that he had heard "there's several Clerks wanting" under TJ's appointment, that he was out of employment, and that he was willing to have "the Salary thats annex'd to any of those offices" placed in the hands of trustees to be withheld from him until his conduct should be fully approved (RC in DLC: Applications for Appointment under Washington; endorsed by TJ as received 30 Nov. 1790 and so recorded in SJL).

To James Anderson

SIR   Philadelphia Dec. 2. 1790.

The letter of April 29. with which you were pleased to honour me, did not come to my hands till the 25th. of October. The plan of the publication it proposes, appears to me judicious, and that such a depository well filled will be very useful. I sincerely wish it all the success which it's great merit deserves. I am far from presuming that I could in any situation contribute towards it any thing worthy the notice of the public. But my present situation is peculiarly unfriendly to literary pursuits, as it occupies my whole time and would still do the same could I double the hours of the day. Should it however permit me to be useful to you in any way, or should any circumstances restore to me that leisure which alone could enable me to indulge my preference for these pursuits, I shall avail myself with pleasure of the permission of your correspondence. The peice now inclosed is not offered for your collection; having been printed in the journals of Congress, it has not the novelty which would be required to place it in that. It is merely a homage of which I ask your personal acceptance. I shall be happy if you will permit me to become a subscriber to the Bee, and as probably other subscriptions might be obtained here, which may render it necessary for you have a correspondent in this city, I shall punctually pay into his hands the price of subscription. Your correspondents at Glasgow will seldom fail a week of occasions of sending me your papers by vessels from that port to this directly. The address by which they will find me is 'Thomas Jefferson Secretary of state. Philadelphia.' Should they go to any other port of America, it will involve delay, expence of postage and hazard. I have the honour to be with great respect & esteem Sir Your most obedt. & most humble servt, TH: JEFFERSON

PrC (DLC); at foot of text: "Doctr. James Anderson at the printing house of Mandell & son, Edinburgh. To the care of Archibald M'Ausland & co. Greenock." On Anderson's PLAN OF THE PUBLICATION, see note to Anderson to TJ, 29 Apr. 1790. TJ instructed him as to the form of address not only because it was the form stripped of honorifics that his family and others were told to use, but because Anderson had misdirected his letter to TJ as "Secty. of State near Petersburgh Virginia—author of several performances." See Short to TJ, 29 Dec. 1790, for his comment on TJ's insistence on a simple style of address.

From Augustine Davis

Richmond, 2 Dec. 1790. In response to Remsen's letter of the 23rd. he is at a great loss to make an accurate estimate, not knowing the number or the length of the laws to be passed, "unless I charge so much per square (calculating 22 lines to the square) in which case I think *One Shilling* per square will be a reasonable charge, which is two thirds less than the printers in this place have for publications that are made charge of." However, if he is favored with the publication of the laws, he would be satisfied with such compensation as TJ or Congress may think proper—"or with the same that may be charged by the Printer who may publish them in the State of Pennsylvania."

RC (DNA: RG 59, PDL); endorsed by TJ as received 11 Dec. 1790 but recorded in SJL under the 10th. For TJ's determination of the price, see Remsen to the printers, 10 Jan. 1791.

From William Hay

DEAR SIR   Richmond Dec. 2d. 1790.

A Difference of Opinion having arisen between Doctr. Currie and me respecting the Encyclopedie methodique, we are desireous you should decide it, as you are possessed of our Letters to you concerning it. I alledge on my part, that I am not obliged to take the Work, but on the Terms of the original Subscription, that is to say, at 751 Livres. On these Terms I received of Doctr. Currie the Livraisons which you had forwarded to him, and those afterwards sent in by you. I agreed to furnish to Doctr. Currie such standard Books in the English Language as he should chuse to that amount, and had they been commissioned then from England, I should certainly have confined myself to 751.ᵗᵗ Altho' I do not consider Doctr. Currie in any Respect culpable for the improper Conduct of the Editors, yet I conceive I am under no Obligation to pay him or them one hundred Guineas instead of less than one third of the Sum, or to enter into a Litigation with the Editors to force a Complyance with their original Contract. If from the fault of the Editors Doctr. Currie cannot put me in possession of the Work, my contract with him is disolved and he must look to them for Redress. I cannot afford the price they ask. If they are entitled to it, Doctr. Currie if he is obliged to pay, will never feel it.—However if you could relieve the Doctr. and me, by getting any other person to take the Work, you would greatly oblige us. The half V, I mentioned to you, was missing, is the second Part of Tome III of Arts and Trades. Perhaps it is not yet published. If it is, it never came to Hand. This half Volume must be procured thro' your Aid, whoever of us is considered the proprietor. Wishing to hear from you I am with great Respect Dear Sir Your most ob. Sert.   WM. HAY

RC (MHi); endorsed by TJ as received 28 Dec. 1790 and so recorded in SJL.

From William Short

Since my arrival here, I have written to you in date of the 25th. and 26th. ulto. One of these letters was sent through our bankers here, the other by the English packet. I write at present to inclose you a letter to the Secretary of the Treasury. As it is committed immediately to the hands of an American who sails immediately from this port for Boston, I have spoken without reserve on several subjects which I could not have ventured to have done if the letter had been committed to other hands or to the post. I take it for granted you will have a communication of it and therefore I say nothing to you respecting it.

I have no information from Paris of any thing having been yet decided concerning the tobacco—or whale-oil. Every thing seems to be quiet there at present. The ecclesiastical sales continue with uncommon success. The King has received the resignation of the Garde des Sceaux, and appointed in his place Duport du Tertre, an obscure advocate, who had been Lieutenant de Maire. He has been forward in the revolution and is brought in entirely by the Marquis de la fayette, who has been for some time trying to effect it. He hopes to do an agreeable thing to the people by bringing into high employment one of an inferior order, but I fear it will excite more envy than satisfaction.

The Austrian troops have taken possession without resistance of the town of Namur and the states have submitted. The Belgick army has retired towards Brussels. Genl. Schoenfeldt has resigned as well as a great number of other foreign officers. Every thing there is in confusion. The Congress and States of Brabant and Hainault seem to be in their agony and yet they excite the people to resist and promise them that their patriotism and exertions will be crowned with success. The Maréchal Bender is expected daily to march and take possession of Brussels which is the center of opposition. The Congress and States sent to him some days ago to ask a truce until the Emperor's answer could be had to a resolve they had unanimously taken to proclaim his third son Grand Duke of *la Belgique*. It is not known whether the truce was granted, but it is not supposed by any body it will stop the march of the Austrian troops.—All the democratic party wish for their arrival and desire to accept the terms offered by the Emperor.

This country is marching a considerable number of troops to the frontiers of Brabant. The garrison of this place which has not quitted it since its surrender to the Prussian troops are now under marching orders. It is not apprehended however that it is in consequence of any hostile designs.

We have here as yet no news of the opening of the English Parliament except the King's speech, which you will certainly receive before this letter. Every thing seems to augur well[1] for the Minister. I beg you to be assured of the sentiments of affectionate attachment with which I am, my dear Sir, your friend & servant,

W: SHORT

PrC (DLC: Short Papers); complimentary close and signature lacking, being supplied from TR (DNA: RG 59, DD); at head of text: "No. 49." Recorded in SJL as received 8 Apr. 1790. Enclosure: William Short to Alexander Hamilton, 2 Dec. 1790 (Syrett, *Hamilton*, VII, 175-87); this long and extraordinarily interesting letter describing Short's negotiations in Amsterdam may or may not have been communicated to TJ by Hamilton as Short supposed. In it Short reported that he had come to an agreement with the houses of W. & J. Willink and N. & J. Van Staphorst & Hubbard to open a loan for 2,500,000f. at a commission of 4% and interest at 5% but to delay the opening of the loan to a more auspicious time. Both these houses and their brokers convinced Short that "if Congress was in absolute want of the money they would set the loan on foot and had no doubt of having it filled before the expiration of the term generally allowed in these cases—that it was however certain it would at present go on slowly and heavily, and might thus be injurious to the future views of Congress as it appeared from their acts they would have occasion to make a series of loans—that it would therefore be best to postpone opening the loan until the beginning of february at which time such a loan would be desired on the market and greedily sought after—that if any favorable circumstances should turn up sooner, which however they did not foresee, they would in that case give notice of it and advise the loan being brought on the market." Short's letter concluded with a frank appraisal of the characteristics of the two houses that had so long served as agents for the United States, and of their standing among Amsterdam bankers.

[1] PrC ends at this point.

From Benjamin Vaughan

Decr. 2, 1790.

There is nothing new. Peace seems established. The Belgic provinces cannot hold out. Some have been alarmed about French affairs, but I have *good* reason to think they go on as usual. The inclosed is submitted to you. A Copy has been sent [to the] Bp. of Autun.

BV.

RC (DLC); addressed; postmarked; endorsed by TJ as received 19 Jan. 1791 and so recorded in SJL; MS slightly torn.

English Objections to a Universal Standard derived from Nature

Two very able persons, the Bp. of Autun and Mr. Jefferson, have proposd for France and America respectively, that an universal standard of measures, and thence of weights, for all nations, should be derived from permanent data furnished by nature; and for this purpose, that recourse should be had to the length of a pendulum vibrating seconds in a given degree of latitude, and in a given temperature.

This respectable proposition has excited the following observations.

1.° It does not appear likely to be encouraged in England, if one may judge from the opinions of some considerable persons in that country, who will naturally be called upon to make a report concerning it, should the plan be proceeded in.—It is much more practicable in their judgment, to have correct copies of an arbitrary standard, than correct deductions from the pendulum in question.

2.° To the objection, that the measures of the *antients* have been lost from having been arbitrary, there seems an easy reply. Let the moderns agree upon an arbitrary standard, and disperse many copies of it in different nations, and as the world has fewer barbarous and more civilized nations in it than formerly, there can be no expectation that all of these copies will be lost. In any event, the loss would only affect posterity in matters of curiosity; and a new standard might be instituted to supply that, which had become extinct from a decay of civilization and of mutual intercourse.

3.° The supposed convenience of having a natural standard which shall be discoverable in *distant* countries, is still more easily controverted. The figure of the earth is so imperfectly ascertained, that no experiments with the pendulum can be depended upon, unless repeated in the given latitude (suppose 45.° North) where the standard is to obtain its origin; and since civilized observers and accurate instruments are necessary for the preliminary experiments, wherever such observers exist who shall feel interested in connecting themselves with the customs of Europe, it will be more possible (even in the proposed latitude) to procure the exact copy of an arbitrary standard from Europe, than accurate instruments and experiments.

4.° When a natural standard is attained by the process in question, the communication of it for use must depend upon *copies* taken from it and these copies are liable to all the difficulties of copies made after an arbitrary standard.

5.° The great motive for adopting a natural standard in preference to one that is artificial, seems to be to incline all nations more readily to a change of the present discordant system. But the great task will be to make nations *abandon* what they have been accustomed to, not to make them *adopt* one new standard in preference to another equally new.[1] Besides, it will not be difficult to fix upon an arbitrary standard which shall imply no undue preference to any nation or nations in the choice of it.

6.° If it is of any particular use to have the arbitrary standard compared with one that is natural, many individuals or learned bodies can perform this task with ease and are likely to do it spontaneously; which will always be a guide to distant countries and to future ages in recovering the dimension of the arbitrary standard, should it ever be necessary to seek after it through that medium.

7.° Modern workmanship is so accurate and the precautions to be taken so well known, that where the dimension of length only is concerned, it is nearly as easy to make many commensurate standards, as a simple standard. Hence the advantage of having many copies of the original standard declared of equal authenticity with the original standard itself, deposited in different countries, rather than of relying upon one standard deposited in one or a few countries. This will guard against accidents, frauds, and jealousies; and be of farther use by calling for frequent revisions and comparisons, when the average of the majority of copies will suffice to settle every dispute.

8.° An arbitrary standard has this additional advantage: that it may in some degree be accommodated to what is in actual use; as well as that it may be settled without delay, without expence, with little labour, and cannot in the result be followed by any controversy: nor need the adjustment of the standard in this arbitrary mode, be attended with more disputes than in the mode proposed; for it is to be observed, that after the length of the pendulum shall have been ascertained, the subsequent application of that dimension to *practice*, both with regard to measures of length and of capacity and to weights, is equally arbitrary in both cases.

9.° On the whole, it is to be hoped that at least some uniform standard will soon be adopted; for though the common people may not easily change their habits at once, yet they will gradually do so, when they see merchants, learned men, sovereigns, and public bodies, using an uniform set of measures and weights. But supposing each nation to retain its antient customs in some of its concerns internally, it will yet be of use to have a standard of agreement with foreigners, which shall render superfluous to every man the knowledge of more than *two* standards, namely, the local one of his native country and the general one adopted for foreign use: It would be like the case of a native and a learned language. Men would also attain the further convenience of forming ideas of the quantum of measures and weights as expressed by foreigners, with more facility and truth, when the standard was such as they were themselves often in the habit of employing.

MS (DLC); entirely in Vaughan's hand, with the exception noted below.
1 These two words interlined in TJ's hand.

To Madame de Bréhan

DEAR MADAM   Philadelphia Dec. 3. 1790.

The letter of May 11. with which you were so good as to honour me, did not come to hand till the 14th. of October when

I was on a visit to Virginia, from whence I returned to this place a few days ago only. Accept my sincere regrets at the perverse arrangements of fortune which seems to have made a point of disappointing all my wishes to be near you, and every occasion even of seeing you. She has equally sported with your sensibility in placing you here during the contests excited by our change of government, and when all was become quiet here you have been transferred to be the spectators of the greater confusions of another revolution. Are you sure that your destiny will not prepare such another scene for you at Berlin?—I am glad that the difficulties of accomodating yourself to the habits and manners of a foreign country (which I foretold to you, and you would not believe) were at length passed, and that you found our country, all circumstances considered, not a disagreeable one. If your separation from it occasioned regret in your mind, be assured that much has been felt by your acquaintances here, who are deeply impressed by the information that the destination of the Count de Moustier is changed. I cannot make up my mind to the idea that I am no more to see you, and am determined to hope that, some time or other, either you will come to America, or I go to Europe, and be again indulged with your society, which had been among the most solacing of my prospects on changing my residence from the seat of your government to that of ours. Continue my dear Madam to honour me with your friendship and to believe that among those who love you most there is no one who feels a higher respect or more sincere attachment for you than him who has the honour to be Dear Madam Your most obedient & most humble servt,   TH: JEFFERSON

PrC (DLC).

To Moustier

DEAR SIR   Philadelphia Dec. 3. 1790.

I am afraid I have suffered in your opinion from the delay of acknowleging the receipt of your several letters into which I have been led by unavoidable circumstances. The truth is that since my arrival in America (now exactly a twelvemonth) I have been able to pass not one third of that time at the seat of government, one half of which was lost by an illness during which I was incapable of doing any thing, and the residue so engaged by accumulated business as to oblige me to suspend my private correspondencies.

I beg you to be assured that yours is valued by me too much to have been suspended under any other circumstances. I am just now returned from Virginia to this place, where the members of government are now assembling to begin it's administration here, and I avail myself of the first moments to recall myself to your recollection. Fortune seems to have arranged among her destinies that I should never continue for any time with a person whose manners and principles had excited my warm attachment. While I resided in France, you resided in America. While I was crossing over to America, you were crossing back to France: when I am come to reside with our government, your residence is transferred to Berlin. Of all this, Fortune is the mistress: but she cannot change my affections, nor lessen the regrets I feel at their perpetual disappointment.—I am sincerely sorry at the delays which the settlement of your constitution has experienced. I suppose they have been rendered unavoidable by difficulties, and hope all will end well. They have certainly prolonged the risk to which the new work was exposed from without as well as within. I think it would be better to wind it up as quickly as possible to consider it as a mere experiment to be amended hereafter, when time and trial shall shew where it is imperfect. Our second experiment is going on happily; and so far we have no reason to wish for changes except by adding those principles which several of the states thought were necessary as a further security for their liberties. All of these as proposed by Congress will certainly be adopted, except the 2d. which is doubtful, and the first which is rejected. The powers of the government for the collection of taxes are found to be perfect, so far as they have been tried. This has been as yet only by duties on consumption. As these fall principally on the rich, it is a general desire to make them contribute the whole money we want if possible. And we have a hope that they will furnish enough for the expences of government and the interest of our whole public debt, foreign and domestic. If they do this for the present, their increase, from the increase of population and consumption (which is at the rate of 5. percent per annum) will sink the capital in 13. or 14. years, as it will operate in the way of compound interest. Independent of this prospect, which is itself a good one, we make the produce of our land office, and some other articles, a sinking fund for the principal. We are now going on with a census of our inhabitants. It will not be completed till the next summer: but such progress is already made as to shew our numbers will very considerably exceed the former estimates. I shall be happy to hear of your health and welfare every where, and that you will continue persuaded of the sentiments of respect and esteem with which I have the honor to be, Dear Sir, your most obedt. & most humble servt.,   TH: JEFFERSON

PrC (DLC).

This and the foregoing letter to Madame de Bréhan affected to place upon fate a responsibility belonging largely to TJ, who had been the principal mover of Moustier's recall. That act, inspired by reports from Madison, arose from the fear that Moustier might adversely affect relations with France (TJ to Jay, 4 Feb. 1789). The effusive protestations of friendship in these two letters, like the reluctant award of the diplomatic medal to Moustier, were prompted by the same fear, being essentially official rather than personal expressions. TJ was well aware that Moustier had left "not . . . a single friend" in the United States and was so concerned over his rumored return that he urged Lafayette's intercession to prevent it (TJ to Short, 6 June 1790).

Jefferson's Opinion on Proposal for Manufacture of Woolen Textiles in Virginia

[3 Dec. 1790]

The house of delegates of Virginia seem disposed to adventure 2500.£ for the encouragement of this undertaking: but the Senate did not concur. By their returning to the subject however at a subsequent session, and wishing more specific propositions, it is probable they might be induced to concur if they saw a certain provision that their money would not be paid for nothing. Some unsuccessful experiments heretofore may have suggested this caution.

Suppose the propositions brought into some such shape as this. The Undertaker is to contribute £1000, the State £2500. viz.

The Undertaker having lain out his £1000. in the necessary implements to be brought from Europe, and these being landed in Virginia, as a security that he will proceed, let the state pay for the first necessary purposes then to occur   £1000.

Let it pay him a stipend of £100. a year for the first three years   300.

Let it give him a bounty (suppose 3d.) on every yard of woollen cloth equal to good plains, which he shall weave for 5. years not exceeding 250£ a year (20,000 yards) the 4. first years, and 200£ the 5th   1200

————

2500.

To every workman whom he shall import, let them give, after he shall have worked in the manufactory 5. years, warrants for acres of land and pay the expences of survey, patent, &c. [This last article is to meet the proposition of the Undertaker. I do not like it because it tends to draw off the manufacturer from his trade. I should better like a premium to him on his continuing in it. As for instance that he should be free from state taxes as long as he should carry on his trade.]¹

The President's intervention seems necessary till the contract shall be concluded. It is presumed he would not like to be embarrassed afterwards with the details of superintendance. Suppose in his answer to the Governor of Virginia he should say

That the Undertaker being in Europe, more specific propositions can not be obtained from him in time to be laid before this assembly:

That in order to secure to the state the benefit of the establishment, and yet guard them against an unproductive grant of money, he thinks some plan like the preceding one might be proposed to the Undertaker:

That, as it is not known whether he would accept it exactly in that form, it might disappoint the views of the state were they to prescribe that or any other form rigorously; consequently that a discretionary power must be given to a certain extent.

That he would willingly co-operate with their Executive in effecting the contract, and certainly would not conclude it on any terms worse for the state than those before explained. and that the contract being once concluded, his distance and other occupations would oblige him to leave the execution of it to the Executive of the state.

MS (DNA: RG 59, MLR); entirely in TJ's hand; undated, but entry in SJPL under 3 Dec. 1790 reads: "Opinion Th: J. on establishment of a woollen manufactory in Virga."; at head of text: "On the proposition for establishing a woollen manufactory in Virginia"; endorsed by Tobias Lear: "Report of the Secy of State. NB. After this report was given in the Secty of State thought upon further Considerations that the President had better not have any further agency in the business."

This near approach to a government subsidy of the proposed textile mill could scarcely have been unrelated to the disappointment felt both by Washington and TJ at the frustrated over-ture made to the British ministry through Gouverneur Morris (see TJ's report, 15 Dec. 1790). In the summer of 1789 one T. Howell wrote Washington: "I flatter myself you'll readily excuse the Liberty I take in addressing you, when you understand that the following thoughts are the result of a strong attachment to the freedom of America, and a desire of transplanting a manufactory which in time will be found of the greatest consequence. Last year I visited the Continent of America, with a full determination to become a Settler, but finding the Government not in so settled a State as I expected obliged me to abandon the enterprize for that present and wait to see the result of the New Government that was then forming, with a full determination, when permanently fixed, to make an offer of my service to the State of Virginia, to introduce the Woolen Manufactory on the present most approved plans now working in England and in my own manufactory. The great objections made by some that Manufactorys can not at present be introduced with advantage into America, are the Country being thinly settled and labour at present too high. The great improvements which have been made in England in the Woolen and Cotton business by Water-Engines is an amazing saving in Labour as much as three fourths through the whole process and in some departments as much as nine tenths. But supposing the number of young white people that will be Requisite for a large Manufactory can not be easily obtain'd I would propose that those Gentlemen who are disposed to emancipate their Negroes would appoint some of their younger ones for that business and give them their freedom after a service of seven years as an Apprentice, then there will be little doubt but they will remain in the business and become useful Members of Society. This I only propose Sir if there should be a scarcity of hands, but from the population I observed when in America, there will be little to be fear'd from that. As this is a business that will require a large Capital to proceed on a scale that would be likely to turn out to profit, I shall propose to sink of my own real property one thousand pounds in the Trade and with me shall import Engines for cording and machines for slabing and spinning with every other apparatus necessary for the business, with a sufficient number of my best Workmen to take under their care those young people who might be willing to be instructed in the several departments of the business.—From the State I shall expect as a Reward for so great a Risk and to make good the Losses that will arise while the Manufactory is in its infant State, a certain Stipend for a given time and a right to a certain quantity of Land a part of which I shall give to my Men as an Encouragement for them to embark in the Undertaking, under certain restrictions that they shall remain in the Manufactory at least 7 years. A House and building [. . .] for the work must be found. &c. &c." If these plans thus outlined were not acceptable, he would be glad to know on what terms the state would give encouragement. Howell added: "My reasons for giving the preference to Virginia are the western part seems natural to grass and the wool which I have seen growing in that part was good and might be greatly improved, provided there was proper encouragement given to the Farm[ers] they might grow wool of the first quality and in a short time be able to furnish the other States with Woolens. . . . As the nature of this business in its present stage will not suffer me to appear in publick in it so as to refer you to any House in America (tho' known) to be inform'd who I am, but if I shall have any occasion to write on this subject again, shall take care to send such a proof that will remove every scruple respecting my abilities and such testimonies of my conduct that I flatter myself thro' such a channel I can not fail in obtaining your patronage (which with God's blessing) I doubt not of success" (T. Howell to Washington, Hay, Wales, 14 July 1789; DNA: RG 59, MLR).

Washington at once transmitted this letter to Gov. Beverley Randolph. He was uncertain whether such a plan was practicable for Virginia, but he was in no doubt at all about the importance of encouraging the production of wool. On his recent tour through New England he had been greatly impressed by the fact that, through legislative encouragement, the farmers of Connecticut had increased the numbers of sheep in two years by one hundred thousand. He said nothing about Howell's suggestion of an apprenticeship to freedom that might appeal to "those Gentlemen . . . disposed to emancipate their Negroes," but the advantages otherwise seemed to him promising: "If a greater quantity of Wool could be produced, and if the hands (which are often in a manner idle) could be employed in the manufacturing it; a spirit of industry might be promoted, a great diminution might be made in the annual expences of individual families, and the Public would eventually be exceedingly benefitted." He added that, if Randolph should see fit to lay the subject before the legislature or if any private company engaged in the business, "the necessity of keeping the Manufacturer's name concealed would undoubtedly occur: as a premature knowledge of it might not only frustrate the success of the Project, but also subject the Person principally concerned to the most distressing consequences" (Washington to Randolph, 22 Nov. 1789, *Writings,* ed. Fitzpatrick, xxx, 462-3).

The wish had the effect of a command. The matter was placed before the General Assembly and on 17 Dec. 1789 a committee headed by Edmund Randolph reported to the House of Delegates that the circumstances of the state forbade this opportunity to be neglected: "By these actual Circumstances your Committee mean an absolute necessity arising from the Nature of the Property in Virginia to endeavour to make the coarse cloathing at least; the intervals which the Hands employed in Agriculture occasionally find; and the Ability for the young and old who are disqualified for the severer Toils of the field to be useful in manufactures." The arguments of efficiency so adaptable to "the Nature of the property in Virginia" were calculated to impress any planter, but the committee could not decide how far "Schemes of this Kind ought to be extended." Virginia was not populous, there were not any proper ranges for large flocks, and the exhortation to farmers and planters to pay strict attention to the increase of sheep—an indispensable condition to such a plan—was the extent of legislative encouragement that could be offered. The committee thought that "machines which facilitate the manufacture of Woollens are probably obtainable." They therefore "Resolved that it be recommended to the Good people of this Commonwealth, to attend to the raising of Wool by every possible means . . . that the Executive open a correspondence with the President of the United States on the foregoing Subject, and that it be lawful for them to bind this Commonwealth in the Sum of   thousand pounds, and the further sum of five hundred pounds per Annum for three years for the prosecution of a Woollen Manufactory on such Terms as they shall approve." The House of Delegates approved the report, but the Senate rejected it (Beverley Randolph to Washington, 11 Jan. 1790, enclosing copy of the resolutions of the Senate and House of Delegates of 17 and 19 Dec. 1789, DNA: RG 59, MLR).

On 8 Nov. 1790 Gov. Randolph wrote the President about the "proposal of a foreign gentleman to establish a Woolen Manufactory," informed him that the legislature had again

taken the matter up, and stated that he had been directed to open correspondence on the subject (RC in DNA: RG 59, MLR). It was this letter that Washington turned over to TJ for his opinion. The arguments and their applicability to the "Nature of the property in Virginia" were as clear to him as they had been to the President. He knew that the machines were available. One had actually appeared in the great Federal Procession in Philadelphia in July 1788 and, as the British intelligence agent George Beckwith reported in 1790, a model of Arkwright's spinning machine was in the office of the Secretary of State, presumably having been submitted in an application for a patent. TJ could also appreciate the advantages for the commercial policy of the United States as well as for the plantation economy: he had already taken pains to let it be known to the British ministry by indirection that a remarkable spirit of invention had developed (TJ to Vaughan, 27 June 1790). A few months later when Alexander Hamilton called a meeting of New York and Philadelphia entrepreneurs at New Brunswick to unfold to them his plan for the Society of Useful Manufactures, he displayed the same Arkwright model along with a number of others and rested his argument on the proposition that such a plan was essential in order to place the United States in a position of equality in negotiating with maritime powers on matters of commerce (Beckwith to Grenville, 10 Aug. 1791, PRO: FO 4/12, f. 164-8). This was the exact reversal of the position originally taken by Hamilton in the autumn of 1789, when, in order to promote a closer commercial connection with England, he had assured Beckwith that the American economy was agricultural and would long remain so as an outlet for British manufactures. If even Hamilton had come around to this position by the summer of 1791, it is not surprising that TJ late in 1790, when he was about to review Gouverneur Morris' frustrated efforts to negotiate in London, should have looked with favor upon a scheme promising such dual advantages both to the Virginia economy and to the national commercial policy. Furthermore, it was clear from the correspondence between Washington and the governor of Virginia what the President's inclinations were. There seemed no reason to oppose the plan.

Yet, as the endorsement given to the report by Lear indicates, TJ altered his opinion after handing in the report. Washington thereupon turned to Edmund Randolph for his opinion, as TJ may have suggested. Randolph thought the "plan for opening a contract with the woollen manufacturer . . . proper in itself, and likely to be approved by the legislature of Virginia." But he then added: "I must confess, that I have paid more attention to the propriety of the President, undertaking a correspondence with the British Artist. I am told and believe, that it is felony to export the machines, which he probably contemplates to bring with him. Permit me therefore to submit to your consideration, whether the continuance of your agency in this affair may not be somewhat objectionable? The project has been announced to Virginia; and the executive of that state can easily transact this business for themselves" (Randolph to Washington, 10 Jan. 1791; DNA: RG 59, MLR). Washington thereupon declined to have any further agency in the matter as being improper for him while he remained in the presidency. "I am told," he wrote Gov. Randolph, that it is a felony to export the Machines which it is probable the Artist contemplates to bring with him, and it certainly would not carry an aspect very favorable to the dignity of the United States for the President in a clandestine manner to entice the subjects of another Nation to violate its Laws." He added that he had laid the subject before the Secretary of State and the Attorney General and that they were "both of the same sentiment . . . and for the reason mentioned." Nevertheless the President pointed out that his agency was not "*absolutely necessary*" to the success of such a plan, that the necessary facts had been communicated, and that this left it "with the State of Virginia to do whatever may be thought best in the affair." Lest even this be thought too non-committal, Washington concluded: "Impressed as I am with the utility of such an establishment, I shall ever be ready to give it every aid that I can with propriety; and I am certain that your Excellency and the Legislature will impute my conduct on this occasion to its true motive" (Washington to Randolph, 13 Jan. 1791, *Writings*, ed. Fitzpatrick, XXXI, 193-4). The agency was closed, but the interest in keeping open a plan for such a useful establishment was manifest. The governor and legislature of Virginia were left to wrestle with the delicate problem of whether an act unsuited to the dignity of the head of a nation was compatible with that of the government of a state.

There can be no doubt that the Secretary of State was responsible for the closing of the door and on this ground of the national dignity. Four years earlier he had declined to give an official recommendation even to a French manufacturer of textiles when no question of enticement to a violation of laws was involved. On that occasion Washington had submitted the proposal to the governor of Virginia, an office then occupied by Edmund Randolph. But the temperamental and easily-affronted Frenchman had left the country in disgust. Both Washington and Randolph were obviously impressed by the more practical plan of the Welsh manufacturer, as the letters of the former and the report of the latter to the Virginia legislature prove. (See Gilles de Lavallée to TJ, 14 Aug. 1785; TJ to Lavallée, 11 Sep. 1785; Thomas Digges to TJ, 12 May 1788, note; Digges to TJ, 28 Apr. 1791; Washington to TJ, 12 July 1791.)

The matter was all the more troublesome for Washington because the resolution of the Virginia House of Delegates declared that the proposed woolen manufactory was of such importance as to warrant "conclusive measures on the part of the General Assembly" and directed the governor to open correspondence with the President so as to bring the negotiations with the proposer "to some definite shape" (JHD, Oct. 1790 session, 1828 edn., p. 6). The author of the resolution was Henry Lee, whose scheme for an industrial center at the Great Falls of the Potomac would meet with discouragement from Washington within a few weeks because of his decision to locate the Federal City on tidewater (see Editorial Note, documents on the Federal District, under 24 Jan. 1791). This may help to explain why, after TJ had registered his disapproval, Washington turned to the Attorney General for advice (Lear to Attorney General, 8 Jan. 1791, DNA: RG 59, MLR).

[1] Brackets in MS.

From Richard Harison

S<small>IR</small>   New York December 4th: 1790

In consequence of the request, contained in your Letter of the
12th. of August last, I have entered into an Examination of the several legislative Acts and judicial proceedings in this State which may
probably have been considered by the British Government as Infractions of the Treaty, between the United States, and Great
Britain.—A variety of Circumstances, particularly the necessity
of my own absence, and that of some of the public Officers, from
this Place for a considerable time have rendered it impossible for
me to be earlier in laying the result of my Enquiries before you.
I hope however that no Inconvenience has arisen from such a Delay,
which though unavoidable, has given me much Pain, and militated
with the Inclination I have to be as serviceable to the Public as
my Abilities will permit.

The Acts of the Legislature of New York, which upon any
Constitution may be esteemed repugnant to the Treaty of Peace
are but few in number. They consist of

1st. The Act relative to debts due to Persons within the Enemy's
lines passed the 12th day of July 1782, with it's subsequent Modifications.

2. The Act for granting a more effectual relief in Cases of certain Trespasses, passed 17th. of August[1] 1783, afterwards extended but in 1787, varied and in part repealed and

3. The Act to preserve the Freedom and Independence of the
State, commonly called the Discrimination Act, passed the 12th.
May 1784, and since repealed.

[1. The Act relative to Debts due to Persons, within the Enemy's
Lines appears to have passed even before the provisional Articles
were concluded between Great Britain, and the United States. It
cannot therefore be considered as an Infraction of a Treaty, not
existing until several Months after, which at most could only be
contemplated as probable, and was perhaps considered as barely
possible.

Whatever therefore might be the nature or Tendency of this
Act, it's Origin was not exceptionable as interfering with any
national Compact. The Act besides a temporary restraint upon
commencing any Suits by Persons, who had been with the Enemy
(which was removed soon after the peace) subjected such Persons
to the Loss of Interest upon their Debts from 1st. January 1776;

Marginal notes: New Edit. of Laws of N York by Messrs. Jones and Varick, Vol. 1. p. 82. — Same Book 1. Vol. p. 93.

made them liable to any farther abatement, even of the principal, which Referees might think proper; and obliged them to recieve the Balance in public Securities.

The Operation of this Act, became soon after the peace a Subject of much Complaint, grounded upon that Article of the Treaty which forbids any Impediment to the recovery of the full value in Sterling money of all bonâ Fide Debts, and that which declares that no Person shall suffer any future Loss in his Person, Liberty, or Property.

With regard to British Creditors, who were supposed to be the proper Objects of the 4th. Article of the Treaty, the Superior Courts of the State soon restrained the operation of the Act, and I do not know a Single Instance where they have been held to be affected by it.]² But with regard to that Class of American Citizens, who either voluntarily united themselves to Great Britain in the late Contest, or remained within the Enemy's Lines, rather than desert their Property, there is no doubt that the Act has had it's full Operation; and these Persons have at all times complained that their Losses have been sustained "in consequence of the Part which they had taken in the late War."

It would be extremely difficult if not impracticable, to collect every Instance in which Creditors of the latter descriptions, have been sufferers in consequence of this Act. Proceedings under it have been had in almost all the Courts of the State, and it would be necessary to search the Records of every County to particularize them. Besides which, many Creditors have been induced to compound with their Debtors, from the Threats that have been used, or the Apprehensions they have entertained upon this Subject— so that the effect of the Act has been more extensive than could be evidenced by any judicial Proceedings.

New Edit. of the Laws of N York Vol. 1. p. 186. Same Book Vol. 2d. p. 166.

The Act in question was explained and extended by an Act passed the 27th Novr: 1784 and amended by another passed the 20th. April 1787.

Same Book Vol. 2d. p. 470.

By the latter Law, and by one passed the 3d. March 1789, the Debtor was precluded from the right of payment in public Securities, but was discharged from Interest between the 1st. of January 1776, and the 1st. May 1786, and thus a particular Class of Creditors, was deprived of Interest upon their Debts not only during the war but for several years after it was terminated.

I do not pretend to determine how far the Operation of these Laws is to be considered as contrary either to the Letter or Spirit of the definitive Treaty; nor whether that Treaty can be construed as affording Security with respect to their Debts, to any but *real British Subjects.*

But altho' British Creditors have not been held to be within the Laws, yet it is a well known Fact that they have not recovered any Interest upon simple Contract Debts, for the Period of the War, where the Debtor had been resident without the British Lines. The right of British Creditors to recover such interest was the sub- ject of serious discussion in the Supreme Court of the State, some time in the year 1786 or 1787 where the Treaty of Peace was re- lied upon by their Counsel as conclusive in their favor. It was urged on the other Hand, that the War had been a general Calamity, during which the Parties could not have access to each other; and even[3] if they could that not only the Law of Nations, but the ex- press Regulations, both of Congress and the British Parliament had declared any intercourse between them to be highly criminal. That the American Merchants had suffered to a prodigious Extent in consequence of payments made to them in a depreciated Currency, and that it would be unjust in the Extreme to charge them with damages merely for omitting what they could not perform with- out a Violation of their Duty.

Upon this Occasion the reasoning of the Defendant's Counsel was prevalent. The Jury (which was special) disallowed the Claim of Interest during the War, and their Determination was sanc- tioned by the Judgment, if not by the avowed approbation of the Court. In Consequence it has become a general Rule to deduct Interest from British Debts for about Seven years, but the deduc- tion has not been acquiesced in without frequent Complaints on the Part of the Creditors or their Agents.

2. I proceed now to the Act generally called the Trespass Act.

This Act was intended to afford a Remedy to those American Citizens, whose property had been injured or made use of whilst in the Possession of the Enemy. It declares that all those who had left their Places of abode on account of the invasion of the Enemy and had not afterwards voluntarily put themselves into the Enemy's Power, may bring Actions of Trespass against those who have occupied injured or destroyed their Estates *within the Enemy's Power* or against any Persons who have purchased or recieved their Effects.[4]

It is evident that the general Expressions in this Law seem in- tentionally to have been adopted in order to comprehend every possi- ble Case in which the Estate or Effects of the Persons described in the

Exrs. of Neate vs. Sands

[127]

Act, had been in the Possession of others within the British Lines. No Exception is made for Persons compelled to act by the Mandates of British Officers; for Cases where Property was changed by the Laws of War among civilized Nations; nor even in favor of those who being subjects of the British Crown, had acted as open Enemies in the Line of their duty.

Hence a variety of Suits has been prosecuted upon this Act since the return of peace against British Officers for Acts of Hostility or Depredation; against Persons impressed or hired to cut or cart Wood for the British Troops; against Persons who had been employed as Artificers to take down Buildings; against Commissaries of Cattle; and against Merchants even of the British Nation who having joined the Enemy for the purposes of trade, were Occupants under their Authority of Houses deserted by the Citizens of America.

It may perhaps be questioned how far many of these Cases were upon sound Construction within the Purview of the Act, and perhaps also the Judges might have been justifiable in qualifying the general Expressions made use of by a tacit Exception of those Actions which were done by the Enemy *as such*, or had an immediate Relation to the War.

In the cause of Rutgers vs. Waddington. Accordingly a decision was had in the Mayors Court of New York, that a British Merchant, who had hired a House from Officers appointed by the British General, and paid rent for it, should not be charged under the Act, by the American owner for the same occupation.

Still, however, as the Principles upon which this Decision was founded had been doubted, and the Act expressly forbid "any military Order or Command of the Enemy" being pleaded or given in Evidence many Persons were subjected to the payment of large Sums (as they supposed) on account of the part which they had taken in the War, and contrary to the Treaty of Peace which they

New Edit. of Laws of N York by Messrs. Jones and Varick, Vol. 2d p. 134. In the several Causes of John Anthony, Nichs. Anthony and Nichs. Anthony Junr. vs. Anthony Van Dam tried in 1789 and 1790. insisted must from it's very nature imply an Indemnity for Acts done in a State of Hostility.

The latter Part of the Trespass Act was repealed on the 4th. of April 1787, but the Supreme Court of the State have nevertheless sustained Actions, even where it appeared that Property had been seised and sold by the direction of the Quarter master General of the British Army.

3. The Act commonly called the discrimination Act passed the 12th. of May 1784. has also been complained of as an Infraction of the Treaty, because Numbers of Persons coming within the

description of American Refugees were thereby banished, or disqualified from electing or being elected to Offices. This Act was virtually repealed in some respects by the Act respecting Elections passed 13th February 1787. and in the whole by an Act passed 12th. March 1788.

New Edit. L. of N York Vol. 2. p. 27. Same Book Vol. 2d. p. 357.

Having thus recapitulated all the Laws of New York, which I apprehend may have been considered by the British Nation as Infractions of the Treaty it is proper that I should mention an Act passed the 22d. February 1788, whereby all Acts and parts of Acts repugnant to the Treaty are repealed. If therefore any Infraction of the Treaty has taken place since that Period in consequence of the Laws of the State, it must be attributed not to the Legislature, but either to the judicial or executive Powers.

Same Book 2d. Vol. p. 256.

For my own part I do not know of any Act by the Executive of this State which can with propriety be complained of as contrary to the Treaty between Great Britain and the United States.—With respect to the Acts of the Judiciary (besides those which I have mentioned) it has been a Subject of Complaint that Judgments have been given in several Instances upon the Confiscation Act since the Peace.—This Act is contained in the first Volume of the New Edition of New York Laws at page 39. &ca. and the Judgments uniformly pursued the Directions there given. I have procured from the Clerk of the Supreme Court a List of all the Judgments given since the date of the provisional Articles which you will find inclosed.[5]

I have now Sir complied as far as was practicable with your Commands except that part of them which relates to the furnishing a Collection of the State Laws. Upon that Subject I have already mentioned what I had been able to procure, but I did not chuse to send the Books without your Approbation. Indeed I supposed that the Removal of the Public Offices might render the delay acceptable.

If I can be further serviceable in this or any other matter that regards the general Service, you will be pleased to command me, and to believe that I am, with the utmost Deference and respect Sir your most obedt. and most humble Servant,

RC (DNA: RG 59, MLR); in clerk's hand, unsigned; endorsed by TJ as received 18 Dec. 1790 and so recorded in SJL. Dft (NHi); with numerous deletions and interlineations, some of which—together with clerical errors in RC—are indicated in notes below. FC of Extract (DNA: RG 59, SDR); at head of text: "No. 45. Extract of a letter from Richard Harrison . . . to the Secretary of State, dated New York December 4th. 1790," consisting of that part of the text indicated in note 2 below and enclosed in TJ to Hammond,

29 May 1792, as enclosure No. 45. PrC of Extract (DLC); in another clerk's hand.

¹ Thus in MS. Dft reads "March," the correct date.

² Matter in brackets (supplied) comprises that part of the text of the Extract enclosed in TJ to Hammond, 29 May 1792.

³ This word supplied from Dft, having been omitted by the clerk.

⁴ At this point in Dft the following is deleted: "The Remedy of this Act was afterwards extended in 1784 to absent Defendants, and great Numbers of Suits at Law have been commenced and prosecuted. Some of which are depending even at the present Hour and a Variety of Decisions has taken place in Consequence of it at different Times."

⁵ At this point the following in Dft is deleted: "But whether these or any of them are to be considered as Infractions of the Treaty."

From Meriwether Smith

DEAR SIR   Bathurst, Virga. 4th. Decbr. 1790.

I have received your favor of the 2d. of November to-day; and I thank you for your Attention to my Request in taking Care of the Letter to Mr. Short. You are pleased to add Assurances of your Esteem and Attachment. Your friendship, independently of any particular Advantage which might flow from it, will ever be esteemed by me, but if it should happen that you might do me a particular Service, it would confer upon me a new obligation. Were I seriously to attempt it, I believe I should not find it difficult to be elected into the Congress; but that might further embarrass my Affairs already too much deranged by my Absence from them in unprofitable pursuits during the late War, and I have not the Vanity to think that I could be of real Service to my Country. Nothing is so desirable to me as a peaceful Retirement. But that is not my portion. And tho' I never was sollicitous for Offices, especially of a pecuniary Nature, I could have no Objection to one which might assist me in the payment of my debts, provided I might render an equivalent in Services useful to the State. Wherein I might be useful none can better judge than yourself. I know that to speak of poverty and to desire favors of a friend, is often a sure means of losing his friendship, but let not that affect you. You will not find me troublesome. My Expectation is not great, neither are my desires extravagant. And tho' I get nothing by it, it will not lessen my Esteem for you.

You have, no doubt, seen the Resolves of the Assembly of Virginia. They may require a justificative declaration, as they wear the appearance of Hostility, and I hear such an one is to be presented at Philadelphia. What the Event may be I cannot pretend to judge. But an Imperium in imperio is a refinement which even

Paley's philosophy will hardly support. One party charges the Congress with an *unconstitutional* Act; and both parties charge it with an Act of injustice. The last Resolve was proposed as a Substitute to the first, but that failing, it seems to have been afterwards adopted as coming from the opposite party, to strengthen the first.

I am happy in [being] able to return you Assurances of the Esteem & attachment with which I have the honor to be, Dear Sir, Your most obedient & most humble Servant. M. SMITH.

RC (DLC: Applications for Office under Washington); endorsed by TJ as received 17 Dec. 1790 and so recorded in SJL.

The first of the famous RESOLVES OF THE ASSEMBLY OF VIRGINIA was adopted on 3 Nov. 1790 and declared that the act for assuming the state debts was "repugnant to the Constitution of the United States, as it goes to the exercise of a power not expressly granted to the General Government." Two days later a second resolution expressed "marked disapprobation" of that part of the act limiting the United States in its redemption of the national debt as being "dangerous to the rights and subversive of the interest of the people." The Virginia remonstrance was adopted on 17 Nov. 1790 (JHD, Oct. 1790, 1828 edn., p. 35, 44, 80-1, 141, 150). Davis' *Virginia Gazette* for 17 Nov. 1790 presented the form of the resolutions as originally introduced. Hamilton viewed these resolutions as "the first symptom of a spirit which must either be killed or will kill the constitution" (Hamilton to Jay, 13 Nov. 1790, Syrett, *Hamilton*, VII, 149-50). Fenno's *Gazette of the United States* and other Federalist papers resorted to ridicule. *The American Mercury* declared Virginia to be "stark mad with the assumption" (Bache's *General Advertiser*, 28 Dec. 1790 and 24 Jan. 1791; *Conn. Courant*, 6 Dec. 1790).

To Noah Webster, Jr.

SIR   Philadelphia Dec. 4. 1790.

Your favor of Oct. 4. [i.e. 14] came to my hands on the 20th. of November. Application was made a day or two after to Mr. Dobson for the copies of your essays, which were recieved, and one of them lodged in the office. For that intended for myself be pleased to accept my thanks. I return you the order on Mr. Allen, that on Dobson having been made use of instead of it. I submit to your consideration whether it might not be adviseable to record a second time your right to the Grammatical institutes in order to bring the lodging of the copy in my office within the 6. months made a condition by the law? I have not at this moment an opportunity of turning to the law to see if that may be done: but I suppose it possible that the failure to fulfill the legal condition on the first record might excite objections against the validity of that.

In mentioning me in your essays, and canvassing my opinions, you have done what every man has a right to do, and it is for the good of society that that right should be freely exercised. No republic is more real than that of letters, and I am the last in principles, as I am the least in pretensions to any dictatorship in it. Had I other dispositions, the philosophical and dispassionate spirit with which you have expressed your own opinions in opposition to mine, would still have commanded my approbation. A desire of being set right in your opinion, which I respect too much not to entertain that desire, induces me to hazard to you the following observations. It had become an universal and almost uncontroverted position in the several states, that the purposes of society do not require a surrender of all our rights to our ordinary governors: that there are certain portions of right not necessary to enable them to carry on an effective government, and which experience has nevertheless proved they will be constantly incroaching on, if submitted to them. That there are also certain fences which experience has proved peculiarly efficacious against wrong, and rarely obstructive of right, which yet the governing powers have ever shewn a disposition to weaken and remove. Of the first kind for instance is freedom of religion: of the second, trial by jury, Habeas corpus laws, free presses. These were the settled opinions of all the states, of that of Virginia, of which I was writing, as well as of the others. The others had in consequence delineated these unceded portions of right, and these fences against wrong, which they meant to exempt from the power of their governors, in instruments called declarations of rights and constitutions: and as they did this by Conventions which they appointed for the express purpose of reserving these rights, and of delegating others[1] to their ordinary legislative, executive and judiciary bodies, none of the reserved rights can be touched without resorting to the people to appoint another convention for the express purpose of permitting it. Where the constitutions then have been so formed by Conventions named for this express purpose they are fixed and unalterable but by a Convention or other body to be specially authorised. And they have been so formed by I believe all the states except Virginia. That state concurs in all these opinions, but has run into the wonderful error that her constitution, tho made by the ordinary legislature, cannot yet be altered by the ordinary legislature. I had therefore no occasion to prove to them the expediency of a constitution alterable only by a special convention. Accordingly I have not in my notes advocated that opinion, tho it was and is mine, as it was and is theirs. I take that position as admitted by them: and only proceed to adduce arguments to prove that they were mistaken in supposing their constitution could not be altered by the common legislature. Among other arguments I urge that the Convention which formed the constitution had been chosen merely for ordinary legislation, that they had no higher power than every subsequent legislature was to have, that all their acts are consequently repealable by subsequent legislatures, that their own practice at a subsequent session proved they were of this opinion themselves, that the opinion and practice of several subsequent legislatures had been the same, and so conclude 'that their constitution is alterable by the common legislature.' Yet these arguments urged to prove that their constitution *is* alterable, you cite as if urged to prove that it *ought not to be* alterable, and you combat them on that ground. An argument which is good to prove one thing, may become ridiculous when exhibited as intended to prove another thing. I will beg the favor of you to look over again the passage in my Notes, and am persuaded you will be sensible that you have misapprehended the object of my arguments, and therefore have combated them on a ground for which they were not intended. My only object in this is the rectification of your own opinion of me, which I repeat that I respect too much to neglect. I have certainly no view of entering into the contest whether it be expedient to delegate unlimited power to our ordinary governors? My opinion is against that expediency. But my occupations do not permit me to undertake to vindicate all my opinions, nor have they importance enough to merit it. It cannot however but weaken my confidence in them when I find them opposed to yours, there being no one who respects the latter more than Sir Your most obedt. & most humble servt,   TH: JEFFERSON

RC (NN); at foot of text: "Mr. Noah Webster. At Hartford"; endorsed in part: "Remarks on powers of legislatures, in answer to some principles advanced in my Essays. NW. See page 59 my Essays." PrC (DLC).

TJ erred in supposing Virginia was the only state that had not had its constitution drawn by a convention especially charged with the task. Of those constitutions drawn during the Revolution, only that of Massachusetts of 1780 had been framed by a constitutional convention. This set the example and when it was reinforced by the immense influence of the Federal Convention of 1787, other states—as Pennsylvania and Georgia had done in 1790—followed the precedent.

The brief exchange with TJ that Noah Webster initiated in the fall of 1790 threw into brilliant relief two opposed and quite irreconcilable concepts of American government (Webster to TJ, 14 Oct. 1790). Both men stood on republican ground and neither yielded an inch to the other. Webster, dogmatic and crotchety, had formed a low opinion of TJ's compatriots in Virginia that was strengthened by his reading of *Notes on Virginia*. On his journey through the middle and southern states to lecture, to promote the sale of his *Grammatical institute of the English language*, and to advocate copyright legislation—a subject on which his views were also antipodal to those of TJ—Webster concluded that "Virginians have much pride, little money on hand, great contempt for Northern people, and amazing fondness for Dissipation." To these deficiencies he added another of perhaps equal gravity in his eye: "They do not understand Grammar" (E. E. F. Skeel, ed., *Notes on the life of Noah Webster*, p. 144). In Philadelphia during the meeting of the Federal Convention, Webster borrowed Francis Hopkinson's copy of *Notes on Virginia* and spent the next day extracting notes from it (same, p. 218). Four months later, as editor of the short-lived *The American Magazine*, he opened fire with a series of articles over the pseudonym *Giles Hickory* (*The American Magazine*, I [New York], p. 13-15 [Dec. 1787]; p. 75-80 [Jan. 1788]; p. 137-45 [Feb. 1788]; p. 204-10 [Mch. 1788]). These pieces were published over Webster's own name in the volume that he submitted for copyright under the title *A collection of essays and fugitiv writings. On moral, historical, political and literary subjects* (Boston, 1790), in which chapters III-VI form a reprinting with some changes of the 1787-1788 articles (see Sowerby, No. 4928). In these essays, which were undoubtedly stimulated in part by Webster's reading of *Notes on Virginia*, he pronounced the opinion that bills of right might be proper enough against kings or barons but were an absurdity in a free government; that the supreme power and indeed *"all* the authority of the State" was, and necessarily had to be, vested in the elected representatives; and that in fact the right of election was "the *only* legislativ or constitutional act, which the people at large can with propriety exercise" (*Essays*, p. 45, 49, 59). He admitted, with perhaps less diffidence than his repeated assertion of an idiosyncratic position would seem to warrant, that these views were repugnant to the accepted prejudices and principles of his countrymen and that it was "a favorite idea in this country, bandied about from one demagogue to another, that *rulers are the servants of the people* (same, p. 45, 49, 80).

The prevailing sentiments of his countrymen that Webster regarded as false, confused, or absurd were grasped by no one more immediately or more tenaciously than by the one whom he selected as his particular target.

To Webster's major contention TJ merely replied that his opinion was against the expediency of delegating "unlimited power to our ordinary governors." But what really disturbed him, quite understandably, was Webster's egregious insistence that he had argued for perpetual and unalterable constitutions. The grammarian's logic that led Webster to classify the author of *Notes on Virginia* with "other advocates for *unchangeable Constitutions*" also enabled him to deny that he had made so palpable an error (same, p. 62; Webster to TJ, 12 Dec. 1790). The misconception must have been particularly galling to one who had so recently embraced the doctrine that the earth belongs in usufruct to the living and that it should be made explicit in the fundamental law of the nation (TJ to Madison, 6 Sep. 1789). The brief exchange was futile and TJ sensibly ended it with silence. But it did illuminate brilliantly and with classic simplicity the enduring difference between a doctrinaire schoolman and a realistic statesman. TJ continued to expound and to act upon the principles of his countrymen. Webster, for his idiosyncratic essays, received the high accolade of a modern student of political theory, who declared that he was the one who "grasped more fully the interconnectedness of *all* the political and constitutional developments of the 1780's" than any other (Gordon S. Wood, *The creation of the American republic* [Chapel Hill, 1969], p. 376; emphasis added).

But on one point at least Webster and TJ were in full accord. At Williamsburg, Webster spent a few hours with George Wythe and pronounced him "a great man for Virginia, and a sensible man anywhere" (Skeel, *Notes*, p. 144n). The first adjective he would never bestow upon TJ, even among Virginians, and he soon earned for himself the unenviable title of being the first Federalist to ridicule him as a man of science (TJ to Madison, 10 Jan. 1791). These and other experiences must have influenced TJ and Madison to make Connecticut one of the primary objects of their northern journey in the spring of 1791 in order to discover from their constituency whether the schoolmen and the members of Congress from that state were truly representative.

¹ TJ first wrote: ". . . constitutions:

and the people naming Conventions to reserve those rights and to delegate others," and then altered the passage to read as above.

From Benjamin Russell

Boston, 5 Dec. 1790. In response to Remsen's inquiry he informs TJ that the laws of the second session printed by him [in the *Massachusetts Centinel*, which on 16 June 1790 became the *Columbian Centinel*] amounted to 372 squares. "The square, in Typographical language, is 20 lines of Long-Primer matter—the line being 20 *ms* long—and in that proportion of shorter or longer lines, larger or smaller types. Inclosed is a *square* of matter of the Centinel—the lines being but 18 *ms* long, it takes almost 23 lines to make a square."[1] The total, "at *half a dollar* a square," amounted to 186 dollars. "The price paid for publishing the Laws of this Commonwealth in Long-Primer squares, has been reduced, on account of the competition of the Printers for the Printing-work of government, which in some of its branches, is lucrative, from One Dollar to Half a Dollar. The price, therefore, that I have inserted, is regulated by the price given by this State—Your Honour's information will enable you to judge whether it is too high or not high enough." But, while compensation was "[not the] first object . . . and while I earnestly solicit the continuation of your patronage, I shall rest satisfied, should I be so fortunate as to obtain it, with such allowance as you shall think just to make"; Captain Patrick Phelon of the customs is authorized to receive his allowance.

RC (DNA: RG 59, PDL); slightly mutilated. Recorded in SJL as received 15 Dec. 1790. Enclosure not found.

The above was in response to Remsen's inquiry of 23 Nov. 1790. While TJ bestowed upon Andrew Brown's *Federal Gazette* the privilege of publishing the statutes in Philadelphia rather than upon John Fenno's *Gazette of the United States*, which had enjoyed the patronage for a brief time in New York, he continued to permit the Federalist Benjamin Russell to print the laws in Boston (see note on TJ's arrangement with Fenno, under 20 Mch. 1790; Rush to TJ, 15 Aug. 1790).

Russell was informed by two Massachusetts representatives, Benjamin Goodhue and Fisher Ames, of his "appointment to publish the Laws &c. of the United States for the Eastern States." With "emotions of gratitude and respect," he had asked to be informed of his duties (Russell to TJ, 12 June 1790, DNA: RG 59, PDL). For TJ's solution to the question of price, see Remsen to the printers, 10 Jan. 1791.

[1] These two sentences were written at foot of text and keyed to the first reference to squares by an asterisk.

From C. W. F. Dumas

MONSIEUR   Lehaie 6e. Dec. 1790

Je commence cette Dépeche par la chûte, aujourd'hui avérée, des plats tyrans Van der Noot, Van Eupen, &c. Si leur regne ephémere ne s'est pas étendu jusqu'ici, ce n'est ni leur faute, ni celle de certains personnages qui n'osent plus les patroniser trop ouvertement, sans laisser néanmoins de nourrir encore quelque apparence de leur inclination pour eux. On cache mal le dépit qu'on a, de ce que sagement l'Empereur ne veut rien avoir à faire avec leur prétendu Haut et Puissant Congrès souverain, qui vient d'expirer à Bruxelles, mais seulement avec les Etats de chaque Province séparément; comme aussi de ce que les opérations des troupes Autrichiennes ne sont pas subordonnées à la Dictature d'un prétendu Congrès-Médiateur, subordonné lui-même, dit-on, à certaine grande personne qui se flattoit d'engager ainsi l'Empereur à une garantie réciproque de la révolution opérée ici il y a 3 ans.

du 7e. Mr. De Mercy a reçu un Courier, qui lui apprend la soumission, non seulement du Brabant, mais aussi de la Flandre et du Hainaut. Limbourg et Namur avoient déjà fait la leur. Ainsi tout est dit: et il n'est plus question de la Médiation ni de la Garantie de l'Angleterre, de la Prusse et de cette République. Par conséquent, le coup est manqué.

En Angleterre on n'en est encore qu'aux complimens avec le nouveau Parlement. Après cela, on leur fera croire, s'il leur plait, que les Cabanes de Nootka et les Baleines qui se laisseront prendre loin de possessions Espagnoles, valent 4 millions Sterling, comme aussi, que l'arc toujours plus tendu de leur crédit est un garant plus sûr des $5\frac{1}{2}$ milliards tournois qu'ils doivent, que les biens nationaux ne le sont en France des $4\frac{1}{2}$ milliards tournois que celle-ci doit.

A tout prendre, l'Empereur paroît avoir fait une sage paix à Reichenbach, et je crois voir venir le temps où il s'en trouvera mieux que ceux qui la lui ont fait faire. Cela ne m'empeche pas d'applaudir aussi au refus de la Russie de faire sa paix sous garantie, comme à un coup de politique très fine. Le temps développera mon idée.

Le Décret de l'Assemblée Nationale en France du 27 Nov., pour assermenter le Clergé, a reveillé plus que jamais l'attention des amis et des ennemis de cette révolution-là. L'hiérarchie proteste, le Pape, dit-on, s'en mêlera aussi; mais les François, Dieu merci, ne sont pas des Brabançons.

La Banque d'Amsterdam est encore à $\frac{1}{4}$ p % au-dessous du pair, après avoir été jusqu'à 2 p % au-dessous. Les uns attribuent ce discrédit à la décadence du Commerce; d'autres, à une raison qu'il seroit imprudent d'écrire; d'autres, à l'émigration de nombre de rentiers qui, depuis la révolution appellée bénie ont, dit-on, exporté peu à peu 100 millions de florins.—Quoiqu'il en soit, la chose est sans exemple dans l'histoire de cette republique.

du 15e. Dec. Mr. De Mercy et les Ministres des 3 Puissances médiatrices, dont la médiation est devenue inutile, viennent, par manière d'acquit de ce qui avoit été conclu à Reichenbach, de si[gner] une courte convention, par laquelle elles garantissent la Constitution des Belges sur le pied de ce qu'elle étoit sous l'Empereur Charles VI. Nous pourrons avoir cette Piece demain ou après-demain; ainsi j'attendrai, pour l'expédition de ma Dépeche, ce complément de la Pacification Belgique.

Permettez-moi, Monsieur, un mot encore sur le Chapitre des Paquebots réguliers Américains. Pour que ce moyen de Correspondance avec l'Europe fût entierement en la puissance des Etats-unis, l'on pourroit avoir 3 malles séparées dans chaque Paquebot, et par conséquent 3 messagers qui, dès leur arrivée à Helvoet, partiroient, l'un pour Paris par Ostende et Dunkerque, l'autre pour Londres par Harvich ou Douvres, et le troisième par Rotterdam et Lahaie &c., à Amsterdam, et reviendroient à bord avant l'expiration du mois, avec les Dépeches des Agens Américains, &c., dans ces Places respectives.

Je finis la présente par l'invocation de la bénédiction divine, à l'occasion du prochain renouvellement d'année, sur les Etats-unis, sur leur Auguste Congrès et Administration, et sur la personne et famille de Votre Excellence, de qui je suis avec le plus vrai respect, Le très-humble, très-Obéissant & fidele Serviteur

C W F Dumas

P.S. Un rentier de mes amis, qui a des Effets Américains dans son Portefeuille, m'apprend que ceux de la Dette liquidée à Amsterdam, sont montés à 1025; et que ceux du Congrès sont toujours au pair avec le comptant, ce qui n'est le cas d'aucun autre Emprunt en ce pays.

RC (DNA: RG 360, PCC No. 93); at head of text: "No. 71"; endorsed by TJ as received 14 Apr. 1791 and so recorded in SJL. FC (Dumas Letter Book, Rijksarchief, The Hague; photostats in DLC).

From John Sitgreaves

Sir   New Bern December 6th. 1790

I had the honor to receive your Letter of the 12h. of August requesting me to furnish you with Copies of the several Legislative, executive and Judicial Acts of this State respecting the Debts and other property of British Subjects and American Refugees; in compliance with which I now inclose you, Sir, all the Acts of the General Assembly of this State, by which the real and personal Estates of the persons therein described as well as the Debts due to them have been confiscated, the several Acts passed to carry into Effect the first mentioned Acts, together with such Acts and parts of Acts as tend to disable or prohibit persons of that description from commencing Suits or obtaining Judgements in the Courts of this State, and the Act declaring the Treaty of peace with Great Britain to be part of the Law of the Land. Under some one or other of those Acts the greater part of the people of this State who were indebted to British Subjects or American Refugees paid to the Commissioners of confiscation the Debts due by them agreeable to the directions of those Acts.

I have not of my own Knowledge known nor have I been able to learn that there has been any Order or proclamation of the executive or any decision of the Judiciary of this State which related to the persons or property of British Subjects or American Refugees.—I have not heard of any Suit being commenced in any of the Courts of this State in which the force or extent of the Treaty was drawn in question, except one lately commenced by a Refugee on which no decision is yet made.

The Laws of this State made during the Revolution were so irregular and confused and many of those of particular Sessions so extremely scarce, that it was thought necessary to revise them. This has been done under the able directions of Judge Iredell, and will (I am informed by the Printer) be published in the course of two or three Months. It will commence with the Laws passed in 1715. which are the first known in this State and will end with the acts which may be passed by our Legislature now in Session and will contain all the *public Acts* in force in this State. As I conceived none but such was desired by you Sir, and as those passed since the Year 1775. are in a very perplexed State, I have thought it proper to delay sending you any until the Revisal is compleated, which shall be forwarded so soon as it is ready for binding and if Sir you also wish to have all those which have heretofore been printed I will procure and send them by the first Opportunity that offers after I receive such intimation.

I am to apologize Sir for delaying to forward the inclosed Copies till this time as you wished to have had them in October. A Desire to give you the fullest Information on the Subject of your Letter induced me to wait until now for Answers from the different Offices of this State which are dispersed in different parts of it at great distances from each other to Letters which I had written and which have not yet been answered.

I should very much regret the delay that has been thus occasioned, if the Interests of Government or its Business should be thereby injured or impeded, or the wishes of Mr. Jefferson frustrated.

I have the Honor to be with great regard and respect Sir Your most obedient and most Humble Servant, JNO: SITGREAVES

RC (DNA: RG 360, PCC No. 76); endorsed by TJ as received 3 Jan. 1791 and so recorded in SJL. The enclosed copies of Acts of the North Carolina legislature are to be found in DNA: RG 360, PCC No. 76, f. 176-234.

From David Hartley

DEAR SIR   Golden Square Dec 7 1790

I have lately had some conversation with Mr. Bolton of Soho near Birmingham relative to a proposed recoinage of the Copper money of this Country, for which he is at present in negotiation with the British ministry. Upon this occasion he has shewn to me from the Charles town Gazette of april 14 1790 the report which you have presented to Congress upon a similar point in your States, by which I find that he or his friend Mr. Mitchell, has had a similar negotiation with you. Mr. Bolton is a very excellent mechanic and has many excellent artists in his employ, and would I doubt not execute such an undertaking to his own honour, and to the satisfaction of your Country. The same apparatus may serve in the first instance for both Countries. It has cost a very large sum of money to Mr. Bolton. I conceive that his views and yours are not at all inconsistent, but perfectly coincident.

By the first part of your report you seem entirely to approve of Mr. Bolton as the undertaker. But you object to a foreign dependence for the supply of your coinage. This objection appears for the reasons assigned to be very forcible and decisive. The right of sovereignty in Coinage is most essential in Gold and Silver. But it is not so essential in Copper. Copper is not esteemed in this country as Coin. It is only esteemed as a convenient merchandize of exchange. Several companies in this Country coin their own medals in copper as pence and half pence, and give and receive them in the intercourse of payments. I understand that Mr.

Boltons proposition to you is upon similar ground to this. He proposes as a manufacturer and merchant to supply your Country in this first instance with your subaltern copper money, but he has not the most distant view that the sovereign mint for gold, and Silver in your states should be established at his Soho. He proposes merely in this first instance that he should supply you with the merchandize of the Copper money which you now want for immediate use, and that he should execute this by means of the apparatus which he has provided for such purposes in this country. After that he proposes to transfer all his apparatus to your Country if you desire to become purchasers, and in the mean-time, in the course of the proposed coinage for you, he will be very ready to instruct any workmen from the united States who shall be sent to him by public authority, in the arts and use of his mint so that even your first copper coinage may be executed by the handicraft of your own Countrymen. His mint is fundamentally improved in all the most essential points, which upon the completion of the first essay and necessary instructions, will be transplanted for ever after for the adoption and use of the sovereign power of your Country.

Mr. Bolton will transmitt to you his proposals specifically, by the next mail subsequent to the date of this letter, which I have taken the liberty of addressing to you, because I think it a point of justice which is due to an eminent manufacturer as such, and much more so in consideration of his universal and approved character for liberality and honor in all his mercantile transactions. To this I shall only add one personal motive for myself which is to take this opportunity which incidentally offers itself of reviving to your recollection the name and memory of an old friend and fellow labourer with you in the common causes of peace and friendship between our two Countries. I am Dear Sir with the greatest regard Ever most sincerely yours,   D HARTLEY

P.S. Mr. Bolton informs me that he is now making specimens of guineas by the approbation of government which have the following properties, viz. 1st. They are equally expressive of the devise with common guineas. 2dly. Altho the head is in *bas relief* yet it does not rise above the general surface of the piece, and these are no prominent parts nor roughnesses because the letters arms and inscriptions are *en creux* and resemble engraving and yet they are of a very fine polish, on the edges and on both the sides. 3dly. The Coins are perfectly round and of equal diameter so that when twenty of them are heaped upon one another they resemble a polished solid cylinder of gold. Thus they will be less subject to loss of weight by common wear and tear and perfectly being of one diameter and thickness they may be easily distinguished from base or diminished guineas by means of a small gauge contrived for that purpose which may be carried in the pocket with as little inconvenience as a half crown piece. The polish is curious and not produced by the twist of the parisian press which is found by experience to deprive the die of its sharpness and spirit by the stricking of a few pounds weight of the coin, altho it will strick specimens very beautifully.

RC (DLC); endorsed by TJ as received 19 Jan. 1791 and so recorded in SJL, though given the erroneous date of 1 Dec. 1790, which was evidently the date of a (missing) Dupl, since a Tr (Birmingham, England, Assay Office), bears this date.

Hartley erred in saying that he had seen TJ's report on coinage in the CHARLES-TOWN GAZETTE of 14 Apr. 1790: that was the date of the report itself. In reading the report Boulton understood clearly enough that the "Artist" TJ alluded to was Jean Pierre Droz, hence the effort to prove the superiority of his own methods over those of THE PARISIAN PRESS (see the Report of 14 Apr. 1790; TJ to Grand, 23 Apr. 1790; TJ to Hamilton, 24 Nov. 1790). This appeal through one known to be an advocate of amicable relations between the United States and Great Britain was evidently Boulton's first effort to detach himself from the intermediation of John H. Mitchell of Charleston (see Michell to Tucker, 22 Mch. 1790, Vol. 16: 342-4). Hartley had been sent to Paris in 1783 as minister plenipotentiary for negotiating the definitive treaty of peace and "for opening, promoting and rendering perpetual the mutual intercourse of trade and commerce" between the two countries. When the second of these objects was not attained—the American envoys having no powers to treat—he remained in Paris awaiting the arrival of such powers. TJ evidently met him first on 31 Aug. 1784 when the American Commissioners informed him that they were empowered to enter into a treaty of amity and commerce with Great Britain (American Commissioners to President of Congress, 11 Nov. 1784). A letter from TJ to Hartley of 30 Apr. 1792, perhaps in response to the above, is recorded in SJL but has not been found.

To Mary Jefferson

MY DEAR POLL   Philadelphia Dec. 7. 1790

This week I write to you, and if you answer my letter as soon as you recieve it, and send it to Colo. Bell at Charlottesville I shall recieve it the day before I write to you again, which will be three weeks hence: and this I shall expect you to do always so that by the correspondence of Mr. Randolph, your sister and yourself I may hear from home once a week. Mr. Randolph's letter from Richmond came to me about five days ago. How do you all do? Tell me that in your letter, also what is going forward with you, how you employ yourself, what weather you have had. We have already had two or three snows here. The workmen are so slow in finishing the house I have rented here that I know not when I shall have it ready except one room which they promise me this week, and which will be my bedroom, study, dining room and parlour. I am not able to give any later news about peace or war than of October 16. which I mentioned in my last to your sister. Wheat h[as] fallen a few pence, and will I think continue to fall, slowly at first and rapidly after a while. Adieu my dear Maria, kiss your sister for me, and assure Mr. Randolph of my affection. I will not tell you how much I love you, lest by rendering you vain, it might render you less worthy of my love. Encore Adieu.

Th: J.

RC (Mrs. Francis Shine, Los Angeles, 1946); addressed: "Miss Maria Jefferson Monticello." PrC (ViU).

MR. RANDOLPH'S LETTER was that of 11 Nov. 1790, received on 3 Dec. Discussions of house-construction, the question of war, and the price of wheat in a letter to a twelve-year old daughter assume proper proportion only in the light of TJ's plan for a regular rotation of letters to the three persons at Monticello, each being for a particular person but also intended for all.

From Joseph Fenwick

SIR   Bordeaux 8 Decemr. 1790.

Annexed are duplicates of the two last letters I had the honor to write you. Since, we are assured of a peace between the Southern Powers of Europe, tho' as yet they have not began to disarm their Navies in this Country or in Spain but have ceased to encrease them.

The Commerce of France exists now in a very loose situation the National Assembly not having as yet fixed the basis on which it is to be conducted. Their Committee of commerce has reported a Tarif for the Import and Export and have reported in favor of a prohibition of all foreign Oils I suppose to oblige the Dunkirk Nantuckettmen. On the Tarif of duties, the general commerce of the nation has been consulted, who have remonstrated for a more or less revision from all the trading Towns. I hope I shall obtain a general remonstrance from this Town against the prohibition of American oils as the one I have presented to the Chamber of Commerce was favorably received by them and is now in the hands of a comittee to revise. I also proposed a Petition against the exclusive privileges given the Nantuckett Company but the Chamber of Commerce thought that unnecessary, not doubting but their privileges woud fall of course with all others in the Kingdom of a partial nature and have confined the memoir on that business to the suspension of American Oils untill the french fishery shou'd be in a situation to supply the necessary quantity for the consumption of the Country.

I have wrote on the subject of oils, at same time exposing the situation, and manner in which the Nantuckett company carryed on the Fishery, to all the American Consuls and Vice Consuls as well as our Correspondents in the different ports of France concerned in trading to America, praying them to endeavor to prevail on the merchants of their respective Towns to remonstrate against the prohibition of American Oils, and in favor of a free Tobacco Trade, what success it will have I can't say.

As the general regulations of Commerce of this Country are yet in embryo, I have nothing further to remark on that subject without anticipating the disposition of the National Assembly. I am in Correspondence with Mr. Short on the subject and shall obey whatever he may please to suggest. I send you by this opportunity a few of the latest Gazettes and have the honor to be with the highest respect Sir Your most obedient and most humble Servant, JOSEPH FENWICK

RC (DNA: RG 59, CD). Dupl (same). Recorded in SJL as received 19 Mch. 1791.

From Thomas Thompson

Madeira, 8 Dec. 1790. He had the honor of being introduced to TJ on his arrival from France, yet supposes "the general tribute of Affection with which your Fellow Citizens celebrated your return, left but little opportunity to note the respects of a stranger." Offers his services "as a zealous and faithfull Servant to the Public, in the capacity of Consul or Agent at Lisbon," for which he deems himself fitted so far as "a competent knowledge of the language and springs of Action of the Portuguese Nation may be necessary; acquired during a residence of Seventeen years in mercantile business in this Island. And as the manner and language of the Spaniards and Portuguese assimilate, I shoud esteem an appointment to either Lisbon or Cadiz as a high honour. But from the influence of my friends with people high in Office at the Court of Lisbon, and my own personal connections, I shoud I think have it in my power to serve the Public better in that City.— The liberality of Virginia has number'd me among her Citizens for these last Seven years, where as a Planter I have thro' the Medium of Taxes contributed my mite to the Public Revenue. I have not been fortunate enough to render my Country any service, but pledge myself to exert my best endeavours to advance her interest and reputation."

RC (DLC: Applications for Office under Washington); endorsed by TJ as received 11 Feb. 1791 and so recorded in SJL.

From George Washington

[Before 8 Dec. 1790]

The P——— requests that Mr. J——— would give the letter and statement herewith sent from the S. of War a perusal, and return it to him in the course of the day with his opinion as to the propriety of the manner of making the communication to Congress; and whether it ought not, at any rate, to be introduced in some such way as this (if it is to pass thro him to Congress) "Pursuant to directions I submit," &ca.—or (if it is to go immediately from the War department to that body) "I lay before Congress by direction of the P. of the U. S. the following Statement" &ca.

Dft (DNA: RG 59, MLR); written on verso of address-leaf of one of TJ's letters to the president, addressed by him: "The President of the United-[states]"; docketed by Washington: "To Mr. Jefferson & Colo. Hamilton"; not recorded in SJL or SJPL.

The enclosed letter and statement from the Secretary of War concerned the expedition against the Miami Indians and presented a far more serious problem than one of form. Long before he left Mount Vernon, Washington had become deeply concerned, both because Knox had not kept him informed and because he apprehended failure. In a private letter to Knox he said that, whatever the outcome, the motives for undertaking the expedition would have to be "laid fully before Congress" and that the report should be ready "at the *opening* of the Session" (Washington to Knox, 2 Sep. 1790), *Writings*, ed. Fitzpatrick, xxxi, 143). Knox, detained in Boston, had just sent the latest news from the West. He reported that Harmar, in a letter of 2 Sep. 1790, had said that he needed about 2,500 to 3,000 men to succeed—a force about double the number of militia and regulars he commanded. Knox did not enclose this letter and he sought to soften its impact by saying

that the contractors had informed him ample supplies of provisions had been furnished, together with horses and other necessities. He enclosed without comment copies of a letter from St. Clair, dated at Marietta, 19 Sep. 1790. St. Clair had arrived there on the 13th, only three weeks after leaving New York and after encountering great difficulty in mustering militia from Pennsylvania. He reported that the President of Pennsylvania had paid no attention whatever to the President's intimations and that the county lieutenants were also apathetic, in consequence of which there was a deficiency of some 200 men from that state. The ammunition and quartermaster stores had not arrived and the Indian depredations were occurring daily, but he hoped the whole of the troops would arrive at the rendezvous at Fort Washington as scheduled. Meanwhile, in accordance with the President's instructions, he was that day sending a message to the commanding officer at Detroit to notify him that the expedition was not aimed at the British posts (Knox to Washington, 25 Oct. 1790, enclosing copies of St. Clair to Knox, 19 Sep. 1790, and to Major Murray, same date; DLC: Washington Papers).

Washington was greatly disturbed by this premature disclosure, not knowing that Hamilton had already informed Beckwith of the purpose of the expedition (Washington to Knox, 4 Nov. 1790, *Writings*, ed. Fitzpatrick, XXXI, 143; Vol. 17: 131-4). It was almost six weeks after Harmar's troops advanced from Fort Washington that Knox reported he had received no news of it (Knox to Washington, 10 Nov. 1790, DLC: Washington Papers). A few days later Washington revealed forebodings that had become certainty with him. Reports about Harmar's drunken conduct, disputes over command, and failure to gain the confidence of westerners had caused him to give up *"all hope* of Success." He was prepared for the worst—"for expence without honor or profit" (Washington to Knox, 19 Nov. 1790, *Writings*, ed. Fitzpatrick, XXXI, 156). Such a dire prospect made it all the more urgent that the reasons for authorizing the military operations be given to Congress as soon possible.

The question of the manner of transmitting this information to Congress was resolved before Washington delivered his annual message. In that document, after explaining that defensive measures against Indian aggressions had proved ineffective, he added: "The event of the measure is yet unknown to me. The Secretary of war is directed to lay before you a statement of the information on which it is founded, as well as an estimate of the expence with which it will be attended" (same, XXXI, 166). On the same day Knox, in "obedience to the orders of the President of the United States," transmitted to both houses the statement alluded to in the above memorandum. It contained documents attesting to Indian depredations on the frontiers and letters, instructions, and reports concerning the military operations, together with an estimate of the cost of the expedition (ASP, *Indian Affairs*, I, 83-104; JHR, I, 333; JS, I, 220). The documents were carefully selected and judiciously edited. Nothing was included in Knox' report about St. Clair's letter about the President of Pennsylvania, the deficiency of militia from that state, or the absence of ammunition and stores. St. Clair's premature disclosure was hidden by words attributed to him but not to be found in his letter: "I am directed to write to the commanding officer at Detroit. I have enclosed a copy of that letter" (ASP, *Indian Affairs*, I, 96). Harmar's

letter asserting the need for more troops was not included, though the contractors' anticipatory statement that the "expedition cannot fail from any default of ours" was included. The whole of this document, whose contrived presentation cannot be fully tested because many of the originals have been lost by fire, sought to justify both the launching of the offensive campaign and its undeniably anticipated failure. The matter had not been "laid fully before Congress." Privately TJ revealed that he thought Knox' report "not very methodically related" (TJ to Randolph, 16 Dec. 1790).

In this instance the bad news of Harmar's defeats on 18 and 22 Oct. 1790 travelled with inexplicable slowness, requiring almost two months to cover the distance that St. Clair had so recently travelled in only three weeks —as the governor assumed would be true in this instance (see St. Clair to Sargent, 27 Nov. 1790, Carter, *Terr. Papers*, II, 312-13). The official accounts arrived in Philadelphia on the evening of the 13th. The next day Washington transmitted Knox' letter and the dispatches to Congress without comment. One of the dispatches was from St. Clair to Knox of 6 Nov. 1790 in which he said that, in a letter of the 29th, he had informed him "generally of the success that attended General Harmar"—an official letter that Knox included neither in his communication of the 8th nor in this one. In St. Clair's opinion the savages had "got a most terrible stroke" and Harmar, while admitting heavy losses, declared that "the head quarters of iniquity were broken up" (ASP, *Indian Affairs*, I, 104-6). The President and heads of departments were well aware of the humiliating end of the expedition, but the revelation to Congress was an implicit assumption of success that could not withstand investigation.

TJ and Hamilton must have concurred in advising Washington that Knox' letter and statement should be sent directly to Congress by him under the President's orders, though no written response from either has been found. But whatever TJ might have felt about this mere matter of form, there is no doubt of his views of offensive campaigns against forest enemies of the sort Hamilton, Knox, and St. Clair, with Washington's approval, had launched late in August (Vol. 17: 131-4). "The federal council," he soon wrote, "has yet to learn by experience, what experience has long ago taught us in Virginia, that rank and file fighting will not do against Indians" (TJ to Innes, 7 Mch. 1791). This was precisely the advice that Virginians and Kentuckians had been giving to the President and the Secretary of War for well over a year—advice disclosed in the documents accompanying the justifying statement that Washington had ordered him to prepare (see Editorial Note, group of documents on new approaches to Spain, under 10 Mch. 1791).

From Tobias Lear

[*Philadelphia*], *10 Dec. 1790.* By the President's command he transmits resolutions of the Convention of Kentucky for forming that district into a separate state, and an application for its admission into the union, together with a letter from the President of the Convention to the President of the United States.

FC (DNA: RG 59, SDC); at head of text: "United States"; at conclusion Lear signed himself "S.P.U.S."; not recorded in SJL. Dft (DNA: RG 59, MLR); dated 9 Dec. 1790; signed by Lear as "Secy. to the Presidt. of the U.S."; at foot of text: "⟨Henry Remsen Jr. Esq. Principal Clerk in the Office of State⟩ The Secretary of State."

For enclosures, see group of documents on Vermont and Kentucky, under 4 Mch. 1791.

From Robert R. Livingston

DEAR SIR   New York 10th. Decr 1790

The enclosed was written long since and accidentaly detained at New York. I send it now to shew that I have not been inattentive to the letter you favoured me with and somewhat to shorten what I am now to tell you of the result of the experiment you encouraged me to make. In order to gain room for affixing the hollow cylinder or tub to the spindle of the mill it was necessary to make a new cog wheel and lanthorne this was a work of some expence and considerable time in the country where I could get but one mill wright and he conceived that I was doing a very foolish piece of work, and felt a reluctance in being so ill employed.

I had calculated upon having the smallest tub[1] three feet every way clear of the wood, my mill wright however not comprehending that the small quantity of water which would then be in the larger tub[2] could have much effect in floating the stones resolved to serve me against my will by so reducing the size of the cylinder as to admit more water. As he did not finish till the day I was to embark for New York it was too late to get it altered. The tub affixed was two feet eight inches below three feet above and two feet ten inches deep. Two inches were above the water. The

Millstones was 4 feet six inches and weighed as near as I could compute between twelve and thirteen hundred weight. I first graduated the gate, and set the mill in motion with a small force of water, without puting any water in the outside vessel, it ground ½ a bushel of rice in twenty four minutes. Water was then put in the outer tub and the mill being set in motion with the same force of water, it ground ½ a bushel of rice in 18 minutes. Here was a clear saving of one quarter but as the water wheels and cog wheels were very large and heavy I found the friction on the gudgeons to be some thing more than one fourth of the force *then* applied, but stating it at one fourth as this was equal on both, the saving in the friction of the stones and spindle will be about one third. If in addition to this the gudgeons should also be floated by hollow cylinders affixed to each end of the shaft (the friction of which may by this means be reduced almost to nothing, especialy if a horizontal wheel should be used) the difference will be still more considerable. My mill did not permit me (on account of the smallness of the tub) to ascertain how much lighter the pressure might have been made without injuring the flower. It had however this advantage, the meal came out perfectly cool and tho the stones were let down so as to run upon each other, which would have spoiled the meal in any other mill, two millers, both prejudiced against the scheme, declared it to be perfectly good and light.[3]

This experiment serves to account for what has often perplexed me. Two mills of the same construction driven by the same force of water will frequently differ from each other both in the quantity and quality of the flours they make in a given time. This I conceive to be owing to the greater or less spring in the bridge tree, but as this is uncertain and incapable of being reduced to any rule I have contrived a mode of applying my principles to it in such a manner as to be useful to mills already erected without altering a single wheel.[4]

Let two thick planks be joined together by leather, elastic yarn or in any other way which will make them water tight and suffer them to play half an inch. In the upper board insert a tube whose length shall be proportioned to the size of the board and the weight of the stone, place this upon the bridge tree of the mill, and let the spindle run on its pivot in the upper board: by filling this tube with more or less water that degree of weight which is calculated to make the best flower will be obtained, and much water be saved, for tho' the friction on the spindle will not be less, yet that on the face of the stones, which is most important, will be greatly diminished. I regret that I had it not in my power to make farther experiments with my mill from the delay in finishing it and the necessity I was under of embarking the river being full of ice and my family on board waiting for me.—I must tell you however that they are all in arms against me and that without your interposition I do not know how I shall compose them. They alledge that my politicks have half ruined them, diminished my fortune, wasted my time and occasioned the loss of my house by *fire* and that now my mechanicks will render *water* equally injurious to them and distroy our mills which stand on large streams by giving an additional value to others in this neighbourhood, which would not before come in competition with them.[5] I have promised by means of a patent to make them some compensation and as I am now satisfied that the invention is both new and useful; I take the liberty to tax your friendship to have one expedited for me as the basis for an application abroad in behalf of a friend who is very apprehensive (as the thing is now well known and talked of) that some other person may take advantage of any delay and avail himself of my labours.[6] I do myself the honor to enclose an official application. The thing is so entirely simple that I have not thought model necessary, a slight drawing will make it sufficiently intelligible. I ought to ask your pardon for the lenght of this Letter, but I well know that whatever comes to you in the shape of an useful improvement will meet with, tho' it should be too imperfect to reward your attention. I have the honor to be Sir with the highest esteem & respect Your Most obt hum: Servt,

R R LIVINGSTON

RC (DLC); endorsed by TJ as received 15 Dec. 1790 and so recorded in SJL. Dft (NHi); with minor variations in phraseology in addition to those differences noted below. Enclosures: (1) Livingston to TJ, 1 Oct. 1790. (2) The enclosed "official application" for a patent has not been found. TJ recorded both enclosures in SJL as received the same day, the second as being dated at New York 9 Dec. 1790 and as being addressed "to board of arts."

On Livingston's idea of reducing friction in grist and other mills, see his letters to TJ of 1 Aug. and 1 Oct. 1790, together with TJ's reply to the first of 8 Aug. 1790. The draft of a letter from Livingston to TJ, undated but written at Clermont probably late in Oct. or early Nov. 1790, is related to this correspondence. No recipient's copy of it has been found and none is recorded in SJL. The letter, therefore, was probably never sent. It reads as follows: "Fearing that in consequence of the removal of Congress I shall not have the pleasure of finding you at New York on my return to it I take this meathod to communicate an Idea which I had intended to have made the subject of a conversation when we met in the hope that you may find leisure to give me your sentiments about it and if it shall seem new to you and as free from objections as it appears to me encourage me to proceed in trying its success or if any objections strike you that you will communicate them to me that I may either relinquish my scheme or improve it from your hints.—The application of water to mills appear to me extreamly imperfect. In the overshot mill which is the best from the line of its direction and the short time that it remains in the basket a very considerable part of the force is lost. In Barkers mill this defect is in some sort remedied but not wholly. This mill even with Rumseys improvement has one defect which will forever render it useless. The weight of the Stones with all the machinery of the mill resting upon the end of the spindle must alway wear it away if sharp and have a considerable degree of friction to over come besides that the mill will want the spring necessary to making light flower and from the position of the weight in the arms will have a little vibratory motion that will deaden this meal in grinding and for these reasons I suppose has never gone into use. To remedy these defects in both mills I would propose 1st. That the wheel should be a perpendicular cylinder whose hight should be proportioned to the head of water that round this on its circumference should be a set number of spiral chanels about 3 inches by two at the top and contracted to one inch at the bottom out of which the water should issue as in Barkers mill. The water should stand in penstock over it and the wheel be so nicely fitted to it as that no water should escape at the sides. The wheel would have the following advantages 1st. by shutting or opening any number of the spiral chanel no more water need be applied than is sufficient to give the force required. 2d. The water acting upon the wheel in its whole passage none of its force could be lost as in the overshot wheel while the length of time that it is confined in the wheel will add to its centifugal force and expel it from the appertures with more velocity than from Barkers mill over which it would also have the advantage of a regular motion by the uniform distribution of the weight. But what I consider as the greatest improvement and which may be applied to Barkers mill or even to those of common construction is the mode in which I would propose to take of[f] the whole friction except that which arose from the Vibration of the [. . .] and the rubing of the stones on each other. I would place at the bottom of and so fixed with the spindle on which the whole machinery rests as to turn with a strong hollow cylindrical box whose solid contents should be two

feet or more if necessary. Thro this the spindle should pass into an open vessel in which should be placed the shel on which the spindle turns. This vessel should be so large as not to [exceed] the inner one by ¼ of an inch at the bottom and round the sides. This vessel should be filled with quick silver which would lessen the weight of the mill stones &c. in proportion to the size of the box. If as is proposed it contains two solid feet the weight would be reduced 1894 ℔. the whole weight of a very large mill stone and this water wheel &c. not being above 2200 so there would indeed be some friction from the mercury but this would I conceive be very triffling as the box need not be above a sixth part of the diam[et]er of the wheel so that its motion would not be rapid. I am not Mathe[mati]cian enough to tell whether this diminution of the weight would greatly lessen the force of the stones, but I should presume not from the manner in which grain is ground. I am satisfied however that the flower made by rubing and without much pressing would be lighter and finer than if it was crushed between two heavy mill stones" (Dft in NHi; punctuation supplied in some instances for the sake of clarity).

BARKERS MILL: A very simple reaction-type water turbine having a vertical shaft with two horizontal arms, at the ends of which are tangential orifices facing in opposite directions so that when water under pressure is introduced into the shaft, a torque is produced by the reaction of its discharge from the orifices. Such relatively inefficient turbines were commonly used for very light powers such as required by the carriage return system of up-and-down sawmills and driving small grist mills (communication from Robert M. Vogel, Smithsonian Institution, 27 Mch. 1964). See also William Waring, "Investigation of the Power of Dr. Barker's Mill, as improved by James Rumsey," Am. Phil. Soc., *Trans.*, III (1793), 185-93, and Barnes Riznik, "The Introduction of the Tub Wheel and Water Turbine in New England, 1790-1840," *Technology and Culture*, x (1969), 199-201.

A memorandum in Remsen's hand in DLC: TJ Papers, 59: 10189, undated, reads as follows: "Mr. Chancellor Livingston of New York, to be informed in answer to his application, that he must furnish a model of his improvements, and a more ample speci-fication than that accompanying his letter. That specification is merely an explanation of the drawings.—The drawings themselves should be more complete." See TJ to Livingston, 4 Feb. 1791, in which the substance of this memorandum is incorporated.

1 Dft reads: "inner tub."
2 Dft reads: "outer tub."
3 Dft reads: ". . . advantage that tho' two millers were present both prejudiced against the scheme they could not with all their efforts tho' the stones were so let down as to run upon each other spoil or deaden the flow'r."
4 Dft reads: ". . . I have thought of a way of giving the benefit of my tub mill (except that which arises from tak-ing of the friction on the spindle) to any mill without altering the wheels."
5 Dft reads: ". . . injurious to me and them and occasion the destruction

of our mills as we possess no less than 8 upon never failing rivers in the neigh-bourhood of others on small streams whose value will (as they suppose) be increased at our expence."
6 Except for complimentary close, Dft concludes with the following: ". . . I have promised by means of a patent to make them some compensation, and accordingly inclose an application for that purpose which you will do me the favor to promote principally as I wish to make it the basis of an application in behalf of a relation in Europe which I have an opportunity of doing by means of a Gentleman who is going shortly. I flatter myself that you should not find it inconvenient to expedite the patent as I run some risk of be[ing] anticipated by some of the many people who have examined the mill I have erected. I have every reason to believe upon the most diligent search that the Idea I have stated is entirely new."

To Joseph Nourse

SIR   December 11th. 1790

In compliance with your letter of November 10th. I have now the honor to enclose you an estimate of the expenses of the Depart-ment of State for one year from the 1st. day of January 1791, as nearly as I can foresee them.

I am with great respect &c.

FC (DNA: RG 59, PCC No. 120). Enclosure (same): "Estimate of the expences of the Department of State for one year from the 1st. day of January 1791," as follows:

"The Secretary of State's Salary		3500 dolrs.
one Chief Clerk		800
Three Clerks	@ 500 each	1500
Clerk for foreign Languages		250
Office keeper and Messenger		200
Stationary of all kinds		150
Firewood		66
Newspapers from the different States, supposed 17 at 4 dollars		68
A Collection of the Laws of the States to be made, and already begun, suppose		200
Gazettes from abroad, & to be sent abroad		25
Laws of the United States to be published in five papers at about 100 dolrs. each publication		500
Laws of the 2d. Session published in four papers at 118 dollars each		472
Office Rent at Philadelphia		187.50
Ditto at New York, supposing the house there not to be let, or if let, the Rent not recovered, for the office is responsible		150
Whole amount of the expenses of the Department of State, at home		8068.50
Expenses of the same, as fixed by law, abroad		40000.
		48,068.50"

Nourse's letter of 10 Nov. 1790 (missing) was received on that date (SJL). For a general note on departmental personnel, services, and operating costs for the period 1790-1793, see group of documents at 12 Aug. 1790 (TJ 17: 343-87).

From Richard Stockton

SIR   No. 83 Walnut Street 11th. Decr 1790

I have had the honor of recieving your letter of the 12th. of August last.

In compliance with your request I have purchased for the Use of the United States the most complete collection of "the printed Laws and ordinances ancient and Modern" of New Jersey from its first settlement to the present time which could be procured.

The old books are scarce, and only to be had at private sale and at a high price.—The Collection of the late Judge Brearley afforded me an opportunity which seldom presents itself.

You will observe that the Laws already in your office are also included in the enclosed list. The Gentlemen who had the disposal of the books refused to divide the set. I have the books in this City with me, and wait your directions where to send them. An order upon the Collector at Burlington will answer for the payment of the purchase money.

[I am happy in being able to inform you that no Laws have been enacted in New Jersey contravening the treaty of peace.

The only Judiciary decision asserting the rights of British Subjects in the State Courts was the opinion of a Single Judge (without the point coming solemnly before the Court upon argument) delivered in a charge to a Jury—by which he directed the Jury to make a deduction of Interest upon an old bond during the period of the late war.

How far this may be Said to infringe the rights of british Subjects you will Judge. I have the honor to be with great respect Sir Your most obedient and most humble Servant,

RD STOCKTON
Atty. of the New Jersey District][1]

P.S. Mr. Stockton leaves town on Monday morning.

RC (DNA: RG 59, MLR); addressed "The Honorable Secretary of State Philadelphia"; endorsed by TJ as received 12 Dec. 1790 and so recorded in SJL. FC of Extract (DNA: RG 59, SDR); at head of text: "No. 42. Extract of a letter from Richard Stockton . . . to the . . . Secretary of State, dated 11th December 1790"; comprising that part of text indicated in note 1 below and sent to Hammond by TJ as enclosure No. 42 in his letter of 29 May 1790. PrC of Extract (DLC); in another clerk's hand.

[1] Matter in brackets (supplied) comprises the text of Extract enclosed in TJ to Hammond, 29 May 1790.

From Thomas Appleton

Paris, 12 Dec. 1790. From late arrangements made relative to the manufactory at Rouen, his residence there in future will be unnecessary. He requests TJ's support in his application as consul at Lisbon. "The great commerce which exists between the United States and Portugal has Decided my establishment there (if the appointment can be obtained). The position Appears the most eligible and the extent of the commercial intercourse, wou'd I imagine make an appointment as Necessary as at any part of Europe. . . . My father will pursue the form that might be requisite. Hoping for your unfailing influence in this Affair I shall wait your Excellency's reply."

RC (DLC: Applications for Office under Washington); endorsed by TJ as received 21 June 1791 and so recorded in SJL.

To Richard Stockton

Sir   Philadelphia Dec. 12. 1790.

I am much obliged by your attention in procuring a set of the laws of New Jersey. Your letter of yesterday, not being handed to me till this morning, and no body being in the Treasury offices on Sunday, I cannot procure you the necessary order for the money till tomorrow. It shall be done as early in the day as the attendance of the officers of the treasury and their forms will admit. As soon as obtained I will send it to No. 83. Walnut street, where you will recieve it yourself if there, or leave orders with some one if you shall be gone.

The volumes you have been so good as to purchase will be received at any time you please by Mr. Henry Remsen, chief clerk at my office on Market street near 8th. on the North side.—I have the honour to be with great respect Sir Your most obedient and most humble servant,   TH: JEFFERSON

PrC (DLC); at foot of text: "Richard Stockton esq. Atty for the U.S. district of New Jersey."

On 15 Dec. 1790 TJ wrote Stockton: "Mr. Jefferson's compliments to Mr. Stockton, and is sorry that the necessary consultations to accomodate to the forms of the treasury this class of accounts (of which Mr. Stockton's happened to be the first that came in) prevented his sending him the inclosed Bank post note for 30½ Dollars, the amount of his account for the purchase of the law books of his state. He observes that the collector of the customs named in his letter will give him cash for this bill" (PrC in DLC; not recorded in SJL).

From Noah Webster, Jr.

SIR   Hartford Decr 12th 1790

By the last mail I had the honor of recieving yours of the 4th current. I am much obliged by the polite manner in which you express your sentiments of my opinions, and by your frendly suggestion respecting a second recording of my Institute. On examining the date of my first record, I find the six months not yet elapsed—the date is June 22—so that by forwarding a copy with this, it will reach you before the expiration of 6 months, viz. the 22d Instant. As soon as you recieve it, Sir, I will thank you for a certificate dated prior to the 22d. A more correct copy may afterwards be lodged in your office in exchange for this.

There seems, Sir, to be some misapprehension between us, respecting the opinions advanced in your Notes and my Essays. You suppose I have mistaken your arguments respecting the Constitution of Virginia or at least the design of them—On reviewing your arguments and my answer, I do not find the ground of the supposition. I must have understood your design as now explained, for I begin my remarks on your argument, with a passage of yours in which you express the same opinion as is contained in your letter. You repeat in your letter the opinion advanced in the Notes, that "there are some fundamental rights which a state ought not to place in the power of an ordinary legislature." It is *this opinion* which I have combated in my Essays. However it is not material—if I have mistaken your design, I hope I have not given any false coloring to your argument.

I will not trouble you with a controversy on a political question, to which I am wholly incompetent. A respect for your talents would prevent me, were there no other consideration. My opinion on the great question between us is simply this—That a state is a corporation whose power is always *equal*, but cannot be exercised but by *delegation*—That the *will* of the state exists no where but in the *resolves* of its delegates, because the *opinions* of the members of the corporation can be no where else *combined*—That the *will* of the state however, thus declared by the *decrees* of its delegates, is the only *rule of action* for the state—That this *will* is always *equal to itself* and of *equally binding force* whether denominated *constitution, law, statute* or *ordinance*—That the members of the corporation cannot express the *will* of the *corporation*, without a meeting for the purpose, and as this is impossible, no instructions of *individual members* can be *binding* upon the *delegation*; consequently no *specific powers* can be *delegated*, nor *specific rights reserved* by the state; for the *will* of the *state* exists only in the *will* of the delegation—That both policy and right require that the *delegation* should at all times possess the *whole power* of the *state* for the purpose of *preventing all possible wrong* and *obtaining* all *possible good*—That *every right* claimed by a citizen of a free government is liable to vary with circumstances; *except what rest wholly on the moral law*; that therefore *every right*, created by political law, should be always subject to be modified by the power that created it, viz. the *will of the state*, which is always the *will of the delegation.*—That in short, the *election* and *organization* of the *body* which is to express the *will of the state*, is the *only power* which the *people* and a *convention can exercise*, and the *only power* which an ordinary legislature *can not*.

Are my ideas too speculative? Perhaps so, but I have lived the most of my life in a state where they are mostly realized. The constitution of Connecticut is however a very bad one; not because the legislature *cannot* reform it; but because they *dare* not. An idea of some constitutional powers, paramount to their own, in the government, together with habit; prevents a reformation of the worst evils that can befal a government: a union of the legislativ with the judicial powers and a want of a supreme executiv. A bold stroke will be necessary to cut up the evil—and a bold stroke will, ere many years, be made for the purpose.

Excuse, Sir, the length of this letter, and give yourself no trouble in replying. Your office has a demand upon your attention which no individual has a right to interfere with.

Enclosed is a Copy of the "Little Readers Assistant" which I beg leave to lodge in your office, in compliance with the copy right act of Congress having lately recorded the title for securing the property. As a school book, it is getting into use, and tho it may never be so generally used as the Institute, yet it may diffuse some useful truths; which is my primary object in all my publications. The farmers catechizm at the end, I design to improve in a future impression. I am, Sir, with perfect respect your most obliged and hum Servant   NOAH WEBSTER JNR

RC (DLC); endorsed as received 18 Dec. 1790 and so recorded in SJL.

From John Telles

Philadelphia, 13 Dec. 1790. Having made application through Robert Morris for consulship at Portugal, offers himself as candidate. "I have been in this Country near 30 years in business; preserving always a fair Character." Is married and has a family, met with heavy losses during war through depreciation, and by this was forced to go to Europe for five years where he formed respectable connections in Portugal. Since his return he has done considerable business with that country. "I had large Orders from that Government for supplys of wheat, which I have complyed with. My friends there also obtained a License from her Majesty for the Importation of a large Quantity of flour, and forwarded me Orders to execute the same, which I did; but the Prices falling there, the Contractors ungenerously rejected several Cargoes, and ordered my Bill on London for their Cost, to be Protested." It is still necessary for him to go there. From his knowledge of the law and language of Portugal as well as his "long experience of the Trade and Interest of the United States and particularly their Intercourse with that Kingdom," he thinks he could give satisfaction in the post and also, from his connections with the Portuguese court, he could "arrange and settle any Matters depending between the Respective Countrys (if any should exist) than A Stranger thoroughly unacquainted there."—He will not trouble TJ with recommendations from Pennsylvania and neighboring states, but has relied upon his friend Robert Morris, who has known him since he arrived in America. He refers TJ also to his friend John Swanwick.

RC (DLC: Applications for Office under Washington); endorsed by TJ as received 14 Dec. 1790 and so recorded in SJL.

From James McHenry

DEAR SIR   Baltimore 14 Decr. 1790.

If I may intreat you to take the trouble to read the inclosed memorial you will see how greatly I have been injured by the French marine minister's non-compliance with an engagement with the late house of John McHenry & Co. It gives me sensible pain to be obliged to make use of this mode of solicitation for attaining so clear a piece of justice, but I do it because I know of no other likely to answer any efficient purpose. I have further to beg of you (should it not be foreign to the duties of our charge des affaires to lay it before the minister), that you would suggest to him what you think proper to be done on the occasion. The Marquiss de la Fayette I expect will throw in his help, so that putting all together I flatter myself with success. Your assistance in this affair will I assure you lay me under a lasting obligation. Having to discharge the debts of the late partnership makes this an object of some importance to me. May I hope that you will favor me with a line, and believe me to be with profound respect and real esteem your most ob. st.   JAMES MCHENRY

I beg you will be so kind as to order one of your clerks to direct the packet to Mr. Short whose Christian name I do not recollect.

RC (DNA: RG 76, British Spoliation Claims); endorsed by TJ as received 17 Dec. 1790 but not recorded in SJL.

From John Swanwick

SIR   Philadelphia [14] December 1790

I have on few Accounts Regretted more an Indisposition, which has Confined me some days at home, than as it prevented my having the honour of waiting upon you, to assure you of the Ardency of my Wishes during your Residence in this City, to be usefull to you in whatever Matters of a Commercial Nature you might have Occasion for information from one who probably is inferior to none in this Country for the extensiveness of his Occupations in this way; and Conceiving the Nature of your department as necessarily connected with a pretty wide Range of Intercourse with Foreign Nations, it will give me always great pleasure, if any thing of this kind may be facilitated by the extensive Scene of Correspondence I have habitually with the Countries to which our Connections most Immediately point.

So much I have taken the liberty to say in Answer to a Message I had the honour to Receive a few days since from you, enquiring for a Person skilled in Foreign Languages. Since then a Mr. Kullen has here presented himself to me for Employment, well recommended from New York and by Mr. Soderstrom from Sweden; Mr. Kullen is a Swede by Birth, and he tells me Master of the French, Spanish, English, and Swedish Tongues; his expectations seem moderate, and would probably meet your views, and of his Talents to translate or do any thing necessary to the Maintenance of a Correspondance in those Tongues I am well assured; you can think of him if he would have any Chance to Answer your Views, he had best know it soon, as he purposes I hear to Return speedily to New York and from thence to sail to the Bahamas, where he has Connections, who have offered him terms to go there, which he must embrace, however unwillingly, if he finds no encouragement to wait on further expectations in America. After his Return to New York, he will be however ten or fourteen days there, in the course of which a Letter from hence might produce his Return and Settlement here.

I have now to mention another Circumstance which Respects my Friend Mr. John Telles a Merchant of this City who I hear is soliciting the American Consulage at Lisbon. If a long residence here with an unblemished Character—if a general acquaintance with the American Trade—if good Connections at Lisbon, many of them of great Influence at that Court; if the Strictest honour and Integrity can Recommend him to this Office, I am sure he will not apply for it in vain. And certainly much more usefull must he be (possessing both Languages and esteemed at both sides of the Water) to our Commerce than Persons comparatively Strangers to it. He is Married in America and has lived here with little interruption these 27 or 30 Years; and was in very flourishing Circumstances, by means of the Assistance of his powerfull Patrons in Lisbon, when the late disasters happened to him, that now Occasion in him the Wish to visit Lisbon to see justice done at once to himself and to Maintain in it the honour of a Country of which he has become a Citizen by all possible ties; Birth only excepted. He will probably shew you a State of his Case the hardship of which perhaps merits even publick Notice from America, at the Court of Portugal; the fact simply and briefly stated is this: A Certain Antonio Joze Ferreira, a Great Favourite at that Court, (at a time when last year, they expected a great want of the first staff of life) obtained a License to Import exclusively into Lisbon, about 80000. bbls Flour from the United States: (this Article having since the War with Great Britain been prohibited the free Importations it formerly had into Portugal). This Mr. Ferreira ordered Telles & Co. to ship half this flour from hence, expressly stating, that he did so, under her Majestys License to him. The price was not limited, the time of dispatch was in his Orders, the 20th April 1790 or *days more* a Vague and Indefinite mode of expressions under which Mr. Ferreira Shelters himself to refuse all the Flour shipped from hence after the 21st. April, tho' much of it was bought, and the Ships Chartered long before, tho' Rains and Inevitable Accidents Retarded the dispatch; and tho' all was got away and Bills of Lading Signed by the 23rd and 30 April 5th and 6th of May the last but 16 days after the 20th April, which were surely warranted by the clause of *Days more* after the 20 April in his orders; Thus Situated these Supplies, or about

15000 bbls of them, were (tho' intended for the relief of the Subjects of her Most Faithfull Majesty and ordered under her immediate Licence) cruelly thrown on the Skipper's hands, not allowed even the benefit of Sale for the Market at Lisbon, but sold for exportation in 15 Days out of her Majesty's Dominions by Her orders. Some of the Flour was sent back, Some sent to France, Mr. Telles's Bill for £ Stg. 30000 Protested in London, tho' he had thereon the Guarantee of Messrs. John Gore & Co. (one of the first Houses there) for their payment. Thus has he been sacrificed, and the Mercantile Interest of this City and New York, put in danger of loosing at least 100 to 150,000 Dollars. I have for my own part, no doubt, a jury of Middlesex will make Messrs. Gore & Co. pay at last; but I have always thought that this in all it's respects was a Matter whereof our Government might well have Remonstrated to the Court of Lisbon, and perhaps by doing this strenuously, this whole Sum might yet be saved to the Commercial Interest of our Country. Be this as it may, there is no doubt Mr. Telles's going to Lisbon in a Publick Character, would have the best Effect on these Affairs of his; and could prove injurious to Nobody. A Committee of his Creditors have signed for him a Circular Letter; he will shew you that fully evinces their Sense of his honour and Integrity; and he must I think prove in all Respects equal to the Consul, it has pleased Her Faithfull Majesty to send to these United States, whose presentation was lately Announced, and who by the by, is involved in *somewhat* similar Circumstances, as to the other half of the Flour shipped at same time by his House.

I beg you will excuse these few thoughts on these Subjects and believe me always with the highest deference & Regard for you. Sir Your most hble Servt, J. SWANWICK

RC (DLC: Washington Papers); in clerk's hand, except for corrections and signature; endorsed by TJ as received 14 Dec. 1790 and so recorded in SJL. TJ's MESSAGE to Swanwick may not have been written; none is recorded in SJL. The consul-designate from Portugal who was also involved in the shipment of flour was Ignatius Palyart. On this affair and the way in which the MERCANTILE INTEREST OF THIS CITY AND NEW YORK responded, see note on consular documents grouped under 21 Feb. 1791.

The Northwest Territory

EDITORIAL NOTE

> If a poor man ... should ask of me, where shall I go in order to live more at my ease, without the aid of oxen and horses? I would say to him, go upon the banks of some rivulet on the Plains of Scioto; there you will obtain permission of the savages of the neighbouring villages to scratch the surface of the earth, and deposit your rye, your corn, your potatoes, your tobacco, &c. leave the rest to nature; and, during her operations, amuse yourself with fishing and hunting.

The words were those of Crèvecoeur and Jefferson had encountered them in France in a copy of the Rev. Manasseh Cutler's *An explanation of the Map which delineates that part of the Federal lands, comprehended between Pennsylvania West Line, the rivers Ohio and Sioto, and Lake Erie . . . now ready for settlement.*[1] This glowing pamphlet, echoing 17th century tracts that depicted an idyllic American wilderness beckoning Europeans to begin afresh in a new land, was addressed first of all to the officers and soldiers of New England, inviting them to escape poverty and distress in an asylum beyond the Alleghenies.

[1] This pamphlet (Salem, Dabney and Cushing, 1787; Newport, Peter Edes, 1788) is generally attributed to Cutler, who arranged to have it printed. Besides extensive extracts from Crèvecoeur's letters, its chief sources were Thomas Hutchins' *Topographical description of Virginia* (London, 1778) and Winthrop Sargent's letters and reports, parts of which were published in Massachusetts newspapers because, Cutler wrote, "So good an authority has produced conviction in the most sceptical, and has had more influence than every thing else" upon prospective adventurers (Cutler to Sargent, 6 Oct. 1786, MHi: Sargent Papers). See Sowerby, No. 4041; Burnett, *Letters*, VIII, 620n.

One leader in the promotional effort even thought it expedient for their ends to bring into question the rhetoric of the Revolution: "We are in this Commonwealth," wrote Cutler in 1786, "on the very borders of complete anarchy. . . . It seems to be more problematical than ever whether mankind are in a state for enjoying all the natural rights of humanity and are possessed of virtue sufficient for the support of a purely republican government. Equal liberty in Civil Community appears finely on paper, but the question is, can it be realized? . . . One thing I am persuaded of—that these commotions will tend to promote our plan and incline well disposed persons to become adventurers, for who would wish to live under a Government subject to such tumults and convulsions?"[2] The versatile minister continued to live in his native state while urging others to leave it, addressing his appeals to a predominantly military audience headed by prominent members of the Cincinnati and employing such unclerical methods as the manipulation of members of Congress and the making of dubious alliances with some of the chief speculators of New York and Boston.

But convulsions in France of an infinitely greater magnitude than the fleeting discontents in Massachusetts promised even more bountiful rewards for the promoters. Joel Barlow, who had probably given Cutler's pamphlet to Jefferson along with a copy of *Articles of an Association by the name of the Ohio Company*, arrived in Paris in the autumn of 1787 and caused a translation of the tract to be published.[3] Its audience, slow to be aroused until William Playfair came on the scene in 1789, was a strange mixture of aristocrats, artisans, peasants, and, as Gouverneur Morris expressed it, "the inhabitants of the Rue d'Honoré and others who might think proper to go to that land of Promise." Morris thought the promise lay chiefly in the claims of the speculators and that the scheme would prove injurious both to those who joined them and to the reputation of America.[4] The ensuing pamphlet and newspaper furor that took place in France in the spring of 1790, embroiling the Scioto affair in French political turmoils, was undoubtedly prejudicial to good relations between the United States and France.[5]

But the promoters' description of the Scioto region as "one of the

[2] Cutler to Sargent, 6 Oct. 1786; Samuel Holden Parsons to Sargent, 26 June [1786] (MHi: Sargent Papers).

[3] It is not known whether TJ owned the first edition of the *Articles* (Worcester, 1786) or the second (New York, 1787). See Sowerby, No. 4042. John Browne Cutting urged that Barlow show TJ a letter from Muskingum predicting that that region would "soon not only be the glory of America, but the envy of the world" (Cutting to TJ, 16 Sep. 1788).

[4] Morris to TJ, 24 Dec. 1790. This letter arrived on 12 Mch. 1791, just as TJ was embarking on the new policy of firmness toward Spain because of discontents in the West. See Editorial Note on New Approaches to Spain, 10 Mch. 1791; see also, Playfair to TJ, 20 Mch. 1791; Playfair to Hamilton, 30 Mch. 1791 and [Sep.-Dec. 1791], Syrett, *Hamilton*, VIII, 227-33; IX, 253-5.

[5] Durand Echeverria, *Mirage in the West* (Princeton, 1957), p. 134-6, summarizes the outburst of pamphleteering over the affair and points out that Moustier, denouncing the scheme to the National Assembly as fraudulent, called for legislative prohibitions against such emigrations. Moustier's letter was read to the National Assembly on 2 Aug. 1790 (*Archives Parlementaires*, XVII, 505). See also Otto's dispatches 21 Jan., 11 May, 10 June, 12 Aug., 12 and 18 Nov. 1790; and 7 May 1791 (DLC: Henry Adams Transcripts).

finest conquests that could ever be presented to man" had a foundation
of such substantial truth as to make their unnecessary adornments
seem comparatively trivial. Within a very short time, the pamphlet
declared, this region would become the center of power, wealth, "and
the future glory of the United States." Titles to land could be acquired
peaceably and legally from the aborigines. The deep alluvial soil would
produce wheat, rye, corn, oats, barley, hemp—even cotton, indigo, and
rice—and all of the fruits known to the temperate zone. Its tobacco
was superior to that of Virginia, its yield of wheat greater than in any
other part of America. Innumerable herds of deer, elk, buffalo, and
bear were sheltered in its groves, "an unquestionable proof of the great
fertility of the soil." Turkeys, geese, ducks, swans, pheasants, and
partridges were more plentiful than domesticated poultry in the older
American settlements. The rivers were not only highways for export-
ing surplus crops to the outer world but were also teeming with suc-
culent fish. Great forests offered inexhaustible sources of naval stores,
thus assuring that shipbuilding would be a primary industry, yet the
hardwoods and conifers were so towering and so devoid of underbrush
that a laborer might clear an acre of land in a single day merely by
girdling. Each sugar maple would produce ten pounds of sugar equal
in flavor and whiteness to the finest Muscovado and a few trees would
supply the wants of a family. There were lead and coal mines, but
agriculture alone would cause the value of lands to double within eight
years. Nature's bounty had been matched by legislative wisdom. The
new ordinance for the government of the region called for the institution
of schools and a university, thus affording an unequaled opportunity
to build a new society, with "no inveterate systems to overturn . . . no
rubbish to remove" before foundations could be laid. Within two
decades the preponderant part of the American population would be on
these western waters. Indeed, if one might "indulge the sublime contemplation of beholding the whole territory of the United States settled
by an enlightened people, and continuing under one extended government," the seat of empire itself would be located on the Ohio river
and the Federal City be established not far from the Scioto lands.[6] The
radiant dream shone forth not merely in Crèvecoeur's ecstatic phrases.
It was given verisimilitude in the carefully qualified affidavit of the
Geographer of the United States, Thomas Hutchins, who declared that
in respect to soil, products, and general advantages for settlement this
description of the marvelously favored land was indeed "judicious, just,
and true."[7]

It was not long after Barlow arrived in Paris and published these
enticing accounts of the Scioto lands that Jefferson, perhaps with truth,

[6] Cutler's *An explanation of the map*; quotations from Crèvecoeur's letters appear at p. 20-3.
[7] Affidavit by Hutchins, 28 Oct. 1787 (same, p. 23). Hutchins, having due
regard for his public responsibility, probably gave even this qualified affidavit
with some reluctance. During the preceding year he had been pressed by Henry
Knox to have his friend Sargent appointed surveyor in preference to others whose
claims, having precedence over his, did not prevail (Knox to Sargent, 28 May
and 4 June 1786; Hutchins to Knox, 7 June 1786, the last written in confidence
and under injunctions of secrecy lest it be construed as showing partiality; all
in MHi: Sargent Papers).

denied having knowledge of anyone offering American lands for sale. During his stay in France and afterward he consistently advised aliens seeking property in the United States to go there before purchasing. As antidote both to promoters' wiles and to purchasers' credulity, he had caused Benjamin Franklin's *Avis à ceux qui voudraient s'en aller en Amérique* to be printed.[8] He knew, as did Franklin, that discontented Europeans under the spell of speculators' extravagant claims would only find new frustrations amid the realities of the American frontier. It was shortly after he became Secretary of State that he learned of Barlow's first shipload of French emigrants, of their unhappy plight, and of the resultant storm of hostility in France toward the Scioto exploiters "as a parcel of kidnappers."[9] The obviously adverse effect of this on relations between the United States and her European ally thus presented a problem to Jefferson that touched both his public duty and his private concern.

These were the beginnings of a mania for speculation that ran unchecked in many areas from 1787 to 1792. Its interconnected operations, carried on by a handful of men in a few coastal centers and based almost invariably on a pyramid of public securities, inevitably affected policy on the government of the West, thereby in another and deeper sense involving Jefferson's most profound convictions as well as his official responsibility. As principal architect of the national domain, he had felt the weight of the speculator's hand on legislation even before he departed for France in 1784.[10] Barlow's activities only added to the evidence long since discernible in communications he had received from America that, in Washington's words, "local politics and self-interested views obtrude themselves into every measure of public utility."[11] One such evidence appeared shortly thereafter when Edward Carrington sent Jefferson a copy of the Northwest Ordinance of 1787, accompanied by a laudatory estimate of it as being much superior to the older arrangement for the territories. That plan, Carrington thought, might have created disgust among westerners, besides "ultimately inconvenient for the Empire"—inconvenient, presumably, for the effective manipulation of power at the center.[12] As author of the displaced Ordinance of 1784, Jefferson responded to this encomium on the new territorial system with eloquent silence.[13]

---

[8] TJ to La Vingtrie, 12 Feb. 1788 and note on the printing of Franklin's *Avis*.

[9] Short to TJ, 10 Feb. 1790.

[10] TJ to Harrison, 3 Mch. 1784; TJ's report on petition of Zebulon Butler, under 21 Jan. 1784; TJ to Huntington, 17 Jan. 1781; note on Virginia's cession of territory northwest of the Ohio [1 Mch. 1784]; note and documents on TJ's plan for government of the western territory [3 Feb.-23 Apr. 1784]; note on Virginia's claim to western territory, Vol. 6: 647-55.

[11] George Washington to David Humphreys, 25 July 1785 (Washington, *Writings*, ed. Fitzpatrick, XXVIII, 204).

[12] Carrington to TJ, 23 Oct. 1787.

[13] TJ professed to be much pleased with the new mode of disposing of public lands, which Carrington had said would perpetuate the old plan but through "contracts for large Tracts . . . to companies of adventurers" (TJ to Carrington, 21 Dec. 1787). He even declared to William Carmichael that the land Ordinance of 1785 was "a very judicious one" and that the domestic debt would soon be extinguished with public securities given in exchange for lands (TJ to Carmichael, 18 Aug. 1785 and 15 Dec. 1787). But such opinions, expressed to one corre-

It was James Monroe, however, who had been the first to suggest to him that the earlier measures were impolitic, that their tendency was to strengthen western interests instead of making these subservient to national purposes, and that the proper remedy called for a reduction in the number of new states contemplated in 1784 and a greater measure of control by Congress.[14] Later, as chairman of the committee that reported a plan of territorial government in 1786, Monroe had been even more explicit. This plan, he wrote, would in effect provide "a colonial government similar to that which prevailed in these States previous to the revolution, with this remarkable and important difference that when such districts shall contain the number of the least numerous of the 'thirteen original States for the time being' they shall be admitted into the confederacy."[15] To Jefferson, who regarded colonial systems as characteristic of monarchical government and therefore incompatible with republican principles, the mere hint that Americans were seeking a guide to territorial policy in the example of the colonies prior to the Revolution was enough to obliterate any reassurances to the contrary.

If Jefferson's response to Carrington was silence, that to Monroe

---

spondent who had been deliberately chosen as a channel of information about proceedings in Congress and to another who was employed chiefly as an indirect means of conveying favorable impressions of the United States to the Spanish government, reveal more about TJ's relations with them than about his real convictions on the subject. His warning to Monroe against land-jobbing and favoritism and against the features of the plan that would place the interests of the states and the nation in conflict instead of making them "joint in every possible instance in order to cultivate the idea of our being one nation," seems to be a closer approximation of his actual views (TJ to Monroe, 17 June 1785; see also, TJ to Madison, 20 June 1787, and his warning to Washington against "a spirit of gambling," TJ to Washington, 1 Jan. 1788).

14 Monroe to TJ, 19 Jan. 1786.

15 Monroe to TJ, 11 May 1786 and 16 July 1786. See also, Monroe to John Jay, 20 Apr. 1786 (Burnett, Letters, VIII, 342). For a closely reasoned and carefully documented legal and historical comparison of the Ordinances of 1784 and 1787, see Francis S. Philbrick, ed., The Laws of Illinois Territory, 1809-1818, in Colls., IHi, xxv, Law Series, v, Introduction, ccl-cccliv. Philbrick challenges the enduring mythology of the ordinances as compacts, assigns them to their proper status as mere legislative enactments, and concludes that the liberal provisions of TJ's Ordinance of 1784 were replaced by those of the Ordinance of 1787 which, deliberately and for a variety of reasons growing out of an illiberal reaction to the generous impulses of the Revolution, established a colonial system "hardly distinguishable from that from which the Revolution had just freed the confederated states" (same, p. cclxxxii). See also, by the same author, The Rise of the West (New York, 1965), p. 120-33. The chief distinction, however, was that pointed out by Monroe.

The important but relatively neglected field of territorial history is beginning to receive the attention it deserves from scholars of competence who are investigating changing patterns of structure and operation and who also recognize the spirit of innovation and idealism that fostered a territorial system appropriate for a republic (Jack E. Eblen, The first and second United States empires: governors and territorial governments 1784-1812 [Pittsburgh, 1968]; "The Northwest Ordinance and the Principle of Territorial Evolution," an essay by Robert F. Berkhofer, Jr., in a forthcoming report of proceedings of the Conference on the History of the Territories sponsored by the National Archives, 3-4 Nov. 1969). But the revisionist interpretations which emphasize a lineal evolution and minimize or reject the views of Philbrick and others who have perceived a marked shift in policy between Jefferson's Ordinance of 1784 and Dane's of 1787 are not convincing.

was so immediate and so forthright as to amount almost to a rebuke for defecting on a fundamental matter of principle. Under the plan of 1784, Jefferson replied, the western inhabitants would have a just share of their own government. They would remain attached to the union in bonds of pride and affection. But under the substituted plan, "we treat them as subjects, we govern them, and not they themselves; they will abhor us as masters and break off from us in defiance." As for the purpose implicit in the new proposals—that of disposing of the western territory so as "to produce the greatest and most benefit to the inhabitants of the maritime states of the union"—this came as a harshly grating echo of theories that had been advanced by protagonists of the British colonial system since the 17th century. Jefferson dismissed such an inconsonant policy with the simple declaration that good faith forbade the national legislature even to discuss it. He thought the question, viewed in its just form, quite otherwise: "How may the territories of the Union be disposed of so as to produce the greatest degree of happiness to their inhabitants?" This, he thought, could best be done by creating units of moderate size. Considering the American character generally and that of westerners in particular, Jefferson believed it both impolitic and a reversal of the order of nature to make "small states on the ocean and large ones beyond the mountains." Events would prove, he predicted with accuracy, that there would have to be a division of the western territory into states of small or moderate size. If anticipated, this would make it possible for them to be arranged "so as to produce the best combination of interest."[16] To James Madison, who would soon write the classic proposition that a republic could be maintained over a vast extent of territory through a diversity of interests, Jefferson also declared that this change in policy was a reversal of the natural order of things. The moment westerners discovered that their interests were being sacrificed to those of the eastern states, he warned, the question of their separation and independence would be determined.[17]

Yet the reversal of policy had taken place. It came in the wake of a storm of protest by westerners fearful that the eastern states were prepared to sacrifice their foremost interest—the navigation of the Mississippi.[18] Virginia delegates in Congress, though at times troubled about the aims of their northern colleagues, had given active support to this new policy. Richard Henry Lee explained their role in terms that might have been uttered by a Massachusetts delegate. "It seemed necessary," he wrote Washington, "for the security of property among uninformed, and perhaps licentious people as the greater part of those who go there are, that a strong toned government should exist, and the rights of property be clearly defined."[19] Again, echoing fears engendered by Shays' rebellion and other popular tendencies, he declared

16 TJ to Monroe, 9 July 1786.
17 TJ to Madison, 16 Dec. 1786.
18 See Editorial Note on New Approaches to Spain, under 10 Mch. 1791.
19 R. H. Lee to George Washington, 15 July 1787 (Burnett, *Letters*, VIII, 620). The Virginia delegates reported to Governor Edmund Randolph, not surprisingly, that they conceived the Ordinance of 1787 "to be much better than that . . . formerly made" (3 Nov. 1787, same, VIII, 672-3).

the new territorial government to be "much more tonic than our democratic forms on the Atlantic are."[20] It is little wonder that Nathan Dane of Massachusetts praised Lee for his assistance or that Edward Carrington of Virginia, subscribing for five shares in the Ohio Company and sharing his colleague's suspicions of the licentious character of frontiersmen, should look forward eagerly to the time when Massachusetts and Connecticut would introduce into the Northwest Territory "a description of men who will fix the character and politics throughout the whole territory, and which will probably endure to the latest period of time."[21] The sentiment was echoed by Dane, who thought that the region, being settled by easterners, would have "full an equal chance of . . . adopting Eastern politics."[22] This combination of interest, achieved through collaboration and compromise chiefly by the delegates of Massachusetts and Virginia, was scarcely what Jefferson had had in mind.

Monroe was correct in saying that the essential principle of the Ordinance of 1784 had been preserved. It is understandable, however, that Jefferson should have been deeply disturbed by the shift in policy. The idea of self-government for the territories was one that he had espoused even before the Declaration of Independence and he was fully aware that its survival was no more assured than that of the union itself. In 1780 when it was first proposed in Congress that the national domain be settled and divided "into distinct republican states, which shall become members of the federal union, and have the same rights of sovereignty, freedom and independence, as the other states," the vote was evenly divided.[23] On that ballot this magnanimous principle, the single most creative addition to the American concept of federalism being evolved in this remarkable decade of political innovation, was submerged in the contests brought on by pressures from the great land companies. The Ohio Company of Associates had itself grown out of a plan of 1783 for the creation of a self-governing state having its own constitution, laws, and representatives in Congress, but its subsequent change in character resulting in control by a few land speculators presaged and primarily caused a comparable shift in Congress toward a colonial system.[24] Such was the strength of the tendency toward separatism, illiberal reaction, and interested views that the essential element in territorial policy, much to the alarm of Monroe and others, was threatened even after it had been affirmed in the Ordinance of 1784.[25] But survive it did against all hazards, and thus the nation seemed to stumble into acceptance of the proposition that, thenceforth, all of its accumulating parts would participate equally as members of the same political society and under the guarantee of republican forms of government. This was something the world theretofore had not wit-

20 R. H. Lee to [William Lee], 30 July 1787 (same, VIII, 629-30).

21 Carrington to Monroe, 7 Aug. 1787 (same, VIII, 631).

22 Nathan Dane to Rufus King, 16 July 1787 (same, VIII, 622).

23 See note, Vol. 6: 582; JCC, XVII, 808; XVIII, 915-6.

24 "Propositions for settling a new state by such officers and soldiers of the federal army as shall associate for that purpose," together with their petition, 16 June 1783, and related documents (Cutler, Cutler, p. 156-77).

25 Monroe to TJ, 19 Jan. 1786 and 16 July 1786; Monroe to Madison, 19 Dec. 1785 (Burnett, Letters, VIII, 277).

nessed, and those who so hesitantly embraced the principle could scarcely have been expected to foresee how, under its generous sway, the boundaries of a republican empire of unprecedented size would go on expanding even into an age of nationalist aspirations that would cause all other imperial systems to recede or crumble.

Nevertheless, if a legislator of Monroe's character could seek a model in the British colonial system and if others favored more tonic forms than the democratic governments of the Atlantic states, the great danger that Jefferson feared was still present. The proposition that good faith forbade the national legislature even to discuss had been, at least in part, written into law. Jefferson had by no means modified the views he expressed so forthrightly in Paris and now, four years later, he was able to see in almost every aspect of the national administration further confirmation of his fear that the people on the western waters, aware of the neglect of their interests, would bring about the catastrophe of separation. Believing that the greater power given to Congress by the Northwest Ordinance of 1787 was at the expense of the right of self-government possessed by the inhabitants of the territories, he could have been expected to examine with care the manner in which this power was exercised by men not of their choosing.

For almost another century it would be the responsibility of the Secretary of State to make such an examination of territorial proceedings and to report upon his findings.[26] As Jefferson contemplated the documents pertaining to the Northwest Territory on which the first discharge of this duty would be based, his concern over the new system of territorial administration could not have been alleviated by its marked military cast or by its involvement in large-scale land operations. Nor could it have been diminished by the testimonials of good will toward Winthrop Sargent, Secretary of the Northwest Territory, that were published at this time in a Philadelphia newspaper and signed by leading French inhabitants of his jurisdiction. For it was clear that the document could only have been made public by the Secretary himself, that he was a leading figure in the Ohio and Scioto companies, and that both of these interlocking enterprises were in serious difficulty.[27] On almost every score the first secretary of the first territorial government gave the appearance of being more concerned with his private land speculations than with his public responsibility. These, though they were adversely affecting foreign relations, were carefully kept within the private domain except in so far as the public authority could be found useful to them.

The report and accompanying mass of documents that Winthrop Sargent sent to the President fell upon the Secretary of State at a time of confusion in his household and of exigent pressures in foreign affairs.[28] The documents were indeed so voluminous that only one copy

[26] The Department of State relinquished its responsibility for territorial matters to the Department of the Interior in 1873 (Oliver W. Holmes, "Territorial Government and the Records of its Administration," in *The Frontier re-examined*, ed. John Francis McDermott, p. 104).

[27] *General Advertiser*, 10 Dec. 1790, address of the citizens of Vincennes to Sargent, 23 July 1790, commending the measures he had taken as acting governor and his adjustment of their claims.

[28] See note to TJ to Short, 7 Nov. 1790.

was prepared for the use of both houses of Congress.[29] Jefferson's first report to the President briefly summarized the categories of land claims of the inhabitants of Vincennes that required legislative attention. The House deferred to the Senate, which referred the matter to Strong, Ellsworth, and Maclay.[30] Experienced as he was in land affairs, Maclay found the business tedious and drafted a report differing from that of Strong. "I stood ready to condemn my own when there was a shadow of objection," the Pennsylvanian declared, "but even this would not excite a particle of candor" on the part of the New Englanders, who seemed to him to have an "amazing predilection . . . for each other."[31] This apparently was the only difference, for Strong's bill authorizing the governor to make grants to those claiming possession by virtue of occupation, improvement, militia service, and other rights became law without evident opposition.[32] The need to settle such cases by legislative authority was clear, but a territorial system that had shifted in emphasis from local to central control brought in its train old and familiar inconveniences. St. Clair soon observed that, from "the very great Distance that Country is . . . from the Seat of Government, there seems to be a necessity for the Titles of Confirmation being made within the Territory or at least . . . put on record there."[33] He had assumed that he had authority to issue patents under the resolution of Congress of 1788. Sargent, acting on the same assumption, had indeed assured the inhabitants of Vincennes that patents to confirm ancient claims and possessions would issue as soon as surveyors' returns were made.[34] Yet the Attorney General soon ruled that no such local authority existed.[35]

St. Clair's report as governor brought a far more voluminous group of documents and an even more complicated set of land claims from the Mississippi settlements of Kaskaskia, Prairie du Rocher, and Cahokia.[36] Again Jefferson made a prompt and brief classification of the types of claims, correlated some with his report on those of Vincennes, described others differing from all such groups and from each other, pointed to an inconvenient result of Congressional action in establishing a line of division, and concluded with one of the few

[29] At the foot of Tr of Washington's message to Congress transmitting TJ's report and its enclosures (DLC: Washington Papers), Lear wrote the following: "NB. As the foregoing Report and Papers were very voluminous, one Copy only was made out, and that delivered to the House of Representatives with a request to the Speaker that they might be communicated to the Senate." This was done (JHR, I, 342).

[30] See Document II; JHR, I, 342; JS, I, 226, 227, 230.

[31] Maclay, *Journal*, ed. Maclay, p. 364-5.

[32] JHR, I, 352, 394, 404, 407, 408; JS, I, 231, 232.

[33] St. Clair to the Attorney General, ca. Jan. 1791. See note, Document VII. Carter, *Terr. Papers*, II, 319n., assigns the probable date of December on the assumption that St. Clair was in Philadelphia at that time. But he only left the Northwest Territory "about the 20th." of December and arrived in Philadelphia on 15 Jan. 1791 (*Federal Gazette*, 21 Jan. 1791; Carter, *Terr. Papers*, II, 471; Maclay, *Journal*, ed. Maclay, p. 377).

[34] Sargent to the inhabitants of Vincennes, 18 July 1790 (see note on enclosure 5, Sargent's report of 31 July 1790; Document I).

[35] Document VII.

[36] Document VIII and enclosures.

aspects of the assignment that could have given him satisfaction—that of drawing attention to St. Clair's recommendation of "the Expediency of having a printing press established at Marietta."[37] Jefferson prepared messages of transmittal and the President sent the report to Congress, but many years passed before claims under the various categories of right—still further complicated by speculative intruders—were conclusively settled.[38] In selecting extracts from St. Clair's report for the eyes of Congress, Jefferson with characteristic prudence excluded some topics—the failure to establish courts of justice, the departure from the strict letter of the law in dividing the county of St. Clair into districts, the illicit commerce with the Spanish side of the river, the British traders' access to the fur trade of the upper Mississippi through Prairie du Chien, the migrations from the American side inspired in part by the prohibition of slavery, the part played by such a land speculator as George Morgan in encouraging these migrations, the instructions for interdicting illicit trade through Peoria with resultant doubts about the legality of requiring passports, and the depredations of Spaniards in taking stone and wood and in hunting buffalo on American territory.[39] These matters, Jefferson no doubt felt, belonged either to the territorial legislature as to matters of police, to the executive department as to relations with Spanish authorities, or to the judiciary as to the construction of the article in the Ordinance of 1787 prohibiting slavery. He marked some of the passages in St. Clair's report for the particular attention of the President, who he knew would be officially and personally interested in the description of the settlements and waterways, in the recommendations for enlarging American access to the trade of the western regions, and in the effect this might have ultimately upon the Potomac route—and, of course, upon the national capital—that had so long engaged his interest.[40]

Exigent as were the pressures upon him, Jefferson in mid-December gave the voluminous executive proceedings an immediate and far from perfunctory scrutiny. This was to be expected and he at once extracted from the record those actions which manifested the kind of executive usurpation that he feared would result from a territoral system imitative of the one Americans had lived under prior to the Revolution. He ignored St. Clair's departure from the letter of the law in dividing the county into divisions in anticipation of legislative approval, for this administrative expedient was designed to establish courts of justice, to make jury service practicable, and to avoid the confusion that would result from a strict application of laws framed without due regard for local circumstances. He even passed silently over St. Clair's presumptive construction of the article in the Ordinance of 1787 prohibiting slavery, for in the absence of Congressional and judicial determination this also could be regarded as an appropriate

[37] Document IX and enclosures.
[38] Documents X and XI; JHR, I, 382; JS, I, 273; report of U.S. Land Commission, 31 Dec. 1809 (ASP, *Public Lands*, II, 123-241; J. F. McDermott, ed., *Old Cahokia*, p. 94-6).
[39] Documents VIII and IX.
[40] Document X.

executive ruling in the face of an urgent and equally unanticipated situation.[41] But for the governor and the secretary as acting governor to issue orders and proclamations regulating the conduct of citizens—this was another matter altogether, touching not only the fundamental distinction between the territorial system he had advocated and the one that had taken its place but also contravening the basic assumption on which the American republic rested. What made these executive regulations all the more reprehensible to him was that they tended to subject civilians to military authority. Jefferson had been profoundly disturbed by the alteration that had taken place between 1784 and 1787 in the governing principle of the territorial system, but now in practice as in theory, as it must have seemed to him, legislative authority in the Northwest Territory was being encroached upon in a manner reminiscent of the actions of those royal governors that had been so warmly condemned in the Declaration of Independence.

Jefferson, of course, was aware of St. Clair's letter to the President of some months earlier in which he had acknowledged that such regulations could not properly be established save by law. Frankly conceding that he had gone beyond his proper powers, St. Clair had rested his justification upon "the necessity of the Case, and . . . the Good of the People."[42] This time-honored doctrine of necessity buttressed by purity of intent was one that Jefferson himself had employed as governor of Virginia and would resort to again in the exercise of presidential authority.[43] But in this instance his condemnation of St. Clair's exercise of legislative power was immediate and emphatic. As he expressed it in his private register of public reports, such regulatory edicts were simply "against law."[44] He employed the same phrase in an equally emphatic though less succinct commentary that he sent to Washington with extracts of the executive proceedings showing the nature of the orders. Holding it to be the duty of government to protect its subordinate members from encroaching upon each other and to shield the citizens against actions *ultra vires*, he urged that the opinion of the Attorney General be obtained. He suggested that if Randolph agreed with his view—as Jefferson no doubt was certain would be the case—the ruling be communicated to the governor of the Northwest Territory for his future conduct.[45]

This was the first real challenge to methods of territorial administration since the establishment of the Northwest Territory.[46] Jefferson's

[41] St. Clair's interpretation of Article VI of the Ordinance of 1787 prohibiting slavery is found in his letter to Washington of 1 May 1790 (Carter, *Terr. Papers,* II, 248; see II, 49n. for a succinct note on early legislative and judicial constructions).

[42] St. Clair to Washington, 1 May 1790 (same, II, 246-7).

[43] "A strict observance of the written laws," TJ wrote in 1810, "is doubtless *one* of the high duties of a good citizen, but it is not the *highest.* The laws of necessity, of self-preservation, of saving our country when in danger, are of higher obligation. . . . When the army was before York, the governor of Virginia took horses, carriages, provisions and even men by force, to enable that army to stay together till it could master the public enemy; and he was justified" (TJ to Colvin, 20 Sep. 1810).

[44] Entry in SJPL under 14 Dec. 1790.

[45] Document III.

[46] Charles Thomson in 1789 had called Sargent's attention to resolutions of

rejection of a justification resting on necessity and the peremptory manner of his challenge must have arisen from a conviction of the importance of curbing at the outset any tendency toward arbitrary methods. This must have seemed to him all the more necessary because the principle of local autonomy that he advocated would presumably have caused the territorial government to be better adapted to local circumstances, thus avoiding the inconveniences that resulted in this and other instances from a retrogressive and imitative colonial system.[47] Further, the very characteristics of settlement in the Northwest that had elated Edward Carrington both as politician and as investor in the land company in which the governor and the secretary were shareholders would have caused Jefferson to be alert to the danger that private aims would injure the public interest. Under the circumstances and in view of the fundamental distinction that he observed between the two concepts of territorial government, Jefferson must certainly have reached an accord with Randolph before he made his recommendation. This inference is supported by what followed.

Washington, long convinced that the inhabitants of the frontier were generally a low order of people defiant of external authority who required the discipline and order of firm government, lacked both Jefferson's confidence in the men on the western waters and his concern about the alteration that had taken place in the character of the territorial system. On reading the extracts of executive proceedings that Jefferson had sent him, his "mind naturally recurred" to the letter in which St. Clair had justified his conduct.[48] He apparently sent his secretary to discuss the matter with the Attorney General. Randolph made some inquiries and Lear, to obtain the answers, went to the office of the Department of State to consult the territorial papers. There he "was informed that the Secy. of State had taken the necessary measures to satisfy the Atty. Genl. upon those points."[49] A week later Washington requested a formal opinion from the Attorney General.[50] No text of the ruling appears to have survived, but there can be little doubt that Randolph concurred with Jefferson. Washington perceived the force of the latter's argument, but did not embrace its conclusion. He wrote St. Clair, but did not transmit the opinion of the Attorney General as a guide for future conduct as Jefferson had suggested. Indeed, he did not make it an official matter at all, but imbedded his observations in what he was careful to describe as a private and friendly letter. Assuring St. Clair that he was fully cognizant of the extenuating circumstances set forth in his letter, he based his gentle

Congress and suggested that these required Indian affairs to be reported with the executive proceedings (Thomson to Sargent, 11 Mch. 1789, Carter, *Terr. Papers*, II, 189). John Jay advised St. Clair about proceedings against John Connolly in the absence of federal laws against treason (St. Clair to Jay, 13 Dec. 1788; Jay to St. Clair, 28 Jan. 1789, same, II, 166, 188). But no challenge had theretofore been made to executive proceedings.

[47] For an analysis of other problems and inconveniences resulting from the shift in territorial policy represented in the Ordinance of 1787, see Philbrick, ed., *Laws of Illinois Territory 1809-1818*, ccclxxxvii-cccclxxvii.

[48] Washington to St. Clair, 2 Jan. 1791 (Carter, *Terr. Papers*, II, 320).

[49] Lear to Randolph, 21 Dec. 1790 (DNA: RG 59, MLR).

[50] Lear to Randolph, 28 Dec. 1790 (same).

admonition not on fundamental principle but on the adverse political consequences that might flow from mistaken or malicious views of a "momentary stretch of power":[51]

The imperfect State in which the Legislation of the North Western Territory is, the want which the Executive has often felt of the necessary coadjutors to adopt even the most urgent laws, and the peculiar situation of a frontier Country, are circumstances which may not strike every one who will observe that the Executive has gone beyond its proper powers. It therefore becomes a matter of high importance that the utmost circumspection should be observed in the conduct of the Executive; for there are not wanting Persons who would rejoice to find the slightest ground of clamour against public Characters; and paying no regard to the absolute necessity of the case which caused a momentary stretch of power, nor the public good which might be produced by it, they would seize the occasion of making impressions unfavorable to Government and possibly productive of disagreeable effects.

I have therefore thought it best to give you this intimation in a private and friendly letter, that by circumspection malice itself may be disarmed.

Washington had put the justification in terms even stronger than those employed by St. Clair, finding in local circumstances both an absolute necessity and the cause of the imperfect state of legislation. No copy of this private letter found its place among the territorial records beside the journal of executive proceedings and the extracts that had evoked so emphatic a recommendation from the Secretary of State. Its influence being confined to the privacy of St. Clair's personal papers, among which it remained, it could not become a guiding precept for future governors of territories. Washington's sympathetic warning observed the letter of Jefferson's recommendation, but in spirit it coincided perfectly with the concept of territorial administration that had prevailed over the one he believed most consonant with republican principles.

Winthrop Sargent, who had departed from the Northwest Territory when St. Clair returned there in mid-September and who arrived in Philadelphia just as Congress opened, was himself both victim and beneficiary of distant and centralized territorial administration. Obliged by law and by St. Clair's absences to serve for considerable periods as acting governor and also expected to act as secretary for Indian affairs, he was not given any adjustment in salary for these functions and even his repeated appeals to the Board of Treasury for reimbursement of advances made for printing, stationery, the territorial seal, and such official necessities had been met by silence.[52] Sargent ap-

51 Washington to St. Clair, 2 Jan. 1791, with "(Private)" at head of text (FC in DLC: Washington Papers; Washington, *Writings*, ed. Fitzpatrick, xxxi, 190-1, and Carter, *Terr. Papers*, ii, 320, present text from RC).
52 Sargent to Washington, 1 Aug. 1790 (Document v, enclosure).

pealed to Washington in a letter that, as he later explained, had been written before he left the territory but omitted from the official proceedings "by some mistake."[53] The explanation is not convincing. The question of adequate compensation, quite understandably, had long been a matter of concern to Sargent. The letter appealing to Washington showed on its surface that he intended it to be placed before Congress. His covering letter of explanation, emphasizing that he desired only such attention to it as Washington might think proper, suggests that Sargent omitted his appeal from the considerable bulk of official proceedings not by oversight but in order to single it out for attention, perhaps in the hope that a matter remediable only by legislation might be laid before Congress under the potent signature of the President. If so, the effort failed. There is no evidence that Washington responded in writing, but he must have communicated informally either through Lear or Jefferson, perhaps about mid-December when the former sent to the latter the omitted letter and its covering note to be placed among the territorial records.[54] For it is certain, as Sargent himself later testified, that he discussed the question with the Secretary of State at some time during the crowded days at the end of the year. The interview must have been brief and circumspect, not alone because of the pressures and the nature of the problem, for Jefferson and Sargent, as each must have perceived at once, stood on vantage points that separated them far more than did their offices.

In some respects the Secretary of the Northwest Territory and the Secretary of State to whom he was required to report had much in common. Both were members of the American Philosophical Society. Both shared a common interest in botany, horticulture, geology, meteorology, and western antiquities. Both had a humanitarian concern for the American Indian. But an immense chasm separated them in their political attitudes and in their grasp of the implications of self-government. This profound difference was epitomized in their views of the public domain and in their concepts of public office. Whereas Jefferson, as a matter of principle, had purposely refrained from engaging in land speculation lest his private interests conflict with his duty as legislator, Sargent, like Robert Morris and many other enterprising contemporaries, sought and utilized public office in such a way as to advance private interests. Indeed, at the very time of his meeting with Jefferson, Sargent was mingling private and public matters in a manner characteristic of those who had brought about the alteration in the territorial system. He later claimed that near the end of 1790, as he inaccurately put it, he had "obtained permission to come on to Philadelphia to urge in person this Suit" for increased salary.[55] But this only concealed the primary object that he had in view.

For the fact is that he had absented himself from his post on the eve of a critical expedition against the Indians in order to travel first to New York and Boston to consult William Duer, Richard Platt,

[53] Sargent to Washington, 13 Dec. 1790 (Document v, enclosure).
[54] Document v.
[55] Sargent to Randolph, 20 May 1794; Sargent to Washington, 30 Dec. 1793 (Carter, *Terr. Papers*, II, 463, 480).

Royal Flint, and Andrew Craigie about the pressing state of their speculations. Late in 1789 one of his closest associates in speculation, Richard Platt, treasurer of the Ohio Company and fellow member of the Society of the Cincinnati, had sent him—*"for your eye only"*—a report from Joel Barlow about his European agency for the Scioto Company. The urgent communication went by express and contained an astonishing command from a private citizen to a public official. Because of the magnitude and suddenness of the development, Platt wrote, Sargent should come to New York without fail during the winter: "You not only *must, but shall come,*" he added, and then explained that, in order to induce others to invest, Sargent should execute a power of attorney authorizing Platt to dispose of such proportion of shares of the Ohio Company as would be an adequate reimbursement of his advances—though the power of attorney of Sargent himself would be used only as an inducement and then would be nullified. Platt repeated the injunction: *"You must and shall come on this winter."*[56] Behind this peremptory command lay a maze of concealed operations, shiftings of securities and certificates, and manipulations of the affairs of the Ohio and Scioto companies that were not penetrated by contemporaries and have not been adequately analyzed since.[57] But the letter was only the first of the alarms that disturbed Sargent's dreams of wealth in the fabulous valley of the Ohio.

In mid-summer of 1790 William Duer himself wrote "most pressingly" to urge Sargent to come to New York on the Scioto business. He was supported in this by Platt, who was concerned but professed to know little about it save that it was a matter of great magnitude that required "the best possible Management."[58] This was understandable. There had recently arrived in the United States several hundred French emigrants who believed they had purchased lands but in fact had not even acquired rights to participate in the single asset of the Scioto Company—an option to buy five million acres adjacent to the lands of the Ohio Company. Joel Barlow, who had kept his principals in the speculation informed of his actions but had received neither support nor directives from them, had executed the contract with a French company as a desperate alternative but with ardent optimism.[59]

56 Platt to Sargent, 15 Nov. 1789 (MHi: Sargent Papers). See note 59.

57 B. H. Pershing, "Winthrop Sargent: A Builder in the Old Northwest," Ph.D. dissertation, Chicago, 1927, is reproduced in the Microfilm Edition of the Winthrop Sargent Papers (MHi, 1965), of which the *Guide*, ed. Frederick S. Allis, Jr., p. 9-20, contains an excellent brief analysis of Sargent's character and career. A. B. Hulbert's "Andrew Craigie and the Scioto Associates," Am. Ant. Soc., *Procs.*, new ser., XXIII (1913), 222-36, and his "The methods and operations of the Scioto group of speculators," MVHR, I (1915), 502-15; II, 56-73, are useful studies based on a thorough examination of the sources that place the onus for secrecy and lack of good faith on Duer, Flint, and Craigie while exempting Cutler and Sargent. See also Davis, *Essays in the earlier history of American corporations*, I, 213-53, and T. T. Belote, "The Scioto Speculation and the French Settlement at Gallipolis," *University Studies*, Cincinnati, ser. II (1907), III, p. 1-82. A fresh study of these interconnected ventures, with particular attention to their impact upon domestic and foreign affairs, is much needed.

58 Platt to Sargent, 14 July 1790 (MHi: Sargent Papers).

59 Barlow revealed to Sargent months after his arrival in Europe that he had experienced "neglect and want of Confidence" at the hands of his principals, and

The clamors of the ill-prepared and misled French settlers presented only one menacing aspect. Another circumstance disturbing to the little group of speculators was the rise in value of the public securities with which the Ohio and Scioto purchases were made, a development presaging that the contract of the former would not be fully met and that of the latter not at all.[60] Instruments had been drawn up in the spring of 1790 to meet the crisis and Cutler had signed one of them authorizing Duer, Flint, and Craigie to seek deeds from the United States, to carry into effect the contract made by Barlow with the Compagnie du Scioto, and to do whatever else was necessary to establish title to the lands on the Ohio and Scioto rivers.[61] Sargent refused

---

added: "I have not received a Syllable since I have been in Europe on the Subject of my Mission." He announced that the contract with the Compagnie du Scioto would be completed in a few days, urged Sargent to hold fast to the contract with Congress and not to "let the despair of any of the Concern induce you or them to give up anything. All will be easy if you have but patience" (Barlow to Sargent, 25 July 1789, MHi: Sargent Papers).

[60] Platt anticipated in 1789 that the rise in the value of securities would prevent the Ohio Company from raising funds to complete its second payment on the contract. He told Sargent that if the Company ended up with less than a thousand shares, as he was certain would be the case, Sargent should insist on his getting ten shares since, "out of zeal for the Company *and particularly your agency*," he had assumed for many who would not reimburse him (Platt to Sargent, 12 Oct. 1789, MHi: Sargent Papers).

[61] Three documents were drawn up: (1) a power of attorney from Cutler and Sargent to Duer, Flint, and Craigie authorizing them to seek deeds from the United States to the Scioto lands described in the contract of 27 Oct. 1787, signed by Cutler alone and dated Apr. 1790; (2) articles of agreement between Cutler and Sargent on the one hand and William Duer on the other, dated 20 Apr. 1790 and signed by Cutler and Duer, setting up a trust to execute Barlow's contract for "the sale of the said Tract of land . . . lately made in Europe," to seek deeds from the United States, to make conveyances, to negotiate other contracts with the federal government or other corporate bodies, to make dividends, and to deposit receipts in the banks of Boston, New York, Philadelphia, "or the National Bank of the United States, should any such be established," to examine the accounts of the agent in Europe, and so on, with Duer, Flint, and Craigie to be designated as the first trustees; and (3) a power of attorney from Sargent to Cutler authorizing him to act in his place in all matters respecting the foregoing articles of agreement, not dated and not signed (MHi: Sargent Papers). The effect of these instruments, had Sargent executed the last, would have been to place upon the Scioto group the responsibility for supporting the settlement agreed upon by their agent—a responsibility which, by Sargent's refusal to sign, fell upon the shareholders of the Ohio Company, among whom in Sargent's agency were several officials in the Treasury and War departments: Alexander Hamilton (5 shares) and Henry Knox, Joseph Nourse, and Henry Kuhl who held one share each (names listed in Sargent's copy of *Articles of an Association by the name of the Ohio Company* [Worcester, 1786]; copy in MHi: Sargent Papers).

In his reply to the charges of the French emigrants, Sargent, placing entire responsibility upon Duer and resting upon purely legal defenses, exposed the true object of his mission: "when I was over the mountains . . . in the Winter of 1790 I learned so much as to be convinced that you must be distressed beyond [Duer's] or any individual capacity to relieve and would therefore have prevailed upon him to come forward with an ingenuous representation to Congress which I then imagined and am now convinced must be your dernier resort—but from some European expectations he declined it. It was my intention to have urged this advice until I had succeeded or come forward myself with the business but my public duties suddenly called me to the Territory—tho' not before I had reason to believe your situation would have been laid before Congress in that session"

to join in this. As he later explained it, the business had been prosecuted "contrary to the original Plan, which was only to use or mortgage the Lands of which the Company had obtained Preemption, without taking upon themselves any of the Risks attending Settlement."[62] These risks were a natural consequence of the actions of Sargent and his Scioto associates from 1787 on in engaging in that form of speculation which Senator Maclay dismissed with contempt as *"dodging"*—selling in Europe before buying in America.[63] But Sargent stubbornly refused to accept the implications of the risk he had embraced at the outset.

This refusal to accept any of the responsibilities of settlement—that is, to support Barlow, whom he had recommended for the agency—was the obstacle to be overcome during the period when Sargent was at the seat of government ostensibly seeking only an increase in salary. Cutler informed him a month before the interview with Jefferson—Sargent was then in Boston—that he had made an offer to Duer and his associates of one-third of his and Sargent's moiety in return for a guarantee against loss on the speculation. Cutler thought that if Duer declined, others might be found who would engage in it, or, if not, favorable accounts from France might accomplish the result before the speculation became known. To show his confidence in Sargent, he gave him a power of attorney to handle his share of the moiety and added:[64]

(Sargent to the inhabitants of Gallipolis, 23 Nov. 1792, Carter, *Terr. Papers*, II, 419-20). In other words, he was attending the third session of the First Congress in an effort to place upon the public the consequences of his own private speculations, while exculpating himself and avoiding all risks by placing the legal and moral responsibility upon others. Manasseh Cutler thought this defense against the charges of the French emigrants "a fair, candid, and perfectly just representation" (Cutler to Sargent, 8 Mch. 1793, MHi: Sargent Papers). But the character of the two men had been impeached long before by their associates in the Ohio Company and, shielding themselves while impeaching *their* friends Duer and Barlow, they steadfastly proclaimed their own honor and rectitude of conduct ("Your Character and mine was highly impeached," Cutler wrote Sargent on 19 Nov. 1788, same). Sargent also sought privately to point suspicion toward Cutler (see note 64).

[62] Sargent's memorandum concerning the Scioto undertaking, dated at Marietta, 17 Mch. 1791, saying what he later said to the allegations of the citizens of Gallipolis—that he had declared to Duer, Cutler, and Platt at the home of the last in 1787 that he would only authorize Platt to advance an equal moiety of £500 to sustain the agency in Europe and that Duer, by some flattering letters from Barlow, had been "induced to depart from our original Intention and involve himself in all the accumulated Expenses of Settlement." He not only placed entire responsibility upon Duer but expressed his belief that Manasseh Cutler and Rufus Putnam had encouraged him in this course. He also stated that he had refused to sign new instruments of indemnification against loss "because *they* now refuse any Engagements for taking the Risks of the Expences of the Adventure upon themselves" (MHi: Sargent Papers). See foregoing note. The memorandum, set down immediately upon his return to Ohio, was intended to exculpate himself and was the basis of his later reply to the inhabitants of Gallipolis.

[63] Maclay, *Journal*, ed. Maclay, p. 216.

[64] Cutler to Sargent, 16 Nov. 1790 (MHi: Sargent Papers). Sargent later informed Flint, who was the trustee designated by Cutler and himself, that he thought "there was something like a System proposed and adopted by Duer and Cutler" and that, while he had been informed of the powers vested by Cutler in

There will be a degree of hazard untill the business is absolutely closed. If you can not accomplish it, I wish you to put the matter in train to be done in your absence. Flint and Platt will, no doubt, afford their aid. I am disposed to make great sacrifice of my part of the concern, if it can not be otherwise obtained, to screen myself from loss on my own share. But if you give up any part of my interest, I wish you previously to consult and obtain the approbation of Flint, to whom I have written on this subject. . . . After all the trouble, anxiety and abuse I have received, it would give me pain to give up, unnecessarily, my share in a speculation that should eventually prove profitable. But, on the other hand, it would give me much greater pain to find myself completely ruined by a failure.

The French emigrants on the Scioto might focus their bitterest recriminations upon the Secretary of the Northwest Territory, but Sargent, who at the moment he met the Secretary of State held the key to the prosecution of the Ohio and Scioto interests before Congress, was ready to let the burden of the settlers' plight fall upon shareholders of the Ohio Company. This was a counsel of prudence that enabled him to avoid ruin as well as risks. For in another year Duer, Flint, and Macomb were in debtors' prison and Platt was a ruined man who expected any day to exchange his domestic "palace . . . for a jail."[65] Sargent escaped obloquy as well. But his reply to the French emigrants was more convincing to his collaborator Cutler than it could be to a dispassionate reader even of the imperfectly preserved and carefully screened record.

For these two key figures in the Ohio and Scioto ventures were as deeply involved as Duer, Flint, and Craigie in the negotiations with the Board of Treasury, in the seeking of influence in Congress, in the agency of Barlow, in their concealments from those they had induced to invest in the Ohio Company and from each other, and in their confusing manipulation of the closely-managed affairs of both companies. Even Edward Carrington, whose aid in Congress had been so beneficial and who repeatedly urged Sargent to manage his shares as he would his own, was unable to elicit responses to his inquiries.[66]

---

the trustees for receiving deeds from Congress "and indeed negotiating the whole Business of our Purchase or Preemption right with *that body*," this was all he had known (Sargent to Flint, 14 Apr. 1791, same). This scarcely comports with the information in the above letter, in which Cutler also informed Sargent that he had left with Duer, Flint, and Craigie the instruments recited in that possessed by Sargent and that they could not therefore refuse to execute the one they had forwarded. Cutler advised Sargent to execute it and leave it with Flint, without even consulting Duer. As for Sargent's proposal of Barlow for the European agency in place of Flint, who had first been considered, Duer had in the beginning hesitated to act upon it (Duer to Sargent, 17 Feb. 1788, same).

[65] Platt to Sargent, 10 May 1792 (MHi: Sargent Papers).

[66] When Carrington accidentally fell in with Captain Guion who was accompanying the French emigrants to the Scioto, he wrote Sargent: "Upon what footing stands this Transaction? Write me—is it a partial concern or does the advantage extend to the whole Company? I have repeatedly requested you upon every occasion to turn the Interest I hold in the Company in any way that you may judge for my advantage" (Carrington to Sargent, 28 July 1790; see also his letters of 10 Jan. and 8 June 1789, 10 Mch. 1793, and 12 Feb. 1794, the last

Equally involved with Duer and others in seeking the government's support of their exploitation of the national domain, they were distinguished from them by the disingenuousness of their defense. Warned at the very outset of the impossibility of keeping the Scioto venture secret, of the consequences of confusing the two enterprises, and of being accused of breach of trust, they plunged ahead.[67] When the exposure came, Sargent, in a haughty and indignant letter rejecting the imputation that the funds or credit of the Ohio Company had been manipulated, defended the Scioto associates on the ground that they were entitled to greater advantages because they had made advances beneficial to the Ohio Company.[68] But the advances, except for pledges toward the expenses of the agency in France, had not been made by Sargent and Cutler. They were eager to be involved in the dealings with government and speculators and continued so long after the outbreak of rebellious murmurings among the Ohio shareholders and after the French emigrants began their recriminations. But what they consistently avoided were the risks and responsibilities entailed in the contract they had agreed to conceal from their friends and fellow shareholders.

Sargent, thus preoccupied with negotiations among the small group of speculators in the hope of realizing the dream without incurring the risks, provided the only account of the interview with the Secretary of State. That account was biassed but also revealing. Speaking for the President, so Sargent later reported, Jefferson stated that his proper recourse lay with Congress—not because Washington did not deem his appeal reasonable, but because "it was improper that any pecuniary Concerns should originate with him." Then Jefferson went further and made a comment whose intent may have been lost upon Sargent. Had Sargent been absent from the capital, Jefferson reportedly said, means would have been found to bring the matter to the attention of Congress. But since he was already there, "he had better take measures for that purpose himself."[69] Sargent obviously accepted this as meaning that Jefferson supported the justness of his claim, which may indeed have been the case. But Jefferson's observation lends itself even more plausibly to the supposition that he may have been hinting that such a matter of personal interest as a salary increase was not sufficient justification for a public official to absent himself from his post at a critical time. In any case, Sargent had no alternative but to accept the negative response. He cast the letter to Washington in the form of a memorial to Congress and then remained in Philadelphia for several weeks hoping for approval and attending to his negotiations with Duer, Platt, and others.[70] When he left Ohio in mid-September

---

alluding to Sargent's charge of mismanagement in the affairs of the company and stating that he had heard this from others but had himself been "really indifferently informed"; MHi: Sargent Papers).

[67] Rufus Putnam to Sargent, 8 Oct. 1787 (same).

[68] Ebenezer Hazard to Sargent, 19 Aug. 1788; Sargent to Hazard, 14 Aug. [i.e., Sep.] 1788 (same).

[69] Sargent to Randolph, 20 May 1794 (Carter, *Terr. Papers*, II, 480).

[70] The memorial, submitted to the House of Representatives on 29 Dec. 1790 by John Laurance in Sargent's behalf, was referred to the Secretary of the

he had indicated to St. Clair that he intended to return by Christmas. But by that time the governor himself had departed and the Northwest Territory was left without any executive officer. Early in January the inhabitants of Marietta assembled and addressed an appeal to Congress. Militia from Pennsylvania and Virginia could not be called to protect them from Indian incursions, they declared, and the national government had not afforded them protection for several months. With the governor and secretary both absent, they wrote, the situation was one of the "utmost danger."[71] Washington peremptorily directed Sargent to return to his post without delay.[72] He arrived there at the beginning of spring, having been absent from his post for upwards of half a year for no other avowed purpose than to prosecute his appeal for increased salary.[73]

Such in brief, was the man who came before the Secretary of State late in 1790—the very personification of those aspects of the altered territorial system that had evoked Jefferson's emphatic warning to Monroe and had aroused his profound concern lest the men on the western waters be alienated and bring on the most dreaded of evils, disunion. For Sargent was not only a reflection of those "swarms of officers" emanating from the center of power under British rule that had been indicted in the Declaration of Independence: he was also the prototype of a long succession of territorial governors, secretaries, and judges who followed thereafter under a colonial system that had been deliberately imitative of the one that had prevailed before independence. The dangerous consequences of such a departure that Jefferson had predicted must have seemed visible to the Secretary of State as he contemplated the man who shared executive power over citizens of the frontier but had not been given that power by them. But, as Monroe had pointed out, the essential principle of Jefferson's territorial system had been preserved. In part because of this the intangible bonds were strong enough to survive even the injuries of those who gave precedence to private over public interest when the two came into conflict.

Treasury (JHR, I, 344; printed in Carter, *Terr. Papers*, II, 318 Hamilton reported on 31 Jan. 1794 (same, II, 473-4).

[71] Petition from the inhabitants of Marietta, 6 Jan. 1791 (*Federal Gazette*, 21 Feb. 1791).

[72] Sargent, in a later letter to Washington, expressed it in circumspect terms: "your pleasure for my immediate return . . . was signified to me" (Sargent to Washington, 30 Dec. 1793, Carter, *Terr. Papers*, II, 463). It is possible that the presidential command was transmitted through the Secretary of State.

[73] Sargent left Philadelphia on 1 Feb. 1791 and arrived in Ohio at the beginning of March (Sargent to Uriah Tracy, 10 Mch. 1794, enclosing documents in support of his memorial, MHi: Sargent Papers; Carter, *Terr. Papers*, III, 334).

I. Tobias Lear to the Secretary of State

SIR   United States December 8th. 1790

In obedience to the Commands of the President of the United States I have the honor to transmit herewith sundry communications of the proceedings of Government in the western Territory from Jany to July 1790 made by the Secretary of the said Territory to the President of the U.S. upon which the President requests your opinion as to what should be done respecting them.

I have likewise the honor to transmit, by the President's order, a Letter and packet from the President of the National Assembly of France directed to the President and Members of the American Congress. This direction prevented the President from opening them when they came to his hands; and he yesterday caused them to be delivered to the Vice-President that they might be opened by the Senate. The Vice-President returned them unopened, with an opinion of the Senate that they might be opened with more propriety by the President of the U.S. and a request that he woud do it and communicate to Congress such parts of them as in his opinion might be proper to be laid before the Legislature.—The President therefore requests that you would become acquainted with their Contents[1] and inform him what (if any) should be laid before Congress. Another Letter from the National Assembly addressed particularly to the President is enclosed herewith for your perusal. The President has the translation of this letter. With the highest respect I have the Honor to be Sir Yr. most obedt. St.,

TOBIAS LEAR
Secy. to the Presdt. U.S.

Dft (DNA: RG 59, MLR). Tr (same). Recorded in SJL the same day. For the enclosures from the National Assembly of France, see TJ's report to the President, 9 Dec. 1790. For the enclosures respecting the Northwest Territory, see notes to Winthrop Sargent to the President, 31 July 1790, following.

[1] In Dft the preceding five words are interlined in substitution for "open and inspect the Letter and packet," deleted.

ENCLOSURE

Acting Governor of the Northwest Territory to the President

Vincennes, County of Knox
July 31st. 1790.

SIR

The Absence of the Gouvernour having made it my Duty to carry into Effect as far as possible the Resolution of Congress of the 29th. of August 1788 respecting the Inhabitants of Post Vincennes, I beg Leave to report, *not only* my Proceedings under that Resolution, but some Circumstances which, in my Opinion, ought at this Time to be communicated as very materially concerning the Interests of the United States as well as Individual Settlers.

The Claims and Pretensions of the People have very generally been exhibited, but notwithstanding they were early advertised upon this Business by Proclamation of Governour St. Clair given at Kaskaskias, March last, and have since been repeatedly called upon by me, yet I have no Doubt there are a few Instances of Inattention and Neglect, which I have provided for by the Publication No. 8, a Copy of which is herewith annexed.[1]

For all the Possessions which appear to have been made by French or British Concessions I have issued Warrants of Survey as by the last Page of No. 2, No. 3, 4, 5, 6, and 7 of the Land Records, for the County of Knox. Copies of all which accompany this Report.[2]

I have also directed that the four hundred Acre Lots to be given to every Head of a Family should be laid off for the Persons named in No. 1 and 2 and allotted, Excepting those, that might fall to the Absentees mentioned in the Pages b and c of No. 2, which are to be retained as *there* set forth until the Pleasure of Government is known.

I beg Leave Sir to observe that there are a few Instances where the ancient Inhabitants (by removing from Vincennes to the Illinois Country or from that Country to this Place) can not be included under the Description of Persons entitled to Donation Lands, and they *humbly solicit* that Congress would be graciously pleased to consider their Situation and admit them to participate in the general Bounty.

I think it necessary here to remark Sir that although the Lands and Lots which have been ordered to be surveyed, appear from very good oral Testimony to belong to those Persons under whose Names they are respectively entered, either by original Grants to them made, Purchase or Inheritance Yet there is scarcely one Case in twenty where the Title is complete, owing to the desultory Manner in which public Business has been transacted, and some other unfortunate Causes.—The original Concessions by the French and British Commandants were generally made upon a small Scrap of Paper, which it has been customary to lodge in the Notary's Office, who has seldom kept any Book of Record, but committed the most important Land Concerns to loose Sheets, which in Process of Time have come into the Possession of Persons that have fraudulently destroyed them or, unacquainted with their Consequence, innocently lost, or trifled them away, for by French Usage they are considered as Family Inheritance, and often descend to Women and Children.—In one Instance, and during the Government of Mr. St. Ange here, a Royal Notary run off with all the Public Papers in his Possession, as by a Certificate produced to me, And I am very sorry further to observe that in the Office of a Mr. Legrand which continued from the Year 1777 to 1788, and where should have been the Vouchers for important Land Transactions, the Records have been so falsified, and there is such gross Fraud and Forgery as to invalidate all Evidence and Information which I might otherwise have acquired from his Papers.

In Addition Sir to the ancient Possessions of the People of Vincennes under French and British Concessions, there is about one hundred and fifty Acres of Land constituting a Part of the Village and extending a Mile up the Wabash River in Front of their improved Claims, *which* was granted by Mr. St. Ange to some of the Pyankeshaw Indians;

allotted into small Divisions for their Whigwhams and by them occupied and improved until the year 1786 when the last of them moved
off, selling individually as they took themselves away their several
Parts and Proportions. The Inhabitants now hold this Land, parcelled
out amongst them in small Lots, some of which are highly improved
and have been built upon before and since 1783. But imagining that a
Confirmation of any Indian Purchase whatever might virtually involve
some future Questions of Magnitude in this Territory, I have postponed all Order upon the Subject until the Pleasure of Congress can
be known. In the mean Time giving to the Claimants my private Opinion that they would be permitted to retain them, either by free Gift or,
for some small Consideration.

A Court of Civil and criminal Jurisdiction established at this Place
by J. Todd, Esqre. under the Authority of Virginia in June 1779 and
who Eked out their Existence to the Summer of 1787, have during that
long Period continued to make large Grants of Lands, *even* by their
own Acknowledgements, and without more Authority for so doing
than is set forth in No. 9.[3] Many of the Concessions which have been
exhibited to me in their Name, They deny to have had any Knowledge
of, and indeed there are some Reasons to conclude they may have been
Forged in the Office of the Mr. Legrand before mentiond, who was a
Servant of the Court and in whose Hand Writing the Deeds have all
been made out.

I cannot find from any Informations I have been able to acquire
that Mr. Todd ever delegated any Power of granting Land in this
Country, or, in Fact, that he was endowed with it himself.—On the
contrary, I find by the Acts of Virginia of 1779, that the Lands Northwest of the River Ohio were expressly excepted from Location, And
that it was declared no Person should be allowed Preemption or any
Benefit whatever, from settling on this Side the said River, And the
Governour was desired to issue his Proclamation requiring all Persons
to remove themselves and, in Case of Disobedience, to make use of
an armed Force, this not to extend to French and other old Inhabitants
actually settled on or before that Time in the Villages of Post
Vincennes and upon the Mississippi. It appears, however, by a Proclamation of Mr. Todd's No. 10, given[4] at Kaskaskias the 15th. Day of
June 1779, that a Kind of Authority was meant to be implied somewhere in the Country to grant Lands not only upon the River Bottom
and Prairies under the French Restrictions, but in *large Quantities*
and with more Latitude at a Distance therefrom. And twenty-six
thousand Acres have been granted away from that Time to 1783
inclusive, and to the Year 1787 (when General Harmar checked the
Abuse) twenty-two thousand more, generally in Parcels of four
hundred Acres, tho' some are much smaller and do not exceed the size
of House Lots. The Court has also granted to Individuals, in some
Instances, Tracts of many Leagues square, but a Sense of the Impropriety of such Measures has prevented the bringing forward those
Claims.—Notwithstanding that some of the four hundred Acre, and
smaller Lots, were possessed on and before 1783, yet the Authority
whence they were derived has been such that I could not consider them
as *rightful* CLAIMS; They are however Sir in a few Instances under

considerable Cultivation and Improvements, and some of the Plantations and many of the small Lots which have been granted by the Court since that Time are now cultivated in Tillage, and have been possessed by the present Claimants at much Expense. But by far the greatest Number of them were obtained at the Cost of Office Fees only and remain to this Hour in a State of Nature, or with no other Alteration than has been necessary to convert them into Sugar Camps.

Upon the Subject of those Lands Sir, A Petition has been presented to me by, and in Behalf of Eighty Americans, setting forth that they were induced to come into this Country by the Court of Post Vincennes with every Assurance of their Authority to make Grants, that in good Faith of this they have formed their Establishments at considerable Expense and must be involved in Ruin unless the Generosity of Congress shall permit their holding them.

The French Inhabitants have also petitioned me upon the Subject of Court Grants; some of which are now under Cultivation at no small Expense and Labour. I beg Leave Sir to lay the Situation of those People before Government, most respectfully representing that the Welfare and Prosperity of a Number of Industrious and good Citizens in this Territory must depend very much upon their Order.

A Petition has also been presented by the Inhabitants of Vincennes, praying a Confirmation of their Commons, comprehending about 2400 Acres of good and 3000 Acres of sunken Lands. They have been, it appears, thirty Years under a Fence which is intended to confine their Cattle within its Boundaries and keep them out of their wheat Fields. For, contrary to the Usage of Farmers generally, the Cattle are here enclosed, and the cultivated Lands are left at large, excepting on those Parts which immediately approach the Common. But this Fence, and quiet Possession under the French and British Governments they seem to imagine entitles them to a good prescriptive Right. It has been the Usage of the Commandants here to make all their Grants in Writing, and as this has not been produced or any Evidence of it I think it my Duty to refer the Matter to Congress as I am not authorized to decide upon it.

One other Petition, Sir, I am constrained to introduce. It has been signed by 131 Canadian, French and American Inhabitants, all enrolled in the Militia, setting forth that many of them were Heads of Families soon after the Year 1783, that from their Situation they are liable to and willing to perform an extraordinary Proportion of Military Duty, And soliciting that Congress would be pleased to make them a Donation of Lands.—In Justice to the Petitioners I think it incumbent on me to observe, that the commanding Officer of the regular Troops here has been obliged in some Instances to demand their Services for Convoys of Provisions up the Wabash River; and from the Weakness of the Garrison and the present Difficulties of Communication with other Posts, and the Ohio, that he may have frequent Occasion for their Aid, which I have no doubt will be yielded at all Times, with the greatest Cheerfulness.

[Before I close this Letter Sir, I must take the Liberty of representing to Congress by Desire of the Citizens of this Country, and as a Matter which I humbly conceive they should be informed of, that there are, not only at this Place, but in the several Villages upon the Mississippi considerable Claims for Supplies furnished the Troops of Virginia before, and since 1783, which no Person yet has been authorized to attend to, and which is very injurious to the Interests and Feelings of Men who seem to have been exposed to a Variety of Distresses and Impositions by Characters pretending to have acted under the Order of that Government.][5]

The People of Vincennes have requested me to make known their Sentiments of Fidelity and Attachment to the Sovereignty of the United States and the Satisfaction they feel in being received into their Protection, which I beg Leave to communicate in their own Words, by the Copy of an Address presented me on the 23d. Inst:

If in this long Letter of Report and Representation I may appear to have tediously dwelt upon the Claims and Pretensions of the People of this Country, I request Sir, that it may be attributed to that Desire which I feel at all Times, faithfully to execute the Attentions necessary to Individual Interests and the great Duty I owe to Government.—

With every Sentiment of Respect To your Excellency and Congress I have the Honour to be Sir Your most obedient Humble Servant

WINTHROP SARGENT

RC (DNA: RG 59, NWT, M/470); at head of text TJ penciled the following directions to Remsen: "Copy this in its entirety except Nos. 8. 9. and 10." (for TJ's instructions about these exceptions, see notes to Enclosures 2 and 4 below; for "Nos. 8. 9. and 10." see Enclosures 5, 6, and 7 below). Tr (DNA: RG 46, Senate Records, 1st. Cong., 3rd. sess.); entirely in Sargent's hand; at head of text: "Copy of a Letter from Winthrop Sargent Esquire to the President of the U. S." FC (OHi: Journal of Executive Proceedings, NWT); differs in some particulars from RC as indicated in textual notes below (for a description of the manuscript of this journal, see Carter, Terr. Papers, III, 263, note). Tr (DNA: RG 59, MLR, in Remsen's hand).

Enclosures: (1) Copy of Journal of Executive Proceedings in the Northwest Territory from "Jany. 1st. 1790 to June the 11th. by Order of his Excellency Arthur St. Clair And to the last of June (in the Absence of the Governour) under Direction of the Secretary" (Tr in DNA: RG 59, NWT, M/470; in Sargent's hand, with signed caption on cover as partially quoted, also signed and attested by Sargent at end of text; full text from FC in O printed in Carter, Terr. Papers, III, 294-315). For extracts from Journal made by TJ and transmitted to the President, see Enclosure, Document III. Both this

copy of the Journal for the first six months of 1790 and that for July (see following note) were forwarded with the above letter from Vincennes on 2 Aug. 1790 (same, III, 329).

(2) Copy of Journal of Executive Proceedings in the Northwest Territory "for the Month of July (in the Absence of the Governour) under the Order of the Secretary" (Tr in DNA: RG 59, NWT, M/470; in Sargent's hand, with seal and signed caption on cover as partially quoted, also signed and attested by him at end of text; full text from FC in O printed in Carter, Terr. Papers, III, 316-29). Above the seal on cover of Tr, TJ penciled the following direction to Remsen: "The proceedings of July 18. from this quire are to be copied as No. 8. No other part is wanting."

(3) Warrants of survey and instructions from Arthur St. Clair to Antoine Girardin, 29 May 1790, directing him to survey for the inhabitants of Cahokia lands possessed by them "on or before the year 1783 in order that the same may be confirmed to them . . . as soon as may be that Patents of confirmation may issue" (Tr in DNA: RG 59, NWT, M/470; attested by Sargent as "From the Land Records No. 1 for the District of Cahokia," accompanied by names of claimants and descriptions of claims; full text in Carter, Terr. Papers, II, 263-76).

(4) Warrants of survey and instruc-

tions from Winthrop Sargent to Samuel Baird as "From the Land Records No. 1 for the Town of Vincennes and County of Knox" (Tr in DNA: RG 59, NWT, M/470; entirely in Sargent's hand; bearing at head of text: "Town at Post Vincennes July the 13th 1790" and at its close: "Vincennes July 31st. 1790. Winthrop Sargent"; another Tr in DNA: RG 46, Senate Records, 1st Cong., 3rd. sess.). At head of text TJ wrote the following instructions in pencil to the departmental copyists (first line only partly legible): "Copy this page [separately and then page?] by page that the numbers may answer. Add as No. 8. proceedings of July 18. from the Journals. 9. and 10. from the end of the report of July 31." The complete text of this document is printed in ASP, *Public Lands*, I, 11-15, but with a confused numbering of the enclosures. It is partially printed in Carter, *Terr. Papers*, II, 285-7, but on the mistaken assumption that at least two different documents were involved—that is, the instructions issued by Sargent to Baird on 13 July 1790 and those issued on 31 July 1790. But the latter date, set down at the close of the document, refers (i) to the time at which the different instructions were copied off so as to form a single enclosure in the above letter to the President written on the same day, and (ii) to the time at which Sargent delivered to Baird the final instructions and warrants that had begun to be drafted on or soon after 18 July 1790 (same, III, 329). There were, in fact, three separate instructions from Sargent to Baird embraced in this transcript, each of which is signed, the first and last of which have separate salutations, and only the first of which bears a date unequivocally attached to it.

Neither the nature of this transcript nor the allusion in the above letter to No. 1, "No. 2, No. 3, 4, 5, 6, and 7"— to say nothing of the penciled notations by TJ concerning "Nos. 8. 9. and 10." (notations that are not noted in either of the printed texts)—can be understood without reference to the fact that this is a single document of seven folded sheets, each having four pages and bearing at the top of its first page a number corresponding to that in Sargent's numerical sequence. His No. 1 and the first page of No. 2 embrace the first instructions of 13 July 1790 to Baird containing "an accurate List of the Heads of Families settled at

Post Vincennes on or before the year 1783" and giving him warrant to survey donation lots for the persons named. It also gave him assurance that "Patents will issue as soon as your Returns are made into my Office." This is the only part of the enclosure printed in Carter, *Terr. Papers*, II, 285-7. The first and second pages of sheet No. 2 are, as Sargent indicated, designated respectively as "b" and "c." These pages embrace the second set of instructions and concern settlers who came "certainly within the Letter of the Resolution of Congress" as being entitled to donation lands, but who had become absentees. In this second directive, which is undated, Sargent instructed Baird to lay off the lots of the fifteen listed absentees for "their Use and Benefit if Congress shall so direct, or otherwise to revert to the United States." The fourth page of No. 2 contains the third directive to Baird, also undated. It directed Baird to survey, at the expense of the owners, the lands of those inhabitants claiming "Possessions . . . by French or British Concessions." This instruction and its accompanying list of names embrace all of the remainder of the enclosure as described by Sargent—that is, "the last Page of No. 2, No. 3, 4, 5, 6, and 7" (full text with names printed in ASP, *Public Lands*, I, 12-15).

(5) This is the enclosure designated by Sargent and by TJ as "No. 8." It was a public notice by Sargent to the inhabitants of Vincennes, dated 18 July 1790, stating that those who had not produced evidence of their claims should do so within sixty days; that warrants would be issued to Baird for making surveys; that patents to confirm "ancient claims and Possessions" would be made out as soon as the surveyor had filed his returns; and that, in cases where records of early concessions had been lost and evidences of assignment were missing, it would be necessary to produce the testimony of some of the old inhabitants, since it was "not impossible that 'a Confirmation to such Claimants might be an Act of very great Injustice'" (Tr in DNA: RG 59, NWT, M/470, from Journal of Executive Proceedings "for the month of July"; another Tr in DNA: RG 46, Senate Records, 1st. Cong., 3rd sess.; text from FC in O printed in Carter, *Terr. Papers*, III, 322).

(6) This is the enclosure designated by Sargent and by TJ as "No. 9." It is

a letter from François Bosseron and other magistrates of Vincennes to Sargent, dated 3 July 1790, informing him, in response to his inquiry as to the reasons the court had assumed authority to make grants of land, that they had done so because the commandants had "always appeared to be vested with the powers to give Lands" and because the deputy of Colonel Todd, J. M. P. Legras, had "verbally informed the Court of Post Vincennes that when they should judge it proper to give Lands . . . they might do it" (Tr in DNA: RG 59, NWT, M/470; at head of text: "No. 9"; another Tr in DNA: RG 46, Senate Records, 1st. Cong., 3rd. sess.; full text printed in Carter, *Terr. Papers*, II, 232-3).

(7) This is the enclosure designated by Sargent and by TJ as "No. 10." It is a copy of a proclamation by John Todd, Jr., dated 15 June 1779, enjoining all persons from making further settlements in Illinois county except on the method employed by the French inhabitants and declaring that this was necessary to ascertain the vacant lands as well as to guard against trespass from the "Number of Adventurers who will shortly over run this Country" (Tr in DNA: RG 59, NWT, M/470; at head of text: "No. 10."; full text printed in Carter, *Terr. Papers*, III, 326-7, note: see also Todd to TJ, 19 Aug. 1779).

(8) Address of Antoine Gamelin and others (judges and militia officers of Vincennes) to Winthrop Sargent, 23 July 1790, on behalf of the citizens of the town, expressing their personal respect, their "full approbation" of measures taken by Sargent in respect to their government and the adjustment of their claims, and their attachment to the United States: "While we deem it a singular blessing to behold the principles of free government unfolding among us, we cherish the pleasing reflection, that our posterity will also have cause to rejoice at the political change now originating. A free and efficient government, wisely administered, and fostered under the protecting wings of an august Union of the States, cannot fail to render the citizens of this wide extended Territory securely happy in the possession of every public blessing.—We cannot take leave, Sir, without offering to your notice a tribute of gratitude and esteem, which every citizen of Vincennes conceives he owes to the merits of an officer who has long commanded at this post. The unsettled situation of things for a series of years previous to this gentleman's arrival, tended in many instances to derange, and in others to suspend the operation of those municipal customs by which the citizens of this town were used to be governed. They were in the habit of submitting the superintendence of their civil regulations to the officer who happened to command the troops posted among them. Hence, in the course of the late war, and from the frequent change of masters, they laboured under heavy and various grievances. But the just and humane attention paid by Major Hamtramck, during his whole command, to the rights and feelings of every individual craving his interposition demands and will allways receive our warmest acknowledgments.—We beg you, Sir, to assure the supreme authority of the United States of our fidelity and attachment; and that our greatest ambition is to deserve its fostering care, by acting the part of good citizens" (Tr in DNA: RG 59, NWT, M/470; full text printed in Carter, *Terr. Papers*, II, 291-2).

(9) Winthrop Sargent to Gamelin and others in response to the foregoing, [25 July 1790]: "Next to the Happiness which I derive from a Consciousness of endeavouring to merit the approbation of the sovereign Authority of the United States by a faithful discharge of the important Trusts committed to me, Is the grateful Plaudit of the respectable Citizens of this Territory. And be assured Gentlemen that I receive it from the Town of Vincennes upon this occasion with singular Satisfaction. In an Event so very interesting and important to every Individual as is the Organization of civil Government I regret exceedingly that you have been deprived of the Wisdom of our Worthy Governour. His extensive abilities and long Experience in the Honourable Walk of Public Life might have more perfectly established that System which promises to you and Posterity such great Political Blessings.—It is certain Gentlemen that the Government of the United States is most congenial to the dignity of human Nature, and the best Possible Palladium for the Lives and Property of Mankind.—The Services of Major Hamtramck to the Public, and his humane attention to the Citizens while in Command here have been highly meritorius. And it is with great Pleasure that I have officially expressed

to him my full approbation thereof.—Your dutiful sentiments of Fidelity and Attachment to the General Government of the United States shall be faithfully transmitted to their August President" (Tr in DNA: RG 59, NWT, M/470; full text printed in Carter, *Terr. Papers*, II, 292-3). Both the identity of the covering letter of transmittal and the date of Sargent's response to the address have been brought into question (same, II, 291, note 71; 292, note 80). But the fact that the above letter to the President mentions the address, while its text is on a leaf conjugate with that on which the text of the response appears, sufficiently establishes its character as an enclosure. The address and the response were both printed in Bache's *General Advertiser* for 10 Dec. 1790 and the date of the latter is there given as 25 July 1790. Since the response to the address

bears no date in the copy transmitted to the Department of State, it is clear that it was Sargent himself who supplied the texts to Bache.

For another letter that was intended to be enclosed with the above but, according to Sargent, was omitted by mistake, see Document v, note.

1 FC reads: ". . . provided for by the Publication of the 18th."
2 This sentence does not appear in FC.
3 FC reads: ". . . No. 9 annexed to the Land Records."
4 FC reads: "It appears however by Proclamation No. 10 (annexed to the Land Records) and given by Mr. Todd. . . ."
5 Passage in brackets (supplied) comprises the extract enclosed in TJ to Washington, 14 Dec. 1790 (see Document IV below).

II. Report of Secretary of State on Lands at Vincennes

The Secretary of state having had under his consideration the Report, made by the Secretary of the government North West of the Ohio, of his proceedings for carrying into effect the resolution of Congress of Aug. 29. 1788. respecting the lands of the inhabitants of Post Vincennes, makes the following REPORT thereon to the President of the United States.

The Resolution of Congress of Aug. 29. 1788. had confirmed in their possessions and titles the French and Canadian inhabitants and other settlers at that post, who, in or before the year 1783. had settled there, and had professed themselves citizens of the U.S. or any of them, and had made a donation to every head of a family, of the same description, of 400. acres of land, part of a square to be laid off adjoining the improvements at the post.

The Secretary of the North Western government, in the absence of the Governour, has carried this resolution into effect, as to all the claims to which he thought it could be clearly applied. There remain however the following descriptions of cases on which he asks further instructions.

1. Certain cases within the letter of the resolution, but rendered doubtful by the condition annexed to the grants of lands in the Illinois country. The cases of these claimants, fifteen in number, are

specially stated in the paper hereto annexed No. 2. and the lands are laid off for them, but remain ungranted till further order.

2. Certain persons who, by removals from one part of the territory to another, are out of the letter of the Resolution, but within it's equity, as they concieve.

3. Certain heads of families, who became such soon after the year 1783. who petition for a participation of the donation, and urge extraordinary militia service to which they are exposed.

4. 150. acres of land within the village, granted, under the former government of that country, to the Piankeshaw Indians, and on their removal sold by them in parcels to individual inhabitants, who in some instances have highly improved them both before and since 1783.

5. Lands granted both before and after 1783. by authority from the Commandant of the post, who, according to the usage under the French and British governments, thinking himself authorised to grant lands, delegated that authority to a court of civil and criminal jurisdiction, whose grants before 1783. amount to 26,000 acres, and between that and 1787 (when the practice was stopped) to 22,000 acres. They are generally in parcels from 400. acres down to the size of house lots; and some of them under considerable improvement. Some of the tenants urge that they were induced by the court itself to come and settle these lands, under assurance of their authority to grant them, and that a loss of the lands and improvements will involve them in ruin.—Besides these small grants, there are some much larger, sometimes of many leagues square, which a sense of their impropriety has prevented the grantees from bringing forward.—Many pretended grants too of this class are believed to be forgeries, and are therefore to be guarded against.

6. 2400 acres of good land, and 3000 acres of sunken do. held under the French, British, and American governments, as Commons for the use of the inhabitants of the village generally, and for 30. years past kept under inclosure for these purposes.

The legislature alone being competent to authorize the grant of lands in cases as yet unprovided for by the laws, the Secretary of state is of opinion that the Report of the Secretary of the North-Western government, with the papers therein referred to, should be laid before Congress for their determination. Authentic copies of them are herewith inclosed to the President of the United States.

[TH: JEFFERSON
Dec. 14. 1790.]

MS (DNA: RG 59, MLR); entirely in TJ's hand; date and signature have been removed, being supplied from PrC (DLC). FC (DNA: RG 59, Record of Reports of Thomas Jefferson). Tr (DNA: RG 46, Senate Records, 1st. Cong., 3rd. sess.). Entry in SJPL reads: "[1790. Dec.]14. Report Th: J. on Resolution Congr. respecting lands of St. Vincennes." Enclosures: (1) Winthrop Sargent to the President, 31 July 1790. (2) "Warrants of Survey and Instructions to Samuel Baird Esquire . . . July 1790." (3) "No. 8. Proceedings of July 18th from the Journals." (4) "No. 9." Bosseron and others to Sargent, 3 July 1790. (5) "No. 10." Proclamation of John Todd, Jr., 15 June 1779 (Tr of all enclosures in DNA: RG 46, Senate Records, 1st. Cong., 3rd. sess., bearing "Attest Samuel A. Otis Secy."; for text of Enclosure I and notes on others, see Document I and notes to its enclosures 4-7. See ASP, *Public Lands*, I, 9-16.

III. Report of Secretary of State on Executive Proceedings in Northwest Territory

The Secretary of state having had under his consideration the journal of the proceedings of the Executive in the North-Western territory, thinks it his duty to extract therefrom, for the notice of the President of the U.S. the articles of Apr. 25. June 6. 28. and 29. copies of which are hereto annexed.

Concieving that the regulations, purported in these articles, are beyond the competence of the Executive of the said government, that they amount in fact to laws, and as such could only flow from it's regular legislature, that it is the duty of the General government to guard it's subordinate members from the encroachment of each other, even where they are made through error or inadvertence, and to cover it's citizens from the exercise of powers not authorized by the laws, the Secretary of state is of opinion that the said articles be laid before the Attorney General for consideration, and, if he finds them to be against law, that his opinion be communicated to the Governour of the North-Western territory for his future conduct.

TH: JEFFERSON

Dec. 14. 1790.

MS (InHi). PrC (DLC). FC (DNA: RG 59, Record of Reports of Thomas Jefferson). Tr (DNA: RG 59, SDC), Entry in SJPL reads: "[Report Th:J.] on Proceedings of Govr. of N.W. territory against law."

ENCLOSURE

Executive Proceedings of the Northwest Territory

April 25th. 1790.

The Governor was pleased to issue the following Order, vizt. All the inhabitants are forbidden to entertain any Strangers, white, indian or negro, let them come from whatsoever place, without acquainting the Officer commanding the Troops of the names of such Strangers, and the place from whence they came. And every Stranger arriving at Cahokia, is ordered to present himself to the said Officer within two hours after his arrival, on pain of imprisonment.

June 6th. 1790.

The Governor, at Kaskaskias, was pleased to make the following Proclamation, vizt.

The practice of selling spirituous liquors to the Indians in the Villages being attended with very ill consequences, it is expressly prohibited; and all and every person transgressing this order, will be liable to be tried and fined at the pleasure of the Court of Quarter sessions of the peace: And as it may be necessary that spirituous liquors should be vended in small quantities to white travellers and others; to prevent all danger of imposition and extortion, no person whomsoever shall sell in any of the Villages or their environs, spirituous liquors to any white person, traveller or inhabitant in any quantity less than one quart at one time, without obtaining a licence from the Governor, which licence shall not be granted but upon the recommendation of the Justices of the Peace, in their Court of Quarter Sessions, and on his or their giving security in the sum of two hundred dollars, to abide by all the regulations made by Law respecting retailers of spirituous liquors, and the orders of the said Court of Quarter Sessions in the premises in the mean time. And for every offence he or they shall be liable to prosecution by indictment and fine at the pleasure of the Court, and to the forfeiture of their bonds. Nor shall any person undertake or exercise the calling or Occupation of an Innholder or Tavernkeeper, without obtaining in the Same manner, and under the same restrictions and penalties, a licence for so doing.

Proclamation.

Whereas his Excellency Arthur St.Clair esqr. the Governor and Commander in Chief of this Territory, did by Proclamation given at Kaskaskias the 10th. instant, strictly prohibit all persons not citizens of the United States or the Territory, from hunting or killing any kind of game within the same, either for the flesh or skins, upon penalty *not only* of forfeiting the flesh and skins which they might acquire, but also prosecution and punishment as trespassers. And it appearing to me to be particularly essential to the interests of this Country, that an observance of the order and prohibition should be obtained, I do hereby call upon all civil and military Officers, who now are or hereafter may be appointed, to use their best endeavours for detecting and bringing to Justice every person who shall violate the same. And Whereas it appears to me to be expedient that Government should receive information of all characters, foreigners and others, coming into the Territory, I do hereby order and direct that every person arriving at *this*, or any of the military posts of the United States within the same, should present himself to the commanding Officer of the Troops in two hours next after his arrival; and the Inhabitants are hereby forbidden to entertain such characters, whether whites, indians or negroes, without immediate information thereof to the said commanding Officers.

Given under my hand and Seal at the town of Post Vincennes and County of Knox this 28th. day of June A.D. 1790, and of the Independence of the United States the Fourteenth.

(signed) Winthrop Sargent.

June 29th. 1790.

It is to be considered as a standing Order hereafter, that no person enrolled in the Militia shall leave the Village or Stations for a longer absence than twenty four hours, without informing him (Major Hamtramck) or the commanding Officer for the time being, of their intention. And all intelligence or discoveries of Indians to be immediately reported.

(signed) Winthrop Sargent.

MS (DNA: RG 59, MLR); in Remsen's hand; at head of text: "Extract from the Journal of the Proceedings in the Executive Department of Government in the territory of the United States North west of the Ohio, reported to the President of the United States by Winthrop Sargent Secretary." PrC (DLC). FC (DNA: RG 59, Record of Reports of Thomas Jefferson). Tr (DNA: RG 59, SDC).

IV. Secretary of State to the President

Sir   Dec. 14. 1790.

I have the honour to inclose you the copy of a paragraph from the report of the proceedings of the Executive of the North-Western government, which may perhaps need the attention of the Secretary at war.—I am, with the most profound respect & attachment Sir Your most obedient & most humble Servant,

TH: JEFFERSON

PrC (DLC); at foot of text: "the President of the U.S."; entry in SJPL reads: "Winthrop Serjt. on claims against Virginia." FC (DNA: RG 59, Record of Reports of Thomas Jefferson). MS (DNA: RG 59, MLR); in Remsen's hand; at head of text: "Extract of a Letter from Winthrop Sargent to the President of the United States, dated Vincennes County of Knox July 31st. 1790." PrC (DLC). FC (DNA: RG 59, Record of Reports of Thomas Jefferson). For identification of enclosed extract, see note 5 to enclosure in Document I.

V. Tobias Lear to the Secretary of State

SIR   United States Decr. 16th. 1790

By the President's Command I have the honor to transmit the enclosed letter from Winthrop Sargent Esqr Secy of the Western Territory, to the President of the United States: which the President requests may be put with the communications from the Western Territory.—I have the honor to be with the highest respect Sir. Yr most Ob. St.

TOBIAS LEAR

S. P. U. S.

RC (DNA: RG 59, MLR). Not recorded in SJL. Enclosure: Winthrop Sargent to the President, 1 Aug. 1790, explaining that the duties of the governor, which he was required by law to assume at certain times, involved additional expenses for which no provision had been made and which his private finances could not defray; that, as Secretary, he had made applications to the Board of Treasury for reimbursement of advances made "for Stationary, Printing, Public Seal &ca." and these had all been met by silence; that the division of the Territory into counties and divisions, all of which needed to be supplied with copies of laws, proclamations, and ordinances, made it impossible for any one person, "tho' devoting his whole Time," to perform this duty; that Governor St. Clair had informed him it was expected he should also consider himself "as Secretary to the Indian Commission—a Business which in the Western Territory will probably for a long Time demand much Attention"; that when the superintendency of Indian affairs was given to the governor, his salary had been increased; that it was therefore to be presumed some further provision should be made for the office of secretary "if, contrary to the original System, it is to comprehend and include the Records of In-

dian Business"; and that, since more important concerns might prevent St. Clair from expressing himself on the subject as intended, he begged leave by this opportunity to lay before Congress both the matter of an increase in salary and the question of his advances, for "such Provision as they may deem meet" (RC in DNA: RG 59, NWT, M/470; Tr, MHi: Sargent Papers; text in Carter, *Terr. Papers*, II, 295-6); this appeal was in substantially the same language Sargent used in his memorial to Congress on 29 Dec. 1790 (same, II, 318-19; JHR, I, 344). On 13 Dec. 1790 Sargent sent this communication to Washington with the following comment: "The enclosed Letter, which I intended should have accompanied my last Official Communications from the Western Territory, has by some mistake been omitted.—Permit me now Sir to lay it before you requesting, *only*, as much Attention to it as your Excellency may deem proper" (DNA: RG 59, NWT, M/470). For a comment on Washington's response, see Editorial Note. In an undated memorandum Remsen recorded the addition of Sargent's letters of 1 August and 13 December 1790 to the documents transmitted by Lear on 8 December 1790 (same; see Document I).

VI. The President to the Senate and the House of Representatives

GENTLEMEN OF THE SENATE AND HOUSE OF
REPRESENTATIVES.   United States December 23rd 1790

It appearing by the Report of the Secretary of the Government North West of the Ohio, that there are certain cases respecting grants of land within that territory, which require the interference of the Legislature of the United States;—I have directed a Copy of said Report and the Papers therein referred to to be laid before you; together with a copy of the Report of the Secretary of State upon the same subject.

GO: WASHINGTON

RC (DNA: RG 46, Senate Records, 1st. Cong., 3rd. sess.); in clerk's hand, signed by Washington. The fact that this message was prepared by TJ is proved by entry in SJPL reading:

"[1791. Dec.] 14. Report Th: J. on Resolution Congr. . . . Communication for Congress on that subject." For enclosures see Document II and its enclosures.

VII. Governor of the Northwest Territory to the Secretary of State

SIR   [Philadelphia] febry. 2d. 1791

A few days I submitted to the Attorney General the form of a Patent for the confirmation of the Lands held by the Inhabitants on the Missisippi and at Post St. Vincennes. I had conceived myself authorised By the Instructions of Congress of the 29th. of August [1788][1] to grant such Patents of confirmation and that it was expected from me but the Attorney is of Opinion that the Instructions does not give the Power, that no Power to that End is in Existence, and consequently, a Law for the purpose is necessary. I would beg the favor Sir that you will bring the Subject before Congress, for it is of importance that those People be quieted in their Possessions as soon as possible. With great Respect &c.

Dft (O: St. Clair Papers); at foot of text: "Mr. Jefferson Esqr. Secretary of State." Entry in SJL indicates that RC (missing) was written from Philadelphia and received the same day.

The opinion of the Attorney General has not been found. St. Clair's request

for it appears in an undated letter written probably in late Jan. 1791: "I shall be very much obliged to you Sir for your Advice about the Possessions of the ancient Settlers on the Missisippi, and that if you think it necessary, you would bring the doubtful points I have mentioned before the President of the united States, and permit me to observe, Sir, that when the very great Distance that Country is and ever will be from the Seat of the Government, there seems to be a necessity for the Titles of Confirmation being made within the Territory or at least a Provision that they may be put on record there" (Dft in O: St. Clair Papers; full text in Carter, *Terr. Papers*, II, 319-20, where the conjectured date is assigned to 1790 and probably to December; in view of the above letter to TJ, however, a later date would seem more plausible). Randolph may have given his opinion in conversation as he had done earlier on the question of the distinction between laws enacted and laws adopted by the territorial legislature (same, II, 319). He also no doubt suggested that the matter of obtaining legal authority for issuing patents confirming the titles of Illinois inhabitants should be laid before the Secretary of State, hence the above letter.

1 Preceding ten words are placed in inverted order to accord with markings on Dft indicating that St. Clair wished RC (missing) to read as above.

VIII. Governor of the Northwest Territory to the Secretary of State

SIR   Philadelphia February 11th. 1791

I beg leave to present the enclosed report of my proceedings in the country on the Mississippi[1] in the course of the last year, and to request that you will please to lay it before the President of the United States.[2] A part, if not the whole of them, has no doubt been transmitted by the secretary of the territory from time to time; but as I was directed to report them to Congress,[3] they are now collected into one view. I am sensible Sir, that it may have been expected to have been done earlier, but the situation[4] I have been in ever since last June during which time I have been obliged to travel near upon five thousand miles, either upon horseback, or in an open boat and separated from my papers prevented it.[5]—I have the honor to be with great respect Sir, Your most obedient servant   AR. ST. CLAIR

Tr (DNA: RG 59, NWT, M/470); clerical omission in text supplied as indicated in note 4 below. 1st Dft (O: St. Clair Papers); mutilated but containing some deletions in phraseology proving that it was the composition draft. 2d. Dft (O: St. Clair Papers); differing slightly from 1st Dft and from Tr as indicated in notes below. Not recorded in SJL or SJPL.

1 2d. Dft reads ". . . proceedings in the Illinois country."

2 2d. Dft reads: ". . . request that you will lay it before Congress."

3 2d. Dft reads: ". . . as I am directed by the Resolution of Congress of the 28th. of August 1788 to report

specially they are now collected into one View."

4 Preceding two words omitted by clerk and supplied from 2d. Dft.

5 2d. Dft contains the following passage amended in part or deleted from (missing) RC: ". . . near upon five thousand Miles, either in an open Boat or upon Horseback, and often separated from my Papers rendered it impossible. The enquiring into the Claims and Titles of the People of that Country which are all in french and the necessity of translating every public communication into that Language, without any Person to assist me, for no Person that had a competent knowledge of both was to be found, was a

very laborious Business will account for some of the Papers which accompany the Report appearing in that language, and that I had not always Leisure to make the translations into English will be an excuse for that impropriety."

ENCLOSURE

Report of Governor of the Northwest Territory

Pursuant to the Resolution of Congress of the 28th. of August 1788, and in Obedience to the Instructions of the President of the united States of the 6th. of October 1789, I embarked at Fort Harmar for Kaskaskia on the 20th. day of December following and arrived on the 5th. day of March 1790. The great length of time consumed in this Voyage was owing to a delay met with at the Falls of Ohio for want of Provisions for the Escort—to being afterwards frozen up in the Mississippi for fifeteen days; and to being again obliged to stop to repair the Damage sustained by the Vessel, which was hurried by the impetuosity of the Stream upon a sunken Tree in the middle of the River, where the Danger of being cast away was very narrowly escaped.

Immediatly on my Arrival the County of St. Clair was erected by Proclamation:—a Placart was published requiring the Inhabitants to exhibit a State of their Claims to Lands in that Quarter, and a List of the Heads of Families. It was a considerable time before any Claims were presented, owing partly to the Ignorance of the People, very few of whom are able either to read or write; and partly to their being entirely unacquainted with the English Language:—they were at length brought forward, and such of them as were found to come within the Resolution of Congress are contained in the Paper marked No. 1.—No. 2 is a List of the Inhabitants, and No. 3 a copy of the Placart.

No Plan of the Town of Kaskaskia could be found either in the public Offices or in the Hands of Individuals. I was therefore obliged to order one to be taken (of which No. 4 is a copy) as it would otherwise have been impossible to describe the Lotts which were to be confirmed. [Mr. Samuel Baird was appointed to do that Duty, as well as to survey the Lands held by the People, and to run the Lines that had been directed by Congress to embrace the Donations. On an Examination of the Claims, however, it was found that many Grants of Land had been made which would fall to the eastward of the Line, to be drawn from the Mouth of the River au Marie; and as all Grants that proceeded either from the Government of France, that of Great Britain, or of the State of Virginia on or before the Year 1783 were to be confirmed, the running of that Line was delayed until Congress should be informed that it would not take in all the Claims, and therefor appeared to be incurring an unnecessary Expense.][1] [Orders of Survey were issued for all the Claims that appeared to be founded agreeably to the Resolution of Congress, and Surveys were made of the greater part of them—a Part only of those Surveys, however, have been returned because the People objected to paying the Surveyor; and it is too true

[194]

that they are ill able to pay. The Illinois Country, as well as that upon the Ouabash, has been involved in great Distress ever since it fell under the american Dominion:—with great cheerfulness the People furnished the Troops under General Clarke and the Illinois Regiment with every thing they could spare, and often with much more than they could spare with any Convenience to themselves:—most of the Certificates for those Supplies are still in their Hands, unliquidated and unpaid; and, in many Instances where Application for payment has been made to the State of Virginia, under whose authority the Certificates were granted, it has been refused.—The Illinois Regiment being disbanded, a Set of Men, pretending the authority of Virginia, embodied themselves; and a scene of general Depradation and Plunder ensued:—to this succeeded three successive and extraordinary Innundations from the Mississippi which either swept away their Crops or prevented their being planted:—the loss of the greatest part of their Trade with the Indians, which was a great Resource, came upon them at this juncture, as well as the hostile incursions of some of the Tribes which had ever before been in friendship with them; and to these was added the loss of their whole last Crop of Corn by an untimely frost:—extreme Misery could not fail to be the Consequence of such accumulated Misfortunes. The Paper No. 5 contains the Orders for a Compensation to the Surveyor; and No. 6 is the Representation of the People praying to be excused from paying it.]²

[A Gentleman, of the name of Todd, had been appointed by the Governor of Virginia Lieutenant of the County of Illinois, and some few grants of Land are said to have been made by him, altho' by his Instructions, which he put upon record at Kaskaskia, he has no Authority to that purpose, but seems rather to have been restrained:—A Copy of these Instructions were transmitted by the Secretary. On Mr. Todds leaving that part of the Country a Person by the Name of De Numbrun was substituted, who made Grants of Land without number: The Power of granting Lands was also assumed by the civil Courts that had been established, and that assumed Power they used very liberally, still pretending, however, that they had been authorised so to do by Mr. Todd, who is stiled Grand Judge for the united States. —It is most probable that such Power was never delegated to the Courts by Mr. Todd; at least it does not appear. All those Grants have been rejected; but I beg leave to suggest, that it might be proper to allow a right of preemption to those who have actually settled and made improvements under them. Some of the Parties seem, respectively, to have had two different Objects in view—the Applicants, the engrossing Lands for a very small Consideration; and the Grantors the accumulation of perquisites: the Courts and sub Lieutenants having exacted four Dollars for each Grant.

There are a number of american Settlers in possession of such Grants, whose claims have been equally rejected. Their Case seems to be a hard one. Not doubting the authority of the Courts which they saw every day excercised, they applied for Lands and obtained them, and made Settlements in consequence, distinct from those of the french; but having removed into that Country after the Year 1783 they do not come within the Resolution of Congress which describes who are to

be considered as ancient Settlers and confirmed in their Possessions;—
As Americans they have been the peculiar Objects of Indian Depredation, while their Neighbours the french, from having had much intercourse with the Indians, and frequently intermarrying with them, until
very lately were generally safe;—they have in consequence been driven
off of the Lands they had improved and have lost both their time and
their labour. No. 7 is a Representation from them upon this Subject.][3]
[Having finished the Business at Kaskaskia, as far as it was possible at that time, on the 5th. day of April I embarked, and proceeded
up the Missisippi to Cahokia, having stopped at Fort de Chartres, and
visited the Village of the Prairie du Rocher which is about a League
distant from it, in Land, on the way. Mr. Baird had been directed to
make the Surveys there, as well as at Kaskaskia, and the same
Objections to paying for them were raised there as at the latter place.
No. 8 is a power to certain of the Inhabitants to make Representations
to me on the Subject, which was done.][4] [No. 9 is a Plot of the
reserved Tract including Fort Chartres. It is however to be observed
that part of this Tract appears to have been granted when the Country
was in possession of the French.][5]
From the Mouth of the Kaskaskia River, which is a very beautiful
stream that takes its rise a great way in the Country, and is navigable
by Boats for a considerable distance, and on the west bank of which
the Town is situated, the Missisippi is very rapid as indeed it is from
the mouth of the Ohio to that place, with a great many very difficult
and dangerous passes: every where indeed the Current in the middle
of the stream, is too strong to be overcome by Oars; Boats are therefore obliged to keep as close to the shore as possible, and then in many
places cannot ascend without towing. The navigation of course might
be very easily interrupted, or prevented altogether, were the Spaniards
or the Indians disposed to attempt it; and the more so as, in some of
the most difficult places, it is necessary to keep the spanish Shore on
board; a Communication however from Fort Massac on the Ohio (or
even some distance above it) with Kaskaskia, by Land, may easily be
opened:—The distance is from fifty to sixty Miles. The Country is
high and the Soil proper enough for a Road, and no considerable
Water intervenes but the River au Vase, which is generally fordable at
large Riffle which presents itself directly in the Course:—the tedious
and dangerous navigation of the Missisippi would be thereby avoided.
Above the Missouri River, the Missisippi becomes comparatively a
gentle and pellucid Stream, whereas below it is at all Seasons extremly
turbid. Above the Illinois River it is truly a gentle Stream, its current,
as I have been informed no where exceeding three Miles an hour.
The Village of Cahokia is situated on a small Creek of the same
name, in a fertile plain and about half a League from its Mouth;
but being surrounded with Marshes, it is very unhealthy in the latter
part of the Summer and the Autumn. The River however affords a
safe and convenient harbour for Boats. It discharges itself nearly opposite to the spanish Village of St. Louis, and is navigable for two
Miles beyond the Town. Half a League lower down the Country and
about an equal distance from the Missisippi is the small Village of the
Prairie du pont, which is generally considered as part of Cahokia.

Here, as at Kaskaskia, no Plan of the Town was to be found, and of course I was obliged to order one to be taken, but a copy of it does not accompany this Report, as by some accident it has been left behind. The Villages at the Prairies du Rocher and du Pont do not appear to have been ever laid out. The People have built upon the Lands their Lands, which have generally small fronts, in a contiguous, but irregular manner, which has given to those Places something of the appearance of Towns. [The same steps were taken to obtain a knowledge of the Lands that were claimed by the People here as at Kaskaskia, and after due Examination Orders of Survey for such as fell within the Resolution of Congress were put into the hands of Mr. Girardin, the only Person that could be found in all that Country who understood any thing of Surveying. There are a good many Persons in that Quarter also whose Claims have been rejected, who, nevertheless, may be properly considered as having an equitable Right, at least to the preemption.][6]

Previous to the issuing any Orders of Survey at Cahokia, it became necessary to decide upon a Claim, set up by the Seminary of Quebec, to a piece of Land four Leagues square, granted, many Years ago, by the Officers then commanding in the Country for the King of France, to the Missionaries of Cahokia and Tamarois. The Bounds of this Concession embraced all the Settlements at Cahokia and the Prairie du Pont, and they had been made, generally, with the consent of the Missionaries for the time being, so long as the Mission subsisted; when it had dropped settlements (within the Bounds) had been permitted by military Officers, both french and English. After a very careful Examination into all the Circumstances it appeared that the Mission of Cahokia and Tamarois had been dropped before the Country was ceded to Great Britain, that it had never been reestablished while it remained under the Dominion of that Power, and that it did not exist now; the present Curé not being a Missionary, but a Parish Priest supported by the Inhabitants, and, that the pretensions of the Seminary of Quebec were futile and groundless. It was therefore considered as a Tract of Land that had reverted for want of Heirs, and was by Proclamation, of which No. 10 is a Copy, reunited to the Domain of the united States; and the Inhabitants were put upon the same foot as the other ancient Settlers. The Survey, mentioned in the Proclamation to have been ordered, was not made because, it afterwards came out, that the King of France had disaproved of the Grant and resumed the Soil. No. 11 is the deposition of Joseph La Bussiere the Notary who published the Edict of the french King respecting it; and No. 12 a Remonstrance of the Inhabitants respecting a sale that had been made of a part of it, by an Attorney for the Seminary of Quebec. No. 13 the Letter from the Superior of that Seminary mentioned in the Proclamation.

[No Returns of Survey from Cahokia are as yet come to hand and it is probable that not many have been made, as the same Objections to paying for them were raised here as elsewhere, and the Inhabitants of that Place are joined in the Remonstrances which have been made by those of the other Villages.][7]

It was not possible to establish the Courts of Justice, nor the Militia, in the County of St. Clair until Cahokia had been visited, and then it was difficult to establish them conformably to the Law; and no Alteration in the Law could take Place at that time because the Judges, who form a part of the Legislature, were not present. The Difficulty arose from these Circumstances: The Villages and Settlements were at a great distance from each other, not any of them were sufficiently peopled to admit of being made a distinct County, the whole afforded barely a sufficient number of Persons who were in any degree qualified to fill the necessary Offices; Justice could not have been administered had the Sessions of the Courts been confined to any one Place, even the most central; for besides the distance, there was considerable danger in passing and repassing. Under these Circumstances no Person would have been found who would have taken upon himself the Office of a Magistrate; neither could the attendance of Juries have been compelled, and the greatest confusion must have ensued. The Judges of the County Court of Common Pleas were by Law limited to five and not less than three. The Expedient therefore of dividing the County into three districts was fallen upon, tho not stricly warranted by Law, and the Judges so distributed as to make the holding of that Court Practicable; and it was ordained that a Session of that Court, of the General Sessions of the Peace, and of the Probate, should be held in each district, but all as Sessions of the same Courts respectively; and the Prothonotary of the Common Pleas, the Clerk of the Peace and the Judge of Probate were directed to appoint deputies and open Offices in each District. The Proclamation for this Measure has been transmitted by the Secretary of the Territory and is in the Office of the Secretary of State. The Measure has since received the Sanction of the Legislature.

By the Ordinance for the Government of the Territory the Laws and Customs which had prevailed among the ancient Settlers are to be continued so far as respects the Descent and Conveyance of real property; the mode of conveyance was an Act before a Notary, and filed in his Office, of which an attested Copy was delivered to the Party. To fulfill that part of the Ordinance it was necessary that Notaries public should be appointed, and one was commissioned at Kaskaskia, one at the Prairie du Rocher, and one at Cahokia. The Inhabitants of the County were also formed into a Regiment of Militia and Commissions issued for a Lieutenant Colonel and all the subordinate Officers.

[The Donations to the ancient Settlers have not been laid out because, at Kaskaskia and the Prairie du Rocher no Person could be found to do it. At Cahokia an Authority was given to Mr. Girardin for that purpose, but nothing, I presume, has been done in consequence of it, for the Alteration that was made in the location of these Donations by the Act of 29th. of August, from the west to the east side of the Hills or ridge of Rocks, throws them at such a distance from their present possessions, (the Hills being of a considerable breadth and not very fit for Cultivation) that, in the existing Circumstances of the Country, they could not possibly occupy them. They humbly pray that the location pointed out by the Act of the 20th. of June 1788 may be restored.]⁸ [No. 14 is a representation respecting their common. What they set forth is true both with respect to their having been long in the occupation of it and the Quality of what they ask for upon the Hills.]⁹

[Great Numbers of People have abandonned the Illinois Country and gone over to the spanish Territory. A Claim however is still kept up by them to their ancient possessions; but it is to be remarked that very few Grants were made by the french in fee simple. When any Person quitted their possessions, the Soil seems to have reverted of course to the Domain of the King, and was regranted at the pleasure of the Officers commanding. It is presumed that, strictly, the Possessions of all those who have so expatriated themselves are fallen to the united States, had they even been granted originally in fee simple, and may be disposed of as they shall see fit, but the loss of the People is severely felt;—may I be permitted to suggest that a Law declaring those Possessions escheated unless the former owners return and occupy them within a certain time would not be an improper Measure.]¹⁰

[At Kaskaskia the Jesuits held valuable Possessions. The Buildings are gone entirely to ruin, but the Lands are still of some value. On the suppression of the Order in France the Officers of the french King disposed of their property at that place by public Sale, but before the Sale took place the Country had been ceded to Great Britain, a circumstance that was not known there. The british Officer who took possession for that Crown considered the Sale as illegal, and laid hold of the Property; and the purchaser, a Mr. Beauvais, and his Descendants, have been kept out ever since. A son of Mr. Beauvais now lays claim to it in virtue of the purchase, and throws himself upon the United States to be confirmed in what yet remains of the property, for which his Father paid a very large sum of Money.]¹¹

The Commerce of the Illinois Country is of some importance in itself, but more so when considered as connected with the spanish side of the Missisippi. The Villages on that side of the River having been originally settled by the french, and under the same Government as that part which is now in the possession of the united States, the connection between them is still very intimate, and favors a commercial intercourse which, tho' illicit, might be carried on by the Citizens of America without risque. It is carried on at present without risque, but is, unfortunately, almost entirely in the hands of the british. Even much the greatest part of the merchandize for the trade of the Missouri River is brought from Michilimackinac by that of the Illinois, partly by the spanish Subjects themselves, and partly by british Traders. The manner is this. The spanish Subjects either introduce them at once, in consequence of a secret convention with their commandants, or they are brought down to Cahokia and landed there, and afterwards, carried over to St. Louis as opportunities can be found. What is brought by the british Traders, the spanish Subjects purchase and pay for on the american side, taking all the risque that attends the introducing them into their own Country upon themselves. The Furs, in which these Goods are generally paid for, Deer Skins answering better than Furs at the new Orleans market, are carried to Canada by the same Communication, that is to say up the Illinois River; up the Chicagoo; and from thence, by a small portage into the Lake Michigan, and along that Lake to Michilimackinac; or from the Chicagoo up the

River au Plein and by a portage into the same Lake. In the spring of the Year the Waters of the Michigan and the Chicagoo rise each to such a height that the intermediate Space is entirely overflowed, and is passable by the Vessels in use there, which are bark Canoes, but which carry a very considerable Burthen, and are navigated by three or by five Persons.

The Commerce of that Country is of some Importance also as an Object of revenue, for, if the Impost on Importations was extended to it, some Money would be produced by it; but the principal advantage would be that it would contribute to turn the Trade into the Channel of the united States. There is no doubt that the Furs of that Country might be brought up the Ohio River at as little, or even a less, Expense as attends the carriage of them to Canada. It has been tried by one Person, a Mr. Vigo, and found to answer, altho' the Goods he carried out were transported by Land from Philadelphia to Pittsburgh, and loaded with an Impost the Competitors were free from, they came to Market on better terms than those from Canada. Could those also be subjected to it, a decided advantage would be given to the american Trader.

There is another Communication between Canada and the Missisippi by the Ouisconsin River, a little above the mouth of which is the Prairie du Chien:—At that place there was a considerable Town while the Country was in the hands of the French: It has gone to ruin, but by that Communication the british carry on all the Trade of the upper part of the Missisippi, and at the Prairie du Chien they assemble twice in every Year in great Numbers; frequently, as I have been informed, to the amount of five or six hundred Persons. It would certainly be for the national honor that an Establishment that would command that Communication was made; but the great Distance and the Difficulties that might attend the supporting it, will probably prevent it at present.

An Establishment at the mouth of the Illinois River would also be very useful, both with respect to the Trade of that River and of the Misouri, but its being regularly innundated once or twice a Year forbids it; there is however an excellent Situation some distance lower down, and nearly opposite to the Misouri, at a Place called Payisa, that would answer: the Situation is high, the Air pure and healthy, and the Soil good, and across the Country, it is not more than three Miles distant from the Illinois River. It was the Opinion of the best informed Men I conversed with at Cahokia and from St. Louis, that if a Town were laid out there, and a small military Post erected it would be peopled immediatly, and St. Louis soon fall again into the same unimportant Situation it held before the Misfortunes of the Illinois Country; At present however St. Louis is the most flourishing Village of the Spaniards in the upper part of the Missisippi, and it has been greatly advanced by the People who abandonned the American side:—to that they were induced partly by the Oppression they suffered, and partly by the fear of losing their Slaves, which they had been taught to believe would be all set free on the Establishment of the american Government. Much pains had indeed been taken to inculcate that belief, (particularly by a Mr. Morgan of new Jersey), and a general desertion of the Country had like t[o have b]een the Consequence.—The construction that was given to that part of the Ordinance which declares there shall be neither slavery, nor involuntary servitude was, that it did not go to the Emancipation of the Slaves they were in possession of, and had obtained under the Laws by which they had formerly been governed, but was intended simply to prevent the introduction of others. In this Construction I hope the intentions of Congress have not been misunderstood, and the Apprehensions of the People were quieted by it; but the circumstance that Slaves cannot be introduced will prevent many People from returning who earnestly wish to return, both from a dislike to the spanish Government, and that the Country itself is much less desirable than on the american side. Could they be allowed to bring them back with them, all those who retired from that Cause would return to a Man.

There is a small Settlement up the Illinois River at the old Pioria Town. A Person of the Name of Mayet had been appointed commandant of the Militia there by General Clarke, and had continued in that Station until my arrival. As he was found to have considerable Influence with the Savages and had conducted himself with some degree of approbation, it was thought best to continue him, and a Commission of Captain in the Militia was given to him with the Instructions marked No. 15. Should it ever be thought proper to interdict the Communication with Canada by the Illinois River, there is no Place, at present in the possession of the united States, that would answer the End so well as this at the old Pioria Town:—The River is very narrow, and, the Channel lying close to the shore, every Boat is obliged to pass within small Musquet shot. It did not appear proper for me to interrupt that Communication at that time; for tho, on the principle of reciprocity, it would be perfectly justifiable in the united States they should be prepared to fill up the void that would thereby be created. The Savages, the Inhabitants and the Spaniards would at once be cut off from a very necessary Commerce;—It was for that Reason that Mayet was directed to suffer Persons to pass and repass who were furnished with passports. Several of the spanish Merchants applied for and obtained them, under the express Condition that they were not to attempt any trade with the Indians. This seemed to be all the hold that could then be well taken of it, and it held out the Idea that the Direction and restriction of the Communication was in the contemplation of Government.—By the Ordinance for regulating Indian Affairs no Person was to be allowed to travel thro' the Indian Nations without having received the approbation of the Superintendant. The Passports above alluded to were founded on that Clause of the Ordinance; but, by the Law lately enacted for regulating the Trade and intercourse with the Indians, it has not been reordained. A Doubt arises whether the Ordinance is not repealed by the Law, and that consequently any Person may travel thro the Indian Nations without asking permission of any one.

[A Contract subsists between Flint and Parker and the late Board of Treasury for a great Tract of Land in the Illinois Country.—No part of the Contract has I believe been complied with on their parts, and probably never will; but if it is not attended to, before a Law passes for erecting an Office for the Sale of the Lands, it may create embarrassments hereafter.][12]

The Papers No. 16 are the Orders for erecting Prisons and an assignment of Lotts to build them upon. The Lott at Cahokia had been reserved when the Town was first laid out, for public Use, and to that of Kaskaskia no Person laid Claim. No. 17 is the copy of a Proclamation forbidding Strangers to hunt in the Territory, and No. 18 another to prevent the cutting and carrying away building Timber and fire Wood to the spanish side. They were occasioned by the Representations of the People, that very great Injury was done to Individuals, and to the public, by the spanish Subjects cutting down and carrying away the Timber, while they were not allowed to bring even a Stone (which are plenty on that side and scarce on this) from that Shore; and that great Numbers of them assumed the Liberty of hunting Buffaloe for the Market of new Orleans, to the prejudice of the Citizens, who were not allowed to fire a Gun, upon any account whatever, on the spanish side. It would have been much more proper that many of those matters, which have been attempted to be regulated by Proclamation, should have been provided for by Law, but the Absence of the Judges prevented it.

Having had occasion to make some Representations to the spanish Commandant at St. Louis and Ste. Genevieve, altho they are not of much importance, yet I believe it is proper to submit the Letters that passed between us; they are contained in the bundle marked No. 19.— No. 20 is a Proclamation of the Governor of New Orleans: Since that, I am informed another has appeared permitting the Importation of every thing the growth of the Countries bordering upon the Missisippi and Ohio Rivers to that City, on the payment of fifteen per Cent ad valorem. I have not been able to obtain a Copy of it.

[When the two Emissions of Paper Money were called in by Congress, a considerable Sum of those Emissions were lodged in the Office of a Notary public at Kaskaskia, by the Direction of the Lieutenant of the Country of Illinois. There it yet remains, and the owners have received no satisfaction for it of any kind. They complain of this, and it would seem not without reason.][13]

There is some Obscurity in that part of the Ordinance which describes the Persons who are to be considered as ancient Settlers. The words are "who on or before the Year 1783 professed themselves citizens of the united States or any of them." A Doubt arises to what part of the Year the word *on* refers. Does it include the whole Year, or is it confined to the first day of it? Congress may perhaps think proper to give it a determinate application.

[Among the Claims for Land that have been rejected, there are several that are founded on purchases made from individual Indians, and the conveyances set forth that they were inherited from their parents, and were not the property of the Nation. It could not however be discovered that any Division of the Lands of the Kaskaskia Indians had ever taken place among themselves, and the Chief of that Nation has applied to be confirmed in a Tract of Land of about five or six thousand Acres, where their Village was situated not long ago; and which would take in the parcels that have been sold and applied for as above:—On this Claim no Decision has been made. It appeared to be a subject that ought to be referred to Congress, but I may be allowed to observe, if one Indian sale is approved, it is probable that a great many will be brought forward.][14]

At the Falls of Ohio, when on the way to Kaskaskia, information was received that the Inhabitants at Post St. Vincennes were in danger of perishing for want of Corn, their whole Crop of the last fall having been destroyed by an untimely frost. I immediately wrote to Major Hamtramack, and requested him, if he found the Case to be as it had been represented, to send, to the Agent of the Contractors for supplying the Troops, for as much as would be absolutely necessary for their preservation. No. 21 is an extract from the Letter to him on the Subject. It appeared to be a duty incumbent upon me to preserve the Lives of the Citizens of the Territory, and I flatter myself that the Measure will meet the approbation of the Legislature.

The Papers No. 22 and 23 are lists of the Heads of Families at Cahokia and the Prairie du Pont and [No. 24 is the Request of a Mr. Gibaut for a small Peice of Land that has been in the Occupation of the Priests at Cahokia for a long time, having been assigned to them by the french, but he wishes to possess it in propriety; and it is true that he was very useful to General Clarke upon many Occasions, and has suffered very considerable losses. I believe no Injury would be done to any One by his request being granted, but it was not for me to give away the Lands of the united States.][15]

[Before I close this Report it may be necessary to mention the necessity there is for a printing press in the western Territory. The Laws adopted or made by the Legislature are declared to be binding upon the People until they are disapproved by Congress. There is no way of giving them any publicity but by having them read at the Courts, and but few People become thereby acquainted with them. Even the Magistrates who are to carry them into Execution are strangers to them, for the Secretary does not conceive it to be his duty to furnish them with Copies: Indeed the Business of his Office increases so fast that it would be impossible to do it. Besides they are in English, and the greatest part of the Inhabitants do not understand a word of it. The translation of them therefore seems to be necessary, and that a sufficient number of them should be printed in both languages, and that can only be done in the Territory where the original Rolls are deposited.—Every public Act and communication of what kind soever I was myself obliged to translate into french, and having no Person to assist me, it made the Business extremly troublesome and laborious.][16] The Situation of Indian Affairs rendering it necessary that I should return to the Seat of Government I did by Letter resign the Government of the Territory into the hands of Mr. Sargent on the   day of   [17] and embarked for the Head Quarters of General Harmar to consult with him, on my way, upon the Measures that would be necessary and practicable for the defence of the Country.

Some Apology seems to be necessary for some of the Paper[s] that accompany the Report appearing in the french Language. The Originals of all of them, which required publication, wer[e] published in English as well as in french. All the communications with the Indians which were numerous had to be translated into that Language on account of the Interpreters, as well as their Answers into English. From June until my arrival in the City I have been in constant motion, either on horseback or in an open Boat where the Copying of Papers was impossible, had I not been separated from them; and they did not come to hand here till very lately. In that time I was obliged to travel about four thousand Miles.—The necessity that this Report should be made before the present Session of Congress ended seemed to forbid any farther delay and will I hope excuse that impropriety.

AR. S. CLAIR,
Governor of the Territory of the united States north west of the Ohio

Postscript.

In the course of the last Fall a considerable number of french Emigrants have been introduced into the Territory, and on my last return from Fort Washington I found about four hundred of them at a place they have named Gallipolis, three Miles below the mouth of the great Kenhawa on the opposite side of the River. They were living in Barracks that had been provided for them by the Scioto Company, but did not seem to be at all usefully employed, and were much discontented. It was not half an hour after my Landing that the Paper marked No. 25 was put into my hands by a Number of Persons deputed for the purpose. No. 26 is my Answer. The Regulations there promised have not yet taken place from the want of proper information with respect to the Characters best fitted to fill the civil and military Offices. I had desired a List from some of the principal Persons themselves and one also from an Agent of the Scioto Company who resides with them, to have an opportunity of comparing them, not choosing to rely altogether upon the recommendations of either, but they were not sent forward, and the Communication was cut off by the Ice. About one hundred more of those Emigrants, are at the Muskingham, and one hundred at Buffaloe Creek in Pennsylvania, waiting the opening of the Season to establish themselves near the Scioto.

MS (DNA: RG 59, NWT, M/470); entirely in St. Clair's hand; at head of text: "Report of the Governor of the Territory of the united States north west of the Ohio"; endorsement carries a similar description; undated, but enclosed in St. Clair to TJ, 11 Feb. 1791. Tr (DNA: RG 59, NWT, M/470). Not recorded in SJL or SJPL. Extracts of the text that TJ enclosed in his report of 17 Feb. 1791 (Document IX) are indicated in textual notes 1-17 below (see explanation at beginning of textual notes).

Enclosures (all in DNA: RG 59, NWT, M/470): (1) List of lands claimed by inhabitants of Kaskaskia (full text in Carter, *Terr. Papers*, II, 253-7).

(2) List of 57 heads of families at Kaskaskia, of whom 7 had arrived after 1783 (full text in same, II, 257-8).

(3) Proclamation issued at Kaskaskia by St. Clair on 7 Mch. 1790 announcing his authority to carry into effect the provisions of the resolution of Congress of 20 June 1788 and requiring the inhabitants "to exhibit in the Office of the Secretary of the Territory forthwith an exact Statement of Lands and Lots they now possess or lay claim to" under French, English, or Virginia grants, so that, if such claims were found authentic, confirming pat-

ents might be issued and "all Cause of Litigation be taken away" (full text in same, III, 296-7).

(4) Plan of the Town of Kaskaskia made by Samuel Baird (not found).

(5) Arthur St. Clair to the inhabitants of Prairie du Rocher, 5 June 1790 (see Enclosure V, Document IX).

(6) Petition of Pierre Gibault and others to St. Clair, 9 June 1790 (see Enclosure VII, Document IX).

(7) Memorial of James Piggot and others to St. Clair, 23 May 1790 (see Enclosure II, Document IX).

(8) Gabriel de Cochy and other inhabitants of Prairie du Rocher to Jean Baptiste Barbau, Sr. and Antoine de Louviere é Cuyers authorizing them to make a representation in their behalf to St. Clair, "to the end that he may see fit to cast an eye of compassion on the distress which is desolating this district, which prevents nearly all of them from paying the costs of surveying . . . without abandoning their land" (French text and translation printed in Carter, *Terr. Papers*, II, 278-9, but with erroneous caption). The representation by the two agents to St. Clair, if made in writing, has not been found.

(9) Map of "the reserved Tract including Fort Chartres" (enclosed with TJ's report of 17 Feb. 1791; see Document IX and illustration in this volume).

(10) Proclamation of 22 Apr. 1790 annulling—subject to "the Pleasure of Congress in the Premises"—claim of the Seminary of Quebec under a grant of 22 June 1722 to a tract of Land "four leagues in a Square," concerning which a power of attorney was issued to Pierre Gibault on 14 Aug. 1768 by the Bishop of Quebec and registered in the recorder's office at Cahokia. St. Clair announced in the proclamation that, though the inhabitants had come to believe the tract granted the missionaries was four leagues square, he had directed it to be surveyed as "Four Leagues in a Square" as expressed in the grant (i.e., a tract one league square) and bounded so that "if any Person thinks himself aggrieved . . . he may know precisely how to make his Complaint in Order to be redressed" (full text in Carter, *Terr. Papers*, III, 297-301).

(11) Deposition of Joseph La Bussière (Labuxière), 29 May 1791, to the effect that, about 33 or 34 years earlier, at the request of the French commandant and the commissioner of the Illinois country, he had published at the church door in Cahokia the king's declaration forbidding the missionaries to make further grants of land (French text and English translation in same, II, 261-2).

(12) Remonstrance of Baptiste Cabassier and 34 other inhabitants of Cahokia to St. Clair, 12 May 1790, urging that he prevent Pierre Gibault from engaging in an illicit sale of their property under a pretended power of attorney, an action prompted by "a cupidity and hardness of heart which have caused Mr. Gibault to wish to deprive us of our property, which we have had to sweat blood to establish" (French and English translation in Carter, *Terr. Papers*, II, 249-51).

(13) Letter of the Superior of the Seminary of Quebec to the church wardens of Cahokia, 6 Aug. 1789, responding to theirs of 6 June 1787, informing them that the power of attorney issued in 1768 to Pierre Gibault was "no longer valid at the seminary" though recorded at Cahokia; that in order to bring the land claims to a satisfactory conclusion it would be necessary to convey the property to the vestry of the parish; that, by such a notarial act, the titles to the property could be conveyed to them; that they would not make such a conveyance "without some legal arrangement"; and that the "negroes formerly belonging to the mission have gained their liberty by prescription and we by no means join in your intention of forcing them into slavery. Providence has bestowed on them this precious gift of liberty and God forbid that we should consent to their being deprived of it" (French text and English translation in Carter, *Terr. Papers*, II, 199-202).

(14) G. Aubuniere and others to St. Clair, 28 Apr. 1790 (see Enclosure III, Document IX).

(15) Instructions from St. Clair to Jean Baptiste Maillet (Mayet), 1 June 1790, appointing him to the command of Peoria and instructing him to do his best to keep the Indians in peace, to arrest and send to Cahokia anyone attempting to carry on trade with the Indians without a license, to restrain any traveler from attempting without a pass from the governor to "go thro' the Country by the Illinois River," and, as soon as possible, to send to him or to the commandant of militia at Cahokia any intelligence of hostile designs on the part of the In-

dians, defending the people of Peoria as best he could until aid could be sent (full text in same, III, 309-10).

(16) Orders of St. Clair of 6 June 1790 to the inhabitants of Kaskaskia to provide themselves with a prison as soon as possible, since nothing was "more necessary for the happiness of society than the proper administration of justice, the prevention of crimes or the punishment thereof in cases where it is impossible to prevent them, and that good citizens be protected in their lives, and their property; advantages which cannot be hoped for if the officers of justice are not supported and furnished with everything necessary for the enforcement of the laws, and in order to put judicial sentences and decrees of magistrates into full effect" (French text and English translation in same, II, 277; on the same day St. Clair directed a prison to be built at Cahokia; same, III, 308).

(17) Proclamation by St. Clair of 10 June 1790 forbidding all persons not citizens of the United States to hunt or kill any kind of game in the Northwest Territory "either for the Flesh or the Skins" under penalty of forfeiting both flesh and skins to the informer, as well as being subjected to punishment as trespassers (full text in same, III, 310-1).

(18) Proclamation by St. Clair of 10 June 1790 forbidding all persons from cutting timber and firewood on lands of the United States and transporting it to Spanish territory (see Enclosure, Document III).

(19) Correspondence between St. Clair and Henri Peyroux de la Coudreniere, Spanish commandant at Ste. Genevieve, and between St. Clair and Manuel Perez, Spanish commandant at St. Louis, 30 Mch. 1790-26 May 1790, principally concerning recovery of slaves (French texts and English translations in Carter, *Terr. Papers*, II, 231-40).

(20) Proclamation of Esteban Miró, Governor of Louisiana and West Florida, 2 Sep. 1789, to give effect to the king's orders permitting subjects and citizens of other countries to emigrate to Louisiana and West Florida by way of the Mississippi with their stock, slaves, and possessions, "promising to each family a tract of land from 240 to 800 acres in proportion to their numbers, free from all expense, as also exemption from taxation, and the private exercise of their religion," on condition that those accepting the offer take an oath of allegiance and become

actual settlers. The proclamation was accompanied by Miró's announcement of 6 Sep. 1789 setting forth the rights, privileges, and immunities to be granted to emigrants (texts of both documents in same, II, 213-15).

(21) Extract of letter from St. Clair to Hamtramck, 23 Jan. 1790 (see Enclosure VI, Document IX).

(22) List of 51 heads of families at Cahokia (text in Carter, *Terr. Papers*, II, 259).

(23) List of 50 heads of families and bachelors at Prairie du Pont (text in same, II, 260-1).

(24) Memorial of Pierre Gibault to St. Clair, 1 May 1790 (see Enclosure IV, Document IX).

(25) Petition of French emigrants at Gallipolis to St. Clair, ca. 16 Nov. 1790 (not found).

(26) St. Clair to French emigrants at Gallipolis, 21 Nov. 1790, expressing his pleasure at their arrival in the territory, his distress over their disagreeable situation, his belief that patience and perseverance would overcome their difficulties, and his assurance that he would use his best endeavors to assist them in finding "in this land of liberty that happiness which is the reward and the incentive to an active life." On the particular cause of their complaint St. Clair wrote: "I am altogether unacquainted with the nature of the contract that has been made with the Scioto company, or what may be the specific pretentions of individuals.—The laws of the country will however compel justice to be done, and those laws will be extended to you as early as it is possible.—They can know the Scioto Company as an individual only, and their course must be general, you will therefore readily perceive the impossability of a person being appointed to judge expressly between the Colonists and that company. Courts will be established where justice will be duly, and regularly administered according to the laws, and where neither favour nor influence will have any weight; and it will be among the first matters I shall attend to, after my arrival at Marietta, to make those arrangements for your security and peace; but as they must all pass through the Secretary's office they cannot be taken earlier" (text printed in Carter, *Terr. Papers*, II, 311-2).

In each of the textual notes below it is to be understood (1) that all brackets in text are supplied from TJ's penciled markings in MS; (2) that all identifications of these bracketed passages are made from penciled letters inserted by him in margin of MS to designate those parts of the text desired for inclusion in the appendix to his own report of 17 Feb. 1791 (Document IX); and (3) that, in doing so, he naturally made appropriate changes of phraseology in the text, of which one example is given in note 1. The lettered marginalia in MS do not proceed in alphabetical sequence because, for the sake of clarity and brevity, TJ wished to correlate these passages with the categories of land claims described in his report on Vincennes of 14 Dec. 1790 (Document II). Three copies of his report were prepared for the President, the Senate, and the House (Document X). In all of these, of course, the extracts were copied by the departmental clerks in alphabetical sequence (see text in ASP, *Public Lands*, I, 19-20).

1 Extract **I** (see preceding general note for explanation of this and fol-

lowing textual notes). TJ altered text of MS to read: "Mr. Samuel Baird was appointed to survey the lands held by the people of Kaskaskia. . . ."

2 Extract **M.**
3 Extract **B.**
4 Extract **N.**
5 Extract **G.**
6 Extract **E.**
7 Extract **O.**
8 Extract **K.**
9 Extract **C.**
10 Extract **H.**
11 Extract **D.**
12 No letter appears to be discernible in margin, but this passage is Extract **L.**
13 Extract **P.**
14 Extract **A.**
15 Extract **F.**
16 Extract **Q.**
17 Blank in MS. St. Clair turned his duties as governor over to Sargent on 11 June 1790 (Carter, *Terr. Papers*, III, 311-13).

IX. Report of Secretary of State on Lands at Kaskaskia, &c.

The Secretary of State, having received from Arthur St. Clair, Esquire, Governor of the North-Western Territory, a Report of his Proceedings for carrying into Effect the Resolve of Congress of August 29th. 1788, respecting the Lands of the Inhabitants of Kaskaskia, La Prairie du Rochers, and Kahokia, which Report was enclosed to him in a Letter bearing Date of the 10th. Instant, and observing therein several Passages proper to be laid before the Legislature, has extracted the same, and thereupon makes, to the President of the United States, the following—

REPORT.

In that which he made on the 14th: of Decr: 1790, relative to the Execution of the same Resolution of Congress at Post Vincennes, he brought under certain general Heads of Description the Claims to Lands at that Place, which had not been provided for by the said Resolution of Congress. To keep the Subject simplified as well as short, he will observe that the Cases at Kaskaskia, described in the Extract marked **A.** belong to the fourth Class of the said Report for St. Vincennes, that those at Kaskaskia of the Extract **B.** belong to the fifth Class of the Report for St. Vincennes, and that those of Kahokia in the Extract **C.** belong to the sixth Class of the same Report, and may be comprehended in the Provision to be made for them.

The Extracts marked **D. E. F. G.** and **H.** describe other Cases out of the Provision of the Resolution, which have arisen at Kaskaskia and Kahokia, differing from each other as well as from all the former Classes.

The Extracts marked **I. K.** state that the Line which by the Resolve of Congress of June 20th: 1788 had been so described as to place the Lands to be allotted to the Inhabitants of Kaskaskia and Kahokia in a fertile and convenient Situation, had been so shifted by the Resolution of August 29th. 1788 as to throw those Allotments into Parts too distant and dangerous to be cultivated by them, and pray that the Line of June 20th. may be re-established.

The Extract **L.** brings into view the Purchase of Flint and Parker in the Illinois country, which may need Attention in the Formation of a Land Law.

The Extracts **M. N. O.** with the Papers they refer to contain the Reasoning urged by the Inhabitants of Kaskaskia, Prairie, and Kahokia against the Demand of the Expenses of certain Surveys made of their Lands neither at their Desire nor for any Use of theirs.

P. explains certain Demands for the revoked Emissions of continental Money remaining in the office of a Notary public of Kaskaskia, and **Q.** the Expediency of having a printing press established at Marietta.

Which several Matters the Secretary of State is of opinion should be laid before the Legislature for their Consideration.

TH: JEFFERSON
Feb. 17. 1791.

MS (DNA: RG 46, Senate Records, 1st Cong., 3rd. sess.); report and enclosures in hands of various clerks, except for date and signature in TJ's hand. PrC of another of the three copies of report and enclosures sent to the President on 17 Feb. 1791 (DLC). FC (DNA: RG 59, Record of Reports of Thomas Jefferson, p. 256-85). Entry in SJPL reads: "1791. Feb. 17. Report Th: J. on resolution Congress respecting lands Kask."

ENCLOSURE I

Extracts from the Report of the Governor of the Territory of the United States North-West of the Ohio

*[Text omitted here since extracts **A** through **Q** are identified in the notes to St. Clair's report (see textual notes to Enclosure, Document* VIII*). As indicated in the above report, TJ arranged the extracts not*

in the sequence in which they occurred in St. Clair's report but selectively in order to correlate these passages with the categories of land claims described in his report on Vincennes (see Document II*).]*

Tr (DNA: RG 46, Senate Records, 1st. Cong., 3rd. sess.); in clerk's hand. PrC of another of the three copies sent to the President on 17 Feb. 1791 (DLC); in clerk's hand. FC (DNA: RG 59, Record of Reports of Thomas Jefferson, p. 259-71).

E N C L O S U R E I I

Memorial of James Piggot and others to Arthur St. Clair

Great Run May 23d. 1790.

We your Petitioners, beg leave to represent to your Excellency the state and circumstances of a number of distressed but faithful subjects of the united States of America, wherein we wish to continue, and that under your immediate Government; But unless our principal agrievance can be removed by your Excellency's encouragement, we shall despair of holding a residence in the State we love. The Indians who have not failed one year in four past to kill our people, steal our horses and at times have killed and drove off numbers of our horned cattle, render it impossible for us to live in the Country any way but in Forts or villages, which we find very sickly in the Missisippi bottom. Neither can we cultivate our land but with a guard of our inhabitants equipt with arms, nor have we more tillable land for the support of seventeen families than what might be easily Tilled by four of us, and as those lands whereon we live are the property of two individuals, it is uncertain how long we may enjoy the scanty privileges we have here; nor do we find by your Excellency's Proclamation that those of us which are the major part, who came to the Country since the year 1783 are entitled to the land we improved at the risk of our lives, with a design to live on. These with many other difficulties which your Excellency may be better informed of by our Reverend friend Mr. James Smith, hath very much gloomed the aspect of a number of the free and loyal subjects of the United States. In consideration of which your Petitioners humbly request, that by your Excellency's command, there may be a village with inlots and outlots sufficient for families to subsist on laid out and established in or near the Prairie de *moriway*. We know the other american settlers near the Missisippi to be in equal deplorable circumstances with ourselves, and consequently would be equally benefited by the privileges we ask; and that those of us that came to the country and improved land since the year 1783 may be confirmed in a right of preemption to their improvements, is the humble request of your Petitioners; and we as in duty bound shall ever pray.   (signed) JAMES PIGGOT
(and 45 others)

Tr (DNA: RG 46, Senate Records, 1st. Cong., 3rd. sess.); in clerk's hand; at head of text: "No. 7" (i.e., enclosure No. 7 in St. Clair's report; see Document VIII above, enclosure); at head of text: "To his Excellency Arthur St. Clair Esqr. Governor and Commander in Chief of the Territory of the United-States North west of the River Ohio." PrC from another of the three copies sent by TJ to the President on 17 Feb. 1791 (DLC). Tr (DNA: RG 59,

Record of Reports of Thomas Jefferson, p. 271-3). Tr (DNA: RG 59, NWT, M/470); containing names of all 46 signers, including James Henderson, Daniel Boone, and William Murry (names given in full in Carter, *Terr. Papers*, II, 253).

ENCLOSURE III

Memorial of G. Aubuniere and others to Arthur St. Clair

SIR   Cohos 28th. April 1790.

The Inhabitants of the Villages of the Cohos and *Prairie du pont* take the Liberty of informing you that in Consequence of the connection which you have been pleased to make of the Seigniory of the Cohos with the Domain of the States in which are included the Lands and commons set apart for their Cattle which they have possessed for several Years, which Lands you have led them to hope would be continued to them. It is found that, by adding this Seigniory to the Domain, they are deprived of a sufficiency of Land on which to support their Cattle; and of Wood not only for building but for Fuel.

It is for these Reasons, Sir, that they have recourse to your Clemency and bountiful Authority, that you may be pleased to grant them a sufficient Common surrounding their Lands, which shall commence by a Line drawn between the Land called Ottach at the End of the Morass along the Coasts, running at two thirds of a League above the Coasts to the Misissipi, and taking the said Line above the Coasts, in returning N.E. ¼ North to the End of the Bounty Lands granted to them by Congress, and which are bounded by a Strait Line drawn from the Misissipi to that running two Miles above the Coasts. This small Portion of Land above the Coasts *n'étant remplie d'entonoirs et bas fonds* which render it unfit for cultivation, at the same Time it is of great Utility to them on account of the Wood, which they cannot do without.

We request you, Sir, that when you shall be pleased to put us in Possession of the 400 acres of Bounty Land which the Congress has granted to each Family, you will order a certain Breadth of Front in order to furnish each with 400 acres from the Mississippi to the Line which shall run two miles above the Coasts, observing that if these 400 acres were given by a Square of 20 Acres, some of them would be found to fall totally in Morass, others in Wood, and others in Meadow, and that each Person may suffer no Injury, lots may be cast for each Parcel.

We, who are faithful Subjects of the United States, expect every Thing from your Equity.   (signed) G. AUBUNIERE
                                        (and 13 others)

Tr (DNA: RG 46, Senate Records, 1st. Cong., 3rd. sess.); in clerk's hand; at head of text: "No. 14" (i.e., enclosure No. 14 in St. Clair's report; see Document VIII above); at head of text: "Translation. To M. St. Clair Governor-General, civil and Military of the Illinois Country." PrC of another of the three copies sent by TJ to the President on 17 Feb. 1791 (DLC). Tr (DNA: RG 59, Record of Reports of Thomas Jefferson, p. 274-6). Tr (DNA: RG 59, NWT); in French, accompanied by English translation, containing names of all 14 signers (names given in full in Carter, *Terr. Papers*, II, 242).

G. AUBUNIERE: Carter, unable to identify this person among census records and lists of land claimants, con-

jectured plausibly that the above spelling may have been a clerk's erroneous transcription of the name of one Gabriel Aubuchon who was in Kaskaskia in 1787 (same, II, 242, note 9, citing C. W. Alvord, ed., *Kaskaskia Records*, in Ill. Hist. Soc., *Colls.*, V, 417).

ENCLOSURE IV

Memorial of Pierre Gibault to Arthur St. Clair

Kahokia 1 May 1790.

The undersigned Memorialist has the Honor to represent to your Excellency.

That from the Moment of the Conquest of the Illinois by Colo. George Rogers Clark, he has not been backward in venturing his Life on the many Occasions in which he found that his Presence was useful and sometimes necessary. And at all Times sacrificing his Property, which he gave for the Support of the Troops at the same Price that he could have received in spanish Dollars, and for which, however, he has received only paper Dollars, of which he has had no Information since he sent them addressed to the Commissioner of Congress, who required a Statement of the Depreciation of them at the Belle Rivière in 1783, with an express promise in Reply, that particular Attention should be paid to his Account, because it was known to be no way exaggerated.

In reality he parted with his Tithes and his Beasts only to set an Example to his Parishioners, who began to perceive that it was intended to pillage them and abandon them afterwards which really took place. The want of seven thousand eight hundred Livres, of which the nonpayment of the american Notes has deprived him the use, has obliged him to sell two good Slaves, who would now be the Support of his old age, and for the want of whom he now finds himself dependent on the Public, who altho' well served, are very rarely led to keep their Promises, except that Part, who employing his Time in their Service, are supported by the secular Power, that is to say, by the civil Government.

The love of his Country and of Liberty have also led the Memorialist to reject all the advantages offered to him by the Spanish Government. And he endeavored by every means in his Power, by Exertions and Exhortations, and by Letters to the principal Inhabitants to retain every Person under the Dominion of the United States, in Expectation of better Times, and giving them to understand that our Lives and Property being employed twelve Years in the Aggrandisement and Preservation of the Conquests of the United States, would at last receive an Acknowledgment and be compensated by the enlightened and upright Ministers who sooner or later would come to examine into, and relieve us from our sad situation. We begin to see the Accomplishment of these Hopes, under the happy Government of your Excellency, and, as your Memorialist has reason to believe, from

Proofs which would be too long to explain here, one of the Number who has been the most forward in risking his Life and Fortune for his Country.

He also hopes that his Demand will be listened to favorably. It is this. The missionaries, like Lords, have at all Times possessed two Tracts of Land near this Village, one three Acres in Front which produces but little Hay, three quarters being useless by a great Morass —the other of two Acres in Front, which may be cultivated, and which the Memorialist will have cultivated with Care, and proposes to have a Dwelling erected on it, with a Garden and Orchard, in Case his Claim is accepted. Your Excellency may think perhaps that this might injure some of the Inhabitants, but it will not. It would be difficult to hire them to cause an Enclosure to be made of the size of these Tracts, so much Land have they more than they can cultivate. May it please your Excellency then to grant them to the Memorialist as belonging to the Domain of the United States, and to give him a Concession to be enjoyed in full Propriety in his private Name, and not as to a Missionary and Priest, to pass to his Successor, otherwise the Memorialist, not wishing to labor for others, would not accept it. It is for the Services he has already rendered and those which he still hopes to render as far as Circumstances may offer and he may be capable, and particularly on the Bounty with which you relieve those who stand in need of Assistance, that he founds his Demand. In hopes of being soon of the number of those who praise Heaven for your fortunate arrival in this Country, and who desire your Prosperity in every Thing, your Memorialist has the Honor of being with the most profound Respect Your Excellency's Mo: obt: & mo. humble Servant

P. GIBAULT
Priest

Tr. (DNA: RG 46, Senate Records, 1st. Cong., 3rd. sess.); in clerk's hand; at head of text: "No. 24." (i.e., enclosure No. 24 in St. Clair's report; see Document VIII above); at head of text: "Translation. To his Excellency Arthur St. Clair, Major General of the Army of the United States, Governor of the Territory possessed by the United States North west of the River Ohio &c. &c." PrC from another of the three copies sent to the President by TJ on 17 Feb. 1791 (DLC). Tr. (DNA: RG 59, Record of Reports of Thomas Jefferson, p. 276-80).

ENCLOSURE V

Arthur St. Clair to the Inhabitants of Prairie du Rocher

BY THE GOVERNOR.—   Kaskaskias June 5th. 1790

Mr. Beard, the Surveyor appointed to survey the Lands held by the Inhabitants at the Prairie du rocher, having executed that business as far as claimants appeared, is to be paid for his services at the rate of two dollars and a half per mile, reckoning upon one line in the length of each survey, and two dollars for each Lot in the Village. When that expence is defrayed, new concessions will be made out for the Proprietors as soon as possible.   (signed) ARTHUR ST. CLAIR

Tr (DNA: RG 46, Senate Records, 1st. Cong., 3rd. sess.); in clerk's hand; at foot of text: "To the inhabitants of the Prairie du Rocher." PrC from another of the three copies sent to the President by TJ on 17 Feb. 1791 (DLC). Tr (DNA: RG 59, Record of Reports of Thomas Jefferson, p. 281).

ENCLOSURE VI

Arthur St. Clair to John Francis Hamtramck

[Fort Steuben, 23 Jan. 1790]

"It is with great pain that I have heard of the scarcity of Corn which reigns in the settlements about the Post. I hope it has been exaggerated, but it is represented to me that unless a supply of that article can be sent forward, the people must actually starve.—Corn can be had here in any quantity, but can the people pay for it? I entreat [you] to enquire into that matter, and if you find that they cannot do without it, write to the Contractor's agent here to whom I will give orders to send forward such quantity as you may find to be absolutely necessary. They must pay for what they can of it, but they must not be suffered to perish, and though I have no direct authority from the Government for this purpose, I must take it upon myself."

Tr. (DNA: RG 46, Senate Records, 1st. Cong., 3rd sess.); in hand of clerk; at head of text: "Extract of a Letter to Major Hamtramck at Post St. Vincennes, dated from Fort Steuben the 23d. January 1790." PrC from another of the three copies sent to the President by TJ on 17 Feb. 1791 (DLC). Tr (DNA: RG 59, Record of Reports of Thomas Jefferson, p. 281-2). The full text of St. Clair's letter is printed in St. Clair Papers, ed. Smith, II, 130-2.

In his reply to the above, Hamtramck wrote St. Clair on 19 Mch. 1791: "I have this day sent a boat to the Falls for 800 bushels of corn, which I shall deliver to the people of the village, who are in a starving condition; so much so that on the 16th instant a woman, a boy about thirteen, and a girl of about seven years were driven to the woods by hunger, and poisoned themselves by eating some wild roots, and have died of it" (same, II, 132).

ENCLOSURE VII

Memorial of Pierre Gibault and others to Arthur St. Clair

County of St. Clair   June 9th. 1790.

The Memorial of the Inhabitants of Kaskaskia, la Prairie du Rocher, and Kahokia, County of St. Clair.

Humbly Sheweth,

That by an Act of the Congress of 20th. June 1788, it was declared that the Lands theretofore possessed by the said Inhabitants should be surveyed at their Expense, and that this Clause appears to them neither necessary nor adapted to quiet the Minds of the People. It does not appear necessary, because from the Establishment of the Colony to this Day, they have enjoyed their Property and Possessions without Disputes or Lawsuits on the Subject of their Limits; that the Surveys of them were made at the Time the Concessions were obtained from their ancient Kings, Lords, or Commandants; and that each of them knew what belonged to him, without attempting an Encroachment on his neighbor, or fearing that his neighbor would encroach on him. It does not appear adapted to pacify them, because instead of assuring to them the peaceable Possession of their ancient Inheritances, as they have enjoyed it till now, that Clause obliges them to bear Expenses, which, in their present Situation, they are absolutely incapable of paying, and for the failure of which they must be deprived of their Lands.

Your Excellency is an Eyewitness of the Poverty to which the Inhabitants are reduced, and of the total Want of Provisions to subsist on. Not knowing where to find a morsel of Bread to nourish their Families, by what Means can they support the Expense of a Survey which has not been sought for on their Parts, and for which it is conceived by them there is no Necessity? Loaded with misery and groaning under the Weight of Misfortunes, accumulated since the Virginia Troops entered their Country, the unhappy Inhabitants throw themselves under the Protection of your Excellency, and take the Liberty to solicit you to lay their deplorable Situation before Congress. And as it may be interesting for the United States to know exactly the Extents and Limits of their ancient Possessions, in order to ascertain the Lands which are yet at the disposal of Congress, it appears to them, in their humble Opinion, that the Expense of Survey ought more properly to be borne by Congress, for whom alone it is useful, than by them who do not feel the Necessity of it. Besides, this is no Object for the United States; but it is great, too great for a few unhappy Beings who your Excellency sees yourself are scarcely able to support their pitiful Existence.

To these Motives they venture to add that of the Generosity worthy of a Great People: the taking upon them a Burthen too heavy for a small Number of unhappy Individuals will give lustre to their Dignity.

They venture to hope that the paternal Goodness of your Excellency towards your adopted Children will induce you to present their humble Supplication to the Honble. Congress, and that you will second it with your Protection.

They will ever pray to Heaven for the Preservation and Prosperity of your Excellency.

(signed) P. GIBAULT, Priest
(and 87 others)

Tr (DNA: RG 46, Senate Records, 1st. Cong., 3rd. sess.); in clerk's hand; at head of text: "(No. 6)" (i.e., enclosure No. 6 in St. Clair's report; see Document VIII above); at head of text: "Translation. To his Excellency Arthur St. Clair Esqr. Governor and Commander in Chief of the Territory of the United States North west of the River Ohio." PrC from another of the three copies sent to the President by TJ on

17 Feb. 1791 (DLC); endorsed by Remsen: "February 17th. 1791. Recorded and Examd." Tr (DNA: RG 59, Record of Reports of Thomas Jefferson, p. 282-5). Tr (DNA: RG 59, NWT, M/470); with all 88 names of signers (these names are printed in Carter, *Terr. Papers*, II, 280-1, with corrections of many of the copyist's errors).

Map of the Reserved Tract including Fort Chartres

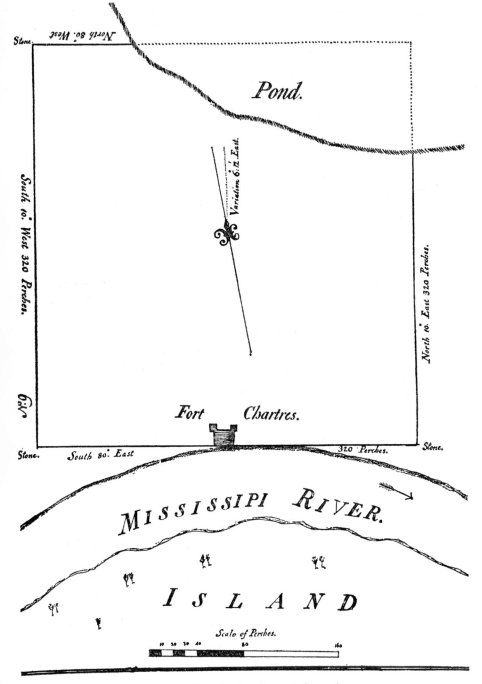

X. Secretary of State to the President

Feb. 17. 1791.

The Secretary of state has the honor to send to the President three copies of a report and message relative to Kaskaskia, Kahokia and Prairie, to wit, one for each house, and one to be retained by the President.

He sends also the original report which contains some things worthy the President's reading, tho not mentioned in the report. The passages reported on are marked with a pencil.

RC (Roger W. Barrett, Chicago, 1947). Not recorded in SJL or SJPL. For the passages on St. Clair's original report that TJ marked for the President's attention, see Editorial Note.

XI. The President to the Senate and the House of Representatives

GENTLEMEN OF THE SENATE, AND HOUSE OF REPRESENTATIVES.

United States February 18th, 1791.

I have received from the Secretary of State a Report on the Proceedings of the Governor of the Northwestern Territory at Kaskaskia, Kahokia, and Prairie, under the Resolution of Congress of August 29th. 1788, which containing Matter proper for your Consideration, I lay the same before you.

Go: WASHINGTON

RC (DNA: RG 46, Senate Records, 1st. Cong., 3rd. sess.); in clerk's hand; signed by Washington; endorsed. Dft (DLC); in clerk's hand; undated and unsigned (enclosed in TJ's memorandum to the President, 17 Feb. 1791). Entry in SJPL reads: "[1791. Feb. 17. Report Th: J. on resolution Congress respecting lands Kask.] Message accompanying it." Enclosure: TJ's report to the President, 17 Feb. 1791 (see Document IX), with its enclosures.

XII. Governor of the Northwest Territory to the Secretary of State

SIR

Philadelphia March 11th. 1791.

When I had the honor to make the report of my proceedings in the Illinois country, the plan of the town of Cahokia had not come to hand.—I have since received three copies, one of which I have transmitted to your office.—I have the honor to be with great respect Sir, your most obedient servant   AR. ST. CLAIR

FC (DNA: RG 59, NWT, M/470). Not recorded in SJL or SJPL. No copy of the plan of Cahokia has been found, but see J. F. McDermott, *Old Cahokia* (St. Louis, 1949).

XIII. Population of the Northwest Territory

The Number of Souls in the Territory of the United States North West of the River Ohio A. D. 1790

In the Seven Ranges of Townships	
Ohio Company Purchase	1000
The French Settlement Opposite Kanhawa	
Symmes Settlements	1300
Clarksville at the Rapids of Ohio	60
Vincennes on the Aubache inclusive of	
River du Chy Station	1000
Kaskaskias	315
Cayhokia	365
At the grand Ruifseau Village of St. Phillip	
Prairie du Rochers	240
	———
	4280

In the Town of Vincennes upon the Aubache are about 40 American Families and 31 Slaves, included in the above Estimate. Upon the Mississippi also 40 American Families and about 73 Slaves which are likewise included.

Upon the Spanish Side of the Mississippi above the Confluence of the Ohio are

At Genivieve, Saline and		
a small new Village	850	the
half of which are Blacks.		
St. Louis	720	of which
120 are Blacks.		
A small Settlement 12 Miles West.	100	
A Settlement 20 Miles up the Missouri River	150	
	———	
	1820	

MS (DLC); in Winthrop Sargent's hand, except for totals which were inserted in pencil by TJ. Printed in *New-York Journal*, 31 Jan. 1791. St. Clair estimated the population of THE FRENCH SETTLEMENT, left blank in Sargent's tabulation, at "about four hundred" (see enclosure, Document VIII). A census of 1791 showed a total of 347 persons, 237 males and 110

females. Half of these were between
20 and 40 years of age, almost a third
were between 1 and 20, and 29 were

infants (J. Guion, "Etat de la population de la Colonie françoise," 20 May
1791, MHi: Sargent Papers).

To James Madison

For Mr. Madison from Th: J.   Dec. 15, 1790.

Extract from a letter of the house of Van Staphorsts.

'So far from Mr. Dohrman having made us any remittance for our friend Mr. Mazzei, that gentleman is greatly in our debt, and we fear will not be able to stand the return of a large amount of bills he drew on Europe on speculations of corn, but which did not arrive. What funds he had in the hands of his London correspondents are attached by his brother Dohrman & Garron of Lisbon. We send out our power of attorney to Leroy & Bayard to recover our demand and would recommend Mr. Mazzei to send his to his friend Madison or any other person he may chuse there.'

Mazzei in his letter to Th: J. goes on. ['My *power of attorney* is already in existence, wherefore it would be superfluous for me to send another. The only thing lacking is to confirm my claims against this fellow Dohrman. My friend Madison in his letter of 10 Dec. 1788 said to me 'he has at my request concurred in an instrument which pledges his Western grant of land as an eventual security for the debt.' I place my hope therefore in your well-known friendship for me, in case he should not be able to be paid, at least to insure that my interests will not be prejudiced by the other creditors. But you would need to be good enough to take my well-being really to heart, and not rely at all on Dohrman's promises. He made a draft in Europe on account of cargoes of grain which he later sold in America, and without even giving notice of this. Such conduct casts grave doubts on his character. Certainly, prudence cannot counsel putting any faith in him.']¹

PrC (DLC); entry in SJL reads: "Madison James (on Mazzei's affairs)."

The letter from the HOUSE OF VAN STAPHORSTS may have been written in the third person and addressed to Mazzei or sent to one of several friends involved in his affairs. It is clear that Mazzei quoted it in his (missing) LETTER TO TH: J. of 3 Sep. 1790 and that

all of the above consists of an extract from that letter, written in reply to TJ's of 5 Apr. 1790 and received on the day that TJ sent this extract to Madison (entry in SJL reads: "[Dec. 15] Mazzei Philip Paris, rue du Regard. No. 30. Sep. 3.").

¹ All of that part of the extract from Mazzei's letter enclosed in brackets (supplied), except the quotation from

Madison's letter of 10 Dec. 1788, is in Italian and has been translated by   Archibald T. MacAllister.

From James Monroe

DEAR SIR   Phila. Decr. 15. 1790.

I send you the letters mention'd last night, among which you will find two, from Mr. Fitzhugh and Mr. Page each, cover'd by one from the old gentleman his father recommendatory of young Mr. Mortimer. He is extremely anxious to have him admitted into your office and under your care. The young man appears to be amiable in temper and manner, sensible, prudent, and is well esteem'd among his acquaintance in these respects: but the two gentlemen who have mention'd him to you are better acquainted with his merit than I am, and to their subscription no addition will be requir'd from me. I told him it was probable the duties of your office had forc'd on you before this the disposition of appointments of this kind, so that altho he most earnestly wishes it yet he is in some measure prepar'd to receive a negative. With real esteem & regard I am sincerely yr. friend & servt.,

JAS. MONROE

RC (DLC); endorsed by TJ as received the same day, but recorded in SJL, along with enclosures, under 14 Dec. 1790. Enclosures: (1) Charles Mortimer to TJ, Fredericksburg, 27 Nov. 1790: "I would not for any Consideration presume to trouble you with this address, or the Enclosed letters, were it not for my Sons Ardent desire and Inclination to be under your Pa-tronage.—It was his Misfortune to grow up at and during the War, when we could not get proper Tutors to prepare him for a Learned profession therefore he was bound and bred to Mercantile Buisness under Messrs. Barclay Merchts in Phila. who will vouch for his character, good Moralls and Mild Disposition. And it was my Misfortune to loose by Depreciation some Considerable Debts by the War, and tho Even now I have a Capital due me by Bonds, to set him up in a Midling line, I can't get paid without Distressing Gentlemen and compell sales which is Disagreeable to my feelings as money can't be raised. Therefore if in your Department his Services Could only get a tolerable Maintenance and some Improvement it would make me happy.—

My worthy friend Colo. Monroe is well acquainted with us, and can recommend him to your notice.—He has a knowledge of Accounts and something of the French language and with your Instruction be Usefull to you and himself. I am with profound Respect, Your Most Obt. Hble. Servt." (RC in DCL: Applications for Office under Washington; endorsed by TJ as received 14 Dec. 1790). (2) William Fitzhugh to TJ, Chatham, 15 Nov. 1790; recorded in SJL but not found. (3) Mann Page to TJ, Mannsfield, 27 Nov. 1790, reading in part as follows: "My Friend and Neighbour Doctr. Mortimer has brought up his only son with much Attention to the mercantile Business. . . . He is fearful that Want of Employment may beget Idleness and Dissipation; and is particularly desirous of placing him under your Patronage. . . . I can venture to recommend him as a young Gentleman of docile Disposition, of amiable Manners, of Application to Business, and of moral Character" (RC in DLC: Applications for Office under Washington; endorsed by TJ as received 14 Dec. 1790).

Commercial and Diplomatic
Relations with Great Britain

EDITORIAL NOTE

*. . . with those who respect their own dignity
so much, ours must not be counted at nought*
—Secretary of State to Morris, 12 Aug. 1790

In a remarkable series of reports to the President and to the House of Representatives during six crucial weeks of the third session of the First Congress—on trade with the Mediterranean, on the related problem with Algiers, on the status of the fisheries, on the emerging difficulties over impressment, on the French representation on the tonnage acts, on the consular establishment, even on the idea of a universal standard of weights and measures—Jefferson exhibited a strategy so concentrated in aim and so varied in form that no one could have failed to discern its major thrust even if he had sought to conceal it. In all of these state papers his fundamental purpose, not unfriendly to Great Britain and not subservient to France, was to insure that declared principles of amity and justice prevail in American relations with the rest of the world, in commerce as in all else. The commercial policy embodied in these reports was one Jefferson had long advocated, both before and during his mission to France. Indeed, its essential elements were formed before the Revolution and were articulated in his *Summary view of the rights of British America*. In that statement he argued that the colonists derived from natural law the right to carry on "a free trade with all parts of the world" and that justice required Great Britain to eliminate from her navigation acts restrictions on the colonists which interfered with their exercise of that right. In 1774 a just regard for the "reciprocal advantages of their connection" could alone prevent the dismemberment of a well-poised empire: in 1790 commercial arrangements "on principles of reciprocal advantage" could alone forestall economic retaliation.[1] In both instances

---

[1] See text from MS of *Summary view*, Vol. 1: 123, 135; also Document v in the present series. The policy TJ advocated was substantially the same as that urged by Hamilton in the eleventh *Federalist*, but soon abandoned by him (see Editorial Note to group of documents on the French representation on the tonnage acts, under 18 Jan. 1791).

TJ later pencilled letters opposite the SJPL entries for these reports in such a way as to indicate, perhaps, that he had grouped them intentionally. The entries, including one of an important British state paper, read: "28. [Dec.

Jefferson's aim was reciprocity. In neither was the warning heeded. In the attack on this central problem of foreign affairs, as Alexander Hamilton and his supporters in the Senate suspected, James Madison was an indispensable collaborator of the Secretary of State. The mission of Gouverneur Morris to test the disposition of the British government on the execution of the terms of the Treaty of Peace, on reciprocal trade arrangements, and on the establishment of diplomatic relations was one Hamilton had helped originate. But in its denouement it proved to be the most effective weapon available to the two collaborators in their interconnected administrative and legislative strategy. It would be implausible in the extreme to suppose that Jefferson and Madison did not concert their plans as they rode northward together for the third session of Congress, confident as they were that the general assent of the public would be given to commercial policies thus far thwarted chiefly by the Senate. Jefferson, concerned about expansion of trade into the Mediterranean, had already informed Washington that the situation of the Algerine captives required attention. He and Madison both assisted in preparing the President's annual message calling for protection of American commerce and fisheries against European restrictions. The response to the message, drawn by Madison, aroused opposition but, as adopted, required the House of Representatives to take some action in matters of commerce and navigation. This victory in a matter of form, followed immediately by the French representation on the tonnage acts, signalled the opening of the contest.[2]

These legislative portents caused George Beckwith to call at once on Hamilton to express his concern. Knowing that the British agent was perfectly aware of the political divisions in the government and also that he was "no stranger to the opinions of the gentleman who drew up" the response, Hamilton gave him a sobering prediction. From such discordant sentiments, he said, "it is difficult not to do something on this subject, and I think in the course of the present Sessions we shall adopt the idea furnished by your Navigation Act, the effect of which will be to restrain your shipping from being the carriers to our Markets of other produce or manufacture than that of your own dominions (in all parts of the world) or of carrying from hence, excepting to your possessions."[3]

1790] (a) Report Th: J. on our citizens in captivity in Algiers. (b) do. on Mediterranean trade. . . . 17. [Jan. 1791] (c) Message to Congress on French representation against foreign tonnage. . . . 18. [i.e., 28 Jan. 1791] (d) Report of Privy Council of Gr. Br. relative to US. Abstract of do. . . .1 Feb. [1791] (e) Report Th: J. on the Cod and whale fishery. French arret of Dec. 29. 87. on American commerce. Other arrets on same subject. Th: J. to Sp[eaker] H. R. inclosing report. G. W.'s approbation of the Report." (The entry for "Report of Privy Council" proves that SJPL, covering TJ's tenure as Secretary of State from 11 Oct. 1789 when Washington first selected him for the post to 31 Dec. 1793 when he resigned, was not compiled from day to day, as was SJL, but was set down subsequently as a record of his chief public papers of the period.)

[2] Brant, *Madison*, III, 324-5; TJ's suggestions for Washington's message, 29 Nov. 1790; for a discussion of the French representation against the tonnage acts, see Editorial Note to the group of documents under 18 Jan. 1791.

[3] Beckwith's report of the conversation is dated "Philadelphia January 19th. 1791" (text enclosed in Beckwith to Grenville, 23 Jan. 1791, PRO: FO 4/12; printed in Syrett, *Hamilton*, VII, 440-1).

This was far more disquieting than Madison's discriminatory proposals that had caused the ministry to send Beckwith hurrying to America in 1789 with the threat of retaliation. But that night the December packet arrived from England and the next day Beckwith asked Hamilton whether this had produced any alteration in his views. "We learn by many private letters from London received last night," Hamilton replied, "that your Administration have declared their intention of appointing a Minister to this country. . . . It will, I hope, pave the way for a future good understanding and put an end to the suggestions of that party with us, who wishing well to a French interest, take every occasion to insinuate that we are held in no consideration by the English government.—Upon the subject of commerce and navigation, which I mentioned to you yesterday, I think I can assure you that nothing will take place during the present session, to the injury of your trade."[4] Beckwith reported these opinions to Grenville as coming from "the gentleman head of a great executive department whose communications have formerly been made known." His conversations, he added, "lay open the state of party as actuated by a wish to advocate an English or a French interest, in matters of commerce and navigation."[5] Grenville could have had no difficulty in identifying the head of the department who had thus labelled the opposing forces and described their aims in a manner nowhere disclosed in the reports of the French *chargé* to Montmorin. Clearly, at this critical juncture, the two great powers of Europe were served by emissaries of very different degrees of initiative and perspicuity. They also had quite different modes of access to the councils of the American government, the one clandestine and the other official. While Hamilton and his followers in the Senate and House had kept Beckwith well informed about their own views of policy and about what they conceived to be the aims of a French interest led by the Secretary of State, Jefferson had thus far scrupulously abstained from divulging such confidences and imputations of motive to Otto.[6]

But the bland assurance offered by Hamilton after the arrival of the London packet, professing a confidence the circumstances could not justify, has misled historians more than it did the discerning British agent. It has been generally assumed that the British government had decided to send a minister to the United States before the move for a navigation bill emerged in the third session; that the timely arrival of news of this decision prevented its enactment; that, thus fortified by the independent action of the British ministry, Hamilton brought his influence to bear in the House of Representatives and caused the bill "mysteriously" to vanish overnight; that the actual arrival of George Hammond as minister in the autumn of 1791 thwarted efforts in the Second Congress to counter British restrictions on American com-

[4] Beckwith's report of this second conversation is dated "Philadelphia January 20th." (same).

[5] Beckwith to Grenville, 23 Jan. 1791 (PRO: FO 4/12).

[6] See Editorial Note to group of documents on the French Representation on the tonnage acts, under 18 Jan. 1791.

merce; and that, indeed, Jefferson himself had lost confidence in the outcome before the new minister arrived in the United States.[7]

Since all of these assumptions are contradicted by the evidence and since Madison's efforts were the legislative counterparts of Jefferson's administrative strategy, both the assumptions and the related measures must be examined. While the conflict over the French representation on tonnage duties reveals the nature of the breach in the government most clearly, Madison's effort to achieve a commercial policy based on principles of reciprocity and Jefferson's reports addressed to the same end were the measures that focused public attention on the struggle.

I

Hamilton himself was acutely aware of the fact that the news of an appointment of a minister to the United States was only private rumor which, lacking official confirmation, could have no effect on the legislative situation.[8] Leeds and Pitt, to be sure, had at first offered excuses to Gouverneur Morris when he brought up the subject of an exchange of ministers, then had seemed disposed to designate one, and finally had expressed a qualified "intention of so doing."[9] But this was neither assurance nor evidence that a decision had been reached. Bemis, while careful to point out that the news received by Hamilton was by no means official, was at pains to show that the decision to dispatch a minister was made "before revival of the movement in Congress for navigation laws" and adduced two evidences that he regarded as conclusive proof: first, Beckwith's dispatches and, second, the report of the Committee of the Privy Council for Trade and Plantations of 28 January 1791, "submitted . . . as explained therein . . . *for the instruction of the Minister who was about to depart for America.*"[10]

[7] Bemis, *Jay's Treaty*, p. 85, 111, 112, 114-15, 116-17, 119-20, presents the accepted view. DeConde, *Entangling alliance*, p. 75-9, adheres closely to Bemis' account and Malone, *Jefferson*, II, 333-5; III, 158, accepts the view that Hamilton blocked retaliatory measures. Setser, *Reciprocity*, p. 110-11, 113, states flatly that the failure of the navigation bill "to be enacted early in 1791 was due to the decision of the British government to send a minister to Philadelphia" and that TJ, even when prepared to submit his report early in 1792, apparently had little hope of favorable action. Yet all present evidence showing that the actual decision came after the reports of Beckwith, Bond, and others had transmitted to the ministry their own sense of alarm. Neel, *Phineas Bond*, p. 75-9, emphasizes and indeed exaggerates Bond's influence on the report of the Lords of Trade of 28 Jan. 1791 and takes this to be the equivalent of the decision to negotiate, yet surprisingly neglects to mention the impact of Bond's dispatches of 3 Jan. and 14 Mch. 1791 on Grenville. Two recent works that accept the prevailing view are Charles R. Ritcheson, *Aftermath of revolution: British policy toward the United States 1783-1795* (Dallas, 1969), p. 116-18 (hereafter cited as Ritcheson, *British policy*) and Jerald A. Combs, *The Jay Treaty* (Berkeley, 1970), p. 57-8.

[8] "There is as yet no certainty of the mission from England, which must precede one from this Country," he wrote Angelica Church on 31 Jan. 1791 (Syrett, *Hamilton*, VII, 608).

[9] See Documents II and VI.

[10] Bemis, *Jay's Treaty*, p. 111, 116, 119. The emphasis is that of Bemis and the paraphrase is not precise. What Leeds had said was that it was the "*intention* forthwith to send to America a person, authorized . . . to treat . . . on commercial as well as other matters; and . . . that this committee should . . . report, what are the proposals, of a commercial nature, proper to be made by the gov-

But Beckwith's dispatches, like his conversations with the Secretary of the Treasury, prove only that he was as much in the dark about the ministry's intentions as Hamilton or anyone else in America. As for the famous *Report on the Commerce and Navigation between His Majesty's Dominions and the Territories belonging to the United States of America*—a climactic application of the theories of Sheffield and the prejudices of Hawkesbury advanced at the moment the assumptions of mercantilism were coming under systematic attack by Adam Smith, David Hume, and others[11]—it was in fact a recommendation, not a decision. As Leeds' secretary told Morris a month before the report was submitted, an appointment of a minister would indeed have been "improper untill they should have determined what such Person was to do."[12] The recommendations of this report of the Lords of Trade and Plantations, drawn up principally by Lord Hawkesbury, only sought to define the limits of policy.

In doing so, it exhibited a remarkably complacent view of existing relations with the United States. Based in large part on the testimony of merchants of London, Liverpool, Bristol, and Glasgow, it regarded with satisfaction the powers granted by the new Constitution. These, it declared, were founded in justice and promised to relieve British trade of many of the burdens placed on it by the individual states. Such acts of injustice had been "condemned by the united voice of America assembled in Convention" and it was reasonable to suppose that the Congress would not imitate them. Indeed, the authors of the report found that impost duties were no higher and tonnage duties were actually less than those that had been imposed by the separate states. Since most of the raw materials furnished by the former colonies could

---

ernment of this country to the . . . United States" (*A Report of the Lords of the Committee of Privy Council . . . on the commerce and navigation between his Majesty's Dominions, and the Territories belonging to the United States of America. 28th January, 1791*, reprinted in *Collection of interesting and important reports and papers on the navigation and trade of Great Britain, Ireland, and the British Colonies in the West Indies and America* [London, 1807], p. [45]-154, [i]-xxxix; the passage quoted is at p. 48-9; hereafter cited as *Report*; emphasis added). For comment on the 1791 printing and reprinting of the *Report*, see note 133 below. The intended appointment was that of Andrew Elliot and this was laid aside when the war crisis of 1790 subsided (Morris to TJ, 28 Dec. 1790).

The report of the Lords of Trade, ordered by the Privy Council on 30 Sep. 1790 at the height of the war crisis, and the intended appointment of a minister were inspired in part also by alarmed appeals from the West Indies. The government of Bermuda, merely on the basis of newspaper reports that a discrimination in tonnage duties was in contemplation, said that this "alarm . . . prompted the speediest application to his Majesty's ministers" (Henry Hamilton to Grenville, 23 June 1790. PRO: FO 4/8, f. 340-3, enclosing memorial of council and assembly. Hamilton also wrote to Hawkesbury).

11 Sheffield's *Observations on the commerce of the United States* (London, 1783), like Charles Jenkinson's reports of 1784 and (as Lord Hawkesbury) of 1791, was a blueprint for policy, not a systematic formulation of the doctrine of mercantilism. As Jacob Viner, "The Economist in History," *American Economic Review*, LIII (May, 1963), p. 3, points out, the incoherent body of projections and practices known as mercantilism was a folk-doctrine with which the name of no theorist of the first rank was connected until the attacks of Smith and others began.

12 Morris to TJ, 28 Dec. 1790.

be obtained elsewhere and since, after they had become independent, their shipbuilding had declined, their fisheries had been almost destroyed, and their benefits from the circuitous trade through the West Indies had been entirely lost, the commercial connection was more important to the United States than to Great Britain. Nevertheless, such was her concern for maintaining sea power, Great Britain had always placed the interests of navigation above those of commerce when the two collided and had never suffered other nations to levy tonnage duties on British vessels without immediate retaliation. The report conceded that the government might ultimately have to resort to counter-regulations, but at present only the merchants of Liverpool favored the traditional response. Those of London, Bristol, and Glasgow, revealing their general satisfaction with the existing and prospective trade relations with America, thought that it would be better to negotiate first and then, if necessary, resort to retaliation.

The Lords of Trade, mindful also of the preponderant claims of navigation in the British system, agreed. Great Britain, they pointed out, had prudently submitted to the measures of the different states, hoping that time would diminish their hostile spirit and that circumstances might arise "to detach them from their new connections." The report therefore recommended "that his Majesty . . . enter into an open negociation with the United States, particularly as Congress appears inclined to it." But on the subject of navigation only one proposition could be offered—that impost and tonnage duties levied on British ships in American ports be the equivalent of those imposed on American vessels in the ports of Great Britain. If it should be proposed, as all assumed would certainly be the case, that this "principle of equality" be extended to the British colonies in America and in the West Indies, the Lords of Trade declared that "this *demand cannot be admitted even as a subject of negociation*."[13] In brief, so advantageous was the existing state of trade and so slight the future threat, Great Britain could confidently forego the customary retaliation and seek instead, with the aid of friendly supporters in the American government, to persuade the United States not to engage in commercial warfare.

Far from being a determination of policy or even evidence that the decision to designate a minister had been made, the report was only a proposal to suspend retaliation while negotiating on a basis wholly irreconcileable with the ideas of reciprocity entertained by Jefferson and Madison. Leeds' secretary had hinted to Morris in December that nothing would be determined until spring.[14] His caution was well advised. Even after a few copies of the report had been printed for the use of the cabinet, these were recalled "by a sudden order of Council" and the rumors that a minister would be appointed soon died away.[15] One reason for this was the growing demand for retaliation on the part of English shipowners. "They growl," Joshua Johnson reported to Jefferson early in 1791, "and say, unless Govern-

13 *Report*, p. 135; emphasis in text.
14 Morris to TJ, 28 Dec. 1790.
15 [William Temple Franklin] to [Tench Coxe], 15 June 1791 (MHi: Knox Papers). Joshua Johnson first reported that 50 copies were being printed and later gave the figure as 100 (Johnson to TJ, 18 Apr. and 10 July 1791).

ment retaliates, and levy's either Duty, or Tonnage, that they will be ruined, and the Americans run away with all the carrying trade."[16] Another and related reason was the division within the British government, a fact confirmed both by its hesitant actions and by reports of competent observers over a period of many months. Jay as well as Jefferson drew inferences of such indecision from the dispatches of Gouverneur Morris.[17] So did Hamilton, who pointedly informed Beckwith of Morris' report "that there is a great diversity of opinion in your Cabinet on the subject of American commerce, *as well as in a higher quarter, that, in short, the K[ing] is much opposed to it, but that the Q[ueen] is more favorably inclined . . . as well as Mr. Pitt himself.*"[18] Such opinions, Beckwith reported, carried much weight in America.

These divisions persisted. Late in 1790 the American consul said it was reported a minister had been appointed. But more than four months afterward when he demanded a categorical answer from Leeds' secretary, he was given only another declaration of intent coupled with an explanation of the difficulty of finding a proper person.[19] Rumor brought forth successively the names of Elliot, Peale, Walpole, Fraser, and finally Hammond. The first was Andrew Elliot, a well-connected Scot, former lieutenant-governor of New York, and brother-in-law of William Eden, head of British secret intelligence.[20] The choice of such

[16] Johnson to TJ, 26 Feb. 1791. Johnson repeatedly urged an American navigation act.

[17] Jay wrote to Washington on 13 June 1790: "The silence of the british Cabinet on the subject of Mr. Morris's letters marks their *Indecision*. It may arise from Doubt of what may be the opinion of Parliament, on some of the commercial, and perhaps other Points; and the Expediency of observing the Caution and Delay which such doubts may prescribe" (DNA: RG 59, MLR; emphasis in text). The observation shows that Washington had disclosed Morris' letters to Jay, one of the originators of the mission. Morris' reports of division in the cabinet led TJ in December to believe the "issue uncertain" (Document II). See also Johnson to TJ, 18 Apr. 1791.

[18] Hamilton's remarks were quoted in an appendix to Beckwith's report to Grenville of 3 Mch. 1791 (PRO: FO 4/12; endorsed as received 1 May). The passage in italics (supplied) does not appear in the official report. In a private communication of the same date, marked "*Secret*," Beckwith indicated that the blank "in the ninth page of the Appendix" was to be filled with the words quoted above and italicized (Beckwith to Grenville, 3 Mch. 1791, Grenville Papers in the custody of George G. Fortescue, Esq., Boconnoc, Lostwithiel, Cornwall, whose courtesy in granting the Editor access to these important family archives is gratefully acknowledged. These papers are hereafter referred to as Grenville Papers, Boconnoc; they have recently been placed in the custody of the British Museum).

[19] Johnson to TJ, 30 Nov. 1790; 26 Feb., 26 Mch., and 18 Apr. 1791.

[20] Andrew Elliot had been collector of customs in New York before the Revolution and during the British occupation of the city he served as lieutenant-governor, superintendent of police, and deputy receiver of quit-rents. He was son of Sir Gilbert Elliot of Minto (1722-1777) and brother of the diplomat, Gilbert Elliot (1751-1814), who was closely attached to his brother-in-law William Eden (Namier and Brooke, *House of Commons*, II, 390; Eugene Devereux, "Andrew Elliot," PMHB, XI, 129-50; Bemis, *Jay's Treaty*, p. 84n.; Van Doren, *Secret History*, 105, 112, 323, 364; Morris to TJ, 28 Dec. 1790; [William Temple Franklin] to [Tench Coxe], 15 June 1791, MHi: Knox Papers). It was Joshua Johnson who mentioned Peale and Walpole (Johnson to TJ, 30 Nov. 1790; 26 Feb., 26 Mch., 18 Apr., and 2 July 1791). See also TJ to Nelson, 29 Mch. 1791; TJ to Washington, 17 Apr. 1791.

a person suggests something of the desire of Pitt and Grenville to maintain private communications with friends in the United States, as does the ultimate appointment of George Hammond, a minor figure in the diplomatic service who had no known connection with America. For despite Pitt's assurance to Morris that the determination to send a minister would be announced by an official letter to the President, this formality was not observed. When the decision was finally made in the spring of 1791, Grenville gave oral assurances through a private American citizen and Pitt employed clandestine channels to make a more explicit communication to Hamilton and others.[21] Some months later Joshua Johnson, who had not yet been informed of the decision, reported to Jefferson that the matter was still in agitation and expressed the view that, from "the apparent fickelness of this Government, little Dependence can be placed in either their actions, or declarations."[22] It is therefore plausible to suppose that one reason for putting aside Elliot, who was familiar with American affairs but too obviously identified with Loyalist and intelligence operations, was the desire to name someone for the post who would serve as envoy less in fact than in form. Certainly the channels opened up by Beckwith continued to be employed by the British minister to the United States. The inference is supported not merely by the circumstances attending his appointment, but also by the declaration made in 1793 by one of Pitt's supporters in Parliament that the British government "considered Colo. Hamilton and not Mr. Hammond as their effective minister."[23]

Yet, even if British councils had been united and if a formal and official notification of the decision to establish diplomatic relations had arrived during the third session, this in itself could not have provided the answer to the central question. A realization of the promised exchange of ministers could have afforded but a slight element of hope, vastly diminished by what had already been learned of the disposition of the British government. On reading Morris' dispatches, Jefferson concluded that the ministry did not "mean to submit their present advantages in commerce to the risk which might attend a discussion of them, whereon some reciprocity could not fail to be

[21] William Stephens Smith to George Washington, 6 June 1791 (DNA: RG 59, MLR); John Maunsell's authorization from William Pitt, ca. June 1791 (DLC: Hamilton Papers). See below for further discussion.

[22] Johnson to TJ, 10 Aug. 1791.

[23] TJ's memorandum of a conversation with John Beckley, 7 June 1793. Beckley had just returned from New York, where he saw Sir John Temple, who permitted him to read a letter from Sir Gregory Page-Turner (1748-1805), an admirer and supporter of Pitt. Beckley reported that the letter contained the passage as given above, together with other assertions "that the government were well apprised of the predominancy of the British interest in the US." and considered "Colo. Hamilton, Mr. King and Mr. W. Smith of S. Carolina as the main supports of that interest. . . ." Beckley also reported that Temple had read to him, but had not allowed him to hold, a letter from Grenville to the same general purport.

Temple was certainly in error in saying that Page-Turner had been a member of parliament for twenty-five years (he acquired his seat in 1784, almost certainly by purchase; Namier and Brooke, *House of Commons*, III, 244). But there is no reason to doubt the general accuracy of the account: after all, Hawkesbury's *Report* revealed that as early as 1790 the British government had not been deceived about the leading defenders of its interest in the United States.

demanded."[24] Had he been able in January of 1791 to obtain a view of the report of the Lords of Trade, he would have found therein a most emphatic confirmation of the accuracy of his analysis. When, after extraordinary pains, the American consul in London finally got possession of the report for a few hours, lamenting that it was impossible for him to procure a copy for the Secretary of State, he correctly assessed its meaning: "I see, if they make that the Basis of Mr. Hammond's negotiation, that nothing will be done."[25] By then Jefferson himself was in possession of an extract of the report containing its most important elements and therefore knew precisely the ground whereon the British minister to the United States stood. Fully realizing the great value of this document in mobilizing support for Madison's navigation bill in the ensuing Congress, he sought to acquire the complete text. "I should not think," he wrote the consul, "50. or 100 guineas misspent in getting the whole of the original from what I know already of it."[26] This instruction phrased as an opinion was written only four days after Jefferson penned the letter to Edward Rutledge that has been offered as the sole evidence of his presumed discouragement resulting from the appointment of a minister.[27] It

[24] See Document II.

[25] Johnson to TJ, 10 July 1791.

[26] TJ to Johnson, 29 Aug. 1791.

[27] TJ's letter to Rutledge of 25 Aug. 1791—usually (as in Ford, v, 375) misdated the 29th—must be read in context. The two men had a deep friendship and respect for each other. They were in fundamental agreement on public measures, particularly with respect to commerce and relations with Great Britain. Rutledge, who applauded TJ's efforts to enable the United States to gain release "from the Trammels of British Commerce . . . by opening new Ports" in the Mediterranean, was bitterly hostile whereas TJ was resolute but in firm control of his emotions. The fact that London merchants exacted £3 sterling per barrel of rice for commissions, freight, duty, and other expenses represented nothing but a form of tribute to Rutledge, whereby American wealth was levied upon "to extinguish those Debts of Britain . . . contracted by her wicked war" (Rutledge to TJ, 28 Apr. 1790). Learning of the inquiries sent out in preparation for the report of the Lords of Trade, he argued that with a navy the United States could threaten the West Indies and dictate a commercial treaty—if not "at present, yet at a period not far distant" (Rutledge to TJ, 20 June 1790; TJ to Rutledge, 4 July 1790). Hence when TJ received Rutledge's letter introducing (and warning against) Robert Goodloe Harper whom he suspected of intent to probe the "Views and Designs of Government" in foreign affairs, he answered the same day. To Rutledge's real discouragement about his inability to break the unanimous front presented by the South Carolina delegation in opposing Madison's discrimination policy, TJ responded with a feigned attitude of submission and of being obliged to "turn the left cheek to him who has smitten the right," a wholly uncharacteristic gesture for him on a matter of fundamental public policy. The real object of his response is not to be found in this but rather in the portrayal of the difficulties—South Carolina's fear of New England shipping and the wild speculation brought on by fiscalism blocking "the tide of public prosperity almost unparaleled in any country"—and in the appeal for reinforcements with which to meet them: "Would to god yourself, Genl. Pinckney, Majr. Pinckney would come forward and aid us with your efforts" (TJ to Rutledge, 25 Aug. 1791). Rutledge, glowing with resentment at a subservience in measures so different from the posture of 1776, rightly grasped the essence of TJ's meaning by offering personal and professional excuses for not coming forward (Rutledge to TJ, 7 Oct. 1791).

Others, accepting the submissive gesture literally, have missed that meaning. Bemis, *Jay's Treaty*, p. 113, and Setser, *Reciprocity*, cite only TJ's letter as

therefore throws a revealing light on that misconstrued communication, the main thrust of which was to prod the South Carolinian to action. The affected air of hopeless resignation was Jefferson's way of stimulating Rutledge to oppose his influence to that of William Loughton Smith, an ardent supporter of Hamilton in the House and a bitter foe of Madison's navigation bill. The authorization of bribery in a fairly substantial sum also suggests that Jefferson's use of the consular service for espionage purposes—a fact which must have been known to the British secret intelligence—may have given Pitt and Grenville an additional incentive for keeping up the hidden communications with Hamilton and his supporters.

But the conclusive reason for rejecting the supposition that the navigation bill was defeated by Hamiltonian influence, aided by the presumed decision to appoint a British minister, is that the concerted strategy of Jefferson and Madison reached its culmination only in the final days of the session, some weeks after Hamilton had given his confident assurance to Beckwith. It has been supposed that this resulted from the cumulative effect of Jefferson's various reports and that the navigation bill was reported by the committee to which these reports had been referred.[28] But this, as the legislative history of the reports and the bill reveals, is not supported by the evidence. Chance as well as calculation helped the two collaborators. Jefferson's report on the mission of Gouverneur Morris was the most effective single factor in throwing their opponents on the defensive.

II

Until the middle of February the legislative contest was one in which Madison's forces, aided though they were by Jefferson's timely reports, lost more ground than they gained. The House, after some debate, had approved without amendment Madison's draft of the response to the President's message which declared that it would be incumbent on that body "to consider in what mode . . . commerce and agriculture can be best relieved from an injurious dependence on the navigation of other nations" and that the Mediterranean trade demanded and would receive attention.[29] It then directed a committee of twelve to bring in a bill or bills for the encouragement of the navigation of the United States. At the same time it called upon the Secretary of State to report on trade with the Mediterranean, an action that could scarcely have caught Jefferson by surprise since he handed in an

evidence of his attitude. Malone, *Jefferson*, II, 335, citing only Bemis and Setser, agrees that TJ had become discouraged. Actually he had anticipated the position reflected in Hawkesbury's *Report* even before the President asked his opinion on Morris' dispatches. "Whenever their avarice of commerce will let them meet us fairly halfway," he wrote another South Carolinian soon after arriving in Philadelphia, "I should meet them with satisfaction, because it would be for our benefit: but I mistake their character if they do this under present circumstances" (TJ to Kinloch, 26 Nov. 1790).

[28] Bemis, *Jay's Treaty*, p. 112; DeConde, *Entangling alliance*, p. 78.

[29] Washington's address was given 8 Dec. 1790. Madison, Ames, and Tucker were appointed to prepare the response. On the 11th Madison's draft of the response was debated and adopted. (JHR, I, 331-2, 333, 334-5; Brant, *Madison*, III, 325).

elaborate report within a fortnight and buttressed this with the report on the Algerine captives.[30] In each of these skirmishes at the opening of the session Madison's forces prevailed.

But there followed a long lull, during which no navigation bill was reported and no action taken on Jefferson's reports, with the Senate being as obdurate as Hamilton in refusing any of his proposed accommodations to France on the relatively insignificant tonnage question. Indeed, in the House none of his reports was accorded the attention of being referred to a committee. Those on the Mediterranean trade and on the Algerine captives were tabled, without further action, though the former was sent to the Senate for its information.[31] These facts, together with the indifference of the New England shipping and commercial interests to the fate of the fisheries, may help to account for the extraordinary force of the report on that aspect of the American economy. This document, analyzing the effect of British regulations, was a vigorous and amplified version of the argument Jefferson had employed so unsuccessfully with Hamilton and the Senate in respect to the French tonnage claims. France, the report argued, was the only nation that could take the surplus of American whale oil. A particular interest there—the Nantucket whalemen settled at Dunkirk and their connections within the French government—had been perpetually soliciting its exclusion. A timely dispatch from William Short indicated that they might succeed and Jefferson enclosed an extract to reinforce his argument.[32] But there was at least ground for hope that the present government would view the United States "not as rivals, but as co-operators against a common rival." With amicable dispositions on both sides, an accommodation of interests might be achieved. This, however, should be sought not in the interest of the fisherman alone. France was a customer for five-eighths of American whale oil, two-thirds of her salt fish, one-fourth of her tobacco, three-fourths of her livestock, a large proportion of her rice, and millions of bushels of wheat, rye, and barley, nearly the whole of which was carried in American vessels. A valuable consumer and a free market, France would in time become an important one for American ships, ship timber, potash, peltry, and other articles.

The argument was addressed directly to the shipbuilding and carrying interests that had been the principal northern protagonists of the tonnage acts. Great Britain, Jefferson conceded, had a right to confine her markets to herself, but "ours cannot be denied of keeping

[30] JHR, I, 337-8; see TJ's reports under 28 Dec. 1790. The best account of the opposition to Madison's response is in Bache's *General Advertiser*, 13 Dec. 1790. Smith of South Carolina offered a non-committal amendment because Madison's words bound the House "to an obligation of taking such measures as almost to exclude foreign vessels." His colleague Tucker supported him. But Madison argued, in part, that under threat of war "it was of the utmost importance that the American navy be put upon so respectable a footing as not to need foreign aid for the exportation of her produce." Smith's amendment was defeated.

[31] See Editorial Note to group of documents on the French representation on the tonnage acts, under 18 Jan. 1791; JHR, I, 345, 346. For Senate action in committing the reports see Editorial Note to group of documents on Mediterranean Trade and Algerine Captives, 28 Dec. 1790.

[32] TJ to President of the Senate, 2 Feb. 1791, enclosing extracts from Short to TJ, 21 Oct. 1790.

our carrying trade to ourselves. And if there be any thing unfriendly in this, it was in the first example." Furthermore, the British ministry had shown no disposition to adjust this or any other matter by arrangements of mutual convenience. Hence the unilateral regulations "they have begun for mounting their navigation on the ruins of ours can only be opposed by counter-regulations on our part."[33] This was precisely the argument that Hamilton himself had employed in the eleventh *Federalist*, but Jefferson identified the principal obstacle far more explicitly than he had done. The report on the fisheries, like the report on the French tonnage claims, was only another variation on the central theme—another effort, carefully timed, to persuade by fact and reasoned argument those who stood on the other side of the fundamentally divisive issue of American relations with Europe. It also, as if in warning, contained the first unequivocal statement by any official of the government about what was known and yet to be disclosed concerning the disposition of the British government. The action of the House of Representatives in ordering the report to "be sent to the Senate for their information" must have proceeded from something more than routine formality.[34] The Senate at least directed that it be printed, but neither house revealed any desire to act on its recommendations or on those advanced in Jefferson's other reports.

Less than a month remained in the session. If the result of the overture to England were to be made known at all, the time had clearly arrived. But it is necessary to point out that no compulsion lay upon the President to make a revelation of failure, since it has been assumed that he delegated the direction of the mission to the Secretary of State, that Jefferson submitted a report on it in December, and that Washington allowed it to remain on his desk for two months before informing Congress.[35] But the fact is that Washington had appointed Morris as his own private agent, had received all of his dispatches, and had shared the first of them with Jefferson only for his perusal.[36] It was not until the beginning of the third session when legislation on American commerce and navigation was in agitation that the President turned over to the Secretary of State the complete record of Morris' agency, including copies of the letters of credence and instruction, and asked for his opinion as to what measures needed to be taken.[37] There was nothing in the request that indicated a need or an intention to place the matter before the Congress or even before the Senate. Nor was there anything in Jefferson's report calling for action by the legislative branch. That report could scarcely be described as hostile to Great Britain and still less could a presumed hostility be accepted as the cause of Washington's delay in informing Congress.[38] On the

[33] Report on the fisheries, 1 Feb. 1791.

[34] JHR, I, 370; the Senate directed that 200 copies of the report be printed (SJ, I, 238, 239).

[35] Bemis, *Jay's Treaty*, p. 110; DeConde, *Entangling alliance*, p. 78.

[36] Washington to TJ, 19 June 1790.

[37] See Document I.

[38] For a different interpretation, see Malone, *Jefferson*, II, 331-2, who also seems to imply that Washington weighed the differing opinions of Hamilton and TJ and then accepted the view of the latter as to the result of Morris'

contrary, it rested its recommendation on a sense of respect for the national dignity. The next move, Jefferson suggested, should be left to Great Britain because the overture had removed all doubt about her intentions and because it would be "dishonourable . . . useless, and even injurious" for the United States to renew proposals for a treaty of commerce or for an exchange of ministers.[39] Washington was in full agreement: the analysis confirmed the opinion that he himself had already formed.[40] If, therefore, there was a difference in this matter between the President and the Secretary of State, it was only as to whether or when the information should be divulged. On this point the record is silent.

But it is implausible to suppose that the fact, the timing, and particularly the form of the disclosure were unrelated to the long delay of the House of Representatives in bringing forth a navigation bill. Not only had Jefferson's reports met with legislative inattention: Madison's forces, rallied so hopefully at the beginning of the session, were in disarray. Hamilton's proposal for a national bank, arising out of no such deep-rooted compulsions as the demand for countervailing measures against European trade restrictions, had received prompt attention while Madison's navigation bill languished in a committee dominated by bank supporters.[41] In the House on the 8th of February the advocates of the bank overwhelmed a sectional minority led by Madison. The next day Jefferson brought forth for the President's consideration drafts of the two messages on Morris' mission to England. With one or two amendments in phraseology, Washington gave his approval.[42] Two days later a petition of several masters of vessels in Charleston, South Carolina, called upon Congress to relieve them from sufferings caused "by the preference given in that place to foreign vessels in the carrying trade." The petition was referred to the dormant committee that had been directed almost two months' earlier to bring in a bill

mission. DeConde, *Entangling alliance*, p. 78, goes further and states that "Hamilton and Jefferson differed completely on . . . the kind of message the President should send to Congress dealing with the failure of the mission." But there is no evidence that Washington consulted Hamilton on the point.

[39] Document II.

[40] Washington's concurrence was expressed both in the sanction he gave to TJ's letter of 17 Dec. 1790 to Morris and in one he himself wrote on the same day: "An official letter from the Secretary of State of this date, acknowledging the receipt of your public dispatches, will discover to you my sentiments on the views and intentions of the british Cabinet. If the exigencies of the national affairs of that kingdom should excite dispositions in it favorable to a commercial treaty with the United States, and to the fulfilment of the treaty of peace, its Ministers will, of themselves, come forward with propositions. Until these are apparent to them, and press, I am satisfied from the communications you have had with them, that it is not only useless, but would be derogatory to push them any farther on the first point or to say anything more on the latter, until we are in a situation to speak with more decision" (Washington to Morris, 17 Dec. 1790, *Writings*, ed. Fitzpatrick, XXXI, 172-3). See also Washington to Morris, 7 July 1790 (quoted in Document I).

[41] Two-thirds of the members of the committee of the House that had been directed to bring in a bill for the encouragement of navigation were bank supporters, their names being italicized in the following list: *Boudinot*, Jackson, Tucker, Ashe, Parker, *William Smith*, *Clymer*, *Vining*, *Benson*, *Sherman*, *Goodhue*, and *Foster* (JHR, I, 337-8).

[42] Documents IV, V, and VI.

respecting trade and navigation.[43] On Saturday the 12th of February, that committee was discharged of its responsibility.[44] If a final proof of legislative mood were needed, this action provided it. On the ensuing Monday the President placed before the Congress the explosive information about Morris' abortive agency.

Jefferson's draft of the President's covering message to both houses employed language that would make the reason for this extraordinary disclosure impossible to mistake. The information was communicated because it "might at some time have influence on matters under . . . consideration" by Congress. This message—which of course would be reported in the press—was brief and restrained, using phraseology drawn in part from Washington's instructions to Morris. From informal conferences with the British ministry to discover their disposition "to fix the commerce between the two nations on principles of reciprocal advantage," Washington could infer no such disposition for "arrangements merely commercial."[45] The austere brevity of the communication could scarcely avoid stirring public and legislative imaginations alike, conveying the impression that the friendly overture of the young republic had been rebuffed by the unacceptable demands if not haughty indifference of a mighty power. But in his draft of the message to the Senate—which of course would not be made public —Jefferson was far more explicit. Its opening words signalled the belief that "the possible event of a refusal of justice" by Great Britain had indeed occurred. Its closing announcement that the ministry's views had been "sufficiently ascertained" and that Morris had been directed to discontinue his communications confirmed the impression. The message duly noted that the British government had expressed an intention to send a minister to the United States, but this became a fact of relative insignificance in light of the conclusion that justice in respect to commerce and the execution of the Treaty of Peace was not obtainable except on terms that were unacceptable. To reinforce this explicit communication Jefferson attached corroborative selections from the letters of Gouverneur Morris, an envoy whom "the mercantile Senators" could scarcely disown.[46]

It would be difficult to exaggerate the impact of this disclosure upon Senators and Representatives who had been so prompt to support Hamiltonian measures and so dilatory with respect to commercial legislation. For this was not the report of the Secretary of State that had been allowed to lie on the desk of the President for two months because of its capacity to inflame national feelings. On the contrary, it was an instrument carefully designed and deliberately chosen at this particular moment to meet an exigent legislative situation. Jefferson was unquestionably responsible for the form it took, and perhaps also influenced the choice of the time to wield it. But to his words Washington gave the full force of his approval, prompted no doubt by his own views of policy as much as by any persuasion the Secretary

[43] JHR, I, 374, 375; text of petition in ASP, Finance, I, 108; Bond to Leeds, 14 Mch. 1791 (AHA, Ann. Rept., 1897, p. 475).
[44] JHR, I, 376.
[45] Document V.
[46] Document VI, enclosures.

of State might bring to bear. For the fact is that the President's own personal and official influence was committed when he urged Congress in serious and explicit terms to consider what encouragement to navigation was expedient in order to "render . . . commerce and agriculture less dependent on foreign bottoms."[47] During the ensuing eight weeks he had witnessed the failure of a committee to prepare such legislation after being directed to do so. He scarcely needed the final affront of the discharge of the committee by the House to inform him that there were some legislators, especially in the Senate, who were determined to block any measure that might give offense to Great Britain. His own mounting sense of impatience at their inattention to his recommendation as well as his deep-seated sense of national dignity could well have moved him to respond at once and in unmistakable terms to this challenge to executive leadership. But there can be no doubt that, on the political uses of the disclosure, the President and the Secretary of State were in full accord.

Nor can there be any doubt that the effect upon the opponents of the navigation bill was shattering. The House immediately referred the President's message to a new committee. In its number and composition this committee bore the appearance of being less favorably disposed than the one that had been discharged. Of its seven members all save Madison had been ardent supporters of the bank bill and other Hamiltonian measures.[48] Yet within the week Madison's navigation bill was approved by the committee and reported to the House.[49] Nor is it surprising that the President's announcement, coupled with the appearance in the press of the text of a navigation bill modelled on the British act, should have alarmed George Beckwith and sent him hurrying to Hamilton and to those in the Senate with whom he had confidential relations.

In an interview that Hamilton granted at the agent's request, Beckwith guessed or had been informed that the message was based on Morris' communications and that these were not of recent date. He therefore had been induced to speculate upon the motives that led the President to delay the disclosure to this particular time. With proper expressions of respect, he nevertheless could not avoid the suspicion that it either stood alone or was designed to connect this matter with other public questions before Congress, particularly in the House of Representatives—such as the Indian war or the "application from another Foreign Power." Speaking as if for the government, Hamilton sought to reassure him about the treaty obligation to France on which the tonnage application was based. "We do not view it here,"

[47] Washington's annual message, 8 Dec. 1790 (JHR, I, 331-2; Washington Writings, ed. Fitzpatrick, XXXI, 167).

[48] The other members were Goodhue, FitzSimons, Bourn, Laurance, Vining, and William Loughton Smith (JHR, I, 377-8, 379).

[49] Goodhue reported on 21 Feb. 1791 (JHR, I, 385; the text of the bill as reported is in ASP, Foreign Relations, I, 128; it appeared in the Federal Gazette, 23 Feb. 1791, the New-York Journal, 28 Feb. 1791, and other newspapers). This was at the time the House was locked in disagreement with the Senate over the excise bill (see Editorial Note to group of documents on the location of the Federal District, under 24 Jan. 1791) and four members of the committee were among the minority in that contest (JHR, I, 383-4, 386-7).

he said, "as binding us down to grant any peculiar advantages to that Power, to the exclusion of other Nations." He also declared that the President, while agreeing with Morris that no commercial treaty was attainable with England, was not influenced by any prejudices whatever. "I am sure he is not led to make these communications to the Legislature at this time, from any idea of assimilating this with other questions," he added, "yet I do not pretend to say that such views may not have struck the minds of certain persons, who have recommended this measure."[50] He believed that no animosities toward England would be aroused and he was certain that "in the Senate . . . none will be effected."

But the assurance was not convincing. In the face of Washington's unequivocal explanation that he had disclosed his assessment of the disposition of the British ministry because this might "at some time have influence on matters under . . . consideration" by Congress, the attempt to absolve the President and fix the blame elsewhere could only imply that Washington did not intend what his language so plainly said or that he was the imperceptive dupe of others. That Hamilton was far more concerned about the effect of the message than he affected to be is shown by his candid statement to Beckwith that Morris' dispatches had revealed a serious division in the British government. It is equally apparent in his ultimate desire, disclosed in this interview for the first time, to have some publicly acceptable pretext for disrupting the alliance with France. "I tell you candidly as an individual," Hamilton declared, "that I think the formation of a treaty of commerce, would by degrees have led to this measure, which undoubtedly that Party with us, whose remaining animosities and French partialities influence their whole political conduct, regard with dissatisfaction." Thus did the President's announcement, terminating his approach to Great Britain out of a sense of national decorum, wring from a member of his cabinet this anguished hope expressed in private to her agent that the prospect of detaching the United States from her ally might induce the ministry to do what Washington had publicly declared it would not do. Such was the measure of Hamilton's concern over an announcement which made vastly more difficult the realization of those partialities that guided his own political conduct.

Beckwith, though he erred in thinking that Washington would employ so powerful an instrument to affect so slight an issue as the French tonnage claims, was deeply concerned. Convinced that the

---

[50] Conversation on 16 Feb. 1791 between Beckwith and Hamilton as reported by the former and enclosed in his dispatch to Grenville of 3 Mch. 1791 (PRO: FO 4/12; full text printed in Syrett, *Hamilton*, VIII, 41-5). Beckwith was told about the message by a member of the Senate before it became public. He also enclosed a copy of the bill in his dispatch, as did Bond in his dispatch to Leeds of 14 Mch. 1791 (AHA, *Ann. Rept.*, 1897, p. 476). The substance of the message to the Senate was also revealed to Théophile Cazenove, who gave a garbled and inaccurate report of it. On the reference of the subject to TJ—possibly echoing Hamilton, with whom he was intimate—he wrote: "They think a minister from England will soon arrive and all can be arranged so as to avoid a war of commerce" (Cazenove to his principals in Amsterdam, 24 Feb. 1791, Cazenove Letterbook; because of what had happened to his friend Count Andriani, Cazenove warned against letting his secret political information be known in America. See Rutledge to TJ, 30 Mch. 1791).

message was "an attempt to check the growing friendship . . . likely to take place between us, to prevent possibly a mutual ministerial appointment, and to give a bias to a French interest," he felt compelled to speak out, regardless of his previous determination to remain silent on political matters. In order to make his views known "where they ought to be," he told Hamilton that he would send him a written communication which he could use in any way he saw fit. The letter that he wrote carefully excluded all of the confidential exchanges with Hamilton, all references to party divisions in the government, all inquiries into motives, all allusions to Morris and his communications.[51] In reporting to Grenville, Beckwith said that he had taken care in drafting this communication to abstain from "any expressions which might furnish the smallest pretext for complaint on the part of those who were pushing a French interest." The central theme of the letter concerned the commercial relations of Great Britain and the United States, their ancient friendships and mutual interests. Emphasizing Great Britain's friendly dispositions as evidenced by her liberality in granting commercial privileges, Beckwith appealed to these traditional bonds of friendship and interest to sustain the "natural habits of commerce . . . where even distance is advantage, and where the immense commercial capital of the one Country, feeds the enterprize of the other." These views, echoing Hamilton's own conception of the complementary economies of the two countries that he had previously expressed to the agent, had not been presented by Beckwith during the interview. On the contrary, far from repeating his earlier concern about a navigation bill aimed at Great Britain, he had by his own account fixed his attention on the Indian war and the French tonnage claims as motives for the President's disclosure. The contrast between the private interview and the written communication suggests the possibility that the agent may have been prompted by Hamilton to emphasize the commercial relations of the two countries, just as he himself had done in the private conversation. But in any case the chief purport of the communication was to counter the implication in Washington's announcement that the disposition of the British government was not friendly. Whether he inspired its form or not, Hamilton informed Beckwith that the letter had been "immediately laid before the President."[52]

Beckwith's letter intended for Washington's eyes was carefully drawn to avoid giving offense. But to others in private conversation, so the agent informed Grenville, he deemed it necessary "to hold a different language." The speedy emergence of the navigation bill undoubtedly prompted him to do so. In the privacy of his conversations with Hamilton and others Beckwith bluntly declared "that if the Party who seemed to be pressing violent measures, conceived that the trade to The States was indispensible to Great Britain, it became necessary

[51] Beckwith to Grenville, 3 Mch. 1791 (PRO: FO 4/12, enclosing copy of Beckwith to Hamilton, 17 Feb. 1791). But see Syrett, *Hamilton*, VIII, 51, wherein Beckwith's letter to Hamilton is described as "almost a verbatim report of the conversation" held on the 16th.

[52] Beckwith to Grenville, 3 Mch. 1791 (PRO: FO 4/12); in this letter Beckwith was able to transmit copies of the President's messages to the House and to the Senate, though the latter was not available to the public.

. . . to say plainly that the fact was not so." The confident assertion was betrayed by the threatening language in which it was conveyed, but, recalling his warning of 1789, Beckwith reminded his friends in the cabinet and in the Congress that the ministry had been prepared then to meet discriminatory legislation in kind. An unidentified member of the House of Representatives—Thomas FitzSimons, almost certainly[53]—told Beckwith that the bill reported on the 21st of February was carried in committee by a single vote and represented "a navigating, as well as . . . a discriminating system." The Representative also declared that he was opposed to the timing as well as the precipitation with which the measure was urged. "I object to it also," Beckwith quoted him as saying, "because I know it to be a French project, some time in agitation . . . pressed in order to prevent discussion.—Mr. Jefferson . . . is at work in every profitable way." He deemed it unwise to close the door on negotiations for a commercial treaty with England by such a premature and violent step and also thought the United States not in a situation to sustain a struggle of trade warfare with the British Empire. "I shall leave no exertions untried," he promised, "to overset this business at the present moment."[54]

The issue was joined in the House on the 23rd of February. On a motion to refer the navigation bill to the committee of the whole, Beckwith was told, there arose "an irregular . . . and warm discussion," followed by adjournment. The next day the bill was referred to the Secretary of State, who was directed to "report to Congress the nature and extent of the privileges and restrictions of the commercial intercourse of the United States with foreign nations," together with such measures as he should think proper for improving American commerce and navigation.[55] Far from demonstrating "the proven influence of Hamilton," this action, like the committee report itself, was in fact a victory for Madison, however narrow the margin. It left the initiative with the Secretary of State, not with the Secretary of the Treasury, and this may have been all that Madison and Jefferson hoped to achieve once the bill was reported. With only eight legislative days remaining in the session, they were well aware that the Senate could easily block the measure by amendment or by inaction even if it were to be adopted by the House. Under these circumstances, it is plausible to suppose that Madison deliberately refrained from forcing the issue upon a Congress already torn by bitter debates over the bank and excise bills.

One reason for doing so could have been to nullify such impugning of motives as had been advanced by Beckwith's informants—that the

[53] The member of the House was quoted by Beckwith as saying: "Excepting Mr. Goodhue of New England, I believe I am more deeply engaged in trade and have more property in it, than all the rest of our House put together. . . . I have no trade but a West India one, and that, wholly with the French, Dutch, and Danish islands." The description seems to apply only to FitzSimons. He and Goodhue were both members of the committee (see note 48).

[54] Beckwith to Grenville, 3 Mch. 1791 (PRO: FO 4/12, Appendix i).

[55] JHR, I, 388. The French *chargé* reported that the "English party" had done its best to have the matter referred to the Secretary of the Treasury, but had failed (Otto to Montmorin, 6 Mch. 1791; DLC: Henry Adams Transcripts).

navigation bill was being "pressed in order to prevent discussion."[56] The Jeffersonian strategy, if one may judge by the whole tenor of his conduct toward legislative bodies, was the exact opposite of this. On the day that his report on the French claims was sent to the Senate, Jefferson warned Otto that there would be delays, more especially because of "the Connection of the Subject with others depending before them, and which consistence may require to be carried on at the same time."[57] After Congress had adjourned, he explained that the general subject of navigation had been postponed merely for want of time. "I may safely say for the new Legislature," Jefferson confidently assured the *chargé*, "that the encouragement of that intercourse [with France] for the advantage of both parties will be considered as among the most interesting branches of the general subject committed to them."[58]

The conflict, as Jefferson perceived, was not merely between those like Hamilton who favored closer ties with England and those like Madison and himself who sought a greater degree of economic independence. It was also and more fundamentally a contest over the proper means of legislating in a republic, a profound and irreconcilable opposition between the Hamiltonian belief in the legitimacy of

[56] Beckwith to Grenville, 3 Mch. 1791 (PRO: FO 4/12, Appendix i), quoting the one identified above as FitzSimons. On 15 Apr. 1791 TJ met with John Vaughan and others at the American Philosophical Society and the next day Vaughan embodied in a letter to his brother what the Secretary of State almost certainly inspired him to write: "There is some opposition to the pursuing the Idea of a Navigation Act in this Country, but I doubt much whether the opposition will prevent its taking place. I am happy that it has been postponed untill the fall . . . as it will give ample time for discussion. The Ideas of the Leading Men are I believe to make a treaty which may *be the Interest of both parties*; but if something is not done towards a Treaty it will in all probability be impossible to prevent the advocates of a Navigation Act similar to yours from carrying into effect what they have in view. The country is beginning to feel its Strength and the good effect of an energetick Government. It is indeed almost impossible to describe the difference of its situation since the change of System. Some may presume and wish to carry matters too far, but the good sense of the Majority may check and will certainly do it if a favorable disposition is discovered [wanting]—even a negative conduct may have a very bad tendency" (John Vaughan to Benjamin Vaughan, 16 Apr. 1791; Tr in PPAP with one word left blank by copyist and conjecturally supplied in brackets; emphasis in original). See note 58.

The views expressed coincide exactly with TJ's views, including the supposition that he, too, desired a full public discussion of the measure. As the only member of the government's "Leading Men" in attendance at the meeting the evening before this letter was written, TJ would have acted with characteristic indirection in expressing these views in the hope that they would be transmitted. For another example of his use of indirection of this sort involving Benjamin Vaughan, see TJ to Vaughan, 27 June 1790, note.

[57] Secretary of State to Otto, 19 Jan. 1791 (Document XI in group of documents on French representation on tonnage duties, under 18 Jan. 1791).

[58] Secretary of State to Otto, 29 Mch. 1791 (same, Document XIII). Phineas Bond, a not unprejudiced witness, reported that the timing of Washington's message had been imputed to the desire "*to prevent any hasty measures* which might interrupt the commercial intercourse with Gr. Britain and to give the members of the legislature during the recess an opportunity to consider and digest the plans the most expedient for the encouragement of the fisheries and the promotion of the general navigation of the United States (Bond to Leeds, 14 Mch. 1791, AHA, *Ann. Rept.*, 1897, p. 476; emphasis supplied).

manipulation and overt appeals to self-interest and the Jeffersonian insistence on a full, open, and informed discussion of public issues. After the victory in the committee and the resultant publication of the navigation bill in the press, Jefferson rested his hopes on the popular response with his usual confidence in the outcome. This opportunity to define the issue in all of its moral and political ramifications and to focus public attention upon it may have been all that was intended at this critical juncture.

Thus when Washington lent his support to the strategy of Madison and Jefferson by disclosing his appraisal of the disposition of the British ministry, the opposition was definitely placed on the defensive. The best proof of this is to be found not in Jefferson's hopes for the next Congress, which continued unabated, but in the mounting sense of alarm among the supporters of the Secretary of the Treasury and among the agents and consuls of Great Britain. Their concern over the rising influence of the Secretary of State, transmitted to the British ministry, brought an end both to its indecision and to the sense of complacency voiced in Lord Hawkesbury's report.

III

This growing fear that Jefferson's influence over foreign policy had gained the ascendancy is clearly reflected in Beckwith's reports to Grenville. On the very day that Washington sent to the Senate Gouverneur Morris' account of his conversations with Pitt and Leeds, one frightened Senator told the British agent that this was done "at the instigation . . . of Mr. Jefferson, and in order to induce us to favor a French interest." He not only revealed the substance of Morris' dispatches but also delivered an urgent warning. "I am very explicit with you on this subject," the Senator said, "and I wish to impress you with . . . my conviction that there is an absolute necessity of following up this business during the summer; a delay I do assure you will at least be dangerous, and may throw us into a French interest. The arguments of that party go to this, that you are monopolizing the commerce of the whole world, as well as the navigation, and that policy dictates our forming a league with France and Spain to counterbalance it.—It occurs to me that if France shall adopt any hostile regulations in navigating or commercial matters, in consequence of our not giving in to their notions of the treaty, such a step must tend to promote an English interest."[59] It was then that Beckwith hastened to the Secretary of the Treasury, drafted his polite letter for the eyes of the President, and began to speak bluntly to those who were anxious to promote an English interest. The chorus of Senatorial voices in that quarter, as Beckwith observed to Grenville, repeated the theme over and over: Jefferson was "making every possible exertion to turn the commerce of this Country into the scale of France." They would

[59] The Senator was unidentified but the force of the language suggests that it was William Samuel Johnson, with whom Beckwith had long been on intimate terms and who in 1789 had been identified as "No. 1" among those whom he was in the habit of consulting (Beckwith to Grenville, 3 Mch. 1791, PRO: FO 4/12, Appendix d).

oppose this. If France should retaliate because of the rejection of their construction of the treaty, this of course would "naturally strengthen an English interest."[60]

The Senators' conversations, even as filtered through the reports of the British agent, reveal their apprehensions as well as their aims. "I do not think a treaty of alliance [with Great Britain] practicable at this moment," one Senator declared. "I am of opinion that a Majority of the sensible cool headed Men in this country would prefer it, but Mr. Jefferson's influence and his exertions would defeat it.—Why should not your Administration be disposed to form a treaty with us of a commercial nature? *It would infallibly lead to the other, and completely undermine the French interest.*[61] Beckwith, an acute and well-informed observer, was so concerned that he took the unusual step of submitting his own recommendation to Grenville. "I have grounds to believe from an Authority which I cannot question, although I am forbid to disclose it," he wrote Grenville in an obvious allusion to Hamilton, "that so dissatisfied is the government . . . with certain recent proceedings of the Court of Madrid, that they would break with them tomorrow, if their condition admitted of it." A treaty of commerce would indeed strike a blow at the French interest, but it would not be achieved if an alliance were to be insisted upon. "I am fully persuaded," he concluded, "if a negotiation does not take place this summer, our commerce will not remain on its present footing, beyond the month of November next."[62] Beckwith described the situation as critical.

Other British emissaries echoed his concern. Phineas Bond would not hazard an opinion as to what legislation the next Congress might enact, but he stated unequivocally that "the influence of the executive Government will certainly be exerted to favor a commercial connection with France." He was aware that Jefferson and Hamilton, when consulted by the committee of the House to whom Washington's message of the 14th had been referred, had given "extremely discordant opinions." But he feared the influence of the Secretary of State and his very strong desire to favor trade with France at the expense of Great Britain, as evidence of which he cited the report on fisheries—a report "couched in a language of severity not practiced between nations at Peace with each other."[63] Others were even more emphatic. The secret agent Allaire warned that if care were not taken Great Britain would lose her privileged position in American trade. Sir John Temple, believing a war of tonnage and other restrictions imminent, reported

[60] Beckwith's report stressed the relation between the French protest and Washington's message of the 14th, "two events . . . so materially connected with [Great Britain's] future commercial and political interests." He stressed also the authenticity of his information and "the repetitions by different gentlemen in confirmation of the same facts," advanced in "regular communications made . . . from day to day during the different stages of the business, from unquestionable sources" (Beckwith to Grenville, 3 Mch. 1791, PRO: FO 4/12; the above quotation is from Appendix d).

[61] Beckwith's conversation on the 26th with a member of the Senate, almost certainly Johnson (same, emphasis added).

[62] Beckwith to Grenville, 3 Mch. 1791 (PRO: FO 4/12).

[63] Bond to Leeds, 3 Jan., 14 Mch. 1791 (AHA, *Ann. Rept.*, 1897, p. 467-8, 470, 474-5, 477.

with concern that "the Secretary of States Party and Politicks gains ground here, and I fear will have influence enough to cause Acts and Resolves . . . disagreeable to Great Britain, to be passed early in the next session of Congress."[64] None of the British agents and consuls expressed satisfaction that the navigation bill had been referred to Jefferson and none considered that a Hamiltonian victory had been achieved by this action. All voiced their apprehensions with varying degrees of emphasis.

Such estimates of the rising influence of the Secretary of State were well founded. Jefferson himself, acutely conscious of the propitious moment, took advantage of it in an extraordinary move to gain European support for his policy. Knowing that French retaliation over the tonnage duties would indeed strengthen an English interest, he told Otto that, as confirmed by reports from all parts of the country, a navigation act would be adopted at the next session and that the President and himself intended to have it framed so as to accord reciprocal rights of citizenship in matters of commerce to nationals of France and the United States. He also warned the *chargé*, in a confidential message really intended for Montmorin, that this would be difficult to accomplish if French merchants induced the National Assembly to engage in commercial reprisals.[65] This was an understandable effort to forestall a recognized danger. But his next move was a proposal for concerted action by France, Spain, and Portugal in support of the American policy. He forwarded a copy of the navigation bill to William Short and urged him to have it translated, printed, and circulated among members of the National Assembly, together with such explanatory comment as needed—but without revealing the quarter whence it came. If Short could think of a better way to determine whether that body would enact a similar measure, he should adopt it.[66] To this call for undiplomatic involvement in the internal legislation of another country, Jefferson added variations when he sent copies of the bill to Carmichael at Madrid and to Humphreys at Lisbon. To Humphreys, who enjoyed the confidence of the Secretary of State less than he did that of the President, he briefly stated the aim and advised him to rely on the counsel of De Pinto concerning the possibility of like action by Portugal.[67] To Carmichael, in whose reliability he had little if any confidence, he was full and explicit. Being virtually certain that the letter would be read by the Spanish authorities before it came to Carmichael, he was at pains in directing him how to communicate the navigation bill to the ministry and to explain its purpose. The bill, he said, had been committed to the Secretary of State to study and it would be brought forward at the next session as a first step, aimed at but not unfriendly to Great Britain. Far from being a design to prompt other nations in matters lying within their

---

[64] Peter Allaire to George Yonge, 21 Mch. 1791 (PRO: FO 4/10; for note on Allaire, see Editorial Note to group of documents on war crisis of 1790, note 121; Temple to Leeds, 19 Mch. and 23 May 1791, PRO: FO 4/9).

[65] Otto to Montmorin, 10 Mch. 1791, reporting TJ's confidential conversation (DLC: Henry Adams Transcripts).

[66] TJ to Short, 15 Mch. 1791.

[67] TJ to Humphreys, 15 Mch. 1791.

province to decide, Jefferson wrote, this was only an informal communication of American intent to make more secure "the freedom of the ocean . . . to all the world."[68] The letter to Carmichael, like the confidential explanation to Otto that was meant for Montmorin, was actually phrased for the eyes of Floridablanca.

This effort to concert measures affecting the European balance of power was in reality an extension of the domestic strategy Jefferson and Madison had devised. Just before sending these instructions to the three American emissaries, Jefferson invited Madison to join him in "a wade into the country"—the March day was wet underfoot but clear overhead—and to dine with him afterwards. He also urged Madison to take up quarters at his residence in Market street, in order among other considerations to be rid of the British agent Beckwith.[69] This was the day after Jefferson gave Carmichael emphatic and unequivocal instructions concerning the new policy toward Spain, a position to which Madison also contributed in important ways but one Washington embraced with some hesitation.[70] Thus to the difficulty with France over tonnage was added the serious problem with Spain over the navigation of the Mississippi, both of these thorny issues becoming critical at a moment when the effort to counter British commercial restrictions seemed about to succeed at home. Under such circumstances it would have been surprising indeed if Jefferson had not devised such an external counterpart of his and Madison's strategy. If the governments of both nations could be persuaded that their commercial interests coincided with those of the United States, these points of friction might be smoothed over at the same time that the policy of commercial reciprocity gained powerful European support. With the British navy so recently mobilized for a war against Spain, Jefferson naturally stressed the impact an American navigation bill would have on the sea power of her rival. Informal as it claimed to be and devoid as it was of any proposal of joint undertakings, this was nevertheless an unprecedented declaration to France, Spain, and Portugal that the United States, in daring to risk commercial warfare with England, was actually doing battle in their behalf against the traditional foe. The young nation had sought to usher in a new era of commercial relations based on principles of universal reciprocity.[71] Now, forced to pick up England's weapon to turn it against her, she would do so not in quest of monopoly or power or imperial dominion but in order to make more secure the freedom of the seas for all nations. This was a liberal impulse, but the weapon was an old one, fabricated amid the contests of European power politics.

It is scarcely credible to suppose that Jefferson could have taken this unusual step without the knowledge and consent of the President. The navigation bill, Jefferson announced to Carmichael in unqualified terms, was "the measure we propose to take." In this he spoke first

[68] TJ to Carmichael, 17 Mch. 1791.

[69] TJ to Madison, 13 Mch. 1791.

[70] See Editorial Note to group of documents on new policy toward Spain, under 10 Mch. 1791.

[71] See TJ's draft of a model treaty of commerce, 1784 (Vol. 4: 463-90); Setser, *Reciprocity*, p. 52-98; Felix Gilbert, *To the Farewell Address*, p. 44-75.

for himself, making the initial disclosure of his intent in a matter committed to him for study. But he also spoke for the administration and —such was his confidence in favorable action by the next Congress— for the government as a whole. There is no reason to suppose that in this instance Jefferson departed from his customary practice of submitting drafts of letters for approval or that, once he proposed the idea, Washington failed to give it his sanction. For at this time the two men acted with such a harmony of views as would never prevail again. On such issues as the permanent seat of government, the Mississippi question, the cases of impressment, the proceedings in the Northwest Territory, the French tonnage claims, the Algerine problems, the relations with Great Britain—indeed on all important matters during the final session of the First Congress they saw eye to eye, excepting only their official divergence on the constitutionality of the national bank. "[My] system," Jefferson later wrote in the most candid letter he ever addressed to Washington, "was to give some satisfactory distinctions to [the French], of little cost to us, in return for the solid advantages yielded us by them; and to have met the English with some restrictions which might induce them to abate their severities against our commerce. I have always supposed this coincided with your sentiments."[72] The supposition, for this brief period at least, was unquestionably valid. Jefferson therefore had cause for confidence that his policy would prevail at home even if it should fail to inspire concerted action abroad.

IV

The view expressed by one Senator to Beckwith that this policy included "the forming a league with France and Spain" was an exaggeration that testified to his apprehensions. But rumors of the possibility that the United States might turn to other European powers added their weight to reports of Beckwith and others that came to the British ministry in the spring of 1791 about the rising influence of "the French party" led by the Secretary of State. The most exigent pressures however, were brought to bear by the mercantile and speculative connections of those Americans who hoped for an alliance with England. Self-interest on both sides of the Atlantic as well as political and other motives operated to bring this hidden channel of communications into play. The particular instrument employed on this occasion was Colonel William Stephens Smith, son of a wealthy New York merchant, Revolutionary officer of repute, son-in-law of the Vice-President, former aide to the President, kinsman of prominent Loyalists through his mother, and a man respected for his integrity by both Thomas Jefferson and George Hammond, though "not untinctured with vanity and affectation."[73] Smith, who had been secretary

[72] TJ to Washington, 9 Sep. 1792.
[73] The quotation is from Hammond to Grenville, 5 Apr. 1792, "Private" (Grenville Papers, Boconnoc); for TJ's characterization of Smith, see TJ to Madison, 30 Jan. 1787, postscript of 5 Feb. 1787. Washington himself had recommended Smith to Congress at the close of the war (Smith to the President of Congress, 14 Jan. 1785, DNA: RG 360, PCC No. 92, M/247). John Jay, who had a high opinion of Smith's talents, had prompted his mission as courier to Portugal in 1787—an episode perhaps intended to bring him into official notice

of legation when Adams was minister to England and had sought to remain there afterward as *chargé des affaires*—or "as much higher" in rank as Congress might have been disposed to admit[74]—spent the first three months of 1791 in London on a mission that merits more scrutiny than it has received.

Smith and his friends, who included Alexander Hamilton and Henry Knox and once had embraced Thomas Jefferson, declared often and indeed with suspicious reiteration that his journey to England had been undertaken solely for private reasons. Both he and they also encouraged the belief that Grenville, taking advantage of his presence in London, paid markedly polite attention to him, expressed an insistent desire for an interview, and persuaded him to convey a message to the President testifying to the friendly disposition of the British government and announcing its decision to send a minister to the United States. The fact of the interview and the message may be credited. But every other circumstance surrounding this extraordinary mission suggests that the exact reverse of the impression Smith and his friends sought to create is a closer approximation to actuality.[75] Private motives may have entered into the calculations that brought Smith to London, among them the desire to sell New York lands and to speculate in public securities.[76] He and his friends also, unquestionably, hoped that this mission would place him in the forefront of those to be considered for the post of minister to England when one should be appointed.[77] But the circumstances under which he took his departure, his actions while in London, his subsequent behavior, and the attendant moves of Robert Morris, Rufus King, and other supporters of Hamiltonian measures make inescapable the conclusion that he was the deliberately chosen and confidential agent of the friends of the British interest in America and that his mission was directed primarily toward public objects.

---

and one in which Smith amplified a minor role in characteristic terms (Smith to Jay, 2 Aug., 12 Sep., 16 and 17 Oct. 1787, same; Jay to Adams, 6 Feb. 1787, same, RG 59, PCC No. 121; Jay to Smith, 6 Feb. and 12 May 1787, same).

[74] Smith to TJ, 29 Jan. 1787. Smith, who had known Washington since 1776, applied early in his administration for "any appointment either at home or abroad" and indicated his preference for a diplomatic post by enclosing testimonials from John Jay as Secretary for Foreign Affairs and from "the Court of Lisbon" (Smith to Washington, 12 May 1789, DLC: Washington Papers).

[75] For a different interpretation, see Bemis, *Jay's Treaty*, p. 118-19; Channing, *History*, IV, 121. Ritcheson, *British policy*, p. 119-21, accepts and indeed extends the prevailing view of Smith's mission. Holding that the move originated in London, that Grenville received Smith several times, that he extended "extraordinary courtesies" to him, and that he gave him a final honor by delaying the Falmouth packet, Ritcheson concludes that "the British Foreign Secretary was deeply intent on relaying a message through Smith to the United States government" and that Smith and his friends, despite exaggerated claims of success, did help stem a "rising tide of anti-British sentiment in the United States."

[76] Richard Platt to Alexander Hamilton, 8 June 1790 (Syrett, *Hamilton*, VIII, 453-4; K. M. Roof, *Colonel William Smith and Lady*, p. 210-11, 212).

[77] See notes 81 and 142. Smith was in fact recommended for the post on his return (Richard Platt to Alexander Hamilton, 8 June 1791, Syrett, *Hamilton*, VIII, 453-4). Late in 1791 the *Courier de l'Europe* published a rumor that Smith had been appointed minister to England (Gouverneur Morris, *Diary*, ed. Davenport, II, 338).

This is quite understandable. The adverse effects of Gouverneur Morris' reports had become a matter of concern to Hamilton, Jay, and others some time before the third session of Congress opened. Hamilton himself, a leader in promoting that mission, had been so disturbed over its outcome that he had attempted to discount its effect by discrediting the agent, but had failed to convince Washington.[78] For a year and more he and his supporters in Congress had tried to convey to the British ministry through Beckwith a sense of their need for some decisive evidence of its friendly disposition and its willingness to negotiate about commercial affairs. Yet, wholly preoccupied with European affairs, the ministry had communicated only its initial warning that commercial discrimination would bring on retaliatory measures. Under these circumstances, it would have seemed obvious that a more direct channel was required to impress upon Pitt and his colleagues the urgency of the situation, and equally so that an emissary highly connected with Washington and Adams, having strong predilections for the English nation, and acquainted with influential personages there would be a fit choice for the purpose. But this very fact goes far to explain why a mission devised to counteract that of Gouverneur Morris should have been characterized to the point of excess as one of a purely private nature.

Just before Congress met, Smith applied to the President for permission to leave his post as federal marshal to go to England, with the avowed intention of returning by the March packet. Although he told Washington that private affairs of his family forced him to leave, his decision to depart by a vessel sailing within a week was made with the utmost haste. "The President I flatter myself will excuse me not addressing him sooner on this Subject," he wrote, "when I assure him that I had no Idea of the necessity of the movement nor in the least contemplated it, previous to yesterday noon."[79] Rufus King conveyed the appeal and explained the nature of Smith's private objects. Washington, in a friendly note written the day before he delivered his annual address to Congress, granted the request.[80] Hamilton assured Beckwith that Smith went "on private business altogether," partly for himself and partly for his father-in-law. But the decision to undertake the journey had been so precipitate that John Adams clearly had not been consulted and Abigail Smith was little better informed. Both were concerned.[81]

[78] See Editorial Note to documents on the war crisis of 1790 (Vol. 17: 96-102).

[79] Smith to Washington, 1 Dec. 1790 (DNA: RG 59, MLR). Smith said that Rufus King would explain the nature of the affairs that obliged him "to leave . . . Country and friends." On the concern of his wife and John Adams, see Abigail Adams Smith to John Adams, 7 Jan. 1791 (MHi: AM); K. M. Roof, *Colonel William Smith and Lady*, p. 211. See note 81.

[80] Washington to Smith, 7 Dec. 1790 (DLC: Washington Papers; *Writings*, ed. Fitzpatrick, XXXI, 164).

[81] Beckwith's report of conversations "with a gentleman in Office" on 15 June 1791, in which Hamilton is quoted as saying that he had told the agent "during the winter" that Smith had gone on private business (enclosed in Beckwith to Grenville, 31 July 1791, PRO: FO 4/12; text printed in Syrett, *Hamilton*, VIII, 475-7, with notes indicating two variations from the account sent by Beckwith to Dorchester on 27 July 1791). Abigail Smith wrote to her father that

Whatever the private objects, Smith obtained an interview with Grenville through confidential channels opened up by Robert Morris. Through his land speculations Morris was able to put Smith in touch with two of the principal members of the Pulteney Associates, William Pulteney and Patrick Colquhoun. Pulteney was a Scottish advocate, a friend of Adam Smith and David Hume, and an independent in Parliament who had sought to conciliate the rebellious colonies but supported the prosecution of the war in order "to protect our American friends from the tyranny and oppression of Congress . . . friends he believed were very numerous."[82] His brother, George Johnstone, had known Robert Morris in America and Pulteney, once an impecunious younger son but now immensely wealthy, was able to purchase Morris' holdings in the Phelps and Gorham purchase because he had married the heiress to the great Pulteney fortune. He was an invariable supporter of Pitt.[83] Colquhoun, also a Scot, had been engaged in mercantile affairs in Virginia before the Revolution. Later, as one of the leading merchants of Glasgow and the most prominent spokesman for the English textile industry, he had become one of Morris' correspondents. Eminently respected for his integrity, acumen, and writings on public affairs, he had also won the esteem of the most powerful political figure of Scotland, Henry Dundas, who was "on the closest terms, public and private, with Pitt."[84] During the war crisis of 1790 Dundas had recommended Colquhoun to Grenville as "a man of intelligence in the American trade and connexions . . . who might be of some use in some parts of the negotiations going forward" with Gouverneur Morris.[85] Thus, with ready access to such men as Pulteney and Colquhoun, Smith could communicate with the second man on the government side in the House of Commons. Gouverneur Morris, even when armed with a letter from Washington, had not been able to command such a hearing as William Stephens Smith achieved through these three redoubtable Scotsmen.

she hoped the voyage was not undertaken without due consideration and then added: "I wish it may succeed equal to his expectations. Those friends to whom he communicated the object, have approved of it. *But if he had been treated by those in Power as he was entitled to expect he would not have been compelled to have undertaken it*" (Abigail Adams Smith to John Adams, 7 Jan. 1791, MHi: AM; emphasis added).

82 Speech in the House, 6 Nov. 1780, calling for punishment of those who stigmatized the war as unjust (Namier and Brooke, *House of Commons*, III, 343, citing Debrett, *Parliamentary Register*, I, 31).

83 Pulteney was the son of Sir James Johnstone (Namier and Brooke, *House of Commons*, III, 341-3).

84 For Patrick Colquhoun (1745-1820), see DNB. The opinion quoted about Henry Dundas (1742-1811), later Lord Melville, is that of Namier and Brooke, *House of Commons*, II, 354-7. For almost a year, perhaps at the instigation of Robert Morris and others, Colquhoun, acting through Dundas, had pressed Grenville to have the government reach an accord with the United States. Echoing the views later expressed by Hamilton and Johnson to Beckwith, he argued that limited admission of American vessels to the West Indies would benefit both nations, that it was important to open diplomatic relations, and that a treaty of commerce would lead to a closer political connection (Colquhoun to Dundas, 3 Apr. 1790, enclosing his observations on the state of commerce with the United States; same to same; 12 and 23 Apr. 1790, with a memorandum arguing the reciprocal advantage of opening the West Indies; all in Grenville Papers, Boconnoc).

85 Dundas to Grenville, 6 Aug. 1790 (Grenville Papers, Boconnoc).

While Smith was still on the Atlantic, a New York newspaper announced that the President had sent him abroad on public business.[86] Similar conjectures appeared in the London press. "Smith says he is only here on his private affairs," wrote his friend Francisco de Miranda to Henry Knox; "this may be so; perhaps what he calls his private affairs may have a public tendency, but the people here will not believe it—they cast a friendly eye to you and will be pleased if S—'s Visit should terminate in a public station.—I send you a paragraph in the papers of yesterday on this subject; at which he laughs and says it is not such thing."[87] Later the Venezuelan adventurer, who commented on Smith's activities to Hamilton as well as to Knox, reported that his ideas had produced a change in sentiment favorable to the United States, that both of them had talked much with persons of influence who seemed aware of the change, and that he thought it a pity not to take advantage of this new atmosphere by establishing a good intelligence—presumably an exchange of ministers—between the two countries.[88]

But what Smith later reported to Washington was that he had "noticed a very great change in the Public opinion" concerning America since he had left England. "I have received more Polite attention as an American from some of the first characters . . . during the Last Winter," he wrote, "than for the whole three years of my public residence." A short time after his arrival he had been "very earnestly solicited to wait on the Minister Mr. Pitt or Lord Grenville" but had "pointedly declined, upon the Principle of . . . appearing in London, in no other Capacity than that of a private Gentleman, pursuing his private affairs." He was told that the ministers had "expressed a great desire" to see him, but he persisted in his refusal since he thought such an advance would be "a greater commitment" of his country than any private individual had a right to make. Yet on one condition he would consent:[89]

'. . . I observed, if any of the Gentlemen in the administration of England wished to see me, and they thought proper to communicate in writing that wish, and had been led to suppose that a private individual of that country merited such a mark of their attention, The great respect I entertained of the present administration would not permit me to pass by the communication unnoticed.'

[86] Smith's wife noted this in another comment revealing her husband's diplomatic ambitions: "A paragraph in this days paper mentions that he has been sent by the President on Public Service, which shows the Worlds opinion that he ought to have been attended to in past appointments (Abigail Adams Smith to John Adams, 7 Jan. 1791, MHi: AM). Short told TJ that the firms representing the United States in Amsterdam were "in general perfectly informed of every thing that passes in America," but did not know of Smith's mission (Short to TJ, 16 Jan. 1791).

[87] Miranda to Knox, 2 Feb. 1791 (MHi: Henry Knox Papers). Later, in a letter that contained nothing else, Miranda asked that Knox provide Smith with "a copy of that small *Cypher* I gave to you at Boston" (Miranda to Knox, 9 Apr. 1791; same).

[88] Miranda to Hamilton, 5 Apr. 1791 (Syrett, *Hamilton*, VIII, 245-6).

[89] Smith to Washington, 6 June 1791 (DNA: RG 59, MLR).

This suggestion, if ever relayed to Grenville, was naturally ignored. Some time elapsed with nothing Smith could report save "numberless visits and invitations" which so far interfered with his private affairs as to prevent a return by the March packet. Nevertheless, "having perfectly embraced the objects" of his visit, he engaged passage in the April packet.[90] This brought results:[91]

> After I had taken leave of my friends accordingly, Mr. Colquhoun a Gentleman at the Head of the manufacturing interest of England, and from whom I had received many marks of friendship and civility, then called on me and said 'since I had been in London he had had several interviews with Mr. Dundas, and other Gentlemen in administration, who he knew would be disappointed if I left London without their seeing me, that the present convulsed state of European affairs so fully engrossed their attention, that they had frequently lamented that it had not been in their power to pay me those civilities which (they were pleased to say) from various circumstances they thought me entitled to.' He then read me a copy of a note which he had sent to Mr. Dundas.

Smith not only requested a copy of the note but also betrayed his inexperience by sending it to Washington. For what Colquhoun's communication proved beyond doubt was that the insistence upon an interview came not from the ministry but from Colquhoun himself. He had written to Dundas earlier and had received no response. Now, on the 4th of April, he wrote again with an urgency tinged with acerbity:[92]

> Mr. Colquhoun begs leave to remind Mr. Dundas of the circumstances he had the honor to mention to him in his note of last Monday—namely, that Colo. Smith has fixed positively to return to America on Tuesday next or Wednesday at farthest. Did not Mr. Colquhoun firmly believe that much useful information to Government would be derived from an interview with this Gentleman, previous to his departure, he would not have presumed to have mentioned this matter again, which he does entirely without Colo. Smith's knowledge.—He has no hesitation to avow his anxiety upon a measure that appears to him of such infinite consequence to the Country, nor his fears that an opportunity extremely critical may be lost by the delay even of a very few days.

This missive, echoing the insistent pleas from the friends of an Anglican interest in America, was written at a time when the ministry was not only wholly engrossed in European affairs but also deeply divided. Indeed, the situation was so serious that on the last day of March, with Leeds well aware he was about to be sacrificed as Secretary for Foreign Affairs but adamant in his refusal to sanction the ministry's

[90] Smith stated that he had told the President in his letter requesting leave that he would return by the April packet. But both in that letter and indeed in this very report he showed that it was his intention to return on the March packet (Smith to Washington, 1 Dec. 1790 and 6 June 1791, DNA: RG 59, MLR).
[91] Smith to Washington, 6 June 1791 (DNA: RG 59, MLR).
[92] Colquhoun to Dundas, 4 Apr. 1791 (copy enclosed in Smith to Washington, 6 June 1791, DNA: RG 59, MLR).

vacillating posture towards Russia, the cabinet had debated the issue until one in the morning. Pitt himself, according to Leeds, even hinted at resignation.[93] Yet it was during this week of crisis that Grenville, who was about to succeed Leeds, granted an interview to Smith. Further, he accepted the extraordinary conditions that were stipulated by the American—or, more likely, by his astute Scottish advisers. But Colquhoun's acerbity and Dundas' aggressiveness—"the most impudent fellow he ever knew," the Lord Chancellor had recently remarked of him[94]—may have been self-defeating. At any rate, Smith now turned to Pulteney to achieve his object.

On the evening of the 5th, the day before he planned to leave for Falmouth to catch the packet, Smith said that he had called on Pulteney at his home in Piccadilly. "Our conversation," he reported later to Washington, "was chiefly political and without entering into a detail of it I shall only say, that I flatter myself that I had constantly in view the honor and dignity of my Country, her attachment to peaceable systems and the reluctance that she would feel at being obliged (from the injustice and cross-grained Politicks of Britain) to take any steps in the vindication of her own honor or the security of her frontiers, which at the present juncture might tend further to embarrass England and perhaps finally force America to throw herself into a Political scale decidedly inimical to the interests of Great Britain."[95] This too revealed more than Smith could have intended, but he went on to inform Washington that Pulteney had "expressed great anxiety" at his leaving before the ministers had had an opportunity to see him and had pressed him so insistently to delay his departure until the May packet that Smith promised to consider it and to write him the next morning. The letter that he wrote on the 6th was obviously intended not for Pulteney but for the eyes of a minister, yet Smith innocently supplied a copy of that, too, to Washington. It began by quoting Pulteney as saying to him " 'that the Gentlemen at the head of the administration of this Country are very desirous of seeing me, as they are investigating those points which may promote a friendly intercourse between Great Britain and the United States of America; but that the pressure of European affairs at the present moment renders it impossible for them immediately to attend to the subject, and therefore as they wish an interview previous to my departure, it would be very agreeable to them, if I could make it convenient to postpone my departure untill the May Packet." This, if it accurately reflected the conversation of the night before, made of Pulteney only a channel to transmit a ministerial desire—not, as Smith had reported to Washington, the originator of the suggestion of a delayed departure.

But what followed was even more extraordinary. "If the Ministers

93 "Political Memoranda of Francis Fifth Duke of Leeds," ed. Oscar Browning, *Camden Society Publications*, xxxv (1884), 148, 154, 155, 157, 160-1.

94 Thurlow's remark was caused by Dundas' suggestion that the Chancellor give a dinner, at which Pitt and Grenville would be present, for the avowed purpose of having Thurlow express before them his opinion on the question of the election of Scottish peers. Thurlow bluntly replied that he would readily give him a dinner, but no opinion on a matter still *coram judice* (same, xxxv, 149-50).

95 Smith to Washington, 6 June 1791 (DNA: RG 59, MLR).

of England perfectly understand, that in communicating with me, they communicate with a private Citizen of America," Smith wrote to Pulteney, "I can have no objection to the proposed interview. . . . But having visited England with the knowledge and approbation of The President of the United States, and having communicated to him my intention of returning in the April packet, I cannot consider myself justified in overstaying that period upon any pretext whatsoever." He would therefore be obliged to depart as planned. "But at the same time, Sir," Smith immediately added, "I would suggest that as I propose sailing in a Vessel under the perfect command of Administration, if (as I have been led to suppose) they wish to see me previous to my departure, and should think proper to detain the Packet untill the object they have in view is answered, and untill my arrival at Falmouth, no arrangements of mine shall interfere with their wish."[96] This audacious suggestion, couched in language contrived to lend the President's sanction to Smith's object by a discreet omission of the reason it had been given, carried the hint that a refusal would in some sense imply an affront to his office. If the interview had indeed been a ministerial proposal instead of his own, Smith must have been aware that a mere letter to Washington by the April packet would have provided sufficient justification for a postponement of his return. The reason for his emphatic refusal to allow any pretext whatever to interfere with his promise to the President is also robbed of its value by the fact that he had already overstayed his leave.[97] Thus the remarkable communication to Pulteney, which in one paragraph insisted upon Smith's status as a private citizen and in the next tried to take on a quasi-public coloring, would appear to be a last gamble to achieve what he had first attempted and failed to get—something in writing from a member of the cabinet that he could take back to the United States. If so, it succeeded.

Pulteney conveyed the letter to Grenville that same day and returned with the response by three in the afternoon. With characteristic coolness of judgment and conciliatory manner, Grenville met both of Smith's stipulations:[98]

[96] Smith to Pulteney, 6 Apr. 1791 (DNA: RG 59, MLR; endorsed: "No. 2. Copy from Colo. Smith to Mr. Pulteney"; in Smith's hand).

[97] See note 90. Furthermore, Smith told the President that he had left his office in charge of his brother, Justus B. Smith and then added: "should this . . . arrangement not be agreeable to The President and he shoud think proper to appoint some other Gentleman to fill his office previous to my return, I shall as I have been accustomed to do, bow with respect to his arrangement" (Smith to Washington, 1 Dec. 1790, DNA: RG 59, MLR). Richard Platt, who should have known, declared at the time that Smith had "previously resigned his office" (Platt to Samuel Webb, 8 Dec. 1790, quoted in K. M. Roof, *Colonel William Smith and Lady*, p. 210).

[98] Grenville to Pulteney, 6 Apr. 1791 (DNA: RG 59, MLR; endorsed: "No. 3. Copy Colo. Smith [thus in MS] to Mr. Pulteney"; emphasis supplied). Smith told Washington that, when Pulteney delivered Grenville's note, he asked him whether the packet would be detained; he said that Pulteney then returned to Grenville and was back again at five o'clock with the minister's second note. But this communication, which Smith also sent to Washington, is not dated the 6th (see note 91). Washington returned the originals of Grenville's two notes after taking copies of them (Washington to Smith, 13 July 1791, *Writings*, ed. Fitzpatrick, XXXI, 311).

I mentioned to you when I last had the pleasure of seeing you here [he wrote Pulteney], that I had felt desirous of a proper opportunity of conversing with Colo. Smith respecting the present situation of Affairs between this Country and the United States of America, as being persuaded that such a conversation would afford me much useful information. As it does not fall within the duties of my Department to conduct or direct the details of any Negotiation which *may be* entered into between the two Countries, it will I am persuaded be easy for you to explain to Colo. Smith . . . that such a conversation could not be considered as being in any manner a ministerial one.—If under these circumstances it should be convenient to him to allow me the honor of seeing him here on Saturday morning between twelve and one, I shall be at home and disengaged.

The reason given for viewing the meeting as not ministerial was scarcely convincing. Grenville was not only the one to whom Beckwith was now submitting his reports on American affairs: he was also increasingly relied upon by Pitt in matters of foreign policy, even in critical issues about which Leeds himself was kept in ignorance.[99] He must also have known that in a few days he would become Secretary for Foreign Affairs. His letter, of course, expressed nothing beyond the desire to obtain useful information. But he had granted the interview and the next day he gave orders for the detention of the packet.[100] When Smith requested a copy of the letter, Pulteney gave him the original and a copy of the note about the packet. Smith transmitted both to Washington as evidence of the changed attitudes he had discovered in England. But the account of what transpired at the interview was his own, set down only after he had returned to the United States. That, too, revealed more than he could have intended.

According to Smith's relation, Grenville received him cordially, thanked him for acceding to the "request" for an interview, and declared it to be his wish, privately and officially as well as one pervading the cabinet, "that some amicable arrangements might take place between the two Countries and their Mutual interests be examined with a friendly eye, and every point between them, explained and adjusted upon principles equally advantageous." The rising dignity of the United States, its foundation well laid in a firm, wise, and liberal Constitution, had caused the people of England to share this disposition of government. Grenville was quoted as having early expressed a wish to see Smith, but the ministry had been too engrossed in European affairs to think of other matters. He hoped that America nourished equally friendly sentiments and that "some means might be fallen upon at Least to unite them again in the bonds of friendship." Smith, acknowledging his gratitude for the extremely polite gesture to a private citizen of the United States and for the detention of the packet, replied that the amicable disposition of his country could not be doubted. She had

---

[99] E. D. Adams, *The influence of Grenville on Pitt's foreign policy* (Washington, 1904), p. 5.

[100] Grenville to Pulteney, 7 Apr. 1791 (DNA: RG 59, MLR; endorsed: "No. 4. Copy from Lord Grenville to Mr. Pulteney").

manifested this by sending a minister to England, but he had been obliged to return home, his mission a failure and he "not very favourable impressed with Ideas of the friendly intentions of England, towards the United States." The ostensible reason publicly given, Grenville would recall, was one "not . . . overcharged with delicacy"—that is, that the American government was not sufficiently coercive to enable it to meet its engagements. Other nations of Europe had not acted on this premise. Hence the United States had no alternative "consistent with that dignity of Character, which it was her intention to support, but to wait untill England by her Minister informed her that she was satisfied with the Ability, and Honourable intentions of the government and rulers in America to fulfill their engagements, and that she was disposed to enter into an investigation of the affairs of the respective nations, and to make such establishments as might appear consistant with the real interests of each." As a private gentleman cognizant of the disposition of his countrymen, Smith could assure Grenville that as soon as this step should be taken "England . . . would meet with every return of civility from the Government of the United States of America, that could be wished." But, lest the ministers delude themselves, he seriously doubted that any other step would lead to this result. They could not expect a second advance, considering the result of the first and the cause of its termination.

Grenville declared that the ministry had already determined to send a minister to the United States, that Elliot had been named but had declined within the past few days, that a proper character was then being sought, "and that as soon as they had fixed upon the Gentleman, no time would be lost in his making arrangements for an immediate departure." He could not say when this would be, but he thought that the person selected might be expected in America within two or three months. Grenville then asked Smith, according to the latter, what sort of person would be acceptable "and by what means a good understanding might be speedily produced, supposing it probable that opposition was to be expected from those attached to a french party, who he had been informed were very strong in America." Since the minister appeared "disposed to enter with great freedom, and with a very flattering degree of Confidence into this Conversation," Smith replied, he would advance his ideas without reserve. Most of the difficulties between the two countries proceeded from a total want of just information regarding American affairs and the principles that governed its people. Also, former administrations had perhaps been too easily disposed to believe that "nothing honourable, great or dignified could possibly issue from thence. . . . The particular class of Character in England who advocated this opinion, and the information of those on the other side the Atlantic upon which it was founded could not be unknown to his Lordship."

As for Grenville's first question, Smith answered that the minister sent to America should be "a man of a fair mind and unblemished reputation, one whose character had never been committed in the late Contests" between the two countries and who therefore would be capable of making "honourable and Just statements to the British court" about the United States. In brief, "a purely British Character" was the only kind of diplomat suitable. As for Grenville's hint about a French party, the existence of parties in the United States "might be readily allowed without the shadow of reflection" and this should clearly enter into calculations.[101] But in doing so it was necessary to contrast the conduct of England and France, since each of the contending parties in America looked to the country it favored in its effort to gain the ascendancy. France, despite her supposed confusion, was aware of the growing importance of the United States as a consumer of her manufactures and, in addition to her past acts of friendship, had manifested a desire for a closer connection by the recent appointment of Ternant as minister, "a Gentleman of abilities and popular in America." But while she was strengthening her friends in America by acts of kindness, England "was decidedly loosing ground by that species of (perhaps) unintentional neglect, which in the present state of political contention, if not soon remedied, might be productive of much injury, if not annihilation to the British interest in America." That party, joined by those who placed the American character first and had no partisan preferences for France or England, desired England to come forward by her minister and manifest a desire to discuss all points of difference arising out of the Treaty of Peace, to adjust these on principles of justice and good faith, and to negotiate a treaty of commerce. By this means only could "*the duties on British Goods and British Shipping . . . be fixed, never to exceed a certain rate*," the collection of debts facilitated, the transactions of merchants aided, the power of consuls defined, and many other useful regulations established which would probably "*secure to Great Britain a preeminence in the American trade, over every other Country in Europe and to render those advantages permanent*."[102] This argument, identical with that advanced in Hawkesbury's *Report*, was reinforced with an urgent warning: "many Circumstances in the affairs of the United States of America pressed exceedingly at present for an almost immediate decision on the part of Great Britain before new difficulties arose, from some loose operating causes or from the intrigues of rival nations."

But it would also be of advantage to the British interest in America, Smith reiterated, if *all* public characters sent to that country as well as the minister of Great Britain "were men whose characters had not been committed in the Late war." Above all, the minister and the consul-general should be "pure British Characters":

. . . as the connection between Great Britain and America must be principally commercial, a Character should be fixed on for Consul General, who had not only some Local Knowledge of the commerce of America but also Local and if possible practical knowledge of the trade of Great Britain and the other countries in Europe so far

---

[101] Smith at first wrote "there were *two* parties in America" and then deleted "two" in order to permit the addition of a third category: "That class of Americans who had attached themselves singly to the American Character unbiassed by french or english systems . . . independent of Party." The alteration significantly provided an alignment in which the President himself, rising above partisan considerations, could be included.

[102] Emphasis added.

as related to their commerce and intercourse with the United States. Such Characters would acquire a preeminence over most foreign Consuls, while it would enable them, by prudence and good judgment, to reconcile to the American mind, many apparent difficulties which without extensive commercial Knowledge it might be often impossible to overcome. . . . [In] a country like America, which was entirely agricultural and commercial and where the trade was carried on by British merchants and natives of Great Britain in every state in the Union, it would seem to be a matter of the greatest consequence to england, to establish an accurate consular system with a superintending consul of extensive knowledge and Abilities whose attention would of course be directed to the rise and progress of the Trade between the two countries, and who by the exercise of good Judgement and watching every event, might be able to suggest useful hints for rendering the intercourse more beneficial between two Countries whose Language, manners, Education, and taste so perfectly assimilate as those of Great Britain and the United States of America.

It is not surprising that, according to Smith, this won Grenville's perfect agreement. It not only stated the case wholly from the point of view of British policy: it also betrayed the acute embarrassment felt by the English interest in America because of those former Loyalists who occupied British consular posts in the United States—John Temple, Phineas Bond, John Hamilton, and George Miller, not one of whom could be regarded as "a pure British Character." It also perhaps revealed to Grenville himself that the specifications for a proper person to fill the office of consul general seemed drawn to fit none other than Patrick Colquhoun, who soon and unsuccessfully solicited that post through Henry Dundas.

Indeed, so effectively did Smith present the British side of the argument that Grenville spoke candidly and as a minister about his displeasure over the hostile measures being taken by the United States against the Indian tribes. This had caused a serious decline in the English fur trade during the last two seasons, with resultant effect on important commercial and manufacturing interests, and would bring about its destruction unless the difficulties were accommodated. Such an important trade, he emphasized, had a bearing on the occupation of the western posts and the security of the Canadian frontiers. The reports in American newspapers that the Indian depredations were countenanced by England had given him uneasiness. He could assure Smith that the English cabinet "disclaimed the Idea in the present Situation, but it was his duty to make this impression, that England could not with perfect indifference see a tribe of indians extirpated . . . without endeavouring in some degree to shelter them, but he flattered himself, with the expectation that America would not proceed to too great extremities on this subject."

This aroused the patriotic and professional feelings of Smith, but he restrained himself and met the thrust by suggesting that the minister sent to negotiate would find the British fur trade better promoted and the frontiers better protected if his country's troops were withdrawn into their proper limits. The American government, he believed, had too much confidence in the British ministry to suspect them of countenancing the incursions of the Indians, but newspaper printers drew other conclusions when British provisions were found in the haversacks of Indians slain in battle. As for American conduct toward the savages, it was "more strongly marked with Justice and benevolence than that of any power who had ever yet come in contact with them." Her treaties and efforts at conciliation proved this. But when, in order to protect her frontiers, war was forced upon her, she would continue it to the point of extirpation if necessary, regardless of the possibility that England might side with the Indians.

When Grenville expressed an interest in the Indian treaties, Smith promised to send copies that had been left with Colquhoun. This closed the interview except for some desultory discussion about the Canadian bill introduced the day before. Grenville was quoted as saying that he had sought the interview so that Smith on his return might communicate to the President the "friendly dispositions of the Ministers of Great Britain and of the Nation at Large towards him and the Country over which he presided." There were several other points, Smith assured the President, that were brought forward in a less pointed manner by Grenville as well as by other persons with whom he talked and these points, to which they were much attached, no doubt would be included "in the propositions which may be expected on the arrival of the English Minister." Such matters, no doubt, would call for consideration before his arrival. After this discreet avoidance of the genuine obstacles to negotiation, Smith closed his report to Washington with a virtual admission of his own predilections:[103]

> The President will doubtless perceive, that the Language adopted by me . . . was perfectly consiliatory, and as far as my knowledge of the sentiments of the people goes, I took the Liberty of concluding that they were favourable to a Liberal Commercial connection with Great Britain and considered myself as conforming to their dispositions in using such a stile of expression as appeared to me calculated, to excite favourable dispositions in the person to whom my discourse was addressed. If however my Zeal on any of the points here stated may have carried me on the one side or the other, too far, it must be recollected that it can in no point of view be considered as a committment of my country or the opinion of its rulers, but merely a commitment of the opinion of a private individual who as he thinks it his duty to do, freely submitts them to the perusal of the President of the United States, and with as much Candour as they were given to Lord Grenville *when sought for by him.*

Full the report certainly was—fifteen closely written pages in all— but not candid and, on essential matters, not truthful. This is proved conclusively by two documents that Smith prepared prior to his interview with Grenville. The first was cast in the form of a letter to

---

[103] Smith to Washington, 6 June 1791 (DNA: RG 59, MLR, with copies of enclosures mentioned in preceding notes; emphasis added).

Patrick Colquhoun and was clearly composed in collaboration with him. Written on the day that Colquhoun made his pressing appeal to Dundas, it announced Smith's intention to depart on the April packet, expressed pleasure at the "many civilities and attentions . . . shewn . . . *an American*," and voiced the hope of "a private Gentleman, somewhat acquainted with the dispositions of his countrymen" that differences between the two nations could be adjusted. Echoing Hamilton's assurances to Beckwith, he said that British creditors would find that "an uniform system of Jurisprudence operates decidedly thro' that extensive continent, and that the doors of justice . . . are as widely open as in any Country in the World." He rejected the charge that the United States had first violated the Treaty of Peace, pointing out that her minister had made the first overture for amicable arrangements and that, after three years of solicitation, he had been "induced to retire from the Court . . . not very favourably impressed with Ideas of its friendly dispositions." If the threat of war in Europe should cause England to abandon this chilly and repellant attitude, he as a friend could give assurance that "the more friendly those decisions are, towards America, the more acceptable they will be to the people of that Country, whose language, manners, education and taste lead them to nourish partialities, which nothing but systems of injustice and false pride can counteract."

Smith then advanced a pointed suggestion. The United States, he declared, was not jealous of England's naval strength but pleased with it. Soon she would be able to supply all of the hemp, pitch, tar, and iron that England could possibly need, thus freeing her of dependence for naval stores on the caprice of European politics. Again echoing Hamilton's words to Beckwith, he pointed out that the interests of the United States and Great Britain were complementary, since as a source of raw materials and as a market for British manufactures the former could produce a favorable balance of trade for the latter of upwards of £4 million sterling annually. "I would only therefore ask any impartial investigator of this subject," Smith concluded, "whether it is not an object of great national importance, that this Country should cherish a friendly intercourse with the United States of America, and whether there exists any other country in the world, from whence such evident advantages may be derived from a commercial intercourse . . .?"

This letter from "a private Gentleman" to a friend who had shown him civilities was obviously written by Smith under the conviction that he would have to depart without gaining an interview with Grenville. It was plainly intended for the eyes of the ministry and Colquhoun promptly turned it over to Dundas, who succinctly expressed the object of those who had sent Smith on his mission in the endorsement that he gave to it: "Letter from Colo. Smith . . . stating the points likely to promote a Closer connection between Great Britain and America."[104] But the letter also served as a source for Smith's draft of his report to Washington, both in phraseology and in substance. It is possible that, during the interview with Grenville, Smith did speak as bluntly about

[104] Smith to Colquhoun, 4 Apr. 1791 (MiU-C: Melville Papers; entirely in Smith's hand except for endorsement quote above).

infractions of the Treaty of Peace and about American overtures as he wished Washington to believe he did. This seems implausible both because the letter was demonstrably the source of some expressions in the report to the President and because the granting of the interview opened the door for a very different kind of communication. Smith entered it with a memorandum addressed to political realities. This document wasted no time in circumlocution but began abruptly with one of the topics that Smith, in his report to Washington, said Grenville had initiated:

It is well known that there are two parties in the American government; composed of the principal leading men in the Country—one set of Individuals very powerful and indeed respectable in favour of France and another in favour of England. The French party is of course solicitous to strengthen itself by the assistance and countenance of France, in order if possible to acquire the ascendancy, while the English party is equally solicitous to acquire a preeminence in the Country through the medium of the same countenance and attention from England. The National Assembly of France, perfectly aware of this circumstance, and of the growing consequence of America as a source for the consumption of Manufactures, (notwithstanding the reported confusion of their affairs,) have already manifested a desire to cultivate a close friendship and connection with America, by the appointment of a very popular character as Minister to the United States—a gentleman of great abilities, well acquainted with America and the characters who govern it, and extremely popular from the circumstance of his having served with the reputation of a gentleman and a soldier in the American Army through the war.—While France is thus strengthening her party in America by acts of kindness and attention to the United States, England is losing ground, by that species of uniform, but perhaps unintentional neglect which in the present state of political contention (if not soon remedied) may be productive of much injury to the British interest in America.

Smith then declared that the friends of this interest desired "most anxiously to see England come forward by her minister and manifest a desire" to settle all differences. This done, there could be expected "a closer connection and more friendly intercourse, thro the medium of a Treaty of Commerce, by which those disagreeable fluctuations in the tonnage on British ships and duties on British manufactures may be done away, and the subjects of Great Britain treated in America in all respects *as the most favoured nation*, which is not the case at present, and cannot be expected until there is a Commercial Treaty between the two countries." There was nothing in this analysis of the political cleavage about the third party uncommitted to either France or England that Smith inserted in his report to the President, stamping it as a remark he made to Grenville. Nor was there in that report any reference to the declared aim of treating British subjects "in all respects *as the most favoured nation*." But, aside from such discrepancies, Smith fabricated his report directly and in large part literally from this memorandum that he had prepared before the interview, giving to it the false character of a response to Grenville's suppositious question about "a french party . . . he had been informed were very strong in America."

So also with respect to the question Smith attributed to the Secretary for Foreign Affairs about the kind of minister likely to prove acceptable to the United States. On this head the memorandum spoke with urgency for the British interest in America—and also for Colquhoun's ambition to be appointed minister or consul general with quasi-diplomatic powers:

> There are several combined circumstances in the affairs of the United States, which press exceedingly at the present moment, for an almost immediate decision on the part of Great Britain before new difficulties arise, from the intrigues of rival nations. It would be of infinite advantage to the British interest in America if the Ministers and Consuls sent to that Country, were men whose characters had never been committed in the late war, but more particularly that the office of Minister and Consul General should be conferred on *pure British Characters*. As the connection between Great Britain and America must be principally commercial, it may be thought of consequence that the Minister should be a commercial character, unless that part of the negotiation should be committed to a Consul General having occasional or permanent Diplomatic powers to a certain extent in the absence of the Minister. With this view a character should be fixed on for Consul General who has not only some local knowledge of the Commerce of America, but also local and if possible practical knowledge of the trade of Great Britain and the other countries of Europe, so far as relates to their Commerce and intercourse with the United States. . . . It doubtless must appear a matter of the greatest consequence to establish an accurate Consular system with a Superintending Consul of extensive knowledge and abilities, whose attention would be directed to the rise and progress of the trade between the two countries.

Such an official, watching events, might be able to suggest "useful hints for rendering the connection closer between two countries who[se] Language, Education, manners, and dispositions so perfectly assimulate as those of Great Britain and the United States." But as Smith copied the language of the memorandum in his report to the President, he altered the key phrase here as elsewhere to conceal what he had actually written for Grenville's eyes: as altered, the useful hints might render "the intercourse more beneficial" between two countries so closely akin. Grenville received the memorandum on the day of the interview, hence it must have been handed to him by Smith.[105]

But the true nature of Smith's report to Washington is not to be gauged by such contrived differences between its phraseology and that of the memorandum given to Grenville, significant as some of these are. It is to be found rather in the gross discrepancy between what had actually occurred and what Smith tried to convince the President had

105 Memorandum by Smith, unsigned and undated (PRO: FO 4/9, f. 222-3; entirely in Smith's hand except for endorsement reading: "Memo. of Colo. Smith Recd. 9th April 1791"; emphasis in original).

taken place. He represented himself as the recipient of flattering attentions from the ministry and as having been prevailed on to consent to
official consultations for the object of conveying to the President "the
friendly dispositions of the Ministers of Great Britain." But in fact, as
Smith proved by the documents he transmitted as well as by the letter
to Colquhoun and the memorandum for Grenville, the single interview
granted to him came as a result of his appeals and the importunations
of Colquhoun, aided by the influence of Pulteney and Dundas. He represented the Secretary of Foreign Affairs as raising questions about the
kind of minister who should be appointed and about the opposition to
be expected from a party favorable to France. But in fact the two documents that Smith used as the basis of his report show that, on these as
on other points touching the primary purpose of his mission, it was he
and not Grenville who introduced the topics. Quite understandably, he
concealed these two revealing documents from Washington. In brief,
presenting a posture of supplication to the British government and
one of a wholly different character to his own, Smith convicted himself
of the same sort of calculated deception that Hamilton had practised
some months earlier in reporting his conversations with Beckwith.
Inexperienced, even less adept at intrigue, and urged on by an ambition
that was easily manipulated on both sides of the Atlantic, Smith ironically revealed the true character of his mission by too literal a fidelity to
the concealed documents and by his very zeal to demonstrate skill in
diplomacy.

For, falsified as it was, his report yet disclosed that he had
spoken in behalf of "the British interest in America," identifying their
views with the sentiment of the people of the United States. With one
exception, all that he said had long since been urged upon the ministry
by Hamilton, Johnson, Schuyler, Paterson, and others in their conversations with Beckwith. That exception, which emphasized the disadvantages they labored under by the presence of former Loyalists in
consular posts, only betrayed their anxiety over the rumored appointment of so well known a Tory as Andrew Elliot. There was, to be
sure, an urgency and explicitness in the appeal Smith made to Grenville beyond what Hamilton said to Beckwith, but this was implicit in
the fact that he undertook the journey. Smith did not define the circumstances that "pressed exceedingly at present for an almost immediate
decision" and he was obviously unaware of the meaning that the
President could not fail to read into this statement. But the suppliant
words betrayed at once his own partisanship and the purpose for which
his principals had sent him abroad. In arguing that the United States
might be, and could only be, bound by treaty not to augment duties
on British ships and goods, he echoed—as Colquhoun, Pulteney, or
Dundas must have told him—the central argument advanced in
Hawkesbury's report as the reason for negotiating instead of retaliating.
Thus Smith exposed the very point he had sought to conceal. Throughout the report he also seemed convinced, or wished to persuade Washington, that the minister to be appointed would be authorized to negotiate. This was a hope that Hamilton had expressed to Beckwith and
perhaps was one of the objects of Smith's mission. But Grenville could

not have given such an assurance when the determination of the basis of negotiation had yet to be made. Almost certainly he would not have done so if it had been.

In his behavior after returning to America as well as in his report to Washington, Smith not only disclosed the real origin and aim of his mission: he also continued to demonstrate his lack of fitness for the diplomatic post he so much desired.

V

Yet assurances that an envoy might be expected soon had been given and when Smith landed in New York on the 5th of June he was obviously elated with the result of his mission. So were his principals. He or they succeeded in giving an adventitious value to Grenville's attentions by creating the impression that the minister himself not only had sought the interview but was so eager to obtain it that he had delayed the packet—a mistaken impression accepted both then and since as valid.[106] With documents to display, Smith revealed them to a small and sympathetic circle in New York and Philadelphia long before the President had a chance to see them. Richard Platt was one who accepted them as evidence both of the ministry's good will and of Smith's diplomatic skill. Explaining the private objects of the mission in a way that conflicted with Smith's own account to the President, Platt urged Hamilton to advance Smith for the post of minister to England in preference to Gouverneur Morris, William Bingham, or Robert R. Livingston. "I wish you will give the thing a fair revolution in your mind," he wrote, "and contrast a patriotic polish'd man, with others who may be led astray by contracted habits, fatuous prejudices and party views, however celebrated they may be for science and Literature."[107] The point of the allusion cannot have been lost.

In glowing terms Smith informed Colquhoun that the friendly assurances given by Grenville had caused the tide to turn. "I can assure you," he wrote, "that never was anything more fortunate and timely, for, from other quarters, other impressions were rapidly gaining ground, springing from other representations than those I was authorized to make and which I flatter myself will overturn those false statements, and contribute to produce on our part every friendly disposition which our trans-Atlantic friends could wish America to nourish. It was surely a most critical period, and fully justified my decision and rapid movements. . . ."[108] If these unguarded words show that the real object of the mission was to counteract the effect of Morris' reports,

---

[106] Bemis, *Jay's Treaty*, p. 118. See also Johnson to TJ, 18 Apr. 1791.

[107] Richard Platt to Alexander Hamilton, 8 June 1791 (Syrett, *Hamilton*, VIII, 453-4). Platt said that he and Smith had "been foiled" in their object of speculating in government securities. But Smith told Washington that he had "perfectly embraced the objects" of his visit.

The fear that TJ might be appointed minister to England was an old one. "It is evidently the object of several gentlemen," wrote Nathan Dane in 1787, "to put the affairs of our Legation at London into the hands of Mr. Jefferson. This is a thing we can by no means agree to" (Nathan Dane to Rufus King, 12 Aug. 1787, Burnett, *Letters of Members*, VIII, 637).

[108] Smith to Colquhoun, 17 June 1791 (extract in Grenville Papers, Boconnoc).

Colquhoun's amplification of Smith's optimism sought to convince Grenville that the Secretary of State had been effectively thwarted. Jefferson was a man of considerable abilities and personal weight, Colquhoun reported, and he and Madison and other leaders had been zealously pursuing every measure that could give them a paramount influence and enable them to favor France and injure Great Britain. But fortunately, while Jefferson's report on the navigation bill was being prepared, "Colonel Smith arrived at the critical moment and . . . exerted the influence he justly possesses in that country in preventing the mischief which had arisen and was likely to result from former misrepresentations." The friends of the British interest in America had thereby increased. "Nothing," Colquhoun added, "could be more grateful to these leading members in the American Government who are favourable to the interest of this country than Colonel Smith's communications of the good dispositions of this country from such respectable authority; and it is supposed that the President and Mr. Secretary Hamilton are among the number who will feel satisfaction at the prospect of an opportunity being soon given for settling all matters at variance between the two countries by means of friendly discussions."[109] Such were the distortions of the aims of the Secretary of State and of the position of the President which arose in the same quarters that had first inspired the mission of Gouverneur Morris, then sought to discredit it, and finally contrived that of Smith to counteract its effect.

Before the week was out Smith hastened on to Philadelphia, being convinced, so he informed Colquhoun, "of the importance of an immediate communication of those friendly impressions made by Lord Grenville on the 9th of April." But he had already written his extended report to the President and besides, as all readers of the newspapers knew, Washington was still on his journey to the southward. The Vice-President was in Braintree. The Secretary of State was also known to be on his travels in New England—and it is abundantly clear in any event that Smith had no intention of reporting to him.[110] His haste in proceeding to Philadelphia at this time can only have been for the purpose of reporting to the commanding figure at the head of the friends of the British interest in the United States, Alexander Hamilton.

Smith arrived in the capital on Sunday the 12th, alighted from his carriage among a group of friends about to dine at the home of Tench Coxe, and spent the day conversing with them.[111] He permitted at least the inner circle to read his report to the President and he also sent a copy of it to John Adams. "Mr. Jay, Hamilton and King were much pleased with the contents of it," Smith wrote to his father-in-law. "But

[109] Colquhoun to Grenville, 29 July 1791, enclosing the extract from Smith's letter (Grenville Papers, Boconnoc; emphasis added). Evidently Smith, flattered by the reception of his friends, assured Colquhoun that the President as well as Hamilton was pleased—an assurance soon robbed of all value.

[110] Smith to Colquhoun, Philadelphia, 17 June 1791 (Grenville Papers, Boconnoc). On the day that he wrote, Philadelphia papers carried information that Washington had arrived in Mount Vernon (N.Y. Daily Advertiser, 20 June 1791). TJ's absence in New England was also reported in the press (same, 6 June 1791). Smith, of course, knew that his father-in-law was in Braintree.

[111] Tench Coxe to John Adams, 15 June 1791 (MHi: AM; endorsed by Adams, at a later date, "Tench Coxe . . . Mercy on him! If possible.").

I believe," he wrote later in a revealing and apparently unique attribution of partisanship to Washington, "The President, Mr. Jefferson and Mr. Maddison would have rather I had stayed at home." He wished much to see Adams, he wrote, in order to tell his long story and to talk freely about domestic politics, but his public and private affairs were so pressing that he was unable to accompany his wife on her visit to Braintree. He referred Adams to her for details and offered a suggestion: "perhaps you will get more if you appoint under the small seal that able negotiator Mrs. A[dams]. She by gently speaking, sweetly smiling and calmly pursuing the subject, may find out what carried me to Europe, what I did while there, and what engages me here at present, more important than the office I hold."[112] Immersed in high politics and ambitious for a diplomatic post, the returning emissary could scarcely restrain his desire to disclose the real object of his mission.

But the gratification felt by his principals was not unqualified, as Hamilton revealed in a conference with Beckwith three days after Smith arrived in the capital. He told the agent that the intelligence derived from the interview with Grenville was in general "pleasing and promising" and that it placed in a decided light the determination of the ministry to "enter on the consideration of Commercial subjects between the Two Countries." Neither conclusion, particularly the latter, could have been warranted by a close reading of Smith's letter to Washington and Hamilton may have been less pleased than he led Beckwith to believe. What unquestionably did disturb him was Grenville's candid comment on American hostilities against the Indians. This, he told Beckwith, might be interpreted either as the expression of a wish or as the declaration of an intent to take part in the conflict. He said that he would feel "extremely concerned" if this comparatively trivial war, which the United States was obliged to prosecute because the safety of its frontiers required it, should nullify the "fair prospect of a happy settlement of the affairs of the Two Countries."[113] Just as Jefferson for a similar purpose had sent an urgent message to Montmorin through Otto, so Hamilton now appealed to Grenville through Beckwith not to undermine the position of the American friends of England by taking the side of the Indians.

The elated spirits of the defenders of the British interest were effectively dampened by other developments. Coxe thought the change in public sentiment reported by Smith was encouraging, but he believed the British government was pursuing an unvaried commercial policy.

112 Smith to Adams, 5 Aug. 1791 (MHi: AM).

113 Beckwith's report of conversation with Hamilton on 15 June 1791, enclosed in his letter to Grenville of 31 July 1791 (PRO: FO 4/12; text in Syrett, *Hamilton*, VIII, 475-7).

It is indicative of the concern of Hamilton during the "critical" weeks before Smith arrived that he revealed both to TJ and to Washington discouraging reports of the "misguided opinions of the British administration" (Hamilton to Washington, 11 Apr. 1791, quoting a letter from Rufus King, Syrett, *Hamilton*, VIII, 277; TJ to Washington, 17 Apr. 1791, enclosing a copy of the same letter, which Hamilton must have disclosed to him, and expressing the view that the reported appointment of a minster was "without foundation"). See also note 139 below.

"The late total prohibition of our piscatory articles, the advance of the importing prices of grain, and the prevention of the discharge of vessels which arrived when their ports are not open for that article," he wrote John Adams, "are as perfectly in the spirit of commercial monopoly, as their antecedent regulations."[114] Also, almost two months elapsed before Grenville took any action toward the appointment of a minister, a delay which naturally brought concern to those who had been encouraged by his assurances. On the first of May he received Beckwith's dispatch describing the situation as critical and enclosing copies of the navigation bill and Washington's message of the 14th of February. Yet it was not until the 24th that, in a burst of belated urgency, he informed Hammond of his appointment and directed him to "use the utmost expedition" in returning to England so as to be able to proceed to America without loss of time.[115] Two days later the Lords of Trade, spurred on by reports from British consuls in the United States, urged "that as little Time as possible . . . be lost, in taking proper means for counteracting . . . those Members of Congress, whose Interest or Inclination it may be to support any Propositions which may be unfriendly to the Commerce and Navigation of this Country."[116] A "pure British Character," to be sure, had been chosen as envoy, perhaps in deference to the urgent insistence from America. The issue was being confronted with determination at last, not because of the channels opened up by Robert Morris for Smith's inexpert negotiations but because of the impetus given an American navigation bill through Washington's disclosure of his appraisal of the disposition of the British ministry. But the fundamental decisions as to whether, where, and on what terms to negotiate were still to be made.

Proof of this is to be found in another and more authoritative communication that came to the friends of England in the United States while the ministry's plans for counteracting their opponents were being matured. This arrived through still another channel of political intelligence—one more direct, more clandestine, and more demonstrably traceable to the fountainhead of the British interest in the United States than that employed by William Stephens Smith. This one came into being in June 1790 when Henry Knox held a long and confidential conversation with Major General John Maunsell, who was about to sail for England. Maunsell, a British army officer who had married into a prominent New York family and had once been supported by Hamilton in his petition for the right to purchase lands in the state, was chosen to approach William Pitt himself. Piercy Brett, a British naval captain who was unknown to Knox, also joined later in the concealed correspondence.[117] The letters exchanged by the three men

114 Tench Coxe to John Adams, 15 June 1791 (MHi: AM).
115 Grenville to Hammond, 24 May 1791 (Grenville Papers, Boconnoc). On the probable reason for this delay, see note 133.
116 Stephen Cottrell to Grenville, 26 May 1791 (PRO: FO 4/10).
117 John Maunsell (1724-1795) served as lieutenant-colonel of the 27th regiment during the French and Indian War, for which he received grants of land in New York and Vermont. In 1763 at Trinity Church in New York he was married to Elizabeth Stillwell, widow of Captain Peter Wraxall. At the outbreak of the Revolution he returned to England, warmly commended by Cadwallader

were sent under covers addressed to Mrs. Maunsell, who remained in New York and forwarded them in both directions. On the day after Maunsell arrived in London, Brett opened the correspondence with comment on the Spanish crisis while the general was "dressing to pay his respects at St. James's."[118] Maunsell himself wrote a month later to say that the subject of their confidential discourse engaged his "constant and most serious attention."[119] Brett, whose political information the general described as "correct and extensive," wrote on the same day.[120] Some weeks later Maunsell had a private interview with Pitt and supposed that he would be sent for again in a few days.[121] Late in

Colden to North and Dartmouth, and served during the war in Ireland. He was made major-general in 1781 and returned to New York in 1784 (*Magazine of American History*, XXVII [1892] 419-28; Charles Maunsell, *Maunsell Family*, II, 557; *Papers of Sir William Johnson*, ed. A. C. Flick, II, 425; IV, 418; V, 182-3; VIII, 657; Syrett, *Hamilton*, IV, 1-2; the best sketch of Wraxall, a figure of importance in the province, is that of C. H. McIlwain in the introduction to his edition of Wraxall's *An abridgment of the Indian Affairs*, p. ix-cxviii). Freeman, *Washington*, VI, 264n., 334n., describes Maunsell as an "unofficial observer" and as an adviser to both governments, who "on several occasions . . . acted as arbiter." Maunsell did express a desire to be presented to Washington and he brought a parcel for him from the Spanish ambassador in London, but there is no evidence that the President knew about the well-concealed correspondence or that Maunsell ever acted as an adviser to the American government, to say nothing of being an arbiter. Piercy Brett belonged to a well-connected naval family, being the nephew of Sir Percy Brett (1709-1810) and the son of William Brett, also a captain in the navy. He is listed as a captain in 1787 (DNB). His cousin, Henrietta Brett was the wife of George Bowyer (1739-1799), a supporter of Pitt —and of the navy—in the House of Commons (Namier and Brooke, *House of Commons*, II, 109).

118 Brett wrote that matters were kept so secret no reports could be credited. But while presenting conflicting views—that Spain intended war, that she had no serious intention of quarreling—he seemed in guarded language to suggest that France was in no situation to assist Spain and that in any case the National Assembly was "decidedly against taking any part against England" (Brett to Knox, 7 July 1790, MHi: Knox Papers).

119 Maunsell to Knox, 4 Aug. 1790 (same).

120 Brett to Knox, 4 July [*i.e.*, Aug.] 1790 (same). Brett also wrote this letter at Maunsell's request. The political situation was still so enveloped in clouds of doubt and uncertainty that "the keenest and clearest eyes can see nothing through them." What negotiations were going on were kept "an impenetrable secret" by Pitt. Yet parliament had been prorogued to the 12th of October so that, it was said, the minister could meet them with peace in his pocket.

121 Maunsell to Knox, 1 Sep. 1790 (same). Like Brett, Maunsell professed not to penetrate the political clouds: "we really are in a curious situation. Arming with great expedition, and in great force, but for what purpose we realy can't tell." Also like him, he then seemed to convey reliable views: "As no war is declared, [the fleets] can't fight, except in a very civil, good humored way. Some people think, all this preparation for war, is to have some influence, on the French revolution, or the disturbed politicks of Europe. Time will tell us more." Maunsell concluded by saying he would turn his pen over "to our friend Brett, who will make better use of it than I can." No letter from Brett of this date has been found, but he did write by the November packet saying that the cloud would be lifted at the meeting of parliament (Brett to Knox, 3 Nov. 1790, MHi: Knox Papers).

Evidently Knox's only reply to Brett was one thanking him for his first letter and saying that he would be grateful for those in future (Knox to Brett, 10 Sep. 1790, MHi: Knox Papers). In a letter to Maunsell thanking him for his and Brett's letters, Knox echoed the cloudy refrain employed by them: "There is a mist on the affairs of France that we cannot penetrate. Time the great elucidator of events must be resorted to on the occasion" (Knox to Maunsell, 6 Apr. 1791, MHi: Knox).

November, some hint of the nature of the subject of Knox' confidential conversation appears in Maunsell's assurance that the Spanish affair had so engaged Pitt's attention that he had had no time to consider other matters. But now that this was settled, the general wrote, "Something in the Diplomatic line with the United States of America, as well as a commercial Treaty, will I suppose be an object of his consideration, as soon as he setts Parliament going. I shall, when any thing of that kind is taken in hand, make you acquainted therewith."[122]

The communications were finally extended to include Knox' brother William, consul at Dublin, and these letters were also exchanged under hidden covers. It is possible that the correspondence conveyed intelligence that does not appear on its surface, though it is more likely that it contained little of significance simply because the ministry, preoccupied with European crises, could not resolve its differences and reach a decision about its American policy. But, late in June 1791, just as Maunsell was departing for America, he was handed a document that revealed a great deal. It was ostensibly written by the general, in part in the third person, but it carried the authority of the first minister of England:[123]

> Mr. Pitt has authorized me to acquaint the Ministers of the United States of America that Great Britain is anxious to establish and preserve the stri[c]test Amity and friendship, with the United States, and that a person properly Authorized will shortly be sent out for the discussion of matters that may require it, in order to make the necessary arrangements for the above purpose.
>
> Mr. Pitt has likewise Authorized Genl. Maunsell to procure for, and transmit to him, what were the wishes and demands of America.
>
> As the President has in his message to the Senate and Assembly of 14th Feby 1791 mentioned that soon after he was called to the Administration he found it important to come to an understanding with the Court of London respecting its disposition to enter into commercial arrangements with the United States on the principles of reciprocal advantages &c. as mentioned in that message for this purpose authorized 'informal conferences with the British Minister from which he does not infer any disposition on their part to enter into any Arrangements merely Commercial.'
>
> General Maunsell tho' not Deplomatically employed hopes that the United States will from the message he brings be satisfied of the

[122] Maunsell to Knox, 29 Nov. 1790 (same); Maunsell said that Brett did not write "a scrip of a pen" by this packet. In this letter the general gave Knox directions how to send his letters to Brett "safely and post free." This and other letters show that one object of concealment was merely to take advantage of Brett's naval connections to obtain free postal service (William Knox to Henry Knox, 13 Jan.; 13 and 18 Feb. 1791; 7 Apr. 1791). But it is equally clear that its principal aim was the transmission of political intelligence through "safe" channels.

[123] Manuscript, undated and in a hand other than Maunsell's, is in DLC: Hamilton Papers. William Knox was with Maunsell in London at the time this paper was handed to him. He wrote to his brother: "General Maunsell tells me he has business to communicate to you, which will take him to Phila. soon after his reaching N. York" (William Knox to Henry Knox, 27 June 1791, MHi: Knox Papers).

friendly dispositions of the court of London and that this information will satisfy the Government of the United States that the Disposition of Great Britain is favorable to a friendly Intercourse with the United States.

Aside from revealing the impact made by Washington's message of the 14th of February on the ministry, the significance of this astonishing communication lies in the strong light it throws on Knox' confidential conversation with General Maunsell in the summer of 1790. At that time the first discouraging reports from Gouverneur Morris had not yet arrived in the United States. But Thomas Jefferson had assumed office and long before that his diplomatic efforts to counter British trade restrictions by opening other markets in Europe had made him an unpleasing choice as Secretary of State to such men as Alexander Hamilton, John Jay, Robert Morris, William Samuel Johnson, and others. Considering him to be implacably hostile to England, they and others repeatedly warned Beckwith that he would do all he could to prevent rather than promote friendly relations with England. On the same unwarranted assumption, Hamilton had urged that the negotiation of differences be carried on in America, where the influence of the Secretary of State might be held in check.[124] Maunsell's reports to Knox show that, like Gouverneur Morris, he had been urged to raise questions about an exchange of ministers and the negotiation of a treaty of commerce. But the document that he brought from Pitt reveals that he had also been charged with the task of opening a direct line of communication between the British ministry and the friends of England in the United States. For the wishes and demands that Pitt authorized the general to procure and transmit to him were not those that would be conveyed from the Secretary of State through official channels. They were such as would come from the one who was beginning to be called "the American Pitt" or "the Premier" directly to his presumed counterpart in the British cabinet. This extraordinary document was in substance if not in form a letter of credence accrediting its bearer not to the head of state but to the Secretary of the Treasury. All of the evidence suggests that the Maunsell mission, originating less than three months after Jefferson assumed office, had as its primary goal the establishment of a concealed line of communication that could be employed to thwart the officer chosen by the President for the conduct of foreign affairs. If so, it was only one further example of the continuing intrigue by which Hamilton and his supporters sought to control foreign policy.[125]

Maunsell sent Pitt's authorization to Knox immediately on landing at New York and soon hastened on to Philadelphia himself. Knox handed the document over to the Secretary of the Treasury for whom

---

[124] Beckwith's report of a conversation with Hamilton on 15 July 1790, enclosed in Dorchester to Grenville, 25 Sep. 1790 (PRO: CO 42/69).

[125] See Editorial Note to group of documents on war crisis of 1790 (Vol. 17: 35-108). The editor of the *Vermont Gazette*, 7 Feb. 1791, wrote: "We are informed, from respectable authority, that in the political circles in the city and province of Quebec, the honorable Alexander Hamilton . . . is held in the highest estimation, being supposed equal to the celebrated Mr. Pitt, and superior to the prime minister of any other court in Europe."

it was intended.[126] To this extent the mission had succeeded. Nevertheless, it cannot have brought any measure of encouragement to the friends of an English connection. On the contrary, its carefully worded message revealed that the minister to the United States would be competent only to discuss matters of difference and to make "necessary arrangements," not actually to conduct a negotiation. It was only another reiteration of such assurances of amity as Leeds had given Morris and Grenville had given Smith. Furthermore, by the time Maunsell arrived in late August, those who had initiated his mission had other and even weightier reasons for being discouraged, the first of these resulting from the fact that undercover intelligence could work both ways.

VI

For simultaneously with the arrival of the general there came to Philadelphia at least two summaries of the report of the Lords of Trade setting forth Hawkesbury's uncompromising defence of the navigation system, all variant but all containing its salient features. This very important and highly secret state paper was made available to the American government not by Maunsell or Smith but by William Temple Franklin, who also had ambitions for diplomatic appointment and who felt even more neglected by the administration than did the son-in-law of John Adams. Franklin, too, was in London in the spring of 1791. Just a few days before the interview between Grenville and Smith took place, he informed Jefferson that the report had been handed in to the privy council, that he had been "promised a sight of it," and that he would later provide him with a particular account.[127] Subsequently, after a few copies had been printed for the use of the cabinet and Franklin had been permitted to see one for a few days, they were by "a sudden order of Council . . . called in again." The person who had lent it to him—almost certainly it was William Pulteney—was obliged to surrender his copy and requested its return. But he himself had made an extended abstract of it and he made that available to Franklin, who incorporated it in a long letter to Tench Coxe, Assistant Secretary of the Treasury. "I am enabled to give you the following report," Franklin wrote, "which may perhaps be inter-

[126] Maunsell landed in New York on 20 Aug. 1791, informed Pitt of his arrival, and promised to submit further reports. He told Knox: "The enclosed was put into my hands for you at my departure [from London on 29 June 1791] . . . Some matters of an interesting nature connected with the discourse we held togather previous to my departure for London in June 1790, having occur'd, makes it necessary for me to have an interview with you. . . . I wish it so happened that I could have the pleasure of paying my respects to the President, at the same time. I beg you will not mention my intention of calling on you" (Maunsell to Pitt, 31 Aug. 1791, PRO: Chatham Papers, 30/8; Maunsell to Knox, 22 Aug. 1791, MHi: Knox Papers). Maunsell promised to continue sending Brett's information from London (Maunsell to Knox, 3 Sep. and 22 Dec. 1791, same). But after Hammond arrived the channel was no longer needed.

[127] Franklin to TJ, 6 Apr. 1791. Franklin hoped to be made minister to France or England (Franklin to TJ, 13 Oct. 1790; TJ to Franklin, 27 Nov. 1790; Franklin to Washington, 13 Oct. 1790, DNA: RG 59, MLR; Washington to Franklin, 25 Oct. 1790, same).

esting to yourself and Mr. Hamilton to whom I request you will communicate it with my respectful Compliments."[128] Coxe presumably complied, though neither the letter nor a copy of it has been found among the Hamilton papers. But he also interpreted the request broadly and had the departmental clerks make additional copies. One of these he sent to the Vice-President. "By this days mail," he wrote Adams, "I received a very lengthy letter from one of our Countrymen in England in which he furnishes me with the substance of a report from a Committee of the privy council relative to the American commerce."[129] The same day Coxe sent another copy to the Secretary of State and identified the source of his information: "Mr. Coxe has the honor to enclose to Mr. Jefferson, a letter from Mr. W. T. Franklin, which it is interesting that he should see, if he is not possessed of the information. He begs the favor of Mr. Jefferson's shewing it to the hon. Mr. Madison."[130]

Jefferson in turn abstracted the letter and had his chief clerk, Henry Remsen, Jr., make copies for further distribution. His abstract was thrice removed from the original source, but it contained the essential elements, being in fact identical with that part of Franklin's letter which conveyed the substance of Hawkesbury's report. Jefferson, however, did give it characteristic editing that excluded all extraneous matter. He concealed the fact that the summary of the report was derived from Franklin through Coxe, thus avoiding the evocation of personal and political animosities their names might arouse. He condensed the substance of the opening paragraph of Franklin's letter to a mere descriptive title: "Abstract of a report of a Committee of the Privy Council, made to the Privy Council, and handed to the King, [*it was drawn by Ld. Hawkesbury.* . . .] communicated in a Letter dated London 15th June 1791." He omitted Franklin's concluding paragraph expressing regret at not being able to send the full text and describing his summary as "a pretty exact Sketch of the report." He also excluded a final expression of opinion that was fully validated by the abstract itself: "I am however informed that the disposition to treat with us on the principles laid down is not diminished."[131]

In the absence of the original of Franklin's letter it cannot be de-

[128] [William Temple Franklin] to [Tench Coxe], London, 15 June 1791 (Tr in hand of John Meyer, clerk in Treasury Department; unsigned and unaddressed; 31 numbered pages in two separate places in MHi: Knox Papers, pages 1-4 being at XXVIII, 108 and pages 5-31 at XLVII, 176; this copy lacks the tables in Appendix that are to be found in TJ's abstract of Franklin's letter).
[129] Tench Coxe to John Adams, 27 Aug. 1791 (MHi: AM).
[130] Tench Coxe to TJ, 27 Aug. 1791 (DLC; endorsed as received 27 Aug. 1791 and so recorded in SJL; this is the whole of Coxe's note).
[131] Three copies of TJ's Abstract have been found: (1) MS, 24 pages, in Remsen's hand, except for the words in caption in italics (supplied) which were interlined by TJ (MHi: AM); (2) Tr of the foregoing, which incorporates without interlineation the words supplied by TJ (DLC: Washington Papers); (3) PrC of MS, which also contains TJ's interlined words attributing authorship to Hawkesbury (DLC: TJ Papers, 64: 11159-82). From this it would appear that TJ prepared MS for the President; that Washington, after causing Lear to retain a copy of it, sent it to Adams. There is no evidence that Washington shared it with other heads of departments. TJ, of course, kept the press copy for his own use and may have made another from MS for Madison.

The Comtesse de Tessé's parting gift to Jefferson in 1789.
(See p. xxxiii-xxxiv.)

William Stephens Smith (1755-1816).
(See p. xxxiv-xxxv.)

Mr James Ferguson. Mr Henry Dundas.

Henry Dundas, first Viscount Melville (1742-1811), conversing with James Fergusson (1769-1842). (See p. xxxiv-xxxv.)

Patrick Colquhoun (1745-1820).

Frederick Augustus Conrad Muhlenberg (1750-1801).
(See p. xxxv-xxxviii.)

Abraham Bedford Venable (1758-1811).
(See p. xxxv-xxxviii.)

James Monroe (1758-1831).

Oliver Wolcott, Jr. (1760-1833).
(See p. xxxv-xxxviii.)

William J. Vredenburgh (1760-1813).
(See p. xxxv-xxxviii.)

1792. Dec. 13. the President called on me to see the model & drawing of some mills for sawing stone. after shewing them he in the course of subsequent conversation asked me if there were not some good manufactories of Porcelaine in Germany, that he was in want of table china & had been speaking to mr Shaw who was going to the East Indies to bring him a set, but he found that ~~so~~ it would not come till he should be no longer in a situation to want it. he took occasion a second time to observe that Shaw said it would be 2. years at least before he ~~sho~~ could have the china here, before which time he said he should be where he should not need it. — I think he asked the question about the manufactories in Germany merely ~~to have an~~ to have an in -direct opportunity of telling me he meant to retire, or within the limits of two years.

Dec. 17. the affair of Reynolds & his wife. — clingham Muhlenb. clerk. testibus F.A. Muhl. Monroe. Venable. — also Wolcott at ~~for~~ Wadsworth. ~~thence to J.M. E.R. Beckley & Webb.~~

~~[several heavily obliterated lines]~~

1793. Jan. 15. M. Blacon, member from Dauphiné, of the 1st. National assembly of France is here. he was one of those who met at my house in Paris when the Monarchical patriots (afterwds called Feuillants) and the Republican patriots (afterwards called Jacobins) were about to form a schism. at a dinner at mr Hammond's to-day he recalls to my mind the names of all the members of both parties who met, to wit, la Fayette Duport, Barnave, Alex. La Meth, Blacon, Mounier, Maubourg, & Dagout. the result of that conference was that they made mutual sacrifices of opn. & prevented the schism. the Republicans gave up their opposition to ~~a king~~ the Monocrats their to a single branch of legislature.

Jan. 16. at a meeting of the board for the sinking fund, in a conversation after busi- -ness was over, mr Adams declared that 'men could never be governed but by force' that neither virtue prudence wisdom nor any thing else sufficed to restrain their passions, that the first National convent. of France had establd. a constn. had excluded themselves from it, admn. for certain time, a new set of successors had come, had demolished their constitution put to death all the leading characters concerned in making it, were now proceedg. to make a new constn. & to exclude themselves for 6. years from it, admn. that their successors would in their turn demolish, hang them, & make a new constn. & so on eternally, till a force would be brought into place to restrain them. — E. R. took notice of this declaration.

13890

Jefferson records the Reynolds affair and then obliterates the passage.
(See p. xxxv-xxxviii.)

William Temple Franklin (1762-1823).
(See p. xxxviii-xxxix.)

termined whether certain emphases were given to its text by Franklin or by Coxe. Several examples of a device frequently employed by Coxe—an index finger drawn in the margin—appear in Jefferson's abstract. These were probably contributed by Coxe, since they do not appear in Knox' copy of the letter. But the emphasis given to a key passage whose meaning no one in government could have failed to grasp is found in all texts, hence was literally transcribed in Jefferson's copy: "The new system adopted by Congress is certainly more favorable than before for cherishing the hopes of an amicable adjustment, as it appears evident '*a party is formed in favour of Great Britain*,' and as the ruling powers in America appear more favourable than heretofore, it would certainly be wrong in this government to proceed to any acts of retaliation." Jefferson's contribution to this passage in the copy that he prepared for the President was to place a revealing "qu:" in the margin opposite the underscored words, less perhaps to call attention to a fact of which Washington could not have been ignorant than to raise a question about the manner in which the presumed disposition of "the ruling powers in America" had become known to the British ministry.[132] The tiny marginal comment, far from reflecting any doubt as to the accuracy of the assertion about a party favorable to Great Britain, seems to be an early hint of the suspicion soon to become a certainty—that the secrets of the cabinet were being made available to the British ministry primarily to thwart any measure of the American government that might prove objectionable to the British government.

But this important passage was certainly edited with care by someone *before* the copy of Franklin's letter came to the Secretary of State. This was evidently done in order to quiet the very suspicions that Jefferson's query seems to reflect and the altered phraseology must have been that of Coxe, acting either voluntarily or under the direction of the Secretary of the Treasury. For what neither he nor Hamilton knew was that Franklin had also sent Jefferson a far more extended summary of Hawkesbury's report and in that the passage about the means by which Great Britain hoped to influence American legislation was set forth in explicit and unexpurgated form:[133]

[132] TJ's query appears in all of the texts described in the foregoing note, but it does not appear in that incorporated in Franklin's letter to Coxe (see note 128). Emphasis in original.

[133] This copy, consisting of 55 pages, is, with one exception, in Blackwell's hand and bears this caption: "Report of a Committee of the Lords of the Privy Council on the Trade of Great Britain with the United States. January 1791" (DLC: TJ Papers, 60: 10326-10353; PrC in same, 60: 10354-10408; emphasis in original; TJ collated Blackwell's transcript with its [missing] prototype and on page 6 [f. 10328v] he wrote: "for omission here see page 52"; the matter omitted by the clerk—tables showing the increase of imports from the British West Indies and the remaining colonies in America since the war—was added on page 52 with the note that it "ought to have followed page 6."). This abstract, more than twice as long as that sent by Franklin to Coxe, was transmitted to TJ in the following letter: "Thinking the Information in the inclosed Paper would be interesting to you, I take the Liberty of sending it to you.—It is the most accurate and compleat Account that has yet appear'd.—I am Dr. sir, respectfully & affectly. Yrs, W. T. Franklin" (Franklin to TJ, 3 July 1791; addressed, post-

Government has indeed been not altogether deceived. The new system is certainly more favorable to British navigation, and there can be no doubt from the proceedings of Congress, and from all that passed in their debates during the two last Sessions, particularly in the *American Senate that a party is already formed in favor of a connection with Great Britain*, which by moderation on her part, may perhaps be so strengthened, as to bring about in a friendly way, the objects in view. It would indeed be extraordinary, if after having submitted to a more disadvantageous situation than the present, Great Britain should commence a Commercial hostility at a time the American Government appears more favorably disposed towards

---

marked ["NEW]-YORK, Sept. 2," and directed "By Capt. Jones via N. York"; entry in SJL shows that it was received at Monticello on 20 Sep. 1791).

It is clear from this that, within a fortnight after he had dispatched his letter to Coxe, Franklin had been given access to Hawkesbury's *Report* in its final form. His "Paper" not only incorporated the whole, including the Appendixes: it also contained matter inserted at the end of the *Report* "under the title of 'Accounts received since the Report was printed, with observations on them.'" These additional documents were: (1) Hamilton's abstract of exports, Aug. 1789 to 30 Sep. 1790; (2) TJ's account of grain and flour exported to France in 1789, as taken from TJ's report on the fisheries; and (3) TJ's account of the number of vessels entering the ports of France from the United States in 1789, from the same report. These documents, among others, were sent by Beckwith to Grenville in his letter of 3 Mch. 1791, received in London on 1 May 1791.

This fact, together with a comparison of the known texts of the report of the Lords of the Committee for Trade, is instructive. A manuscript copy of the report as presented on 28 Jan. 1791, lacking the Appendixes, is in PRO: PC 1/19/A24/3, bearing an endorsement showing that it was read on 1-2 Mch. 1791 and "Approved." An identical copy, having a similar endorsement, is in PRO: FO 4/9, f. 85-153. An incomplete but congruent copy in the British Museum, Add. MSS. 38350:234-247 and 38376:112-117, bears directions to the printer and is accompanied by three pages of corrected proofs showing that the original title was *A Report of The Lords of the Committee of Privy Council, appointed for all Matters of Trade and Foreign Plantations, on The American Trade. 28th January 1791*—a title corrected on this proof to that given in note 10 above. The first printing of the *Report* thus took place after 2 Mch. 1791. When Beckwith's letter was received on 1 May 1791, the printed copies were recalled by "a sudden order of Council" so that Hawkesbury might compare his own commercial statistics with those just received from America. The new figures did not disturb the complacency of the Lords of Trade, even though those supplied by Hamilton and TJ were so discordant as to cause considerable comment (see Editorial Notes, French protest on tonnage acts, 18 Jan. 1791, and TJ's report on fisheries, 1 Feb. 1791). The newly-arrived documents and commentary were placed at p. 102-17 of the final printing of the *Report*, with the original Appendixes A-D following at p. i-xli. Two copies of this final printing, one bearing on its cover the seal of George III, are in the British Museum. It was an abstract based on this final form of the *Report* that Franklin was able to send to TJ early in July. This chronology of the printing, recall, and reprinting of the *Report* affords a plausible explanation for Grenville's delay until late May in taking action on Hammond's appointment after having received Beckwith's letter describing the situation as critical.

It was TJ's copy of Franklin's more "accurate and compleat Account" that Worthington C. Ford found in the Jefferson Papers in the Department of State and published as *Report of a Committee of the Lords of the Privy Council* (Washington, Department of State, 1888), p. 5-63, a title which has misled some into thinking that this was in fact the text of the *Report* itself. Photocopies of all versions have been deposited by the Editors in the Princeton University Library.

her. On the other hand, it would be imprudent, as yet, to place too much confidence on their supposed good intentions 'till experience shews whether Congress is inclined to persist in them, and influence enough to carry laws founded on them into execution throughout the United States.

Jefferson sent his abstract of Franklin's briefer version of the report to the President. This copy was then given to John Adams, presumably by Washington himself. There is no evidence that Jefferson revealed either that or the longer summary to his colleagues in the cabinet, though he must surely have disclosed both to James Madison. Apparently no *précis* of Hawkesbury's report came to Washington from the other heads of departments. Knox presumably obtained his copy of Franklin's letter either from Coxe or from Hamilton. Robert Morris and doubtless other key figures were also in possession of the information.[134]

Thus, just at the moment when George Hammond was handed his instructions in London, every member of the administration had acquired the substance of the highly secret state paper on which those instructions were based—one that Jefferson accurately called "a document of authority."[135] Through a guarded communication within the administration that itself revealed the deep political cleavages, all knew beyond question what slight hope there was for any negotiation involving genuine reciprocity. All knew that negotiation had been chosen in preference to retaliation chiefly if not solely in order to achieve the goals of British policy through those in the American government who were friendly and who, if supported, could be depended upon to oppose measures inimical to Great Britain. This unexpectedly revealed

---

[134] Robert Morris also gained "through the channel of a friend some particulars relative to the report of the Privy Council." The channel may have been Hamilton, Knox, Coxe, or Franklin himself. On the same day that Coxe received Franklin's summary of the report, Morris grimly wrote Colquhoun: "it seems . . . that your Govt. want better information from this country than they possess" (Morris to Colquhoun, 27 Aug. 1791, extract enclosed in Colquhoun to Grenville, 15 Nov. 1791, Grenville Papers, Boconnoc).

[135] This allusion appears in TJ's report on commerce, 16 Dec. 1793, in connection with his argument that four-fifths of the rice and tobacco imported into Great Britain from America before the war were re-exported. The argument was one that TJ had long advanced, but now in the autumn of 1791 as he was in the midst of preparing his report for the Second Congress he was able to rest it on an authoritative British document "composed . . . from the books of their customhouses."

Hammond was given a copy of Hawkesbury's *Report*. His instructions, drafted by Hawkesbury himself, described it as "a clear statement of the principles on which these Instructions are founded, and all the arguments by which the Justice and policy of them are to be defended." Hammond was told to consider the Report "as a Paper delivered to you in confidence, and on no account communicate it to any one else, as there are Matters in it, which are proper only for the Information of a person, to whom the management of so delicate and important a Business is confided, and ought not to be known by the persons concerned in the Government of the United States" (Hawkesbury's draft of instructions for Hammond, prepared at Grenville's request and dated 4 July 1791, AHA, *Ann. Rept.*, 1936, "Instructions to the British Ministers to the United States 1791-1812," ed. Bernard Mayo [Washington, 1941], p. 5n, 6; cited hereafter as Mayo, *IBM*).

document therefore held implications of the highest importance, both for the foreign policy of the United States and for her internal politics. The President and the Secretary of State were now aware that, for upwards of a year, the British ministry had been confident that a pro-British party existed in America, that it was centered in the Senate, and that its leaders desired a closer connection with Great Britain. They knew, too, that the ministry could not have derived this knowledge from "debates . . . in the *American Senate*" which the people were not privileged to hear. Such knowledge, obviously, had been received through hidden channels of communication reaching into that closed chamber. And none in the administration can have been unaware of the identity of the leader of those in the Senate who were "*in favor of a connection with Great Britain.*"

The shattering effects of these disclosures on the eve of the opening of the Second Congress can be gauged as much by the silence of Hamilton and his followers as by the comments of others. Tench Coxe expressed his opinion candidly to Adams if not to his superior. "It is a very poor state paper as to the information and reasoning it contains and winds up with a sufferance of the present state of things," he wrote. "The West India trade and that to their Northern Colonies are stated as objects on which the British government ought to refuse even *to treat.*"[136] This was the heart of the matter, but in his reply Adams made no comment, not even to acknowledge the receipt of so important a document. Jefferson saw, as any detached judge could have seen, that there was even less ground for optimism in Hawkesbury's recommendations than had been revealed by the mission of Gouverneur Morris. "Some new indications of the ideas with which the British cabinet are coming into treaty confirm your opinions, which I knew to be right," he wrote Morris, "but the Anglomany of some would not permit them to accede to."[137] Hamilton, though silent, was too astute not to see that this was a document that could not be discredited, especially when confirmed by private intelligence from London. "I fear there is no Disposition at present in our Ministers to treat properly with America," John Barker Church wrote to him early in August. "Lord Hawkesbury is lately admitted into the Cabinet, and his Prejudices are strong against you, and the Enthusiasm for maintaining the Navigation Act is such that there is not a Shadow of probability they will in any Shape relax."[138] Nothing could reveal the impact of the report of the Lords of Trade on Hamilton more effectively than the fact that he transmitted this part of Church's letter to Washington, as if to disabuse him of any suspicion that his Secretary of the Treasury had been too plainly identified with the Senate partisans of the English interest.[139] This, for Hamilton, was clearly a time for silence and discretion.

[136] Coxe to Adams, 27 Aug. 1791 (MHi: AM).
[137] TJ to Morris, 30 Aug. 1791.
[138] Church to Hamilton, London, [2 Aug. 1791] (Syrett, *Hamilton*, IX, 4-5).
[139] Hamilton to Washington, London, [6 Oct. 1791] (same, IX, 289). See also note 113 above.

EDITORIAL NOTE

VII

For the greatest disarray in the Hamiltonian ranks had already been caused by the President himself. On his return to the capital in July, Washington received Smith's lengthy report of his conversation with Grenville. His reply demolished whatever trace of elation remained among those who had promoted the mission and had been credulous enough to hail its outcome as a success. It was all the more crushing because, in phraseology as well as substance, it repeated what had been said in the message to Congress on the 14th of February. "Very soon after I came to the government," Washington's reply read, "I took measures for enquiring into the disposition of the British cabinet on the matters in question between us: and what you now communicate corresponds very exactly with the result of those enquiries."[140] When Smith, a young man of volatile temper, read these chilling words from the man whom he had hoped to impress with his skill in diplomacy, his elation dissolved in anger. He vented his resentment in the drafting of an intemperate response and—as if to identify beyond doubt the true fountainhead of his mission—hastened to Hamilton for advice, showing him the draft just as he had shown him the text of his report to the President. Hamilton possessed sufficient detachment of judgment and knowledge of Washington to know that Smith's irate expression of resentment was extremely imprudent. He therefore urged him to take no notice of the President's response but to allow the matter quietly to work "its own operation on the Minds of the Government." Smith accepted this sane counsel with reluctance, but he did discard the letter and derived such satisfaction as he could by sending a copy of it to John Adams.[141] Thereafter, disappointed and embittered, he placed the onus on Jefferson and dissembled his feelings toward Washington.[142]

[140] Washington to Smith, 13 July 1791 in TJ's hand (Dft in DLC: Jefferson Papers; Tr in DLC: Washington Papers; *Writings*, ed. Fitzpatrick, XXXI, 311).
[141] On Smith's "excessive inflammability of temper," of which he himself was sensibly aware, see TJ to Madison, 30 Jan. 1787, postscript of 5 Feb. 1787. Smith's account of Hamilton's dissuading him from sending the angry response is set forth in his letter to Adams, 5 Aug. 1791 (MHi: AM), in which he also says that he only replied to Washington: "I have the honor to acknowledge the receipt of the Presidents Letter of the 13th of July in answer to the Communications I thought it my duty to make on the 6th of June after my return from Europe." No copy of this curt acknowledgement has been found. See also Adams to Smith, 19 June 1791; Otis to Adams, 16 June 1791; Adams to Knox, 19 June 1791 (MHi: AM).
[142] In a private letter to Grenville, Hammond reported: "Colonel Smith, whom your Lordship saw in London, having conceived some disgust against Mr. Jefferson and the President, and imagining that his communications had not been treated with the respect they merited, has resigned a very lucrative situation under this government, and is now on his voyage to England. As he may probably endeavor to throw himself in your Lordship's way, I take the liberty of apprising you that, although his abilities are rather contracted, and he is not untinctured with vanity and affectation, I firmly believe him to be a man of unimpeachable integrity, and possessing a strong predilection for England" (Hammond to Grenville, 5 Apr. 1792, Grenville Papers, Boconnoc).
Both Smith's wife and John Adams had been pleased when Smith, no doubt on Hamilton's recommendation, was appointed while still in England as supervisor of excise for the New York district at a salary of $800 plus .5% commission (JEP, I, 81; Syrett, *Hamilton*, VIII, 187; IX, 427; K. M. Roof, *Colonel Smith and*

There can be little doubt that his animus would have been increased and Hamilton's discomfiture made more acute if either could have known that the response which the President signed was drafted by the Secretary of State.

This, of course, meant that Jefferson had read Smith's report and its accompanying documents. He could not have failed to observe the inconsistencies and to penetrate the unwitting disclosures of an inexpert and overzealous emissary. Nor could he have lacked the discernment to see that Smith had acted as spokesman for the partisans of the British interest in America and that the only significant revelation in his report was not Grenville's message but his own appeal for support against those of opposite political convictions in the United States. The nuances of Jefferson's careful and characteristic phrasing of the President's response take on added meaning in the light of this knowledge. The repetition of the opening phrases of the message to Congress of the 14th of February was therefore deliberate, and this much Hamilton if not Smith might have grasped. As an intentional reminder of Washington's public appraisal of the attitude of the British government, it was also a reaffirmation of confidence in his own emissary. It was a subtle rebuke to those engaging in hidden intrigue to the confusion of American diplomacy and the compromising of national dignity, perhaps also an admonition against the danger of permitting partisan advocacy to intrude itself into the conduct of foreign policy. These meanings in their fullest amplitude cannot have been perceived by Smith or by his principals who had initiated his mission and had laid the foundation for its failure. But no one could have read Washington's emphatic appraisal without knowing that Smith had achieved nothing except to expose himself and Hamilton to well-grounded suspicions about the true origin and purpose of his swift journey to London.[143]

Lady, p. 211-12). In a confidential exchange with Knox, Smith showed that he still hoped to be minister to England. When Knox told him that "certain principles of policy will dictate a different arrangement from the one you contemplated" and enjoined him not to reveal this—the appointment of Pinckney—"directly or indirectly . . . now or hereafter to any person on earth," Smith said that he was satisfied. He added: "I think I discharged faithfully the duty I owed my Country, my friends and myself; others may enjoy the fruits, without exciting my envy, or any passion that an honourable mind could revolt at" (Smith to Knox, 3 and 7 Dec. 1791; Knox to Smith, 4 Dec. 1791, MHi: Knox Papers). Smith resigned in dudgeon early in 1792, assuring Washington that he was retiring from public employment and would not "discover a disposition to return to it" under the existing administration. Washington accepted the offensive resignation in good grace. Later, in again applying for office, Smith said that the "late change in administration" had removed all of his personal objections to a public station (Washington to Smith, 10 Feb. 1792; Smith to Washington, 11 July 1794, DLC: Washington Papers). No change, of course, had occurred except for TJ's resignation. See note 165.

[143] In private matters, however, Smith had accomplished something. He had succeeded in selling some lands and in obtaining the means to speculate further. He borrowed $100,000 for Robert Morris from William Pulteney and his associates. And he persuaded an English artisan, Thomas Marshall, to emigrate; Hamilton engaged his services for the Society for Establishing Useful Manufactures (Tr of indenture between Smith and Morris concerning the loan, 30 Aug. 1791, DLC: Hamilton Papers; K. M. Roof, *Colonel William Smith and*

Yet Hamilton, however sensible his advice to Smith, was not one to allow an issue of such moment passively to work its own operation on the minds of government. Even after the rebuff by Washington his effort to fix responsibility for the message of February 14th on the partisan activities of the Secretary of State persisted. Again the channels opened up by Robert Morris were utilized. Late in July Beckwith informed Grenville that two letters from London had been received in Philadelphia and that both contained "the strongest assurances of the liberal and enlightened views of The Cabinet toward this Country, and of the misinformation upon which the public message of last spring was founded."[144] These letters, written by Patrick Colquhoun, were addressed to Smith and to Morris. The latter informed Colquhoun that he had communicated "to the President . . . and to the Ministers" that paragraph of his letter pertaining to Washington's message and to the decision to send a minister to the United States. They were, he said, "well pleased."[145] The letter to Smith was also revealed to the President, perhaps by Morris or Hamilton. But the persistent credulity of those who wished to believe was weakening. Beckwith reported to Grenville that "a gentleman in Office"—his usual manner of designating Hamilton—had asked whether these opinions were those of an individual or whether they might "be considered as proceeding from a superior authority."[146] The agent, who did not disclose what answer he gave to Hamilton, obviously intended the inquiry for himself as well. But, professing an assurance that his letter to Grenville betrayed, he told the President's secretary that his own communications from London confirmed the accounts in these two letters.[147]

Colquhoun, however, was as much in the dark as Beckwith and kept pressing upon Grenville the urgent need to send a minister before the opening of Congress. Late in the summer, still proclaiming Smith's mission a triumph in countering misinformation "industriously disseminated by the French party" and in bolstering the British interest in America, he yet warned that "their success . . . will depend much on the appearance of a British minister in America before Mr. Jefferson's report can be made in October next." Should "any accident" prevent his appearance, Colquhoun was prompted to write Grenville, a navigation act undoubtedly would be enacted. But if a prudent, well-informed, conciliatory person "whose name and character had not been known in the transactions of the war, should come as minister, it was "the decided opinion of the British interest in America that . . . everything favourable would result"—despite the fact that Americans hoped for privileges it would be difficult if not impossible for Great Britain to grant.[148] Colquhoun also tried to arrange an interview between the

Lady, p. 212; Bond to Leeds, 3 May 1791, AHA, *Ann. Rept.*, 1897, p. 483-4; Gouverneur Morris, *Diary*, ed. Davenport, II, 326; Marshall to Hamilton, 9 July 1791, Syrett, *Hamilton*, VIII, 556-7). See note, TJ's opinion on textiles, 3 Dec. 1790, for comparison with Hamilton's action in this respect.

144 Beckwith to Grenville, 31 July 1791 (PRO: FO 4/12).
145 Morris to Colquhoun, 28 July 1791 (extract enclosed in Colquhoun to Grenville, 24 Sep. 1791, Grenville Papers, Boconnoc).
146 Beckwith to Grenville, 31 July 1791 (PRO: FO 4/12).
147 Lear to Washington, 19 June 1791 (DLC: Washington Papers).
148 Colquhoun to Grenville, 5 Aug. 1791 (Grenville Papers, Boconnoc).

minister and John Browne Cutting, a friend of Smith and, like him, anxious to promote a closer connection with Great Britain. But this effort, too, brought a stinging backlash. Landing in New York in October, Cutting told Colquhoun he was amazed at the phenomenal progress being made in the United States. But this had produced sentiments that the friends of the British interest had not conveyed to the ministry:[149]

> The people feel themselves free and happy. I regret to add that most of those with whom I converse express an utter indifference, and even a repugnancy to a commercial treaty with Great Britain. I hope to find a different disposition elsewhere. But I much fear Mr. Hammond will come out too late.

This, written from the very capital of the partisans of Great Britain, was a measure of the distance that separated them from the political realities of the nation—a fissure soon to be thrown into brilliant relief by the American version of the "contest of Burke and Paine."[150]

VIII

Far from being discouraged, therefore, Jefferson could look forward even more confidently than in the spring to increased support for the navigation bill. He was in fact at work on his report at the very moment that the British ministry itself provided the most authoritative confirmation of the views he had expressed and the President had made public on February 14th.[151] It was thus ironic that, of the various approaches to the British government made by Hamilton and his supporters through Morris, Smith, and Maunsell, the only one that provided reliable and incontrovertible intelligence was the one that Hamilton sought to discredit. The irony is heightened because it was Washington's disclosure of views based on Morris' information that was chiefly responsible for the decision of Pitt and Grenville to send a minister to the United States. This is not to say that the President's open assertion of national dignity triumphed where covert supplication and intrigue had failed. The British response, it seems clear, was grounded in the fear inspired by the disclosure and by official and private reports from America that the United States might indeed resort to the means which Jefferson, disinclined as he was to make use of it, believed infallible.[152]

[149] Colquhoun to Grenville, 8 Aug. and 15 Nov. 1791, enclosing in the latter extract of a letter from Cutting to Colquhoun, dated at New York, 12 Oct. 1791 (same). In October Colquhoun—or perhaps Hammond—also transmitted an unsigned memorandum from his correspondents in the United States warning that TJ's report on commerce was expected to be acted upon promptly at the next session and that the merchants in America universally desired the early establishment of a commercial system between the two countries (Extract, Oct. 1791, Grenville Papers, Boconnoc).
[150] See note to TJ to Jonathan B. Smith, 26 Apr. 1791; the quotation is from Monroe to TJ, 25 July 1791.
[151] TJ to Ross, 26 Aug. 1791. See also note 27.
[152] TJ's outline of policy, 12 July 1790 (enclosure to Document I in group of documents on war crisis of 1790).

Even so, Hamilton and the friends of the British interest were the beneficiaries. George Hammond, commissioned to delay rather than to negotiate, provided exactly the opportunity needed at a time when the intrigues of the Secretary of the Treasury had come dangerously near exposing him. For the new minister, like Maunsell who was no longer needed, was in effect if not in form accredited to Hamilton and—as his instructions specified—to "all moderate Men who wish for a Connection with Great Britain." Hammond was particularly directed to address himself "to the members of the American Senate, who have more than once already shewn a Disposition to restrain the impetuosity of the House of Representatives."[153] But Hamilton, the acknowledged leader of the well-disposed Senators, evidently felt the circumstances required even more caution than he had exercised with Beckwith. He first transmitted to Washington private news of implacable British attitudes.[154] The information added nothing at all to what was already known on better authority by the entire administration. But the supererogatory act did seem to imply that the Secretary of the Treasury wished it to be understood that the President's position was also his. If so, the gesture was proved deceptive by all that followed. With Washington and Jefferson both absent, Hamilton called the next day on Jean Baptiste Ternant, the newly-arrived French minister.

The conference lasted for almost four hours. Hamilton spoke at length of the importance the United States attached to its commerce with the French West Indies. When Ternant pointed out that favors extended had been met with actions of a wholly contrary tendency on the part of the United States, his visitor "did his utmost to prove . . . that imperative circumstances on which depended the success of the new Constitution had prevented Congress from granting the exceptions it had intended from the beginning to extend to French commerce." The reasons he advanced were the familiar ones that Senators had already given to Otto.[155] But he also led Ternant to believe that, if it should be proved American ships arriving from a foreign port were exempt from tonnage duties in French ports, he would succeed in obtaining exemption for French ships in American ports and even in getting reimbursement of duties already paid.[156] When his attempt to discover the nature of Ternant's instructions failed, Ham-

[153] Mayo, *IBM*, p. 12.

[154] See above, at notes 138 and 139. It was also at this time that Earl Wycombe, son of the Marquis of Lansdowne whom TJ had known in Paris, arrived by the same packet that brought Maunsell. The general assumed that either Knox or TJ would present Wycombe to the President. But the young man had expressed a desire to see only "New England, the President, and Premier" and it was Hamilton who made the presentation by letter—a matter worthy of note only because Hamilton, at this particular moment, made a point of recalling "the friendly dispositions and liberal policy" of Wycombe's father, as if to emphasize the contrast with the disposition shown in the letter he had sent to Washington three days earlier (Maunsell to Knox, 3 Sep. 1791, MHi: Knox Papers; Nathaniel Hazard to Alexander Hamilton, 11 Oct. 1791; Hamilton to Washington, 11 Oct. 1791, Syrett, *Hamilton*, IX, 365, 369-70).

[155] See Editorial Note to group of documents on the French representation on the tonnage acts, under 18 Jan. 1791.

[156] See, for comparison, Hamilton to TJ, 11 and 13 Jan. 1791 (Documents VI and VIII in the same group).

ilton suggested that it would be possible to eliminate all difficulties by a new treaty. He said that he eagerly desired this to take place and, if it did, he would himself propose all of the exceptions that the new treaty might require or that reciprocity could justify. The wary diplomat pointed out that it was important for the United States first of all to demonstrate its fidelity to the terms of the existing treaties. On that, he said, "would probably depend the conclusion of the new one that he *appeared* to desire."[157]

Hamilton then turned to American relations with England. He declared the United States would insist on the admission of American ships to the British West Indies and would make this a condition *sine qua non* in negotiating a commercial treaty. If, as was expected, England should propose a treaty of alliance and make that a condition of negotiating on commerce, the proposition would be rejected. The Secretary of the Treasury voiced this opinion not only for the government, but for himself as well. "Mr. Hamilton," reported Ternant in summing up the interview, "made the greatest protestations of attachment to France, and he tried hard to convince me of his opinion that the true interest of the United States excluded any other political alliance than the one they had with us. But I had the impression he had not come entirely on his own, and that the President might have charged him to have a few discussions with me. We parted as great friends, with a mutual promise of seeing each other often, and always to keep loyalty and frankness in our talks."[158]

But loyalty and frankness were exactly the elements lacking. Everything that Hamilton had expressed to the French minister stood in stark contradiction to all he had been saying to Beckwith for two years. It was also contradicted by the whole tenor of his policy. With one exception—the proposal of a new treaty with France, which was clearly disingenuous—it placed him in a position indistinguishable from that of the Secretary of State. The move, therefore, may have been intended in part to allay suspicions. If so and if Hamilton assumed Jefferson would exchange confidences with Ternant as he himself had done with Beckwith and soon would with Hammond, he misjudged his colleague in this as in other respects. Jefferson, who learned of the conversation only when Hamilton finally divulged it, was even more reserved with the new minister than he had been with Otto—so much so that Ternant complained of the fact in his dispatches.[159] Further, it was this very proposal of a new commercial treaty

157 Emphasis added. Here and elsewhere Ternant indicated the wariness with which he received Hamilton.
158 Ternant to Montmorin, 9 Oct. 1791 ("Correspondence of French Ministers 1791-1797," ed. F. J. Turner, AHA, *Ann. Rept.*, 1903, II, 57-60; cited hereafter as *Turner, CFM*).
159 Ternant to Montmorin, 24 and 27 Oct. 1791 (same, p. 61-2, 67). At Mount Vernon and again at Georgetown, where TJ and Ternant were thrown together for some time with ample opportunity for confidential discussion, the minister was able to draw from him only the following, which he said were TJ's own words and which he believed to be his true sentiments: ". . . if the drafting of a treaty of commerce were to depend on him, he would cause it to consist of but a single article which would provide for the reciprocal naturalization of the nationals of France and the United States so as to place them on a

that gave Jefferson one of his first proofs that cabinet secrets were being conveyed by the Secretary of the Treasury to the British minister. It was also this that led him to believe the proposal only a stratagem to pave the way for a similar overture by the government to Hammond.[160] All of the evidence suggests that Jefferson's suspicions on both counts were even better founded than he knew. Once again the passion for intrigue had produced a contrary effect.

But not an end to such characteristic and calculated efforts to dominate foreign policy. The next move, inspired by the fear of Jefferson's impending report calling for a navigation act, was made through Phineas Bond and George Hammond. On the day following Hamilton's call on Ternant, Bond was able to provide Grenville with an account of views of the friends of the British interest that stood in marked contrast to the assurances given by their leader to the French minister. The consul first revealed that the report of the Lords of Trade was "fully *understood* by the ministers of the United States."[161] He reported that this document, about which he himself had not been informed until then, had led some in administration to conclude that the attitude of Great Britain in commercial matters was "not very favorable." But those who theretofore had regarded admission to the West Indies as the indispensable basis for a treaty, particularly the New Englanders, might consider as an equivalent the privilege of selling American-built ships to British subjects. Bond was aware that any tampering with the navigation system, besides opening the door to fraud and evasion, "might be attended with consequences very dangerous to Britain's political weight." Yet the leading men with whom he had conversed were concerned for the future. They did not think the United States "in a situation to enter *at this time* into a treaty offensive and defensive with Gt. Britain: the honor of the Government they say is pledged to fulfil their engagements with those powers who, in the hour of difficulty, interposed their aid."[162] Any hastily arranged "departure from these engagements . . . would blast the credit of the new Government in the opinions of all mankind." But, the leading men said, "in a series of time the advantages of a commercial connexion with Gt. Britain would be so extensively felt that every part of the Union would see the expediency of the closest alliance between the two countries."[163] The impact of the report of the Lords of Trade, transmitted to the British consul by someone among the very few in government who were privy to it, thus enabled Bond to give unusual meaning to this dispatch. Those who knew at last that access to the West Indies would be flatly refused now offered an equivalent that they hoped would gain the votes of New England shipping interests. Their appeal for some small temporary concession in order to

---

footing of perfect equality as to commerce in the ports of the two nations in Europe and in every other part of the world" (same, p. 61-2). This was TJ's consistent position.

160 TJ's memorandum of cabinet consultations late Dec. 1791, "written Mar. 11. 1792."

161 Emphasis in original.

162 Emphasis added.

163 Bond to Grenville, 8 Oct. 1791 (AHA, *Ann. Rept.*, 1897, p. 492-3).

attain the larger goal in future negated all that had been said to Ternant. It was couched in language almost identical with that expressed by Hamilton to Beckwith earlier in the year.[164] This ultimate goal—the destruction of the French alliance and the substitution of one with Great Britain in its place—was apparent also in the initial advice offered by its proponents to the new British minister.

Hammond arrived in Philadelphia on 20 Oct. 1791, two days before the Secretary of State returned to the capital and four days before the session opened. He had been instructed not to present his credentials until a minister to England had been appointed, but his consultations with the persons of influence whom he had been directed to cultivate led him to conclude that a delay could have serious political consequences. He therefore departed from the literal requirements of his orders and assumed his public station after Jefferson has assured him that the President had offered the ministerial post to an unnamed person.[165] Hammond explained the circumstances in his official dispatch. But in a private letter to Grenville he enlarged upon the political factors. His duties, he wrote, lay with the Secretary of State whose political principles were not unknown to the Secretary for Foreign Affairs. There was therefore no reason to expect from him "a favourable, perhaps not a faithful or candid exposition of the motives" for delay. The resultant insinuations Jefferson's adherents might have thrown out in Congress "the friends of a British interest might have found it difficult to repel." His advisers reported that Jefferson had consistently encouraged the belief that England would never send a minister or "evince a desire to enter into a fair commercial arrangement." Consequently, since he was expected shortly to make his report on commercial policy, nothing would be more embarrassing to him than for the new minister to make his actual appearance on the scene, prepared "to enter into the immediate discussion of arrangements, commercial as well as political, upon fair and honourable principles of mutual benefit."[166] These political considerations, Hammond concluded, were not mere speculative opinions of his own: one or two Senators had

[164] See above at notes 50 and 51 for a partial quotation. The earlier conversation between Hamilton and Beckwith took place on 16 Feb. 1791 and the parallel passage is in Syrett, *Hamilton*, VIII, 44.

[165] Joanne L. Neel, *Phineas Bond*, p. 86, states that Bond called on TJ on 21 Oct. 1791 and informed him that Hammond could present his credentials only when the United States had named or invested "some Person" as minister to Great Britain. TJ arrived on Saturday the 22d and, after both he and Hammond had missed each other in personal visits, the two men entered into the "previous explanations" Bond had said were necessary. But it was not until about the 6th of November that the President discussed with TJ the choice of minister to London. The decision, which was made by Washington, occurred three days later. The identity of the person chosen was evidently kept in such secrecy that it was known only to the President and the Secretary of State (TJ to Pinckney, 6 Nov. 1791; TJ to Short, 9 Nov. 1791; Washington to TJ, 9 Nov. 1791). On the 11th Hammond presented his credentials to the President and thus TJ's information to him that an offer had been made was probably given on the preceding day. Under these circumstances the secret was sufficiently revealed to enable Knox to tell Smith that the choice had not fallen on him (see note 142).

[166] Hammond to Grenville, 16 Nov. 1791 (Grenville Papers, Boconnoc). The warning that TJ would immediately present his report at the opening of Congress had already been received by Grenville when Hammond wrote. See note 149 above.

urged them upon him and had voiced their apprehensions. The approach to Hammond and the expressed anxieties reveal, in this concern over a delay in the mere ceremony of the presentation of credentials, how deep and growing was the fear of the navigation bill that Jefferson intended to recommend.

But once again the effort to block his report through intrigue did not succeed. Jefferson, more concerned with substance than form, seized the initiative. If, as he soon obliged Hammond to concede, the minister lacked express power to arrange a treaty, some steps by the United States might be "necessary in consequence of it."[167] The warning was made good before the year was out when he announced to the President in Hamilton's presence that he was ready to submit his report and that it could not avoid a recommendation of retaliation against Great Britain. In view of the long series of intrigues to forestall such an event, each ending in frustration or worse, there is little reason to doubt the accuracy of Jefferson's statement that Hamilton "opposed it violently."[168] Retaliation, the Secretary of the Treasury argued, would prolong Great Britain's hold on the western posts. Jefferson conceded the force of this. He agreed that, if the discussion of infractions of the Treaty of Peace afforded a glimmer of hope for an amicable adjustment of differences, he would withhold the report on commerce until the next session. Having long since anticipated this discussion, he had already given to Hammond his own summary specification of British actions deemed in contravention of the treaty.[169] Hammond had not only been given particular instructions and detailed information about unfulfilled treaty stipulations, chiefly those pertaining to debts and Loyalists' claims: he had also been enjoined to consider this as the first and leading object of his mission and to "lose no time in stating these Particulars" to those with whom he was to treat.[170] He could not, therefore, have been unprepared. Only a few days after Jefferson delivered his list of supposed infractions, Hammond apologized for not having submitted his own counter-allegations. Yet, after Jefferson had agreed to postpone his report on commerce pending the discussion, two full months elapsed before the British minister met his responsibility—and then only after Washington became impatient and directed that he be given a jog. From this and other circumstances Jefferson was finally led to conclude, with better justification than he realized, that Hamilton "communicated to Hammond all our views and knew from him in return the views of the British court."[171] But what he did not know was that the Secretary of the Treasury had given Hammond the impression that it was the mere exchange of ministers between the two countries that had caused him

[167] TJ to Hamond, 29 Nov.; 5, 13, and 15 Dec. 1791; Hammond to TJ, 30 Nov.; 6 and 15 Dec. 1791. This initial exchange is printed in ASP, *Foreign Relations*, I, 188-90.
[168] TJ's memorandum "written Mar. 11. 1792."
[169] TJ to Hammond, 15 Dec. 1791.
[170] Mayo, *IBM*, p. 14.
[171] TJ's memorandum "written Mar. 11. 1792."; TJ said that he jogged Hammond at the President's assembly on 21 Feb. 1792. Hammond complied within a fortnight (Hammond to TJ, 5 Mch. 1792).

to postpone his report.[172] Hammond's credulity in accepting and passing on to his government such a misconception is a measure of his failure to understand the man with whom it was his duty to treat. But the error was less his than that of the men of influence and their leader in the administration whom he was officially required to cultivate.

For theirs was the more egregious credulity. Their pursuit of a policy of subservience was grounded in the belief that the continued existence of the new government depended on its fiscal arrangements and that these required opposition to any measure disturbing to trade with Great Britain. That belief was unshaken even by actions of the British ministry which betrayed its fear that the Secretary of State might be able to make good the threat of a navigation act. It could not be disturbed by the manifest evidences that the remarkably expanding American economy and the enterprising spirit of its commerce, now invading the oriental markets of European nations, could not long be kept in a state of quasi-colonial dependence. Indeed, so profound was the credulousness born of fiscalism that those under its sway believed what Hamilton told Beckwith and what he or one of his followers told Bond—that, once the French connection had been broken, "every part of the Union would see the expediency of the closest alliance" between England and the United States. This was the ultimate aim, with the insubstantial arguments of fiscalism and the inept use of deception being the means.

Yet, in the face of intrigues whose variety and extent Jefferson could not have perceived, he did withhold his report at the moment his opponents in the administration and in the Congress feared it most. With a candor and conciliation that were never reciprocated, he held in abeyance the threat of retaliation because of the possibility, however slight, that "some changes might take place . . . which might call for corresponding changes in measures."[173] Such forbearance during diplomatic discussions was characteristic, but it was also decisive. With the passing of this auspicious moment came the gradual shift of Washington's influence, permanently and for reasons still awaiting adequate explanation, to the Hamiltonian side of the scales. Once, aroused by the persistent tactics of delay in resolving the differences between England and the United States, Washington seemed about to embrace a position more friendly to the French alliance—one that Jefferson called the polar star of his system.[174] But this, too, was an evanescent moment and the recommendations set forth in Jefferson's generously delayed report came nearest to being realized only after his tenure as Secretary of State had ended.[175]

Meanwhile, through the instrumentality of the British minister and by a continuing use of intrigue and deception, Hamilton was able to

[172] Hammond to Grenville, 9 Jan. 1792 (DLC: Henry Adams Transcripts).
[173] TJ to Speaker of the House, 20 Feb. 1793.
[174] TJ's memorandum of conversation with the President, 27 Dec. 1792.
[175] Malone, *Jefferson*, III, 153-9, presents a cogent analysis of factors influencing TJ's presentation of his report on leaving office and concludes that the actions of the British government before and after this left "no doubt that the threat of retaliatory commercial legislation would have been an effective weapon in diplomacy." His conclusion is amply supported by the evidence.

nullify Jefferson's influence over foreign policy and even to prevent the employment of the threat that had so clearly proved its effectiveness. But the treaty of 1794 which embodied the policy of subservience and of which he was the chief architect did not bring forth from every part of the nation the desire for a closer alliance with England. Instead, it rent the fabric so violently that, as it seems in the perspective of time, only those intangible bonds of union in which Jefferson placed his reliance could have preserved it. The policy of subservience could perhaps postpone but not prevent war. And it helped to make inevitable the ultimate repudiation of its advocates by the electorate. Thus the ligaments of interest, enmeshing their great protagonist and his followers in a web of credulity, proved to be both fragile and dangerously misleading. After two years of suppliant effort by those who sought to correct what they conceived to be partisan and purposeful misinformation, the British ministry had been misled into supposing its friends in America more numerous and the nation more pliable than was the case—even, perhaps, to believe that an alliance was possible.[176] But neither the President nor the Secretary of State, unwitting victims of calculated deception though they were, had been misled. Both understood the national character and cherished its dignity.

[176] William Gordon read in the London press what he regarded as ministerial news about Hammond's alleged commission to conclude "a treaty of *offensive* and *defensive* Alliance" as well as a commercial treaty. He sent an explosive protest to John Adams and expressed the hope that Hammond would be told "in the plainest American English, that the motto of the United States is—Peace and Commerce with all the World upon a principle of reciprocity, and that they are determined to be the dupes of no power on earth" (Gordon to Adams, 15 Sep. 1791, MHi: AM). The American consul in London reported at the same time that the British believed the United States would "readily come into any measures . . . and that a Treaty, offensive and defensive" could be concluded (Johnson to TJ, 12 Sep. 1791). Maunsell, in transmitting a letter from Brett shortly after this, asked about Hammond's mission: "Is there a likelyhood of the bands of friendship and steady alliance being tyed between the United States and Great Britain, commercial and political? thro' the mission of our Ambassador" (Maunsell to Knox, 9 Feb. 1792; Brett's letter has not been found).

I. The President to the Secretary of State

DEAR SIR   Decr. 11th. 1790

Herewith you will receive the Powers and Instructions with which Gouvr. Morris Esqr. is invested and his Communications consequent thereof.—You will give them the consideration their importance merit, and report your opinion of the measures proper to be taken thereupon.

The following extract from one of my *private* letters to Mr. Morris contains all the notice I have *yet* taken of his public communications.—I give it that you may have the whole matter before you.

"New York July 7th. 1790

This letter will be short; the intention being little more than to acknowledge their receipt of your several favors from London; dated the 7th. and 13th. of April and 1st. and 2d. of May respecting the business which had been entrusted to you of a public nature; and of your other let[ters] of the 12th. of April and 3d. of May which more immediately relate to my private concerns.—Permit me to thank you, my good Sir, for the attention you have paid to the latter; and as far as your intercourse with the British Ministry had gone, to assure you of my entire approbation of your conduct with respect to the former.—I shall wait the answer which your address of the 30th. of April will extort from the Duke of Leeds (if he does not mean to be silent) before I shall write more fully to you on that head."[1]

Go: WASHINGTON

RC (DLC); endorsed by TJ as received 11 Dec. 1790 and so recorded in SJL. Dft (DLC: Washington Papers). FC (DNA: RG 59, SDC). Entry in SJPL reads: "G.W. to Th: J. on the powers and instructions to Gouvr. Morris."

The whole of Morris' correspondence pertaining to the London mission is printed in Sparks, *Gouverneur Morris*, II, 3-56. On 19 June 1790 Washington had sent to TJ the earlier part of Gouverneur Morris' reports, but without specifying what these were (see that letter for Morris to Washington, 1 May 1790, together with notes and summaries of Morris' correspondence with the Duke of Leeds). In the above, as we know from TJ's report of 15 Dec. 1790, Washington included his letter of credence and his letter of instructions to Morris of 13 Oct. 1789, texts of which are in Washington, *Writings*, ed. Fitzpatrick, XXX, 439-42. Extracts of salient parts of these, along with others of Morris' letters of 7 and 13 Apr. and 2 May 1790, are quoted in the Editorial Note to documents relating to the war crisis of 1790. Washington also included with the above Morris' two letters of 22 Jan. 1790. The first of these, dated at Paris, acknowledged receipt of the President's two letters of 13 Oct. 1789 and promised to depart for London as soon as possible. Morris added: "When last in that city, I saw the Duke of Leeds twice at the French Ambassador's, and from some slight circumstances was induced to believe, that the British court are better disposed towards a connexion with the United States, than they were some eighteen months ago. The principal difficulty will, I imagine, arise from the personal character of the King, which is of that perseverance, and from the personal dislike, which he bears to his former subjects" (Sparks, *Gouverneur Morris*, II, 6). The second of these two letters was private (Morris, *Diary*, ed. Davenport, I, 376-7). Morris' letter of 24 Sep. 1790 evidently had not arrived at the time the above was written, though this cannot be certainly established since Washington did not follow TJ's habit of recording the date of receipt of his letters. It may be that it had been received and was omitted because it dealt with the impressment of seamen and was therefore not strictly within the sphere of Morris' authority (see note, Morris to TJ, 24 Dec. 1790). All other letters from Morris to Washington reporting on the London mission that TJ certainly had before him in drafting his report, and therefore were enclosed in the above, are printed below.

[1] This is not the whole of Washington's letter of 7 July 1790: another paragraph followed that dealt with private matters (Washington, *Writings*, ed. Fitzpatrick, XXXI, 68-9).

Gouverneur Morris to George Washington

SIR   London 7 April 1790

I arrived in this City on Saturday Evening the twenty eighth of March and called the next Morning on the Duke of Leeds Minister for foreign Affairs. He was not at Home, I therefore wrote to him a Note Copy whereof is enclosed as also of his Answer received that Evening. On Monday the twenty ninth I waited upon him at Whitehall and after the usual Compliments, presented your Letter telling him that it would explain the Nature of my Business. Having read it, he said with much Warmth and Gladness in his Appearance "I am very happy Mr. Morris to see this Letter and under the Presidents own Hand. I assure you it is very much my Wish to cultivate a friendly and commercial Intercourse between the two Countries *and more*, and I can answer for the Rest of his Majesty's Servants that they are of the same Opinion." "I am happy my Lord to find that such Sentiments prevail, for we are too near Neighbours not to be either good friends or dangerous Enemies." "You are perfectly right Sir and certainly it is to be desired as well for our mutual Interests as for the Peace and Happiness of Mankind that we should be upon the *best* Footing." I assured him of our sincere Disposition to be upon good Terms and then proceeded to mention those Points in the Treaty of Paris which remained to be performed: and first I observed that by the Constitution of the United States which he had certainly read all Obstacles to the Recovery of british Debts are removed, and that if any Doubts could have remained they are now done away by the Organization of a federal Court which has Cognizance of Causes arising under the Treaty. He said he was very happy to receive this Information, that he had been of Opinion and had written so to Mr. Adams that the Articles ought to be performed in the Order in which they stood in the Treaty. Not chusing to enter into any Discussion of his Conduct in Relation to Mr. Adams, I told his Grace that I had but one Rule or Principle both for public and private Life, in Conformity to which I had always entertained the Idea that it would consist most with the Dignity of the United States first to perform *all their* Stipulations and then to require such Performance from others, and that (in Effect) if each Party were on mutual Covenants to suspend his Compliance expecting that of the other all Treaties would be illusory. He agreed in this Sentiment, upon which I added that the United States had now placed themselves in the Situation just mentioned: and here I took Occasion to observe that the Southern States who had been much blamed in this Country for obstructing the Recovery of british Debts, were not liable to all the Severity of Censure which had been thrown upon them. That their Negroes having been taken or seduced away, and the Payment for those Negroes having been stipulated by Treaty they had formed a Reliance on such Payment for Discharge of Debts contracted with british Merchants both previously and subsequently to the War. That the Suspension of this Resource had occasioned a Deficiency of Means, so that their Conduct had been dictated by an overruling Necessity. Returning then to the main Business I observed that as we had now fully performed our Part it was proper to mention that two Articles remained to be fulfilled by them viz. that which related to the Posts and that regarding Compensation for the Negroes. Unless indeed they had sent out orders respecting the former subsequent to the Writing of your Letter, and I took the Liberty to consider *that* as a very probable Circumstance. He now became a little embarrassed, and told me that he could not exactly say how that Matter stood. That as to the Affair of the Negroes he had long wished to have it brought up and to have Something done, but Something or other had always interfered. He then changed the Conversation but I brought it back, and he changed it again. Hence it was apparent that he would go no farther than general Professions and Assurances. I then told him that there was a little Circumstance which had operated very disagreably upon the Feelings of America. Here he interrupted me "I know what you are going to say. Our not sending a Minister. I wished to send you one but then I wished to have a Man every Way equal to the Task. A Man of Abilities and one agreable to the People of America, but it was difficult. It is a great Way off. And many object on that Score." I expressed my Persuasion that this Country count not want Men well qualified for every Office, and he again changed the Conversation. Therefore as it was not worth while to discuss the Winds and the Weather I observed that as he might probably chuse to consider the Matter a little and to read again the Treaty and compare it with the American Constitution. He said that he should and wished me to leave your Letter which he would have copied and return to me. I did so telling him that I should be very glad to have a speedy Answer and he promised that I should.—Thus Sir this Matter was begun but nine Days have since elapsed and I have heard Nothing farther from the Duke of Leeds. It is true that Easter Hollidays have intervened and that public Business is in general suspended for that Period. I shall give them sufficient Time to shew whether they are as well disposed as he has declared and then give them a Hint. Before I saw him I communicated to the french Embassador *in Confidence* that you had directed me to call for a Performance of the Treaty. He told me at once that they would not give up the Posts. Perhaps he may be right. I thought it best to make such Communication because the Thing itself cannot remain Secret and by mentioning it to him we are enabled to say with Truth that in every Step relating to the Treaty of Paris we have acted confidentially in Regard to our Ally. With sincere Respect I am Sir your obed. Servant

GOUVR. MORRIS

Dupl (DLC: Washington Papers); at head of text: "*Duplicate*." Enclosure: Gouverneur Morris to the Duke of Leeds, 28 [i.e., 29] Mch. 1790: "Mr. Morris had the Honor to wait upon his Grace the Duke of Leeds this Morning, but had not that of seeing him.—He presents his most respectful Compliments and will be happy to know the time when it will be most convenient for his Grace to receive certain Communications which Mr. M. is directed to make to his Majesty's Ministers by the President of the United

States of America" (dated at "froomes Hotel Covent Garden 28 March 1790"; Tr in DLC: Washington Papers, in Morris' hand, followed by his Tr of Leeds' response: "The Duke of Leeds presents his Compliments to Mr. Morris, and will be glad to see him at the Office ToMorrow and Half past two. Whitehall Sunday 28 [i.e., 29] March 1790").

ENCLOSURE II

Gouverneur Morris to George Washington

SIR   London 29 May 1790

I do myself the Honor to enclose a Copy of my Letter of the first Instant. On the Night of the fourth there was a hot Press here which has continued ever since, and the declared Object is to compel Spain to atone for an Insult offered to Great Britain by capturing two Vessels in Nootka Sound. Permit me to observe incidentally that it would not be amiss for the American Captain who was a Witness of the Whole Transaction to publish a faithful Narrative. The general Opinion here, is that Spain will submit, and that Spain only is the Object of this Armament. But I hold a very different Faith. If Spain submits she may as well give up her american Dominions, for the Position advanced here is that Nations have a Right to take Possession of any Territory unoccupied. Now without noticing the Inconsistency between this Assertion and those which preceeded the War of 1755 when France built Fort Duquesne upon Ground unoccupied by british Subjects, it cannot escape the most cursory Observation that the british sitting down in the Vicinity of Spanish Settlements will establish such a System of contraband Traffic as must ruin the Commerce of Cadiz, and the Revenue now derived from it by the spanish Monarch.—In former Letters I have communicated in some Measure my Ideas upon the second Opinion. I shall not therefore recapitulate them, but only in general notice that the Armament against Spain, should Spain shrink from the Contest, will undoubtedly be sent to the Baltic with decisive Effect. You will observe also that the Ministers count upon the Nullity of France, of which I shall say a Word presently.

In Consequence of the Orders for impressing Seamen a number of Americans were taken, and the Applications made for their Releif were in some Instances ineffectual. On the Morning of the twelfth Mr. Cutting called to inform me that he was appointed Agent to several of the American Masters of Ships; I gave him my Advice as to the best Mode of Proceeding and particularly urged him to authenticate all the Facts by Affidavits, assuring him that if he was unsuccessful I would endeavor to obtain the Assistance of such Persons as I might be acquainted with. On the seventeenth Mr. Payne called to tell me that he had conversed on the same Subject with Mr. Burke, who had asked him if there was any Minister, Consul or other Agent of the united States, who could properly make application to the Government: to which he had replied in the Negative, but said that I was here who had been a Member of Congress and was therefore the fittest Person to step forward. In Consequence of what passed between them he urged me to take the Matter up, which I promised to do. On the eighteenth, I wrote to the Duke of Leeds requesting an Interview. He desired me to come at three oClock of the next Day, but his Note was delivered after the Hour was passed, and very shortly after it came another Note giving me another Appointment for the twentieth.

Upon entering his Closet he apologized for not answering my Letters. I told him that I had in my Turn an Apology to make for troubling him with an Affair on which I was not authorized to speak. He said I had misunderstood one Part of his Letter to me, for that he certainly meant to express a Willingness to enter into a Treaty of Commerce. I replied that as to my Letter I supposed he would answer it at his Leizure, and therefore we would wave the Discussion. That my present Object was to mention the Conduct of their Press Gangs who had taken many american Seamen and had entered American Vessels with as little Ceremony as those belonging to Britain. "I beleive my Lord this is the only Instance in which we are not treated as Aliens." He acknowledged that it was wrong, and would speak to Lord Chatham on the Subject. I told him that many disagreeable Circumstances had already happened, and that there was known to expect many more in a general Impress thro the british Dominions. That Masters of Vessels on their Return to America would excite much Heat "and *that*, my Lord, combined with other Circumstances, may perhaps occasion very disagreable Events; for you know that when a Wound is but recently healed 'tis easy to rub off the Skin." He then repeated his assurances of Good Will, and exprest an anxious Wish to prevent all Disagreement; observing at the same Time that there was much Difficulty in distinguishing between the Seamen of the two Countries. I acknowledged the Inconveniencies to which they might be subjected by the Pretence of British Seamen to be americans, and wished therefore that some Plan might be adopted which, founded on good Faith, might at the same Time prevent the Concealment of british Sailors, and protect the Americans from Insult. As a Means of accomplishing that End, I suggested the Idea of Certificates of Citizenship, to be given by the Admiralty Courts in America to our Seamen. He seemed much pleased and willing at once to adopt it, but I desired him to consult first the King's Servants in that particular Department, and having again reminded him that I spoke without Authority, took my Leave, but at his Request promised to visit him again the next Day.

The Morning of the twenty first I found him sitting with Mr. Pitt, to whom he presented me. The first Point we took up was that of the Impress. Mr. Pitt exprest his Approbation of the Plan I had proposed to the Duke, but observed that it was liable to Abuse notwithstanding every Precaution which the Admiralty Offices in America could take. I acknowledged that it was, but observed that, even setting aside the great political Interests of both Countries, it was for the commercial Interest of Britain rather to wink at such Abuse; for that if they should be involved in a War *with the House of Bourbon* our Commerce with Britain must be in American Bottoms, because a War Premium of Insurance would give a decided Preference to the Manufactures of other Countries in our Markets. But that no Wages could induce

American Seamen to come within the british Dominions, if they were thereby liable to be impressed. Mr. Pitt replied to this, that the Degree of Risque, and consequently the Rate of Insurance, must depend upon the *Kind of War*. Not taking any direct Notice of this Expression, I observed that Notwithstanding the wretched State of the *french Government* there still existed much Force in that Country, and that the Power of commanding human Labor must also exist somewhere; so that if the Government could not arm their Fleets there would still be many Privateers, and that (in Effect) the slenderest Naval Efforts must involve merchant Vessels in considerable Danger. Returning then to the Consideration of the principal Point, we discussed the Means of carrying the Plan into Effect, and for that Purpose I recommended that his Majesty's Servants should order all their marine Officers to admit as Evidence of being an american Seaman, the Certificate to that Effect of the Admiralty in America, containing in it a proper Dexcription of the Person &c., but without excluding however other Evidence; and observed that in Consequence of the Communication that such Orders were given the executive Authority in America, without the Aid of the Legislature, by Directions to the several Admiralties might carry the Plan into Effect, so far as relates to those Seamen who should apply for Certificates. I am induced to beleive that this Measure if adopted, will not only answer the desired End, but be productive of other good Consequences in America, which I will not now trouble you with the Detail of.

This Affair being so far adjusted, we proceeded to new Matter, and they both assured me that I had misapprehended the Duke's Letter in Regard to a Treaty of Commerce. I answered coolly that it was easy to rectify the Mistake, but it appeared idle to form a new Treaty untill the Parties should be thoroughly satisfied with that already existing. Mr. Pitt then took up the Conversation and said that the Delay of Compliance on our Part had rendered that Compliance less effectual, and that Cases must certainly exist where great Injury had been sustained by the Delay. To this I replied that Delay is always a Kind of Breach, since as long as it lasts it is the Non Performance of Stipulations. I proceeded then to a more exact Investigation of the Question. And first, as I knew them to be pestered with many Applications for Redress by those who had and those who pretended to have suffered, I attempted to shew what I verily beleive to be the Fact viz. that the Injury was much smaller that was imagined, because among the various Classes of American Debtors, those only could be considered who had the Ability and not the Will to pay at the Peace, and were now deprived of the Ability. These I supposed to be not numerous, and as to others I stated Interest as the natural Compensation for Delay of Payment, observing that it was impossible to go into an Examination of all the incidental Evils. In the second Place I desired him to consider that we in Turn complained that the british Government had not, as they ought, paid for the Slaves which were taken away. That we felt for the Situation they were in of being obliged either to break Faith with the Slaves whom they had seduced by the Offer of Freedom, or to violate the Stipulations they had made

[289]

with us upon that Subject. That we were willing therefore to waive our literal Claims, but had every Right to insist upon Compensation, and that it would not be difficult for the Planters to shew that they had sustained an annual Loss from the Want of Men to cultivate their Lands, and thereby produce the Means of paying their Debts. Mr. Pitt exclaimed at this as if it were an exagerated Statement. I at once acknowledged my belief that in this, as in all similar Cases, there might be some Exageration on both Sides "but Sir what I have tends to shew that these Complaints and Enquiries are excellent if the Parties mean to keep asunder: if they wish to come together all such Matters should be kept out of Sight, and each Side perform *now*, as well as the actual Situation of Things will permit." Mr. Pitt then made many Professions of an earnest Desire to cultivate the best Understanding, &ca. &ca. &ca. On the Whole he thought it might be best to consider the Subject generally, and to see if on general Ground some Compensation could not be made mutually. I immediately replied "If I understand you, Mr. Pitt, you wish to make a new Treaty instead of complying with the old one." He admitted this to be *in some Sort* his Idea. I said that even on that Ground I did not see what better could be done than to perform the old one. "As to Compensation for Negroes taken away, it is too trifling an Object for you to dispute; so that Nothing remains but the Posts. I suppose therefore you wish to retain those Posts." "Why perhaps we may." "They are not worth the Keeping, for it must cost you a great Deal of Money, and produce no Benefit. The only Reason you can have to desire them is to secure the Fur Trade, and that will center in this Country let who will carry it on in America." I gave him the Reasons for this Opinion, which I am sure is well founded, but I will not trouble you with them. His answer was well turned. "If you consider these Posts as a trivial Object, there is the less Reason for requiring them." "Pardon me Sir, I only state the retaining them as *useless to you*, but this Matter is to be considered in a different Point of Light. Those who made the Peace acted wisely in separating the Possessions of the two Countries by so wide a Water. It is essential to preserve this Boundary, if you wish to live in Amity with us. Near Neighbours are seldom good ones, for the Quarrels among Borderers frequently bring on Wars. It is therefore essential for both Parties that you should give them up; but as to us it is of particular Importance, because our national Honor is interested. You hold them with the avowed Intention of forcing us to comply with such Conditions as you may impose." "Why Sir as to the Consideration of national Honor we can retort the Observation, and say our Honor is concerned in your Delay of the Performance of the Treaty." "No Sir, Your natural and proper Course was to comply fully on your Part, and if then we had refused a Compliance, you might rightfully have issued Letters of Marque and Reprisal to such of your Subjects as were injured by our Refusal. But the Conduct you have pursued naturally excites Resentment in every American Bosom. We do not think it worth while to go to War with you for these Posts, but *we know our Rights, and will avail ourselves of them when Time and Circumstances may suit.*"—Mr. Pitt asked me if I had Powers to treat. I told him I had not and that we could not appoint any Person as Minister, they had so much neglected the former Appointment. He asked me whether we would appoint a Minister if they did. I told him that I could almost promise that we should, but was not authorized to give any positive Assurance. The Question then was how to communicate on this Subject. I suggested, that since much Time might be unnecessarily consumed by Reason of the Distance and Uncertainty of Communication, it would perhaps be expedient for them to appoint a Minister and delay his Departure untill you should have made a similar Appointment. Mr. Pitt said they might communicate to you their Intention to appoint &ca. I told him that his Communication might encounter some little Difficulty, because you could not properly hear any Thing from the british Consuls, those being Characters unknown in America. His Pride was a little touched at this. "I should suppose Mr. Morris that Attention might as well be paid to what they say, as that the Duke of Leeds and I should hold the present Conversation with you." "By no Means Sir I never should have thought of asking a Conference with his Grace, if I had not possessed a Letter from the President of the United States, which you know my Lord I left with you, and which I dare say you have communicated to Mr. Pitt." He had. Mr. Pitt said they would in like Manner write a Letter to one of their Consuls. "Yes Sir, the *Letter* will be attended to, but not the Consul, who is in no Respect different from any other british Subject; and this is the Circumstance which I wished you to attend to." He said, in Reply to this, that Etiquette ought not to be pushed so far as to injure Business, and keep the Countries asunder. I assured him that the Rulers of America had too much Understanding to care for Etiquette but prayed him at the same Time to recollect, that they (the british) had hitherto kept us at a Distance, instead of making Advances. That you had gone quite as far as they had any Reason to expect, in writing the Letter just mentioned, but that from what had passed in Consequence of it, and which (as he might naturally suppose) I had transmitted, we could not but consider them as wishing to avoid an Intercourse. He took up this Point, and exprest again his Hope that I would remove such an Idea, assuring me that they were disposed to cultivate a Connection &ca. To this I replied, that any written Communications which his Grace of Leeds might make, should be duly transmitted, but I did not like to write meer Conversation, because it might be misconceived, and disagreable Questions afterwards arise, whereas written Things remain and speak for themselves. They agreed to the Propriety of this Sentiment. I observed farther, that our Disposition towards a good Understanding was evidenced, not only by your Letter, but also by the Decision of a Majority of the House of Representatives against laying extraordinary Restrictions on british Vessels in our Ports. Mr. Pitt said that, instead of Restrictions, we ought to give them particular Privileges in Return for those which we enjoy here. I assured him that I knew of none except that of being imprest, a Privilege which of all others we least wished to partake of. The Duke of Leeds observed, in the same Stile of Jocularity, that we were at least treated in that Respect as the most favored Nation, seeing that we were treated like themselves. But Mr. Pitt said seriously, that they had certainly evidenced Good-Will towards us, by what they had done respecting our Commerce. I replied therefore, with like Seriousness, that their Regulations had been dictated by a View to their own Interest, and therefore as we felt no favor, we owned no Obligation. The Subject being now pretty well exhausted, they promised to consult together and give me the Result of their Deliberations. This I am yet to receive, but I learn that Mr. Grenville has this Day consulted some Persons skilled in the Fur Trade, and that from his Conversation it seemed probable that they would give up the Posts. My Information is good.

I have already said, that the Ministers here count upon the Nullity of France. They do not however expect that She will violate her Treaty with Spain, and therefore they are rather I beleive in Hopes that Spain will submit to such Terms as they may impose. How far they may be bound to aid Prussia, seems as yet to be doubtful, but for my own Part I beleive that a War is inevitable, and I act on that Ground. If it does not take Place, they will I think desire such Things of us as a Treaty of Commerce as we shall not be disposed to grant: but if it does happen, then they will give us a good Price for our Neutrality, and Spain I think will do so too, wherefore this appears to be a favorable Moment for treating with that Court about the Mississippi.

Before I close this Letter, already too long, I must entreat Permission to make one or two explanatory Observations. It is evident that the Conduct of this Government towards us, from the Time of my first Interview with the Duke of Leeds, has depended on the Contingency of War or Peace with the neighbouring Powers; and they have kept Things in Suspense accordingly. When therefore they came a little forward, it proved to me their Apprehension of a Rupture. I have some Reason to think that they are in greater Danger than they are themselves aware of, and I have much Cause to suspect that they meditate a Blow in Flanders in which it is not improbable that they will be foiled and disappointed. Beleiving therefore that I knew their Motives, it only remained to square my Conduct and Conversation accordingly. And here you will consider, that the Characteristic of this Nation is Pride; whence it follows that if they are brought to sacrifice a little of their self Importance, they will readily add some other Sacrifices. I kept therefore a little aloof, and did not, as I might have done, obtain an Assurance that they would appoint a Minister if you would. On the contrary it now stands on such Ground that they must write a Letter making the first Advance, which you of Course will be in Possession of, and to that Effect I warned them against sending *a Message* by one of their Consuls.—With perfect Respect I have the Honor to be Sir your most obedient & humble Servant

GOUVR. MORRIS

Dupl (DLC: Washington Papers); at head of text: "Duplicate." Enclosure: Morris to Washington, 1 May 1790, printed above as enclosure to Washington to TJ, 19 June 1790. Text as printed in *ASP, Foreign Relations*, I, 125, has a postscript not in Dupl: "P.S. May 30th. It is utterly impossible for me to copy the letters which I intended to enclose. It is now near one o'clock in the morning, and Mr. Williams sets off at eleven."

Gouverneur Morris to George Washington

SIR   London 3 July 1790

This Letter will accompany Copies of what I had the Honor to write on the first and twenty ninth of May. I have heard nothing since from the Duke of Leeds. On the tenth of June the King prorogued the Parliament, which was dissolved on the eleventh. The Elections will be compleated in about ten Days, and then the Ministers will feel themselves more at Liberty to avow their Intentions than they are at present. They will have a great Majority tho perhaps weaker by half a dozen than in the last House, but the immense patronage which must result from a War will soon overballance that Difference. I was told on the tenth that the Duke of Leeds is to remove from the Office of Secretary of foreign Affairs and is to be succeeded by Lord Hawksbury formerly Charles Jenkinson. He is an able Man, strongly opposed to America and it is said from Inclination, but perhaps it is from the Desire to please his royal Master. Such an Appointment would look like a Bar to any friendly Communication with us, but I incline to think otherwise. He will at least be an efficient Minister, and whatever *he* agrees to will go smoothly thro the Cabinet, whereas the present Man is evidently afraid of committing himself by saying or doing any Thing positive. On the seventeenth of June I learnt a Conversation which had recently passed with Mr. Grenville about the Posts, from the Complection of which I conclude that they are nearly determined to give them up. In the Course of that Conversation (in which the Minister was collecting Information from a Gentleman acquainted with the Country and its Trade) he said, that the Americans had made some Overtures for a commercial Treaty which might perhaps take Place and that he wished to be prepared in Case that Matter should be brought forward which appeared however to be uncertain. He mentioned at the same Time but meerly as Matter of common Report, that the Spaniards had agreed to give us the Navigation of the Mississippi. I am therefore confirmed in my Opinion that if they get engaged in a War they will be glad to form a friendly Connection with us. And as to the Contingency of War, I was informed on the twenty first of June that about three Weeks before that Period they had sent an Express over Land to India probably with Instructions to prepare for if not to commence Hostilities. This added to many other Circumstances leaves but little known to doubt of their Intentions. Prussia has been arming and negotiating and seems as if desirous to gain Time till this Country can act.

The Fleet which lay at Spithead had sailed some Days since for Torbay, and is to be joined, it is said, by a Dutch Squadron who come forward in the Quality of Allies to great Britain. The Idea of calling upon an Ally to assist a British against a Spanish Fleet seems to be a little extraordinary. But it would not be extraordinary that a Dutch Squadron should go into the Baltic and assist the Swedes against Russia.

We are now so near the Moment when the Curtain is to be drawn up that I will not trouble you with my Conjectures about the Scenes which are to be displayed. France I am persuaded will not remain an idle Spectator. I am with perfect Respect Sir your most obedient & humble Servant

GOUVR. MORRIS

Dupl (DLC: Washington Papers); at head of text: "Duplicate."

ENCLOSURE IV

Gouverneur Morris to George Washington

SIR   London 16 August 1790

I had the Honor to write to you on the third of July of which Letter I now enclose a Copy. I have patiently waited since that Period for the Answer which had been promised on the twenty first of May to my Letter of the thirtieth of April. Had any Circumstance turned up which would in my opinion have justified a new application it should have been made, but this has not been the Case. You will have seen the Declaration and Counter Declaration of the spanish and british Courts exchanged at Madrid the twenty fourth of last Month. These leave the material Ground of Controversy in it's original State and the armaments go on with unremitting Diligence. The Event seems to turn upon the Ability and Inclination of France whose Condition is far from desirable, but I shall not attempt to describe it because I have no Doubt that Mr. Short being on the Spot will transmit much better Information than I can pretend to. The poor King of Hungary pressed by Prussia and distracted by the interior Commotions of his various Dominions and unsupported by France has been obliged to accede to Terms of Pacification by no Means desirable. This leaves Britain and her friends more at Liberty to press the other Powers. The Proceedings of the Congress have of Course been very secret and if they had not a meer private Individual in this Country could not acquire an early Knowlege of them. There is however one Circumstance which let Things terminate as they may will I conceive have considerable Consequences. The King of Prussia has endeavored to obtain from Poland the Cession of Thurn and Dantzig. These Countries are you know already surrounded by his Dominions except towards the Sea and if he had succeeded or should succeed he will not only become at once a naval Power but will hold in his Hand the Key to the great Granary of Europe. This at a Period when from the Extension of Commerce and Manufactures in other Countries the Want of Bread is often feared and sometimes felt will give him immense advantages both in Peace and War besides those of rendering his Dominions more compact and of encreasing his Revenue. It is, I think, hardly possible that Britain and Holland should have wished for his Success, and if his Failure should be owing to their Resistance it may at no distant Period give Rise to new Connections and Alliances in the North. In the Baltic they have been very busy. The Seasons give but little Time there for any other naval War than that which Man must wage with the Elements. They make therefore the best or (if you please) the worst Use of their Time. Little however has been effected except the Havock of the human Race which is not over numerous in that Quarter. The King of Sweden with infinite Gallantry places himself in Situations where he can gain little and may loose all. Hitherto he has extricated himself by downright fighting and as it is too late for effectual Interference from England or Holland probably both Sides having sung Te Deum will take Breath and may perhaps be content to try what Negotiation can do next Winter.

I have little Doubt but that the Ministry here would have agreed to comply with the Treaty of Peace had they found themselves engaged in a War which they have been upon the Brink of for some Months and I presume that in Proportion as the Clouds shall disperse they will be less tractable. I have taken Patience and remained here tho I had many private Reasons for going to the Continent but as I did believe that by being on the Spot I might be useful especially if a favorable Occasion should offer I thought it my Duty to stay. From some Circumstances too slight to be worth mentioning I incline to think that such Occasion is not far distant, but never perhaps were the Affairs of Europe in a Situation which admits so little of forming any solid opinion; and this from the spreading of what is called the french Disease in other Words Revolt. Hungary Part of Germany Italy and Saxony with France and Flanders are already in different Stages of that Disease. Poland is constitutionally afflicted with it. In Sweden and Holland slight Circumstances would bring forward Seeds which have long been sown, and no Man can tell or even guess how far it may extend or What may be the Consequences. This Country is free from the Contagion and likely to continue so. Indeed the English seem in some Respects to have changed Sentiments and Manners with the french. They are as far gone in Loyalty as their Neighbours in Republicanism. Happy America where alone (I verily believe) both Freedom and Virtue have their real and substantial Existence.

I wait with anxious Expectation to hear what Congress may have done in Relation to this Country as well as upon the important Subject of Finance: for that also would have no small Influence on the british Cabinet. Having long been in the Habit of contemplating public Credit as the most certain and abundant National Resource they will naturally and indeed necessarily take up their Opinion of us on that Ground. And if at the same Time their mercantile Interest should *feel* that we have a Government it might produce a general Conviction that we are not to be trifled with. Incidental Circumstances among foreign Nations may give us momentary Advantages and doubtless it is the Duty of all public Servants to watch those moments and turn them to the best Account. But it is by the Solidity of our domestic System alone that we can become permanently and intrinsically respectable. Consequently it is by that alone that we can hope for permanent and useful Connections. And altho we ought not from such Considerations become supine or inattentive to the Measures of the greater maritime Powers (which would indeed be very imprudent) yet we may certainly repose with greater Confidence on the Good Faith of others when they see and above all when they *feel* the Value of our Friendship.

I pray your kind Excuse Sir for giving Vent to these Ideas which are as much the Sentiments of my Heart as the Dictates of my Understanding. As Conclusions of Reason they have naturally been adopted by every thinking Man in America, but he must come out of it perhaps if he would have their Emportance deeply impressed by the Impulsion of daily Experience.

FC (DLC: Gouverneur Morris Papers); at head of text: "George Washington Esqr. Public."

ENCLOSURE V

Gouverneur Morris to George Washington

SIR   London 18 September 1790

I had the Honor to address you on the 16th. of August, and stated as nearly as I could the Situation of Russia and Sweden. This Situation has produced a very natural Effect. Sweden being unsupported by her Allies, and Russia having Nothing to gain by farther Fighting but a Part of the finland Deserts not worth fighting for, they have struck a Bargain of Peace immediately without the Interference of any one else. This leaves the Russian and Turk to pursue their Game single-handed. The Ministers of Britain are by no Means well pleased that they were not consulted by the Swede, and I think it probable thay if Russia makes Peace with the Turks, it will be without the Mediation of Prussia or England. For as Things are situated it seems impossible for those Powers to do the Empress any Mischief before next Spring.

The national Assembly of France have also adopted as a national Compact the old family Compact with Spain, and they are arming as fast as their disjointed Condition will admit. At the same Time the general Opinion of this Country seem'd to be that the Ministry would obtain very honorable Terms from Spain whereas the Ministers themselves were as I beleive much embarrassed as to the Line of Conduct which they should pursue. To support the high Tone in which they first opened would probably bring on a bloody War for an empty Sound. To recede would expose them to severe Animadversion at Home and a Loss of Reputation abroad. These Circumstances appearing to me favorable, I wrote the Letter of which No. one is a Copy. It is calculated first to operate upon an Administration which I beleived to be divided in Regard to America, and a Sovereign who hates the very Name, while he prides himself upon his Piety and moral Fame. Secondly it was intended as a Ground of future Justification for any Measures which Congress might think proper to adopt. And thirdly it had I own a special View to the Nature of this Government and People; for if they do eventually get engaged in War, and feel a little from our Coldness, and if in Addition thereto the commercial Men find any Ground of Complaint, it will make them so eager to rectify their Mistake as to give us considerable Advantages.

[296]

In Answer to this Letter I received that of which Number two is a Copy. This was written in his own Handwriting and as it is said therein to be not ministerial but confidential we must so consider it. Consequently it is not a public Paper. The Inference to be drawn from it is that the Council could not agree as yet upon the Answer to be given. Hence I concluded that those who pursuing the true Interests of Great Britain wish to be on the best Terms with America are outnumbered by those whose sour Prejudices and hot Resentment render them averse to every Intercourse except that which may immediately subserve a selfish Policy. These then do not yet know America. Perhaps America does not yet know herself. They beleive that british Credit is essential to our Commerce. Useful it certainly is at present, but let our public Credit be well established and supported, and in a very few Years our commercial Resources will astonish the World. We are yet but in the seeding Time of national Prosperity, and it will be well not to mortgage the Crop before it is gathered. Excuse I pray Sir this Digression. The Matter of it is not wholly inapplicable.

A Copy of my Answer to the Duke and his Reply are in the Papers No. 3 and 4. In Consequence of the latter I waited upon him the fifteenth Instant, and I saw at once by his Countenance that he felt himself obliged to act an aukward Part. I waited therefore for him to begin the Conversation which he did by saying he understood I was going to America. I told him he had mistaken my Letter for that by *the Continent* I meant the Continent of Europe. After some Pause he said that he hoped soon to fix upon a Minister to America. That they had a Person in Contemplation who was not however absolutely agreed on. I did not ask who it was. After a farther Pause he said that *in order to save Time* and obviate Difficulties the Intention was to send over a Gentleman with a common Letter of Recommendation but having Letters of Credence in his Pocket. I exprest my perfect Approbation of this Expedient. He told me that he was earnestly desirous of a real bona fide Connection not meerly by the Words of a Treaty but in Reality. I met these by similar Professions but took Care to confine them to a commercial Intercourse for mutual Benefit on liberal Terms. He told me that as to the two Points of the Treaty there were still Difficulties. He wished they could be got out of the Way. He then hesitated a little and dropt the Conversation. Having waited some time for him to resume it and being convinced by his Silence that it was intended to hold a Conference and say Nothing, I determined to try for Information in a different Way. I began therefore by expressing with an Air of serious Concern my Conviction that their Detention of the Western Posts would form an insurmountable Barier against a Treaty with us. Knowing so well as he did the nature of popular Governments, he would not be surprized that some in America should oppose a Treaty with Britain from serious Doubt as to the Policy of the Measure and others from private Reasons, and he must see that holding those Posts would form an Argument for one and a Pretext for the other. Finding that he felt this, I added that their Conduct in this Respect gave serious Alarm to reasonable well meaning Men. Some beleived their Design was to deprive us of our

Share in the Fur Trade which they considered as a serious Injury, but others were convinced that holding those Posts was attended with great and useless Expence to Britain which the Benefits of the Fur Trade by no Means compensated, and even that she would derive those Benefits whether that Trade were carried on thro the Medium of Canada or of the United States. Hence they inferred some other, and consequently some hostile Views. So that every Murder committed by the Indians was attributed to british Intrigues; and altho some Men of liberal Minds might judge differently their Arguments would have little Weight with the many who felt themselves aggrieved. He owned that there was Force in these Reflections. I told him farther that I did not presume to judge of the great Circle of european Politics, but according to my limited Comprehension was led to suppose that they would not act with the same decisive Energy towards their Neighbours while they doubted of our Conduct. He said I was perfectly right, and he said so in a Manner which shewed that this had been urged and felt during the late Negotiations. I proceeded therefore a little farther, premising that this Conversation was meerly from one Gentleman to another, and prayed him to consider that in a War between Britain and the House of Bourbon (a Thing which must happen at some Time or other) we can give the West India Islands to whom we please without engaging in the War ourselves, and our Conduct must be governed by our Interest. He acknowledged that this was naturally to be expected, and it seemed from his Manner that the same Thing had been represented before but not in such strong Colors. I observed that those Preferences which we had a Right to give in our own Ports, and those Restrictions which we had a Right to impose, would have a most extensive Operation. Assured him of my sincere Beleif that their exclusive System as far as it related to the Commerce of their Islands had a Tendency to injure that Navigation which it was their Object to encrease, because if we met them on equal Ground of Restriction they would loose more in one Way than they gained in another. That they had many large Ships employed in carrying the single Article of Tobacco; and if we should pass a Navigation Act to meet theirs they could not bring us a Yard of Cloth which contained spanish Wool and so of other Things. I thought I could perceive that Considerations like these had already given them some Alarm. I therefore said that I supposed his People had transmitted Information of the Attempts made in Congress to adopt such Regulations. He said they had. I observed that not having yet received the Laws passed by Congress I could not say exactly what had been done. That I hoped Things were yet open for Treaty. *That doubtless there were many Persons in this Country who to gratify their Resentment occasioned by Losses or Disappointments in the American War would be glad to urge on a State of commercial Hostilities*, but this would prove perhaps a loosing Game to both. He really thought it would. Having gone as far in that Line as was useful, I took a short Turn in my Subject and said I had waited with great Patience during the Negotiations they were carrying on, because I supposed *they would naturally square their Conduct towards us by their Position in Respect to other Nations.*

I made this Observation in a careless Manner as a Thing of Course but immediately fixing my Eye upon him he shewed that it was exactly the Circumstance they had wished to conceal. I added that finding the northern Courts were at Peace, and *supposing they had come to their final Decisions with Respect to the House of Bourbon,* I thought it probable that they were prepared to speak definitively to us also. Here I waited for his Answer which indeed I did not expect to receive. He was pretty sufficiently embarrassed, and from his Look and Manner I collected quite as much as he was willing to communicate. After some little Sayings of no Consequence he asked me what the united States would think of the undefined Claim of Spain to America. Having no Objection to take that Information from his Questions which could not be drawn forth in his Answers I told him that it would make no Impression on our Minds. That the Spaniards being in Fact apprehensive of Danger from us were disposed to make Sacrifices for our Friendship. That the Navigation of the Mississippi, hitherto the Bone of Contention, was I beleived given up by them already or soon would be so, and as for their Claims they never would affect us and therefore we did not care any Thing about them. That the Reason for withholding that Navigation, hitherto, was the Fear of contraband Trade, and for the same Reason they must in my Opinion sacrifice the last Man and last Shilling upon the Question about Nootka Sound. He said he had always thought the Danger of contraband ought to be considered in dealing on this Subject, for that Nations like Individuals ought to treat with Candor and Honesty. We had a good Deal of Conversation on that and other Topics in which America was not directly concerned, and then I told him that if they came to any Determination in Regard to us speedily I should wish to be apprized of it. He assured me that I should, and offered to make his Communications to you thro me, and for that Purpose to address his Letters to me in Paris, but for Reasons communicated in a former Letter, I thought it best to decline this Offer, and therefore observed that his own Packets would give him a speedier and more certain Means of Conveyance. I then took my Leave.

I have troubled you Sir with the leading Features of this Conversation that you might the better judge of the Conclusions I draw from it. I think the Cabinet is divided on the Question of War or Peace. If France appeared strong enough to excuse *a retrograde Manoeuvre* I beleive they would discover all at once that Spain has better Reasons to than they had been before apprized of, and therefore *on Principles of Justice* and having received the strongest Assurances of brotherly Love from the catholic King the Defender of the Faith would disarm. His Ministers will not treat with us at present, unless they could see their Way to an offensive and defensive Alliance, which we shall be in no Hurry to contract. Should War break out, the anti american Party will I beleive agree to *any* Terms, for it is more the Taste of the Medicine which they nauseate, than the Size of the Dose. Mr. Pitt I beleive wishes a Continuance of Peace. Observe that he is rather the Queens Man than the King's, and that since his Majesty's Illness she has been of great Consequence. This depends in part on a medical

Reason. To prevent the Relapse of Persons who have been mad, they must be kept in constant Awe of somebody; and it is said the Phisician of the King gave the Matter in Charge to his royal Consort who performs that, like every other Part of her conjugal Duty, with singular Zeal and Perseverance. He and all those who are in Possession of his entire Confidence, wish it is said for War; which gives you know great Patronage, and by the Encrease of Taxes and Offices, encreases the Influence and Power of the Crown. The King *and his friends* are also violently indisposed to America.

Things being so situated, and having Business on the Continent, I shall leave this City in a few Days and shall perhaps write a farther Letter of Lamentations to the Duke of Leeds before I go. I intend to write such a Letter to you on the whole Business, as may in Case of Need be laid before the Legislature, and consequently before the Public.

I long since expressed my Opinion to you Sir that the appearances of Prosperity here were fallacious. In Nothing are they more so than in the Affairs of the India Company, which are deplorably bad, and they are now engaged in a War with Tippoo Saib which, terminate how it may, must make them worse.

It is Time to close this lengthy Epistle. Let me therefore entreat you to receive the Assurances of that sincere Respect & Esteem with which I have the Honor to be &c. &c.

FC (DLC: Gouverneur Morris Papers); at head of text: "George Washington Esqr. Public." Enclosures: (1) Morris to Leeds, 10 Sep. 1790, recalling the conversation with Leeds and Pitt and the promise of a reply to his own letter of 30 Apr. 1790, stating that he had "waited patiently in this city to the present hour, though called by many affairs to the continent," and advising that he could not much longer delay his departure. He then added: "I was led to believe, my Lord, that a friendly connexion might have taken place between this country and that of which I have the honor to be a citizen. How far it might be useful to Great Britain, I presume not to conjecture; being perfectly convinced, from the wisdom and extensive information of his Majesty's ministers, that the best rule for private judgment must be derived from their conduct. But, my Lord, I candidly own, that such connexion appears to be of great consequence to America; and therefore the hope of becoming instrumental in the accomplishment of it was most pleasing; nor am I ashamed to avow my concern at the disappointment. Your Grace will readily recollect the purport of the letter, which you did me the honor to write on the twenty-eighth of April, and that

mine of the thirtieth entreated a communication of the nature and extent of that redress, which his Majesty's ministers expected from the specific points of the treaty of peace, and the kind and measure of compensation they would require in case, as had been supposed, the specific performance on our part were now impracticable. Months having elapsed in silence, your Grace will, I hope, pardon me for observing that the pointed avowal of a determination to withhold performance, unless upon certain conditions, the communication of which is withheld, might be construed into unconditional refusal. Your personal integrity and honor, my Lord, the acknowledged justice of his Majesty, and the pride of British faith, prohibit me from harboring that idea. But it may perhaps be entertained by my countrymen, and if it should, it may lead to measures, which in their consequences may eventually induce the two nations to seek rather the means of reciprocal injury, than of mutual advantage. I humbly hope that this may never happen. The sentiment of America has long been conciliatory, and I should feel inexpressible satisfaction if your Grace would supply me with the means of restoring activity to her friendly dispositions" (FC in DLC:

Gouverneur Morris Papers). (2) Leeds to Morris, 10 Sep. 1790, acknowledging his letter and adding: "I well remember the nature of the conversation you allude to, as well as the particular points upon which the two countries mutually complain of a non-observance of treaty. Each party may perhaps have reason for complaint. I can assure you, Sir, I sincerely lament it. I am not entering into a ministerial discussion upon the subject of our not being already further advanced, in what we are both interested in, a real *bonâ fide* intercourse of friendship, but am only acknowledging, confidentially, my own private opinion, and what it has not been hitherto in my power to remedy. I shall, I trust, be enabled very soon to address myself upon a new subject to General Washington; and in the mean time, shall be very happy to see you, Sir, before your departure for America" (FC in DLC: Gouverneur Morris Papers). (3) Morris to Leeds, 13 Sep. 1790, saying that he had left town on the 12th before Leeds' letter of the 10th was received, that he had "this Instant returned," and that he would wait upon Leeds at such time as he should designate (FC in DLC: Gouverneur Morris Papers). (4) Leeds to Morris, 14 Sep. 1790 (FC in DLC: Gouverneur Morris Papers), appointing the time of the interview on the following day. Enclosures 3 and 4, being immaterial, were not included in Washington's message to the Senate (see Document VI, note).

II. Report of the Secretary of State

The Secretary of state having had under consideration the two letters of Oct. 13. 1789. from the President of the U. S. to Mr. Gouverneur Morris, and those from Mr. Morris to the President of Jan. 22. Jan. 22.[1] Apr. 7. 13. May. 1. 29. July 3. Aug. 16. and Sep. 18. referred to him by the President, makes the following REPORT thereon.

The President's letters of Jan. 22.[2] authorized Mr. Morris to enter into conference with the British ministers in order to discover their sentiments on the following subjects.

1. Their detention of the Western posts contrary to the treaty of peace.

2. Indemnification for the negroes carried off against the stipulations of the same treaty.

3. A treaty for the regulation of the commerce between the two countries.

4. The exchange of a Minister.

The letters of Mr. Morris beforementioned state the communications, oral and written, which have passed between him and the ministers and from these the Secretary of state draws the following inferences.

1. That the British court is decided not to surrender the posts in any event; and that they will urge as a pretext that tho our courts of justice are now open to British subjects, they were so long shut after the peace as to have defeated irremediably the recovery

of debts in many cases. They suggest indeed the idea of an indemnification on our part. But probably were we disposed to admit their right to indemnification, they would take care to set it so high as to ensure a disagreement.

2. That as to indemnification for the negroes, their measures for concealing them in the first instance were so efficacious, as to reduce our demand for them, so far as we can support it by direct proof, to be very small indeed. It's smallness seems to have kept it out of discussion. Were other difficulties removed, they would probably make none of this article.

3. That they equivocate on every proposal of a treaty of commerce, and authorize in their communications with Mr. Morris the same conclusions which have been drawn from those they had had from time to time with Mr. Adams, and those through Majr. Beckwith: to wit, that they do not mean to submit their present advantages in commerce to the risk which might attend a discussion of them, whereon some reciprocity could not fail to be demanded. Unless indeed we would agree to make it a treaty of *alliance*, as well as of *commerce*, so as to undermine our obligations with France. This method of stripping that rival nation of it's alliances they tried successfully with Holland, endeavoured at with Spain, and have plainly and repeatedly suggested to us. For this they would probably relax some of the rigours they exercise against our commerce.

4. That as to a Minister, their Secretary for foreign affairs is disposed to exchange one, but meets with opposition in his cabinet, so as to render the issue uncertain.

From the whole of which the Secretary of state is of opinion

That Mr. Morris's letters remove any doubts which might have been entertained as to the intentions and dispositions of the British cabinet.

That it would be dishonourable to the U.S. useless, and even injurious, to renew the propositions for a treaty of commerce, or for the exchange of a minister: and that these subjects should now remain dormant, till they shall be brought forward earnestly by them.

That the demands of the posts, and of indemnification for the negroes should not be again made till we are in readiness to do ourselves the justice which may be refused.

That Mr. Morris should be informed that he has fulfilled the object of his agency to the satisfaction of the President, inasmuch as he has enabled him to judge of the real views of the British cabinet, and that it is his pleasure that the matters committed to him be left in the situation in which the letter shall find them.

That a proper compensation be given to Mr. Morris for his services herein, which having been begun on the 22d. of January and ended the 18th. of September, comprehend a space of near 8. months: that the allowance to an Agent may be properly fixed any where between the half and the whole of what is allowed to a Chargé d'affaires; which, according to the establishment of the U.S. at the time of this appointment was at the rate of 3000. Dollars a year: consequently that such a sum of between one and two thousand dollars be allowed him as the President shall deem proper, on a view of the interference which this agency may have had with Mr. Morris's private pursuits in Europe.

TH: JEFFERSON
Dec. 15. 1790.

MS (DNA: RG 59, MLR); docketed by Lear. Tr (DNA: RG 59, SDC). Entry in SJPL reads: "[Dec.] 15. Opinion Th: J. on Gouvr. Morris negociation with Gr.Br."

1 The repetition of the date was intentional. See note and enclosures to Document I.

2 Thus in MS. TJ meant to allude to Washington's letter of credence and his letter of instructions to Morris, both dated 13 Oct. 1789.

III. The Secretary of State to Gouverneur Morris

DEAR SIR   Philadelphia December 17th. 1790.

Since mine to you of August 12th. yours of July 3d. August 16th. and September 18th. are come to hand. They suffice to remove all doubts which might have been entertained as to the real intentions of the British cabinet on the several matters confided to you. The view of Government, in troubling you with this business, was either to remove from between the two Nations all causes of difference, by a fair and friendly adjustment, if such was the intention of the other party, or to place it beyond a doubt that such was not their intention. In result, it is clear enough that further applications would tend to delay, rather than advance, our object. It is therefore the pleasure of the President that no others be made: and that in whatever state this letter may find the business, in that state it be left. I have it in charge at the same time to assure you that your conduct in these communications with the British ministers has met the President's entire approbation, and to convey to you his acknowledgments for your services.

As an attendance on this business must at times have interfered with your private pursuits, and subjected you also to additional expenses, I have the honor to enclose you a draught on our bankers in Holland for a thousand dollars, as an indemnification for those sacrifices.

My letter of August 12th. desired a certain other communication to be made to the same Court if a war should have actually commenced: if the event has not already called for it, it is considered as inexpedient to be made at all.

You will of course have the goodness to inform me of whatever may have passed further since the date of your last.

In conveying to you this testimony of approbation from the President of the United States, I am happy in an occasion of repeating assurances of the sentiments of perfect esteem and respect with which I have the honor to be Dear Sir &c.

FC (DNA: RG 59, PCC No. 121).

IV. The President to the Secretary of State

Feby 9th. 1791

The messages to the two Houses, as altered, are quite agreeable TO   GW.

Whether, as it is equally known to both houses, that we have no person in a public character at the Court of London it is best that the word "informal" should remain in the message to the Ho: of Representatives, or not, Mr. J. may decide by the fair copy he shall send to   GW

RC (DLC); addressed by Washington: "Mr. Jefferson Secy State"; endorsed by TJ as received 9 Feb. 1791, but not recorded in SJL.

For the alterations in the messages to the two Houses, see notes to Documents V and VI.

V. The President to the Senate and the House of Representatives

Feb. 14. 1791.

GENTLEMEN OF THE SENATE AND OF THE HOUSE OF REPRESENTATIVES

Soon after I was called to the administration of the government

[I found it important to come to an understanding with the court of London on several points interesting to the U.S. and particularly to know Whether they were]¹ disposed to enter into arrangements, by mutual consent, which might fix the commerce between the two nations on principles of reciprocal advantage. For this purpose I authorised informal² conferences with their ministers; and from these I do not infer any disposition on their part to enter into any arrangements merely commercial. I have thought it proper to give you this information, as it might at some time have influence on matters under your consideration.

Dft (DLC); entirely in TJ's hand, with deletions and interlineations as indicated below. This and following document are integral and endorsed by Remsen: "Communication to the Senate and House of Representatives." Tr (DLC: Washington Papers. Entry in SJPL reads: "[Feb.] 14. Message to Congr. on our affairs with Gr. Br. & G. W.'s approbation." The official text (JHR, I, 377-8; SJ, I, 269) is identical with Dft as altered.

¹ TJ first wrote and then deleted: "I took measures for obtaining information Whether the court of London was," substituting therefor the matter in brackets (supplied).

² This word interlined and then placed in parentheses (by Washington who queried its use in his memorandum to TJ; Document IV). TJ deleted the parentheses, allowing it to stand in the final version.

VI. The President to the Senate

[GENTLEMEN OF THE SENATE   [14 Feb. 1791]

Conceiving that in the possible event of a refusal of justice on the part of Gr. Britain, we should stand less committed should it be made to a private rather than to a public person, I employed Mr. Gouv. Morris, who was on the spot, and without giving him any definite character, to enter informally into the conferences before mentioned. For your more particular information I lay before you the instructions I gave him, and those]¹ parts of his communications wherein the British ministers appear either in conversation or by letter. These are, two letters from the D. of Leeds to Mr. Morris, and three letters of Mr. Morris giving an account of two conferences with the D. of Leeds, and one with him and Mr. Pitt. The sum of these is that they declare without scruple they do not mean to fulfill what remains of the treaty of peace to be fulfilled on their part (by which we are to understand the delivery of the posts and payment for property carried off) till performance on our part, and compensation where the delay has rendered performance now impracticable: that on the subject of a treaty of commerce they avoided direct answers so as to satisfy

Mr. Morris[2] they did not mean to enter into one unless it could be extended to a treaty of alliance offensive and defensive, or unless in the event of a rupture with Spain.

As to the sending a minister here, they make excuses in the first conference, seem disposed to it in the second, and in the last express an intention of so doing.

Their views being thus sufficiently ascertained, I have directed Mr. Morris to discontinue his communications with them.

Dft (DLC); with deletions and interlineations as indicated below. Tr (DLC: Washington Papers). See note to foregoing document. The official text (JEP, I, 73) agrees with Dft as altered.

Enclosures: (1) Washington to Morris, 13 Oct. 1789 (credentials). (2) Washington to Morris, 13 Oct. 1789 (instructions). (3) Morris to Washington, 7 Apr. 1790. (4) Leeds to Morris, 28 Apr. 1790. (5) Morris to Washington, 29 May 1790. (6) Morris to Leeds, 10 Sep. 1790. (7) Leeds to Morris, 10 Sep. 1790. (8) Morris to Washington, 18 Sep. 1790. All of the enclosures, together with the texts of both of the President's messages, are printed in ASP, *Foreign Relations*, I, 121-7. For messages from Morris not sent to the Senate, see enclosure to Washington to TJ, 19 June 1790, and enclosures III and IV to Document I

in the present series.

[1] The passage in brackets (supplied) is written on a slip pasted over a cancelled passage, which reads: "Gentlemen of the Senate—For your further and more particular information I lay before you the instructions I gave to Mr. Gouverneur Morris (the person whom I employed for the purpose before mentioned) and those." This passage was not cancelled in TJ's usual manner of making deletions and hence must have been done by Washington. This is the most important of the alterations that Washington approved in his memorandum to TJ (Document IV).

[2] This passage at first read: ". . . they made evasive answers which satisfied Mr. Morris" and then was altered by deletion and interlineation to read as above. This was perhaps one of the alterations suggested by Washington.

To James Brown

DEAR SIR   Philadelphia Dec. 16. 1790.

I have just desired Capt. Maxwell at Norfolk to forward to you 6. packages of furniture arrived there for me, the numbers and contents as below stated. I must beg the favor of you to receive them and pay the river freight &ca., from Norfolk for which I have desired Capt. Maxwell to draw on you. They are to be forwarded to Monticello; when a good opportunity offers. If my own waggons run at present, be so good as to reserve them for them. If not perhaps Mr. Lewis could have them taken up on good terms by the return waggons which carry my own tobacco. There is no hurry about them, and they are very heavy. I am with great esteem Dear Sir Your most obedt. humble servt.,   TH: JEFFERSON

T. I. No. 77. A marble pedestal.

78. Part of the same.

81. A chest of drawers.

82. Another chest of drawers.

83. The two marble tops of the chests of drawers.

84. The driver's seat of a chariot.

PrC (MHi). The marble pedestal was that given by Madame de Tessé to TJ. See illustration in this volume. See note to Short to TJ, 7 Nov. 1790.

From Childs & Swaine

Philadelphia, 16 Dec. 1790. In response to Remsen's of the 23rd, they will be perfectly satisfied with such compensation as the Secretary of State deems reasonable. "If, however, it is necessary to mention a price, we are willing to receive payment either by the session, or by the printed page of the Acts. If paid by the page, we ask one dollar; if by the session, one hundred dollars."

RC (DNA: RG 59, PDL); addressed to Remsen. Not recorded in SJL. For TJ's determination of the price, see Remsen to the printers, 10 Jan. 1791.

To James Maxwell

DEAR SIR   Philadelphia Dec. 16. 1790.

Having desired that some part of my furniture should come from Paris immediately to Virginia I took the liberty of desiring Mr. Short to consign it to you. I now learn by a letter from Monsr. La Motte merchant at Havre that he has shipped them on board the John Capt. Bushnell bound for Norfolk, where I suppose them arrived, as his letter purports to come by the same vessel. There should be six packages, the numbers and contents of which I shall state at the end of this letter. They are subject to no duty, as being a part of my furniture, the residue of which, 78. packages in number came here and were duty free. La Motte does not say where the freight was to be paid. If in America, I will pay it on sight on your draft or the captain's. I must trouble you to forward them to Richmond to Mr. James Brown merchant there, who will pay the river freight for them.

Permit me at the same time to ask you to procure for me 3. or 4. casks of the best Hughes's crab cyder, such as may do honour to our country, which is famed for that article; and to forward it to me here at the season you think best, either in casks or bottled as shall be best for the liquor. Your draught on me for the amount shall be paid on sight. I believe there are very frequent vessels coming here from Norfolk. I am with great esteem Dear Sir your most obedt. humble servt., TH: JEFFERSON

PrC (MHi); a PrC (MHi) lists the contents of the six cases, above TJ's signature, and may have been a part of this letter; it agrees with the list in TJ to Brown of this date. See note,

Short to TJ, 7 Nov. 1790. La Motte's letters informing TJ of the consignment were those of 13 and 22 Sep. 1790, recorded in SJL as received 15 Dec. 1790 but not found.

To Thomas Mann Randolph, Jr.

DEAR SIR   Philadelphia Dec. 16. 1790.

I am now to acknowledge the receipt of your favor of Nov. 11. I have yesterday received a letter from Mr. Mazzei authorizing the immediate sale of Colle, and shall therefore write to Mr. Lewis on the subject. I sincerely wish you may be able to get some of Mr. Carter's land adjoining. But I should think it worth your while to go further than 300 acres, and that by a negociation with Dobson you might obtain so much time as to render the paiments easy. But of all this you are best judge.—I send herewith some seeds which I must trouble you with the care of. They are the seeds of the Sugar maple and the Paccan nuts. Be so good as to make George prepare a nursery in a proper place and to plant in it the Paccan nuts immediately, and the Maple seeds at a proper season. Mr. Lewis must be so good as to have it so inclosed as to keep the hares out. There is also in the same tin box some seeds of the Cypress vine for Patsy.—You will see in the inclosed papers the official account of the Western expedition: not very methodically related. I have just received letters from France by which I am informed that the crops of wheat all over Europe have been so abundant that we shall find no market there this year. I am still of opinion therefore that that article will fall early in the spring with us. The papers will inform you that it is still a French crown here. Present me most affectionately to my dear daughters & believe me to be Dear Sir Yours cordially, TH: JEFFERSON

RC (DLC); addressed: "Thomas M. Randolph junr. esq. Monticello." Mazzei's letter, dated at "Paris rue du Regard, No. 30," 3 Sep. 1790, is recorded in SJL as received 15 Dec.

1790 but has not been found. For some of the reasons why TJ thought the official report of the expedition against the Indians deficient, see note to Washington to TJ, under 8 Dec. 1790.

From Robert Crew

SIR   London Decr 17th 1790

I enclose to you four newspapers, which contain some parliamentary debates, which it may be agreeable for you to receive.— I shall be glad to have the honour of receiving your commands in any thing it may be in my power to serve you. I am with the greatest respect Sir Your most obedt Servt,   Ro CREW

RC (DLC); endorsed by TJ as received 17 Mch. 1791 and so recorded in SJL. Enclosures not identified, but perhaps copies of *The Times* (London) for 14-17 Dec. 1790 containing proceedings of Parliament on the first four days of the session. The item that may have interested TJ most was the attack on Pitt's policy toward Spain led by Charles James Fox and supported by Charles Grey, who produced statistics showing the high cost of supporting the southern whale fishery. Grey was accused by ministerial supporters of viewing the matter in a narrow fiscal sense instead of considering the fishery as a nursery for seamen and hence essential to England's maritime strength.

Robert Crew was a Virginian who had settled in London in 1784 as a tobacco merchant (Crew to TJ, 5 Oct. 1784). He evidently returned to America but was back in London by 1790 and in "a comfortable situation in mercantile business" (Crew to Short, 5 Jan. 1790 and 7 Jan. 1791, OCHP:

Short Papers; the first of these letters announced TJ's safe arrival on the *Clermont* at Norfolk on 25 Nov. 1789). On 1 Jan. 1793 Crew began a partnership with Thomas Allport for importing tobacco (Crew & Allport to TJ, 10 Dec. 1792; printed form showing typical charges per hogshead plus commission of 2 ₩ % on tobacco received and 5% on goods shipped). In announcing this fact to TJ, Crew sent a paper containing Grey's motion for an address to the king against the war with France and added: "This government offer 7/₩ bus. for American wheat that may touch in England for orders, in order to prevent the French from being supplied. At the same time British Wheat is only 5/10 ₩ bush." (Crew to TJ, 1793). Ten years later Crew sent TJ a patented churn capable of "saving much time and labour" and suggested that TJ might wish to have his workmen "construct others from the pattern for the public benefit" (Crew to TJ, 18 July 1803). The only extant letter from TJ to Crew appears to be that of 10 Sep. 1789.

The Impressment of Hugh Purdie and Others

I. JOHN BROWNE CUTTING TO THE SECRETARY OF STATE
[17? JULY 1790]

II. SECRETARY OF STATE TO JOHN BROWNE CUTTING, 17 DEC. 1790

III. SECRETARY OF STATE TO JOSHUA JOHNSON, 17 DEC. 1790, WITH DOCUMENTS ON THE CASE OF HUGH PURDIE AND OTHERS

IV. SECRETARY OF STATE TO THE PRESIDENT, 23 DEC. 1790

V. SECRETARY OF STATE TO JOSHUA JOHNSON, 23 DEC. 1790

VI. SECRETARY OF STATE TO JAMES MAURY, 23 DEC. 1790

EDITORIAL NOTE

In mid-December, at Washington's request, Jefferson reviewed the entire correspondence relating to the abortive mission of Gouverneur Morris. He concluded and the President agreed that any further initiative for a commercial treaty and an exchange of ministers would have to come from England.[1] This, however, was far from being a policy of passive waiting on the decisions of a foreign ministry. Its positive manifestations are to be found in thrusts on several fronts—in Jefferson's report on fisheries suggesting retaliatory measures against a nation "mounting their navigation on the ruin of ours," in his renewed attempt to legislate a commercial system "founded in universal reciprocity," in his promptings born of delusive hope that France, Spain, and Portugal might be induced to follow this example, in the effort to expand American commerce in the Mediterranean by confronting the Algerine menace, and in the determined move to give the commerce of the western settlements open access to the sea.[2] To these essentially indirect measures Jefferson now decided to add an explicit and formal protest on an issue destined to endure as an outstanding cause of hostility between the United States and Great Britain until, after more than two decades, it was finally if tacitly resolved by war—the impressment by the British navy of seamen claiming to be citizens of the United States.

This was an explosive issue. Appealing to deep-seated emotions, magnified now by powerful sentiments of nationalism, it was one that had angered Americans since long before the Revolution.[3] It was also

[1] See group of documents on commercial and diplomatic relations with Great Britain, under 15 Dec. 1790.

[2] See report on fisheries, 1 Feb. 1791; group of documents on commerce at end of Jan. 1791; TJ to Carmichael, 17 Mch. 1791; TJ to Humphreys, 15 Mch. 1791 and 11 Apr. 1791; report on Algerine captives and on Mediterranean commerce, 28 Dec. 1790; documents on new approaches to Spain, 10 Mch. 1791.

[3] Impressment of sailors, ships' carpenters, and laborers in Boston in 1747 caused a riot of three days (J. F. Zimmerman, *Impressment of American seamen* [New York, 1925], p. 11, citing Thomas Hutchinson, *History of Massachusetts*, II, 286-90). Colonials were exempt from impressment under a statute (6 Anne, c. 37, s. 9, repealed in 1768) cited by John Adams in Rex v. Corbet (see note 7 below).

an issue that brought into conflict fundamental principles of government, thus in still another area making visible with acute clarity the widening cleavage between old-world ideologies and those of the new era Americans believed themselves to be entering. The doctrine of an indefeasible allegiance of which the individual could divest himself only with the consent of his sovereign was almost universally adhered to by European nations and had been imbedded in the common law of Great Britain for centuries.[4] With the Declaration of Independence and its revolutionary idea of the sovereignty of the individual, however, the countervailing doctrine of the right of voluntary expatriation emerged as a logical necessity. It is not surprising that traditionalists in American jurisprudence such as Marshall, Story, and Kent should have continued until well into the 19th century to concur with Blackstone in upholding the common law doctrine.[5] But Thomas Jefferson, as author of the document that announced the proposition of government by consent, had embraced immediately the doctrine that would be most appropriate for a republic. Indeed, as early as 1774 he had asserted that "right, which nature has given to all men, of departing from the country in which chance, not choice, has placed them"— an assertion of the natural right of expatriation repeated in almost identical terms in his naturalization bill of 1779. His commitment to the principle was also exemplified in 1788 when he negotiated the Consular Convention with France and persuaded Montmorin to drop the inappropriate clause in that of 1784 "which declared the indelibility of the character of subject."[6] Yet the opposed theories, enduring

[4] Zimmerman, *Impressment*, p. 21-2; ASP, *Foreign relations*, II, 148-9.

[5] J. B. Moore, *Digest of international law* (Washington, 1906), III, 552-86. Chief Justice Ellsworth in 1799 in the case of Isaac Williams declared that the common law had been left untouched by the Revolution and that even the "most visionary writers . . . do not contend for the principle in the unlimited extent, that a citizen may at any and at all times, renounce his own, and join himself to a foreign country" (Wharton, *State trials*, 654). Marshall declared in 1814 that he had "never entertained a *scintilla* of doubt" on the subject (Marshall to Pickering, 11 Apr. 1814, quoted in Beveridge, *Marshall*, IV, 54). This judicial embrace of the common law doctrine was offset by a single Kentucky court decision of 1839 which alluded to the right of expatriation as "a practical and fundamental doctrine of America" (J. B. Moore, *Principles of American diplomacy* [New York, 1918], p. 274). It was also in marked contrast to popular feeling and to informed exposition of the American doctrine in pamphlets and newspapers during public discussion of the issue (see, for example, George Hay, *Treatise on expatriation* [Washington, 1814]; surprisingly, TJ seems not to have had a copy of this pamphlet). TJ excoriated the federal judiciary not merely for its view of the right of expatriation but also, even more vigorously, for accepting the common law generally and thereby making a "sweeping pretension to a system of law for the US. . . . infinitely beyond their power to adopt" (TJ to Randolph, 18 Aug. 1799). See note 6.

[6] See Vol. 1:121; 2:476-8. With Montmorin TJ avoided discussion of conflicting principles by arguing that arrest of passengers would violate American bills of rights and these, being fundamental, could not be obstructed by any convention (TJ to Montmorin, 20 June 1788; TJ to Jay, 14 Nov. 1788). TJ's acceptance of what he described simply as "our principle" governing expatriation (TJ to Gallatin, 12 July 1803) was immediate, unreserved, and grounded on natural law. As he later expressed it: "I hold the right of expatriation to be inherent in every man by the laws of nature, and incapable of being rightfully taken away from him even by the united will of every other person in the nation" (TJ to Gallatin, 26 June 1806). See also TJ to Morris, 16 Aug. 1793.

relevant as they have continued to be, led to conflict between the two nations only because Great Britain sought to enforce the common law doctrine on board American vessels navigating the high seas. In this first approach to the issue of impressment, however, Jefferson appealed neither to "the universal laws of nature," as American citizens soon would on this problem, nor to the freedom of the seas. He called instead for protection of American seamen in British ports under "the laws of hospitality in usage among nations."

The incident on which he rested his protest involved one of the thousands of individuals caught in the dragnet of the press gangs during the war crisis of 1790. During late summer and autumn reports of "multiplied acts of violence" of the sort had come to the Secretary of State from several sources. He had kept the President informed, but both men were aware of the thorny realities of the problem and of the need for caution in raising the issue. Given the similarity in laws, language, and inherited customs, proof of nationality was difficult and fraud on both sides was easily and frequently practiced. Press gangs on shore, armed with cutlasses and admiralty warrants, may not have been "gentlemen of the purest honor and most polish'd deportment" and naval officers at sea were undoubtedly at times arrogant and even brutal in pressing sailors into service.[7] But British subjects no less than American citizens were challenging the practice with growing insistence.[8] Blackstone himself, while recognizing its sanction at common law, regarded impressment as defensible only out of public necessity.[9] Even Admiralty officials, increasingly harassed by the problem of recruitment, did not embrace the policy from choice.[10] Nor, as reports coming to Jefferson indicated, were they wholly intransigent in judging claims of American nationality. This fact, together with the explosive nature of the issue and its possible effect on the mission of Gouverneur Morris that had not yet been officially ended, suggested the wisdom of withholding any formal protest until overwhelming proofs of flagrant abuse were at hand. Such proofs seemed undoubtedly present in the case of one Hugh Purdie, whose impressive affidavit and related correspondence reached Jefferson just two days after the President had

[7] The quotation is from Document I. Perhaps the most dramatic example of naval arrogance meeting with determined resistance is that of 22 Apr. 1769 on the high seas off Marblehead when Lieutenant Henry Panton of H. M. frigate *Rose* intercepted and searched the American brig *Pitt Packet* and was killed with a harpoon wielded by one Michael Corbet (Case No. 56, Rex v. Corbet, *Legal papers of John Adams*, ed. Wroth and Zobel, II, 276-335). Adams defended Corbet and won acquittal.

[8] Daniel A. Baugh, *British naval administration in the age of Walpole* (Princeton, 1965), p. 147-240, found vociferous opposition to impressment in England in the 1740's coming from all quarters of society. The first carefully reasoned challenge to impressment on grounds of incompatibility with the rights of Englishmen was evidently that in a series of letters signed *Maynard* published in the London *Public ledger* on 7, 10, 18, and 21 Jan. 1777, the authors of which have been identified as James Oglethorpe and Granville Sharp (Paul Conner, " 'Maynard' unmasked: Oglethorpe and Sharp versus the press gangs," Am. Phil. Soc., *Procs.*, 111 [Aug. 1967], 199-211, with texts of the letters).

[9] Blackstone, *Commentaries* (Chicago, 1872), I, 267-8. See also J. R. Hutchinson, *The press gang afloat and ashore* (London, 1913), p. 1-18.

[10] Zimmerman, *Impressment*, p. 13, citing various authorities; Baugh, *British naval administration*, p. 149-50.

requested his opinion on Morris' mission.[11] As he read the documents concerning these two matters, the Secretary of State must have found in them ample confirmation of the attitudes of hostility toward the United States that he had experienced at first hand in London some four years earlier. His decision to protest the Purdie case was immediate and he chose it from the great mass of impressments because he considered it to be one in which the insult to the United States had been "the most bare-faced, the most deliberately intentional, and the proof the most complete."[12]

I

There were plausible reasons for such a confident conclusion. Hugh Purdie's sworn affidavit was so literate and so circumstantial in its verifiable assertions as to extend the mantle of credibility to the whole, including his patriotic indignation at aspersions on the name of Washington. The affidavit even incorporated the text of a certificate of birth from the Rev. John Bracken, rector of Bruton parish. From this and accompanying documents it appeared that Purdie was a native Virginian of about 24; that he was a son of Alexander Purdie of Williamsburg, who until his death in 1779 had been postmaster, bookseller, and printer of the *Virginia Gazette*; that he had served as an apprentice under David Ross, the Richmond merchant; and that William Short remembered him as a fellow student at the College of William and Mary. Among other verifiable statements in Purdie's affidavit was his assertion to the commander of the *Boreas* that Lord Fincastle and his two brothers, sons of the Earl of Dunmore, had been his "ancient school fellows" and could vouch for his birth as an American.[13] It is almost certain that Jefferson himself had known young Purdie, for he had been a frequent patron of the printing and bookselling establishment of his father. As governor, he could possibly have known him in Richmond during the time Purdie was apprenticed to Davis Ross.

Furthermore, John Browne Cutting, through whom the relevant documents were transmitted, was a person in whom Jefferson reposed some confidence and with whom—as with his brother, Nathaniel Cutting—he had enjoyed friendly relationships in France. Though some Americans in Europe were inclined to be skeptical about John Browne Cutting's right to call himself Dr. Cutting, there is reason to believe that he was a thoughtful as well as an ardently patriotic American.[14]

[11] Cutting to TJ, 4 Oct. 1790, enclosing Purdie's affidavit and other documents pertaining to the case, was received by TJ on 13 Dec. 1790 (SJL). This letter has not been found, but texts of its enclosures are printed below (Document III). Among the documents TJ had under consideration at the time this letter arrived was Gouverneur Morris' letter of 29 May 1790 reporting his protest to Leeds about the press gangs and mentioning the fact that on the 12th Cutting had informed him of his being appointed "Agent to several of the American Masters of Ships" (Washington to TJ, 11 Dec. 1790, Enclosure II).

[12] Document V.

[13] Enclosure XI, Document III.

[14] Cutting was introduced to TJ by John Adams, who said simply that he needed no other recommendation "than his own Genius," and by William Stephens Smith, who described him "as a Gentleman of genius and merit" (Adams to TJ, 16 Sep. 1787; Smith to TJ, 18 Sep. 1787). Among the many

For some months during the war crisis of 1790 he had inundated Jefferson and others, including John Adams and William Short, with long accounts of his efforts to assist suffering American seamen and of his frustrations in dealing with Admiralty officials.[15] Late in the summer he wrote to Adams:[16]

> If ever there was a time when the volunteer exertions of a citizen of America became a duty incumbent upon him in a foreign realm, that period has existed here. For many weeks past I have not been absent a single day from the Admiralty, sundays only excepted. . . . I have not yet leisure to transmit either to yourself or to Mr. Jefferson a full detail of facts.

In an earlier letter explaining why he had taken upon himself such arduous labors, Cutting wrote:[17]

> I cou'd not endure to see my fellow citizens first subjected to the outrages of british press gangs and then drag'd on board british ships of war to be scourged at the mere will and base discretion of every mean or malignant petty officer of the navy into the performance of services which our native seamen dread and detest. In this crisis I came forward and did and have done and am continually doing all that a zealous persevering individual cou'd or can do in his private capacity.

But Cutting's motives, like the national character of which he was so inordinately proud, appear to be a mixture of both idealism and materialism. His characterization of British seamen who accepted the authority of press warrants through habits of submission and of others "nurtur'd in the western hive of Liberty . . . [who] entertain'd ideas of personal freedom the most fervent and exalted" was plainly calculated to impress the Secretary of State. Jefferson in fact construed Cutting's

letters exchanged between Cutting and TJ, see especially Cutting's of 22 Sep. 1789. Gouverneur Morris seemed to regard Cutting as a busybody, noted his "vaunting account of his services [in behalf of the seamen] . . . and of his Disinterestedness," and spoke of his "ferreting the Admiralty about Mr. Purdie" (Morris, *Diary*, ed. Davenport, I, 128, 207, 473, 482, 514, 518, 523, 531, 535, 542, 549, 557, 605-606; II, 95, 205, 207). See also, note to TJ to Washington, 7 Feb. 1792.

15 On 31 May 1790 Cutting informed Adams that he had written to Mr. Jefferson very fully about impressments. Again on 5 July 1790, urging the need for some criteria to discriminate between British and American sailors, he wrote: "But as I have repeatedly written both to yourself and Mr. Jefferson on this subject, I shall not trouble you with a fresh repetition of what I considered it my duty at the time zealously to represent" (MHi: AM). Cutting wrote TJ soon after 12 May 1790 when he was designated as agent for some American captains (see Vol. 16: 415, note). But the only letters recorded in SJL as received by TJ are those of 11 June, 16 July, 7 and 11-12 Aug., and 4 and 6 Oct. 1790 (received respectively on 28 Aug., 4 Oct., 20 Nov., 25 Oct., 13 Dec., and 29 Nov. 1790). No text of any of these letters is known to exist save that here printed as Document I. Cutting wrote to Short on 30 Apr., 23 May, 2, 9, 11 June, 4 and 18 July, 8 and 29 Aug., 18 Sep., and 18 Oct. 1790 (DLC: Short Papers). He transmitted several of Short's replies to TJ (see Vol. 16: 415 n.; 508-509 n.). See note, TJ to Washington, 7 Feb. 1792.

16 Cutting to Adams, 11 Aug. 1790 (MHi: AM).

17 Cutting to Adams, 17 July 1790 (MHi: AM).

actions as arising out of feelings of humanity and patriotism.[18] But such sentiments were in this instance evidently alloyed with the hope of office if not of gain. In a letter to John Adams, Cutting admitted the intrinsic difficulty of proving citizenship in some cases and suggested that, while an effective solution to the problem could probably not be devised by the United States, a palliative would be the appointment of a consul capable of substituting for private efforts "prudence and management sustain'd by a suitable authority from the American government." He concluded with a hint of his own qualifications for the post.[19]

Whatever the amalgam of motives, there can be no doubt about the zeal with which Cutting labored in the summer of 1790 in behalf of American sailors. In his *Facts and observations . . . in a letter addressed to the Secretary of State*, a pamphlet privately printed by Cutting in 1795, he estimated that of some thirteen thousand seamen said to have been impressed in 1790 more than two thousand were American citizens. He pointed out that many of these had embarked on British bottoms at the end of the war, being unable to get employment in the American fisheries or shipping; that there was scarcely a British vessel that had not a portion of Americans enrolled among its crew; and that some four to five thousand American seamen were employed on vessels entering the port of London every year, many of them able-bodied seamen such as would bring the highest bounties, being sons of substantial citizens of the United States, principally from New Hampshire, Massachusetts, New York, Maryland, and Virginia.[20] Cutting described the hot presses of 1790 in which "almost every vessel in the Thames was stripped of it's crew; and the American, indiscriminately with the British, mariners, forced into the . . . fleet."[21] He gave a harrowing account of sailors herding together for common defense, but discovered, overpowered, "or barbarously hunted, like wild beasts, from covert to covert . . . and hundreds of them overcome by force," imprisoned, and subjected to insult and punishment for refusing to swear allegiance to the crown.[22]

Cutting's *Facts and observations* provides the fullest and most detailed account of his labors and of the manner in which he became involved. In this justificatory piece he declared that Captain Nathaniel Colley of the *Clermont*—the mariner whose table had so impressed Jefferson on his return voyage from France that he ordered two copies for himself—had come to him asking advice and assistance, since embarrassed American commanders who had lost their crews had found their own efforts unavailing in the absence of an American consul. Cutting decided to risk everything in behalf of his countrymen:[23]

Unaided and almost unknown, an alien in a foreign land, I undertook to assert the independence of our nation, and the rights of its

18 See Documents I and II.
19 Cutting to Adams, 17 July 1790.
20 Cutting, *Facts and observations, justifying the claims of John Browne Cutting* . . . [Philadelphia, 1795], p. 8-10, 13. The title reveals the correct form of Cutting's middle name, hitherto given as Brown.
21 Same, p. 8.
22 Same, p. 11.
23 Same, p. 14.

citizens: I undertook to do so, because it was solicited, because it was necessary; because it was honorable; but, I now confess, that the extent and duration of the undertaking, and the reception that my services have been doomed to meet, convince me that I ought rather to have satisfied myself, as other worthy citizens more wisely did, by deploring, yet submitting to the persecution.

The bitterness of the veiled allusion to Gouverneur Morris and others was engendered by subsequent experience, but there is no doubt that Cutting's commitment was wholehearted.

Sometime before the 12th of May Cutting convened a group of American captains, received special authorization to represent them, and obtained from them lists of crews and their places of origin. Resolutions granting such authority were adopted at another meeting in July by eight commanders who gathered at the Maryland Coffee House. Their style, at least in the first two resolves, betrays Cutting's authorship:[24]

1. That an american mariner in Great Britain in being exposed to all the rigour of british press warrants, in being liable to the assaults and outrages of a british press gang, and in being eventually liable to be compelled into a foreign service (except each commander of the vessel from which he is thus forced, can trace him to that very ship whither he is dragged for confinement, and will positively swear that he is a native and subject of the United States of America) must be considered in an unsafe and truly alarming condition, a situation, not only inviting to a temporary violation, but hazarding a total subversion of his most precious rights.

2dly. That the consequences resulting from this unprotected situation of the said citizens are so irksome to the feelings and detrimental to the interests of american mariners and commanders, that in the opinion of those present, since no minister or consul of their nation is on the spot, to whom under such difficulties they might with more propriety resort, with complaints and for redress—it is expedient that they now have recourse to some other fit person of the same country, desiring them in their behalf to cause these grievances to be made known to the government of the United States.

3dly. That the thanks of this meeting be cordially given to John Brown Cutting Esquire for those able and patriotic efforts which have already much contributed, and by being continued may in the opinion of this meeting still materially contribute, to soften the situation, or procure the discharge of many american citizens, who have been or now are unjustly impress'd as subjects of this kingdom: and that he be and hereby is intreated to continue those efforts: and likewise that he be earnestly requested on the part of this meeting, to convey to the government of the United States these facts touching the past and present situation of the american mariners here,

[24] This meeting evidently took place on 22 July 1790 (Cutting, *Facts and observations*, p. 52). Among those who signed were J. Swift, John Osmand, Tristram Barnard, and William Billings. This undated text, entirely in Cutting's hand, was enclosed in his letter to Adams, 17 July 1790 (MHi: AM). Another copy was doubtless sent to TJ in Cutting's missing letter of 16 July 1790.

which any of the american commanders have communicated or shall communicate to him for this purpose, together with such other truths pertinent to the subject as he may otherwise acquire.

Cutting undoubtedly transmitted copies of this and similar authorizations to the Secretary of State, though such enclosures have disappeared from view with most of their covering letters.

As a result of his voluntary endeavors, Cutting soon found his lodgings "filled every morning, with numbers of those distressed and terrified clients" and he became acquainted "with all their arrests, and all their necessities."[25] His *Facts and observations* lists the names of more than seven hundred persons whom he described as "Some of the American Seamen, succoured and Liberated from British Impress, in the Year 1790." In addition it presents the names of ships, masters, and sailors involved in a number of the cases in which his persistent visits to the Admiralty—with his "pockets full of affidavits and memorials," as well as coins for the clerks—resulted in success. Among these was the case of Hugh Purdie.

II

Late in July, Purdie, on board H.M.S. *Crescent* at Torbay, addressed the following statement to John Adams "or his successor" as minister:[26]

You will find I am a native of Virginia by a certificate in my possession; but am deprived of my liberty by being impressed into the service of his britannic Majesty. My late father bore considerable posts under the constitution during the late war. He was printer to the public and post master general to the State of Virginia, but by too great faith in the paper currency of the state, reduced those of his family who survived the fatigues of the war to service employments for their subsistence. I have urged the faith of treaties and the consequence of a violation in vain. I must therefore humbly solicit your protection or assistance in procuring my discharge.

I have already acquainted Mr. Ebenezer Hazard, a friend of mine in New York, of my being impress'd, and doubt not he will make use of his influence in that quarter. . . . P.S. At the time of my discharge I think it but reasonable they shou'd find me a passage from some port, from whence I may get home, with payment for my detention. Shou'd it be requisite I can get some in London to prove with my own oath I never was in England and ever denied any allegiance to its government.

This letter was "erroneously brought by the postman to Mr. Cutting and by him honestly open'd and answer'd on the 27 July 1790."[27]

25 Cutting, *Facts and observations*, 19-24, 35.
26 Purdie to Adams, undated, entirely in Cutting's hand (MHi: AM). This was enclosed in Cutting to Adams, 11 Aug. 1790 (MHi: AM). Another copy was no doubt sent to TJ in Cutting's missing letter of 7 Aug. 1790.
27 Caption by Cutting at head of Purdie's letter to Adams (see preceding note). The substance of Cutting's reply is summarized at end of text.

Cutting urged Purdie to set forth the facts in writing and to refer him to persons in London who would be able to provide corroborative testimony. To this the sailor replied immediately:[28]

I Hugh Purdie do solemnly swear that I was born in the City of Williamsburg, Virginia, that my age is twenty three years and four months, my height five feet eight inches and three fourths that I have dark brown hair and light coloured eyes.

I shipped on board the ship Russel the 10th of last August in Norfolk Virginia as second mate of said ship which belonged to Newbury Port bound to Havre de Grace or elsewhere. We arrived at Portsmouth in England the 14 Sepr. following, from whence we were ordered by William and James Douglas, merchants in America Square to London, where we discharged our cargo, but in our passage down the river had the misfortune to have the ship stopped. Being desirous of seeing the world as much as possible, I determined on staying in London: but had the misfortune to lose what money I had shortly after my discharge . . . from Capt. Holland dated the 10 October. On application to the above merchants you will have the above particulars.

Purdie then gave a brief account of shipping on the West Indiaman *Boyd*, of being obliged to complete the return voyage to England, and of being impressed and sent on board *Astrea*, then to *Wasp*, and finally to *Crescent*. He knew of no one in London who could positively corroborate his statements save a Loyalist named Gutridge. But he urged Cutting to lay his case before Congress and concluded: "My father was well known to that honourable body, as his son is to the members for Virginia. . . . Col. [Josiah] Parker, Member for Virginia, is my particular friend and acquaintance, and you will greatly add to the obligation I already feel myself under to you by addressing him.—Pray excuse the incorrectness of the above, as the boatswain pipes and I must away or incur the usual epithet of rebellious rascal."

Cutting immediately wrote to William Short, obtained additional affidavits, and pursued this and other cases at the Admiralty. For more than a week in mid-August he sought an audience with Pitt, his importunations being in vain until he asked for a return of his memorials and affidavits because one of the cases was that of "a young man, well known to persons of the first consideration in his own country." The allusion was obviously intended as a hint that the Virginia sailor was known to the Secretary of State if not to the President of the United States. This produced an interview with Pitt the very next day. A few hours later a letter arrived from the Admiralty saying that orders had been issued for the discharge of Purdie and three other seamen. But the fleet, including *Crescent*, had sailed two days earlier.[29]

The fleet returned to Spithead on the 14th of September. On the

28 Purdie to Cutting, 30 July 1790 (MHi: AM, entirely in Cutting's hand). This text was enclosed in Cutting to Adams, 11 Aug. 1790 (MHi: AM). Another copy was no doubt sent to TJ in Cutting's missing letter of 7 Aug. 1790.
29 Cutting, *Facts and observations*, p. 24-5.

17th Cutting received two letters from Purdie, the second revealing the fact that he had been put in irons and was to be punished. Cutting rushed off to see "a gentleman . . . known to the British ministry as possessing, in a great degree, the confidence of our government"— Gouverneur Morris. On the 17th Morris repaired to Whitehall, asked an interview with the Duke of Leeds or with the Under Secretary, stated the facts of the case to the latter, and obtained his assurance that the matter would be promptly taken up with the Admiralty. The next day Cutting was busy "ferreting the Admiralty about Purdie" and was able to inform Morris that orders for the sailor's release had been issued. As late as the 22d, however, he still did not know what response the captain of *Crescent* had made to these new orders. But the sailor was scourged anyway. As Cutting later expressed it:[30]

This ill-fated man had been led to the gangway on the preceding morning, and without trial, amidst insults and scoffings, was doomed to suffer a severe and ignominious punishment. His offense, as it is set forth in a plain and honest narrative, written by himself, and attested on oath, consisted in a decent and dignified resentment of the obloquy and derision cast upon his nation, the government, and its chief magistrate. The corrupt system, the brutal individual that could regard such conduct as criminal, cannot fail to meet an honorable contrast, in the meritorious construction which the same conduct will receive, from the pure and enlightened mind of every American patriot. Policy required, however, that I should suppress every sentiment of sympathy and indignation, till I had accomplished my principal object.

As he remembered it later, Cutting continued to pursue this object until, within a few days, he was given Captain Young's letter accusing the sailor of mutinous conduct.[31] But the fact is that Purdie had been flogged on the afternoon of the 15th and released on the 16th—that is, about the time that Cutting received news of the impending punishment. The release, therefore, was in response to the orders that had been issued in August.

Nevertheless, Cutting's ferreting at the Admiralty had been useful, for the flogging of Purdie was the crucial point on which Jefferson rested his protest. In his view the letter from the commander of *Crescent*, confessing knowledge of orders to release the sailor and yet arguing that discipline made it "impossible . . . to avoid whipping a free American," was sufficient in itself to supersede all other testimony.[32] But Jefferson's real object was not so much to score a point as to make an example of the naval commander lest his act, accepted without protest and without reprimand, breed further violations and thus exacerbate even more the already strained relations between the two countries. Purdie's appeal to patriotic sentiments in this case,

---

30 For Purdie's two letters, see Document III, Enclosures V and VI. Cutting, *Facts and observations*, p. 24-5, 27; Morris, *Diary*, ed. Davenport, I, 605-606. Purdie claimed that he was released on the 17th, but it seems plausible to accept Captain Young's statement that it was on the 16th.
31 Cutting, *Facts and observations*, p. 27.
32 Document III.

heightened by allegations of the contemptuous attitudes of British naval officers toward Americans as rebels, sufficiently illustrated the inflammatory ingredients of this issue.

Success in obtaining orders for the release of Purdie and many others led Cutting, so he declared in *Facts and observations*, to form a daring and ambitious plan to smuggle American sailors from England to France. According to his later account he was able, with the cooperation of the master of a smuggling vessel and three agents, to transfer from different ports in England a group of at least 947 American sailors, most of whose names he published. This operation, he pointed out, required secrecy for its success and "it's unlawfulness exacted caution."[33] To finance these and other aspects of his efforts, Cutting relied on some of his own funds and on loans from William Short, Daniel Parker, Nathaniel Appleton, and others.[34] He regarded the resolutions of the captains who met at the Maryland Coffee House as being "not merely a tribute, but as a species of warrant or commission."[35] Later, at the end of the war crisis, a number of other captains gave their particular testimony to the public press:[36]

We the Subscribers feel ourselves in duty bound thus publickly to acknowledge for ourselves and in behalf of the Mercantile and Maritime interest of these United States the particular obligations we and they in general, are under to MR. JOHN BROWN CUTTING, a citizen of America now in London, for his unwearied applications and constant success, in effecting the release of all the American Seamen who were suffering by an indiscriminate Press which existed in all the ports of Great Britain, from the month of April, until the time of our departure, and we doubt not that other Masters of American Ships, will be equally ready to make known the grateful sense we all entertained of MR. CUTTING's friendship.

Thus in these months of arduous effort, declared Cutting:[37]

I had stood alone, devoting every moment of my time, every faculty of my mind, every shilling of my property, and every resource of my credit, to an object, which I considered, both as an important public service, and a private indispensable duty. I had punctually and circumstantially communicated to our government, the predicament in which I had been fortuitously placed, and the measures which I had resolutely pursued. The public gazettes of America, as well as of England, had announced the success of my agency, and the gratitude of those who had been relieved by it.

[33] Cutting, *Facts and observations*, p. 36. An affidavit by one James Donnaughey of 12 Feb. 1793, given on oath before Thomas Pinckney, states that he was engaged by Cutting to enlist the aid of one Maclane in the smuggling operations (Tr in hand of Timothy Pickering, CSmH: Pinckney Papers). See note, TJ to Washington, 7 Feb. 1792.
[34] Cutting, *Facts and observations*, p. 54-7.
[35] Same, p. 52-3.
[36] Dated at Boston 23 Oct. 1790 and published in the *Columbian Centinel* of the 27th over the names of Tristram Barnard, Edward Davis, Charles C. Russell, Richard S. Tibbits, Samuel Calder, and Fitzwilliam Sargeant.
[37] Cutting, *Facts and observations*, p. 16.

EDITORIAL NOTE

But during the whole of this period and for some time thereafter, Cutting added, he had received no word of approbation or of sanction from his government. This silence he found "inconceivably painful and mortifying" and his prospects of being indemnified gloomy. But when in due course a letter arrived from the Secretary of State acknowledging Cutting's fatiguing exertions and closing with "sentiments of great esteem and attachment," his spirits were elevated. "Supported by such applause," Cutting declared, "it cannot any longer be doubted but that it was necessary and laudable to interpose for the relief of our maritime fellow-citizens." He thought it fair to construe Jefferson's letter "as giving, retrospectively, the sanction of government to my agency."[38]

III

Cutting's letter of 4 Oct. 1790 contained a summary of his conversation with Pitt and enclosed affidavits and other documents relating to Purdie's case. Immediately upon receiving this inflammatory packet, Jefferson placed it before the President. In recommending that Purdie's case be made the basis of a formal protest, he characteristically employed a gesture of indirection which enabled him to make use of blunter language than would have been permissible in a formal diplomatic exchange. He did so by drafting a dispatch to the American consul in London directing him to lay the facts before the Duke of Leeds under "the express command of the President"—and to reveal these private instructions as of his own volition, not as prompted by the administration.[39]

These draft instructions thus calculated for the eye of Leeds were under consideration by the Secretary of State and the President for a full week. In the absence of Washington's diary for this period, it is not possible to say what his attitude was in the beginning. The President must, however, have suggested some alterations in the draft since, some days later, Jefferson submitted another and final version that was approved.[40] It is scarcely plausible to suppose that Washington sought to add force to the expressions employed. It is more likely that in this instance he endeavored to soften the language, just as he did in the case of Jefferson's dispatch to Carmichael outlining in emphatic terms the new policy of firmness toward Spain.[41] The significant point, however, is that Jefferson initiated the idea of making a formal protest and that the President was persuaded to give his approval in the emphatic terms of an express command.

Despite the indubitable fact of Purdie's American citizenship and the admission by the commander of *Crescent* that the sailor had been flogged after orders for his release as an alien had been received, Jefferson abandoned the case when the American consul informed him that Hugh Purdie had turned violently against Cutting, that he had refused the offers of Joshua Johnson to obtain passage for him back

[38] Same, p. 16-18. The letter was that of 17 Dec. 1790 (Document II).
[39] Document V.
[40] Document IV.
[41] Editorial Note to group of documents on new approaches to Spain, under 10 Mch. 1791.

to Virginia, and that he had in brief proved himself to be "a profligate and worthless Man." This, even if true, had no relevance to the issue. But Johnson also reported that he had known of no instance of mistreatment of American sailors and that he had met with "every assurance and Friendly disposition in this Government towards that of the United States."[42] Such a disposition assuredly had not manifested itself in commercial policy or in the manner in which Gouverneur Morris had been received. But the judicious restraint of the consul exactly suited Jefferson's own style of diplomacy. He therefore readily acquiesced in consigning the case of Hugh Purdie to oblivion. "We would chuse never to commit ourselves," he wrote, "but when we are so clearly in the right as to admit no doubt."[43]

Involvement with Purdie's voluntary protector proved not so easy to terminate. Jefferson recommended what he considered to be a liberal compensation for the expenditures and labors of John Browne Cutting in behalf of American seamen.[44] But Cutting advanced his claim with such an expansive regard for round figures and with such inadequate documentary support as to make it relatively easy for Federalist opponents later to suggest that his true object was not unmixed with avarice. Cutting was deeply hurt by the charge and countered with every proof that could be mustered for an operation which, involving secrecy, petty bribery, and even violation of the law, was understandably deficient in vouchers and receipts. He also defended his honor with courage and pertinacity. Indeed, though impressment of American sailors continued for two decades to exacerbate relations between the United States and Great Britain, it disappeared as an issue long before the claim of John Browne Cutting was adjudicated. Even in old age Jefferson was called upon to lend his voice to the indemnification of "an honest fellow citizen, who has not only lost his money in public service, but whose probity has been questioned by violent factionists on account of that very patriotism."[45] He, too, ceased to exist before the persistent claimant ended his dogged pursuit of justice.[46]

Jefferson properly regarded the documents pertaining to Gouverneur Morris' mission and to Cutting's efforts to relieve impressed sailors as being concerned with matters of "capital importance."[47] In carrying out these interconnected decisions he exhibited the same spirit of candor, courtesy, and willingness to accord motives of justice to others that characterized all of his diplomacy. When he framed the instructions to the American consul that reflected this habitual approach, neither he nor Washington had received Gouverneur Morris' report of his actions in the case of Hugh Purdie, though this must have arrived shortly thereafter. This report would only have confirmed the prudence of both decisions.

Morris was willing to concede that British ministers seemed de-

[42] Johnson to TJ, 27 Mch. and 10 Aug. 1791. See also, Johnson to TJ, 26 Feb. 1791.
[43] TJ to Johnson, 29 Aug. 1791.
[44] 7 Feb. 1792.
[45] Cutting to TJ, 22 June 1824 and 9 July 1824; TJ to Cutting, 2 July 1824.
[46] For note on the history of Cutting's claim for reimbursement, see TJ to Washington, 7 Feb. 1792.
[47] Document VI.

sirous of avoiding just grounds for complaint and he recognized that in an operation necessarily left to agents who were apt to be neither scrupulous nor delicate, the system was "as barbarous in the execution, as in the principle it is violent and despotic." He also declared that his own position on the question was the disagreeable one of being liable to censure for neglect or to the imputation of seeking employment, a dilemma he resolved by deciding on each case as it arose. He reported that when Cutting came to seek his aid in saving Purdie from an ignominious punishment, he went at once to Whitehall to wait on the Duke of Leeds or Under Secretary Burgess. But the very next morning another appeal came to him from Captain Samuel Makins, who told him that his vessel had been intercepted at the mouth of the channel by a British frigate and that some of his sailors had been "induced to enter into the British service . . . by ill usage, threats, and particularly by the assurance, that having nobody here to speak for them, their case was desperate, and therefore they might as well take the bounty as let it alone, for go they must."[48]

On being informed by Captain Makins that he not only had failed to obtain satisfaction at the Admiralty but had been insulted there, Morris dispatched a letter to Duke of Leeds. In this he stated three facts: (1) that an American ship had been intercepted and detained on the high seas by a British vessel of war; (2) that, while she was in the port of London, seamen had been taken from her and detained despite their oaths of citizenship; and (3) that others on board a British ship of war had been detained despite claims of the American master to whom they were bound. As to the first, Morris emphasized the serious consequences that might flow from the act of interrupting a vessel in its voyage by calling to Leeds' attention "that sentiment, which was excited by the conduct of a Spanish frigate in Nootka Sound." This was a remarkably blunt allusion to a scarcely comparable incident, particularly in view of the fact that the war fever had not yet wholly subsided in England. As to the second point, Morris suggested that Great Britain's insistence that none but native-born Americans be exempt from impressment would raise questions "of a most delicate nature." This comment came near charging Great Britain with a breach of the Treaty of Peace, for by that treaty "the sovereign . . . relinquished all rights over those [subjects] then in America, who chose to take the benefit of it." If this compact could thus be set aside in the case of a mariner, Morris declared, many others might no longer rely on it. On the third point, the cumulative belligerency of Morris' hints reached new heights: "I pray leave to submit to your Grace, whether it is consistent to claim British seamen, who have contracted to serve in American vessels, and yet withhold American seamen, who have contracted to serve in British vessels. Pardon me for adding, that this would justify a practice, which I hope may never take place, of manning the privateers of your enemies with the seamen of America."[49]

[48] Morris to Washington, 24 Sep. 1790 (DLC: Morris Papers). Morris, *Diary*, ed. Davenport, I, 605-606, 608, 610, 611.
[49] Morris to Leeds, 24 Sep. 1790 (DLC: Morris Papers). As further examples of Morris' posturing displomacy, see his public letters to TJ of 24 and 28 Dec.

Morris' vigorous protest to Leeds, like most writings from the same facile pen, was expressed with grace and force. But it was also theatrical. Its essentially bellicose tone provided ample proof of the fact that, however talented in business or brilliant in repartee Gouverneur Morris might be, his gifts did not include a mastery of the arts of diplomacy. By the effrontery of making, at the very opening of a diplomatic exchange, unmistakable allusions to the possibility of armed conflict, he not only insured a dignified silence on the part of the Duke of Leeds. He also exposed himself to the suspicion of being less intent upon accommodation with the Foreign Secretary of Great Britain than on creating a favorable impression upon the President of the United States.

But the American Secretary of State had no need of this further demonstration of a style of diplomatic discourse that was fundamentally antagonistic in approach. Evidence of the fact was sufficiently exhibited in the correspondence that Washington had placed in his hands two days before news of Hugh Purdie's impressment came to him. This illuminating glimpse of the manner in which Morris conducted negotiations in behalf of a sovereign state was not the cause of the termination of his agency. But, all other factors aside, Jefferson could only have welcomed the opportunity to cancel a mission that had been conducted in a manner offensive even to those who had sponsored the emissary.[50] His own style of diplomacy was respectful in approach, conciliatory in manner, and based upon the assumption that mutual trust should exist until proved ill-founded. This was a diplomacy that by no means excluded the quality of firmness and, both in this and in all other respects, it exactly coincided with his concept of the relations that should prevail among individuals of honor and civility. Joshua Johnson had been bred in the same society that had instilled these concepts of personal and national behavior in him and the Secretary of State was quite willing to entrust to him the handling of such an inflammable issue as that involving the case of Hugh Purdie and other impressed seamen. Later, when Gouverneur Morris was made minister to France, he had no such congenial alternative.

1790, through which it is easy to see that Leeds, quite understandably, had relegated further discussions with the American agent to Under Secretary Burgess. It is perhaps significant that TJ not only did not respond to these letters but did not even acknowledge their receipt.
[50] See Vol. 17: 97-105.

I. John Browne Cutting to the Secretary of State

DEAR SIR   [London, 17? July 1790]

The moment I had sealed the letter which I wrote you in such haste yesterday, I proceeded to the Admiralty with my pocket full of affidavits and memorials and smoothing my passage through

[324]

the offices of the clerks *by putting my hand into a smaller pocket* (as all who are anxious for speedy success in any Admiralty-suit ought to do or they will repent the omission) I soon reached the upper regions of office, where I was permitted to state the grievances of the commanders of american vessels and their impress'd seamen.

I address'd myself more particularly to Mr. Ibbetson one of the joint secretaries to the Admiralty, cogently representing the violation of their rights, the damage in their property, the coarse contumatious treatment, and in some cases the personal outrages, which my countrymen had suffered, ever since the commencement of the late impress, but more especially on the night of the 15th instant, when mates apprentices and seamen were seiz'd indiscriminately, their certificates of citizenship and of discharge as being americans, signed by officers of rank in the british navy—disregarded or torn out of their possession—several of these mariners confined in the unwholesome hold of a british Hulk or Tender and their american commanders insulted when they went on board to succour or to claim them.

Suggesting what just cause of Umbrage regular complaints of such facts from american citizens might give to the government of their own country, I aver'd my persuasion that to minister occasion for such complaints cou'd not in the present crisis of european affairs be desirable to the british government. Yet supposing that no just cause of offence was either wish'd or meant to be given, still it might be foreseen that the operation of such harsh usage, on the part of their subordinate agents whether inflicted accidentally by mistake or maliciously by design, must in the end prove detrimental to leading commercial interests of Britain, and thence tend directly to diminish the present exhuberance of her national revenues Since if the american seamen were deter'd from venturing into british ports, fearful of insult from the press-gangs or of being forced into a foreign service, the consequence wou'd be that many american articles of export—or at least some of them of no small importance—Tobacco for instance, an article of so great fiscal fertility as to yield vast sums both in customs and excise—must chiefly be conveyed to other foreign markets instead of this. Nor are these, continued I, the only circumstances that render this wrongful taking or even temporary detention of american seamen in Britain highly impolitic. In former wars when british seamen were taken from the employment of the merchant into the service of the sovereign, foreign seamen from Holland, Denmark or Sweden might always be hired to replace them: but these being now wholly absorbed in manning the fleets of their own nations respectively, the service of the anglo-american seamen, and of course their perfect exemption from the touch of a british press-gang, appear materially if not indispensably necessary to a continuance in its present extent of the foreign commerce of Great Britain.

Observing from the attention that these remarks seemed to gain for me that I touched a nerve of exquisite sensibility, and which vibrated to the hearts of those whom I wished to move, I proceeded directly to the point of my present aim—namely to obtain a positive order to the british regulating Captains to discharge the american seamen who had been impress'd on the 15 instant.

Among these I ought to mention the case of two by the names of Stephens and Cunningham, both of Boston to whose birth and citizenship Capt. Tristam Barnard of the ship Mary had sworn prior to the time when they were taken. These men dreading the despotism of the press gangs and understanding from some quarter that there was a method of proving their citizenship which being adopted wou'd screen them, had made out a written description of themselves on oath stating that they were natives and citizens of the United States. Capt. Barnard had certified in writing on the same paper that what these men thus affirmed was according to the best of his knowledge the real truth, and subscribed to an oath of it before a magistrate. When the press gang boarded the Mary on the 15th this paper was produced as proof that ought to exempt Stephens and Cunningham from being impress'd. Instead of this these certificates were torn out of their possession. Nor wou'd the regulating Capt. return them again even to Capt. Barnard, who said if he cou'd not get his men, yet he claim'd his certificates as a property for which he had paid the magistrate a valuable consideration. The two men were hurried on board the Enterprize, an old frigate moored off the Tower and which serves as a common receptacle for those miserable mariners who are impress'd in the river Thames until they are examin'd and sent down to the fleet. Thither Barnard pursued them and enquir'd of the regulating Captain what oath he must take to entitle him to get back his two american seamen. The answer given was—You cannot and shall not have them except You positively swear that they were born in and are subjects of the United States of America. Barnard who is a sturdy citizen and a man of sense began to expostulate with this officer on the unreasonable rigour of the terms of such an oath, and asked how any man under any circumstances cou'd with strict propriety swear to the birth of another, when that other perhaps was older than himself? However in the sequel Barnard did take the oath observing that tho there was hardship and absurdity in exacting it in so rigid a form yet honestly believing as he did that Stephens and Cunningham were american citizens he wou'd venture to swear for them. When he return'd again with this affidavit to claim his seamen, he tells me they came upon deck out of the hold of the Hulk pale and feeble, complaining that they had eaten nothing for four and twenty hours, and he assures me the tears gushed out of their eyes at the sight of him. Provoked by a combination of circumstances so trying, and the officer now incensing that provocation with reproaches of what he had said the day before concerning the rigour and absurdity of an oath which he had since taken notwithstanding: Barnard became so irritated as to retort and to say, that true it was he had taken the oath and upon the construction he gave it and under the same circumstances shou'd take it again yet he was nevertheless of a similar opinion as to the irrational and preposterous rigour of the terms of it, and he still thought such an oath if interpreted strictly no man cou'd with propriety take. Hereupon the officer flatly refused to release the two seamen, alledging that what Barnard now said invalidated the oath which he had before taken.

While I was writing to you yesterday Barnard called upon me with this complaint, intreating my aid and advice as a fellow citizen. I immediately threw his narrative into the form of a memorial to the Lords of the Admiralty, and accompanying with a new affidavit of the birth and citizenship of Cunningham and Stephens (to which the Mate of the Mary had also sworn) and producing both, with many others at the Admiralty as above mention'd, took occasion therefrom to bring before their Lordships the very irksome and unhandsome predicament in which the american mariners were involved 1st. By the narrow and rigourous rule of evidence laid down by their Lordships as the sole standard of proof to ascertain american citizenship, and 2dly By the rigid interpretation, or (what I affirmed was more analogous to the present case) mis-interpretation of that rule by those who applied it under the orders of their Lordships.

I embraced this opportunity likewise to unfold and expatiate upon the various methods of management by which the efficacy

of some letters directing the discharge of american seamen, which their Lordships had granted me on memorials and the requisite proof prior to those which I now presented, had been heretofore done away—contrary I did not doubt to the intent of the board of Admiralty. I instanced the case of William Ingersoll, of the ship Marietta, who being impressed early in June, his commander Fitzwilliam Sargent, had immediately sworn that he was born in and was a subject of the United States of America, thereby furnishing accurately the full evidence exacted by the board to entitle him to an immediate discharge, yet before that letter cou'd be had or was sent, Ingersoll was hurried out of the department of the regulating Captain and sent down to some ship at Sheerness which we cou'd not identify. That still anxious for the relief of a friendless and unprotected citizen I did again in behalf of Capt. Sargent—who had meanwhile been obliged to sail for America without his townsman—represent these facts and ask another letter to the commanding officer at Sheerness for the discharge of Ingersoll. But a similar disappointment had baffled this new effort. Admiral Dalrymple not finding Ingersoll on board of any ship under his command, conceived he must have been turned over to the fleet at Torbay. I hoped however their Lordships wou'd allow me to persist and press for a fresh letter to the commanding Admiral at Torbay. For such liberal sentiments I was sure actuated their Lordships as wou'd incline them to dispense with a rigid adherence to official forms, when it threaten'd to frustrate by delay, the chief purpose for which it might be presumed those forms were instituted—namely a prompt and effectual administration of national justice, especially to foreigners. Nor cou'd I distrust their disposition to countenance even the unauthorized efforts of an american citizen in his social capacity as such: when it was evident he cou'd be stimulated by no sinister views, but was moved solely by an ardent and very natural anxiety to assist in extricating his fellow citizens from a condition which they loathed and deprecated: a condition which tho' rendered tolerable to british seamen through habits of submission of the excessive authority of press warrants, was considered as peculiarly odious and even intolerable to those, who having been nurtur'd in the western hive of Liberty and cherishing a natal love for its sweets, entertain'd ideas of personal freedom the most fervent and exalted; such as might be expected to animate minds which had never yielded to force, nor been subdued by violence. That their Lordships wou'd I know make due allowance for the dominion and strength of national prejudices; especially those prejudices, which if they seemed exotic or looked unlovly in the eyes of foreigners, were nevertheless most dear to the natives in whose country they flourished and in whose affections they were rooted. That a genuine magnanimity wou'd induce them as readily to listen to reasonable suggestions and just claims from a private individual as to weightier remonstrances or more positive demands from a public minister, particularly at a moment when it must be seen, that suggestions and claims thus brought forward, constituted a very needful, tho' I owned but a puny substitute for that sort of requisition, which might at once without wearying their Lordships have met and resisted those unintentional incroachments on the rights of my countrymen. On the whole substance therefore of the present application it wou'd be disrespectful and irreverent in me to question that new orders woud issue from their Lordships, to the regulating Captains and to other officers in the impress service, requiring them to be gentler and more cautious in impressing american seamen from american vessels; and milder in their after treatment of them (where they did impress) on board the british Hulks and Tenders; and finally that all those who had already been sworn to or discharged as americans might again be discharged—particularly Ingersoll, Cunningham and Stephens.

In reply I was told there was much difficulty in discriminating an american from a british seaman: that many british attempted to pass for americans. But that with regard to any ill-treatment offered the americans in any shape I must surely have been misinformed: that the officers employed in the impress-service were gentlemen of the purest honor and most polish'd deportment, tho' it was possible in some cases they might have construed the oath more rigorously than their Lordships wished or intended: that in the instance of Cunningham and Stephens it seemed as if they had; that these two men upon the evidence I brought forward, ought to be discharged and that a letter to this effect shou'd be forthwith prepar'd; and likewise a fresh letter written to Admiral Barrington at Torbay for the release of Ingersoll.

Tr. (MHi: AM); in Cutting's hand, enclosed in his to Adams of 17 July 1790 (same); at head of text: "Copy of a letter to Mr. Jefferson). 18 July 90"; accompanied by copies of documents on Purdie case, all in Cutting's hand. Despite the endorsement, this letter must have been begun on the 17th; that of the 16th (missing) is recorded in SJL as received on 4 Oct. 1790 but the above letter is not recorded in SJL.

See also, Cutting's *Facts and observations*, p. 28-9.

II. Secretary of State to John Browne Cutting

DEAR SIR   Philadelphia December 17th. 1790

Your favor of June 11th. came to hand August 28th. Those of July 16. August 7. 11. October 4. and 6. at subsequent periods. —They should not have thus long have remained unacknowledged but for the idea, which has been constantly kept up, that you were on the verge of your departure for this country. Even so late as the date of your last, Mr. Barrett says in a letter to me that "Mr. Cutting will hand to me certain papers," from which I supposed you actually arrived for some days. Finding it is not the case, I can no longer defer informing you that your several letters have been laid before the President of the United States, and assuring you of the sense entertained of the zeal you have shewn, and the services you have rendered in the cases of our impressed seamen. Mr. Johnson had been appointed Consul for the United States in the port of London in July, a month before the receipt of your first letter on the subject of our seamen; and it has been unfortunate for you that his commission was so long getting to hand, and consequently left you so long exposed to the fatiguing exertions which your humanity and patriotism have led you to make for the relief of so many of our countrymen.

I perceive by your last letter, and indeed it was obviously to be expected, that these solicitations had occasioned you some special expences. It is the duty of the public servants to desire as particular a statement of these as you can give, and where you cannot be particular, that you give the best general estimate you can of their amount, in order that they may be reimbursed. In the mean time, I enclose you a draft on our bankers in Holland for fifty pounds sterling, the sum presented to our mind by the copy of a letter enclosed in your last. I presume that very soon after the date of your last, Mr. Johnson will have relieved you from all further trouble in this line.

With a repetition of thanks for your exertions on behalf of our countrymen, I am with sentiments of great esteem and attachment, Dear Sir Your most obt. & most hbl. Servant,

TH: JEFFERSON

Dupl (DLC: Short Papers); in Remsen's hand except for signature; at head of text: "Duplicate"; addressed in TJ's hand: "John Brown Cutting esquire London," with the following on cover: "Received & Left by Sir Your Obt. &. Hble. Serv. Joshua Johnson 30 June 1791." FC (DNA: RG 59, PCC No. 121).

III. Secretary of State to Joshua Johnson

Philadelphia Dec. 17. 1790.

Tho not yet informed of your reciept of my letter covering your commission as Consul for the United States in the port of London, yet knowing that the ship has arrived by which it went, I take for granted the letter and commission have gone safe to hand, and that you have been called into the frequent exercise of your office for the relief of our seamen, upon whom such multiplied acts of violence have been committed in England, by press-gangs, pretending to take them for British subjects, not only without evidence, but against evidence. By what means may be procured for our seamen, while in British ports, that security for their persons which the laws of hospitality require, and which the British nation will surely not refuse, remains to be settled. In the mean time there is one of these cases wherein so wilful, and so flagrant a violation has been committed by a British officer on the person of one of our citizens, as requires that it be laid before his government, in friendly and firm reliance of satisfaction for the injury, and of assurance, for the future, that the citizens of the U.S. entering the ports of Great Britain, in pursuit of a lawful commerce, shall be protected by the laws of hospitality in usage among nations.

It is represented to the President of the U.S. that Hugh Purdie, a native of Williamsburgh in Virginia, was in the month of July last, siesed in London by a party of men, calling themselves press-officers, and pretending authority from their government so to do, notwithstanding his declarations, and the evidence he offered of his being a native citizen of the United states, and that he was transferred on board the Crescent, a British ship of war, commanded by a Capt. Young. Passing over the intermediate violences exercised on him, because not peculiar to his case (so many other American citizens having suffered the same) I proceed to the particular one which distinguishes the present representation. Satisfactory evidence having been produced by Mr. John Brown Cutting, a citizen of the U.S. to the Lords of the admiralty that Hugh Purdie was a native citizen of the same states, they, in their justice, issued orders to the Lord Howe, their admiral, for his discharge. In the mean time the Lord Howe had sailed with the fleet of which the Crescent was. But, on the 27th. of August, he wrote to the board of Admiralty that he had recieved their orders for the discharge of Hugh Purdie, and had directed it accordingly. Notwithstanding these orders, the reciept of which at sea Capt. Young acknowleges, notwithstanding Capt. Young's confessed knowlege that Hugh Purdie was a citizen of the U.S. from whence it resulted that his being carried on board the Crescent, and so long detained there, had been an act of wrong, which called for expiatory conduct and attentions, rather than new injuries on his part towards the sufferer, instead of discharging him, according to the orders he had recieved, on his arrival in port, which was on the 14th. of September, he, on the 15th. confined him in irons for several hours, then had him bound and scourged in presence of the ship's crew under a threat to the executioner, that, if he did not do his duty well, he should take the place of the sufferer. At length he discharged him on the 17th. without the means of subsistence for a single day. To establish these facts, I inclose you copies of papers communicated to me by Mr. Cutting, who laid the case of Purdie before the board of Admiralty, and who can corroborate them by his personal evidence. He can especially verify the letter of Capt. Young, were it necessary to verify a paper the original of which is under the command of his majesty's ministers: and this paper is so material as to supersede of itself all other testimony, confessing the orders to discharge Purdie that yet he had whipped him, and that it was impossible, without giving up all sense of discipline, to avoid whipping a free American citizen. We have such confidence in the justice of the British government, in their friendly regard to these states, in their respect for the honour and good understanding of the two countries, compromitted by this act of their officer, as not to doubt their due notice of *him*, indemnification to the sufferer, and a friendly assurance to these states that effectual measures shall be adopted in future to protect the persons of their citizens while in British ports.

By the express command of the President of the U.S. you are to lay this case, and our sense of it, before his Britannic majesty's Minister for foreign affairs, to urge it on his particular notice by all the motives which it calls up, and to communicate to me the result.—I have the honor to be with sentiments of the most perfect esteem, Sir, Your most obedient & most humble servt.,

Th: Jefferson

RC (DNA: RG 59, CD). FC (DNA: RG 59, PCC No. 121). The actual date of this letter, in its final form, should have been 23 Dec. 1790 (see TJ to Washington, 22 Dec. 1790).

John Browne Cutting to the Lords Commissioners of the Admiralty

St. James's Square Augt. 10th. 1790.

To the Right Honble. the Lords Commissioners of the British Admiralty.

The Memorial of John Brown Cutting respectfully sheweth.

That your memorialist is a native and Citizen of the United States of America, and has been intreated by four of his fellow Citizens to represent that they are truly such, and to ask your orders for their discharge from onbound his Britannic Majesty's ships the Edgar and Crescent.

Your memorialist having first taken great pains to satisfy himself that Hugh Purdie, Thomas Henderson, Isaac Crapper and George Sheldrake, are really Americans, and not British mariners, now submits the best testimony of the fact which can be had here, not doubting that it will be pronounced sufficient to entitle them to that interference of your Lordships which is thereupon respectfully claimed and solicited for the said foreigners by their countryman, Your Lordships most obedient servant.   JOHN BROWN CUTTING

FC (DNA: RG 59, PCC No. 121). Enclosures: (1) Copy of affidavit of Thomas Longman, bookseller of Paternoster Row, London, dated 5 Aug. 1790, stating that he had received letters from Alexander Purdie of Williamsburg, that he had been satisfactorily informed that he had a son who was a mariner, and that from evidence recently received he does not doubt that Hugh Purdie is his son and a citizen of Virginia. (2) Copy of undated affidavit of John Randolph Grymes, formerly of Middlesex county, Virginia, and now a resident of London and a subject of the realm, stating that he had known Alexander Purdie and believes Hugh Purdie to be his son. (FC of both enclosures in DNA: RG 59, PCC No. 121).

William Short to John Browne Cutting

Paris 11th August 1790

I am happy to be able to add to the testimony of Purdie's being a Citizen of the United States. I remember perfectly being at College at Williamsburg with a person of that name, and that he was son of the Postmaster General at that place. I not only recollect the name and knew the family while at College, but I recollect also the person of Purdie so as to be able to swear to his identity if I should see him. However as this cannot be done, I mention it merely to shew you my full persuasion of the Purdie in question being a Citizen of the United States, since he states himself as being of a particular family and description, and I know that such a family and of such a description existed.

FC (DNA: RG 59, PCC No. 121); at head of text: "Extract of a letter from William Short Esqr. in Paris to Mr. Cutting in London dated 11th. August 1790."

John Browne Cutting to J. Hunt

SIR   [18 Aug. 1790]

I entreat the favor of you to return by the bearer that memorial and those papers, which, on behalf of Purdie and other impressed American mariners, I put into your hand on the 10th instant.

I vainly flattered myself so far as to expect the indulgence of being heard five minutes by the Earl of Chatham himself in their behalf; especially as one of them is a young man well known to persons of the first consideration in his own Country, through whom the Government of it will doubtless be apprised of his present condition.

It is with much regret that I abandon the prospect of contributing to the meliorization of it, by a statement of facts to the Lords of the British Admiralty. I have the honor to be &c.

FC (DNA: RG 59, PCC No. 121); at head of text: "Copy of a note from Mr. Cutting to J. Hunt Esqr. private Secretary to the Earl of Chatham dated 18th August 1790." To this Cutting received the following reply: "Mr. Hunt presents his compliments to Mr. Cutting. He has communicated his letter to the Earl of Chatham, who will be happy to see him tomorrow at half past twelve o'clock" (dated "Admiralty 18th August 1790"; same).

Philip Stephens to John Browne Cutting

SIR   [Admiralty Office, 19 Aug. 1790]

Having laid before my Lords Commissioners of the Admiralty your Memorial of the 10th instant requesting the discharge of the four men named in the margin, natives of America and subjects of the United States of America, who have been impressed and put on board his Majesty's Ships the Edgar and Crescent, I am commanded by their Lordships to acquaint you that they have given orders for the discharge of the said men. I am Sir, Your very huml Servt.

PH. STEPHENS

FC (DNA: RG 59, PCC No. 121); at head of text: "Copy of a letter from Philip Stephens Esqr. Secretary to the Lords Commissioners of the British Admiralty, to Mr. Cutting dated Admiralty Office 19th August 1790"; at foot of text: "Hugh Purdie, Thomas Henderson, George Sheldrake, Isaac Crapper."

Hugh Purdie to John Browne Cutting

SIR   Crescent Spithead Septemr. 15th. 1790.

The fleet under the command of Earl Howe arrived last night, and I am sorry to acquaint you that the Captain of the Crescent does not seem disposed to order me on shore so soon as I could wish, therefore must intreat of you to forward my discharge by the earliest opportunity. The cruize has been extremely tedious which makes me more desirous than ever of my freedom. With hearty wishes for your health and thanks for the trouble you have been at, I subscribe myself, your obliged humble Servant H. PURDIE

FC (DNA: RG 59, PCC No. 121).

ENCLOSURE VI

Hugh Purdie to John Browne Cutting

Crescent Septemr. 15th.
SIR 12 O'clock.

My situation at this instant makes me shed tears plentifully. I must proceed to inform you that in delivering my letter to you dated this day, to one of the bargemen, I inadvertently handed it through one of the ports not knowing it was a crime. The Gunner, who is not a commissioned Officer, immediately ordered me to be whipped. I said on coming on the ships forecastle that shortly I expected to be on shore out of the way of such treatment. He immediately saluted my ears with the gentle epithet of d—d rebellious american son of a bitch, and to hell with me and my Mr. Washingtons. I said no more, being inwardly tortured, but walked along the gangway. The Gunner followed me and gave me so violent a blow on the head as to knock me into the waist, just brushing the butt of an eighteen pounder in my descent. I was immediately ordered into irons. In a moment the order was obeyed; and I now remain for punishment. Try dear Sir, if possible to respite me from this horrid treatment until I can have a fair and impartial trial. I am sensible you will be affected by this detail from your oppressed fellow Citizen. HUGH PURDIE

FC (DNA: RG 59, PCC No. 121).

ENCLOSURE VII

Hugh Purdie to John Browne Cutting

SIR [*Crescent*, 16 Sep. 1790]

These lines will inform you that at four o'clock on the 15th. September 1790 I was released from my irons and brought to the quarter deck, where by the advice of some who were my friends, I plead hard for a Court Martial where evidence might be taken on both sides. Contrary to their expectation it was denied me: and the Captain ordered me one dozen lashes with a rogues cat o' nine tails, with a threat to the boatswain's mate, that if he did not do his duty well, he should take my place. The bare idea of the cause for which I have been punished, I am fully sensible must strike deep into the hearts of Americans, who cannot but honor the glorious name which occasioned the quarrel between the Gunner of the Ship and myself. For my part I ever thought it beneath the character of a Washington to mention his name in such company. But to hear it spoken of with derision, demanded as I thought an answer, which was no other than that if he the Gunner was in London, we should be more perhaps on an equality. This word has occasioned the punishment I am so fully sensible of as scarcely to be able to pen this letter. If you can do any thing for my redress in England, I doubt not your endeavors. Mr. Gist, merchant in London, may perhaps befriend me on the occasion, together with Mr. Longman my late fathers correspondent. With sincere wishes for your health and expectation of shortly hearing from you, I remain your obliged and very humble servant.   HUGH PURDIE

P.S. This will be perhaps the last; if so, conclude, what I cannot but expect will be the case, a villanous scheme for my life.

FC (DNA: RG 59, PCC No. 121); at head of text: "From the same to the same [Purdie to Cutting], dated Crescent Spithead September 16th. 1790."

E N C L O S U R E   VIII

John Browne Cutting to Hugh Purdie

DEAR SIR   [London, 17 Sep. 1790]
This moment your two letters of the 15th. inst. are put into my hands. The proper steps for efectuating your immediate release are taken. I send you this line merely from the possibility that the Post may arrive an hour or two sooner than the order for your discharge.
Say nothing, fear nothing. In less than twenty four hours a positive order for your liberation will arrive. Meanwhile I am affectionately yours.   J. B. CUTTING

FC (DNA: RG 59, PCC No. 121); at head of text: "From Mr. Cutting to Hugh Purdie dated 17th of September 1790."

E N C L O S U R E   IX

John Browne Cutting to Philip Stephens

[London, 22 Sep. 1790]

Mr. Cutting's compliments to Mr. Stephens, on whom he waits agreeably to appointment, to ask if any reply from the commander of the Crescent (concerning Hugh Purdie) has yet been given to the letter which Mr. Stephens was pleased to say he had written, and the purport of the answer to which, should be communicated to Mr. Cutting on tuesday morning.
Mr. Cutting would also wish to be informed if any report has been made by the board of Admiralty in the case of the crew of the American Ship Thomas (E. Vickery commander) delivered in yesterday morning.

FC (DNA: RG 59, PCC No. 121); at head of text: "Copy of a Note from Mr. Cutting to Mr. Stephens dated 22d. September 1790."

William Young to Philip Stephens

DEAR SIR   [Crescent, 19 Sep. 1790]

I have just received your letter and am sorry you should have had the trouble of writing in favor of a man who so very little deserves it. Lord Howe gave me at sea, an order to discharge Hugh Purdie as soon as I came into any port in England. We came to Spithead on tuesday evening, and my intention was to discharge him the next morning; but in the morning he behaved in a manner so mutinous towards the Gunner, that it was impossible, without giving up all sense of discipline to avoid punishing him. He was punished immediately and discharged the next day. His complaint of having been beaten and abused as an American, is absolutely false. I think I can assert that until the day he was punished he was not once struck from the day of his being sent on board the Crescent till the day of his leaving her; though I have learnt that he was generally so disrespectful and disobedient that had the officers informed me of his conduct instead of very improperly concealing it, he would certainly have been punished much oftener than he was. I am with great regard and esteem, your faithful humble servant.   WILLIAM YOUNG

FC (DNA: RG 59, PCC No. 121);   to Philip Stephens Esqr. Secretary to
at head of text: "Copy of a letter from   the Admiralty, dated Crescent Spithead
William Young Esquire Commander   19th September 1790."
of the British Ship of War the Crescent,

Affidavit of Hugh Purdie

MIDDLESEX ⎫
  to wit ⎰   [1 Oct. 1790]

I Hugh Purdie do solemnly swear to the truth of the facts following. I was born in the City of Williamsburg in Virginia, my age is twenty three years, my height five feet eight inches and three quarters, my eyes are of a light colour and my complexion of a dark brown. On the 10th. day of August 1789 I shipped as second mate in Norfolk in Virginia on board the ship Russell. This ship commanded by Captain Holland arrived at Portsmouth about the 14th. day of September following, from whence we were ordered to London, where the cargo was discharged; but on her passage out of the River Thames having run down a barge, she was libelled and detained. On the 10th. day of October 1789 Captain Holland gave me a written discharge in these words. "These are to certify that Hugh Purdie is lawfully discharged from the Ship Russell, this tenth day of October as witness my hand. John Holland. Test. Jonathan Moulton." Finding myself at this time out of employment and there being no American ship in the port of London, on board which I might work my passage home, Captain Holland spoke to Capt. John

Young of the ship Boyd, a British merchantman bound to the Island of St. Christophers, with whom I shipped as a seaman for that Island, having previously informed him that I was a native and citizen of the United States of America. On my arrival at St. Christophers, being desirous to get home from thence, I applied to Captn. Young for my discharge, entreating him to let me go to the Island of St. Eustatia for this purpose. Captn. Young said I had signed articles obliging me to perform the whole passage, and that he had given bond in England under considerable penalty to return every seaman thither whom he had brought out from thence. Understanding the case to be so, and knowing I had signed articles for the voyage, I made myself easy in performing them. The Boyd arrived off Foulstone the 5th. of June 1790, and on that day I was impressed and sent on board the British frigate Astra commanded by Admiral King; as soon as I was on board this frigate I addressed myself to the commanding Lieutenant, assuring him I was not a British subject, but an American Citizen, that I was willing to make oath of it, and that I had written certificates to prove that I was such; and to convince him that I was quite in earnest I did there on the spot formally deny all and any allegiance to the British King, a crime that I supposed would be punishable as treason in a British seaman. He answered, I was as much an Englishman as himself and as much bound to serve his Majesty, and should be made to do so; and he ordered me below with the British seamen, with whom I was shortly after regulated and sent on board the wasp sloop of war. The wasp went round to Spithead, and shortly after I was draughted into the British frigate Crescent commanded by William Young Esqr. To him within a day or two afterwards I addressed a letter nearly in the following terms. "Sir. I am sorry to inform you I cannot content myself on board a King's Ship. I am a native of Virginia and never was in England 'till very lately. I have some property in Virginia and should be sorry to risk it's being confiscated, which in case of war and fullfilment of the articles of confederacy by Congress it might be, if I fight against my Country or the friends of my Country. In time of peace I might be willing to gain experience in the Ship, but otherwise I should fear the censure of a numerous acquaintance who would execrate my name. I served my apprenticeship to David Ross & Co., merchants of Richmond, Virginia, who promoted me at the age of sixteen. Captain Nelson of the Boreas knows I am an American, he seized a ship, a few years since, on board which I was; besides a written certificate in my possession, proving that I am an American. Lord Fincastle and the Honble. Alexander and John Murray, sons of John Earl of Dunmore, my ancient school fellows, can sufficiently vouch for my birth, and their father knows the post which my father held under Congress. I hope your honor will give me leave to address Mr. Adams on the occasion, who I make no doubt will at least endeavour to remove me. I have the honor to be Sir, your obedient humble servant. Hugh Purdie." To this letter I received no answer but this, "Captn. Young will consider of it." I afterwards spoke to Captn. Young several times on the same subject and always received the same answer. Feeling my situation painful in every respect, and

[338]

very much wishing to get from onboard, I wrote a letter to Mr. Adams, superscribing it to him or successor, in London, and enclosed it to a Bookseller who had been my late fathers correspondent: he answered me on the 27th. of July that he had with much difficulty found out a Mr. Cutting who had opened my letter, and was exerting himself in my behalf; and he enclosed a letter to me from Mr. Cutting with instructions to make a written declaration descriptive of my birth, person and other particulars, and to request of Captn. Young, or any commissioned officer onboard, to administer an oath to me of the truth thereof, or to allow me to go on shore to swear before a proper magistrate. I did as Mr. Cutting directed, and applied to Captn. Young, entreating him to swear me, or to suffer me to make oath before a proper magistrate on shore. He denied my request, and in a haughty manner desired me never again to trouble him more on the subject, but to go about my business and to do my duty, or it would be worse for me. Upon this I wrote to Mr. Cutting and enclosed him the written declaration and informed him of my condition, relying wholly on the goodness of this Gentleman, though an entire stranger to me. I wrote him on the 30th. of July, on the 9th., 13th. and 15th. of August, begging him to free me from the state of oppression and servitude I then was in, and enclosed him the certificate of my birth in the words following: "These may certify that Hugh Purdie was born in the parish of Bruton, James City County, Virginia, A.D. 1767, March 17th. as by the parish register, John Bracken minister of the Gospel, by desire of the bearer and the act of Congress requiring the same, this 27th. day of September 1788." This same certificate I had offered to the British officer who impressed me: he would not look at it but threatened to shoot me through the head if I did not immediately get into the boat, nor would Captn. Young of the Crescent ever examine it. In the meantime I was known by the greater part of the crew, and most of the officers to be an American, and when I was ordered to do duty in my watch, the words used were "call the yankee." Late in August the Crescent sailed with the rest of the fleet from Torbay on a cruise, and returned to Spithead the 14th. September following in the evening; the next morning I wrote a line to Mr. Cutting, expressing my impatience to get on shore, and entreating him to forward my discharge; this letter I inadvertently handed through one of the ports to the bargeman, not knowing it was a crime to do so. The Gunner, a Mr. Aylward, seeing me hand it out, sent the boatswain's mate to thresh me in; this boatswain's mate came behind me while leaning out of the port and without saying a word before he struck, struck me several times with a rattan. I turned around and asked "what he meant by that" He said he had orders for it. I said "I saw no officer on the quarter deck." He then said the orders came from the Gunner. I went immediately to the Gunner and told him "I thought he might have spoken to me before he ordered me to be struck, that had I been in his situation and he in mine I should have treated him with more mildness," He began to upbraid me immediately in the most furious manner, calling me "a damned rebellious American son of a bitch, and to hell with me and my Mr. Washingtons." I replied that if we were on shore we would be more upon an equality." He then told me all my Mr. Washingtons would not save me now, and that ["] if I said another word he would run his fist down my throat." Being irritated by such usage, I passed on towards the quarter deck to complain of it to a commissioned Officer. The Gunner followed me and gave me so violent a blow on the head as to knock me into the waist of the ship, just brushing the butt of an eighteen pounder in my fall. I got up as soon as I could and went aft to complain to Lieutenant Champaign on the quarter deck. I told my story, and the Gunner his; upon which the Lieutenant went immediately into the Cabbin to inform Captain Young, who was then dressing to go on board another Ship; he came up, and having heard the Gunner's complaint of me, ordered me to be put in irons immediately, and the order was instantly obeyed; at 4 o'clock in the afternoon of the same day Captn. Young returned onboard the Crescent, I was released from my irons and ordered on the quarter deck. He again heard the story of the Gunner; when the Gunner came to mention that part of the quarrel between us wherein he had spoken of Mr. Washington, I interrupted him, and observed "that I could not bear to hear that name spoken of contemptuously, otherwise I should not have answered the Gunner as I did. ["] I likewise told Captn. Young that if I had offended against the criminal law of England I might be accountable for it, but owing no allegiance to the British King, I was not liable to arbitrary punishment; yet still if I had offended against any law I desired to be now tried by a Court martial onboard the Crescent, where evidence might be taken and heard on both sides. Contrary to the expectation of several persons onboard who seemed to pity my hard condition (among whom I ought to mention the third Lieutenant, who afterwards when I was turned on shore destitute, kindly gave a little money), Captain Young answered that "the less I said the better it would be for me." And commanding the whole crew to be called around me, ordered me to the Gangway, and ordered me to be whipped one dozen lashes upon my bare back with a rogues cat o' nine tails; and he told the boatswain's mate, who was to whip me with this infamous instrument of punishment, that if he did not do his duty well he should take my place; accordingly I was lashed with the greatest severity, and so excruciating was the pain that though I tried to endure it without making a noise, I could not help shrieking out after the sixth or seventh lash; and when this scourging ceased, though ready to faint, and my whole back being in a terrible condition, I refused the aid of the surgeon at the moment; but the surgeon came to me in the evening and finding me in tears and great agony, administered to me a dose of opium and put some cooling ointment on my back. He humanely repeated the same on the next evening, namely the 16th. of September, and on the 17th. of September, and not before, Captain Young had me called and told me I was discharged by order of the Lords of the Admiralty. Soon after Captain Young went on shore and left for me a certificate in the following words "This is to certify that Hugh Purdie, a native of Williamsburg in Virginia, was discharged from the Kings Ship Crescent which I command, by order of the Lords Commissioners of the Admiralty. Given on board the Crescent at Spithead the 17th. of September 1790. William Young." And on the back of the same certificate, in the same hand writing "Hugh Purdie is about five eight inches high with a sallow complexion and long brown hair." On quitting the Ship, having previously expended what money I possessed, I asked if I was to get no pay for my service during the months I had been onboard. I was answered "Yes, when the Ship is paid off." Thus I was impressed, detained against my will, and against proof of my being a foreigner, and forced to do duty as a British seaman on board the Crescent, and after Captain Young, through the kind exertions of Mr. Cutting at the Admiralty, had a positive order to discharge me as an American subject and native (of such facts I was apprized at sea early in September) nevertheless I was ignominiously punished on the angry accusation of Mr. Aylward the Gunner, without the sentence of a Court martial or even a full hearing of my own story.

HUGH PURDIE

FC (DNA: RG 59, PCC No. 121); at foot of text: "Sworn before me this 1st. day of October 1790. Wm. Hyde."

IV. Secretary of State to the President

Thursday. 3. aclock. P.M.
Decr. 23. 1790.

Th: Jefferson has the honour to inform the President that a gentleman leaves town early tomorrow morning for New-York from whence a vessel sails on Monday for Liverpool, on board which will go a passenger who may be trusted with any letters for London.

Th:J. proposes to make up his packet to-night. Can the President give him previously a half hour, for the communication of the letter to Johnson in it's final form, and for another subject? He will be at Mrs. House's till five aclock where he will receive his orders, or as he returns from thence home.

RC (DNA: RG 59, MLR); addressed: "The President of the United States"; endorsed by Lear. Not recorded in SJL or SJPL.

Neither of the two men who eventually conveyed the packet of dispatches

has been identified. TJ obviously took great care to see that its contents (which included also Washington's letter of 17 Dec. 1790 to Gouverneur Morris) escaped the view of the British ministry (see TJ to Maury, 23 Dec. 1790).

V. Secretary of State to Joshua Johnson

DEAR SIR   Philadelphia Dec. 23. 1790.

The vexations of our seamen and their sufferings under the press-gangs of England have become so serious, as to oblige our government to take serious notice of it. The particular case has been selected where the insult to the U.S. has been the most barefaced, the most deliberately intentional, and the proof the most complete. The inclosed letter to you is on that subject, and has been written on the supposition that you would shew the original to the Duke of Leeds and give him a copy of it, but as of your own movement, and not as if officially instructed so to do. You will be pleased to follow up this matter as closely as decency will permit, pressing it in firm but respectful terms on all occasions. We think it essential that Capt. Young's case may be an example to others.— The inclosed letters are important. Be so good as to have them conveyed by the surest means possible. I am with great esteem Dear Sir Your most obedt & most humble servt,

TH: JEFFERSON

RC (Charles H. Collins, Colorado Springs, Colo., 1949). FC (DNA: RG 59, PCC No. 121). Enclosure: Document III and its enclosures.

VI. Secretary of State to James Maury

DEAR SIR   Philadelphia Dec. 23. 1790.

The enclosed letters are of capital importance, and as the ship which carries them goes to your port, I take the liberty of putting them under cover to you, and begging your attention to their being conveyed safely, and clear of the inspection of Government, which I know makes free with foreign letters. Pressed hard to get these despatches ready in time, I leave to your friend Mr. Madison to give you the news if he can find any for you, and shall only add assurances of the sincere esteem and attachment with which I am Dear Sir &c.

FC (DNA: RG 59, PCC No. 121). Enclosures: (1) Documents II, III, and v. (2) Secretary of State to Gouverneur Morris, 17 Dec. 1790.

From David Humphreys

SIR   Madrid Dec. 18th. 1790.

It was not until the 3d of this Month that I was able to obtain my Passports and have every thing in readiness to leave Lisbon; nor until yesterday to arrive here, although I travelled constantly from daylight to dark, making only one stop of about an hour in the middle of the day. After much difficulty, delay and vexation the papers are delivered safely to their Address. I shall not write any thing from this place which I am not willing should be known to this Court, as I am almost certain the letter will be opened in the Post Office, notwithstanding it goes under cover to Mr. Bulkeley Merchant in Lisbon. Hereafter I shall have the honor of explaining myself with more freedom, and in the mean time I have that of being, With every sentiment of respect and esteem, Sir, Your Most obedt. & Most hble. Servt.,

D. HUMPHREYS

P.S. I have just seen the King of G. Britain's Speech to Parliament, in the Leyden Gazette. You will doubtless receive it before this can reach you. The *Convention*, which is printed here on a Single sheet in Spanish and French, is circulated but partially.

RC (DNA: RG 59, DD); at head of text: "(No. 9)"; endorsed by TJ as received 28 Feb. 1791 and so recorded in SJL. FC (DNA: RG 59, DD).

From Robert Patterson

SIR   [Philadelphia] Dec. 18th. 1790.

You will not, I am persuaded, be displeased with any hint, though from one who has not the honour of being personally known to you, which aims at public utility.—

The advantages which must accrue to the community, from the establishment of *uniform weights and measures* throughout the United States, are obvious at first view.—I would beg leave to suggest what appears to me a matter very proper to be connected with the above. I mean some alteration in our Calendar.

There are many weighty reasons why the number of months in the year should continue the same as at present, but none, except that of arbitrary custom, why the number of days in each month should not be as nearly equal as possible. As that matter now stands, a species of injustice is unavoidable, in many of our public as well as private transactions; particularly in the payment of interest, Salaries, house rent, &c. where months, quarters or half years are taken into account. For instance, as much interest is allowed for the month of February of 28 days, as for the month of January, which is more than $\frac{1}{10}$ part longer; and as much salary or house-rent for the first half of the year, as for the second; though, in common years, the one has *three days* less than the other.

This arbitrary inequality among the months has produced another irregularity. The intercalary day, in leap years, is in reality due (so to speak) at the end of the preceding year, and yet the payment is unjustly deferred two months, for the sake of adding it to the short month of February.

The following arrangement appears to me liable to no possible objection, except that of its being an innovation; and this, I apprehend, can have little weight with the people of the United States, who have, in many instances of much greater magnitude, broken off the shackles of former prejudice, and dared to think and act for themselves.

Jany.	30		July	30	
Feby.	31	91	Aug.	31	91
March.	30		Sep.	30	

Apl.	31		Oct.	31	
May.	30	92	Nov.	30	91
June	31		Dec.	30	

In leap years Dec. 31.—And consequently the last quarter 92. According to the above, not only the month, but also the quarters and half years, are as nearly equal among themselves as it is possible for them to be, and the intercalary day, in leap years, is thrown in at the *end* of the year where it ought to be.—

In Europe they have, or have had, their *old stiles*, and *new stiles*, and why may not we have our *American stile*. The addition of A.S. to our dates, till such time as other nations shall adopt the same stile with us, would render our chronology sufficiently inteligible.—I am Sir, with all possible respect your obedt. Servant,   ROBT. PATTERSON

RC (DLC); addressed: "The Honble Thomas Jefferson Esqr. Secretary of State Present"; endorsed as received 18 Dec. 1790 and so recorded in SJL.

From John Parish

SIR   Hamburgh 21st. December 1790

On the 1st. Instant, I had the honour to receive a packet containing Your very obliging favours of the 17th. June and 26th. August accompanying a Commission from the President of the United States appointing me as Their Vice Consul for the Port of Hamburgh.

I am highly sensible of the Honour and preference intended me on the present Occasion, and no less so for the obliging and handsome manner in which You have been pleased to announce this Appointment. It has long been my wish to be named your Consul here; you may therefore suppose the Reluctance with which I am obliged to decline acting under the present Commission. I will explain to You my Reasons.

The maritime powers have all Consuls. They are honorary Appointments, confer'd solely on Merchants residing here, and they appoint their Vice Consuls, who are considered as Subordinate Characters, and generally young men of no importance.

The Senate receive Credentials, only from Consuls; so that although I might have announced to them my Appointment as Vice Consul, they could not, in their Official Capacity, have received it with that Distinction which is shown to Consuls on such an Occasion. And although you have been pleased to explain away the subordinate part of a Vice Consul, still, *here* they are only a kind of Substitute, and no Man of Character known to exercise this function. For those Considerations only, I must beg leave to decline the Appointment, although I am no less impressed with the Sense that it was intended as a Mark of Distinction to me, and I beg the favour of You, Sir, to express these my Sentiments in the most delicate manner to the President, for whose publick and private Virtue the World have so high a Veneration.

It would give me pain, if I thought my present Reasons for declining the Appointment, should not be found to have sufficient Weight; but I hope after the Explanation I have given, You will see their propriety.

That the Publick however may not suffer in the intermediate time, I shall take upon myself the functions of the office, conformable to the Instructions laid down in your letter of the 26th. August and should your Government still be pleased to appoint me as their Consul here, I shall consider it an Honour to act in that Capacity without fee or reward; in which Case, it may be as well to let the Commission run for the free Imperial Cities of Hamburgh, Lubeck and Bremen. They are so contiguous, as easily to be comprehended under one District, and they are invariably Joined in the Consular Appointments here.

Flattering myself with the hopes of an answer I have the honour to subscribe myself most Respectfully Sir Your most obedient & very humble Servant,   J. PARISH

RC (DNA: RG 59); slightly mutilated; at foot of text: "Thomas Jefferson Esqr. [M]inister for Foreign Affairs for [the] United States of America. Philadelphia." Recorded in SJL as received 10 Apr. 1791.

From Benjamin Hawkins

Senate Chamber 22nd decr. 1790

A committee of the Senate are in want of an act of the general assembly of the state of Rhode Island and Providence Plantations passed in Jany. 1790 intituled "An act to incorporate certain persons by the name of the river machine company, in the town of Providence and for other purposes therein mentioned";—An act of the general assembly of the State of Maryland, at their session in april 1783, intituled "An act appointing wardens for the Port of Baltimore town in Baltimore County" One other act passed in novr. 1788 intituled "A suppliment to the act last named;—And also an act of the State of Georgia "for levying and appropriating a duty on tonnage, for the purpose of clearing the river Savannah, and removing the wrecks and other obstructions therein."

If you have all or any of the said acts, I request you send them by the messenger, the bearer of this. Adieu

BENJAMIN HAWKINS

RC (DNA: RG 59, MLR); addressed: "Mr. Jefferson, Secretary of State"; in margin TJ wrote: "If Mr. Remsen has any of these acts he will be pleased to deliver them to the bearer taking his receipt on this letter. Th: J."; at foot of text is the receipt signed by Cornelius Maxwell for "one Law of State of Georgia passed 5 Augt. 1782 and seven others passed in 1784"; below this George Taylor, Jr. noted that these laws were returned on 28 Dec. 1790. Not recorded in SJL.

To George Washington

December 22nd. 1790

Th: Jefferson has the honor to inform the President that his letter to Gouverneur Morris is dated December 17th.—He encloses him a letter from Mr. James Brown just now received.

Tr (DNA: RG 59, SDC).

Washington's inquiry, if in writing, has not been found and neither it nor the above is recorded in SJL. Evidently Washington made the inquiry in order to give his own letter to Morris the same date as that of TJ's letter. See note to Washington to TJ, 11 Dec. 1790.

The enclosed letter from Brown was dated at Danville, Ky., 1 Oct. 1790, and recorded in SJL as received 22 Dec. 1790. It has not been found but undoubtedly was Brown's declination of the office of Attorney for Kentucky. William Murry was appointed to the vacancy on 26 Feb. 1791 (JEP, I, 42, 77; TJ to Murry, 26 Feb. 1791, transmitting commission; Tr in DNA: RG 59, PCC).

To Thomas McKean

SIR   Philadelphia December 23d. 1790.

As you have been so friendly as to transmit to the President of the U.S. the papers of Philip Wilson, I take the liberty of availing myself of the same channel to convey to him the opinion of the Attorney general in answer to his application. I do this the rather as not knowing how to address to him. I have the honour to be with real marks of the highest respect & esteem Sir Your most obedt. & most humble servt,   TH: JEFFERSON

PrC (DLC); at foot of text: "the honble. T. McKain." Enclosures not found.

On 21 Dec. 1790 Tobias Lear wrote TJ: "By the President's Command, T. Lear has the honor to enclose to the Secretary of State the report of the Attorney General upon the papers of Philip Wilson, and respectfully to suggest to the Secretary of State whether it would not be proper to transmit a copy of the report, together with the papers, either to Judge McKean, through whom Mr. Wilson's papers were forwarded to the President, or to Mr. Wilson himself. And in case they should be transmitted, that the Secretary of State would, as to him appears most proper, either send them from himself or return them to be sent from the President" (RC in DLC, endorsed by TJ; Dft in DNA: RG 59, MLR, written by Lear on verso of address-leaf bearing in TJ's hand: "The President of the United States"; not recorded in SJL).

The PAPERS returned by TJ concerned the American ship *Mentor*, built and owned by Philip Wilson, a Philadelphia merchant and American citizen then residing in London. *Mentor* was pursued, run ashore, and destroyed on the Delaware coast near Cape Henlopen by two British ships, *Centurion* and *Vulture*. This occurred on 1 Apr. 1783, after the period set for the cessation of hostilities, and Wilson in 1785 petitioned the British government for reparation to the extent of about £18,000. William Scott, King's Advocate-General, ruled and a committee of the Privy Council agreed that the claim was valid. But no settlement was made and in 1788 a suit brought by Wilson against the captain of *Centurion* was dismissed by the High Court of Ad-

miralty (Wharton, *Dipl. Corr.*, VI, 96-9, 224, 251, 252, 258; *Mentor*, 165 *English reports* 141 [1799]; J. B. Moore, *International adjudications* [New York, 1931], IV, 192; Pinckney to Grenville, 8 June 1793, enclosed in Pinckney to TJ, 27 Aug. 1793). Wilson thereupon sought American assistance, appealing first to Thomas McKean, Chief Justice of Pennsylvania. "The reason of Mr. Wilson's application to me," McKean wrote in forwarding the petition to the President, "respecting an affair I never before heard of, I cannot tell, unless he believes that from a little knowledge I had of his seeming, if not real attachment to the American Revolution, I would interest myself in his behalf, or that humanity would urge me to it. He had two brothers, officers in the British Army during the war, and yet appeared to be anxious for our success, and I believe was active, tho' particulars have escaped my recollection. He has no other claim upon me" (McKean to Washington, 12 July 1790, PHi: McKean Papers, enclosing letter from Wilson to McKean, Westminster, 11 Mch. 1790, not found). Randolph's opinion evidently indicated that the appeal lay properly to the British government. But Wilson continued to seek American assistance. He wrote several letters to Washington which the President turned over to the Secretary of State. Assuming that similar cases might arise, TJ instructed the American minister in London to make the matter an official concern. Pinckney, moved by Wilson's acute distress and by his refusal to accept a settlement of £2,000 offered on grounds of compassion, arranged a loan of £100 and otherwise confused the issue by urging that Congress afford temporary relief. His discussions with Grenville were without result (TJ to Pinckney, 11 June 1792; 16 Mch. and 4 June 1793; Pinckney to TJ, 29 Aug., 5 Oct., 9 Nov., and 13 Dec. 1792, enclosing Wilson to TJ, 3 Dec. 1792; and 27 Aug. 1793, enclosing Pinckney to Grenville, 8 June 1793; Washington to Secretary of State, 18 July 1796, *Writings*, ed. Fitzpatrick, xxxv, 145). See also Wilson to TJ, 16 July 1791; 28 Nov. 1791; and 28 Mch. 1792.

Living in dire need in London and having legally declared himself a pauper, Wilson petitioned the King asking that the powers of the Commissioners to settle American claims be enlarged so as to admit an investigation of that of *Mentor*. His wife also joined in the affecting plea to the English authorities. Both appeals were unavailing (Wilson's petitions to the King, 8 Mch. 1796, 7 Dec. 1797, and Mch. 1798; Wilson to Stephen Cottrell, Secretary to the Privy Council, 14 Dec. 1797, 26 and 28 Apr. 1798; printed *Declaration and case of Philip Wilson*, 8 p. [London], 1797; Cottrell to Wilson, 22 Dec. 1797; and six letters of Mrs. Eleanor Wilson, Feb.-Apr. 1798, all in unbound papers of the Privy Council, PRO: PC 1/41).

In 1797 and again in 1798 Wilson also petitioned Congress for relief and indemnification, but with similar lack of success. In 1798 he brought suit against Admiral Digby, commander of the British squadron on the American station at the time *Mentor* was destroyed. Scott, now judge of the High Court of Admiralty, was obviously moved by compassion for the plaintiff. But he found it unprecedented that a suit brought against one of the captors, dismissed, and not appealed should have been followed ten years later by another against "a person totally ignorant

of the whole transaction." He lamented that Wilson's "distress of fortune prevented him for proceeding further" in the case against the captain of *Centurion*, but ruled that to hold Digby responsible would be contrary "to every principle of law and justice by which the proceedings of this Court have been directed, ever since it has borne the shape of an established Court of Justice" (*Mentor*, 165 *English reports*, 141-3 [5 Feb. 1799]). Wilson then returned to the United States, being again in Philadelphia early in 1801 (SJL entry for 28 Mch. 1801 shows that TJ received a letter from him [missing], dated there 25 Mch. 1801). He began a long and equally unsuccessful effort to obtain compensation from the American government for commodities seized in 1778 for use of the army. His petition on this claim was before Congress constantly from 1805 until his death about 1811, when his widow and son took up the matter and pursued it at least until 1838. They were no more successful than he had been (see JHR for 4th, 5th, 6th, 7th, 8th, 9th, 10th, 11th, 23rd, and 24th Congresses; JS for 4th, 5th, and 11th Congresses; *Annals*, VII, 504, 508; XXII, 102-3).

From an early period of life Wilson had "made the stepping of Masts, and form of Vessels for Fast Sailing" his special study. But in 1802 when he offered the results to the United States government for naval use, his presentation was unfortunately ironic. *Mentor* had not been able to outrun *Centurion* and *Vulture*, but it was "the pursuit of *Superior Velocity*, in the Sailing of Shipping," this hapless student of naval architecture wrote, that "caused me to build that Ship" (Wilson to TJ, 13 and 15 Apr. 1802).

From Robert Powell and Charles Fierer

HOND. SIR   George town the 23th Dec 1790

Pardon us Sir, for the Liberty we take in Addressing you on a Subject which has already put us under many Obligations to you and which will always be Remembered with the utmost Gratitude. When we last had the Honor of Conversing with you on the Subject Respecting the Establishment of a Glas Manufactory in the State of Virginia, we had a Prospect of Raising a Sufficiant

Sum of Money for that purpose, by disposing of a part of our real property; in this negotiation (though then shure of Success) we have however failed, and sooner than we expected received twelve Manufactorers which, with a considerable expence we procured in diferent parts of Europe, and for which we have now to pay £20 a piece for their passage, the difficulty of procuring Money in this Country on a Short notice, the danger we are in of keeping our hands unemployed for a long time, or perhaps of loosing them altogether Obliges us to fall upon the inclosed plan to raise the Sum which would enable us to Compleat the works we have begun with a promising prospect.

We are Conscious Sir, that business of this kind do not come with in the limits of the department over which you preside, but we hope from favors already received you will Condecent to be the protector of an undertaking which in a further day may prove beneficial to our Country.

As the Success of our Plan for raising this Sum by Subscription must all together depend upon the reception it meets with from the first Characters of the State of Virginia now Assembled at Philadelphia we humbly beg you Sir, to continue your good wishes towards our undertaking in this critical moment.

Should the Presedent and yourself honor the paper with your names there would (agreeable to the Opinion of our friends in Virginia) be no doubt of Success. Mr Roger West a Neighbor and Acquaintance of the President is one of the Security for the repaiment of the Money. He has wrote to Mr. Lee in Congress on the Subject and promises to Compleat the work if we should meet with some Success in Philadelphia.

Since we had the honor of Seeing you last we have moved our hands on the land we purchased and begun to build, and have no doubt Should we Succeed in raising the Money in Question, to put two furnaces to work by the first day of April next. Mr Nicols continues a friend to our undertaking as well as the Inhabitance on James River.

We beg you will be pleased to favor us, as soon as Convenient, with an answer Addressed to Charles Fierer in George town. We have the honor to remain with the utmost respect Your most O'b & Humb Servants,   ROBERT POWELL

              CHARLES FIERER

RC (MHi); endorsed by TJ as received 30 Dec. but recorded in SJL under 28 Dec. 1790. Enclosure: A printed prospectus for raising "a Sum of Money by Subscription . . . to compleat the Glass-Works . . . begun

on James-river," which Powell & Fierer wrote to inquire about on 26 Jan.
1791 (Powell & Fierer to TJ, 26 Jan.

1791, RC in MHi; endorsed by TJ as
received 29 Jan. 1791 and so recorded
in SJL).

To Martha Jefferson Randolph

MY DEAR DAUGHTER   Philadelphia Dec. 23. 1790.

This is a scolding letter for you all. I have not recieved a scrip
of a pen from home since I left it which is now eleven weeks.
I think it so easy for you to write me one letter every week, which
will be but once in three weeks for each of you, when I write one
every week who have not one moment's repose from business from
the first to the last moment of the week. Perhaps you think you have
nothing to say to me. It is a great deal to say you are all well, or
that one has a cold, another a fever &c., besides that there is not
a sprig of grass that shoots uninteresting to me, nor any thing
that moves, from yourself down to Bergere or Grizzle. Write
then my dear daughter punctually on your day, and Mr. Randolph
and Polly on theirs. I suspect you may have news to tell me of
yourself of the most tender interest to me. Why silent then?

I am still without a house, and consequently without a place to
open my furniture. This has prevented my sending you what I
was to send for Monticello. In the mean time the river is frozen up
so as that no vessel can get out, nor probably will these two months:
so that you will be much longer without them than I had hoped.
I know how inconvenient this will be and am distressed at it; but
there is no help. I send a pamphlet for Mr. Randolph. My best
affections to him, Polly, & yourself. Adieu my dear,

TH: JEFFERSON

RC (NNP).

BERGERE and GRIZZLE were shepherd
dogs. At Le Harve TJ had purchased
a bitch "big with pups" and these were
the survivors. For a comment on Berg-
ère's intelligence, see Randall, *Life*,
II, 15n. The fact that TJ suspected
"news . . . of the most tender interest"
shows that he had observed but had not
discussed Martha's pregnancy during
the autumn. His first grandchild, Anne
Cary Randolph, was born in February
and the news of her birth gave him
intense pleasure (TJ to Martha Randolph, 9 Feb. 1791).—TJ had been
absent less than seven weeks.

From William Short

DEAR SIR   Amsterdam Dec. 23. 1790.

I wrote to you on the 26th. ulto. by the way of the English
packet, and the 2d. inst. by an American vessel which sailed from

this place for Boston. This letter inclosed one for the Secretary of the Treasury, in which I entered into a very lengthy and full detail of several subjects about which he wished to be informed. A duplicate of it has been waiting some time for the departure of another vessel which has been long intending to sail for the United States. Other letters will also go by it for the Secretary of the treasury, as the delay will enable me to add to that already written for this conveyance. I have thought it better to send his letters by this route than by the way of England.

The journals of the national assembly which you will receive regularly by the way of Havre will inform you of the progress of their business. The rapid and successful sales of ecclesiastical property have given a considerable rise to public credit, accelerated the circulation of money and given an air of contentment and prosperity.

The collection of taxes also is become more successful; but the slow advances made towards the finishing of the constitution, the delays which have already taken place and those which are foreseen from the accumulation of business in the assembly, and the facility with which they suffer themselves to be diverted from their main object in order to enter into business of detail; are causes of serious uneasiness to the best informed and best intentioned. It is certain that a majority of the assembly have no desire to separate. This majority is composed of men of different characters and principles, and who desire the continuation of the session from different motives—the ambitious of the popular party who feel that they could in no case govern more despotically—the timorous of the same party who think the present assembly necessary to keep under the enemies of the revolution—the ruined who desire to secure eighteen livres a day to live on—the curates to whom it is necessary to put them at their ease, and the Bishops who have need of it in addition to the pittance allowed them, and who are exempted also during the session from a residence in their bishopricks, at all times disagreeable to them and now insupportable. To these may be added such as see that the continuance of the present assembly is postponing the organisation of government, and who hope that anarchy will disgust the nation against the new system. All parties accuse each other of wishing to delay the completion of constitution, and they are probably all grounded in their accusations.

The Marquis de la fayette and a small number well disposed, well informed and much attached to his principles, wish really to see the present assembly voluntarily separated. He is pursued with much bitterness and hatred by the leaders of the club *des Jacobins,* and the pamphleteers of their party. This gives him the favor in some degree, of the court, but takes from him entirely that of the people, I mean the lowest class of people.

The conduct of the people of that order at Brussels, who from being the most tempestuous supporters of Vander Noot, changed in a few days so as that he was obliged to make his escape to avoid their fury, and who received with open arms the Austrian troops, gave such encouragement to the discontented French who are at Turin that they urged the Count d'Artois and the princes there to enter France immediately at the head of such as would join them. It is thought that the Prince of Condé was of the same opinion. They had agents at Lyons with whom they kept up communication for this purpose. Some of these are arrested, and I am informed by a letter from Paris of the 16th. inst. that the *comité des recherches* were that day to be put in possession of the papers relative to this affair. It is possible it may turn out like many others, meer suspicion which an ignorant or overzealous municipality has magnified into a conspiracy. There is no doubt however of such a plan having been agitated by the Princes and their followers at Turin, and I am well informed from Paris that the Queen took every possible step to deter them from it. It was cause of much uneasiness at court and particularly to the King and Queen. The latter would in such a case be in very real danger, as she is still very obnoxious to the people and their leaders, and considered by them though unjustly, as the soul of all the efforts made against the revolution.

I am informed by the Secretary whom I left at Paris, that the subject of tobacco will be probably discussed about this time in the assembly. He is a well-informed man and enjoys very much the confidence of the Mis. de la f———. By his means I have kept the interests of the U.S. fully in view of the committees since my absence.—You know the question of tobacco was recommitted to the committee of impositions as mentioned in a former letter. This was something gained for us as it was a defeat of their first plan.

I mentioned to you also what had been concerted with the diplomatick committee previous to my departure from Paris. The committee of impositions is now disposed to be still more favorable than the diplomatick committee—viz. to subject the importation of tobacco only to a duty of 2s. 6. deniers a pound. I do not know whether they will make this report but the leading members are for it. They are for approximating as much as possible the second part of the plan which I proposed to them, of admitting the tobacco without duty for the reasons mentioned to you in my No. 46.

With respect to the other branches of our commerce also affairs have taken a much more favorable turn since the conferences mentioned to have taken place previous to my departure. The great object was to remove prejudices and to bring their attention to dwell on the subject, which is no easy matter in the present crisis where there are so many more immediate and pressing interests to attend to.

The plan proposed and which there are hopes of passing, is to continue the dispositions of the *arrêt du conseil* of Dec. 87. for the present. They will probably change the title, and perhaps strike out the clause which suppressed the *10. sous par livre* that were to cease at the end of this month. Every thing will be done however to confirm this suppression and particularly by Dupont who is a warm supporter of the arrêt which he considers as his offspring. He had however abandoned it for a long time, and allowed the committee of commerce to strangle it without interfering. From being a violent economist he had passed for some time no body knows why into the most exclusive system.

You will have seen by the papers that the disturbances in the French islands and particularly Martinique have induced the assembly to decree the sending commissaries with extensive powers for settling these disturbances, and also ships of war with troops. They repent now having given their colonies so much latitude in the formation of their government. Every step they take respecting them at present will be dictated by ill-humour.

The report for explaining and extending the decree concerning the droit d'aubaine passed the committee of domains unanimously some time ago, but it has not yet been produced to the assembly because it is connected with other matters and that no opportunity of introducing the report has presented itself. This is what M. de Vieuzac the reporter of the committee informs me. He is sure there will be no difficulty and promises to present the report the first moment possible.

You have seen long ago the articles of pacification between England and Spain. They seem highly agreeable to Parliament where the Minister, as was foreseen carries every thing before him. The disarming is only to be partial. The debates and the silence of the Minister seem to confirm the opinion that he means to interfere in the spring in the quarrel between Russia and the Porte, if a peace should not take place this winter. Indeed it is impossible that the allies of the Porte can remain longer inactive if they mean to prevent the Empress of Russia extending her conquests to Constantinople. She has already possession of the mouth of the Danube so as to cut off all communication between the black sea and Ismailow—against which place her next attack was intended, and of which she has probably possession before this time.

It is said that the cabinet of St. James is displeased with the dilatory decisions of that of Berlin. It is believed also that a good deal of division exists in the Ministry of the latter.—It is certain that from some cause or other the triple alliance has had much less effect on the affairs of Europe than was expected after the negotiations of Reichenbach.

The affairs of Brabant are terminated certainly against the wishes of the three powers. Their ministers at the Hague signed and presented to the Imperial Ambassador a kind of protestation, which is considered by some as a proof of want of candor and by all as a want of success in their business. The Imperial domination has been every where re-established there to the great joy of all parties except that of Van der Noot and Van Eupen. They had exercised such acts of despotism and cruelty by means of the priests and populace as revolted every body.

The Vonckists, who were for independence and an equal representation in the beginning, and of whom the chiefs had been forced to fly the country, were the only party whose principles were good. They now submit with alacrity to the Imperial government in order to get rid of an aristocratical theocracy supported by bigotry, ignorance and popular fury.

The manner in which this counter-revolution has been effected does much honor to the Count de Mercy, and to the Maréchal Bender who commanded the troops, subject to Count de Mercy's instructions. He is expected here to-morrow on his way to Brussels where he will govern, as it is said during the absence of the former *Gouverneurs-generaux*.

The last advices from the East-Indies shew that Tippo Saib has become very troublesome to the British company. It is thought they will be obliged to go into a serious war with him. This is considered more inconvenient than alarming, as it will prevent ministry receiving such aid from the company as was expected.

Parliamentary debates however, to which I refer you for the minister's plan for covering the expences of the late armament, will in time throw more light on the real situation of East-India affairs.

Nothing new has turned up respecting the business on which I came here since my last. Every thing however promises very fairly and the success then mentioned seems to me out of doubt.

M. Du fresne has said nothing against the mode of paying the latter part of the sum intended to be remitted as mentioned in a former letter. He has acknowledged the receipt of it, and the French bankers here say every body was perfectly satisfied.

The report of this payment has been made to the national assembly by the committee which produced the estimates for the next year, in which this is calculated. It has been stated at different sums by different papers. The true state however is as I mentioned formerly 3,600,000.[tt]

The bankers of the U.S. have received the letter of the Secretary of the Treasury of Nov. 3. My last from him was of Sep. 1. He intended then forwarding me other papers which have not yet come to my hands, but I have as yet had no occasion for them. I beg you to be fully assured of the sentiments of attachment & respect with which I have the honor to be, Dear Sir, Your obedient servant,

W: SHORT

Tr (DNA: RG 59, DD); at head of text: "No. 50. W. Short to the Secty of State." Recorded in SJL as received 12 Mch. 1791.

The SECRETARY whom Short left in Paris was one Raymond. Because of his activities with the committees and especially that of Roederer on tobacco, Governeur Morris regarded him as "a sophistical cunning fellow" and did not know at first that he was Short's secretary (Morris, *Diary*, ed. Davenport, II, 117, 133). When he learned that Short had engaged him, he wrote Robert Morris: "This Mr. Raymond is I am told a young man of Genius, and one on whom Lafayette greatly relies *even for advice.* He is by Birth an Alsatian, but has long resided in this City. He employed himself busily in going about to the various Committees and supposed that he was doing wondrously well; but all this little under work is not worth a farthing, and so Experience has shewn, for in every Instance where our Interests were concerned the Decrees have gone against us" (G. Morris to R. Morris, 13 Mch. 1791, NhHi; Tr through courtesy of E. James Ferguson).

From William Short

DEAR SIR   Amsterdam Dec. 23. 1790

This letter accompanying my No. 50. will be sent by the English packet. By your desire I make use of this conveyance, although from hence it is a very uncertain one as the weather at this season of the year frequently keeps the mail several days at Helvoetsluys and thus prevents letters arriving in time for the Packet. I fear this was the fate of mine of Nov. 26.

I have lately recieved from Paris your letter of Sep. 6. from Philadelphia inclosing a bill of exchange for 589. ℔6s. and a letter for Mr. Fenwick. I read it agreeably to your desire and forwarded it to him with advice that I would accept and pay at sight his bill for the disbursements and charges respecting the wine. No delay can therefore arise on that score. I have already advice of the Champaign you had ordered being already recieved at Havre, and I hope it is now on the sea. I have advice also that the Mis. de la fayette's picture is finished and I have directed it to be sent also to Havre. The price is 16. guineas for the painting, 3½ for the gilt frame; and 12.ᵗ for box and packing. The painter is Boze, who I think has taken by far the best likenesses of the Marquis.

Your letter of the 30th. of Sep. from Monticello arrived here a few days ago by the vessel from N. York. You will easily believe that it has made me repent having abandoned myself so entirely to the impressions under which I wrote one of the letters to which that is an answer. I repent it the more sincerely because I find these impressions were lasting and that several other letters have been written to you by me under their influence. They will continue dropping in upon you from time to time when you are perhaps by no means in a disposition of mind to recieve such letters. I wish most sincerely for that reason they had never been written. It is too late now to recall them or I would do it with all my heart. All that I can do is to beg you will excuse so much importunity, and obliterate it from your memory. I am the more excusable for having so far *forgotten my countrymen* that all the Americans at Paris and some of those in London had fallen into the same forgetfulness and reasoned on that subject as I had done. I might add to them a number of others of other countries but I agree that their mode of reasoning is no example for Americans. I mention this therefore merely as an excuse for what is considered as a forgetfulness. For had I been right in the first supposition the letters I wrote in consequence of it would appear perfectly excusable to all those who know the unbounded confidence with which your friendship had long accustomed me to unfold the most retired thoughts of my mind. As it is therefore I can only beg you to consider the importunate parts of such of my letters as may come to your hands as if they had never been written. It is a new proof to me that it is always wrong to act or write under first impressions. There is one circumstance however in which I certainly cannot be wrong, and of which of course you will allow me to correct you—that is, your opinion that every day increases my attachment to Europe, and renders my future reconcilement to my country more desperate. I feel too strongly the contrary not to assert it with all the sincerity of my heart. I should certainly quit Europe with less reluctance now than a year or two ago, and my reconcilement to my country is an expression which I cannot admit since that would suppose a kind of coolness. On the contrary it is my sincere and devout wish to be there. It has been long my desire to be settled there agreeably to my wishes, and if this had been within my power my absence from thence would have been of a much shorter duration than it has been. Until that does take place I shall consider myself as a traveller and look with a longing eye towards my native home. Could I suppose possible what you seem to think as certain two years hence in the case of my being in America, I declare with the certainty of unerring conviction that I would prefer it to any appointment in Europe. Yet I cannot suppose that a preference would be given to me over such a number of candidates as will certainly present themselves. There is nothing on this side of the Atlantic that I would not quit for it with joy and alacrity.

What you desire me to mention to Tolozan and Sequeville was under the idea that I should be at Paris. Your letter and that of the Secretary of the Treasury directed my staying here three months. It is in conformity to them that I shall not return to Paris before the latter part of Febry, unless called there by business. It will probably therefore not be till after you shall have written me the result of your conversation with the President, that I shall speak to them. You may be assured however that they will neither of them accept the present but on the condition of your doing the same.

The difficulty respecting the house has been removed, as I already informed you by Langeac's agreeing to what he said was verbal between you and him. The congé had been delayed somewhat by these difficulties, but his brother accepted it conditionally. After Langeac's removing the difficulty as his brother insisted on the doctrine of the term, and was confirmed by Mr. Grand and others, I agreed it should count from it. This was July 15. The house however was put into his possession in Nov. although the six months additional do not expire till Jan. 7. You were obliged to deliver the house in the condition you received it. Mr. Grand thought it would be best to have examined and valued such things as were to be done and to pay the money. You know you had no *etat de la maison*. Of course it was necessary to be guided by the one they produced—with which the examination was made and attended by Petit. The estimation after deducting the bars and bells you had put to the windows, and remise doors which they took at evaluation, amounted to I think about 1300. This was examined also by Mr. Grands architect and approved by him, and the sum paid to Mr. Langeac. Mr. Grand paid it and charged it (with the house rent, as you had desired) to Congress.

Petit has gone to Champagne. He persisted in his determination of not going for the wages proposed. I think it very probable that Mde. de Corny's Maitre d'hotel will be glad to go if he is not placed of which I think there is little probability. I will have the enquiry made which you desire. I will thank you however to mention precisely what terms you would be willing to give. I have just learned that De Cornis is dead—his death said to be owing more to mental than corporeal disorder. His fortune shattered by the revolution was the cause of it.

You say my brother was well when you last heard from Kentuckey. I have not heard of or from him since his projected scheme of going down the Mississipi, and I begin to be uneasy about him.—Humphreys wrote me when he first arrived in London. I know not what has become of him since. I hear that Franklin has arrived there also.

I shall forward my account, settled up to July 1. by the vessel which will sail from hence for America, and at the same time add mine with you balanced and of which I shall receive the amount here. You desired two gold medals to be struck of which one was for M. de la Luzerne, the other to be sent to America with the dye. As I suppose one will be wanted for De Moustier also I have directed three to be struck. It will remain with M. Grand for your orders. I suppose the dye is finished about this time. M. de la Luzerne has written me to enquire about this medal and seems to be much flattered with recieving it. I have directed it to be hurried as much as possible. Adieu my dear Sir & believe me most sincerely your friend & servant, W: SHORT

I have directed several pamphlets to be sent you with the papers from Paris—one respecting an uniform standard by a man of letters—one on *monnoies* by Mirabeau—and one on coinage by the Bishop of Autun. Appleton has written to me to beg I would write to you and the Secretary of the Treasury in support of his application as Consul for Lisbon. It is merely to discharge my promise to him, and because it is more easy to write than to explain to him and make him concieve that neither the one or the other will have any influence on the appointment that I trouble you on this subject. I had told him before my leaving Paris that my letter would be of no use; but I could not even make him believe that. The application will be made by his father.

RC (DLC); at head of text; "*Private*"; endorsed as received 12 Mch. 1791 and so recorded in SJL. PrC (DLC: Short Papers).

The pamphlet by the MAN OF LETTERS was Rigobert Bonne's *Principes sur les mesures en longueur et en capacité*, of which the author had already sent TJ a copy (see Bonne to TJ, 27 Oct. 1790, note). Another was Mirabeau's *De la constitution monétaire. Précédé d'observations sur le Rapport du Comité des Monnoies, et suivi d'un projet de lois monétaires* (Paris, 1790). The pamphlet by the BISHOP OF AUTUN was Talleyrand-Périgord's *Opinion . . . sur la fabrication des petites monnoies* (Paris, 1790), printed

by order of the National Assembly. See Sowerby, Nos. 3584, 3585.

Short's papers contain various letters about repairs to Hotel de Langeac and termination of TJ's lease (Grandpierre to Short, 31 July 1790; De Langeac to Grand, 15 Nov. 1790; Grand to Short, 20 Nov. 1790; and Short to Grand, 28 Nov. 1790). For a reproduction of the portrait of Lafayette by Boze, see Vol. 5: 185. It has been generally supposed that only two examples of the gold diplomatic medal were struck and indeed TJ had directed this, one for presentation to La Luzerne and one to be given to Moustier (see Vol. 16: xli). But the above letter shows that Short directed a third to be struck and left with Grand.

From Hugh Williamson

SIR   Chamber of Congress 23rd Decr. 1790.

William H. Hill of the County of New Hanover in the State of N: C: is the Gentleman who was recommended to the President for Attorney by sundry of the Representatives from that State. A Letter for him goes by the Wilmington Mail.—I have the Honour to be Sir Your most obedt. servt.,

Hu WILLIAMSON

RC (DLC); endorsed by TJ as received 23 Dec. 1790 and so recorded in SJL.

Hill was actually nominated by Washington on the 17th and confirmed by the Senate on the 20th (JEP, I, 64). The letter was probably one urging

him to accept. At the same time, on the recommendation of Benjamin Hawkins, Washington nominated John Sitgreaves as judge for the district of North Carolina (Hawkins to Washington, 4 Nov. 1790, DNA: RG 59, MLR; JEP, I, 63).

Gaetano Drago to George Washington

Genoa, 24 Dec. 1790. He had applied to the Congress for consulship at Genoa. "Several friends of Mr. Peter [i.e., Pierce] Butler a Member of the Congress, who are also mine had made me hope that under his Auspices Corroborated by your Excellencies Authority I could hope to obtain my Intent." Encloses his petition and hopes to serve "without any view of Interest, your New Rising Republic" because appointment of a representative there would advance its commerce and also "the probability of making a Truce with the Barbary Regencies by means of a Contribution far inferior to the advantages that would accrue from a free Navigation." Should his appeal be read by "a Person the most Worthy and well deserving of Liberty and the Most Respectable in the Annals of Our Age," he would regard it as one of the happiest events of his life.

RC (DLC: Washington Papers); addressed: "The Most Illustrious General Washington President of the Most Honorable Congress at Philadelphia"; endorsed by TJ as received 30 June 1791 and so recorded in SJL. Enclosure: Drago's petition to "The Most Illustrious and Most Honorable Congress," Genoa, 4 May 1789, applying for appointment as consul "on the encouragement of a Worthy Merchant of Boston" [Richard Codman] and stating: "Our Republick which receives with pleasure the Representatives of all Powers would look with pleasure on a Minister of the New State, the Republican Constitution of which has so much Analogy with its own" (same).

Drago had previously sent a copy of his petition to TJ, whom he met briefly at Genoa in 1787 (Drago to TJ, 4 May and 22 June 1789). Later he sent a copy of the same petition to the American consul at Liverpool, James Maury, having procured an introduction "through some particular friends" at that place. He claimed that Maury promised to sponsor his candidacy, but when nothing happened he again turned to Pierce Butler, despite the warning of the latter and others that his foreign birth interposed an obstacle. Indeed, he presumed there would be some "expense of Office fees . . . in procuring the Commission, &ca." and he authorized Butler to disburse such costs to the extent of £50 to £60 sterling and draw on him at Amsterdam for the advance (Drago to Butler, 30 July 1790, DLC: Washington Papers). See also Drago to TJ, 11 Mch. and 13 July 1793. There is no evidence that TJ made any direct response to these persistent appeals.

From Matthew McAllister

SIR   Savannah December 24th. 1790

It has given me some pain that I have not been able to procure and forward the proceedings and laws required by your favor of the 12th. of August last earlier. This delay I hope may be attributed principally to two causes—the difficulty in making the collection required, here—and the distance between this place and the Seat of our Government. The volume of State Laws you will herewith receive have been picked up from individuals, with some assistance from my own set. They are not to be procured at any one place or office. There are but few Acts wanting to make this Vol. a complete set of the State Laws. All that have any relation to the business in question I beleive are contained in it.

The Statutes not in print I have not been able to get copies of, but have added a list of them. I did not thing it adviseable to have them bound which could be done when the remaining acts were collected.

Very soon after the receipt of your Letter I did myself the honor to write by Captn. Carpenter via New York stating some difficulties and requesting a little information. The Captain has returned and tells me that he believes a Mr. Fisher Merchant of that place took the Letter and promised to deliver it, a copy of which is inclosed. The Executive proceedings relative to the business are marked No. 2.—The Judiciary Decisions No. 3.—Some Affidavits No. 4.

From the general terms of one part of your Letter, I have taken the liberty Sir to make and transmit such a statement of the business and have offered such remarks pro and con as occurred marked No. 1. Persuaded at the same time of it's deficiency, and trespassing perhaps unnecessarily on the indulgence, by it will be perceived the number of Cannon taken here and at Sunbury in this State by the British Troops, and by Major Habersham's Certificate No. 5. the quantity left when they evacuated this State.

Any number of Affidavits similar to the inclosed may be obtained if necessary.—The papers do not go forward under the highest proof of their authenticity, should it be necessary, it can be easily done on notice.—You will be pleased to fill up the blanks in the inclosed account as may appear just and reasonable, some small charges against me are inclosed—a draft on the Collector here will answer, or on the Treasury as may be most convenient. The Bearer of this, My Brother, will wait on you with the Papers. —I have the honor to be with great respect Sir, Your most obedient & most Hble Servant,   MATT. McALLISTER

RC (DNA: RG 360, PCC No. 76); endorsed by TJ as received 29 Mch. 1791 and so recorded in SJL. None of the enclosures has been found save three receipts covering the "small charges" for procuring copies of Georgia statutes (same, p. 169). See TJ to Temple, 11 Aug. 1790, and enclosures.

From Gouverneur Morris

DEAR SIR   London 24 December 1790

I did not receive your Letter of the twelfth of August untill Yesterday Afternoon or I should have made an earlier Reply. I am very happy to find that you approve of the Ground on which the InterChange of Ministers with this Country was placed and the Judgment formed Respecting the Posts. I am led to fear that my Conduct in Regard to our impressed Seamen has not been equally fortunate, but I hope the Interference will be excused. Having no other Guide than my own Sense of our Interest and Honor it is not improbable that I may have missed my Way. It was with much Anxiety that I took any one of those Steps to which I found myself impelled.

My Letters to the President subsequent to the Month of May will have communicated my Conduct and the Opinions by which it was directed. I flatter myself that on the Subject of an Alliance with this Country they will be found conformable to the Sentiments which you express and which will ever I hope govern the Councils of our Country.

It was my good fortune also to anticipate your Ideas respecting the Designs of Britain upon the Spanish Possessions, and therefore whenever they mentioned to me the Claims of Spain as highly interesting to us, I declared (but as my private Opinion only) that we should view those Claims of exclusive Right with perfect Indifference from a Conviction that it never would be exercised to our Prejudice. This was with the double View of keeping up their Disquietude about Connections which we might form with Spain, and of preventing them from having any Shadow of Pretext to embroil us with that Court hereafter, should the existing Dispute be amicably adjusted.

Before I dismiss this Subject, indulge me with your Pardon for hinting an Idea on which I have formed no decisive opinion, but which may perhaps merit some Consideration. Spain from the Situation of France, the Sense of her own Weakness, and the Effects of her late Treaty with Britain, may perhaps wish for an effectual Guarantee of her transatlantic Dominions; and perhaps she may deem that which we can give more important than what Britain holds out. Perhaps she might incline to give Something valuable for our Friendship and Protection.

The Convention between Britain and Spain having been compleated, and a Bill for the Government of Quebec being in Agitation, I thought it might be well to pass a few Days here: and therefore having private Business sufficient to prevent the drawing of any direct Conclusions of a public Nature, I came hither on Sunday the twelfth Instant. I made the needful Enquiries respecting the Quebec System, and on the fourteenth called at Whitehall. The Duke of Leeds being absent, I left a Card and on the eighteenth paid his Grace another Visit. The Council was then breaking up, and as he had much to do, he sent Mr. Burgess to me with an Apology. This Gentleman gave me a Deal of civil Nothingness. Was glad that our Difficulties about the Impress were at an End. Had during my Absence received frequent Applications from Mr. Cutting, and in Consequence of what passed between us had paid every Attention to them. Administration had every Desire I could wish for Treaty. Many Cabinet Councils had been held upon it. A great many Difficulties had arisen in fixing on the Persons to whom the Management should be committed. This Matter however was adjusted. A Reference had been made, above three Months since, to Lord Hawkesbury. His Lordship very diligent, but his Report not yet made. When received no Time would be lost in setting all the different Engines at Work. Hoped we should soon have Residents with each other &ca. &ca. &ca. I heard him quietly out, and then replied that I was sorry to have interrupted his Attention to other Affairs. Having been called by private Business to London I thought it my Duty to let them know I was alive. If his Grace wished to see me I would wait on him at such Time as he might indicate. My Stay here would be short. I should write to America before my Departure, and if I learnt Nothing more than that things remained in the same State of Uncertainty in which I had left them I should say so. It was for them and not for me to consider what Consequences Delay might produce to the british Commerce.

The Reputation of the United States rises fast, and altho our Enemies make Objections to the funding System, yet that step towards the Establishment of public Credit has produced a sensible Effect on those opinions which no Administration will wholly disregard.

FC (DLC: Gouverneur Morris Papers); at head of text: "Thomas Jefferson Esqr. Public." Recorded in SJL as received 12 Mch. 1791. For comment on this letter, see Editorial Note on commercial and diplomatic relations with Great Britain, under 15 Dec. 1790.

From Gouverneur Morris

DEAR SIR London 24 December 1790

Your Letter of the twelfth of August was highly pleasing to me, among other Reasons because it releived me from a painful Situation. I wished to have expressed to you my Congratulations on your safe Arrival, and on the domestic Event which shortly succeeded. I wished also to express to you as an American my Satisfaction with your official Appointment, and as a Man my Esteem Respect and Affection. The Presidents Letter to me prevented all this. I could not write to you and not mention the Course of the Business, and I could not write to you about the Business without appearing to assume a diplomatic Existence. This may have been a false Delicacy, but this is the Fact. I will not now pester you with Professions of Regard, but on every proper Occasion I expect to shew that I am not wholly unworthy of your friendly Notice.

When I was last in England Mr. Cutting applied to me for a Loan of Money, having he said been put to great Expence in the liberating of impressed Americans. I told him I would lend Money to Nobody, because I would not hurt the Feelings of any of my Countrymen by a particular Refusal, and had been obliged to reject already some Applications of that Sort. I told him farther that the regular and proper Expence should be born by the Owners of the several Ships Whose Seamen were taken, and that he ought to have had the Concurrence of their Correspondents here. That I feared he would now find it difficult to recover his Money, but as the Principle was laudable, if he would make out an Account of his Expenditures I would examine it, and pay such Part as seemed to me Right, and take my Chance of receiving it again from the United States. This Proposition did not meet his Wishes at all. He therefore offered to give a Bill on you for a certain Amount, which he desired me to advance. This I refused with some Asperity, as it was taking a Liberty with you which he could not justify. I have not seen him since, and only mention these Things now, lest by some of the many Accidents to which human Affairs are liable they should be presented to you or others in a different Light.

There is another Matter also in which I found myself obliged to offend some of my Countrymen. Mr. Barlow and Major Blagden had formed a Plan for colonizing the Banks of the Scioto with the Inhabitants of the Rue d'Honore, and others who might think proper to go to that Land of Promise. And indeed a Land of Promise they made it: promising freely what in the Nature of Things could never be performed. I saw that this Scheme might in it's Event prove injurious both to the Parties engaged in it and to the Reputation of America. When it became a Subject of Conversation in Society, I thought it incumbent on me to undeceive those who imagined the Government of America was concerned, and those also who supposed that I might be interested. Many Adventurers called on me for Information. Not to have told them the Truth when they asked Information which was to decide their Fate, would have been in my opinion criminal. I have some Reason to believe that this necessary Conduct has given Offence, and may have occasioned Misrepresentation. I therefore give you the Facts. I treated both the Plan and the Authors of it with as much Delicacy as I could, but I could not support what I could not approve.

The public Letter accompanying this will communicate all the Information I possess respecting the Business entrusted to me. I will add here my Conviction that the present Minister will do nothing effectual for some Time to come. Their European Affairs are not yet fully adjusted, and I think they will not be able to agree on a System to be pursued for America. In the mean Time we are growing into Notice, and encreasing in our Importance. If at the critical Moment we make them feel that the adoption of Measures like their own will greatly injure their Navigation and Trade, then and not till then will they become seriously desirous of fair and honorable Connection. This Moment is not yet arrived. We must wait both the Developement of their Intentions, and of our Means and Resources. We must wait also the Fate of France, and the new Connections and Alliances to be grounded thereon in Europe. It is in my opinion a happy Circumstance that our Hands are not now tied, and I hope we shall be cautious indeed as to all future Engagements.

P.S. Thanks for your Report: perhaps from Paris I shall trouble you with some Ideas on the Subject of it.

FC (DLC: Gouverneur Morris Papers); at head of text: "Thomas Jefferson Esqr. Private." Recorded in SJL as received 12 Mch. 1791. For comment on this letter, see Editorial Note, the impressment of Hugh Purdie and others, under 17 Dec. 1790.

Henry Remsen, Jr. to Tobias Lear

Philadelphia, 24 Dec. 1790. Enclosing a duplicate commission for Edward Church, made out by order of the Secretary of State because Mr. Church left England about the time the original was dispatched from New York and did not receive it. The "Year of Independence" not added to the duplicate because not in the original.

RC (DNA: RG 59, MLR); dated "Friday noon" and endorsed as received 24 Dec. 1790.

From Sir John Sinclair

Whitehall, London, 25th. Decemr. 1790.

Sir John Sinclair's best Compliments to Mr. Jefferson, had the pleasure of receiving his report, upon the subject of establishing an uniformity in the Weights, Measures, and Coins of the United States; the principles of which evidently proves, Mr. Jeffersons thorough acquaintance with that important branch of Police. He embraces the earliest opportunity of sending Mr. Jefferson a very interesting Letter upon the subject, by a very respectable Mathematician, who has been among the first to prove, that the Linear Measure of England, the Averdupois Weight, and the Winchester measure of Capacity, are very intimately connected together and may be ascertained from the same standard.

Dr. Rotheram, in the Postscript, has very properly remarked, that the English and Americans, *as brethren*, should use the same Weights and Measures. Sir John Sinclair finds with infinite regret an idea very prevalent in England, that if the late rupture with Spain, had ended in War, the Americans were rather inclined to consider the Spaniards as their Brethren, than the English. It would give him much satisfaction, had he it in his power to contradict, with some degree of Authority, what he hopes is an ill-founded, and injurious aspersion: for surely the interests of America and of England, are, or ought to be, the same, and he wishes that societies were established on both sides of the Water, for the purpose of promoting so desirable a connexion.

He is at present endeavouring to establish a Society, for the purpose of improving British Wool, and he has the honor of sending Mr. Jefferson, a Copy of the printed Papers upon the subject; together with a Specimen of the Wool of the Shetland Islands, which is reckoned the finest produced in any part of the British Dominions. He also begs to inclose a Circular Letter to the Clergy of Scotland, and his Statistical queries, which are likely to furnish materials for a very curious account of that part of Great Britain.

He begs to be particularly remembered to Mr. Adams, Mr. Morris, and Mr. Laurens, and should be happy at any time, to have the pleasure of hearing from Mr. Jefferson or them.

He sends two Copies, of the Papers abovementioned, lest by any mistake or misfortune, one of the Copies should not find its way to New York.

RC (DLC); endorsed by TJ as received 4 Apr. 1791 and so recorded in SJL. Enclosures: (1) John Rotheram, *Observations on the proposed plan for an universal standard of weights and measures; in a letter to Sir John Sinclair, bart.* [Edinburgh, 1790?]; see Sowerby, No. 3757. (2) *Report of the Committee of the Highland Society of Scotland, to whom the subject of Shetland wool was referred. With an appendix containing some papers, drawn up by Sir J. Sinclair and Dr. Anderson in reference to the said report* [Edinburgh, 1790]. (3) *Address to the public, respecting the proper system to be pursued for the improvement of British wool* [Edinburgh, 1790?]. (4) Printed copies of Sinclair's circular and queries addressed to the more than nine hundred members of the Kirk of Scotland asking them to report information on commerce, population, history, soil, climate, minerals, natural productions, manufactures, mills, language, schools, inns, artisans, eminent men, charity, manners, and many other subjects, all of which came to public attention in

the work for which Sinclair is chiefly remembered—*The statistical account of Scotland* (Edinburgh, 1791-9; Sowerby, No. 3591). In TJ's papers there are two specimens of wool preserved—one "sent . . . by Mr. Hackley" and another "Specimen of Mr. [James] Bowdoin's Wool, from American Sheep raised on his Island of 'Naushan'" (DLC: TJ Papers, 235: 42262-3)—but evidently that sent by Sinclair was not.

The British Wool Society, founded in Jan. 1791 with Sinclair as chairman, was an unsuccessful product of the founder's boundless energy and enthusiasm. One of those who emphatically disagreed with Sinclair about the quality of wool produced by the Shetland breed—a term covering "anything sheep-like found in those islands"—was Sir Joseph Banks, who both suspected Sinclair's devotion to science and denigrated the hairy Shetland breed as "your aborigines" and "those Scotts Goats" (Rosalind Mitchison, *Agricultural Sir John* [London, 1962], p. 101-19, 121-36).

From José Ignacio de Viar

SIR   New York 25th. Decr. 1790

My present indisposition of Rehumatic pains deprives me of the pleasure of seeing you for Christmass, as I wished; for which Reason I benefit of the only means of writing to wish you with all happiness the Compliments of the Season.

I am with sentiments of the most perfect Respect & esteem, Sir Your most obedient, and most humble Servant

JOSEPH IGNATS. VIAR

RC (DNA: RG 59, NFL); endorsed by TJ as received 28 Dec. 1790 and so recorded in SJL.

From Gouverneur Morris

DEAR SIR   London   28 Decr. 1790

This will accompany what I had the Honor to write on the twenty fourth. In the Afternoon of that Day I received a Note from Mr. Burgess appointing an Hour of the twenty fifth for an Interview with the Duke of Leeds. I attended, but something or other kept his Grace away. The twenty sixth I received a note apologizing for the Disappointment and requesting my Attendance the twenty seventh. I waited on him again. A Note had been sent informing me that a severe Indisposition kept the Duke at Home, but this I did not receive in Season to prevent the Visit. Mr. Burgess therefore mentioned to me the Contents of it. The Duke it seems wished if I had any Communications to make before I went to Paris that they should come thro Mr. Burgess. I told him that, as he well knew, I had to make none and only put myself in the Way of receiving them. He said the Business remained as it was when he last spoke to me; that he could now say however the Duke had a Person in his Eye to be sent to America. I told him carelessly that I had heard Mr. Elliott was appointed. He said no Appointment had been made; it would be improper untill they should have determined what such Person was to do. I smiled at this and he was a little confused. He said they wished to make their Communications thro me and hoped I should be again in London *next Spring*. I told him that perhaps I might, but that was of no Consequence, they could easily find a Channel of their own.

There was Nothing in this which at all surprized me. It needs no Comment and is indeed exactly what I expected. *Next Spring* they will know better what to look for from their present Negotiations. Their intended Appointment of Mr. Elliot was during the Heighth of the Armament. He, on being spoken to, thought the Affair was concluded and mentioned it to his Friends. One of them told me of it. At that Time he was to have gone out immediately, but the whole Affair is now suspended.

FC (DLC: Gouverneur Morris Papers); at head of text: "*Public.*" Recorded in SJL as received 13 Mch. 1791. See Editorial Note on diplomatic and commercial relations with Great Britain, under 15 Dec. 1790.

Reports on Mediterranean Trade and Algerine Captives

EDITORIAL NOTE

We ought to begin a naval power, if we
mean to carry on our own commerce. Can
we begin it on a more honourable occasion
or with a weaker foe?
—*Jefferson to Monroe, 11 Nov. 1784*

For two and a half centuries after the brothers Barbarossa of
Algiers had ceased to terrorize the Mediterranean, the great powers
of Europe stood silent and subservient before their petty successors,
allowing and even encouraging them to carry on their piracies because,
as makeweights in the grand scales of politics, their usefulness seemed
to counterbalance their cost in lives, tribute, and national honor. On
their side the chieftains of the Barbary states, employing weapons
forged in contests older than the Crusades, made the capture and enslavement of Christians one of their principal means of aggrandize-
ment from the twelfth century onward. Their shrewd, calculated
policy carried out under the waning suzerainty of the Ottoman Empire
was based on two cardinal assumptions. By concluding peace only with
some and usually with the most formidable of the European nations,
they were at liberty to prey upon the commerce of others—a strategy
which bore most heavily upon the little states of the Mediterranean and
the Baltic. By permitting others and particularly the great powers to
be carriers of their produce, they at once provided a shield for it and
made themselves invulnerable to privateering. They could therefore
devote their energies at sea exclusively to predatory and piratical
activities.

Emboldened by success in forcing the most powerful monarchs of
Europe to become their tributaries, the Barbary states did not hesitate
to break their treaties on flimsy or contrived pretexts and then to exact
huge sums to have them renewed, while the ascent of a successor dey
or the reception of a new ambassador became the occasion for exacting
ceremonial gifts, a special form of tribute which naturally increased

[369]

the frequency of such events. Even after England acquired Gibraltar in 1704 and her powerful navy patrolled the Mediterranean as a virtual British sea, she found it expedient to continue as a tributary nation, paying ransom for her enslaved subjects and suffering the indignities heaped upon her admirals and consuls. France, so Lafayette thought, stood "upon a much more decent footing with those pirats than Any other Nation."[1] But the gradations of decency among states that accorded tacit sanction to piracy were exceedingly minute and France, having almost a monopoly of the carrying trade of the Barbary states, was no less an accessory because she elected to regard her contributions as voluntary. All of the leading maritime nations of Europe, without exception, were implicated in this long, dismal reckoning of values.[2]

Natives of Massachusetts as well as Virginia had experienced enslavement by the Algerines as early as the seventeenth century. But in the years before the Revolution, despite such occasional harassments, American colonists enjoying the protection of British passes to the Mediterranean had been able to develop a substantial trade with such ports as Barcelona, Marseilles, Leghorn, and Tangier. On the basis of official records which considerably discounted the actual values of commodities, the total exports to these regions from British America

---

[1] Lafayette to the American Commissioners, 8 Apr. 1785.

[2] The pioneer work on the background of Mediterranean piracy and the activities of the Mathurins, an order founded in the twelfth century for the redemption of captives, is Pierre Dan, *Histoire de Barbarie et ses corsairs* (Paris, 1637). For British relations with Barbary, see [Joseph Morgan], *Several voyages to Barbary* (London, 1736); R. L. Playfair, *The scourge of Christendom* (London, 1884), an account based on archival sources that included, as the most important record of the final years, archives of the American consulate in Algiers, rescued "from the oblivion of a garret at Marseilles" in consequence of Playfair's inquiries; and Stanley Lane-Poole, *The Story of the Barbary corsairs* (New York, 1890). Studies of American relations either reflect disproportionate emphasis on naval matters or exhibit the kind of partisan bias found in Henry Adams' *History* or do both. Gardner W. Allen, *Our navy and the Barbary corsairs* (Boston, 1905) is exact and detailed but concerned primarily with naval operations. Harold and Margaret Sprout, *The rise of American naval power* (Princeton, 1939; revised 1942), is a pioneering study of naval policy but it exaggerates sectional differences and partisan cleavages. Marshall Smelser, *The Congress founds the navy 1787-1798* (Notre Dame, 1959), regards the establishment of the navy as an exclusive achievement of the Federalists but, like others, fails to provide a satisfactory explanation for the vacillation of Hamilton, Jay, and other Federalists on the naval question or for the failure to employ naval force against the Algerines after it had been created. The first corrective to this sectional and partisan overemphasis was that of Julia H. MacLeod, "Jefferson and the Navy: A Defense," *Huntington Library Quarterly*, VIII (Feb. 1945), 153-84. This revisionist interpretation is also reflected in the specialized studies by Louis B. Wright and Julia H. MacLeod, *The first Americans in North Africa* (Princeton, 1945) and by James A. Field, Jr., *America and the Mediterranean world* (Princeton, 1969). The most useful general account of American policy is Ray W. Irwin, *The diplomatic relations of the United States with the Barbary powers* (Chapel Hill, 1931). A more recent and more restricted treatment is H. G. Barnby, *The prisoners of Algiers: an account of the forgotten American-Algerian war 1785-1797* (London, 1966), a work based largely on British archival sources and valuable for its description of the status of the Algerine slaves and the traffic in their redemption. In its treatment of American policy and its context of domestic politics, however, it is both superficial and inexact.

in 1770 amounted to £707,000 sterling.[3] Jefferson estimated that in the pre-war years some 1,200 seamen and upwards of 100 ships totalling 20,000 tons were annually engaged in this commerce, accounting for one-sixth of the wheat and flour and one-fourth of the dried and pickled fish exported from American ports.[4] So knowledgeable a merchant as Stephen Higginson considered the Mediterranean market to be "as profitable to us as any part of our European trade."[5] Exports of rice and lumber from the South, grain and flour from the middle colonies, and rum and fish from New England caused the interests of every section to be affected. The most important single article in this trade was salt fish, of which the choice grades were sent to Catholic markets in Portugal, Spain, and the Mediterranean.[6] Tobacco, which Jefferson estimated on the basis of Alexander Cluny's *The American traveller* to amount annually to £1,305,000 out of a total of £4,244,000 sterling for all American exports before the war, did not enter at all in the direct trade with the Mediterranean.[7]

In the years following the Treaty of Paris, when American trading vessels were penetrating the China Sea and indeed all the seas of the world except the Mediterranean, the question was whether the young nation would respond to this exclusion in the acquiescent manner of Europe or whether in this as in other respects it would, as David Hartley predicted, lay the foundations for "great events in the new page of life." Hartley in 1783 warned his English compatriots that, soon or late, "the American principle of equal reciprocity and the restrictive principle of the British Acts of Navigation must come to issue."[8] In the interconnected problems of American trade with the Mediterranean and relations with the Barbary states, as elsewhere, the issue was joined almost at the moment the prediction was made. But in the ensuing search for a solution to these problems in which the stagnant fisheries and crippled shipping of New England were vitally affected, it is an ironic fact that it was a tobacco planter of Virginia who took the lead both in championing these interests and in opposing the idea of having the new republic become a tributary to pirate states. Jefferson, whose system in the new page of life called for peace and harmony with all nations, was from the very beginning an advocate of force against the Algerines. He rejected the posture of subservience born

[3] Irwin, *Barbary powers*, p. 17-19, citing G. L. Beers, *Old colonial system*, I, 123-6, and D. Macpherson, *Annals of commerce*, III, 458, 572, 573.

[4] See Document III in the present group. Richard O'Bryen estimated that before the war "Americans used to employ 200 sail of merchantmen in the streights trade, and . . . reap great advantages by it" (O'Bryen to TJ, 28 Apr. 1787).

[5] Stephen Higginson to John Adams, 8 Aug. 1785 (MHi: AM).

[6] See TJ's notes on northern commerce, May-July 1784 (Vol. 7: 344). After the treaty with Morocco mules became a significant import, stimulated perhaps by Washington's interest in these animals which became widely known to the public when the King of Spain presented an ass to him that soon became famous under the name of Royal Gift (Freeman, *Washington*, VI, 58-9, 297n.; the best account of Royal Gift is J. H. Powell, *General Washington and the Jack Ass* [New York, 1969], p. 176-90).

[7] See group of documents on American commerce, at end of Jan. 1791. TJ, with reason, considered Cluny to be more reliable than Sheffield.

[8] David Hartley to C. J. Fox, 20 May 1783, quoted in Richard B. Morris, *The Peacemakers* (New York, 1965), p. 431-2.

of European power politics as being incompatible with honor, justice, and the national interest.[9]

Historians generally and too readily have accepted the premise that the government under the Articles of Confederation did not make use of naval force against the Algerines because it lacked the power to do so. Some, while recognizing Jefferson's insistence upon the necessity of a navy if the United States were to be a carrier of its own produce, have seen the development of a coherent naval policy as an achievement of the commercial and financial interests of the North against the opposition of an agrarian South and West—as a triumph of Hamiltonian Federalists over Jeffersonian Republicans.[10] Others, though avoiding such exaggerated sectional and partisan interpretations, have yet concluded that the problem posed by the Barbary states could be attended to only after the fiscal deficiencies of the Confederation had been remedied by the Hamiltonian system.[11] But partisan and sectional differences, genuine as they were and much as they affected foreign policy, do not provide a wholly satisfactory gauge of the depth of the cleavage. Such differences on policy were indeed generally submerged in the growing recognition of the need for centralized power over commerce. "If we mean to be a commercial people or even to be secure on our Atlantic side," wrote Alexander Hamilton in phrases that echoed those of Jefferson six years earlier, "we must endeavour as soon as possible to have a navy."[12] Others of Hamilton's persuasion professed a desire to use force in combating the Barbary menace. "If our Government could draw forth the Resources of the Country which . . . are abundant," declared John Jay in 1786, "I should prefer War to Tribute, and carry on our Mediterranean Trade in Vessels armed and manned at the public Expence."[13]

But the insubstantial nature of such an apparent concurrence of views was soon demonstrated by events. Those who had pleaded the presumed impotence of the Confederation as a reason for preferring tribute were now confronted with Jefferson's recommendation of force.[14] The power to draw forth the resources of the nation had been granted, but it was no more employed to suppress Algerine piracy than it was to alleviate the plight of the fisheries or to achieve through navigation laws that genuine reciprocity for which Hamilton had also argued eloquently in the eleventh *Federalist*.[15] On each of these issues the Hamiltonian position, theretofore almost indistinguishable from

[9] TJ to John Page, 20 Aug. 1785; TJ to Adams, 11 July 1786; TJ to Monroe, 11 Nov. 1784, 11 Aug. 1786.

[10] C. O. Paullin, *The navy in the American Revolution*, p. 81-5; Harold and Margaret Sprout, *The rise of American naval power*, p. 14-15, 18, 24, 26-32; Smelser, *The Congress founds the navy*, p. 27, 53-4, 58, 84, 116-17, 126, 145-6, 164-6. See note 2 above.

[11] Field, *America and the Mediterranean world*, p. 34; Irwin, *Barbary powers*, p. 52-3.

[12] *Federalist* No. 24 (Syrett, *Hamilton*, IV, 422); see also *Federalist* No. 34 (same, p. 472). For TJ's earlier statement on the need for a navy, see *Notes on Virginia*, ed. Peden, p. 176. See also TJ to Monroe, 9 Feb. 1785.

[13] TJ to Jay, 14 Dec. 1786.

[14] Document III.

[15] See Editorial Note, group of documents on French protest of tonnage acts, under 18 Jan. 1791.

that of Jefferson, was promptly abandoned when the powers of the new government came to be wielded. Jefferson's policy, grounded on principle as well as on a realistic grasp of the problem, remained unaffected by changes in the structure of government or in the nature of constitutions. His consistency arose from a profound belief in republican principles and from an unswerving confidence in the new "empire for liberty," whatever the form of its organic law.

Thus to the obvious partisan and sectional differences over the creation of a naval establishment and its use in reopening the Mediterranean to American trade were added more fundamental divergences affecting matters of much greater moment than even the valuable commerce interdicted by a group of weak and predatory states. These concerned not only the search for economic independence and the relation of the United States to the dominant powers of Europe. They touched also the nature and direction of the new society that was being created and the differing ways in which its dignity, its justice, and its national interest were conceived.

I

Acquiescent as European nations were before the Barbary states, no minister of the time could have based his policy on an open espousal of piracy or even, as Vergennes said of Great Britain, dare to obstruct concerted plans for its suppression for fear of the scandal that would ensue.[16] But one member of the British parliament whose devotion to the navigation system was strong enough to overcome his discretion was Lord Sheffield, who bluntly declared the Algerines to be beneficial to the national interest. His words were all the more forceful because they were embedded in his *Observations on the commerce of the American states*, a work which caused Edward Gibbon to say that the "Navigation Act, the palladium of Britain, was defended and perhaps saved by his pen."[17] The essence of its argument was that an independent America carried no threat to England "except as to the carrying trade, the nursery of seamen, and this it is in our power to prevent to a considerable degree. . . . *We must therefore retain the carrying trade wherever we possibly can.*"[18] In elucidating this essential doctrine, Sheffield added:[19]

It is not probable the American States will have a very free trade in the Mediterranean; it will not be the interest of any of the great maritime powers to protect them there from the Barbary States. If they know their interests, they will not encourage the Americans to be carriers. That the Barbary States are advantageous to the maritime powers is certain. If they were suppressed, the little States of Italy, &c. would have much more of the carrying trade. The French never shewed themselves worse politicians, than in

16 TJ to Jay, 23 May 1786.
17 Quoted in DNB sketch of John Baker Holroyd (1735-1821), first Earl of Sheffield.
18 Sheffield, *Observations on the commerce of the American states* (London, 1783), p. 187; emphasis in original.
19 Same, p. 204-5.

encouraging the late armed neutrality . . . [which would have been] as hurtful to the great maritime powers, as the Barbary States are useful. The Americans cannot protect themselves from the latter; they cannot pretend to a navy.

As Americans read this unblushing recommendation that piracy be reckoned as a factor in determining national policy, many came to think open acquiescence nothing more than covert encouragement. Benjamin Franklin quoted London merchants as saying, no doubt in unwitting paraphrase of a remark attributed to Louis XIV, "that if *there were no Algiers, it would be worth England's while to build one.*"[20] Ralph Izard in 1785 declared that he would rather go to war with Great Britain than with Algiers if it were proved, as reported, that she had "encouraged the piratical states to attack our Vessels."[21] John Adams suspected that one object of the Tripolitan envoy's mission to London in 1786 was "to obtain aids from England to carry on War against us" and he was certain that "there are not wanting persons in England, who will find means to stimulate this African to stir up his Countrymen against American Vessells."[22] Richard O'Bryen, the leading figure among the American captives in Algiers and one whom Jefferson regarded as a man of sense, thought England would obstruct any efforts at peace with the Algerines, unless given such concessions in trade as would not be "consistent with the honor and dignity of the United States of America and as becoming a free and independent people." O'Bryen believed that a considerable revenue from the sale of thousands of Mediterranean passes and exorbitant insurance premiums paid by Americans were also factors influencing British attitudes. He was certain that France, possessing almost all of the commerce of the Barbary states and being the chief carrier of their produce, was equally interested in preventing a peace with the pirates.[23]

The actions of both powers tend to confirm the suspicions. In the case of Great Britain this is exemplified in the manner in which its consulate at Algiers—the first to be instituted by England—was administered. The British subject who had proved most friendly to the interests of the United States and particularly to the American captives was one John Woulfe, a Jewish merchant and convert to Christianity who enjoyed the confidence and respect of the Dey. He had come to Algiers in 1777 as vice-consul under assurances that he would succeed to the consulship, but the appointment went to Nathaniel Davison. In 1783 Davison, refusing to tolerate insults and believing that two good frigates would be more than a match for any force the Algerines could muster, hauled down the British flag and departed. The Dey turned to Woulfe to act as intermediary and he advised the British government

[20] Benjamin Franklin to Robert R. Livingston, 25 July 1783; emphasis in original (*Rev. dipl. corr.*, ed. Wharton, VI, 587). Louis XIV is said to have remarked: "If there were no Algiers, I would make one" (Lane-Poole, *Barbary corsairs*, p. 257).
[21] Ralph Izard to TJ, 10 June 1785.
[22] John Adams to John Jay, 17 Feb. 1786 (MHi: AM).
[23] O'Bryen to TJ, 25 Sep. 1787.

to dispatch a frigate to inquire into the cause of Davison's leaving. This was done, the investigation proved abortive, and Woulfe was left in charge of the consulate. But Davison was not reappointed and neither was Woulfe given the post. The appointment went instead to Charles Logie, who was reported to be an habitual drunkard and of such unsavory reputation that none of the other consuls would associate with him. He was also suspected in 1785 of prompting the Algerines to venture into the Atlantic soon after Spain concluded a treaty with the pirates. This led to the capture of the schooner *Maria* of Boston and the ship *Dauphin* of Philadelphia, along with twenty-one prisoners. Logie at first displayed such "Peculiar Humanity" to the prisoners as to gain their favorable attention.[24] But, becoming their bondsman, he made some of them his personal servants, subjected them to other indignities, and thus transformed their initial attitude into one of permanent suspicion, distrust, and contempt. Logie showered attentions on the inept American agent, John Lamb, who associated with him on terms of such intimacy as to convince O'Bryen that all of the secrets of the mission were known to the British consul.[25] After negotiating the short-lived truce of 1793 between Portugal and Algiers that had such disastrous effects on American shipping, Logie was recalled and given a pension of £400 for life. He was succeeded by an even more dubious character, one Charles Mace, a former clergyman who had abandoned the cloth for various speculative enterprises. Mace brought about such a weakening of relations between Great Britain and Algiers that he was obliged to flee the wrath of the Dey, who regarded him as "better suited for looking after goats in Corsica than to be consul of the English in Algiers."[26]

The appointment of such men as Logie and Mace, coupled with the rejection of one who had befriended America and another who urged the use of British naval force, suggests that Whitehall at least gave tacit sanction to Sheffield's doctrine of tolerance toward the Algerines. Certainly England possessed abundant means for compelling respect and enforcing peace in the Mediterranean if policy had dictated its use.

So also did France. Her disinclination to assist the United States in gaining a competitive position in the Mediterranean markets may have been understandable but it was also beyond doubt. The French

24 Petition of O'Bryen and others to Congress, 28 Aug. 1785 (DNA: RG 360, PCC No. 42, VI, f. 117); Jay recommended that the American minister in London be directed to "signify to his britannic Majesty the Sense they entertain of the Humanity and Generosity of his Consul" (JCC, XXX, 12). O'Bryen to TJ, 25 Aug. 1785.

25 O'Bryen to TJ, 8 June 1786; see also, Carmichael to TJ, 18 July 1786, 15 Oct. 1787; Lamb to the American Commissioners, 20 May 1786. In the opinion of the surgeon of the British consulate at Algiers, Dr. Warner (or Werner), Logie was "a drunkard, and his wife a prostitute" (TJ's memorandum of Warner's testimony, ca. Jan. 1788); TJ thought Warner's testimony on other matters was "full, clear, and consistent" (Document II). See also Playfair, *Scourge of Christendom*, p. 215-22. But Logie filled his dispatches with savage attacks on the doctor and accused *his* wife of being a prostitute (see Barnby, *The prisoners of Algiers*, p. 34-5, 71, 74, 80, 110, 134, 139, 142). Barnby's estimate of Logie is more favorable than that of others, but he ranks Mace as both inept and incompetent (same, p. 132, 155, 192, 214).

26 Playfair, *Scourge of Christendom*, p. 224, quoting the Swedish consular diary.

chargé in the United States was only rephrasing a sentiment expressed much earlier by De Choiseul when he said that the Americans were "the most formidable rivals of any nation which wishes to conserve or augment its navigation."[27] France naturally refused in the treaty negotiations of 1778 to supply the protection against piracy that was once provided by England. But even her pledge in Article VIII of the Treaty of Commerce to employ her "good offices and interposition" with the Barbary states proved to be empty of value. The American Commissioners—no doubt suspecting this to be the case—raised a test case as soon as the treaty was signed. The response of the French government was evasive.[28] Later, when the expiration of the Treaty of 1684 between France and Algiers seemed to offer a favorable opening, another effort was made. This was undoubtedly inspired by Jefferson. The letter that he drafted pointedly recalled the earlier appeal to the terms of Article VIII and then went considerably beyond a mere request for French interposition. Since neither Adams nor Franklin agreed with Jefferson in his advocacy of force against the Algerines, it is clear that this démarche represented his hope rather than their conviction. If France should choose hostilities instead of a costly renewal of the treaty with Algiers, the Commissioners' letter to Vergennes suggested, "Congress would probably prefer joining in the war, rather than treat with the Nations who so barbarously and inhumanly commence hostilities against others who have done them no injury."[29] This not only carried a delicate imputation: it also advanced a proposal which could have committed the United States. But the effort failed. Thenceforth Jefferson placed no reliance on the treaty pledge. In his report to Congress in 1790 he did not even offer it as an available alternative, though the French *chargé* was concerned to know whether Article VIII would be invoked.[30] France had proved herself no more disposed than England to open up the Mediterranean for the benefit of the United States. But the unsuccessful appeals had at least confirmed the opinion expressed by Jay and widely held in the United States "that European commercial Nations never rejoice to see a Rival

[27] Otto to Montmorin, 4 Aug. 1790 (DLC: Henry Adams Transcripts). De Choiseul, thirty years earlier, had written: "Make no mistake about it, the true balance of power now rests in commerce—and in America" (translated from De Flassan, *Histoire générale et raisonnée de la diplomatie française ou de la politique de la France*, VI [Paris, 1811], 160). Jefferson made a similar observation in *Notes on Virginia* and so did Hamilton in the eleventh *Federalist* (see Note 12).

[28] Arthur Lee, Benjamin Franklin, and John Adams to Vergennes, 28 Aug. 1778; Sartine to Vergennes, 21 Sep. 1778; Vergennes to American Commissioners, 27 Sep. 1778; American Commissioners to Vergennes, 1 Oct. 1778 (*Rev. dipl. corr.*, ed. Wharton, II, 698, 731, 746, 747).

[29] Adams to Franklin and TJ, 20 Mch. 1785; American Commissioners to Vergennes, 28 Mch. 1785, enclosing copies of letters mentioned in preceding note. See also TJ to Adams, 24 Sep. 1785.

[30] See Document III; Otto to Montmorin, 10 Dec. 1790 (DLC: Henry Adams Transcripts). Otto was in doubt as to the kind of policy the United States would adopt: "The resource of tribute succeeds better with the pirates, but is too expensive for the United States." Yet within a few years European nations became alarmed because the American payments of tribute were so lavish as to threaten established methods of dealing with the Barbary states (Irwin, *Barbary powers*, p. 80).

at peace with those Pirates."[31] The young republic would have to solve the problem as best it could.

The solution through concerted action that Jefferson proposed has been regarded as visionary and impracticable, not only because the maritime powers of Europe would not countenance it but also because the government under the Articles of Confederation could not sustain it.[32] But Jefferson was acutely cognizant of both the European and the American obstacles. He neither underestimated their formidable nature nor was he deterred by their existence. The plan that he devised—first in the overture to France, then in indirect approaches to Spain and Portugal, and finally as the elaboration of a strategy suggested by D'Estaing[33]—was based on two departures from previous European experience that were themselves a tacit commentary upon the magnitude of the obstacles. First, since it was unrealistic to expect cooperation from the great powers, it would be necessary to seek a coalition of those little states that had been victimized over the centuries—"Portugal, Naples, the two Sicilies, Venice, Malta, Denmark and Sweden."[34] Second, the sporadic expeditions, sieges, and bombardments that had proved so costly and so ineffectual in the past would give way to a strategy of the constant cruise and the permanent blockade, aimed not at a retaliation against piracy but at its destruction. Jefferson thought that if such a plan could be begun with only two or three states, it would prove so effective that every other power in Europe would soon support it—except, of course, France, England, and perhaps Spain and Holland. It was not within the choice of the Americans, he declared, to decide whether they would "pay money to cover their trade against the Algerines." Even if they did nothing, they would still have to pay great sums either in insurance or in negotiating for peace.[35] Their only choice in fact lay between a form of blackmail that was as costly as it was demeaning and an expedient which promised to be both effectual and compatible with the principles of an enlightened nation.

The readiness of the smaller powers to cooperate in such a proposal was an encouraging sign. So also were Lafayette's enthusiasm for the "Antipiratical Confederacy" and D'Estaing's hope that America would set an example for Europe by rejecting its traditional policy of sub-

[31] Jay to TJ, 14 Dec. 1786; Jay to TJ, 25 Nov. 1788; Report of Jay on petition of John Lamb, 10 Feb. 1785 (DNA: RG 360, PCC No. 81; M/247).
[32] L. M. Sears declared flatly that the "project was too visionary to be realized" (DAH, III, 371). See also, Irwin, *Barbary powers*, p. 47-50; Field, *America and the Mediterranean world*, p. 34-6; Allen, *Barbary corsairs*, 39-42, 43; Smelser, *The Congress founds the navy*, 38-9; Malone, *Jefferson*, II, 30-1. See note 39, below.
[33] TJ to Monroe, 11 Nov. 1784 (which contains the earliest suggestion of the plan that TJ formally drafted two years later); 6 Feb. 1785; 10 May 1786; American Commissioners to Vergennes, 28 Mch. 1785; TJ to Carmichael, 18 Aug. 1785; TJ to Adams, 27 Nov. 1785; 11 July 1786; TJ's proposal for concerted action against the Barbary states, July-Dec. 1786 (Vol. 10: 560-70). TJ's suggestion to Carmichael—that is, to Floridablanca through Carmichael—that "the interests of Spain and America may call for a concert of proceedings against" Algiers possibly helped stimulate Spain's friendly assistance in the negotiations with Morocco.
[34] TJ, Autobiography (Ford, I, 93).
[35] TJ to Monroe, 11 Aug. 1786.

servience.[36] Lafayette recognized that it would be extremely difficult "to Make it Agreable to this Ministry that I should meddle with the War."[37] But Jefferson had anticipated this and informed Vergennes of his plan even before some of the envoys of smaller states expressed apprehension that France would oppose it. In approaching Vergennes he characteristically avoided any insinuation of doubt about French conduct by asking whether England would interfere. " 'She dares not to do it,' " replied the minister.[38] But if England dared not for fear of affronting Europe, such a restraint would presumably operate just as effectively on France. Hence Jefferson, doubtful of the neutralism of France, must have hoped only to confine her opposition to covert means. These, though difficult to counter, were limited by the fear of exposure. Vergennes verified Jefferson's unexpressed doubts by issuing a blunt warning to Lafayette to take no part in the enterprise. Thirty years afterward Lafayette proudly pointed to his advocacy of a proposal that "at the time appeared romantic." Defending himself as a prescient statesman, he later came to believe that "Vergennes, in the name of the courts of Versailles and London, destroyed my edifice."[39] But the edifice was not created by him, and Jefferson, its real architect, was not so malleable. Far from being destroyed by the kind of hidden opposition he had already anticipated, the proposal required for its next stage of development only a resolution of Congress giving it official sanction. To achieve this Jefferson held the nail for Lafayette to drive, as he had done so often in the effort to obtain French concessions on trade. Vergennes' warning to desist came after the marquis had already done all that he could do for the scheme.

One reason why Jefferson resorted to this strategy of indirection in seeking the approval of Congress was that he and John Adams were divided in their views about policy toward the Barbary states, though not about the importance of the Mediterranean trade. Adams, more sanguine than Jefferson in estimating the value of this commerce, declared in 1786 that the United States could have 200 ships engaged in it and that their freight revenues alone would amount annually to £200,000 sterling. He also agreed that the Algerine menace provided a good excuse for beginning a navy. But he preferred to purchase peace and argued that it was poor economy to sacrifice a trade worth "a Million annually to save one Gift of two hundred thousand Pounds."[40] The argument was as valid for war as for tribute, but when Jefferson proposed an alliance with Portugal against the Algerines, Adams made no response. Shortly thereafter Abdurrahman, an envoy of Tripoli, appeared in London and Adams thought this offered an oppor-

[36] Lafayette to TJ, ca. 6 Mch. 1786, enclosing his to Knox, 6 Mch. 1786, and "a paper from the Count D'Estaing," 4 Mch. 1786 (DNA: RG 360, PCC No. 150; M/247); D'Estaing to TJ, 17 May 1786.

[37] Lafayette to TJ, [23 Oct. 1786].

[38] TJ, Autobiography (Ford, I, 93); TJ to Jay, 23 May 1786.

[39] Gottschalk, Lafayette, p. 266, states that Lafayette conceded later that the plan "appeared romantic." But in 1816 Lafayette cited his stand on this proposal among other "choses qui paraissaient alors romanesques" only to suggest that "il ne faut pas supposer les gens aveugles, parce qu'ils voient plus loin ou autrement que notre société habituelle" (Mémoires, III, 222-3; VI, 5).

[40] Adams to TJ, 3 July 1786.

tunity to treat with all four of the Barbary states. He dispatched an urgent appeal to Jefferson to come to London partly to conclude the treaty with Portugal but primarily to negotiate with the Tripolitan. "There is nothing to be done in Europe, of half the importance of this," he wrote, "and I dare not communicate to Congress what has passed without your Concurrence."[41]

But in fact Adams had already given Jay both a full account of his conferences with Abdurrahman and an eloquent plea for the policy of purchasing peace. This, he advised, might cost £60,000 sterling annually—"an enormous sum . . . but infinitely less than the expense of fighting."[42] A few days later he estimated the initial cost of peace with all of the Barbary states at £200,000, suggested that a loan of two million florins be negotiated in Amsterdam, and predicted that a perpetual treaty would give an instant rise to the reputation of the United States all over the world and make its "commerce, navigation, and fisheries . . . extend into the Mediterranean, to Spain and Portugal, France and England."[43] He apparently did not reflect that the same sum applied to the support of a fleet far less costly than that maintained by the United States during the revolution might, in collaboration with other powers, be more effective and less humiliating than the kind of perpetual peace that had been so repeatedly broken in the past. But such was his recommendation to Congress at a time when to Jefferson the very thought of paying tribute to Algiers caused his faculties to be "absolutely suspended between indignation and impotence."[44] Since Adams had already declared his own sentiments while seeking a concurrence of opinion, Jefferson had little room for choice. Their commission was a joint one and the resultant dispatch, which concealed their individual preferences, was an obvious compromise. It merely stated that they found the cost of a perpetual peace greater than anticipated and that they would not proceed to negotiate without further instructions. Adams almost certainly drafted this dispatch, for it graphically described the corsairs' method of fighting as having an awesome ferocity born of religious frenzy and encouraged by promise of rewards both temporal and eternal. This was not only irrelevant: it also could scarcely have been calculated to sway Congress toward war.[45] Besides demonstrating Jefferson's customary avoidance of a clash of opinions that would only have nullified each other, the consultation in London served chiefly to indicate the prudence of an indirect approach to Congress.

Jefferson must have anticipated this result. As he made clear to

41 TJ to Adams, 27 Nov. 1785; Adams to TJ, 21 Feb. 1786.
42 Adams to Jay, 16 Feb. 1786 (DNA: RG 360, PCC No. 84; M/247). Adams had long since made it clear that each of the states was interested in this valuable trade; that so long as the great powers of Europe "submit to be tributary to these Robbers, and even encourage them," it would be unwise and imprudent of the United States "to entertain any Thoughts of contending with them"; and that this was a matter of great importance demanding the immediate attention of Congress (Adams to Jay, 15 Dec. 1784; 9 Mch., 13 Apr. 1785; same).
43 Adams to Jay, 22 Feb. 1786 (same).
44 TJ to Nathanael Greene, 12 Jan. 1786.
45 American Commissioners to Jay, 28 Mch. 1786.

Jay, his primary object in going to London was to conclude the treaty with Portugal. Perhaps, as he had already suggested to Adams, he hoped to insert in its provisions an agreement for concerted action against the Algerines.[46] Before departing from Paris, he had also discussed his coalition plan with Lafayette and no doubt had inspired him to recommend it to General Knox.[47] Soon after his return he renewed his discussions with Lafayette and D'Estaing, approached some of the envoys of nations at war with the Algerines, drafted the proposed convention, and sent copies of it to the Russian minister and the Portuguese ambassador.[48] He of course gave his colleague in London an opportunity to associate himself with the effort. But Adams professed resignation—"your Plan of fighting will no more be adopted than mine of negotiating"—and declared that neither Congress nor the American people would support an indefinite commitment to war. "A disposition seems rather to prevail among our Citizens to give up all ideas of Navigation and naval power," he wrote, "and lay themselves consequently at the Mercy of Foreigners, even for the price of their produce."[49] Yet a few months earlier he had stoutly urged an American navigation act and had declared it visionary to think of avoiding commercial connections with Europe since the American people were "as aquatic as the tortoise and sea fowl."[50] Against Adams' stubborn adherence to his position, it was vain for Jefferson to argue that a purchased peace would not be kept, that constant cruising would soon turn the people of Barbary from piracy to agriculture, and that justice, honor, and the natural interest dictated a course that would compel the respect of Europe. Adams agreed only that, after the failure of Lamb's inglorious mission, negotiations with Algiers should not be renewed.[51] Clearly, if Congress were to be induced to propose a concert with other warring powers, the persuasion could not come from ministers so divided.

After agreeing to await further instructions, Jefferson in his dispatches did not emulate Adams in urging adoption of his view. He did, however, mention to Jay—in a deceptively casual report of his conversation with Vergennes that did not disclose its full meaning or extent—the blockading strategy that De Massiac had employed and D'Estaing had recommended. But to Monroe in Congress he gave an unequivocal endorsement of the scheme, urged its adoption as an effective means of putting an end to piracy, and welcomed it as an excuse for creating a naval establishment that would enable the Confederation to show its teeth in domestic affairs.[52] Jefferson also stoked the fires of Lafayette's ambition by holding forth the promise of glory as leader

[46] TJ to Jay, 12 Mch. 1786; TJ to Adams, 27 Nov. 1785.
[47] Lafayette to TJ, ca. 6 Mch. 1786.
[48] TJ to Jay, 23 May 1786; D'Estaing to TJ, 17 May 1786; TJ to Monroe, 11 Aug. 1786; TJ to the ambassadors of Portugal and Russia, 1 Dec. 1786 (missing); TJ's plan for concerted action, July-Dec. 1786 (Vol. 9: 560-70).
[49] Adams to TJ, 31 July 1786.
[50] Adams to Jay, 6 Dec. 1785 (DNA: RG 360, PCC No. 84; M/247).
[51] TJ to Adams, 11 July 1786.
[52] TJ to Jay, 23 May 1786; TJ to Monroe, 11 Aug. 1786.

of the combined force, a post for which he had originally considered John Paul Jones. Under this stimulus and undoubtedly at Jefferson's prompting, Lafayette informed Washington of the difference of opinion between Adams and Jefferson, declared himself in agreement with the latter, and urged that Congress authorize their ministers in Europe to make the proposal to "Naples, Rome, Venice, Portugal, and some other powers."[53] Long in the habit of sending communications to the Secretary for Foreign Affairs that curiously blended personal and political affairs, Lafayette sent a similar but more cautious plea to John Jay. He concealed the differing views of Adams and Jefferson behind the impersonal acknowledgment that there might be "a Diversity of Opinions" over the question of war or tribute, but declared that there could "in No Mind be Any doubt about the Advantages of a third Measure—Viz a Confederacy of Six or Seven Powers, Each of them Giving a small quota, the Reunion of Which would Insure a Constant and Sufficient Cruise Against those Pirats." Deliberately creating the impression that the proposal originated with himself, Lafayette stated that it was "not as yet very well diggested in My Head." He appealed to interested motives by announcing his intention "to Manage the Armament so as to Use American flour, fish, and naval stores" and concluded by urging that Congress "Empower their Ministers to Stipulate for such an Arrangement."[54]

By remaining discreetly in the shadow of the marquis, Jefferson revealed his awareness of the real difficulty. Late in life he ascribed the failure of the scheme to the inability of the Confederation to meet its financial engagements.[55] But until his draft of the "articles of a special confederation" could be formally placed before those governments at war with the Barbary states and until it had been accepted by them, no appropriation of funds would be necessary. Given the powerful influence of American revolutionary principles that many in Europe applauded and defenders of the old order feared, Jefferson may have hoped at least to force the issue into the open. The mere declaration by the United States that war was preferable to a humiliating acquiescence in piracy, as his own experiences in France would have justified him in believing, might have caused the foundations of the old policy to begin to crumble under the pressure of sheer moral force. The opportunity to turn a new page in this dismal chapter of the book of life was now in the hands of the American Congress. But there, too, lay a more formidable obstacle than the proposed confederacy had encountered in Europe.

[53] Lafayette to Washington, 22 Oct. 1786 (*Letters of Lafayette to Washington, 1777-1799*, ed. Gottschalk, p. 315).

[54] Lafayette to Jay, 28 Oct. 1786 (DNA: RG 360, PCC No. 156; M/247). In his first letter after returning to France in 1784 Lafayette had informed Jay that the American ministers would write about the Algerine business and that he had promised to provide them with such information as he could collect (Lafayette to Jay, 19 Mch. 1785). See also Lafayette's letters to Jay on political and personal matters, 18 Apr., 11 May, 15 Apr., 4 and 6 Sep. 1785; 11 Feb. 1786; 3 May and 18 Oct. 1787 (same).

[55] TJ, Autobiography (Ford, I, 94).

II

When Congress received letters in the autumn of 1785 announcing Algiers' declaration of war against the United States and conveying the surmise that "some European powers have influenced . . . the Algerines to check the progress of the American Navigation," John Jay based his report on the assumption that Americans aspired to "naval Strength and maritime Importance."[56] He bluntly declared to Congress that "the time is come for the final and decided Determination of this Question vizt. Whether it would be more wise in the United States to withdraw their Attention from the Sea, and Permit Foreigners to fetch and Carry for them; or to persevere in concerting and pursuing such measures as may conduce to render them a maritime Power?" This vigorous report has been regarded as the initiation of the only serious effort under the Articles of Confederation to reestablish the navy and its failure has been ascribed to the impotence of the government and the opposition of delegates from the South.[57] There is no doubt that Jay raised an important question and did so in forthright terms. But the political context of his report requires closer scrutiny.

It is true that Jay, like Hamilton, attached high value to the Mediterranean trade. He was also acutely sensitive to the plight of the Algerine captives. More than once he declared his preference for war over tribute.[58] The response to Algiers' declaration of war that he urged upon Congress was firm and unequivocal: "both the Honor and Interest of the United States demand that decided and vigorous Measures be taken to protect the american Trade and meeting these predatory Enemies in a proper Manner." Indeed, his report went further and recommended that "a Minister . . . be sent to Portugal, and instructed, among other things, to negociate for such an Alliance, as may provide for a Co-operation of Forces and Mutual Defense against the common Enemy, and restrain both Nations from making a separate Peace." To accomplish this and to make it the interest of other nations to end the war, Jay even went so far as to suggest a system of ex-

[56] The surmise was that of John Bondfield, who first transmitted information of Algiers' hostility (Bondfield to Jay, 28 July 1785, enclosing a letter from De Soulanges, commandant at Toulon, to the Directors of Commerce of Toulon, 14 July 1785; DNA: RG 360, PCC No. 92; M/247). John Paul Jones also forwarded information from De Soulanges (Jones to Jay, L'Orient, 6 Aug. 1785; De Soulanges to the judges and consuls of Nantes, 14 July 1785; same). Jones expressed the opinion that the late peace with Spain influenced Algiers to declare war and that this would "produce a good effect, if it Unites the People of America in measures consistent with their National Honor and Interest and rouses them from that ill judged security which the intoxication of success has produced since the Revolution." Both points were reflected in Jay's letter to the President of Congress, 13 Oct. 1785 (JCC, XXIX, 833-4). Jay reported on 20 Oct. 1785 (JCC, XXIX, 842-4).

[57] Harold and Margaret Sprout, *The rise of American naval power*, p. 18.

[58] Jay to Adams, 14 Oct., 1 Nov. 1785 (*Correspondence and public papers of John Jay*, ed. Johnston, III, 172-3; 175-6); Jay to TJ, 19 Jan., 14 Dec. 1786; Jay to Lafayette, 16 Feb. 1787 (DNA: RG 360, PCC No. 121; M/61); Jay's report on consular establishment, 19 Sep. 1785 (DNA: RG 360, PCC No. 81; M/247); Jay to the President of Congress, 3 Aug. 1786 (same); Jay's report on petition of Hannah Stevens, 1 May 1787 (same).

clusive and reciprocal trade arrangements with Portugal that anticipated
the similar overtures made by Jefferson in 1791.[59] His proposal of an
"Alliance . . . for a Co-operation of Forces and mutual Defence against
the common Enemy" was in fact essentially the same idea that Jefferson was already exploring in Paris.

Yet it is an instructive indication of the relations of the Secretary
for Foreign Affairs with the American minister to France that Jefferson
learned of these views on fundamentally important aspects of foreign
policy not through official communications but from a private letter
written by Jay to John Paul Jones. According to Jones, Jefferson
joined him in applauding "the noble Sentiments" of firmness and
national dignity that it voiced.[60] Jay's letter happened to arrive just as
Jefferson was discussing with Jones and Lafayette his own plan for
cooperative action against the Algerines. But instead of expressing to
Jay his approbation of ideas so exactly congruent with his own, he
maintained an official silence in his dispatches and persisted in his
strategy of making an indirect approach to Congress through Lafayette.
The noble sentiments had not misled him: he was well aware that,
far from being in accord, he and Jay had quite different views of
what the honor and national interest of the United States required.

This is not surprising. At the beginning of 1786 Jefferson could
scarcely have forgotten that, only six months earlier and in a private
letter, Jay had asked him whether he thought the United States
should engage in a carrying trade for all or for none of its products.
The very inquiry and the privacy in which it was put implied a
doubt about the ground on which Jay would soon rest his recommendations for promoting "naval Strength and maritime Importance." But
what that report took to be an assumption Jefferson regarded as an
intractable reality. The American people, he responded to Jay, had
already decided this question. His own preferences inclined him
toward an agrarian rather than a commercial society, but since the
course had been settled by the people, those responsible for forming
policy should "in every instance preserve an equality of right to them
in the transportation of commodities, in the right of fishing, and in the
other uses of the sea." This would bring on insults, violations of property, and frequent wars. For protection, the nation of necessity would
require some naval force. "This alone," Jefferson concluded, "can
countenance our people as carriers on the water, and I suppose them
to be determined to continue such."[61] The vigor of the response and the

[59] Jay's report on Algiers' declaration of war, 20 Oct. 1785 (JCC, XXIX,
842-4).
[60] Jones to Jay, Paris, 7 Jan. 1786 (DNA: RG 360, PCC No. 168; M/247),
acknowledging Jay's letter reporting that he had that day transmitted to Congress Jones' information about Algiers' declaration of war and adding: "To what
Measures it may give occasion is as yet uncertain. I flatter myself they will be
such as the Honor and Interest of the United States demand.—It would not in my
opinion become either to return an unprovoked Declaration of War by overtures
for peace, and Offers of Tribute" (Jay to Jones, 13 Oct. 1785; NNC: Jay
Papers).
[61] TJ to Jay, 23 Aug. 1785; Jay received this letter at least four months
later and may have responded to it in his letter of 30 Dec. 1785 (missing). Jay
to TJ, 14 June 1785; this letter (missing) no doubt reflected the kind of

elaboration of the argument would scarcely have been needed if Jefferson had felt that he and the Secretary for Foreign Affairs were in agreement. His own answer to the question had been formed long before he went to Europe.[62]

But even as this surprising inquiry came to him Jefferson was experiencing "infinite uneasiness" about the puzzling manner in which Congress' determination to press negotiations with the Barbary states was made known. He knew such orders had been given and even the amount of money that had been appropriated.[63] Yet in the ensuing months reliable travelers—including some who bore letters of subsequent date from Jay himself—had come and gone without bringing the necessary commissions, instructions, and letters of credence. Jefferson was so acutely distressed at this extraordinary delay that at last he proposed to Adams that they proceed without waiting for the instructions and that Thomas Barclay be sent on the mission. Adams agreed and Jefferson immediately prepared the draft treaty and necessary documents, dispatching them to London by special messenger. At that moment John Lamb arrived. Jay himself had taken almost a month to prepare the dispatch after Congress had ordered it and Lamb, the bearer he chose in preference to all others, had required an additional six months to deliver it.[64]

Although Jefferson had expected such orders even before he learned of Congress' authorization, he could not have known that this action resulted from the memorial of John Lamb himself. Nor could he have been aware that this document was drafted by Alexander Hamilton and supported by John Jay. In words chosen for him by Hamilton, Lamb had declared to Congress that he believed the national interest required

inquiries Jay advanced in his report of 17 May 1785 on the model treaty of amity and commerce transmitted by the American Commissioners, "such as, Whether American Exports shall be wholly, or how far, confined to American Bottoms? Whether any, and what distinction, shall be made in that Respect, between the vessels of one foreign Nation, and another?" (DNA: RG 360, PCC No. 81; M/247). Jay concluded that it was inadvisable to make any further treaties until these questions of policy had been determined. What Jay was arguing against, in reality, was the fundamental policy set forth in the Plan of 1776, reaffirmed in that of 1784—in the preparation of which TJ had a leading part—and also embodied in the Model Treaty of 1784 that he drafted (report of committee headed by TJ, 20 Dec. 1783; JCC, XXVI, 355-6; XXVII, 368-72; Charles Thomson to TJ, 16 May 1784; TJ's draft of model treaty, 4 Sep.-10 Nov. 1784 [Vol. 7: 463-90]). Jay's report manifested a growing opposition to the system of commercial treaties and contrasted with TJ's aim, which was to employ the treaty power so as "to take the commerce of the states out of the hands of the states, and to place it under the superintendance of Congress, so far as the imperfect provisions of our constitution will admit, and until the states shall by new compact make them more perfect" (TJ to Monroe, 17 June 1785).

[62] *Notes on Virginia*, ed. Peden, 175-6; TJ to Washington, 15 Mch. 1784. See preceding note.

[63] Adams to TJ, 29 May 1785; Foster to TJ, 26 Mch. 1785; Lee to TJ, 16 May 1785; TJ to Hardy, 11 May 1785 (missing, but see entry); TJ to Monroe, 5 July 1785; TJ to Adams, 22 June 1785.

[64] TJ to Adams, 5 and 28 July; 6, 14, and 17 Aug.; 19 and 24 Sep. 1785; TJ to Jay, 30 Aug., 11 Oct. 1785. Congress authorized new powers on 14 Feb. 1785; Jay sent instructions to the American Commissioners on 11 Mch. 1785; Lamb arrived in Paris on 18 Sep. 1785.

the formation of "some treaty of Amity and Commerce with the States of Barbary"; that, having concluded from "the general sense of persons" with whom he had conversed that it was the intention of Congress to initiate such negotiations, he offered his services in conducting them; that he possessed "no other inducements to this trust than his zeal for the service of the United States and his knowledge of the Country acquired by an intercourse of five years"; and that the only reward he desired was "to have the sanction of the United States and the necessary powers to treat."[65] Lamb came armed with testimonials from influential political and commercial figures in New England, including the governor of Connecticut and a former president of Congress—Samuel Huntington, Benjamin Huntington, Samuel Holden Parsons, Josiah Platt Cooke, and others. Parsons described Lamb as "a Gentleman on whose Fidelity, understanding and mercantile Abilities great Confidence is plac'd by his Acquaintance." He then added: "As we have yet no Treaty with those People it becomes necessary for him to have some Congressional Authority to warrant his proceedings. He will explain to you his views."[66] But these views were carefully excluded from the memorial that was prepared for Lamb. Hamilton's authorship was also concealed. This suggestive fact was hidden from most members of Congress—perhaps from all save one or two—behind the screen of Lamb's meticulous copy of Hamilton's original draft. The document that Congress received had every appearance of being the composition of John Lamb himself.

This memorial of an obscure Connecticut merchant disclosed no new urgency, no fact unknown to Congress, not even an estimate of the cost of the proposed negotiation. Yet when required to report upon it, John Jay gave it an endorsement that revealed his awareness of the undisclosed purposes. Agreeing that the national interest required "Treaties of Peace and Amity . . . with the Piratical States of Barbary," he argued that presents to a considerable amount would

[65] Hamilton's rough draft of the petition, undated and with several deletions and interlineations, is in DLC: Hamilton Papers; it is, of course, a far more literate document than Lamb could have produced. Lamb's transcript, also undated, is a scrupulously exact copy of the text prepared by Hamilton (DNA: RG 360, PCC No. 42, IV, f. 368, endorsed by Charles Thomson: "No. 2. petition of Capt. Lamb. Read 9 Feby 1785"). Accompanying this is the following testimonial, dated Norwich, Connecticut, 19 Nov. 1784 and signed by Samuel and Benjamin Huntington: "The Bearer Capt. John Lamb of Norwich . . . is Recommended as a person of Integrity and Ability in Trade. Any Favours shewn him by Authority will doubtless be Improved by his faithfull Endeavours to promote the Trade and Commerce of America." Subjoined to this is an official attestation by the governor of Connecticut, Matthew Griswold: "This Certifies that the foregoing . . . is According to my Apprehension a True and Just Representation of the Character of Capt. John Lamb . . . and I heartily Concur with Those Gentlemen in the Recommendation . . . Given under my hand and Seal . . . the 27th Day of November 1784" (same, f. 376).

John Lamb of Norwich is not to be confused with John Lamb (1735-1800), an ardent patriot and Revolutionary soldier of New York whom Washington appointed collector for the port of New York (Lamb to Washington, 22 May 1789; JEP, I, 10, 12).

[66] Samuel Holden Parsons to Abiel Foster, 1 Jan. 1785 (DLC: printed in Burnett, *Letters of Members*, VIII, 73n.), enclosed in Foster to TJ, 26 Mch. 1785. See preceding and following notes.

be necessary, the most suitable of which would be naval and military stores; that Lamb would be a proper person to carry on the negotiations under the American commissioners in Europe; and that, since the commercial nations of Europe would not be pleased to see American ships navigating the Mediterranean, the negotiations should be "prosecuted under all the Advantages which can be derived from the Character and Talents of those Plenipotentiaries, aided by the Powerful influence of present, and the Hope of future Gratuities."[67] The recommendation of tribute instead of war was the exact opposite of what Jay would advocate so vigorously in the following autumn. He did not reckon the cost of negotiating, but on Livingston's motion the wholly inadequate amount of $80,000 was authorized, Jay was directed to press upon the ministers the need of "prosecuting this important business," and in the ensuing months one delegate after another enjoyed the complacent feeling that effective measures for opening the Mediterranean to American ships had been taken.[68]

[67] Report on Lamb's petition, 10 Feb. 1785 (DNA: RG 360, PCC No. 81; M/247). In transmitting the report, Jay enclosed a private letter from Samuel Huntington to himself which reads in part: "[Capt. Lamb] is desirous to obtain some Aid from Congress as a Protection, and willing to do any national Service for us in his Power.—[He] is a Gentleman of Fidelity and mercantile Knowledge, especially in the Marine Department, of an enterprising Genius and intrepid Spirit. He hath suffered much in the late War in the Cause of his Country. I wish him success in his proposed Plan, and take the Liberty to recommend him to your favorable Notice further to communicate his Views and Wishes.— Whether any Negociation between these States and the Emperor of Morocco is now in a Train, I am uninformed; but presume yourself must be Acquainted. A free and safe Navigation to his Dominions must be very advantageous to these States, if it can be obtained on just and liberal commercial Principles" (Huntington to Jay, 10 Jan. 1785, DNA: RG 360, PCC No. 42, IV, f. 372-3; in Remsen's hand, as "Copied from the Original"). Since Lamb was directed by Huntington to Jay, it appears that the latter, after learning of "his Views and Wishes," must have induced Hamilton to lend his good offices in drafting the petition, which was then presumably presented by Lamb himself, perhaps through Joseph Platt Cooke of Connecticut (see Foster to TJ, 26 Mch. 1785). The petition, accompanied by the testimonials of Samuel and Benjamin Huntington and Matthew Griswold, was read in Congress on 9 Feb. 1785 and on the 10th was referred to Jay, who reported the next day. Only then did he disclose Huntington's private letter, in which, he said, "Mr. Lamb is mentioned in very honorable Terms. From this and his other recommendations, there is Reason to entertain a very advantageous Opinion of his Character" (Jay to the President of Congress, 10 Feb. 1785, DNA: RG 360, PCC No. 80; M/247).

[68] Jay's report was referred to Monroe, Livingston, and Johnson; Livingston reported on 14 Feb. 1785 (JCC, XXVIII, 55n., 64n., 65-6); N. H. delegates to Meshech Weare, 27 Feb. 1785; N. C. delegates to Alexander Martin, 1 Mch. 1785; Penna. delegates to John Dickinson, 9 Mch. 1785; Grayson to Madison, 1 May and 27 June 1785; Lee to Fitzgerald, 4 May 1785; Lee to TJ, 16 May 1785; S. C. delegates to William Moultrie, 10 Aug. 1785 (Burnett, *Letters of Members*, VIII, p. 47, 50, 60, 64, 111, 139, 156, 180). Rufus King seems to have been alone in thinking that the sums required to treat were "far more extensive than those entertained by Congress" (King to Gerry, 1 May 1785, same, VIII, p. 108).

Early in 1785, acting on the memorial of such leading merchants as Jonathan M. Nesbitt, Thomas FitzSimons, Mordecai Lewis, George Clymer, and Clement Biddle, the President of Pennsylvania urged that Congress, on a matter of extreme importance, "speedily to conciliate the states of Barbary . . . by presents . . . as practised by most of the Commercial Nations in Europe." The Pennsylvania

Why, then, this recommendation of tribute by one who professed a preference for war? The powerful political support for an unknown merchant, the concealment of authorship of his memorial, the disclaimer of all compensation for an arduous undertaking, and the action taken by Congress without waiting for the advice of ministers whom it already had authorized to treat—all of these factors made it patently clear that private objects were being sought under cover of public authority. Not until a year later did Jefferson obtain a glimpse of the nature of those objects. It then appeared that the plan concerted by the influential supporters of Lamb was to take the 32-gun Continental frigate *Alliance*—the only ship of the revolutionary navy that had not yet been sold—and present her to the Emperor of Morocco, the most friendly of the Barbary rulers. The negotiation was to be conducted by Lamb as agent, sent directly from the United States.[69] Since *Alliance* was owned by the public, the promoters evidently hoped to profit from an appropriation that would cover the cost of fitting her out and lading her with the naval stores that, as Jay suggested, would make the most suitable kind of presents. This aim was deflected when Congress rejected Jay's recommendation of Lamb. Despite this rebuff, Jay chose the unsuccessful memorialist as the bearer of his important letter to the American ministers and the sponsors of Lamb continued their patronage by urging testimonials upon Jefferson and Adams in the hope of gaining what Congress had refused.[70] Their aims respecting *Alliance* also persisted but in a different form.

For immediately after Congress appropriated funds for the Barbary negotiations, David Howell of Rhode Island moved that *Alliance*, widely esteemed for her speed, beauty, and victorious record, be sold.[71] Such an effort had been made the year before, but a committee representative of all sections of the nation declared that "the honour of the flag of the United States and the protection of its trade and coasts from the insults of pirates" required that the frigate be repaired and fitted for service. Their report was approved.[72] Howell's motion met a

---

delegates replied that "a Gentleman well recommended for his integrity and personal knowledge" had been sent with dispatches and might "be employed to carry into effect the wishes of Congress at the Court of the Emperor of Morocco." They urged that the news be kept secret since Great Britain might use her influence to prevent the treaties (*Penna. Archives*, ed. Hazard, x, 411, 418, 705-706).

[69] Monroe to TJ, 19 Jan. 1786.

[70] Jay to the American Commissioners, 11 Mch. 1785; Foster to TJ, 26 Mch. 1785.

[71] JCC, XXVIII, 228; the motion, drawn by Howell, is in DNA: RG 360, PCC No. 36, f. 559; M/247. The best account of *Alliance* is that of Louis H. Bolander, "The Frigate *Alliance*, the Favorite Ship of the American Revolution," *U. S. Naval Institute Procs.*, LXIII (Sep. 1937), 1249-58. Of *Alliance* Gardner W. Allen declared: "With this frigate as the flagship of a small squadron, with John Paul Jones in command, the insolence of the Barbary pirates might have been checked at the outset, saving much blood and money and avoiding humiliation" (*A naval history of the American Revolution*, II, 615-16).

[72] Report of committee (Ellery, Morris, Osgood), 27 Mch. 1784. This report was referred to Lee, Gerry, and Read, who reported on 30 Mch. 1784 that the embarrassed state of finances required that both *Alliance* and *Washington* be sold. But on 8 Apr. 1784 Congress authorized only the disposal of *Washington* (JCC, XXVI, 171, 210; DNA: RG 360, PCC No. 28, f. 221, 225; M/247).

different fate, but only after delay and opposition showing that such feelings about this sole remaining vessel under federal registry still persisted. A committee headed by Rufus King reported on Howell's motion on 3 June 1785, recommending that *Alliance* be sold. Only four delegates, three of them from the South, voted against the recommendation. Congress directed that the purchaser be given the option of paying in specie or in public securities and the Board of Treasury delegated the supervision of sale and delivery to John Barry, late commander of the frigate. On 5 August, without disclosing the identity of the buyer, Barry reported that *Alliance* had been sold at public auction for £9,750.[73] This was approximately one-tenth of the estimated cost of building such a frigate and the purchaser was also allowed to give promissory notes pledging payment in depreciated public securities in four instalments. Within six months the owner of *Alliance* was boasting of her as "one of the Finest Frigates in the World."[74]

This transaction extended over a period of four months, during which time nothing was heard of John Lamb. But just six weeks after the sale took place—ample time for an eastward passage—he finally made his appearance in Paris. The striking coincidence in dates and other circumstances suggest that the effort to sell *Alliance* accounted for Lamb's otherwise unexplained delay in delivering urgent orders of Congress. His mercantile if not his political sponsors may have hoped to purchase the frigate for depreciated securities and then sell her back to the government for specie under the fund authorized for the Barbary negotiations. If so, they again suffered disappointment, for there were others who had a similar, though public, object in view. This proposal came with the immense patronage of Benjamin Frank-

[73] The committee (King, Howell, Pinckney), appointed 4 Apr. 1785, reported on 23 May that the Board of Treasury be authorized to sell *Alliance* "for Specie or public securities at public or private Sale" and on 28 June 1785 Congress approved Pinckney's motion that payment in specie or securities be at the option of the buyer (JCC, XXVIII, 228, 390, 422-3, 484; DNA: RG 360, PCC No. 36, II, f. 559; No. 28, f. 213; No. 36, III, f. 53).

The Board of Treasury authorized sale in instalments (Commissioners to President of Congress, 5 Aug. 1785; Barry to Commissioners, 4 Aug. 1785; DNA: RG 360, PCC No. 140, II, f. 45; M/247; see also expenditures of Marine, same, No. 141, II, f. 241, showing allowance of $586.82 to Barry for pay and sundry disbursements on *Alliance* to 3 Aug. 1785). The amount received for *Alliance* was reported to Congress as $26,000 in public securities (JCC, XXIX, 615). There has been confusion about the disposition of *Alliance*. Bolander states that she was bought by John Coburn and a Mr. Whitehead who soon sold her at a handsome profit to Robert Morris (*U.S. Naval Institute Procs.*, LXIII [Sep. 1937], 1258). It has also been stated, erroneously, that the frigate was transferred to France (*Am. Neptune*, XXII [Oct. 1962], 271). John F. Watson, *Annals of Philadelphia* (Philadelphia, 1860), II, 339, states that *Alliance* was bought by Benjamin G. Eyre, shipbuilder of Kensington, who sold her to Robert Morris). A letter from Charles Biddle would seem to suggest that the initial buyer was the state of Pennsylvania (see below, note 75). Whatever the intermediate transfer, Morris soon acquired the redoubtable frigate and employed her in the East India trade.

[74] Charles Biddle to Benjamin Franklin, 5 Jan. 1786, enclosed in Franklin to Jay, 12 Jan. 1786 (DNA: RG 360, PCC No. 80; M/247). A Marine estimate made in 1783 of the cost of building, equipping, and manning a 40-gun frigate was $300,000; *Alliance* carried 36 guns (DNA: RG 360, PCC No. 144; M/247).

lin, recently elected President of Pennsylvania, and in the form of a letter to John Jay covering one to himself from Charles Biddle, Vice-President of the state. Biddle suggested that nothing the United States could possibly employ in treating with Algiers would be so effective as the gift of *Alliance* laden with naval stores. Such a present, he added, would be worth more to the pirates than five times her value in specie and payment could be made in public "paper . . . which [would] make the Purchase Easy to Congress and be of an advantage to this State."[75] Franklin, who had just returned from Europe, gave his full support to the plan. If Congress intended to send an envoy from America, he wrote, nothing would be more likely to procure him a welcome reception than the gift of *Alliance*. If Jay should be of the same opinion and if he saw no impropriety in it, he requested that the matter be laid before Congress.[76] This was essentially the same kind of proposal that Jay himself had supported only the year before. But since that time Algiers had declared war and Jay had welcomed the chance to adopt a vigorous policy. "If we act properly," he wrote in a private letter to John Adams, ". . . it may lay the foundations for a navy, and tend to draw us more closely into a federal system."[77] Yet, three months later, confronted with an opportunity to acquire a newly repaired *Alliance* on terms that amounted to a mere transfer of credit, Jay declined to embrace the offer either for war or for tribute. Despite Franklin's deferentially expressed but unmistakable intent, he did not even submit the proposal to Congress.

On Lamb's arrival, Jefferson was sufficiently sensitive to the political influences back of Jay's choice of messenger to acquiesce in what he assumed to be the desire of Congress. But his acquiescence was more apparent than real. He would not consent to any change in the plan to send Barclay to Morocco and he proposed that Lamb be given the agency to Algiers, a virtually hopeless assignment even with half of the appropriation allotted to it. Further, Jefferson urged and Adams agreed that Lamb be prevented from drawing for funds through the Amsterdam bankers and that he be given a reliable secretary who could inform the ministers of "anything . . . amiss."[78] Despite Jefferson's assertion that he was unable to gauge Lamb's abilities or integrity, these precautions betray his lack of confidence in the man and perhaps also his suspicion about the concealed purposes that had elicited such powerful political sponsorship. The manner in which Lamb conducted himself from the moment he sought this important public trust to the time it was withdrawn from him amply justified his intuitive distrust. Lamb's arrival in Algiers in what was believed to be an American-built vessel suggests that commercial objects were still being pursued. The American captives in Algiers could scarcely believe that Congress would send "such a man to negotiate so impor-

75 Biddle to Franklin, 5 Jan. 1786 (DNA: RG 360, PCC No. 80; M/247). Biddle suggested this as a mode of enabling Pennsylvania to meet the late requisition of Congress, for which public securities were not acceptable (see note 73).

76 Franklin to Jay, 12 Jan. 1786, enclosing Biddle's letter (same).

77 Jay to Adams, 14 Oct. 1785 (*Correspondence and public papers of John Jay*, ed. Johnston, III, 172-3).

78 TJ to Adams, 6, 14, 17 Aug.; 19, 24 Sep. 1785; TJ to Jay, 11 Oct. 1785.

tant an affair . . . where it required the most able Statesman and Politician."[79]

Hamilton and Jay may have been deliberately deceived about the character of this inept emissary, but neither could have been unaware of the private aims that caused him to be brought forward. Both lent their support to this imposition on the public and Jay did so even after his recommendation of the man had been rejected by Congress. It is scarcely surprising, therefore, that those delegates who had sponsored Lamb received "now and then a Shrug and Sneer" even before the failure of the mission was known.[80] This, together with information from Adams and Jefferson showing the inadequacy of the appropriation, prompted some in Congress to reassess their attitudes. William Grayson, who disliked "the scandalous example of Europe" but preferred tribute to war, now began to favor a loan in Holland that would provide ample funds for negotiation. After a long delay, the committee considering Jay's report on the need of a naval force recommended that Congress borrow or otherwise obtain "considerable sums of money for the express purpose of procuring peace" and that, if the overture should be rejected, these resources be employed "in protecting the Commerce of these States."[81] When Congress received the compromise dispatch from Adams and Jefferson with its realistic estimate of the cost of negotiating peace, Pinckney moved that they be authorized to borrow three million florins. Grayson felt certain the motion would be approved.[82]

In 1785 when Jay submitted his vigorous response to Algiers' declaration of war, the French *chargé* thought the universal conviction favored negotiation, with annual tribute in the form of tobacco and naval stores.[83] But now, in the face of a growing determination to borrow funds for negotiation or for war, Jay abandoned the position

---

[79] O'Bryen, Coffin, and Stephens to TJ, 8 June 1786. For further evidence of Lamb's private objects, see below at note 154.

[80] Stephen M. Mitchell to Jeremiah Wadsworth, 3 May 1786 (Burnett, *Letters of Members*, VIII, 350). For other evidences of the shift from complacency to concern on the part of members of Congress, tinged with suspicions of the role of Great Britain in causing the failure of Lamb's mission, see Lee to Madison, 16 Feb. 1786; Gorham to Bowdoin, 5 Apr. 1786; entry in Rodney's diary, 2 May 1786; King to Gerry, 14 May 1786; Sedgwick to Strong, 6 Aug. 1786; Md. delegates to the governor of Maryland, 7 Aug. 1786 (same, VIII, 308, 337, 347-8, 360, 416).

[81] The committee on Jay's report of 20 Oct. 1785 (Johnson, Monroe, Pinckney, Kean, and Dane) was not appointed until 29 Mch. 1786, when the mood of Congress was quite different from what it had been early in 1785. The committee report, submitted 5 Apr. 1786, also urged that "the federal Government . . . turn their earliest attention to the Marine department" (JCC, XXX, 144n., 152-3; DNA: RG 360, PCC No. 25, II, f. 459; M/247). No action was taken, though almost every member of Congress spoke when the report was under discussion on 2 May 1786 (Rodney's diary, Burnett, *Letters of Members*, VIII, 347-8). Another committee on this committee report was appointed 8 Aug. 1786, to be succeeded by still another on 11 Sep. 1786 and renewed on 12 Feb. 1787 (JCC, XXXI, 505n., 645n.; XXXII, 42n.).

[82] JCC, XXX, 307n.; 311-12; Jay to President of Congress, 23 May 1786 (DNA: RG 360, PCC No. 80; M/247). Grayson to Madison, 28 May 1786; Grayson to Washington, 27 May 1786 (Burnett, *Letters of Members*, VIII, 372, 374).

[83] Otto to Vergennes, 8 Oct. 1785 (Bancroft, *History of the formation of the Constitution*, I, 460).

he had previously assumed. He not only withheld from Congress the offer of *Alliance*: he also submitted a report strongly opposing the Pinckney resolution. He declared himself very dubious about it on grounds of policy and he also questioned whether such a loan could be obtained. Even if it were feasible, he thought it improper to make the attempt since the government could not depend on the states and therefore could not pledge the public faith for repayment of specific sums. But the significance of his report lies not so much in this departure from ground theretofore occupied as in the reasons which prompted it. The people, Jay argued, would never provide public revenues except by constitutional coercion or by "the dictates of reason." Since the former was not possible, the people might be moved by other compulsions. They would feel more disposed to purchase peace while experiencing the evils of the war than they would "to repay borrowed sums when all their fears and dangers from Sallee rovers, Algerine Corsairs, and the pirates of Tunis and Tripoli" had vanished. Hence Congress should inform the states what sums would be required to purchase treaties and should declare that until requisitions for this object were met "the depredations of the barbarians will . . . continue and increase."[84] This argument for a kind of coercion through deliberate inaction reflected a belief that the dictates of reason could be brought into play by aroused fears or appeals to self-interest. It was, of course, as valid a basis for the use of force Jay had so recently advocated as it was for purchasing peace in emulation of the example of Europe. But the inconsistency concealed a deeper purpose than the mere desire to compel compliance with the requisitions of Congress.

This latent intent becomes clearer in light of the response Jay made to Jefferson's proposal for a special confederacy embracing the very objects Jay professed to seek—the creation of a navy, the response with force to Algerine insults, the repudiation of Europe's acquiescence in piracy, the defense of American trade in the Mediterranean, and the espousal of those noble sentiments of national honor Jay had voiced to John Paul Jones. But when Lafayette suggested that the American ministers be authorized to propose such a league, Jay forwarded his letter to Congress without comment.[85] The next day he replied to Lafayette and again expressed his preference for war. "What Plan or System Congress will adopt," he wrote, ". . . is not yet decided. The one you Suggest has Advantages. The great Question I think is, whether we shall wage War or pay Tribute? I for my Part prefer War, and consequently am ready for every proper Plan of uniting and multi-

---

[84] According to Thomson's Resolve Book (DNA: RG 360, PCC No. 190; JCC, XXX, 312n.) Jay reported on 30 May 1786, but this fact is not recorded in the journals of Congress. The letter of the American Commissioners of 28 Mch. 1786 was evidently referred to the committee and its successors, to whom was referred Jay's report of 20 Oct. 1785. Since, as the endorsement on the copy of that letter shows, the original was not returned or reported upon (JCC, XXX, 307n.; see also note 81), Jay's report, dated 29 May 1786, must have suffered the same fate. It is not to be found among his official reports in DNA: RG 360, PCC No. 81; M/247; the text is printed in *Dipl. Corr., 1783-89*, I, 606-8.

[85] Jay to the President of Congress, 15 Feb. 1787, enclosing that of Lafayette to himself, 28 Oct. 1786 (DNA: RG 360, PCC No. 80; M/247).

plying their Enemies."[86] The opportunity to declare this preference again and in a public report soon presented itself in a manner which suggests that Jefferson also employed other indirect means of bringing the plan before Congress. This may have resulted from the outline of its features that he gave to James Monroe.[87] It was also undoubtedly influenced by the bitter hostility Virginians and Kentuckians felt toward Jay because they feared he was prepared to yield the right of navigating the Mississippi. In any event the scheme that seemed to offer the most practicable mode of coping with the Barbary pirates and of creating a naval establishment now came not from the commercial North but from the agricultural South. It encountered Jay's firm opposition.

Virginia had instructed her delegates in Congress to take up the question of relations with Barbary and on 27 July 1787 they advanced Jefferson's proposal for a confederacy that they later described as "a measure which appears . . . practicable, which would be . . . honorable to the Union, and in which the states are . . . materially interested."[88] William Grayson, who had once disagreed with Jay on the use of force and was hostile to him on other grounds, brought the measure forward in such detailed terms as to suggest that he had somehow acquired a copy of Jefferson's draft of the proposed convention. His motion called for authorization to be given to Jefferson alone, not jointly to him and Adams as Lafayette had suggested. It directed the American minister to France "to form a Confederacy with the powers of Europe who are now at War with the piratical states . . . or may be disposed to go to war with them." It prohibited any of the contracting powers from making a separate peace, called for mutual guarantees against renewed aggression, and required express stipulations for the assignment of quotas in men and shipping, for the ascertainment of cruising stations at different periods, and for the establishment of the general command. Some indication of Congressional support for the proposal may be found in the fact that the blanks providing for a limitation of the quota of the United States were filled so as to provide for "one frigate and two sloops of war"—Jefferson had suggested "a couple of frigates" to Monroe—but afterward this restriction on the number of vessels was eliminated. The motion to refer the matter to the Secretary for Foreign Affairs was opposed by three delegates.[89]

Jay reported in less than a week, rejecting the measure he had so recently led Lafayette to believe consonant with his own views. He called attention to the opinion expressed in his 1785 report that it would always be more for the honor and interest of the United States

<hr>

[86] Jay to Lafayette, 16 Feb. 1787 (DNA: RG 59, PCC No. 121; M/61).

[87] TJ to Monroe, 11 Aug. 1787.

[88] Virginia delegates to Gov. Randolph, 3 Nov. 1787 (Burnett, *Letters of Members*, VIII, 670-4).

[89] Grayson's motion was introduced 27 July 1787 (JCC, XXXIII, 419-20; DNA: RG 360, PCC No. 81). Those voting against the reference were Yates of New York and Smith and Schureman of New Jersey. Two years earlier Grayson had written; "The Secy for foreign affairs is for war with these pirates; but I cannot see the policy of this, and think we had better follow the scandalous example of the European powers, and make peace with them as soon as we can" (Grayson to Madison, 14 Oct. 1785; Burnett, *Letters of Members*, VIII, 235).

to prefer war to tribute. Nevertheless, he felt that the proposed confederacy was rendered unseasonable by the inefficiency of the national government and the inadequacy of the public revenues. He refrained from any discussion of the merits of the proposal or its promise of lessened costs through concerted action, but evidently still thought in terms of the considerable naval force he had recommended in 1785: "a vigorous Effort to revive our Navigation and meliorate our finances, should at least accompany any Exertions to establish a naval Force; for otherwise that Force will be languid and incompetent to its Object." Even if such a confederacy could be achieved, he thought it highly probable that the quota of the United States would be much greater than could be met. With the offer of *Alliance* still undisclosed, he doubted that Congress could build, equip, and keep manned even three frigates. Nor would it become the dignity of the nation "to take the Lead in forming such a Confederation, unless they were prepared to support such spirited Propositions by spirited and important Operations." Hence he thought it would be "most prudent for Congress to delay entering into the proposed, or indeed any other Engagements, until the Means of executing them appear to be clearly within their Reach."[90]

The Virginia delegates reported the rejection of the plan, expressed their regret that a measure so prudent could not be adopted, and explained that "the desperate prospect of the United States being enabled to comply with their Stipulations in such a Confederacy, has obliged Congress to decline any Overtures towards this desirable Object."[91] This explanation, resting on the undeniably distressed state of the public finances, had a plausibility that caused Jefferson late in life to accept it as valid. Without exception, historians have also embraced it.

But such an explanation is not wholly convincing, especially as viewed in light of the changing postures of the Secretary for Foreign Affairs and his avoidance of any public comment on the merits of the plan. Had Jay consistently supported his declared preference for war, he might have pointed out that the estimated cost of maintaining *Alliance* on cruise for a year with a complement of 250 men was not much more than the amount that Congress, acting on his recommendation, had appropriated for tribute in response to Lamb's memorial.[92] Jay himself had urged in 1785 that the United States create a navy of five 40-gun frigates, in addition to subsidizing the arming of merchantmen. This was a more costly and formidable force than Jefferson contemplated for the combined fleet of the proposed concert of powers. Yet when support for vigorous measures seemed to be growing in Congress, Jay receded, doubting that a loan could be obtained, though John Adams—at Jefferson's urging and in order to save the nation's credit—soon borrowed a million guilders in Amsterdam even

90 Jay's report on Grayson's motion is dated 2 Aug. 1787 (DNA: RG 360, PCC No. 81, III, f. 139; M/247; JCC, XXXIII, 451-2).
91 Virginia delegates to Gov. Randolph, 3 Nov. 1787 (Burnett, *Letters of Members*, VIII, 670-4).
92 A Marine estimate of 1783 calculated this cost at $120,000, including recruitment bounties; the appropriation for negotiating treaties with the Barbary states was $80,000 (DNA: RG 360, PCC No. 144; M/247).

without authorization from Congress. Jay had also recommended a broad offensive and defensive alliance with Portugal against the Barbary pirates and regarded this as one of several warlike measures demanded by "the Honor and Interest of the United States."[93] Yet when asked to report on a far more limited and less costly plan for concerted action, he privately conceded its merit and then publicly rejected it because he thought it incompatible with the national dignity for the government to advance a proposition it might not be able to support. Clearly, if the United States lacked the power to draw forth the resources of the nation in 1786 when Jay opposed Pinckney's motion, it lacked the power to do so in 1785 when he called for a formidable naval establishment. Whatever he may have accepted later as explanation for the rejection of his plan, Jefferson at the time anticipated the argument that would be employed and refused to be swayed by it. "It will be said there is no money in the treasury," he wrote. "There never will be money in the treasury till the confederacy shews it's teeth."[94] Coercive power was indeed lacking, but so also was the will to use the means that were available.

In this perhaps lies the key to Jay's inconsistency. Believing that the people would respond only when made to feel the need for a stronger government, he rested his hope in mounting adversity. "Good will come out of evil; these discontents nourish federal ideas," he declared of European restrictions on American trade. So also the declaration of war by Algiers would tend to draw the nation "more closely into a federal system."[95] Where Jefferson was willing even to exceed the limits of delegated authority by using the treaty power to augment national control over commerce, Jay would make no further treaties until the system had been defined.[96] Even while the Federal Convention was sitting he declared that reason and public spirit would "require the Aid of Calamity to render their Dictates effectual."[97] This trust in the uses of adversity was made explicit when he advised Congress to warn the states that the Algerine depredations would continue until funds needed to purchase peace were forthcoming. Such a reliance for the framing of policy was, of course, rooted in a distrust of the people. Jay realized fully that the resources of the nation were abundant and that the enterprise of Americans was astonishing. Yet he found "Reason to fear that too much has been expected from the virtue and good Sense of the People."[98]

[93] Jay's report of 20 Oct. 1785 (JCC, XXIX, 842-4; DNA: RG 360, PCC No. 81; M/247); on Adams' negotiation of a new loan see TJ to Adams, 2 Mch. 1788; TJ to Jay, 16 Mch. 1788.

[94] TJ to Monroe, 11 Aug. 1786.

[95] Jay to Adams, 14 Oct. 1785 (*Correspondence and public papers of John Jay*, ed. Johnston, III, 172-3). See also Jay to Lafayette, 15 July 1785 (same, III, 160-2).

[96] TJ to Monroe, 17 June 1785; TJ to Adams, 28 July 1785. TJ had also suggested earlier that whatever sums were needed to gain free access to European seas should be levied on commerce with European powers, in a specifically designated impost, in order to signify to them "that they protect these enormities for their own loss" (TJ to Greene, 12 Jan. 1786). On Jay's report on the model treaty drafted by TJ, see note 61 above.

[97] Jay to TJ, 24 Apr. 1787.

[98] Jay to TJ, 9 Feb. 1787.

Jay was far from alone in finding merit in a policy of calculated inaction born of distrust. George Washington, who was even more anxious than he to suppress the Mediterranean pirates by force, asked how it was possible "in such an enlightened, in such a liberal age . . . the great maritime powers of Europe should submit to pay an annual tribute to the little piratical states of Barbary?" He considered it "the highest disgrace on them to become tributary to such banditti, who might for half the sum that is paid them be exterminated from the Earth."[99] Yet when Lafayette laid before him Jefferson's plan for concerted action, his response was substantially the same as that voiced by Jay: it was vain to look for respect abroad, vain to complain of restrictions on commerce, and "vain . . . to talk of chastising the Algerians, or doing ourselves justice in any other respect, till the wisdom and force of the Union can be more concentrated and better applied."[100] Washington indeed fortified the fears of Jay in a remarkable exchange of letters that coincided with the latter's retreat from his advocacy of war against the Algerines.

Early in 1786 Jay informed Washington of a plan being concerted for a general convention to revise the Articles of Confederation. He wondered whether the people were ripe for it or whether the system proposed, which he did not describe, could "only be expected from calamity and commotion."[101] Though Washington concurred in the sentiments, he feared that the people were not ready, not "yet sufficiently *misled* to retract from error." But he thought the fabric was tottering, public virtue almost lost, and the structure foredoomed if nothing were done.[102] Jay, encouraged, disclosed his apprehensions of an approaching crisis or revolution: "The mass of men are neither wise nor good, and the virtue like the other resources of the country, can only be drawn to a point and exerted by strong circumstances ably managed, or a strong government ably administered."[103] Washington agreed that the government was probably formed on "too good an opinion of human nature" and that coercive power was necessary to make men adopt measures for their own good.[104] Jay beheld an opening and boldly seized it. "Shall we have a king?" he asked—and then hastened to answer: "Not in my opinion while other experiments remain untried." But he had dared to raise the question and he went on to put others of compatible tenor. Should there be an upper legis-

[99] Washington to Lafayette, 15 Aug. 1786 and 25 Mch. 1787 (Washington, *Writings*, ed. Fitzpatrick, XXVIII, 521; XXIX, 185).

[100] Washington to Lafayette, 15 Aug. 1787 (same, XXIX, 260).

[101] Jay to Washington, 16 Mch. 1786 (DLC: Washington Papers). Jay did not describe the plan for a general convention or say where or by whom it was originated. He could not have had in mind the Virginia resolution which led ultimately to the Annapolis Convention of 1786, for that called only for a meeting of commissioners to discuss the question of uniform trade regulations (see note, Madison to TJ, 22 Jan. 1786). He perhaps referred to some such plan for a convention as Hamilton had drafted in 1783 and had then "abandoned for want of support" (Hamilton's resolution, July 1783, Syrett, *Hamilton*, III, 420-6).

[102] Washington to Jay, 18 May 1786 (Washington, *Writings*, ed. Fitzpatrick, XXVIII, 431), emphasis in original.

[103] Jay to Washington, 27 June 1786 (DLC: Washington Papers).

[104] Washington to Jay, 1 Aug. 1786 (Washington, *Writings*, ed. Fitzpatrick, XXVIII, 502).

lative chamber with members having life tenure? Should all state officials, military and civil, be commissioned and removable by the national government?[105] The drift of the questions was clear, evidencing Jay's conviction that "a national Government as strong as may be compatible with Liberty, is necessary to give . . . Security and Respectability."[106] Without dissociating himself from their plain tendency, Washington avoided the specific questions. "But," he asked in a highly significant response, "is the public mind matured for such an important change as the one you have suggested? What would be the consequences of a premature attempt? My opinion is, that this Coun-

---

[105] Jay to Washington, 7 Jan. 1787 (DLC: Washington Papers).

[106] Jay to Adams, 4 July 1787 (DNA: RG 59, PCC No. 121; M/61). Jay's bold question did not arise in a vacuum. It was just at this time that George Beckwith was told by an informant—almost certainly William Samuel Johnson—that there was not a gentleman from New Hampshire to Georgia who was not in favor of exchanging the existing government for a monarchy; that this view was held by the most powerful group, including some of the ablest men in the states; that they desired to form a government as nearly resembling that of Great Britain as possible; that they had "cast their eyes to . . . one of the King's Sons"; that they had fixed upon two gentlemen to go to Europe for this purpose "when they judge that matters are ripe for it"; and that Washington had been "lately sounded upon the subject" (Beckwith's report, enclosed in Dorchester to Sydney, 10 Apr. 1787, PRO: CO 42/50, f. 92, 94-9). The informant detailed two reports about Washington's attitude; first, that he was determined not to return to public life; second, that he looked forward "to the supreme power" and had prompted the Rev. David Griffith to sound the country "on this very subject." Griffith, former surgeon and chaplain of the Third Virginia Regiment and one for whom Washington had high regard, had spent some time in New York in the winter of 1786-1787 and had "mixed much with men in office"—of whom Jay must certainly have been one (Beckwith's report, same; Washington, *Writings*, ed. Fitzpatrick, XXVIII, 400-1). A few months later when Hamilton, "for reasons of some moment," made an effort to discover the author of a reported plan to bring over Frederick, Duke of York, as head of an American monarchy, Humphreys replied that this was not a novel idea, that its aim was "to feel the public pulse and to discover whether the public mind would be startled with propositions of Royalty," and that the day before a dinner the duke had been offered as the first toast, "half jest, half earnest" (see note 11, Editorial Note, French protest on the tonnage acts, under 18 Jan. 1791; Humphreys to Hamilton, 1 Sep. 1787, Syrett, *Hamilton* IV, 240-2). In London a leading New York Loyalist, William Smith, anxiously "nursing up the British interest in the old Colonies," succinctly characterized such hopes on both sides of the Atlantic. Disapproving Mirabeau's attack on the Cincinnati, he yet took comfort in the thought that its effect would be "an Increase of Ferments between the Parties in America who were republicans against the Men of Property, all wishing a new Revolution either for a Government on the British Model or the antient union" (Smith, *Diary*, ed. Upton, I, 98, 124). The division was not so simple and the aims in part mistaken, but the probings in America and especially in New York unquestionably existed. All of this lends support to the view recorded by TJ that the Annapolis Convention of 1786 had been divided "on the question of a republican or kingly government" but that, "so general thro' the states, was the sentiment in favor of the former, that the friends of the latter confined themselves to a course of obstruction only, and delay, to every thing proposed. They hoped that, nothing being done, and all things going from bad to worse, a kingly government might be usurped, and submitted to by the people, as better than anarchy . . ." (Ford, I, 158).

Such was the climate in which Jay's question was put, a fact which adds significance to Washington's response that the existing structure of government was like a house ready to fall and that it was not likely any change of conduct could remedy its defects.

try must yet feel and see more, before it can be accomplished."[107] Much as Washington and Jay sympathized with the Algerine captives, much as they deplored the Barbary depredations, much as they proclaimed the dishonor of becoming tributary to pirate states, they were united in the conviction that this obstacle to American trade in the Mediterranean was one means—though but one of several—by which the people might be made to feel and see more clearly the need for a government of coercive powers.

Whatever may have been the influence of a deliberate choice of inaction until the means of execution came clearly within reach, a government competent to draw forth the resources of the nation was soon created. Against slight opposition, the article in the Constitution authorizing the establishment of a navy—a provision carried over in altered phraseology from the Articles of Confederation—escaped that "spirit of censure, which . . . spared few other parts" of the fundamental law.[108] The premise on which the policy of inaction rested had now been removed. This afforded a better means of gauging the cleavage between those who, regardless of the state of the fisc or the structure of government, rejected the European posture of subservience and those who professed a desire to make no engagements until a government of coercive authority could gain the acceptance of the American people.

When the government of the Confederation was about to expire, John Jay provided a revealing forecast of the manner in which the means would be used. "I wish the Porte could be sounded on this Subject," he wrote to Jefferson. "Overtures for a Treaty from us to that Court, made at *this Period*, would probably be grateful, and might eventually terminate all our Difficulties with Algiers, &ca., especially as the Emperor of Morocco will promote it."[109] He had no doubt

---

[107] Washington to Jay, 10 Mch. 1787 (Washington, *Writings*, ed. Fitzpatrick, xxix, 176). Washington's response on this occasion invites comparison with his firmness in putting an end to the Newburgh conspiracy of 1783, an unequivocal intercession which inspired TJ to say "that the moderation and virtue of a single character has probably prevented this revolution from being closed as most others have been by a subversion of that liberty it was intended to establish" (TJ to Washington, 16 Apr. 1784). At that time also external grievances were manipulated by Morris, Hamilton, Knox, and others to augment the powers of the national government, as Richard T. Kohn, "The Inside History of the Newburgh Conspiracy: America and the Coup d'Etat," WMQ, 3rd ser., xxvii (Apr. 1970), 187-220, has brilliantly demonstrated. But three years later, lacking the direct authority he then possessed and troubled as most great military leaders have been by the turmoil and confusion of free institutions, Washington was far less decisive. His reponse could not have failed to raise hopes among those who desired to go as far as possible in emulation of the British form of government, even to the establishment of a monarchy (see preceding note). But the elevated public debate of the next two years concerning the principles and structure of government proved what severe limits the national character imposed upon such unrealistic hopes.

[108] James Madison in *Federalist* No. 41 (*The Federalist*, ed. B. F. Wright, p. 298). Madison attributed this to the "palpable necessity of the power to provide and maintain a navy" and echoed TJ in observing that "The batteries most capable of repelling foreign enterprises on our safety, are happily such as can never be turned by a perfidious government against our liberties" (see TJ to Monroe, 11 Aug. 1786).

[109] Jay to TJ, 25 Nov. 1788; emphasis in original.

forgotten that Jefferson had already given him Vergennes' opinion of such an approach: it would require costly presents at Constantinople and would not "procure . . . peace at Algiers one penny the cheaper."[110] But on his own initiative and with the means clearly in prospect, Jay now proposed overtures that would lead to tribute, not war.

III

The first matter of business that Jefferson discussed with the President on assuming office was the situation of "the unfortunate Christians in Captivity among the Barbarians."[111] Washington had long been deeply concerned, the more so because impostors were beginning to mulct the families of missing sailors whom they reported as captured. Officious individuals were also bringing forward schemes for redemption of the captives that threatened to interfere with the agency of the Mathurins that Jefferson had already authorized under injunctions of the strictest secrecy. One such proposal came from a well-connected Virginian and former Revolutionary officer, John Skey Eustace, who busied himself in the summer of 1789 by preparing an elaborate questionnaire on the history of the various national orders of redemptioners and on the cost of liberating slaves. Eustace presented this to an officer of the order at Bordeaux and forwarded the resultant answers and other documents to John Jay. This added nothing useful to the information already available and the unauthorized negotiation, undertaken without the knowledge or approval of the American minister in France, paralleled the plan already under way. Jay thanked Eustace for his "interesting Letter . . . accompanied with several Papers" and promised to turn it over to the new Secretary of State, being persuaded he would "avail himself of the Information it contains."[112]

[110] TJ to Jay, 23 May 1786.
[111] Entry of 23 Mch. 1790 (Washington, *Diaries*, ed. Fitzpatrick, IV, 106).
[112] On Washington's reaction to impostors, see his letters to Thomas Thomson, 21 Aug. and 18 Sep. 1788; to Matthew Irwin, 20 July 1789; and to Matthew Whiting, 18 Nov. 1789 (Washington, *Writings*, XXX, 56-7, 357-8, 458-9; texts of the letters to Irwin and Whiting are in DNA: RG 59, MLR; Thomson to Washington, 12 Aug. 1788; D. Horton to Whiting, 25 Sep. 1789; Whiting to Washington, 25 Oct. 1789, DLC: Washington Papers; see also TJ to the President of Pennsylvania, 24 June 1790, enclosing an account of a sailor calling himself Archibald Ross).
John Skey Eustace to John Jay, 15 July 1789, with various enclosures as numbered by Remsen: (1) Account of the three orders of redemptioners, dated Paris, 27 June 1789; (2) 16-page printed *Discours* of the Archbishop of Paris before the National Assembly, 26 June 1789; (3) 8-page printed *Arrêtés de la Nation*, 15 July 1789, both of these pamphlets being inscribed to Jay by Eustace; (4) Eustace to Audibert, 8 July 1789 and Audibert to Eustace, 10 July 1789, together with an 8-page questionnaire including Audibert's answers; in French, together with translations; (5) printed text of *Copie de la lettre de Mgr. . . . de Castries, au Provincial de la merci* [of Toulouse], 7 Nov. 1784, together with translation; (6) translation of an account of 316 French slaves redeemed at Algiers in 1785, including "three Gentlemen" (DNA: RG 59, MLR, misfiled at 1 Jan. 1791); Washington to Eustace, 23 Nov. 1789 (same); Jay to Eustace, 7 Oct. 1789 (same, PCC No. 121); Short to Eustace, 30 Oct. 1789 (DLC: Short Papers).
These and other unauthorized interventions in foreign affairs by private

Another letter awaiting Jefferson's attention was one that had been sent to Jay early in 1790:[113]

> Mr. Gerry, with his respects to the Secretary of State, encloses two letters, the substance of which has this morning been communicated to the President of the United States, and relates to some American prisoners at Algiers. The President has desired that the papers may be enclosed to the Secretary of State, and is disposed to do whatever may be requisite on his part to afford relief to the unhappy sufferers, adding at the same time, that by letters from Mr. Jefferson dated in August last, our Bankers at Holland had given information of their having money in their hands appropriated amongst other purposes, to the one mentioned.

The first enclosure was a letter from James Anderson of Greenock to Thomas Russell of Boston covering the second, which was from the British consul at Algiers, Charles Logie. Anderson cautioned Russell that it might be improper to publish Logie's letter but gave him full liberty to make every other use of it to facilitate the release of the prisoners. "The whole sum wanted for their redemption," he added, "cannot be an object of hesitation to the States of America."[114] Logie's letter was in response to an inquiry forwarded by Anderson concerning John Robertson, one of the captives whose family in New England was reported to be in distressed circumstances. Logie was willing to intercede not only for Robertson but also for the others. "If you can by writing to your friends in America be of any service to those poor people," he urged, "God will reward you for it. I can say that they are all good worthy people and in a most dismal situation. There are fourteen prisoners in all, Americans, English, Scotch and Irish . . . and all Slaves as subjects of the States of America." Logie suggested that funds be deposited in London in order to save exchange. Those contributing could be assured that he would draw for no more than the exact sum paid out in ransom and fees. In the case of Robertson, he concluded, this would amount to not more than £500 sterling. While the scarcity of slaves and the liberality of Spain and other countries since 1785 had caused a very considerable increase in ransom costs, this was a very high figure—greater by far than the current estimate by O'Bryen or the limit of £150 allowed by Jefferson to the Mathurins. But Logie, as "an act of humanity," declared that he would not charge a commission or other expenses.[115] This effort to solicit American funds for the release of Robertson failed. But in a subsequent attempt that provides some gauge of the price when not affected by anticipated contributions of wealthy American merchants,

individuals, whether arising from interested or altruistic motives—see, for example, Cathalan's not disinterested proposal enclosed in his letter to TJ, 22 Jan. 1791—only complicated the issue. TJ ignored all such efforts, well knowing that "the more all voluntary interpositions are discouraged, the better for our unhappy friends" (TJ to Short, 25 Apr. 1791).

[113] Gerry to Jay, 21 Jan. 1790 (DNA: RG 59, DL; M/40).

[114] Anderson to Russell, Greenock, 4 Oct. 1789 (same).

[115] Logie to Anderson, Algiers, 24 June 1789 (same). There were fifteen prisoners in Algiers at this date, not fourteen as Logie states.

Logie did succeed in obtaining the release of one Charles Colvill. The total cost in his case was far lower than that estimated for Robertson: it came to only £300 even when augmented by "additional and unavoidable expences." Colvill was "a Scotch boy."[116]

The accumulated letters and appeals, awakening humane impulses that overlooked interested motives, brought no solutions but may have given new stimulus to Jefferson's sense of urgency. In France, to support the effort of the Mathurins, he had "let it be reported and believed at Algiers that Congress would not redeem" the captives —an assumed mask of inhumanity that had drawn upon him "the most afflicting reproaches."[117] Now in conversations with Washington

[116] Short to TJ, 7 July 1790; in dollar equivalents TJ estimated Logie's figure for Robertson at $2,137.50 and the actual cost of Colvill's ransom at $1,481 (TJ's memorandum of costs of ransom, 1785-1790; MS in DLC: TJ Papers, 59:10110). It is very doubtful whether Logie's efforts proceeded from purely humanitarian considerations.

There has been confusion about dates, position, number and names of captives, and other details surrounding the capture of *Maria* and *Dauphin*—a confusion arising from contemporary records as well as subsequent writings (see, for example, Barnby, *The prisoners of Algiers*, p. 1, 40, 41; Smelser, *The Congress founds the navy*, p. 35; Malone, *Jefferson*, II, 27, 28, 32; Allen, *Our navy and the Barbary corsairs*, p. 13-14). The schooner *Maria*, Isaac Stephens master, owned by William Foster & Co. of Boston, bound from Boston to Cadiz, was taken off Cape St. Vincent on 24 July 1785. The ship *Dauphin*, Richard O'Bryen master, owned by Matthew and Thomas Irwin & Co. of Philadelphia, bound from St. Ubes to Philadelphia, was taken eighty leagues northwest of St. Ubes on 30 July 1785. *Maria* had on board Captain Stephens, Alexander Forsyth, mate, and a crew of four; *Dauphin* had on board Captain O'Bryen, Andrew Montgomery, mate, a crew of eleven, and two passengers (Captain Zaccheus Coffin and a Frenchman, Jacobus Tessanier), in all twenty-one persons (O'Bryen to TJ, 24 Aug. 1785; O'Bryen, Coffin, and Stephens to Congress, 28 Aug. 1785, DNA: RG 360, PCC No. 42, VI, f. 117). TJ himself erred in giving the total and Jay, in investigating the case of Whiting (see note 112 above), informed Washington that only the names of captains and mates were known (TJ to Eppes, 11 Dec. 1785; Jay to Washington, 16 Nov. 1789; DNA: RG 59, MLR). Jay was evidently misled by his clerks, for the original petition of the three captains provides the names of all officers and members of the crews; the office report, prepared by the usually reliable Remsen and based on departmental records, contained other errors as well (MS in Remsen's hand, enclosed in Jay to Washington, 16 Nov. 1789; same).

This and other documents also misled TJ in giving the date of capture of *Maria* as 25 July 1785 and the position of *Dauphin* as "50. Leagues Westward of Lisbon" instead of "Eighty Leagues to the Nwd. of St. Ubes" (Document IV; petition of O'Bryen and others, 28 Aug. 1785, DNA: RG 360, PCC No. 42, VI, f. 119). By 1790 *Dauphin* was occasionally called *Dolphin*, an error that still persists (see Document IV, enclosure 8; the perpetuation of this error was insured by its inclusion in ASP, *Foreign Relations*, I, 103).

A list of names of prisoners prepared by TJ and based on O'Bryen's petition to Congress of 26 Dec. 1789 showed that the number had been reduced at that time to fifteen (MS in TJ's hand, DLC: TJ Papers, 232:41545, where TJ gives the date of the petition as 20 Dec. 1789; see O'Bryen to TJ, 12 Dec. 1789). At the time TJ prepared his report the number was fourteen, owing to the ransom of Colvill (James Simpson to [Washington], 25 Aug. 1790; see Document IV, enclosure 8). None of the six who had died in the plagues of 1787 and 1788 (including Captain Coffin) or the one who had been ransomed was captured with *Maria* (see Johnson to TJ, 25 Feb. 1791, for the names of those who died in the plague). Only eight of the twenty-one captured were native-born Americans.

[117] Document IV; TJ to Jay, 4 May 1788; Jay to the President of Congress, 12 Sep. 1788 (DNA: RG 360, PCC No. 80; M/247; JCC, XXXIV, 523-4).

and others and in assessing the evidence found in the departmental files, he had additional reason to feel more acutely the prisoners' anguish and his own compatriots' feelings:[118]

O Lord how Long wilt thou turn a Deaf Ear to our Calamites and Make Congress and Commonwealth the instruments of Cruelty O Lord hear our petitions and prayers . . . only one Cargo of tobacco would Redeem us all or a Small Lottery in Each State and Many ways Might be pointed out No body to is Disposed for Charity untill we are no More and then thay will Say thay are Sorrey the poor man is Dead god be mercifull to his Soul But take Care you Dont bring on judgments I Could fill a Number of Sheets But to No affect only Realize My Situation a Starveing family My Self a Slave that has Lived a freeman. . . .

It is not surprising that Jefferson's instructions to Short about the Algerine business took on a new urgency. "Do not let it languish a moment, nor leave us a moment uninformed of any thing relative to it," he wrote. "It is in truth a tender business, and more felt as such in this than in any other country."[119]

But the cold reality of commerce was also involved. Within a few days after Jefferson assumed office a letter was transmitted to him from a merchant in Maryland who urged the familiar device for achieving a purchased peace:[120]

From fifty to one hundred Vessells, would be immediately employed in the Mediterranean, if we could send there with safety. If that trade could be opened to our Ships it would give a Spring to the New England Fisheries, as well as open a market for our produce. I hope this Session of Congress will not pass over, without taking into consideration that very important business. It is presumed that a sum of money not exceeding, Twenty or thirty thousand dollars properly applied to the Bey of Algiers, might gain us permission to navigate those seas with safety. Perhaps a handsome ship laden with Naval Stores, would effect the treaty.

At Present we are compelled to send to Britain for Ships to carry american produce into the Mediterranean Sea, a market always open and Suited for us.

Such mercantile hopes were stimulated by American traders who were now profiting from the treaty negotiated with Morocco by Thomas Barclay. In 1789 one of them, William Cowell of the schooner *Machias*, carried a cargo of iron and $2,000 in specie to

[118] Petition of Isaac Stephens to Congress, 9 Feb. 1788 (DNA: RG 360, PCC No. 59, I, f. 319-22).

[119] TJ to Short, 26 July 1790; soon after his first consultation with Washington, TJ had shown him his letter of 6 Apr. 1790 to Short urging him to press the negotiations (Washington, *Diaries*, ed. Fitzpatrick, IV, 113).

[120] "Extract of a letter from a Merchant in Maryd. March 28th. 1790" (DLC; in an unidentified hand; endorsed by TJ: "Mediterranean trade"). The writer has been identified by the Library of Congress as William Brown of Annapolis. If this attribution is correct, then the recipient may have been Charles Carroll, who acted as a channel of communication between TJ and Brown early in 1790 (see TJ to Brown, 18 Apr. and 13 June 1790).

Morocco, made a ready sale, and returned with 70 mules "very well contented with his voyage."[121] But Sidi Mahomet, the Emperor who had agreed to the treaty for a remarkably low sum and without a pledge of annual tribute, was becoming impatient because no envoy laden with presents had arrived from the United States. When this came to the attention of the Secretary for Foreign Affairs, Jay dispatched an urgent explanation to the American agent, Francesco Chiappe, and accompanied it with a communication from the President to the Emperor.[122] Unfortunately these letters arrived two months after the death of Sidi Mahomet—an event which of course required the sending of an envoy "to compliment the new sovereign with the usual gifts and confirm the good peace and harmony."[123] Half of the period of four months allotted for the confirmation of the treaty had already expired. But through his own timely entreaties and the distribution of further gifts, Chiappe explained, the new Emperor had agreed to allow an additional four months. Chiappe also gave some indication of what the successor of Sidi Mahomet hoped for: the Spanish envoy was expected at Tangier aboard a frigate "bearing a

[121] Giuseppe Chiappe to Thomas Barclay, 28 Mch. 1789 (DNA: RG 59, DL; M/41).

[122] Thomas Barclay to John Jay, 20 July 1789, forwarding one from Giuseppe Chiappe to Barclay, 28 Mch. 1789, which enclosed one from Francesco Chiappe to himself, 11 Feb. 1789; G. Chiappe to President of Congress, 25 Apr. and 18 July 1789 (RC's and translations in DNA: RG 360, PCC No. 98, M/247; DNA: RG 59, AL, M/40, M/41); Jay to F. Chiappe, 1 Dec. 1789; Jay to G. Chiappe, 1 Dec. 1789 (DLC: Washington Papers; DNA: RG 59, FL, M/61; same, RG 59, PCC No. 121); Washington to the Emperor of Morocco, 1 Dec. 1789 (Washington, *Writings*, ed. Fitzpatrick, XXX, 474-6); Jay to Carmichael, 7 Dec. 1789; Jay to Short, 11 Dec. 1789; Jay to Gouverneur Morris, 15 Dec. 1789 (same; DLC: Washington Papers). Jay's urgency and extraordinary care in sending these communications through three separate channels stands in marked contrast to his handling of the instructions of Congress sent through Lamb to the American Commissioners. Washington read and approved the dispatches on the day they were submitted to him (Washington to Jay, 1 Dec. 1789; DNA: RG 59, MLR; Washington, *Diaries*, ed. Fitzpatrick, IV, 56).

[123] Francesco Chiappe received the packet from Jay on 11 June 1790, either from Carmichael or Short, for Morris detained the one sent to him because he feared "Chiappe . . . might be one of the many cut off" by the new Emperor. Morris also stated: "At present it would seem that every Thing is in Confusion at Morocco. The Crown is contested, and the Ultimate Possession must be decided by Arms. Should the present cruel Occupant be successful He may perhaps cancel every Thing which has been done by his late Father for he entertains it is said an Attachment to a System of Politics directly the Reverse of that which was adopted by his Predecessor" (Morris to Jay, London, 7 July 1790; RC in DLC; endorsed by TJ as received 14 Oct. 1790 and so recorded in SJL). TJ was at Monticello when he received Morris' letter, but he did not include it among those he sent to Washington on 27 Oct. 1790 "containing the substance of such letters, received since the 14th. of Sep. 1790. as the President might wish to have communicated to him." The prediction proved to be accurate. Francesco Chiappe to John Jay, 3 Aug. 1790 (RC in Italian, DNA: RG 360, PCC No. 98; M/247; endorsed by TJ as received 1 Dec. 1790 and so recorded in SJL); Francesco Chiappe to George Washington, 3 Aug. 1790, responding for the Emperor to Washington's letter of 1 Dec. 1789 and assuring him that the monarch would not take it ill if the arrival of the American ambassador were delayed four months later than the arrival of the other ambassadors (RC in Italian, DNA: RG 59, MLR; sent by Lear to TJ, 1 Dec. 1790; same, RG 59, SDC).

great Gift" thought to amount to 150,000 piastres.[124] This information came to Jefferson only after the additional period of grace had expired.

The Algerine captives had repeatedly petitioned Congress and had made a direct appeal to Washington even before he was elected President. But, aside from authorizations by Congress in 1787 and 1788 for their redemption and subsistence, no action was taken until shortly after Jefferson became Secretary of State. Acting on the latest appeal of the captives, the House of Representatives on 14 May 1790 referred the petition to the Secretary of State "with instruction to examine the same and report his Opinion thereupon to the House."[125] It is scarcely plausible to assume that this directive about a matter in which Jefferson had been so long and deeply interested did not involve the kind of close collaboration that existed between him and Madison on related problems of commerce. It is still less so to accept at face value his explanation for the delay of several months in submitting his findings. The delay, it seems clear, was a calculated result of that collaboration.

It is significant, first of all, that at the third session Jefferson did not submit his report to the House of Representatives as required by its resolution, but to the President, who immediately transmitted it to both the House and the Senate.[126] His explanation for the delay was that, at the time the House asked him to report on the captives, "there still existed some Expectation that certain Measures . . . employed to effect their Redemption, the Success of which depended on their Secrecy, might prove effectual." These expectations, however, had been so far weakened by information received during the recess as to make it his duty to lay a full statement before the President.[127] But this explanation begged the question. If news arriving during the recess had weakened expectations, it had also undermined the grounds given for postponement—the need for secrecy. How, in any case, did this news transform an obligation to respond to the House of Representatives into a duty to report to the President? Jefferson had indeed received three dispatches from William Short that held out very little hope of success. But these did not come to hand until late October and, discouraging as they were, it is extremely doubtful that they had done anything to alter his expectations.[128] The fact is that, much as Jefferson respected Père Chauvier for his discretion, good judgment,

<hr />

124 Francesco Chiappe to John Jay, 4 Sep. 1790 (DNA: RG 59, MLR; recorded in SJL as received 1 Dec. 1790, with duplicate received 2 Mch. 1791); see TJ to Chiappe, 13 May 1791.

125 Richard O'Bryen to George Washington, 22 Sep. 1788 (DLC: Washington Papers), appealing to him on behalf of the prisoners; text of resolution of 14 May 1790, signed by John Beckley (DNA: RG 59, MLR; *Annals*, II, 1572; JHR, I, 216).

126 TJ submitted his report (Document IV) on 28 Dec. 1790 and Washington two days later transmitted it to both houses for such provision as to them should "seem most expedient" (JHR, I, 345).

127 Document IV.

128 Short to TJ, 14 and 25 June; 7 July 1790; see Document IV, note to enclosure 3.

and humanitarian instincts, he had little hope even at the time he left France that the Mathurins would succeed. When he finally directed his report to the President, he appended to it extracts from Short's dispatches as evidence of the weakened expectations. But in doing so he discreetly omitted from one of them an observation proving that his own discouragement had not originated during the recess of Congress. "You will recollect," Short observed in the passage that Congress did not see, "the little hope which you had of its success before your departure."[129]

There were other examples of judicious editing that Jefferson gave to the evidence submitted with his report. In preparing it he went through his correspondence for the preceding five years and compiled two memoranda. The first and longer of these was an abstract of communications about the naval strength of the Barbary states and the amounts of ransom paid or estimated. This information he utilized both in his report on the Algerine captives and in that on trade with the Mediterranean.[130] The second memorandum was based in part on the first and contained some information omitted from his report to the President. One of these omissions showed that in 1786 "the Government of Naples redeemed @ 4032.^{tt} tournois, average" or about $700. Another was a note of an article under a Venice dateline from the *Gazette de France* of 20 April 1790: "the Emperor has notified the European consuls that he will offer Algiers 500 Doll. apeice for all Christian slaves."[131] The inclusion of such evidence, otherwise of no significance, would have weakened in some degree the principal argument of the report concerning the price of ransom—that it was already exorbitant and the trend upward. This was an argument generally supported by the evidence, but Jefferson apparently sought by such omissions to strengthen it and thus draw attention to his own preference for the use of force in approaching two interconnected problems. As the report shows in its concluding paragraph, the liberation of the captives was intimately connected with the liberation of Mediterranean commerce. Since both distresses proceeded from the same cause, both might "very probably" be relieved by the same measures—measures which, in serving this dual purpose, might benefit from aroused humanitarian impulses as well as from economic motives.

Jefferson's strategic coupling of these two problems seems to offer the most satisfactory explanation for the postponement of the report and for its being directed to the President instead of the House of Representatives. Such a strategy promised, in addition to its appeal to humane and interested motives, the immense advantage of placing the recommended solution under the patronage of the President. Late in October Jefferson sent to Washington the full texts of Short's three discouraging reports on the efforts of the Mathurins, suggested that

[129] Short to TJ, 7 July 1790; in acknowledging this and other dispatches, TJ instructed Short to "pursue the redemption of our captives through the same channel, till some better means can be devised" (TJ to Short, 23 Jan. 1791).

[130] Abstract of TJ's correspondence from 14 Aug. 1785 to 9 July 1790 pertaining to Algerine prisoners and Barbary affairs (3-page MS in TJ's hand, DLC: TJ Papers, 232: 41540-1).

[131] Memorandum concerning Algerine captives, 1785-1790 (MS in TJ's hand, DLC: TJ Papers, 59: 10110).

the Algerine affairs seemed "to call for some new decision," and then, in company with Madison, stopped by Mount Vernon on his way to Philadelphia.[132] Simultaneously a letter from James Simpson, Russian consul at Gibraltar, appeared in the press providing the latest information about the prisoners. Simpson said he had given particulars to the President, and added: "I continue firmly of opinion that you have but very little chance of peace with Algiers, during the present Dey's life."[133] Jefferson attached Simpson's letter to his report, but, so far as known, his suggestions of items for inclusion in the President's Annual Message did not refer either to the Algerine captives or to trade with the Mediterranean. Alexander Hamilton supplied this stimulus by calling Washington's attention to the "almost total interruption of our Mediterranean Trade from the dread of Piratical depredentations" and the "great importance of opening that trade, and the expediency of considering whether protection cannot be afforded to it."[134]

In his message Washington made no direct allusion to the Algerine captives, but he did call particular attention to the state of trade with the Mediterranean. "So many circumstances unite in rendering the present state of it distressful to us," he advised, "that you will not think any deliberations mis-employed, which may lead to its relief and protection."[135] Within three days the response of the House of Representatives, drafted by Madison, declared that "the present state of our trade to the Mediterranean seems not less to demand, and will accordingly receive, the attention which you have recommended."[136] Four days later the House referred that part of the President's speech to the Secretary of State and within two weeks Jefferson submitted his two interconnected reports, both bearing the same date. In the report on the captives, Jefferson could now do what had not been possible in the previous session—reinforce his argument by linking it with the problem of Mediterranean commerce "now under the Consideration of Congress." Even this stretched the point, for no bill had been introduced, the House had only promised to give attention to the matter, and the Senate had not even done that.[137] But the circumstances surrounding this presidential message and legislative response make it difficult to avoid the conclusion that Jefferson and Madison had collaborated, under benefit of a timely and parallel support by Hamilton.

132 TJ to Washington, 27 Oct. 1790; see Editorial Note to group of documents on commercial and diplomatic relations with Great Britain, 15 Dec. 1790.

133 "Extract of a letter from James Stimpson, Esq. Russian consul at Gibraltar, August 30, 1790" (*Gazette of the United States*, 3 Nov. 1790); see also Document IV, enclosure 8.

134 TJ's draft of items for the President's message, 29 Nov. 1790; Hamilton, notes for consideration of the President, 1 Dec. 1790 (Syrett, *Hamilton*, VII, 173).

135 Annual message, 8 Dec. 1790 (Washington, *Writings*, ed. Fitzpatrick, XXXI, 167).

136 JHR, I, 335; Brant, *Madison*, III, 325; Extract of the speech of the President 8 Dec. and also resolution referring it to Secretary of State, 15 Dec. 1790, both attested by John Beckley (DLC: TJ Papers, 58: 10000 and 10039).

137 The Senate's response to the President, reported by Ellsworth for a committee including King and Izard, merely said: "Impressed with the importance of a free intercourse with the Mediterranean, we shall not think any deliberations misemployed, which may conduce to the adoption of proper measures for removing the impediments that obstruct it" (JS, I, 221).

These exchanges avoided all mention of the plight of the captives, yet gave Jefferson the opportunity which he apparently sought through a deliberate postponement of the report. Washington's silence on that problem, which definitely was under consideration by the House, suggests his awareness that the opportunity would be seized by the Secretary of State.

Measures for the relief and protection of trade in the Mediterranean might, of course, emulate the traditional custom of Europe or they might employ force as Jefferson had long urged. But how could the distress of the captives be alleviated save by ransom? Revealing the coherence of his plan and purpose, Jefferson suggested that force might be countered by force through captures of the enemy for purposes of exchange. The enemy, of course, were Algerines, but Jefferson went further: "Perhaps Turkish Captives may be Objects of greater Partiality with them, as their Government is entirely in the Hands of Turks, who are treated, in every Instance as a superior Order of Beings."[138] The very fact that he advanced such a specific suggestion reflects the intensity of his repugnance to the idea of paying ransom or tribute. But its full significance emerges only in the light of a remarkable document that Jefferson received just before he and Madison met Washington at Mount Vernon.

This document contained the proposal of an anonymous European who was introduced to William Short by Count Volney, whom Jefferson had known in France as a member of the cultivated circle about Madame Helvétius at Auteuil. Volney's auspices merited consideration and the author justified it. He had long resided at Constantinople and Algiers. He was both well-informed and a man of some substance— possibly a Levantine merchant—but his identity is shrouded in the secrecy upon which he understandably insisted. The assumption on which his proposal rested was that the American flag could not enter the Mediterranean until Algiers had been brought to terms and that this could be done only through force—an assumption coinciding perfectly with Jefferson's own objectives. The means suggested by the author was that the United States, directly or through an authorized private company, should send frigates to cruise against Greek and Turkish merchant vessels in the eastern Mediterranean and thus achieve peace with Algiers through pressure upon Turkey. He believed that three frigates would suffice, that the prizes taken would more than offset the cost of such a venture, and that the capture of two Turkish caravels could force the Ottoman Empire to compel both peace and the release of the Algerine captives. His hope, so he assured Short, was that the operation would be entirely mercantile and that those engaged in it should receive all of the profits. He was ready to invest a part of his fortune in what he believed to be "the most expeditious and certain mode of effecting the business at Algiers" and he hoped the United States would countenance it by issuing letters of marque for the purpose. Since privateering against the Barbary states was not feasible, "Congress should not make any scruple in re-

138 Document IV.

imbursing themselves on all the subjects of the Grand Seignior."[139] In forwarding this extraordinary proposal—which included the suggestion that, at certain stages, the commander of the expedition should fly English colors—William Short understated the obvious when he said that there were "several objections which occur at first view."[140]

The United States certainly could not issue letters of marque for preying upon the commerce of a nation with which it was at peace. But this obvious fact only places in bolder relief the use that Jefferson did make of a proposal that could not be publicly countenanced. It is understandable that he should have failed to include in his extracts of the dispatch Short's succinct summary of the proposal, even though the President to whom the report was ostensibly directed had already seen the full text of the letter and also its interesting enclosure. Jefferson probably translated the document himself, mistakenly identifying Volney as the author, and then caused a copy of the translation to be made by his chief clerk, Henry Remsen, Jr. The latter text he gave to the President, who retained a copy of it for his own files and then passed Remsen's copy on to the Vice-President. No copy was retained in the files of the Department of State.[141] This circumstance suggests that Washington and Jefferson had reached an understanding on policy and were also agreed in sharing with Adams a document requiring the utmost secrecy. Naturally Jefferson could not attach such a document to an official report addressed to the President though actually intended for the Congress. But he could and did employ it discreetly with the heads of the administration to reinforce his argument for the use of force. This may have been his primary and perhaps his only object, for he knew at first hand from Adams and from Washington through Lafayette that both men had emphatically declared their preference for war over tribute. But if those behind the closed doors of the Senate should support a policy of force, he may have wished to provide their President with a document showing how the privateering that had had such a strong appeal to New Englanders during the Revolution might be employed with promise of equal profits in the Mediterranean. The United States would still be at peace with Turkey and therefore unable to issue letters of marque against her commerce. But Russia was not. Also, as the Russian ambassador at Paris had indicated to Jefferson, her interests in the Mediterranean and in the possibility of concerted action coincided with those of the United States.

With such possibilities in prospect, the meaning of Jefferson's public allusion to Turkish captives could be illuminated by this secret document showing how measures adopted to alleviate one distress might "very probably involve the Relief of the other." The application of force, public as well as private, might bring peace, profits, and a lucrative trade with the Mediterranean as well as the release of the prisoners. If John Adams should reveal the document to a few of the more influential members of the Senate, humane and interested motives

---

[139] Document I.
[140] Short to TJ, 7 July 1790; this letter was one of those sent by TJ to Washington from Monticello (TJ to Washington, 27 Oct. 1790).
[141] The text retained by Washington (DLC: Washington Papers) is identical with that copied by Remsen from the translation (MHi: AM).

alike might be aroused, combined, and strengthened toward a single end. The anonymous European, who stood ready to disclose his identity if the venture succeeded and who was also willing to serve as negotiator when the regencies had been forced to treat, had provided a timely assistance that Jefferson could not have anticipated when he deliberately postponed his report.

IV

With the plight of the prisoners thus linked to the problem of commerce, Jefferson shaped the report on Mediterranean trade toward his plan for a special confederacy, whose merits Washington, Adams, Jay, and others had acknowledged. As usual, he presented the available alternatives to Congress but left no one in doubt as to where his own preference lay. The sole obstacle to trade with the Mediterranean was the unprovoked war with Algiers and the sole remedy was to bring that to an end. A purchased peace emulating the example of rich and powerful nations would mean, as with them, placing interest before honor. It would also cost enormous sums, with the estimates ranging upwards to a million dollars as calculated by a knowledgeable person whose name Jefferson was not free to disclose.[142] To this would be added costly presents for confirming treaties or for ceremonial occasions. Even so, force would be required to punish infractions since pirates who could make great nations bow in tribute would not hesitate to violate their pledges. The decision between war, tribute, and ransom rested with the Congress. But, balancing the cost of tribute against the cost of force, Jefferson pointed to the danger that Portugal might make peace with Algiers. If this should happen—a point supported by a timely letter from the Russian consul at Gibraltar—American vessels could not approach the coasts of Europe and even the growing trade with Morocco would be lost.[143] Russia, Portugal, and other powers at war with the pirate states could reasonably be expected to join in a concerted operation for applying to the Mediterranean the De Massiac plan of constant cruising that Portugal had successfully demonstrated in recent years in patrolling the straits. By this means, after a few years, the object could be "completely obtained."[144]

Jefferson buttressed his argument for an allied naval force by attaching carefully selected extracts of documents, among them his own letter to Jay with its almost casual comment on the plan of De

[142] This was a Dr. Warner (or Werner), a surgeon to the British consulate in Algiers (see TJ's memoranda of conversations with Warner, ca. Jan. 1788; Barnby, *The prisoners of Algiers*, p. 142-3).

[143] Document IV, enclosure 8; "Extract of a letter from James Stimpson . . . August 30, 1790" (*Gazette of the United States*, 3 Nov. 1790). Robert Morris also turned over to TJ a letter from John Bulkeley of Lisbon, reporting that "them rovers cruise in the straights with impunity, as they have nothing to dread but the Portuguese Cruisers." He said that Admiral José de Mello commanding the Portuguese fleet was "a warm friend to the American Constitution" and without this protection the coasts outside the straits "would be infested with them Plunderers." TJ did not receive the letter until after the session ended (John Bulkeley to Robert Morris, undated but endorsed by Remsen as received 6 Mch. 1790, DNA: RG 59, MLR).

[144] Document III.

Massiac. But he discreetly omitted Lafayette's letter of 1786 arguing the merits of "the Antipiratical Confederacy." To have employed it might have brought embarrassment to the marquis and also to American relations with France. But again, as in 1786, Jefferson rested on his own muted statement and allowed others to press the case for him. He included extracts from two letters written by Adams to Jay, the first of which reckoned the cost of peace with the Barbary states as "not much less than two hundred thousand pounds Sterling." The second estimated that additional presents could cost as much as £60,-000 annually, which Adams regarded as "an enormous sum . . . but infinitely less than the expence of fighting."[145] Jefferson, of course, was aware that the Vice-President would see this testimony and perhaps recall his own declared preference for war over tribute. But Adams' estimates—placed beside the proposal of the anonymous European calling for only three frigates and the plan requiring even less than this through concert with Russia, Portugal, and other powers—threw doubt upon his own assertion that war was "infinitely" more costly than tribute. To drive the point home, Jefferson chose D'Estaing's eloquent tribute to De Massiac's plan. D'Estaing, like Lafayette, wrote as an honorary citizen of the United States and he could speak with far more authority on matters of naval strategy. He gave unqualified endorsement to the idea of a constant cruise and declared that a blockade was both more economical and more certain than bombardment. The latter was like using guineas to break window-panes, which could always be repaired. But if several powers could maintain a constant blockade for only a few years, Barbary piracy would come to an end. Speaking as a citizen of America, a title dear to his heart, D'Estaing declared that this was the sole means of bringing to terms the only people who could "take pleasure in disturbing *our* commerce." He hoped that the United States would set the example for Europe by pursuing this plan "formed on principles of humanity."[146] Jefferson attached the entire text of the letter to his report.

Although he subordinated his own opinions while letting D'Estaing and others speak for him, the issue was as squarely presented as when John Jay made his blunt recommendations in 1785. As evidence of the importance Jefferson attached to the choice of war or tribute he first read the report to the President and then submitted it to him in writing. Washington returned it with the following comment: "There is nothing in the enclosed report that does, in the opinion of the P. require alteration."[147] Jefferson's letter to the Speaker of the House was presented the same day that Washington sent to Congress his message on the Algerine captives. He urged complete secrecy, since publication

145 Document III, enclosures 2 and 5.

146 Document III, enclosure 7 (for original text, see D'Estaing to TJ, 17 May 1786); D'Estaing's eloquent plea echoed that of Lafayette to Knox urging the same point when he expressed his "ambitious and boundless desire that the United States may in every circumstance strike out new and most direct roads to glory and consequence" (Lafayette to Knox, 6 Mch. 1786; DNA: RG 360, PCC No. 150, I).

147 Document I, Washington to TJ, before 28 Dec. 1790 (RC in DLC: TJ Papers, 60: 10411; undated; addressed: "Secretary of State"; not recorded in SJL or SJPL).

might embarrass D'Estaing and since France, England, and other powers at peace with the Barbary states might, as Vergennes had done in 1786, endeavor to block plans for cooperative action. In the House the galleries were cleared when the report was read and in the Senate it was consigned to the deeper secrecy of legislative inaction.[148]

Both of the interconnected reports were tabled and the House of Representatives, despite its assurance to the President that trade with the Mediterranean demanded and would receive attention, took no action beyond sending that report to the Senate. In the Senate, William Maclay immediately grasped its unequivocal intent, though he egregiously mistook the motives that prompted it. "The report," he declared, "seemed to breathe resentment, and abounded with martial estimates in a naval way." Later, he was certain that it was the intent "of the Court to have a fleet and army."[149] The meaning was also grasped by the committee to which the report, along with that on the Algerine captives, was referred. This committee, headed by Jefferson's friend John Langdon, included the Senate's most influential supporters of Hamiltonian measures—Robert Morris, Rufus King, Caleb Strong, and Oliver Ellsworth. It had been appointed initially to consider that part of the President's message that Hamilton had urged upon him— the great importance of the Mediterranean trade and the question of affording protection for it. The committee reported immediately. The "trade of the United States to the Mediterranean cannot be protected but by a naval force," it began boldly—and then retreated into equivocation: "it will be proper to resort to the same as soon as the state of the public finances will admit."[150] Robert Morris himself, under vastly altered circumstances, had advanced such a proposal in 1782 and had then withdrawn it the next year.[151] When the report came under consideration, Maclay suspected a plot to engage in a "distant war with these pirates" in order to increase debts and taxes, which were declared in debate to be the only bonds of Union.[152]

The isolated Pennsylvanian was more certain of it two weeks later when the Secretary of State, having just received several letters from the Algerine captives, forwarded them to the President of the Senate.[153] What these documents did, first of all, was to unveil still further the private objects John Lamb's sponsors had had in view in 1785. The first letter, on the basis of Lamb's purported "Instructions," described these objects in explicit detail: The Americans had little money—and that paper—but the country abounded in masts, yards, spars, tar, pitch, iron and other naval stores; no nation in the world could build

---

[148] Document v; JHR, I, 346; Annals, II, 1838; the report was sent to the Senate with a "confidential communication" from the Secretary of State (JS, I, 227).

[149] Maclay, Journal, ed. Maclay, p. 364. Maclay erred in thinking that the report concerned the Algerine captives: that had already been transmitted by the President.

[150] Langdon reported on 6 Jan. 1791 (JS, I, 222, 227, 230; JEP, I, 73).

[151] C. O. Paullin, Navy of the Revolution, p. 242-51.

[152] Maclay, Journal, ed. Maclay, p. 366.

[153] Document VI; Maclay, Journal, ed. Maclay, p. 375-6. Maclay thought that the former report of the committee had "recommended a war" with Algiers and that TJ's communication had the same design.

"such fine and fast sailing Cruisers as the Americans"; if the Algerines —"a brave people like themselves"—should make peace, they could be supplied with American Cruisers and naval stores very cheaply, at prices to be fixed by treaty; and these stores and swift vessels would be advantageous to the Algerines if they should be at war with the Dutch, the Danes, or the Swedes. O'Bryen, the letter asserted, had read Lamb's "Instructions" several times. Far more knowledgeable about Algerine affairs than the envoy, he knew that even such persuasive arguments would require an opportune moment and a privacy unpenetrated by the consuls of England, France, and Spain. Such a moment arrived in the spring of 1790 when two of the American captives in the Dey's palace were able to convey the propositions to the new General of Marine and Secretary for Foreign Affairs. In reporting this, O'Bryen described the source of his information as being *"partly* the Instructions of the American Ambassador" who came to Algiers in 1786.[154] As adapted by him from a remembered or transcribed copy withheld until "good Fortune and favorable Opportunities" should occur, these, therefore, were the private instructions framed for a public emissary to cover concealed objectives—objectives that, however unwittingly, had been countenanced by Hamilton, Jay, and others. This was the exact opposite of Jefferson's proposed confederacy that sought to end both piracy and the indignity of being tributary to it. It was in effect a proposal to form a league with pirate states and to insure their capacity to continue depredations on the trade of the small powers of the Baltic and the Mediterranean. The engine for achieving this would be the conversion of public funds into tribute in the form of cruisers and naval stores, at prices to be fixed in treaty by an envoy negotiating both for the public and for well-concealed private interests.

Jefferson, characteristically, allowed this disclosure of the partial "Instructions of the American Ambassador" to stand uncorrected. As a prisoner O'Bryen consistently urged negotiation and tribute rather than force, but his letters brought such timely support for Jefferson's policy as to render any mere gesture to set the record straight both imprudent and gratuitous. For the Algerine captive now made explicit what the report on Mediterranean trade silently passed over: that the United States had "three powerful Enemies in Algiers"—France, Spain, and, most inveterate of all, England. To this was added the argument long since advanced by John Adams that a closed Mediterranean involved a levy on trade: O'Bryen estimated that Americans paid upwards of £1,000,000 sterling annually to Great Britain for insurance. But the essence of his communications was that the situation of France, Spain, and England made it difficult for them to oppose American negotiations for peace; that the Algerine minister, favorably impressed by the belated revelation of these instructions of the American emissary, was inclined toward peace with the United States; and that his own price for influence with the Dey and Divan would be

---

[154] Document VI, enclosure I. For Lamb's official instructions, see Documents II and III in group of documents on the missions to the Barbary states, under 12 Oct. 1785.

only "an American built Schooner of 12 Guns." Spain, having just purchased "a very dishonorable and impolitic Peace" at exorbitant cost, was reported to be in such difficulty with Algiers that the treaty would not be renewed after the death of the Dey who had agreed to it. Moreover, Spain was reported to be "arming to support the Grand Duke of Tuscany"—one of the small powers Jefferson hoped to include in the confederacy—and the Algerine minister was quoted as saying that any nation taking the side of Russia would become an enemy of Algiers.[155] Under such circumstances the moment for proposing a concerted action would appear to have been far more auspicious than when Jay recommended an alliance with Portugal in 1785. The object of O'Bryen's letters, as William Maclay perceived, was to show that a peace might be obtained on easy terms "by furnishing . . . naval stores."[156] But in their new sense of urgency, in their pointing to the preoccupations of France, Spain, and England elsewhere, and in their fresh evidence of the costliness, the instability, and the humiliation of a purchased peace, the letters gave strong and timely support to Jefferson's proposed use of naval force.

The letters were referred to Langdon's committee and its own report on Mediterranean trade was recommitted. A week later Langdon reported to the Senate in executive session. His committee recommended that the President be authorized to take such measures as he might deem necessary for the redemption of the captives, provided the cost did not exceed $40,000 and that measures be taken to confirm the treaty with Morocco at a cost of not more than $20,000. The Senate approved the measure after deleting the limitation on negotiations with Morocco. On the same day the committee resubmitted its report calling for a naval force as soon as the public finances would admit.[157] Maclay considered this as intending to declare war against the Algerines and "vociferated against the measure" to such an extent that he thought he had offended his colleague, Robert Morris. This would suggest that Morris, now the owner of the frigate *Alliance*, was among those in the Senate whom Maclay described as favoring a fleet and the expenditure of "half a million dollars rather than redeem these unhappy men."[158] The report was recommitted and Langdon's committee was given an enlarged directive to "consider the subject, and report generally thereon."[159]

In a message drafted by Jefferson, Washington called for restoration of the stricken provision of funds for confirmation of the Moroccan treaty. The Senate acquiesced by passing a bill appropriating $20,000 for this purpose. It also authorized the President to borrow this sum and pledged the good faith of the nation for its repayment.[160] At the same time the Senate advised the President to suspend efforts to

[155] Document VI, enclosure II.

[156] Maclay, *Journal*, ed. Maclay, p. 376.

[157] JS, I, 234; JEP, I, 72.

[158] Maclay, *Journal*, ed. Maclay, p. 383. "This thing of a fleet has been working among our members all the session," Maclay added; "I have heard it break out often."

[159] JS, I, 237-8; JEP, I, 73.

[160] Documents VII and VIII; JEP, I, 75.

ransom the prisoners until the situation of the treasury should warrant it. A motion to augment by $40,000 the appropriation of the bill for confirming the Moroccan treaty, probably offered by Maclay, was defeated. The reason given for suspension of efforts at ransom was that large expenditures had been authorized for protection of the western frontiers. But, in the closing hours of the session, the necessity for secrecy in an appropriation bill involving both houses was undoubtedly an important factor.[161] Even the equivocal resolution calling for a naval force to protect trade with the Mediterranean when the public finances permitted was allowed to die in committee. With these hesitant measures, there disappeared the auspicious moment that had brought into conjunction "good Fortune and favorable Opportunities."

V

When Louis Guillaume Otto reported Washington's Annual Message, he amplified in glowing terms its description of the rich harvests, the expanding commerce and industry, the rising credit and respectability of the nation, the revenues in excess of those predicted by the Secretary of the Treasury, and the other evidences of peace, prosperity, and tranquillity under an administration crowned with success beyond all expectations.[162] The means thought lacking in 1785 when Jay called for a strong naval establishment and a far-reaching alliance with Portugal were now abundantly present. The opportunity to abandon what John Adams considered a policy of poor economy was at hand: once the sole obstacle had been removed, the Mediterranean promised to be "an extensive Field of Commerce and Wealth to America," as both the perceptive prisoner in Algiers and the Secretary of the Treasury recognized.[163] With the grant of coercive authority to draw forth the resources of the nation, the good faith pledged to redeem a loan for placating the new Emperor of Morocco could as readily have been pledged for one authorizing concerted action to put an end to piracy and tribute. "Now . . . the business is complete," William Samuel Johnson had exclaimed in great joy to William Maclay on passage of the excise bill: "We have a revenue that will support the government and every necessary measure of Government." Maclay warned him that an opposition dangerous to government might be aroused through "overexertion to obtain support."[164] This was prophetic, but the powers granted and the resources available were not utilized.

"Not exercising the powers we have," Fisher Ames declared in the

---

161 JEP, I, 77-8; JS, I, 294, 298, 302, 306, 309; JHR, I, 400. The importance of secrecy is indicated both in TJ's communication of his report on trade with the Mediterranean and in subsequent developments (see Washington to TJ, 10 Mch. 1792; TJ to Washington, 1 Apr. 1792; Washington to the Senate, 8 May 1792). Maclay, unjustly and in terms of extreme harshness, blamed the President for the postponement of efforts to ransom the Algerine captives (Maclay, *Journal*, ed. Maclay, p. 408-9).

162 Otto to Montmorin, 10 Dec. 1790 (DLC: Henry Adams Transcripts).

163 Document VI, enclosure I.

164 Maclay, *Journal*, ed. Maclay, p. 390.

debate on the national bank bill, "may be as pernicious as usurping those we have not."[165] He was making the valid point—one Madison himself had advanced in *The Federalist*—that the former government had often exercised implied powers and could scarcely proceed without doing so. The redemption of the captives in Algiers, he suggested, was not expressly granted though irresistibly implied. But in this debate as elsewhere during this session, the eloquent champion of Hamiltonian measures was as silent as the Secretary of the Treasury himself about the need for a naval establishment and for protection of trade with the Mediterranean. The nation was now in a far better situation to support a maritime force than it had been during the Revolution. But thenceforth, for the remainder of this divisive decade, those who wielded the powers of government and who have been credited with laying the foundations of the American navy applied those powers in emulation of the discredited example of Europe.

It was in vain that Jefferson in 1792 again summarized the alternatives for the President. He conceded that the cost of naval force would be considerable—$400,000 at the outset and $125,000 annually thereafter—but argued that the examples of De Massiac and more recently of the Portuguese had proved the practicability of the constant cruise and that, with the reasonable prospect of cooperation with Portugal, Naples, Genoa, and Malta, this would be "the most honourable and efficaceaous way of having peace."[166] In 1793 when the British consul, Charles Logie, promoted a truce between Portugal and Algiers, the result was a disaster—a trebling of insurance, the capture of more than a hundred seamen, and the seizure of some eleven American vessels in the Atlantic.[167] There was an outcry of indignation throughout the United States against Great Britain. Old resentments over commercial restrictions, impressment of seamen, and limitation of the maritime rights of neutrals were stirred afresh by the suspicion that the Algerines had been unleashed against American vessels on the high seas. This widespread conviction, though denied by the British Secretary for Foreign Affairs, was nevertheless well-grounded.[168] War with Great Britain was threatened and at last, such

[165] *Annals*, II, 1905.

[166] TJ to Washington, 1 Apr. 1792, enclosing his remarks on ransom and peace with the Algerines.

[167] TJ's report showed that for some time there had existed apprehensions about a truce between Portugal and Algiers (Document III). Richard O'Bryen warned that there would be "fatal consequences" for the United States, resulting in a vast expense in building and equipping eight or ten cruisers; TJ sent this emphatic warning to the Senate as soon as the Second Congress opened (TJ to the President of the Senate, 9 Dec. 1791, enclosing O'Bryen to Congress, 28 Apr. 1791). Barnby, *The prisoners of Algiers*, p. 111, lists the eleven American vessels captured in the short-lived truce in the autumn of 1793, along with a total of 105 seamen (see also James Simpson to Secretary of State, 21 Oct., 21 and 27 Nov. 1793).

[168] On the question of British complicity in the truce, see Humphreys to Secretary of State, 17 Jan. 1793; Pinckney to Secretary of State, 25 Nov. 1793. Irwin, *Barbary powers*, p. 58-60, 67-8, noted the conflicting testimony and the absence of conclusive proof of Grenville's disavowal of British initiative or intent to injure the United States; but the question was set at rest by Barnby, *The prisoners of Algiers*, p. 103, who explains the instructions to Logie as arising

was the demand from all sections of the nation, a naval force of six frigates was authorized. Even so, there was no deflection in the prevailing policy toward Algiers. To the cost of a navy was now added the cost of becoming a tributary nation, more than a million dollars being expended for the purchase of peace in addition to the costs of ransom and annual payments of tribute.[169] None of the frigates built in the war-fever of 1794 was employed against the Algerine pirates. But when that crisis resulted in the treaty which strained to the breaking point the bonds between France and the United States, they did find employment against the former ally.

Just before the third session of the First Congress opened, Mrs. Henrietta Colden revealed her son's ambition to serve in the American navy which, in youthful enthusiasm, he already envisioned as "riding triumphant on the Ocean, and giving Laws to Europe." In the meantime, the doting mother revealed, he would be glad to serve as mate on one of the revenue cutters. This remarkable appeal for patronage, couched in such effusively patriotic terms as to arouse wonder, was surprisingly addressed not to the Secretary of the Treasury but to the Secretary of State. Jefferson responded while his reports were being considered. In "our infant attempts at a marine," he wrote, "I had indeed expected that some vessels of greater dignity would be agreed on."[170] The expectation was fully justified by the arguments that had been advanced by Morris in his report of 1782, by Jay in that of 1785, and by Hamilton in *The Federalist*. But the will to create a navy and to use it against the Barbary states was as lacking after the powers had been granted as it was before. The state of the treasury and the cost of wars with the Indians—ineptly directed and vastly augmented by favored contracts for military arms and supplies—cannot provide a satisfactory explanation for this abrupt abandonment of a position previously defended with reason and eloquence. Like the similar abandonment of arguments in the eleventh *Federalist* for achieving commercial reciprocity, this had deeper roots in the fundamental cleavage in American politics.

Late in life Jefferson explained Hamilton's opposition to a navy at this period as being based on his "known anxieties for a close connection with Great Britain, to which he might apprehend danger from collision between their vessels and ours."[171] The closer connection with Great Britain and the avoidance of war with her at all costs was one side of the coin: the other was a determination from the very

from the need Great Britain had for a naval base at Algiers to oppose French Mediterranean power.

[169] The cost of the treaty with Algiers alone, including naval stores and the estimated cost of a frigate, was set by the Secretary of the Treasury at $992,463.25 (report of Oliver Wolcott, 4 Jan. 1797, cited with list of payments by Irwin, *Barbary powers*, p. 80-1).

[170] Mrs. Colden to TJ, 25 Nov. 1790; TJ to Mrs. Colden, 20 Jan. 1791. TJ's expectations, together with Maclay's fears of a growing sentiment for a navy, find confirmation in a remarkable letter from John Barry, late commander of *Alliance*. Barry was evidently so convinced of the correctness of information given him that it was "in contemplation to have a few Ships of War built" that he offered suggestions—interestingly enough to TJ rather than to the Secretary of War—about the design of the vessels (Barry to TJ, 14 Feb. 1791).

[171] TJ to Adams, 1 Nov. 1822.

outset to destroy the alliance with France.[172] The policy of subservience toward Great Britain merged imperceptibly with that of subservience toward African piracy, each lending strength to the other. Thus, despite the words that the Secretary of the Treasury wrote for the President's message calling for protection to trade with the Mediterranean, his position on this aspect of foreign policy was in effect if not in principle scarcely distinguishable from that of Lord Sheffield. This added greatly to the ultimate cost in money and resources. But the real levy was upon the national character in committing the young republic to the example of those rich and powerful nations that, in this instance, counted "their Interest more than their Honor."[173] It was not until the executive power fell into his own hands that Jefferson was able to put into effect the policy he had advocated from the beginning and thus to inaugurate a new era in the history of the great sea where commerce originated. All nations, as he intended, were beneficiaries of this policy compounded of altruism, interest, and respect for the national character.

[172] See Editorial Note, group of documents on commercial and diplomatic relations with Great Britain, under 15 Dec. 1790.

[173] Arthur Chuquet, in his preface to Emile Dupuy's *Américains et Barbaresques* (Paris, 1910), p. iv, made this overly generous appraisal: "La conduite des Américains dans l'Afrique du Nord offre un contraste frappant avec celle des autres États à la même èpoque. On ne peut s'empêcher de la louer et de l'admirer. Le théâtre des opérations est très éloigné des États-Unis; les ressources de l'expédition sont restreintes; la marine américaine naît à peine; les puissances se montret sourdement hostiles. Mais la froide ténacité des Yankees surmonte tous les obstacles. Ils donnent l'exemple à la vieille Europe." But the example was not so unflawed, since during three administrations the practice set by Europe was followed by the United States.

I. A Proposal to Use Force against the Barbary States

Paris July 12th. 1790.

Means which the Congress may make use of, in order to force the Regencies of Barbary to make peace with them.

The Flag of the United States cannot be displayed 'till after the Congress shall have made Peace with the Regencies of Barbary. The consideration of the advantages which the Anglo-Americans would derive from this Navigation, have already induced the Congress to attempt Negociations with this haughty Regency, which dictates to the other two the Conduct they are pursue.[1] But these advances have been rejected, because the Algerines who renounce a War ordered by Islamisme and their particular statutes against Christians, only from Fear or the Convenience of a Majority,[2] are at the present Moment very far from contracting new Alliances.

The Congress can then flatter themselves by force only, to obtain peace with them, and now is the time to make use of it; for if the Portuguese should cease to guard the straight of Gibraltar with the same Care[3] and success, the Vessels of the United States could not without great danger even approach the coasts of Europe.

But what is the Plan which the Congress can follow to bring about an accommodation? The States are so far distant that it is impossible to think of a bombardment. Since the inexcusable errors committed by the Spaniards before Algiers, the bombardment of this Place requires double the precautions and forces[4] that were formerly requisite. In all the Attacks, badly conceived and still worse executed, the Algerines have learned to fortify the weak parts of their Cities, and have provided themselves with one hundred sloops,[5] gunners and bombadiers, against whom it will be proper to guard.

Nor is it even very certain that a cruise pursued with rigour, would render the pirates of Barbary more docile to receive propositions for Peace. Besides the support of the naval forces destined to pursue them, would occasion to Congress a very great annual expence, for which all the return would be, the doubtful hope of a remote accommodation.

Naples for some years has always had at sea, frigates and chebecks to protect commerce and cruise against the Barbarians.[6] The efforts of all these armaments have hitherto been unsuccessful; but I conceive that more experience and more information in the conduct of the Officers, who commanded these Vessels, would eventually ensure more success. I am not less certain that neither Algiers nor Tunis think[7] of making peace with that Power, as long as these means are pursued.

However the Congress have no other measures left, but there exists between them and Naples this essential difference; that is to say, the Cruise which can only be an expence to Naples may become a very lucrative and advantageous object for the United States. Their position and distance enable them in making War on the Barbarians, to attack an enemy possessed of a rich booty,[8] without fearing resentment or any reprisal from him, and it is probable that the damages which they may do, will determine him in a little time to solicit an accommodation, which will be so much the more binding,[9] as his own interest will have sealed the condition.

Algiers, Tunis and Tripoli are only Provinces of the Ottoman Empire, and altho' the Porte has for a long time ceased to send

Pachas there, the Sultan of Constantinople is always considered by them as the Sovereign Lord—his will is there respected—his orders executed. He gives the title of Pacha to two of the train of Chiefs which are at the head of the Regencies every two years. He sends an Officer to them with an honorary vest as a sign of confirmation of the dignities and power with which he has invested them. This ceremony which keeps alive the remembrance that they are only his subjects, is considered as an augmentation of pay for the Militia, who from Duty as well as interest are entirely devoted to him. The money in these three States is struck in his name. Every Friday they have public prayers in the Mosques for his prosperity. In a word, every disobedience to his orders would be there regarded as a rebellious act pregnant with the most serious consequences.

It is above all in the Regency the most formidable for Christianity—in the Kingdom, where the Militia is the most numerous and the Grand Seignior has the most power; because the Turks, of which that Militia is composed, ever look upon themselves as subjects of the Empire, and preserve for their Sovereign the greatest respect and most profound devotion.

The connections of the Barbarian Regencies with the Porte are not confined to simple respect and deference. On the accession of a new Sultan they are bound to send him an Embassy with rich presents and slaves. Constantinople on her part gives them from time to time, Vessels proper for cruising and warlike stores.[10] She permits them to recruit throughout the Provinces, and if the Metropolis is at war, the Regencies must take part in the quarrel, and send to her succour all their maritime force.

The Ottoman Porte has probably withdrawn its Pachas from Barbary, only to be able to alledge to the complaints of her Allies, the pretext of her inability to suppress excesses, which she applauded in secret, and artfully encouraged.[11] But Russia has known how to develope[12] the dark springs of this policy;[13] and at the time of her last Treaty of Peace of Cainardy, she stipulated that the Grand Seignior should be responsible for the injuries and damages that her subjects might suffer from the Regencies of Barbary.

The Emperor from this example obtained the same conditions. A capija Bacha sent by the Porte with a Khat-i-cherif, caused all the vessels and slaves to be restored, which the Corsairs had taken under the Austrian flag. The Emperor without making a particular Treaty of peace with the Regencies of Barbary, without even the expence of supporting a Consul with them, finds his merchant-men more respected than those of more formidable maritime powers.

At the Peace which will follow this present War, the Heir of the Austrian States and the Empress of Russia will without doubt exact the same advantages; and it is pretended that the King of Prussia, in gratitude for the efforts he made to prevent the ruin of the Turkish Empire, has already obtained the safety of his flag in the Mediterranean.

Hence it follows that Algiers and Tripoli are always part of the Ottoman Empire, and that Congress should not make any scruple in reimbursing themselves on all the subjects of the Grand Seignior for the unprofitable cruises[14] which their vessels shall make on the coasts of Barbary. The Turks and the Greeks have many coasting vessels in the Archipelago.[15] It is also probable that this Navigation will be much encouraged in the issue of the present War, and the numerous prizes which the United States[16] may take from them, will not only largely pay the expences of the armaments, but make the Porte[17] feel that it is important for her to cause a cessation of hostilities, against which she has no means of reprisal. Congress with regard to Turkey will find them-selves in a much more advantageous situation, than that of the States of Barbary with regard to the commercial Powers of Europe, as the latter are not sheltered from bombardments, and on the contrary the enemies of Congress have not even an idea of the route to the States.

In commencing hostilities it is of importance to strike a great blow, and as, in order to succeed the destination of the armaments must be kept secret, it is proper that Congress should defray the expences the two first years: They might afterwards abandon this advantageous cruise to mercantile speculation, and the following is the plan they may pursue.

A Frigate* of 40 guns and two others of less force should be armed, preferring in the choice of these Vessels the fastest sailers, that they might on occasion avoid a too unequal combat. It appears to me that these are sufficient, either to destroy the Barbary Corsairs, or to cruise in the Levant.[18] They should sail from the American Continent soon enough to arrive at Lisbon about the vernal equinox. There the armaments should take in such refresh-

---

* *Note.* It would be best if the first battery was of at least 18 pounders; that caliber has the advantage in fighting at a distance, the turkish Vessels, which in the principal combats exhaust their powder and their ardor, and miss, from their inexperience in levelling, almost all their objects.

ments as they may stand in need of, and might announce, without affectation, that they are bound on a cruise against the Barbarians. The Commandant alone should be informed of the real design.

From the vernal equinox to the end of June the three frigates should keep on the coasts of Spain, Provence, Italy or Barbary, according to the information they may have of the cruise of the Pirates, who then make their first appearance. If they possess themselves of any of their Chebecs, they could send them to Malta to sell the slaves.

About the first of July they go to Malta, to repair and take in refreshments and pilots acquainted with the Mediterranean and Levant. They also there reinforce their crews, for the purpose of manning without weakening themselves, the important prizes which they may make. According to the richness of the cargoes, Malta, Leghorn and Genoa are the places to which they should be sent. If the Commandant should find a good Galliot to be sold at Malta, it would be well to purchase it, as well for the purpose of chase,[19] as to take the Turkish and Grecian batteaux which ply along the coasts. This Galliot might be armed in the Maltese mode, which is well constructed for embarkation.[20] From Malta, without having divulged his project, the Commandant might go directly into the road of Damietta, bearing in his route English colours. He would there find two Caravels of the Grand Seignior, taking in rice and linen for the coast of Syria. (I suppose the Turkish war will then be terminated.) These Caravels have half their crews on shore four leagues distant from their vessels, and their lower batteries out of order. The three american frigates would then be able to carry them off.

If when the Commandant shall arrive in the road of Damietta, the two Caravels should have already sailed, he might pursue them on the coast of Syria, and find them in the road of Caiphe, or Seyde, or Baruthe or Tripoli, and always anchored so far from the land that the forts cannot protect them.

In case he should have the good luck to take them, he could conduct them to Malta or Cagliari, and from thence with the approbation of Congress,[21] send[22] one of the Turkish Officers of the Vessels with a letter, in which he should propose to the Porte the restitution of these Caravels on the following conditions.

1st. That the Grand Seignior shall make peace with Congress without requiring any present.

2d. That he oblige Algiers to restore to the United States, the

Anglo-Americans which they hold in bondage, and to pay the value of the vessels and cargoes which they have taken from them.

3d. That he compel the Regencies of Barbary to respect for the time to come[23] the flag of the United States.

It is beyond a doubt that the Porte, who never piques herself on honor except when her interest is in question, would accept with resignation such generous offers.

But in case the two Caravels should not be taken, then the armaments of Congress might fix their cruise on the route of Alexandria, and paying due respect to Europeans vessels which form caravans, should confine themselves to stopping all the Turkish and Grecian Vessels they came across. In a little time they would acquire booty sufficient to compensate Congress amply for the expence of the expedition, independent of the shares of the crews. [The Grecian seamen should be landed at the first island, and the Turks guarded in order to be sold at Malta, which is destitute of slaves since the redemption by the late Emperor of Morocco. A common man now sells there for 100 louis d'or.

The armaments of Congress will recollect that it would be imprudent to enter the straights of Rhodes, Slancho and Chios, where the Ottoman fleet resort during the fine weather. On the approach of Winter there is no other danger in the Archipelago than the shoals and winds, the fleet having then returned to Constantinople.][24] From towards the first of October until the beginning of December, the Commandant of the naval forces of the United States must endeavour to be on the coasts of Barbary, in order to pursue the Corsairs, which during that period make their second sally. In calm seasons, the vessels which the Regencies of Algiers and Tunis send to sea consist of Galliots or other rowing Vessels.

The person who gives these ideas, with the sole motive of being useful to a wise and enlightened Nation, has requested the Minister of the United States residing at Paris not to mention his name, but if his project be adopted, if every thing succeeds agreeable to his wishes, if, in fine, the success of the armaments recommended lead near to a peace, the only end which a friend of humanity has in view, then he shall be very glad to be known, because from the knowledge he has of the Eastern languages he may still be useful in the formation of Treaties. He requests Congress to be well assured, that no person will labour for their interests with more zeal and disinterestedness than himself.

N. B. The present existing Marine of Algiers is composed of

1 Corvette of 30 guns, 6 pounders, given by France.

5 Chebecks, one of which of 30 guns in the actual service of the Grand Seignior in the Archipelago.

1 small new Chebeck built at Bougie.

2 Galliots, which go out in calm weather, and

1 Frigate of 40 guns of 18[25] pounders, which will be finished in September.

The naval forces go out together from the Port of Algiers, and afterwards separate.

Tr (MHi: AM); entirely in hand of Henry Remsen, Jr., from translation of MS (DLC); in French; in clerk's hand, with corrections by William Short; at head of text TJ wrote: "[p]ar M. Volney." Another Tr, made from that by Remsen (DLC: Washington Papers). See Editorial Note.

It is evident that the author, however familiar he may have been with "the Eastern languages," was not at ease in French. The clerk who transcribed the missing prototype compounded the original errors and made two lengthy omissions, which Short inserted in MS (see notes 13 and 24 below). The translation—very probably made by TJ himself—is not exact (see notes below). TJ erred in supposing that, as indicated by his notation on MS, the document was written by C.F.C. Volney. It was, on the contrary, written by an unidentified person whom Volney introduced to Short (see Short to TJ, 7 July 1790, public).

1 MS: "qu'elles ont à tenir."
2 MS: ". . . qui ne renoncent que par Crainte où par une Convenance majeure a la guerre Contre les Créthiens ordonnées par l'islamisme et leurs statuts particuliers."
3 MS: "la même exactitude."
4 MS: "le double de Précautions, de préparatifs et de Soins."
5 MS: "chaloupes."
6 MS: "les barbaresques."
7 MS: "ne penseront pas."
8 MS: "un Ennemy sur lequel il y a des riches Captures à faire."
9 MS: "plus Solide."
10 MS: "et des munitions de Guerre."
11 MS: "et qu'elle encourage même Sous le manteau."
12 MS: "deviner."
13 In MS this entire clause is interlined in hand of William Short, proving that MS was copied from some other text.
14 MS: "la Course Stérile."
15 MS: "batiments marchands qui font le Cabotage dans L'archipel."
16 MS: "que les Corsaires des Etats unis."
17 MS: "Payeront, non Seulement avec usure les frais des Armements; mais elles ne tarderont pas de faire sentir à la Porte. . . ."
18 MS: "dans les mers du Levant."
19 MS: "tant pour Servir de Mouche." One meaning of "Mouche" is dispatch-boat; hence the author may have meant that the Galliot would be used for intelligence purposes.
20 MS: "qui sont trés au fait du maniement de ces Embarcations."
21 MS: "avec l'autorisation prévue du Congrez."
22 MS: "à Constantinople."
23 MS: "dorénavant."
24 Matter in brackets (supplied) was omitted by clerk in transcribing MS and Short inserted the passage in margin.
25 MS reads "12."

II. Secretary of State to the President

Dec. 28. 1790.

The Secretary of State has the honor of presenting to the President a copy of the Report he read to him on the Mediterranean trade, the original of which he has made up for the Speaker of the house of representatives.

RC (DNA: RG 59, MLR); docketed in Lear's hand. Not recorded in SJL or SJPL. Enclosure: Document III, following.

III. Report on American Trade in the Mediterranean

The Secretary of State, to whom was referred, by the House of Representatives, so much of the Speech of the President of the United States, to both Houses of Congress, as relates to the Trade of the United States in the Mediterranean, with Instructions to report thereupon to the House, has had the same under Consideration, and thereupon makes the following REPORT.

The Loss of the Records of the Custom-houses in several of the States, which took place about the Commencement, and during the Course of the Late War, has deprived us of official Information, as to the Extent of our Commerce and Navigation in the Mediterranean Sea. According to the Best which may be obtained from other Sources meriting Respect, it may be concluded that about one Sixth of the Wheat and Flour exported from the United States. and about one Fourth in Value of their dried and pickled Fish, and some Rice, found their best Markets in the Mediterranean Ports: that these Articles constituted the principal Part of what we sent into that Sea: that that Commerce loaded outwards from Eighty to one hundred Ships, annually, of Twenty thousand Tons, navigated by about Twelve hundred Seamen. It was abandoned early in the War: and, after the Peace which ensued, it was obvious to our Merchants that their Adventures into that Sea would be exposed to the Depredations of the piratical States on the Coast of Barbary. Congress too, was very early attentive to this Danger, and, by a Commission of the 12th. of May 1784, authorized certain Persons, named Ministers Plenipotentiary for that Purpose, to conclude Treaties of Peace and Amity with the Barbary Powers: and, it being afterwards found more expedient that the Negociations should be carried on at the Residences of those Powers, Congress, by a further Commission, bearing Date the 11th. of March 1785, impowered the same Ministers Plenipotentiary to appoint Agents to repair to the said Powers, at their proper Residences, and there to negociate such Treaties. The Whole Expenses were limited to Eighty thousand Dollars. Agents were accordingly sent to Morocco and Algiers.

Before the Appointment of the one to Morocco, it was known that a Cruiser of that State had taken a Vessel of the United States, and that the Emperor, on the friendly Interposition of the Court of Madrid, had liberated the Crew, and made Restitution of the Vessel and Cargo; as far as their Condition admitted. This was a happy Presage of the liberal Treaty he afterwards concluded with our Agent, still under the friendly Mediation of Spain, and at an Expense of between Nine and Ten thousand Dollars only. On his Death, which has taken Place not long since, it becomes necessary, according to their Usage, to obtain immediately a Recognition of the Treaty by his Successor, and consequently to make Provision for the Expenses which may attend it. The Amount of the former furnishes one Ground of Estimate: but the Character and Dispositions of the Successor, which are unknown here, may influence it materially. The Friendship of this Power is important, because our Atlantic, as well as Mediterranean Trade, is open to his Annoyance, and because we carry on an useful Commerce with his Nation.

The Algerines had also taken two Vessels of the United States, with Twenty one Persons on board, whom they retained as Slaves. On the Arrival of the Agent, sent to that Regency, the Dey refused utterly to treat of Peace on any Terms, and demanded 59,496 Dollars for the Ransom of our Captives. This Mission, therefore, proved ineffectual.

While these Negociations were on Foot at Morocco and Algiers, an Ambassador from Tripoli arrived in London. The Ministers Plenipotentiary of the United States met him in Person. He demanded for the Peace of that State Thirty thousand Guineas, and undertook to engage that of Tunis for the like Sum. These Demands were beyond the Limits of Congress, and of Reason, and Nothing was done. Nor was it of Importance, as Algiers remaining hostile, the Peace of Tunis and Tripoli was of no value; and when that of the former should be obtained, theirs would soon follow.

Our Navigation then into the Mediterranean has not been resumed at all since the Peace. The sole Obstacle has been the un-provoked War of Algiers; and the sole Remedy must be to bring that War to an End, or to palliate it's Effects.

It's Effects may perhaps be palliated by ensuring our Ships and Cargoes destined for that Sea, and by forming a Convention with the Regency, for the Ransom of our Seamen, according to a fixed Tariff. That Tariff will, probably, be high, and the Rate of Insurance, so settled, in the long run, as to pay for the Vessels and Cargoes insured, and Something more. What Proportion will be captured, nothing but Experience can determine. Our Commerce differs from that of most of the Nations with whom the predatory States are in Habits of War. Theirs is spread all over the Face of the Mediterranean, and, therefore, must be sought for all over it's Face. Ours must all enter at a Streight only five Leagues wide, so that their Cruisers, taking a safe and commanding Position near the Streight's Mouth, may very effectually inspect whatever enters it. So safe a Station, with a Certainty of receiving, for their Prisoners, a good and stated Price, may tempt their Cupidity to seek our Vessels, particularly. Nor is it certain that our Seamen could be induced to engage in that Navigation, though with the Security of Algerine Faith that they would be liberated on the Payment of a fixed Sum. The temporary Deprivation of Liberty, perhaps Chains, the Danger of the Pest; the Perils of the Engage-ment preceding their Surrender, and possible Delays of the Ran-som, might turn elsewhere the Choice of Men, to whom all the Rest of the World is open. In every case, there would be Embar-rassments, which would enter into the Merchant's Estimate, and endanger his Preference of foreign Bottoms, not exposed to them. And, upon the Whole, this Expedient does not fulfil our Wish of a complete Re-establishment of our Commerce in that Sea.

A Second Plan might be, to obtain Peace by purchasing it. For this we have the Example of rich and powerful Nations, in this Instance counting their Interest more than their Honor. If, con-forming to their Example, we determine to purchase a Peace, it is proper to inquire what that Peace may cost. This being merely a Matter of Conjecture, we can only compare together such Opinions as have been obtained, and, from them, form one for ourselves.

Mr. Wolf, a respectable Irishman, who had resided very long See No. 1. at Algiers, thought a Peace might be obtained from that Regency, and the Redemption of our Captives included, for Sixty or Sev-enty thousand Pounds sterling. His Character and Opinion, both, merited Respect. Yet, his Estimate being the lowest of all who have hazarded an Opinion on this Subject, one is apt to fear his Judgment might have been biassed by the Hope he entertained that the United States would charge him with this Negociation.

Captain Obrien, one of our Captives, who had been in Algiers four Years and a half at the Date of his last Letter, a very sensible Man, and to whom we are indebted for very minute Information, supposes that Peace alone might be bought for that Sum, that is to say for Three hundred and twenty two thousand Dollars.

No. 2. 3.   The Tripoline Ambassador beforementioned, thought that Peace could be made with the three smaller Powers for Ninety thousand Pounds sterling, to which were to be added the Expenses of the Mission, and other incidental Expenses. But he could not answer for Algiers: they would demand more. The Ministers Plenipotentiary who conferred with him, had judged that as much must be paid to Algiers as to the other three Powers together: and, consequently, that, according to this Measure, the Peace of Algiers would cost from an hundred to an hundred and twenty five thousand Pounds sterling, or from four hundred and sixty to five hundred and seventy five thousand Dollars.

The latter Sum seemed to meet the Ideas of the Count de Vergennes, who, from a very long Residence at Constantinople, was a good Judge of whatever related to the Porte, or its Dependencies.

A Person, whose Name is not free to be mentioned here, a Native of the Continent of Europe, who had long lived, and still lives at Algiers, with whom the Minister Plenipotentiary of the United States at Paris had many and long Conversations, and found his Information, full, clear, and consistent, was of Opinion the Peace of Algiers could not be bought, by the United States, for less than a Million of Dollars.

And when that is paid, all is not done. On the Death of a Dey (and the present one is between seventy and eighty Years of Age) respectable Presents must be made to the Successor, that he may recognize the Treaty, and very often he takes the Liberty of altering it. When a Consul is sent or changed, new Presents must be No. 4. made. If these Events have a considerable Interval, Occasion must be made of renewing Presents. And, with all this, they must see that we are in Condition to chastise an Infraction of the Treaty; consequently some marine Force must be exhibited in their Harbour, from Time to Time.

The late Peace of Spain with Algiers is said to have cost from Three to Five Millions of Dollars. Having received the Money, they take the Vessels of that Nation on the most groundless Pretexts; counting that the same Force which bowed Spain to so hard a Treaty may break it with Impunity.

Their Treaty with France, which had expired, was, about two Years ago, renewed for Fifty Years. The Sum given at the time of Renewal is not known. But Presents are to be repeated every Ten Years, and a Tribute of One hundred thousand Dollars to be annually paid. Yet, perceiving that France, embarrassed at Home with her domestic Affairs, was less capable of acting abroad, they took six Vessels of that Nation in the Course of the last Year, and retain the Captives forty-four in Number, in Slavery.

It is the Opinion of Captain OBrian that those Nations are best treated, who pay a smaller Sum in the Beginning, and an annual Tribute, afterwards. In this Way, he informs us that the Dutch, Danes, Swedes, and Venetians pay to Algiers, from Twenty four to thirty thousand Dollars a Year each; the two first in naval Stores, the two last chiefly in Money. It is supposed that the No. 5. Peace of the Barbary States costs Great Britain about Sixty thousand Guineas, or Two hundred and eighty thousand Dollars a Year. But it must be noted that these Facts cannot be arithmetically advanced, as, from a principle of self-condemnation, the Governments keep them from the public Eye as much as possible.

Nor must we omit finally to recollect that the Algerines, attentive to reserve always a sufficient Aliment for their Piracies, will never extend their Peace beyond certain Limits, and, consequently, that we may find ourselves in the Case of those Nations to whom they refuse Peace at any Price.

The third Expedient is to repel Force by Force. Several Statements are hereto annexed of the naval Force of Algiers, taken in No. 6. 1785. 1786. 1787. 1788. and 1789, differing in small Degrees, but concurring in the Main. From these it results that that they have usually had about nine Chebecks of, from ten to thirty six Guns, and four Gallies, which have been reduced by Losses to six Chebecs and four Gallies. They have a forty Gun Frigate on the Stocks, and expect two Cruisers from the Grand Seignior. The Character of their Vessels is that they are sharp-built and swift, but so light as not to stand the Broadside of a good Frigate. Their Guns are of different Calibers, unskilfully pointed and worked; the Vessels illy manœuvred, but crowded with Men, one third Turks, the Rest Moors, of determined Bravery, and resting their sole Hopes on boarding. But two of these Vessels belong to the Government; the Rest being private Property. If they come out of

Harbour together, they separate immediately in Quest of Prey; and, it is said, they were never known to act together in any Instance. Nor do they come out at all when they know there are Vessels cruising for them. They perform three Cruises a Year, between the Middle of April and November, when they unrig, and lay up for the Winter. When not confined within the Streights, they run Northwardly to the Channel and Westwardly to the western Islands.

They are in Peace, at present, with France, Spain, England, Venice, the United Netherlands, Sweden, and Denmark: and at War with Russia, Austria, Portugal, Naples, Sardinia, Genoa, and Malta.

Should the United States propose to vindicate their Commerce by Arms, they would, perhaps, think it prudent to possess a Force equal to the Whole of that which may be opposed to them. What that equal Force would be, will belong to another Department to No. 7. say. At the same Time, it might never be necessary to draw out the Whole at once, nor, perhaps, any Proportion of it, but for a small Part of the Year: as it is reasonable to presume that a Concert of Operation might be arranged among the Powers at War with the Barbary States, so as that, each performing a Tour of a given Duration, and in given Order, a constant Cruise, during the eight temperate Months of every Year, may be kept up before the Harbour of Algiers, till the Object of such Operations be completely obtained. Portugal has, singly, for several Years past, kept up such a Cruise before the Streights of Gibraltar, and, by that Means, has confined the Algerines closely within. But two of their Vessels have been out of the Streights in the last five Years. Should Portugal effect a Peace with them, as has been apprehended for some Time, the Atlantic will immediately become the principal Scene of their Piracies: their Peace with Spain having reduced the Profits of their Mediterranean Cruises below the Expences of Equipment.

Upon the Whole, it rests with Congress to decide between War, Tribute, and Ransom, as the Means of re-establishing our Mediterranean Commerce. If War, they will consider how far our own Resources shall be called forth, and how far they will enable the Executive to engage, in the Forms of the Constitution, the co-operation of other Powers. If Tribute, or Ransom, it will rest with them to limit and provide the Amount, and, with the Executive, observing

III. REPORT ON TRADE

the same constitutional Forms, to take Arrangements for employing it to the best Advantage.

TH: JEFFERSON Secretary of State

Dec. 28. 1790.

PrC (DNA: RG 59, MLR); in clerk's hand, except for signature and date, which are in TJ's hand. Another PrC (DLC). MS (DLC); in TJ's hand, dated but not signed (fair copy of previous and missing draft). FC (DNA: RG 59, Record of Reports of Thomas Jefferson). Entry in SJPL reads: "[Dec. 28. Report Th: J.] on Mediterranean trade." Numbers in margin are in PrC and correspond with numbers of enclosures.

Enclosures: (1) "Extract of a letter from Richard O'Brian, one of the American Captives at Algiers to Congress, dated Algiers, December 26, 1789," reading: "It was the opinion of Mr. John Wolf, who resided many Years in this city, that the United States of America may obtain a peace for one hundred Years with this Regency for the sum of sixty or seventy thousand pounds sterling, and the redemption of fifteen Americans included. Mr. Wolf was the British Chargé d'affaires in Algiers, and was much the friend of America: but he is no more.—I have now been four years and a half in captivity, and I have much reason to think that America may obtain a peace with Algiers for the sum of sixty five or seventy thousand pounds, considering the present state of Algiers: That this Regency would find it their interest to take two or three American cruisers in part payment for making a peace, and also would take masts, yards, plank, scantling, tar, pitch, and turpentine and Philadelphia iron, as a part payment: all to be regulated at a certain fixed price by treaty."

(2) Extract of a letter from John Adams to John Jay, London, 22 Feb. 1786, reading: "On Monday evening another conference was held with the Tripolitan Ambassador. When he began to explain himself concerning his demands, he said they would be different, according to the duration of the treaty. If that were perpetual, they would be greater: if for a term of years less: His advice was that it should be perpetual. Once signed by the Bashaw, Dey, and other officers, it

would be indissoluble, and binding forever upon all their successors. But if a temporary treaty were made, it might be difficult and expensive to revive it. For a perpetual treaty, such as they had now with Spain, a sum of thirty thousand guineas must be paid upon the delivery of the articles signed by the Dey and other officers. If it were agreed to, he would send his Secretary by land to Marseilles, and from thence by water to Tripoli, who should bring it back by the same route, signed by the Dey &c. He had proposed so small a sum in consideration of the circumstances, but declared it was not half of what had been lately paid them by Spain. If we chose to treat upon a different plan, he would make a treaty perpetual, upon the payment of twelve thousand five hundred guineas for the first year, and three thousand guineas annually, until the thirty thousand guineas were paid. It was observed that these were large sums, and vastly beyond expectation, but his Excellency answered, that they never made a treaty for less. Upon the arrival of a prize, the Dey and the other officers were entitled by their laws to large shares, by which they might make greater profits than these sums amounted to, and they never would give up this advantage for less. He was told that, although there was a full power to treat, the American Ministers were limited to a much smaller sum; so that it would be impossible to do anything until we could write to Congress, and know their pleasure. Colonel Smith was present at this as he had been at the last conference, and agreed to go to Paris, to communicate all to Mr. Jefferson, and persuade him to come here, that we may join in further conferences, and transmit the result to Congress. The Ambassador believed that Tunis and Morocco would treat upon the same terms, but could not answer for Algiers. They would demand more. When Mr. Jefferson arrives, we shall insist upon knowing the ultimatum, and transmit it to Congress. Congress will perceive that one hundred and twenty thousand guineas will be indispensable, to conclude with the four powers, at this rate, besides a present to the Ambassadors, and their incidental charges. Besides this, a present of five hundred guineas is made upon the arrival of a consul in each State. No man wishes more fervently that the expence could be less, but the fact cannot be altered, and the truth ought not to be concealed. It may be reasonably concluded, that this great affair cannot be finished, for much less than two hundred thousand pounds Sterling."

(3) Extract of a letter from TJ to John Jay, 23 May 1786; extract is there identified in note 1.

(4) Extract of letter from Richard O'Bryen to TJ, 28 Apr. 1787; extract is there identified in note 1. Extract of letter from Richard O'Bryen to TJ, 13 June 1789; extract printed there comprises all of text of letter that has been found.

(5) Extract of letter from John Adams to John Jay, 16 Feb. 1786, reading: "The American commerce can be protected from these Africans, only by negociation or by war; if presents should be exacted from us as ample as those which are given by England, the expence may amount to sixty thousand pounds sterling a year, an enormous sum to be sure, but infinitely less than the expence of fighting: two frigates of 30 Guns each, would cost as much to fit them for the sea, besides the accumulating charges of stores, provisions, pay, and clothing. The powers of Europe generally send a squadron of men of war with their ministers, and

offer battle at the same time that they propose treaties and promise presents."

(6) "Several statements of the Marine force of Algiers, public and private," drawn from John Lamb to American Commissioners, 20 May 1786; Paul R. Randall to his father, 2 Apr. 1786 (TJ erred in giving the date as 27 May 1786; see enclosure, Randall to American Commissioners, 14 May 1786); Richard O'Bryen and others to TJ, 8 June 1786; Richard O'Bryen to TJ, 25 Sep. 1787; a statement of 5 Feb. 1788 "by the ⟨person spoken of without being named⟩ Inhabitant of Algiers spoken of in the Report" showing a force of "9. vessels from 36 down to 20. Guns, 4 or 5. smaller," and indicating that "about this date the Algerines lost 2 or 3 Vessels, stranded or taken"; and "the latest statement," furnished by O'Bryen in Dec. 1789, reading: "1. ship of 24. guns received lately from France. 5. large cruisers . . . 3. gallies and 60 Gunboats. In the fall of 1789 they laid the keel of a 40. Gun frigate, and they expect 2 Cruisers from the Grand Seignior" (MS in TJ's hand, undated, DLC: TJ Papers, 53: 8984-5).

(7) Translation of D'Estaing to TJ, 17 May 1786. Texts of all of the foregoing enclosures are in DNA: RG 59, Record of Reports of Thomas Jefferson, which is the source of preceding quotations save for that of enclosure 5; PrC of texts in another clerk's hand in DNA: RG 59, MLR; and another PrC in DLC.

IV. Report on American Captives in Algiers

The Secretary of State, having had under Consideration the Situation of the Citizens of the United States in Captivity at Algiers, makes the following Report thereupon to the President of the United States.

When the House of Representatives, at their late Session, were pleased to refer to the Secretary of State, the Petition of our Citizens in Captivity at Algiers, there still existed some Expectation that certain Measures, which had been employed to effect their Redemption, the Success of which depended on their Secrecy, might prove effectual. Information received during the Recess of Congress, has so far weakened those Expectations as to make it now a Duty to lay before the President of the United States, a full Statement of what has been attempted for the Relief of these our suffering Citizens, as well before, as since he came into Office, that he may be enabled to decide what further is to be done.

On the 25th. of July 1785, the Schooner Maria, Captain Stevens, belonging to a Mr. Foster of Boston, was taken off Cape St. Vincents, by an Algerine Corsair: and five days afterwards, the Ship Dauphin, Captain Obrian, belonging to Messrs. Irwins of Philadelphia, was taken by another Algerine, about 50. Leagues Westward of Lisbon. These Vessels, with their Cargoes and Crews, twenty one Persons in Number, were carried into Algiers.

Congress had, some Time before, commissioned Ministers Plenipotentiary for entering into Treaties of Amity and Commerce with the Barbary Powers, and to send them proper Agents for preparing such Treaties. An Agent was accordingly appointed for Algiers, and his Instructions prepared, when the Ministers Plenipotentiary received Information of these Captures. Though the Ransom of Captives was not among the Objects expressed in their Commissions, because at their Dates the Case did not exist, yet they thought it their Duty to undertake that Ransom, fearing that the Captives might be sold and dispersed through the interior and distant Countries of Africa, if the previous Orders of Congress should be waited for. They therefore added a supplementary Instruction, to the Agent, to negociate their Ransom. But while acting thus without Authority, they thought themselves bound to offer a Price so moderate as not to be disapproved. They, therefore, restrained him to Two hundred Dollars a Man; which was something less than had been just before paid for about Three hundred French Captives, by the Mathurins, a religious Order of France, instituted in ancient Times for the Redemption of Christian Captives from the infidel Powers. On the Arrival of the Agent at Algiers, the Dey demanded Fifty nine thousand four hundred and ninety six Dollars for the Twenty one Captives, and could not be brought to abate but little from that Demand. The Agent, therefore, returned in 1786, without having effected either Peace or Ransom. In the Beginning of the next Year, 1787, the Minister Plenipotentiary of the United States at Paris procured an Interview with the General of the religious Order of Mathurins, before mentioned, to engage him to lend his Agency, at the Expence of the United States, for the Redemption of their captive Citizens. He proffered, at once, all the Services he could render, with the Liberality and the Zeal which distinguish his Character. He observed

No. 1.

that he had Agents on the Spot, constantly employed in seeking out, and redeeming the Captives of their own Country; that these should act for us, as for themselves; that Nothing could be accepted for their Agency; and that he would only expect that the Price of Redemption should be ready on our Part, so as to cover the Engagement into which he should enter. He added that, by the Time all Expences were paid, their last Redemption had amounted to near Two thousand five hundred Livres a Man, and that he could by no Means flatter us that they could redeem our Captives as cheap as their own. The Pirates would take Advantage of it's being out of their ordinary Line. Still he was in Hopes they would not be much higher.

The Proposition was submitted to Congress, that is to say, in February 1787, and on the 19th. of September, in the same Year, their Minister Plenipotentiary at Paris, received their Orders to embrace the Offers of the Mathurins. This he immediately notified to the General, observing, however, that he did not desire him to enter into any Engagements, till a sufficient Sum to cover them should be actually deposited in Paris. The General wished that the whole might be kept rigorously secret, as, should the Barbarians suspect him to be acting for the United States, they would demand such Sums as he could never agree to give, even with our Consent, because it would injure his future Purchases from them. He said he had Information from his Agent at Algiers, that our Captives received so liberal a daily Allowance as to evince that it came from a public Source. He recommended that this should be discontinued, engaging that he would have an allowance administered to them, much short, indeed, of what they had hitherto received, but such as was given to his own Countrymen, quite Sufficient for physical Necessaries, and more likely to prepare the Opinion that, as they were subsisted by his Charity, they were to be redeemed by it also. These Ideas, suggested to him by the Danger of raising his Market, were approved by the Minister Plenipotentiary, because this being the first Instance of a Redemption by the United State, it would form a Precedent; because a high Price given by us, might induce these Pirates to abandon all other Nations in pursuit of Americans, whereas the contrary would take place, could our Price of Redemption be fixed at the lowest Point.

To destroy, therefore, every Expectation of a Redemption by the United States, the Bills of the Spanish Consul at Algiers, who had made the Kind Advances before spoken of, for the Sustenance of our Captives, were not answered. On the Contrary, a Hint was given that these Advances had better be discontinued, as it was not known that they would be reimbursed. It was necessary even to go further, and to suffer the Captives themselves and their Friends to believe, for a while that[1] no Attention was paid to them, no Notice taken of their Letters. They are still under this Impression. It would have been unsafe to trust them with a Secret, the disclosure of which might forever prevent their Redemption, by raising the Demands of the Captors to Sums which a due Regard for our Seamen, still in Freedom, would forbid us to give. This was the most trying of all Circumstances, and drew from them the most afflicting Reproaches.

It was a Twelvemonth afterwards before the Money could be deposited in Paris, and the Negociation be actually put into Train. In the meantime the General had received Information from Algiers of a very considerable Change of Prices there. Within the last two or three Years the Spaniards, the Neapolitans, and the Russians had redeemed at exorbitant Sums. Slaves were become scarce, and would hardly be sold at any Price. Still he entered on the Business with an Assurance of doing the Best in his Power, and he was authorized to offer as far as Three thousand Livres or Five hundred and fifty five Dollars a Man. He wrote immediately to consult a confidential Agent at Marseilles, on the best Mode of carrying this Business into Effect; from whom he received the No. 2. Answer No. 2. hereto annexed.

Nothing further was known of his Progress or Prospects when the House of Representatives were pleased, at their last Session, to refer the Petition of our Captives at Algiers to the Secretary of State. The preceding Narrative shews that no Report could have then been made without risking the Object, of which some Hopes were still entertained. Later Advices, however, from the No. 3. Chargé des Affaires of the United States, at Paris, inform us that these Measures, though not yet desperate, are not to be counted on. Besides the Exorbitance of Price, before feared, the late Transfer of the Lands and Revenues of the Clergy, in France, to the Public, by withdrawing the Means, seems to have suspended the Proceedings of the Mathurins in the Purposes of their Institution.

It is Time, therefore, to look about for something more promising, without relinquishing, in the meanwhile, the Chance of Success through them. Endeavours to collect Information, which have been continued a considerable Time, as to the Ransoms which would probably be demanded from us, and those actually paid by other Nations, enable the Secretary of State to lay before the President the following short View, collected from original Papers now in his Possession, or from Information delivered to him personally.

Passing over the Ransoms of the Mathurins, which are kept far below the common Level, by special Circumstances;

In 1786, the Dey of Algiers demanded from our Agent 59,496 No. 4. Dollars for 21 Captives, which was 2,833 Dollars a Man. The Agent flattered himself they could be ransomed for 1200 Dollars apiece. His Secretary informed us, at the same Time, that Spain No. 5. had paid 1600 Dollars.

In 1787, the Russians redeemed at 1546 Dollars a Man.

In 1788, a well informed Inhabitant of Algiers, assured the Minister Plenipotentiary of the United States, at Paris, that no Nation had redeemed, since the Spanish Treaty, at less than from 250 to 300 Pounds sterling, the medium of which is 1237 Dollars. No. 6. Captain Obrian, at the same Date, thinks we must pay 1800 Dollars, and mentions a Savoy Captain, just redeemed at 4074 Dollars.

In 1789, Mr. Logie, the English Consul at Algiers, informed a Person who wished to ransom one of our common Sailors, that he would cost from 450 to 500 Pounds Sterling, the Mean of which is 2137 Dollars. In December of the same Year, Captain Obrian No. 7. thinks our Men will now cost 2920 Dollars each, though a Jew Merchant believes he could get them for 2264 Dollars.

No. 8. In 1790, July 9th. a Mr. Simpson, of Gibraltar, who at some particular Request, had taken Pains to find for what Sum our Captives could be redeemed, finds that the Fourteen will cost 34,792$\frac{28}{38}$ Dollars, which is 2485 Dollars a Man. At the same Date, one of them, a Scotch Boy, a common Mariner, was actually redeemed at 8,000 Livres, equal to 1481 Dollars, which is within 19 Dollars of the Price Simpson states for common Men: and the Chargé des Affaires of the United States at Paris is informed that the Whole may be redeemed at that Rate, adding Fifty per Cent on the Captains, which would bring it to 1571 Dollars a Man.

It is found then that the Prices are 1200. 1237. 1481. 1546. 1571. 1600. 1800. 2137. 2264, 2485. 2833. and 2920. Dollars a Man, not noticing that of 4074. Dollars, because it was for a Captain.

In 1786, there were 2200 Captives in Algiers, which in 1789 had been reduced by Death or Ransom to 655. Of ours six have died, and one has been ransomed by his Friends.

From these Facts and Opinions some Conjecture may be formed

of the Terms on which the Liberty of our Citizens may be obtained.

But should it be thought better to repress Force by Force, another Expedient, for their Liberation, may perhaps offer. Captures made on the Enemy, may perhaps put us into Possession of some of their Mariners, and Exchange be substituted for Ransom. It is not, indeed, a fixed Usage with them to exchange Prisoners. It is rather their Custom to refuse it. However such Exchanges are sometimes effected, by allowing them more or less of Advantage. They have sometimes accepted of two Moors for a Christian, at others, they have refused five or six for one. Perhaps Turkish Captives may be Objects of greater Partiality with them, as their Government is entirely in the Hands of Turks, who are treated, in every Instance as a superior Order of Beings. Exchange, too, will be more practicable in our Case, as our Captives have not been sold to private Individuals, but are retained in the hands of the Government.

The Liberation of our Citizens has an intimate Connection with the Liberation of our Commerce in the Mediterranean, now under the Consideration of Congress. The Distresses of both proceed from the same Cause, and the Measures which shall be adopted for the Relief of the one, may very probably involve the Relief of the other.

TH: JEFFERSON Secretary of State.
Dec. 28. 1790.

MS (DNA: RG 46, Senate Records, 1st. Cong., 3rd. sess.); in clerk's hand, except for signature, title, and date in the hand of TJ, who also supplied "No. 1." in margin when the clerk inadvertently omitted it. PrC (DNA: RG 59, MLR). Another PrC (DLC). MS (DLC); in TJ's hand, dated but not signed (fair copy of previous and missing draft). FC (DNA: RG 59, Record of Reports of Thomas Jefferson). Entry in SJPL reads: "[Dec.] 28. Report Th: J. on our citizens in captivity in Algiers." Numbers in margin are in MS and correspond with those of enclosures.

Enclosures: (1) John Lamb to American Commissioners, extract, 20 May 1786 (see note 3 there for identification of extract). (2) "Answer of the Agent of the Mathurins to his General" [Perrin to Chauvier], 19 Aug. 1789, printed as enclosure to TJ to Jay, 19 Sep. 1789, where Tr in English

is identified as enclosed in above report. (3) Extracts of letters from Short to TJ, 14 June, 25 June, and 7 July 1790 (the first misdated in above report); see under respective dates for identification of extracts. (4) Extract of a letter from Lamb to TJ, 29 Mch. 1786; see note 1 there. (5) Extract of a letter from Paul R. Randall to his father (incorrectly identified in PrC and FC of above report as addressed to TJ), 2 Apr. 1786; printed as enclosure to Randall to American Commissioners, 14 May 1786, where extract is identified in note 1. (6) Extract of a letter from O'Bryen to TJ, 2 June 1788. (7) Extract of a letter from O'Bryen to TJ, 12 Dec. 1789 (only the texts of extracts of enclosures 6 and 7 as printed under their respective dates have been found). (8) "Extract of a letter from James Simpson [to George Washington] dated Gibraltar Aug. 25. 1790," reading: "Having lately been desired to enquire by means of my correspondents at Algiers how many Americans remained there, and the sum would be demanded for their Ransom, I take the liberty of inclosing for your information copy of the return made me, and to say that as the Gentleman encharged me to make this enquiry, wrote in a stile as if the generous and humane Idea of Ransom flowed from a private source, I much fear as the sum demanded is considerable, I shall not have the happyness of being encharged by them with directions for carrying it into execution" (RC in DNA: RG 59, CD; endorsed by TJ, with extract bracketed by him and having caption as quoted in his hand at head of text; FC in DNA: RG 59, Record of Reports of Thomas Jefferson). Enclosed with this was Simpson's "List of American Prisoners at Algiers 9th July 1790 with the sums demanded by the Regency for their ransom," reading as follows:

"Crew of the Ship Dolphin captured 30th July 1785.

Richard O Bryan	Captain	ransom demanded Zs	2000
Andrew Montgomery	Mate		1500
Jacob Tessanier	French passenger		2000
William Paterson	Seaman (Keeps a Tavern)		1500
Philip Sloan	"		725
Peleg Lorin	"		725
John Robertson	"		725
James Hall	"		725

Crew of the Schooner Mary taken 25th July 1785.

Isaac Stephens	Captain		2000
Alexander Forsyth	Mate		1500
James Cathcart	Seaman (Keeps a Tavern)		900
George Smith	"	(in the King's house)	725
John Gregory	"		725
James Hermit	"		725
		Algerine Sequines	16,475

Duty on the above sum, 10 Pr.%   1647½
Sundry gratifications to Officers of the Dey's household and
Regency, equal to 17⅙ Zs. each person   240⅓

34,792.— $\frac{28}{38}$ Mexican dollars @ 38 Mozunas each are   Zequins 18,362. $\frac{5}{6}$ —"

(MS in DNA: RG 59, CD. Tr of all of foregoing enclosures with TJ's report in DNA: RG 59, Record of Reports of Thomas Jefferson; MS in various clerks' hands in DNA: RG 46, Senate Records, 1st. Cong., 3rd. sess., with captions "No. 1." through "No. 8." inserted in TJ's hand. PrC in DNA: RG 59, MLR. Another PrC in DLC).

1 At this point TJ wrote and then deleted: "their case was desperate."

V. Secretary of State to the Speaker of the House of Representatives

SIR   Philadelphia Dec. 29. 1790.

I have now the honour of submitting to the House of Representatives a Report on the navigation and commerce of the United states in the Mediterranean, which they were pleased to refer to me.

I think it my duty to suggest to the consideration of the house whether it may not be proper to forbid any copy of this report, either printed or manuscript, to be taken; and whether the habitual permission, to persons not of the house, to take notes of what is passing, should not be suspended on this occasion. An unreserved communication, which may be proper, and necessary, for the information of our own government, may be improper and even injurious if handed to the government of other nations. I submit to the judgment of the house whether some parts of this report may not be of that nature.

I have the honour to be with the most profound respect Sir Your most obedient & most humble servant, TH: JEFFERSON

PrC (DLC); at foot of text: "The Honble. the Speaker of the house of representatives." FC (DNA: RG 59, Record of Reports of Thomas Jefferson). Entry in SJPL reads: "[Dec. 28] Th: J. to Sp. H. R. on [Mediterranean trade]."

VI. Secretary of State to the President of the Senate

SIR   Philadelphia Jan. 20. 1791.

I have the honor to inclose you a letter from one of our captive citizens of Algiers, if I may judge from the superscription, and from the letters from the same quarter which I have received myself. As these relate to a matter before your house, and contain some information we have not before had, I take the liberty of inclosing you copies of them.—I have the honour to be with sentiments of the most profound respect & attachment, Sir Your most obedient & most humble servt.,   TH: JEFFERSON

RC (DNA: RG 46, Senate Records, 1st. Cong., 3rd. sess.); at foot of text: "The President of the Senate" (entry in SJL describes it as to "Adams V. P. of the Senate"). PrC (DLC). FC (DNA: RG 59, Record of Reports of Thomas Jefferson, p. 142). Enclosures (in addition to that first mentioned, not otherwise identified): (1) O'Bryen to Carmichael [11 or 15 May 1790],

printed below. (2) O'Bryen to Carmichael, 17 May 1790, printed below. (3) O'Bryen to TJ, 12 July 1790.

The above letter and its enclosures were laid before the Senate on 21 Jan. 1791 and referred to the committee appointed to report on trade with the Mediterranean (JS, I, 234).

ENCLOSURE I

Richard O'Bryen to William Carmichael

                                         City of Algiers June the 24th.
ESTEEMED SIR   [i.e., 11 or 15 May][1] 1790.

I have the Honor of informing you that good Fortune and favorable Opportunities offering, the following particulars were communicated to his Excellency the Effendi Vickelhadge General of the marine and Minister for foreign Affairs for this Regency by two of my Brother Sufferers in the Dey's Palace, viz. George Smith and Philip Sloan— the 1st. is Chamberlain to the Vickelhadge, the 2d. is Capt. aproa of the Dey's palace.

"That the United States of America abounds in masts, yards, Spars of all sizes fit for vessels; and Plank and Scantling, Tar, Pitch, and Turpentine and Iron. That these articles are cheaper in America than they are in any part of Europe.

"That there is no nation in the world that builds such fine and fast sailing Cruisers as the Americans—that the Americans never did the Algerines any Injury, that they never fitted out Cruisers against them, and always wished to make an honorable Peace with this Regency, as the Americans considered the Algerines to be a brave People like themselves.

"That the Americans have but little money, and that the Currency of the Country, is paper money, but that America abounds in Maritime Stores—that if the Algerines would make a Peace with America they may be supplied with American Cruisers at a very cheap Rate, and also with all the Productions of America which this Regency may want for their marine, and as the Americans have no money to give for a Peace they would give Masts, Yards, Spars, Plank, Scantling, Tar, Pitch, Turpentine, and Philadelphia Iron, and by being at Peace with America, the Algerines would be supplied with Cruisers and Stores, and need not be at the Trouble and Expense of building Cruisers in Algiers, and of Course would take many Prizes, and could pay all their attention to their marine in constructing Gun Boats to protect the City.

"That these propositions were partly the Instructions of the American Ambassador who came here in 1786 and intended only to ascertain our Ransom, and try to make a Peace on honorable Terms with this Regency, and to see if this Regency would not take for our Ransom and for the Peace in lieu of money American Masts, yards, Plank, and Scantling, Tar, Pitch, and Turpentine all to be agreed on at a certain fixed Price by Treaty, but that Mr. Lamb could speak nothing but English and the french Consul and Conde D'Espilly, the Spanish ambassador would not take the Trouble to explain Mr. Lamb's Propositions, as the Terms of the Peace would be advantageous to the Algerines, and that the french and spaniards advised Mr. Lamb to return to America that the Algerines would not make a Peace with the United States of America.

"That America is one thousand Leagues Distance from Algiers— that the Commerce of America is chiefly to the West India Islands, and from one State to another—that our chief Commerce is our coasting Trade, and that we have but little Trade to Europe, particularly to the Mediterranean and Ports adjacent, that the American Cargoes are of but little Value, and consist of Wheat, Flour, Salt, Pork and Fish, and a few Cargoes of naval Stores, that these vessels are manned with fewer Sailors than those of any other Nation, that they sail faster, and consequently are less liable to be captured, and of course little profit the Algerines can derive by being at War with the Americans who wish to make an honorable Peace with this Regency, and that in Case the Algerines should be at war with the northern nations of Europe, the Algerines may be supplied with maritime Stores by the Americans, and that if the Regency would not find it to their advantage to sell the Americans Passports for the Mediterranean and Ports adjacent, or elsewhere at a certain reasonable Price and on Conditions to be fixed by Treaty which conditions would exclude and prevent any pretext of Quarrels or Embroylas, and as it would be the Interest of America to encourage her Trade in the Mediterranean so on the Increase of America more passports would be required and the greater the advantage would be to the Algerines. This would open a Channel for this Regency, having a Resource for supplying their marine in Case they should be at war with the Dutch, Danes, or Swedes, the Nations that supply the Algerines at present, and that the Americans will as liberally reward any Person that is their Friend and Advocate in making the Peace as their Circumstances will admit.

These Propositions were explained to his Excellency the minister for foreign affairs at sundry Times from the 7th. to the 13th. of May 1790.

The Vickelhadge asked how these Propositions of the American Ambassador were known to us. He was answered that Captain OBryen read Mr. Lamb's Instructions several Times, and he explained them to us. His Excellency the Vickelhadge said that when Mr. Lamb was in Algiers in 1786, that at that Period this Regency was settling the Spanish Peace, and that the American Ambassador was by no means a suitable Person as he spoke nothing but English, and they knew nothing of his Propositions, that after the Americans had freed themselves from the British, that the British Nation had demanded as a Favor of this Regency not to make a Peace with the Americans, and that some Time before the American Ambassador came, the French and Conde D'Espilly tried all their Influence against the American's obtaining a Peace. That these three Nations were and are the Enemies of America, and that he would explain all more particularly to the American Ambassador if he came to make a Peace, but that those Nations had no Influence over the Algerines, and that nothing should prejudice this Regency against the Americans, if they came to make a Peace.

The Vickelhadge said he believed this Regency would make a Peace with America on as easy Terms as possible, considering the present Times, and as the Americans had no money to give for a Peace, we must give the Productions of America, vizt. Tar, Pitch, Turpentine, Masts, Yards, Spars, Plank and Scantling, and Cruisers american built.

The Vickelhadge said as he intended to be the Friend and Advocate of America in making a Peace with this Regency, he would expect for his Weight, Trouble, and Influence, an American built Schooner of 12 Guns, which of course would not cost much, that he would pave the way with the Dey and Divan, so that America would succeed, and that he would recommend it strongly to the Dey to make a Peace with America, and that he knew the former Vickelhadge was promised by and through Mr. Lamb and Wolf more than the amount of a Schooner, but that he would esteem and do more for getting an American Schooner, than he would for Sacks of money, that he or this Regency did not want Money, they only wanted American Cruisers and naval Stores for their Marine.

The Vickelhadge said that he wished much to know about getting the Schooner. To this question I returned for answer, that it was impossible for us to say positively, but that we would write to the american Divan, or to Congress, and to the American Ambassador at Madrid. He asked when the American Divan met to do Business, and respecting our Form of Government, and was answered that last March Congress met, and that our Government is founded on Liberty and Justice. The Vickelhadge said that a few months ago the Portuguese asked for a Peace and that it was refused them. He said he hoped if the Americans sent an Ambassador to Algiers to make the Peace, that they would send a Man that could speak the Spanish or Italian Language. He ridiculed much the sending a man to make the Peace that no one could understand what he had to say, and said that the Conde D'Espilly was a bad and false man.

Indeed I hope Congress will appoint a proper Person to negociate the Peace, and I should certainly recommend Mr. Faure as a good Assistant; I think you may confide in him. But all I now mention is entirely unknown to any Person in this Country excepting the Vickelhadge and I and my two brother-sufferers in the Dey's Palace, and I hope all will be managed with that good Policy and Secrecy that such important Business requires, as no Person here has any Idea that the Americans are thinking of a Peace.

It will be very requisite for you to give an Answer as soon as possible and as fully as your Situation will admit of, writing by two Conveyances, and what you would wish to communicate or say in Answer to the Vickelhadge, write it separate from other Particulars, which you would think proper to communicate to me, as I would wish, (if you think proper) to communicate your Answer, thro' the same Channel to the Vickelhadge, directing to me, under cover to the care of Monsieur Faure, to avoid any Suspicions.

I hope Congress will give the Ambassador they send to Algiers as extensive Powers as possible, and should the Terms of the Peace be too great, that his Instructions will admit him to see on what Terms he could procure 150 Passports of Algiers, for as you will conceive that until you give some Answer and impower some Person to act that it is impossible to know exactly on what Terms america may obtain Peace, or what the Heads of the Treaty may be. I think all wears a favorable aspect.

I have stated the Particulars communicated to the Vickelhadge, and his answers, and submit all with much Respect to your Consideration. Indeed it would have been impossible to have brought the Affair to its present Meridian in any other manner, for depend the Vickelhadge would not have listened to propositions different from what have been communicated, and I have the Pleasure to add that about a month ago the Noznagee asked the Capt. Aproa, one of my Crew, why the Americans did not try for a Peace.

I hope no american vessel will be captured, for depend it would be very prejudicial towards obtaining a Peace. It would occasion the Terms to be greater than they would be if none were captured, and would be a Clue for the Enemies of America to persuade the Algerines that much was to be got by being at war with the United States of America.

And I take the Liberty of mentioning that a few Lines from you to the Spanish,[2] would be requisite, as he thinks you are displeased with him respecting the affair of our Disbursements, so as not to have any Enemies to America in this Quarter. This in a great measure would lull him and Consul Logie asleep.

You will recollect, Sir, that I wrote you that all Nations pay ⅓ or ¼ more than they used to pay, or is agreed on by Treaty, owing to the spanish Peace, which has hurt all Nations here except the British. And some Hints from you to Congress would be requisite on this Subject.

I am sorry to hear that you have taken a Tour to France, for you will not receive this Letter as soon as I could wish. I write under cover to Messrs. Etienne Drouilhoult and Compy. Banquiers at Madrid, and as the Port is to be embargoed in a few Days, and the Vessel, a Danish Ship bound to Spain, Time will not permit me to write more particularly or correctly, and I hope you will receive this Letter, as I believe it will be some Time before I shall have another opportunity of writing to you.

You will observe that the Vickelhadge sways the whole Regency as he thinks proper, and that his Influence is very great. For by his Recommendations to the Bey of Tunis, the present Vickelhadge of Tunis was appointed to that office; and the Vickelhadge of Algiers has a Brother at present a great man at Constantinople. Great Care should be taken not to lose the Friendship of the present Noznagee (the Prime Minister) the Head of Opposition, for by making these two great Men the Friends of America, any Thing can be done in this Regency. The plain Question is will America give Cruisers and Maritime Stores to this Regency to make a Peace; otherwise the Algerines can get Cruisers (to take Americans) from other Nations. They have Money sufficient to build a large Fleet, but at present all their Cruisers are gone up the Levant except two, and three Gallies, so that this Regency are much in want of Cruisers; and I dare say never a more favorable opportunity offered, or will offer for America than the present, which bids fair to open an extensive Field of Commerce and Wealth to America.

I would have wrote you concerning the Morocco affair, but I suppose you have heard all sometime past. I hope we shall keep our Peace with Morocco, for the Situation of West Barbary is such as to be very detrimental to American Commerce, if we unfortunately should lose the Peace with the new Emperor. I need not mention to you the distressed and suffering Situation of my Brother Sufferers in the Marine. Esteemed Sir, Your most obedient most humble Servant,

RICHARD O'BRYEN

Tr (DNA: RG 46, Senate Records, 1st. Cong., 3rd. sess.); in hand of George Taylor; at foot of text: "To William Carmichael Esqr. american Ambassador at Madrid." Below the text O'Bryen appended the following note to William Short: "NB. The Copy of this Letter I sent to Mr. Carmichael. It was dated May the 15th. 1790, and not being certain where he was, I thought it of sufficient Importance to write to you, so that should Mr. Carmichael be in France, as Report says, you will give him these Letters to read, keeping the same Time copies, and transmit such Parts thereof to Congress as you think requisite, or to Mr. Jefferson—the same Time acknowledge the Receipt of these Letters as soon as possible, so that I may know you have received them" (on date of this document, see note 1 below). PrC (DLC). FC (DNA: RG 59, Record of Reports of Thomas Jefferson).

1 Date in RC refers to the date of O'Bryen's transmission of the copy to Short, not the date of the original letter to Carmichael. In O'Bryen's appended note to Short (see above) he gave the

date of the original letter as 15 May but in the text of the letter of 17 May 1790 (see Enclosure II below) he stated that he had written Carmichael on "the 11th. Inst." Since Taylor transcribed both texts it cannot be determined whether he made a copyist's error or whether O'Bryen himself erred. The earlier date seems more plausible. It was probably because of pressure of business that TJ included O'Bryen's note to Short without explaining it and that in his file record of the report both of O'Bryen's letters are recorded in improper sequence, as if their actual dates were respectively 17 May 1790 and 24 June 1790, an error repeated of course in ASP, Foreign Affairs, I, 116-20.

2 That is, the Spanish consul at Algiers.

ENCLOSURE II

Richard O'Bryen to William Carmichael

Esteemed Sir   City of Algiers May the 17th. 1790.

I had the Honor of writing you a Letter dated the 11th.[1] Inst. and as Time permits I shall mention other particulars. The Vickelhadge being further sounded relative to a peace with America, says that if the Americans wish to make a Peace with this Regency, why do they not send an Ambassador, or empower some Person to act for them, and I cannot help repeating to you that the Foundation of all Treaties, in this Regency, should be laid by some Person in Algiers, and I am convinced that no Person is more capable than Monsr. Faure. Depend, Sir, you may confide in him, and by empowering Monsr. Faure the Affair would be done with that secrecy which is requisite, considering that America has three powerful Enemies in Algiers vizt. French and Spaniards, and the most inveterate is the English. But as british Affairs are very unsettled at present, british Influence cannot be very great. And the French have just emerged from having very nearly lost their Peace, and the present Situation of France is such that I believe they cannot afford to give money to this Regency to corrupt the Algerines to the Prejudice of America.

When the English Consul signified to the Dey and Regency, that Spain was arming to support the Grand Duke of Tuscany, the Vickelhadge said that any Nation that took the part of the Russians or Imperialists, that Nation had no longer a Peace with this Regency. So that I assure you that if the Spaniards arm in favor of the Grand Duke, they are no longer at Peace with Algiers. The spanish Consul said that Spain had armed a small Fleet, as Customary to exercise the officers of their marine, and if the Armament was any way extra, it was perhaps on Account of some Disturbance in spanish America. The

Vickelhadge said Miramus. So that considering the present Situation
of the three Enemies of America in this Quarter, and this Regency
in want of Cruisers I cannot percieve that ever a more favorable Opportunity offered for America to make a Peace than the present, and
I must observe that those Nations, the Dutch, Danes, Swedes, and
Venetians have their Peace on a more solid Basis than the Spanish
Peace, for the annual Tribute those Nations pay is the Bait that keeps
their Peace, and not any sentiment of national Honor, or regard to
Treaties, but the view of the Tribute annually and for their own Convenience, in being supplied annually with naval and military Stores.

Spain made a very dishonorable and impolitic Peace. What makes
the Algerines adhere to it, is owing to the vast Sums of Money and
Presents given, which are sufficient to almost tempt these People to
adore Lucifer and depend that when the Dey goes to his long Home
it will be difficult for the Spaniards to keep their Peace, &c. as they
gave a great Sum of money for their Peace, and a second great Sum
not to be tributary. These People say at present that they have got all
from Spain that they can get, and that it is prejudicial to this Regency
to keep the Peace with Spain. But it would be too barefaced for the
present Dey and Ministry to break the Peace or Treaty, inasmuch as
they themselves made it or agreed thereto.

Indeed America should always to be ready to embrace every opportunity of trying for a Peace, and even if refused the second Time, notwithstanding good Policy requires that always some Person should
be empowered. For depend it is very prejudicial to America in not
having a Peace with the Barbary States, and I compute that the Insurance paid on American Bottoms, and Merchandize amounts annually
to upwards of one million Sterling, which Sum the British Nation gets
by insuring American Property on Account of our not being at Peace
with the Barbary States.

You will observe that the Spaniards gave the former Vickelhadge
thirty two thousand Dollars for bringing the Subject of the spanish
Peace before the Dey and Divan, and they gave very valuable Presents,
so that considering from the 1st. of June 1785 to May 1790, it is
generally said here that the Spanish Peace and Ryalas or Presents and
Redemptions have cost Spain full 4½ millions of Dollars. And as I
often wrote you, that there is no doing Business with these People
without first giving Presents, it being the Custom of this Country,
therefore I think that the Vickelhadge's Demand of an American
Schooner of 12 Guns was by no means high. For as you will observe
that he would promise and engage to be the Friend and Advocate. So
that if the Americans did not succeed, the Vickelhadge of course would
not expect to get the Schooner, but still it would be requisite to reward him for his Trouble and good Intentions, so as to keep him the
Friend of America on another Occasion. But all in a great Measure
depends on the Vickelhadge. The Dey is led by him in every respect,
and by liberally rewarding him, the Terms of the Peace would not be
very high, for all depends on his Representations to the Dey, and no
one dare oppose him.

But to keep the Peace hereafter, much Attention should be paid to
the prime Minister. Indeed no one can say with any Degree of cer-

tainty who may be the Dey's Successor, and a Peace made by one Party in opposition to the Other, cannot be said to be on a firm Basis or lasting; for if the Party in Opposition once gets the Helm of State, they will not consider themselves bound to keep the Peace made by the other Party, and there is a great Party that disapproved of making a Peace with Spain. Many respectable Turks here say that it was nothing but Bribery or a Torrent of Corruption, which the Algerine Ministry could not resist that obtained Spain a Peace. Indeed it was by no means the Voice of the People—Fine. . . .[2]

RICHARD O'BRYEN

Tr (DNA: RG 46, Senate Records, 1st. Cong., 3rd. sess.); in hand of George Taylor; at foot of text O'Bryen's note to Short (see note 2 below). PrC (DLC); in TJ's hand at head of text: "letters received and communicated after the report was given in." FC (DNA: RG 59, Record of Reports of Thomas Jefferson). Not recorded in SJL, but enclosed in Short's public dispatch of 3 Oct. 1790 which TJ received on 11 Jan. 1791.

[1] Thus in Tr; in the note Short appended to the copy of that letter (see note to Enclosure I above), O'Bryen stated that the date was "May the 15th."

[2] At this point in text there is the following: "NB. These are the Copies of the Letters I wrote to Mr. Carmichael, which you will please to signify to him if he is in Europe." This note, of course, was directed to Short (see above).

VII. Senate Resolution on the Algerine Captives

In Senate Feb. 1. 1791.

The Committee to whom was referred that part of the speech of the President of the U.S. at the opening of the session which relates to the commerce of the Mediterranean, and also the letter from the Secretary of state dated 20th. Jany. 1791. with the papers accompanying the same reported, Whereupon

Resolved that the Senate do advise and consent that the President of the U.S. take such measures as he may think necessary for the redemption of the citizens of the U.S. now in captivity at Algiers, provided the expence shall not exceed 40,000 Doll: and also that measures be taken to confirm the treaty now existing between the U.S. and the emperor of Morocco.

MS (DLC); entirely in TJ's hand. This is the text as adopted. For the resolution as introduced, see JEP, I, 72. See also Editorial Note above.

VIII. The President to the Senate

GENTLEMEN OF THE SENATE   [22 February 1791]

I will proceed to take measures for the ransom of our citizens in captivity at Algiers, in conformity with your resolution of advice of the first instant, so soon as the monies necessary shall be appropriated by the legislature and shall be in readiness.

The recognition of our treaty with the new Emperor of Marocco requires also previous appropriation and provision. The importance of this last to the liberty and property of our citizens induces me to urge it on your earliest attention.

Dft (DLC); entirely in TJ's hand; undated; the message, dated "United States, *February 22d, 1791*," appears as TJ drafted it in JEP, I, 75. Entry in SJPL indicates that TJ drafted the message on the day the resolution of 1 Feb. 1791 was adopted, but this was probably an error.

It is to be noted that, though some funds had been allocated for the ransom of the captives from the loan of 1788, Washington declined to move without a further appropriation. TJ probably persuaded him to adopt this position, as he did later when redemption of the prisoners and a treaty with Algiers were again under consideration. TJ argued then that, regardless of the manner of getting funds, both houses should be informed in advance lest the Senate decline to ratify and the House to appropruate after the event. Washington agreed. The issue was complicated by the need for secrecy (see TJ's memorandum, 11 Mch. 1792).

From William Short

DEAR SIR   Amsterdam Dec. 29. 1790

I wrote to you on the 23d. inst. by the English packet my *No. 50* and a private letter. In the latter I acknowleged the reciept of your two letters, of the 6th. of Sep. containing a bill of exchange of 589.ᵗ 6s. and of the 30th. of the same month from Monticello. I mentioned then what I beg leave to repeat now that the reciept of that letter had made me repent most sincerely the manner in which I had written to you more than once on a subject which interested me most sensibly, and which had made me forget the limits which I ought to have prescribed to the overflowings of my mind. I mentioned in that letter also that I was the more sorry for this as I found that that transgression had been continued in several of my succeeding letters, and that I feared your patience would be at length exhausted and make you recieve them in a disposition of mind different from that which it is my first desire to preserve. I should be inconsolable for having written these letters if I thought you would persist in the error into which I see they have led you—You say that I have forgotten my countrymen altogether as well as the nature of our government. I might here plead the general issue, but waving that, as it would be too long and too little satisfactory probably, I will observe in justification that what is here taken for forgetfulness is common to every American in Paris and several in London. Their conversation and their letters to me were uniform on that head and so decidedly so that every observation which I made in attenuation of their certainty was considered merely as a *façon de parler*. I do not pretend here to say that their way of seeing was just, I only mention it to shew that I might have fallen into the same error without an entire forgetfulness of my countrymen and their government. I do not quote also M. de Mo-m-in [Montmorin], the corps diplomatique at Paris and the rest of my acquaintance there, because their manner of viewing such things is no model certainly for Americans and never will be one for me. Be all this as it may however I am ready to declare that one of my reasons for wishing to remain at Paris was that I believed most sincerely either on good or bad ground, that I could be useful there, that I acknowlege that my opinion is by no means an impartial, probably not a just one, and that I shall be the first to imitate at an humble distance, the example of the Lacedemonian, and instead of repining at my own want of success, find my consolation in the hope of seeing another more useful. He will certainly have a more perfect intimacy with the circumstances of the U. S. which alone, it is thought, can enable one to know and pursue their interests. Under that idea the absence of seven years is certainly sufficient. I had thought however that a residence in Europe on the contrary gave a more perfect acquaintance with such circumstances of the U. S. as are necessary for advancing their interests here, because from hence the U. S. are generalized and always examined under the idea of their relations with foreign countries. The ideas thus acquired are unfettered by those of detail and locality, and the present system of intercourse across the ocean is such that I should have thought that, although a person resident at Williamsburgh would have a more perfect acquaintance with the state of Virginia and perhaps the minute details of other states, yet one resident at London, Paris, or Amsterdam would be better acquainted with the U. States, or such of their circumstances as are necessary to be known in order to pursue their interests in Europe.—But I find that I have fallen into a common error of correcting one fault by committing another. After having wearied your patience by the repetitions of my former letters I am now exhausting it by endeavouring to justify them. I will say no more than to insist on your correcting your opinion in which I do assure you most positively you are mistaken '*that every day increases my attachment to Europe* and *renders my future reconcilement to my own country more desperate.*' I know and feel fully the value of my attachment to Europe, and I aver that it is not it which principally induces me to desire to continue some time longer on this side of the Atlantic but my wish to postpone my return to America under present circumstances, and until they should be somewhat changed, for the reasons mentioned in my former letters. I aver with equal sincerity that I should prefer what you seem to think certain two years hence in the case of my being in America, to any thing in Europe. It is what would crown my wishes, but it is so far beyond my hopes that should I return at present it cannot be with a view to it, but with a determination founded on mature deliberation to go and fix myself in the western country. It is not ambition however that will carry me there, but a desire to settle myself as nearly as possible agreeable to my wishes.

We have recieved here an account of Monro's being chosen for the Senate, as well as the resolution of the assembly respecting the assumption. Both these circumstances shew that the disposition is antifederal as I am told Monroe is considered of that class. This renders more probable also the continuance of Monro's colleague as I should imagine. On what can be founded the opinion that he will be dropped? Don't these circumstances remove the foundation that there was?

I mentioned to you also in my last letter that Langeac had removed the difficulty I apprehended respecting the *congé* of the house—and that that affair was finally settled, possession having been given him in Nov. last. After having the *etat de la maison* examined and the articles necessary for putting it in the situation in which you recieved it, estimated, and then examined, and approved by M. Grand's architect—after deducting some articles which you had had made, such as bars and bells &c.—the balance was paid by M. Grand to M. Langeac's brother. It was about 1300.^{tt} This as well as the whole of the house rent which has been paid since your departure, except 300.^{tt}, was charged by M. Grand as you desired to the U. S. The 300.^{tt} were for your saddle horse sold to Langeac before I recieved your letter desiring the house rent should not go into your account. As M. Grand had no account open I think with Congress except the 66,000.^{tt} which you had ordered to be deposited there these sums have been paid I believe out of it.

I inclose at present my account with Congress settled up to July 1. as you had desired. It is divided into two accounts, 1. That as your secretary balanced finally. It ends Sep. 24. 89. because the year ended then and my account as Chargé des affaires begins from thence merely to avoid a fraction of two days as you did not leave Paris till the 26th. In this account I think there can be no difficulty as it consists merely of my salary and postage, the first fixed by M. Grand agreeably to M. Franklin's and in consequence of your letter, the second paid by me as contained in my servant's account of expences, the only evidence that can be given or required. This sum amounting to 429.ᵗ 4ˢ. is extracted from these accounts for four years.—2. My account as Chargé des affaires. It is stated in florins because my bills were paid me sometimes in assignats which I was obliged to sell for cash, and sometimes in cash with the *agio* deducted by M. Grand, so that if stated in Livres I should have a difficulty in fixing this matter and should be obliged to be satisfied with an *a peu pres*, taking the *agio* on an average of 5 p. cent agreeably to M. Grands letter which has guided me in my account with you as you will see.—Besides I should not precisely know what part of the sum had been paid away by me in assignats though that would be very inconsiderable as most objects of detail are necessarily paid for in cash, and further for several months I recieved only cash from Mr. Grand, he deducting the agio so that during that space I had no assignats to pay. After that I recieved assignats from him and paid them in the few cases in which I could. On the whole I suppose the account is within a very few guilders of being the same as far as I have been able to settle it by conjecture in assignats, specie and florins and stating their proportions. To avoid complication and because I suppose it equally just as my salary is fixed in dollars, I have stated the value of these dollars in florins agreeable to what Mr. Hubbard tells me is the rule. This I have charged to Congress and given them credit for my draughts on their bankers in florins. The postage, pamphlets &c. agreeably to account sent, amount to 537.ᵗ 9. This was necessarily paid in specie and of course settled by average agreeably to M. Hubbard's opinion as to the exchange and Mr. Grand's as to the *agio* of the assignats. I wrote to him to enquire this in order to settle my account with you herewith sent.—The remaining article of my account with Congress to July 1. may perhaps meet with some difficulty. It is the ƒ665.12.8 or 1500.ᵗ with which Nomeny run off. You desire me to ascertain what part was destined for Congress on the best evidence that I can. I had thought at first it would be easy to do this, but on turning to my accounts I find it more difficult than I had imagined from the manner in which these monies were paid. At the beginning of every month it was my custom to draw for nearly equal sums. Out of it I paid regularly your servants wages, such things as were necessary for public use, which consisted then in the medal boxes making by Upton, and my own expences. As the house was much exposed I made it a point to keep no money by me, and particularly as I generally returned home late, and until then the room where I lodged might be easily entered. Petit was my *caissier*. I took money from him in detail. He purchased and paid for such things as were wanted. He was often in advance and when my bill at the beginning of the month was more than sufficient the rest remained in his hands. Hence it is impossible to ascertain with precision what part of the 1500.^{tt} stolen was destined to public use, or what part of the 1500.^{tt} drawn for four days afterwards to replace it was actually applied to that use. I see from my journal only that about 350.^{tt} or 60.^{tt} are all that could possibly have been appropriated of those 1500.^{tt} to my particular purposes, but I cannot say that the whole or what part of this sum was thus appropriated. However if this matter is to be settled with Congress as with an individual, I acknowlege that the *onus probandi* lies on me and that I can only claim strictly what I can shew to have been destined for their purposes; and this I repeat it is impossible for me to do with precision for the reasons abovementioned. There is another view in which this subject presents itself. It is certainly the intention of Congress that I should recieve the salary destined to me. I cannot be said to recieve what does not come into my hands and what was carried off in this manner by an unforeseen accident. It may be said it is by my own fault as I might have gone to the bankers myself and recieved it. I cannot suppose this a matter of indispensable necessity. I did what is generally done. I sent a person of confidence to recieve it. This confidence was founded on his supposed probity, and his having been frequently trusted with money, and even with larger sums. But even if I had gone myself and recieved this money and had been robbed of it on the way on my return home, or if I had deposed it in a place of security and this had been forced, I should think a sovereign whose intention is that a given sum should be really recieved would be disposed to take the matter in consideration and make up the loss sustained without the fault of the person sustaining it. I do not say this is a matter of right, but the case with me seems to approach much nearer the degree which may be called of right. However I do not depend on my judgment as I am interested. I give the reasons for which I have charged the whole of the bill and I ask the favor of you to be so good as to say in explanation of the charge, to the person who is to settle the account, whatever you may think proper. After that they may settle it as they please. But it is necessary that some explanation should be given of the charge as it stands in my account.—I inclose you also your account balanced. The bill which I recieved from you, and the price of the Mis. de la fayette's picture are not contained in it as the former is for your wine and the latter will be joined to some trifles that I shall have to pay for you for the dress from Houdon, echelle de bibliotheque &c. This account is dated Dec. 30. because that will be the date of my order on the bankers here for the balance which I shall give them to-morrow. That part which is on public account will appear and of course will be re-imbursed you. The medal boxes being made by your order I have thought it best finally that you should account with Congress for them. They are now safely deposited at M. Grands waiting for their or your orders. I inclosed you in my letter of Nov. 7. the account of which this is the continuation. For greater security a copy is added on the back of this account. The articles purchased since, are contained in Petits account and receipt of the 14th. of Nov., of which I send you the original having not taken the precaution, as it was the moment of my departure from Paris, to make him give me a duplicate of this, as of his other accounts sent you formerly.—All this account was paid in specie except perhaps a very small part to Upton. In order to induce him to work it was necessary to advance him money in detail and of course in specie, and giving him a larger sum in advance would have been the means of preventing him from continuing the boxes. Servants wages were of course paid in specie and besides there were then no assignats below 200.^{tt} I wrote to M. Grand to know what was the average from Nov. 89. to Aug. 90. of the relative value of livres in specie at Paris compared with florins. His answer is confined only to the average price for that time of assignats and specie. It was necessary to know also the average exchange. This has been supplied by Mr. Hubbard whom I desired to examine the rate of exchange for that time. I send you his note on the subject.

I mentioned to you in my last that the Champagne was recieved at Havre. I have since heard nothing further of it, but I hope it has been long sent off from thence. M. Fenwick I hope will soon dispatch the Bordeaux. I have written to him that I would pay immediately his disbursements on that account. M. Vernon was with him when he last wrote me on the 18th. He was then to embark in a fortnight for Norfolk, Virga.

I inclose you three letters. One for the Secretary of the Treasury. I have always directed to him agreeable to the old and honorable stile—because he has never said any thing to me respecting it, and because as much as I despise these kinds of things when merely relative to myself, I adhere to them when relative to others whose value of them I cannot estimate. I should hope however that the address which you have adopted would be approved of by him and all those whose examples have weight. Example is a much better and more sure method of curing the folly of ridiculous titles than a decree of the national assembly. By a letter from London we are told that they have very late American intelligence there and that it is expected the present session of Congress will be warm and violent on the subject of additional taxes and that other States will join Virginia though on different principles against the late funding bill.—The *club des Jacobins* at Paris it is said is forming into two factions. This gives some additional force to the Mis. de la fayette. Adieu my dear Sir, pardon the lengthy details of this tiresome letter—and particularly the cause which has given rise to them—and believe me with sincerity your friend & servant, W: SHORT

RC (DLC); at head of text: "*Private*"; docketed by TJ in pencil (perhaps some time after the receipt of the letter): "relative to our accounts"; endorsed by TJ as received 14 Apr. 1791 and so recorded in SJL. Enclosures:

(1) Short to Hamilton, 18 Dec. 1790, with its enclosures (Syrett, *Hamilton*, VII, 348-68). (2) Short's ACCOUNT . . . DATED DEC. 30 (see note, Short to TJ, 7 Nov. 1790, for this and Petit's account).

From William Short

DEAR SIR   Amsterdam Dec. 30. 1790

I had the honor of writing to you on the 23d. by the way of the English packet which will sail in a few days. This letter inclosing one for the Secretary of the treasury, will be sent by an American vessel which sails for New-York to-morrow.

The national assembly did not resume the subject of tobacco as was expected when I last wrote. Their business and their manner of proceeding, as I have frequently mentioned to you, renders it impossible even for themselves to say one day what will be the deliberation of the next. I still hope however that so far as their deliberations concern the objects of our commerce they will be not much longer delayed as it is certain their dispositions are more favorable to us on those subjects now than they were some time ago. I have no reason to suppose that those favorable dispositions will be changed, but with such an assembly nothing is stable.

With respect to their islands the disorder and confusion which prevail there will necessarily postpone the regulations of their commerce on which the assembly is to decide after having heard the wishes of the colonies expressed by their respective assemblies legally chosen. The national assembly as you have been already informed have thought it necessary that troops should be sent there. If it becomes indispensable to make use of them to re-establish order, the assembly urged by the deputies of the maritime towns and provinces will be disposed to treat them as a conquered country and dictate severe terms as to their commercial privileges. But if matters are amicably settled, their privileges will in time be augmented, viz. as soon as the revolution shall be so fully established in France as to render the support of those engaged in the Westindia commerce, less necessary to it. This is the opinion of the deputies of the colonies and those who have large possessions there, with whom I was acquainted at Paris. They felt that the members of the national assembly from Bordeaux, Nantes and the provinces adjoining them were essential to the revolution and of course that every thing would be sacrificed to them by an assembly whose first object was to effect the revolution.

The reporter of the committee for the abolition of the *droits d'aubaine* in the foreign possessions of France has given me repeated assurances since I left Paris, by the secretary whom I left there, that he waited only for an opportunity of presenting it to the assembly. The delay has been much longer than I could have expected. He assured me himself that he would present it long ago and that there was not the smallest doubt of its passing the assembly with the same ease as the committee. I shall continue to press him on the subject as it is the most sure, perhaps the only means of obtaining what we desire. Should the proposition come from us and go to them through the minister it is possible in their disposition with respect to the islands and their constant jealousy of ministerial communications that it might be rejected. I communicated to you some time ago the proposals of *Drost* made through Mr. Grand. I see that something has been said in the national assembly about employing him in a new partial coinage. I do not know whether it will be done, but this will probably induce him to apply soon for an answer from you.

The opinion of England and Prussia interfering in the Spring in the quarrel between Russia and the Porte is confirmed every day. This adds strength to another that Russia is now endeavouring to induce the Turk to accept a peace without their mediation. She presses this by daily successes and it is thought that Ismailow is before this added to her conquests on the Danube.

The Emperor has taken on himself the execution of the decree of the chamber of Wetzlaer. His troops have not yet entered Liege, but the Magistrates have sent the act of their submission to his will in which they throw themselves on his justice for the redress of their grievances. I beg you to accept assurances of the sentiments of attachment with which I am dear Sir, your most obedient servant,

W: SHORT

PrC (DLC: Short Papers); at head of text: "*No. 51.*" Recorded in SJL as received 14 Apr. 1791. FC (DNA: RG 59, DD).

From C. W. F. Dumas

MONSIEUR La Haie 31e. Dec. 1790

Je n'ai rien, pour le coup, à ajouter à ma dernière du 6 au 15 courant, que j'ai portée moi-même à Rotterdam, et remise en mains propres de Wm. Stuard, Capitaine de la Fregatte *the Willink*, parti de là pour Baltimore, sinon de relever une faute essentielle commise à la hâte d'après un Rentier au sujet du prix courant des Obligations de la Négotiation des fonds liquidés. Au lieu de ƒ1025, c'est ƒ1250 que coute aujourd'hui une de ces Obligations de ƒ1000 de Capital, de la Négociation de Mess. v. Staphorst, &c.: car c'est à 25 p% au-delà du Capital qu'on les achette; et celles de la Négociation du Courtier Stadnitsky sont encore plus haut, leur cours actuel étant à 27 p% au-dessus du Capital.

Les circonstances où se trouve l'Europe paroissent toujours très-critiques, tant par rapport au Nord, et à la part qu'y prendront, plus ou moins forcément, d'autres Puissances, qu'eu égard aux grandes Indes.

La Banque d'Amsterdam reste au-dessous du Pair. On continue de garnisonner l'intérieur de l'Etat, et demain il retentira de bénédictions! Grace à Dieu, celles dont jouissent les Etats-Unis, et leur Administration, sont réelles et journalières. Je suis avec grand respect, De Votre Excellence, Le très-humble, très-obéissant & fidele Serviteur

C W F DUMAS

RC (DNA: RG 59, PCC No. 93); at head of text: "No. 72. Dupl. A S.E. Mr. Ths. Jefferson Esqr. Minre. d'Etat & des Affes. Etr. en Congrès des Et. Un. d'Amérique." Recorded in SJL as received 14 Apr. 1791. FC (Dumas Letter Book, Rijksarchief, The Hague; photostats in DLC).

Coinage and the Unit of Money

I. NOTES ON BILLON AS REPORTED TO THE
NATIONAL ASSEMBLY, 1790
II. THOMAS JEFFERSON TO ALEXANDER HAMILTON,
29 DECEMBER 1790
III. THOMAS JEFFERSON TO ALEXANDER HAMILTON,
24 JANUARY 1791

EDITORIAL NOTE

In late November Jefferson received newspapers from William Short that seemed to provide a means for opening up the subject of coinage with the Secretary of the Treasury, then engaged in preparing his report on the establishment of a mint.[1] In the *Gazette Nationale* of 3 Aug. 1790 that Short had sent, he observed a report by Naurissat on billon which so impressed him that he made detailed notes of it.[2] The printed text of the report he then dispatched to Hamilton with an open hint of his willingness to make further exchanges of information.[3] The subject was one in which he had long been interested and it was closely connected with his hope for the establishment of a symmetrical system of weights, measures, and money based on an invariable standard, about which he would soon make a supplementary report to Congress.[4]

Jefferson's approach to Hamilton in an effort to reach an accommodation in advance of legislation on the mint is revealing. In 1784 he had consulted Robert Morris before drafting his own propositions on coinage. This, like the overture to Hamilton, was perhaps primarily to neutralize political opposition, for Jefferson was well aware of the obstacles to innovation that existed in the circles of finance and commerce. His own plans for an American currency had been developing at least since 1776 when he first proposed the decimalized dollar.[5] Robert Morris thought decimal reckoning desirable, though not necessary, and he made his proposed unit of money the common denominator of the thirteen currencies already in existence. This half-measure born of conservatism was so impractical that the price of a horse would have required "a notation of 6 figures . . . 115,200" and the public debt of 80 millions would have been expressed as 115,200,000,000.[6] Also, Jefferson could not have been unaware of the persistent interest in contract coinage, despite the fiasco of the copper coinage of 1787 with its speculative intrigues involving William Duer, Royal Flint, and others.[7] Viewing coinage as an attribute of sovereignty, he hoped

[1] Short to TJ, 4 Aug. 1790, informing him that newspapers would probably go by the same vessel. Hamilton was directed to prepare a plan or plans for a mint immediately after TJ's report on copper coinage was submitted (JHR, I, 194; Vol. 16: 341).
[2] Document I.
[3] Document II.
[4] Editorial Note, TJ's report on copper coinage, 14 Apr. 1790; report on weights and measures, 4 July 1790.
[5] Vol. 1: 516; Vol. 7: 152.
[6] TJ Autobiography, Ford, I, 74.
[7] Don Taxay, *The U.S. Mint and coinage* (New York, 1966), p. 26-43.

to make the unit of money integral with a decimalized system of weights and measures that would be uniquely American in its simplicity, convenience, and adaptability to general usage among nations. Six months earlier he had sent Hamilton a copy of his report on weights and measures in the hope that he would agree to the suggested alteration in the money unit. Hamilton was not then opposed and indeed expressed himself as favorable to the idea of a "general standard among nations."[8]

Now Jefferson renewed his approach, prompted no doubt by the fear that Hamilton's opinion had changed and that the forthcoming report on the mint would be more derivative than innovative. The recently-received report from France recommending billon could have been only an excuse for making the overture, for Jefferson himself had already urged the convenience of billon in his report on copper coinage. His more recent report on weights and measures had recognized the value of the money unit as established by Congress in 1786 at 375.64 grains of pure silver, but he had proposed a "very minute alteration" that would increase its weight a third of a grain in order to link the currency with his system of weights and measures.[9] This time Hamilton evidently did not respond to the appeal for "unreserved communications" and sent Jefferson a copy of his report only after it had been completed and sent to the House of Representatives.

Jefferson affected to have gained "a great deal of satisfaction" from reading it.[10] This no doubt was true with respect to the retention of the dollar as the money unit, the decimal reckoning, the bi-metallic standard, and the ratio between gold and silver. But in fractional currency Hamilton provided nothing between the dollar and the tenth of a dollar, which would have been awkward in practice. He rejected the idea of billion and his copper cent—a cumbersome coin weighing two-thirds as much as the dollar—was inconvenient. His smaller copper coin did not adhere to decimal notation but was equated with the English farthing. These and other derivative features could have given Jefferson little satisfaction. But on the devaluation of the dollar from 375.64 to 371.25 grains of silver, his disagreement with the report, though candidly stated, was more fundamental than his polite response to Hamilton indicated. He was as aware as Hamilton of the truism in James Steuart's *Principles of political economy* that "every variation . . . upon the intrinsic value of the money-unit, has the effect of benefiting the class of creditors, at the expence of the debtors, or vice versa."[11] But this drastic departure from the value already fixed by Congress would not only affect the discharge of the national debt and therefore involve the national honor: it would also collide with Jefferson's dream of a unified system of weights, measures, and coins. Later, after Jefferson had unpacked his *Encyclopédie* and had gained more accurate information about the value of the Spanish dollar at various periods, he thought that Hamilton's proposition to draw "5

8 TJ to Hamilton, 12 June 1790; Hamilton to TJ, [16] June 1790.
9 Vol. 16: 346-7, 662.
10 Document III.
11 Quoted in Syrett, *Hamilton*, VII, 463.

cents out of every dollar" was really equated with the depreciated Spanish dollar of 1772, having 370.95548 grains of silver as compared with its former value of 376.72824 grains. Since he believed this depreciated dollar could not have circulated in America during the Revolution sufficiently to have caused it to be taken as a standard, Jefferson concluded that the American debt was contracted when the dollar was at the higher valuation before 1772.[12] The premise was arguable, but the conclusion testified both to his regard for the public faith and to his wish to keep the currency integrated with his proposed system of weights and measures.

Hamilton, as Jefferson knew, had arrived at his valuation of 371.25 grains by a reliance on the crude methods of assaying prevalent in the United States at the time.[13] In an attempt to verify the result of 371 grains shown by the assay, Hamilton emulated the practice of American merchants in paying in fine gold for the actual weight of dollars in circulation. This figure—24.75 grains of fine gold per dollar—at a ratio of 15 to 1 provided his valuation of 371.25 grains, whereas the minted weight of the Spanish dollar was nearer to the value established by Congress in 1786 than to that of the assay.[14] Hamilton conceded in his report that Jefferson's "small alteration" in the value of the dollar to link it with a uniform system of weights, measures, and coins might be desirable. But he thought it certainly not advisable to do so by "so considerable a change in the money unit, as would be produced by the addition of five grains of silver to the proper weight of the dollar."[15] The crude methods of assaying and the fundamental error of basing "the fine weight of the new American dollar on that of a worn Spanish one" left him in no doubt as to what the proper weight was.[16] Jefferson's argument, of course, rested on the same faulty foundation of the dollar as valued in general usage. But rather than sacrifice the idea of a uniform national system of weights, measures, and coins he was willing, if necessary, to give up the dollar as the unit of money and to adopt instead either an ounce of pure silver or an ounce of standard silver.[17] Neither Hamilton nor the Congress was ready for such an innovation.

When the House sent Hamilton's report to the Senate on 7 Feb. 1791, it was referred to a committee composed of Morris, Izard, Monroe, and Schuyler. Morris did not report until the hectic hours at the close of the session.[18] "The resolution of the Mint," wrote Maclay, "was foully smuggled through. . . . The plea of want of time prevails, and every one that attempts to speak is silenced with the cry of question and a mere insurrection of the members in support of the demand."[19] Maclay was certain that a resolution was brought forward

---

[12] See group of documents on weights, measures, and coins at end of 1791.
[13] Syrett, *Hamilton*, VII, 468-9.
[14] Taxay, *U.S. Mint and coinage*, p. 49.
[15] Syrett, *Hamilton*, VII, 605.
[16] Taxay, *U.S. Mint and coinage*, p. 49.
[17] Document III.
[18] JS, I, 239, 292. Hamilton's report was laid before the House on 28 Jan. 1791 and sent to the Senate 5 Feb. (JHR, I, 366, 370).
[19] Maclay, *Journal*, ed. Maclay, p. 409, 410.

because unanimous consent was required for reading bills out of order. He hoped the House would raise the questions he was unable to debate in the Senate. Even at this late hour in the session serious opposition did arise in the House. The resolution was adopted, though by the very small majority of 25 to 21. The roll call vote revealed the familiar partisan and sectional alignments.[20]

Jefferson's report on weights and measures was taken up by the House in December and transmitted to the Senate. In January he sent to both houses the addendum and correction to his report.[21] He was evidently so sanguine about legislative action that he explored with David Rittenhouse the question of how to preserve the standard of measure. Rittenhouse was very dubious about the possibility of protecting and using a standard of any given length. None, he pointed out to Jefferson, had been preserved from ancient times nor could the United States "transmit them to posterity with sufficient authenticity, or to different Countries for general use."[22] The doubts may not have been resolved, but Rittenhouse as usual cooperated with Jefferson by pointing out that the cellars of the American Philosophical Society might be used for "the purpose of which we are speaking."[23] The

[20] JHR, I, 341, 356-7; JS, I, 225, 233.

[21] See Documents VIII and IX with TJ's report on weights and measures under 4 July 1790.

[22] Rittenhouse to TJ, 4 Jan. 1791. In transmitting his report (TJ to Speaker, 4 July 1790), TJ had referred to the speech of Sir John Riggs Miller in the House of Commons that he had just read in a London paper. Miller supported the propositions of the Bishop of Autun (see Sowerby, No. 3761), called for a standard so nearly the same "at all times and in all places . . . as to afford no temptation or encouragement to buy with one weight or measure and to sell with another," and urged the seconds pendulum as a standard common to Great Britain and all Europe. This was not only completely in accord with TJ's recommendation: it also had the merit of being a British rather than a French argument and thus, given the determination of Hamilton and his supporters to break the alliance with France and to form a closer connection with England, of being more persuasive with those in the centers of finance and commerce who had opposed the adoption of a metric system. For this reason it is virtually certain that TJ employed Miller's speech to prepare the public mind for his report. Early in September he was in Philadelphia and undoubtedly in touch with Benjamin Franklin Bache, whose *General Advertiser* was launched on 1 Oct. 1790. A week later *A Subscriber*, pointedly connecting Miller's speech with TJ's allusion to it in his letter to the Speaker, submitted it for publication. It appeared in the issues of 7 and 9 Oct. 1790. It is plausible to assume that in this as in other instances TJ made information on matters of public concern available to Bache just as he had done earlier with John Fenno and would do later with Philip Freneau, Samuel Harrison Smith, William Duane, and others (on TJ's relations with Fenno, see under 20 Mch. 1790; on his relations with Bache, see note to Remsen's letter to Russell, 23 Nov. 1790). But if TJ was *A Subscriber*, his effort was partially offset when Bache printed the Rev. George Skene Keith's criticism of TJ's report just as the debate on it arose in the House (*General Advertiser*, 21 Dec. 1790; see note to TJ to Madison, 10 Jan. 1791). Keith sent various copies of his pamphlet to prominent Americans, including Washington (Keith to Washington, 1 July 1791, DLC: Washington Papers).

[23] TJ to Rutherford, 25 Dec. 1792; report of the committee of the Senate, 5 Apr. 1792 (JS, I, 420).TJ thought that variations in length of the pendulum rod because of temperature could be "got over by placing it in a cellar deep enough to be of the mean temperature of the earth. 20. feet deep suffices" (TJ's note on "The rival propositions," DLC: TJ Papers, 62: 10809).

purpose Jefferson had in mind was clearly to preserve and protect the standard of measure against changes in temperature. The standard he later described as "an uniform cylindrical rod of iron, of such length as, in latitude 45.° in the level of the ocean, and in a cellar or other place of uniform natural temperature, shall perform it's vibrations . . . in one second of mean time."[24]

But the explorations were premature and the cellars of the Society were soon rented by John Vaughan for the storage of wine.[25] No action was taken on Jefferson's report at this session and the resolution on the interconnected problem of the mint only authorized the President to procure such artisans and apparatus as would be needed. This responsibility Washington delegated to the Secretary of State and Jefferson continued his efforts to bring Droz to America.[26] The issue would be joined in the next session over the bill to establish regulations governing the mint. When the time came, Jefferson was ready with still another proposal to accommodate the unit of money to his integrated system of weights and measures. But the Federalists of the Senate debased the dollar even more than the Secretary of the Treasury had proposed.

[24] Minutes of the Society, 23 Apr. 1790 and 18 Feb. 1791 (Am. Phil. Soc., *Procs.*, XXII, part III [July, 1885], 182, 189).

[25] TJ to Short, 25 Apr., 29 Aug., and 24 Nov. 1791; Short to TJ, 26 June, 20 July, 24 Aug. 1791; see group of documents on weights, measures, and coins at end of 1791. Robert Leslie, as well as others, supposed that the Secretary of the Treasury would execute the duties authorized by the resolution on the mint; he offered his services in constructing a plating mill, a coinage apparatus, and a machine for impressing the edges (Syrett, *Hamilton*, VIII, 168; Mitchell to TJ, 23 Sep. 1791).

[26] See group of documents on weights, measures, and coins at end of 1791.

I. Notes on Billon as reported to the National Assembly

[1790]

La monnoie de Billon is composed of ⅘ copper and ⅕ silver which makes it intrinsically worth 11ᵗ-10 the marc. [Les cloches, the bells of the kingdom become useless, will weigh 184,000,000 ℔ and be worth 184. millions of livres as metal]

A proposal is made to mix arsenic with the copper of Billon to brighten the colour, but it will add 60 percent to the expence, therefore rejected. Copper costs but 25 sous. This new metal would be 40 sous.

The committee proposes that the new Billon shall be composed of ⅙ silver and ⅚ copper, that is to say

	₶	s.	d.
à deux deniers de fin, valant, au prix du tarif	8.	18.	2.
les cinq sixièmes de cuivre valant @ 25 sous la livre		10.	4.
total de la valeur intrinseque	9.	8.	6.
frais de fabrication	1.		
Cachets à 6 pour cent		12.	6.
benefice pour le tresor public		19.	
total de la valeur numeraire	12.	0.	0.

Ainsi les pieces de 5 sols seront à la taille de 48 au marc. celles de 2 sols à la taille de 120. celles de 18 deniers à la taille de 160.

Le remede sur le fin ou d'alloi sera de trois grains, et le remede de poids sera de trois pieces sur les pieces de 5 sols, de 8 pieces sur celles de 2 sols, et de 12 pieces sur celles de 18. deniers.

Ces remedes sont une marge indispensablement necessaire aux Directeurs des monnoies, pour la fabrication de toutes sortes d'especes, et sont tous reversibles au profit du tresor public, dans la proportion.

MS (DLC); entirely in TJ's hand; at head of text: "Notes on Billon from the report of the Committee of Finances to the National Assembly in the Gazette Nationale. Aug. 3. 1790."

II. Thomas Jefferson to Alexander Hamilton

[29 Dec. 1790]

Th: Jefferson presents his respectful compliments to the Secretary of the treasury, and his condoleances on the accident of the other evening, which he hopes has produced no serious loss.

He incloses to the Secretary of the Treasury a report of a committee of the National assembly of France, on the subject of Billon, containing more particular information as to that species of coin than he had before met with. If the metal be so mixt as to make it of ⅕ of the intrinsic value of the standard silver coin of the U.S. the Cent of billon will be a little smaller than the present 16ths. of dollars, and consequently be more convenient than a

Copper cent. This he submits to the better judgment of the Secretary of the Treasury, and hopes he will consider the liberty taken as an advance towards unreserved communications for reciprocal benefit.

PrC (DLC). Enclosure: *Rapport fait à L'Assemblée Nationale, au nom du comité des Finances, par M. Naurissart. Monnoie de Billon* (10 p., Paris, 1790). The report was presented on 16 Jan. 1790 and ordered to be printed by the National Assembly (*Archives Parlementaires*, XI, 225-6).

III. Thomas Jefferson to Alexander Hamilton

DEAR SIR [24 Jan. 1791]

I return you the report on the mint which I have read over with a great deal of satisfaction. I concur with you in thinking that the unit must stand on both metals, that the alloy should be the same in both, also in the proportion you establish between the value of the two metals. As to the question on whom the expence of coinage is to fall, I have been so little able to make up an opinion satisfactory to myself as to be ready to concur in either[1] decision. With respect to the dollar, it must be admitted by all the world that there is great incertainty in the meaning of the term, and therefore all the world will have justified Congress for their act of removing the incertainty by declaring what they understood by the term. But the incertainty once removed, exists no longer, and I very much doubt a right now to change the value, and especially to lessen it. It would lead to so easy a mode of paying off their debts. Besides, the parties injured by this reduction of the value would have so much matter to urge in support of the first point of fixation. Should it be thought however that Congress may reduce the value of the dollar I should then be for adopting for our unit, instead of the dollar, either one ounce of pure silver, or one ounce of standard silver, so as to keep[2] the unit of money a part of the system of measures, weights and coins. I hazard these thoughts to you extempore and am dear Sir respectfully & affectionately TH: JEFFERSON

I enclose you two letters just received from France.

RC (CtY); undated, but date established from entry in SJL concerning a letter to Hamilton "(on the mint)." PrC (DLC); lacks postscript.

[1] TJ first wrote "any" and then deleted it.
[2] Preceding four words interlined in substitution for "making," deleted.

From Tench Coxe

Sir [1790]

I have the honor to send you a very interesting report made in March last by a Comme. of the British Privy Council upon the subject of their corn trade. The two first paragraphs of the 7th page appear to merit particular attention, and more especially the last of them against which you will observe I have placed an index ☞.

The paragraph in page 22, marked with an index favors exceedingly the opinion that the Barley in the French return, was fraudulently introduced into France from England and The paragraph at the top of the page 23 marked also with an index shows the footing on which foreign corn is judiciously proposed to be introduced. The restriction, which I mentioned to have been informed of, is, I presume a confinement of this accomodation to the importing in *British* Ships.

This paper was sent to me this morning by Mr. Vaughan with a request that I would return it as soon as possible. I conceive it so important that it should be laid before you, that I have ventured to send it to you. If Mr. V. applies to me for it I will take the liberty of sending for it unless you shall have previously returned it to me.

I have the

RC (DLC); in the hand of Tench Coxe, undated and not recorded in SJL, but perhaps written in late summer or early autumn of 1790. The text is incomplete, but apparently lacks only the remainder of the complimentary close and the signature. Enclosure: Hawkesbury's *Representation of the Lords of the Committee of Council . . . upon the present state of the laws for* regulating the importation and exportation of corn (London, 1790). The particular copy that Coxe marked was evidently returned to John Vaughan. TJ also received a copy from John Browne Cutting, which was perhaps enclosed in one of his several missing letters written in 1790 (see Sowerby, No. 3591). See TJ to Carroll, 4 Apr. 1791.

From William Lewis

Sir   Philadelphia January 1st. 1791.

In consequence of your Letter of the 12th. of August last, I am about to lay before you the Information which it calls for, so far as I have been able to collect it. As I do not take your meaning to be, that I should confine myself to such matters as I might think exceptionable, I shall mention all such as have fallen within my knowledge, that "May be considered by the British

Nation as an infraction of the Treaty," and submit them, with some remarks of my own to your consideration.—On conversing with the British Consul for the State of Pennsylvania I found, that he was possessed of a printed statement, which had been prepared by a Committee of British Merchants, appointed for the purpose of enumerating the Infractions of which they complained, and I hoped to derive some useful Information from it, but I could not be favoured with a sight of it. Recollecting that he had in March 1788 presented a memorial on the same subject, to the President and supreme executive Council of this Commonwealth, and supposing it to contain so much of the printed Statement as relates to Pennsylvania; I procured a Copy of it, which shall, with some explanatory observations be laid before you. The memorial was transmitted by the President and Council to the Legislature. On the first day of March A.D. 1788, a Committee of the House, appointed in consequence of a Resolution of Congress, made a Report, which was soon after adopted, that having "Examined into the subject matter of that part of the said message, which recommends to the notice of this House the resolution of Congress passed March 21st. 1787, and suggests the propriety of passing a declaratory Act to answer the end intended by the said resolution, they cannot find that there is any act or acts, or any part or parts of any act or Acts, passed by the Legislature of Pennsylvania, now in force, which are repugnant to the treaty of peace between the united States and his Britannic Majesty, or to any articles thereof, or that at all tend to restrain, limit, or in any manner impede, retard or counteract the operation and execution thereof, or to explain the same."

On receiving your Letter, I sent an extract of so much of it as relates to this business, to the President and Council, and requested to be furnished with Copies of all Proclamations, orders, minutes and Proceedings of Council (if any such there were) which might be supposed by the people of Great-Britain to have been in violation of the Treaty, between that nation and the united States, and I was soon after furnished by them with the following Resolution, to wit,

"Resolved that the Secretary be desired to inform the Attorney of the united States for the District of Pennsylvania, that the supreme executive Council of this Commonwealth, having never been inattentive to any National Engagement, are not informed that any proclamation, order, minute, or proceeding of their Body, has been, or can be in any degree supposed by the people of

Great-Britain, to be in violation of the Treaty between that Nation and the United States."

These Documents shew the Sentiments of the executive and legislative Authorities of Pennsylvania with respect to their observance of the Treaty with Great-Britain, and from what follows, you will be able to form an accurate Judgment thereon. I shall begin with the memorial, and as it relates to matters with which you may not be fully acquainted, I shall endeavour to give the necessary Information respecting them.

The first complaint which it contains is, that the Legislature of Pennsylvania have not passed an act in pursuance of "The recommendatory Resolve of Congress to the different States of the Union, to repeal all Laws repugnant to the Treaty of peace." Had the Legislature of Pennsylvania conceived the meaning of that Resolution to be, that such repealing Laws should be passed by States in which no repugnant Law existed, and within which such repealing Law could not possibly operate, I am confident that it would have readily been complied with; but as they did not understand it in this Sense, and were informed by their Committee that no such repugnant Act existed in Pennsylvania, they passed no Law in consequence of it.

The memorial admits, that the Report of the Committee "Is founded in the strictest Truth" and that "There is no Law at present existing in this State repugnant to the Treaty of peace," but adds that "The position must be taken in this qualified Sense, that no Laws exist here which contravene the Treaty of peace, provided the Treaty be the scale by which the Laws are to be construed, and explained; for there certainly are Laws now existing, the construction of which if confined to the mere letter of the Laws themselves, would essentially affect the rights of British Subjects; Whereas by referring to the Treaty to qualify such Laws, no impediment could arise, but every just right might be prosecuted according to the Spirit and Meaning of the Treaty." If what is here assumed for fact is realy so, the reasoning on it may be just, but if the Instances brought to prove it, have not that effect, and if no others exist, the conclusion cannot be warranted.

The first one mentioned by the Consul is "The present situation of the Bankrupt Laws of this State" which are said "In some Instances to press hard upon the Interest and Security of all foreign Creditors, but they particularly affect the British Creditors by reason of their very extensive Dealings" And that "One essential Inconvenience arises from a late Determination of the Commissioners of Bankruptcy by which they excluded the agents of foreign Merchants from any right to vote in the choice of the assignees of the Bankrupt. But one Instance is here mentioned of the "Bankrupt Laws pressing hard upon the Interest and security of British Creditors" and I cannot possibly immagine another, nor see any weight in this. I do not know that the Creditors of a Bankrupt in England ever had the Right of choosing Assignees under the Laws of that Country, until it was given them by a Statute of the 5th. of George the 2nd. c.30. § 26th. which declares, that this right may be exercised by their Agents or Attornies, whose powers are authenticated in the special manner therein mentioned. No part of the British Bankrupt Laws has ever been held to extend to Pennsylvania, and of course no right could be derived here under this Statute. The first Bankrupt Law that we ever had in Pennsylvania was passed on the 16th. of September 1785. It gave to Commissioners to be appointed by the President or Vice-President of the Supreme executive Council the right of disposing of the Bankrupt's estate for the benefit of his Creditors, but did not enable the Creditors to choose Assignees. This power was first given them by the 11th. Section of an Act passed on the 15th. of March 1787, and as it makes no mention of their voting by Agents &c. the question referred to by the Consul arose under it. It was further objected to their right of voting, with equal and perhaps greater weight, that admitting the Creditors right of voting by their Agents, the powers of the Agents were in the Instance referred to, which was that of Col: Dean, given for other purposes, and did not extend to this, nor were they authenticated as the Statute of George the 2nd. required. On one or both of these objections the Agents were excluded from voting, and not because the Creditors were British Subjects, for had they belonged to any nation, or to a neighbouring State, or even been Citizens of Pennsylvania, the questions and the Decision must have been precisely the same: so that I am altogether at a loss to conceive, how this can be an Infraction of the Treaty, or have any relation to it.

And I am if possible at a still greater loss to conceive how "The operation of the Laws of Attachment of this State" should have been thought of as an evil to be complained of by the Consul; for he admits the wisdom and justice of our Law as to "Domestic Attachments" as they are called, and that which relates to foreign ones, was passed in the year 1705. It gives the same right to all Creditors, of all denominations and of all Countries, that it does to the Citizens of Pennsylvania, tho' it must be admitted, that British Creditors, by availing themselves of their early knowledge of the failure of British Merchants who trade to this Country, send here, and attach their property before the failures are generally known, and thereby derive greater advantage from this Law than all the world besides. The Act complained of may be found in pa. 44. of the first volume of Pennsylvania Laws.

"The Settlement of Interest on Debts due to British Merchants antecedent to the late Troubles" is the next matter mentioned by the Consul, and this is said to be "Of considerable consequence to them, and is presumed by him to be of so much Importance as to require some particular legislative Interposition to define its nature and extent."

[The Legislature of the year 1788, did not think themselves authorized by any principles of sound policy or good Government, to pass a Law to define the nature and extent of Contracts entered into more than a dozen years before and it is reasonable to presume that such a Law would have been complained of as an Infraction of the Treaty. Every person has been left to pursue his remedy at Law, without any particular act being made for the allowance or abatement of Interest, and as the question has altogether depended on the Laws of England, the Consuls acknowledgement that "The Channels of Justice flow with great purity and Impartiality in Pennsylvania, and that the Laws are faithfully and diligently administered" Seems to be a full refutation of his own objection. Since however the objection is so much insisted on, I will take the liberty of mentioning some facts, a knowledge whereof may be necessary to form a Judgment respecting it.

I beleive it is truly stated by the Consul, that "The terms of Contracts between British and American Merchants are for the most part of this sort. Goods are sent hither to be paid for in one year; after which Interest becomes due at the yearly rate of 5 ⅌ Cent." This having been a long established usage, it has so far received the sanction of our Courts, as that Interest has been allowed in such cases from the end of the year, but as there is no possitive Law for the allowing of Interest on an account; as the claim of Interest by British Merchants from their American Debtors, was founded on this usage alone; and as no Instance had before happened of the Intercourse between the People of Great-Britain and of America being interrupted by War; Our Courts held the Case to be a new one, to which the usage did not extend, and as there was neither Law or usage for allowing Interest during the War; that is from the Battle of Lexington in April 1775 until the provisional Articles between the united States and his Britannic Majesty in November 1782, it has been generally disallowed during that period. If the Debt had been contracted more than a year before the Battle of Lexington, Interest has been allowed, I beleive in all cases, from the time of the Debt becoming due, until the Battle of Lexington, and from the provisional Articles, until the time of payment. The Rule has been reciprocal. It prevailed in a trial in our Supreme Court wherein a Citizen of a neighbouring State was Plaintiff and a British Subject defendant, altho' the Debt had been contracted long before the War. It has been observed in other Cases, and I very much doubt if a different one has prevailed at Westminster-Hall in actions brought on running Accounts.]¹

What is said by the Consul with respect to the Law of Alienage, seems to bear so very little relation to the Treaty, that I should have supposed it to have been mentioned under an Idea, that England ought, as the most favoured Nation to have some exclusive Grant of Priviledges: were it not for the following words contained in the memorial "If the *Faith of Treaties* enjoins the mutual security of Rights, the justice of this Government will encourage every fit means to effectuate this essential purpose."— I will only add, that whatever our Law of Alienage may be, we received it from England, with this difference that by an Act entitled "An Act to enable Aliens to purchase and hold real Estates within this Commonwealth"—passed the 11th. Day of February 1789. All Foreigners or Aliens not being the subjects of some sovereign State or Power at War with the United States of America are declared capable until the first day of January Anno Domini 1792 to purchase Lands, Tenements, and Hereditaments within this Commonwealth and to hold the same to them their heirs and assigns for ever.

And with this farther difference, that in Pennsylvania a Mortgage being a mere Security, on which the Remedy is a Scire facias to effect a Sale of the Land for the payment of the Debt, it may be taken by a Foreigner as well as by a Citizen of Pennsylvania and has always been considered as personal Estate.

I am afraid that I have wearied your patience, by paying an over minute attention to this long memorial, which I might perhaps have considered as merely containing Hints for the improvement of our Laws, so as to become peculiarly favourable to the people of Britain, did it not conclude with some observations respecting "National Character and national Justice" And an express

Declaration that "The suggestions are built on the broad principles of commutative Justice, and the solemn stipulations of Treaties, applied to the particular objects of the Representation."

The British Consul considers the 14th. § of an Act entitled "An act for the Attainder of divers Traitors &c." passed the 6th. of March 1788² and the 4th. § of a Supplement thereto, passed the 29th. of March 1779. as an Infraction of the Treaty. The first of these Acts is in pa. 98 of the 2nd. Vol. of the Pennsylvania Laws, and the Supplement is in pa. 177 of the same Book. The Reasons assigned by him are, if I rightly comprehend them

1. That a British Subject, who has a lawful title to the Lands seised as the property of an attainted Traitor, or who is his Judgment or mortgage Creditor, will be suddenly barred of his right by the opperation of these Sections, if he does not exhibit his claim in the manner therein mentioned.

2. That these sections are calculated to draw the Decision of questions affecting the rights of British Subjects from the proper Tribunals to summary ones, and to subject them to new and unusual modes of Trial.

3. That if a British Subject who is a Creditor of any such attainted Traitor, establishes his claim, he is not under these Acts intitled to payment in gold or silver.

Remarks

1. I have not heard of any such case as is here mentioned having occurred, nor of facts that can give rise to any thing of the kind; from which I conclude, that they were mentioned as possible cases, under supposed Circumstances.

2. These acts authorized the President or Vice-President (I say *authorized*, because we have no such officers at present) to call on such offenders only, as should aid the enemy by joining the army &c., to surrender themselves under the Penalty of attainder, and not upon all offenders; and as the Treaty put an end to the War, so it put an end to all attainders under these acts, and consequently no new case can arise.

3. The 8th. Sect. of the Supplement pa. 179. restores the Remedy by Ejectment to all persons, except such as claim by a Title derived under the person attainted.

4. The 10th. Sect. of the Supplement pa. 180. gives the right of Trial by Jury, to all Claimants, so that the course of justice is the same as in other cases.

5th. The 4th. and 5th. Sects. of the Supplement pa. 178. extends the time limited by the 14th. Section pa. 107 of the first Act for exhibiting of claims—And in addition to this, most, if not all Countries have their Laws for limiting the time within which actions shall be brought. They have them in England and we have them here, and I cannot see how a reasonable time limitted by the Legislature for closing all claims on the Person attainted, and bringing the balance into the Treasury, can be a violation of any Treaty; But it is a full answer to the objection

6th. That the British Creditor may still have his remedy by action against the Person attainted, and the reasoning used by the Consul would put an End to all the Laws of Forfeiture, since there cannot be a Doubt, but that the Legislature of any State, might at any time, after the Treaty as well as before, prohibit the Commission of any offence, under the penalty of any particular Sum, or of the Forfeiture of all the offender's Estate, without making any provision for the payment of his Debts. Of this the English Law affords abundant proof. Hence it appears that these acts, instead of being Infractions of the Treaty, give rights to the British Creditors, which they would not have otherwise had, and leave them the choice of accepting of them or not as they think proper.

These remarks will I hope be excused, since they have arisen from a desire to save you the Trouble of a tedious perusal and consideration of the Several Acts.

Tender Laws as they are called, having given rise to complaints against some or all of the States, it may afford you satisfaction, at the expence of but little trouble, to have a short statement of them, as they have existed in Pennsylvania.

The 2nd. and 3rd. Sects. of an act entitled "An act for making the Continental Bills of Credit, and the Bills of credit emitted by resolves of the late assemblies legal tender, and for other purposes therein mentioned," passed the 29th. of January 1777. made "The Bills of Credit *emitted and made current* by the Continental Congress, and the Bills of Credit *made current* by the Resolves of the late assemblies of Pennsylvania, and certain other Bills therein mentioned["] a legal tender, under the penalty of forfeiting the Debt by a refusal, pa. 7 of the 2nd. vol. of Pennsylvania Laws.

As this act only mentioned "The Bills of Credit *emitted and made Current*" it was held not to extend to such bills as were emitted by future Acts of Congress, or of our State Legislature, and therefore subsequent Laws were enacted, declaring them to be a legal Tender, but for want of sufficient accuracy of expression by the Legislature, such subsequent Emissions, were for the most part only made a legal tender for the purpose of stopping Interest, and not of forfeiting the Debt by a Refusal. It is not necessary to refer you to the several Acts, nor to some others that were afterwards made to suspend their operation: For a Law passed on the 21st. of June 1781 repealing "So much of all the Laws of this Commonwealth as declare all or any of the above mentioned Bills of Credit a legal tender, or as impose any forfeiture for refusing to take them["]—2. vol. State Laws 493.

Should it appear to you, on comparing the 6th. Sect. of the Act of the 29th. of January 1777 with the 2nd. Section of that of the 21st. of June 1781. that the latter does not repeal the former, and of course that the legal Exchange between Great-Britain and America remains as it was fixed by the first Act, at 155 ℔ Cent, I answer that a solemn determination to the contrary took place several years ago in our Supreme Court, since which, the Judges have refused to let the question be argued, and the exchange has been regulated, both in and out of Court by the current price of Bills. I mention this, because there may perhaps appear to be some grounds for a contrary opinion.

On the 16th. of March 1785 a Law was passed for emitting £150000. in Bills of Credit, but as they were only made receiveable in the payment of Taxes, and of other Debts due to the State, no British Creditor can, or ever could be injured by this Act.

As the acts for emitting Bills of Credit, and making them a Tender for different purposes, are very numerous, I have made this short statement, which gives a full view of all that can be necessary for you to know respecting them.

The following Remarks will shew, the restrictions which have been laid at different periods by acts of the Legislature, on the Recovery of Debts.

The 6th. 7th. 8th. and 9th. Sections of the abovementioned Act of the 21st. of June 1781 Entitled "An act for the repeal of so much of the Laws of this Commonwealth as make the Continental Bills of Credit &c a legal tender" &c, restrain under the Limitations therein mentioned, the issuing of Executions for the principle of any Debt, until two years from the passing of the said Act. 2 Vol State Laws 495. 496.

This Act was passed during the War, and had no exception

in favour of British Subjects, tho' there was one in the 9th. Section of it against them.

Before the two years had expired, to wit on the 12th. of March 1783, Another Act was passed extending the Restriction for one year longer, that is to say, until the 21st. of June 1784, and from thence until the end of the next sitting of Assembly. 3 Vol of Pennsylvania Laws 138.—There was no Exception in this Act in favour of British Creditors, and as the end of the next sitting of Assembly after the 21st. of June 1784, was on the 24th. of September in the same year, it expired on that day. From that time until the 23rd. of December in the same year, there was no existing Law in Pennsylvania, laying any restraint on the Recovery of any Debts whatever, but on the last mentioned Day, another Law was enacted respecting Debts contracted before the 1st. Day of January 1777, and subjecting the Recovery thereof to considerable Restraints, with an exception in favour of all British Creditors, whose Debts had been contracted before the 4th. Day of July Anno Domini 1776.

Hence it appears—

1st. That the impediment to the recovery of all Debts contracted before the 1st. Day of January Anno Domini 1777, created by the act of the 21st. of June 1781, and continued by that of the 12th. of March 1783. continued, (if the Treaty did not prevent it) until the 24th. day of September Anno Domini 1784.

2. That a new impediment (if the Treaty did not prevent it) was created by the Act of the 23rd. of December Anno Domini 1784, to the Recovery by British Creditors of their Debts contracted between the 4th. Day of July Anno Domini 1776. and the 1st. Day of January 1777, which continued until the 23rd. of December 1787—3 Vol Penna. Laws pa. 412.

As commerce between England and Pennsylvania had ceased before the 4th. Day of July 1776; it can hardly be supposed, that any such Debts as are last mentioned, were contracted between that period and the first Day of January 1777. Of course there could not have been any Impediment to the recovery of them and I am confident that no such Case ever occurred.

Whether British Creditors ever met with any Impediment under the act of the 21st. of June 1781, or that of the 12th. of March 1783 in the recovery of their Debts, I will not undertake to say. I was in full practice at the Bar during the Continuance of both these acts, and recollect no Instance of the kind, so that it is not likely that the Court was ever called upon to determine whether they or the treaty should prevail. In other cases, [the Judges have uniformly and without hesitation declared in favor of the Treaty, on the Ground of its being the Supreme Law of the Land. On this ground, they have not only discharged attainted Traitors from Arrests but have frequently declared that they were entitled by the Treaty to Protection.][3]

I do not know whether I have answered your views or not. My object has been, on the one hand to avoid reasoning on general principles, and on the other to enable you to avail yourself of any local knowledge which I may possess. I beleive that I have omitted nothing which can be "Considered by the British Nation as an Infraction of the Treaty."

Should any further Information be thought necessary, I shall be happy in having an opportunity to communicate it.

[I am with the highest Esteem Yr. Mo: Obt. & very Hble. Servt. WM. LEWIS][3]

RC (DNA: RG 59, MLR); endorsed by TJ as received 3 Jan. 1791 and so recorded in SJL. FC of Extracts (DNA: RG 59, SDR); in clerk's hand, consisting of three extracts (see notes 1 and 3), over the first of which is this caption: "No. 60. Extra of a letter of March 15th. 1788. from the British Consul at Philadelphia, to the Governor of Pennsylvania" and over the last two of which is the following: "Observations on the preceding Extract by William Lewis, Esqr. Attorney of the district of Pennsylvania for the United States." These extracts comprise the whole text of enclosure No. 60 in TJ to Hammond, 29 May 1792. For other texts of extracts as set forth in enclosures Nos. 1-60, see notes to that letter.

Despite his elaborate effort, Lewis failed to supply one document central to the purpose of TJ's inquiry—the resolution of the General Assembly of 3 Mch. 1787, the text of which (enclosure No. 43 in TJ to Hammond, 29 May 1792) he was obliged to obtain from the journals of that body rather than rely upon the partial quotation given above. Congress' resolution of 21 Mch. 1787 was carefully designed to obviate the kind of action already taken by Pennsylvania. That resolution was based on the explicit assertion that no state could rightfully impede or interpret the terms of the Treaty of Peace as the supreme law of the land. Congress requested each state to pass a general law repealing all statutes held to contravene the treaty, not specifying particular acts by title. The object, of course, was to make such a comprehensive repeal specifically binding upon courts of law and equity (JCC, XXXII, 124-5). In the meager selection from Lewis' letter that TJ was able to use in his reply to Hammond, the attorney did point out that Pennsylvania courts had recognized the supremacy of the treaty.

1 Matter in brackets (supplied) is the whole of the first extract indicated in note above.

2 Thus in MS, an error for 1778.

3 Matter in brackets (supplied) is the whole of the last two extracts indicated in note above.

From George Buchanan

At this particular Period, when some of the Medical Faculty may expect to meet with advantageous appointments, I hope you will excuse the liberty I have taken Sir, in addressing you a few lines.

I find that a Bill is Brought into Congress for the establishment of Marine Hospitals, and for the benefit of my Family would wish to be made Physician of the one to be established in Baltimore; I know of no person Sir, whose Interest upon that occasion I would rather solicit than Yours; Your friendship and attention Sir, upon former occasions, I have been highly Honored with, and if, at this time I could meet with your protection and Interest, I should ever esteem myself under obligations to you: There are many Candidates from this Place, but none of them have ever received a regular Medical Education, and Dr. Wynkoop whom I understand has been very industrious, must, if he succeeds, inevitably appoint some other Person to do the Business, for his Bad Health will never Permit him to do his duty.[1] He is too bad even to attend to private Practice. I mention this Sir not so much to forward my own Election, as to have a respectable appointment to our Hospital.

Your voice with the President Sir, I am confident would have weight and if, before it is too late, you would do me the Honor of mentioning my name to him, or any others in whose Hands the appointment lay, I should ever feel myself much endebted to you.— I have the Honor to be Sir, with much respect your very Humble servant   Geo Buchanan

RC (DLC: Washington Papers); endorsed by TJ as received 4 Jan. 1791 and so recorded in SJL.

[1] At this point Buchanan placed an asterisk and at foot of text wrote: "has a consumption."

From David Humphreys

Madrid January 3d. 1791.

I have had, Sir, many conversations with Mr. Carmichael on the subject of your letter to him. If it had arrived early in summer, he thinks we might have obtained all our wishes. Then the critical state of affairs induced the Comte de Florida Blanca to throw out those general assertions that we should have no reason to complain of the conduct of this court with respect to the Mississippi, which gave rise to the report its navigation was opened.

That minister had intimations from del Campo of the conferences between Mr. Morris and the Duke of Leeds which occasioned him to say with warmth to Mr. Carmichael now is your time to make a treaty with England. Fitzherbert availed himself of those conferences to create apprehensions that the Americans would aid his nation in case of war. Long time the conduct of Spain was fluctuating and undecided. After a variety of circumstances (which Mr. Carmichael has explained in dispatches that have miscarried and which he will repeat in others by me) a convention was formed whereby the British gained substantially every thing they at first demanded. Want of money to support a war and the queen's intrigues together with advice from the Compte Montmorin that peace was essential for France were probably the principal causes which compelled Spain to yield the point after each side had tried which could hold out longest. The preparations cost Spain sixteen million dollars. Thus the crisis most favorable for the attainment of our wishes is past. Unless there is some secret article in the convention by which England guarantees the possessions of Spain in America, resentment may remain[1] in the Spanish court for having been obliged to receive the Law. They may also desire to be in readiness for events. How far these or other motives may operate in producing a change of system with respect to the United States remains to be learnt from an adherance to the latter part of your instructions to Mr. Carmichael.

The fact is clear that the United States are daily gaining political consideration in Europe. Spain, guided by narrow policy towards it's colonies, fears the consequence of our encreasing strength and resources. The Compte de Florida Blanca has been so long and so obstinately opposed to the admission of foreign vessels into the gulf of Mexico, that the most he can ever be persuaded to do will be to suffer some body else to negociate, to whom, if there be blame for inconsistency in policy the fault may be imputed. But the compte not being well with the queen, loses credit; and recent circumstances indicate that he is but the ostensible, while le Rena ([2]at the head of the finance) is the real Minister. Mr. Carmichael thinks, that if the compte will not consent to open a negociation with liberal views, it may be possible to displace him and find a successor of better dispositions: that is if the queen lives, but she is apprehensive of dying in childbed next month, which event would give the compte more weight than ever. Campomanes, who is at the head of the judicatures, Compte D'Aranda and many others entertain just ideas with respect to our country.

The first is high in influence and secretly an enemy of the Compte de Florida Blanca; the last, at the head of opposition, will not come into Office himself, but in case of a change of administration, some of his friends will succeed. Mr. Carmichael, being on terms of intimacy with the first characters here, is certainly capable of effecting more at this court than any other American.

He is heartily desirous of accomplishing the object in view at all events and fully determined to return to America in twelve or eighteen months at farthest. He has expressed that intention repeatedly. [Were he]³ to be invested with full powers, perhaps he would be able to do something before his departure from this Continent. Of this however you will judge best from the tenor of his future communications and other circumstances. Nothing has passed between him and me on that subject. But I question whether this court after having sent Gardoqui to treat in America will ever send any other minister there for that purpose. Even if they would I believe more advantages might be gained by negociating here than there.

The British ambassador has conferences with the minister almost every day, which excites jealousy in the representatives of some other powers.

Something also gives uneasiness to this court. Affairs do not go well. Frequent councils are convened. The government is feeble, jealous, mercenary and unpopular. The king is a well disposed, passionate, weak man. The queen (a shrewd, well instructed woman, addicted to pleasure and expence) governs the kingdom. She is not beloved. Nor did either of them receive the usual acclamations of the people when they returned from their country residence last fall. The queen has even been insulted, which makes her appear rarely in public. For this offence twelve washerwomen have been confined and their husbands banished the kingdom because they petitioned for their release. Several natives of distinction have lately been exiled from the capital to the provinces, among others the comptesse of Galvez. Compte Segur, a Frenchman accused of being the author of a libel against the queen, within a week past died of rigorous confinement. This government, alarmed at the success of the revolution in France, shews great distrust and hatred of the French. Several have been arrested at midnight and hurried out of the country. People begin to think and even to speak in private circles freely. In some provinces dissatisfaction prevails on account of new taxes. Three regiments are just sent into Gallicia to quell those disturbances, where an attempt was made to assassinate the new General on the road. General Lacy (who commands at Barcel[ona] and has been obliged to menace the city by turning the cannon against it) is continually writing to court for men and military supplies. Tho' the Spaniards in many places retain the appearance, habits and manners of a people who have but lately lost their liberty; yet affairs are not ripe for reformation from want of leaders, information and means of combination. The utmost diligence is used to suppress intelligence from other countries. Notwithstanding I had the necessary passports, at the frontier town I was delayed a day and not permitted to proceed, until the Officers of police had put my letters under cover to the police in Madrid. This having been done in my presence, they delivered them to me, with an apology for the strictness of their orders. On my arrival at Madrid, I went directly to Mr. Carmichael and upon his application to the Compte de Florida Blanca, the letters (which had remained in my trunk under the seal of government) were returned unopened into my hand. But notwithstanding all precautions, letters, newspapers and pamphlets come from France into this kingdom. Interesting paragraphs are copied, circulated and read with avidity.

Projects have certainly been meditated for attempting a counter revolution in France from Turin and other quarters at the same time. They proved abortive. Tho', I believe, the designs were previously known at this court, no aid was given. In France the finances have a good aspect and the revolution is becoming confirmed. It is thought the Compte de Artois and Most of the refugees will return within the time limited by the decree of the national assembly. I have the honor to be your most obedient servt.

D. HUMPHREYS

RC (DNA: RG 59, DD) at head of text: "No. 10"; entirely in code, being decoded in part interlineally and verified by the Editors, employing Code No. 8; endorsed by TJ as received 31 Mch. 1791 and so recorded in SJL. Tr (DNA: RG 59, DD); at head of text: "No. 10. (in Cypher)"; varies from decoding as indicated below, as does another Tr accompanying it.

For extracts from this letter trans-

mitted by TJ to Washington, see TJ to Washington, 2 Apr. 1791.

1 The cypher calls for the following reading: "may remai govern in"; both Trs decipher it thus.

2 The following symbols are deleted in RC: 925. 719. 240. [1351?]. 688. 24. (a man of better experience).

3 The words in brackets are supplied, not having been encoded but obviously intended to be.

From Tobias Lear

United States Jany 3d. 1791

By the President's command T. Lear has the honor to transmit to the Secretary of State to be lodged in his Office one exemplified Copy of an Act of the Legislature of the State of New Jersey for vesting in the United States of America the Jurisdiction of a Lot of Land at Sandy Hook in the County of Monmouth, and a letter which accompanied said Act from the Goverr. of the State of New Jersey to the President of the United States.—By the President's Command—TOBIAS LEAR—S. P. U. S.

RC (DNA: RG 59, MLR); not recorded in SJL. FC (DNA: RG 59, MLR); written on verso of address leaf bearing the following in Edmund Randolph's hand: "The President of the United States."

From David Rittenhouse

DR SIR   Jany. 4th. 1791

Under the Building lately erected by the Philosophical Society there are very large and deep Cellars. Suppose in the midst of one of them, another of 12 or 15 feet deep and 16 feet square was dug and walled and arched over would it not answer the purpose of which we were speaking. A considerable part of the Expence would be saved, and whatever reasonable compensation should be made to the Society wou'd I think be very acceptable. I am a little apprehensive of one inconvenience, whether the Cavern be made there or elsewhere, I mean Mephitic Air taking possession of it, but this may be guarded against. The prodigious extent of those under the Observatory at Paris perhaps secures them from anything of that sort.—I am Dr. Sir, with great respect Yours &c.

D. RITTENHOUSE

RC (DLC); endorsed by TJ as received 4 Jan. 1791 and so recorded in SJL. For an explanation of the purpose of which Rittenhouse and TJ were speaking, see Editorial Note to group of documents on coinage and the unit of money at end of 1790.

To Mary Jefferson

Philadelphia Jan. 5. 1790. [i.e., 1791]

I did not write to you, my dear Poll, the last week, because I was really angry at recieving no letter. I have now been near nine weeks from home, and have never had a scrip of a pen, when by the regularity of the post, I might recieve your letters as frequently and as exactly as if I were at Charlottesville. I ascribed it at first to indolence, but the affection must be weak which is so long over-ruled by that. Adieu. Th: J.

RC (ViU); addressed: "Miss Maria Jefferson Monticello." PrC (same).

From Alexander Donald

My Dear Sir   London 6th. January 1791.

The last letter I had the honour of receiving from you was dated the 29th August. I am disapointed at not having the Pleasure of hearing from you by the Decemr. Packet. I hope you will write me by the January one, and that you will be so good as send me an introductory letter to M. de la Hante in Paris, if it is not already on the way. Mr. Short writes me that this letter would probably be of great service to me and I am fully convinced of the Justness of his observation. If I receive the above letter soon, it is very probable that I may go over to Paris, and have the honour of delivering it myself.

I am just returned from a visit to my Friends in the North. I was fortunate in having very good weather. Indeed we have not experienced any cold this winter. Hitherto the weather has been very mild, but we have had very heavy gales of wind accompanied with much rain, which I think must prove injurious to the Crops of wheat. So much the better for America. For if the Crops in Europe are materially injured, there will be a demand for all your Surplus grain, and at good prices.—I fear the intelligence of the Spanish Convention would reduce prices all over your Continent. I wish therefore from my Heart that it had not taken place.

The Empress of Russia appears determined to drive the Turks out of Europe, and to keep possession of all her Conquests in despite of the Spirited remonstrances of the King of Prussia. This will probably induce him to take an active part against her in the Spring and if so, this Country will be obliged to send a respectable Fleet into the Baltick to protect the Dominions of Prussia from the insults and ravages of the Russian Fleets. Admiral Lord Hood is appointed to the Command of this Fleet which will probably consist of 15. or 20 Sail of the Line, and suppose will be joined by a proportionate Squadron from Holland. Russia cannot long withstand the joint efforts of the three Powers, especially as she must be pretty well exhausted already by her long exertions against Turkey.

You will hear before you receive this, that the Flemings have again come under the dominion of Austria. Peace is also restored to the Principality of Liege, and the Regent Prince de Rohan has absconded, as well as many of the Principal Patriots. I cannot help thinking that it is at least Problematical how matters may end in France. The National Assembly are still sitting, I think their time is out in May next. I am inclined to think that the present members will not resign their seats at that time. But a few months will determine this. You will receive a letter from Mr. Short by this Packet, who can give you much better information on French Politicks than I can.

I have sent an order to Mr. Brown to buy one Hundred Thousand Bushels of wheat provided it can be bought in my limits, which are the highest that I think can be prudently given. This order may be of some service to many of my Old Friends. Every market in Europe (except France) is glutted with Tobacco and the prices have in consequence fallen very low. France is not able to buy, having nothing to pay except Assignats, which the People on this Side the Channel have not a very high opinion of. I am sorry to see that the N. A. have permitted the Cultivation of Tobacco in France. It will reduce the demand for it from America, but this I presume you will be much pleased with, as I observe that you are opposed to the Culture of it in America, and so would I, if I could see any other thing they could raise whereby their lands would be equally productive.

I am ashamed to say that I have left in Virga. the letter wherein you was so good as give me the Prices for the different kinds of French Wines. If it was not giving you too much trouble I will thank you much for a Copy of it, and a few lines of introduction to your wine merchant in Bourdeaux.

I will be extremely happy if you will put it in my power to be serviceable to you. Wishing you many returns of this Season, I remain with great respect & esteem My Dear Sir Your obliged & obt. Servt.   A. DONALD

RC (DLC); endorsed as received 12 Mch. 1791 and so recorded in SJL.

From Benjamin Vaughan

DEAR SIR   London, Jany. 6, 1791.

There is little doubt entertained, that we have dictated to Russia to come to terms with Turkey, a summons to which I do not see how the Empress can refuse obedience. But in return, she will remember the insult, as will her successor the fact, that the navy of England is always to be guarded against. This datum is now so well understood through Europe, that it seems likely to make us as odious as before the war with America.

There seems another continental object for our court in Poland; but it is so ridiculous, that I presume it will be given up.—After these affairs are over, Mr. P's reign is supposed likely to be very short.

There is every appearance, that the French Revolution has consolidated itself in its present stage. Nevertheless, from the late efforts of the Aristocrates, some local tumults are still likely to occur, which however will be of no moment as to the final event. I have the honor to be, Dear sir, Your sincere & respectful humble servt.   BENJN. VAUGHAN

I send this letter through my brother, not knowing where you may be at its arrival.

RC (DLC); at head of text: "For Thomas Jefferson Esq: secretary of State"; endorsed by TJ as received 13 Mch. 1791 and so recorded in SJL.

To William Lindsay

SIR   Philadelphia Jan: 10. 1791.

I have duly recieved your favor of Dec. 11. and return you many thanks for the advance you were so kind as to make for the freight of my furniture which I now inclose to you, that is to say fifty dollars thirty six cents. Having seen the arrival of the vessel announced I immediately wrote to Capt. Maxwell to ask the favor of him to do for me what was necessary. Your letter came to hand before an answer could have come from him. I wrote at the same time to Mr. James Brown merchant at Richmd. to recieve the furniture and pay any expences on it. I have his answer that he will do it. So that I have only to ask the favor of yourself or Capt. Maxwell to send them to Richmond to Mr. Brown who will answer your draught for every expence.

I was sensible that the novelty of the case, on my arrival in Virginia with my baggage, laid you under doubt as to the duties. On my arrival here I mentioned it to the Secretary of the Treasury, that if my baggage was liable to duty I would remit it to you immediately and set the thing to rights. He said it was not liable, and that you had done right. Between 70. and 80. packages of my furniture from Paris are lately landed here, and are duty free. With a due sense of your obliging conduct I am Sir your most Obedt. & most humble servt.   TH: JEFFERSON

PrC (MHi).

TJ's letters to Maxwell and Brown of 16 Dec. 1790 crossed one in the post from Lindsay, dated at Norfolk 11 Dec. 1790, which enclosed "a Bill of Lading for sundry Packages imported . . . in the ship John, Charles Bushnell Master from Havre de Grace . . . as also an Account of the freight." Lindsay informed TJ that he had paid the freight, and added: "As the Goods are deposited in the Publick Store I wish you to appoint an Agent here in order to ascertain the Contents and Value that they may be entered at the Custom house according to Law" (RC in MHi; endorsed by TJ as received 22 Dec. 1790 and so recorded in SJL; enclosures not found). Brown acknowledged TJ's letter from Richmond on 28 Dec. 1790, promised to forward the packages to Monticello, and hoped TJ had "received the Books as ℔ the Linnet in good order" (RC in MHi;

endorsed by TJ as received 4 Jan. 1791 and so recorded in SJL). Maxwell replied from Norfolk on 3 Jan. 1791 that on the ship John's arrival he had been so unwell as to be incapable of attending to any business and had asked Lindsay to receive the shipment, adding: "as he supposed the goods subject to duty, and were accordingly stored with him, who answered to You the Letter Adresd to me by Monsr. La Motte. . . . Your request in respect to the Hughes's Crabb Cyder shall be paid particular atention to, and the best I can procure shall be sent you. At present all business by Water is stopt from the severity of the weather, people walking A Cross from this to Portsmouth on the Ice" (RC in MHi; endorsed by TJ as received 17 Jan. 1791 and so recorded in SJL). An entry in Account Book shows that TJ enclosed in this letter a post bill of $50.36 to reimburse Lindsay for "freight of some of my furniture."

To James Madison

TH: J. TO J. M.   Jan. 10. 1791.

Will you be so good as to let me know how much I am in your debt for travelling expenses and the horse. My monstrous bill of freight rendered the question useless till now. I send you a moment's amusement at my expence in the Connecticut paper. I suppose it is from some schoolmaster who does not like that the mysteries of his art should become useless.

RC (DLC: Madison Papers); addressed: "James Madison esq." Not recorded in SJL. Enclosure: printed below.

TJ's assumption was right: the author of the squib in the *Connecticut*

Courant was Noah Webster, who one day would be called schoolmaster to the nation. The satire on the report on weights and measures was only a forerunner of the Federalists' later ridicule of TJ's salt mountains and horned toads, being an inferior example of the productions of one of the Hartford Wits. During 1790 Webster wrote a number of anonymous essays for the *Connecticut Courant*, employing *The Prompter* as his signature. These satirical efforts, imitative of Franklin's *Poor Richard*, were proclaimed by the author to be "full of common sense, the best sense in the world" (E.E.F. Skeel, ed., *Notes on the life of Noah Webster* [New York, 1912], I, 297-8; II, 534). They were first published in 1790 and went through many editions. Webster silently dropped "A Pendulum without a Bob" from the collected edition. See note to TJ to Webster, 4 Dec. 1790.

A more serious criticism of TJ's recommendation of the rod pendulum came from a Scottish clergyman, George Skene Keith, who sent him a copy of his *Tracts on weights, measures, and coins* (London, 1791). TJ appears not to have acknowledged this, though he did thank James Somerville for a copy received later (Keith to TJ, 1 July 1791; TJ to Somerville, 1 Dec. 1791, acknowledging Somerville's [missing] letter of 22 Nov. 1791 from Baltimore, recorded in SJL as received 24 Nov. 1791; see Sowerby, No. 3766). A favorable comment on TJ's report on weights and measures, signed W. W., appeared in Bache's *General Advertiser* for 21 Dec. 1790. A more recent criticism of TJ as being naïve, not to

say intransigent, in his response to Rittenhouse's comments appears in Brooke Hindle's *Rittenhouse*, p. 309-16. The fundamental point on which Rittenhouse and TJ differed was not the shape of the pendulum, though TJ did recommend the uniform cylindrical rod as proposed by Robert Leslie. His basic aim was to choose motion rather than a linear standard and to fix upon some one latitude for determining the length of the second pendulum (or the second rod) in the hope that it might "become a line of union with the rest of the world." Rittenhouse publicly supported TJ's report. But in his correspondence with TJ and especially in his criticism of Skene's pamphlet he seemed to prefer the linear standard that France later adopted (Hindle, *Rittenhouse*, p. 313; TJ to Rittenhouse, 8 June 1792; Rittenhouse to TJ, 11 June 1792). This adoption brought disappointment to TJ's hopes. While it is true that his report was the work of a statesman rather than a scientist, it does not follow from this that he was imperceptive or that he was insistent in the advocacy of "his own creation." Neither the cylindrical rod nor the choice of latitude was original with him, as he was careful to point out (Vol. 16: 651, 652). See also TJ's comparison of the "rival propositions" (undated but after 12 Jan. 1792, DLC: TJ Papers, 60: 10809-17).

ENCLOSURE

The Prompter, No. III
A Pendulum without a Bob

This must be a queer thing indeed. But the bob is of no use. The Secretary of State, in his report to Congress, on the subject of coins, weights and measures, has discarded the bob; and Mr. Jefferson's mathematical abilities no man will dispute.

But what of a Pendulum without a bob? The Prompter answers, great effects indeed may be produced by it. This pendulum is to regulate the *measures, weights* and *coin* of the United States.

In a pendulum, with a spherical bob, it is difficult to ascertain the exact *center of osullation*; but in a cylindrical rod of uniform size, the *center of osullation* is just *two thirds of the length* from the *point of suspension*; (the very spot where the boys try to hit a ball with a hickory stick.) Now to apply the rod. Such a rod, vibrating seconds in the latitude of 45.° must be 58. inches and 7 tenths in length, nearly. Divide this rod into 587 equal parts, we have a *line*, ten lines make an inch, ten inches make a foot &c. This is an excellent method of measuring: *decimal arithmetic* being the easiest in nature. Besides, the rod will be a standard permanent and invariable, for a rod that will *vibrate seconds* must always be of the same length. Add to this, foreigners may learn our measures precisely by procuring a similar rod, and how gloriously convenient would it be for all nations to use the same measures.

But let us see how this bobless pendulum can regulate *measures of capacity, weights and coins.* A pendulum to vibrate seconds, must always be of the *same* length; divided into *equal* parts, those parts must always be of the *same* length. Then we have an *inch*—this is all we want—10 cubic inches may make a measure called a *gill* or a *metre*—10 metres a pint—10 pints a pottle or gallon—10 gallons a bushel or a cubic foot. How simple is this!

Then for weights: a *cubic inch of clear rain water* must, all the world over, be of equal weight—say then, a cubic inch of water is an *ounce*—10 ounces a pound—10 pounds a stone—10 stones a kental—10 kentals a hogshead.

Now for coins—let the dollar weigh an ounce (a cubic inch of rain water, which is nearly its present weight) which may be divided into ten parts for *dimes*—and these into tenths for *cents,* &c.

The Prompter is not jesting. It is a serious fact, that the Report of the Secretary of State, of which this is an epitome, is ingenious beyond any thing on the subject now extant. A *pendulum without a bob,* an invariable standard, may regulate the measures, weights and coins of all nations by one single principle.

Text from *Connecticut Courant,* 3 Jan. 1791.

From George Mason

Dear Sir   Virginia Gunston-Hall January 10th. 1791.

As I well know Your Attachment to the sacred Cause of Liberty must interest You in the Success of the French Revolution, it is with great pleasure I can inform You, that it is still going on prosperously; notwithstanding the Evils which have been predicted from the large Emissions of Paper Money. I have a Letter from my Son John, dated as late as the 10th. of Novemr. in which he informs me, that the Sales of the Church and Crown Lands are going on successfully, in every Part of the Kingdom; and the Paper Money absorbed by them, as fast as it comes into Circulation; being publickly burnt as it is taken in; and that from the Experiments already made, it is generally thought the Proceeds of the public Lands will be more than three times the Amount of the Paper ordered to be issued; in Consequence of which, Exchange with foreign Countrys (which had been so extreamly low) is beginning to look up again.

The public Lands, in the different Districts, are laid off in Lotts, numbered and valued, by Commissioners on Oath, and after having been advertised six weeks (one lott at a time in each District) it is sold to the highest Bidders. The first lott in the City of Bourdeaux consisting of nine Houses or Tenements, was sold on the 5th. of Novemr. A prodigious Croud of People attended, and many Purchasers, bidding with great Alacrity, 1, 2 and 3 thousand livres at a time above each other, and the Lott sold, upon an Average, at about 50 ₩ cent. above it's Valuation; and by Advices from Paris, and other Parts of the Kingdom, the Sales were going on every where, in nearly the same Proportion.

This is a most fortunate Event for the French Revolution; it is a Proof of great and general Confidence; and I hope will give the finishing Stroke to it. There is something very extraordinary in these Sales. It was natural to suppose, that the Distrust of many in the new Government, the religious Scruples, or Superstition of others, with respect to the Church Lands, and the great Quantity of Land brought suddenly to Market, wou'd have occasioned very low Sales; against the last, however, the Mode of selling has wisely guarded. Nothing has yet been decided upon the Subject of the Farm; a late Plan has been proposed, with Respect to Tobacco, which they term, a regie, a Sort of second Farm in the Hands of the Nation; the Nation proposing to take into their Hands, exclusively, the Purchase and Sale of Tobacco; whether this will be adopted, or the Trade made entirely free, is yet uncertain.— The Crop of Wheat in France has turn'd out much shorter than was expected, and foreign Supplies will again be wanted. A Scarcity has already begun to be felt in Bourdeaux, and a Company has been lately formed there, of some of the most wealthy Merchants, under the Auspices of the Municipality, in which 700,-000ᵗ has been already subscribed, to purchase wheat abroad, for the Consumption of the City, and orders given for the Purchase on the Baltic; but this is an Object of only a few weeks Consumption; the Dayly Consumption of the City being computed at 1,800 Boisseaux.

By the last Couriers from Paris, they were informed in Bourdeaux, that the Spanish Ambassador had announced to the King, the signing at Madrid an Arangement between the Courts of Madrid and London, which will put a Stop to the Hostilities, for which they have been so long, and so vigorously, preparing; that Spain is to cede to Great Britain a right to trade, and make Establishments in the Bay of Nootka; but not a word of the reimbursment of Expences; which Great Britain held, at first, as a sine qua non. This News was believed, but not absolutely confirmed.

My Son John was admitted, about the latter End of last Summer, a Member of the great Constitutional Committee for the City of Bourdeaux, an Appointment with which I am very well pleased; not only as it shows that he is well known and esteemed in the City, but as it will make him acquainted with some of the first Characters in that Part of the Kingdom, and will be the Means of much Information and Improvement. He intends, after visiting most of the principal Manufactories in France, to imbark for America in May next, and if he meets with a good Ship for that Port, to come first to Charles Town in S.C. but as he purposes to establish a House, in the Commission Line, upon Potomack River, I believe I shall advise him to take the french and spanish west Indies, in his way. Their House in Bourdeaux will still be continued, under the Management of Mr. Fenwick. John is very anxious to know the place where the Seat of the General Government will be fixed, as it will in some Measure determine the place of his Establishment; and desires to know my Opinion, whether Congress can ever be got out of the Whirlpool of Philadelphia? I shall answer him, that it is my Opinion it can not, for half a Century to come.

There is a particular Circumstance, tho' its Consequences have been little attended to, or thought of, which is continually sapping and contaminating the Republicanism of the United States, and if not timely altered, will corrupt the rising Generation. It may be, and I believe will be, a Work of Difficulty to prevent it's baneful Influence; but it surely ought to be attempted. I hope I shall have the Pleasure of seeing You at Gunston, when You return to Virginia, and wish to have some Conversation with You on the Subject. I am, with the most sincere Regard and Esteem, dear Sir, Your affecte. Friend & Obdt. Servt.,   G. MASON

P.S. I beg the Favour of You to present my best Respects to our Friend Mr. Madison. He is one of the few men, whom from a pretty thorough Acquaintance, I really esteem; tho' I have been apprehensive some late Difference (and it has only been a late one) on political Questions had caused a Coolness between Us. I am sure it has not on my Part; for if I know my own Heart, I have more Liberality, than to think the worse of a Friend for a Disagreement on any theoretical Opinions; and I well know that the iniquitous Attempts too frequently made in any Assembly, are almost enough to shake any Man's democratical principles.

RC (DLC); endorsed by TJ as received 17 Jan. 1791 and so recorded in SJL.

Despite Mason's professed belief that the seat of government would remain in Philadelphia for half a century, it seems clear that the principal object of this letter was to obtain access to the most closely held secret of the moment—that concerning the exact location of the Federal District, not disclosed until two weeks after the inquiry was made. The nature of the particular CIRCUMSTANCE . . . SAPPING AND CONTAMINATING THE REPUBLICANISM OF THE UNITED STATES remains conjectural, despite TJ's specific query in his response of 4 Feb. 1791. For the "surmise that it had reference to the power of the Federal Courts," which seems implausible, see Kate Mason Rowland, *The Life of George Mason* (New York, 1892), II, 333. Another conjecture has been advanced in *The Papers of George Mason*, ed. Robert A. Rutland, III, 1218-19n. On the basis of TJ's letter to Washington of 23 May 1792, Rutland believes that Mason was concerned about "the speculation in public securities touched off by the Assumption Act." But what distressed Mason was clearly "a particular Circumstance" whose consequences had been little noticed and this certainly could not be said of either assumption or speculation. In his remarkable summary of the direction and tendency of administration that had left "the public mind . . . no longer confident and serene," TJ pointed to the obvious fact that evidences of the change—of which speculation was only one and not the most fundamental aspect—had been "hackneyed in the public papers in detail" (TJ to Washington, 23 May 1792). He could scarcely have done otherwise. TJ himself had long been aware of the divisive effects of assumption and speculation and in fact had anticipated opposition in the South by trying to prepare Mason and others for a palatable compromise (TJ to Mason, 13 June 1790). Only a few weeks before Mason wrote the above letter the Virginia resolutions and remonstrance against assumption had reverberated in the press. The first wave of speculation,

now subsided, had been in anticipation of assumption and at this time the full tide of the script mania had not yet arrived. Being well aware of Virginia sentiment on national measures and their apparent tendency, TJ, as his response shows, was naturally puzzled as to what could have caused so grave a concern to be expressed in such guarded terms.

It seems clear, therefore, that Mason did not have in mind any subversive effects of major measures of the national government, for these measures had been challenged in Congress, in the press, and in private correspondence. A plausible explanation for his apprehension would appear to arise, as did so many of his views and concerns, closer at home. Perhaps it arose out of his long-standing battle with the "Alexandria Faction," whose leaders he accused of frustrating the will of the General Assembly, of engendering and perpetuating party and faction, of corrupting and perverting the administration of justice, of being able "without Fear of Controul or Punishment, to oppress the People," and of "continually gaining Strength by the Power of appointing Militia Officers, Commissioners of the Tax and other money-jobs" (see Vol. 17: 458n.; Mason to Johnston, 3 Nov. 1790, Mason, *Papers*, ed. Rutland, III, 1208-10; petition to the General Assembly, 11 Nov. 1790; same, 1211-16). Believing this, Mason may very well have persuaded himself that such a self-perpetuating oligarchy, if left unchallenged, would contaminate local government with the same kind of corruption that TJ saw in operation in the national legislature. He may have feared that its baneful influence, working through intimate connections of family and place, would nourish a system to which youth would become habituated. Thus the rising generation would become corrupted and perpetuate oligarchical rule. If this concern for the preservation of republican principles in local government was indeed the thing that disturbed Mason, he would have found TJ in full accord with the object, though certainly not sharing his alarmed conclusion that the greater of the discernible dangers to republicanism lay in the unit of government closest to the people.

Whatever it was that distressed Mason, it seems safe to conclude that it was something differentiated from the general climate of opposition in Virginia to the assumption, the excise, the bank, and the general measures of the national government apparent to every observer. Both the President and the Secretary of State appear to have been so conscious of the local cast of Mason's political position and of his personal interests that this almost certainly was permitted to have a major if not a decisive role in the decision to locate the Federal District on tidewater (see Editorial Note, group of documents on location of the Federal District, under 24 Jan. 1791). The danger that Mason perceived, it seems clear, arose from a source close at hand.

Henry Remsen, Jr., to the Printers of the Laws

SIR   Philadelphia, Jany. 10. 1791.

I have the pleasure to send you herewith enclosed, a bank post note for 88 dollars and 50 cents, being the compensation the Secretary of State has determined to allow for the publication in your paper of the Acts passed at the Second Session of the Congress of the United States.

In fixing the compensation at this sum, the Secretary was governed by the several proposals he had received. One gentleman offered to take for the work 50 cents per page of the folio printed volume: another 100 cents; but the others left it with him to name the price. He therefore thought it best to adopt a mean, which might not produce either too great gain or loss, and fixed three quarters of a dollar as the uniform allowance for every page of the folio printed volume. On receiving this I must beg the favor of your transmitting to the Secretary a bill and receipt agreeably to the annexed form. I am Sir &c,

                                        HENRY REMSEN JUNR.

FC (DNA: RG 59, PCC No. 120); at head of text: "To the Printers who publish the Laws of the United States."

Benjamin Russell, editor of the *Columbian Centinel*, acknowledged Remsen's "Bank Post Note for 88 Dols. 50 Cents" in a letter to TJ of 22 Jan.

1791 (RC in DNA: RG 59, PDL; endorsed by Remsen as received 3 Feb. 1791). See Remsen to the printers, 23 Nov. 1790; Brown to TJ, 26 Nov. 1790; Davis to TJ, 2 Dec. 1790; Russell to TJ, 5 Dec. 1790; Childs & Swaine to Remsen, 16 Dec. 1790.

From George Wythe

G.W. TO T.J.   Williamsburgh, 10th of January, 1791.

When you can attend to trifles, tell me your opinion, in general, of the drawing inclosed with this; particularly, should not parties appear before the judge? Is not the skin of Sisamnes, whose story, you know, Herodotus relates, added by Mr. West to the original design, an improvement? On the reverse, are not the words 'state of Virginia,' on the exergon, since within it are represented Patomack, &c. a tautology? And, if so, what ought to supply their place? Return the drawing at your leisure. If any makers or sellers of instruments for philosophical experiments be in Philadelphia, desire one of them to send me a bill of his articles, with their cost. I wish you felicity perpetual.

RC (DLC); endorsed by TJ as received 2 Feb. 1791 and so recorded in SJL. Enclosure not found.

SKIN OF SISAMNES: The allusion is to the 25th chapter of the 5th book of Herodotus: "[Darius] left as general of all the troops upon the sea-coast Ortanes, son of Sisamnes, whose father King Cambyses slew and flayed because that he, being of the number of the royal judges, had taken money to give an unjust sentence. Thereupon Cambyses slew and flayed Sisamnes and cutting his skin into strips, stretched them across the seat of the throne whereon he had been wont to sit when he heard causes. Having so done Cambyses appointed the son of Sisamnes to be judge in his father's room and bade him never forget in what way his seat was cushioned" (*History of Herodotus*, ed. George Rawlinson, 4th. ed., III [New York, 1880], 228). On the seal for the Court of Chancery, see TJ to Wythe, 14 Mch. 1791.

To William Brown

SIR   Philadelphia Jan. 11. 1791.

It is many days since I received the favor of your letter. I have been, and still am likely to be so pressed with business, at least during the earlier part of the session of Congress, as to give me time only to mention to you, that I have brought with me the papers in the affair between us, from my own house, where it was impossible for me to look into them. As there are many of them, and they will probably take me a day, I apprehend it will be some time, perhaps even some weeks before I can give them a day. They shall have the first in my power to spare, and it shall be a part of the business to give you immediate notice of the result. I do not foresee any room for difference of opinion unless it be in the price of the tobacco. However I can at present say no more than that I wish to do full justice and to receive it, and that you shall hear from me as soon as I can write fully. I am with great regard Sir Your most obedt humble servt,   TH: JEFFERSON

PrC (MHi).

Brown's letter was that of 23 Dec. 1790, recorded in SJL as received 28 Dec. 1790 but not found. TJ settled the disagreeable business with characteristic generosity. See TJ to Brown, 18 Apr. and 13 June 1790; 17 Mch. and 4 Apr. 1791; TJ to Carroll, 4 Apr. 1791.

To James Currie

DEAR SIR   Philadelphia Jan. 11. 1791.

As you were so good as to assist me in the purchase of the horse from Mr. Braxton, I take the liberty of sending the inclosed under your cover, and of leaving it open for your notice. I have ventured to trouble you with the taking in and cancelling my promisory note.

You will have seen in the public papers a letter of the D. of Leeds as is said, announcing peace. This is the only scrip from Europe to this effect, and it has stood alone this fortnight or three weeks without confirmation or contradiction.

The farmers here are probably unreasonable in refusing the market price (a French crown) for their wheat. However the prospect in Europe is not as unfavorable as the mercantile extracts pretend. There will be a want of wheat in France at a reasonable price. The price in Marseilles is very good, and likely so to continue, as the house of Cathalan authorize me to assure. A great demand from the same country for tobacco must come a little sooner or a little later. It would have come by this time had it been decided who is to buy. With sentiments of the sincerest esteem I am Dear Sir your affectionate friend & servt,

TH: JEFFERSON

PrC (DLC). Enclosure: TJ to Carter Braxton, 11 Jan. 1791, reading: "An extraordinary press of business for several days past has forbidden my turning my attention to any thing of a private nature. This has occasioned me to pass over the exact day by which I should have remitted to you the sum of thirty five pounds for a horse of yours I purchased from your son. I now inclose you a bank post note for one hundred and sixteen dollars and two thirds, for which the nearest Collector of the customs will give you cash, by an arrangement between the bank and Treasury. I hope this short and unintentional delay will not have subjected you to any inconvenience. . . . P.S. Will you be so good as to deliver my promisory note to Doctr. Currie?" (PrC in MHi).

To Thomas Mann Randolph, Jr.

DEAR SIR   Philadelphia Jan. 11. 1790 [i.e., 1791]

I have this day recieved your favor of Dec.   It is the first and only news I have had from home since I left it. I have written some scolding letters on this account. I am very sorry for the discontinuance of the Charlottesville post, and will contribute any thing reasonable for it's reestablishment provided it goes *from Charlottesville* to Richmond directly, and returns there in like manner. In the mean time I pray that a letter may be written to me once a week. This job can be divided among you so as to bring it on each but once in three weeks, which I will repay weekly. I do not ask long letters when there is no subject for them, but only to know how you all do. These letters may always find a conveyance from Charlottesville to Richmond.

I think the price of wheat unjustifiably low at Richmond. It has been constant here at a French crown. This price has been occasioned by the West India demand, and as all the country North of Baltimore is now shut up by the ice, I think the demands must now center in the Chesapeak, consequently that the harvest of Virginia will be from this till the ice breaks up here. There will be little demand in Europe this year; but there is some in France, tho' their crop was good.

A letter in the public papers supposed from the D. of Leeds to the Mayor of London announces peace. It has appeared here this fortnight, without contradiction or confirmation. It is rather believed than otherwise.

Congress have before them two important propositions. The one for the establishment of a bank, the other of a tax on ardent spirits, which they call an excise, tho' not resembling the excise in the odious method of collection. Moral, as well as fiscal reasons procure it advocates.

Mrs. Monroe set out for New York yesterday, to continue there till March. Her little daughter went thro' the small pox so easily as merely to satisfy them she had it. Present my sincere love to my daughters and believe me to be dear Sir yours affectionately,

Th: Jefferson

RC (DLC). PrC (same); mutilated. Randolph's FAVOR OF DEC. (blank in MS) was that of 27 Dec. 1790, recorded in SJL as received 11 Jan. 1791 but not found.

To David Ross

Dear Sir   Philadelphia Jan. 11. 1791.

I have this day recieved your favor, covering copies of the accounts, and your observations on them. The rapid reading I have been able to give them does not satisfy me that there can be any just measure of dealings between man and man but real money. However, these papers are long and the subject intricate. They will take me a considerable time to examine and weigh, probably several days. My occupations during the session of Congress are so unremitting that I foresee little prospect of being able to turn to any thing else which would require time, till they rise, which must by the constitution be about the close of the next month. I will then lay the last hand to the business, so as to prepare it either for a settlement between ourselves, if I see that our opinions can approach on the subject, or otherwise I should propose to refer it to the arbitration of some of the judges of our state. I wish to do you full justice. I am persuaded you wish the same to me. Ideas habitual on the one side, not so on the other, prevent us from seeing the same thing in the same light. It is a difference of reason, and will I am sure be conducted and finished with reason and candour. In the meantime it cannot influence those sentiments of esteem & regard with which I am Dear Sir Your sincere friend & servt,   TH: JEFFERSON

PrC (MHi). Ross' FAVOR of 3 Jan. 1791, recorded in SJL as received 11 Jan. 1791, has not been found. He also wrote TJ on 12 and 22 Nov. 1790, but these too are missing. See TJ to Francis Eppes, 25 July 1790 and 31 Oct. 1790.

From John Bradford

Lexington [Ky.], *12 Jan. 1791.* Remsen's letter requesting "one copy of the Kentucky news papers" to be sent by post to Secretary of State and to commence from 1 Oct. 1790 did not come to hand until 20 Dec., hence he "could not procure papers farther back than Novr. 27." There being no direct communication between that place and Philadelphia, he "will send them by every Opportunity."

RC (DNA: RG 59, PDL); endorsed: "Staunton Forwd. by P. Hieskell"; endorsed by Remsen as received 28 Feb. 1791. Remsen's letter was that of 15 Sep. 1790. Bradford was editor of *The Kentucky Gazette,* the only paper then being published in Kentucky.

To James Madison

MY DEAR SIR   Jan. 12. 1791.

It being impossible to entertain a doubt that the horse I bought of you was fairly sold, and fairly bought, that his disorder was of the instant, and might have happened years after as well as when it did, so as to exonerate you as is justly established, from all responsibility, I should as soon think of filching the sum from your pocket, as of permitting the loss to be yours. I therefore send you a check on the bank for 95.26 Dollars including the two balances. Yours affectionately   TH: J.

RC (DLC: Madison Papers). Not recorded in SJL.

The sudden death of the horse TJ had purchased from Madison the previous autumn and the efforts of the two steadfast friends to come to terms about its value—problems further complicated by the matter of settling for expenses shared on their journey southward—provide an illuminating episode concerning the relations of mutual trust and generosity existing between them. TJ paid an advance of $50 on 26 Dec. 1790 on the expenses. This, Madison felt, overpaid the account for traveling costs and refunded $23.26. TJ insisted on paying the exact cost of the horse, $83.33. This, together with the expense account of $38.66, made TJ's total indebtedness $145.26. Deducting the advance, he sent with this letter a remittance of $95.26 (Account Book, 12 Jan. 1791; Brant, *Madison*, III, 321-2, and Ketcham, *Madison*, p. 318, reckon otherwise).

From Edward Telfair

SIR State-House, Augusta, 12th. January 1791

I have been favored with your address of the 27th. October last, notifying the King of Spain's orders "not to permit, under any pretext, persons held in slavery within the United States" to "introduce themselves as free persons into the province of Florida." The early attention, in this particular, paid to the protection of the property of the Citizens of this State, residing on and near the southern frontiers, will be contemplated with much pleasure and satisfaction, especially as it gives room to anticipate, future measures will be taken by which every existing difficulty relative to the perfect security of that species of property already alluded to, may be removed. I have now before me a concurred Resolution of the General Assembly, requesting that "the utmost influence with the President be used to procure a restoration of the negroes who have taken refuge in the Spanish provinces of East and west Florida since the peace of 1783" and, here it may be observed, that the General Assembly were deeply impressed with the importance of this very interesting measure, in as much as they have instructed the State representation to extend that influence, and report thereon to the Government of this State; due representations to His most Catholic Majesty on the Subject of restitution, will no doubt have the desired effect: a respectable galley of considerable force being stationed in the River St. Mary, appears to be one of the best expedients for the prevention of future grievances of this nature and at the same time might in some degree prevent abuses in the revenue of the United States.

Were a conference held with the Governor of East Florida, it might perhaps appear that his power so far extends as to suffer, in the future the Citizens of the United States, to claim, recover and remove within the limits of the said states any persons held in Slavery on satisfactory proof of ownership being produced. I have the honor to be Sir Your most Obedt. Servt.

EDWD. TELFAIR

RC (DNA: RG 59, MLR); at foot of text: "The Secretary of the United States"; endorsed by TJ as received 4 Mch. 1791 and so recorded in SJL. See Editorial Note and Document III in group of documents on refugee slaves and the Mississippi Question, under 12 Mch. 1791.

From John Churchman

South 2nd. Street No. 183.
1 mo. 13th. 1791

The Committee of the House of Representatives to whom was referred my memorial, having made a Report in favor of the Penalty being made larger for such as shall Copy Charts, Maps &c. for a given time, but have said but little in favour of the Proposed Voyage to Baffins Bay, as there has arisen a doubt with some individuals whether the encouragement of an expedition of this sort might not be inconsistent with the Spirit of the Constitution, these matters are left to be decided by the House. Altho I am well aware, of the time of the Secretary of State being very precious, yet if liesure will only admit of writing an Opinion on the Propriety of such a Voyage, from the great confidence of the Members on the Knowledge of the Secretary in the whole Circle of Sciences, I am sure it would have great weight with them. I am encouraged to mention this matter from a conversation with some of them. It would have been very agreeable to me had the Memorial been referred in this line at first, but as the Committee have already reported, I suppose it might be rather indelicate and out of order in this stage of the Business to request such a thing directed to the House. The expence of the voyage is supposed to amount to about 3000 Dollars. If the members of the House could be convinced of the probability of such a Trip turning out useful to the Public, I have good reason to think that they would not hesitate to give their consent, but as some of them profess not to have studied subjects of this nature, they seem to be at a loss to make up their minds. I am sorry to be the cause of this trouble, and it would give me pain to make an improper request. Should there be a freedom to write a little note on this subject by the Bearer, or before the Report of the Committee has a second reading, I shall place this favour on the Catalogue of those which with gratitude I have already received. A Committee of the Marine Society here have reported in favour of the Chart &ca. I am with the greatest Sentiments thy Sincere Friend. J. CHURCHMAN

RC (DLC); endorsed by TJ as received 13 Jan. 1791 and so recorded in SJL.

To James Bringhurst

SIR   Philadelphia Jan. 15. 1791.

I have taken time to examine the account you presented me and to endeavor to recollect the particulars. I had always believed I had paid off the whole of it. I recollect sending a sum of money by Genl. Nelson for that purpose, and I have among my papers in Virginia his letter mentioning the payment of it, so that I was under a full impression of it's being entirely discharged. I have since that been in Philadelphia months at a time, and should not have failed to have called on you if I had had the least idea I was still in your debt. I do not say this to draw a doubt over the exactness of your account. It is more presumable in my mind that the inexactitude has been in Genl. Nelson or myself. Still every prudent man wishes to see his own statement of an account before he closes it. These papers are all preserved at my house in Virginia. But I cannot get a sight of them till I go there, which will not be till the summer. To the delay of 14. years then, which has proceeded from the want of a notification of it, I must still propose a further of some months: more for the sake of satisfying my own mind than from any expectation that the error may be with you instead of me. You shall hear from me as soon as I am enabled to examine into it. I am Sir Your very humble servt. TH: JEFFERSON

P.S. I return the note.

PrC (MHi).

James Bringhurst was a Philadelphia ironmonger from whom, beginning in 1775, TJ purchased a pistol, various bolts and locks, and sundries. He settled his account in full up to 20 May 1776. A year later he sent a bill of exchange for £160 Pennsylvania currency by Benjamin Harrison, a delegate to Congress whom he mistook in the above letter for Thomas Nelson. There was evidently a debit balance amounting in 1790 to $27.80 and on 17 Aug. 1791 TJ settled the account (Account Book).

To Sharp Delany

SIR   Philadelphia Jan. 15. 1791

I have been in daily expectation of recieving the invoice wherein the prices of the paper will be stated, as Mr. Short assured me it should come in his next letter. But I have not yet recieved it. If it be necessary however for the regularity of your accounts, I think we can come at it nearly. The invoice of the articles which came with them, states 150.[1] rouleaux of paper. Turning to a paper I had, I find that I paid once in Paris 2 livres 10. sols for a single rouleau. Buying by the quantity will make it come much cheaper. As it is all very plain paper, I do not expect it will cost me more than 2. livres a rouleau which will be 300. livres the whole. If you think proper to settle the duty on that price or any other you think more probable, I shall be glad to pay it immediately, and if the price should be found to have been settled too low when my account comes, I will pay the difference. If you will be so good as to let me know the amount of the duty on the wine and paper, I will call with it or send it to you. I am with great esteem Sir Your most obedt. humble servt.   TH: JEFFERSON

PrC (MHi).

The above was in response to Delany's request of 12 Jan. 1791 reading: "I am closing my last Quarters Accounts, which obliges me to request, that you may furnish the Office with the Value of the Paperhangings in Your Entry" (RC in DLC, endorsed by TJ as received 14 Jan. 1791 and so recorded in SJL). ENTRY refers to TJ's customs declaration for wines and wallpaper imported on *Henrietta*, Benjamin Wickes, master, which arrived from Le Havre in October. This declaration, dated 22 Oct. 1790 and signed by TJ, reads in part:

"Twelve Cases Containing Fifty six dozen & Eight Bottles Wine	}	Galls. 145 - 10 -	14.50
		Bottles 18.00 - 5pCt. -	0.90
61. One Case Containing 145 Rolls Paper Hangings	}	Livres 300	
		adv. 30	
		———	
		330	
		Doll. 61.05 - 7½ -	4.58
			———
			19.98
		disct. 10pct.	1.99
		dollrs.	17.99"

(MS in ViU; in clerk's hand, countersigned by Sharp Delany). The declaration contains this marginal note: "a seperate entry for 65 packages furniture &c." An entry in TJ's Account Book for 4 Feb. 1791 shows that he gave Delany an "order on bank for 28.39 duty and portage of wines and papers." See Short to TJ, 7 Nov. 1790.

[1] Thus in MS. The invoice for Case No. 61 in TJ's shipment of furniture shows that 145 rolls were received (see note, Short to TJ, 7 Nov. 1790).

From James Fanning

SIR   Paris the 15th. January 1791

The proofs I have been honour'd with of your Excellency's kindness embolden me to trouble you at this distance to pray your advice and assistance to preserve a property, for my family, which I think well worth looking after; as I receive no manner of account about it give me leave to lay before you my Situation with regard to that property. A grant was made me of 2000 acres of Land in West Florida, and to my Brother Mathew Fanning a like grant of 2000 acres in the Same Country. His Excellency Peter Chester Esqr. Capn. Genl. and Govr. in chief of that province renew'd on the 9th. October 1779 two different warrants, which he had issued out on the 20th Novr. 1778 address'd to Elias Durnford Esqr. Surveyor Genl., to measure and lay out to the said Mathw. Fanning 2000 acres on the north side of Bayou Pierre, and to lay out to me 2000 acres on the north west side of Bayou Pierre; I have in my possession the warrants sign'd by the Govr. Genl. and the plats sign'd by the Surveyor Genl. and the field works. What was survey'd for my Brothr. is situated (according to the plat) on the north side of Bayou Pierre, bounded on the southwest by lands survey'd to Coll. Willm. Steel, southeast by Bayou Pierre and on the other side by (then) vacant Lands, distant from the Natchez about 40 miles; and the field work says: "Mathew Fanning's 2000 acres of Land beginning at an Iron wood, standing on the north side of Bayou Pierre, it being the last bounded tree of James Fanning's Land, running thence to said Fanning's Land." What was Survey'd to me is Situated on the north west side of Bayou Pierre, distant from the Natchez about 41 miles, bounded on the south west by the Land Survey'd for my said Brothr. Mathw. Fanning, south east by Bayou Pierre, on all other sides by (then) vacant Land: the field work of what was Survey'd to me Says: "James Fanning's 2000 acres of Land beginning at a dog wood, standing at the north side of Bayou pierre Nt. 30 Wt. from an Iron wood, the upper boundery of Robert Fendals, the breath of the creek being the distance between the boundery and the Iron wood of Robert Fendal."—On the 29th. Decemr. 1784 I sent a letter of attorney (by the advice of Mr. Gallwey of Nantes) to Messrs. Shoolbred & Moody of Charlston to act for me in regard to the Lands above mention'd, My Brother having made over to me his 2000 acres; I am stil in the situation your Excellency left me as to them Gentlemen, (Messieurs Shoolbred & Moody) thats to say, without a line from them. In January 1788 your Excellency was so good as to forward a letter for me to their Excellency's the Delegates of Georgia in congress at Philidelphia. In february the same year I wrote to the Honble. Major Genl. Wayne of Savanna in Georgia and enclosed to him a letter

from the Marquis de La Fayette, wherein the Marqs. requested
him to favour me with his protection and advice. I have not been
honour'd with an answer from the Genl. nor did I ever get a
line on this subject since Mr. Arthur Neil (who acted for me)
quitted Pensacola, but thro your Excellency, who had the goodness
to forward to me in Augt. 1788 a letter from the Honble. Abraham
Baldwin Esqr. dated New York the 20th. April of said year, in
answer to one your Excellency forwarded for me to the Delegates
of Georgia in Congress. In that letter he's pleased to inform me:
that in 1785 a petition was preferred to the Legislature of Georgia
in behalf of the Inhabitants who are settled in that part of the state
where my Lands lie, in compliance with which a Law was made
securing to the Settlers the improvements which they had made on
vacant Lands; but nothing had then as yet been done respecting the
Surveys made in that Country under the British Government.
He adds that many of the Citizens of that State, and of several
other states in the Union have rights to land there in the same
situation as mine, and he had no doubt but that proper attention
wou'd be paid to all such rights, as soon as it wou'd be thought
expedient to open an office for the issuing of grants for those Lands,
but he did not expect it wou'd be done soon. He says that my warrants and surveys are all the security that can be had till patents are
issued, that in the meantime my Attorneys wou'd probably give
notice to the Inhabitants of that Country of my surveys with the
necessary descriptions, that then there wou'd be little danger of
their Settleing upon them as they will know they can obtain no
pattents and will therefore loose the labour of their improvements.
This most Worthy Gentleman had the goodness to write to Messieurs Shoolbred & Moody to know whether they had received my
instructions and consider'd themselves as my Attorneys. Their answer to him dated the 28th. Augt. 1788, wherein they own the
receipt of my letter of Attorney and say it was impossible then to
render me any Service, with his letter on the Subject to your Excellency, you were pleased to forward to me. What surprises me
is that Messieurs Shoolbred & Moody never wrote me a line so
that I don't know if they gave notice to the Inhabitants of my
Surveys. May I entreat your Excellency's advice how to act? For
Messieurs Shoolbred & Moody conduct themselves in such a manner towards me as convinces me that it's not agreeable to them to
be troubled with my affairs. I cannot blame them. I am a Stranger
to them. I only wish they had been so kind as to have favoured me
with a line; as unfortunately I have no acquaintance in the Country

I am totally at a loss what to do. I must then reiterate my request to your Excellency for your advice. Mr. Short will be so good as to forward to me your letter. The anarchy and confusion is such all over this kingdom that there's no security in the provinces, and a moment may come when there will be as little in the Capital. Towards the end of this month I shall remove with my family to Flanders or to England and wait to see the return of peace and order. Every day numbers of family's are quitting the Kingdom. Wherever I shall be I shall retain the highest sense of the obligations I owe your Excellency, happy if ever in my power to convince you of the infinite respect with which I have the honour to be Sir Your Excellency's most obliged & most obedient humble Servt.,   JA: FANNING

RC (DLC); endorsed by TJ as received 19 June 1791 and so recorded in SJL. See TJ to the Georgia delegates in Congress, 7 Feb. 1788; Abraham Baldwin to TJ, 20 Apr. 1788; TJ to Fanning, 29 July 1788.

From Joseph Fenwick

SIR   Bordeaux 15 Jany. 1791.

The above is a copy of my last. Since we are assured of Peace between the maritime powers of Europe.

The National Assembly has not yet pronounced definitively on any comercial regulations with foreign powers.

The Committee who the Fish oil business was refered to have reported in favor of the admission of American oils, but the Chamber of Commerce will not I believe send forward a member on the business to the Assembly, contenting themselves with writing to their deputies expressing their sentiments thereon. Mr. Short writes me he has now great hopes that the Tobacco business will be decided on favorable to the American commerce. The Oil he is more dubious of.—With the greatest respect I have the honor to be Sir Your most Obdient & most humble Servant,

JOSEPH FENWICK

RC (DNA: RG 59, CD); endorsed by TJ as received 5 Apr. 1791 and so recorded in SJL. Enclosure: Dupl of Fenwick to TJ, 8 Dec. 1790.

From David Humphreys

SIR   Madrid. Jan: 15th: 1791.

I have employed my time here in communicating according to instructions the sentiments of the President on the navigation of the Missisipi, and other important points. Mr. Carmichael's ideas are just; his exertions will be powerful and unremitting to obtain the accomplishment of our desires before his departure from this country: the task will now be difficult, if not impracticable, from the Opinions which are impressed on this Court. I fear these are rather rivetted than impressed to the very substance of their former jealous policy. I learn from other good authority, as well as from Mr. Carmichael, that all the representations of Gardoqui, (when minister in America) tended to excite a belief that the most respectable and influential people throughout the United States did not wish to have the navigation of the Missisipi opened for years to come, from an apprehension such event would weaken the government, and impoverish the Atlantic States by emigrations. It was even pretended that none but a handful of settlers on the Western Waters, and a few inhabitants of the Southern States would acquiesce in the measure.

At present affairs here are guided more by intrigue than reason. So that no one can answer for the consequence of a negociation. Means are used to bring our subject with advantage into discussion. The king is just gone to hunt for ten days; play is usual after the holidays; his prime minister and the family Ambassadors only attended him. Nothing can be ascertained until his return.

It is not improbable a change of ministry may soon take place. The situation about the court becomes every day more critical. Nor is it less so in the country. The night before last twenty two French and Italians were sent from Madrid under guard, out of the kingdom for speaking too freely; as was one Spanish Marquis to a distant province.

The Austrian Netherlands have entirely submitted to the Emperor. The people of Liege are in the way to do the same to their Bishop. In the North, the empire of Russia has gained farther advantages. A peace in that Quarter is expected.

In France the refusal of a great part of the Bishops to take the Oath, and the report of plots occasion considerable agitation. Still the constitution strengthens. I have the honor to be, with great respect, Your most obedient Serv'nt,   D. HUMPHREYS

RC (DNA: RG 59, DD); entirely in code and decoded by the Editors, employing Code No. 8; at head of text: "No. 11"; endorsed by TJ as received 30 Mch. 1791 and so recorded in SJL. Tr (DNA: RG 59, DD); in clerk's hand, except for one line in TJ's and endorsement of date of receipt. An-

other Tr (DNA: RG 59, DD); this decoded text agrees with foregoing except that it is entirely in clerk's hand.

For an extract of this letter that TJ transmitted to Washington, see TJ to Washington, 2 Apr. 1791.

From Henry Knox

DEAR SIR   Sunday 16 January 1791

Among the other objects to be considered tomorrow, it is the desire of the President that the memorial of a frenchman, an inhabitant of the Western territory upon an injury which he suffered from the Commandant of a Spanish post should also be reported upon. The memorial is lodged in your office with your last report. Will you please to bring it with you?—I am Dear Sir Your sincerely & affectionately   H KNOX

RC (DLC); endorsed by TJ as received 16 Jan. 1791 and so recorded in SJL.

THE MEMORIAL OF A FRENCHMAN was that of Joseph St. Marie, whose trading goods had been seized on the east bank of the Mississippi in 1787 (see Editorial Note, group of documents on the new policy toward Spain, under 10 Mch. 1791).

From Martha Jefferson Randolph

Montecello January 16th 1791

I very much regret not having answer'd yours My Dearest Papa sooner, but being misinformed with regard to the Charlottesville post which we heard was discontinued has till now prevented my writing and not as you supposed having nothing to say. It is unlucky that the matrasses can not be sent now as we shall soon be in great distress. Aunt Fleming and probably one of her sons being expected here shortly I must accept of Mrs. Lewis's kind offer who in returning one of the beds I sent home offered a second if necessary. I have reason to think my self far advanced in her good graces as she has really been friendly. Martin has left us and not relying much in the carefullness of the boys particularly when left to them selves I took an account of the plate china and locked up all that was not in imediate use. Not recollecting that there was a set of queens ware here I sent to Richmond for some by which means the china was preserved entire except our beautiful cups which being obliged to leave out are all broke but one. The spoons &c. that are in use are counted and locked up night and morning so that I hope to keep them all to gather till your return. It was very troublesome in the begining tho now I have the boys in tolerable order every thing goes on pretty well. I have wrought an entire reformation on the rest of my household. Nothing comes in or goes out without my knowledge and I believe there is as little

[499]

waste as possible. I visit the kitchen smoke house and fowls when the weather permits and according to your desire saw the meat cut out. I can give but a poor account of my reading having had so little time to my self that tho I really have the greatest inclination I have not as yet been able to indulge it. Polly improves weekly in her spanish which she reads with much more facility than when you went away. She was surprised that I should think of making her look for *all* the words and the parts of the verb also when she made nonsence but finding me inexorable she is at last reconciled to her dictionary with whom she had for some time past been on very bad terms. She has been twice thro her grammar since your departure. As for the harpsicord tho I put it in fine order it has been to little purpose till very lately. I am in hopes she will continue to attend to that also. She is remarkably docile where she can surmount her Laziness of which she has an astonishing degree and which makes her neglect what ever she thinks will not be imediately discovered. I have entered into all these details because however trifling they would appear to others, to you my Dear Papa I think they will be interesting. I received a kind invitation from Aunt Eppes to spend the month of February at Eppinton but Mrs. Fleming's being here at that time will render it useless. The morning of the 13th at 10 minutes past four we had an earthquake which was severe enough to awaken us all in the house and several of the servants in the out houses. It was followed by a second shock very slight and an aurora borealis. I am extremely obliged to you for the cypress vine which with a bundle of seeds I found in rumaging up some drawer in the chamber, written on the back *cupressus Patula* and some others. I intend to decorate my windows this spring. You promised me a colection of garden seeds for a young Lady in the west indies [*Bruni*] for whom also I will send you a letter to be forwarded to her with them. Adieu My Dearest Father. Mr. Randolph and Polly join in love. Believe me ever your affectionate child.   M. RANDOLPH

RC (MHi); addressed: "Thomas Jefferson Secretary of State Philadelphia"; postmarked: "RICHMOND, Jan. 25" and "FREE"; endorsed by TJ as received 2 Feb. 1791 and so recorded in SJL.

From William Short

DEAR SIR   Amsterdam Jan. 16. 1791.

This letter containing one for the Secretary of the Treasury will be sent by an American vessel that is going down to Texel where she will wait only for a change of the wind. She will find there all the other vessels by which I have written since my arrival here, constant contrary winds having prevented any vessel from leaving that place since the month of November. I wrote also by the English packets of Dec. and Jan. which I am happy to learn did not experience a similar delay.

By private letter I have this moment recieved from Paris I learn that one of the Algerine captains who took the American ships was there, and the writer congratulated me on our prisoners being on the point of being released. Whether this Algerine captain is a supposed personage, and whether there is any foundation for the hope of the release of our prisoners I cannot say, as the letter goes no further and I have no information of any kind respecting the matter. I inclosed you from Paris a letter which I had received from one of the prisoners in which he spoke of a negotiation begun for this purpose by order of Congress, but I never heard any thing else respecting it before or since. I shall be exceedingly happy if it is so as I am persuaded there is no hope of any thing being done for the present at least by the Mathurins.

I wrote to you some time ago respecting the money which had been deposed at Mr. Grand's for this purpose. Should you have no intention of applying it immediately as was intended I cannot help repeating the propriety of using it in the payment of the arrears of interest due there to the foreign officers. The certainty of the U.S. being able to command in future whatever sums they want for the Algerine business renders such a deposit useless at present. As the principal of the debt due to these officers is inconsiderable, as it bears an interest of six p. cent, and particularly as these officers spread through various parts of Europe, do a real injury to the credit of the U.S. by their clamours, it would be good policy perhaps to appropriate a part of the monies now in the hands of the agents here and which are remaining unemployed to the final discharge of the debts. I submit this to your consideration to suggest it if you think proper to the Secretary of the Treasury.

[You know that the assembly some time ago formed a central committee in order to examine what they had done and what they had still to do as *pouvoir constituant*. This was considered as a means of ascertaining the end of the present session. By the report which this committee has made it was proposed that the assembly should devote their morning sessions to the objects therein determined as being either constitutional or essential to the support of the constitution. The Lameths and about thirty of their party opposed the report in the most unreserved manner. The report however passed by a very great majority and gave great pleasure to the well disposed, because they considered it as fixing the term of the session within a short period. It proves however in fact that there is no hope of this term arriving within any certain time, since the objects there prescribed for the present session cannot be completed so as to be reduced to any calculation. Supposing it possible that the assembly should adhere to this report it is impossible to conjecture when the business could be finished, but it is evident they will not adhere to it so long as they suffer their attention to be called to all objects of importance of a Judiciary or administrative nature, and this they seem as much disposed to now as ever—some because they do not wish the assembly to end, others because they fear it, and many because they hope that the anarchy and despotism which will necessarily prevail as long as the present assembly lasts will disgust the nation with the present order of things. I think it very probable that such numbers will become dissatisfied ere long with the *pouvoir constituant* as will point out to them the necessity of giving place to a succeeding legislature, but I do not think there is any danger of their attachment to a free government being altered. So that supposing no foreign interference, of which I see no good grounds for apprehension, I continue to think that the present revolution will end by establishing the principles of liberty and a good constitution in France. It is under this idea that I suppose a little experience will show them the monstrous defects in the present organisation of the powers of government and will teach them also the manner and the necessity of correcting them.

The uneasiness which prevailed for some time on account of the refugees at Turin and the persons arrested at Lyons seems to have subsided. It is certain that the conduct of the people at Brussels had so roused their hopes that they wished the Princes to enter France immediately. These or at least the Count d'Artois refused such a rash senseless project, and since then nothing more seems to have been said about it.

Apprehensions of disorder from the clergy were for some time more founded, and even yet it is not known what will be the issue in the provinces where there is much bigotry still remaining. As the clergy or at least the discontented amongst them will endeavour to persuade the people that this is an overthrow of religion effected by the influence of the protestants in the assembly, they will create disorders perhaps in some places, but in general the

spirit of the revolution is yet a torrent which bears down everything before—and it so happens that that part of the clergy which
opposes the decree that creates these apprehensions, is the same
which has been uniformly in opposition to all the decrees of the
assembly. I suppose you know that the dispute is about the right
of the assembly to change the limits of the dioceses without the
consent of the Pope. A few Jansenists decided every thing in the
ecclesiastical committee whose plans were all adopted by the assembly: they established what they called the civil constitution
of the clergy by changing totally the ecclesiastical system. This
gives new vigour to the Roman catholic religion and will probably
postpone its end in France. These changes are altogether to the
disadvantage of the richer part of the clergy and of course opposed
by them. The same committee unnecessarily conformed the dioceses
to the departments, and it is this which is the pretext for the
present opposition.—All the higher clergy except two have so committed themselves by their opposition that they have no decent
means now of retracting unless the consent of the Pope should
arrive in an answer which is expected daily. There is little hope
of his consenting. The inevitable consequence seems to be that
all the refusing Bishops and Curates will be displaced and their
successors named agreeable to the new mode of election.

Nothing further has been done by the assembly respecting
tobacco since my last though the discussion is expected to be renewed daily. Before I left Paris I wrote to Marseilles, Bordeaux
and Havre in order to desire the consuls to endeavour to have
favorable representations made respecting the American commerce to the Assembly. Mr. Fenwick of Bordeaux informs me that
the chamber of commerce of that place is well disposed particularly
with regard to the oil business and that they propose instructing
their deputies to have it subjected to a much lower duty than that
of the arrêt du conseil. I learn from the committee of commerce
of the national assembly also that the new tariff they are about to
propose is now under press, that by it the duty on our oils is much
lowered and other foreign oils prohibited. This is very different
from their first report and tariff which were printed. I think it
probable that the assembly will adopt it in the lump from mere
lassistude, the necessity of fixing something and the impossibility
of examining every article of the tariff separately. All the foreign
merchants settled in the different ports and their connexions in
and about the assembly will oppose violently the exclusion of
foreign oils.

You are informed of the disturbances which still rage in the French islands as the means adopted by the National Assembly for appeasing them by commissioners and an army.—A mulatto of the name of Auger, said to have embarked in France for the U. States, and gone from thence to St. Domingo, put himself at the head of a party and gave much alarm for a short time. He has been obliged to fly to the Spanish part of the island where he is arrested by the order of that government.][1]

We are in daily expectation of the news of Ismailow being taken by the Russians. When the last accounts came away they were bombarding it in all quarters. Prince Potemkin is certainly trying at the same time to negotiate a separate peace with the Porte through the Visir who is at the head of the grand army. Prussia is trying to counteract this by keeping up the hopes of the Porte of effectual relief in the Spring. Negotiations connected with this business are active in several other parts of Europe. It is said that there are some indications of Spain's joining the English and Prussian mediation, but this merely from a desire to procure peace for the Turk and not from any attachment to these cabinets.—It is believed also that a negotiation is now carrying on by them with Denmark in order to facilitate the entrance of the fleet which England seems decided to send into the Baltic in the Spring. Admiral Hood is designed to command it and to those ships still kept in commission will be joined the fleet of Admiral Cornish after whom an express was sent immediately on the arrangement with Spain, in order to recall him from the West Indies.

You will easily conceive that this complication of interests and powers gives rise to such a variety of combinations that it is difficult to ascertain the result with any kind of precision. We may conjecture reasonably however that it will produce peace either by the separate negotiation between the Russian and Turk during the winter or by the interference of the mediating powers in the spring.

[For authentic information with respect to the British affairs in the East Indies I refer you to the debates of the house of commons, the Minister having promised to lay before them all the papers they wished for. His triumph on his refusal to communicate those respecting the Spanish negotiation prevents our knowing any thing more than what is contained in the convention signed by the two powers. From the terms in which it is couched it would seem there was wide field for dispute still left between them. The situation and disposition of France will be probably the measure of the

Spanish conformity to this convention which was extorted from them. I know not how this convention will have affected the U.S. as I do not know what is the system they would have observed in the case of a rupture. As far as I can judge however from such circumstances as came to my knowledge at Paris I think Spain would have been very tractable; and if she has serious thoughts of breaking with England in any short time I suppose she would be well disposed still to favor the wishes of the U.S.—The extract of your letter to Mr. Carmichael which you sent me has been kept entirely to myself. He has never mentioned to me whether he has received the letter itself, but I take it for granted it would have been sent by a sure conveyance.][1]

I learn accidentally in the moment from London that Colo. W. S. Smith has arrived in England and is still at Bath where he has been these ten days. It is conjectured that his object was to demand a surrender of the forts and that the convention with Spain is the cause that he has stopped in his way. I find that the Agents of the U.S. here who are in general perfectly informed of every thing that passes in America do not yet know of Colo. Smith's having left it, or at least they have said nothing to me about it, so that I suppose his departure was either very sudden or secret.

I have just received also from London the President's speech at the opening of Congress. It was waited for here with much impatience. I have communicated it to the agents who seem perfectly satisfied with it. As they think it will be of service, they intend having it published in some of the papers of this country. The remonstrance of the Pennsylvania public creditors which accompanied the Speech is approved of also by these gentlemen, but it will not be published. We are anxious to see what Congress will do respecting it, and the resolutions of the States opposed to the assumption.

[I think I mentioned to you some time ago that Mr. Swan of Boston had made a contract with the French ministry for ship timber. He intends I believe to contract with them also for supplying their marine and garrisons with salt provisions. These are such important articles that it is much to be desired that no mismanagement should take place in future. You know how much one of them has already suffered from this circumstance. Mr. Swan seems fully sensible of this, but I am not sufficiently acquainted with his commercial character to know how far he may be relied on. He has made proposals also to the Spanish ministry for furnishing salted provisions and taking payment in the debt of the U.S. to that country. The proposals are relished there and they desire him to go to Madrid for the purpose of concluding something. I know not whether he will go, but this shews that in proper hands something might be done respecting it which would be a means of adding to the debouché for those articles. The admiralty of this country are endeavouring to collect information with respect to our ship timber and particularly the live-oak. They have applied to Mr. Willink respecting it. Unfortunately the carpenters of the U.S. are in the habit of employing timber in an unseasoned state. This has already thrown our shipping into a discredit which will prevent that art becoming an important addition to our commerce unless the evil can be remedied by some means or other. Some houses here had ordered ships to be built in America by way of experiment. They have turned out so badly notwithstanding the cheapness of the first cost, that they have abandoned the prosecution of this object, and this has induced others to follow their example without the expence of an experiment.

Samples of the sugar of the maple tree refined at N. York have been sent to several houses here. One of them has conceived such hopes from them that they intend to send refiners there and endeavour to introduce this article into the commerce between this place and the U.S. I suppose however that it will be some time before enough is made for our own consumption, and that until then it cannot become an article of exportation.]¹—I have the honor to be with sentiments of the most perfect attachment & respect, Dear Sir, your obedient humble servant

W: SHORT

P.S. Jan. 17. I have just received a letter from Mr. Carmichael of Nov. 14. It came to Paris by Mr. Littlepage who gave it to the Marquis de la fayette. Between the two after being lost for some time, it has got to my hands. The letter is short as I am referred to the bearer for more particular information with respect to the politics of that court. I think it proper however to send you the following extract. "I can only say that from the characters who surround the throne here its system must be weak perhaps wicked with respect to those it may think weaker than itself. For what we lose on one side in opinion we seek to gain on the other though prudence nor magnanimity have nothing to say with the motive." He adds also "I thank you for your American information for I have none for a long time." You may be able perhaps to judge from this, if you have not better information, whether he has received your letter of August. I should infer from it that he had not.

I inclose you a report of the committee of imposition by which you will see their plan for the present year. It was ordered to be printed by the assembly. After much delay it has been published. You will see that their sentiments are totally changed with respect to tobacco. The discussion will certainly be not much longer delayed. At least we may be as sure of it as we can be of any movement of the assembly.

PrC (DLC: Short Papers); at head of text: "*No. 52*"; at foot of text: "Thomas Jefferson Secretary of State." Tr (DNA: RG 59, DD). Another Tr (same); at head of text: "Extract of a letter from William Short Esquire to the Secretary of State dated Amsterdam Jany. 16th. 1791"; text consists of those passages indicated in note 1 below. Recorded in SJL as received 20 Apr. 1791. Enclosures: (1) Report of Roederer's committee, *Rapport fait au nom du comité de l'imposition, con-* *cernant le revenu public provenant de la vente exclusive du tabac* (Paris, 1790). See Sowerby, No. 2581. (2) Short to Hamilton, 15 Jan. 1791 (Syrett, *Hamilton*, VII, 427-34).

1 The three passages enclosed in brackets (supplied) comprise the text of Tr described above. These extracts were enclosed in TJ to Washington, 24 Apr. 1791 (DLC: Washington Papers).

From Jean Baptiste Guide

EXCELLENCE   Nice 17. Janvier 1791

J'eus le Bonheur en 1788 de faire icy la conoissance Personelle de Votre Excellence et de Lui exprimer Mon désir de former des Liaisons de comerce avec Les etats unis de L'amerique.

Votre Excellence eut la bonté de me faire passer de Paris quelques notions relatives à mon projet et j'eus L'honeur de l'en remercier en L'assurant que je n'attendais qu'une Occasion favorable.

Je viens de me décider d'envoyer à Baltimore un petit Brigantin que j'ai, Doublé a neuf en Cuivre, nomé L'Antoinette, sous Pavillon Savoyard. J'y ai mis une Cargaison en Marchandises et en Piastres d'Espagne, pour avoir le retour en Tabac et autres articles du Continent.

Mon frere puïne, Pierre Guide, qui a travaille longtemps dans ma Maison, ayant eu dessein de passer en Virginie pour conoître le Pays, je Lui ai donné la Gestion entiere de mon expedition.

Venant d'aprendre que Votre Excellence a ete appelée de Paris dans Sa Patrie et placée au Ministere des affaires etrangeres, J'ose demander à Votre excellence Ses Bontés pour mon expedition et pour mon frere Pierre qui aura L'honeur de lui presenter cette Lettre.

Le Zelle que j'emploie à entamer les premieres Liaisons directes entre Nice et Les pays des etats unis me flattent que Votre Excellence voudra bien acorder sa protection et Sa Bienveillance à mon frere qui s'efforcera de les meriter.

Votre Excellence me fit La Grace de me dire que le Pavillon françois etait un des plus favorisés pour les droits dans Les ports des etats unis. Je ne puis et n'ai voulu me servir que de cellui de mon Souverain. Je demanderai à Votre Excellence de me procurer toutes Les douceurs possibles. Agravé deja par le risque des barbaresques, j'ai besoin de quelque facilité. Votre Excellence sait mieux que Perssonne le courage que donne au negotiant Les succès des premières operations.

Mon frere a quelqu'envie de se fixer à Baltimore ou Philadelphie. Il me renvera alors Le navire et attendra des nouvelles expeditions. En cédant à ce projet qui me separe d'un frere que j'aime infiniment, ma Consolation serait de le Savoir honnoré des Bontés de Votre Excellence et d'y trouver des moyens à multiplier mes raports d'affaire avec Le Continent.

Le cap. Fr. Baret, né à la martinique, Mais sujet naturalisé du Roi de Sardaigne, commande Mon Brigantin. C'est un marin qui a du merite et que j'ose recomender à Votre Excellence.

Je Suplie Votre Excellence de me permettre de lui offrir mes Services dans ce Pays. Je m'estimerai fort heureux de pouvoir m'ocuper à remplir Ses ordres com'encor à me rendre utile dans L'occasion aux Sujets des etats unis qui pourraient avoir des interets icy. C'est Dans ces dispositions que je me proteste avec un Profond Respect De Votre Excellence Le tres humble & tres obeissant Serviteur BTE. GUIDE

P.S. Mon Navire pars de Marseille où je l'avais envoyé doubler en Cuivre. Il reviendra icy à droiture et desormais il faira directement les Voyages de Nice au Continent et Vice-versa. Mon frere aura des Lettres pour Votre Excellence de nos parens M. Cathalan et des Pieds d'olivier.

RC (DLC); endorsed by TJ as received 30 Apr. 1791 and so recorded in SJL.

One of the letters that Pierre Guide bore with him was that from Stephen Cathalan, Jr., dated at Marseilles 22 Jan. 1791 introducing "Mr. Pierre Guide, Brother to Mr. Jan. Bste. Guide Merchant of Nice, with whom you was acquainted at your Passage at that Place" and stating: "he intend to remain in the U.S. of America to open a Trade between U.S. and Nice, if the Success of the voyage of the Vessel he goes on, belonging to his Brother, Proves Satisfactory.—I Beg you to Protect him, with your kind advices, and render him the assistance he may have occasion for; what you will do in his Favour, will be considered by me as a Great Favour Confered on myself"

(RC in DLC, endorsed by TJ as received 30 Apr. 1791 and so recorded in SJL).

From James Monroe

DEAR SIR   Phila. Jany. 17. 1791.

I wrote you soon after my arrival here relative to the wishes and pretentions of a Mr. Mortimer, son of Dr. M. of Fredbg., to an appointment in your office. As I understood mine was accompanied with letters from Mr. Fitzhugh and Mr. Page I suppos'd an answer would have been communicated to these gentlemen. Latterly I have received several applications on that subject from the Doctor and his friends. I have therefore to request that you will enable me give him satisfactory information on that point. I have just received a letter from Colo. Bell who informs that Mr. and Mrs. Randolph are well. Sincerely I am your friend & servt.

JAS. MONROE

RC (DLC); endorsed by TJ as received 17 Jan. 1791 and so recorded in SJL.

From John Sevier

SIR   Congress Chamber 17 Jany. 1791.

Mr. Pery who was appointed one of the Judges of the territory So. of Ohio I am informed have declined the Acceptance of that office. I therefore presume the President will find it expedient to supply the vacancy by another Appointment.—Permit me to Name to the Honble. the Secreatary of State, Waightstil Avery Esquire as a proper person to fill this important office. His competent Abilities integrity, And Uprightness, together with his enterprise And General Acquaintance with the People of the Territory. The favourable Opinions entertained of this Gentleman by those People, would perhaps render this appointment as pleasing as any that could be made.—I have the honor to be with due respect yours respectively,   JOHN SEVIER

RC (DLC: Washington Papers); at foot of text: Honble Secy. of State"; addressed: "Honble. Mr. Jefferson Secreay. of State Philadelphia"; endorsed by TJ as received 17 Jan. 1791 and so recorded in SJL.

For circumstances surrounding the judicial vacancy in the Southwest Territory and the appointment of Joseph Anderson to fill it, see Editorial Note and group of documents relating to the subject, at 4 Mch. 1791.

From William Short

DEAR SIR   Amsterdam Jan. 17. 1791.

My last private letter to you was of the 29th. ulto. It is still at the Texel with all the letters I have written to you and the Secretary of the Treasury by that way since my arrival here. The wind has remained constantly since the month of Nov. so as to prevent any vessel sailing from that place.—In my last I enclosed you my account with yourself of which I have received the balance from Messrs. Willink & V. Staphorst, my accounts with the U.S. as your secretary, and as chargé des affaires to the 1st. of July last. I explained fully the several articles of these accounts which required it.

In the same letter as well as in that of the 23d. ulto. sent by the English packet I told you how sorry I was to have gone into such unreserved details in my letter to which yours of Sep. 30 was an answer. I do not repeat the same here because I do not wish to weary you with apologies on a subject which must already have been matter of more than sufficient ennui to you, as I find it was repeated in several of my letters before I knew the effect it would produce. I am sorry it is so different from what I had improperly suffered myself to hope for, and do assure you that I blame myself so much that I hope at least for your excuses, if there can be any excuses for having written so often and so much on a subject which concerned merely myself. It is to avoid adding to it that I say nothing more in extenuation at present. Begging you however to be fully persuaded that you were mistaken in what you say about my attachment to Europe, to be assured that I should prefer being there on the terms you mention if they could be hoped for, to being any thing in Europe, and to believe that my desire to remain here some time longer proceeded from a belief that I could be useful and a desire to be so, and also from the impossibility which I foresaw of settling myself agreeably to my wishes in America.

It has been hinted to me here that there was an idea of appointing Mr. Van Staphorst Consul for the U.S. at this place and that he had declined it from a desire not to have any thing to do with the present government here. If so I think he was right. I cannot help adding however in case this idea should still exist that I fear such an appointment would do more harm than good, as it would certainly excite the jealousy and ill humour formerly subsisting between the two houses employed here by the U.S. and which seems at present to be done away. I know not who could be appointed as Consul here but I think it better even to have none than to rouse old differences between the two houses.

The agents here have learned from their correspondents that the Secretary of the Treasury has been endeavoring to find bills and intends to draw for the money in their hands. Supposing it would be too late I have not written to him respecting it, but I think it would be well for him to consider whether it would not be more advantageous to have coin sent from hence for several reasons and particularly the following. 1. Bills to that amount must tend to keep the exchange low in America and be prejudicial to commerce. 2. Coin sent would turn out as well and probably better than bills drawn payable in London on account of the difference of exchange between this place and that. 3. The advantage of increasing the quantity of circulating specie by importing it into a country where it is wanted. The Secretary will always know three months beforehand the sum he will want and that will give him time or nearly to have it sent from hence. The insurance is inconsiderable.

The Marquis de la fayette has been lately indisposed and confined to his bed for the first time during the revolution. No danger is apprehended. His party strengthens in proportion as the *Club des Jacobins* divides. A new club under the title of *Monarchique* has been formed in Paris. They would probably have sunk into oblivion if the municipality of Paris to please the *Jacobins* had not taken on themselves to forbid their assembling. This act of municipal tyranny, founded on the club's having distributed bread to the poor of the different quarters of the capital at a cheap rate, has much encreased their importance and the number of its members. I do not think however it will last long, as the municipality is sensible of having done wrong and will do nothing more to prevent their assembling. The members are composed of men of heterogeneous principles.

I have received no letter from you since that of Sep. 30. I shall write to you again in a few days by the English packet as the last post by which one can be sure of that conveyance will leave this place the 25th. In the mean time be assured of the sincerity with which I am my dear Sir your friend & servant

W: SHORT

RC (DLC); at head of text: *"Private"*; endorsed by TJ as received 20 Apr. 1791 and so recorded in SJL. PrC (DLC: Short Papers).

From Giuseppe Chiappe to the President

EXCELLENCE

Le 18e. Janvier 1791
à Mogador

J'ay eû l'honneur d'êcrire a Vôtre Excellence voye de Cadix et de Madrid le 13e. et 28e. du Mois de May de l'année qui vient de terminer, àffin de l'informer sur tout ce qui s'étoit passé rapport a la Mort inopinée du Feu Roy Sydy Mohamet Ben Abdalla et sur l'installation de son successeur Sydy Mulay Liazid (q.D.g.). J'ay appris ensuite de mon Frere Francisco qu'il avoit obtenu un Delai sur l'Ambassade, pour que le tems ne fut si pressé a la Nation pour concurrir au nombre des autres a l'Homage qu'on se dispose de prêter au Nouvel Empereur, qui fait toujours connoitre d'avence les dispositions pacifiques, par les quelles il se propose de reçevoir amicalement tous les Representants. Mon dit Frere Francisco aussi bien que mon Frere Geronimo a Tanger doivent avoir continuées regulierement leurs informations, parce qu'ils ont êtés Jusqu'appresent plus a portée de les perçevoir, s'étant S.M.I. detenue fort long tems dans ces Contrées du Nort. La presente va sous Couverte du Consul Général a Londres, qui Je ne doute pas voudra l'encheminer au plus vîte et par le Canal mieux connu, et c'est pour continuer a V.E. les nouvelles qui pourront servir de lumieres, et continuer les apparences d'une solide Paix que Dieu benisse. Le Monarque est passé a Mequinez, d'ou il se propose de venir pour le Poiàleons a l'autre Capitale de Maroc. Mon Frere Francisco a été ordonné de le suivre, ce qui contribuira beaucoup a entrettenir la bonne Armonie sur l'attente de l'Ambassade qui ne devroit pas tarder, et que Je suppose deja en route. Dernierement l'Embassadeur de Portugal êtoit arrivé a Gibraltar aussi bien que celuy d'Engleterre, et celuy de Raguse, et on les attend incessamment a la Cour. Ils suivront bien tôt les autres, et Je souhaitte que celuy des Etats Unis puisse les devencer pour prouver a S.M.I. l'empressement qui les anime a se procurer son Amitié, et sa correspondence. J'ose me flatter d'y pouvoir concurrir par mes services et Je ne manquerois pas d'y contribuer personellement aussi-tôt que J'aurois l'honneur de me presenter a Sa Divine Majesté Impériale, de qui dans sa Minorité J'ay toujours reçues des marques non equivoques de sa bienvaillance et de sa valable protection. Mes Amis encore a la Cour ne desisteront pas de se prêter a moi leur assistence pour seconder mes desirs et toutes mes expositions pour la bonne issüe. Le 30e. de 9bre. passé la Fregatte Americaine nomée Thomas Wilson, son Cape. Euphrahim Waite, avec 16. Personnes d'Equipage y compris le Capn. est arrivée a cet Port venant de Philadelphie en droitture pour charger de Mules, et le 13. du Courant elle est repartie avec 68. Mules pour l'Isle de Tabago. Nôtre Gouvernement l'a très-bien reçue et fetée, et de ma part Je l'ay assiduement assistée en preference, selon que mon devoir le demende. Je voudrois bien que les affaires encouragent reciproquement le Comerce, pour que Je puisse me rendre utile a l'Illustre Nation que Je serve, et prouver a V.E. la haute consideration avec la quelle J'ay l'honneur d'être trés-respectueusement De Vôtre Excellence Le très-Hle. & Très-Obt. Serviteur

GIUSEPPE CHIAPPE

RC (DNA: RG 360, PCC No. 98); at foot of text: "A Son Excellence Monsieur le President du Congres Unis de l'Amerique a la Nouvelle Jorck"; endorsed by TJ as received 30 June 1791 and so recorded in SJL. For Chiappe's letter of 13 May 1790, see Short to Jay, 23 May 1790, note; that of 28 May 1790 has not been found.

From Miroménil

A Paris ce 18. Janv. 1791.

J'ay recü, Monsieur, la lettre que vous m'avés fait L'Honneur de m'Ecrire Le 6. de 7bre. dernier de la Part de M. votre President General Washington, qui desir avoir 20. Douzaines de Bouteilles des Grands Vins Nommé *Segur* du Medoc. La Renommée de ce General est trop Connue de la france pour ne pas faire desirer à tout bon françois, de saisir toutes Les occasions de pouvoir Luy donner des preuves de Respect, et d'Empressement à Exécuter ses ordres. Je vous suplie, Monsieur, de Luy presenter cet Hommage de ma part et de reçevoir Personnellement, toute ma reconnoissance de m'avoir mis à même de faire ce qui peut vous estre agréable, et à ce respectable General.

J'Etois en éffét Proprietaire depuis 1765. d'une partie de ces grands vins, par ma premiere femme, nommée Ségur, que J'ay perdü en 1774. Elle me Laissa 2. filles que J'ay marié en 1786. et auxquelles J'ay rendüe Le bien de Leur Mère. Ainsy la terre de La Tour en Medoc dont elles Jouissent en Commun appartient Aujourd'huy à Leurs Maris. Mais Néanmoins J'ay Conservé une corespondance d'Amitié et de Reconnoissance avec le Sr. Domenger qui en est le regisseur, auquel Je vais envoyer votre Lettre, en le Chargeant de Mettre à Execution une Commission qui me devient précieuse par l'envie que J'ay de plaire au General Washington. J'auray soins aussy d'En prévenir Mrs. Le Comte de La Pallu et

Marquis de Beaumont, mes Gendres, qui sûrement ne seront pas moins Empressés que moy de Donner Leurs ordres en Conséquence, et Je Crois pouvoir vous assurer de l'Exactitude que l'on Mettra, pour La qualité du vin, et pour que vos vües soient entièrement remplies.

Je vais aussy prier MM. Fennwick, Masson & Comie. de Bordeaux qui m'ont Ecrit et envoyé votre Lettre Le 7. de ce mois, de vous faire passer ma réponse, et de les prévenir que le Sr. Domenger aura L'Honneur de Les voir et de s'aranger avec Eux.—Soyés bien persuadé, Monsieur, du tres sincere attachement avec Lequel J'ay L'Honneur d'estre votre tres humble et tres obeissant Serviteur

LE CTE. DE MIROMÉNIL, M[aréch]al de Camp

RC (ViWC); endorsed by TJ as received 21 June 1791 and so recorded in SJL.

To James Monroe

MY DEAR SIR   Philadelphia Jan. 18. 1791.

I have been constantly afflicted at my inability to acknowledge the reciept of Dr. Mortimer's letters and of those of my friends Mr. Fitzhugh and Mr. Page: but I have for some weeks past been forced by other business to suspend answering any letters whatever, unless indeed of indispensable magnitude, and even now I must beg you to make the answer for me. When I came into office, I found the clerkships all filled by gentlemen who had been in them several years, and who to the title of possession added that of irreprocheable conduct. I have therefore not had a single appointment to make. This answer has been given to near an hundred letters which I have had to write in reply to applications of this nature. I wish with all my soul I could have obliged my friends on this occasion. Your taking the trouble to write thus much, and apologize for my not writing will oblige Dear Sir Your sincere friend & servt.,   TH: JEFFERSON

PrC (DLC); at foot of text: "Colo. Monroe."

From Timothy Pickering

SIR   Philadelphia January 18. 1791.

As I shall leave town before the papers relative to an intended sale in France of Virginia lands, will be ready to be executed, I

[514]

have committed the conduct of the business, so far as it respects myself, to my friend Mr. Samuel Hodgdon. He will wait on you with the papers, when completed, to receive such certificate as you shall think proper to give relative to him, Mr. Levi Hollingsworth, and myself, respecting the above proposed sale of our lands in Virginia.

As the matter has been suspended longer than I expected, permit me to remind you, that as Mr. Hodgdon and Mr. Hollingsworth were not personally known to you, I requested Mr. Peters, who has many years been acquainted with them, to accompany me to your house and give you his opinion of their characters. This he was kind enough to do; and the opinion he expressed concerning them appeared to be satisfactory to you.—With great respect, I am Sir, your obliged and most obedient Servant,

TIMOTHY PICKERING

RC (DLC); endorsed by TJ as received 24 Feb. 1791 and so recorded in SJL. For TJ's cautious affidavit, see 4 Mch. 1791.

Representation by France against the Tonnage Acts

EDITORIAL NOTE

C'est surtout M. Jefferson qui prend le
plus interêt au succès de cette grand revolution. Il m'a dit souvent, que les travaux de
l'Assemblée Nationale serviront á regenerer
non seulement la France, mais les Etats
unis, dont les principes commençoient á se
corrompre. Presque tous les Whigs ou les
veritables Republicains de ce pays sont du
même avis. . . .

Otto to Montmorin, 23 July 1791

The importance of the union in a commercial sense, Alexander
Hamilton wrote in the eleventh *Federalist*, was one of those arguments for the proposed constitution on which there was least room
for a difference of opinion and to which, in fact, a general assent had
been given. Few informed readers could have disagreed with the assertion and none could have misunderstood him when he said that
the maritime powers of Europe, uneasy before the enterprising spirit
of American commerce, might foster divisions in order to achieve
"the threefold purpose of preventing our interference in their navigation, of monopolizing the profits of our trade, and of clipping the
wings by which we might soar to a dangerous greatness."[1] A few

---

[1] *The Federalist*, ed. B. F. Wright, p. 137. Hamilton's use of the phrase "clipping the wings" recalls the story told by Benjamin Rush several times about a
British minister who reportedly said to Henry Laurens before the war: "*You spread
too much canvas upon our seas, and we are determined to clip it.*" In the same
connection Rush quoted a British officer after Yorktown: "Your independence I
fear will be established, but remember it must be acquired for you upon the
ocean" (Rush, letters to *Penna. Journ.*, 4 July 1782; to James Madison, 30 Jan.

weeks earlier Hamilton had lamented the degradation of the national character brought on by the inability of the government, confronted with exclusions and restraints imposed on American trade by European powers, to adopt "those defensive regulations, which would be likely to produce a greater reciprocity of privileges."[2]

Such arguments for granting to the government a power to defend its economy had indeed been given a general assent, beginning with the propositions of 1784 for a rigorous navigation law and reaching a final confirmation in the Convention of 1787.[3] John Adams' dispatches from London had been filled with urgent pleas for retaliatory duties, for an American system of navigation, and for a stronger government to enforce its terms.[4] Jefferson, in the absence of legislative authority, had deliberately sought to utilize the treaty power to give central direction to commercial policy, "so far as the imperfect provisions of our constitution will admit, and until the states shall by new compact make them more perfect."[5] Rufus King, John Jay, James Madison, James Monroe, and others of varying political attitudes and backgrounds had joined in the effort to find some means of removing the shackles from American commerce. John Jay was not the only one who realized that uneasiness induced by trade restrictions "promotes the System of perfecting our Union and strengthening the fœderal Government."[6]

But, like most of their compatriots, all would have attached to

1806; and to John Adams, 27 June 1812, *Letters of Benjamin Rush*, ed. L. H. Butterfield, I, 274-5, 277n.; II, 914, 1144).

[2] Unsigned piece by Hamilton, N.Y. *Daily Advertiser*, 21 July 1787 (Syrett, *Hamilton*, IV, 230).

[3] The address of 1784 asked for authority to enable Congress to "make it the interest of every nation to enter into equal treaties with us" (TJ to Harrison, 30 Apr. 1784). It also outlined a measure substantially like that of 1791 and rested its appeal on the same argument advanced by Hamilton in the *Federalist*. TJ was a member of the committee and it is plausible to suppose he had a hand in drafting the basic assumption of the address: "It will certainly be admitted, that unless the United States can act as a nation and be regarded as such by foreign powers, and unless Congress for this purpose shall be vested with powers competent to the protection of commerce, they can never command reciprocal advantages in trade; and without such reciprocity, our foreign commerce must decline and eventually be annihilated" (printed report of committee, 22 Apr. 1784, DNA: RG 59, PCC, M/247; JCC, XXVI, 269-71).

[4] John Adams to Robert R. Livingston, 14 July 1783; 3 May, 10 and 26 June, 6 Aug., and 24 Nov. 1785; 4 Jan. 1786 (Wharton, *Dipl. Corr.*, I, 487-8; II, 377-8, 385-7, 423, 537, 558-9; VI, 541-2).

[5] TJ to Monroe, 17 June 1785. TJ was not sanguine about the results to be achieved through such use of the treaty power and in this remarkable letter he seemed rather to be urging Monroe and his colleagues in Congress toward the creation of the "more perfect" compact of the states. He was less explicit with John Adams (TJ to Adams, 7 July 1785).

[6] Jay to TJ, 15 June 1785; Washington thought British restrictions would "immediately produce powers in Congress to regulate the Trade of the Union" which might otherwise not be obtained in half a century (Washington to Lafayette, 25 July 1785, *Writings*, ed. Fitzpatrick, XXVIII, 206-7). King told Otto Congress would be willing to exclude Great Britain entirely from American commerce if France would grant concessions in their West Indies. On the same condition Jay suggested a new treaty with France obligating the United States to levy extraordinary duties on British goods and shipping (Otto to Vergennes, 20 May, 13 Aug., and 22 Sep. 1786, Arch. Aff. Etr., Corr. Pol., E.-U., XXXI-XXXII; photostats in DLC). See also Harrison to TJ, 16 Apr. 1784; Madison to TJ, 25 Apr. 1784; Setser, *Reciprocity*, p. 52-98.

Hamilton's words their commonly accepted meaning, assigning chief blame for exclusions and restraints not indiscriminately to the maritime powers of Europe but to Great Britain and the mercantilist principles of Sheffield and Hawkesbury she had embraced. Some would have recognized that she thereby made them two of the most effective architects of the American Constitution since, as Fisher Ames pointed out, it "was dictated by commercial necessity more than any other cause."[7] England's commercial rigor toward her former colonies, however plausible in theory or rooted in imperial necessity, had in fact provided for Americans the unifying effect of external force almost equivalent to that once produced by military power. There were, of course, other and powerful impulses toward a more effective union, chief among them the common experience of a war fought for separate nationality and the elevated principles offered in justification. But the threat posed by England to the economy of the new nation was the most immediate and the most exigent single force.

The American people, the French minister to the United States observed in 1789, had undergone a genuine moral and political revolution in the preceding three years. Thenceforth their legislation would be directed toward the central object of diminishing the preponderant influence of England over their commerce. But this could not be achieved suddenly. Patience as well as encouragement would be required of France because conflicting interests and deep-rooted predilections would make it difficult to sever old connections and establish new ones. Congress, when it had finally broken the chains, would be able to deal more freely in its relations with other powers.[8] With the passage of the tonnage acts of 1789 and 1790 and the resultant French protest, Moustier's observations received ample confirmation. The tonnage duties paid by France were trivial in her fiscal scales and unimportant in those of the United States. But neither the conflict over Hamiltonian finance nor even that over the permanent residence of the government which exacerbated all other major issues could throw quite so revealing a light on the nature of the divisions in the American political fabric as did this relatively unimportant question—an illumination all the more significant because the discussions were, for the most part, hidden from public view. When Otto, the French *chargé d'affaires*, submitted the French representation on the tonnage acts late in 1790, the most important result he achieved was to illustrate the two fundamentally different ways in which Americans regarded the nature of their moral and political revolution.

I

A general assent to the proposition and a common grasp of what Hamilton's language meant could not long conceal the profound differences of will and purpose that were concealed by the apparent con-

[7] 28 Apr. 1789, *Annals*, I, 221.
[8] Moustier to Necker, 12 May 1789; Moustier to Montmorin, 1 June and 2 July 1789 (Arch. Aff. Etr., Corr. Pol., E.-U., xxxiv; photostats in DLC); Otto to Montmorin, 28 Sep. 1790 and 6 Jan. 1791 (DLC: Henry Adams Transcripts; Setser, *Reciprocity*, p. 91-2).

sensus. For no sooner had the power over commerce been granted than Hamilton and others of his persuasion reversed the arguments they had previously employed. Every attempt to exercise that power they now characterized not as a defensive measure to achieve commercial reciprocity and to restore the dignity of the national character, but as the initiation of commercial hostilities that might bring on actual warfare if not the dissolution of the union. Ardently committed to the idea of an energetic government that would not hesitate to intervene in the economy, they now declined to use the weapon that had been fabricated. They also succeeded, after bitter contests, in preventing Madison and Jefferson from laying hands on it. This abrupt shift in position did not convert the believers in a strong government and in a liberal construction of delegated powers into their opposites. It did not make Madison, much less Jefferson, the advocate of an American system of mercantilism and it did not deprive Hamilton of his claim to be regarded as its fountainhead in the new world.[9] But it did sharply distinguish arguments of coherence and consistency from those of mere political expediency. On the one side it ranged those who stood with Jefferson, whose system of policy respecting trade and its relation to the national purpose was the same in 1793 that it had been in 1783, being fortified both by the liberal principles of the Revolution and by the wisdom embraced in Choiseul's dictum of an earlier day that the European balance of power lay in America and in commerce.[10] On the other side it placed those who, like Hamilton, had argued from the same postulates in 1787 but who in 1789, rather than point the weapon toward the nation against whose measures it had been provided, chose a continuation of the posture of impotence and acquiescence—at least with respect to Great Britain.

[9] The hypothesis that the central characteristic of American history from 1763 to 1828 was the development of an American mercantilism is set forth in W. A. Williams, "The Age of Mercantilism: An Interpretation of the American Political Economy," WMQ, 3rd. ser., XV (Oct. 1958), p. 419-37. By a redefinition of the term Hamilton's mercantilism becomes "latent and limited" while it was "Jefferson and the other agrarians who did develop an American mercantilism." William D. Grampp, "A Re-examination of Jeffersonian Economics," *Southern Economic Journal*, XII (Jan. 1946), 263-82, reprinted in *Thomas Jefferson A Profile*, ed. Merrill D. Peterson (New York, 1967), p. 135-63, provides a more satisfying analysis of TJ's economic views and policies.

[10] "Make no mistake about it," wrote Choiseul in 1759 as French foreign minister, "the true balance of power now rests in commerce—and in America" (De Flassan, *Histoire générale et raisonnée de la diplomatie française, ou de la politique de la France*, VI [Paris, 1811], 160, cited by Felix Gilbert, *To the Farewell Address*, p. 106). Merrill D. Peterson, "Thomas Jefferson and Commercial Policy, 1783-1793," WMQ, 3rd. ser., XXII (Oct. 1965), 584-610, reprinted in *Thomas Jefferson A Profile*, ed. Peterson, p. 104-34, presents a convenient summary and recognizes that TJ was "a principal architect and executor" of the commercial Plan of 1784, but claims too much in supposing it was this that "had given coherence and direction to all his work and thought on national affairs" in the decade preceding 1793 (p. 108). The system, which TJ cannot fairly be said to have regarded as his own personal or partisan possession (as Peterson does, p. 132), was important to him as a means, but it was not all. Its principles were in fact derivative. What gave coherence and direction to TJ's thought and actions on national affairs in this decade and throughout life, in commerce as in all other concerns public and private, were the overriding moral propositions set forth in the Declaration of Independence.

The departure of Hamiltonians from the ground previously occupied thus revealed the profound disjunctions afflicting the American body politic. These cleavages were indeed so deep and unalterable
as to threaten the existence of the union, not so much because two
quite opposite systems of commercial policy were locked in conflict or
because of the very real danger of intervention, subversion, or even
war from one or another of the European powers. The danger lay
rather in Hamilton's want of confidence in the people, in their spirit,
in their institutions, and, above all, in their declared principles of government. Hamilton at least had the candor to admit more openly than
any other contemporary that, along with his doubts about the new
system of things, he entertained a very different set of political principles. At the moment the Constitution was proposed, he thought its
adoption doubtful, the dismemberment of the union likely, the resultant
existence of monarchies and republics side by side possible, and a
"reunion with Great Britain . . . not impossible, though not much to
be feared." A good administration under Washington might, however, "conciliate the confidence and affection of the people and perhaps
enable the government to acquire more consistency than the proposed
constitution seems to promise for so great a country."[11] If the author
of the eleventh *Federalist* had read the tenth by Madison, he evidently
did not share its estimate of the sources of strength in a republic
covering an extensive territory. The want of confidence, the misreading of the national character, the trust in a revered military hero and
in energetic leadership—these traits of one who came to dominate
policy under Washington brought on a steadily mounting disaffection
of the people and with it a genuine danger of the dissolution of the
union. The abrupt abandonment of a position previously assumed on
commercial policy was the opening signal, inviting consequences quite
the opposite of the conciliating effects Hamilton had anticipated.

It is important to note, however, that the old arguments had been
surrendered and the new ones assumed by spokesmen for commercial
and shipping interests some time before Hamilton came into the government. Indeed, a large measure of his power and success in wielding
it derived from the fact that there were many others who shared his
doubts about the experiment in republican government, who admired
English institutions and ways of ordering society, and who saw not
much to fear in a reunion—especially since independence had brought

11 Hamilton's "Conjectures about the new Constitution," [17-30 Sep. 1787],
Syrett, *Hamilton*, IV, 276-7. These conjectures are all the more interesting because,
at this time, Hamilton made a serious effort for "reasons of some moment" to
discover the author of a letter about a "mission . . . originated in Connecticut"
to invite the second son of George III (Frederick, Duke of York) to become
monarch of the United States—a plan that was soberly entertained by some
(Hamilton to Wadsworth, 20 Aug. 1787; Wadsworth to Hamilton, 26 Aug. 1787;
Humphreys to Hamilton, 1 Sep. 1787, Syrett, *Hamilton*, IV, 236, 237, 240-2).
A few months earlier an informant—almost certainly William Samuel Johnson—
had given George Beckwith some hints of such a plan (see note 106, Editorial
Note, Mediterranean trade and Algerine captives, under 28 Dec. 1790). It was
Johnson's fellow townsman Hezekiah Wetmore who was active in circulating the
anonymous letter about which Hamilton inquired. On Wetmore's relations with
Johnson during the war, see George C. Groce, Jr., *William Samuel Johnson*,
p. 106.

a clipping of commercial wings from without and threats of retaliation from within. Their convictions were made manifest the moment the House of Representatives was organized in 1789 when James Madison urged upon his colleagues an immediate step to obtain "supplies for the federal treasury, and a speedy rescue of our trade from its present anarchy." The expedient that he proposed was the identical schedule of imposts that Congress had recommended to the states in 1783. To this he proposed to add only "a clause or two" on tonnage duties, copied directly from the Virginia statute, so as to discriminate in favor of those nations having commercial treaties with the United States. This plan could be put into operation immediately, he declared, thus producing considerable revenue from the spring importations that would otherwise be lost. His first argument was that such a measure would meet the public expectations, that the propositions of 1783 had been given general approval, and that the new government, in its first act, should "revive those principles of honor and honesty that have too long lain dormant."[12] Empty as the treasury was, however, the anticipated duties on the spring importations were lost in the ensuing collision of special interests. Ames of Massachusetts, deploring the thousands of hogsheads of tobacco rotting in southern warehouses, asked for high tonnage duties so that New England could build ships to take them to market. Tucker of South Carolina, knowing that British bottoms had a virtual monopoly in carrying southern produce, urged low rates lest agriculture be taxed to support eastern commerce and shipping. FitzSimons of Pennsylvania, viewing the spectacular growth of manufactures in his state since the war, called for protective duties for infant manufactures on a greatly extended list of imports. All protested their concern for the national interest and for liberal principles of commerce.[13]

Local, regional, and national interests could be accommodated with relative ease, however, compared with the difficulty presented by Madison's discriminatory tonnage clauses. There was general agreement that American ships should be favored as against those of all other nations, but the cleavage between those who wished to exercise the mandate that had been given by the nation and those who now attacked the position they once occupied was irreconcilable. When Madison declared that "the public sentiments of America" would be favorable to such discrimination, John Laurance of New York immediately challenged him. How, he asked, "is the public sentiment, in this case, to be collected?" Had the nations in treaty given advantages entitling them to a preference? If so, let the obligation be discharged. If not, let the national interest and not sentiments of gratitude determine, since, "nations as well as individuals, are guided by the principle of interest." Madison, Laurance pointed out, had not contended that discrimination was a treaty obligation. He had claimed that France had been persuaded by the American minister to relax her rigid system, but an alteration had since taken place and the privilege

12 *Annals*, I, 102-3, 110-14, 115.
13 *Annals*, I, 105, 107, 109-10, 111-12, 115, 117-19, 168-9, 177-9, 179-81, 186-7, 191, 201-2, 234-5, 236-7, 241-2, 244, 245-6, 255-9, 272, 278-9, 290, 416.

withdrawn. The argument that Great Britain had too great a monopoly of American trade and that this called for government intervention so that other nations could engage in competition for direct participation in it was irrelevant. This was not a point for government to settle. If merchants found it to "their interest or convenience to form connexions with the subjects of one nation in preference to another, why should the Government interfere to dissolve it? They should be left to themselves, like the industrious bee, to gather from the choicest flower the greatest abundance of commercial sweets." Such intervention, improper in itself, might in fact produce disastrous consequences. The nation against which such a regulation was directed might retaliate and—such was her power—might even destroy that part of the carrying trade which still remained in American hands.[14] Here, in a single speech delivered before Washington had even been inaugurated, Laurance articulated most of the arguments that thenceforth would be employed to defend the newly disclosed concepts of policy toward England and France.

Even so, the arguments were not powerful enough to persuade members of the House of Representatives to disregard what they conceived to be the public expectations. Madison thought the known sentiments of the people at large would make it very offensive to them to find Great Britain placed on the footing of the most favored nation "by the first act of a Government instituted for the purpose of uniting the States in the vindication of their commercial interests against her monopolizing regulations."[15] Abraham Baldwin took the same position in an angry reply to Laurance:[16]

> . . . the gentleman from New York . . . wants evidence of what the public sentiment is. I think . . . we have a strong proof . . . in the very existence of the House. This sentiment [was] . . . the cause of the revolution under which we are about to act. The commercial restrictions Great Britain placed upon our commerce in pursuing her selfish policy, gave rise to an unavailing clamor, and excited the feeble attempt which several of the State Legislatures made to counteract the detestable regulations of a commercial enemy; but these proving altogether ineffectual to ward off the effects of the blow, or revenge their cause, the convention at Annapolis was formed for the express purpose of counteracting them on general

[14] *Annals*, I, 183-4.

[15] Madison employed these words in his letter to TJ, 30 May 1789, but they only echoed his forceful argument in replying to Laurance: "We have now the power to avail ourselves of our natural superiority, and I am for beginning with some manifestation of that ability, that foreign nations may or might be taught to pay us that respect which they have neglected on account of our former imbecility. This language and these sentiments are the language and sentiments of our constituents. The great political revolution now brought about, by the organization of the new Government, has its foundation in these sentiments. . . . But permit me to ask . . . if it is not the same thing whether we want the power or the will to compel them to do us commercial justice?" (*Annals*, I, 209-10, 255-6). Madison's forceful reasoning compelled Laurance to fall back on the artifice adopted by the Senate—that of proposing more stringent measures—despite his argument that the United States was in no condition to engage in commercial war with Great Britain (*Annals*, I, 201-2, 246, 255-6).

[16] *Annals*, I, 187-8.

principles. This convention found the completion of the business impossible to be effected in their hands; it terminated . . . in the convention who framed the present constitution, which has perfected a happy revolution in politics and commerce.

The general expectation of the country is, that there shall be a discrimination; that those nations who have not yet explained the terms on which an intercourse shall be carried on, or who have by establishing regulations bearing hard upon such intercourse, may know our ability and disposition to withhold, or bestow advantages according as we find a principle of reciprocity prevail.

Madison's calm arguments and Baldwin's expostulations, both grounded in the same view of national policy that Hamilton had set forth in the eleventh *Federalist*, almost prevailed against the contrary attitude which Madison considered to be "impolitic in every view that can be taken of the subject."[17] The House of Representatives, he reported to Jefferson, had agitated the question with determination and was "almost unanimously in favor of some monitory proof that our new government is able and not afraid to encounter the restrictions of Britain."[18]

But something more fundamental than the interests of those engaged in commerce and shipping was involved in this breach in the old general assent. Madison and Jefferson were as well aware as Sheffield or Laurance that habits of commerce, long credit terms offered by British merchants, the Algerine pirates, and other harsh realities kept a major part of American exports channelled through England to the markets of France and other countries. They also fully understood the risks involved. But these realities were made far more formidable by the ties of consanguinity and affection which drew many of their former allies over to the new policy toward Great Britain. Such was the power of these intangible bonds that a member of Congress from the South or West, in New York, could easily "believe himself not in the capital of the American empire, but in Quebec, Halifax, Shelburne, or some other British town." Sheridan and Fox themselves, a correspondent of a Philadelphia newspaper declared, "could not have plead the cause of the British commerce with more zeal than some gentlemen have done on the floor of Congress."[19] John Laurance, born a Briton, vestryman of Trinity Church, trustee of Columbia College, and, like Hamilton, an able lawyer whose professional and public acts faithfully reflected the constituency he represented, may well have believed that a commercial discrimination against nations not in treaty with the United States might prove injurious to the national interest. But others closer to the feelings of Americans who lived beyond the large commercial centers had other views of him and the policy he advocated. Laurance, declared Senator Maclay, was "a mere tool for British agents and factors."[20]

But if Laurance was overwhelmed by the vigor of Madison's leader-

[17] Madison to Edmund Randolph, 31 May 1789 (DLC: Madison Papers).
[18] Madison to TJ, 27 May 1789.
[19] *New-York Journal*, 29 June 1790.
[20] Maclay, *Journal*, ed. Maclay, p. 47.

ship in the House, the situation was just the reverse in the Senate. There Maclay was almost alone in supporting the old position against a Senate majority. Going well beyond Madison, he argued that a failure to discriminate violated both the spirit of the treaty with France and the specific terms of its Article V. He warned his colleagues against the danger of French retaliation, but Ellsworth scoffed at such fears and pledged his word that France would never be heard from on the subject. Maclay thought the Senate utterly indifferent to the merits of the argument. Its amendments to the House bill abolishing discrimination he dismissed as villainous.[21] But when the House refused to agree to such amendments the Senate, faced with a formidable opposition in and out of Congress, was obliged to resort to legislative artifice. Embracing the arguments of the opposition as its own, it now declared that a discrimination in tonnage duties in the mild form proposed by Madison was but a trifling compensation for injuries received and that "a bolder stroke at once" should be made. It therefore appointed a committee to draw up a bill that would "effectually cure all disadvantages and carry the remedy to every particular disease and retaliate on every nation, exactly in kind."[22] Nothing more was heard of the bill.

This maneuver, which Maclay accurately saw as a mere strategy to defeat the proposed discrimination, succeeded. It not only undermined Madison's position in the House: it also won over the President. While the bill was under debate, David Stuart had written him that a discrimination in tonnage duties would be highly approved by all save British merchants, but that people were asking what inducement the British could have "to enter into any treaty at all with America, when her commerce is as much favored without one, as that of any nation which has a treaty?"[23] Washington concurred. The failure to make such a discrimination was indeed so contrary to his ideas of justice and policy, he wrote, that he had seriously considered withholding his signature from the bill, being induced to sign it only when assured by some members of the Senate that a more effective measure was being prepared.[24] The character of the assurance as a mere subterfuge was made transparent in the next session, when Madison renewed the contest with such vigor and increased popular support that Jefferson thought success was assured.[25] But again the Senate blocked the way, with such members of the committee of the previous session as Morris, Ellsworth, and King no longer talking of bold retaliation against every nation. The tonnage act of 1790, much to Maclay's wonder, was in large part a repetition of that of the preceding year. Washington signed it apparently without qualms about the new policy that had been introduced, so different from his

21 Same, p. 78.

22 Same, p. 96-7; Madison to TJ, 30 June 1789; SJ, I, 34-5, 36, 37, 38, 41, 53; Setser, *Reciprocity*, p. 106-7.

23 Stuart to Washington, 14 July 1789 (DLC: Washington Papers).

24 Washington to Stuart, 26 July 1789 (Washington, *Writings*, ed. Fitzpatrick, XXX, 363).

25 TJ to Randolph, 30 May 1790; see also Editorial Note to group of documents on American commercial policy, under 18 June 1790.

own views of justice and also from what the eleventh *Federalist* had forecast.[26]

The British merchants trading in America, long used to a discrimination in tonnage and other duties imposed by some states, had little need to protest the "small favor" Madison had proposed for nations in treaty with the United States. Their cause was ably upheld by Americans whose interests were congruent and whose sympathies toward England, like their trade and other connections, had resumed the old channels. The issue far transcended questions of revenue and regulation of commerce, important as these were. It was one which touched the most profound feelings of Americans about themselves, about their government, and about their relation to the two principal powers of Europe. Its outcome sharply and decisively deflected American policy from the path that had been indicated by what Baldwin termed "the happy revolution in politics and commerce." The defeat of Madison's proposal—perhaps as mild an assertion of national dignity and as restrained an effort to induce Great Britain to negotiate on the basis of reciprocity as could have been devised—was the opening thrust of a new system of which the acknowledged protagonist was the Secretary of the Treasury, who by no means shared the President's view that the tonnage act of 1789 was contrary to justice and policy.

The response to Madison's defeat was immediate at home and abroad. In Virginia, even so staunch a Federalist as Edward Carrington found it "incomprehensible" that England should have been placed on the footing of the most favored nation.[27] In England, the ministry was so concerned about the mere raising of the threat of discrimination that it sent a direct and secret warning to those in the government it regarded as friends to the English interest, particularly the Secretary of the Treasury.[28] In France, just before he left Paris, Jefferson received Madison's coded message conveying the disquieting news that the Senate had confirmed Great Britain "in the enjoyment of our trade as she may please to regulate it and France discouraged from her efforts at a competition which it is not less our interest than hers to promote."[29] He responded the next day, predicting that such a measure would place a damper on the extremely friendly dispositions of the National Assembly toward the United States. "To say in excuse that gratitude is never to enter into the motives of national conduct," he wrote, "is to revive a principle which has been buried for centuries with it's kindred principles of the lawfulness of assassination, poison, perjury, &c. All of these were legitimate principles in the dark ages which intervened between antient and modern civilisation, but exploded and held in just horror in the 18th century. . . . Let us hope that our new government will take some other occasion to shew that they mean to proscribe no virtue from the canons of their conduct with other nations. In every other instance [it] . . . has ushered itself to

26 Maclay, *Journal*, ed. Maclay, p. 310; see Vol. 16: 516-17.

27 Carrington to Madison, 12 and 27 May 1789 (DLC: Madison Papers).

28 George Beckwith's report of "Conversations with different persons," enclosed in Dorchester to Grenville, 25 Oct. 1789 (PRO: CO 42/56, f. 278, 280-310; Vol. 17: 52-5).

29 Madison to TJ, 27 May 1789.

the world as honest, masculine and dignified."[30] National honor and dignity, as Madison had pointed out in the very beginning of the debates and as Hamilton had argued in the eleventh *Federalist*, required such a policy. But the tonnage acts signalled a continued acquiescence in the clipping of the wings of American commerce by Great Britain and the beginning of an attitude of coldness toward France, whose dispositions had never been more friendly than at the beginning of her own revolution.

Jefferson's estimate of the French response to this shift in attitude proved to be more accurate than Ellsworth's prediction. Nevertheless, such views continued to be voiced. Even after the representation against the tonnage duties had been made, Hamilton expressed doubt that it was based on serious instructions from the ministry, despite the fact that William Short had given him ample warning about the complaints of French merchants. To this Short added his own fear that the tonnage acts would damage the friendly relations with France, perhaps to the extent of preventing such a general diffusion of American commerce as would make it "less dependent on any particular country."[31] Such observations on policy may not have pleased Hamilton, but the warning was well-grounded. Merchants of Le Havre promptly protested the tonnage duties and late in 1789 the ministry faced the problem. Montmorin, while convinced that the legislation was in conflict with the treaty of commerce, urged restraint upon the merchants. But in 1790 Ruellan of Le Havre sent out two ships, assuming they would be treated as American vessels were in France. He had long been engaged in the tobacco trade, favored by Virginia and Maryland laws that encouraged direct access to the French market. He was therefore vexed to find that his ships were on the same footing in American ports with those of Great Britain. What was even more galling, the new federal regulations required payment of tonnage duties at each port entered. Ruellan's captains paid under protest at Alexandria and Norfolk and the merchant asked the ministry to demand restitution. He also urged retaliation in the form of a similar levy on American ships then in French ports.[32] The result was a sharp division in the ministry.

Montmorin at first was successful in persuading his colleagues that the more prudent course was to open discussions with the United States. The tonnage acts, he declared in his instructions to Otto, violated both the letter and the spirit of the treaty. While such a clear contravention of its terms authorized a similar action by France, the ministry thought it more in keeping with the relations of two friendly allies to make a representation and to request that French vessels be exempt from the duty.[33] These views were set forth in a dispatch expressing friendly assurances and offering congratulations to the President on the brilliant marks of confidence shown by the peo-

---

[30] TJ to Madison, 28 Aug. 1789.

[31] Short to Hamilton, 3 Aug. 1790 (Syrett, *Hamilton*, VI, 517).

[32] La Luzerne to Montmorin, 3 Jan. and 21 Aug. 1790; Lambert to Montmorin, 5 Aug. 1790 (Arch. Aff. Etr., Corr. Pol., E.-U., XXXV; photostats in DLC).

[33] Montmorin to Otto, 10 July 1790 (same).

ple to him and to the new government. Otto's representation was also to be accompanied by the reply of the King to Washington's letter of recall as well as by Montmorin's to Jefferson, both expressing friendship and attachment to the alliance.[34] The French response to the act that placed the ally on the same footing with the former foe was, thus far, both temperate and amicable.

But the clamors of the French mercantile interests could not be stilled. William Short, still assuming that the object of American policy was to promote commerce between the two nations, warned even before learning of the tonnage act of 1790 that the French merchants were especially aroused by the levy imposed for each port entered. "Any example of this kind set by us," he wrote, "will certainly be followed here, as soon as they can find time to attend to their commercial regulations."[35] Moustier, who had so recently been such an enthusiastic advocate of trade with the United States, took the initiative. He regarded the tonnage acts as an imitation of the monopolizing spirit of the English navigation system and as so burdensome to French commerce as to amount to a prohibition. He found it shocking that Congress had paid no attention to its treaty obligations and that, in return for French favors, the United States had seized the first moment of its enjoyment of power over commerce to place France and England on an equal footing. This, he thought, called for retaliation. He therefore proposed that he, Necker, and La Luzerne, together with the deputies of the National Assembly for commerce and colonies, be designated as a committee to draw up a countervailing system of restrictions. He warned that the merchants would not only ask the National Assembly to provide a remedy for the future but would also demand restitution of duties already paid. To insure a real rather than a nominal reciprocity, he proposed that a new treaty of commerce be negotiated.[36]

Montmorin, unable to resist the mounting complaints of the merchants, discussed Moustier's plan with La Luzerne, minister of marine, and Lambert, comptroller general. La Luzerne agreed that it was best to suspend decision until Otto reported the results of his discussions with the Secretary of State. Lambert, whose favorable dispositions toward American trade had been demonstrated in his relations with Jefferson as minister to France, now took up the cause of the clamoring merchants. Montmorin told him bluntly that a demand for restitution of duties paid by Ruellan at Norfolk and Alexandria would be "as impolitic as it is premature."[37] But in the end he was obliged to yield and to instruct Otto to present this claim in addition to the representation against the tonnage acts. The mercantile interests of France, aided by such former friends of American commerce as Moustier and La Luzerne, were demanding and would soon receive the same sort of retaliatory measures that Madison and others in the United States

[34] Montmorin to Otto, 11 Sep. 1790 (same).

[35] Short to TJ, 4 Aug. 1790.

[36] Moustier to Montmorin, 24 July 1790 (Arch. Aff. Etr., Corr. Pol., E.-U., xxxv; photostats in DLC).

[37] Montmorin to La Luzerne and Necker, 6 Aug. 1790; La Luzerne to Montmorin, 21 Aug. 1790; Montmorin to Lambert, 15 Aug. 1790 (same).

had urged as a counterbalance to the mercantilist policies of Great Britain.

Otto, just before acting on his instructions, saw in the President's message to Congress a veiled proposal to give greater protection to American navigation. He considered this to be the wish of the most influential persons in the United States. "It is inconceivable," he added, "that some men, otherwise very informed and sagacious, could persuade themselves that they could push their jealousy of European powers to the highest pitch without experiencing a similar treatment by them. In seeking to engross all, might they not lose all? The desire they manifest of favoring no foreign power, of carrying their own exports and imports, does it not suppose in other nations a default of interest, of feeling, and of dignity that the modern history of Europe does not authorize one to admit? This passion for relating all to themselves is the great although perhaps the only defect in American politics. Mr. Jefferson is no more exempt from it than those who have never seen Europe."[38] The observation, in its failure to discern the nature of divisions already apparent, tells much about the observer.

II

Louis Guillaume Otto, to whom fell the responsibility of presenting his country's case, had known the Secretary of State since 1783, both in France and in the United States. Their relationship was personally cordial and officially correct. When Otto was named *chargé* in 1785, Jefferson welcomed him as a colleague and recommended him to his compatriots as amiable in disposition, always reasonable, and "affectionate to America."[39] The estimate seems just. Otto was friendly to the United States and even ranked it as second in his affections to his country.[40] He was well received and highly regarded in the circles in which he moved. He was elected to the American Philosophical Society and given an honorary doctorate of laws by the College of Providence.[41] Historians have appraised him as an able, informed, discerning, and even astute observer of the American scene.[42] But penetration and intellectual acumen were not listed by Jefferson among Otto's other admirable qualities. The silent omission seems to be sustained by the record.

38 Otto to Montmorin, 10 Dec. 1790 (DLC: Henry Adams Transcripts). All quotations from Otto's dispatches save the epigraph at head of Editorial Note have been translated.

39 TJ to Monroe, 17 June 1785; TJ to Otto, 26 May 1785 (missing); Otto to TJ, 1 June 1785.

40 For biographical information on Louis Guillaume Otto (1754-1817) see *Biographie universelle*; J. P. Mitchell, *St. Jean de Crèvecoeur* (New York, 1916); and Margaret M. O'Dwyer, "A French Diplomat's View of Congress," WMQ, 3rd. ser., XXI (July, 1964), 408-44, the last containing translations of a selection from Otto's dispatches.

41 Otto was elected a member on 19 Jan. 1787; the only meeting he attended was that of 19 Aug. 1791 when TJ escorted him and Ternant (Am. Phil. Soc., *Procs.*, XXII, part III [July, 1885], 147, 195).

42 O'Dwyer considered Otto to be "able and astute," citing other commendatory appraisals by Irving Brant, Samuel E. Morison, and Bradford Perkins (WMQ, 3rd ser., XXI [July, 1964], p. 410n.); DeConde, *Entangling alliance*, p. 168, described him as "capable."

There were no patricians in America, Otto observed, but there were *"gentlemen"* who by reason of wealth, talent, education, family, or place" had risen to preeminence and among whom intimate bonds existed that enabled them to influence affairs.[43] By inclination as well as office the French diplomat gravitated to this social and political elite. In 1787 he married a member of the manorial Livingston family.[44] Perhaps with an eye on ministerial rank, he informed Montmorin that this would multiply his connections with many influential persons, including governors, delegates in Congress, and members of the Federal Convention.[45] Indeed, in this congenial atmosphere Otto was reported already to act as a minister plenipotentiary and to live in the style of a nobleman, with numerous servants and attendants.[46] It is true that he accorded Jefferson first place as a friend of France and came to agree with him that New York seemed more a suburb of London than an American city.[47] Yet this was the environment that he preferred and it was from the confines of this community of wealth, fashion, and position that he viewed the progress of the young republic through several momentous years. Hamilton, Knox, Jay, and other leaders, including certain members of the Senate, were for long his primary and often confidential sources of information about public affairs. It is thus not surprising that Montmorin should have praised Otto for the exactness of his dispatches.[48] The amiable *chargé*, less acute as analyst than as reflector, did submit from his confined vantage point a series of important reports. But much of their value derives from the official intelligence, the partial views, and the sometimes undisclosed aims of his informants, against which he was insufficiently guarded.

In 1786 Otto could report that England had more partisans in America than was supposed, though Henry Knox, who had often discussed the matter with him, saw less possibility of a reunion than ever.[49] He also discovered in this center of commerce that Americans were "governed by that pecuniary interest which ordinarily directs

---

[43] Otto to Vergennes, 10 Oct. 1786 (Arch. Aff. Etr., Corr. Pol., E.-U., XXX; photostats in DLC).

[44] Otto married Elizabeth, daughter of Peter Van Brugh Livingston, early in 1787. She died the same year and her funeral was a public event, the cortege being composed of the governor, members of Congress, and other dignitaries, with flags in the city and harbor at half-staff. On 13 Apr. 1790 Otto married Crèvecoeur's daughter; TJ attended the wedding (Mitchell, *Crèvecoeur*, p. 279-82).

[45] Otto to Montmorin, 19 May 1787 (Arch. Aff. Etr., Corr. Pol., E.-U., XXXII; photostats in DLC).

[46] Cutler, *Manasseh Cutler*, I, 300.

[47] Otto to Montmorin, 12 July 1790 (DLC: Henry Adams Transcripts).

[48] Montmorin to Otto, 31 Aug. 1787 and 26 Feb. 1799 (Arch. Aff. Etr., Corr. Pol., E.-U., XXXIII, photostats in DLC). Nevertheless, in such an example of his reporting as that on the opening of debates in the House of Representatives on the tonnage bill of 1790, Otto was so imprecise as to mislead Montmorin into thinking that the United States had granted an exemption to France (Montmorin to Otto, 13 Nov. 1790, same, XXXV; Otto to Montmorin, 20 May 1790, DLC: Henry Adams Transcripts).

[49] Otto to Vergennes, 4 Dec. 1786 (Arch. Aff. Etr., Corr. Pol., E.-U., XXXII; photostats in DLC).

the politics of a mercantile republic."[50] But, having learned the dangers of democracy, they had been prudent enough to provide in their constitutions "a kind of elective nobility and . . . an elective king."[51] Under the former government they had filled the executive offices with men of proved integrity who guarded financial secrets so well that it was impossible for any malversation to take place—this at a time when Duer, Cutler, Sargent, Platt and others were conducting their operations with official cooperation.[52] So also under the new government, whose administrators understood well the finesse needed to manage a people jealous of their liberty. Thus Henry Knox had deliberately carried the democratic argument against a standing army to such an extreme and had so frightened the people with the specter of a permanent militia as to prepare the public mind for the establishment of a regular army, a proposition that would have been almost unanimously rejected if the administration had had the imprudence to advance it in the first place.[53] As for the Scioto Company, Otto at first was extremely hostile to its efforts to persuade French subjects to give up their homes and seek liberty in an American wilderness. But soon, on information elicited from such informed sources as William Duer and Richard Platt, he reported that the company was doing its utmost to provide the immigrants with food, labor, cabins, and instruction in frontier survival, all at its own expense. On the same basis he also placed blame elsewhere: Joel Barlow, representing the company in Paris, had shown bad faith in failing to make remittances and Robert Morris' agents in France had tried to discredit the Scioto venture so as to benefit his own land speculations. Further, as Otto naively echoed one who enjoyed the confidence of the President, Washington had given his assurance—in secret—that he would extend his own personal protection to the company since its settlements would enhance the value of his own western lands.[54] The *chargé* was so much impressed by the efficient measures of the administration that he was convinced Indian hostilities were no longer to be feared. The troops, in fact, were intended to preserve harmony and restrain the Americans, since it was generally agreed among those in the capital that the frontier settlers were "the scum of mankind and infinitely more ferocious, more perfidious, and more intractable than the savages themselves."[55] Such views of the Scioto Company and of the western inhabitants, reflecting credit upon those who supplied the information and blame on

[50] Otto to Montmorin, 30 Oct. 1789 (DLC: Henry Adams Transcripts).

[51] Otto to Montmorin, 25 Dec. 1789 (same). Otto thought that the tendency of the state and national governments was toward "an elective aristocracy and even a monarchy," since the lower house represented *passion* and the upper house *reason*, so that eventually all of the governments in the United States would "consist of three branches: monarchy, aristocracy, and democracy."

[52] Otto to Vergennes, 10 Feb. 1787 (Arch. Aff. Etr., Corr. Pol., E.-U., XXXII).

[53] Otto accepted without question this supposed legislative manipulation because his informant was none other than Secretary of War Henry Knox (Otto to Montmorin, 20 Jan. 1790; DLC: Henry Adams Transcripts).

[54] Otto to Montmorin, 21 Jan., 11 May, 10 June, 12 Aug., and 12 Nov. 1790; 7 May 1791 (same).

[55] Otto to Montmorin, 20 May 1790 (same).

those at a distance, surely did not originate with the Secretary of State.

Alexander Hamilton, under the indispensable aegis of Washington, was the cabinet officer whose talents most impressed Otto. His genius would restore national credit and, by assuming state debts and fusing all private interests, would achieve his aim of making one consolidated nation out of twelve republics. Otto thought Hamilton's arguments could not be refuted, but, falling back on the opinions of persons expert in such matters, he confessed that it was impossible for him to determine the accuracy of his calculations.[56] He believed the Secretary of the Treasury was doing everything possible to persuade the American people to accept direct taxation and had written for this purpose a series of newspaper articles over the pseudonym *The Observer*.[57] Through his foresight and magic use of the sinking fund he had brought securities almost to par in a few months. Already he was being called "the American *Necker*." As for the debt owed by the United States to France, Hamilton was well aware that many Americans viewed it as a bond between the two countries and would regret to see it pass into other hands. Yet, as Otto discovered in the course of particular interviews on the subject, he certainly intended to transfer the debt to Holland or perhaps even to England. But this was for the laudable and understandable object of obtaining a lower rate of interest —and it was not impossible this could be as low as three percent, given the great increase in American credit.[58] As for Hamilton's views

[56] Otto to Montmorin, 15 Jan. and 12 Aug. 1790 (same).

[57] Otto to Montmorin, 30 Oct. 1789 (same). *The Observer*, author of a series of eighteen pieces on credit and taxes printed in the *Gazette of the United States*, 28 Oct. 1789—17 Feb. 1790, as taken from *The American Mercury* (Hartford), was certainly not Hamilton (Jeremiah Wadsworth to Alexander Hamilton, 17 Dec. 1789, Syrett, *Hamilton*, VI, 15, 16n.).

[58] Otto to Montmorin, 30 Oct. 1789; 15 Jan., 24 June, 24 and 25 Dec. 1790 (DLC: Henry Adams Transcripts). In the first of these dispatches Otto reported on a "particularly embarrassing" approach by Hamilton to Moustier on the question of the debt to France: "Mr. Hamilton . . . had sent a confidential note to Moustiers informing him that the principal object of the next session of Congress would be the arrangement of finances and inquiring whether his Majesty was disposed to give a new proof of his generosity by renouncing for five or six years the partial reimbursements stipulated by the two contracts and meanwhile accept regular payments of interest due or falling due. Moustiers had responded that, if this request were to be made officially, he thought it would be received favorably and that he would be able to give the American government information of it certainly soon after his arrival" in France. This response, Otto reported, had given much satisfaction, but the debates in the National Assembly had raised alarm in America. He was convinced the "heads of American finance" intended to transfer the debt to Holland. Moustier informed Otto privately that he had reported Hamilton's confidential inquiry and believed that the favor would be granted. Otto announced this to Hamilton: "He received this information with gratitude and began to dwell on the natural ties which exist between France and the United States, ties which necessarily would become stronger because of the proofs of generosity and attachment which France never ceased to provide." Otto, who had once believed that the debt was the only dependable bond between the two countries and who now suspected Hamilton of wishing to transfer it to obtain lower interest charges, took this moment to raise the question. Hamilton responded with such "incoherence and vagueness" as to confirm his suspicions (Otto to Montmorin, 28 Aug. 1788, Arch. Aff. Etr., Corr. Pol., E.-U., XXXIII; photostats in DLC; Otto to Montmorin, 24 June 1790, DLC: Henry Adams Transcripts).

toward France, there could be no doubt that he, like all members of the President's cabinet, was strongly predisposed toward that nation and deeply imbued with the necessity of maintaining amicable relations. He had told the *chargé* in one of his interviews that he was attached to the alliance, that the bonds between the two countries were natural, and that these ties would be strengthened. Otto was convinced of his sincerity.[59]

Otto's view of the tone and character of the administration also reflected the position of Hamilton and Knox in the cabinet and of those members of the Senate with whom he was on terms of confidentiality. From this vantage point the administration was above all one of united councils—this at a time when even so casual and imperceptive a visitor as Count Andriani was able to discern the political differences that existed—and it was also moderate, elevated, effective, and "one of the most virtuous and most active that has perhaps ever existed."[60] Otto perceived a vast difference between its character and that of the Congress. While the administration was united in cherishing the French alliance as the foundation stone of American independence and possessed extended and even noble aims, its good intentions were at times almost nullified by the legislative branch, composed for the most part of men given to intrigue whose sole object was to advance their personal interests and to cultivate popularity by shifting the burdens of the people to foreigners.[61] Over this government Washington presided, adding luster to its unassailable virtue and giving to its proceedings such a pure and universal confidence as no citizen of a free country had ever enjoyed. In his early morning inspections of his household and of all bureaus of government, he left domestic and civil servants with the conviction that nothing escaped his penetration and vigilance. After the first session of Congress, he required all departments to supply him with plans and proposals for the next, which would decide the fate of the union.[62] Thus the President, aware that it was almost impossible for legislators to be sufficiently informed in all of the grand operations of government, introduced the practice of having heads of departments draft proposals which he sent to Congress on his own initiative, leaving to that body the function of discussion and enactment.[63] Endowed with the attributes of a sovereign and venerated as such, Washington also accepted the burdens of monarchy. The Society of the Cincinnati had resolved to celebrate his birthday annually in order to make him resemble in everything the king of England.[64] He was a perfect judge of men and so the strange choice of his secretaries, none of whom was esteemed, was thought to arise from his wish to convince the public that he did everything himself, with none other holding the pen or the staff of command. Nor was he content merely to set the example of zeal, promptness, and

[59] Otto to Montmorin, 24 June and 28 Sep. 1790 (same).
[60] Otto to Montmorin, 12 Aug. 1790 (same).
[61] Otto to Montmorin, 28 Sep. 1790 (same).
[62] Otto to Montmorin, 14 Nov. 1789; 12 and 20 Jan., 31 Mch., 10 and 13 June, 12 July, 12 Aug., 28 Sep., 10 and 12 Dec. 1790 (same).
[63] Otto to Montmorin, 12 and 20 Jan. 1790 (same).
[64] Otto to Montmorin, 31 Mch. 1790 (same).

exactitude in the conduct of public office. When, for instance, Jefferson arrived in Virginia instead of New York and displayed no readiness to report upon his long mission in France or to accept the post to which he had been appointed, Washington immediately dispatched an express commanding him to repair to the capital "without even giving him time to see his plantations in Virgina."[65] He seemed in all things, Otto concluded, "to wish to resemble Caesar, whose *Commentaries* are constantly on his table. But in some respects he transcends his model and the public scarcely notices some little blemishes which humanity has left on one of its masterpieces and which the American patriot likes to cover with a thick veil."[66]

It is difficult not to regard such views of Washington and his administration as derivative in large part from the Secretary of the Treasury, who considered Caesar to be one of the greatest figures of history. So also with Otto's observations about the signs of an emerging opposition in the southern states, whose reserved powers—a defect that the framers of the Constitution had not been able to attack openly— left a vast area in which "those petty little tyrants" could obstruct the best efforts of the administration.[67] It is especially difficult not to associate Hamilton with Otto's immediate access to the closely guarded secret of Humphrey's mission or with the mistaken explanation of the agency undertaken by Gouverneur Morris. When, to the discomfiture of Hamilton and his supporters, Washington divulged the latter secret, Otto's report placed the responsibility for originating the mission squarely upon Robert Morris. The Secretary of the Treasury had taken the lead in urging that an agent be sent to London and that Gouverneur Morris be chosen for it, whereas, so far as the evidence reveals, Robert Morris was not even consulted about the matter, much less being its originator. The report submitted by Otto to his government also included a characterization of Gouverneur Morris which coincided in its essentials with that given by Hamilton to Washington a few months earlier.[68] It seems equally probable that Hamilton was the source of Otto's information—obtained a full month before the report proposing a national bank was submitted to the House of Representatives—that this institution would undoubtedly be

---

[65] Otto to Montmorin, 10 Dec. 1790 (same). The message Otto alluded to was not sent by express and, of course, was quite different in tone from what his informants wished him to think (Washington to TJ, 30 Nov. 1790; see also Washington to TJ, 21 Jan. 1790, the letter which was sent by express). In the same climate of opinion the public address to TJ by the Virginia House of Delegates (*Gazette of the United States*, 2 Jan. 1790) brought unfavorable comparison with that to Washington by the legislature of New York. "These addresses," Otto wrote, "are of great importance in giving distinction to the principal personages. But in order to make them more effective it would perhaps be prudent if they were employed with less prodigality." TJ's merits and services were very great, he said, but more gradations should be placed between "the respect due the head of state and that shown to a servant of the public" (Otto to Montmorin, 12 Jan. 1790, same).

[66] Otto to Montmorin, 13 June 1790 (same).

[67] Otto to Montmorin, 1 Nov. 1790 (same).

[68] Otto to Montmorin, 6 and 10 Mch. 1791. On Hamilton's characterization of Gouverneur Morris in comments made to Beckwith and to Washington, see Editorial Note to documents on the war crisis of 1790 (Vol. 17: 96-102).

established at Philadelphia; that, to judge of the general dispositions of the government, its operations would be intimately connected with those of the bank; and that soon the two would be so interconnected as to render one unable to subsist without the other.[69] The general dispositions of the government as to such an agency cannot have included the views of the Secretary of State, but they certainly represented those of the creator of the Bank of the United States, who regarded it as "a political machine of the greatest importance to the State."[70]

The French *chargé*, of course, sought to inform rather than mislead his government. Nor did the restricted vantage point from which he reported on American affairs entirely warp his perspective. He was not uncritical of the Secretary of the Treasury, especially after Madison opened the debate on his funding plan.[71] He also firmly opposed the Secretary of State on the question of the consular appointments to the French West Indies, while at the same time paying full tribute to him as a declared friend of France. A few days after Jefferson assumed office, Otto gave this appraisal of his public posture:[72]

> Mr. Jefferson . . . has already given a public proof of his modesty and of his good dispositions towards France. The citizens of Alexandria having publicly thanked him for the commercial advantages he had obtained from our Government, he replied: 'Truth and candor oblige me to declare that you owe these encouragements *only* to the friendly dispositions of a nation which, on all occasions, has shown itself ready to adopt measures which could strengthen the reciprocal bonds of interest and friendship.' In no instance does Mr. Jefferson disavow these sentiments. In respect to resources, wealth, science, friendliness, and good dispositions toward Americans, he puts France above all other nations and he never wearies in praising her or in drawing true and lively pictures of Britain's prejudices, of her pride and vainglory, and of her animosity towards Americans. In accepting the post of Secretary of State, Mr. Jefferson acceded to the will of the President and the public rather

[69] Otto to Montmorin, 15 Nov. 1790 (DLC: Henry Adams Transcripts). These views were set forth in a discussion about the permanent residence. Otto concluded that the capital could never be removed to the Potomac because of the bank and that this helped explain southern opposition to the bill—a view elaborated at length by John Meyer, Hamilton's clerk ("Memoirs of the Life of Alexander Hamilton" by John Meyer, DLC: Hamilton Papers). Since Otto was in New York at this time and Hamilton in Philadelphia, it is likely that Otto's information came indirectly from Schuyler or others whom Hamilton consulted about his report—as he did, for example, with Robert Morris and Thomas FitzSimons (Hamilton to Morris, 9 Nov. 1790, Syrett, *Hamilton*, VII, 146). During the debates on the bank bill and just after Madison's speech of two and a half hours against it, Théophile Cazenove reported that "those who desire that the seat of government be on the Potomac are united against the Bank." This, he said, had united "the opposite party" and he predicted that the bill would pass. Cazenove was on friendly terms with Hamilton and may have been reflecting his views (Cazenove to his principals, 5 Feb. 1791, Cazenove Letterbook).
[70] Hamilton's Report on a National Bank was submitted on 14 Dec. 1790 (same, VII, 305-42, at p. 329).
[71] Otto to Montmorin, 1 and 30 Mch. 1791 (DLC: Henry Adams Transcripts).
[72] Otto to Montmorin, 31 Mch. 1790 (same).

than follow his own inclination, which was to return to France. He has made his first appearance here with the simplicity of a true Republican. His modesty and his amiability have won the hearts of those who have seen him for the first time, while confirming the esteem of his old friends. Of all Americans who have been to France, Mr. Jefferson, after Dr. Franklin, is the only one who frankly shows the gratitude for the civilities accorded him there. These feelings are all the more gratifying, Sir, as the most influential persons place great confidence in him and think that if the United States had the misfortune to lose the President, the Secretary of State would be more likely to succeed him than any other. . . . Mr. Jefferson, like all southerners, is republican in mind and heart, and also expresses more gratitude than is generally the case in a free country. We thus have reason to felicitate ourselves on seeing at the head of foreign affairs a man so just and helpful as Mr. Jefferson, and I believe that on all occasions we can rely on his friendship.

Otto's esteem for the Secretary of State remained constant, but it is clear that their relationship was not one of intimacy. During the debates on the tonnage act of 1790, Otto seemed quite unaware of the part that Jefferson and Madison played. He was in fact convinced that the amendment to exempt nations in treaty with the United States was offered only in order to defeat the measure.[73] He was concerned enough to initiate a formal discussion of the consular appointments for San Domingo and Martinique, but not to make an official matter of the tonnage question, despite his belief that the failure to grant an exemption collided with the treaty of commerce.[74] Instead, he expressed his views in private and, so far as his dispatches reveal, derived his information about legislative intent from those Senators with whom he was in the habit of conversing. Later, on receiving Montmorin's instructions to take up the matter officially, he explained that his protest of the similar acts of New Hampshire and Massachusetts in 1785 had made him reluctant to raise the question. But that experience served chiefly to indicate how much he had been impressed by the political environment in which he moved.[75] It had also helped prepare him for something less than full understanding of the views of the Secretary of State. As much concerned about the enterprising spirit of American commerce as any European cabinet minister, Otto regarded the United States as the mercantile rival of all other nations.

[73] Otto to Montmorin, 28 Sep. 1790 (same).
[74] Otto to Montmorin, 6 June 1790 (same).
[75] Otto to Montmorin, 28 Sep. 1790 (same). In reporting the failure of the Senate to admit the discriminating clause, Otto informed Montmorin that he had upheld the French case in private conversations and would await instructions. "The case," he added, "is entirely similar to the one in 1786 in which by order of the Court I demanded and obtained the revocation of the laws of New Hampshire and Massachusetts" (Otto to Montmorin, 12 Aug. 1790, same). Since this was so, Otto's explanation of his failure to initiate a formal move—that mercantile interests had prevented a modification of the state laws and that their repeal had caused the English consul to thank him for services rendered his nation—appears contrived and was certainly defensive. It also reflects Otto's New York perspective on actions taken in New Hampshire and Massachusetts.

Like Moustier, he was moving perceptibly away from the idea of reciprocity and toward a system of retaliation.[76] In this respect, since he understood his own nation better than he did the American republic and its divided councils, his predictions about future commercial relations proved to be well founded.

Thus the most conspicuous characteristic of the dispatches of this amiable French diplomat, from the beginning of the new government to the end of the First Congress, is their reflection of views derived not from the Secretary of State with whom his business lay but from those quarters supporting the policies of the Secretary of the Treasury, who himself had a leading part in creating such impressions. This is not surprising. The dispositions of the government as reflected by Otto are consonant with the differing styles of official conduct of Alexander Hamilton and Thomas Jefferson. In his ambition to gain a dominant influence over policy, Hamilton had not hesitated to carry on private and confidential discussions with the agent George Beckwith, as he would later with the British minister, intervening secretly and divisively in matters within the province of the Department of State.[77] It is therefore understandable that, immediately on taking office, he should have initiated confidential conversations with Moustier and later with Otto about the United States debt to France. It was also characteristic that he should have sought to convince the official representatives of France of his and the entire administration's unswerving loyalty to the alliance—at the same time that he covertly revealed to the agent of Great Britain his ultimate goal of destroying it.[78] It was equally characteristic that Jefferson, while maintaining cordial personal relations with Otto, should have been officially reserved with him as he later was with Ternant, withholding comment on the position of the government until it had been defined and defending it thereafter with fidelity. Having publicly avowed his friendship for France and his gratitude for her commercial concessions, he had no need to dissimulate or engage in confidential and unofficial exchanges with her representative. He also kept at a distance because his tastes and interests differed markedly from those of the *chargé*. In the spring and summer of 1790, with Otto maintaining his accustomed style of living, Jefferson took one brief glimpse of the social and political attitudes of a city "steeped in Anglicism" and then withdrew. He lived, wrote Otto's father-in-law, in a mean house in Maiden Lane and confined himself to official duties because he disliked the stiff style and etiquette of New York. Otto himself had the courtesy to regard this rather as true republican simplicity.[79]

But there would come a time, as the discussions on the tonnage

[76] Otto to Montmorin, 4 Aug. 1790 (same).

[77] See Editorial Note to group of documents on the war crisis of 1790, under 12 July 1790.

[78] For comment on Hamilton's contradictory statements to Ternant and to Beckwith concerning the French alliance and on TJ's reserved attitude toward Ternant, see Editorial Note to group of documents on commercial and diplomatic relations with Great Britain, under 15 Dec. 1790.

[79] St. Jean de Crèvecoeur to William Short, ca. 15 July 1790 (DLC: Short Papers); Otto to Montmorin, 31 Mch. 1790 (DLC: Henry Adams Transcripts).

question brought on a confrontation of far greater import at the close of the first Congress, when Jefferson deemed it imperative to speak to the *chargé* with less reserve and to provide him with another view of American political realities.

III

Determined to remain in New York City until he received directions for removing the legation to the seat of government, Otto was still there when Montmorin's instructions on the tonnage acts arrived about the first of December. Since this was obligatory, he immediately set out for Philadelphia to confer with the Secretary of State and also— as his orders did not require—to probe "the dispositions of the most influential members of both houses of Congress."[80] He arrived just at the opening of the session. His analysis of the President's annual message, his account of the reaction to the French tributes to Franklin, his view of the "haughty republicanism" of Philadelphia, his opinion that the endurance of the government depended on the life of Washington, his belief that Jefferson concurred in the aim of seeking a much higher scale of duties to protect American navigation—all indicated that, up to the moment of opening the discussions, Otto continued to receive his impressions from the accustomed quarters.[81] Having reported such views to the ministry, he then met with the Secretary of State. At Jefferson's suggestion, the interview took place at his residence, not at the departmental offices.[82]

Montmorin's instructions required that the claim be presented in friendly terms, as befitted an ally. Otto made the effort, but his own style of diplomacy intervened. He began by pointing out that he had refrained from questioning the tonnage duties until required to do so. Jefferson himself knew at first hand, he said, that his government had manifested its friendly dispositions in commercial matters, especially in respect to trade with the islands and in spite of strong protests from mercantile interests. Having observed that the Confederation, weak as it was, had interceded to obtain the repeal of the tonnage acts of New Hampshire and Massachusetts, it was all the more surprised to find Congress imposing such duties in violation of the treaty it had upheld as against inferior legislatures. Nevertheless, it was not seeking favors—it was only requesting an exemption clearly stated in the treaty. To this Otto added a blunt warning. The United States was naturally expected to meet its contractual obligations but, beyond this, it should be extremely circumspect with regard to its engagements to France because of the prevailing situation in the realm and the influence that commercial interests would undoubtedly have on its legislation.

"Mr. Jefferson," Otto reported to Montmorin, "affected to be surprised with this opening and not to recall Article V of the treaty." He

[80] Otto to Montmorin, 12 Dec. 1790 (same).
[81] Otto to Montmorin, 10 and 12 Dec. 1790 (same).
[82] Otto said that he wrote on arrival in Philadelphia asking for an interview and that TJ in reply asked him to come to his residence. Neither letter has been found and neither is recorded in SJL.

had been absent when the act of 1789 was passed, he said, but all reports had led him to believe the Congress disposed to grant exemption to French vessels, not because of treaty obligations but from simple motives of attachment. This desire, however, had been frustrated for a number of reasons, particularly the inconvenience of being exposed to the claims of the Dutch and other nations in treaty with the United States. "As for the French merchants," Jefferson replied to Otto's warning, "I know from certain information that they only enjoy influence in the National Assembly because they are needed to maintain a majority, but that in a short while after the revolution their influence will fall, because in such a country as France the landed interest must always dominate that of commerce." This astonished Otto, who tried without success to persuade the Secretary of State of his error. Indeed Jefferson went further and declared that the discussion over tonnage would never have taken place if the French ministry had listened to his proposition "*to make a reciprocal naturalization of the citizens of the two nations.*" Otto's retort to this far-reaching exercise of the treaty power—which Jefferson had indeed advanced as a serious proposition—was tinged with sarcasm.[83] The plan would no doubt have been adopted, he replied, if the United States had possessed a sugar island as rich as San Domingo and as near to France as it was to North America. Jefferson grasped the meaning perfectly, Otto reported, but persisted in his illusory belief that French restrictions on trade with the colonies would be removed and that Americans would be able to send flour directly to San Domingo instead of by way of Bordeaux. "There is nothing more bizarre," he exclaimed, "than to impose this circuitous and costly detour on a necessary article of food. The prosperity of your colonies depends on an immediate change. This would bring a low cost of subsistence, which in turn would cause the population and the productivity of San Domingo to double. If you fear that we might export your sugar, our government would undertake to see that our merchants do not bring in any of that contraband commodity. In concert with your consuls, we would be careful to execute such laws as might be made on the subject."

To Jefferson's effort to enlarge the subject of discussion, Otto replied that he had received no instructions on the matter and was absolutely ignorant as to the principles of colonial regulation the new regime might adopt. His own private opinion had always been that distant possessions could interest France only when they yielded advantages proportionate to costs. He had often heard a very different kind of doctrine advanced in the United States, but the arguments used to support it had left him unconvinced. Otto himself then brought up another topic. The recent consular appointments to the French islands appeared to him contrary to accepted principles and, he believed, would produce a disagreeable sensation in France. During the course

[83] Otto to Montmorin (DLC: Henry Adams Transcripts; emphasis in original). TJ made his proposal to Vergennes in the discussion of the tonnage acts of New Hampshire and Massachusetts. Privately to Adams he advanced a much more general proposition (Vergennes to TJ, 30 Oct. 1785; TJ to Vergennes, 20 Nov. 1785; TJ to Adams, 28 July 1785, enclosure).

of the conversation, Otto informed Montmorin, he had felt it necessary to disabuse the Secretary of State of an error he shared with many Americans—"that when France achieves tranquillity, the new legislature will accord to foreigners the liberty of an unlimited commerce; that it will open the ports of its colonies without distinction; and that in a true cosmopolitan fashion it will treat all the world as brothers."[84] The error was genuine enough but Jefferson, having experienced at first hand the weight of mercantile influence on the politics of France, was less confident that the French landed interest would decide future policy than Otto believed him to be.

With this parting exchange the interview came to a close, having lasted just an hour. The next day Otto sent to the Secretary of State the written representation as requested.[85] In this he paraphrased Montmorin's instructions but, as his own personal admonition, he also added that his government could indeed have brought about a reciprocity of tonnage duties if it had not chosen first to make a representation of the matter. Such an opening of the official discussion was worthy of Gouverneur Morris, whose conversations with the Duke of Leeds six months earlier so closely paralleled it both in matter and in style. Otto did both Jefferson and Washington the justice to say that, had it depended on them, France would enjoy in the United States everything stipulated by treaty and also some advantages granted as favor. But, forgetting the role he had previously assigned to the President as initiator of legislation, Otto now reported him to be so strictly confined to the mere execution of laws as to be scarcely permitted an opinion of his own. He thought the Secretary of State even more closely circumscribed. In France, Jefferson could and often did employ the language dictated by his affections, but now he was imprisoned by legislators concerned only with the immediate interests of their constituents, who were little disposed to respect treaties or bonds of friendship. Clearly, as viewed through the single lens provided by Otto, this was an exchange of diplomatic formality without a trace of evidence that any political confidences had been extended by the Secretary of State. Otto's impression of him and of the dispositions of the government as seen from his accustomed vantage point had not changed. As soon as he dispatched the official note, he hastened back to the congenial environment of New York, there to remain for most of this crucial session of Congress.[86]

---

84 Otto to Montmorin, 13 Dec. 1790 (DLC: Henry Adams Transcripts).

85 See Document I.

86 TJ having informed him that Moustier, assigned to Berlin, would not return to the United States, Otto explained that he felt it necessary to terminate the discussions at once and prepare for whatever change might be made in the legation. His dispatch following the brief trip to Philadelphia was devoted to high praise for Hamilton's report on a national bank: "The reputation of Mr. Hamilton has never been so well established since the publication of this report, which has been read with avidity by all classes of citizens" (Otto to Montmorin, 24 Dec. 1790, DLC: Henry Adams Transcripts). He was equally extravagant in his admiration for Hamilton's use of the sinking fund to raise the value of public securities by buying at the price asked rather than at market value. But he had a sharp exchange with Tench Coxe, whom he described as the "first assistant and right arm of Mr. Hamilton." When Coxe suggested that in the

It is obvious that Jefferson purposely delayed his response. Its timing and nature would depend upon the consultations he wished to have first with Madison, then with the Secretary of the Treasury, and finally with the President. He was also at the moment engaged in his report on Morris' fruitless mission and he could scarcely have failed to discern the favorable opportunity thus presented to connect the two matters for strategic purposes, as Hamilton and others later and with good reason suspected him of doing. Perhaps to gain time, he asked Otto whether exemption from the *petit cabotage* in France, as stipulated in the treaty, applied only to vessels of the United States.[87] This not only confirmed Otto in his belief that the discussions would be deliberately prolonged: it also convinced him that Jefferson was adroitly seeking grounds for defense in case Congress persisted in refusing an exemption of tonnage duties to French vessels. Otto declared these suspicions to Montmorin in explicit terms. In the face of such a subterfuge, he was unwilling to furnish an opponent with arms that would later be used to attack him. He therefore had confined his reply to the letter, the sense, and the expressed intent of Article V of the treaty. For the same reason he had not touched upon a sort of hidden impost that he regarded as an equally reprehensible violation of its terms.[88]

It was just at this moment that Otto, all of his suspicions at the alert, received new orders directing him to ask restitution of duties paid by the merchant Ruellan.[89] This fortuitous development seemed to present an excellent opportunity for forcing the Secretary of State to abandon any dilatory tactics he might have conceived. Otto therefore acted at once and presented in almost peremptory terms the demand that Montmorin had regarded as both impolitic and premature. Interest no less than justice, he wrote, should cause the United States to exempt French vessels. The mounting protests, he warned again, could bring on reprisals that would bear more heavily on American ships than on those of France. Further delay on this important matter—the hint betrayed his desire to let his suspicions be known to Jefferson as well as to Montmorin—would only augment mercantile clamors for a remedy. Otto concluded with a hope that was virtually a stipulation —that he be given a response satisfactory to his government and that this be done before the departure of the packetboat, scheduled for the end of the month.[90] The blunt demand for restitution, the reiterated

---

coming year the United States hoped to make a general refunding of the foreign debt, to set a unique example of rectitude and fidelity in meeting engagements, and thus to repay the generosity of France to America in her hour of need, Otto replied to this "false magnanimity" with chilling dignity (Otto to Montmorin, 25 Dec. 1790, same).

[87] See Document II. Montmorin expected TJ to raise this question.

[88] Otto thought the change in the impost act from a 10 percent discount favoring American vessels to a 10 percent surcharge on duties paid by foreign vessels was a disguised tonnage duty (Otto to Montmorin, 6 Jan. 1791, DLC: Henry Adams Transcripts). See Document IV.

[89] Montmorin to Otto, 10 July and 11 Sep. 1790 (Arch. Aff. Etr., Corr. Pol., E.-U., xxxv; photostats in DLC); Otto to Montmorin, 6 Jan. 1791 (DLC: Henry Adams Transcripts).

[90] See Document V.

warning of retaliation, the insistence upon an immediate and favorable response were thoroughly characteristic of Otto's manner of carrying on a negotiation. Again the comparison with Gouverneur Morris seems inescapable. Both emissaries appeared to find the role of adversary more congenial than that of diplomat. Both seemed more concerned to impress a superior with detailed accounts of ripostes and rebuttals than in reaching an accommodation. Both were engaged in matters touching the commercial policy of the new government that fell simultaneously into the hands of the Secretary of State.[91] For him this was a fortunate circumstance. The ministry's support of Ruellan may have seemed impolitic and premature to Montmorin at Versailles, but to Jefferson at Philadelphia the demand could scarcely have been received at a more opportune moment. Its language was as exactly suited to his purpose as if it had been deliberately contrived with that end in view.

When this second and more emphatic note arrived, Jefferson had already had the advantage of close and confidential discussions with Madison in their effort to concert executive and legislative action. Unfortunately, less is known of their collaboration at this time than during the years when an ocean separated them. But the single document concerning their deliberations on the tonnage question makes it abundantly clear that, from the beginning, Jefferson's strategy was to aim directly at the Senate and particularly at those in that body whom the British ministry as well as William Maclay regarded as spokesmen for the British interest. There is no reason to suppose that Madison was not in full agreement with this plan, for the "mercantile Senators" and their supporters had been the chief obstacle to his own efforts in previous sessions to enact the kind of legislation called for by Hamilton in the eleventh *Federalist*. To achieve his object Jefferson deliberately chose to submit to Washington a report instead of a draft of a reply to Otto, since he could have no assurance that the latter would be laid before the Senate. By drafting a report ostensibly for the eyes of Washington alone but actually for the attention of such men as Ellsworth, King, Schuyler, and Morris, he would be able both to "speak without reserve" and to fortify his arguments about the value of American trade with France.[92] More important, this would endow his words with the immense weight of the President's official and personal influence. The thrust that Jefferson gave to the draft of a covering message from the President to the Senate was even bolder. This document, adding strength to the report by its enclosure of copies of the French decrees granting commercial favors to the United States, was far from being a routine note of transmittal. It was a categorical request for advice in the conduct of foreign affairs that could not be

91 For comment on Gouverneur Morris as diplomat see Editorial Note to documents on the war crisis of 1790 (Vol. 17: 96-102). See also Washington to TJ, 19 June 1790; Document I in grouped documents on commercial and diplomatic relations with Great Britain, under 15 Dec. 1790; Bemis, *Jay's Treaty*, p. 66-9, 84-5.

92 See Document III. It is evident from this letter, however, that Madison was inclined to accept the French position. TJ feared the consequences of such a construction—that is, that other nations might claim most-favored-nation treatment.

evaded. Would the Senate, the message asked, consider the matter and enable the President to give such a response as would "best comport with the justice and the interests of the United States"?[93] Jefferson's strategy, then, was to place the issue squarely up to the body that until now had proved itself to be so sensitive to warnings of commercial reprisal from England and so indifferent to friendly overtures from France. But would Washington agree to lay the report before the Senate? Would he do so by asking such a direct and unavoidable question?

Before facing this formidable hurdle, Jefferson paid a silent but eloquent tribute to the influence of Hamilton by seeking his concurrence. If the Secretary of the Treasury could be convinced that it was good policy to make some friendly gesture to France, the difficulty of persuading the President and especially the recalcitrant members of the Senate would be vastly diminished. No text or record of any written communication from Jefferson to Hamilton submitting the draft report for his consideration is known to exist. Presumably, then, the effort to achieve unity in the cabinet on this issue was initiated in a personal interview. Given the fundamentally different convictions of the two men about the controlling principles of government, the effort was foredoomed to failure. On this issue they were agreed only in their legal interpretation of the treaty obligation. But in rejecting Jefferson's suggestion that a solution not required by treaty might be provided by legislation, Hamilton argued that there was "a want of reciprocity in the thing itself . . . in a circumstance which materially affects the general policy of our navigation system."[94] Assuming an agreement on policy that was in fact belied by his answer, he failed to define the nature of the American navigation system or to indicate the legal basis of its existence. But he rejected the proposal on the ground that the national interest could be made to suffer because more American than French vessels were involved in trade between the two countries.

Jefferson received this negative response on the 12th of January. It was on that very evening that Otto's brusque demand for restitution of duties arrived from New York, employing precisely the same argument of national interest to which Hamilton had appealed. France, Otto hinted in his reiterated warning, had it in her power to compel reciprocity and in that case the United States would suffer most because her vessels greatly outnumbered those of France in the trade between the two countries. The argument was so apt and its tone so threatening that Jefferson sent it to Hamilton immediately, without waiting to have it translated for the President. His covering note, a final effort to achieve agreement in the cabinet, put the issue to the Secretary of the Treasury just as his draft of the President's message did to the Senate. Could Hamilton suggest any better mode of dealing with a matter likely to become serious?[95] Jefferson, of course, made no allusion to Otto's unwitting use of Hamilton's argument to support a contrary conclusion. But this unexpected assistance from the *chargé*

93 See Document X.
94 See Document VI.
95 See Documents V and VII.

made no difference. In his second and equally negative response to Jefferson's appeal for cooperation, Hamilton fell back on innuendo. Discounting the genuineness of the demand, he expressed doubt that Otto had acted on serious instructions from the ministry and suggested that, on the contrary, his representation was a mere expedient to gain advantage at a time when the subject of navigation was being discussed in Congress.[96] The implication was almost as pointed as if Hamilton had named Jefferson and Madison as manipulators of Otto, employing such tactics as he himself had used and would continue to use with representatives of both France and Great Britain.

Hamilton's response revealed his posture as well as his suspicions. In this, his first unequivocal alignment with views of policy enunciated in the first session by Laurance and other friends of the British connection, the Secretary of the Treasury repeated their familiar arguments—professions of belief in unrestricted trade with all the world and warnings about commercial and other forms of warfare. He could offer no solution except to suggest a new treaty with France that would "extend reciprocal advantages and fix them on a permanent basis."[97] This, like his later restatement of the proposal to Ternant, could have deceived no one. Jefferson could scarcely have deluded himself with the hope that the Senate, which only a few days earlier had turned its back on friendly overtures from France involving nothing more than ceremony, would sanction a treaty of enlarged commercial advantages such as Hamilton professed to favor.

But the attempt to achieve unity in the cabinet had at least defined the unyielding reality of the breach. Perceiving its true nature, Jefferson rested his case on the fulcrum of the European balance of power. France was not only an ally and a valuable consumer of American produce: she paid for it in hard money which the American people then poured "into the coffers of their enemies."[98] This, not the relatively trivial amount of tonnage duties, was the crux of the matter and it involved immense political as well as economic consequences for the United States. Five years earlier Jefferson had employed the same line of reasoning with Vergennes.[99] But arguments that were persuasive with the French ministry lacked the power to convince in the American cabinet. Hamilton, so his language declared, was opposed to any measure which might "lead to commercial warfare with *any* power."[100] The favor to France, he thought, might be taken by others as proofs of an unfriendly temper. Here he spoke from experience born of the British ministry's emphatic warnings of 1789 against discrimination.[101] But he also spoke without sufficient regard for the implication of his words. For at the heart of Otto's protest was its overt warning of

[96] See Document VIII.

[97] See Document VIII; on Hamilton's suggestion of a new treaty in his interview with Ternant, see Editorial Note to group of documents on commercial and diplomatic relations with Great Britain, under 15 Dec. 1790.

[98] See Document IX.

[99] TJ to Vergennes, 15 Aug. 1785.

[100] Emphasis supplied.

[101] Document VIII. On Beckwith's warning in 1789, see Editorial Note to group of documents on war crisis of 1790 (Vol. 17: 52-5).

retaliation. The threat of reprisal, long since predicted by Jefferson and more recently by Short, had now become a reality because of the tonnage acts of 1789 and 1790. What Hamilton's response meant, therefore, is not to be found in the language employed but in the attitudes thus inadvertently revealed. What these attitudes proclaimed in flat contradiction of the words was that the threat of French retaliation leading possibly to commercial warfare was one that could be accepted with equanimity, not only without concern but without the slightest effort to alleviate resentment. The commercial warfare to be dreaded was not that with "any power" but only that with Great Britain. The disclosure may have been inadvertent but it was also unmistakably clear.

With these two rejections of Jefferson's appeals, Hamilton buried with finality the doctrines of the eleventh *Federalist* and stood forth at last as the leader of those in the Senate who, long since, had consigned them to oblivion. Having good reason to fear that the appeal would fail, Jefferson may in fact have intended to force into open view such a glaring discrepancy between professed policies and undisclosed partialities, both within the hidden councils of the administration and behind the closed doors of the Senate. There is no evidence that Jefferson revealed his exchange with Hamilton to the President and it may be safely assumed that he did not.

IV

It would have been surprising indeed if Hamilton had not suspected that Otto was brought forward at this expedient moment on leading strings held by the Secretary of State. For when Washington adopted without revision Jefferson's draft of the message to the Senate on the tonnage issue, fortune was beginning to smile on the converging lines of strategy devised by Jefferson and Madison to achieve a navigation bill. George Beckwith as well as Hamilton and his supporters in the Senate suspected the two matters were purposely connected.[102] Other and less calculated developments did nothing to dispel the suspicions.

Late in January Jefferson received from William Short as apt and effective an argument on the French tonnage claims as if the Secretary of State had himself shaped the dispatch—as indeed, in a sense, he did. Some in the National Assembly, Short reported, thought the United States so attached to England that it was futile for France to encourage American trade. Others, citing the impost and tonnage acts and complaining bitterly about being placed on the same footing with England, believed the decrees favoring tobacco and oil had not been met with reciprocal advantages. In reporting these increasing signs of hostility, Short also indicated how France could attract American exports to the extent of about ninety million livres annually and, in doing so, pay for the greater part of it in manufactures on

---

[102] Document x. The supposition that Washington had asked TJ to report on the French representation (Freeman, *Washington*, VI, 294) is unfounded (see Document III). On the views of Beckwith and others on the connection between this message and the navigation bill, see Editorial Note to group of documents on commercial and diplomatic relations with Great Britain, under 15 Dec. 1790.

equal or even better terms than those offered by England. He also enclosed a copy of the report of the committee on commerce and warned of retaliatory impost and tonnage duties. Grazing interests and those connected with the Nantucket whalemen settled in France— both groups being represented on the committee—had become alarmed by the low prices of American salt provisions and by competition from the fisheries. They demanded heavy duties on these articles and were deaf to humanitarian considerations.[103]

It is easy to imagine the gratification with which Jefferson received this timely dispatch. He immediately made an extract of it and sent it to the Senate over his own signature.[104] But in doing so he was careful to choose those parts that would be most useful in achieving his strategic objectives. Short's opinions that the delegates in the National Assembly were extremely ignorant in matters of commerce, that a disinterested ministry would not adopt a narrow policy on salt and fish products, that the advantages of a closer political and commercial connection would soon become apparent to French legislators, that France would then be disposed to agree to such terms as the United States might propose, and that, when the auspicious moment arrived, definitive stipulations could be made for gaining admission to the French West Indies—all of these sanguine predictions Jefferson carefully concealed from the eyes of the Senators. Through such calculated editing of the dispatch, Short's analysis became in fact if not in form an argument of the Secretary of State, stripped of all elements that could be grasped by those eager for any reason to delay action.

Jefferson's report, characteristically, had outlined various legislative alternatives, but the policy he preferred was as clear as the argument he used to support it. Some gesture of friendship toward the ally was required by both justice and the national interest. If an act were to be passed putting French vessels on the footing of those of American citizens, declaring explicitly that this was done in response to privileges extended by France to American tobacco and products of the fisheries, other nations could not claim such a status without granting equivalents. Such a measure might render French favors more secure, whereas a refusal of the French claim might produce a contrary result—as Otto's notes and Short's dispatch strongly hinted.[105] These arguments and the direction in which they so clearly pointed became those of the administration by the mere reference of the report to the Senate. But the question was whether that body would again differ with Washington on a measure that he believed to be dictated by policy as well as justice. The friends of the British interest in the Senate were well aware that a refusal to accept the French interpretation of the

103 Short to TJ, 21 Oct. 1790.

104 TJ to President of the Senate, 2 Feb. 1791 (extract is identified at note 3, Short to TJ, 21 Oct. 1790, and text is printed in ASP, *Foreign Relations*, I, 120-1). Although Washington's message, TJ's report, and Otto's communications of 13 Dec. 1790 and that of 8 Jan. 1791 were recorded in full in the Executive Journal (JEP, I, 66-71), the Secretary of the Senate merely noted that "A letter from the Secretary of State enclosing an extract . . . was read" and that it was ordered "the letter and enclosure lie for consideration" (same, I, 73). Maclay made no mention of the receipt of the letter and extract.

105 Document IX.

treaty might bring on a hostile response from the ally and thus tend to strengthen relations with Great Britain. George Beckwith was told by one Senator—perhaps William Samuel Johnson, since the agent identified him as a friend—that this move was "an attempt of Mr. Jefferson . . . and of the French party connected with him to favor France, and to try to bring forward the discriminating system of duties in a different mode." Another Senator told Beckwith that the communication from the President was of such a nature as to demand a reply. "We shall be perfectly polite . . . to avoid giving offence," he added, "but we do not . . . think we are bound to give that nation any exclusive advantages in matters of trade; a certain description of persons in our house are disposed to accompany our reply with something of this nature. But we have a majority against it." It is clear from the repeated assertions made to Beckwith that those in the majority believed "that the President's submitting these papers . . . at this moment [was] at the instigation of Mr. Jefferson."[106]

The report, together with Otto's notes and the French decrees, was referred to a wholly unsympathetic committee—Morris, King, Izard, Strong, and Ellsworth. Maclay thought some who had fought discrimination formerly had recanted in debate in order to be appointed.[107] A week later Morris handed in the report against the French claims and once again Maclay found himself almost alone in opposition, pitted against an intransigent and not altogether candid majority. He tried repeatedly to obtain a view of Jefferson's report and its accompanying documents. But Otis, secretary of the Senate, put him off with various excuses. While the British agent was kept fully informed by both the Senators and the Secretary of the Treasury, Maclay never saw any of the documents except the statement of alternatives at the close of Jefferson's report.[108] He had suspected during the first session that some of his colleagues had hoped to destroy the confidence between the United States and France and now he was certain of it. Morris pleaded with him to join in the effort to postpone the discussion and Jefferson called on him in person. But the extent of Maclay's embittered isolation from his colleagues and from the administration is revealed in his conviction that even Jefferson countenanced the affront to France and that the vote against discrimination in the tonnage act of 1789 was the work of the President, designed to facilitate a connection with Great Britain.[109]

Senate action on the committee's report was delayed until the 26th of February, with only four legislative days left in the session. A bitter debate between Maclay and Ellsworth ensued. The Pennsylvanian opposed all of Jefferson's alternatives as well as his construction of the treaty, called upon the Senate to observe its letter and

[106] George Beckwith to Grenville, 3 Mch. 1791, Appendix (a), dated 3 Feb. 1791, and Appendixes (c) and (d), dated 15 Feb. 1791 (PRO: FO 4/12).
[107] JEP, I, 66-71; Maclay, *Journal*, ed. Maclay, p. 380.
[108] JEP, I, 72; Maclay, *Journal*, ed. Maclay, p. 380, 381, 382, 390, 392.
[109] Same, p. 394-5, 397. Maclay's embittered and erroneous conjecture led DeConde, *Entangling alliance*, p. 150-1, to the unwarranted conclusion that the Hamiltonians at this time had succeeded in enlisting "the powerful backing of the President" in this beginning of their effort to undermine the French alliance.

spirit, and urged that the injury done France be remedied by a repeal of the tonnage acts. "I have ever thought," he declared, "that a liberal and manly policy, more conformable to the genius of the people, was the surest method of engaging and preserving the esteem of that magnanimous nation. And the alternative might be war and confusion." This goaded Ellsworth beyond endurance:[110]

> A burst of abuse now flowed forth against the French by Ellsworth in the most vituperative language that fancy could invent. Selfishness, interested views, their motive, to dismember the English empire. *Divide et impera* their motto. Nay, slay the British subjects with the sword of their fellows. No gratitude in nations, no honor in politics. None but a fool would expect it. Serve yourself the first article in the creed of politics. No return due to them. Ridicule, not thanks, would attend acknowledgments. . . . [Ellsworth] fell on me with the most sarcastic severity. No confusion anywhere but in the speaker's head. Alas, how shall I write it? I almost lost my temper and, finding no protection from the Chair, left the room.

But a moment's reflection restored his composure. He returned to the chamber, heard Rufus King join Ellsworth in sentiment, and then found himself gazing upon the full length portraits of the King and Queen of France that Congress had requested in 1779 in order that "the representatives . . . may daily have before their eyes the first royal friends and patrons of their cause." Maclay knew that it was useless, but he could not remain silent:[111]

> Nations being composed of individuals, the virtue, character, and reputation of the nation must depend on the morals of the individual, and could have no other basis. Gratitude, generosity, sensibility of favors, benignity, and beneficence had not abandoned the human breast. In fact, these were the conditions on which the human race existed . . . these passions, so far as they respected the French nation, were deeply engraved on the bosom of every American revolutionist. I knew there were characters of a different kind in America, but for them we cared not. . . . I was convinced the sense of America had been fairly expressed by Congress on the resignation of General Washington, when the epithet of 'magnanimous nation' was applied to them.

This eloquent response, echoing Jefferson's letter to Madison on learning of the passage of the tonnage act of 1789, touched the deepest moral implications of the political cleavage in the nation—the manner in which the national character was conceived. Maclay opened a volume of the *Journals* of 1783, turned to the report of a committee of three, and found that "language labored and seemed to fail in expressions of

110 Maclay, *Journal*, ed. Maclay, p. 405.
111 TJ was a member of Congress when the portraits were presented at Annapolis on 6 Apr. 1784. They were moved with other government property to New York, then to Philadelphia, and finally to Washington, but in 1941 Burnett wrote: "where they now are, if indeed they still exist, no man knoweth" (Burnett, *Continental Congress*, p. 604). The quotation is from Maclay, *Journal*, ed. Maclay, p. 405-6.

gratitude to our ally." But, while confronting his opponents with their own words to reveal the extent of their reversal of position, he was charitable enough to withhold in debate the names of the committee whose encomiums he quoted—Madison, Ellsworth, and Hamilton.

But opposition, as Maclay well knew, was in vain. "I was the only one," he recorded in his diary, "who voted boldly and decidedly against" the report of the committee.[112] In that report, ironically, those who had accused the Secretary of State of bending every effort to promote a French interest now employed as their own the same construction of the treaty that he had set forth in his report to the President. But they rejected his recommendation that the defense of this construction be accompanied by an explanation couched "in as friendly terms as possible." The resolution as adopted over Maclay's single dissent merely advised that "an answer be given to the Court of France, defending, in the most friendly manner, this construction in opposition to that urged by the said Court."[113] But this, like the resolution of the House of Representatives requiring the Secretary of State to report on American commerce, left the initiative in his hands. He did not hesitate to provide the kind of explanation that he was afraid the French ministry would not receive from its own representative.

During almost all of the time that these interconnected legislative and executive moves took place, Otto had been absent in New York. There he received and answered Jefferson's letter informing him that the President had laid the tonnage question before the Senate. He accepted this procedure as a matter of course, being persuaded that the concurrence of that body was necessary "in everything relating to foreign affairs."[114] He was totally unaware of the nature or even the existence of the report of the Secretary of State, to say nothing of the strategy that gave rise to it. In his first dispatch from Philadelphia, written the day after the session ended, Otto praised Jefferson's report on the fisheries and said that it had produced a great

---

[112] Same, p. 402.

[113] JEP, I, 77; Lear to TJ, 27 Feb. 1791. It may be noted that Maclay provides the only known text of the report as submitted by Morris for the committee. As reported, this passage read: ". . . do advise an answer to be given to the Court of France, defending this construction in opposition to that urged by the said Court, and at the same time explaining in the most friendly terms the difficulties opposed to the exemptions they claim." The report was then amended to read as above. Maclay "contended against the alternatives of the Secretary of State as exceptionable, and opposed the whole, but all in vain" (DLC: MS Journal of Maclay).

[114] Otto to Montmorin, 29 Jan. 1790 (DLC: Henry Adams Transcripts), enclosing copies of TJ's letter of 19 Jan. 1791 and of his response of 21 Jan. 1791 (Documents XI and XII). George Beckwith was also under the impression that all foreign dispatches were laid before the Senate as a "Council of State" and asked Grenville to protect his confidences with its members as well as those "in another quarter" (that is, Hamilton in the cabinet) so as to keep the substance of these conversations from "being known hereafter in The American States" (Beckwith to Grenville, 11 Mch. 1791, PRO: FO 4/12). It was this dispatch, clearly based on information provided by the Hamiltonians, that analyzed party divisions in the government and accused Jefferson of giving to all communications from abroad a partisan emphasis, so that "whatever passes from him to The President becomes tinged with a French influence."

sensation in the capital—but that nothing worthy of being reported had transpired during the deliberations of Congress.[115] Beckwith, Bond, and others had long since provided the British government with perceptive analyses of the state of party divisions and, now that the Senate had followed Hamilton's lead, Jefferson concluded that the time had come to give the *chargé* a clearer view of the issues.

Within a few days of his arrival, Otto was reporting to Montmorin that, while it was impossible for him to discover in what manner and through which channels proposals for a rapprochement with England had been made, the friends of France had chosen this moment to bring forward a navigation act. The English party had risen in vain against this measure and had done its best to persuade the House to place it in the hands of the Secretary of the Treasury. In this it had failed and the report would be made by Jefferson, whose sentiments were generally known:[116]

> There is no doubt but that the Secretary of State will present this question in its true light and that he will not lack votes. . . . This discussion of the navigation act, joined to the debates caused by Mr. Jefferson's report on the fisheries, has divided the American government into two parties, one of which, directed by Messrs. Hamilton and R. Morris, tends to favor England and the other, under the auspices of Mr. Jefferson and his friends, leans strongly toward France. The latter party included more than two-thirds of the House of Representatives, but in the Senate the balance is so equal that it swings alternately to one side and the other. If they were able to open the doors of that chamber, the English party would no longer dare show itself.

So much Otto may have gathered merely from being at the seat of government, where the party cleavage was discernible to all informed persons. But Jefferson, speaking privately and confidentially, now focussed attention not on the political divisions at home but on the danger from abroad. He did inform the *chargé* that he and the President were "extremely embarrassed" at their inability to persuade the majority of the Senate to share the sentiments of attachment that the administration had for France. But, according to Otto's account of the interview, he spoke for a united administration and at no time indicated that his colleague in the cabinet was of a different persuasion or that the majority of the Senate accepted him as their leader. His concern lay elsewhere. Otto was now able to report such confidences of the Secretary of State as he had not theretofore been privileged to hear:[117]

115 Otto to Montmorin, 4 Mch. 1791 (DLC: Henry Adams Transcripts).

116 Otto to Montmorin, 6 Mar. 1791 (same). See Editorial Note to documents on commercial and diplomatic relations with Great Britain, under 15 Dec. 1790.

117 Otto to Montmorin, 10 Mch. 1791 (same). A clearer contrast between the relations of TJ and Otto and those of Hamilton and Beckwith could not be provided than the difference between this dispatch and that written the next day by Beckwith. The latter was in effect not only Hamilton's accusation against his colleague for exercising undue partisan influence over the President by giving a French caste to all foreign intelligence (see note 114), but also an urgent appeal through Beckwith to the British ministry to permit negotiations for a

I have not yet responded to your Memoir [he quoted Jefferson as saying] . . . because I wished to prepare you in advance for the letter I am obligated to write to you and to indicate the circumstances in which it is important for you to cause it to be considered by your government.

It is a fact that an exemption of the tonnage duty is not expressly stipulated in the treaty of commerce. You think that it is implied by the terms of Article V. But the Senate has judged differently and it is my duty to adopt its decision. Yet even admitting that the exemption you ask be implicitly accorded by Article V, it would be easy to prove that it is not in the interest of France to demand it. . . . It is not in consequence of the treaty that the President and the numerous friends of France desire to manifest their gratitude: its favors may become available to every nation. Our object is to establish a navigation act in which the exemptions, being applicable only to France, will put her on the footing of the only favored nation without giving to other nations any right to demand the same favors. You know that, in excluding every ship coming from a port where ours are not admitted and all merchandise imported in the ships of a nation which does not produce such merchandise, we shall single France out, so to speak, for she alone receives our ships in her colonies. She alone sends us merchandise of her growth and manufacture. The House of Representatives having charged me to make a report on this subject has sufficiently declared its opinion, for my sentiments are known. I have particularly declared them in my report on the fisheries. Finally, you may be certain, this great stroke will be carried in the next session.

There is only one thing to fear and it is my duty to explain myself to you. I am so deeply imbued with the importance of a connection and a perfect understanding between our two nations that I regard it as an essential object of the executive power to restrain the force of the mercantile interest, which is often too powerful in legislative bodies. I fear that in consequence of the refusal of the exemption of tonnage duties demanded by His Majesty, your government will only think of reprisals and of depriving our vessels of the advantages they enjoy in France. Although such a reciprocity might be just, it would be impolitic. The English would indubitably engross our coastal trade in France and in addition my compatriots would acutely feel the deprivation of favors which they believe they possess by virtue of treaty stipulations. Hence every measure which might tend to bring the two nations together would become more difficult to propose and to effect.

At the present moment we are certain that a great majority of the public is in favor of France and the House of Representatives is equally well disposed. It only remains then for us to conquer the Senate and we can only succeed there when we are able to make them open their doors. The mystery with which it covers its delib-

treaty of commerce to be carried on in the United States so that such supposed influence could be nullified—in brief, to enable Hamilton to do what he accused TJ of doing (Beckwith to Grenville, 11 Mch. 1791, PRO: FO 4/12).

erations serves to veil personal interests which rule there in all their vigor. Great efforts have been made in this session to render its deliberations public. These will probably succeed in the next session.

No longer did Jefferson affect confidence that the landed interest of France would always dominate commercial policy. Being certain of the feelings of friendship and gratitude the American people had for France, he had no anxiety about the fate of the navigation bill at home. But this unprecedented act of private disclosure revealed the depth of his fear that retaliation by the French government would produce exactly the result sought by Hamilton and those who desired a closer connection with England. This fear was merely confirmed, not aroused, by the dispatches of William Short describing the pressures exerted by *les Nantuckois* of Dunkirk, by those interested in the tobacco monopoly, and by the graziers and landed proprietors of France. Short's sanguine and ill-founded predictions had been kept from the Senate, but Jefferson was not misled by them. His own experience of the difficulty of introducing American whale oil, tobacco, and salt provisions into the French market told him how hardly won and precariously held were the favors granted by royal decree. The private explanation to Otto arose out of his acute awareness that private interests in France, retaliating against their counterparts in the United States, might jeopardize the great object now almost within grasp. But this was offered not to enlighten the *chargé*. The confidential discourse was in fact an urgent message to Montmorin about American political realities.

This extraordinary step, together with other circumstances, makes it plausible to suppose that Jefferson supplied Otto with an *aide-mémoire* so that the French ministry could have no possible misconception of what was meant. The candor that was the hallmark of his diplomatic relations with Montmorin would naturally have prompted him to reveal his purposes to that minister with the utmost precision. He also understood the character of the *chargé*. It may or may not be significant that Otto recorded Jefferson's words as if they were a direct quotation: the text could have been a summary or a paraphrase of what was expressed in conversation. But it is important to note that the words quoted were entirely characteristic of Jefferson, both in style and in substance. They were concentrated upon a single point, defined with clarity and precision. They contained no hint that the administration was deeply divided, no trace of the kind of personal and partisan imputations that Beckwith's informants had employed with respect to the Secretary of State. Montmorin, even as a witness to the erosion of executive authority in revolutionary France, might not be able to understand how the President could take one view of policy and the Senate another—and also make it prevail. But at least he could not mistake the goal to which the administration was committed.

The supposition that the words attributed to Jefferson were put in writing by him and handed to the *chargé* becomes a virtual certainty in light of the effort made by Otto "to interpret this private discourse of Mr. Jefferson." His explanation, thoroughly characteristic of all of his reporting, stands in marked contrast to the statement attributed to the Secretary of State. The Senate was averse to granting any exclusive favors to France, Otto explained to Montmorin, because some of its members were speculators in public securities and others were engaged in a direct commerce with England. The most remarkable Senator in the latter group was "Robert Morris, English by birth . . . a man of the greatest talent, whose commercial speculations are no more limited than his ambition. He directs the Senate as he formerly did American finances by making his politics keep step with his commerce."[118] Also, after consulting some Senators and Representatives, Otto penetrated the "mystery" of the mission of Gouverneur Morris. Its original instigator was Robert Morris, who persuaded the President to send out this feeler in the hope that it would result in an alliance with England. The dispatches of the emissary, however, had produced a contrary effect. The Senate and the House had almost unanimously rejected the idea of an alliance as incompatible with the obligation of the United States to France. For the same reason they had welcomed the proposal of an act of navigation. But Morris' influence in the Senate was increasing day by day and would be greater if it were not that he plead too openly the cause of England. The warmth with which Morris was opposed on the tonnage issue was only a political trick to induce France to respond in kind, thus aiding negotiations already begun to form an English alliance. Robert Morris was entirely devoted to the emissary, being attached to him both in business and by sentiment. Gouverneur Morris, Otto concluded, possessed very great talents and was indeed one of the most eloquent and witty men in the country, having an unusual ability in conceiving new projects and persuading others to like them. But he was not trusted by his countrymen.

Otto's explication of Jefferson's statement, compounded as it was of surmise, contradiction, and actual misinformation about Robert Morris' connection with the mission to England, about the unanimous rejection of an alliance that had not been proposed, and about the welcome accorded the move for a navigation act, abundantly justifies the belief that it was his own and that it derived from his accustomed sources of information, not from the Secretary of State. Certainly Jefferson could have had no reason to obscure the central point of his message with such a mixture of conjecture, misstatement, and impugning of individual motives, some of it perhaps contrived with deliberate intent to mislead. It was enough for him, characteristically, to inform the French foreign minister simply and unequivocally that a navigation bill was in prospect, that it would almost certainly pass at the next session, that a formidable obstacle existed in the Senate because its

[118] Otto to Montmorin, 10 Mch. 1791 (DLC: Henry Adams Transcripts). Otto attributed Robert Morris' effort to break the connection with France, in part at least, to his resentment over the decision not to renew his tobacco contract (see also TJ to Monroe, 18 Dec. 1786). He also attributed to Morris the defeat of the bill to give effect to the Consular Convention of 1788 and quoted him in an angry outburst on the last day of the session: "France has too much influence in the House of Representatives. It is necessary for the dignity of the Senate to prove that we are not under the same influence. We insist on the rules of the Senate [requiring unanimous consent]. It is important to show that we are independent" (Otto to Montmorin, 12 Mch. 1791, same).

doors were closed, that this could undoubtedly be remedied soon, but that, most important of all, the fair promise of attaining the goal might be frustrated if hostile measures should be taken in France. All of the circumstances suggest that this direct statement embedded in its contrasting context may indeed be regarded as an authentic expression of the Secretary of State, either as transcribed literally from an *aide-mémoire* or as recorded with almost exact fidelity by the auditor.

During this interview, so far as the record discloses, Jefferson never revealed to Otto that he had drawn up a report to the President, much less that its interpretation of the treaty was the one adopted by the Senate and that, appropriately revised, it was actually the response of the government to his two communications. Originally conceived as an instrument for the President to use against intransigent Senators, that report now became a means of isolating them in the eyes of the French ministry. The fact concealed from Otto was only a concurrence of legal opinion, for Jefferson arrived at his construction independently, expressed it candidly, and both Hamilton and the Senate embraced it. But he did improve the uses of such concealment by representing himself as duty bound to defend the Senate's interpretation, thereby magnifying the onus borne by that body. He also delayed his written communication for almost three weeks. Otto drew the intended inference: the Secretary of State was laboring to defend a construction imposed on him by the Senate. "You will note in the attached letter," he reported to Montmorin, "the embarrassment the Executive of the United States finds itself in reconciling its sentiments and its professions of friendship with the forced interpretation that the Legislature has insisted on giving to our treaty of commerce. Whatever may be the efforts of Mr. Jefferson to give a favorable sense to Article V, it is evident that our construction is the only one that is admissible in sound logic."[119]

There was no need to try to persuade a Secretary of State who to all appearances was only executing orders. But Otto wrote or consulted with several leading Senators to convince them their interpretation was illogical, a fruitless effort of which he gave Montmorin an elaborate account. Those whom he consulted replied with arguments that had been well rehearsed in the first session. If it were only a question of favoring France, motives of equity and gratitude would justify the exemption. They had never been more embarrassed, one Senator explained, than on the response to be made to the French claim. But to grant it would bring on a thousand other embarrassments: the demands of other nations in treaty with the United States, the danger of commercial war with England, and, especially, the risk of touching any branch of revenue at a moment when the least shock would upset the national finances. Northern Senators assured Otto of their readiness

[119] Otto to Montmorin, 1 Apr. 1791 (same), enclosing TJ's response (Document XIII). It is clear that none of the Senators revealed to Otto the fact or the substance of TJ's report as enclosed in the President's message. Since all proceedings on the tonnage claim were recorded in the Executive Journal, not even the journal entries appeared in the press. Otto may have acknowledged TJ's reply of 29 Mch. 1791 in a letter of 29 Apr. 1791, recorded in SJL as received the next day. No text of this letter has been found.

to give France proof of their gratitude, but their southern colleagues would not consent to an exemption except on terms injurious to their own navigation. Southern Senators, avowing equal sentiments of affection, were opposed to tonnage duties but unable to satisfy northerners without it. Otto, full of sympathy for Jefferson for having to defend an interpretation born of such conflicting interests, informed Montmorin that he would answer him only to correct several mistakes he had permitted to slip into his argument. The Secretary of State had only concealed authorship of a legal opinion, but the Senators hid their inner convictions behind protests of friendship for France. None gave the faintest echo of the abuse of France or the ridicule of moral considerations in the affairs of nations such as Ellsworth had voiced in anger behind closed doors, certain that his words would not appear in the public press.

In another confidential conversation a few weeks later, Jefferson gave Otto such a reassuring glimpse of the administration's goal as to cause him to resort to the use of code in reporting it to Mortmorin, apparently the only time he ever did so:[120]

> Mr. Jefferson assured me in this conference that the news coming to him from all parts confirms him in the opinion that Congress will adopt a navigation act in the next session, and that this act will be very favorable to France. The plan of the President and of Mr. Jefferson is to grant naturalization to French citizens in America in matters respecting commerce; but I foresee that this plan will experience great difficulties. Some particular favors will also be accorded French wine and brandy. Mr. Jefferson begged me to inform you confidentially of these views, the execution of which will require very much address and perseverance.

This was a hope Jefferson had long cherished and one that he would soon repeat to the new French minister to the United States.[121] With the friends of the British interest now clearly on the defensive, it might even become a reality. Having just returned from the tour that he and Madison had made through New York, Vermont, and Connecticut, Jefferson certainly could have found no reason to doubt that the New England shipping interests would continue to support a strong navigation act and that the farmers of the rich Connecticut valley would be as deeply concerned as ever about retaining access to the French West Indies. Washington was away on his southern tour, but Jefferson could look forward with confidence to his favoring such a bold stroke as some Senators had pretended to have in view in 1789, the promise of which had gained Washington's reluctant consent to an act he considered unjust and impolitic. Aided by the President's powerful influence and by the growing momentum of the effort to compel the Senate to open its doors, the strategy promised to succeed even if the National Assembly should react with hostility to the denial of the French interpretation of the treaty.

[120] Otto to Montmorin, 4 Apr. 1791 (DLC: Henry Adams Transcripts).
[121] TJ's remarks to Ternant on the point are quoted in Editorial Note to group of documents on commercial and diplomatic relations with Great Britain, under 15 Dec. 1790, note 159.

But Jefferson's fear of a hostile response was only too well founded. Even at the moment he confided his anxiety to Otto, the decrees that he regarded as the sheet anchor of the American connection with France had begun to give way. Already the National Assembly had passed decrees discriminating almost prohibitively against the importation of tobacco in American ships.[122] Montmorin had brought his influence to bear even without the urging of the Secretary of State. But his efforts were unavailing against the claims of special interests and, without Jefferson in France to hold the nails for him to drive, Lafayette was indecisive.[123] American firms were beginning to circumvent the new tobacco regulations even before Otto's report of the confidential conversation came to Montmorin. On the very day that he received it, William Short reported the effective termination of favors previously granted to whale oil, tobacco, and American built ships.[124] Jefferson grasped the consequences of this action more clearly than any other political leader because he had sought longer and more consistently than any other to avoid it. The blow was a bitter one and, so Otto reported, opened the eyes of some of the most intelligent Americans. They now began to feel that the Senate had been wrong in being so intractable on the tonnage question, fearing that changes would be carried further—even to the extent of depriving Americans of their advantages in the French Antilles.[125] But the realization came too late. By mid-summer Jefferson was warning of the possibility that Congress, far from singling France out for particular favor, might adopt retaliatory measures against her. At the end of the year the two nations were virtually engaged in commercial hostilities, the beginning of a rift that would end at last with the dissolution of the alliance.[126] The French response was by no means the cause and the commercial policy of the new regime did not originate in a mere difference over tonnage duties.

The dispute over the tonnage acts involved such a relatively trivial sum—about thirty-four thousand livres per year or slightly more than the combined salaries of the two cabinet officers around whom the storm gathered—that some Senators joined Hamilton in wondering why France should have made an issue of it.[127] Whence, then, arose their fear that so slight a burden could threaten the public credit? Even Hamilton, in arguing that this factor had to be taken into account, conceded that the obstacle was not insuperable.[128] The intransigent refusal to accommodate the ally, the resolute avoidance of responsibility for achieving a solution, the bland dismissal of the alternatives suggested by the Secretary of State—these attitudes added to the very

122 Setser, *Reciprocity*, p. 119-22; DeConde, *Entangling alliance*, p. 152-5.

123 Short to TJ, 18, 22, 25 Feb.; 4, 12 Mch. 1791; Morris to TJ, 26 Feb. 1791; Short to Montmorin, 6 Apr. 1791 (Arch. Aff. Etr., Corr. Pol., E.-U., xxxv; photostats in DLC).

124 Otto to Montmorin, 17 June 1791 (DLC: Henry Adams Transcripts); Short to TJ, 10 June 1791.

125 Otto to Montmorin, 7 May 1791 (DLC: Henry Adams Transcripts).

126 TJ to Short, 28, 29 July; 29 Aug. 1791; Setser, *Reciprocity*, p. 122; DeConde, *Entangling alliance*, p. 154-7.

127 Otto to Montmorin, 1 Apr. 1791 (DLC: Henry Adams Transcripts).

128 Document VI.

triviality of the sums involved suggest that the real stakes were much greater, that the actual grounds for inaction and opposition lay elsewhere, and that the explanations given by Hamilton to Jefferson and by the Senators to Otto were, at best, disingenuous efforts to conceal their ultimate aims. Those aims, though latent, had not been disclosed when the government of the Confederation had supported France on such an issue at a time it lacked authority. But they could not be concealed now that the nation possessed full power over commerce. For what was the difference, Madison bluntly asked his colleagues in the House, between the lack of power and the lack of will to use it?[129]

Hence none of the divisive questions agitated in full view of the public—the impost, the assumption, the excise, the national bank, the permanent seat of government—could cast quite so brilliant a light on the nature of the fundamental cleavage in government as did this slight matter of tonnage duties, debated within the cabinet and behind the closed doors of the Senate. While such issues laid the foundations for a growing and ultimately irresistible opposition, they were all domestic in character and were fought out mainly on lines of economic and sectional interests. The conflict over the use of the commerce power as an instrument of foreign policy not only embraced these same political alignments: it also involved two opposing points of view concerning the relations of the United States with the rest of the world and particularly with respect to the European balance of power. To these basic economic and sectional alignments it thus added the variant ways in which Americans conceived of their national character, the differing concepts of the meaning of their own revolutionary experience. The Secretary of the Treasury and the Secretary of State embodied these opposites and ultimately became their symbol.

It is generally supposed that their first clash came over the national bank and that the crucial division over foreign policy emerged with the outbreak of war between France and England in 1793, bringing with it "the first serious and long continued dissension in the Cabinet" and the resultant formation of political parties.[130] But political parties, in the sense that the American people divided on great issues affecting their nationhood and their form of government, had existed from the beginning of the revolutionary movement, as John Adams and others well understood. And in large measure external forces—armed conflict followed by commercial restrictions, political colonialism followed by economic dependence—had supplied the cohesion necessary for the pivotal decisions. The author of the eleventh *Federalist* advanced the proposition to which the people gave general assent when he called for "one great American system, superior to the control of all transatlantic force or influence, and able to dictate the terms of the connection between the old and the new world!"[131] But now that the national government had been clothed with authority, external forces served to divide rather than to unite. The gravitational pull of

[129] See note 15 above.

[130] Joseph Charles, *Origins of the American party system* (1961), p. 41; Felix Gilbert, *To the Farewell Address*, p. 116, 120; Paul A. Varg, *Foreign Policies of the Founding Fathers*, p. 70-1, 72, 79, 83.

[131] *The Federalist*, ed. B. F. Wright, p. 142.

the two great powers of Europe first rent the government and then the nation, bringing to the American people their most divisive experience since their separation from the British empire.

Hamilton based his unwillingness to use the power that had been granted on a denial of the mandate for which he had pleaded. He was not the first to do so, but he was the most daring and the most resourceful. He was also the most deceptive. It was not to his colleague in the cabinet or to the President but to the British secret agent that he first revealed his ultimate goal. *"In the present state of things,"* he confided to George Beckwith while the Senate was delaying action on the French claim, "nothing has happened between us and France, to give a tolerable pretence for breaking off our treaty of alliance with that Power and immediately forming one with you. A regard for National decorum puts such a decisive step as this out of our reach."[132] Out of reach, that is to say, until a tolerable pretext could be found that would make it possible to preserve the outward form if not the inner reality of national dignity. But the objective had been defined with unmistakable clarity: the ultimate destruction of the alliance with France and the formation of one with England.

In this lies the key to the profound conflict over foreign policy in the last decade of the century, of which the cleavage within the government over the insignificant favor claimed by France was only the herald. The tolerable pretext would be sought in season and out with unflagging determination by the Secretary of the Treasury—in private communications to the British and French ministers, in the struggle over neutrality, in the bitter conflict over the treaty of 1794, in the attempt to deny the right of a legitimate opposition to exist and to be heard, and at last in the mobilization of the military power of the nation against the former ally. Even Otto soon became aware of "those pretended friends of France . . . assiduously spreading their calumnies and false insinuations" in the American press. Yet, in an unwitting tribute to the reserve and official conduct of the Secretary of State, he remained to the end of his mission under the delusion that the administration was united in its sympathy for the aims of the French revolution and in its fidelity to the alliance.[133]

But if the author of the eleventh *Federalist* had forsaken the ground on which he formerly stood, calling for an end to the degradation of the national character in terms he knew would gain the general assent of his countrymen, he could find justification for a continued acquiescence in the policy of Great Britain in his own philosophy as expressed in the eighth number. "Safety from external danger," he wrote in that, "is the most powerful director of national conduct. Even the ardent love of liberty will after a time, give way to its dictates. . . . To be more safe, [the people] at length become willing to run the risk of being less free."[134] The safety of his system, he believed, required a continued subservience to British policy even if it meant a loss of some

132 Report of conversation with Hamilton on 16 Feb. 1791, enclosed in Beckwith to Grenville, 3 Mch. 1791 (PRO: FO 4/12; text printed in Syrett, *Hamilton*, VIII, 41-5; emphasis added).
133 Otto to Montmorin, 22 July 1791 (DLC: Henry Adams Transcripts).
134 *The Federalist*, ed. B. F. Wright, p. 120.

economic freedom and with it the dignity of a free nation. Jefferson found the most potent springs of national conduct elsewhere—not in external danger, not even in preserving the alliance with France or in redressing the European balance of power, but in the character and spirit of the American people. This was the real nature of the cleavage in government—one resting at last on fundamental moral principles—that was illumined so brilliantly by this trivial matter of tonnage duties. The issue, as Jefferson clearly saw, was "an important one."[135]

[135] Document III.

I. Louis Guillaume Otto to the Secretary of State

MONSIEUR   À Philadelphie le 13e. Dec. 1790.

Pendant le long séjour que vous aves fait en France, vous aves eu Lieu de vous convaincre des Dispositions favorables de Sa Majesté pour rendre permanens les Liens qui unissent les deux Nations, et pour donner de la Stabilité aux Traités d'Alliance et de Commerce qui forment la Base de cette Union. Ces Traités ont été si bien maintenus par le Congrès formé sous l'ancienne Confederation qu'il a cru devoir interposer son Autorité toutes les fois que des Loix faites par des Etats individuels paroissoient en enfreindre les Dispositions, et particulierement lorsqu'en 1785 les Etats du New-Hampshire et du Massachussets avoient imposé des Droits de Tonnage extraordinaires sur les Bâtimens etrangers sans en exempter ceux de la Nation Françoise. Les Reflexions, que j'ai l'Honneur de vous adresser dans la Notte ci-jointe, étant fondées sur les mêmes principes, j'ose croire qu'elles meriteront de la Part du Gouvernement des Etats Unis l'Attention la plus serieuse.— Je suis avec Respect, Monsieur, Votre très humble et très obéissant Serviteur   L. G. OTTO.

Tr (DNA: RG 46, Records of the U.S. Senate); in Taylor's hand, "(Copy)" at head of text. Tr (same); English translation in Remsen's hand.

PrC of first Tr (DLC). Translation of letter and enclosure printed in JEP, I, 70-1. Recorded in SJL as received 13 Dec. 1790.

ENCLOSURE

Louis Guillaume Otto to Thomas Jefferson

À Philadelphie le 13e. Decembre 1790.

Le Soussigné, Chargé des Affaires de France a reçu l'Ordre exprès de sa Cour de representer aux Etats Unis que l'Acte passé par le

Congrès le 20e. Juillet 1789, et renouvellé le 20e. Juillet de l'Année courante, qui impose un Droit de Tonnage extraordinaire sur les Bâtimens etrangers, sans en excepter les Navires François, est directement contraire à l'Esprit et au But du Traité de Commerce qui lie les deux Nations, et dont Sa Majesté a non seulement scrupuleusement observé la Teneur, mais dont Elle a etendu les Avantages par plusieurs Règlemens très favorables au Commerce et à la Navigation des Etats Unis.

Par l'Article 5e. de ce Traité les Citoyens de ces Etats sont declarés exempts du Droit de Tonnage imposé en France sur les Bâtimens etrangers, et ils ne sont assujettis à ce Droit que pour le petit Cabotage; on a reservé au Congrès la Faculté d'etablir un *Droit equivalent à ce dernier*; Stipulation fondée sur l'Etat où etoient les Choses en Amérique lors de la Signature du Traité; il n'existoit à cette Epoque aucun Droit de Tonnage dans les Etats Unis.

Il est evident que c'est la non-existence de ce Droit et le Motif d'une parfaite Reciprocité stipulée dans le Préambule du Traité qui ont déterminé le Roi à accorder l'Exemption contenue dans l'Article 5e.; et une Preuve que le Congrès n'avoit point l'Intention de porter atteinte à cette Reciprocité, c'est qu'*il s'est borné à se reserver la Faculté d'etablir sur le petit Cabotage un Droit equivalent à celui qui se perçoit en France*. Cette Reserve auroit été completement inutile, si aux Termes du Traité le Congrès s'etoit cru en Liberté de mettre un Droit de Tonnage *quelconque* sur les Bâtimens François.

Le Soussigné a l'Honneur d'observer que cette Atteinte portée à l'Article 5e. du Traité de Commerce auroit pu autoriser Sa Majesté à modifier proportionellement les Faveurs accordées par le même Article à la Navigation Américaine, mais le Roi, toujours Fidèle à ses principes d'Amitié et d'Attachement pour les Etats Unis, et voulant confirmer de plus en plus les Liaisons qui subsistent si heureusement entre la Nation Françoise et ces Etats, a trouvé plus conforme à ces Vues d'ordonner au Soussigné de faire des Representations à ce Sujet, et de demander en faveur des Navires François une Modification de l'Acte qui impose un Droit de Tonnage extraordinaire sur les Bâtimens etrangers. Sa Majesté ne doute pas que les Etats Unis ne reconnoissent la Justice de cette Reclamation et ne soient disposés à remettre les choses sur le Pied où elles etoient lors de la Signature du Traité du 6e. Fevr. 1778.   L. G. OTTO

Tr (DNA: RG 46, Records of the U.S. Senate); in Taylor's hand, "(Copy)" at head of text. Tr (Arch. Aff. Etr., Corr. Pol., E-U.; photostats in DLC). Tr (DNA: RG 46); English translation in Remsen's hand. PrC of first Tr (DLC).

II. Secretary of State to Louis Guillaume Otto

Dec. 29. 1790.

The Secretary of state presents his respectful compliments to the Chargé des affaires of France. It is not till now that his other occupations have permitted him to enter on the consideration of his letter of the 13th. inst. Will he be so good as to inform him whether other, the most favoured nations, pay the tonnage of 100 sols, on arriving in any part of France, *from a foreign port*, or whether this exemption is peculiar to the vessels of the U.S.? Mr. Jefferson not being able as yet to have access to his own books and papers which might inform him of this fact, hopes Mr. Otto will be so good as to supply that resource by his friendly information of this fact which may throw light on the 5th. article of the treaty.

PrC (DLC). Tr (DLC: Henry Adams Transcripts); in French, quoted in Otto to Montmorin, 6 Jan. 1791.

III. Thomas Jefferson to James Madison

Saturday morning [1 Jan. 1791]

I intended to have called last night and left with you the inclosed draught of a letter to Otto but it was so cold I could not give up my hack. I recieved yours soon after I came home. Of the two constructions I observe you lean more to the 2d. and I more to the 1st. on account of the consequences to which the 2d. may be pursued. My first idea was to write this letter to Otto and previously communicate it to the President, and he perhaps to the Senate. But I have concluded to throw it into the form of a report to the President, to be submitted to the Senate. This will permit me to speak without reserve, to admit the force of the 2d. construction, and to enforce the proposition I suggest in the close, by shewing what valuable branches of our commerce hang on the will of the French nation. I shall see you at dinner, and be glad to exchange further thoughts on the subject which is an important one.

RC (DLC: Madison Papers); undated and not recorded in SJL; at foot of text Madison wrote, perhaps late in life: "Jany. 1. 1791." Madison's letter has not been found and is not recorded in SJL.

IV. Louis Guillaume Otto to the Secretary of State

[New York, 6 Jan. 1791]

L'exemption du droit de fret accordée aux Etats unis par l'art. 5 du traité de commerce a été stipulée dans plusieurs traité conclus entre la France et d'autres Puissances. Les Principes de reciprocité qui forment communement la base des traités de commerce ont engagé à differentes epoques le Gouvernement Francois à stipuler cette exemption soit parceque l'autre Puissance contractante offroit un equivalent ou que le droit de fret n'etoit pas etabli dans ses ports. Telle etoit entre autres la situation des Etats Unis lors de la conclusion du traité; on ne connoissoit alors en Amerique aucun droit de fret, ses ports etant ouverts indistinctement à toutes les nations amies ou neutres. Il a donc fallu etablir en France une *reciprocité* à cet egard en stipulant pour les batimens Americains la même liberté de commerce, dont les Francois jouissoient en Amerique. L'art, 5. du traité y a pourvû, mais en exceptant les droits imposés en France sur le *petit Cabotage* il a reservé au Congrès la faculté de prelever sur les navires François un droit equivalent en *pareil cas.*

Tr (DLC: Henry Adams Transcripts); text taken from Otto's dispatch No. 52 to Montmorin, 6 Jan. 1791, and recorded with same date in SJL as having been received on 10 Jan. 1791.

V. Louis Guillaume Otto to the Secretary of State

MONSIEUR   A New York le 8. Janv. 1791

J'ai L'honneur de vous adresser ci-joint une Lettre du Roi au Congrès, et une autre que vous ecrit M. de Montmorin. Vous y trouveréz l'Expression sincere des Sentimens que vous avéz inspirés à notre Gouvernement et des Regrets du Ministre de ne plus être immediatement en relation avec vous. Ces Sentimens sont partagés par toutes les Personnes qui ont eu l'Avantage de vous connoitre en France.

Je suis peiné, Monsieur, d'avoir à vous annoncer en même Tems que les Plaintes de nos Negocians, au sujet des Droits de Tonnage, se multiplient, et qu'elles ont non seulement fixé l'attention du Roi, mais celle de plusieurs Departemens du Royaume. J'ai reçu de nouveaux Ordres de demander aux Etats Unis une Decision à ce Sujet, et de Solliciter en Faveur des Négocians lézés la Restitution des Droits qui ont dejà été payés. Je vous prie instamment, Monsieur, de ne pas perdre de vue un Objet qui, comme j'ai eu l'Honneur de vous le dire verbalement, est de la plus grande Importance pour cimenter les Liaisons futures de Commerce entre les deux Nations.

En examinant plus particulierement cette Question, vous trou-

veréz peut être que les motifs de convenance sont aussi puissans que ceux de Justice pour engager les Etats Unis à donner à Sa Majesté la Satisfaction qu'elle demande. Il entre dans les Ports de France au moins deux fois plus de Bâtimens Américains qu'il ne vient de Bâtimens François dans les Ports Americains. L'Exemption du Droit de Tonnage est donc evidemment moins avantageux pour les François que pour les Navigateurs des Etats-Unis. Quoiqu'il en soit, je puis vous assurer, Monsieur, que les Delais d'une Decision à cet egard ne pourront que multiplier les Difficultés en augmentant les justes plaintes des Négocians François. Je vous prie en Consequence de me mettre en Etat de donner à ma Cour une Reponse satisfaisante avant l'Expedition du Paquebot qui partira vers la Fin de ce Mois. J'ai l'Honneur d'être, avec un respectueux Attachement, Monsieur, Votre très humble et très obeissant Serviteur
L. G. OTTO

Tr (DNA: RG 46, Records of the U. S. Senate); in Taylor's hand, "(Copy)" at head of text. Tr (same); English translation, also in Taylor's hand. PrC of both of preceding (DLC). English translation printed in JEP, I,

71. Recorded in SJL as received 12 Jan. 1791. Enclosures: (1) Louis XVI to president and members of Congress, 11 Sep. 1790 (see TJ to Washington, 9 Dec. 1790). (2) Montmorin to TJ, 31 July 1790.

VI. Alexander Hamilton to Thomas Jefferson

DEAR SIR   Philadelphia January the 11th 1791

I have perused with attention your intended report to the President; and will, as I am sure is your wish, give you my opinion with frankness.

As far as a summary examination enables me to judge, I agree in your interpretation of the Treaty. The exemption sought does not appear to be claimable as a right.

But I am not equally well satisfied of the policy of granting it on the ground you suggest. This, in my mind, stands in a very questionable shape. Though there be a collateral consideration, there is a want of reciprocity in the thing itself; and this in a circumstance which materially affects the general policy of our navigation system. The tendency of the measure would be to place French Vessels upon an equal footing with our own, *in our ports*, while our Vessels in the *ports of France* may be subjected to all the duties which are there laid on the mass of foreign Vessels—I say the mass of foreign vessels because the title of "most favoured nation" is a very extensive one—the terms being almost words of course in Commercial Treaties. And consequently our own Vessels in the carrying Trade between the United States and France would be in a worse situation than French Vessels. This is the necessary result of equal privileges on on[e] side, and unequal on the other, in favour of the Vessels of France.

Though in the present state of the French Navigation little would be to be apprehended from the Regulation; yet when the probable increase of that Navigation under a free Government is considered it can hardly be deemed safe to calculate future consequences from the actual situation in this respect.

And if the principle of the Regulation cannot be deemed safe in a permanent view, it ought not to be admitted temporarily; for inconvenient precedents are always embarrassing.

On the whole I should be of opinion that the introduction of such a principle without *immediate* reciprocity, would be a high price for the advantage which it is intended to compensate.

It will no doubt have occurred to you that the fund has been mortgaged for the public Debt. I do not however mention this as an insuperable objection but it would be essential that the same act which should destroy this source of revenue should provide an equivalent. This I consider as a rule which ought to be sacred, as it affects public Credit.—I have the honor to be With the sincerest esteem & regard Dear Sir Your Obed. Serv,   A. HAMILTON

P.S. If you have any spare set of the printed papers, I should be obliged by having them.

RC (DLC); endorsed by TJ as received 12 Jan. 1791 and so recorded in SJL.

VII. Thomas Jefferson to Alexander Hamilton

DEAR SIR   January 13. 1791

I inclose you copies of the printed papers you desired: also a letter I recieved last night. This paper I will thank you to return by the bearer when you shall have perused it, as it is yet to be translated and communicated to the President. It is evident that this matter will become serious, and tho' I am pointedly against admitting the French construction of the treaty, yet I think it essential to cook up some favour which may ensure the continuance of the good dispositions they have towards us. A nation which takes one third of our tobacco, more than half our fish oil and two thirds of our fish, say one half of the amount of these great staples and a great deal of rice and from whom we take nothing in return but hard money to carry directly over and pour into the coffers of their enemies, such a customer, I say, deserves some menagemens. I would thank you sincerely to suggest any thing better than what I had thought of. I am Dear Sir Yours affectionately & respectfully,   Th: Jefferson

PrC (DLC); at foot of text (torn but decipherable from remaining ascenders of letters): "Secretary of the Treasury." Recorded in SJL but TJ failed to write the figure "13" in the proper place, thus making it appear that this entry pertained to a letter of 11 Jan. 1791. The above is clearly a response to Hamilton's letter of the latter date, received on 12 Jan. FC (DNA: RG 59, PCC No. 120); misdated 1 Jan. 1791, thus misleading even careful scholars (Ford, v, 267-8; Syrett, *Hamilton*, vii, 408). Enclosures: (1) Otto to TJ, 8 Jan. 1791 (Document v, above). (2) Printed text of Lambert to TJ, 29 Dec. 1787, including text of *arrêt* of that date. (3) Printed text of *arrêt* of 7 Dec. 1788, both this and preceding enclosure having French and English texts (see Vol. 12: 471n. and Vol. 14: 269n. for description).

VIII. Alexander Hamilton to Thomas Jefferson

Dear Sir   Jany 13. 91.

I thank you for the printed papers you have been so obliging as to send.

I cannot forbear a conjecture that the communications of the Chargé des affaires of France are rather expedients to improve a moment, in which it is perceived questions concerning navigation are to be discussed than the effects of serious instructions from his Court.

Be this as it may I really have not thought of any substitute for your proposition to which objections do not lie. And in general I have doubts of the eligibility of *exparte* concessions, liable to be resumed at pleasure. I had rather endeavour by a new Treaty of Commerce with France to extend reciprocal advantages and fix them on a permanent basis. This would not only be more solid but it would perhaps be less likely than apparently gratuitous and voluntary exemptions to beget discontents elsewhere; especially (as ought to be the case) if each party should be at liberty for equivalent considerations to grant like privilege to others. My commercial system turns very much on giving a free Course to Trade and cultivating good humour with all the world. And I feel a particular reluctance to hazard any thing in the present state of our affairs which may lead to commercial warfare with any power; which as far as my knowledge of examples extends is commonly productive of mutual inconvenience and injury and of dispositions tending to a worse kind of warfare. Exemptions and preferences which are not the effect of Treaty are apt to be regarded by those who do not partake in them as proofs of an unfriendly temper towards them. With respect & Affection I remain Dr Sir Yr Obedt,   A. HAMILTON

RC (DLC); endorsed as received 13 Jan. 1791 and so recorded in SJL.

IX. Report of the Secretary of State to the President

The Secretary of State having received from the Chargé des Affaires of France a note on the Tonnage payable by French vessels in the ports of the United States has had the same under his consideration, and thereupon makes the following REPORT to the President of the United States.

The Chargé des Affaires of France, by a Note of the 13th. of December represents, by order of his Court, that they consider so much of the Acts of Congress of July 20th. 1789 and 1790 as imposes an extraordinary Tonnage on foreign vessels, without excepting those of France, to be in contravention of the 5th. Article of the Treaty of Amity and Commerce between the two Nations; that this would have authorised on their part a proportional modification in the favours granted to the American navigation: but that his sovereign had thought it more conformable to his principles of friendship and attachment to the United States to order him to make representations thereon, and to ask, in favour of French vessels, a modification of the Acts which impose an extraordinary Tonnage on foreign vessels.

The Secretary of State in giving in this paper to the President of the United States, thinks it his duty to accompany it with the following observations:

The 3d. and 4th. articles of the Treaty of Amity and Commerce between France and the United States, subject the vessels of each nation to pay, in the ports of the other, only such duties as are paid by the most favoured Nation: and give them reciprocally all the

privileges and exemptions, in navigation and commerce, which
are given by either to the most favoured Nations. Had the contracting parties stopped here, they would have been free to raise
or lower their Tonnage as they should find it expedient; only taking
care to keep the other on the footing of the most favoured nation.

The question then is whether the 5th. Article, cited in the note,
is anything more than an application of the principle comprised in
the 3d. and 4th. to a particular object? Or whether it is an additional stipulation of something not so comprised?

I. That it is merely an application of a principle comprised
in the preceding Articles, is declared by the express words of
the Article, to wit, "*Dans l'exemption ci-dessus* est *nommément
compris*" &c. "*In the above exemption* is *particularly comprised*
the imposition of 100. sols per Ton established in France on foreign
vessels." Here then is at once an express declaration that the exemption from the duty of 100 sols, is *comprised* in the 3d. and
4th. Articles; that is to say, it was one of the exemptions, enjoyed
by the most favoured nations, and, as such, extended to us by those
Articles. If the exemption spoken of in this 1st. member of the
5th. Article was *comprised* in the 3d. and 4th. Articles, as is
expressly declared, then the reservation by France out of that exemption (which makes the 2d. member of the same article) *was
also comprised*: that is to say, if *the whole* was comprised, *the
part* was comprised. And if this reservation of France in the 2d.
member was comprised in the 3d. and 4th. Articles, then the
counter reservation by the United States (which constitutes the
3d. and last member of the same Article) was also comprised.
Because it is but a corresponding portion of a similar whole on
our part, which had been comprised by the same terms with theirs.

In short the whole Article relates to a particular duty of 100
sols laid by some antecedent law of France on the vessels of foreign nations, relinquished as to the most favoured, and consequently to us. It is not a new and additional stipulation then, but a
declared application of the stipulations comprised in the preceding
Articles to a particular case, by way of greater caution.

The doctrine laid down generally in the 3d. and 4th. Articles,
and exemplified specially in the 5th. amounts to this. "The vessels
of the most favoured nations, coming from foreign ports, are
exempted from the duty of 100. sols: therefore you are exempted
from it by the 3d. and 4th. Articles. The vessels of the most-
favoured nations, coming coastwise, pay that duty: therefore you
are to pay it by the 3d. and 4th. Articles. We shall not think it

unfriendly in you to lay a like duty on Coasters, because it will be no more than we have done ourselves. You are free also to lay that or any other duty on vessels coming from foreign ports: provided they apply to all other nations, even the most favoured. We are free to do the same, under the same restriction. Our exempting you from a duty which the most favoured nations do not pay, does not exempt you from one which they do pay."

In this view it is evident that the 5th. Article neither enlarges, nor abridges the stipulations of the 3d. and 4th. The effect of the Treaty would have been precisely the same had it been omitted altogether; consequently it may be truly said that the reservation by the United States in this article is completely useless. And it may be added with equal truth that the equivalent reservation by France is completely useless: as well as her previous abandonment of the same duty: and in short the whole article. Each party then remains free to raise or lower it's Tonnage, provided the change operates on all nations, even the most favoured.

Without undertaking to affirm, we may obviously conjecture, that this Article has been inserted on the part of the United States from an over-caution to guard, *nommément, by name,* against a particular aggrievance, which they thought they could never be too well secured against: and that has happened, which generally happens; doubts have been produced by the too great number of words used to prevent doubt.

II. The Court of France however understands this Article as intended to introduce something to which the preceding Articles had not reached; and not merely as an application of them to a particular case. Their opinion seems to be founded on the general rule, in the construction of instruments, to leave no words merely useless, for which any rational meaning can be found. They say that the reservation by the United States of a right to lay a duty equivalent to that of the 100 sols, reserved by France, would have been completely useless, if they were left free, by the preceding articles, to lay a Tonnage to any extent whatever. Consequently that the reservation of a part proves a relinquishment of the residue.

If some meaning, and such a one, is to be given to the last member of the Article, some meaning, and a similar one, must be given to the corresponding member. If the reservation by the United States of a right to lay an equivalent duty, implies a relinquishment of their right to lay any other, the reservation by France of a right to continue the specified duty to which it is an equivalent, must imply a relinquishment of the right on her part to lay or continue any other. Equivalent reservations by both, must imply equivalent restrictions on both. The exact reciprocity stipulated in the preceding articles, and which pervades every part of the Treaty, ensures a counterright to each party for every right ceded to the other.

Let it be further considered that the duty called *tonnage* in the United States is in lieu of the duties for anchorage, for the support of Buoys, Beacons, and Lighthouses, to guide the mariner into harbour, and along the coast, which are provided and supported at the expence of the United States, and for fees to measurers, weighers, gaugers &c. who are paid by the United States; for which articles, among many others (light excepted) duties are paid by us in the ports of France under their specific names. That Government has hitherto thought these duties consistent with the Treaty; and consequently the same duties under a general, instead of specific names, with us, must be equally consistent with it; it is not the name, but the thing which is essential. If we have renounced the right to lay any port duties, they must be understood to have equally renounced that of either laying new or continuing the old. If we ought to refund the port duties received from their vessels since the date of the act of Congress, they should refund the port duties they have received from our vessels since the date of the Treaty; for nothing short of this is the reciprocity of the Treaty.

If this construction be adopted then, each party has forever renounced the right of laying any duties on the vessels of the other coming from any foreign port, or more than 100 sols on those coming coastwise. Could this relinquishment be confined to the two contracting parties alone, the United States would be the gainers, for it is well known that a much* greater number of American than of French vessels are employed in the commerce between the two countries: but the exemption, once conceded by the one nation to the other, becomes immediately the property of all others, who are on the footing of the most-favoured nations. It is true that those others would be obliged to yield the same compensation, that is to say, to receive our vessels duty free. Whether

* By an official paper from the Bureau of the balance of commerce of France, we find that of the ships which entered the ports of France from the U.S. in the year 1789. only 13. amounting to 2105. tons were French, and 163. making 24,172. tons were American.[1]

we should gain or lose in the exchange of the measure with them, is not easy to say.

Another consequence of this construction will be that the vessels of the most favoured nations, paying no duties will be on a better footing than those of natives, which pay a moderate duty, consequently either the duty on these also must be given up, or they will be supplanted by foreign vessels in our own ports.

The resource then of duty on our vessels for the purposes either of revenue or regulation, will be forever lost to both. It is hardly conceivable that either party, looking forward to all these consequences, would see their interest in them.

III. But if France persists in claiming this exemption, what is to be done? The claim indeed is couched in mild and friendly terms; but the idea leaks out that a refusal would authorise them to modify proportionally the favours granted, by the same article, to our navigation. Perhaps they may do what we should feel much more severely; they may turn their eyes to the favours granted us by their Arrets of December 29th. 1787 and December 7th. 1788. which hang on their will alone, unconnected with the Treaty. Those Arrets, among other advantages, admit our whale oils to the exclusion of that of all other foreigners, and this monopoly procures a vent for seven twelfths of the produce of that Fishery, which experience has taught us could find no other market. Near two thirds of the produce of our cod fisheries too have lately found a free vent in the Colonies of France.* This indeed has been an

	Cod fishery	Whale fishery	Both fisheries
France & the French West Indies The rest of the world	586,167 dollrs. 307,097	131,906 dollrs. 101,306	718,073 dollrs. 408,403
Whole produce	893,264	233,212	1,126,476

irregularity growing out of the anarchy reigning in those Colonies. Yet the demands of the Colonists, even of the Government-party among them, (if an auxiliary disposition can be excited by some marks of friendship and distinction on our part) may perhaps produce a constitutional concession to them to procure their provisions at the cheapest market; that is to say, at ours.

* Abstract of the produce of the Fisheries exported from the United States from August 20th. 1789 to August 14th. 1790, in which is omitted one quarter's exportations from Boston, Plymouth, Dighton, Penobscot, Frenchman's Bay, Machias, and New York, of which the returns are not received.

Considering the value of the interests we have at stake, and considering the smallness of difference between foreign and native Tonnage, on French vessels alone, it might perhaps be thought adviseable to make the sacrifice asked; and especially if it can be so done as to give no title to other the most favoured nations to claim it. If the act should put French vessels on the footing of those of natives, and declare it to be in consideration of the favours granted us by the Arrets of Decr. 29th. 1787, and December 7th. 1788, (and perhaps this would satisfy them), no nation could then demand the same favour, without offering an equivalent compensation. It might strengthen too the tenure by which those Arrets are held, which must be precarious, so long as they are gratuitous.

It is desirable, in many instances, to exchange mutual advantages by Legislative Acts rather than by Treaty: because the former, though understood to be in consideration of each other, and therefore greatly respected, yet when they become too inconvenient, can be dropped at the will of either party: whereas stipulations by Treaty are forever irrevocable but by joint consent, let a change of circumstances render them ever so burthensome.

On the whole, if it be the opinion, that the 1st. construction is to be insisted on, as ours, in opposition to the 2d. urged by the Court of France, and that no relaxation is to be admitted, an answer shall be given to that Court defending that construction, and explaining in as friendly terms as possible, the difficulties opposed to the exemption they claim.

2. If it be the opinion that it is advantageous for us to close with France in her interpretation of a reciprocal and perpetual exemption from Tonnage; a repeal of so much of the Tonnage law will be the answer.

3. If it be thought better to waive rigorous and nice discussions of right, and to make the modification an act of friendship and of compensation for favours received, the passage of such a bill will then be the answer.

TH: JEFFERSON

Jan. 18. 1791.

MS (DNA: RG 46, Records of the U. S. Senate); in hand of Jacob Blackwell except for date, signature, and matter indicated in note 1 below. PrC (DLC: TJ Papers, 69: 11968-79); lacking signature and date but not TJ's note as indicated in note 1 below. Entry in SJPL, immediately following that of 17 Jan. 1791 for the draft of the President's message to Congress on "French representation against foreign tonnage" (see note, Document x), reads: "[1791. Jan.] 18. Report Th: J. on same subject, and Otto's letters."

1 This note, keyed to text by asterisk, is in TJ's hand.

X. The President to the Senate

GENTLEMEN OF THE SENATE [17 Jan. 1791]

I lay before you a representation of the Chargé des affaires of France, made by order of his court, on the acts of Congress of the 20th. of July 1789. and 1790. Imposing an extra tonnage on foreign vessels, not excepting those of that country, together with the Report of the Secretary of State thereon: and I recommend the same to your consideration, that I may be enabled to give it such answer as may best comport with the justice and the interests of the United States.

PrC of Dft (DLC); in TJ's hand. Entry in SJPL reads: "[1791. Jan.] 17. Message to Congress on French representation against foreign tonnage." RC (DNA: RG 46, Records of the U.S. Senate); in Lear's hand, signed by Washington, dated "United States January 19th 1791." FC (DLC: Washington Papers). Enclosures: (1) Otto to Secretary of State, 13 Dec. 1790 and 8 Jan. 1791. (2) Report of Secretary of State, 18 Jan. 1791. (3) Printed text of Lambert to TJ, 29 Dec. 1787, with English and French texts of arrêt of that date. (4) Printed text of arrêt of 7 Dec. 1788, with translation of same in Taylor's hand. All of the foregoing are in DNA: RG 46, Records of the U.S. Senate (see Vol. 12: 466-70; Vol. 14: 268-9). The above message and accompanying documents were received by the Senate on 19 Jan. 1791 and are printed in JEP, I, 66-71.

XI. Secretary of State to Louis Guillaume Otto

SIR Philadelphia January 19th. 1791.

It was not in my Power to proceed on the Subject of your Representation of December 13th. till your Favor of January 6th. ascertained a Fact, which I thought material to be known. I have laid the whole before the President of the United States, who, this Day, submits it to the Consideration of the Legislature. Their Forms, their Deliberations, will occasion necessary Delay; and this may, perhaps, be increased by the Connection of the Subject with others depending before them, and which consistence may require to be carried on at the same Time. I can hardly, therefore, flatter myself with the Hope of communicating to you the Result so early as the sailing of your next Packet. But you may be assured that it shall be done as soon as that Result shall be known to me.

Permit me to acknowledge here the Receipt of your Letter of January 8th:, to express by Sense of the friendly Sentiments it conveyed to me from his Majesty's Minister, and Assurances of my sincere Attachment to a Nation whose Prosperity I ardently wish, from a Sentiment of Affection, as well as from a Conviction that that of my own Country is intimately bound up with it. Be pleased to accept yourself, Sir, assurances of the Respect and Esteem, with which I have the Honor to be, Sir, Your most obedient and Most humble Servant,   TH: JEFFERSON

PrC (DLC); in clerk's hand, except for signature. FC (DNA: RG 59, PCC No. 120). Tr in French (DLC: Henry Adams Transcripts); quoted in Otto's dispatch No. 53 to Montmorin, 29 Jan. 1791, consisting only of the passage "Their Forms . . . shall be known to me."

XII. Louis Guillaume Otto to the Secretary of State

[New York, 21 Jan. 1791]

J'ai reçu la lettre que Vous m'avés fait l'honneur de m'ecrire le 19. de ce mois. La demarche que Vous avés bien voulu faire pour engager la Legislature des Etats unis à prendre en consideration la demande que j'ai eu l'honneur de Vous soumettre au nom de Sa Majesté sera d'autant plus utile, que les plaintes multipliées des Negocians et Capitaines François ne peuvent manquer de decourager entierement notre navigation dans les ports des Etats unis. Les Capitaines des deux paquebots François qui se trouvent ici viennent de me representer qu'ils ont payé près de 400. piastres de tonnage et que vû le peu de commerce que font ces batimens, dont l'un est même sur son lest, leurs armateurs seront nécéssairement ruinés en peu de tems. Il paroit, Monsieur, que, dans tous les cas, des batimens fretés uniquement pour la correspondance publique entre les deux Nations devroient être exempts du droit de tonnage, mais comme j'ai lieu de croire que la Legislature jugera convenable d'avoir egard aux reclamations de Sa Majesté, en exemptant les batimens françois collectivement de tout droit de tonnage je ne fais mention de nos paquebots que pour Vous faire connoitre Monsieur un nouvel inconvenient qui resulte de la Loi du Congrès.

Ayant reçu l'ordre de me transporter à Philadelphie en attendant la nomination du Ministre qui doit succeder à M. de Moustier, j'aurai l'honneur, Monsieur, de Vous communiquer differens autres objets qu'il sera interessant de regler.

Les sentimens d'affection que Vous temoignés pour la Nation Françoise ne peuvent surpasser les regrets de mes compatriotes de ne plus Vous voir chés eux. Je saisis avec empressement cette occasion de Vous en donner de nouvelles assurances et je me feliciterai en tout tems d'être l'organe de la haute opinion, qu'ils ont conçue

de Vos talens et de cette politique franche qui a dirigé Votre conduite. Vous me trouverés toujours pret, M., à seconder les dispositions que Vous avés pour resserrer les liens qui unissent les deux
Nations, et pour ecarter les difficultés qui pourront naitre momen-
tanement des differens raports où se trouvent les Administrations
respectives,—J'ai l'honneur d'etre &c

Tr (Arch. Aff. Etr., Paris, Corr. Pol., E.-U., xxxv; photostat in DLC); at head of text: "Newyork, avec le No. 53. —Copie d'une Lettre de M. Otto, Chargé des affaires des France à M. Jefferson, Secretaire d'Etat des Etats-unis; en datte du 21 Janv. 1791." Recorded in SJL as received 26 Jan. 1791.

XIII. Secretary of State to Louis Guillaume Otto

Sir   Philadelphia March 29th. 1791.

The note of December 13th. which you did me the honor to
address to me on the Acts of Congress of the 20th. of July 1789
and 1790. fixing the tonnage payable by foreign vessels arriving
from a foreign port *without excepting those of France*, has been
submitted to the Government of the United States. They consider
the conduct of his most Christian Majesty in making this the subject of fair discussion and explanation as a new proof of his justice
and friendship and they have entered on the consideration with
all the respect due to whatever comes from his Majesty or his
Ministers, and with all the dispositions to find grounds for an
union of opinion which a sincere attachment to your nation and a
desire to meet their wishes on every occasion could inspire. But
the 5th article of the Treaty of Amity and Commerce is not seen
here exactly in the point of view in which your note places it.

[The 3d. and 4th. articles[1] subject the vessels of each nation to
pay in the ports of the other, only such duties as are paid by the
most favoured nation: and give them reciprocally all the privileges
and exemptions in navigation and commerce, which are given by
either to the most favoured nations. Had the contracting parties
stopped here, they would have been free to raise or lower their
tonnage as they should find it expedient; only taking care to keep
the other on the footing of the most favoured Nation.

The question then is whether the 5th. article, cited in the note,
is any thing more than an application of the principle comprised in
the 3d. and 4th. to a particular object? or whether it is an additional stipulation of something not so comprised?

[573]

I. That it is merely an application of a principle comprised in the preceding Articles, is declared by the express words of the Article, to wit, *"Dans l'exemption ci-dessus* est *nommément compris"* &c. *"In the above exemption* is *particularly comprised* the imposition of 100. sols per ton established in France on foreign vessels. Here then is at once an express declaration that the exemption from the duty of 100 sols is *comprised* in the 3d. and 4th. articles; that is to say, it was one of the exemptions enjoyed by the most favoured nations, and, as such, extended to us by those articles. If the exemption spoken of in this 1st. member of the 4th. article was *comprised* in the 3d. and 4th. articles, as is expressly declared, then the reservation by France out of that exemption (which makes the 2d. member of the same Article) *was also comprised*: that is to say, if *the whole* was comprised *the part* was comprised. And if this reservation of France in the 2d. member was comprised in the 3d. and 4th. articles, then the counter reservation by the United States (which constitutes the 3d. and last member of the same Article) was also comprised. Because it is but a corresponding portion of a similar whole on our part, which had been comprised by the same terms with theirs.

In short the whole article relates to a particular duty of 100. sols laid by some antecedent law of France on the vessels of foreign nations, relinquished as to the most favoured, and consequently to us. It is not a new and additional stipulation then, but a declared application of the stipulations comprised in the preceding articles to a particular case, by way of greater caution.

The doctrine laid down generally in the 3d. and 4th. articles, and exemplified specially in the 5th. amounts to this. "The vessels of the most favoured Nations, coming from foreign ports, are exempted from the duty of 100 sols: therefore you are exempted from it by the 3d. and 4th. articles. The vessels of the most-favoured Nations, coming coastwise, pay that duty: therefore you are to pay it by the 3d. and 4th. Articles. We shall not think it unfriendly in you to levy a like duty on Coasters, because it will be no more than we have done ourselves. You are free also to lay that or any other duty on vessels coming from foreign ports, provided they apply to all other Nations, even the most favoured. We are free to do the same, under the same restriction. Our exempting you from a duty which the most favoured nations do not pay, does not exempt you from one which they do pay."

In this view it is evident that the 5th. Article neither enlarges, nor abridges the stipulations of the 3d. and 4th. The effect of the

Treaty would have been precisely the same had it been omitted altogether; consequently it may be truly said that the reservation by the United States in this article is completely useless. And it may be added with equal truth that the equivalent reservation by France is completely useless: as well as her previous abandoment of the same duty: and in short the whole article. Each party then remains free to raise or lower it's tonnage, provided the change operates on all nations, even the most-favoured.

Without undertaking to affirm, we may obviously conjecture, that this article has been inserted on the part of the United States from an over caution to guard, *nommement, by name,* against a particular aggrievance, which they thought they could never be too well secured against: and that has happened, which generally happens; doubts have been produced by the two great number of words used to prevent doubt.

II. The Court of France however understands this article as intended to introduce something to which the preceding articles had not reached; and not merely as an application of them to a particular case. Their opinion seems to be founded on the general rule, in the construction of instruments, to leave no words merely useless, for which any rational meaning can be found. They say that the reservation by the United States of a right to lay a duty equivalent to that of the 100. sols, reserved by France, would have been completely useless, if they were left free, by the preceding articles, to lay a tonnage to any extent whatever. Consequently that the reservation of a part proves a relinqueshment of the residue.

If some meaning, and such a one, is to be given to the last member of the article, some meaning, and a similar one, must be given to the corresponding member. If the reservation by the United States of a right to lay an equivalent duty, implies a relinquishment of their right to lay any other, the reservation by France of a right to continue the specified duty to which it is an equivalent, must imply a relinquishment of the right on her part to lay or continue any other. Equivalent reservations by both, must imply equivalent restrictions on both. The exact reciprocity stipulated in the preceding articles, and which pervades every part of the Treaty, ensures a counter right to each party for every right ceded to the other.

Let it be further considered that the duty called *tonnage* in the United States is in lieu of the duties for anchorage, for the support of Buoys, Beacons, and Lighthouses, to guide the mariner into harbour, and along the coast, which are provided and supported at the expence of the United States, and for fees to measurers, weighers, gaugers &c. who are paid by the United States; for which articles, among many others (light excepted) duties are paid by us in the ports of France under their specific names. That Government has hitherto thought these duties consistent with the Treaty; and consequently the same duties under a general, instead of specific names, with us, must be equally consistent with it; it is not the name, but the thing which is essential. If we have renounced the right to lay any port duties, they must be understood to have equally renounced that of either laying new or continuing the old. If we ought to refund the port duties received from their vessels since the date of the act of Congress, they should refund the port duties they have received from our vessels since the date of the Treaty, for nothing short of this is the reciprocity of the Treaty.

If this construction be adopted then, each party has forever renounced the right of laying any duties on the vessels of the other coming from any foreign port, or more than 100. sols on those coming coastwise. Could this relinquishment be confined to the two contracting parties alone it's effect would be calculable:[2] But the exemption once conceded by the one nation to the other, becomes immediately the property of all others, who are on the footing of the most favoured Nations. It is true that those others would be obliged to yield the same compensation, that is to say, to receive our vessels duty free. Whether France and the United States[3] would gain or lose in the exchange of the measure with them, is not easy to say.

Another consequence of this construction will be that the vessels of the most favoured nations, paying no duties will be on a better footing than those of natives, which pay a moderate duty. Consequently either the duty on these also must be given up, or they will be supplanted by foreign vessels in our own ports.

The resource then of duty on vessels for the purposes either of revenue or regulation, will be forever lost, to both. It is hardly conceivable that either party, looking forward to all these consequences, would see their interest in them.][4] So that on the whole, Sir, we consider the 5th. article of the Treaty merely as an illustration of the 3d. and 4th. articles, by an application of the principles comprised in them to the case stated in that, and that a contrary construction would exceedingly embarrass and injure both the contracting parties. We feel every disposition on our part to make considerable sacrifices where they would result to the sole benefit of your nation: but where they would excite from other nations corresponding claims, it becomes necessary to proceed with caution. You probably know, Sir, that the general subject of navigation was before our Legislature at their last Session, and was postponed merely for the want of time to go through it before the period arrived to which the constitution had limited their existence. It will be resumed at the meeting of the new Legislature, and from a knowledge of the sincere attachment of my Countrymen to the prosperity of your nation, and to the increase of our intercourse with it, I may safely say for the new Legislature that the encouragement of that intercourse for the advantage of both parties will be considered as among the most interesting branches of the general subject submitted to them. From a perfect conviction of the coincidence of our interests nobody wishes more sincerely to cultivate the habit of mutual good offices and favours than he who has the honor to be with sentiments of the greatest respect and esteem Sir Your most obedient and most humble Servant.

PrC (DLC); in clerk's hand, unsigned. FC (DNA: RG 59, PCC No. 120). Tr (Arch. Aff. Etr., Paris, Corr. Pol., E.-U., XXXV; photostat in DLC); in French.

As indicated in Editorial Note above, TJ made a few appropriate changes in the text of his report to the President (Document IX) and utilized this for his response to Otto. The texts of the two documents are the same except as indicated in textual notes below.

1 TJ here omitted the words "of the Treaty of Amity and Commerce between France and the United States" that appear in his report.

2 TJ here omitted the following passage that appears in his report: ". . . the United States would be the gainers,

for it is well known that a much greater number of American than of French vessels are employed in the commerce between the two countries." The footnote to this passage was of course also omitted.

3 In report the beginning of this sentence reads: "Whether we would . . . ."

4 The passage in brackets (supplied) containing the statement of the case and the analysis of the meaning of Article V is exactly the same as that in the report to the President except as indicated in the preceding notes. Omissions and variations preceding and following this passage were such as were required to convert a report to the President to an appropriate response to the French government.

To Jacob Hiltzheimer

SIR   Philadelphia. Jan. 19. 1791.

Convenience obliged me to detain the within till the beginning of this month, but the subsequent delay has entirely proceeded from the circumstance of your account's having escaped my eye, and my mind being totally occupied by other objects which have for some time forbidden me to think of any thing private. Accept this apology for the delay and assurances of the esteem with which I am Sir Your most obedient humble servt.,   TH: JEFFERSON

PrC (MHi); after PrC was executed, TJ wrote at foot of text: "Mr. Jacob Hiltzheimer, covering an order on the bank for 60.10 Dollars." TJ's entry in

Account Book for this date reads: "gave Hilzheimer order on bank for 60.1 in full keeping horses—his servants 1 D."

To Henrietta Maria Colden

MADAM   Philadelphia Jan. 20. 1791.

I am sure I shall have appeared very inattentive to the honour of the letter you were pleased to write me, but I have not been so in what was essential. The truth is that I have been obliged by an extraordinary press of business, to suspend all private correspondencies for some weeks past. But immediately on the reciept of your letter I laid the wishes of your son before the head of the department to which it belonged, and also before the head of all the departments. I am in hopes it will appear to others, as it does to me that Mr. Colden will be an acquisition to our infant attempts at a marine. In this persuasion, I shall not fail to render him any service I can. I had indeed expected that some vessels of greater dignity would be agreed on; but as yet this has not taken place.— I congratulate you Madam on the late pacification. Tho' we should of right have had nothing to do with this war, yet when neighbors' houses are afire, our own is always in danger.—We have been told here of the sufferings of New York for want of fuel and bread with more than charitable concern. I hope they have been less than fame has made them, and that they are at an end. I have the honour to be with sentiments of the most perfect respect & esteem, Madam, your most obedient and most humble servt.,

TH: JEFFERSON

PrC (DLC).

For a comment on the surprising fact that Mrs. Colden applied to TJ for an appointment of her son on one of the revenue cutters rather than to Hamilton, see note to Mrs. Colden to TJ, 25 Nov. 1790 and Editorial Note to the group of documents on Mediterranean trade, under 28 Dec. 1790.

To Francis Eppes

DEAR SIR   Philadelphia Jan. 20. 1791.

I was in hopes that before this I could have invited Jack to come on, and had a lodging ready for him. But the house I agreed for, to be delivered to me completely finished on the 1st. day of October, is still full of workmen. I have got one room in it, in which I am obliged to sleep, to eat, and to do business with all the world, and the workmen say it will still be six weeks before they can put me at my ease. Sometime in March therefore I am in hopes I shall be ready for Jack. In the mean time the season would be almost too rigorous to attend lectures which are given mostly in the night and distant from my habitation.—Peace is at length established between Great Britain and Spain. The merchants write that this has had an unfavourable effect on American produce. Wheat is here at a French crown. But it will be lower as soon as the farmers can come to market. There will be a considerable demand for it in France, particularly in the Southern parts. I see you are making lusty preparation for Hanson in February. Will you be so good as to let me know, after your sale is over, how much it averages a head, as also the proportion of tithables and not tithables. It will enable me to decide what I must do in the same way the ensuing fall. Mine will only be supplementary to my lands. Present me most affectionately to Mrs. Eppes and the young people. I hope when I come to Virginia again I shall be able to see her and you. As soon as my workmen permit me you shall again hear from me. I am with great sincerity dear Sir your affectionate friend & servt.,   TH: JEFFERSON

PrC (ViU).

YOUR SALE: On 5 Jan. (as well as 12 and 19 Jan.) 1791, the *Virginia Gazette, and General Advertiser* carried the following advertisement: "On the first day of February next, will be sold, on two years credit, at my planta-tion in Cumberland county, (three miles above Col. Skipwith's mill) ONE HUNDRED NEGROES. *Bond on good security will be required, and all bonds not punctually discharged, to bear interest from their dates.* FRANCIS EPPES. —Chesterfield county, Dec. 15, 1790."

To Martha Jefferson Randolph

MY DEAR DAUGHTER   Philadelphia Jan. 20. 1791.

Mr. Short in a late letter says that your acquaintances in Panthemont complain excessively of your inattention to them and desired him to mention it. Matters there are going on well. The sales of the church lands are succeful beyond all calculation. There has been a riot in Paris in which M. de Castrie's houshould furniture was destroyed. I am opening my things from Paris as fast as the workmen will make room for me. In a box lately opened I find a copy of the octavo edition of the Encyclopedie, and a complete copy of Buffon's works with Daubenton's part which I had written for to present to Mr. Randolph. But I do not know when I shall be able to send any thing forward from the slowness of workmen in making houseroom for me to open my things and for the ice in the river.—The cold of this place has made me wish for some stockings of cotton and hair's fur knit together. I do not recall whether Bet can knit. If she can do it well, it might be a good employment for her sometimes. If she cannot, I wish a good knitter could be found in the neighborhood to knit some for me. They should be very large. Present my cordial regards to Mr. Randolph, and kiss Polly for me, telling her I have received not a single letter from Monticello since I left it, except one from Mr. Randolph. Adieu my dear. Your's affectionately,

TH: JEFFERSON

P.S. The inclosed letter is for a neighbor of yours being somewhere on the waters of Buckisland. It is from her sister who is in Paris, the wife of one of the Duke of Orleans's grooms. He was of General Phillips's army.

RC (NNP). PrC (MHi).

In ViU: TJMF there is a MS list of the names and ages of sixty-one of Martha's schoolmates at the Abbaye de Panthemont, undated but evidently drafted in 1786 since Martha's age is given as 14 (Mary's name was interpolated later without an age being given). An endorsement by M.J.T. Burke states that an asterisk had been placed opposite the names of Martha's intimate friends. These were, with their numbers preceding and their ages following:

19	D'haricourt	22
23	Bellecour	14
26	Bruni	14
30	Varcourt	13
34	D'harincourt	6
35	Annesley	16
36	Hawkins	17
37	Liniere	15
60	Memene Bellecour	
61	Izi D'Orgemont	

From William Green

SIR, London January the 21. 1791.

I have the honour to address you upon a subject of Public Interest to the United States of America; and which as your time must be constantly occupied upon important topics, I shall introduce to your notice with all possible brevity as well as myself, a general Resident and doing business as an American Merchant in the City of New York; which I quitted for a few months in September last, to settle some private affairs which were then pending in Great Britain.

I embarked on board the Brigantine Rachel Captain Nicholas Duff Commander bound to London (an attested Copy of whose affidavit I now inclose herewith as containing material information upon the Subject.) I have only to add that the Vessel has been for many years the property of Citizens of the United States and that I purchased her in August last from Mr. Nicholas Breevoort Merchant also of New York, her former Owner and in whose employ and under the present regulations of Congress she had frequently been admitted to an entry in the Ports of England and Ireland and even so late as May last landed a Cargo at Limerick.

Upon the opening of this business at the British Treasury, I thought it necessary to claim of the British Ministers the right of the United States to naturalize foreign Vessels of any description whenever it might be found necessary or expedient so to do, a right exercised by all independent Nations and particularly by Great Britain, and under this plea contended for the admission of the Rachel to an entry but was delayed from time to time from receiving any Answer, until after the Signature of the Convention with Spain when apparently it being deemed as no longer necessary to temporize upon this question of Commercial Policy, I received on the 24 day of December last a direct Negative; and under the oppressive circumstances in which the Captain had been placed by the Officers of the Customs in this Port his detention was unavoidably such that the Vessel could not depart until the 20th. Instant.

I am a very great loser by the detention of the Vessel as that Affidavit truly states and also in some degree by the fall in the price of her Cargo, which after all I am constrained to hazard at a Market for which it was not originally intended, and where also I may be a great loser, but as it was a question of Commercial Policy interesting to the Union, I conceived it to be my duty as a Citizen not to shrink from it's decision.

I trust you will have the goodness to pardon my adding a few remarks upon this Subject.

It has been for ages the policy of the Nations of Europe, whilst at War to cover their Navigation under the Flags and papers of Neutral Nations, and this is a prime source of the present Wealth of the Dutch and all the Hanse Towns and free Imperial Cities particularly Hamburg whose Flag is generally attended to as much upon the Ocean as if she had Twenty Sail of Line of Battle Ships to protect it from Injury and Insult.

It is not the custom generally in Europe to state in the Lettres de Mer or other Sea papers where the Vessel was or might have been built, but simply to declare her to be the property of a Citizen or Subject of the Government furnishing the papers.

The Custom of inserting the name of the place of built originated in England for Domestic purposes and from thence became adopted in the Colonies.

In future Wars the profit of these usages will center with the American Merchant if he is supported and protected by his Government. At present I humbly recommend an alteration in the form of the Documents furnisht to Ships and Vessels belonging to the United States, and that in the new papers to be given in lieu of the old the place of the original built of the Vessel be left out and that She be simply asserted to be the property of a Citizen or Citizens of the United States.

The obvious motive of this Government is to prevent the American Merchant from availing himself of these advantages by confining all American Commerce to Vessels built in the United States or to Vessels that Great Britain may chuse to deem British Vessels and even the former must be navigated agreeably to Regulations made by this same Government otherways if examined by a British Cruiser near any part of any English Coast they are liable to seizure and confiscation. My personal Inconvenience from this loss is very little when compared with another which I have sustained under the Flag of the United States and which is little short of the amount of Two hundred thousand dollars. It is in order to ascertain under Consular proofs the authenticity of this loss to lay before Congress at my return that I am now in England.— I have the honour to be with the greatest respect and Consideration Sir Your most Obedient Humble Servant,

WILLIAM GREEN

RC (DLC); endorsed by TJ as received 12 Apr. 1791 and so recorded in SJL. Dupl (DLC); similarly endorsed but not recorded in SJL. Enclosure: Affidavit of Nicholas Duff, "Commander of the Brigantine Rachel of and belonging to the Port and City of New York . . . and Registered and Navigated according to the Laws of Congress," stating that *Rachel* sailed from New York on 11 Sep. 1790 with a cargo of pot ash, pearl ash, and staves bound for London; that on her arrival on 22 Oct. 1790 "the Officers of the London Custom House . . . refused to admit her to an entry, under pretence that it was contrary to Law, the said Brigantine having been originally built in the Dominions of the King of France; but informed him it being only a form of Office, so soon as an application was made at the British Treasury, the Lords Commissioners thereof would certainly permit her to enter and discharge"; that, though a speedy answer was from time to time promised, no answer was given until 24 Dec. 1790 when *Rachel* was positively refused entry; and that, by this delay of sixty-three days the owners sustained a loss of £681 sterling, "having lost by her detention a full freight out to Seville and back again to London" (Tr in DLC, dated 17 Jan. 1791 and attested as a true copy by Joshua Johnson on 5 Feb. 1791).

From Stephen Cathalan, Jr.

SIR   Marseilles the 22d. January 1791

I had the honour of Paying you my Respects the 25th. Last Septber, since I am Favoured with your honoured Lines of the 7th. do.

It is To You, Sir, that I owe the Appointment of being Vice-Consul for the U.S. in this Place. I will be ever Gratefull of that Mark of esteem and Friendship confered on me by you, and will endeavour, by my Proceedings, that never you Regret the choice you have made of me.

I have noted, that the tittle of Vice Consul, makes any other difference with that of Consul, but of Being not an American Native. I am well Satisfied as it is; Tittles and Denominations are of a very little consequence in the Fact; to Feel an office with Integrity, Dignity and Proper Knowledge must be the only ambition of the Person appointed and will be mine as much as in my Power.

I will only observe you, that on the Numbers of Foreing Consuls in this Place, many are not Native of the Country they Reppresent, and are appointed as the others natives, *Consuls.* I will be like the Single reppresentent of a Nation, Called vice-Consul, a tittle that is Confounded or Synonim here with that of Chancellor, appointed by his own Consul.

Foreing Consuls makes here a kind of a Body, Paying their visits in a Body to Proper Persons, meeting and Dining together often, their chancellors or vice-Consuls are not admitted in their meetings; when I will be Installed, I will shew them by your Letters the Reasons why I am appointed *Vice Consul,* and hope they will make any difference and admit me. It would be very hard if they should not do it.

I acknowledge that when a Native American will accept that Office, he is Entitled to have the Prefference on any other, but as long as any will offer, the U.S. would be reppresented as the others nations; these are, Sir, Private observations between you and me, Intending not at all ask any alteration on the Resolves of Congress, to whose I Submitt, I will Follow and execute.

The Long detention of the Commissions in the hands of M. de Montmorin, must be attributed to the great alterations made in the French Government. As to the uniform, arms, seall and Legend, I wrotte to Mr. Wm. Short, for some necessary explanations, which he could not Give me, he addressed me, to Comodor Paul Jones at Paris, for the uniform, and to Dupré engravor for the arms. I

[583]

expect their answers, I have wrotte in the mean time to Jos. Fenwick Consul at Bordeaux, who will I hope Give them to me.

This Letter will Go to America by the Sardinian, vessel L'Antoinette Capn. Jos. Barret belonging to Mr. Ju. Bste. Guide, Mercht. of Nice, whom you know. I have Loaded on her 40 young olive Tries of the Best quality, with a chest of olives for Sowing to the address of Messrs. Robt Gilmor & Co. of Baltimore, with orders to forward them by the 1st. opportunity to Charles Town Sth. Caroa. to Messrs. Brailsford & Morris or Mr. Wm. Drayton. They are well Packed in 6 Barrels with Sand &c. and hope will arive in the Good Season, to be planted; you have here inclosed the Memorandum of my Gardner for the manner of Planting them, as well a Bill of Loading. Mr. Pierre Guide Brother to J. Bste. Goes him self in that vessel, and very Gently has Loaded them free of Freight; he intend to Sale her Cargo and Load it in Return with Tobacco for the Farm of Turin, if this Trial Succeeds, he intends to establish him self in America and furnish that Farm with that article; I have taken the Liberty of Giving him a Letter of Introduction for you, and will be gratefull of what you will do in his Favour.

You have the Invoice of the olive tries here inclosed, the amount of which I value on M. Grant Banker at Paris in £162^{tt}. Tourns. I have ordered an other Parcel of olive Trees at Gignac in Languedoc, which will be Loaded for america, via Bordeaux by Jos. Fenwick Consul for U.S. and expect in a day or two receive the Invoice, with advice of their departure by the Canal, for that place.

My Father, Mother, wife and Little Daughter very gratefull of what you have done for me, and of your kind remembrance, assure you with their Respects.

I hope that by this time, with the Last orders my Father has sent to Messrs. Willing Morris & Swanwick of Phila. and under your kind interposition the unhappy affair of Mr. Ths. Barclay may be Settled, which I will [be] happy to Learn, and more to receive the Divi[dends] being in a Great need of Money. I have the honour to be with Respect Sir Your most obedient humble & Devoted Servant   STEPHEN CATHALAN JUNR. or Younger

Please to observe, that I have not Communicated to Gimon Brothers my Refflexion about the Algerine Busisness; with them I keap an other Language.

RC (DLC); addressed: "Thos. Jefferson Secretary of State Philadelphia *Private* Affairs"; endorsed by TJ as received 30 Apr. 1791 and so recorded in SJL; slightly mutilated, two words being supplied from Dupl (DLC), which has one addition to the text under date of 26 Jan. as indicated below and is endorsed by TJ as received 19 June 1791, but is not recorded in SJL. Enclosures: (1) "Memorandum for the Olive Tries Marseilles the 22d. January 1791" stating that, if the trees arrive safely before the end of May, they might be planted in squares of 15 to 18 feet at a depth of one foot; that, if not, the barrels should be placed in a trench together, the hoops and a few staves removed, and kept watered during the summer; that they should be kept out "of the Sun in the Great hot weather" until planted later; that the chest of olives should be planted three feet deep, covered, watered, and opened the succeeding February, after which: "they will take some olives, that they will Break, to see if the almond have firmented; if it has not yet Swelled, they will cover it again and leave it for one year more; they will Sow them, if they have Swelled, at one Inch depth in the Land, recover them with Land, putting on it, horse Dunk one Inch,

watering them with an arrosoir; then they will sprout out in 2 or 3 Months, otherwise it would be only the insuing year" (Tr in Cathalan's hand, signed by him, DLC; PrC in hand of Lambert, undated, DLC). (2) Invoice for "40 young olive Tries, costing with all charges Included on Board . . . £150ᵗᵗ one chest olives for sowing 12ᵗᵗ," dated 20 Jan. 1791 (MHi, in Cathalan's hand and signed by him). Copies of enclosures were transmitted by TJ to William Drayton, 1 May 1790.

On 26 Jan. 1791 Cathalan wrote TJ enclosing an invoice just received from Gignac for "2 Barls. Containing together 20 young olive Trees and 24 very Younger ones," costing 60 livres and, with those sent by *Antoinette*, making a total of 222 livres (RC in MHi; endorsed by TJ as received 30 Apr. 1791 and so recorded in SJL; in Dupl of his letter above Cathalan repeated the substance of this letter of 26 Jan. 1791; Dupl of both invoices in DLC: TJ Papers, 59: 10264).

From Stephen Cathalan, Jr.

SIR   Marseilles the 22d. January 1791.

I had the honour of recieving your Letters of the 17th. Last June and 26th. Last August; this Last came the First to me.

That of the 17th. June advising me that the President of the United States has honoured me with the appointment of Vice-Consul for United States of America in this Port of Marseilles, reached my hands very little Time since. The Commission Inclosed in it, Wilm. Short Esqr. your chargé d'affaires at Paris, took it out from it in order to gett from the French Minister of Foreing Affairs the *Exequatur*; and as I expected from a Day to an other to receive it, and on it make my self acknowlegded towards the Admiralty and the executive Power of this Department; tho' I have not yet received it, I find now that I have too Long time delay'd of acknowleging you the receipt of those two Letters, and Making you, Sir, my sincere thanks for the honour that the President of U.S. has Confered on me, in Appointing me for that honourable office.

I beg you, Sir, to assure the President of United States, that I will use all my endeavours and employ every thing in my Power to render my self worth of the feeling of that office, to the Satisfaction of Congress and the American Individuals, when they will have occasion to avail of my Services.

I will Conform myself in all Points to the Duties and regulations for the exercise of Consular office, mentioned in your Letter of the 20th. Last August, as well as on those that Congress or you will order me to follow, and never Mislead.

Any American Vessels have yet appeared in this, nor any other French Ports of the Mediteranean, since a very Long Time. When Some will appear, I will not fail to give your every Six Months an State of them arranged in the Manner you Prescribe, closed in the Last Days of June and December; as Long as a Treaty between U.S. and Algiers will not take Place, I apprehend that tho' I desire with all my Heart, to be useful to United States, my Services will be of very little use to America.

To Prove you, Sir, how much I wish to contribute with all my Power to their Welfare and Prosperity, I Take the Liberty of Inclosing you in this Packett my Refflexions on Such a Treaty and a Repport of what I have done till now, to prepare the means to make it if Possible.

I leave the whole to your wise Considerations, and if Found by you worth the Serious attention of Congress, I will find my self very happy if my Services in that Line may be accepted.

I will do my self the honor of wearing the Navy uniform you Prescribe, as Soon as I will be Installed in the Vice-Consular Office, and to sustain with Dignity the Respectable Nation I am to Reppresent here.

In Politicks I have no news worth your attention this Moment. You are I doubt not well advised of all what ocurs Dayly at Paris; I will not fail of advising you of what may occur here.

In the Commercial Line, I am of Opinion, that if they Succeed in the Natal. Assy. to Distroy the Farm of Tobacco, that Branch of Trade between France and America will become very active, and that very little Tobacco will be Planted in France, as it will become Dearer and not of a So good quality as your's.

I have obtained Lately at Court, that Foreing Beef and Pork Salted, which could not be interposed at Marseilles Free of Duty, but when destined for our East or West Indies Islands, will now be sold or Shipped for any Foreing Port, without paying the duty of about £12^{tt} ℔ Bal; I sollicited that alteration, Shewing the injustice of being obliged to pay that heavy duty, on a Large Parcel of american Pork, which I had order to Send to Cadiz, finding not an advantageous sale here; by that new regulation I have already shipped them Freely.

I apprehend that as we have suffered Large and heavy Rains during 3 Months which have caused Large innundations of almost all the Rivers of France, we will have a Bad Crop of wheat, this Summer; now American Wheat would obtain £36^{tt} to 37^{tt} ₩ Charge (100 English quarters makes 175 Charges) superfine Fresh Flour £38^{tt} to 40^{tt} ₩ Bal.; the above Prices will rise next Spring and Summer, if unfortunately the young Crop proves bad. I am of oppinion of encouraging the American exports of that Produce, this way, if Prices are Moderate with you.

The Exchange on London is now here at 25d. ½ to ¾ ₩ ecu of 3 Livres. Fish oil For Tannaries is at very high Prices and scarce here, Since the Prohibition of the Foreing whale oil; American whale oil will meet now with fine and advantageous Sales tho' it's quality has not yet been much Liked in France, would it not be Possible to make it as well in America, as that of Portugal. French Baccaloo oil has been sold at 220^{tt} ₩ Cask of about ℔. 500. American whale oil would I dare say obtain now about £30^{tt} pr. ql. of 90 lb. English, if of Good quality. I have the honour to be with respect Sir Your most obedient humble & Devoted Servant   STEPHEN CATHALAN JUNR.

RC (DNA: RG 59, CD); recorded in SJL as received 30 Apr. 1791. Dupl (same); at head of text: "Copy."

ENCLOSURE

Refflexions on a Treaty of Peace between United States of America and Algiers

Marseilles the 20th. January 1791.

It is not to me to Shew to Congress, the Great Advantages it would result to America, by a Peace or a Truce with Algiers.

I have not been authorised to do what I have done till now; it may be desowned, and my too much active Zeal in that affair, may be with Reason Censured.

The Conversing here or at Paris on that subject, with Thos. Jefferson Esqr. Secretary of State, when he was Minister in France, we have seen, with the greatest concern that as long as a Treaty should not take Place with Algiers, the Mediterranean would be shut to the American Colour, and of Course American Trade, which cou'd become very extensive in this Part of the Globe, would remain as it is since the Independency, of very Little Consequence.

When Ths. Barclay Esqr. went to Algiers, to treat for a Peace, Algerians having taken very Little time before two American Vessels, and hoping to have for the Rapacity of their Cruziers, a New and advantageous chance, encouraged I doubt not by the English Consul, treated him with scorn; but Since, Seven Years are elapsed, Algerians have made any other Prizes on the Americans, and have Little hopes of making any others; it appears then that now it is Time to make a New attempt.

Having been honoured by Congress, with the Appointment of Vice-Consul for United States of America in the Port of Marseilles, finding that very seldom I may have opportunities to be useful to the Country which has Adopted me, whishing however to deserve and answer to the confidence Congress has in me, by some Important Services for my own Part, being established in the European Place, the best situated to Correspond with Algiers, and very Intimate with the Single Merchants who have a Factory there, where they remained Long, who are highly considered by the Dey, at Lenght knew by a Long experience the Sprit or the Politick of that country, and the Best Manner of Treating there; I suggested my Ideas in September last to Mr. Willm. Short, chargé d'affaires a Paris. He answered me the 6th. october last.

"I cannot say any thing at present, about the Algerine Business. Still if that house would find out whether the Dey would take a Moderate Price for our Prisonners who are there, it would be an Agreeable Circumstance; if they make inquiries, they Should take care to do it as of their own Accord and not authorised by U. S. Hitherto the Dey has demanded an Exhorbitant Price."

On that kind of encouragement, tho' I don't dissemble to me my little Knowledge in Politick, and the Difficulties I would have to Surmount in a Negotiation for a Peace, I found that American Prisonners could not be treated with advantage for U. S. but in Treating at the Same Time for a Peace.

I then Remitted the 14th. october Last, a Note of which I annex here a Copy No 1. Joined is the Copy of the Answer from Algiers No 2, which I received the 12th. Inst. to which I have repplyed the 15th. do. as ℔ Copy No 3.

I will not fail of advising Ths. Jefferson Secretary of State of the News I will receive on that affair, but I will now Wait the Orders Congress or he will Give me and not Go on Further.

The advantages of a Peace with Algiers will be very great ones if it can be obtained on Moderate Terms.

The Spanish and Italians Markets would be open to the American Codfish or Baccalao, which Could be Sold at under Prices than the English Fishery, that would become a Large Branch of Trade, Yearly extended to the advantage of U. S., when of Course the English Fishery would Lessen by the Concurence. (Tho' Marseilles will remain a Free Port, Foreing Fisheries are and will remain subjected to a Prohibitive Duty, to favor the French fishery).

Wheat and Flour Tobacco and all the others American Products would be carried into the Mediterraneans Ports, on the American Bottoms, at more moderate Freights than on any others.

The American Navy would Soon become Powerfull, their Stocks full of Ships on the Building, which would be sold advantageously in the Mediterranean Ports, when since the Act of the English Parliament, prohibiting the Purchase by their fellow subjects, of the American Built-Vessels, that Important Branch is quite Lost in America.

The American Vessels could be employed on Freight, for any Voyage in Europe in Concurence with the Danish, Dutch, English or Sweedish Vessels; and in Case of Warr between France, England or Spain, if U. S. were Neutrals, their Vessels would be employed as other Neutral Vessels at Very advantageous Freights.

At Lenght can we calculate yet what may Gett U. S. by Such a Treaty in the actual circumstances of F . . . . e, and her C . . . . . es [France and her colonies].

Now it is to be Weighed, what it will cost to U. S. to obtain by a Peace, with Algiers, the above advantages or any others; Congress will Judge in his Wisdom what Sacrifices he will make to obtain it.

As to the means for recover what will be lost, without hurting the Finances of the U. S. by some Moderate Tax, it is not to me to Suggest it to Congress; however as in a Scheme, all what may contribute to it's Success, ought enter in it, I dare yet Give also my Oppinion, on that Point tho' perhaps I go to far out of my Line.

A Small Tax, of a retenûe of about 6 Pence ℔ Pound Currency on the Wages of the Mariners; a Moderate Tax of So much ℔ Ton on any American Vessels Bound to Cadix, and for any Mediterranean Ports; at Lenght a Tax on each Mediterranean Pass, delivered to any American Vessels, which by their destination would be in need of; These three objects I dare Say would not be found heavy or un Popular; the wages and Freights would rise in Proportion to those triffling Taxes, and would Soon cover the Amount of the Expences of that Peace, and in Case that the above taxes would not be Sufficient, a Very Small Duty on the Cargoes exported from U. S. for the Mediterranean would exceed it Soon.

As to the Agents I have employed, and am of Opinion that Congress should employ, if he not prefers employ me by their interposition, they are not very Interested People, but if they Succeed, what Congress will allow them for their Benefit on such a Negotiation, will be more economical to U. S. even in doing it with a kind of munificiency worth of a Powerfull Nation, than the Charges &c. &c. &c. attending an Embassy on that Purpose, of which I dare Say, the Success would be a great deal more uncertain.

What the Dey of Algiers may ask from U. S. may be easily Foreseen, some fine Vessel for Cruizer, or Small Fregatte, well Feeted, Ship Timber, Iron, Ropes, Gun Powder and other things for Ship's use, with some Cash intended for the Liberty of the Slaves; more or Less, are the Basis of Such a Treaty.

If Congress intends on the above to Treat, it will be necessary that he Gives all at wants [once] orders for a Proposal, with the ultimatum at the same Time; because by the Results of the Meetings with the Persons I employ, we find that Success will depend to Lay hold of a favorable opportunity, from the Dey in Getting in the Same Instant

[589]

his first and Last word all at wants, before any Body Can't be inform'd. To find that moment, is the most Difficult Matter.

I have enough Said on that Subject; happy I will be! if my Proceedings may obtain the approbation of Congress; if on the Contrary they deserve Censure, I dare hope to be excused in favour of a too ardent Zeal for my own Part, having sought this Occasion to Shew how I am tied to the welfare and Prosperity of the United States of America.

STEPHEN CATHALAN JUNR.

RC (DNA: RG 59, CD). Dupl (same) at head of text: "Copy." Enclosures: (1) "Copy of a Note remitted by Stephen Cathalan Jr. Vice-Consul for the United States of America to Messrs. Gimon Brothers," Marseilles, 14 Oct. 1790, asking that firm to write to their house at Algiers to find out the names and numbers of American prisoners there and at the same time to inquire of the Dey the lowest price required for their ransom, since until then "il en a demandé un prix exhorbittant, que les Etats unis ne peuvent absolument payer" and if the Dey would set a good price a humanitarian order might raise the sum. Cathalan also pointed out that, since the corsairs had made no other captives among American sailors, it would be better to make peace: "ce peuple," he added, "est encore nouveau et Pauvre, il ne peut Gueres donner, et le Dey ne peût raisonablement exiger des condittions pareilles a celles qu'il a mis aux diverses nations d'Europe qui Frequentent La Mediterannée ou qui y ont Leur Ports"; if the Regency were in fact disposed to make proposals for a treaty with the United States, then Cathalan would seek powers of treating through the agency of Messrs. Gimon & Cie. He inquired of the conditions that would be set for treating and concluded: "Il Parait que Jusqu'a Present, C'est Le Consul d'Angleterre, par ordre sans doutte de cette Puissance, qui doit y avoir mis Les plus Grands obstacles; Le Ressentiment des Anglais contre Les Americains est encore assés fort pour Leur faire sacrifier de L'Argent pour traverser ou rompre toute Negociation, C'est Suivant mon Oppinion Le Point Le plus difficille. L'essential quant a present doit etre de recommander Le Secret, et d'empecher autant que possible que Le Consul Anglais soit Informé" (MS in DNA: RG 59, CD; at head of text: "Algier's Affair No. 1"; in Cathalan's hand; Dupl in same).

(2) "Algier's Answer to the Preced- ing Note, received at Marseilles the 12th January, 1791," unsigned and undated, acknowledging Cathalan's inquiry and stating that they had had an audience with the Dey and "nous serions peutetre venûs a Bout de traitter de suitte et de la Paix et du Rachapt des Esclaves, si nous Eussions été authorisés de faire des Propositions acceptables, Car il y aurait Vraysemblablement plûs d'attention, mais comme nous n'avons pû luy en parler que Vagûement, il a Seulement Repondû qu'il ne pouvait pour le moment entendre a aucun Accomodement." The correspondent of Messrs. Gimon & Cie. added that, although they had acted in secret, there were grounds for believing that several persons at Algiers knew of their activity; that the Dey had sent to them that day to say that he demanded 15,000 sequins or 150,000₶ for the fourteen American slaves, to which 25,000₶ should be added for "Fraix de Rachapt ou Droits de Sortie"; and that "dans quelque temps il pourra S'Expliquer pour la Paix." The correspondent listed names of the captives (garbling these and omitting the name of one) and concluded that, if the United States intended to make some sacrifices to achieve a peace and to redeem the slaves, they would strongly advise them not to send any ambassador "ou autre Personne ad hoc sur le Pays," but instead to treat through someone already established there who had standing enough with the Dey to succeed (MS in DNA: RG 59, CD; at head of text: "No. 2"; Dupl in same).

(3) "Copy of a note remitted the 15th. January 1791. to Messrs. Gimon freres, by Stephen Cathalan Junr., Vice Consul for the united States of america at Marseilles," acknowledging the foregoing and stating that five or six months would be required to receive information on the subject; that, having no order or power to act, he could only give his own opinions; that, in these circumstances, it was advisable not to discuss the business with the

Dey again unless he himself should speak of it first; that, in case he did so, they should say to him that the price of 15,000 sequins in addition to other costs was "furieusement Cher"—that a philanthropic order would never be able to raise a fourth of that sum—that there was no evidence whatever that the United States would ever dream of ransoming the slaves except by making a treaty of peace of which the release of the captives would constitute one of the principal articles—that, although the Americans desired to free their fellow citizens, they would accept the harsh necessity of leaving them in slavery rather than to pay such an excessive price. Cathalan added that, although the number of the slaves was small, the news of their captivity had made such a deep impression on the Americans, who attached such a great price to liberty and who had such a horror of slavery, that since then no captain or crew could be found in all the United States to sail an American ship into the Mediterranean, even if the voyage might have made their fortune; that as long as these fourteen men were detained in Algiers, no other American would sail there—a warning to their compatriots that would be a consolation to the captives in their misery; that, besides, it would be well for the Dey to know that there were not in America, as in Catholic countries, charitable works of redemption which, though doubtless founded on praiseworthy humanitarian motives, had nevertheless contributed to the progressive increase of the demands of the Dey, who knew of the great revenues of these philanthropic orders. Cathalan concluded by saying that he was writing to the United States to inquire whether sacrifices would be made to achieve a peace and the ransom of the captives; that in the meantime, in case the Dey appeared to have pacific dispositions, it would be well for him to make explicit the terms in money and goods that would be demanded; that the treaty would have to be made for at least fifty years; that, from the manner in which he wrote to the United States, he presumed that the negotiation, if it took place, would not be conducted by others sent there; and that "il faut du secret" (MS in DNA: RG 59, CD; at head of text: "No. 3"; Dupl in same).

From Nathaniel Colley

Sir   Norfolk. Jany. 22nd. 1791.

I have shipt by the Bearer Capt. Anderson, your Tables which I had made in London for you Which I hope will meet your Approbation, as I made it a point to find out the Mr. Titt you Recomended me to, he has Remov'd from Cheapside to Hatten Garden. I think they are well made but he has charged too high a price for them. As you see by his Account which I shall Enclose to you as also a Bill of Loading, they are packd up Agreeable to your Directions in Baise and the Box Covered with Oil Cloth. I can find no person here that wants a Bill on philadelphia or I should take the Liberty of Drawing on you for the Amount of the Above.[1] I am just now Setting of with the Brigg for City point to Load again for London Where I shall Esteem it a singular favor to be honoured with A few Lines from you on your Receipt of this, or any other Commissions that you may have to London, as I will most willingly Execute any that's within the Reach of my Power. I shall forward you A Copy of this by Post, for fear of A Miscarriage. I am Sir with the Greatest Respect your Honours Most. Obdt. Hb. Svt.   NATH. COLLEY

P. S. I must beg the favour of your presenting my most Respectfull Compliments to your Daughters if they are at Philadelphia.

RC (MHi); endorsed by TJ as received 11 Feb. 1791 and so recorded in SJL. Dupl (MHi); at head of text: "Duplicate of one sent by Captn. Anderson"; with variations in phraseology, one of which is noted below; addressed and postmarked; endorsed by TJ as received 3 Feb. 1791 and so recorded in SJL, though erroneously assigned the date of 7 Jan. 1791. Enclosures: (1) Account of Samuel Titt, London, 25 Nov. 1790, charging £6 6s. for "a fine Solid Mahagony Secret flap Table Taper feet fluted and Therm'd" and £3 18s. for a small one; to these sums were added the cost of green baise, oil cloth, shipping, exchange for Virginia currency (at one-third discount), customs duties at Norfolk, and freight to

Philadelphia, making the total sum £18 10s. 10d. (MS in MHi; Dupl in same). THERM'D: Therming or thurming—the process of achieving the effect of square moulded work or the tapered form of foot on the square legs of tables (Edwin Foley, *Book of decorative furniture*, London [1911], II, 384). (2) Bill of lading dated at Norfolk 21 Jan. 1791 for "one Box Merchandize" shipped to TJ on *Isabella*, Captain Atcheson Anderson (MS in DLC).

[1] At this point Dupl included the following sentence: "Therefore shall leave it till it may be Convenient for you to Direct me in what Manner will be Most Convenient for you to Remit it."

From C.W.F. Dumas

Lahaie 23d. Janv. 1791.

Depuis ma derniere du dernier Xbre, m'étant adressé au meilleur Banquier d'ici, il me donna les prix courants suivant des Obligations Amsterdamoises de notre Dette liquide, tels qu'il les procuroit, disoit-il, aux rentiers qui lui en demandoient, savoir

de la négociation de Stadnitsky, valant 9 % d'intérêt annuel   128 p.%.

plus recente de Staphorst, de même   —118

plus recente à 7½% d'intérêt annuel   —103

d'autres enfin au pair   —100

Enfin Messrs. v. Staphorst m'apprennent par Lettre du 18 de ce mois que la premiere Négociation de la Dette liquidée, domiciliée chez eux, se vend environ 19 à 20 p% au-dessus du pair; celle du Courtier Stadnitsky, quelque chose de plus, à cause du remboursement plus prochain, et qu'en supposant l'une comportante l'autre à 20% c'est ƒ1200 que vaut maintenant une de ces Obligations originairement de ƒ1000. Le bon vieux rentier qui m'avoit induit en erreur là-dessus l'avoit été lui-même par un fripon de notaire qui faisoit ses affaires et qui vouloit l'engager à vendre comme je vous l'avois marqué d'après le bon homme qui a congédié son fripon, et en me remerciant, m'a assuré qu'il ne vendroit aucun de ces fonds, pas même au prix étonnant que je lui appris, et qu'à mesure qu'ils lui seroient remboursés il acheteroit à leur place de ceux à la charge des Etats-Unis à 5 p% de la negociation du 1er fevrier dernier. Il en a d'ailleurs déjà une vingtaine d'obligations de celles dont l'intérêt se paie au 1er de Juin, qu'il m'a fait voir.

Quant à la Banque d'Amsterdam, voici ce que me marque un brave Négociant patriote de la même ville, que j'avois prié instamment de m'apprendre la vraie raison de sa détresse. "On a beaucoup raisonné sur notre argent de Banque, dont le déclin a été vraiment étonnant, et ne pouvoit ni procéder ni continuer, que d'un vrai discredit, une vraie méfiance. On dit presentement qu'on prendra des mesures pour le faire remonter au pair à l'ouverture de la Banque, qui se fera vers le fin de ce mois, et d'en prévenir tout déclin ultérieur. Nous autres, qui en souffrons, lui souhaittons en cela le succès que nous n'osons espérer."

Je dois à Nos amis d'Amsterdam la communication, plus consolante, de l'excellent discours de notre illustre Président, du 8 Décembre dernier, que j'ai envoyé à Mr. Luzac, avec requisition de l'insérer incessamment, ou, si les affaires du Nord de l'Europe doivent toujours occuper son petit papier, de le remettre de ma part à un Gazettier hollandois. Ils m'ont appris aussi que les deux Ports seuls de N. York et Philadelphie ont produit pendant les 3 mois seulement de Juillet, Août et Septembre, en especes sonnantes payées à l'Union, au-delà de 400,000 Dollars.

Il se confirme que plus de 12,000 Turcs ont été egorgés à Ismaïl, et qu'il y aura guerre entre les Russes et les Prussiens. Je ne crois pas que ces derniers s'y hazardent; et bien d'autres pensent, comme moi, qu'au fait et au prendre ils n'oseront attaquer; ils se flattent, en attendant, de l'assistance de la Grande Bretagne, et (*risum teneamus*) de cette paralitique republique. Je ne pourrois pas encore avec sureté m'expliquer sur son état interne, encore moins sur les 4 personnages (l'Anglois *Grenville* en est un) qui l'ont causé. Tout y est calme, et ne peut que l'être, car tout y est garnisonné.—Le parti qu'a pris la Cour de Turin de chasser tous les François fugitifs, une précaution analogue prise à leur sujet par l'Espagne sur ses Frontieres, ainsi que par Naples, &c., déconcerte toute la Politique de leurs amis ici et ailleurs. On se retranche, on s'amuse à présent, faute de mieux, à faire sonner le plus haut qu'on peut les réclamations et prétentions de quelques petits Prélats et Princes Allemands pour leurs Encensoirs et Fiefs en Alsace et en Lorraine.

Il me tarde d'apprendre l'admission de Kentucke à la 14e. place dans la plus auguste des Confédérations, le succès des Troupes envoyées par notre illustre Président pour châtier les Bandits du Nordouest qui exercent sur vos établissements un brigandage, apparemment attisé par les Anglois, et toutes les autres sages résolutions que va prendre votre troisieme Session, que Dieu benisse avec votre Excellence, dont je suis, avec grand respect, le &c.

FC (Dumas Letter Book, Rijksarchief, The Hague; photostats in DLC); at head of text: "No. 73 à S. E. Mr. Ths. Jefferson Mine. d'Et. &c." Recorded in SJL as received 19 June 1791.

From Mary Walker Lewis

January 23 1791

Permit me to congratulate you my Dr. Sir on Mrs. Randolphs safe delivery of a very fine Daughter and I with candor assure you she is uncommonly well with the sweet little Girl.—Mr. Randolph is not at home but every attention shall be payd to my Dr. friend Mrs. Randolph that is in my power and you will hear from us frequently.—I am with every Sentiment of Esteem and Affection your sincear Friend

M Lewis

RC (MHi); endorsed by TJ as received 7 Feb. 1791. This letter enclosed one from Martha herself, also dated 23 Jan. 1791, and one from Mary dated 22 Jan. 1791, both of which were recorded as received on 7 Feb. 1791.

Neither of these letters has been found, but the text of that from Mary, written at Monticello, is given in Randolph, Domestic Life, p. 193, as follows: "Dear Papa—I received your letter of December the 7th about a fortnight ago, and would have answered it directly, but my sister had to answer hers last week and I this. We are all well at present. Jenny Randolph and myself keep house—she one week, and I the other. I owe sister thirty-five pages in Don Quixote, and am now paying them as fast as I can. Last Christmas I gave sister the 'Tales of the Castle,' and she made me a present of the 'Observer,' a little ivory box, and one of her drawings; and to Jenny she gave 'Paradise Lost,' and some other things. Adieu, dear Papa. I am your affectionate daughter, Maria Jefferson."

Mary's allusion to gifts "is one of the few references to an exchange of Christmas presents among members of the Monticello family" (Bear, Family Letters, p. 70 n.). Her gift to Martha was Thomas Holcroft's Tales of the castle: or, stories of instruction and delight, translated from Madame de Genlis' Les veillées du chateau (London, 1785, 5 vols.). Martha's gift to her was Richard Cumberland's The Observer: being a collection of moral, literary and familiar essays (first published in 1785 in one volume, but Martha may have given Mary the third edition, London, 1790, 5 vols.).

To William Short

Dear Sir   Philadelphia Jan. 23. 1791.

Your letters which have come to hand are as follows

No.	Date	Recd.	Passage Weeks—Days	No.	Date	Recd.	Weeks—Day
29	May 9.	Oct. 14.	22—4	38	Aug. 4.	Nov. 20.	15—3
30	11.	14	22—2	39	22.	23.	13—2
32	23.	25	22—1	40	27	Dec. 15	15—5
33	Jun. 14.	25	19	41	Sep. 5	15.	14—3
34	25.	25	17—3	42	9	Jan. 11	17—5
35	29.	Sep. 26	12—5	43	Oct. 3.	12	14—3
36	July 7.	Oct. 25	15—5	47	Nov. 25.	19.	7—6
37	22.	Nov. 2.	15—	48	26	19	7—5

I think it material to note to you the length of their passage that it may enable you to judge of the best conveyances. The two last have come in 7. weeks 5 and 6 days, one of them by the English packet, and a private one of Sep. 26. by the English packet also came in 4. weeks 5 days. All the rest have been from 12 to 22 weeks. No. 48. by the packet and 47. by an immediate vessel being in hand, I shall probably not receive 44. 45. 46. this month or two yet. Those by the packet bring us what is really new and interesting, the others lose their interest because they come when we are already advanced one, two, three months ahead of them through other channels. Whatever therefore is not really secret had better come by the[1] English packets. M. Dumas now sends me through that conveyance the Leyden gazette. Your No. 31. has never been received.

In my last public letters to you, which were of Aug. 10. 26. 31. I informed you of my intended journey to Virginia, and that I should not write to you again till my return here. No opportunity has occurred since of sending a letter directly, till the present one by the French packet: and Mr. Remsen informs me that none occurred during my absence to send you the newspapers.

The 3d. and subsequent amendments to the constitution have been agreed to by N. Hampshire, Rho. I. New Y., Jersey, Penns. Del. Mar. N. Car. and S. Car. The 1st. by N. Hamp. Rho. I. N. York Jersey Mar. North and S. Carola. and the 2d. by only Jersey Del. Mar. and the two Carolinas. The other states, viz.

Mass. Connect. Virginia and Georgia have not decided on them. Vermont has acceded to the new constitution of the U. S. and is coming forward to ask admission into Congress. Kentuckey has asked the same and a bill for the purpose has passed the Senate and is now before the representatives, where it will meet no difficulty. But they have only asked admission for the year 1792.

The census has made considerable progress, but will not be completed till midsummer. It is judged at present that our numbers will be between 4. and 5. millions. Virginia it is supposed will be between 7. and 800,000.

You will percieve by the papers that the object of our Indian expedition has been so imperfectly obtained as to call for another the ensuing year.—By the present conveyance you will probably receive a proclamation locating the federal territory so as to comprehend Georgetown. It will appear within a day or two.— We must still pursue the redemption of our captives through the same channel, till some better means can be devised. The money however which is in Mr. Grand's hands, will be the subject of a letter to you from the Secretary of the treasury, as soon as he can have an act of Congress authorising the application of it to the debt of the foreign officers.

The most important matters now before Congress are propositions to establish a bank, to establish a land office, and Excise. The latter measure tho severely modified is very unpopular in the middle and Southern states.

Fenno's and Davies's papers will accompany this. These contain all the laws of the last session, and therefore it is thought better to defer sending them to you in a body till an 8vo. edition appears, which is proposed to be printed, as this will be more conveniently conveyed as well as handled. I am with great and sincere esteem Dear Sir Your most obedient & most humble servt.,

TH: JEFFERSON

RC (DLC: Short Papers); endorsed by Short as received 23 Mch. 1791. PrC (DLC). FC (DNA: RG 59, DCI). Tr (DNA: RG 59, PCC No. 121); misdated 23 Jan. 1792, consisting only of that part of the text indicated in note 1 below, and entered in error at the last pages of PCC No. 121, possibly at the time Taylor was about to succeed Remsen as chief clerk. Entered as "public" in SJL. TJ probably forwarded with the above a letter sent him by Thomas Edmunds concerning Short's sisters and friends (Edmunds to TJ, Richmond,

28 Nov. 1790, MHi; endorsed by TJ as received 6 Dec. 1790 and so recorded in SJL). Short's sister, Mrs. Edmunds, had died about a year earlier and he had learned of this and of the situation of his surviving sisters only by accident. In great anxiety because of "this long and unexampled silence," he feared the other sisters had joined his brother in Kentucky (William Short to William Nelson, 21 Feb. 1791, NjP).

1 Text in Tr ends at this point.

From William Carmichael

Madrid 24 January 1791

Colonel Humphreys delivered to me your Letter of the 6th of August on the 18th of the last month; Nothing could equal my astonishment in finding that I have been employing my time in a situation that has been for many years and is agreable so little to my own Credit or to the Satisfaction of my Country.

The only method which I could take in the Moment was to Show to a Man who justly merits the Confidence placed in him, the pains I had taken for Information and how improbable it was that I should spend my time and even my own fortune to procure Intelligence without transmitting the Materials which I obtained with great difficulty and Considerable expence that at least proove my zeal tho' perhaps not my Talents.

The next Object will be to forward Copies of all the Dispatches which I find by your Letter have not reached the Department. I cannot account for the detention of my Letters: I know that I have had powerful Enemies here who from personal motives have in many Instances endeavoured to Injure me.

I discovered that a Servant who had lived with me more than six years had received Money to a considerable Amount from one of these Persons The Ct. Cabarrus. He has paid and is paying dearly the Suborning my Domestics yet more from his own Imprudence than my Efforts.

On the 26th of February I gave an accompt of a friendly conversation which I had with the Ct. de Florida Blanca on that Subject which terminated to our mutual Satisfaction.

The President will have probably communicated to you the Letter I had the honor to write him on the first notice of his nomination: Least that Letter should not have met with better fortune than so many others have done, I inclose a Copy as Also of one I wrote from Aranguez on being advised by you that he had been pleased to continue me in my present Employment.

You will see that I have no Interested motive to Influence my Conduct; I say with Truth that I have now to begin life (so far as the Expression may be applied to Independance and Domestic Ease) and I thought I could have done it with pleasure untill I received your Letters by Colonel Humphreys.

I Announced to the Department of foreign Affairs the time and Manner in which I received the Cyphers sent me. Colonel Humphreys has seen by the Covers of those Cyphers and by Certificates

I took from Persons who were present or who delivered them, that it would have been highly imprudent in me to have made use of them. If they have ever been employed No Letter in Cypher has ever reached me.

I sent duplicates of these Certificates Immediately to the Department and I find that by the List which you sent me of letters received that those have not come to hand.

You will pardon this detail. It is necessary for my own tranquillity which has suffered more than I can Express for several years past and more particularly since I have received your last letter. If my Letters since the 26th of February have reached you, you will be convinced that no one here in the Diplomatic line was so early or better Informed than I have been with respect to the apparent Rupture between this Country and Great Britain. I knew how it would end, because I knew that measures begun in Folly would terminate in Humiliation and that Humiliation may lead to something more.

Something however might have been done in a Moment of projects and apprehension had not a certain negotiation carried on our part at London transpired and which I think was known here rather from British Policy than from the vigilance of the Marquis del Campo. Entirely unaquainted with this Maneuvre altho' in Correspondence with the Person Employed, I was suspected to be in the Secret. This Suspicion banished Confidence, which returns by slow degrees. This Circumstance induced me to drop entirely my Correspondence with G[ouverneur] M[orris]. To Continue it would have done harm and certainly could do no good.

I have seen Extracts of the Presidents Letter communicated to the Duke of Leeds perhaps mutilated or forged to serve here the views of the British Cabinet: I do not yet dispair of Obtaining Copies of those Letters thro the same Channel that I procured the first accompt of the demands of G. B. and the Signature of the late Convention.

You will easily conceive that I must now discretionally obey (from the Change of circumstances) the Latter part of the Instructions given me; But Sir the opportunities of seeing the Minister in the Character I hold are so rare, that there is little room for Insinuation. However Active, However punctual I may be, I must wait untill Every Ambassador, every Minister, even if there was one from the Republic of Ragusa have had their Audience before I can Obtain mine. You will see by the inclosed paper No. 1 the Conversation I have had with the Minister.—I have endeavored

Indirectly to suggest Ideas of the Necessity of a Speedy determination in this Government to Adopt the Measures pointed out by your Last Letters. These Suggestions have been Made to persons who have *Now* and probably will have in future much Influence in this Cabinet If the Queen lives. I shall communicate to you the Effects which my Representations may produce and with Colonel Humphreys Advice and approbation If occasion offers and Circumstances permit I shall decidedly press the business.

This Government is weak, The Ministry is in a ticklish Situation, The Queen Governs and Governs with caprice, The People begin to dispute Their Sovereigns and altho' they have no cheifs to look up to the dissatisfaction is general.

As I have participated to Colonel Humphreys my Ideas and many Ancedotes relative to the actual Situation of Affairs here, I am persuaded he will not fail to communicate to the President or yourself what may be deficient in the Letters I leave for his Inspection.

There is probably something in Agitation here with respect to the Affairs of the North. I shall endeavour to developpe that business. Here they hold themselves in readiness to arm. The Object is doubtful and unnacountable. It is a mixture of haughtiness and timidity. In fact after having blundered into humiliation abroad They wish to Appear respectable at Home. This is an Observation made to me by the Ct. de Camponanes Governor of the Council of Castille, who is with those he can Influence decidedly of opinion that it is the Interest of his Country to form Liberal and lasting Connections with the United States.

I have had the honor in the Course of this Month to write you on our Affairs with Morrocco; with Algiers as I have sent Duplicates of My Letters I flatter Myself they will be received. Relying on the good opinion of me that you have been pleased to express on Many occasions I intreat you to engage the President to permit me to return to my native Country. I shall send you My Accompts as soon as I can put them in order.—I have the honor to be with the greatest Respect Sir Your Most Obedt. and Most Humble sert,   Wm. Carmichael

RC (DNA: RG 59, PCC No. 88); endorsed by TJ as received 31 Mch. 1791 and so recorded in SJL. Enclosure: Carmichael to Washington, 26 Apr. 1790 (DLC: Washington Papers). The shaky handwriting, the blotted and smeared paper, the discursive and rambling style, the un- convincing explanations for the failure at communication—all lend confirmation to the estimate of Carmichael's character given by the British ambassador at Madrid: "on many accounts an amiable and valuable man; but . . . his health is ruined and . . . he has addicted himself entirely to hard drinking" (Humphreys to Washington, 3 July 1792; Humphreys, *Humphreys*, II, 142-8). The fact that Cabarrus was able to bribe one of Carmichael's servants, that Carmichael had taken affidavits as to the condition of the covers of the ciphers at the time they were delivered, and that he dispatched copies of these to Jay afford plausible grounds for assuming that the Spanish government had access to whatever dispatches were sent by him in code—and of course to those which for some years TJ apparently wrote on the basis of this assumption.

To William Short

DEAR SIR   Philadelphia Jan. 24. 1791.

Your several private letters unacknowledged are May 9. June 14. 29. July 7. 11. 16. August 4. 15. 22. Sep. 26. Oct. 3. 27. Nov. 27.[1] Mine to you have been Aug. 9. 12. 25. 31. Sep. 6. 30. of which the two first and two last have not yet been acknowledged. That of Aug. 9. indeed was only a postscript.—To business.

Goldsmith's Encyclopedie I can meddle no further with. Just before I came away, I applied to Royez, from whom Goldsmith was to have them (Goldsmith being then absent) and desired him to furnish them. He put me off from week to week. I told him I was then packing the residue, and if not furnished in time, they could never again be recieved. He admitted at length he could not furnish them, having mislaid the subscription papers, the package was closed, and it was understood between him and me that there was an end of it. I think Frouillé knows all this. The gentlemen for whom they were, will not take them.

I must pray you to keep in mind and execute the commissions for the clock (which must come entirely by water from Paris to this place) and two epreuves d'etains of P. Jones's medal. Also the *President's*[2] *wine*. I have not recieved his bill yet. I hope the *wine* will arrive before the *warm weather*.

The Dutchess Danville's commission shall be carefully attended to. But the river being frozen up there will be no chance of getting the seeds to her as early as I could wish. I must await too a vessel going directly to Havre, as I know the incertainty of every other conveyance. My furniture is arrived here and in Virginia. As far as I have proceeded in opening I find not much broke. Not more than half is as yet opened, as I am in a house not yet finished. No news yet of my carriages. I inclose a letter for Petit, which when you shall have perused, be so good as to seal and deliver him. You will see by that how much I still desire him. I hope he will come, and without exacting such wages as to make him a burthen to me when here. He had 36. Louis at Paris and fed himself. I should think myself well off to get him for that and feed him. I should think him high at 4. Louis a month, and at any rate would not go beyond 5. and even at that I should feel constantly sore under the burthen, always understood that I am to feed him. In fact 60. Louis a year now would be as heavy on me as 150. would have been at Paris. I would not give above 3. Guineas a month were it not that he is familiar to me, and of approved honesty. If he will not come, give him, if you please, a gratuity of 300.^{tt} on my account.

Since *Tolozan* and *Sequeville* are decided not to *accept their presents unless I accept mine, I must yield as theirs is their livelihood.* Be so good then as to *finish that matter by*[3] *the usual exchange of presents in my behalf. Our government* having now adopted *the usage* of *making presents in the like* case, so as to *establish a reciprocity, one of the motives for my refusal is removed, which may be mentioned to them. On recieving therefore the present of congé of usage* be so good as to *give them*[4] *the twelve and eight hundred livres, mentioned in my letter of April 6* and *more* if on enquiry from *Baron Grimm* or any other in whose *information you confide you find that more has been usually given by those of my grade, but do not give less than there mentioned.* I know indeed that *Doctr. Franklin gave considerably more, but that was* because *he was extravagantly well treated on the occasion himself. To face the expence of the presents to Tolozan and Sequeville you must draw on our bankers* in the first instance and as I presume the *King's present will be his picture* or something *set in diamonds, I must get you my dear Sir to have these taken out of the cadre and disposed of advantageously at Paris, London or Amsterdam and deposit the proceeds* with the *Van Staphorsts* & *Hubbard on my account* where it will be *ready to cover* what shall have been *given to Tolozan and Sequeville* and any further *deficiency* which may be produced by the *expences of my return,* or a *disallowance* of any article of *my French accounts. Send to me the cadre, be it picture, snuff box* or what it will, by any *conveyance, but sealed and unknown* to the *person who brings it and above all things contrive that the conversion of the present into money be absolutely secret so as never to be suspected at Court,* much *less find its way into an English newspaper. My letter of September 30 will have explained to you something of your own affair. It has not been mentioned to me since our return to Philadelphia,* and I have thought it better[5] to *let your claim ripen itself in silence. Delay is in your favor. The mission to Amsterdam was to give you prominence. It has had that effect. I now think[6] you may expect the Hague.*

Humphreys is gone to Lisbon, the grade not settled.[7] *The last letter from Carmichael is May 1789. An opportunity has been given* him to *explain this.* I doubt if *he can be long supported* against *his inattention* and the *weight* of the *public opinion. Old[8] servants knowing* and *known* in the *public affairs[9] whose names may add weight* to the *administration will probably be sent to Paris and London.[10] I[11]* have *done what little I could toward getting an appointment rather to please* you than to *serve you. For I see fully* that the *leading interests of your life are lost if you do not come home ere long* and take possession of the *high ground so open to you,* and from whence *you may command* any *post* either at *home or abroad.* Still *I shall* continue to *work in favor of your wishes.* I am with great & constant esteem Dear Sir Your sincere friend & servt., TH: JEFFERSON

P.S. Since writing the above your private letter of Oct. 30. is recieved. Remember me affectionately to Mazzei.

RC (ViW); partly in code; at head of text: "Private"; endorsed as received 31 Mch. 1791. PrC (DLC); first page is in TJ Papers, 60: 10270 and final three pages are in 232: 41496-8 (a confused grouping which accounts for the duplication and misattribution of quotations in Sowerby, Nos. 4197, 4198); lacks postscript. Dft (DLC: TJ Papers, 232: 41495, 41499); consisting of two leaves containing the texts *en clair* for the two principal encoded passages; some of the variations between text *en clair* and encoded passages (in which errors both of encoding and decoding occur) are indicated below. Enclosure: TJ to Petit, 25 Jan. 1791.

For the background of TJ's decision about the presents to TOLOZAN AND SEQUEVILLE see Vol. 16: 356-68 and p. 52, where the text *en clair* pertaining to the presents is reproduced in facsimile. It is clear both from the matter deleted (see note 3) and from a partly legible passage at the beginning of the text *en clair* ("have [. . .] been decided not to let them") that when TJ began this letter he seemed about to take the course indicated by the Constitution, but then decided otherwise. It is also clear that, though he did not know until the decision was made by Washington to appoint Gouverneur

Morris as minister to France, he suspected that this would be done (see notes 8 and 9).

[1] An error for 7 Nov. 1790.
[2] This and subsequent words in italics are written in cipher. Short's interlinear decoding has been collated with the texts *en clair* and verified by the editors employing Code No. 10. For variations between the texts *en clair* and the encoded passages in RC see following notes.
[3] At this point in text *en clair* TJ first wrote and then deleted the following "telling them that rather than leave this court without profiting of the opportunity which usage gives me of leaving them a token of my esteem I submit to the unpleasant task of arranging that matter with Congress disagreeable as it is and undecided."
[4] At this point the text *en clair* has the following words not encoded: "not less than."
[5] At this point in text *en clair* TJ first wrote "to let it lie," then deleted this and substituted "not to introduce the subj," and finally deleted the substitution and interlined the passage as above.
[6] The preceding three sentences are interlined in text *en clair* and this sentence first read "They now con-

jecture you may expect" &c., then was altered to read as above.

7 TJ erred in encoding the preceding four words, thereby causing Short considerable anxiety. Instead of using the symbols 1619. 1287. 1099. 460. 387.' for this passage (taken from the text *en clair*), TJ wrote 1619. 128. 1099. 466. 387.' Given the context and possessing the key, Short should have had no difficulty in overcoming this slight confusion, but he was obliged to wait nine months for TJ's clarification (see Short to TJ, 30 Mch. 1791; TJ to Short, 28 July 1791).

8 In text *en clair* this word is underscored. This entire sentence occurs in text *en clair* immediately after that ending ". . . expect the Hague." TJ

in encoding evidently decided to place it here as a further consideration for Short's feelings in addition to that implicit in the changes indicated in notes 9 and 10.

9 The preceding seven words in text *en clair* are interlined in substitution for the following, deleted: "well versed in the affairs of their country and in the public confidence will."

10 At this point in text *en clair* appears the following clause, not deleted and not encoded: "if a minister comes from the last as is rumoured."

11 At the beginning of this sentence in text *en clair* TJ first wrote and then deleted: "Tho' I suspect an intention of giving you an appointment."

From William Short

DEAR SIR   Amsterdam Jan. 24. 1791.

I hope my letters of the 26th. of Nov. and 23d. of Dec. sent by the English Packets of Dec. and Jan. will be received in good time as they alone can account for the delay of my other letters written both to yourself and the Secretary of the Treasury since my arrival here. These were put on board American vessels sailing from hence immediately for the United States. Constant contrary winds have prevailed since that time so as to prevent any vessel from leaving the Texel, and of course my letters are still there: Those which I have written to you were dated Nov. 25. (sent after an American vessel at the Texel and at the moment of sailing. I know not with certainty whether she got out) Dec. 2. by a vessel bound for Boston. Dec. 29 and 30. Jan. 16. 17. by vessels bound for N. York.—In these I acknowledged the receipt of yours of Sep. 6. 30. the last which have come to my hands.

I am the more sorry for the excessive delay of these letters because in those which were written to the Secretary of the Treasury I entered into very full and particular details concerning the several objects about which he is certainly impatient to be informed. I may add however that no other inconvenience will result from that delay *as*[1] [*no loan is yet opened.*[2] *As far as I can judge it will be found proper*[3] *to postpone it two or three*[4] *weeks longer,* for reasons mentioned in my other letters which are of general application and in this instance particularly *for the greater certainty of a success that may enhance the credit of the United States.*

The reporter of the committee of domaines has at length presented the opinion of that committee respecting the decree on the *droit d'aubaine*, to the Assembly. He had unfortunately connected it with the business of successions, so that an adjournment was insisted on in order that the report might be discussed. It was referred to four different committees. I had put the Mis. de la fayette fully in possession of this subject, and I wrote to him again respecting it immediately on being informed of the turn it had taken. The secretary whom I left in Paris writes me that they are now trying to get the diplomatic committee to ask for a discussion of this report to obtain a decree explanatory merely as to the *droit d'aubaine*. In the present ill humour and jealousy which prevail with respect to their colonies it is difficult to say what they will do but we may be sure that M. de Montmorin will use his exertions to effect what we desire. I apprehend delay however, which no application can prevent, and I always had doubts my self with respect to the success of this business notwithstanding the opinion of the reporter and committee of domaines. I mentioned formerly on what these doubts were founded.

Since the report of the committee of impositions made in the month of Dec. of which you will have seen an extract in the journals of the assembly, and of which I enclosed you a copy in my last, nothing more has been said on tobacco except by a member of the committee of finance. You will have seen that the committee of imposition propose to abandon tobacco as an article of revenue. The member of the committee of finance on the contrary insisted on it; another member of the same committee however insisted on his informing the assembly that what he said was his private opinion and not that of the committee of finance. No body as I have frequently repeated can say with certainty when the assembly will take up any subject, nor what they will decide on it. Their sentiments with respect to tobacco have experienced a manifest alteration since the first report of the committee of imposition respecting it. It is probable now that it will be made an article of free commerce, with a duty on entering the Kingdom.—But should the farm be continued still some modifications may be expected at present in favor of their commercial connexions with the U.S. I forgot to mention above that I had received through Mr. Donald your letter of Nov. 25. respecting this article.

The commercial committee have formed a new tariff which is now under press as they write me, to be presented to the assembly. They not only admit American oils in their plan but put the duties

lower than under the *arrêt du conseil*. It is yet for the assembly
to decide on it. I have already informed you of the stages through
which this business has been carried and the manner in which it
has been done. I hope the means will be approved of, and that the
U.S. will have reason to be satisfied with the result. The delay
is inevitable from the nature and proceedings of the assembly. That
is the cause also of the uncertainty and variation in the opinions
which I have communicated to you from time to time on these subjects.

The resistance of a considerable party of the clergy to a decree
of the assembly for their civil organisation and particularly for
changing the limits of the dioceses, and the violent measures
adopted by the assembly respecting this resistance, or rather non
compliance has been matter of uneasiness for some time.—By a
decree of the assembly all those of the clergy who by a given day
had not taken an oath to maintain the civil organisation of that
body were to be deprived of their ecclesiastical functions and their
successors immediately appointed agreeably to the new mode of
election. That day rigorously has passed and only two bishops
of the assembly have taken the oath. Of the curates of Paris a
majority also had refused but among those who subscribed were
some of the principal and particularly the curate of St. Eustache
the King's confessor, who it is said was converted by the King
himself, who takes every possible means of preventing what might
occasion disorder and who from his uniform conduct merits better
treatment than he sometimes receives.—By a construction of the
decree some delay is obtained for its execution. In the mean time
two of the refusing Bishops have entered into negotiation. They
desire to find some decent means of retracting their refusal. Hitherto they have waited for the consent of the Pope, to obtain which
they had sent an express to Rome. His answer has not yet been
received but it is known by private letters that he is disposed to
accommodation at present though he would not hear of it at first.
I know not yet what effect this will produce on the people in the
provinces. In the capital their love of the revolution so far surpasses
every other passion that all the exertions of the *garde nationale*
have been necessary to prevent their entering the churches and
hanging the refusing curates. They will manifest their dispositions
less violently perhaps in the provinces but in general the spirit of
the revolution will certainly predominate, even if the clergy
succeed to convince them that it is contrary to the spirit of religion.

The funds have risen to an uncommon height owing to the considerable reimbursements made by the emission of assignats. These do not depreciate as might have been expected.—On the whole if there were any probability of the assembly's confining themselves merely to the business of organizing the government so as to put an end to their session and call a new legislature the revolution might be considered as really in a successful state. But the report of the central committee which you will have received, prescribes such a superabundance of matter as necessary to be deliberated on and settled by the present assembly, that its end as well as the term of the completion of the constitution can be reduced to no calculation. All that seems to me certain is that the revolution will in one way or another end by giving a free government to France. This event might be hastened much by the assembly if they would. My former letters will have informed you how little I think it is to be hoped from them and for what reasons.

The Russians as has been expected for some time have taken Ismailow. They stormed it and put the whole garrison to the sword on the 22d. of Dec. This was probably to strike terror into the Turks in order to aid the separate negociation which it is known Prince Potemkin is endeavouring to effect with the Grand Visier. The object is to engage the Porte to accept peace without the mediation of other powers. On the other hand Prussia is active both in negotiation and military demonstration to counteract this project. Preparations are making for sending a large army into Livonia in the spring which has induced the Empress to call off some of the heavy troops from those employed against the Turks. England also keeps an augmented navy in commission. It seems not doubted that the design is to send a fleet into the Baltic as soon as the season will permit it. It is said also that the three mediating powers are negotiating with Denmark to engage that country to be at least indifferent as to the entrance of this fleet: and that there are grounds for hopes of success. Some think also that there are indications which render it probable that Spain will join in the mediation for obtaining peace for the Turk. I have no reason to suppose it other than that arising from the desire which Spain must naturally have to see peace restored to that power. It is supposed if she joins in the mediation it will be merely for that object and not from any disposition to favor generally the system of the mediating powers. Where so many and such opposite principles enter into account it would be temerity to conjecture the particular results without being behind the curtain: and even there probably the schemes are not yet fully ascertained. Every day must necessarily throw new lights on this complicated state of affairs in proportion as the state of negotiation is more advanced.

I think it probable myself that peace will be effected one way or another in the course of the year. The present favorable situation of the Russian army, the dispersed and disheartened situation of the Ottoman, the succour promised by Prussia so long deferred, the little hope of immediate relief from the geographical position of that power, the ardent desire of Russia to effect a peace without mediation and the sacrifices she is disposed to make to effect it; all induce me to believe that it will be brought about in that way. If however the Porte from a well founded confidence in the active interference of the mediating powers should decide still to hold out then it seems that the Empress will be induced to come to terms rather than enter the lists with new and powerful enemies from whom she would have much to fear particularly by sea. Still I find several who think from the character of the Empress that she will resist and try the event of a campaign rather than sacrifice so much success and so much glory in having a peace dictated to her. Her resources at home are without end from her mode of calling them into action, and her credit even here stands high, certainly much higher than it should do. It is supposed also that in this extremity she would be seconded by the Emperor notwithstanding his pacific turn. He would be authorized by treaty to do this, and his present situation would enable him; the disturbances in the various parts of his dominions having been all settled. In Brabant particularly his authority is more firmly settled than if he had come to it by inheritance only, since he enjoys it also by a kind of conquest.

It is the system of the English cabinet which is considered here as the most unaccountable. The commerce of that country is at present in the most prosperous situation since the balance is in their favor with every part of Europe. They have more to gain by peace and more to apprehend from war than any other power and yet they seem determined to risk it. The advantages of their commerce in the Baltic are certain, those in the Levant eventual, still they seem determined to sacrifice one at least for a time in order to grasp at the other. On the whole it is regarded as one of those sacrifices of commerce to politics which France has so often given examples of. Time will shew whether Mr. Pitt or those who condemn him are in the right.][5]

The Imperial troops have entered Liege in execution of the orders of the chamber of Wetzlaer. The inhabitants make no resistance and throw themselves entirely on the mercy of the Emperor. The Prince will be first reinstated unconditionally agreeably to the decree. It is probable there will be some modifications made afterwards. It was thought that the King of Prussia would not have been an indifferent spectator of this event. Letters circulate in public, I know not whether they are authentic, between his minister M. Dohm and the imperial commandant, which shew that the decree of Wetzlaer, and particularly what was agreed on at Franckfort with respect to the disputes at Liege, is not construed in the same way by their respective masters. Be this as it may the fate of Liege will be always rendered subservient to the policy of those courts.

The States of Holland are now in session. The finances of this country are supposed to be in a bad way. New taxes which are always a delicate point and the touchstone of every government are considered at present indispensable. It is foreseen they will produce discontent. What was formerly called here the patriotic party exists no longer as a party, but throughout all the provinces, and particularly in this, they form a large mass of wealthy people. They are ulcerated in the extreme. The Prince and Aristocratical party, though natural enemies are kept allied by these their common enemy. They have in their hands the armed force of this country and are sure of support from Prussia, which is much more than sufficient to keep down all opposition. It is much to be desired for the interest of all those powers who borrow money here that government should remain armed with such an irresistible force as to confine its subjects to objects of peace and commerce. Were a revolution to be attempted it would be carried on, as far as we may judge from their present dispositions, with a destructive rage and dry up the chanels of wealth at this place.

One circumstance which is considered as a strong proof of the want of confidence in the government at least at this place, and so far as relates to the direction of the bank of Amsterdam in the hands of the governmental party, is the low price at which bank money has been for some time.—Instead of being several p. cent above par as has always been the case it has been as low as 2½ below, and when the bank was shut some days ago it was 1. p. cent. It will be opened again in a few days when it is thought that they will have coined a sufficient sum to pay off such as may chuse it though they are not obliged to do it. If they should not do this and not exhibit the real situation of the bank to public view which they cannot be legally compelled to, it is apprehended that their credit will sink lower than it has done. This would have a very unhappy influence on the commercial operations of this place. The best informed seem fully satisfied that the affairs of the bank are in proper order. The malevolent insist that the funds have been diverted for various purposes, and among them is reckoned the payment of what they call the Prussian invasion.

With respect to the East Indies and particularly the British affairs there, I can only repeat here what I mentioned in my last letter, that I referred you for authentic information on that subject to the debates of the house of Commons. The minister triumphed in his refusals to produce any of the papers relative to the Spanish negotiation, but promised to lay before them all those relative to the E. Indies. This letter incloses one for the Secretary of the Treasury and will go by the English Packet.

I beg you to accept with it assurances of those sentiments of respect and Attachment of which I hope you will never doubt and with which I have the honor to be Dear Sir Your obedient & humble servant,   W: SHORT

P. S. Jan. 25. I find by the Leyden gazette of this morning that the letter of M. Dohm mentioned yesterday may be considered as authentic. It was written from Aix la Chapelle Jan. 13. the day after the imperial troops entered Liege accompanied by those of two of the electors. This letter was published and distributed at Liege as soon and perhaps sooner than it was received by the Marechal de Bender, and it is said also that he disavowed by a letter to the imperial commandant at Liege having received such an one. The difference of opinion between them is such as affords full pretext for a quarrel if the cabinets of Berlin and Vienna think proper. M. Dohm insists that the conviction of Frankfort is still in force and that the Imperial troops cannot be employed but to keep order and preserve a statu quo. The ministers of the directors and particularly of the bishop of Liege, say that they are to enforce the decree of Wetzlaer, and to be supported by the troops if necessary. No answer has yet arrived from Vienna in consequence of dispatches sent there from Berlin in which the King of Prussia on the Imperial assistance being required wishing to enter into a friendly explanation, states to the Emperor "que la soumission des Liegeois ne pouvoit être acceptée et realisée que par les Princes directeurs et en consequence des points dont on est *convenu unanimement à Frankfort.*" In a letter from M. Dohm to the States of Liege of Jan. 2. on their submission absolutely to the Emperor's decision there is this remarkable expression "dans l'empire au quel le Pays de Liege appartient, il n'existe aucune, *volonté absolue* qui puisse decider le soit de ses provinces." They are re-establishing the Princes authority at Liege. The people murmur but are controlled by the troops. This affair will be the thermometer of the dispositions of Prussia and Austria relative to each other, and the Liegeois of course will be supported or abandoned according to circumstances. **W. S.**

PrC (DLC: Short Papers); at head of text: "No. 53"; accompanied by text *en clair* of passage to be encoded (see note 1). Tr (DNA: RG 59, DD). Tr of Extract (DLC: TJ Papers, 60: 10855-66); consisting of that part of text indicated in note 3; at head of text: "Extract of a Letter from William Short to Thomas Jefferson Secretary of State dated Amsterdam Jany. 24. 1791." Another Tr of Extract (DNA: RG 59, SDC). Recorded in SJL as received 4 Apr. 1791. Enclosure: Short to Secretary of the Treasury, 25 Jan. 1791, referring him to the above letter to TJ for the situation of European politics, enclosing a general state of exports from St. Petersburg for 1790 and a particular account of those to the United States, pointing out that England employed more ships in this trade than all other nations together "and yet their minister seems decided to take measures in the spring which would at least arrest this business for some time," and informing him in cipher that "the terms on which the loan is to be made are the same with the last except that the commission is to be half per cent lower. It will be opened the middle or latter part of February" (PrC in DLC: Short Papers; text printed in Syrett, *Hamilton*, VII, 454-6). It should be noted, as established by this passage in cipher, that TJ and Hamilton employed the same cipher key with Short—that designated in this edition as No. 10.

The lengthy extract from the above letter was sent by TJ to Washington on 10 Apr. 1791, doubtless in part to carry out the intent expressed in his own letter to Short of 24 Jan. 1791 to do what he could to advance his claims to an appointment "rather to please . . . than to serve" him; for Short's dispatches contained the most acute observations about European politics available to the government at this time—not even excepting those of Gouverneur Morris.

1 This and subsequent words in italics *to the end of this paragraph only* are in cipher, for which the text *en clair* and the decodings represented in Tr and Tr of Extract exist and have been verified by the Editors, employing Code No. 10.

2 At this point in text *en clair* Short first wrote and then deleted: "It was thought at first that one might be opened in the beginning of Febry. but."

3 This word interlined in text *en clair* in substitution for "necessary" deleted.

4 Preceding three words in text *en clair* interlined in substitution for "still some" deleted.

5 The passage enclosed in brackets (supplied) comprises the matter in the extract enclosed in TJ to Washington, 10 Apr. 1791.

APPENDIX

The First Conflict in the Cabinet

> It is essential to the success of the Minister
> of a great Department that he subdivide the
> objects of his care, distribute them among
> Competent assistants and content himself
> with a general but Vigilant superintendence.
> —*Hamilton to McHenry, 30 July 1798*

> . . . the fault is laid on Duer. But *respondeat
> superior.*
> —*William Maclay, 18 January 1790*

Six weeks after Jefferson became Secretary of State, Theodorick
Bland of Virginia introduced resolutions in the House which, as
adopted, called for publication of lists of names and amounts of arrearages in pay due officers and soldiers of the Virginia and North
Carolina lines.[1] The provisions that aroused the most intense opposition required that powers of attorney should be attested by two justices
of the peace and should authorize payment only of specific and stated
sums. Staunch supporters of the Secretary of the Treasury in the
Senate—Ellsworth, Johnson, King, and others—opposed the restrictions. But Richard Henry Lee found the opposition astonishing since
the legislation was only designed to prevent fraud. He was certain
that "a parcel of Scoundrel Speculators went directly after the appropriation of last September and cheated the Soldiers out of 27,000
dollars for less than a penny in the pound."[2] He feared the resolutions
would be defeated, but they prevailed on a critical ballot when John
Adams broke the tie. The soldiers were unaware of the amounts due
them in specie, declared Senator Maclay, and only the speculators
knew in whose hands the lists of names and amounts were lodged.[3]
But none could have doubted that, as Bland cautiously supposed, the
lists had come "from a public office."[4] Maclay flatly asserted that the
"most villainous and abandoned speculation took place . . . from the
Treasury."[5] The hint of official collusion was implicit in the resolutions and was made plainer still by the nature and force of the
opposition.

The issue thus raised, as the Secretary of the Treasury conceded,
was one of inconsiderable magnitude in the number of persons and
the amount of property involved. But in his plea for a presidential

[1] This Appendix continues, on another level, the discussion of the context of
Hamilton's call for a presidential veto of the resolutions of 24 May 1790 and
Jefferson's rebuttal (see Vol. 16:455-70). That phase of this first clash between
the two men, as indicated below, was carried on in terms of high principle.
This one was not.

[2] R. H. Lee to Arthur Lee, 19 May 1790 (Lee, *Letters,* ed. Ballagh, II, 516-7,
misdated 1789; Microfilm Edition of The Lee Family Papers [Charlottesville,
1966]). Lee was a member of the committee to which Bland's resolutions were
referred (JS, I, 143).

[3] Maclay, *Journal,* ed. Maclay, p. 269-70.

[4] *Annals,* II, 1552.

[5] Maclay, *Journal,* ed. Maclay, p. 269.

veto, Hamilton elevated it to the plane of "those great principles, that constitute the foundations of property" and even of government itself. On this exalted level he argued that the resolutions were in the nature of *ex post facto* enactments, that they had the effect of impairing contracts, and that, if fraud had been committed, the power to expose it and to afford remedy was peculiarly judicial in nature and should be exercised without legislative interference. "Nothing . . . but some urgent public necessity, some impending national Calamity, something that threatens direct and general mischief to Society, for which there is no adequate redress in the established course of things," Hamilton argued, could justify such an infringement upon "the established rules of property, which ought, as far as possible to be held sacred and inviolable."[6] A few years later, on an issue involving a vast amount of property and in a defense of the sanctity of contracts that would exert a powerful influence over subsequent judicial construction, Hamilton declared it to be "a contravention of the first principles of natural justice and social policy" for a legislature to revoke a contract even when innocent persons were injured by fraud or corruption in those forming it.[7] Now, resting his technical argument on the laws and usages of the states, he urged that questions of fraud be left to the courts and that the national government set an example by refusing to emulate recent state legislatures in their intermeddling with contractual obligations.

When Washington referred Hamilton's argument to the Secretary of State for his opinion, Jefferson refused to allow the issue to be contested on that ground. He agreed with Hamilton in an almost unlimited condemnation of retroactive laws. "The few instances of wrong which they redress," he declared, "are so overweighed by the insecurity they draw over all property, and even over life itself, and by the atrocious violations of both to which they lead, that it is better to live under the evil than the remedy."[8] But he denied that the resolutions were retrospective, believing the assignments of claims to be invalid under Virginia law and, if fraud had been committed as Hamilton conceded, equally void in equity. This was essentially the same response Maclay had made in the Senate to the contention that the

[6] For Hamilton's request for a veto, see Vol. 16:462-7; Syrett, *Hamilton*, VI, 433-9. The fact that Hamilton volunteered the advice, submitting his request for a veto in a written communication as the means "best calculated to place the subject under the eye of the President with least trouble to him," is proved by his covering letter (Hamilton to Washington, 29 May 1790; same, VI, 447-8).

[7] B. F. Wright, *The contract clause*, p. 22, quoting Hamilton's opinion on the Yazoo claims (and correcting its date to 25 Mch. 1796) from Robert Goodloe Harper's *The case of the Georgia sales on the Mississippi, considered with reference to the law authorities and public acts* (Philadelphia, 1799), p. 88-9. Wright, same, p. 21, 25-6, discusses the influence of Hamilton's opinion on Marshall in the case of *Fletcher* v. *Peck* (1810). A year after this opinion was handed down, according to Timothy Pickering, John Marshall said he thought Hamilton "one of the greatest men that had ever appeared in the public councils of the United States; and that he was as pure as great. In short, that no greater man had appeared in any country" (Timothy Pickering to James A. Hamilton, 4 Jan. 1821; Dft, MHi: Pickering Papers, XLVI, 361; RC, DLC: MacLane-Hamilton Papers).

[8] For TJ's opinion on Hamilton's request for a veto, see Vol. 16:468-70.

resolutions "defaced writings and tore the seals from obligations."[9] The resolutions, Jefferson contended, only placed the government in the position of a court of equity that refused to permit itself to be a handmaid to fraud. Standing before the claimant and the assignee, its decision as to payment was crucial. Being free to award it to one or the other, the question was whether it should benefit him who had suffered from fraud or him who had committed it.

In this first of their conflicts over fundamental principles of administration, Hamilton chose to ignore the suggestion of collusion so clearly discernible in Bland's resolutions. Jefferson made the hint explicit. In a simple, lawyer-like statement of the facts he pointed out that the soldiers' accounts had been examined by the proper officer of government, that a list of the balances due each individual had been made out, and that "this list became known to certain persons before the souldiers themselves had information of it."[10] He went on to point out that it was not honorable to take a legal advantage contrary to justice, but it was "honorable to enforce a salutary principle of law *when a relinquishment of it is sollicited only to support a fraud.*"[11] This extraordinary statement seemed to be an appeal to the President to look further into the office from which the lists had issued. If so, it failed of its object just as Hamilton's appeal for a veto failed. Washington, ignoring the possibility of collusion within his administration, signed the resolutions and thus insulated himself from disclosures that might have been made. This settled the immediate issue but could not stifle the seeds of suspicion that continued to flourish with every confirming event of succeeding years.

"There are those," *A Free Citizen* had exclaimed in defense of another kind of soldiers' claims, "who advocate appeal to the courts of judicature, to redress frauds! Common sense revolts at the subterfuge."[12] Jefferson and members of the Virginia delegation knew what frauds were being concealed behind eloquent appeals to the sacred rights of property. They suspected but did not know then or ever the ramifications of collusion within the offices of the Treasury. Hamilton affected to believe that Congress acted upon "vague suggestions, loose reports . . . and problematical testimony."[13] But, as he well knew, this was not the case.

I

"No remarkable or interesting event hath happen'd in our neighbourhood since you left us," James Monroe wrote to Jefferson in the spring of 1790 in entire innocence of activities there that would soon become a public scandal and, as amplified years later, would almost bring him to the dueling field with Alexander Hamilton.[14] It was only

9 Maclay, *Journal*, ed. Maclay, p. 270. Maclay's legal argument paralleled that of TJ in other respects as well.
10 Vol. 16:468.
11 Emphasis added.
12 *New-York Journal*, 4 Mch. 1790.
13 Vol. 16:464.
14 Monroe to TJ, 20 May 1790.

a fortnight after Jefferson passed through that part of Virginia on his way to take office that Gustavus B. Wallace reported to James Madison the facts that led directly to Bland's resolutions:[15]

> There are a great number of small ballances due to the soldiers and officers of this and the North Carolina line which has been drawn by the paymaster Genl. and still remains in his hands to the Amount as I am inform'd of thirty thousand dollars. There is now in this State, a man from New York by the name of Renolds purchasing their ballances at the rate of 3/ in the pound. He was in this town, shew'd me his list of Names, from the paymasters books, and the ballances due to each man: he has purchased a great many: at the request of some gentlemen in this place I give you this information that if possible this trade may be put a Stop to and the Soldiers get the whole of their money which may be done with ease by publishing the list of names belonging to each State and the Sums due them.

Wallace, a former colonel in the Virginia line, later a member of the legislature, and "generally esteemed a brave and good officer and a worthy man," was clearly not at home with the pen.[16] But his statement of the facts was so succinct and his proposed means of putting a stop to the traffic so sensible that both were utilized when the resolutions were drawn up. Madison, suspecting official misconduct, asked at once for additional information. Wallace complied with facts that also affected the action in Congress:[17]

> Yours of the 10th I receiv'd. Mr. Reynolds is now on his way to Newyork. From what he inform'd me his partner got the Lists from a Clerk of the Treasury. Since I wrote you he receiv'd some other Lists amounting to 3000 dollars, due to the officers of this State. The person that he corresponds with from this place and remits the Soldiers powers of Attorney to is William J. Vriedenburg No. 40 great Dock Street N.Y. What makes the Speculation worse is that he shews a Soldier a list with a smaller Sum than is really due him, and gets a power of an Attorney for the whole that is due him with out mentioning the Sum. There are Soldiers that have £24 due them and some less but in his list [there] appears to be none over Six dollars and this he buys for 1/6 or 2/.

This was another and cruder exploitation by "emissaries . . . exploring the interior and distant parts of the Union in order to take advantage

[15] Gustavus B. Wallace to James Madison, 25 Mch. 1790 (DLC: Madison Papers), dated at Fredericksburg.

[16] The quotation is from an undated and unsigned list of applicants for office in Washington's administration, Wallace being listed as "a former officer and representative in the state legislature" who desired appointment as collector for the port of Rappahannock (DLC: Washington Papers, ser. 7, vol. 29, p. 21). Gustavus Brown Wallace (1751-1802) was the son of Dr. Michael Wallace of "Ellerslie," King George county, and was lieutenant-colonel of the 11th Virginia Regiment (*Fredericksburg Herald*, 24 Aug. 1802; Vol. 3:652).

[17] Wallace to Madison, 20 Apr. 1790 (DLC: Madison Papers). Madison's letter of the 10th, to which this was a reply, has not been found. Vredenburgh's correct address was 46 Great Dock Street.

of the ignorance of holders" that Madison had reported to Jefferson early in 1790.[18] That wave of speculation, Maclay believed, was a villainous business that "spread over the whole continent."[19] It had helped inspire Madison's effort to achieve legislative discrimination among holders of public securities and now, hard on the heels of his disappointment came news of these fresh impositions on veterans of the Revolution and their widows. Madison at the time was smarting under public criticism by those who impugned his motives or criticized his judgment. Even in Virginia such an astute supporter as Joseph Jones, though applauding his justice and humanity, doubted the wisdom of his policy.[20]

But the question of arrearages of pay to Virginia and North Carolina soldiers, however similar in the practices of speculators and in the feelings aroused for innocent victims, was altogether different. The money due had long since been appropriated, the victimization was direct, it was practised upon specific persons, the evidence of official laxity if not collusion was clear, and no question of national policy was at stake. The sense of outrage among veterans and their friends as they gathered on militia and court days was heightened because the agent or agents[21] of the northern broker, operating in isolated rural areas of the South, were at once blatant, secretive, and inept in concealing their deceptions. They did not advertise in the press as did dealers in public securities, but they did let it be known whom they were seeking and what business they were about. As emissaries from the commercial centers of the North, they thus added another item to the accumulating stock of sectional grievances generated by the manner in which federal power was being wielded.

Madison feared that the speculation was widespread. Immediately on receiving Wallace's information he wrote to the governor of Virginia to ask his official aid in stopping the abuse on the scene. But Beverley Randolph, prompted by an aroused public sentiment, had already taken action. He wrote Madison proposing substantially the same remedy that was later incorporated in the resolutions of Congress. On his own initiative he also designated Anthony Singleton, a former officer in the Virginia line and himself a broker in federal

---

18 Madison to TJ, 24 Jan. 1790.

19 Maclay, *Journal*, ed. Maclay, p. 178. Maclay believed that Morris, Fitz-Simons, Wadsworth, and others had been given prior information of Hamilton's report on public credit and that many members of Congress were deeply involved.

20 Jones to Madison, 25 Mch. 1790 (DLC: Madison Papers). Edward Carrington also deplored the frauds and conceded that the situation of the creditors "excited . . . the greatest commiseration." But he thought that courts of equity were the proper source for relief where fraud had been committed and that the officers and soldiers, while considering their case as a hard one, were reconciled to it "as resulting from a State of things beyond the controul of Government" (Carrington to Madison, 27 Mch. 1790, same).

21 Only one of the agents has been identified in the speculation in arrearages (see below), but there were probably several. Benjamin Hawkins of North Carolina, on his way to take his seat in the Senate early in 1790, met two agents having large sums for buying certificates (Maclay, *Journal*, ed. Maclay, p. 179). Those buying up arrearages of pay must also have bought certificates of various sorts.

securities, as agent "to receive powers of attorney from such as will confide in him and cannot conveniently go to New York."[22] This official appointment was announced in the *Virginia Gazette* and Randolph assured Madison that he would "take every possible step to prevent impositions upon the claimants."[23] As soon as the resolutions were adopted, but before they received the President's sanction, Madison forwarded a copy to the governor. The two Virginia senators were aware that he had done so, but they dispatched another copy the same day. "Fortunately," they wrote, "this speculation has not so far been carried into execution as to have drawn from the Treasury the appropriated money, which has furnished the Government an opportunity of so regulating the issues, as that the money should only be paid to the honest proprietors." They urged that the governor give the soldiers "speedy and effectual intelligence of the provisions coming forward in their favor."[24] Even with Randolph's prompt action, however, the door to fraud was not completely closed. A member of the council feared that, because many of the soldiers were dead or scattered over the state, much of the money would not be drawn from the Treasury.[25] Even after reading the announcement of Singleton's appointment and after the resolutions were known in Virginia, so experienced an officer as Thomas Posey had to ask in what form to draw a power of attorney for his own arrearages. But "from what I can learn," he added, perhaps on the basis of rumors spread by the speculators, "there is no money at the seat of government for the purpose."[26] Madison soon predicted, with accuracy, that fraud would be practised in administration of the effects of deceased soldiers. "What a door is here open," he exclaimed, "for collusion . . . if any of the Clerks in the Account offices are not proof against temptation!"[27]

It was this well-founded fear that had led to the move for legislative restraints on the Treasury in the payment of arrearages. Madison had shared Wallace's information with the Virginia delegation and with the Secretary of State. Then, late in April, he came down with influenza. The resolutions were introduced by Bland shortly after Madison resumed his seat, but there can be no doubt that the directing hand was his. Ellsworth, King, Johnson, and other staunch supporters

[22] John Dawson to James Madison, 14 May 1790 (DLC: Madison Papers), acknowledging Madison's of 27 Apr. 1790 (not found). Singleton on 30 Dec. 1789 announced his desire to purchase military certificates of Virginia, "final settlements, commutation certificates, etc. etc." and continued to run the advertisement for several months (*Virginia Gazette*, 8 Sep. 1790).
[23] Beverley Randolph to James Madison, 4 June 1790 (DLC: Madison Papers), acknowledging Madison's of 25 May 1790, which enclosed a copy of the resolutions. Madison said that in substance the resolutions corresponded "with the idea suggested" by Randolph (Madison to Randolph, 25 May 1790, with copy of the resolutions as adopted, CVSP, I, 157-9).
[24] Richard Henry Lee and John Walker to Beverley Randolph, 25 May 1790, explaining that they sent this warning because of the "wonderful and vicious activity of the speculators, and the great dispersion of those who may yet fall victims" (CVSP, V, 159).
[25] John Dawson to James Madison, 14 May 1790 (DLC: Madison Papers).
[26] Thomas Posey to James Madison, 5 July 1790 (same). Posey wrote from Fredericksburg, whence Wallace, a fellow officer, had first reported the speculation.
[27] Madison to TJ, 1 May 1791.

of the Secretary of the Treasury had done their best to weaken the resolutions in the Senate, where the issue was most vigorously contested. But their effort to validate powers of attorney drawn up previously and not in accord with the required form, provided no evidence of forgery or fraud had been adduced within a limited period, met with failure when John Adams broke the tie vote against the amendment.[28] It is not surprising, therefore, that at this time Madison's fight for discrimination among holders of federal securities, his personal solicitation at the Treasury in behalf of individual veterans, and his prompt and successful effort in procuring the resolutions on arrearages caused him to be regarded, particularly among his constituents in Virginia, as "the Advocate of the Oppressed . . . and the Soldier's Friend."[29]

The attempt in the Senate to legitimatize powers of attorney already in the hands of speculators may have been the sort of compromise Hamilton had in mind when he suggested that an unexceptionable measure could be arranged, to the success of which he pledged "his most zealous endeavours." This, he thought, would speedily remove such momentary dissatisfactions as "should happen to exist in particular parts of the union."[30] But when the President signed the resolutions, he closed the door on compromise. This was just as well, for the two views in the cabinet over this initial contest of principles of administration were irreconcilable. The Secretary of the Treasury was now officially directed to take necessary steps to effect payment within the states of Virginia and North Carolina. The President was directed to have transmitted to the governors, for publication, complete lists of the officers and soldiers and the amounts due each individual. Having received in many instances fractional but good specie value for their claims, the veterans were now free to obtain the whole from the Treasury and to learn precisely what sums were due them. The speculators, their investment lost and their powers of attorney invalid,[31]

---

28 The resolutions came before the Senate on 18 May 1790 and were opposed by King, Johnson, and Strong, "with many others . . . in an abandoned and shameless manner" (Maclay, *Journal*, ed. Maclay, p. 268). The next day the resolutions were committed to Ellsworth, Lee, Johnston, Izard, and King. The amendment was Ellsworth's and Maclay thought it "calculated as much as possible to favor the speculation" (same, p. 269). The resolutions were adopted by the Senate on the 21st and by the House as amended on the 24th. On the 28th they were laid before the President and the next day Hamilton submitted his request for a veto (JS, I, 141, 142, 143, 144, 145, 147, 151).

29 Abraham Hunt to James Madison, 9 July 1790 (DLC: Madison Papers). "I shall be one amid the thousands of freeborn Soldiers but too hardly dealt with, who rise up and call Maddison Blessed." Maxcey Ewell, a Virginia veteran who said that he was "turned loose with a wife and a number of small children without Bread Meat or Money," was another soldier whom Madison aided (Ewell to Madison, 21 Feb. 1791, same). Both Madison and TJ personally solicited his claim at the Treasury (Ewell to Madison, 19 Oct. 1790, same; Ewell to TJ, 10 Oct. 1790 and 21 Feb. 1791; TJ to Ewell, 16 Oct. 1790 and 8 May 1791).

30 Vol. 16:467.

31 It should be noted that the requirement for attestation of powers of attorney by two justices of the peace applied only to the particular category of claims covered by Bland's resolutions. Members of Congress—such as Schuyler, Wadsworth, and indeed Madison himself—acted in other respects under powers of attorney given by their constituents with or without attestation (see Thomas Wash to James Madison, 22 Feb. 1791, enclosing a power of attorney attested by one justice of the peace, DLC: Madison Papers).

were understandably vexed. But the doors to the collusion that Madison and Jefferson feared were still open.

II

In their warning to Governor Randolph the Virginia senators declared that "a set of unprincipled speculators had by false statements, fraudulently purchased up the rights of the soldiers" of the Virginia and North Carolina lines.[32] It is certain that a number of persons were involved in the speculation, which was also probably as extensive but perhaps not as complete as the senators' indignation led them to suppose. The names of only two of the speculators are known, the one an agent and the other his principal. Both belonged to that incurably sanguine group of army contractors, commission merchants, dealers in public securities, speculators, and political hangers-on who flocked about the offices of the War and Treasury departments after Congress moved to New York, each eagerly offering his services to the public in hope of profit. The name of the principal is scarcely known to history, that of the agent emblazoned in infamy. The activities of these two, whose partnership in fraud brought on the first conflict between Jefferson and Hamilton, reveal on another level the nature of the contest carried on elsewhere in terms of elevated principle. The two men and their scheme merit closer scrutiny than they have received.

The principal who supplied the funds for buying up claims to arrearages—and who perhaps was himself an agent acting for a group of speculators—was by no means unknown in the social and business circles of New York City. He was William J. Vredenburgh, a young merchant and broker of thirty whose ancestor had come from Holland in the middle of the seventeenth century. The progenitor of the family established himself in Dock Street and four generations of Vredenburghs—merchants, artisans, and holders of minor offices—had lived in the ancestral home until 1785, when it was sold. Vredenburgh had been in the commission business with his father and then, as a partner in the firm of Currie & Vredenburgh, carried on a coastal trade in flour, rum, salt, and other provisions.[33] By 1789,

[32] Richard Henry Lee and John Walker to Beverley Randolph, 25 May 1790 (CVSP, V, 159).

[33] E. Reuel Smith, *Notes on the Vredenburgh and Burnett families* (New York, 1917), p. 10, 11, 14, 15, 16, 19, 20, 21, 22, 29, 30, 32-6, 37, 38, 40, 41, 46, 63, 82-4, 88, 90-102, 112-15, 123-7, 130, 135 (hereafter cited as Smith, *Notes*); E. Norman Leslie, *History of Skaneateles and vicinity 1781-1881* (Auburn, New York [1882], hereafter cited as Leslie, *Skaneateles*; *New York Genealogical and Biographical Record*, XI [1878], 62).

William J. Vredenburgh, son of Johannes Willem van Vredenburgh (1734-1794), was born in New York City in 1760. In 1784 he married Elizabeth Townsend, the daughter of Platt Townsend and Elizabeth Hubbard. He was brought up in the Collegiate Reformed Dutch Church, the oldest in the city, but by 1796 was a pew holder in Trinity Church and later helped to found what became the St. James Episcopal Church in Skaneateles. On the death of his first wife he married Mrs. Mary Rozier Gilzean, widow of a Jamaican doctor who inherited his estate in Cornwall, Jamaica, "and a large amount of debts" (Smith, *Notes*, p. 7, 70-1, 73, 122, 123). Among his other activities, Vredenburgh was an importer of indentured servants of many nationalities and occupa-

after the partnership was dissolved, he was active as a broker dealing in soldiers' claims, state and federal securities, and all sorts of "class rights, Soldiers Bounty Rights of this State, and Land Warrants."[34] He was sufficiently established and prudent enough to survive the crisis of 1792 when Duer, Platt, Flint, and others were ruined or in jail. By 1793 he was engaged in a fairly extensive foreign trade with the West Indies, South America, Europe, and the Orient. He was active in land speculation in western New York and in 1792 was granted 69 patents aggregating 45,600 acres. He settled in that region in 1803, his home site being at what is now the town of Skaneateles, and there he became active in entrepreneurial ventures and Republican politics.[35]

In 1790 Vredenburgh lived with his wife and two daughters in a genteelly furnished house at 46 Dock (later Pearl) street on the corner of Broad opposite Fraunces' Tavern. This location was the very hub of legal, commercial, and governmental activity. Nearby on the same street were the offices of the Secretary of War, the Secretary of the Treasury, the Paymaster General, and other officials. These were such powerful fiscal magnets that when Congress moved to New York in 1786 an optimistic newspaper estimated governmental expenditures of every sort—including especially army accounts—would total "not less than one Thousand Spanish Milled Dollars per day." Simultaneously the public was warned against the artifices of sharpsters who assumed many different shapes, "personating clergymen, gentlemen, men of business, seamen, countrymen, &c."[36] Vredenburgh was at the

---

tions, an enterprise which later earned his family the reputation of having aristocratic leanings because, contrary to the custom of western New York, his imported servants were not treated as members of the family (Smith, *Notes*, p. 46; Leslie, *Skaneateles*, p. 109-10). Vredenburgh died in Skaneateles in 1813.

[34] N. Y. *Daily Advertiser*, 19 June 1790. Vredenburgh is listed as a land broker in *The New-York Directory* for 1791.

[35] In addition to his dealings in land, which included speculation in New York's Military Tract and in the Connecticut Sufferers' Tract, Vredenburgh was concerned in promoting such ventures as saw mills, grist mills, a turnpike, a salt spring, a hotel, a distillery, and an iron furnace. He became a justice of the peace, postmaster, and a member of the state legislature (Smith, *Notes*, p. 19, 20, 21-2, 29, 73, 122, 123, 127, 130). On the political implications of the disposition of New York's vast public domain in which such Clintonians as Vredenburgh benefited, see Alfred F. Young, *The Democratic Republicans of New York*, p. 231-43.

[36] Quoted from a New York newspaper of 31 Mch. and 14 Aug. 1786 in *The New-York Directory* for 1786 (facsimile edition, New York, 1886), p. 120, 166. Late in 1789 the offices of the Secretary, Comptroller, Register, and Auditor of the Treasury moved to the corner of Broad and Great Dock, opposite No. 46 where Vredenburgh lived with his father. The office of the Paymaster-General and Commissioner of Army Accounts was located at No. 14 Great Dock and the offices of the Secretary of War were at No. 47. Contractors for army supplies gave their correspondents Vredenburgh's residence as an address (Peter Anspach to Timothy Pickering, 18 Dec. 1792, MHi: Pickering Papers). For a description of this area as a place "conveniently situated for business," see Noah Webster's account of New York in 1786 (*American Magazine*, I [March, 1788], 220-28; see also Griswold, *Republican Court*, p. 32; Cutler, *Journals*, ed. Cutler, I, 306-9). In 1789 Vredenburgh was captain of the first company of the second regiment of the Light Infantry of New York City and led his company past his home in the procession escorting Washington to Federal Hall for his inauguration (*The New-York Directory*, 1789; Smith, *Notes*, p. 14, 41; Vredenburgh later rose to be major of the first regiment).

center of this burgeoning activity and his agent was one of the sharpsters who had been drawn to it as flies are drawn to sweets.

Vredenburgh himself was respected and his family appears to have
been well connected. His sister was married to the brother of Richard
Varick, then mayor of the city. The family historian asserts that
during their long residence in lower Manhattan the Vredenburghs were
associated with "the Varicks, the Van Dykes, the Hoffmans, the Ten
Eycks, the Clintons, the Roosevelts, and the Hamiltons."[37] In one form
or another such connections did exist. But in 1790 Vredenburgh was a
young man on the rise and not a leading figure in society, finance,
or government. He had no known connections with Henry Knox, Secretary of War. His relations with Alexander Hamilton may have been
limited to professional legal services.[38] This is understandable, for
in politics Vredenburgh was a Republican, being in 1792 a member
of the Clintonian faction who called themselves "The Friends of Liberty
and Good Order."[39] His political sentiments are also discernible in the
names bestowed on two of the vessels he built for trade with France,
The Goddess of Liberty and *France and Liberty*.[40] Vredenburgh must
have been known to Hamilton but he could scarcely have been an
intimate.

Yet it is certain that he possessed connections of sufficient influence
to cause his voice to be attended to on this occasion. After Bland's
resolutions had been reported and before they were adopted, Vredenburgh made a vigorous protest on behalf of himself and others
engaged in the speculation. It is significant that he did not present his
case in a formal petition to Congress but in a private letter. This
communication, addressed to an unidentified recipient, may have been
directed to a member of the House of Representatives—perhaps to
John Laurance, who spoke for the mercantile interest and who repre-

[37] Smith, *Notes*, p. 63, 81, 112-13, 115, 116, 120.
[38] Only two transactions linking Hamilton and Vredenburgh have been found.
The first was merely the delivery of a bond given in 1760 by Benjamin Vredenburgh to Vredenburgh's father and held by Hamilton for Abraham Morris
(receipt in Hamilton's hand, dated 18 June 1785, and signed by William Vredenburgh; DLC: Hamilton Papers). The second occurred in 1797 when William
J. Vredenburgh paid Hamilton a retainer of $20 to represent him in a suit
against Hallett & Bowne for recovery on a policy of maritime insurance issued
by them on the brig *Nancy* (memorandum of Hugh M. Dougan, Associate
Editor, The Legal Papers of Alexander Hamilton). Hamilton won the case before
the New York Supreme Court but had some difficulty collecting his fee. In
submitting his bill of $75, he wrote Vredenburgh: "The argument was success-
ful. The amount was considerable. The points were nice. The . . . charge is
certainly moderate. Under these circumstances Mr. Hamilton is not a little disappointed that so much delay has attended the satisfaction of his demand" (RC,
undated, in Hamilton's hand, made available to the Editors through the courtesy
of the late Sedgwick Smith, The Cove, Skaneateles, New York, a descendant of
Vredenburgh. The Editors are also indebted to Mr. Smith for permission to publish other documents from his family collection, cited below as Vredenburgh
Papers, Skaneateles).
[39] Smith, *Notes*, p. 30. The Republican partisan John Beckley became a
political and family friend of Vredenburgh (Beckley to Vredenburgh, 26 Nov.
1796, 2 Jan. and 23 Feb. 1797, 3 Apr. 1798, 4 May 1799, Vredenburgh Papers,
Skaneateles).
[40] Smith, *Notes*, p. 32-6, where the name of the vessel is given incorrectly as
Prince and Liberty (Vredenburgh Papers, Skaneateles).

sented the district in which Vredenburgh lived. The protest was as vigorous as it was immediate: [41]

Sir,

In perusing Mr. Bland's report respecting arrears of pay due part of the Troops of Va. and N. C. Lines, should it pass agreable to his report, I, as well as others, shall be greatly injured and the Door of Justice shut against me. I am one of those that Speculate in all kinds of Pay and Public Securities, due to officers or Soldiers of any line or State, and have now by me Sixty Assignments amounting in the whole by the Paymaster General's account to 1800 dollars. These assignments are in my favor, regularly executed before a Justice of the Peace and would have been paid long since— but there were a few [. . .][42] that had not come to hand, which I waited for and not wishing to trouble the Paymaster to settle them in small amounts. The above assignments are all that I have or Expect to have—out of which there are several of the Same persons pay that is claimed by other persons in this city and which I shall probably lose as those persons' claims are prior to mine. The objections I have to Mr. Bland's report are 1st. He requires the Transfer to be Executed before two Justices. Mine are before one. 2. A representative—I am only assigne and attorney. 3d. A certain Sum. Mine are for all the pay found due. 4th. Payment to be made within the States of Va. and N. Ca. Mine are from the Paymaster Genl for the time being.

I hope you will Excuse the Liberty of thus addressing you and that you will be of the opinion that Mr. Bland's report, as it now stands, ought not to pass into a Law, or any other that will destroy my right to those Assignments.

I am with respect, Sir, yr most obedt. Servt.

This was an admirably succinct statement, but it omitted one important point that no prudent defender of a speculator in Congress could ignore. Bland in introducing his resolutions had made accusations of fraud and had hinted at collusion in a public office. The unidentified recipient of the letter must have raised the same question, for in a memorandum on the subject Vredenburgh replied to it and provided additional information about the whole enterprise: [43]

Mr. *Bland* states that a *list* of Names of officers and soldiers of the Va. and N. Ca. Lines having pay due them, had been obtained from a Public Officer and Assignments of their pay fraudulently obtained.

Several gentlemen and Myself of this City some time last fall em-

[41] William J. Vredenburgh to ————, undated but ca. 20 May 1790 (Vredenburgh Papers, Skaneateles; the original manuscript is lacking and the text has been taken from E. Reuel Smith's transcript, Note Book, II, p. 23-4, cited hereafter as Smith, Note Book). Smith was not an altogether reliable copyist (see preceding note) but he obviously sought literal exactness.

[42] Smith, Note Book, II, p. 23, indicates an omission, perhaps of a word. Vredenburgh probably wrote "more" or "others."

[43] Smith, Note Book, II, p. 24-6.

ployed a Person in Va. to purchase a certain number of Officers'
and Soldiers' arrears of Pay and Bounty of Lands, due to them from
the U. S. We obtained a list from a Gentleman that had one a long
time before . . . and we heard of Numbers of persons that have
purchased their pay in Richmond and Carolina. It is impossible to
know what particular office Mr. Bland alludes to.

I believe there have been many copies in Circulation and received from different channels. How far Mr. B. can support his
assertions, I know not. I have no doubt that frauds have been
committed in buying and selling soldiers' pay—and where there has
been one instance of soldiers being cheated there have been fifty
instances of soldiers cheating. I bought Soldiers' Bounty Lands at
the same time as I bought their pay by different assignments. I
presented the powers for the Land to the Secty of War who without hesitation issued the Warrants.

Out of the few claims that I have lodged in the Paymaster Genls
office I find there are several that are claimed by others.

There are many persons in this speculation unconnected with
each other and have no doubt but the greater part of the claims
are purchased already &c. &c. Is it any strange thing for soldiers
or even officers to sell pay due them, which they can not get and
which has been due them many years? Have not the soldiers and
officers of the present Army on the frontiers and Elsewhere been
obliged to sell their pay at a very low rate? Some have assigned the
whole to receive a 3rd, 4th, or 5th part immediately. Those very
assignments have been presented to the Paymaster Genl, Examined
and 1/3 part of the sum due actually paid and the rest will be
shortly. The officers lately gone to Georgia were impatient waiting
to receive *the due to them* for their past services, chose to sell their
claims at a low rate. If Mr. Bland wished to prevent the Officers
and Soldiers selling their pay or lands he should have got Congress to have passed a Law for the purpose several years ago.

We have a higher opinion of the Wisdom and Justice of Congress than to believe that they will be guilty of so bare faced a piece
of injustice as to pass a law agreeable to the notions of Mr. Bland.

The law now in agitation is a down right Ex post facto Law
which the Constitution forbids being made.

Vredenburgh's sense of outraged justice equalled that of Madison,
Maclay, and other defenders of the soldiers, but he concealed as much
as he disclosed. He not only did not name the person who had made
official records available to a few for the defrauding of many: he also
tried to suggest the impossibility of discovering the office where
collusion originated. He further sought to direct suspicion elsewhere
by crying fraud on the soldiers themselves—doubtless with good reason in some instances. In confirming the suspicion of members of
Congress that the speculations began soon after the appropriations of
1789, he failed to state that he had sent several lists at different times
to his agent in Virginia. It was the agent, not the principal, who

declared frankly that "his partner got the Lists from a Clerk of the Treasury."[44]

Vredenburgh's vigorous protest of Bland's resolutions suggests that he had a leading if not dominant role in the speculation. So, too, does the prompt attention accorded that protest. In still another memorandum, Vredenburgh wrote:[45]

Upon the Report of the Secretary of the Treasury that Warrants had been granted to Joseph Howell, Jr. P[ay] M[aster] Genl by the late Board of Treasury for four months Specie Pay due for the year 1783 to non commissioned officers and privates of the Virginia Line. On the 29th Sept. 1789 Congress appropriated a Sum not exceeding $190,000 for discharging warrants remaining unpaid. That in consequence of the above said appropriation, I caused to be purchased from said Soldiers at a generous price amounts due them and received their several assignments duly Executed before two witnesses and attested before one of the Magistrates of the County the Soldier was then in:—These assignments were presented to the P. M. Genl in   and acknowledged by him to be duly executed &c. and noted for payment but the State of the Treasury was not then in a situation to pay them. That by a late Resolve of Congress   it appears that   . That in Consequence of this Resolve the P. M. Genl has his doubt whether it does not exclude me from receiving Payment for those assignments in the Manner they now are.

This memorandum not only contradicted the reason given previously by Vredenburgh for failing to collect on the claims: it was also incorrect in its allegation about the state of the Treasury, since warrants for larger sums were being issued and paid in specie at the time.[46] It was drafted shortly after Bland's resolutions became law, perhaps with a view to recovery through litigation. For soon after the passage of the resolutions Vredenburgh requested and obtained from Howell

[44] Wallace to Madison, 20 Apr. 1790 (DLC: Madison Papers). Reynolds later placed the onus on Duer.

[45] Smith, Note Book, II, p. 27. The document that Smith transcribed was perhaps undated, but probably drawn up soon after 7 June 1790. It was clearly a draft, with blanks left for appropriate insertions. Smith preserved the blanks and inserted in the first, in parentheses, the dates 23 Jan., 30 Mch., and 27 Apr. 1790 (see note 47).

[46] For the period in question, see Register's Office, Day Book No. 1, 1789-1791 (DNA: RG 39); Register's Office, Estimates and Statements, Vol. 1 (DNA: RG 53). It is true that the Treasury in the spring of 1790 was so situated as to require a temporary loan (Hamilton to Speaker of the House, 19 and 25 Sep. 1789; Hamilton to Washington, 29 Mch. 1790, Syrett, Hamilton, V, 379-92, 400-08; VI, 328). Even so, the loan was authorized and available for current demands (Washington to Hamilton, 31 Mch. 1790; Willing to Hamilton, 8 Apr. 1790, same, V, 333, 359). The total of arrearages, if demanded at a single time, might have presented embarrassment, but Vredenburgh's three groups of claims, amounting in all to only $1,812.36 and spread over a period of four months, could not have been declined for the reason given (see following note). Among other warrants issued at this time on claims against the government was that for $561.07 on the assignment to Royal Flint, attorney for Mrs. Catharine Greene for the salary of Baron de Glaubeck (see note 203).

certificates showing that, prior to their adoption, he had presented for payment three different groups of soldiers' claims for which he had powers of attorney attested by only one justice of the peace. He had procured sixty assignments in all, coming from soldiers of the Artillery Dragoons, Lee's Legion, Posey's detachment, and other Virginia units, aggregating $1,812.36 in arrearages of pay.[47] This was only a fraction of the total amount of arrearage claims, but all that Vredenburgh himself acquired. He believed that most of them had been bought up by himself and other speculators by the time his agent returned to New York with what proved to be his last group of assignments, soon to be rendered valueless.

But not valueless until after Ellsworth, King, and Johnson in the Senate had echoed the very arguments to defeat the resolutions that Vredenburgh had so succinctly expressed and not until after the Secretary of the Treasury had done likewise in his powerful appeal for a presidential veto. Such astute lawyers as Ellsworth, Johnson, and Hamilton needed no briefing from a speculator about the law of contracts or the constitutional prohibition against retroactive legislation. But their immediate and vigorous response to Vredenburgh's private protest offered striking, if more sophisticated, parallels to the arguments he first employed. The direct or indirect channels of communication between the speculator and those in government who re-

[47] In the Vredenburgh Papers, Skaneateles, are the remnants of three certificates, identical in character, that were issued on 17 June 1790 by Joseph Howell, Jr., Paymaster-General. Each remnant was torn from a sheet that once had at its top a list of names and sums due. These certificates testified that, on 23 Jan., 30 Mch., and 27 Apr. 1790 respectively, Vredenburgh had presented claims of arrearages for payment. Part of the text of the first remnant is lacking, but the second reads: "I do certify that on the 30th of March 1790 the above named William J. Vredenburgh of the City of New York presented to me powers of attorney and assignments of the above named men (late of the Virginia Line) for the specie pay due to them respectively, on account of their pay for the year 1783, which powers of attorney and assignments were on the day aforesaid examined by me and noted in the returns of specie pay due the late Virginia Line, payable to the said Wm. J. Vredenburgh—Certified at the request of the said Wm J. Vredenburgh. Joseph Howell Jun. P. M. Genl." From these fragments and from E. Reuel Smith's transcripts, which lack all save a few names, it appears that the claims presented on 23 Jan. 1790 amounted to $347.06; those for 30 Mch. 1790, $748.30; and those for 27 Apr. 1790, $717—representing, according to Smith, sums from $6.60 to $60 owed to the 60 claimants (Smith, Note Book, II, p. 27).

These certificates were issued ten days after Bland's resolutions became law and after Howell had expressed doubt as to the legitimacy of the accompanying powers of attorney. Had Vredenburgh actually presented the claims on the dates as asserted, he could at least have procured warrants assuring him of payment. His failure to do so and his request for the certificates suggest that, in his effort to establish a retroactive legitimacy of his claims, he found an accommodating officer in the Paymaster-General. This, not surprisingly, happened in other instances when Congressional influence was brought to bear. For example, on a soldier's claim presented by Jeremiah Wadsworth, a clerk in the Auditor's office noted that there was no record of its "having been filed in season." Beneath this were two notes by Oliver Wolcott, as Comptroller: "Col. Wadsworth informs that Mr. Howell will certify that the claim was presented in season" and, as a directive, "Mr. Howell will certify that this was shewn in season." Howell so certified and the claim with the certificate was sent to the Auditor's office (Account of Newton Ramsen, No. 2029, 15 Feb. 1792, DNA: RG 217, M235/4).

sponded to his appeal cannot be traced, but the similarity of the arguments was matched by another striking concurrence. In his plea for a veto Hamilton proposed an alternative solution that would have involved litigation at the seat of government between claimants and assignees, with resultant advantage to the latter. He argued that by this means the aid of government could be lent to counteract the presumed advantage speculators had taken of the soldiers. Yet the first and most egregious advantage the former had over the latter derived from government itself and, by implication, from an act of malfeasance in a public office. So far as the record discloses, however, neither Ellsworth, King, Johnson, nor Hamilton displayed any more desire to pursue this clear trail than had Vredenburgh.

The reticence of the speculator is understandable. But a special responsibility rested upon the Secretary of the Treasury who had argued so eloquently that the character of the national government was committed and that it should set an example consonant with "the dictates of Equity and the Maxims of good government." Hamilton's own character was also involved. If he did not know at the moment that the speculation arose from misconduct within the Treasury, as seems highly improbable, he was soon enlightened. Nevertheless he took no action until, two and a half years later, public disclosure was imminent and he himself was accused of being an accomplice in the speculations of the agent of Vredenburgh. The response that he made was such as to obscure the issue without meeting the charge, besides bringing pain to his family, embarrassment to his partisans, and advantage to such political enemies as did not scruple to accept it. Hamilton's defense met with skepticism at the time but, despite its obfuscating nature, has been accepted at face value by historians since.[48] It has never received the critical examination that it demands.

---

[48] In 1904, in reprinting Hamilton's published defense, Henry Cabot Lodge portrayed James Monroe as the one who had dishonorably forced the disclosure: ". . . Hamilton gave the whole story and all the documents to the world, and killed at a blow the despicable charge that he had been speculating in government claims. In so doing he cleared his name and fame as a public man, but it was at the cost of bitter mortification to himself, and displayed to the public gaze a wretched blot upon his private life. No harder trial and no more honorable act could well be devised than were involved in issuing this pamphlet. The original wrong-doing was terribly expiated, and the atonement to a proud, sensitive man was very hard to bear. The character which suffers most in the business is that of Monroe. On him rests a dark stain of dishonor, of slippery evasion, and of mean revenge, which has never been wiped out, and which apparently can never be lightened or diminished" (Hamilton, *Works*, ed. Lodge, VII [New York, 1904], 370-1n.).

This, in its essentials, was the interpretation that Hamilton himself sought to establish. In one form or another it has been accepted by all Hamilton biographers and has not been challenged even by those generally sympathetic to Monroe and Jefferson, whom Hamilton also implicated. See, for example, among recent works: Nathan Schachner, *Alexander Hamilton* (New York, 1946), p. 364-72; John C. Miller, *Alexander Hamilton* (New York, 1959), p. 332-42; Broadus Mitchell, *Alexander Hamilton*, II (New York, 1962), 326-422; W. P. Cresson, *James Monroe* (Chapel Hill, 1946), p. 155-69; Malone, *Jefferson*, III, 326-34; Merrill Peterson, *Jefferson* (New York, 1970), p. 414-15, 575-6n; Philip M. Marsh, "John Beckley, Mystery Man of the early Jeffersonians," PMHB, LXXII (1948), 57-8, 63-4; Syrett, *Hamilton*, X, 377-8n; XIII, 115-16n. Of accounts in Hamilton biographies the most detailed and the least exception-

III

The agent of Vredenburgh was one James Reynolds, about whose character and career little is known and that little highly unfavorable. In his brief moment on the stage of high politics he was charged with being a blackmailer, a forger, a perjuror, a conniver in his wife's adultery, and a thoroughly profligate person. It must be acknowledged that he, and some of his accusers as well, did not come into court with clean hands. But a few facts emerge from the dismal record to relieve in some slight degree the picture of unmitigated blackguardism.

James Reynolds was the son of one David Reynolds, who had served during the Revolution as an assistant commissary of purchases under Jeremiah Wadsworth of Connecticut and who, at the close of the war or later, appears to have settled at New Cornwall in Orange County, New York.[49] In 1779 James assisted his father in the procurement of supplies for the army, a schooling that led some to riches and others to ruin. David Reynolds was among the latter, for in 1783 he was imprisoned for what he called "publick Debts." He appeared to Wadsworth for relief, finding it hard that his incarceration prevented him from settling his accounts when, as he said, "my hole estate Lies In the hands of the publick."[50] Wadsworth may have intervened for the father, as he did later for the son. If so, it was possibly at this time that David Reynolds found it expedient to cross the Hudson and settle in Orange County.

After the war James Reynolds, having evidently gone to sea for a while, settled in New York City.[51] Hamilton later declared that he never knew Reynolds until the government moved to Philadelphia. But

---

able as to its factual statements is that of Mitchell, but on all essential points its interpretation, though expressing the culpability of Monroe in less extreme language, is in accord with that of Lodge. The least dependable accounts, factually and otherwise, are those of Miller and Schachner, both of whose interpretations are cited by Ammon, *Monroe*, p. x, 95-6, 158-60, as acceptable.

[49] David Reynolds' exact place in the large family of that name in New England has not been established. He was probably the David Reynolds (1738 [or 1741]-1823) who had a son, James Reynolds (b. 1 Nov. 1759), who came from Connecticut, and who settled in Orange County, New York. But it is certain that the David Reynolds who served in the commissary department under Wadsworth was active in procuring supplies in the vicinity of New Cornwall (later Cornwall); that in the latter part of the war he was aided by his son James Reynolds; that the latter, in addition to making trips by land for purchases of beef and other stores, employed a sloop on the Hudson for collecting salt and other supplies; and that his father had charge of some Continental "Store Houses on the North River above West Point" where such supplies were kept (Royal Flint to David Reynolds, 8 Sep., 30 July, and 22 Aug. 1778; David Reynolds to Jeremiah Wadsworth, 19 June, 28 Aug., 7 Nov. 1779; David Reynolds to Royal Flint, 13 Jan. 1780; Jeremiah Wadsworth to David Reynolds, 26 Sep., 4 and 21 Dec. 1779, CtHi: Jeremiah Wadsworth Papers).

[50] Reynolds said that he had been in close confinement on account of some rum purchased of one David Long for Wadsworth's account and claimed that "thare is a Considerable some Due" on his accounts with Wadsworth and another person "Besides the Lether that was Left with the army which I hear has sins ben sold" (Reynolds to Wadsworth, 7 Apr. 1783, same). Reynolds had been the object of complaints on other matters during the war (James Mathews' sworn affidavit against David Reynolds, 23 Oct. 1779, same).

[51] See note 89 below.

in 1787 he was certainly aware of his existence when he reported to Wadsworth that news of a rumored plot to set up a monarchy had come "to one James Reynolds of this city."[52] Others of standing in the city certainly knew him and had some confidence in him. For in 1789, just as so dubious a figure as John Lamb had once enlisted the support of Hamilton, Jay, and leading characters of Connecticut for his mission to Algiers, so James Reynolds was able to obtain significant backing for political preferment. The employment he sought was in the Treasury—not yet established as a department—and one of his supporters was an intimate friend of Alexander Hamilton. Reynolds' petition was addressed to the President and showed that he was informed about proceedings in Congress. Writing a few days before the passage of the bill levying duties on imports, he said he understood "that the Impost will soon be in the possession of the Congress of the United States, and that a regulation will shortly take Place." He asked to be appointed to the "Office of Tide or Land Waiter" and offered to post bond for the faithful performance of his duties if required. He informed Washington that he had been "employed in the Service of the United States in the late War with his Sloop in the North River upwards of two years" and that afterwards he was "employed in the Commissary's Department to the close of the war . . . to the entire approbation of his employers." To his petition was appended a testimonial signed by William Alwen, Robert Troup, Hendrick Wycoff; Robert Boyd, and John Blagge asserting that they were well acquainted with Reynolds and that they recommended him "as an honest industrous Man, well Qualifyed for the Office which he sollicits."[53] Reynolds did not receive that or any governmental appointment, perhaps because other and less flattering testimonials could have been produced. But to this respectable support must be added the fact that he did enjoy the confidence of such a rising young businessman as Vredenburgh. He also possessed candor enough to

[52] Hamilton to Wadsworth, 29 Aug. 1787 (Syrett, *Hamilton*, IV, 236); it is perhaps significant that this information came to Reynolds from one Hezekiah Wetmore, who had formerly been in the Paymaster-General's office. Both Jacob Clingman and Henry Seckel, a Philadelphia merchant, quoted Hamilton as saying that he had known James Reynolds' father during the Revolution. Mrs. Reynolds told Clingman in the autumn of 1791 that her husband had known Hamilton for "some months." Jeremiah Wadsworth said he told Mrs. Reynolds in 1792 that he knew her husband and that his "character was bad" (Wadsworth to Hamilton, 2 Aug. 1797, CtHi: Jeremiah Wadsworth Papers). But this was five years after he had intervened in behalf of Reynolds and his wife.

[53] "The Petition of James Reynolds," submitted "To George Washington Esqr. President and Senate of the United States," 26 June 1789 (DNA: RG 59, MLR; letter and signature in Reynolds' hand; the testimonial is in an unidentified hand). Troup was a lawyer and, like Reynolds' partner Vredenburgh, deeply involved in land speculation in western New York. Boyd was sheriff of the City and County of New York. Wyckoff, Blagge, and Alwen were merchants. Reynolds' addressing the petition as he did suggests that Troup, a lawyer aware of the constitutional role of the Senate in appointments to office, may have advised him as to form. He may have even drafted it for Reynolds to copy in his own hand, just as Hamilton had done for John Lamb in 1785 (see Editorial Note to group of documents on Mediterranean trade and Algerine captives, under 28 Dec. 1790).

provide leading Virginians with accurate and precise information about their partnership in speculation.

In assisting his father in large commissary transactions during the war, young Reynolds must have met a number of officials, contractors, and army suppliers who like himself later turned to speculation, among them William Duer and the ubiquitous Royal Flint. It was possibly in this way, too, that he met his future wife, Maria Lewis—as, for example, when Jeremiah Wadsworth directed David Reynolds to dispatch cattle to Thomas Lewis in nearby Farmington, Connecticut.[54] Less is known with certainty of Maria Lewis Reynolds than of her husband. She has been branded in history as a woman of loose morals, the partner in iniquity with her husband in duping and blackmailing the Secretary of the Treasury. Hamilton said that she introduced herself to him in the summer of 1791 as "a daughter of a Mr. Lewis, sister to a Mrs. G. Livingston of the State of New York."[55] Wadsworth

[54] Wadsworth to Reynolds, 21 Nov. 1779 (CtHi: Jeremiah Wadsworth Papers). Maria Lewis presumably belonged to the Lewis family in the vicinity of Farmington, but her parentage has not been traced.

[55] The quotation is not taken from Hamilton's *Observations on certain documents, contained in No. V and VI of 'The History of the United States for the Year 1796,' in which the charge of speculation against Alexander Hamilton, late Secretary of the Treasury, is fully refuted* (Philadelphia, printed for John Fenno, by John Bioren, 1797 [cited hereafter as *Observations*]), p. 27, where Mrs. Reynolds is represented as "the sister of a Mr. G. Livingston." On the assumption that this was a typographical error rather than the use of *sister* in the contemporary meaning of *sister-in-law*, the quotation has been taken from what appears to be Hamilton's composition draft of *Observations* (MS of 29 numbered pages, in Hamilton's hand, DLC: McLane-Hamilton Papers, cited hereafter as MS of *Observations*).

This manuscript contains many variations, in substance as well as phraseology, proving that it was not the final text used by the printer of *Observations*. In it, for example, Hamilton wrote: "the truth is that I withdrew from office poorer than I went into it and certainly not worth 2000£ in the world. . . . I have never been directly or indirectly interested in the public funds beyond the sum of   dollars and when I framed or proposed my plan was wholly ignorant of the situation of any particular friend or connection of mine in this respect." Hamilton struck the passage, perhaps realizing that with such leading speculators as Duer, Platt, Flint, and even Morris all ruined, poverty was not proof of innocence. The printed version placed the emphasis on the reputation Hamilton certainly carried into office: "I dare appeal to my immediate fellow-citizens, of whatever political party, for the truth of the assertion, that no man ever carried into public life a more unblemished pecuniary reputation . . . a character marked by indifference to the acquisition of property rather than by avidity for it" (*Observations*, p. 6).

In the printed account of his first visit to Mrs. Reynolds, Hamilton mentioned neither the sum he gave nor her appearance. In the draft he wrote: "I put a thirty dollar bill in my Pocket and went to the house. . . . It required a harder heart than mine to refuse [other means of consolation] to < a pretty woman > Beauty in distress." While Schachner, *Hamilton*, p. 366-7, describes Mrs. Reynolds as "a bold, florid, handsome woman" with "coarsely handsome features" and others have drawn similar imaginative portraits, this cancelled passage in Hamilton's draft is perhaps the only reliable comment concerning her features. It is plausible to assume that she was as personally attractive to Hamilton as she evidently was to others, including—if the memoirs of Peter A. Grotjan may be depended on—Grotjan himself and Aaron Burr. According to Hamilton, Wadsworth, and others, Mrs. Reynolds had a highly emotional temperament and was much given to weeping. This, too, seems plausible.

said that she claimed to be "the Sister of Col. [Lewis] DuBois."[56]
Only three persons seem to have voiced the opinion that, far from
being the aggressor, she herself was the victim of a cruel and slander-
ous fabrication. One of these was Jacob Clingman, a clerk in one of the
mercantile firms of Frederick A. C. Muhlenberg, Speaker of the House
of Representatives, who was indicted with Reynolds on a charge of
subornation of perjury to gain administration over the effects of an
allegedly deceased soldier—the kind of fraudulent behavior among the
clerks that Madison had predicted.[57] Another was Peter A. Grotjan,
a Philadelphia merchant who wrote long after the event and in such a
mixture of verifiable fact and implausible recollection tinged with
romanticism as to make his account usable as evidence only with
extreme caution.[58] The third was James Thomson Callender, the
polemicist.

What is known with certainty is that, after the game of purchasing soldiers' arrearages was up and the government moved to Philadelphia, Reynolds and his wife established themselves there. Evidently
hardship pressed upon them, perhaps because Reynolds' activities in
Virginia had given him ill repute among both Federalists and Republicans.[59] In 1791, according to Maria Reynolds, her husband
deserted her, leaving her in distress with a young daughter. She
turned for succor first to Hamilton and later to Wadsworth. Both offered to assist her and both did so. Hamilton, as he confessed later,
gave her money and formed an adulterous relation with her. He also
claimed that when her husband returned late in 1791 and discovered
their affair, he demanded retribution in the form of money. Hamilton

[56] Wadsworth to Hamilton, 2 Aug. 1797 (text from Dft supplied through
courtesy of Pierce W. Gaines, Fairfield, Connecticut). The relationship attributed
becomes intelligible if, according to contemporary usage, *sister* meant *sister-in-
law* (see preceding note).

[57] The testimony of Clingman as recorded by James Monroe, 2 Jan. 1793
(PBL). Mrs. Reynolds later obtained a divorce and married Clingman (John
Beckley to [James Monroe?], 22 June 1793, text from Tr supplied through
courtesy of Pierce W. Gaines, Fairfield, Connecticut; printed in Syrett, *Hamilton*,
XIV, 466-7). Richard Folwell, a publisher who had known Mrs. Reynolds in
Philadelphia, claimed that she married Clingman before obtaining the divorce
and that the Clingmans were living in 1797 in East Nottingham, Cecil County,
Maryland, where they were known to his family (Folwell's testimony, dated 12
Aug. 1797, is in DLC: McLane-Hamilton Papers; the text is printed in Allan
McLane Hamilton, *The intimate life of Alexander Hamilton* [New York, 1910],
p. 473-6). Callender asserted that she and Clingman were living in Alexandria,
Virginia, in 1798 (see below, at notes 171 and 176).

[58] Peter A. Grotjan (1774-1850), a merchant who settled in Philadelphia
shortly before the Hamilton-Reynolds affair became public, claims that a few years
afterward he became the friend of a widow, Mrs. Maria Clement, whom he discovered to be Maria Reynolds. He described her as a person of intelligence,
sensibility, and gentleness of manner. He said that later she agreed "to super-
intend the household affairs of a celebrated old French doctor by the name of
Mathew [or Mathews]" and thereby gained some position of respectability (MS
Memoirs of Peter A. Grotjan, written late in life, PHi).

[59] The views that Madison, Monroe, and others of the Virginia delegation
entertained of Reynolds for his role in exploiting their constituents were shared
for other reasons by Wadsworth, Wolcott, Muhlenberg, and Hamilton, according to their own testimony.

said that he complied to keep the matter secret, but suspected that husband and wife were joined in a conspiracy of blackmail. The only evidence to support these charges of adultery and extortion is that of Hamilton, who exposed both himself and the Reynoldses to the world in the hope that disclosure of his private guilt would "effectually wipe away a more serious stain."[60] The liaison with Maria Reynolds may have lasted longer than a year, though Hamilton's own somewhat indefinite account makes it less. Whatever its duration, there seems little reason to challenge his statement that he was anxious to terminate it.[61]

At the end of 1792 the affair became known to a few in government when Oliver Wolcott, Comptroller of the Treasury, instituted proceedings against Reynolds and Clingman for fraud and subornation of perjury. When the warrant was first issued, Clingman, having heard Reynolds boast of his relationship with the Secretary of the Treasury, said that he urged him to seek Hamilton's aid, that he did so, and that Hamilton advised him to "keep out of the way, a few days, and the matter would be settled." After being taken into custody, Reynolds appealed by letter to Hamilton, who reportedly declined to assist him. He also applied to Andrew G. Fraunces, a clerk in the Treasury Department, who said that Hamilton threatened him with discharge if he did anything in the matter. Clingman then urged Mrs. Reynolds to appeal to Hamilton. She claimed she had already done so, that she had received money from him after her husband's imprisonment, that he had advised her to see Wolcott but under an injunction not to mention his name, that she had nevertheless disclosed it—thereby, she said, surprising the Comptroller—and that he had promised to consult Hamilton. Clingman said that he had asked Mrs. Reynolds for

[60] Hamilton, *Observations*, p. 15. "The necessity of [the confession] to my defence against a more heinous charge," Hamilton explained, "could alone have extorted from me so painful an indecorum."

[61] Monroe's memorandum of 16 Dec. 1792 giving an account of the meeting with Hamilton the night before states that they were shown letters from Reynolds and his wife "commencing early in 1791" (PBL), but the first dated letter presented by Hamilton, the second in the series, is that from James Reynolds of 15 Dec. 1791. Mitchell, *Hamilton*, II, 400, 704, note 2, places the beginning of the affair about the middle of July 1791. According to Hamilton's version, knowledge of Reynolds' character and suspicion of a concert between husband and wife prompted him to end the affair, though her appeals by letter in "tender and pathetic effusions" made this difficult (*Observations*, p. 31-3). In his draft, Hamilton said that he "made no reply" to these letters, but the assertion was omitted from the pamphlet. A more significant omission concerns his receipt of Mrs. Reynolds' letter announcing her husband's discovery of the affair. According to both the draft and the printed text, Hamilton said he doubted whether there had been a discovery by accident or the time had arrived for the "catastrophe of the plot." But in the draft he deleted the following words: "my resolution to end it having now become unequivocal" (MS of *Observations*, DLC: McLane-Hamilton Papers). This, according to Hamilton, was on 15 Dec. 1791, the day he received a letter from Reynolds and discussed the matter with him. Yet the affair continued well into the next year. Hamilton gives the impression that his relations with the Reynoldses were broken off before Reynolds and Clingman were indicted. But he is less clear about the termination than about the beginning of the episode. He certainly met with Reynolds after he was released from prison and he wrote Mrs. Reynolds during her husband's imprisonment.

letters she had received from Hamilton, thinking that "he might probably use them to obtain her husband's liberty." She told him that Hamilton had asked her to burn all that were signed and in his hand, which she had done. On being pressed, she gave to Clingman "two or three" unsigned notes, identifying them as from Hamilton.[62] This suggests that, in his desperation, Clingman himself thought to use the letters as a form of blackmail to escape prosecution. If so, the hapless clerk abandoned such an imprudent compounding of his errors and decided instead to unburden himself to his employer. This was a sensible move for Clingman since Muhlenberg, a former clergyman and a moderate Federalist, was a man generally respected for his honesty, impartiality, and good judgment.[63] But it was fateful for Hamilton.

Muhlenberg responded with characteristic understanding to his clerk's appeal. He agreed to assist Clingman, but "not being partic-

[62] Affidavit of Jacob Clingman, 13 Dec. 1792 (Tr in hand of Bernard Webb, principal clerk of John Beckley, Clerk of the House of Representatives; signed by Clingman, PBL; another Tr, also in Webb's hand, with notation at foot of text in Monroe's hand: "Signed by Jacob Clingman"; endorsed by Hamilton, "No. 4[a]," DLC: McLane-Hamilton Papers; Hamilton's *Observations*, p. 71-9; James Thomson Callender, *History of the United States for the year 1796* [Philadelphia, 1797], p. 212-16, cited hereafter as Callender, *History*).
There are a number of variations in phraseology between the text furnished Hamilton by Monroe (Tr in DLC: McLane-Hamilton Papers) and its signed prototype (Tr in PBL). For example, the former omits the word "soldiers" from the phrase in the latter which reads ". . . a list of soldiers claims." All of these variations seem to have been due to clerical errors. In his *Observations*, Hamilton printed with exactness this and other texts of the key documents furnished him, at his request, in 1792. These documents were numbered 1 to 4 both in the prototypes and in the texts given Hamilton. Clingman's affidavit was No. 4. Nos. 1-3 were, respectively, those described in notes 64, 71, and 73 below. Document No. 5 is a four-page manuscript containing three parts recorded on different dates: (1) Clingman's testimony of 15 Dec. 1792, in the hand of Bernard Webb, occupying two and a half pages; (2) Monroe's record of the interview with Hamilton that evening as set down, in Monroe's hand, on the next day, occupying the bottom of p. 3 and the top of p. 4; and (3) Clingman's testimony of 2 Jan. 1793, also recorded in Monroe's hand, occupying the bottom half of p. 4 (PBL; numbered "5" at head of text). It is important to note that Callender's text appended the names of the three Congressmen to the second part and that of Monroe alone to the third part, a clerical insertion that almost led to a duel because it gave Hamilton the opportunity to focus his attack on Monroe. *There are neither signatures nor initials appended to any part of the original manuscript of No. 5.* Hamilton may have been shown the first part of No. 5 in 1792, but he did not see the second and third parts until Callender published them in 1797.
The texts of documents Nos. 1 to 4 as printed in Callender's *History* were neither the signed prototypes retained by Monroe nor, of course, the derivative copies made by Bernard Webb, annotated by Monroe, and supplied to Hamilton. That Callender used some other text is proved by variants in his *History* in instances in which the signed prototypes and Hamilton's copies are in agreement. For example, the two latter texts agree in the wording ". . . supposes he is gone out of the State," while Callender's text reads: ". . . supposes he is gone out of town." A clerk's copy of all four of these texts, together with the important document No. 5, is in this respect consonant with Callender's variant, but it was not the text used by him (Tr owned by Pierce W. Gaines, Fairfield, Connecticut).
[63] Paul A. W. Wallace, *The Muhlenbergs of Pennsylvania* (Philadelphia, 1950); sketch by George H. Genzmer in DAB.

ularly acquainted with Reynolds in a great Measure declined, so far as respected him." The cautiously chosen words are revealing. While Muhlenberg felt that he could not intercede for a person unknown to him, he did go so far as to ask Aaron Burr to join him in approaching Hamilton, perhaps because Reynolds also came from New York City and may have been known to the Senator. Sometime during the latter part of November the two Congressmen called at the Treasury. Muhlenberg commended Clingman as one who had theretofore sustained a good character. The record is silent as to what Burr might have said. Hamilton, so far as is known, committed himself no further than to signify his willingness to do all that could be done with propriety. It is plausible to suppose that he suggested the matter be taken up with the Comptroller, who had initiated the prosecutions. Certainly Hamilton revealed nothing of his personal involvement with Reynolds or even his professed belief that the man was a profligate character. These disclosures came later, under compulsion. At this stage, it should be noted, partisan motives could not have been involved. Muhlenberg was not investigating but soliciting, his only object being to help a young man who had gone astray. Yet essential information had been withheld by the Secretary of the Treasury who, according to his own later testimony, was in the best position to give it and on whose shoulders rested the responsibility for dealing with corruption in his department.

Muhlenberg next called on Wolcott, having in the meantime and from some unidentified source gained damaging information about Reynolds. This may have come from John Beckley, Clerk of the House of Representatives, or from some member of the Virginia delegation who was aware of Reynolds' speculation in arrearages of pay. Whatever the source, Muhlenberg from that time on flatly refused to extend his concern for the clerk to the accomplice. As he candidly said to Wolcott, "I verily believe him to be a rascal."[64] But Wolcott raised some difficulties even as to Clingman. He yielded no further than perhaps to suggest—as he reportedly did also to Mrs. Reynolds—that he would discuss the matter with Hamilton. It is certain that his response was so indeterminate as to require another interview. At their second meeting Wolcott told Muhlenberg that if "a certain List of Money due to individuals which Reynolds and Clingman were said to have in their Possession" should be delivered up and if Clingman should name the person in the public offices from whom it was obtained, his "request might perhaps be granted with greater Propriety."[65] Information about the unspecified list must have come from Clingman. As the clerk later

[64] Statement of Frederick A. C. Muhlenberg, 13 Dec. 1792 (Tr in the hand of Bernard Webb, signed by Muhlenberg, PBL; another Tr, also in Webb's hand, with notation at foot of text in Monroe's hand: "Signed by Mr. Muhlenberg"; endorsed by Hamilton: "No. 1[a]," DLC: McLane-Hamilton Papers; Tr in hand of Hamilton, *Observations*, p. 63-5; Callender, *History*, p. 209-10).

[65] Same. It is not clear whether one or more lists were surrendered. Muhlenberg mentioned only "a certain list," but Clingman mentioned "the lists of the names of the persons to whom pay is due" and in 1797 Wolcott testified that "the lists" and the letter from Clingman were in his possession (Clingman to Wolcott, 4 Dec. 1792, printed with Wolcott's affidavit of 12 July 1797; Hamilton's *Observations*, Appendix No. xxiv).

testified, the Reynoldses had told him some time since that "he had books containing the amount of the cash due the Virginia line, at his own house at New York, with liberty to copy, and were obtained through Mr. Duer."[66]

Wolcott still had given no assurances. He had only set forth a condition which, even if met, might not end the prosecution. His object was evidently to identify the source of collusion in the Treasury. Except for Jefferson's palpable hint to the President in 1790, this was the first effort within the administration to do so. It is important to note that this move, so far as the evidence shows, was not initiated by the Secretary of the Treasury. Hamilton had not acted in 1790 when Bland publicly intimated that malfeasance existed in a public office. Now, two and a half years later when investigation would almost certainly lead to his own door, he had good reason to wish the matter quietly settled, to have Reynolds released, and to speed him out of the state. Having begun a prosecution for fraud, Wolcott was unexpectedly apprised of misconduct in the Treasury. The opportunity to identify the guilty person or persons was clearly the first but not the last motive that led him to accede to Muhlenberg's appeal. Making no promises, he had nevertheless held out an inducement to gain further information from those under prosecution. Muhlenberg informed his clerk of the stipulated condition.

So, according to Clingman, did Mrs. Reynolds, who told him that Hamilton had said Clingman "should write a letter to Mr. Wolcott, and a duplicate of the same to himself, promising to give up the list and refund the money."[67] There was a significant difference in this stipulation. According to Clingman's reporting of Mrs. Reynolds' conversation, Hamilton said nothing at all about identifying the person from whom the list had been obtained. The omission may have been due to inaccurate reporting, but it is also consistent with Hamilton's previous failure to press an investigation inside the Treasury. Clingman wrote to Wolcott shortly thereafter, pledging himself to meet the conditions. He offered to repay the money, to give up the lists, "and to disclose the name of the person *in the utmost confidence*" from whom they were obtained. He earnestly hoped that this would cause the prosecution to be withdrawn, since otherwise only injury would come to him-

[66] Affidavit of Jacob Clingman, 13 Dec. 1792 (see note 62 for references).

[67] Statement of Muhlenberg, 13 Dec. 1792 (see note 64 for references). In his affidavit of 13 Dec. 1792 Clingman said merely that, in his interview with the Comptroller, Wolcott had stipulated that Reynolds would be released if he would give up a list of soldiers claims. According to Clingman, he had advised Mrs. Reynolds to seek her husband's release because "the money was ready to be refunded" (see note 62 for references). Apparently, then, the only real obstacle was that of identifying the source of collusion. That Wolcott was insistent and that Reynolds and Clingman were reluctant on the point—Wolcott said that they "obstinately refused for some time" to deliver up the lists or name the person—is proved both by the identity of the clerk (see note 126 below) and by Wolcott's affidavit of 12 July 1797 (Hamilton, *Observations*, Appendix No. XXIV).

There is no contemporary evidence that Hamilton emulated Wolcott in trying to trace corruption in the department, though when the affair became public in 1797 he naturally sought to create the impression that he had done so.

self without further advantage to the government.[68] The appeal, bearing evidence of Muhlenberg's prudence and kindly intercession, was made entirely in Clingman's own behalf, with no mention of Reynolds. But Wolcott understood that Clingman spoke also for his accomplice. Muhlenberg was informed that the pledge was met, the action against both men withdrawn, and Reynolds released from jail. This ended Muhlenberg's role as sponsor for his clerk, but not his anxiety.

During the two or three weeks in which these solicitations took place, Clingman volunteered hints to Muhlenberg that "Reynolds had it in his Power very materially to injure the Secretary of the Treasury and . . . knew several very improper Transactions of his."[69] Muhlenberg said he paid little attention until Clingman at last quoted Reynolds as saying that he could hang the Secretary of the Treasury, that Hamilton was deeply concerned in speculation, and that he had frequently advanced money to him. Muhlenberg later explained that such charges gave him considerable uneasiness. This is not surprising. Early in 1790 when speculation in government securities was at its height, with a few benefiting from knowledge of the plans of the Secretary of the Treasury before the public was aware of them, Muhlenberg believed that two of Hamilton's supporters in the Pennsylvania delegation, Morris and FitzSimons, were themselves involved.[70] Now, with Clingman testifying that Reynolds had access to Treasury lists and was making accusations against Hamilton, suspicions flourished. Hamilton's unsigned notes to Reynolds seemed ample confirmation. The Speaker felt it his duty to consult others in Congress and the probability that Reynolds would soon be released prompted him to act at once.

On Wednesday the 12th of December, a week after Clingman agreed to meet Wolcott's stipulations, Muhlenberg took into his confidence James Monroe, Senator from Virginia, and Abraham B. Venable, Representative from the same state. He made available to them Hamilton's notes to Reynolds, revealed what Clingman had reported, and intimated that Reynolds could give them intelligence implicating the Secretary of the Treasury. In doing so, this respected and generally sympathetic supporter of Hamiltonian measures transformed the question into one touching the public interest. From that point on partisan politics could scarcely have been excluded from either side.

IV

Muhlenberg certainly informed Monroe and Venable that Reynolds' release was imminent, for they hastened to the jail that same day. They had been told that Reynolds was from Richmond and was accused of committing frauds on their constituents. They did not identify themselves by name but as members of Congress. On finding Reynolds was not a Virginian, they questioned him about "the other particulars." He informed them that he could reveal "the Misconduct . . . of a

[68] Clingman to Wolcott, 4 Dec. 1792 (Hamilton, *Observations*, Appendix No. xxiv).
[69] Statement of Muhlenberg, 13 Dec. 1792 (see note 64 for references).
[70] Maclay, *Journal*, ed. Maclay, p. 178.

Person high in Office," but would not do so until after his release, which he had been assured would take place that evening. Reynolds left his visitors in no doubt that he had Hamilton in mind, for he said that Wolcott was in the same department and under him. His disclosures echoed much of what Clingman had reported and were patently equivocal. While boasting that the high official was in his power, he declared at the same time that that person had initiated the prosecution to oppress and drive him away, had instigated a merchant to offer bail so as to decoy him into custody, had often promised to give him employment without doing so, and yet now had prompted Wolcott to have him released. Reynolds feared he would not be discharged if he revealed everything he knew, but he promised to communicate the whole at ten o'clock the next morning. At that hour on the 13th Monroe and Venable were informed that Reynolds "had absconded or concealed himself."[71]

This is just what Reynolds' equivocation, added to facts already in their possession, had led them to suspect. Knowing that Clingman had pledged to reveal the name of the person from whom the lists had been obtained, they naturally were not convinced by Reynolds' attribution of the motives that led to his imprisonment and proposed release. Anticipating his flight and the loss of his promised information, they acted at once. After leaving the jail on the 12th, they reported these fears to the Speaker and that same evening Muhlenberg accompanied Monroe to Reynolds' home. They found Mrs. Reynolds alone and had difficulty persuading her to give any information. But having the advantage of the unsigned notes endorsed in Reynolds' hand "from Secretary Hamilton Esqr.," to say nothing of Clingman's disclosures, they at last induced her to talk. What she had to reveal was both informative and free of the equivocations so manifest in her husband's testimony. She admitted that the unsigned notes were Hamilton's and corroborated Clingman's information about her destruction of other communications from him. At Hamilton's request and in the absence of her husband, Mrs. Reynolds acknowledged, she had "burned a considerable number of letters from him to her husband . . . touching business between them, to prevent their being made public." She stated that Hamilton had advised her to go to her friends, had offered to assist her, and—confirming Clingman's report—had urged her husband to "leave the parts, not to be seen here again . . . in which case, he would give something clever." She said that she believed this was because Reynolds "could tell something, that would make some of the Heads of departments tremble." She revealed that Jeremiah Wadsworth had been active in her behalf, at first at her request and then, she thought, with the knowledge and prompting of Hamilton.

This much was merely confirmatory. But then Mrs. Reynolds made a new disclosure. The visit of the Congressmen to the jail had not gone unnoticed and had aroused the concern of Wadsworth and perhaps

71 Statement of Monroe and Venable, 13 Dec. 1792 (Tr in the hand of Bernard Webb, signed by Monroe and Venable, PBL; another Tr, also in Webb's hand, with notation at foot of text in Monroe's hand: "Signed by James Monroe & Abram. Venable"; endorsed by Hamilton: "No. 2[a]," DLC: McLane-Hamilton Papers; Hamilton, *Observations*, p. 65-8; Callender, *History*, p. 210-11).

of Hamilton. Wadsworth, in consequence, had come to Mrs. Reynolds immediately afterward to ask what their object was. He told her "Mr. Hamilton had enemies who would try to prove some speculations on him, but . . . he would be found immaculate." To this, so Mrs. Reynolds informed Muhlenberg and Monroe, she replied that "she rather doubted it." She then showed them two notes. The first was written by Hamilton two days after Clingman's letter to Wolcott. The second, purportedly written that day, was from Wadsworth. Both expressed a desire to relieve her. Mrs. Reynolds denied having had any more recent communications from Hamilton or having received any money from him that day.[72] This closed the interview. Although their suspicions were strengthened, the two Congressmen had gained no conclusive evidence. They set down an account of the interview immediately afterward and the next day signed the clerk's fair copy of it.[73]

On Thursday the 13th, their suspicions further confirmed by Reynolds' flight and broken promise, the Congressmen believed it their duty to probe further. Besides recording their own statements, they had Clingman put his testimony in writing. In this statement, in addition to what he had already told Muhlenberg, Clingman said that he had known Reynolds since September of 1791 and had been on terms of mutual confidence and intimacy with him. He stated that he had found Hamilton at Mrs. Reynolds' early in 1792 and that, on another occasion shortly afterward when Hamilton called and found him there, the Secretary of the Treasury had delivered a note to Mrs. Reynolds at the door, pretending to be merely a messenger conveying it on orders from another. Clingman quoted Mrs. Reynolds as saying that Hamilton had assisted her husband and had received upwards of eleven hundred dollars from him. He said that shortly after Duer's failure Reynolds had told him in confidence that, with Hamilton's

[72] In 1797 Hamilton sought to create the impression that he knew nothing of Wadsworth's intercession until after Reynolds was released from jail. He asked Wadsworth to testify to this fact if his recollection was the same (RC, Hamilton to Wadsworth, 28 July 1797, text supplied through courtesy of Pierce W. Gaines, Fairfield, Connecticut). Wadsworth, while framing his response in an effort to aid Hamilton's defense, avoided any comment on the point (Dft, Wadsworth to Hamilton, 2 Aug. 1797, text supplied through courtesy of Pierce W. Gaines, Fairfield, Connecticut).

[73] Statement of Monroe and Muhlenberg, 13 Dec. 1792 (Tr in hand of Bernard Webb, signed by Monroe and Muhlenberg, in that order, NjMoW; another Tr, also in Webb's hand, with notation by Monroe at foot of text: "Signed by James Monroe & F. A. Muhlenburg"; endorsed by Hamilton: "No. III[a]," DLC: Mc-Lane-Hamilton Papers; Hamilton, *Observations*, p. 68-70; Callender, *History*, p. 211-12, where the name of Venable is mistakenly appended to the document). The clerk's copy furnished by Monroe to Hamilton (Tr in DLC: McLane-Hamilton Papers) departs in one respect from that signed by Monroe and Muhlenberg. In the latter text (and also in that printed by Callender), the final sentence reads: "She denied any recent communications with Mr. Hamilton, or that she had received any money from him today [i.e., 12 Dec. 1792]." In the text employed by Hamilton the final word is "lately" instead of "today." In two other instances in the text signed by Monroe and Muhlenberg (Tr in NjMoW), Webb struck out "today" and substituted "yesterday"—an alteration proving incidentally that the interview was recorded on the 12th, probably by Monroe. Thus the change of the final "today" to "lately" was probably intended.

assistance, he would have made fifteen hundred pounds if Duer had remained solvent three days longer. He also quoted Reynolds as saying that Hamilton had acknowledged a connection with Duer, that he "had made thirty thousand dollars by speculation," and that he had supplied Reynolds himself with money for speculation.

Clingman further testified that he had lent money to Reynolds on assurance it could always be repaid by money acquired from Hamilton and that, on one occasion, he had seen him go to Hamilton's home and get $100 for payment on a $200 loan, the remainder of which came from the same source shortly thereafter. He also stated that, after her husband was in jail, Mrs. Reynolds had gone to Wadsworth because her father-in-law had served under him in the commissary department and that he had agreed to give assistance, saying " 'now you have made me your friend, you must apply to no person else.' " Clingman himself had found Wadsworth at Mrs. Reynolds' on Sunday the 9th and said that the Congressman had promised to do what he could for Clingman and Reynolds' family, provided his name should not be mentioned. On Wednesday the 12th, when Wadsworth called on Mrs. Reynolds, Clingman saw him leave there the note that Muhlenberg and Monroe read soon thereafter. At that time, he said, Wadsworth assured Mrs. Reynolds that "he had seen every body and done every thing." That evening about eight or nine o'clock, Clingman reported, Reynolds was discharged from jail and, about midnight of this day of much comings and goings, Reynolds sent a letter to Hamilton by a female messenger. While he trailed her, Clingman followed him. The two men joined each other before Hamilton's home and waited in the street until the girl emerged. Clingman quoted her as saying, for Hamilton, that Reynolds need not leave town that night but should call on him early the next day. Between seven and eight on the 13th Clingman said that he saw Reynolds enter Hamilton's home, but did not see him afterward and supposed he had left the state. The testimony seems entitled to credence. Indeed Hamilton himself later verified the accuracy of Clingman's statement that he had received a letter from Reynolds the night of the 12th and a visit the next morning.[74]

At this point James Monroe apparently assumed the leading role in the inquiry. "I should have considered myself as highly criminal, advised as I was of your conduct," he later wrote Hamilton, "had I not united in the inquiry into it: for what offence can be more reprehensible in an officer charged with the finances of his country, than to be engaged in speculation? And what other officer who had reason to suspect this could justify himself for failing to examine into the truth of this charge?"[75] Nevertheless, Monroe and his colleagues proceeded with circumspection. By going to the magistrate who committed Reynolds and to the Attorney General of Pennsylvania who

---

[74] Affidavit of Jacob Clingman, 13 Dec. 1792 (see note 62 for references). Clingman's testimony was not sworn before a magistrate, but it concluded with this statement: "The above contains the truth, to the best of my knowledge and recollection, and to which I am ready to make oath."

[75] Monroe to Hamilton, 21 July 1797 (Tr in Monroe's hand, PBL; RC in DLC: McLane-Hamilton Papers; Hamilton, *Observations*, Appendix No. XL).

authorized his release, they could have learned much about the dismissal of the proceedings. But this would have made the affair public. Considerations of delicacy and propriety toward the Secretary of the Treasury and perhaps also prudent avoidance of risk to themselves for acting on inconclusive proofs prompted them to call first upon Hamilton.

It has been generally supposed that they confronted him as inquisitors. No doubt they did hope to gain further information, just as they had used Clingman's testimony to obtain more from Mrs. Reynolds. Political motives must also have intruded, just as such considerations animated Hamilton's effort to conceal his relations with Reynolds. This was to be expected. A harshly partisan political campaign had just taken place, during which John F. Mercer of Maryland openly charged that Hamilton had speculated in public funds and had offered him a bribe to vote for the supplementary assumption bill.[76] Washington regarded this as so serious that he initiated inquiries into the matter, an action that came only a few weeks after Jefferson had advanced charges of equal gravity in a letter to the President himself. The system of the Secretary of the Treasury, Jefferson bluntly declared, "was calculated to undermine and demolish the republic" and, as a means to that end through the corruption and manipulation of the legislative branch, Hamilton had been guilty of "dealing out Treasury-secrets among his friends in what time and measure" he pleased.[77] There was too solid a foundation of fact supporting the latter charge for it to be ignored. With the President showing deep concern for the integrity of his administration and even for the survival of the nation, it is scarcely surprising that the two Virginia Congressmen, aided by the influential and moderate voice of the Speaker, pressed forward along the trail that seemed to inculpate the author of a system so opposed to their own.

Hamilton later charged that "two very profligate men . . . sought to obtain their liberation from prison by the favor of party spirit." This was not only inaccurate as to the status of the men: it also ignored the fact that none of the Congressmen had ever solicited Reynolds' release. As they were quick to point out, it was the Treasury itself

[76] The involved dispute over Mercer's accusations is succinctly set forth in an Introductory Note to Hamilton's letter to Mercer, 26 Sep. 1792 (Syrett, *Hamilton*, XII, 481-90, with other documents there cited), in which he declared his intention of pursuing "means for a full and effectual investigation and vindication" of charges impeaching his rectitude.

[77] TJ to Washington, 9 Sep. 1792. Even before receiving this letter Washington had expressed fear that the "internal dissensions . . . harrowing and tearing our vitals" would disrupt the government unless prevented by mutual forbearance and concessions. "Without these," he added, "I do not see how the Reins of Government are to be managed, or how the Union of the States can be much longer preserved" (Washington to Hamilton, 29 July and 26 Aug. 1792, Syrett, *Hamilton*, XII, 129-34, 276-7; Washington to TJ, 23 Aug. 1792, *Writings*, ed. Fitzpatrick, XXXII, 128-32). Washington, who had no high opinion of Mercer's character, considered his charges so serious that he deemed it "incumbent on Colo. Hamilton to clear it up—or for the President of the U States to take notice of it" (Washington to David Stuart, 21 Oct. 1792; Dft, DNA: RG 59, MLR; text printed, together with Stuart's reply of 5 Nov. 1792, in Syrett, *Hamilton*, XII, 487-8; see Washington to Mercer, 23 July 1792, *Writings*, ed. Fitzpatrick, XXXII, 89-92).

that had compounded with Reynolds "before the inquiry began."[78] In their indignation at this charge by a man who, at the time, had acknowledged the candor of their proceedings as well as the facts on which their suspicions were founded, Hamilton quickly retreated, absolving the Congressmen of partisan motives but ascribing to the two men a desire to gain relief through party favor.[79] This was palpably evasive. But it was a means of escaping the contradiction between Hamilton's public attribution of partisan motives and his private acknowledgment that Muhlenberg, Monroe, and Venable had acted with candor and propriety.

While party animus was increasingly manifest on both sides, the generally accepted view that Monroe and his colleagues confronted Hamilton as prosecutors to gain partisan advantage requires modification. Their object, after giving Hamilton prior notice of what they proposed to do, was to lay the matter directly before the President. This is proved both by their own assertions and by their letter to Washington, dated the day after Reynolds was released from jail. This was probably drawn up on the evening of the 12th after the visit to Mrs. Reynolds, for its purpose was to transmit "some documents respecting the conduct of Colo. Hamilton, in the Office of Secretary of the Treasury." The documents to be enclosed were, of course, Muhlenberg's statement of his role in behalf of Clingman, the account by Monroe and Venable of their visit with Reynolds, the record of the interview with Mrs. Reynolds by Muhlenberg and Monroe set down the night of the 12th, and the affidavit by Clingman that they obtained the next day. They thus adopted a course transferring responsibility from themselves that would either permit Hamilton to exculpate himself or compel his resignation, while at the same time making it possible without public scandal to investigate official misconduct in the Treasury—something Hamilton had consistently failed to do.[80] This prior notice given to him was a just and honorable action that stands in strong contrast to the manner in which the administration later proceeded against and disgraced Edmund Randolph as Secretary of State. Had party spirit alone governed their actions, a Congressional investigation could have exploded the scandal at the

[78] Hamilton's advertisement in *Gazette of the United States*, 8 July 1797; Monroe and Muhlenberg to Hamilton, 17 July 1797 (RC, in Monroe's hand, signed by both men, and endorsed by Hamilton: "xxxiii"; DLC: McLane-Hamilton Papers; Hamilton, *Observations*, Appendix No. xxxiii). Clingman was never jailed on the charge of subornation and Hamilton admitted his error as to him.

[79] Hamilton to Monroe and Muhlenberg, 17 July 1797 (Hamilton, *Observations*, Appendix, No. xxxiv).

[80] [Monroe, Muhlenberg, and Venable] to the President, 13 Dec. 1792 (Tr, unsigned, in hand of Bernard Webb, PBL). The documents to be enclosed were those numbered 1 to 4 as described above in note 62, together with the first part of document No. 5 containing Clingman's further testimony on the morning of 15 Dec. 1792. In preparing to lay the matter before the President, Monroe and his colleagues could scarcely have been unaware that the dispute between Mercer and Hamilton, about which Washington was concerned and which threatened to become an affair of honor, appeared at this time to be reaching a climax (Hamilton to Mercer, 6 Dec. and Dec. 1792; Mercer to Hamilton, Dec. 1792, Syrett, *Hamilton*, xii, 289-91, 390-2; see notes 76 and 77 above).

very moment that Hamilton, under the guise of *An American* and *Catullus*, was attacking the Secretary of State as an enemy of the Constitution, an "intriguing incendiary," and "the patron and promoter of *national disunion national insignificance, public disorder and discredit.*"[81]

The letter to Washington testifies to its authors' conviction that the accusations against Hamilton were well-founded. Its intended enclosures they considered to be of such importance as to merit his attention. "We think proper, however, to observe," they wrote, "that we do not consider ourselves as prosecutors, but only as communicating, for his information, to the Chief Magistrate, intelligence, it highly imports him to know."[82] Clearly anticipating that the matter would be investigated further, they indicated that other information had come to them and was available. They also signified their willingness to testify under oath to such facts as were based on their own knowledge. The letter, which in style betrays the hand of Monroe, was copied fair by a clerk on the 13th. But it was not signed, Washington never saw it, and no investigation ever took place. The nature of the response that Hamilton made when the three Congressmen called on him, though far from erasing suspicions, was such as to close the door to any further proceedings on the basis of decency and civility.

V

While Monroe and his colleagues had obviously decided upon their course of action after the interview of the 12th with Mrs. Reynolds, it was not until the 15th that the confrontation with Hamilton took place. During this interval Clingman, who was now a thoroughly cooperative witness, brought the Congressmen important new evidence. Reynolds, he reported, had unexpectedly returned to town the night of the 13th with a letter to himself, written earlier that day but not sent. According to Clingman, Reynolds tore out part of the letter, threw it into the fire, and handed the mutilated remnant to him. As first published, this note read:[83]

[81] The three numbers of *An American* appeared in Fenno's *Gazette of the United States*, 4, 11, and 18 Aug. 1792 (Syrett, *Hamilton*, XII, 157-64, 188-93, 224). The six numbers of *Catullus* appeared in the same paper on 15, 19, and 29 Sep., 17 Oct., 24 Nov., and 22 Dec. 1792 (same, XII, 379-85, 393-401, 498-506, 578-87). TJ perceived immediately that *An American* was Hamilton in disguise and told Washington so (TJ to Washington, 9 Sep. 1792). See Ammon, *Monroe*, p. 93-5.

[82] [Monroe, Muhlenberg, and Venable] to the President, 13 Dec. 1792 (Tr in hand of Bernard Webb, PBL). No other text of this letter has been found. It was not printed in Callender's *History* or in Hamilton's *Observations*.

[83] Callender, *History*, p. 220-1. The asterisks employed to conceal the identity of the friend who was "treated . . . ill" may have been in the original but more likely were inserted by Callender. The allusion was possibly to the clerk in the Treasury who was dismissed when Clingman and Reynolds revealed his identity, though this seems less plausible than the assumption that Reynolds, taking the blame upon himself, may have referred to "*your* friend," meaning Mrs. Reynolds. But there could be no doubt about the chief point—that Reynolds, after meeting with Hamilton, had claimed that Hamilton promised money to himself and his wife to go away.

My dear Mr. Clingman, I hope I have not forfeited your friendship, the last night's conversation don't think anything of it, for I was not myself. I know I have treated * * * * friend ill, and too well I am convinced [. . . .][84] to have satisfaction from HIM at all events, and you onely I trust too. I will see you this evening. He has offered to furnish me and Mrs. Reynolds with money to carry us off. If I will go, he will see that Mrs. Reynolds has money to follow me, and as for Mr. Francis, he says he will make him swear back what he has said, and will turn him out of office.[85] This is all I can say till I see you.—I am, dear Clingman, believe me, forever your sincere friend, James Reynolds.

Clingman turned this fragment over to the Congressmen. They must have been puzzled as to the cause of its mutilation, but were naturally impressed with its corroboration of previous testimony about Hamilton's desire to have Reynolds and his wife out of the way. This was indeed significant new evidence.

Clingman had other important news, supported by another document that he gave to Monroe and his colleagues. This was a note from the Comptroller of the Treasury which read: "Mr. Wolcott will be glad to see Mr. Clingman tomorrow, at half after nine o'clock. Thursday."[86] At the appointed time on Friday the 14th, Clingman reported, he was interviewed by Wolcott in the presence of Hamilton and "was strictly examined by both respecting the Persons who were inquiring into the Matter and their Object." He said that Wolcott "should not consider himself bound" unless Clingman reciprocated his own candor. This was a clear threat to reopen the proceedings. But the clerk presumably did not reveal or professed not to know the identity of Monroe and Venable, for, he reported, Hamilton had "desired him to go into the Gallery where he would see them and enquire their Names of the Bystanders."

Clingman further reported that, under the strict probing of the

[84] At this point Callender inserted the following editorial note in brackets: "Here about three lines are torn out." The mutilation of the letter is puzzling and Hamilton seized upon this point with vigor. He admitted the genuineness of the letter because it showed the author was motivated by revenge, a deduction plausible enough since the remnant made this clear. But at the same time he thought the "chasm of three lines . . . manifestly essential to explain the sense" and to reveal the cause of resentment. He then used the missing lines to discredit the witness: "The expunging of them is a violent presumption that they would have contradicted the purpose for which the letter was produced.—A witness offering such a mutilated piece discredits himself. The mutilation is alone satisfactory proof of contrivance and imposition. The manner of accounting for it is frivolous" (Hamilton, *Observations*, p. 21, 23). The mutilation of the letter, unexplained except by Clingman's mere statement of how it happened, certainly suggests that Reynolds or Clingman, or both, had something to hide. But, while Hamilton's pointing to this weakness was good forensics, there still remained the clearly expressed "purpose for which the letter was produced"— the charge that Hamilton had offered money to the Reynoldses to induce them to leave town. In his zeal to discredit the testimony, Hamilton obscured but did not deny this damaging testimony.

[85] At this point Callender appended the following note: "The Secretary kept his word. The person here meant was discharged from the treasury office." The clerk was Andrew G. Fraunces.

[86] Callender, *History*, p. 223.

two men, he had admitted giving to the Congressmen Hamilton's notes to Reynolds and that Hamilton had told him "he had done very wrong." He also reported that he had revealed to Hamilton Reynolds' letter of the 13th, mentioning his assertion that he would cause Fraunces to forswear his testimony. Clingman quoted Hamilton as replying that "he would make him unsay any Falsity he had declared" and that Reynolds was "a villain or rascal and he supposed would swear to any Thing." This conversation about Hamilton's connection with Reynolds, carried on in Wolcott's presence, brought forth the remark from Hamilton, according to Clingman, that "he had had some Transaction with Reynolds, which he had before mentioned . . . to Mr. Wolcott, and need not go into Detail." Clingman stated also that Reynolds had said to him: "when he was about to set out to Virginia, on his last trip to buy up cash-claims of the Virginia line, he told Mr. Hamilton that [John] Hopkins [Commissioner of Loans for Virginia] would not pay upon those powers of attorney[87] . . . to which he, (Mr. Hamilton) replied, he would write Hopkins on the subject." Obviously, the Congressmen were given such information as this last because they were following the cold—and by now false—trail of arrearages of pay due Virginia soldiers.

Clingman's new information—its comments on the interview with Hamilton and Wolcott alternating with reports of conversations with Reynolds—was clearly drawn forth in part in response to questions from Monroe, Muhlenberg, and Venable. It also undoubtedly formed the basis for questions that the Congressmen put to Hamilton later that evening, especially on such matters as Reynolds' mutilated letter and Hamilton's meeting with him on the 13th. Clingman's testimony was taken down by a clerk on the 15th. Its opening passage reported that, very early that morning, Reynolds had been received by Hamilton and had found him "extremely agitated, walking backward and forward, striking, alternately, his forehead and his thigh; observing to him, that he had enemies at work, but was willing to meet them, on fair ground, and requested him not to stay long, lest it might be noticed."[88] Clingman said that Reynolds had parted from Hamilton at sunrise. Since Hamilton himself admitted that he had met Reynolds on the 13th, it is reasonable to conclude that Clingman was equally accurate in his second report of another meeting at sunrise two days later. With this account of his interview on the 15th with an agitated Secretary of the Treasury, James Reynolds, a known reprobate who was prosecuted for crime more than once but apparently never convicted, vanished as an identifiable person from the historical record.[89]

[87] That is, the powers of attorney given to Reynolds as agent for Vredenburgh before the passage of Bland's resolutions and not in accord with their stipulations.

[88] Statement of Clingman, 15 Dec. 1792 (see note 62 on document No. 5; see also note 101).

[89] It is possible that Reynolds went back to sea. In Philadelphia in the spring of 1791 the mother of one William Duncan, who had sailed from Philadelphia in 1775 in a vessel that was never heard from again, received a visit from one James Reynolds, who represented himself as one who had come there to look after his family's estate. Reynolds told Mrs. Duncan that "some Years past he went as a Captain in a Vessel from Gibraltar to Algiers, and there saw a Captive named Montgomery, who informed him that he had seen a captive from America named

VI

His disappearance on the very day that the three Congressmen confronted Hamilton, when he might have been examined as an essential witness concerning the validity of Hamilton's account of their relationship, must have struck them at the time as it did others later as corroboration of the suspicion that collusion or worse existed in the Treasury.[90] So, too, must they have been impressed by the significant new information revealed to them by Clingman—the mutilated letter from Reynolds, the note from Wolcott summoning Clingman to the interview with Hamilton, their probing inquiry into the identity of the Congressmen, the report of Hamilton's agitation, and the charge that he had promised to evade enforcement of the legislation on arrearages by writing to the Commissioner of Loans for Virginia. They certainly could not have been unaware of the significance of the fact that Hamilton knew that his notes to Reynolds were in their hands. The probing that had elicited this acknowledgment from Clingman meant that from some other source—possibly from Mrs. Reynolds but, more likely, from Wadsworth—Hamilton had gained this information perhaps as early as the 12th and probably because of it had prompted Wolcott to send for the clerk.

Hamilton was thus painfully aware that his unsigned and in part disguised notes—the most damaging evidence against him—might be

---

William Duncan, but situated so as not to be able to write to his Friends." He suggested that she make inquiries and endeavor to get him released or redeemed (Memorandum sent to Daniel Coxe from Philadelphia, 21 May 1791, and taken by him to the Foreign Office; PRO: FO 4/10, f. 73-4).

The improbability of the story, the impositions being practised at this time on the families of lost seamen by reports of their captivity in Algiers, the concern of the government in preventing such frauds, the presence of Reynolds in Philadelphia at the time, and the verifiable facts given—all present strong presumptive evidence that this James Reynolds and the agent of William J. Vredenburgh were the same person (for similar efforts by impostors, see the case of one Archibald Ross as reported by TJ to the President of Pennsylvania, 24 June 1790). There appears to be no record of an American captive among the Algerine prisoners by the name of William Duncan.

The American captive named Montgomery whom Reynolds saw in Algiers was Andrew Montgomery, mate of the *Dauphin* that was captured in 1785. When John Lamb of Connecticut went to Algiers the next year, he was said to have arrived there in an American vessel (see Editorial Note, group of documents on Mediterranean Trade and Algerine Captives, under 28 Dec. 1790) and one may surmise that this was possibly the voyage of which James Reynolds spoke to Mrs. Duncan in 1791. The coincident circumstance that in 1793 a James Reynolds was captain of the *Belvedere* and that William J. Vredenburgh owned a ship of that name may also support the supposition that Reynolds found it expedient to resume seafaring (Smith, *Notes*, II, p. 32-6). Whether he did or not is of trivial significance compared with the fact that the Secretary of the Treasury, for reasons he never explained, had dealings with him after his release from jail and before his disappearance.

[90] Callender, relying on the promise attributed to Hamilton in Reynolds' letter of 13 Dec. 1792 to Clingman and on the testimony of Mrs. Reynolds, made much of this and assumed as a fact that Hamilton had engaged both Reynolds and his wife to disappear (Callender, *History*, p. 220, 228, 229, 230). After Hamilton published his *Observations*, Callender was even more emphatic in charging Hamilton with failure to explain his meetings with Reynolds (Callender, *Sketches of the History of America* [Philadelphia, 1798], p. 98, 99; hereafter referred to as Callender, *Sketches*).

revealed to the public at any moment. Forewarned by more than two full days, he was too experienced in adversary proceedings not to have anticipated the need to prepare an explanation for their existence and an account of his relationship with Reynolds, whatever the eventuality. The opinion voiced by Mrs. Reynolds and echoed by Clingman that the meetings between Hamilton and Reynolds were for the purpose of concerting such an explanation has a degree of plausibility that cannot be accorded alternative suppositions.[91] This belief gains further credibility because Hamilton, as *Catullus*, had promised to loose on the 15th another of his anonymous shafts at the Secretary of State. But he failed to provide the instalment for Fenno's *Gazette*, thus permitting the inference that he was preoccupied at the time with more pressing concern. As to what these were, there can be little doubt that his relations with Reynolds and his fear that political opponents were bent on destroying him commanded his attention at this moment more than any other public or private matters.[92] At sunrise on the 15th Hamilton was reported to be in a state of unusual agitation. Later that morning he apparently received the three Congressmen with his accustomed poise. The transformation, if such it really was, may have reflected in part his understandable relief on learning that they did not propose to conduct a Congressional investigation. But his self-confident demeanor must have rested at bottom on the knowledge that, having anticipated the need to meet their inquiries, he was now prepared.

The confrontation took place at the Treasury offices. According to Hamilton's later account, Muhlenberg began with the remark that "they *had discovered a very improper connection*" between him and Reynolds. This uncivil opening, he said, provoked him to such strong expressions of indignation as to compel their admission that they did not regard the fact as proven but that, having been given documents of a suspicious nature, they intended to lay them before the President, "declaring at the same time that their agency . . . was influenced by a sense of public duty and by no motive of personal ill will." Hamilton then added: "If my memory be correct, the notes from me were now shewn to me which without a moment's hesitation I acknowledged to be mine." This, he asserted, placed the matter on a different footing. Since he "always stood ready to meet fair inquiry with frank communication," he proposed to meet his visitors at his home that evening because, he said, "it happened . . . to be in my power by written documents to remove all doubt as to the nature of the business." To this the Congressmen agreed. Immediately afterward, Hamilton later said, he had seen Oliver Wolcott, told him for the first time about the affair, and informed him of the meeting with the Congressmen. He also said

[91] Testimony of Clingman, 2 Jan. 1793 (see note 62 for references).

[92] *Gazette of the United States*, 15 Dec. 1792, explaining that the number of *Catullus* promised for that day would not appear. The affair with Mercer was also occupying Hamilton's attention at this time (see notes 76 and 77 above). But Mercer was a far from formidable opponent and he possessed no such evidence as Hamilton knew to be in the hands of Monroe, Muhlenberg, and Venable.

that he had then placed in Wolcott's hands the documents he proposed to present as proof and "engaged him to be present at the intended explanation."[93]

It is probable that Muhlenberg did take the lead at this first meeting. He was the ranking Congressman and in a matter of public concern it would have been his duty to do so. It is also possible, though scarcely plausible, that the disguised notes were then revealed to Hamilton. But it is most unlikely that either the Speaker or his colleagues could have been so imprudent as to advance such a serious charge without being able to prove it. Moreover, their object was mainly to give Hamilton notice of their intent to place the matter before the President. As for Hamilton's later contention that it was on the 15th he first informed Wolcott of his connection with Reynolds—considered also in light of his effort to get Wadsworth to say that he had not been concerned in the matter until after Reynolds' release from jail[94]—this can be accepted as valid only if Clingman's account of his interview with Hamilton and Wolcott on the 14th is disregarded. Nor can the posture of open candor meeting fair inquiry be credited in view of Reynolds' disappearance and Hamilton's subsequent characterization of the inquiry as the product of a spirit of Jacobinism by which the "most profligate of men are encouraged, probably bribed, certainly with patronage if not with money, to become informers and accusers," with the ultimate aim of "undermining all the props of public security and private happiness."[95]

According to Wolcott, who was present at the second interview that evening, the conversation was opened by Monroe, who read Hamilton's disguised notes and also the record of their own conversations with Reynolds and Clingman. Thereupon, Wolcott testified, Hamilton "entered into an explanation and by a variety of written documents, which were read, fully evinced, that there was nothing in the transactions . . . which had any connection with, or relation to speculations in the Funds, claims upon the United States, or any public or official transactions or duties whatever." Wolcott said this was so completely evident that Venable requested Hamilton "to desist from exhibiting further proofs," but he "insisted upon being allowed to read such documents . . . for the purpose of obviating every shadow of doubt respecting the propriety of his Official conduct." The three Congressmen, Wolcott asserted, "severally acknowledged their entire satisfaction, that the affair had no relation to Official duties, and that it ought not to affect or impair the public confidence in Mr. Hamilton's character."[96]

This account loses considerable weight as evidence because it was written five years after the event. There was much left unexplained

93 Hamilton, *Observations*, p. 42-3; emphasis in original.
94 Hamilton to Wadsworth, 28 July 1797 (text from RC supplied through courtesy of Pierce W. Gaines, Fairfield, Connecticut).
95 Hamilton, *Observations*, p. 3-6.
96 Hamilton, *Observations*, Appendix No. XXIV. The documents that Monroe read included those numbered 1 to 4 as described above in notes 64, 71, 73, and 62 respectively. They probably included also the first part of document No. 5 as described in note 62 above.

that did affect Hamilton's official conduct and it can scarcely be supposed that in 1792 the Congressmen could have said there was nothing in the affair to lessen public confidence in his character. At that time the public was wholly unaware of the matter. But the circumstances under which Wolcott wrote the account diminish its evidential value even more. When No. V of Callender's *History of the United States for 1796* appeared late in June, 1797, Wolcott, then in Philadelphia, sent a copy to Hamilton in New York and said that he had been repeatedly called upon for an explanation because of the apparent design to prove that Hamilton had speculated in government funds. To answer such inquiries Wolcott said he had stated in substance that, at the interview in 1792, "an explanation took place . . . when each of the Gentlemen acknowledged themselves perfectly satisfied, and that there was nothing in the affair which could or ought to affect your Character as a public officer or impair the public confidence in your integrity."[97] On the day that Hamilton received this letter, he enclosed a "substance of Declaration" in his letters to Monroe, Muhlenberg, and Venable that, with slight variation, was an adaption of Wolcott's own expressions. The following is the declaration he claimed the three Congressmen had made that evening in December 1792:[98]

> That they regretted the trouble and uneasiness which they had occasioned to me in consequence of the Representations made to them. That they were perfectly satisfied with the explanation I had given and that there was nothing in the transaction which ought to affect my character as a public Officer or lessen the public Confidence in my integrity.

What Hamilton did not know was that, on 4 July 1797, the day before he wrote these words and sent them to Monroe and his colleagues to ask their verification, the sixth number of Callender's *History* came from the press, making public Monroe's own account of the interview. That account, undeniably written the day after the event it recorded, flatly contradicted the general tenor and the specific claims of Hamilton's memorandum. Although the declaration he attributed to the three Congressmen had been taken almost literally from Wolcott's letter of two days earlier and although Monroe's contemporary account was before the public, Hamilton blandly made this affirmation about his borrowed words: "I took the next morning a memorandum of the substance of what was said to me, which will be seen by a copy of it transmitted in a letter to each of the gentlemen."[99] Wolcott's private explanation to anxious Federalists, expressed in the same letter in which he advised against any further public defense, was thenceforth the position that Hamilton was determined

[97] Wolcott to Hamilton, 3 July 1797 (DLC: McLane-Hamilton Papers).
[98] "Memorandum of Substance of Declaration of Messrs. Monroe, Mughlenburgh and Venable concerning the affair of James Reynolds" (MS in hand of Hamilton, endorsed by Monroe: "1797. Note of Col: Hamilton, as to statement of Mr. Muhlenbg and Mr. Monroe," PBL; enclosed in Hamilton to Monroe, 5 July 1797, Dft in DLC: McLane-Hamilton Papers; Hamilton, *Observations*, Appendix No. xxv).
[99] Hamilton, *Observations*, p. 45.

to defend, whatever the cost.[100] He did so with characteristic daring but diminishing credibility.

The following account of the confrontation by Monroe is the only contemporary description of what took place that evening in 1792:[101]

[Sunday] 16th [December 1792]. Last night we waited on Colo. H. when he informed us of a particular connection with Mrs. R. the period of its commencement and circumstances attending it—his visiting her at Inscheps[102]—the frequent supplies of money to her

[100] Wolcott urged Hamilton to judge for himself, but added: "in my opinion it will be best to write nothing at least for the present. . . . I think you may be certain that your character is not affected, in point of integrity and official conduct. The indignation against those who have basely published this scandal is I believe universal. If you determine to notice the affair and I can assist you you may command me, but I doubt the expediency" (Wolcott to Hamilton, 3 July 1797, DLC: McLane-Hamilton Papers).

[101] This account, in Monroe's hand, is appended to the clerk's copy of document No. 5 (see note 62 for references). The sentence in italics (supplied) is the one that Hamilton found particularly objectionable because it conflicted with the statement he had already attributed to the Congressmen. But other parts of No. 5 were also damaging and while Hamilton made allusions to this very important document, he did not print it. Mitchell, *Hamilton*, II, 411, 708, note 41, acknowledging that it was necessary to Hamilton's purpose, thought the omission could have been due to haste in publication. The pamphlet was indeed hastily compiled and there were two other unexplained omissions of documents to which Hamilton referred but did not print (*Observations*, Appendixes Nos. XXXI and XXXII). Also, both Jeremiah Wadsworth's solicited letter and Richard Folwell's volunteered memorandum were omitted even though both endeavored to support Hamilton. It would appear that the omission of these last two was intended, since, in one form or another, both raised doubts about Hamilton's defense. It therefore seems equally plausible to suppose that document No. 5— a far more damaging sequence of testimony—was omitted for the same reason. Callender, to be sure, had printed the whole of it (Callender, *History*, p. 216-18). But if Hamilton had presented the text to his readers, his failure to confront some of the significant evidence against himself would have been all the more glaring. Only a reader familiar with Callender's text of No. 5 could have known that Hamilton did not face at all such testimony as Clingman's account of the interview with him and Wolcott on the 14th, Hamilton's confirmation of Clingman's statement that he had seen Reynolds on the 13th, his reported meeting with Reynolds again on the 15th, and his intimation that Duer was the malfeasant who supplied the lists. He did, however, seek to discredit Mrs. Reynolds' charge against him of conspiring with her husband to fabricate the documents on which his defense rested. In his discussion of this charge, Callender pointedly remarked in a footnote: "The colonel has reprinted the other papers, but leaves out No. v" (Callender, *History*, p. 94).

[102] John Inskeep (1757-1834) was proprietor of The George, an inn at the southwest corner of Second and Mulberry (later Arch) Streets. He became a respected merchant and entrepreneur and in 1800 and again in 1805 was elected mayor of the City (PMHB, XXVIII [1904], 129-35). Monroe may have misunderstood, or Hamilton, hearing the evidence for the first time, may have been confused. All of the evidence indicated that the meetings with Mrs. Reynolds had been at her house. Callender noted the inconsistency and wrote Hamilton: "Permit me to State one palpable mistake, as I judge it to be. In No. 5 of the documents you tell of *visiting her at Inskeep's*. The George was never a house of that sort. Inquiry was made at the time and it was affirmed that neither Mrs. Reynolds nor you had ever been there. Besides, in the letters there is no trace of such a thing. I tell you honestly and as a friend, that this has an air of inconsistency, and I would gladly, if you can give me a reconcilement of it, save you the trouble of inserting one in your second pamphlet, for that you must come out again I firmly believe. I might mention other things, but perhaps have already stretched my letter to a disagreeable length" (Callender to Ham-

and her husband and on that account—his duress by them from the fear of a disclosure and his anxiety to be relieved from it and them. To support this he shewed a great number of Letters from Reynolds and herself, commencing early in 1791.—He acknowledged all the letters in a disguised hand, in our possession, to be his. *We left him under an impression our suspicions were removed.* He acknowledged our conduct toward him had been fair and liberal—he could not complain of it. We took back all the papers even his own notes, nor did he ask their destruction.

Monroe also stated in this memorandum that Hamilton had confirmed Clingman's testimony about his receiving a note from Reynolds late on the night of the 12th, that he had met with him the next morning, and that he had never seen him before he came to Philadelphia. He further noted that Hamilton had told the Congressmen that the prosecution against Reynolds and Clingman had been dismissed "in consideration of the surrender of a list of pay improperly obtained from his office, and by means of a person who had it not in his power now to injure the department, intimating he meant Mr. Duer." Hamilton added that this information came from Reynolds. Presumably no questions were asked about Hamilton's reported meeting with Reynolds at sunrise that day.

This account of the interview was appended to the clerk's copy of the information given in by Clingman on the 15th. But Monroe set it down in his own hand and was guarded in his description of the "particular connection with Mrs. R." This suggests that he sought to protect the privacy of Hamilton's confession. Hamilton himself later claimed there was a mutual agreement to keep it secret. But Monroe's evident surprise that he did not even ask for the destruction of his own notes indicates that there was no such understanding. On the contrary, when Hamilton on the 17th requested copies of all the papers communicated, he only asked that his original notes be detained from the parties of whom they were had, to put it out of their power to repeat the abuse of them. . . ." Monroe complied with the request and gave him the assurance.[103]

---

ilton, 29 Oct. 1797, DLC: McLane-Hamilton Papers; emphasis in original). The point was obvious, but Hamilton ignored the letter.

[103] Hamilton asked for copies of the several papers communicated, "including the notes [of his own], and the fragments of Mr. Reynolds' letter to Mr. Clingman" (Hamilton to Muhlenberg, Monroe, and Venable, [17] Dec. 1792, Hamilton, *Observations*, Appendix No. xxvi; Muhlenberg to Hamilton, 18 Dec. 1792, DLC: McLane-Hamilton Papers: Hamilton, *Observations*, Appendix No. xxvii; Monroe to Hamilton, 20 Dec. 1792, same, No. xxxviii; DLC: McLane-Hamilton Papers). Wolcott told Hamilton he had answered inquirers by saying "no publication [of the fifth number of Callender's *History*] could have been made without a breach of confidence pledged" in his presence on 15 Dec. 1792 by Monroe and his colleagues. Though often asserted as a fact, this is the only categorical statement on the part of anyone that such a pledge had been given. Wolcott did not repeat the assertion in his published affidavit (Wolcott to Hamilton, 3 July 1797, DLC: McLane-Hamilton Papers; Hamilton, *Observations*, Appendix No. xxiv). Hamilton, to be sure, did speak of "the condition of secrecy which was annexed," but offered no evidence (same, p. 49-50).

The copies were delivered to Hamilton by Webb, who, in reply to Hamilton's

But the disclosure of the nature of Hamilton's defense was quickly made through one or more channels. Within two days the news was being whispered about in a widening circle in such a way as to guarantee its public emergence soon or late. This included members of Congress of both parties, among them such friends of Hamilton as Rufus King and Theodore Sedgwick. It is possible that Monroe, having perhaps already revealed to Jefferson and members of the Virginia delegation that inquiries were on foot, disclosed the denouement to them in confidence. Certainly by the 17th the Secretary of State was among those not present at the confrontation who knew the facts. On that day Jefferson set down this memorandum:[104]

> . Dec. 17. The affair of Reynolds and his wife.—Clingham Muhlenb's clerk, testifies to F. A. Muhl. Monroe Venable.—also Wolcott at [and?] Wadsworth. Known to J[ames] M[adison]. E[dmund] R[andolph]. [John] Beckley and [Bernard] Webb.
> *Reynolds was speculating agent in the speculations of Govt. arrearages. He was furnished by Duer with a list of the claims of arrearages due to the Virga. and Carola. lines and bought them up, against which the Resolutions of Congress of June 4. 1790. were levelled. Hamilton advised the President to give his negative to those resolutions.*

Two weeks later Clingman called on Monroe, who now had custody of all the papers, and informed him "that he had been apprized of Mr. Hamiltons vindication by Mr. Walcott a day or two" after the confrontation. He went on to observe "that he communicated the same to Mrs. Reynolds, who appeared much shocked at it and wept immoderately—That she denied the imputation and declared that it had been a fabrication of Colo. Hamilton and that her husband had joined in it, who had told her so, and that he had given him receipts for money and written letters, so as to give the countenance to the pretence—That he was with Colo. H. the day after he left the jail" when it had been supposed he was in Jersey. Clingman expressed the opinion that Mrs. Reynolds "was innocent and that the defense was an imposition."[105] Monroe recorded this significant testimony in his own hand below his account of the interview with Hamilton.

---

question whether others were privy to the matter, named John Beckley. According to the latter, Hamilton asked Webb to tell Beckley that he considered him bound not to disclose it, to which Beckley responded by the same clerk "that he considered himself under no injunction whatever—that if H. had any thing to say to him it must be in writing" (Monroe to Burr, 1 Dec. 1797, PHi; text printed in MVHR, XXXIV [Dec. 1947], 467; postscript is not in Dft of this letter in NjMoW). This statement by Beckley after the event was no doubt to defend himself against the general supposition that he had given the documents to Callender. Monroe said that he had requested Beckley "to say nothing of it and to keep it secret" (same).

104 TJ's memorandum of 17 Dec. 1792. The paragraph in italics (supplied) was scored out by TJ, the name of Hamilton being heavily obliterated. It is clear from this that TJ, Monroe, and others accepted the testimony of Reynolds, as supported by Hamilton at the interview, that Duer was the guilty official.

105 This formed the third part of document No. 5, printed in Callender's *History*, p. 216-18, but not in Hamilton's *Observations* (see note 62 above for description of the whole of No. 5).

It is scarcely credible to suppose that the Comptroller of the Treasury, whose loyalty to Hamilton was beyond question and who had an exact sense of official decorum, could have made the revelation to one against whom he had so recently instituted proceedings for fraud and to whose release from prosecution he had agreed with some reluctance. Wolcott was indeed so circumspect in avoiding comment on the nature of Hamilton's defense that, even five years later when the entire nation was aware of it, his account of the confrontation avoided all mention of Mrs. Reynolds and referred only to unspecified "transactions" that had no relation to Hamilton's public character.[106] But the significant fact about Clingman's testimony is its nature rather than its source. The clerk had been informed by someone in a position to know that receipts and letters had been offered in Hamilton's defense.[107] This much was undeniably true. In addition Clingman had also reported the charge—here advanced for the first but by no means the last time—that documents had been fabricated in a concerted arrangement between Hamilton and Reynolds. This was and would remain an unproven and perhaps unprovable allegation. But all of the prior and subsequent circumstances, as well as the kind of proofs offered by Hamilton, suggest that in this instance Mrs. Reynolds, whatever her other frailties, came closer to supplying a coherent explanation than anyone else. Because it was so congruent with all other circumstances, this testimony created for Hamilton the greatest difficulty when the matter finally became public. To it he devoted the principal part of his published defense.

But, at the time, he quickly resumed his usual confident posture, convinced that he had stifled all suspicions or at least had erected the sort of barrier that would prevent even political enemies from going to the President, much less to the public. This, for the time being, was a safe reliance. Those with whom he dealt, as he himself conceded, were men of fairness and liberality. On the 17th December, therefore, Hamilton as *Catullus* resumed his briefly suspended efforts in the public press to traduce the Secretary of State. On that day, too, an event took place in the Treasury that was concealed, with deliberate intent, both from the inquiring Congressmen and from the public. It delineated the most significant discrepancy between what Hamilton in 1797 asked the public to believe and what, in 1792, he wished those who confronted him to accept. This was central to the only issue that Monroe, Muhlenberg, and Venable had set out to investigate

---

[106] Wolcott's affidavit, 12 July 1797 (Hamilton, *Observations*, Appendix No. XXIV).

[107] Clingman's possession of this information, as Hamilton recognized, had damaging implications. He argued, plausibly enough, that there was "the strongest reason to conclude it . . . not true" that Wolcott had revealed the nature of the defense. He also supposed, less convincingly, that Clingman had *conjectured* the nature of the defense because "as an accomplice, he was privy to the whole affair." From this he concluded that Clingman's entire testimony "fell to the ground" because Mrs. Reynolds' own letters provided absolute contradiction of her "artful explanation" about the fabricated letters and receipts (Hamilton, *Observations*, p. 49-50). In brief, Hamilton sought to demolish the whole of Clingman's testimony by relying for proof upon the very documents whose authenticity had been brought into question. See below for discussion.

—the question whether collusion existed in Hamilton's department and where its source lay.

VII

Writing five years after the event, Hamilton said that Mrs. Reynolds in one of their meetings had told him her husband was engaged in speculation and could give information about misconduct in the Treasury. According to his account, he acted at once:[108]

> I sent for Reynolds who came to me accordingly.—In the course of our interview, he confessed that he had obtained a list of claims from a person in my department which he had made use of in his speculations. I invited him, by the expectation of my friendship and good offices, to disclose the person. After some affectation of scruple, he pretended to yield, and ascribed the infidelity to Mr. Duer, from whom he said he had obtained the list in New-York, while he (Duer) was in the department.—As Mr. Duer had resigned his office some time before the seat of government was removed to Philadelphia; this discovery, if it had been true, was not very important—yet it was the interest of my passions to appear to set value upon it and to continue the expectation of friendship and good offices.

Hamilton clearly intended to cast doubt upon the truth of the charge against Duer, arising from a source he described elsewhere as unreliable and "governed by the double motive of escaping from disgrace and . . . of gratifying revenge." Yet when Reynolds asked for employment as a clerk, Hamilton said that his relations with Mrs. Reynolds led him to use vague expressions that may have been regarded as a promise, even though his knowledge of the man "was decisive against such a request." He offered his refusal to appoint as proof of innocence. "Could I have preferred my private gratification to the public interest," he wrote, "should I not have found the employment he desired for a man, whom it was so convenient to me, on my own statement, to lay under obligations[?] . . . Or is it likely that wanting it, I should have hazarded his resentment by a persevering refusal? This little circumstance shews at once the delicacy of my conduct, in its public relations, and the impossibility of my having had the connection pretended with Reynolds." Toward the end of 1791, according to Hamilton's account, the affair was discovered by Reynolds. He demanded satisfaction but was hesitant in defining its terms. Hamilton reminded him that at their first interview he had "made him a promise of service . . . [and] was

108 Hamilton, *Observations*, p. 29. In his MS of *Observations* Hamilton gave a somewhat different version of the interview: "In the course of it, after having engaged a promise that I would endeavour to serve him as the consideration for the discovery of an important secret, he told me that he was possessed of a list of certain claims upon the Treasury which he had obtained from a person in the department at New York . . . Mr. Duer for the purpose of speculation." As to Reynolds' request for employment, Hamilton wrote: "I parried it by telling him there was no vacancy in my immediate office and that the appointment of Clerks in the other branches was left to the chiefs of the respective branches" (MS of *Observations*, DLC: McLane-Hamilton Papers).

disposed to do it as far as might be proper and within his power." In the end, he concluded, money appeared to be the retribution desired.[109] Thus the discovery that began as a declared effort to trace corruption in the department was forgotten in the purported yielding to blackmail.

This self-defense, benefiting from Hamilton's brilliant experience as a trial lawyer, had cogency enough to mislead Oliver Wolcott, who sought to corroborate its salient points. Wolcott testified that, prior to the confrontation in 1792 and before he knew anything of its cause, he had received a report that Reynolds, in prison, "had threatened to make disclosures injurious to the character of some head of a Department." He said that he communicated this to Hamilton, who advised him "to take no steps towards a liberation of Reynolds while such a report existed and remained unexplained," an assertion which Hamilton confirmed.[110] Wolcott did not identify the source of the report. After the prosecutions were begun, he said, Clingman had confessed to him that he and Reynolds had obtained certain lists from the Treasury. Wolcott asserted that both men for some time obstinately refused "to deliver up the lists or to disclose the name of the person, through whose infidelity they had been obtained." But at length, on Wolcott's promise to "endeavor to effect their liberation from the consequences of the prosecution," the two accused men had been induced to surrender the lists, to repay the sum fraudulently obtained, and to identify the malfeasant in the Treasury. In accordance with his promise, Wolcott said, he informed the Attorney General of Pennsylvania that an important discovery had been made and that a condition had been stipulated "by which it could be rendered useful to the public in preventing future frauds," in consequence of which the prosecutions against both men were dismissed.

While Hamilton had only implied that Reynolds might not have been truthful in placing the guilt on Duer, Wolcott went further, seeking to correct what he called "an injurious mistake":[111]

> . . . nothing occurred at any time to my knowledge, which could give colour to a suspicion, that Mr. Duer was in any manner directly

[109] Same, p. 22, 29-30, 33, 34.

[110] "Notwithstanding the powerful motives I may be presumed to have had to desire the liberation of Reynolds, on account of my situation with his wife," Hamilton argued, "I cautioned Mr. Wolcott not to facilitate his liberation, till the affair of the threat was satisfactorily cleared up. The solemn denial of it in Reynolds' letter No. XLII was considered by Mr. Wolcott as sufficient" (Hamilton, *Observations*, p. 53, Appendixes Nos. XXIV and XLII). This was plausible enough, provided greater credence could be attached to Reynolds' letter than to his contrary assertions to Clingman, Monroe, and Venable. See following note and discussion of that letter below.

[111] Wolcott was here repeating in substance what he had told Hamilton a few days earlier: "It is false that Duer had any hand in the transaction—the lists are in my hands, with *a letter* from Clingman and Reynolds. The Clerk who furnished the lists was notified of the discovery by me and dismissed. His name has hitherto been concealed" (Wolcott to Hamilton, 3 July 1797, DLC: McLane-Hamilton Papers; emphasis supplied). Neither the letter referred to nor the lists can be found in Wolcott's papers. Hamilton, *Observations*, Appendixes XXIV and XLII, prints one letter from Clingman of 4 Dec. 1792 and another from Reynolds of 5 Dec. 1792, both addressed to Wolcott. Wolcott's affidavit (Appendix XXIV) is dated 12 July 1797.

or indirectly concerned with or privy to the transaction. The infidelity was committed by a clerk in the office of the Register.—Mr. Duer resigned his office in March, 1790 . . . the Clerk who furnished the lists was first employed in Philadelphia in January 1791. The Accounts from which the lists were taken, were all settled at the Treasury subsequent to the time last mentioned; on the discovery . . . the Clerk was dismissed, and has not since been employed in the public offices.—The name of the Clerk . . . has not been publicly mentioned for a reason which appears in Clingman's letter but if the disclosure is found necessary to the vindication of an innocent character, it shall be made.

As to the source of collusion, Hamilton agreed fully in placing the guilt upon an unidentified clerk and in justifying the dismissal of the prosecutions on the ground that a greater public interest was being protected. "It was certainly of more consequence to the public," he declared, "to detect and expel from the bosom of the Treasury Department an unfaithful Clerk to prevent future and extensive mischief, than to disgrace and punish two worthless individuals." He appealed to men of candor to draw proofs of his innocence and delicacy "from the reflection that, under circumstances so peculiar, the culprits were compelled to give a real and substantial equivalent for the relief which they obtained from a department, *over which I presided*."[112] Hamilton's eloquent appeal was effective as an exercise in forensics. So also was Wolcott's threat to disclose the name of the guilty clerk if this became necessary to defend an innocent Duer. Unfortunately, their pleas in avoidance, while doing violence to some of the facts, served still further to screen the source of collusion.

The Congressmen who confronted Hamilton in 1792 were men of candor, as their actions proved and as he admitted. Yet nothing in the record suggests that anything was then said to them about an important discovery that would prevent frauds in future. None of the contemporary evidence pointed to a clerk as the guilty party or mentioned his dismissal. All of the testimony—including that of Hamilton, who in this as in other instances relied upon the word of Reynolds when he found it useful to do so[113]—placed the blame upon William Duer.

This is understandable. Duer had been forced to resign from the Treasury in 1790 because he was indeed using public office for private purposes.[114] The Congressmen who began the inquiry knew that the lists of soldiers' arrearages of pay had been obtained while he was in office. From the time he was prompted by the protests of Vredenburgh and others to ask for a veto of Bland's resolutions, Hamilton

112 Same, p. 56; emphasis in text.
113 See Hamilton's statement at the interview as recorded by Monroe, 16 Dec. 1792, in the second part of document No. 5 (see note 62 for references). For another significant instance of his reliance on Reynolds' testimony, see preceding two notes and discussion below. Hamilton and Wolcott not only accepted the testimony of Reynolds and Clingman as to the culpability of the clerk, but by their own admission dismissed him on that evidence alone.
114 Duer continued to be favored by the Treasury and by Hamilton after his resignation (see Editorial Note, group of documents on the new policy toward Spain, under 10 Mch. 1791).

himself had been aware that a list or perhaps several lists had gone from the Treasury into the hands of speculators. This, according to his own account, was more than a year before he allegedly learned of misconduct in his department from his paramour. Obviously, none present at the confrontation in 1792 could have been asked to believe the assertion by Hamilton that Reynolds only exposed the collusion late in 1791, much less to accept the claim of Wolcott that the important discovery had been made only a few days before the confrontation took place. At that time, with Duer in jail in New York and wholly unaware of what was taking place in Philadelphia, it was natural enough for Reynolds to place the blame on him, for Hamilton to let it remain there, and for Wolcott to give his silent acquiescence. Indeed, all of the circumstances as well as the contemporary testimony suggest that this was where the responsibility actually belonged.

But accusations made so easily in private in 1792, however plausible, could not be advanced in public five years later. Duer was still imprisoned and had long since hinted that he, too, might reveal much from a jail cell.[115] Under the altered circumstances, both Hamilton and Wolcott shifted the blame elsewhere.[116] In doing so they were careful to avoid any precise description of the nature of the secrets that had been leaked from the Treasury. Hamilton included in his *Observations* the testimony of Clingman with its allusion to books obtained from Duer, but in his own narrative he does not refer to lists of sums due officers and soldiers of the Virginia and North Carolina lines. Wolcott was equally vague. While he justified the dismissal of the prosecutions on the ground that lists had been surrendered, he cautiously described them only as "lists of the names and sums due to certain Creditors of the United States, which lists had been obtained from the Treasury."[117] The surrender of the lists, of course, could not in itself have prevented future frauds and Wolcott therefore was fully justified in stipulating that the one in the Treasury who gave them up should be identified.

His insistence on this stipulation reflected his own rigorous concept of public office as a public trust. From the time he became Comptroller he had been much concerned about the kind of intermingling of public and private business that had brought about the dismissal of Duer as Assistant Secretary of the Treasury. When a friend sent him a power of attorney authorizing him to make a transfer of government securities, Wolcott returned it with the blunt statement that it would be highly improper for him to accept any agencies from his friends or to be "concerned in any private business relating to the Treasury."[118] He was also alert in detecting forgeries, counterfeits, and fraudulent claims.[119] In 1792 he became particularly concerned about the use

115 Duer was still the recipient of Hamilton's concern and friendship in the form of loans (Duer to Hamilton, 11 Dec. 1797, DLC: McLane-Hamilton Papers).

116 See above, at note 111.

117 Hamilton, *Observations*, Appendix No. XXIV.

118 Oliver Wolcott to John Williams, 31 Aug. 1791 (CtHi: Wolcott Papers).

119 See, for example, Wolcott to John Cochran, 9 Sep. 1791, concerning a counterfeit certificate "most remarkably accurate," except for the wrong watermark (same); see also note 47 above.

of deception in obtaining letters of administration.[120] The extent of the frauds practised in such cases became so great that Wolcott deemed it necessary late in that year to make "a strenuous attempt . . . to discover the authors and bring them to punishment."[121]

It was this determination to make an example of those imposing on the public that led Wolcott to initiate two suits against Reynolds and Clingman, the first for subornation of perjury and the second for defrauding the government. In mid-November he began to gather evidence for the trial of these cases, set for the third Monday of December.[122] Simultaneously James Ewing, Commissioner of Loans for New Jersey, transmitted a certificate that Wolcott discovered to be a forgery. He directed Ewing to make an inquiry about that and also about another case involving one "Spencer" or "Edwards." Ewing's response, evidently lost, was written on the day that Reynolds was released from jail and when it came to Wolcott's hand his zeal to apprehend the culprit had suffered a marked decline. A pursuit of

[120] Wolcott to Hamilton, 3 May 1792 (Syrett, *Hamilton*, XI, 359-60, and references there).

[121] Wolcott to Christopher Gore, 13 Nov. 1792 (CtHi: Wolcott Papers), transmitting a number of powers of attorney that Wolcott had held on presumption of their being forged and asking that Gore, federal attorney for the district of Massachusetts, investigate and begin prosecutions where necessary.

[122] Wolcott to Samuel Emery, 19 Nov. 1792 (same), requesting him either to produce Ephraim Goodenough in court or to procure proofs of his being alive and entitled to the claim involved in the prosecution against John Delabar for allegedly fraudulent administration of his estate. In addition to the suit instituted 13 Nov. 1792 against Delabar, who was charged with perjury and defrauding the Treasury "of a Sum . . . near Four hundred Dollars," two suits were begun against Reynolds and Clingman on the 16th, the first for suborning Delabar to commit perjury and the second for defrauding the government (*Commonwealth* v. *Reynolds and Clingman*, Mayor's Court Docket, 1792-1796, p. 71; Prisoners for Trial Docket, 1790-1797, p. 113, where it is noted that, on the day the warrant was issued, "Clingman got Bail"; City of Philadelphia, Department of Records). The cases were set for trial on Monday, 17 Dec. 1792. While the suits against Reynolds and Clingman were dismissed on 12 Dec. 1792, Delabar was held until 1 Apr. 1793 when Jared Ingersoll, Attorney General of Pennsylvania, ordered his release. This was probably to await proof that Goodenough was alive, as indeed he was. Goodenough, accompanied by Levi Holden, arrived in Philadelphia early in 1793 to give testimony and to receive pay on his certificate. His and Holden's expenses cost the government $174 (Receipt of Holden, 7 Mch. 1793, with itemized costs for "Time and Expenses to Philadelphia and Back to Boston"; Emery to Wolcott, 7 Mch. 1793; Wolcott to the Auditor, 18 Apr. 1793, all in Account No. 3946, Samuel C. Emery, DNA: RG 217, M235/11). Wolcott did not say whether Reynolds and Clingman had *actually* refunded the sum of which they had defrauded the government—only that they had "consented" to do so (Hamilton, *Observations*, Appendix No. XXIV). It is to be doubted whether the refund was made. Goodenough threatened to bring civil suit against "Delabar or his Confederates" to recover $133 depreciation on his certificate (Emery to Wolcott, 7 Mch. 1793, DNA: RG 217, M235/11).

It should be noted that up to this time, since the autumn of 1790, James Reynolds had been defendant in no less than four criminal prosecutions involving charges of larceny or receiving stolen goods, in two of which there were co-defendants. In all of these cases he was acquitted though in two of them a co-defendant was found guilty (Mayor's Court Docket, 1789-1792, p. 195, 196, 200, City of Philadelphia, Department of Records). No record of a criminal prosecution against Jacob Clingman prior or subsequent to the suits against him and Reynolds has been found.

"Spencer" or "Edwards," he replied, would probably be ineffectual. Then, in obvious response to a suggestion from Ewing, he added: "I do not recommend an Advertisement, as it might excite erroneous ideas with regard to your Office and besides is not likely to produce the effect intended." He thought it best to be silent, since he did not apprehend any great danger of fraud from that source.[123]

The letter revealing this changed attitude was written on the day that Monroe, Muhlenberg, and Venable confronted Hamilton. It was also the day that Reynolds vanished from sight. Two years later Ewing brought up the case again in response to an inquiry from one John Peck. "I advise you," Wolcott replied, "to . . . inform him, that the subscription which was made in your office in the name of Samuel Edwards was a fraud, and that subsequent appearances relating to that transaction, have been of such a mysterious nature, that you have transmitted all the papers to this office, where a suitable investigation will take place, and to which he may be referred for a more particular reply."[124] The mystery, which Wolcott and Hamilton alone may have penetrated, still endures.

But it is important to note that, in their effort in 1797 to shift the suspicion of official misconduct from Duer to a clerk, the Secretary and the Comptroller obscured other essential facts. First of all, the prosecutions against Reynolds and Clingman had nothing whatever to do with the question of arrearages of pay for the Virginia and North Carolina soldiers. The dismissal of the proceedings could not, therefore, protect the public against that abuse or indeed against a recurrence of the crimes for which the two men were accused. Adversary proceedings in *Commonwealth* v. *Reynolds and Clingman* would have been the most effective way to establish their guilt or innocence and also to gain information about possible collusion within the Treasury, even as to the question of arrearages. Second, if the lists related to that question, as the Congressmen were led to suppose, their surrender in 1792 could in no sense have been a real and substantial equivalent sufficient to justify a *nolle prosequi*. This was two and a half years after Bland's resolutions had required that such lists be published in the newspapers. Finally, while Wolcott's charge that lists were obtained by Reynolds and Clingman through "the infidelity . . . committed by a clerk in the office of the Register" may be accepted as valid, it is misleading. Wolcott's assertion that the clerk who was dismissed began his employment in the Treasury in January 1791 was correct. But this meant that the clerk was first employed some months after the lists of Virginia and North Carolina soldiers had become public property.

The clerk upon whom both Wolcott and Hamilton placed the blame was concealed even from contemporaries. Callender, who analyzed the testimony more searchingly than any other of the time, suspected that the culprit was Andrew G. Fraunces.[125] This was a plausible surmise, since Fraunces was dismissed from the Treasury early in 1793, but it was ill-founded. The dismissed clerk was Simeon Reynolds, who was almost certainly a kinsman of James Reynolds and who may have

[123] Wolcott to Ewing, 26 Nov., 11 and 15 Dec. 1792 (CtHi: Wolcott Papers).
[124] Wolcott to Ewing, 11 Dec. 1794 (same).
[125] Callender, *Sketches*, p. 100.

gained employment in January 1791 through the favor that Hamilton had led the latter to expect.[126] His dismissal, which Wolcott took to be so firm a ground on which to affirm the innocence of William Duer, took place on the same day that Reynolds and Clingman would have been brought to trial if the prosecutions initiated by the Comptroller had not so unexpectedly implicated his superior officer. Wolcott's exposure of the weakness of his own defense of Duer was perhaps unwitting. But Hamilton's assertion that he first learned of misconduct in the Treasury from Mrs. Reynolds and then sent for her husband is a contrived explanation that cannot be credited.

The conclusion to which these facts points is clear. Jacob Clingman, the cooperative witness whose testimony was frequently sustained by other evidence, was undoubtedly the one who charged Simeon Reynolds with collusion and concealed his name under a stipulation of utmost confidence in his letter to Oliver Wolcott. This essential information, elicited by Wolcott's stern insistence on tracing corruption within the department, was the price Clingman had to pay for getting himself and his accomplice out of the toils of the law. But the unidentified lists, as his letter to Wolcott revealed, gave him and his partner access to the names of such public creditors as Ephraim Goodenough, who was fortunate enough to be paid for recovering his claim, and of others whose poverty and ignorance gave them little protection against "those Vultures who prey upon the unfortunate."[127] The lists were also perhaps such as led to the mysterious trail of "Spencer" or "Edwards." This was a leakage of Treasury secrets that repeated but was quite different from the one that had prompted Bland's resolutions in 1790.

The explanation that Hamilton offered to the Congressmen who confronted him concealed this central fact. It screened a clerk behind the charge against Duer, a current act of malfeasance in the Treasury behind one of the past. Both concealments did violence to Hamilton's professed zeal to investigate official misconduct and to meet fair inquiry with openness and candor. They also meant that the testimony accepted as proof of the culpability of Simeon Reynolds and justification for his dismissal came from a source described by Hamilton as the "two . . . most profligate men in the world," who for this information were freed of prosecution for crimes of which they were admittedly guilty.[128] The concealment of the facts about misconduct then current in the

[126] Simeon Reynolds may have been the son of Gamaliel Reynolds of Norwich, Connecticut. Marion H. Reynolds, *The history and descendants of John and Sarah . . . Reynolds of Saybrook, Lyme and Norwich* (New York, 1928), p. 31, states that this Simeon Reynolds was born in Norwich on 23 June 1763 and was "known to have settled in Philadelphia." The Simeon Reynolds whom Wolcott dismissed first appeared on the Treasury rolls as a clerk in the Register's Office, drawing his quarterly salary of $125 on 31 Mch. 1791 (Account of Joseph Nourse for the Register's Office, 1 Jan.-31 Mch. 1791, No. 1126, DNA: RG 217, M235/2). His final salary payment terminated on 17 Dec. 1792 (same, M235/9, No. 3420).

[127] Robert Denny, Annapolis, to John Wright, 21 Mch. 1794, protesting—with success—in behalf of the heirs of one William Wedge who had been too trusting in granting powers of attorney to a person with no more claim against Wedge than Denny had "against the Dey of Algiers" (Account of William Wedge, 30 June 1794, No. 5430, DNA: RG 217, M235/17).

[128] Alexander Hamilton to John Fenno, 6 July 1797 (*Gazette of the United States*, 8 July 1797).

Treasury suggests that, on being released from prison, James Reynolds had very persuasive reasons for disappearing from the scene and—perhaps as a condition for being permitted to do so—for cooperating with the Secretary of the Treasury. It is certain that he vanished and almost equally so that he was induced to see the advantage in being cooperative.

VIII

It is unnecessary to analyze all of the confused, contradictory, and misleading evidence adduced after the episode became public knowledge. But it is necessary to pursue it to its unedifying conclusion and to face the question of the reliability of the documents offered by the Secretary of the Treasury in defense of his public virtue. This is unavoidable because Hamilton himself was the first to bring on a public discussion of their genuineness and because, in another equally diversionary act, he sought verification in a place scarcely appropriate for weighing documentary evidence—the duelling ground.

While the suspicions that produced the confrontation had not been resolved and while Jacob Clingman, John Beckley, and others continued to concern themselves, the three Congressmen remained quiet about the episode.[129] No apparent use was made of the secret in 1793 when Giles' resolutions sought to lift the veil on some of the mysteries of the Hamiltonian system of public finance. It did not emerge when direct charges were brought by Andrew G. Fraunces, who knew much about what was going on within the Treasury and who, like other clerks, used his position for private advantage.[130] But as partisan

[129] Beckley, in consultation and correspondence with Jacob Clingman, gained information from the latter that he reported first in conversation with TJ and then later in writing, hoping that this would prompt further investigation (TJ's memorandum of conversation with Beckley, 12 June 1793; Clingman to Beckley, 22 June 1793, enclosed in Beckley to [Monroe?], 27 June 1793, both the last and its enclosure being in the hand of Bernard Webb and made available to the Editors through courtesy of the owner, Pierce W. Gaines, Fairfield, Connecticut).

[130] Andrew G. Fraunces was first employed as a clerk of the Board of Treasury in 1785. He became principal clerk soon thereafter and was retained in the Office of the Secretary of the Treasury until dismissed early in 1793, having been until that time regarded first by Duer and then by Hamilton, his immediate superiors, as a reliable subordinate. A measure of the confidence reposed in him is to be found in the assignments given him in addition to regular duties. For example, he was charged with the task of purchasing silks, providing sailors, and fitting out the elaborate barge in which the Board of Treasury, Secretary for Foreign Affairs, and Secretary at War met the President-elect at Elizabeth in 1789; he was sent on a special mission to Virginia in 1788; and an Indian charge of the Continental Congress, George Morgan White Eyes, was put under his care (Account of Fraunces, No. 1306, 24 May 1791, DNA: RG 217, M235/2; same, Pre-Federal Accounting Records, M7/1 and 2, under 10 July 1788 and 4 Feb. 1789). According to the report given to TJ by Beckley, Hamilton dismissed the clerk "to save appearances, but with an assurance of all future service" and accordingly established him in New York (TJ's memorandum of 12 June 1793). The dispute between Fraunces and Hamilton over the claim of Baron de Glaubeck and Fraunces' speculation in certificates took place shortly thereafter and Hamilton denounced his former clerk as "a despicable calumniator" (Hamilton to Fraunces, 1 Oct. 1793, Syrett, *Hamilton*, xv, 354).

But by 1797, while castigating TJ in his *Observations* for having any relations with such a "worthless man," Hamilton himself procured from Fraunces two

animosities became more and more bitter in this divisive decade, it was virtually certain that the hidden documents would emerge. A threat to disclose them was made in 1795 and also, less openly, in the electoral campaign of 1796. James Thomson Callender charged that in that year Noah Webster's *Minerva* had hinted that Hamilton might be an eligible candidate for the presidency. He said that a person in Philadelphia—probably meaning John Beckley, who at the time was cooperating with Callender and also much concerned about the critical New York election—wrote his correspondent in New York warning that if a single paragraph on the subject appeared in the paper, the documents on the Reynolds affair would "instantly . . . be laid before the world." According to Callender, the *Minerva* became silent.[131] Both Hamilton and Webster, each speaking for himself, immediately branded the allegation as "totally *false.*"[132]

Whether or not such a threat had been made in 1796, the documents Monroe and his colleagues had once planned to take to the President were displayed before the nation in June 1797. Simultaneously with the arrival of Monroe in Philadelphia after his recall as minister to France, Callender announced the publication of No. V of his *History of the United States for 1796* containing "some *singular* and *authentic* papers relative to Mr. Alexander Hamilton." Federalist rumors at once attributed authorship of the pamphlet to Beckley. Callender categorically denied that he had written a single sentence of it, but Beckley was undoubtedly the one who made the documents available to him.[133]

---

letters written by TJ in response to his appeals for aid and published them to discredit their author (TJ to Fraunces, 27 and 28 June 1797; Hamilton, *Observations*, Appendixes Nos. XLIV, XLV). Fraunces, in extreme want at this time, obtained "a present relief" from Hamilton, who thus obtained TJ's letters (John Barnes to TJ, 3 Oct. 1797). TJ gave Fraunces a polite response but declined to give either money or a certificate of character, pointedly suggesting that his previous length of service was the best presumption in his favor. While Fraunces wrote TJ on 26, 27, and 28 June 1797, 16 Jan., 22 Feb., and 10 Apr. 1798, he replied only with the two letters published by Hamilton and one other of 6 Nov. 1797 (SJL; none of Fraunces' letters and only the texts of TJ's replies in Hamilton's *Observations* have been found). See note 203.

131 On 23 Oct. 1795 the *Aurora*, reminding Wolcott "of a certain enquiry of a very suspicious aspect, respecting real mal-conduct on the part of his friend, patron and predecessor in office," asked whether the publication of that transaction "would . . . redound to the honour or reputation of the parties" (quoted by Philip M. Marsh, "John Beckley," PMHB, LXXII [Jan. 1948], 62). The anecdote about the 1796 threat appeared in an advertisement in *Gazette of the United States*, 27 June 1797, quoted from Callender, *History*, p. 208. Beckley's intense interest in the New York election is reflected in his letter to Vredenburgh, 26 June 1796 (Vredenburgh Papers, Skaneateles).

132 Webster's sworn affidavit, 12 July 1797 (Hamilton, *Observations*, Appendix No. XLIII; Hamilton to Fenno, 6 July 1797, denounced the anecdote as "wholly false," *Gazette of the United States*, 8 July 1797). Webster asked Timothy Pickering to send for the pamphlet, saying that one copy would suffice for himself and Hamilton "as by the advertisement we see it contains downright *lies*" (Webster to Pickering, 2 July 1797, MHi: Pickering Papers). Wolcott had already sent a copy to Hamilton (Wolcott to Hamilton, 3 July 1797, DLC: McLane-Hamilton Papers).

133 Theodore Sedgwick to Rufus King, 24 June 1797 (*King*, ed. King, II, 193); Wolcott to Hamilton, 3 July 1797 (DLC: McLane-Hamilton Papers); Philip Marsh, "Hamilton and Monroe," MVHR, XXXIV (Dec. 1947), p. 467, quoting Monroe to Burr, 1 Dec. 1797; Callender, *History*, preface.

This he did in the form of a derivative clerk's copy that in one important respect departed from the originals that Monroe had deposited with a "respectable character in Virginia."[134] The person alluded to may have been Thomas Jefferson. Not even the Federalists of the time suggested that he had released the documents or had prompted their publication, but he has since been suspected of having inspired or approved the disclosure.[135] There is no evidence to substantiate this implausible suspicion. "Mr. Jefferson had received a copy of these documents," Callender declared later. "He never shewed them, nor ever spoke of them, to any person. In summer, 1797, when the vice-president heard of the intended publication, he advised that the papers should be suppressed . . . but his interposition came too late. Mr. Hamilton knew that Mr. Jefferson was master of his secret, but had kept it."[136] Such an attitude was entirely characteristic of Jefferson. But Callender belonged to an earthier school of politics.

Even he broached the subject with some diffidence. The style of his *History*, as he explicitly stated, was a direct response to the vituperative journalism of the Federalists, especially that of William Cobbett. Denying that Webster's Connecticut was the true center of republicanism, Callender claimed that honor for Jefferson's state: "The Virginians encourage no newsprinter to balance accounts in black ball with Webster; or to proclaim the people of New England bankrupts, swindlers, conspirators, and traitors."[137] His replies in the first four numbers of his *History* to the writings of *Camillus*, *Phocion*, and *Curtius* concerned such general issues as Hamiltonian finance, Jay's Treaty, and relations with France and England, being relatively free of personal attacks. But with the fifth number Callender took the offensive, his declared motive being to reply in kind to the calumnies heaped upon Monroe.[138] He pointed out that Hamilton's affair with Mrs.

[134] Callender emphasized by repetition that the documents he published were "nothing more nor less than exact copies, from attested originals, of which Mr. Hamilton . . . has been, at his own desire, supplied with an accurate transcript" (Callender, *History*, p. 205-6). But see note 62 above for the significant discrepancy between the text retained by Monroe and that used by Callender.

[135] Writing a year before Marsh proved that Beckley and not Monroe had released the documents, Cresson, *Monroe*, p. 162, stated: "It is not too difficult to link the names of Beckley, Jefferson, and Callender into a chain of evidence that gives us a simple solution of the case." The only evidence presented was a citation of James Schouler, *History of the United States*, I, 373. Schouler had in fact done no more than name "Jefferson, Madison, and Giles, and possibly Edmund Randolph or Beckley" as among the Virginia Republicans who might have given the documents to Callender (same, I, 375, note). Jonathan Daniels, *Ordeal of Ambition* (New York, 1970), p. 85-93, 163-8, goes even further than Cresson in implicating TJ.

[136] Callender, *Sketches*, p. 101-2.

[137] Callender, *History*, p. 54.

[138] Callender noted that Robert Goodloe Harper had publicly accused Monroe of being "guilty of corruption by foreign influence." This, he charged, was only one of hundreds of calumnies showing that the "friends of *order* . . . are resolved to set no limits to their rage and their vengeance. Of course, they cannot expect to meet with that tenderness which they refuse to grant. Attacks on Mr. Munroe have been frequently repeated from the stock-holding presses. They are cowardly, because he is absent. They are unjust, because his conduct will bear the strictest enquiry. They are ungrateful, because he displayed . . . the greatest lenity to Mr. Alexander Hamilton, the prime mover of the federal party. . . . The unfounded

Reynolds had been known at the time to many members of Congress. "If any republican character had been the hero of the story," Callender observed, "it would have been echoed from one end of the continent to the other. Yet that party . . . observed profound silence."[139] This, as prior and subsequent events proved, was a valid observation. Yet the man who made it was the one who broke the silence. A few years later, disappointed in obtaining further patronage from Jefferson, he joined his former enemies in employing the same kind of political scurrility against him.

The fifth number of Callender's *History* contained his prefatory comments and the four documents that Monroe, Muhlenberg, and Venable had prepared to transmit to the President.[140] Hamilton admitted that the documents appeared to be authentic and promised to "place the subject more precisely before the public." He attributed the inquiry of 1792 to political motives by saying that two of the most profligate of men had sought escape from prison "by *the favour of party spirit*." He identified two of the three inquiring Congressmen as his "*known political opponents*," and then added: "A full explanation took place between them and myself . . . in which by *written documents* I convinced them of the falshood of the accusation. They declared themselves perfectly satisfied with the explanation and expressed their regret at the necessity which had been occasioned to me of making it."[141]

Simultaneously Hamilton sent identical but separate letters to the three Congressmen, asking each to attest his version of the interview:[142]

I shall rely upon your delicacy that the manner of doing it, will be such as one Gentleman has a right to expect from another—especially as you must be sensible that the present appearance of the papers is contrary to the course which was understood between us to be proper and includes a dishonourable infidelity somewhere.

He enclosed his memorandum attributing to them perfect satisfaction with his explanation, claiming that it was written down the morning after the interview. On this ground, impossible to maintain in face of

---

reproaches heaped on Mr. Munroe, form the immediate motive to the publication of these papers" (Callender, *History*, p. 204-5).

[139] Callender, *Sketches*, p. 101.

[140] No. v was published on 26 June 1797 and included only documents Nos. 1-4 as described in note 62 above, No. 5 being included in No. vi which appeared on 4 July 1797. All of the numbers were collected and published later that month under the title, *The History of the United States for 1796, including a variety of interesting particulars relative to the federal government previous to that period* (Philadelphia: Snowden & M'Corkle, preface dated 19 July 1797); Evans No. 31906.

[141] Hamilton to Fenno, 6 July 1797 (*Gazette of the United States*, 8 July 1797).

[142] Hamilton to Monroe, 5 July 1797 (Dft, endorsed by Hamilton: "xxv"; DLC: McLane-Hamilton Papers; RC in clerk's hand, signed by Hamilton; addressed: "James Monroe Esqr."; endorsed by Monroe, with note on cover in his hand showing that Wolcott delivered it: "Mr. Wolcott called on Mr. Munroe," PBL). For text of the enclosed memorandum, see above at note 98 (Dft of memorandum, DLC: McLane-Hamilton Papers; Hamilton, *Observations*, Appendix No. xxv).

Monroe's account that was indisputably recorded at the time, he took his stand. Hamilton sought to establish this version by offering them the choice of acknowledging its veracity or of facing him on the duelling ground. Even if this obviously incorrect and belated version were not sustained, the charge of dishonorable infidelity afforded still another ground for challenge.

When Hamilton wrote this letter he had only seen part of the document containing Clingman's testimony on the day of the confrontation in 1792. But when he received the sixth number of Callender's *History* shortly thereafter, his first impulse was to ask Monroe whether that part of "the paper numbered V dated Philadelphia the 15 of December 1792 published partly in the fifth and partly in the sixth number of 'The History of the United States for 1796' and having the signatures of *James Monroe, Abraham Venable* and *F. A. Mughlenberg*" was the copy of a genuine original. As he may have suspected, however, this could have been answered by a simple affirmation. He withheld the inquiry. Meantime, Monroe received his copy of Hamilton's letter just as he was on the point of leaving for New York, perhaps going by the same stage that carried a letter from Wolcott showing what a drastic change the sixth number of the *History* had wrought in him. "I am astonished," he wrote, "at the villany of Munroe —a more base, false, and malignant suggestion than is contained in his note of Jany 2d 1793 was never uttered."[143] With Hamilton already anxious to fix the "dishonourable infidelity" upon Monroe, this letter from one who had previously advised against a published response—added no doubt to the comments of other irate Federalists

---

[143] Hamilton to Monroe, 8 July 1797 (Dft, DLC: McLane-Hamilton Papers). Hamilton said that he had written such a letter "to the gentlemen" but had mislaid the copy (Hamilton, *Observations,* p. 116). Wolcott wrote Hamilton twice on the 7th, the first enclosing No. VI of Callender's *History* and the second acknowledging Hamilton's with the enclosures for Monroe, Muhlenberg, and Venable. In the second Wolcott added: "By what I last sent you, you will see the perfidy of at least Monroe" (Wolcott to Hamilton, 7 July 1797, same).

In his *Observations,* p. 116, Hamilton said he had received replies to his letter of the 5th from Muhlenberg and Venable but, having "no answer from Mr. Monroe," he called on him in New York. This assertion, conveying an impression of evasiveness on Monroe's part that Hamilton tried to deepen in the ensuing correspondence and in his pamphlet, was made within a month of the event when he had at hand all of the documents needed to verify it. Under these circumstances, the statement can only be regarded as a deliberate misrepresentation with the intent of discrediting Monroe. For the fact is that it was impossible for Hamilton to have received replies from Muhlenberg and Venable before he sought the meeting with Monroe. His request was made, and granted, on the 10th of July, the day Monroe arrived in New York (Monroe to Hamilton, 10 July 1797, DLC: McLane-Hamilton Papers). Muhlenberg wrote on the 10th, Venable on the 9th and 10th. Even if Venable's letter of the 9th (a Sunday) went off on the eight o'clock post next morning, it could not have reached New York until the afternoon of the 11th. Hamilton's explosive meeting with Monroe took place at ten that morning. Contrary to the impression he sought to create, therefore, Hamilton got his first response in person from Monroe, not in the letters from Muhlenberg and Venable. Since Hamilton did not print Monroe's response of the 10th and was careful to avoid giving the date of their meeting, only an informed reader of his *Observations* could have detected the misrepresentation. The unwarranted innuendo that Monroe was slow or evasive in responding has continued to be accepted as truth (see, for example, Miller, *Hamilton,* p. 460; Ammon, *Monroe,* p. 158-9).

—must have had a decisive influence. One of such volatile temper as Hamilton, always ready to defend his honor, scarcely needed such promptings.

Immediately on arriving in New York, Monroe received a letter from Hamilton asking for an interview. He granted the request, adding curtly that Hamilton might bring with him whomever he chose. The meeting took place at ten in the morning of the 11th at Monroe's lodgings in Wall Street. John Barker Church accompanied Hamilton and David Gelston, a Republican member of Congress was present as the friend of Monroe. Gelston left a dramatic account of the meeting which described Hamilton as "very much agitated" on entering the room. Hamilton went into some detail about the history of the Reynolds affair, Monroe interrupted him by saying that this was unnecessary, and "some warmth appeared in both Gentlemen." After some explanations on both sides, Monroe pointed out that his initial involvement in the affair was "merely accidental." He said that he knew nothing of Callender's publication until he arrived in Philadelphia and that he was sorry the documents had been made public. He promised a joint reply as soon as he returned to Philadelphia. It was in an atmosphere already tense that Monroe declared he had sealed up his copy of the papers and had had no intention of publishing them. He stated his belief that his copies of the documents were "yet . . . sealed with his friend in Virginia." Hamilton declared this to be a "totally false" representation. Monroe met the insult with indignation: "Do you say I represent falsely you are a scoundrel." Hamilton retorted: "I will meet you like a gentleman." Monroe is reported to have replied with grim quietness: "I am ready. Get your pistols." But both Church and Gelston interceded and brought about some degree of calm. All agreed that any intemperate expression should be forgotten and that those present would proceed to Philadelphia, resuming the discussion there.[144]

Meanwhile, Muhlenberg and Venable had written separate replies. Venable was cautious, recalling that the three men had expressed satisfaction with Hamilton's explanation "in general terms." But he emphatically rejected the idea that he had had any part in the release of Reynolds and Clingman or had been moved "by favour of party spirit."[145] He then departed for Virginia. Muhlenberg replied on the 10th. He regretted Callender's publication, denied that he had had

---

[144] Monroe to Hamilton, 10 July 1797 (same); "Minutes of an Interview between Col. Monroe and Col. Hamilton," 11 July 1797 (PHi: Gratz Collection).

[145] Venable to Hamilton, 9 July 1797 (RC, endorsed by Hamilton: "xxx"; DLC: McLane-Hamilton Papers; Hamilton, *Observations*, Appendix No. xxx). The next day Venable wrote another letter which Hamilton did not publish: "The transaction took place at Mr. Monroes, where I left the papers, since which I have not seen them. The paper alluded to as well as I can recollect was in the nature of a memorandum for our own use, to refresh our memories in case we should ever be called upon, and not intended for any other use. . . . The original I presume is in the possession of Mr. Monroe, as I left them in his house Mr. Mughlenberg being present. I do not know any means by which these papers could have got out, unless by the person who copied them, who had been present during the whole investigation, both before and after my being called on" (Venable to Hamilton, 10 Oct. 1797, DLC: McLane-Hamilton Papers).

any agency in it, and expressed regret at the trouble and uneasiness given Hamilton, assuring him that he had been "perfectly satisfied with the explanation" given. Thus far his acquiescence in Hamilton's version was full and exact. But he ignored Hamilton's assertion that there was nothing in the transaction to affect his official character or lessen public confidence in his integrity. He also reminded Hamilton of his own admission of their fair conduct and his acknowledgment that there had been reasonable grounds for their suspicions.[146]

Monroe arrived back in Philadelphia at noon on the 16th. He informed Hamilton of his arrival and next morning met with Muhlenberg to prepare their joint response. With Muhlenberg already committed, the result was an obviously uncomfortable compromise for him, for Monroe brought their reply closer to actuality. They informed Hamilton that they would give such information as they could, "the original papers having been deposited in the hands of a respectable character in Virginia soon after the transaction took place, and where they now are." This very pointed repetition of the remark that Hamilton had previously declared totally false was followed by the statement that they had had "no agency in or knowledge of the publication of these papers till they appeared." Then came the impossible task of reconciling Muhlenberg's acceptance of Hamilton's version with the statement Monroe had recorded in 1793: "We left him under an impression our Suspicions were removed." Denying the obvious in an effort to conciliate, they said that the same impression left with him was the one they had—that his explanation had removed their suspicions of his involvement in speculation with Reynolds. Had this not been so, they argued, they would not have given him a false impression, neither would they have abandoned the plan to go to the President. This ignored the embarrassing dilemma in which Hamilton's explanation had placed them, but they concluded by expressing resentment at the unjust intimation that they had helped procure the release of Reynolds and Clingman and that in making the inquiry they had been motivated by party spirit. They reminded Hamilton of his own unequivocal acknowledgment of the propriety and candor of their conduct.[147] Far from expressing themselves "perfectly satisfied" as Muhlenberg had done, they had not even given a convincing explanation of the passage that Hamilton found exceptionable.

Yet, replying the same day, Hamilton said that he was pleased both with their explanation of "the ambiguous phrase" and with their confirmation of the fact that his own "explanation had been satisfactory." This was not at all what their tortured construction conveyed, but it was now Hamilton's turn to reconcile his own contradictory assertions. His effort was as unconvincing as theirs. A careful reading of his public statement, he suggested, would show that he at-

[146] Muhlenberg to Hamilton, 10 July 1797 (endorsed by Hamilton: "xxix," same; Hamilton, *Observations*, Appendix No. xxix).

[147] Monroe to Hamilton, 16 [i.e., 17] July 1797 (endorsed by Hamilton: "xxxii," DLC: McLane-Hamilton Papers); Monroe and Muhlenberg to Hamilton, 17 July 1797 (in Monroe's hand, signed by both, and endorsed by Hamilton: "xxxiii," same; Hamilton, *Observations*, Nos. xxxii and xxxiii).

tributed only to Reynolds and Clingman the hope of seeking release through "favour of party spirit" and that he neither said nor implied that their inquiry was so motivated. Hence there could be nothing inconsistent with his admission of their fair and liberal conduct. Furthermore, he said that the admission had been in response to a question and only after they had given "full and unqualified expressions" of their "entire satisfaction with the explanation." This assurance, he claimed, had been given by all three, differing in terms but agreeing in substance.[148] But both the terms and the unqualified nature of the assurances were framed by Hamilton and rested on his word alone. Only Muhlenberg had explicitly, but not completely, supported Hamilton's version. Even he retreated from so unqualified an expression when he signed the letter with Monroe. Yet all, including Monroe, had declared unequivocally that their suspicions had been removed. This obviously was not the unvarnished truth, but it showed how far they were prepared to conciliate.

At this point, mutual concessions having been made, the unsavory episode might well have been brought to an end. Even Hamilton, impetuous as he was, hesitated for a brief moment. He went so far as to draft a letter for publication in the *Gazette of the United States* which would have kept the discussion from sinking to a lower level. He asserted that it had been a general maxim with him not to dignify slander by responding to it and, that, except for the names of Muhlenberg and others attached to the documents, he would have relied in this instance "on those internal characters of falsehood in the story, which could escape no discerning eye." But since he had obtained "from the Gentlemen concerned a full testimony, that they were convinced . . . of the falsehood" uttered against him "and a disavowal of the implication contained in the ambiguous phrase of their Memorandum," he had concluded to dispense with the detailed account he had promised. Instead, he would publish only his letter to them, their response, and some other unspecified documents. "But in addition to this," he wrote, "I have resolved to place in the hands of my friend   a particular narrative of the affair and the original papers which support it, with permission to communicate them to respectable men of whatever political party on whose delicacy reliance may be placed."[149] This, too, attributed expressions to Monroe and his colleagues that their letter did not warrant. But if the decision had been left with Monroe, as his subsequent actions indicate, he might well have regarded this as an acceptable means of disposing of the business. Unfortunately, Hamilton did not accept this generous compromise. Putting aside his draft, he went headlong to meet the accusation that rankled more acutely than any other. The decision was unfortunate, for the more he strove the more he exposed the weakness of his defense.

---

[148] Hamilton to Monroe and Muhlenberg, 17 July 1797 (Dft, undated, endorsed by Hamilton: "xxxiv," DLC: McLane-Hamilton Papers; RC in PBL, endorsed by Monroe; Hamilton, *Observations*, Appendix No. xxxiv).

[149] Hamilton to Fenno, [17 July 1797] (Dft, DLC: McLane-Hamilton Papers; undated, but obviously written on the 17th; see note 151 below).

Five years earlier, outraged by Hamilton's vilification and distortion of Jefferson's letters as American minister to France, Monroe had answered *Catullus* with facts and unassailable dignity.[150] Now, he himself was the chief target of Federalist calumnies because he had interposed himself as an obstacle to the destruction of the French alliance, an objective Hamilton had pursued ever since he came into office in 1789. Humiliated by his recall, on the verge of illness, and wholly preoccupied in preparing a defense of his own public character, Monroe regarded the Reynolds affair as an intrusion upon far more important concerns. He believed—as did many Federalists—that Hamilton had acted very indiscreetly in drawing public attention to it, thus magnifying its importance. Hamilton himself argued that he was forced to make an explanation, a position difficult to sustain in the face of the conciliatory attitude of Monroe and Muhlenberg. The hard choice he offered had been met, though certainly not in the terms he professed to read into the response. He had expressed himself as satisfied, but this was so far from being the case that, in the very act of transmitting the response, he singled out Monroe for personal attack. Monroe was convinced that Hamilton's friends had pressed him to do this, being so anxious to be rid of himself that they were willing to hazard him. From the moment Hamilton turned upon him, Monroe considered himself on the defensive with Hamilton as the aggressor. This onus in an affair of honor Hamilton studiously avoided. But the real significance of the aggression lay in the point that Hamilton sought to establish. All of the evidence indicates that his primary object was not so much to destroy a political enemy, gratifying as that would have been, as to force him to discredit Mrs. Reynolds' charge that the documents had been fabricated.

This objective is apparent in the wholly new grounds for dissatisfaction that Hamilton now chose. Since Monroe was clearly identified as the one who had recorded Clingman's final testimony, Hamilton, inferring from this mere act that Monroe had "meant to give credit and sanction to the suggestion [by Mrs. Reynolds] that the defence . . . was an imposition," demanded an explanation.[151] Even in the face of this far-fetched inference Monroe sought to placate. He replied that, surprised as he was by Clingman's information, he neither meant to give nor imply any opinion of his own as to its contents. "I simply entered the communication as I received it," he concluded, "reserving to myself the liberty to form an opinion upon it at such future time as I found convenient, paying due regard to all the circumstances connected with it." This was as unequivocal an assurance as the one Hamilton had accepted in the joint letter of Muhlenberg and Monroe, but he

[150] The most judicious account of Hamilton's attacks on TJ in 1792 and Monroe's response is that of Malone, *Jefferson*, II, 457-77; see also, Philip M. Marsh, *Monroe's defense of Jefferson and Freneau against Hamilton* (Oxford, Ohio, 1948).

[151] Hamilton to Monroe, [17 July 1797] (Hamilton, *Observations*, Appendix No. XXXV, not dated, but obviously written on the 17th, thus proving that Hamilton's hesitation about continuing the dispute was only momentary; see note 149 above).

found it unsatisfactory. Indeed, drawing still another inference, he thought the recording of Clingman's testimony meant that the suspicions his explanation had removed had been revived. "This," Hamilton declared, making his purpose explicit, "would include the very derogatory suspicion, that I had concerted with Reynolds not only the fabrication of all the letters and documents under his hand, but also the forgery of the letters produced as those of Mrs. Reynolds—since these last unequivocally contradict the pretence communicated by Clingman."[152]

This presented an intolerable choice. Monroe could not admit the validity of Hamilton's inference without being challenged or called upon for proofs. He could not deny it without branding as false Mrs. Reynolds' charge that the letters had been fabricated. In the face of this dilemma he stood on the ground he had already chosen, condensing his reply to a single sentence: "I can only observe that in entering the note which bears my single signature, I did not convey or mean to convey any opinion of my own, as to the faith which was due to it, but left it to stand on its own merits, reserving to myself the right to judge of it, as upon any fact afterwards communicated according to its import and authenticity."[153]

This drew from Hamilton the sharp retort that he had proposed a simple and direct question to which he sought a simple and direct answer, but instead had received one he understood to be negative, "conceived in such circuitous terms as may leave an obscurity upon the point which ought not to have remained." He then declared that Monroe's having *any* communication with Clingman after his own explanation and his "receiving . . . and recording information depending on the mere veracity of a man undeniably guilty of subornation of perjury" were actions highly indelicate and improper. "To have given or intended to give the least sanction or credit, after all that was known to you, to the mere assertion of . . . Clingman, Reynolds, or his wife," Hamilton concluded, "would have betrayed a disposition toward me which, if it appeared to exist, would merit epithets the severest that I could apply."[154] Monroe, greatly angered, retorted that

152 Monroe to Hamilton, 17 July 1797 (same, No. XXXVI; RC, DLC: McLane-Hamilton Papers, addressed: "Alexander Hamilton Esqr. . . . at Mrs. Williams's corner of Spruce and 3rd. Street"; endorsed by Hamilton: "XXXVI"); Hamilton to Monroe, 18 July 1797 (Dft, DLC: McLane-Hamilton Papers, endorsed by Hamilton: "XXXVII" and containing the following deletion: ". . . the very derogatory suspicion < *entertained on the mere assertion of a man guilty of an infamous offence and one of the combination to slander me* >"; RC, NjMoW; Hamilton, *Observations*, Appendix No. XXXVII).
On the day that Hamilton wrote this response, Fenno's paper carried another attack upon Monroe, accusing him as American minister of giving countenance to Thomas Paine, "a vile defamer of the most exalted characters in the nation" (*Gazette of the United States*, 18 July 1797).
153 Monroe to Hamilton, 18 July 1797 (RC, DLC: McLane-Hamilton Papers; addressed to Hamilton "at Mrs. Williams's"; Hamilton, *Observations*, Appendix No. XXXVIII).
154 Hamilton to Monroe, 20 July 1797 (Dft, DLC: McLane-Hamilton Papers, containing numerous alterations; endorsed by Hamilton: "XXXIX"; Hamilton, *Observations*, Appendix No. XXXIX). Hamilton's deletions reveal that the final sentence quoted was a softened expression. As first drafted, it read: ". . . would have betrayed a disposition towards me malignant, dishonorable and even base."

Hamilton's letter itself gave "an indelicate and improper coloring" to the matter. Seeking to restore the discussion to its proper level, he said that their inquiry was begun as a public duty and, as Hamilton had often admitted, was conducted "with *delicacy* and *propriety*," the words being underscored lest the allusion be lost. Monroe reminded Hamilton that he himself had admitted all the facts on which their opinion was founded but had accounted for them "on another principle"; that they had not bound themselves not to receive additional information or even from proceeding further; that they deemed it highly proper to hear what Clingman had to say because Hamilton had acknowledged all of his prior testimony to be true and because, as an interested party, he had a right to be heard; and that he had not been sought out or even informed of Hamilton's explanation by them, but by his own testimony had been given that information by Oliver Wolcott.

Monroe reiterated his earlier statements that the recording of Clingman's testimony was not intended to convey any opinion of his own, as proved by his subsequent refusal to act on it. If the imputations against Hamilton for speculations should be proved by him to be ill-founded, he would be content. He had made no accusation since the interview and offered no opinion on it, but reserved the right to form one after reading Hamilton's defense and was resolved "not to bar the door to free inquiry as to the merits of the case in either view." This came close to being a tacit admission that suspicions had not been allayed, but Monroe, while unyielding, obviously wished to satisfy Hamilton on rational grounds. He concluded with an expression of this desire and also a fair warning:[155]

> This contains a just state of this affair so far as I remember it, which I presume will be satisfactory to you, and to which I shall only add that as on the one hand I shall always be ready to do justice to the claims of any one upon me, so I shall always be equally prepared to vindicate my conduct and character against the attacks of any one who may assail them.

Hamilton, with justice, denied that he had acknowledged the truth of all of Clingman's information, but immediately drew from Monroe's too-inclusive statement the inference that he had intended to support its veracity. Similarly, forgetting that he had already promised to place the matter before the public, Hamilton conceived that there was a design under way to force him to make a formal defense. He held Monroe responsible since he had given countenance to Clingman's testimony and had failed to respect Hamilton's confidence "as a man of honor and sensibility" would have done. Worse, by professing that his opinion would be determined on the basis of Hamilton's defense, he allowed the inference that his suspicions were still alive. This was not precisely what Monroe had said, but the inference was well founded and Hamilton promptly drew another from it—that "nothing . . . but the wretched tale of Clingman" had shaken his original conviction. He concluded, therefore, that Monroe attached a weight to it that

[155] Monroe to Hamilton, 21 July 1797 (RC, DLC: McLane-Hamilton Papers; Tr in Monroe's hand, PBL; Hamilton, *Observations*, Appendix No. XL).

could not be justified under fair principles and that he had been and was then "actuated by motives . . . malignant and dishonourable" toward himself.[156]

This, the most provocative statement in the entire correspondence, was obviously intended to provoke a challenge. Some of Monroe's friends thought he should have issued one and Monroe himself, after he had prepared his public vindication, appeared to doubt whether under other circumstances he could have avoided doing so.[157] But at this moment his great concern was to give an account of his conduct as minister. He waited three days to reply and then wrote: "If it is your object to render this affair a personal one between us, you might have been more explicit, since you well know if that is your disposition, what my determination is, and to which I shall firmly adhere. But if it is to illustrate truth and place the question on its true merits, as I have always been disposed to do, it appears illy calculated to promote that end."[158] Hamilton professed not to understand what Monroe's determination was, though it had been clearly expressed in his letter of the 21st. As for himself, he had given his impressions of Monroe's wholly inadmissible recording of "Clingman's last miserable

[156] Hamilton to Monroe, 22 July 1797 (Dft, DLC: McLane-Hamilton Papers, with numerous alterations; Tr in a clerk's hand, same; Hamilton, *Observations*, Appendix No. xLVI). This letter was delivered the same day by Hamilton's friend, Major William Jackson, who explained that Hamilton had gone to New York because his wife was "in the last stage of pregnancy." He then entered into conversation with Monroe, the result of which clearly manifested Monroe's wish to conciliate. Jackson reported his conclusions to Hamilton: (1) that Monroe thought the correspondence should be withdrawn and destroyed, but did not wish to be considered as making the proposal; (2) that if an inquiry should be addressed to himself, Muhlenberg, and Venable asking whether they meant by recording Clingman's testimony to express an opinion or give any sanction to it, he had no doubt they would say that they had not; (3) that Monroe had never intended to become Hamilton's accuser and was not then so disposed; and (4) that, while he believed his own letters had been respectful, Hamilton's had been "much otherwise." Jackson then urged accommodation: "indeed, my dear Hamilton, unless there are very strong reasons to press you on the subject of publishing, I wish it could be postponed until we meet. . . . I am really of opinion that better effects may result from a declaration on the part of Muhlenberg, Monroe and Venable . . . than from entering into a detailed publication, which . . . would only furnish fresh *pabulum* for the virulent invective and abuse of faction to feed on." In any case, Jackson thought it best to suspend publication until Monroe returned from Virginia, particularly as he had Hamilton's "*gauntlet . . . now before him.*" He concluded: "Let me repeat that your friends and every impartial Man are convinced of your purity as a public Officer, and no one among them can suppose that you are called on to furnish the Presbyterian pulpits with subject matter of declamation, however irrelevant, against the best political interests of our country" (Jackson to Hamilton, 24 July 1797, DLC: McLane-Hamilton Papers; emphasis in original). Neither the accommodating disposition of Monroe nor the sensible counsel of Jackson had effect, perhaps because the latter immediately withdrew it after consulting James McHenry (Jackson to Hamilton, 25 July 1797, same). See notes 159 and 161.

[157] Monroe to Burr, 1 Dec. 1797 (NjMoW); Dawson to Burr, 24 Dec. 1797 (same).

[158] Monroe to Hamilton, 25 July 1797 (Dft, NjMoW; RC, DLC: McLane-Hamilton Papers; Hamilton: "xLVII," same; Hamilton, *Observations*, Appendix No. xLVII). On verso of his draft Monroe wrote, perhaps as a memorandum of his instructions to Burr: "If he chuses need not publish our correspondence and may make the most of our certificate. No occasion for a reply, as it may lead on and irritate."

contrivance," being prepared for any consequences to which this might lead. In the draft of this letter Hamilton first wrote and then deleted a passage revealing clearly enough the object he had in view in continuing to press forward against the prudent counsel of Wolcott, Jackson, and perhaps others. For Monroe to allow any weight whatever to Clingman's testimony, he wrote, "was to admit a probability in a greater or less degree that I had been guilty of an artifice as foolish and rash as it must have been base; since it must have included the fabrication as well of Mrs. Reynolds' as of her husband's letters, the detection of which was the easiest thing in the world." Hamilton crossed out the significant words, declared himself still unsatisfied with Monroe's explanation, and said that he would leave the disgusting subject, allowing the public to decide the issue on the basis of the public explanation to which he had been driven.[159] Monroe replied that his repeated explanations accorded with truth and propriety. "If these do not yield you satisfaction," he wrote, "I can give you no other unless called on in a way which for the illustration of truth, I wish to avoid, but which I am ever ready to meet."[160] This was immediately seized upon by Hamilton as an intended but inexplicit challenge. "On the supposition that it is so intended," he wrote, "I have authorized Major Jackson to communicate with you and to settle time and place."[161]

The Virginian was too familiar with the etiquette of the duelling code to be trapped even on grounds of punctillio. He refused to give Jackson a response but retaliated in kind in a letter to Hamilton. As defender rather than accuser, he saw nothing in the correspondence to induce him to issue a challenge. But if Hamilton's letter was meant as such, then he asked him to say so explicitly, in which case Colonel Burr would give his answer and "make such other arrangements as may

159 Hamilton to Monroe, 28 July 1797 (Dft, DLC: McLane-Hamilton Papers, with deleted passage quoted above; Tr, endorsed by Hamilton: "XLVIII," same; Hamilton, *Observations*, Appendix No. XLVIII). Jackson delivered this letter to Monroe and, reversing his former position, wrote Hamilton: "It appears to me that your publication must go on as Mr. M. did not seem willing to grant the certificate, and I confess I should be unwilling to recommend any compromise short of that" (Jackson to Hamilton, 31 July 1797, DLC: McLane-Hamilton Papers). Monroe had indeed been the first to suggest that a certificate might be given by himself and his colleagues (see note 156 above), but what Hamilton desired, of course, was a statement wholly discrediting Clingman's testimony, including the charge of fabrication.

160 Monroe to Hamilton, 31 July 1797 (RC, DLC: McLane-Hamilton Papers; Tr, endorsed by Hamilton: "XLIX," same; Hamilton, *Observations*, Appendix No. XLIX).

161 Hamilton to Monroe, 4 Aug. 1797 (same, No. L; Dft, DLC: McLane-Hamilton Papers). In delivering the letter Jackson said that Hamilton considered Monroe's response as "an overture to a personal meeting." Monroe asked if this was meant as a challenge, but Jackson declined to answer on grounds of propriety. Monroe then consulted John Dawson, a member of the Virginia delegation, and authorized him to read to Jackson his response to Hamilton ("Note of Mr. Dawson" giving account of his meeting with Jackson, 17 Aug. 1797, NjMoW). Jackson urged Hamilton not to make a direct challenge, since it remained with Monroe to accept or resent the accusation of "malignant and dishonourable" motives (Jackson to Hamilton, 5 and 7 Aug. 1797, same). This was also the advice of McHenry (McHenry to Hamilton [6? Aug. 1797], NjMoW).

be suitable in such an event."[162] Monroe sent the unsealed letter to Burr, together with his correspondence with Hamilton. Contrary to the view that the reply to Hamilton was an evasion and that its covering letter to Burr was an appeal, Monroe explicitly maintained in both the position he had held from the beginning. Considering Hamilton the aggressor, he told Burr that if a challenge had been intended it should of course be accepted and should not be avoided "by any the slightest sacrifice or condescention." Yet, as he had done with Hamilton and Jackson, he allowed Burr ample room for accommodation. He said that he would not give a certificate that did not accord with truth, but he did authorize Burr, in case the discussion took an amicable turn, to hint "that if he chuses, you think all the letters between him and me had better be suppress'd or not published in his publication: since they certainly weaken the ground of Muhlenberg's and my letter to him, which was written in a spirit of conciliation, as well as of truth." Should Hamilton do this, he could "make his inferences from *that*" as he pleased, since they intended to say no more on the subject unless Hamilton attacked them. After the personal issue was settled, but only then, Monroe was willing to say that he had meant only to let Clingman's testimony stand on the credibility of the man, not implying any opinion of his own. But Hamilton, he said, would never ask the question to which this answer could be given, since he was "always endeavoring to get more from me than in conscience, I could give." Monroe then gave Burr this final admonition: ". . . in case he manages his defense so as to make Muhlenberg, Venable and myself, become his accusers in our own defense, he loses the benefit of our certificate."[163] This meant that Monroe was prepared, if forced, to become the aggressor. But, knowing Hamilton and being a man of prudence as well as honor, he confided this to Burr alone.

Burr proved to be an unreliable intermediary. He not only failed to reach an accommodation, but urged Monroe to attest a statement he had thus far refused to make. "If you and Muhlenburgh really believe, as I do, and think you must, that H. is innocent of the charge of any concern in Speculation with Reynolds," he wrote, "it is my opinion that it will be an act of magnanimity and justice to say so in a joint certificate. You expressed to me the same idea when we were here. This is, and should be treated as a distinct thing from any personal impropriety of conduct to you." He enclosed a draft of the proposed joint certificate, urging that, if approved, the signed copy be sent to him by return mail. There was nothing in the correspondence or in Monroe's explicit directions to Burr that could have suggested his agreement with such a proposal. On the contrary, Monroe had told Hamilton himself that he would await his defense before forming an opinion. It seems obvious that Burr's request for such a statement

[162] Monroe to Hamilton, 6 Aug. 1797 (RC, DLC: McLane-Hamilton Papers; Tr, in Monroe's hand, NjMoW; Hamilton, *Observations*, Appendix No. LI).
[163] Monroe to Burr, 6 Aug. 1797 (NjMoW); Burr to Monroe, 13 Aug. 1797 (CSmH; the certificate that Burr drafted is quoted in Mitchell, *Hamilton*, II, 709, note 60).

was prompted by Hamilton's need to include it in his publication. Burr, moving closer to the Federalists just as Muhlenberg had been inclining toward the Republicans, assured Monroe of his "delicate and inviolable" regard to his honor in anything committed to him as intermediary. He enclosed Hamilton's reply, naturally without informing Monroe that he himself had actually helped Hamilton to frame it. Burr said that the reply required no comment since he, as Monroe's emissary, considered the personal affair as closed.[164] His principal certainly did not so consider it.

Monroe was ill when he received this astonishing communication from the man to whom he had confided decisions affecting his life and honor. The enclosed letter from Hamilton was brief:[165]

> The intention of my letter of the 4th instant, as itself imports, was to meet and close with an advance towards a personal interview, which it appeared to me had been made by you.
> From the tenor of your reply of the 6th, which disavows the inference I had drawn, any further step on my part, as being inconsistent with the ground I have heretofore taken, would be improper.

This suggested that, despite Monroe's disavowal, the inference was valid. It also meant that Hamilton had assumed to himself the posture of defense and claimed it as one consistently held. Burr had failed to elicit from him a direct answer to the direct question that he was charged to receive. For this Burr perhaps could not be held culpable. But his condescension to the adversary which Monroe strictly forbade him to make went far beyond the request for a testimonial to Hamilton's innocence. When Monroe, reading Hamilton's final letter, directed him to inform Hamilton that it was unsatisfactory and gave him full power to act in his behalf, Burr did not even deign to respond.[166]

---

[164] Hamilton to Monroe, 9 Aug. 1797 (1st Dft, DLC: McLane-Hamilton Papers; 2d Dft, with alterations noted below, same; FC in Hamilton's hand, same). On verso of the second draft Hamilton noted: "a letter . . . written and delivered to Col. Burr, who advised a revision and alteration as best adapted to some eventual course which might obviate the necessity of publication." The revision suggested by Burr came at the close of the first paragraph. The fair copy of Hamilton's version read: ". . . an advance towards a personal interview, which it appeared to me was intimated in your preceding one." Burr gave Hamilton the benefit of the more emphatic phrasing quoted in the text that Monroe received (see following note).

[165] Hamilton to Monroe, 9 Aug. 1797 (RC, NjMoW: FC, in Hamilton's hand, endorsed by him: "Copy of second letter d[e]l[ivere]d"; Hamilton, *Observations*, Appendix No. LII). This is the final letter in the exchange published by Hamilton.

[166] Monroe to Burr, 1 Dec. 1797, enclosing one of 2 Dec. 1797 to Hamilton (both in NjMoW). After Monroe had finished his *View of the conduct of the Executive* (Philadelphia, 1797), he authorized Burr to deliver the letter to Hamilton and reopen the exchange that had ended so unsatisfactorily for himself. He gave the unsealed letters to TJ, asking him to discuss the matter with Madison and Dawson. They, as well as TJ, advised that the matter be considered as closed. With Hamilton's charge of dishonorable conduct still rankling, Monroe accepted the advice, taking what satisfaction he could from TJ's report that his own publication had evoked "unqualified eulogies, both on the matter and manner, by all . . . not hostile to it from principle" (TJ to Monroe, 27

Nor, it may be presumed, did he inform Hamilton, who proceeded to publish the entire correspondence. Burr thus aided Hamilton in this final letter to convey the impression that Monroe had made an advance, that he had moved decisively to meet it, and that his antagonist had retreated. His political partisans sought to deepen the impression and, in varying degrees, historians have perpetuated it. No account of the episode has recognized that Monroe, always ready to accommodate on just and honorable grounds, steadfastly refused to yield the central point.

This concerned the credibility of the testimony conveying Mrs. Reynolds' charge that the documents had been fabricated. Monroe did not accede to Burr's appeal for a testimonial to Hamilton's innocence, but in responding he did draw up a certificate that reiterated precisely what he had said to Hamilton from the first:[167]

> I hereby certify, that it was not my intention to give any sanction to, or opinion of my own, as to the entry which bears my single signature, in the papers containing an enquiry into Colo. Hamilton's conduct, by Messrs. Muhlenburg Venable and myself in 1792, but that I meant it to stand on the credit of Mr. Clingman only upon whose application the entry was made.

It was Hamilton himself, the actual aggressor, who retreated. He failed to elicit a repudiation of Clingman's testimony even on the duelling ground, which Monroe reminded him more than once was scarcely a place for the illustration of truth. His failure resulted from Monroe's stubborn refusal to yield.

X

Hamilton's other efforts to defend himself against Mrs. Reynolds' charge were equally futile, raising new doubts the more he sought to erase them. While seeking to destroy her allegation by threatening a duel with Monroe, Hamilton simultaneously tried to use her letters as conclusive proof of his own innocence. He first procured a sworn statement from one Mary Williams, keeper of a Philadelphia boarding house, who testified that her acquaintance with Mrs. Reynolds began when she asked lodging and was refused. She swore that she had afterwards seen her frequently, was familiar with her handwriting, and was satisfied that six documents docketed by her were in her "proper handwriting." In his published defense Hamilton rested the authenticity of the letters on Mary Williams' affidavit and declared that they tore up by the roots "the pretence of a contrivance . . . to fabricate the

---

Dec. 1797; Monroe to Dawson, 10 Dec. 1797; Dawson to Monroe, 24 Dec. 1797, the last two in NjMoW). In its dignified and reasoned discussion of general issues, wholly devoid of partisan or personal invective, Monroe's *View* was indeed an intellectual triumph standing in marked contrast to Hamilton's *Observations*, both in the performance and in the result.

[167] MS dated 16 Aug. 1797, signed by Monroe (NjMoW). This was probably enclosed in Monroe's letter of the same date (not found).

evidence."[168] But Hamilton himself recognized the insubstantial nature of such a foundation. Being "somewhat embarrassed to prove Mrs. Reynolds' hand writing," he appealed to Jeremiah Wadsworth just a week after he had procured the affidavit of Mary Williams.

"Thinking it probable, as [Mrs. Reynolds] was a great scribbler, you must have received some notes from her when she applied to you for your assistance," he wrote Wadsworth, "I send you one of her notes to me and if your recollection serves would be much obliged to you to return it with your affidavit annexed." He stated the form of affidavit that he desired.[169] Wadsworth, reciting a long story about going to see Oliver Wolcott and Thomas Mifflin at Mrs. Reynolds' request and discovering that she had already disclosed her relations with Hamilton to them as well as to himself, declined to give the affidavit. "I have not the least knowledge of Mrs. Reynolds' hand-writing," he wrote, "nor do I remember ever to have received a line from her but a letter or two for you which by your request I returned to her." Then, as an afterthought, he added, "if I did they were destroyed."

Wadsworth obviously sought to be helpful in other respects, much as he thought Hamilton ill-advised in publishing his defense. After his interview with Wolcott, he wrote, he informed Mrs. Reynolds that his intercession was at an end and that her husband would have to stand trial. For a part of the time Clingman was present at this meeting. Wadsworth reported that he came away confirmed in his previous opinion that "the whole business was a combination" to swindle Hamilton. Nevertheless, when Mrs. Reynolds subsequently asked him to deliver letters to Hamilton, he did so. But Hamilton refused to receive them and requested that they be returned or destroyed. This part of Wadsworth's draft of the letter to Hamilton obviously gave him much difficulty, but he said when Mrs. Reynolds called upon him once again asking that he appeal to Hamilton to enable her to "go out of Town," he admitted that he again complied. Again Hamilton refused to receive the letters, being decided against having any further cor-

---

[168] Hamilton, *Observations*, p. 50-1; sworn affidavit of Mary Williams, 21 July 1797 (same, Appendix No. XLI). The six documents alluded to were those cited in *Observations* as Nos. "I, VIII, IX, X, XII, and XIII [i.e., XVIII]," the entire number of Mrs. Reynolds' letters printed by Hamilton. Philadelphia directories show that Mary Williams kept a boarding house at 104 Spruce Street from 1797 to 1802; she died in Washington two years later leaving a small estate, the disposition of which involved some undisclosed "indelicate matter" for her executor, William Cranch (William Cranch to George Simpson, 25 Sep., 10 Oct., and 13 Nov. 1804, PHi).

Two observations may be made about this testimony. First, Hamilton lodged at Mrs. Williams' boarding house at the time he asked her to authenticate Mrs. Reynolds' handwriting (see note 152 above). Second, the affidavit was procured on the day Hamilton received Monroe's letter with its pointed hint that the letters from Reynolds and his wife that were read to them in 1792 had not been "proved"—that is, attested (Monroe to Hamilton, 21 July 1797, PBL).

[169] Hamilton to Wadsworth, 28 July 1790 (RC supplied through courtesy of Pierce W. Gaines, Fairfield, Connecticut). The form of affidavit Hamilton suggested read: " 'That you have received letters from Mrs. Reynolds, conceive yourself to be acquainted with her hand writing, and that you verily believe this letter to be of her hand writing.' "

respondence with her or—Wadsworth wrote and then deleted the words —"giving any aid."[170] The labored account was clearly intended to sustain the point Hamilton desired to make: that he knew nothing of Wadsworth's efforts until after the confrontation. What it actually did was to prove just the opposite. Wadsworth's assertions were also contradicted in part by the testimony of Clingman and Mrs. Reynolds, to say nothing of that of Monroe and Muhlenberg. Hamilton omitted the letter from his pamphlet, relying instead on the affidavit of Mary Williams. It is not surprising that he did so. But it is significant that he chose Mrs. Williams as a witness in preference to another.

For just at this moment when Hamilton was having difficulty proving the authenticity of Mrs. Reynolds' handwriting, evidence of exactly the kind he professed to seek was volunteered by Richard Folwell, a Philadelphia publisher who was then as anxious to ingratiate himself with Federalists as he later was with Republicans.[171] This fortuitous development was reported by an excited Edward Jones just two days after Hamilton had sent his appeal to Jeremiah Wadsworth. Folwell's character, Jones wrote, was "sufficiently fair to give weight to his testimony." Folwell, who evidently had been sent to Jones by the editor of the *Gazette of the United States*, said that Mrs. Reynolds had boarded with his mother, that he knew her to be a person of loose morals, that she had been encouraged by her husband to engage in illicit affairs for money, and that he was prepared to testify to what he knew but did not wish to appear as volunteering the information.[172] Jones therefore suggested that Hamilton, without mentioning himself or Fenno, ask Folwell "to make oath to what he knew." But before he finished the letter Folwell appeared with a memorandum setting forth his "most important information." His motives in making the disclosures, Jones declared, were "highly disinterested," but he hoped that his information might be "cloathed in language favorable to his talents as a writer" and "be published in the shape of a letter." Just as Jones was about to sign his letter, Folwell appeared again, this time with documentary evidence of no small importance: a letter to himself from one who signed herself "Maria Clingman." Jones sent a copy of this letter to Hamilton and made the comment that it proved two important facts: her handwriting and her connection with Clingman.[173] This was undeniable and, equally important, Folwell was prepared to offer his testimony under oath. Hamilton's friends were much pleased with this unexpected development. William Jackson, congratulating Hamilton, was concerned because he had not acknowledged the packet containing such important information. Fearing it

[170] Wadsworth to Hamilton, 2 Aug. 1797 (Dft supplied through courtesy of Pierce W. Gaines, Fairfield, Connecticut).

[171] Richard Folwell (1768?-1814) in 1797 published *A short history of the Yellow Fever*, in 1801 issued the authorized Folwell edition of the *Journals of Congress*, and from 1805 to 1813 published a periodical called *The Spirit of the Press*, for which he solicited a subscription from TJ as "the principal Pillar of the public Will" (Folwell to TJ, 22 Aug. 1805). TJ subscribed for eight months.

[172] MS dated 12 Aug. 1797 in DLC: McLane-Hamilton Papers; text printed in A. McL. Hamilton, *The intimate life of Alexander Hamilton*, p. 473-6.

[173] Jones to Hamilton, 30 July 1797 (DLC: McLane-Hamilton Papers).

had gone astray, Jones asked Folwell to write out a second account. For greater security he sent the second one under the frank of the Comptroller of the Treasury.[174]

But Hamilton, as both his silence and his use of the documents prove, did not fully share his friends' pleasure over the effort of Folwell "to see Right prevail, and Innocence protected." He could see at once that Folwell's testimony, which was far from being disinterested, was even more exceptionable than that of Wadsworth. It not only claimed that Reynolds had urged his wife to make assignations with "certain high influential characters . . . to gull Money from them," but asserted that she herself had revealed this to Folwell. There were also obvious inconsistencies in Folwell's statement, as well as clear evidence that he framed his account so as to refute the testimony as published in Callender's *History*, which he said he had read. Much of what he set down was admittedly based on rumor, including the story of a young man reported to have been hanged for perjury in New York who confessed in his dying speech that he had been deluded by Clingman and Reynolds. But Folwell had indeed known Mrs. Reynolds and he did annex to his statement the letter in which she announced her marriage to Clingman.[175] Hamilton, quite understandably, declined to print this farrago of gossip and documented fact. But the omission of far greater significance is that, at a time when he was embarrassed to find proofs of the authenticity of Mrs. Reynolds' handwriting, he made no effort whatever to obtain a sworn affidavit from Folwell testifying to a fact he was supposedly so eager to establish.[176]

Instead of pursuing this obvious course, Hamilton made use of the testimony of a gentleman he deemed unbiased because he had never had any personal or political relations with him. He then paraphrased the letter of the gentleman as saying that, in a conversation with Mrs. Reynolds, she had voluntarily confessed her belief and even knowledge that Hamilton was innocent of all the charges made against him by her husband "or any other person of her acquaintance"; that she had spoken of Hamilton in terms of exalted esteem, declaring in the most solemn manner her extreme unhappiness lest he should think her an accessory to the vindictive acts of her husband; and that, in extreme agitation and unhappiness, she had expressed her fear "that the resentment of Mr. Reynolds on *a particular score* might have urged him to improper lengths of revenge."[177] The undisclosed gentleman was undoubtedly Richard Folwell and the statements must therefore have come from the memorandum in which he first "roughly summoned them up" for Edward Jones. While it was Folwell's express wish to have his state-

174 Jackson to Hamilton, 11 Aug. 1797 (DLC: McLane-Hamilton Papers).
175 Folwell's memorandum, 12 Aug. 1797 (DLC: McLane-Hamilton Papers; A. McL. Hamilton, *The intimate life of Alexander Hamilton*, p. 475).
176 Folwell's first memorandum should have come to Hamilton on or about the first of July, several days before he got Wadsworth's reply. Even if he had not received it then—as he unquestionably did soon thereafter—he still had time to obtain a sworn statement from Folwell after getting his memorandum of 12 Aug. 1797.
177 Hamilton, *Observations*, p. 51-2.

ment published, Hamilton said he had not been allowed to make public use of the letter or to name its author.[178] But he said that he was "permitted to refer any gentleman to the perusal of his letter in the hands of William Bingham, Esquire" and that Bingham had also allowed him to "deposit with him for similar inspection all the original papers" appended to the narrative.[179] After he had received Folwell's second memorandum, Hamilton announced at the close of his pamphlet that, in addition to the original letters from Mrs. Reynolds to himself, two others by her were in the hands of "the gentlemen with whom the papers" had been deposited. Both of these, he said, were signed "Maria Clingman."[180]

Hamilton's *Observations* appeared late in August, being announced by Fenno as "a concise statement of the base means practised by the Jacobins of the United States to asperse the characters of those persons who are considered as hostile to their disorganizing schemes."[181] The publisher's claim only reflected Hamilton's opening passages in which he portrayed himself as the innocent victim of the vilest of all efforts of "the Jacobin Scandal-Club" to accomplish its purposes through its "principal engine . . . calumny."[182] Thus aimed at both parties and persons, the tract appeared at a time when the Federalist press, led by the *Gazette of the United States*, was filled with squibs and articles

[178] Hamilton, *Observations*, p. 52. "The letter from the gentleman above alluded to," Hamilton added, "has been already shown to *Mr. Monroe*." This statement cannot be credited. There is no reference to Folwell's memorandum in any of Hamilton's correspondence with Jackson. Monroe had gone to Virginia before Hamilton returned to Philadelphia to publish his pamphlet, and, in any case, an attempt by Hamilton to prove his innocence by such testimony at a time when he had accused Monroe of motives "malignant and dishonorable" toward himself would have been highly incongruous. It is possible that, with Burr being cooperative—and insensitive—enough to assist Hamilton in drafting his response to Monroe, Hamilton did show Folwell's letter to him and perhaps regarded this as equivalent to showing it to his principal. If so, Burr did not mention it to Monroe (Burr to Monroe, 13 Aug. 1797, CSmH).

[179] Hamilton, *Observations*, p. 52. Bingham later asserted that he knew nothing of this until he saw the statement in print and that he had never received the documents (Mitchell, *Hamilton*, II, 421-2, citing McHenry to Hamilton, 18 Nov. 1799, and a letter from Bingham to Hamilton, 21 July 1801, in which he returned at Hamilton's request "a Packet of Papers which . . . were deposited" with him and had long been in his possession). Hamilton had also told Robert Troup that, in case of his death, the papers should be conveyed by a careful hand to Oliver Wolcott. They have never been found in the papers of Bingham, Hamilton, or Wolcott.

[180] Hamilton, *Observations*, p. lviii. Hamilton's reference to "the gentlemen" with whom the papers had been deposited may have been a typographical error or he may have planned to have Wolcott share custody of them with Bingham. One of the two letters referred to was addressed to a Mrs. Miller, the other to Folwell, and Hamilton said that in the former Mrs. Reynolds announced her marriage to Clingman. This, too, may have been an error. Folwell said that the letter to himself, enclosed in his second memorandum, contained that announcement.

[181] The pamphlet was advertised in the *Gazette of the United States*, 28 Aug. 1797, having been published on the 25th. Fenno carried the advertisement in almost every issue of the paper for the next four months, a fact which suggests that this 1797 edition of the tract was received by a comparatively apathetic public.

[182] Hamilton, *Observations*, p. 3-13.

impugning the character of Monroe.[183] But, whatever else might be said of Hamilton's sensational revelation of his correspondence with the Reynoldses, his defense could not in any proper sense be called concise or convincing. The manner in which the evidence was presented, the misleading account of the exchange with Monroe, the confused chronology of the documents, the irrelevant intrusion and deliberate misconstruction of Jefferson's innocuous letters to Fraunces—all exemplified a surprising incoherence of argument set in a polemical context. On an issue that rested at bottom on the validity of his testimony as compared with that of Clingman and the Reynoldses, Hamilton raised new doubts by the very elaborateness of his defense. He increased these doubts when he rejected their testimony as totally unreliable and at the same time accepted it as conclusive proof when it favored himself. His publisher declared that the letters of James and Maria Reynolds proved "beyond the possibility of a doubt that the connection between [Hamilton] and Reynolds, was the result of a daring conspiracy on the part of the latter and his associates to extort money."[184] Hamilton himself said that Mrs. Reynolds' own letters absolutely contradicted her charge that he and her husband had fabricated evidence to support the allegation of an adulterous relation.[185] But what these documents did, on the contrary, was to expose the transparency of his own defense.

XI

The original manuscripts of the letters from James and Maria Reynolds that Hamilton published have never been discovered. But the printed texts raised immediate doubts as to their authenticity. Two months after the pamphlet appeared, Callender wrote to Hamilton:[186]

As the facts which you . . . bring forward, and the conclusions which you attempt to draw from them do not appear Satisfactory to me, I intend introducing a reply to them in a volume upon your administration that I am now engaged in writing. My object in this letter is, to request that you will give an order to a friend of mine and myself to inspect the papers lodged with Mr. Bingham, that I may judge what credit is due to them. Such an order, I conceive from your own words . . . to be necessary to obtain a perusal of

---

[183] On 31 Aug. 1797, under an Albany dateline, the *Gazette of the United States* published a long attack on Monroe that identified him with plots and conspiracies against the government existing both in a foreign country and "also in the bosom of America." On 2 Sep. 1797 the *Gazette* published a purported letter from an American in Paris to his friend in Philadelphia saying that Monroe's recall was a subject of rejoicing for those Americans in France "still attached to the genuine principles of their government"; that he had invariably followed directions of the Jacobins; and that, on every public occasion, he had vilified "not only our Constitution, as being formed on unequal principles, but the immortal Washington and Adams, as meriting the fate of Caesar and Louis." On 20 Sep. 1797 the *Gazette* referred to Monroe as "this Gallican, Anti-American M——e."

[184] *Gazette of the United States*, 28 Aug. 1797.

[185] Hamilton, *Observations*, p. 50-1.

[186] Callender to Hamilton, 29 Oct. 1797 (DLC: McLane-Hamilton Papers). The friend alluded to was perhaps John Beckley.

them; and if they appear to be genuine, I shall be as ready to confess my conviction to the public, as I was to declare my former opinion. I hope that there is nothing improper in this application. I am sure that I have no personal enmity of you, nor any pleasure in giving you uneasiness. The freedom which I take with all parties ought to have convinced you that I am the 'hireling' of none.

Hamilton did not deign to notice this appeal even with a denial.[187] This is understandable. While he had said that the documents were available for inspection by persons of either political party, he had restricted access to those in whom reliance could be placed. He had further qualified the conditions of access by referring "any gentleman" to William Bingham, being well assured that none would apply. After all, for doing no more than record information from the same sources to which Hamilton now appealed for proof of his innocence, Monroe had been accused of acting on dishonorable motives and of giving countenance to worthless evidence. Hence, just as the nature of Hamilton's explanation to Monroe, Muhlenberg, and Venable had closed the door to further investigation by men of principle, so this offer to make the "original papers" available for inspection erected a similar barrier. Thus protected, Hamilton could be assured that he alone among all of his contemporaries possessed the answer to the question whether the handwriting in the six letters of Maria Reynolds submitted by him was the same as that in the two letters of Maria Clingman produced by Folwell. His urgent attempt to authenticate the former and his avoidance of all effort to prove the latter suggest what that answer was. Many must have surmised its nature. Only Callender, however, in face of the conditions stipulated by Hamilton, was indelicate enough to ask to see the letters and candid enough to articulate the doubt that such a request implied.

But history, long after the passions and polemics of the time have been quieted, requires that any barrier be probed, whatever the cost, when persons have been defamed or truth injured or questions not asked. This requirement, in the absence of all of the original manuscripts, must be met in this instance with an appraisal of the printed texts of the letters of James and Maria Reynolds.[188] This need not be

---

[187] Hamilton docketed the letter: "Impudent Experiment. NO NOTICE."

[188] There were six letters from Maria Reynolds to Hamilton, all save the last of 2 June 1792 bearing no date or only the day of the week (Hamilton, *Observations*, Appendixes Nos. I, VIII, IX, X, XII, and XVIII). James Reynolds' fourteen letters were dated 15, 17, and 19 Dec. 1791; 17 Jan., 24 Mch., 3, 7, 17, and 23 Apr., 2 May, 23 June, 24 and 30 Aug. 1792, with one undated letter between 2 and 23 June 1792. There were in addition five receipts from Reynolds, the first, dated 22 Dec. 1791, for $600; one of 3 Jan. for $400; and three of 3 and 7 Apr. and 24 June 1792 for $90, $45, and $50 respectively, totalling $1,185 (same, Appendixes Nos. II-VII, XI, XIII-XVII, XIX-XXII).

There are several incongruities of dates and chronology in Reynolds' letters that cannot all be explained as mere lapses of the supposed author. The letter of "Sunday Evening 24th March. 1792" should have been dated Saturday or the 25th and that of "sunday evening" 23 June 1792 asking for a loan of $50 should have been dated Saturday or the 24th, as the receipt was. An anachronism in the letter correctly dated "Saturday Evening, 17th December, 1791," cannot be explained as a common error. In it Reynolds said that he had "taken till tuesday

exhaustive or even minutely detailed. Variations in spelling, contractions, and modes of expression were of course matters of common occurrence in letters of even the most sophisticated men of the time, including those of Hamilton himself. Misdating and confusion of days of the week are also errors commonly to be found in the correspondence of the literate and illiterate alike. But, after all due allowance is made, the letters of James Reynolds and his wife as published by Hamilton present a character so immediately recognizable as to place their true nature beyond doubt.

This is discernible in the occasional incongruities of date that cannot all be explained as simple lapses. It is exhibited in the remarkable manner in which, going beyond the range of mere coincidence, the letters address themselves to the specific details of the adverse testimony—for example, the amount of money paid by Hamilton and the allusion to speculating in the Lancaster Turnpike. It is manifest also in the fact that the published letters terminate well before Wolcott instituted proceedings against Reynolds and Clingman, thus leaving unanswered the more important question raised by Hamilton's dealings with Reynolds after he was released from jail. Yet in evaluating the charge that Mrs. Reynolds made and Hamilton spent so much effort trying to refute, one need attend only to the texts of the letters themselves.

In style Maria Reynolds' six notes are brief, demanding, and ardent, exhibiting a dolorous attitude of unrequited passion typical of that genre in an age of sensibility. Mrs. Reynolds was capable of good grammatical construction and her spelling was generally correct. But one of her peculiarities was that she misspelled simple words while handling more difficult ones with ease. She had no trouble with *tortured, happiness, disappointment, anguish, insupportable, language, affliction, inexorable, consolation, existence, complaining,* and *adieu.* But words of one or two syllables gave her much difficulty. She usually but not invariably wrote *se* for *see, rite* for *write, mutch* for *much, moast* for *most, pilliow* for *pillow,* and so on. Mrs. Reynolds also had two other significant traits. First, she could misspell words in ways unusual even for unlettered persons of the day, such as *kneese* for *knees, youse* or *yuse* for *use, greateest* for *greatest, gleme* for *gleam, voed* for *void, intreatee* for *entreat,* and *contennue* for *continue.* Second, she also misspelled some words exactly as her husband did, such as *disstressed* for *distressed, ben* (or *bin*) for *been, togeather* for *together,* and *seturation*

---

morning" to consider what steps to take. But his first letter announcing his discovery of his wife's infidelity had only been written on Thursday the 15th. According to Hamilton's chronology the two men seem to have met three times. Hamilton stated that he sent for Reynolds on receiving his letter of the 15th; that the meeting, as he recalled, took place that day and was inconclusive; and that when he received the letter Reynolds wrote on the 17th—incidentally proposing a meeting at The George on Tuesday the 20th—he called on him that day and insisted on knowing his object, which Reynolds explained in his letter of the 19th. The first payment presumably took place at a meeting of the two men on the 22d when Reynolds gave his receipt for $600. Thus, according to this account, Reynolds declined in two private meetings to state his purpose but was willing to expose himself in writing as a blackmailer—though, implausibly, he did so only in his third letter.

for *situation* (Reynolds gave such variations on the last as *setevation*, *setervation*, *setuvation*, *setivation*, and *sutivation*, a complex of variants accorded by him to no other term).

As published in Hamilton's *Observations*, James Reynolds' letters and receipts fell between 15 Dec. 1791 and 30 Aug. 1792. The correspondence opened with his discovery of the alleged amour and changed in tone from that of an outraged and threatening husband to one of an importunate, obsequious, and wheedling extortionist. Like his wife, Reynolds had difficulty with simple words, spelling *fue* for *few*, *boath* for *both*, and *shush* for *such*. But he could handle polysyllabic words without difficulty, such as *distraction*, *imprudent*, *disagreeable*, and *calculation*, in addition to a number of such words that she also employed, including *consolation*, *insupportable*, and *unhappiness*. Like her also, he had the peculiarity of being able to spell some words in unusual ways and at the same time—often in the same letter—to give its correct form. Thus Maria could write *deer freend* and also *dear sir*, while James could manage such a remarkable variant as *tiremd* and in the same letter give its correct form, *determined*, to say nothing of spelling *determination* correctly at least twice elsewhere. He also wrote *exspess* as well as *express*, while spelling *sespect* in the same letter in which he wrote *suspicion*. On the whole, perhaps because his letters were longer and more numerous, Reynolds outdid his wife in inventive misspellings. Such fractured orthography as *surcomcance* for *circumstance*, *preposial* for *proposal*, *protickeler* for *particular*, and *tiremd* for *determined* would be unusual even in the writing of an unlettered phonetic scribbler of the time. But, sprinkled as these words are rather sparingly through long passages of generally well wrought sentences framed with a due regard for conventional idiom and with the overwhelming majority of the words being in correct form, these idiosyncratic spellings can only be regarded as incredibly naive inventions.

They are not only incongruous in the context in which they appear: they are also not to be found in the letter that Reynolds wrote to Washington in 1789 in applying for office.[189] Nor do they appear in the mutilated letter from Reynolds to Clingman of 13 December 1792. That remnant, though not in perfect form, bears none of the orthographic peculiarities to be found in the letters in Hamilton's *Observations*.[190] It is important to note that Hamilton published a letter purportedly written by Reynolds to Wolcott, bearing a date only a week earlier than that of the fragment. In this letter, characterized by two variants of the peculiar spelling of *situation* and by other misspellings not to be found in his two known letters, Reynolds said his wife had told him a report had come to Wolcott that he had threatened to make "Some of the heads of the Departments tremble" if he were not discharged. He denied that he had ever made such a statement. Like Hamilton denying that he had charged Monroe and his colleagues with partisan motives, he said he had only meant that the clerk in the public office who gave out the lists would tremble on being

189 James Reynolds to the President and Senate, 26 June 1789 (see note 53 above).
190 Callender, *History*, p. 220-1.

discovered. He declared that the charge against him was "tottely Groundless without the least foundation Immaginable" and that if Wolcott would give him "the pleashure of waiting uppon" him the next day he would give him all the information possible. He then went on to explain that he and Clingman had only given a bond of indemnification to the administrator of the estate of the claimant, an action he represented as a mere "Oversight of ours."[191]

This letter cannot be reconciled in spelling, in grammar, or in substance with either Reynolds' mutilated letter or his application for office. It cannot be reconciled with the testimony given by Clingman to the three Congressmen or with the statement made by Reynolds himself to Monroe and Venable when they visited him in jail. Most important of all, it cannot be reconciled with the testimony that Hamilton himself published to show why the proceedings against the two men had been dismissed—that of Oliver Wolcott. In the affidavit that he furnished to Hamilton, Wolcott stated that the two men had consented to surrender the lists, to restore the balance, and to reveal the name of the person who furnished the lists. "This," he testified, "was done conformably to the proposition contained in the letter from Clingman dated December 4, 1792. . . . The original letter and the lists which were surrendered now remain in my possession."[192] He made no mention of a letter from Reynolds written on the following day. There was, in fact, no need for such a letter after the conditions had been met. It was needed only for Hamilton's own purposes.

Thus on every score, even in the absence of the original letters of James and Maria Reynolds, the conclusion is obvious. Mrs. Reynolds' charge that the letters were forged cannot be supported by objective proof. But her testimony in some respects, like that of Clingman, found corroboration in the admissions of Hamilton, the contradictions of Wadsworth, and the facts attested by Muhlenberg and Monroe. Hence her allegation seems to merit consideration, especially since the charges of adultery and complicity in extortion rest solely upon the word of Hamilton. But even if this were not so, the letters that he adduced in support of his accusations against her and her husband are less trustworthy. They exhibit in their texts, in their substantive incongruities, and in their conflict with verifiable evidence overwhelming proofs of their own insufficiency. They are the palpably contrived documents of a brilliant and daring man who, writing under much stress in the two or three days available to him in 1792, tried to imitate what he conceived to be the style of less literate persons. The result was inexpert to the point of naivete, but its character is beyond doubt. The purported letters of James and Maria Reynolds as published in Hamilton's *Observations* cannot be accepted as genuine.[193]

[191] Hamilton, *Observations*, Appendix No. XLII.
[192] Same, Appendix No. XXIV. It should be noted that, immediately after he read No. V of Callender's *History*, Wolcott wrote Hamilton that the lists were in his hands, together "with *a letter* from Clingman and Reynolds" (Wolcott to Hamilton, 3 July 1797, DLC: McLane-Hamilton Papers; emphasis added).
[193] This verdict must be applied also to the letter that Hamilton wrote on "Sunday December 17th 1791," reading as follows: "I am this moment going to a rendezvous which I suspect may involve a most serious plot against me, but

This was recognized at the time, but has been wholly ignored since. Only Callender appears to have given public support to Mrs. Reynolds' charge of fabrication. His analysis of the documents was not full or even exact, but it was penetrating. In his *Sketches of the history of America* published early in 1798, he pointed out the contradictions in Hamilton's argument and then noted the textual incongruities of the letters: "The construction of the periods disagrees with this apparent incapacity of spelling. . . . A few gross blunders are interspersed . . . but, when stript of such a veil, the body of the composition is pure and correct. In the literary world, fabrications of this nature have been frequent." Callender went further: "He who acknowledged the reality of such epistles, could feel no scruple to forge them. The latter supposition is as favourable as the former to his good name." He pointed out that Clingman and Mrs. Reynolds were married and living in Alexandria. "If the letters published by Mr. Hamilton in the name of Maria are genuine," he suggested, "it would be very easy to obtain her attestation of the fact. A justice of the peace . . . could dispatch the business in half an hour. She could be directed to give a sample of her hand; and by comparing this with the letters, it would be ascertained whether or not they really came from her pen. But Camillus dares not meet this test." Callender then addressed Hamilton directly:[194]

The whole collection would not have required above an evening to write. . . . You speak as if it was impossible to invent a few letters.

---

various reasons, and among others a desire to ascertain the truth induce me to hazard the consequence. As any disastrous event might interest my fame; I drop you this line, that from my impressions may be inferred the truth of the matter" (DLC: McLane-Hamilton Papers; not addressed). The mistake in the date (Sunday was the 18th) could have been a common error, but not likely if it were written immediately after Hamilton had received Reynolds' letter of the 17th and, according to his account, went to see him in order to get a decisive answer (see note 185 above). No such letter was written on the 15th, when, according to his own account, Hamilton had already suspected a plot and sent for Reynolds.

The implausible nature of the letter—its laconic announcement and its hint at the possibility of personal danger, a fear that found expression nowhere else in the episode and which Hamilton's actions belied—is confirmed also in the physical characteristics of the document. Being signed yet having no addressee's name, it bears superficially the impression that it might have been either a retained file copy or a letter not sent (Mitchell, *Hamilton*, II, 705, note 8, conjectures that it may not have been sent "because Reynolds was mollified"; but Reynolds' supposed mollification only took place some five days later). The paper, greyish in tint and having a distinctive watermark, is a single sheet of a kind for which no other example has been found in Hamilton's papers for 1791 —or indeed for any other year. Being head of a department in which the detection of forgeries depended on watermarks and other physical characteristics, Hamilton of course was well aware of the ease with which fabrications could be detected (see the cancelled passage in his letter to Monroe, at note 159 above). In this instance he did not make the mistake of choosing a paper with a dated watermark and he was careful not to use the kind to be found in his letters and papers of 1797, the year in which this misdated letter was probably composed. It is significant that Hamilton made no mention of the text and of course did not publish it.

[194] Callender, *Sketches*, p. 93-5, 97-100. Callender told TJ that his sketches had sold beyond all expectation, 700 copies being disposed of in five weeks (Callender to TJ, 21 Mch. 1798).

Yet, upon this very business, you wrote a feigned hand. And what is your molehill appendix, altogether, to the gigantic fabrications of Psalmanazar and of Chatterton? Send for the lady, and let us hear what she has to say. . . . Never pretend that you scorn to confront accusers. The world will believe that you dare not.

Even behind the shield of hypothesis, this was a far bolder attribution of guilt than could be found in Monroe's non-committal responses. Yet Hamilton treated it with silence, just as he had avoided the opportunity presented by Folwell to authenticate Maria Reynolds' handwriting.

This was just as well. Hamilton's friends were deeply mortified by the publication of his pamphlet. "Myself and most of his other friends conceive this confession humiliating in the extreme," wrote Henry Knox, "and such a text as will serve his enemies for a commentary while he . . . lives, and his name is mentioned as a public man for employment."[195] Bishop White declined in public to drink a toast to Hamilton, giving as his reason the disclosures made in the pamphlet.[196] Most of the leaders of both parties maintained an embarrassed silence, though it is clear that nineteenth century screenings of family papers removed many of the comments that must have been exchanged. James Madison, in a letter to Jefferson, appraised the pamphlet without malice but with devastating accuracy:[197]

> The publication under all its characters is a curious specimen of the ingenious folly of its Author. Next to the error of publishing at all, is that of forgetting that simplicity and candor are the only dress which prudence would put on innocence. Here we see every rhetorical artifice employed to excite the spirit of party to prop up his sinking reputation, and whilst the most exaggerated complaints are uttered against the unfair and virulent persecution of himself, he deals out in every page the most malignant insinuations against others. The one against you is a masterpiece of folly, because its impotence is in exact proportion to its venom.

The unfortunate episode produced some veiled allusions in the bitter campaign of 1800 when another tract by Hamilton caused anguish even to his staunchest supporters.[198] But there was little need in that year

195 Henry Knox to David Cobb, 16 Sep. 1797 (MHi: Knox Papers); Cobb admitted that Hamilton had fallen for the present, but cynically declared that he would rise again since purity of character was not necessary for public confidence (Cobb to Knox, 1 Oct. 1797, same); *Patrioticus* in the *New-York Gazette* read Hamilton's pamphlet with "mingled emotions of pity and indignation . . . pity at the weakness of human nature, which in this respect is so conspicuous in that otherwise great personage for writing the defense; indignation at the pitiful malevolence of Mr. Monroe who drove him to it, by cruelly refusing him a certificate to do away an atrocious calumny preferred against him" (quoted in *Gazette of the United States*, 20 Sep. 1797).

196 Callender to TJ, 28 Sep. 1797. "If you have not seen it," Callender added, "no anticipation can equal the infamy of this piece. It is worth all that fifty of the best pens in America could have said against him, and the most pitiful part of the whole is his notice of you."

197 Madison to TJ, 20 Oct. 1797, enclosing TJ's copy of the pamphlet that he had received from Monroe.

198 Jedidiah Morse to Oliver Wolcott, Jr., 27 Oct. 1800 (CtHi: Wolcott Papers), saying he had never doubted Hamilton's integrity or patriotism but

even for political writers of the calibre of James Thomson Callender to discuss the matter. All that such partisans required was a reissue of Hamilton's *Observations*. This was brought out in exact and literal form, the only alterations being two on the title-page that were prompted by a malicious humor: on its recto the work was announced as printed for John Fenno and *Pro Bono Publico*, while on its verso the following appeared in place of the copyright notice: "Copy Right *not* secured according to the Act of Congress."[199]

The humiliation felt by Hamilton's friends was all the greater because his confession left untouched the question which began with an official inquiry in 1792 and ended five years later in personal tragedy. The pain that Hamilton brought to his family and friends by confessing private guilt did not wipe out the "more serious stain": that was simply left untouched. Many indeed shared Jefferson's view that Hamilton's willingness to plead guilty to adultery seemed "rather to have strengthened than weakened the suspicions that he was in truth guilty of the speculations."[200] The answer to such suspicions was hidden on the 15th of December 1792 behind a veil that, even to meet a public duty, men of decency could not lift. "No Body," declared Senator Maclay, "can prove these things, but every body knows them."[201] No one has ever proved them. Even the confession of private guilt remains in doubt, with the word of Hamilton balanced against that of Mrs. Reynolds and the scales perhaps tipped in her favor because the documents he brought forward in proof of adultery do indeed sustain her charge of fabrication.

Yet the question far transcending these in importance was answered with finality. This was a question not of private conduct or even of

---

many men would doubt "his prudence in a former publication" and in that of his *Letter from Alexander Hamilton, concerning . . . John Adams* (New York, 1800); Noah Webster had similar feelings (Mitchell, *Hamilton*, II, 408).

[199] *Observations on certain documents contained in No. V. & VI. of 'The History of the United States for the Year 1796,' in which the charge of speculation against Alexander Hamilton . . . is fully refuted. Written by himself* (Philadelphia, 1800; Shipton-Mooney No. 37571). The reprint was scrupulously exact in reproducing capitalization, punctuation, orthography, italics, and even errors. Apparently the only deviation from the 1797 edition, aside from the changes in the title-page noted above, lay in the effort to correct Hamilton's error in Mary Williams' affidavit referring to one of Mrs. Reynolds' letters as Document XIII, which the 1800 edition mistakenly rendered as XXIII instead of XVIII.

[200] TJ to John Taylor, 8 Oct. 1797. TJ received a copy of the pamphlet on 14 Oct. 1797 along with John Barnes' letter expressing sentiments comparable to his own: "Mr. H. has Assuredly, reduced his Consequence to the most degrading and Contemptable point of view. . . . Such another piece of ridiculous folly: sure, never Man was guilty of . . . as if it were possible . . . to justify his Public Conduct, by a *simple* confession of his Private ridiculous Amour" (Barnes to TJ, 3 Oct. 1797, text supplied through courtesy of Pierce W. Gaines, Fairfield, Connecticut). TJ passed his copy along to Monroe, who carried it with him on a visit to Madison (see note 197 above). While there Monroe saw John Dawson, who told him that Hamilton had been "given up wherever he has been as an immoral man; and that the ease with which he acknowledges himself an adulterer inspires doubts that he was guilty of the other charge also" (Monroe to TJ, 20 Oct. 1797).

[201] Maclay, *Journal*, ed. Maclay, p. 394.

individual malfeasance on the part of a public official. It was a question of derivative principles of administration under which Hamilton sought to make "the System of the British Ministry, the model of his conduct as assumed American Primate—chusing rather to trust to a monied Interest he created, for the support of his Measures, than their rectitude."[202] It was a question of using the powers of government to defend privilege, to bestow favors, to appeal to interested motives, and, in doing so, to ignore the misconduct of those over whom, as he declared, the minister of a great department should exercise "a general but vigilant superintendence." It was, finally, a question of rejecting the fundamental postulate of a society that proposed to abandon the concept of special privilege for a few and to start groping toward the ideal of equality for all.

The answer to this greater question is amply documented in the entire record as well as in the episode which began when Bland's resolutions pointed toward malfeasance in a public office. Hamilton as the embodiment of that answer was perhaps only a surrogate for others less disinterested than he. But in using the reins of interest for the guidance of policy, he made himself culpable on a greater scale than if he had been guilty of the personal speculation of which he was suspected. By so doing, he made the department over which he presided an accessory to the privileged and interested purposes of those within and without who took advantage of the opportunities that he made possible. He created under the sanction of his office an atmosphere in which the activities of such men as Vredenburgh and Reynolds could flourish and be carried on with impunity. Indeed, by lending his assistance to Wadsworth and others in the case of Baron de Glaubeck, he engaged in the same kind of imposition on a veteran of the Revolution as that practised by Reynolds in Virginia, the chief distinction being that the claimant was not mulcted for personal profit but had the greater part of the sum due him transferred by official favoritism to a personal friend.[203] This was exactly the opposite of that

202 Edmund Pendleton to George Washington, 11 Sep. 1793 (*Letters and Papers of Edmund Pendleton*, ed. David J. Mays, II, 613-14).

203 The favoritism shown to the widow of Nathanael Greene involved what TJ referred to as "the infamous case" of P.W.J. Ludwig, Baron de Glaubeck, a foreign officer who served under Greene and was cited for special merit in the engagement at Cowpens (TJ's memorandum of 12 June 1793). In 1785 Greene reported to Congress that, being without funds himself, he had felt obliged as commanding general to endorse bills for Glaubeck, a foreigner who had neither money nor credit. The bills were protested, returning to Greene "with damages and interest to the amount of near a thousand Dollars," which Greene was obliged to borrow (Extract of letter from Greene to the President of Congress, 22 Aug. 1785, DLC: McLane-Hamilton Papers). In 1789, after presenting two petitions to Congress, Glaubeck was allowed pay as captain from 9 Mch. 1781 to 24 Aug. 1782 (JHR, I, 35, 65, 67, 69, 116-17). The special act was passed on the last day of the session and two days later Glaubeck assigned his salary claim of $701.33 to Thomas Bazen, an illiterate merchant of New York City, for £109-4-0 New York currency. Six weeks later Bazen, signing by mark and receiving $273, conveyed his right to Royal Flint as attorney for Mrs. Catharine Greene (Tr of assignment of Glaubeck to Bazen, 1 Oct. 1789, witnessed by Joseph King and Edward Dunscomb; Tr of assignment of Bazen to Flint, 19 Nov. 1789, witnessed by John Stagg, Jr., and William Knox; attestation by Joseph Nourse, 23 Nov. 1793, DLC: Hamilton Papers). On 16 Mch. 1790

posture of governmental neutrality in respect to private obligations which Hamilton had defended so strongly in his appeal for a veto of Bland's resolutions. The reversal is not surprising, for Hamilton, acclaimed as one of the greatest of administrators, often violated his own precepts.

This first symbolic clash between Hamilton and Jefferson thus illustrated in all of its aspects—on the exalted level of "the first principles

---

Glaubeck's account was adjusted at the Treasury, Nourse registered a warrant on the same date, and Flint received a certificate entitling him to receive $561.07 due on the claim (Trs of Eveleigh's Warrant No. 224 and Nourse's certificate, both dated 16 Mch. 1790; attestation by Nourse, 23 Nov. 1793, same). In 1792 Mrs. Greene, having known of the effort made in her behalf, inquired of Hamilton as to the result (Catharine Greene to Hamilton, 26 June 1792, Syrett, *Hamilton*, XI, 571). Her agents, Joseph Anthony & Son, returned the original certificate to the Treasury and on 15 Feb. 1793 a new one was issued for $909.59, including interest of $348.52 (Extract from the Books of the Registered Debt, enclosed in Nourse to Hamilton, 29 Nov. 1793, DLC: Hamilton Papers). This was the amount that Mrs. Greene received.

When Andrew G. Fraunces was dismissed from the Treasury in 1793, he claimed he had been employed by Hamilton and Duer to purchase Glaubeck's assignment and that he had possession of a power of attorney in his own hand with corrections by Hamilton. Fraunces published his charges and Hamilton appealed to Wadsworth, Duer, Flint, and Mrs. Greene for affidavits showing that Glaubeck's claim was not bought for speculation but for Mrs. Greene's benefit (Hamilton to Catharine Greene, 3 Sep. 1793; Hamilton to Wadsworth, 3 Sep. 1793; Robert Affleck to Hamilton, 7 Sep. 1793, Syrett, *Hamilton*, XV, 318-20, 321, 323-4). Wadsworth, who echoed Greene and others in calling Glaubeck "an imposture," had told Mrs. Reynolds that he knew more about the affair than any other person (Wadsworth to Hamilton, 2 Aug. 1797, text supplied through courtesy of Pierce W. Gaines, Fairfield, Connecticut). It was certainly he who, as an executor of Greene's estate, initiated the business. Wadsworth claimed that, after the passage of the bill granting him pay as captain, Glaubeck had promised to apply part of it to the Greene debt but had avoided him. "I went directly to you and asked your Aid," he wrote Hamilton, "as I was satisfied Glaubeck intended to sell his certificate and fly the Country. According to the best of my recollection you drew me a power, but Glaubeck got information that I was after him and kept concealed. Being obliged to leave New York I employed Mr. Flint who told me he could find him, but he sold the certificate I think to Francis who Mr. Flint purchased it of, and Mrs. Greene actually had it" (Wadsworth to Hamilton, 13 Sep. 1793, Syrett, *Hamilton*, XV, 335; see Hamilton's explanation of Fraunces' charges in his letter to Washington, 9 Aug. 1793; also Wolcott to Hamilton, 7 Aug. 1793, same, XV, 197-203, 213-22). Flint's own account of the transaction apparently has not survived.

But Hamilton's exertions to prove that Mrs. Greene actually received the money obscured the real issue. Fraunces himself readily admitted that Hamilton did not intervene for personal advantage and indeed said he knew that "the negotiation was *solely* for the benefit of Mrs. Greene." What he was concerned about was that, having lent his office as a favor to one friend, Hamilton might do the same for another—in brief to cause him to be treated as Glaubeck had been (William Willcocks to Hamilton, 5 Sep. 1793, Syrett, *Hamilton*, XV, 323). Hamilton seems not to have grasped the implications of his involvement in the Glaubeck affair or to have understood, as Wolcott did, the impropriety of acting officially for friends or being "concerned in any private business relating to the Treasury" (see note 118). The committee of the House that reported on Fraunces' memorial found his charges about Hamilton's role in the Glaubeck affair "wholly illiberal and groundless" (Syrett, *Hamilton*, XIV, 462-3n.). But the evidence that Hamilton himself produced proves that in this instance he did allow personal considerations to affect his official decision, which is what Fraunces had charged (*An appeal to the legislature of the United States, and*

of natural justice and social policy" as well as on the sordid level of reality to which the head of a great department permitted it to descend —two fundamentally opposed and irreconcilable ways of looking at government. In this instance as in almost all others, both in principle and in practice, Hamilton took his guidance from the old order, Jefferson from the new.

---

to the citizens individually, of the several states. By Andrew G. Fraunces [New York, 1793; Shipton-Mooney No. 25504]). In his MS of *Observations* Hamilton said that Fraunces had made against him "a formal accusation of criminal conduct in office," but he prudently changed this to "unfaithful conduct" in the printed version (MS of *Observations*, DLC: McLane-Hamilton Papers).

Preliminary indexes will be issued periodically for groups of volumes. Indexes covering Vols. 1-6 and 7-12 have been published. An index covering Vols. 13-18 is in preparation. A comprehensive index of persons, places, subjects, etc., arranged in a single consolidated sequence, will be issued at the conclusion of the series.

THE PAPERS OF THOMAS JEFFERSON is composed in Monticello, a type specially designed by the Mergenthaler Linotype Company for this series. Monticello is based on a type design originally developed by Binny & Ronaldson, the first successful typefounding company in America. It is considered historically appropriate here because it was used extensively in American printing during the last thirty years of Jefferson's life, 1796 to 1826; and because Jefferson himself expressed cordial approval of Binny & Ronaldson types.

Composed and printed by Princeton University Press. Illustrations are reproduced by Meriden Gravure Company, Meriden, Connecticut. Paper for the series is made by Curtis Paper Company, at Newark, Delaware; cloth for the series is made by Holliston Mills, Inc., Norwood, Massachusetts. Bound by the Maple Press Company, Baltimore.

DESIGNED BY P. J. CONKWRIGHT